PHLIP

(Prentice Hall Learning on the Internet Partnership)

is a content-rich, multidisciplinary business education Web site created by professors for professors and their students.

for students

- Interactive on-line study guide
- Internet-based exercises
- Current-events articles and exercises
- On-line study hall
- Writing center

for faculty

- Instructor's Manual and PowerPoint slides
- On-line course syllabus builder
- Faculty resource center
- CME—Course Monitor Edition for on-line course management featuring a roster, announcements, and a grade book

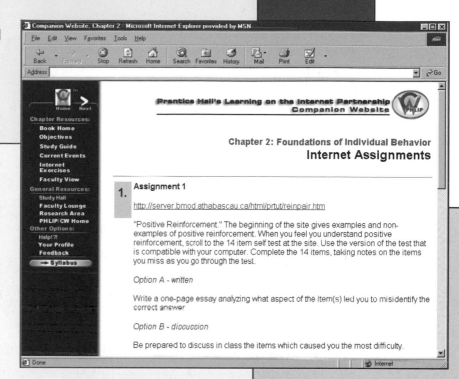

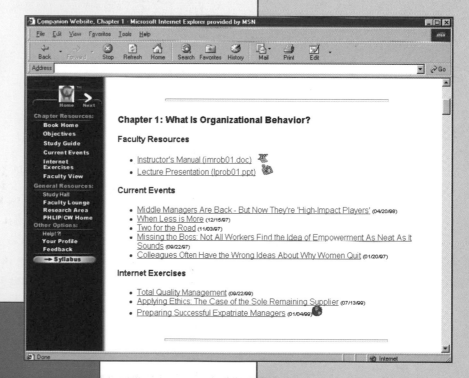

Organizational Behavior

9th Edition

Stephen P. Robbins

San Diego State University

Prentice Hall

Prentice Hall Upper Saddle River, New Jersey 07458

Robbins, Stephen P.
    Organizational behavior/Stephen P. Robbins.—
9th ed.
      p. cm.
    Includes bibliographical references and indexes.
    ISBN 0-13-016680-4
    1. Organizational behavior.   I.   Title.

HD58.7 .R62 2000
658.3   99-049448

Senior Editor: David Shafer
Managing Editor (Editorial): Jennifer Glennon
Editor-in-Chief: Natalie Anderson
Editorial Assistant: Kim Marsden
Assistant Editor: Michele Foresta
Media Project Manager: Michele Faranda
Executive Marketing Manager: Michael Campbell
Associate Managing Editor (Production): Judy Leale
Production Coordinator: Keri Jean
Manufacturing Supervisor: Arnold Vila
Manufacturing Buyer: Diane Peirano
Senior Prepress/Manufacturing Manager: Vincent Scelta
Senior Designer: Cheryl Asherman
Design Manager: Patricia Smythe
Interior Design: Amanda Kavanaugh
Photo Development Editor: Nancy Moudry
Photo Researcher: Melinda Alexander
Cover Design: Laura Ospanik
Senior Print/Media Production Manager: Karen Goldsmith
Composition: UG / GGS Information Services, Inc.

10 9 8 7 6 5 4 3 2 1
ISBN 0-13-016680-4

For my wife, Laura

STEPHEN P. ROBBINS received his Ph.D. from the University of Arizona. He previously worked for the Shell Oil Company and Reynolds Metals Company. Since completing his graduate studies, Dr. Robbins has taught at the University of Nebraska at Omaha, Concordia University in Montreal, the University of Baltimore, Southern Illinois University at Edwardsville, and San Diego State University. Dr. Robbins' research interests have focused on conflict, power, and politics in organizations, as well as the development of effective interpersonal skills. His articles on these and other topics have appeared in such journals as *Business Horizons, the California Management Review, Business and Economic Perspectives, International Management, Management Review, Canadian Personnel and Industrial Relations*, and the *Journal of Management Education*.

In recent years, Dr. Robbins has been spending most of his professional time writing textbooks. In addition to *Organizational Behavior, 9th ed.*, these include *Fundamentals of Management , 3rd ed.*, with David DeCenzo (Prentice Hall, 2001); *Supervision Today!, 3rd ed.*, with David DeCenzo (Prentice Hall, 2001); *Managing Today!, 2nd ed.* (Prentice Hall, 2000); *Management, 6th ed.*, with Mary Coulter (Prentice Hall, 1999), *Human Resource Management, 6th ed.*, with David DeCenzo (Wiley, 1999); *Essentials of Organizational Behavior, 6th ed.* (Prentice Hall, 1999); *Training in InterPersonal Skills, 2nd ed.*, with Phillip Hunsaker (Prentice Hall, 1996); and *Organization Theory, 3rd ed.* (Prentice Hall, 1990). These books are used at more than a thousand U.S. colleges and universities, as well as hundreds of schools throughout Canada, Latin America, Australia, New Zealand, Asia, and Europe.

In Dr. Robbins' "other life," he participates in masters' track competition. Since turning 50 in 1993, he has set numerous indoor and outdoor age-group world sprint records. He has won more than a dozen indoor and outdoor U.S. championships at 60m, 100m, 200m, and 400m, and won five gold medals at World Veteran Championships.

CONTENTS IN BRIEF

CONTENTS

Please note that this icon signals that there is interactive video for the topic discussed in this chapter. The video can be found on the CD-ROM that accompanies this text. For more details, please see Preface pages XXIV and XXV.

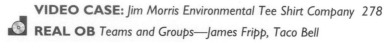

PREFACE

Since its fifth edition, this book has been the number-one-selling organizational behavior (OB) textbook in the United States and worldwide. More than 700,000 students around the globe have studied OB from this text. Part of the book's success, I like to think, has been due to my commitment to keeping it current and relevant to readers. Those were my goals in 1979 with the first edition. Those goals continue to guide me more than 20 years later.

I want to use this preface to highlight those features that adopters continue to tell me they like (and have been retained in this revision), to describe what's new in this ninth edition, to summarize the various supplementary materials that Prentice Hall makes available to complement the text, and to thank those who were involved in making this revision a reality.

Retained from the Previous Edition

- **Writing style.** This book is most often singled out for the writing style. Reviewers and users regularly tell me that it's "conversational," "interesting," "student friendly," and "very clear and understandable." I believe this revision maintains that tradition.
- **Examples, examples, examples.** My teaching experience tells me that students may not remember a concept, but they'll remember an example. Moreover, a good example goes a long way in helping students to better understand a concept. So, as with the previous editions, you'll find this revision packed full of recent real-world examples drawn from a variety of organizations—business and not-for-profit, large and small, and local and international.
- **Comprehensive literature coverage.** Clarity of writing and comprehensive content are often seen as conflicting goals. This book stands as evidence that they needn't be. *Organizational Behavior, Ninth Edition* continues to provide the most complete and up-to-date review of the OB literature.
- **Three-level model of analysis.** Since its first edition, this book has presented OB at three levels of analysis. It begins with individual behavior and then moves to group behavior. Finally, it adds the organization system to capture the full complexity of organizational behavior. Students seem to find this approach logical and straightforward.
- **Integration of globalization, diversity, and ethics.** As seen in Exhibit P-1, the topics of globalization and cross-cultural differences, diversity, and ethics are discussed throughout this book. Rather than presented in stand-alone chapters, they have been woven into the context of relevant issues. I have found that this integrative approach makes these issues more fully part of OB and reinforces their importance.
- **Skill-building emphasis.** "Concepts to Skills" boxes demonstrate the linkage between OB concepts and skill applications. Exercises at the end of each chapter reinforce critical thinking, behavioral-analysis, team-building, and Internet-search skills.
- **Pedagogy.** This edition continues the tradition of providing the most complete assortment of in-text pedagogy available in any OB book. This includes review and critical-thinking questions, point/counterpoint debates,

team exercises, ethical dilemma exercises, Internet search exercises, and case incidents and video cases.

■ **Cutting-edge technology.** This edition expands on the technology initiatives of the previous edition in several ways.

1. Each copy of *OB/9e* includes a free CD-ROM containing video of interviews with real managers dealing with real organizational behavior issues. There are discussion questions and a follow-up with your author, connecting the material in the book to the situation on the CD. Look for the "REAL OB" icon in the book's Contents for easy reference. In addition, there is an Internet connection to the book's Web site <www.prenhall.com/robbins>. Students can access from this Web site an interactive study guide, links to additional OB sites, and up-to-date news articles linked to the text.

2. As with the previous two editions, *OB/9e* is supported by PHLIP— Prentice Hall Learning on the Internet Partnership. This is a faculty-support Web site featuring *Instructor's Manual,* PowerPoint slides, cur-

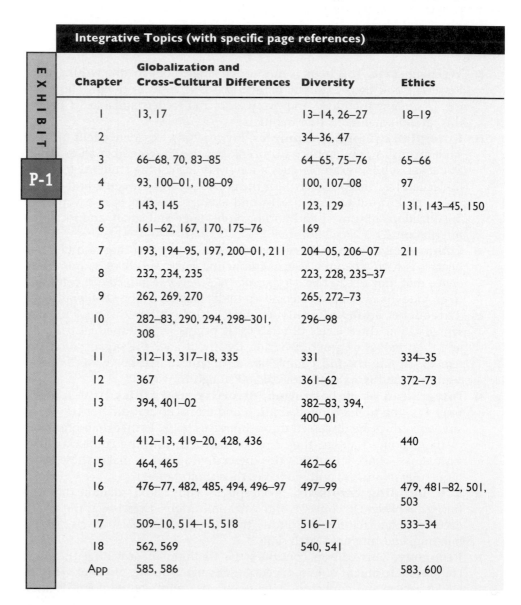

EXHIBIT P-1

Integrative Topics (with specific page references)

Chapter	Globalization and Cross-Cultural Differences	Diversity	Ethics
1	13, 17	13–14, 26–27	18–19
2		34–36, 47	
3	66–68, 70, 83–85	64–65, 75–76	65–66
4	93, 100–01, 108–09	100, 107–08	97
5	143, 145	123, 129	131, 143–45, 150
6	161–62, 167, 170, 175–76	169	
7	193, 194–95, 197, 200–01, 211	204–05, 206–07	211
8	232, 234, 235	223, 228, 235–37	
9	262, 269, 270	265, 272–73	
10	282–83, 290, 294, 298–301, 308	296–98	
11	312–13, 317–18, 335	331	334–35
12	367	361–62	372–73
13	394, 401–02	382–83, 394, 400–01	
14	412–13, 419–20, 428, 436		440
15	464, 465	462–66	
16	476–77, 482, 485, 494, 496–97	497–99	479, 481–82, 501, 503
17	509–10, 514–15, 518	516–17	533–34
18	562, 569	540, 541	
App	585, 586		583, 600

rent news articles, student self-testing materials, and links to related Internet sites.

3. There is also an on-line course for this text. For more information, please contact your local representative, or visit our Web site at <www.prenhall.com/phbusiness>.

4. *The Prentice Hall Self-Assessment Library* (CD-ROM or print version), edited by Stephen P. Robbins, is also available FREE as a value-pack with this text. This product contains 45 self-assessment questionnaires that provide students with insights into their skills, abilities and interests.

New to the Ninth Edition

■ **Contemporary content.** New material on the Hudson Institute's *Workforce 2020* report, organizational citizenship behavior, emotions, trust, virtual teams, team effectiveness, and low- and high-context cultures has been added. Of course, the entire book's research base has been revised and updated for this edition.

I'm most enthusiastic about the new material on emotions introduced in Chapter 4. Anyone who has ever worked in an organization knows that emotions are an intrinsic part of day-to-day life. Yet the topic has been absent from most OB books. The reason has been a lack of substantive research. Fortunately, in the last few years, researchers have discovered emotions as an important OB topic worthy of study. There now exists a rapidly expanding body of research for OB textbook authors to draw upon. And I've done that in this edition. In Chapter 4, you'll find an up-to-date review of the emotions literature as it relates to OB.

■ **"Myth or Science?" boxes.** This new feature presents a commonly accepted "fact" about human behavior, followed by confirming or disproving research evidence. Some examples include "You Can't Teach an Old Dog New Tricks;" "Happy Workers Are Productive Workers;" and "It's Not *What* You Know, It's *Who* You Know." These boxes provide repeated evidence that common sense can lead you astray and that behavioral research offers a means for testing the validity of commonsense notions. These boxes are meant to help you to see how the field of OB, built on a large body of research evidence, can provide valuable insights toward understanding and explaining human behavior at work.

■ **Revised "Point/Counterpoint" dialogues.** Most are new and all have been reduced in length to present more focused arguments.

■ **Internet search exercises.** These exercises are designed to help students learn about resources available on the Internet and to use those resources to answer OB-related questions. For each exercise, students should (a) describe in detail the path they took to develop their answer, including citing their Internet sources and (b) provide their answers to the questions asked. Part (a) reinforces that it's as important to know the paths on the Internet that students take to find an answer as the answer itself.

For students with little or no Internet experience, go to <http://searchenginewatch.internet.com>. This site is a comprehensive source for learning how to navigate around the Internet and how to specifically do Internet searches. For more experienced individuals, we suggest using popular search engines such as AltaVista <www.altavista.com>, Excite <www.excite.com>, Google! <www.google.com>, Lycos

<www.lycos.com>, MetaCrawler <www.metacrawler.com>, and Yahoo! <www.yahoo.com>.

- **Dropped the "Learn about Yourself" exercises.** These exercises are no longer necessary since the *Prentice Hall Self-Assessment Library* is now available *FREE*, in CD-ROM or print format, as a value-pack with this book. Containing 45 self-assessment instruments, the *Self-Assessment Library* does a far better and more comprehensive job of helping students to learn about their skills, abilities, and interests than did these in-text exercises. The *Self-Assessment Library* is organized into three parts: "What About Me?" "Working with Others," and "Life in Organizations." The best part of this tool is that in its CD-ROM format, after each instrument is completed, it is automatically graded and analyzed.

Supplements

This book comes with the most comprehensive and user-friendly supplement package available with any OB text. The following highlights these supplements:

- *Instructor's Manual.* Features teaching tips to accompany boxed text features, critical-thinking exercises, lecture outlines, chapter summaries and much more to help facilitate the teaching process.
- *Test Item File.* Contains a selection of multiple-choice, true/false, scenario-based, and essay exercises of varying lengths.
- **PHLIP–Prentice Hall's Learning on the Internet Partnership.** This content-rich, multidisciplinary business education Web site was created *by* professors *for* professors and their students. PHLIP provides on-line support for faculty and students using *Robbins' Organizational Behavior, Ninth Edition.* Students have access to a student study hall, current events, an interactive study guide, and vital Internet resources. Instructors will find downloadable supplements, on-line faculty support, and a faculty lounge that includes a chat room, a teaching archive, computer tips, and Internet skills.
- *On-line Student Study Guide.* Interactive and exciting! The *On-line Student Study Guide* features multiple-choice, true/false, and Internet-based essay questions that can be scored on-line. Incorrect answers are keyed to the text for student review. There are also numerous links to sites throughout the Internet where additional information on concepts and featured companies can be found.
- **Video package.** This two-video package consists of new part-ending "On Location!" and chapter-ending *Small Business 2000* segments. "On Location!" segments capture live footage of current, relevant companies such as Waterford Crystal, Doc Martin, and Starbucks. *Small Business 2000* segments, aired on PBS, involve interviews of real entrepreneurs and their experiences both creating and maintaining small businesses.
- **Instructor's Resource CD-ROM.** Contains electronic/downloadable versions of the *Instructor's Manual, Test Item File,* and PowerPoint slides.
- **Overhead color transparencies.** Approximately 100 of the most critical PowerPoint slides provided as full-color acetates. To further enhance lectures, teaching notes for each slide are included as a printed, punched, and perforated booklet for insertion into a three-ring binder.
- *Study Guide.* Designed to aid student comprehension of the text, the *Study Guide* contains chapter objectives; detailed chapter outlines; and review, discussion, and study questions.

- ■ ***The Prentice Hall Self-Assessment Library*** **on CD-ROM.** Contains 45 popular questionnaires that give students insight into their skills, abilities, and interests. This CD-ROM can be ordered *free* with the text as a value pack. It also is offered for sale in a stand alone package (ISBN 0-13-021212-1). See your PH sales representative for details.
- ■ **The Robbins'** *OB/9e* **CD-ROM (included free in this book)** Includes video of real managers dealing with real organizational behavior issues in the workplace, discussion questions, and a follow-up by your text's author. Look for the icon in the book's Contents for easy reference.

Acknowledgments

Getting this book into your hands was a team effort. In addition to my contribution, it took faculty reviewers, and a talented group of designers and production specialists, editorial personnel, and marketing and sales staff.

Let me begin my acknowledgments by thanking a number of faculty for providing suggestions on how the last edition could be improved and/or reviewing this revision. This text is an immensely better book because of the comments of the following people: Robert Key, University of Phoenix; William Smith, Emporia State University; Barbara Hassell, Indiana University, Kelly School of Business; Jann Freed, Central College; Stephen Jenner, California State University, Dominguez Hills; and Abigail Hubbard, University of Houston; Melony Mead, University of Phoenix; Philip Roth, Clemson University; and Lehman Benson III, University of Arizona. I also want to single out Professor Lou Marino at the University of Alabama for reviewing, testing, and fine-tuning the Internet Search exercises.

On the design and production side, I want to thank Judy Leale, Cheryl Asherman, Amanda Kavanaugh, Nancy Moudry, and my wife Laura Ospanik. Judy did another superb job of "mothering" this book through the production process. Thanks Judy for putting your heart and soul into this project and for tolerating my continual phone calls and e-mail. Thank you Cheryl for your ideas and support and Amanda for a beautiful interior design, and thanks to Nancy for the terrific photo research. And a very special thanks to my wife Laura, in addition to being the greatest wife in the world, she is also an extremely talented graphic artist. Thanks, honey, for creating this striking cover design.

David Shafer, my editor, again did a masterful job of overseeing the editorial tasks required in a revision. Thanks David for your hard work and support. Along with David, I also want to thank Sandy Steiner, Jim Boyd, Natalie Anderson, Brian Kibby, Jennifer Glennon, Kim Marsden, Michele Faranda, Karen Goldsmith, and Michele Foresta.

Finally, let me thank my marketing manager and the Prentice Hall sales staff for their contribution. To Michael Campbell—let me just say in print what I've told you several times verbally: I sincerely appreciate your continual flow of creative ideas and the enthusiasm you've shown for my projects. And to the terrific PH sales staff, who have been selling my books for more than a quarter of a century: Thank you for the attention you've given this book through its many editions.

Stephen P. Robbins

Stephen P. Robbins

INTRODUCTION

Meet Jason Hershberger (see photo). He got his undergraduate degrees in computer science and geology from the University of Southern California. He earned his M.S. in computer science from USC in 1996 at the age of 23. Since then, Jason has worked for Torrey Science Corporation in San Diego, California. His job encompasses a wide variety of tasks related to the development of modem software. Some of these include designing software, scheduling projects, organizing teams, delegating assignments, providing guidance to team members, and monitoring team results.

"My college course work did an excellent job in helping me become a subject matter expert," says Jason. "But it did very little to help me understand the people factor. I have now learned, through experience, that the primary reason most projects succeed or misfire is due to the people factor. The most difficult part of my job isn't solving technical problems. It's things like handling people with a diverse range of personality characteristics and learning how to communicate with these people. For instance, motivating people to take ownership for their tasks and completing these tasks on schedule has everything to do with my communication skills and very little to do with my technical expertise."

Jason Hershberger has learned what most managers learn very quickly: A large part of the success in any management job is developing good interpersonal or people skills. Lawrence Weinbach, former chief executive at the accounting firm of Arthur Andersen & Co., puts it this way: "Pure technical knowledge is only going to get you to a point. Beyond that, interpersonal skills become critical."[1]

Although practicing managers have long understood the importance of interpersonal skills to managerial effectiveness, business schools were slower to get the message. Until the late 1980s, business school curricula focused almost singularly on the technical aspects of management, empha-

What Is Organizational Behavior?

sizing courses in economics, accounting, finance, and quantitative techniques. Course work in human behavior and people skills received minimal attention relative to the technical aspects of management. Over the past decade, however, business faculty have come to realize the importance that an understanding of human behavior plays in determining a manager's effectiveness, and required courses on people skills have been widely added to the curriculum.

Recognition of the importance of developing managers' interpersonal skills is closely tied to the need for organizations to get and keep high-performing employees. This becomes particularly crucial in a tight labor market.[2] Companies with reputations as a good place to work—such as Hewlett-Packard, Lincoln Electric, Southwest Airlines, and Starbucks—have a big advantage. A recent national study of the U.S. workforce found that wages and fringe benefits aren't the reason people like their jobs or stay with an employer. Far more important is the quality of the employees' jobs and the supportiveness of their work environments.[3] So having managers with good interpersonal skills is likely to make the workplace more pleasant, which, in turn, makes it easier to hire and keep qualified people.

According to the Center for Creative Leadership in Greensboro, North Carolina, about 40 percent of new management hires fail within their first 18 months.[4] When the center looked into *why* these new hires failed, it found that "failure to build good relationships with peers and subordinates" was the culprit an overwhelming 82 percent of the time.[5] Consistent with these findings are surveys that have sought to determine what skills

LEARNING OBJECTIVES

AFTER READING THIS CHAPTER, YOU SHOULD BE ABLE TO

1. Define organizational behavior (OB)
2. Describe what managers do
3. Explain the value of the systematic study of OB
4. List the major challenges and opportunities for managers to use OB concepts
5. Identify the contributions made by major behavioral science disciplines to OB
6. Describe why managers require a knowledge of OB
7. Explain the need for a contingency approach to the study of OB
8. Identify the three levels of analysis in this book's OB model

managers

Individuals who achieve goals through other people.

organization

A consciously coordinated social unit, composed of two or more people, that functions on a relatively continuous basis to achieve a common goal or set of goals.

planning

Includes defining goals, establishing strategy, and developing plans to coordinate activities.

organizing

Determining what tasks are to be done, who is to do them, how the tasks are to be grouped, who reports to whom, and where decisions are to be made.

college recruiters consider most important for job effectiveness of M.B.A. graduates.[6] These surveys consistently identify interpersonal skills as most important.

We have come to understand that technical skills are necessary but insufficient for succeeding in management. In today's increasingly competitive and demanding workplace, managers can't succeed on their technical skills alone. They also have to have good people skills. This book has been written to help both managers and potential managers develop those people skills.

WHAT MANAGERS DO

Let's begin by briefly defining the terms *manager* and the place where managers work—the *organization*. Then let's look at the manager's job; specifically, what do managers do?

Managers get things done through other people. They make decisions, allocate resources, and direct the activities of others to attain goals. Managers do their work in an **organization**. This is a consciously coordinated social unit, composed of two or more people, that functions on a relatively continuous basis to achieve a common goal or set of goals. On the basis of this definition, manufacturing and service firms are organizations and so are schools, hospitals, churches, military units, retail stores, police departments, and local, state, and federal government agencies. The people who oversee the activities of others and who are responsible for attaining goals in these organizations are managers (although they're sometimes called *administrators*, especially in not-for-profit organizations).

MANAGEMENT FUNCTIONS

In the early part of the twentieth century, a French industrialist by the name of Henri Fayol wrote that all managers perform five management functions: They plan, organize, command, coordinate, and control.[7] Today, we have condensed those down to four: planning, organizing, leading, and controlling.

Since organizations exist to achieve goals, someone has to define those goals and the means by which they can be achieved. Management is that someone. The **planning** function encompasses defining an organization's goals, establishing an overall strategy for achieving those goals, and developing a comprehensive hierarchy of plans to integrate and coordinate activities.

Managers are also responsible for designing an organization's structure. We call this function **organizing**. It includes the determination of what tasks are to be done, who is to do them, how the tasks are to be grouped, who reports to whom, and where decisions are to be made.

Every organization contains people, and it is management's job to direct and coordinate those people. This is the **leading** function. When managers motivate employees,

Leading her employees is an important part of Kerren Sargent's job. Sargent (right) owns a Cookies by Design franchise in San Diego. Because her business gets hectic at times, Sargent needs employees who are willing to put in what she calls "a horrendous amount of hours." Good interpersonal skills help Sargent motivate her small staff of 12 employees to satisfy customer demand. Her strong people skills also help her find and keep qualified employees in a tight job market. "I have people who have been with me for four years," she says.

direct the activities of others, select the most effective communication channels, or resolve conflicts among members, they are engaging in leading.

The final function managers perform is **controlling**. To ensure that things are going as they should, management must monitor the organization's performance. Actual performance must be compared with the previously set goals. If there are any significant deviations, it's management's job to get the organization back on track. This monitoring, comparing, and potential correcting is what is meant by the controlling function.

So, using the functional approach, the answer to the question, What do managers do? is that they plan, organize, lead, and control.

MANAGEMENT ROLES

In the late 1960s, a graduate student at MIT, Henry Mintzberg, undertook a careful study of five executives to determine what these managers did on their jobs. On the basis of his observations of these managers, Mintzberg concluded that managers perform 10 different, highly interrelated roles, or sets of behaviors attributable to their jobs.[8] As shown in Exhibit 1–1, these 10 roles can be grouped as being primarily concerned with interpersonal relationships, the transfer of information, and decision making.

Interpersonal Roles All managers are required to perform duties that are ceremonial and symbolic in nature. When the president of a college hands out diplomas at commencement or a factory supervisor gives a group of high school students a tour of the plant, he or she is acting in a *figurehead* role. All managers also have a *leadership* role. This role includes hiring, training, motivating, and disciplining employees. The third role within the interpersonal grouping is the *liaison* role. Mintzberg described this activity as contacting others who provide the manager with information. These may be individuals or groups inside or outside the organization. The sales manager who obtains information from the personnel manager in his or her own company has an internal liaison relationship. When that sales manager has contacts with other sales executives through a marketing trade association, he or she has an outside liaison relationship.

Information Roles All managers, to some degree, collect information from organizations and institutions outside their own. Typically, they get information by reading magazines and talking with other people to learn of changes in the public's tastes, what competitors may be planning, and the like. Mintzberg called this the *monitor* role. Managers also act as a conduit to transmit information to organizational members. This is the *disseminator* role. Managers additionally perform a *spokesperson* role when they represent the organization to outsiders.

Decisional Roles Finally, Mintzberg identified four roles that revolve around the making of choices. In the *entrepreneur* role, managers initiate and oversee new projects that will improve their organization's performance. As *disturbance handlers*, managers take corrective action in response to unforeseen problems. As *resource allocators*, managers are responsible for allocating human, physical, and monetary resources. Last, managers perform a *negotiator* role, in which they discuss issues and bargain with other units to gain advantages for their own unit.

leading

Includes motivating employees, directing others, selecting the most effective communication channels, and resolving conflicts.

controlling

Monitoring activities to ensure they are being accomplished as planned and correcting any significant deviations.

Mintzberg's Managerial Roles

Role	Description	Example
Interpersonal		
Figurehead	Is symbolic head; required to perform a number of routine duties of a legal or social nature	Handles ceremonies, status requests, solicitations
Leader	Is responsible for the motivation and direction of subordinates	Performs virtually all managerial activities involving subordinates
Liaison	Maintains a network of outside contacts who provide favors and information	Acknowledges mail, external board work
Informational		
Monitor	Receives wide variety of information; serves as nerve center of internal and external information of the organization	Handles all mail and contacts categorized as concerned primarily with receiving information
Disseminator	Transmits information received from outsiders or from other subordinates to members of the organization	Forwards mail into organization for informational purposes; makes verbal contacts involving information flow to subordinates such as review sessions
Spokesperson	Transmits information to outsiders on organization's plans, policies, actions, and results; serves as expert on organization's industry	Attends board meetings; handles contacts involving transmission of information to outsiders
Decisional		
Entrepreneur	Searches organization and its environment for opportunities and initiates projects to bring about change	Holds strategy and review sessions involving initiation or design of improvement projects
Disturbance handler	Is responsible for corrective action when organization faces important, unexpected disturbances	Holds strategy and review sessions involving disturbances and crises
Resource allocator	Makes or approves significant organizational decisions	Handles scheduling; requests for authorization; budgeting; the programming of subordinates' work
Negotiator	Is responsible for representing the organization at major negotiations	Handles contract negotiation

EXHIBIT 1-1

MANAGEMENT SKILLS

Still another way of considering what managers do is to look at the skills or competencies they need to successfully achieve their goals. Robert Katz has identified three essential management skills: technical, human, and conceptual.[9]

technical skills

The ability to apply specialized knowledge or expertise.

Technical Skills   **Technical skills** encompass the ability to apply specialized knowledge or expertise. When you think of the skills held by professionals such as civil engineers or oral surgeons, you typically focus on their technical skills.

Through extensive formal education, they have learned the special knowledge and practices of their field. Of course, professionals don't have a monopoly on technical skills, and not all technical skills have to be learned in schools or formal training programs. All jobs require some specialized expertise, and many people develop their technical skills on the job.

Human Skills The ability to work with, understand, and motivate other people, both individually and in groups, describes **human skills**. Many people are technically proficient but interpersonally incompetent. They might be poor listeners, unable to understand the needs of others, or have difficulty managing conflicts. Since managers get things done through other people, they must have good human skills to communicate, motivate, and delegate.

human skills
The ability to work with, understand, and motivate other people, both individually and in groups.

Conceptual Skills Managers must have the mental ability to analyze and diagnose complex situations. These tasks require **conceptual skills**. Decision making, for instance, requires managers to spot problems, identify alternatives that can correct them, evaluate those alternatives, and select the best one. Managers can be technically and interpersonally competent yet still fail because of an inability to rationally process and interpret information.

conceptual skills
The mental ability to analyze and diagnose complex situations.

EFFECTIVE VS. SUCCESSFUL MANAGERIAL ACTIVITIES

Fred Luthans and his associates looked at the issue of what managers do from a somewhat different perspective.[10] They asked the question: Do managers who move up most quickly in an organization do the same activities and with the same emphasis as managers who do the best job? You would tend to think that the managers who were the most effective in their jobs would also be the ones who were promoted fastest. But that's not what appears to happen.

Luthans and his associates studied more than 450 managers. What they found was that these managers all engaged in four managerial activities:

1. *Traditional management.* Decision making, planning, and controlling
2. *Communication.* Exchanging routine information and processing paperwork
3. *Human resource management.* Motivating, disciplining, managing conflict, staffing, and training
4. *Networking.* Socializing, politicking, and interacting with outsiders

The "average" manager in the study spent 32 percent of his or her time in traditional management activities, 29 percent communicating, 20 percent in human resource management activities, and 19 percent networking. However, the amount of time and effort that different managers spent on those four activities varied a great deal. Specifically, as shown in Exhibit 1–2, managers who were *successful* (defined in terms of the speed of promotion within their organization) had a very different emphasis than managers who were *effective* (defined in terms of the quantity and quality of their performance and the satisfaction and commitment of their employees). Among successful managers, networking made the largest relative contribution to success, and human resource management activities made the least relative contribution. Among effective managers, communication made the largest relative contribution and networking the least.

This study adds important insights to our knowledge of what managers do. On average, managers spend approximately 20 to 30 percent of their time on each of the four activities: traditional management, communication, human re-

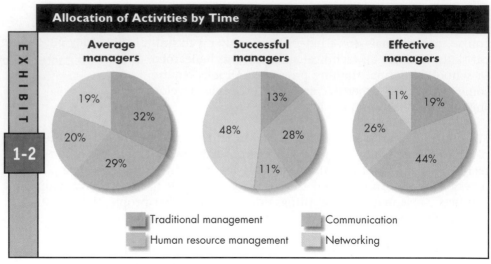

Source: Based on F. Luthans, R. M. Hodgetts and S. A. Rosenkrantz, *Real Managers* (Cambridge, MA: Ballinger, 1988).

source management, and networking. However, successful managers don't give the same emphasis to each of those activities as do effective managers. In fact, their emphases are almost the opposite. This finding challenges the historical assumption that promotions are based on performance, vividly illustrating the importance that social and political skills play in getting ahead in organizations.

A REVIEW OF THE MANAGER'S JOB

One common thread runs through the functions, roles, skills, and activities approaches to management: Each recognizes the paramount importance of managing people. Regardless of whether it's called "the leading function," "interpersonal roles," "human skills," or "human resource management, communication, and networking activities," it's clear that managers need to develop their people skills if they're going to be effective and successful.

ENTER ORGANIZATIONAL BEHAVIOR

We've made the case for the importance of people skills. But neither this book nor the discipline upon which it's based is called People Skills. The term that is widely used to describe the discipline is *Organizational Behavior*.

organizational behavior (OB)

A field of study that investigates the impact that individuals, groups, and structure have on behavior within organizations, for the purpose of applying such knowledge toward improving an organization's effectiveness.

Organizational behavior (often abbreviated as OB) is *a field of study that investigates the impact that individuals, groups, and structure have on behavior within organizations for the purpose of applying such knowledge toward improving an organization's effectiveness.* That's a lot of words, so let's break it down.

Organizational behavior is a field of study. That statement means that it is a distinct area of expertise with a common body of knowledge. What does it study? It studies three determinants of behavior in organizations: individuals, groups, and structure. In addition, OB applies the knowledge gained about individuals, groups, and the effect of structure on behavior in order to make organizations work more effectively.

To sum up our definition, OB is concerned with the study of what people do in an organization and how that behavior affects the performance of the organization. And because OB is specifically concerned with employment-related situa-

tions, you should not be surprised to find that it emphasizes behavior as related to jobs, work, absenteeism, employment turnover, productivity, human performance, and management.

There is increasing agreement as to the components or topics that constitute the subject area of OB. Although there is still considerable debate as to the relative importance of each, there appears to be general agreement that OB includes the core topics of motivation, leader behavior and power, interpersonal communication, group structure and processes, learning, attitude development and perception, change processes, conflict, work design, and work stress.[11]

REPLACING INTUITION WITH SYSTEMATIC STUDY

Each of us is a student of behavior. Since our earliest years, we have watched the actions of others and have attempted to interpret what we see. Whether or not you have explicitly thought about it before, you have been "reading" people almost all your life. You watch what others do and try to explain to yourself why they have engaged in their behavior. In addition, you have attempted to predict what they might do under different sets of conditions. Unfortunately, your casual or commonsense approach to reading others can often lead to erroneous predictions. However, you can improve your predictive ability by replacing your intuitive opinions with a more systematic approach.

The systematic approach used in this book will uncover important facts and relationships and will provide a base from which more accurate predictions of behavior can be made. Underlying this systematic approach is the belief that behavior is not random. It stems from and is directed toward some end that the individual believes, rightly or wrongly, is in his or her best interest.

Behavior generally is predictable if we know how the person perceived the situation and what is important to him or her. While people's behavior may not appear to be rational to an outsider,

What is organizational behavior? It's a field of study that focuses on three levels of behavior in organizations. One level is the individual, such as the Wal-Mart greeter handing out smiley balloons. Another level is the group, such as the three employees of Praxair, a distributor of bottled industrial gases, who meet to discuss their work. The third level is structure, which is depicted here by employees working in cubicles at Bloomberg, a financial media company.

there is reason to believe it usually is intended to be rational and it is seen as rational by them. An observer often sees behavior as nonrational because the observer does not have access to the same information or does not perceive the environment in the same way.[12]

Certainly there are differences between individuals. Placed in similar situations, all people don't act exactly alike. However, there are certain fundamental consistencies underlying the behavior of all individuals that can be identified and then modified to reflect individual differences.

These fundamental consistencies are very important. Why? Because they allow predictability. When you get into your car, you make some definite and usually highly accurate predictions about how other people will behave. In North America, for instance, you would predict that other drivers will stop at stop signs and red lights, drive on the right side of the road, pass on your left, and not cross the solid double line on mountain roads. Notice that your predictions about the behavior of people behind the wheels of their cars are almost always correct. Obviously, the rules of driving make predictions about driving behavior fairly easy.

There are certain fundamental consistencies underlying the behavior of all individuals that can be identified and then modified to reflect individual differences.

What may be less obvious is that there are rules (written and unwritten) in almost every setting. Therefore, it can be argued that it's possible to predict behavior (undoubtedly, not always with 100 percent accuracy) in supermarkets, classrooms, doctors' offices, elevators, and in most structured situations. For instance, do you turn around and face the doors when you get into an elevator? Almost everyone does. But did you ever read that you're supposed to do this? Probably not! Just as I make predictions about automobile drivers (where there are definite rules of the road), I can make predictions about the behavior of people in elevators (where there are few written rules). In a class of 60 students, if you wanted to ask a question of the instructor, I predict that you would raise your hand. Why don't you clap, stand up, raise your leg, cough, or yell "Hey, over here!"? The reason is that you have learned that raising your hand is appropriate behavior in school. These examples support a major contention in this text: Behavior is generally predictable, and the *systematic study* of behavior is a means to making reasonably accurate predictions.

systematic study

Looking at relationships, attempting to attribute causes and effects, and drawing conclusions based on scientific evidence.

intuition

A feeling not necessarily supported by research.

When we use the phrase **systematic study**, we mean looking at relationships, attempting to attribute causes and effects, and basing our conclusions on scientific evidence—that is, on data gathered under controlled conditions and measured and interpreted in a reasonably rigorous manner. (See Appendix B in the back of the book for a basic review of research methods used in studies of organizational behavior.)

Systematic study replaces **intuition**, or those "gut feelings" about "why I do what I do" and "what makes others tick." Of course, a systematic approach does not mean that those things you have come to believe in an unsystematic way are necessarily incorrect. Some of the conclusions we make in this text, based on reasonably substantive research findings, will only support what you always knew was true. But you'll also be exposed to research evidence that runs counter to what you may have thought was common sense. One of the objectives of this text is to encourage you to move away from your intuitive views of behavior toward a systematic analysis, in the belief that such analysis will improve your accuracy in explaining and predicting behavior.

Preconceived Notions vs. Substantive Evidence

Assume you signed up to take an introductory college course in calculus. On the first day of class your instructor asks you to take out a piece of paper and answer the following question: "Why is the sign of the second derivative negative when the first derivative is set equal to zero, if the function is concave from below?" It's unlikely you'd be able to answer that question. Your reply to that instructor would probably be something like, "How am I supposed to know? That's why I'm taking this course!"

Now, change the scenario. You're in an introductory course in organizational behavior. On the first day of class your instructor asks you to write the answer to the following question: "Why aren't employees as motivated at work today as they were 30 years ago?" You might feel a bit of reluctance, but I'd guess you'd begin writing. You'd have no problem coming up with an explanation to this motivation question.

The previous scenarios were meant to demonstrate one of the challenges of teaching a course in OB. You enter an OB course with a lot of *preconceived notions* that you accept as *facts*. You already think you know a lot about human behavior. That's not typically true in calculus, physics, chemistry, or even accounting. So, in contrast to many other disciplines, OB not only introduces you to a comprehensive set of concepts and theories, it has to deal with a lot of commonly accepted "facts" about human behavior and organizations that you've acquired over the years. Some examples might include: "You can't teach an old dog new tricks," "happy workers are productive workers," "two heads are better than one," and "it's not what you know, it's who you know." But these "facts" aren't necessarily true. So one of the objectives of a course in organizational behavior is to *replace* popularly held notions, often accepted without question, with science-based conclusions.

As you'll see in this book, the field of OB is built on decades of research. This research provides a body of substantive evidence that is able to replace preconceived notions. Throughout this book, we've included boxes entitled "Myth or Science?"[13] They call your attention to some of the more popular notions or myths about organizational behavior. We use the boxes to show how OB research has disproved them or, in some cases, shown them to be true. Hopefully you'll find these boxes interesting. But more importantly, they'll help remind you that the study of human behavior at work is a science and that you need to be vigilant to "seat of the pants" explanations of work-related behaviors.

CONTRIBUTING DISCIPLINES TO THE OB FIELD

Organizational behavior is an applied behavioral science that is built upon contributions from a number of behavioral disciplines. The predominant areas are psychology, sociology, social psychology, anthropology, and political science. As we shall learn, psychology's contributions have been mainly at the individual or micro level of analysis, while the other four disciplines have contributed to our understanding of macro concepts such as group processes and organization. Exhibit 1–3 overviews the major contributions to the study of organizational behavior.

PSYCHOLOGY

Psychology is the science that seeks to measure, explain, and sometimes change the behavior of humans and other animals. Psychologists concern themselves with studying and attempting to understand individual behavior. Those who have contributed and continue to add to the knowledge of OB are learning theorists, per-

psychology

The science that seeks to measure, explain, and sometimes change the behavior of humans and other animals.

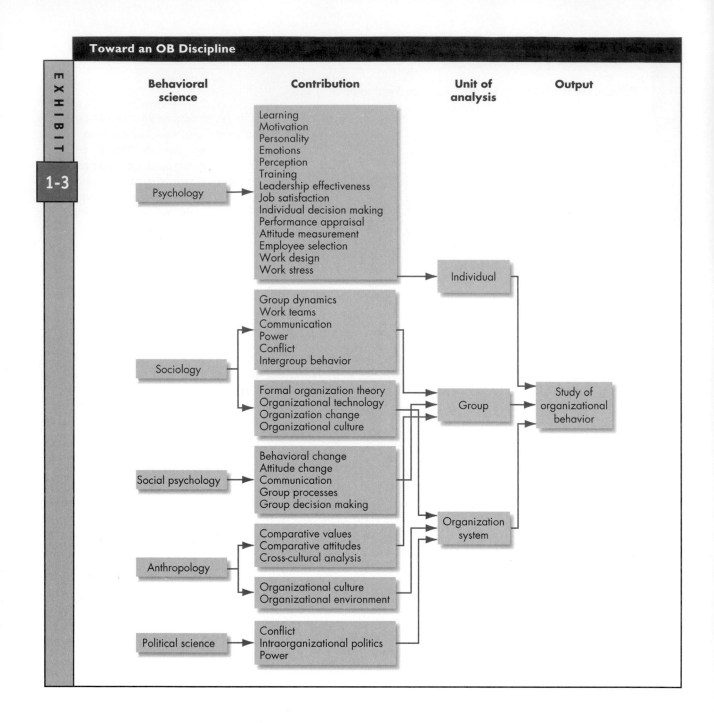

EXHIBIT 1-3

Behavioral science | Contribution | Unit of analysis | Output

Psychology →
Learning
Motivation
Personality
Emotions
Perception
Training
Leadership effectiveness
Job satisfaction
Individual decision making
Performance appraisal
Attitude measurement
Employee selection
Work design
Work stress
→ Individual

Sociology →
Group dynamics
Work teams
Communication
Power
Conflict
Intergroup behavior

Formal organization theory
Organizational technology
Organization change
Organizational culture
→ Group

Social psychology →
Behavioral change
Attitude change
Communication
Group processes
Group decision making

Anthropology →
Comparative values
Comparative attitudes
Cross-cultural analysis

Organizational culture
Organizational environment
→ Organization system

Political science →
Conflict
Intraorganizational politics
Power

→ Study of organizational behavior

sonality theorists, counseling psychologists, and, most important, industrial and organizational psychologists.

Early industrial and organizational psychologists concerned themselves with problems of fatigue, boredom, and other factors relevant to working conditions that could impede efficient work performance. More recently, their contributions have been expanded to include learning, perception, personality, emotions, training, leadership effectiveness, needs and motivational forces, job satisfaction, decision-making processes, performance appraisals, attitude measurement, employee selection techniques, work design, and job stress.

SOCIOLOGY

Whereas psychologists focus their attention on the individual, sociologists study the social system in which individuals fill their roles; that is, **sociology** studies people in relation to their fellow human beings. Specifically, sociologists have made their greatest contribution to OB through their study of group behavior in organizations, particularly formal and complex organizations. Some of the areas within OB that have received valuable input from sociologists are group dynamics, design of work teams, organizational culture, formal organization theory and structure, organizational technology, communications, power, and conflict.

sociology

The study of people in relation to their fellow human beings.

SOCIAL PSYCHOLOGY

Social psychology is an area within psychology, blending concepts from both psychology and sociology. It focuses on the influence of people on one another. One of the major areas receiving considerable investigation from social psychologists has been *change*—how to implement it and how to reduce barriers to its acceptance. Additionally, we find social psychologists making significant contributions in the areas of measuring, understanding, and changing attitudes; communication patterns; the ways in which group activities can satisfy individual needs; and group decision-making processes.

social psychology

An area within psychology that blends concepts from psychology and sociology and that focuses on the influence of people on one another.

ANTHROPOLOGY

Anthropology is the study of societies to learn about human beings and their activities. Anthropologists' work on cultures and environments, for instance, has helped us understand differences in fundamental values, attitudes, and behavior among people in different countries and within different organizations. Much of our current understanding of organizational culture, organizational environ-

anthropology

The study of societies to learn about human beings and their activities.

ments, and differences among national cultures is the result of the work of anthropologists or those using their methodologies.

POLITICAL SCIENCE

political science

The study of the behavior of individuals and groups within a political environment.

Although frequently overlooked, the contributions of political scientists are significant to the understanding of behavior in organizations. **Political science** studies the behavior of individuals and groups within a political environment. Specific topics of concern here include structuring of conflict, allocation of power, and how people manipulate power for individual self-interest.

THERE ARE FEW ABSOLUTES IN OB

There are few, if any, simple and universal principles that explain organizational behavior. There are laws in the physical sciences—chemistry, astronomy, physics—that are consistent and apply in a wide range of situations. They allow

[*"God gave all the easy problems to the physicists."*]

scientists to generalize about the pull of gravity or to confidently send astronauts into space to repair satellites. But as one noted behavioral researcher aptly concluded, "God gave all the easy problems to the physicists." Human beings are complex. Because they are not alike, our ability to make simple, accurate, and sweeping generalizations is limited. Two people often act very differently in the same situation, and the same person's behavior changes in different situations. For instance, not everyone is motivated by money, and you behave differently at church on Sunday than you did at the beer party the night before.

That doesn't mean, of course, that we can't offer reasonably accurate explanations of human behavior or make valid predictions. It does mean, however, that OB concepts must reflect situational, or contingency, conditions. We can say that *x* leads to *y*, but only under conditions specified in *z* (the **contingency variables**). The science of OB has developed by using general concepts and then altering their application to the particular situation. So, for example, OB scholars would avoid stating that effective leaders should always seek the ideas of their followers before making a decision. Rather, we shall find that in some situations a participative style is clearly superior, but, in other situations, an autocratic decision style is more effective. In other words, the effectiveness of a particular leadership style is contingent upon the situation in which it is used.

contingency variables

Situational factors; variables that moderate the relationship between two or more other variables and improve the correlation.

As you proceed through this text, you'll encounter a wealth of research-based theories about how people behave in organizations. But don't expect to find a lot of straightforward cause-and-effect relationships. There aren't many! Organizational behavior theories mirror the subject matter with which they deal. People are complex and complicated, and so too must be the theories developed to explain their actions.

CHALLENGES AND OPPORTUNITIES FOR OB

Understanding organizational behavior has never been more important for managers. A quick look at a few of the dramatic changes now taking place in organizations supports this claim. For instance, the typical employee is getting older; more and more women and nonwhites are in the workplace; corporate downsizing and the heavy use of temporary workers are severing the bonds of loyalty that historically tied many employees to their employers; and global competition is requiring employees to become more flexible and to learn to cope with rapid change.

In short, there are a lot of challenges and opportunities today for managers to use OB concepts. In this section, we review some of the more critical issues confronting managers for which OB offers solutions—or at least some meaningful insights toward solutions.

RESPONDING TO GLOBALIZATION

Organizations are no longer constrained by national borders. Burger King is owned by a British firm, and McDonald's sells hamburgers in Moscow. Exxon, a so-called American company, receives almost 75 percent of its revenues from sales outside the United States. Toyota makes cars in Kentucky; General Motors makes cars in Brazil; and Ford (which owns part of Mazda) transfers executives from Detroit to Japan to help Mazda manage its operations. These examples illustrate that the world has become a global village. In turn, managers have to become capable of working with people from different cultures.

Globalization affects a manager's people skills in at least two ways. First, if you're a manager, you're increasingly likely to find yourself in a foreign assignment. You may be transferred to your employer's operating division or subsidiary in another country. Once there, you'll have to manage a workforce that is likely to be very different in needs, aspirations, and attitudes from the ones you were used to back home. Second, even in your own country, you're going to find yourself working with bosses, peers, and other employees who were born and raised in different cultures. What motivates you may not motivate them. Your style of communication may be straightforward and open, but they may find this style uncomfortable and threatening. To work effectively with these people, you'll need to understand their culture, how it has shaped them, and how to adapt your management style to their differences. As we discuss OB concepts throughout this book, we'll frequently address how cultural differences might require managers to modify their practices.

MANAGING WORKFORCE DIVERSITY

One of the most important and broad-based challenges currently facing organizations is adapting to people who are different. The term we use for describing this challenge is *workforce diversity*. Whereas globalization focuses on differences among people *from* different countries, workforce diversity addresses differences among people *within* given countries.

Workforce diversity means that organizations are becoming more heterogeneous in terms of gender, race, and ethnicity. But the term encompasses anyone who varies from the so-called norm. In addition to the more obvious groups—women, African Americans, Hispanic Americans, Asian Americans—it also includes the physically disabled, gays and lesbians, and the elderly. Moreover, it's an issue in Canada, Australia, South Africa, Japan, and Europe as well as the United States. Managers in Canada and Australia, for instance, are having to adjust to large influxes of Asian workers. The "new" South Africa will increasingly be characterized by blacks holding important technical and managerial jobs. Women, long confined to low-paying temporary jobs in Japan, are moving into managerial positions. And the creation of the European Union cooperative trade arrangement, which opened up borders throughout much of western Europe, has increased workforce diversity in organizations that operate in countries such as Germany, Portugal, Italy, and France.

We used to take a melting-pot approach to differences in organizations, assuming people who were different would somehow automatically want to assimilate. But

workforce diversity

The increasing heterogeneity of organizations with the inclusion of different groups.

Mike Baldwin (center), CEO of Texas-based Virtual Solutions, and his managers accommodate the needs of the company's diverse employees, about half of whom come from outside the United States. Baldwin assigns mentors to new employees to help them adjust to U.S. culture such as understanding American slang. He sponsors international events featuring ethnic potlucks so employees can learn about the cultures of other employees. Baldwin liberalized his firm's vacation policy so employees could travel to their countries during holidays. Effectively managing diversity helps Baldwin retain his highly skilled workers who design and write custom database software.

we now recognize that employees don't set aside their cultural values and lifestyle preferences when they come to work. The challenge for organizations, therefore, is to make themselves more accommodating to diverse groups of people by addressing their different lifestyles, family needs, and work styles. The melting-pot assumption is being replaced by one that recognizes and values differences.[14]

Haven't organizations always included members of diverse groups? Yes, but they were a small percentage of the workforce and were, for the most part, ignored by large organizations. Moreover, it was assumed that these minorities would seek to blend in and assimilate. For instance, most members of the U.S. workforce prior to 1980 were male Caucasians working full-time to support a nonemployed wife and school-aged children. Now such employees are the true minority! Currently, 46 percent of the U.S. labor force are women. Minorities and immigrants make up 23 percent.[15] As a case in point, Hewlett-Packard's workforce is 19 percent minorities and 40 percent women.[16] A Digital Equipment Corporation plant in Boston provides a partial preview of the future. The factory's 350 employees include men and women from 44 countries who speak 19 languages. When plant management issues written announcements, they are printed in English, Chinese, French, Spanish, Portuguese, Vietnamese, and Haitian Creole.

Workforce diversity has important implications for management practice. Managers will need to shift their philosophy from treating everyone alike to recognizing differences and responding to those differences in ways that will ensure employee retention and greater productivity while, at the same time, not discriminating. This shift includes, for instance, providing diversity training and revamping benefit programs to make them more "family friendly." Diversity, if positively managed, can increase creativity and innovation in organizations as well as improve decision making by providing different perspectives on problems.[17] When diversity is not managed properly, there is potential for higher turnover, more difficult communication, and more interpersonal conflicts.

IMPROVING QUALITY AND PRODUCTIVITY

William French manages in a tough business. He's director of manufacturing at Alcatel Network Systems' plant in Raleigh, North Carolina.[18] The plant makes broadband telecommunication and data network products, and those products face a multitude of aggressive competitors. To survive, French has had to cut fat, increase productivity, and improve quality. And he's succeeded. From 1993 to 1997, he cut the cycle time for a typical product by 75 percent, reduced in-plant defects by 40 percent, and drastically increased employee productivity. By using self-directed work teams, streamlining processes, and implementing continuous improvement programs, this Alcatel plant is now a model of manufacturing efficiency.

More and more managers are confronting the challenges that William French is facing. They are having to improve their organization's productivity and the quality of the products and services they offer. Toward the goal of improving quality and productivity, they are implementing programs such as total quality management and reengineering—programs that require extensive employee involvement.

As Exhibit 1-5 describes, **total quality management (TQM)** is a philosophy of management that is driven by the constant attainment of customer satisfaction through the continuous improvement of all organizational processes.[19] TQM has implications for OB because it requires employees to rethink what they do and become more involved in workplace decisions.

In times of rapid and dramatic change, it's sometimes necessary to approach improving quality and productivity from the perspective of "How would we do things around here if we were starting over from scratch?" That, in essence, is the approach of **reengineering**. It asks managers to reconsider how work would be done and their organization structured if they were starting over.[20] To illustrate the concept of reengineering, consider a manufacturer of roller skates in the 1960s. His product was essentially a shoe with wheels beneath it. The typical roller skate was a leather boot with shoelaces, attached to a steel platform that held four wooden wheels. If our manufacturer took a continuous improvement approach to change, he would look for small incremental improvements that he could introduce in his product. For instance, he might consider adding hooks to the upper part of the boot for speed lacing; or changing the weight of leather used for improved comfort; or using different ball bearings to make the wheels spin more smoothly. Now most of us are familiar with in-line skates. They represent a reengineering approach to roller skates. The goal was to come up with a skating device that could improve skating speed, mobility, and control. Roller blades fulfilled those goals in a completely different type of shoe. The upper was made of injected plastic, made popular in skiing. Laces were replaced by easy-close clamps. And the four wooden wheels, set in pairs of two, were replaced by four to six in-line plastic wheels. The reengineered result, which didn't look

total quality management (TQM)

A philosophy of management that is driven by the constant attainment of customer satisfaction through the continuous improvement of all organizational processes.

reengineering

Reconsiders how work would be done and the organization structured if they were being created from scratch.

What Is Total Quality Management?

1. *Intense focus on the customer.* The customer includes not only outsiders who buy the organization's products or services but also internal customers (such as shipping or accounts payable personnel) who interact with and serve others in the organization.
2. *Concern for continuous improvement.* TQM is a commitment to never being satisfied. "Very good" is not good enough. Quality can always be improved.
3. *Improvement in the quality of everything the organization does.* TQM uses a very broad definition of quality. It relates not only to the final product but also to how the organization handles deliveries, how rapidly it responds to complaints, how politely the phones are answered, and the like.
4. *Accurate measurement.* TQM uses statistical techniques to measure every critical performance variable in the organization's operations. These performance variables are then compared against standards or benchmarks to identify problems, the problems are traced to their roots, and the causes are eliminated.
5. *Empowerment of employees.* TQM involves the people on the line in the improvement process. Teams are widely used in TQM programs as empowerment vehicles for finding and solving problems.

EXHIBIT 1-5

much like the traditional roller skate, proved universally superior. The rest, of course, is history. In-line skates have revolutionized the roller skate business.

Contemporary managers understand that, for any effort to improve quality and productivity to succeed, it must include their employees. These employees will not only be a major force in carrying out changes but increasingly will participate actively in planning them. OB offers important insights into helping managers work through those changes.

IMPROVING PEOPLE SKILLS

We opened this chapter by demonstrating how important people skills are to managerial effectiveness. We said that "this book has been written to help managers, and potential managers, develop those people skills."

As you proceed through this text, we'll present relevant concepts and theories that can help you explain and predict the behavior of people at work. In addition, you'll also gain insights into specific people skills that you can use on the job. For instance, you'll learn a variety of ways to motivate people, how to be a better communicator, and how to create more effective teams.

EMPOWERING PEOPLE

If you pick up any popular business periodical nowadays, you'll read about the reshaping of the relationship between managers and those they're supposedly responsible for managing. You'll find managers being called coaches, advisers, sponsors, or facilitators. In many organizations, employees are now called associates. And there's a blurring between the roles of managers and workers.[21] Decision making is being pushed down to the operating level, where workers are being given the freedom to make choices about schedules and procedures and to solve work-related problems. In the 1980s, managers were encouraged to get their employees to participate in work-related decisions. Now, managers are going considerably further by allowing employees full control of their work. An increasing number of organizations are using self-managed teams, where workers operate largely without bosses.

Empowering employees

Putting employees in charge of what they do.

What's going on? What's going on is that managers are **empowering employees**. They are putting employees in charge of what they do. And in so doing, managers are having to learn how to give up control, and employees are having to learn how to take responsibility for their work and make appropriate decisions. In later chapters, we'll show how empowerment is changing leadership styles, power relationships, the way work is designed, and the way organizations are structured.

COPING WITH "TEMPORARINESS"

Managers have always been concerned with change. What's different nowadays is the length of time between changes. It used to be that managers needed to introduce major change programs once or twice a decade. Today, change is an ongoing activity for most managers. The concept of continuous improvement, for instance, implies constant change.

Managing today is more accurately described as long periods of ongoing change, interrupted occasionally by short periods of stability!

In the past, managing could be characterized by long periods of stability, interrupted occasionally by short periods of change. Managing today would be more accurately described as long periods of ongoing change, interrupted occasionally by short periods of stability! The world that most managers and employees face today is one of permanent temporariness. The actual jobs that workers perform are in a permanent state of flux, so workers need to continually update their knowledge and skills to perform new job requirements.[22] For example, production employees at companies such as Caterpillar, Daimler-

Matsushita's New "Temp" Workers

Japanese companies have long offered their employees lifetime jobs. While that still remains the norm, there are signs that the powerful chains that have permanently linked Japanese employees to their employers may be breaking.

Japan prides itself on its lifetime employment practices. It is the backbone of the industrial complex that made Japan a global economic power. It provides companies with incredibly loyal employees, who readily sublimate their self-interests for the long-term interests of their company. However, this system is making it increasingly difficult for Japanese companies to be flexible and respond to changes in global markets.

Matsushita, one of the world's largest electronics companies that markets its products under the Panasonic and National names, is leading the way in creating new options for its white-collar employees. Until recently, like most other large Japanese companies,

Matsushita offered such employees a single benefits package that assumed they would spend their entire working life at the company. But seeking to increase the company's flexibility, and recognizing that younger workers have become more interested in mobility, Matsushita now offers new employees three options. "We want to give more opportunities to our employees to select their course," says the managing director of personnel at Matsushita. "We accept that some will seek work later outside the company, but that's the reality of the changes in Japanese business and in Japanese society."

The company continues to provide a traditional reward package designed for those planning on spending their entire career with Matsushita. When these employees reach the retirement age of 60, they receive a large lump sum. Along the way, they get a bonus twice a year—paid on seniority, not merit—and can participate in programs for housing loans and other company-sponsored investment benefits.

Two new options are called Plan A and Plan B. For employees who have special skills and don't expect to stay for long, there is Plan A. It includes a higher base salary, the opportunity to take advances on their pensions, and bonuses tied to performance rather than seniority. Another feature of this plan is that it allows employees to manage their own pension funds rather than accept a fixed rate of return from Matsushita. Plan B is designed for those who want more flexibility than the traditional plan but less than Plan A.

Changes come slowly in Japan and at Matsushita. Not surprisingly, given Japanese culture, most new Matsushita recruits are opting for the traditional system. Only 8 percent of the 814 new employees hired in spring 1998 selected Plan A. But 31 percent chose Plan B. For Masushita, it's a start at getting employees to lessen their dependence on the company and take a major step toward managing their own careers.

Source: Based on S. Strom, "Japan's New 'Temp' Workers," *New York Times*, June 17, 1998, p. C1.

Chrysler, and Reynolds Metals now need to know how to operate computerized production equipment. That was not part of their job description 20 years ago. Work groups are also increasingly in a state of flux. In the past, employees were assigned to a specific work group, and that assignment was relatively permanent. There was a considerable amount of security in working with the same people day in and day out. That predictability has been replaced by temporary work groups, teams that include members from different departments and whose members change all the time, and the increased use of employee rotation to fill constantly changing work assignments. Finally, organizations themselves are in a state of flux. They continually reorganize their various divisions, sell off poor-performing businesses, downsize operations, subcontract noncritical services and operations to other organizations, and replace permanent employees with temporaries.[23]

Today's managers and employees must learn to cope with temporariness. They have to learn to live with flexibility, spontaneity, and unpredictability. The study of OB can provide important insights into helping you better understand a work world of continual change, how to overcome resistance to change, and how best to create an organizational culture that thrives on change.

STIMULATING INNOVATION AND CHANGE

Whatever happened to W. T. Grant, Woolworth, Gimbel's, and Eastern Airlines? All these giants went bust! Why have other giants, such as Sears, Boeing, and Digital Equipment, implemented huge cost-cutting programs and eliminated thousands of jobs? To avoid going bust!

Today's successful organizations must foster innovation and master the art of change or they'll become candidates for extinction. Victory will go to those organizations that maintain their flexibility, continually improve their quality, and beat their competition to the marketplace with a constant stream of innovative products and services.

Domino's single-handedly brought on the demise of thousands of small pizza parlors whose managers thought they could continue doing what they had been doing for years. Amazon.com is putting a lot of independent bookstores out of business as it proves you can successfully sell books from an Internet Web site. Fox Television has successfully stolen a major portion of the under-25 viewing audience from its much larger network rivals through innovative programming including *The Simpsons*, *Beverly Hills 90210*, and *Melrose Place*.

By encouraging employees to "Think Big," marketing managers Michael Collins and Tim Hill are stimulating innovation and change at SAGA Software. Collins and Hill were hired as change agents to turn around the struggling company that distributed little-known mainframe software and whose employees were content with the status quo. Their job was to increase sales and create a new identity for SAGA. The duo has turned SAGA into a major software player by forming an efficient marketing structure, hiring creative and enthusiastic employees to promote the brand, and developing new products. The results: sales have increased 30 percent since Collins and Hill's arrival.

An organization's employees can be the impetus for innovation and change or they can be a major stumbling block. The challenge for managers is to stimulate employee creativity and tolerance for change. The field of OB provides a wealth of ideas and techniques to aid in realizing these goals.

IMPROVING ETHICAL BEHAVIOR

In an organizational world characterized by cutbacks, expectations of increasing worker productivity, and tough competition in the marketplace, it's not altogether surprising that many employees feel pressured to cut corners, break rules, and engage in other forms of questionable practices.

ethical dilemma

Situation in which an individual is required to define right and wrong conduct.

Members of organizations are increasingly finding themselves facing **ethical dilemmas**, situations in which they are required to define right and wrong conduct.[24] For example, should they "blow the whistle" if they uncover illegal activities taking place in their company? Should they follow orders with which they don't personally agree? Do they give an inflated performance evaluation to an employee whom they like, knowing that such an evaluation could save that employee's job? Do they allow themselves to "play politics" in the organization if it will help their career advancement?

What constitutes good ethical behavior has never been clearly defined. And, in recent years, the line differentiating right from wrong has become even more blurred. Employees see people all around them engaging in unethical practices—elected officials are indicted for padding their expense accounts or taking bribes; high-powered lawyers, who know the rules, are found to be avoiding payment of Social Security taxes for their household help; successful executives use insider information for personal financial gain; employees in other companies participate in massive cover-ups of defective military weapons. They hear these people, when caught, giving excuses such as "everyone does it," or "you have to seize every advantage nowadays," or "I never thought I'd get caught."

Managers and their organizations are responding to this problem from a number of directions.[25] They're writing and distributing codes of ethics to guide employees through ethical dilemmas. They're offering seminars, workshops, and similar training programs to try to improve ethical behaviors. They're providing in-house advisers who can be contacted, in many cases anonymously, for assistance in dealing with ethical issues. And they're creating protection mechanisms for employees who reveal internal unethical practices.

Today's manager needs to create an ethically healthy climate for his or her employees, where they can do their work productively and confront a minimal degree of ambiguity regarding what constitutes right and wrong behaviors. In upcoming chapters, we'll discuss the kinds of actions managers can take to create an ethically healthy climate and to help employees sort through ethically ambiguous situations.

COMING ATTRACTIONS: DEVELOPING AN OB MODEL

We conclude this chapter by presenting a general model that defines the field of OB, stakes out its parameters, and identifies its primary dependent and independent variables. The end result will be a "coming attraction" of the topics making up the remainder of this book.

AN OVERVIEW

A **model** is an abstraction of reality, a simplified representation of some real-world phenomenon. A mannequin in a retail store is a model. So, too, is the accountant's formula: Assets = Liabilities + Owners' Equity. Exhibit 1-6 presents the skeleton on which we will construct our OB model. It proposes that there are three levels of analysis in OB and that, as we move from the individual level to the organization systems level, we add systematically to our understanding of behavior in organizations. The three basic levels are analogous to building blocks; each level is constructed upon the previous level. Group concepts grow out of the foundation laid in the individual section; we overlay structural constraints on the individual and group in order to arrive at organizational behavior.

model

Abstraction of reality; simplified representation of some real-world phenomenon.

dependent variable

A response that is affected by an independent variable.

THE DEPENDENT VARIABLES

Dependent variables are the key factors that you want to explain or predict and that are affected by some other factor. What are the primary dependent variables in OB? Scholars have historically tended to emphasize productivity, absenteeism, turnover, and job satisfaction. More recently, a fifth variable—organizational citizenship— has been added to this list. Let's briefly review each of these variables to ensure that we understand what they mean and why they've achieved their level of distinction.

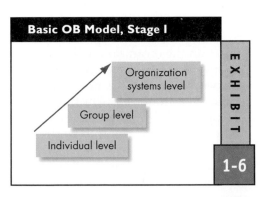

Basic OB Model, Stage I

Organization systems level

Group level

Individual level

EXHIBIT

1-6

productivity

A performance measure including effectiveness and efficiency.

effectiveness

Achievement of goals.

efficiency

The ratio of effective output to the input required to achieve it.

Productivity An organization is productive if it achieves its goals and does so by transferring inputs to outputs at the lowest cost. As such, **productivity** implies a concern for both **effectiveness** and **efficiency**.

A hospital, for example, is *effective* when it successfully meets the needs of its clientele. It is *efficient* when it can do so at a low cost. If a hospital manages to achieve higher output from its present staff by reducing the average number of days a patient is confined to a bed or by increasing the number of staff–patient contacts per day, we say that the hospital has gained productive efficiency. A business firm is effective when it attains its sales or market share goals, but its productivity also depends on achieving those goals efficiently. Popular measures of organizational efficiency include return on investment, profit per dollar of sales, and output per hour of labor.

We can also look at productivity from the perspective of the individual employee. Take the cases of Mike and Al, who are both long-distance truckers. If Mike is supposed to haul his fully loaded rig from New York to its destination in Los Angeles in 75 hours or less, he is effective if he makes the 3,000-mile trip within that time period. But measures of productivity must take into account the costs incurred in reaching the goal. That's where efficiency comes in. Let's assume that Mike made the New York to Los Angeles run in 68 hours and averaged 7 miles per gallon. Al, on the other hand, made the trip in 68 hours also but averaged 9 miles per gallon (rigs and loads are identical). Both Mike and Al were effective—they accomplished their goal—but Al was more efficient than Mike because his rig consumed less gas and, therefore, he achieved his goal at a lower cost.

In summary, one of OB's major concerns is productivity. We want to know what factors will influence the effectiveness and efficiency of individuals, of groups, and of the overall organization.

absenteeism

Failure to report to work.

Absenteeism **Absenteeism** is the failure to report to work. Its annual cost has been estimated at over $40 billion for U.S. organizations and $12 billion for Canadian firms.[26] In Germany, absences cost industrial firms more than 60 billion Deutschmarks (U.S.$35.5 billion) each year.[27] At the job level, a one-day absence by a clerical worker can cost a U.S. employer up to $100 in reduced efficiency and increased supervisory workload.[28] These figures indicate the importance to an organization of keeping absenteeism low.

It's obviously difficult for an organization to operate smoothly and to attain its objectives if employees fail to report to their jobs. The work flow is disrupted, and often important decisions must be delayed. In organizations that rely heavily upon assembly-line production, absenteeism can be considerably more than a disruption; it can result in a drastic reduction in quality of output, and, in some cases, it can bring about a complete shutdown of the production facility. But levels of absenteeism beyond the normal range in any organization have a direct impact on that organization's effectiveness and efficiency.

Are *all* absences bad? Probably not! Although most absences have a negative impact on the organization, we can conceive of situations in which the organization may benefit by an employee's voluntarily choosing not to come to work. For instance, illness, fatigue, or excess stress can significantly decrease an employee's productivity. In jobs in which an employee needs to be alert—surgeons and airline pilots are obvious examples—it may well be better for the organization if the employee does not report to work rather than show up and perform poorly. The cost of an accident in such jobs could be prohibitive. Even in managerial jobs, where mistakes are less spectacular, performance may be improved when managers absent themselves from work rather than make a poor decision under stress. But these examples are clearly atypical. For the most part, we can assume that organizations benefit when employee absenteeism is low.

Turnover **Turnover** is the voluntary and involuntary permanent withdrawal from an organization. A high turnover rate results in increased recruiting, selection, and training costs. What are those costs? A conservative estimate would be about $15,000 per employee.[29] A high rate of turnover can also disrupt the efficient running of an organization when knowledgeable and experienced personnel leave and replacements must be found and prepared to assume positions of responsibility.

All organizations, of course, have some turnover. In fact, if the "right" people are leaving the organization—the marginal and submarginal employees—turnover can be positive. It may create the opportunity to replace an underperforming individual with someone who has higher skills or motivation, open up increased opportunities for promotions, and add new and fresh ideas to the organization.[30] In today's changing world of work, reasonable levels of employee-initiated turnover facilitate organizational flexibility and employee independence, and they can lessen the need for management-initiated layoffs.

But turnover often involves the loss of people the organization doesn't want to lose. For instance, one study covering 900 employees who had resigned their jobs found that 92 percent earned performance ratings of "satisfactory" or better from their superiors.[31] So when turnover is excessive, or when it involves valuable performers, it can be a disruptive factor, hindering the organization's effectiveness.

Organizational Citizenship **Organizational citizenship** is discretionary behavior that is not part of an employee's formal job requirements, but that nevertheless promotes the effective functioning of the organization.[32]

Successful organizations need employees who will do more than their usual job duties and provide performance that is *beyond* expectations. In today's dynamic workplace, where tasks are increasingly done in teams and where flexibility is critical, organizations need employees who'll engage in "good citizenship" behaviors such as making constructive statements about their work group and the organization, helping others on their team, volunteering for extra job activities, avoiding unnecessary conflicts, showing care for organizational property, respecting the spirit as well as the letter of rules and regulations, and gracefully tolerating the occasional work-related impositions and nuisances.

Organizations want and need employees who will do those things that aren't in any job description. And the evidence indicates that those organizations that have such employees outperform those that don't.[33] As a result, OB is concerned with organizational citizenship behavior (OCB) as a dependent variable.

Job satisfaction The final dependent variable we will look at is **job satisfaction**, which we define simply, at this point, as the difference between the amount of rewards workers receive and the amount they believe they should receive. (We expand considerably on that definition in Chapter 3.) Unlike the previous four variables, job satisfaction represents an attitude rather than a behavior. Why, then, has it become a primary dependent variable? For two reasons: its demonstrated relationship to performance factors and the value preferences held by many OB researchers.

The belief that satisfied employees are more productive than dissatisfied employees has been a basic tenet among managers for years. Although

turnover

Voluntary and involuntary permanent withdrawal from the organization.

organizational citizenship

Discretionary behavior that is not part of an employee's formal job requirements but that nevertheless promotes the effective functioning of the organization.

"This is a company that understands that positive emotions can be good for the soul," says Gloria Mayfield Banks, a senior sales director at Mary Kay Cosmetics. Job satisfaction is high at Mary Kay, where rewards like constant praise from co-workers and a generous profit-sharing plan fulfill employees' desires for both quality and quantity of life. Highly satisfied workers is one reason that Mary Kay Cosmetics ranks as one of America's best employers.

job satisfaction

A general attitude toward one's job; the difference between the amount of rewards workers receive and the amount they believe they should receive.

much evidence questions that assumed causal relationship, it can be argued that advanced societies should be concerned not only with the quantity of life—that is, concerns such as higher productivity and material acquisitions—but also with its quality. Those researchers with strong humanistic values argue that satisfaction is a legitimate objective of an organization. Not only is satisfaction negatively related to absenteeism and turnover, but, they argue, organizations have a responsibility to provide employees with jobs that are challenging and intrinsically rewarding. Therefore, although job satisfaction represents an attitude rather than a behavior, OB researchers typically consider it an important dependent variable.

THE INDEPENDENT VARIABLES

independent variable

The presumed cause of some change in the dependent variable.

What are the major determinants of productivity, absenteeism, turnover, OCB, and job satisfaction? Our answer to that question brings us to the **independent variables**. Consistent with our belief that organizational behavior can best be understood when viewed essentially as a set of increasingly complex building blocks, the base, or first level, of our model lies in understanding individual behavior.

Individual-Level Variables It has been said that "managers, unlike parents, must work with used, not new, human beings—human beings whom others have gotten to first."[34] When individuals enter an organization, they are a bit like used cars. Each is different. Some are "low-mileage"—they have been treated carefully and have had only limited exposure to the realities of the elements. Others are "well-worn," having been driven over some rough roads. This metaphor indicates that people enter organizations with certain characteristics that will influence their behavior at work. The more obvious of these are personal or biographical characteristics such as age, gender, and marital status; personality characteristics; an inherent emotional framework; values and attitudes; and basic ability levels. These characteristics are essentially intact when an individual enters the workforce, and, for the most part, there is little management can do to alter them. Yet they have a very real impact on employee behavior. Therefore, each of these factors—biographical characteristics, ability, values, attitudes, personality, and emotions—will be discussed as independent variables in Chapters 2 through 4.

There are four other individual-level variables that have been shown to affect employee behavior: perception, individual decision making, learning, and motivation. Those topics will be introduced and discussed in Chapters 2, 5, 6, and 7.

Group-Level Variables The behavior of people in groups is more than the sum total of all the individuals acting in their own way. The complexity of our model is increased when we acknowledge that people's behavior when they are in groups is different from their behavior when they are alone. Therefore, the next step in the development of an understanding of OB is the study of group behavior.

Chapter 8 lays the foundation for an understanding of the dynamics of group behavior. That chapter discusses how individuals in groups are influenced by the patterns of behavior they are expected to exhibit, what the group considers to be acceptable standards of behavior, and the degree to which group members are attracted to each other. Chapter 9 translates our understanding of groups to the design of effective work teams. Chapters 10 through 13 demonstrate how communication patterns, leadership styles, power and politics, and levels of conflict affect group behavior.

Organization Systems Level Variables Organizational behavior reaches its highest level of sophistication when we add formal structure to our previous knowledge of individual and group behavior. Just as groups are more than the sum of their individual members, so are organizations more than the sum of their member groups. The design of the formal organization, work processes, and jobs; the organization's human resource policies and practices (that is, selection processes, training programs, performance evaluation methods); and the internal culture all have an impact on the dependent variables. These are discussed in detail in Chapters 14 through 17.

TOWARD A CONTINGENCY OB MODEL

Our final model is shown in Exhibit 1-7. It shows the five key dependent variables and a large number of independent variables, organized by level of analysis, that research indicates have varying effects on the former. As complicated as this model is, it still does not do justice to the complexity of the OB subject matter, but it should help explain why the chapters in this book are arranged as they are and help you to explain and predict the behavior of people at work.

For the most part, our model does not explicitly identify the vast number of contingency variables because of the tremendous complexity that would be involved in such a diagram. Rather, throughout this text we shall introduce important contingency variables that will improve the explanatory linkage between the independent and dependent variables in our OB model.

Note that we have included the concepts of change and stress in Exhibit 1–7, acknowledging the dynamics of behavior and the fact that work stress is an individual, group, and organizational issue. Specifically, in Chapter 18 we will discuss the change process, ways to manage organizational change, key change issues for management in the new millennium, consequences of work stress, and techniques for managing stress.

Also note that Exhibit 1–7 includes linkages between the three levels of analysis. For instance, organization structure is linked to leadership and trust. This link is meant to convey that authority and leadership are related; management exerts its influence on group behavior through leadership. Similarly, communication is the means by which individuals transmit information; thus, it is the link between individual and group behavior.

SUMMARY AND IMPLICATIONS FOR MANAGERS

Managers need to develop their interpersonal or people skills if they are going to be effective in their jobs. Organizational behavior (OB) is a field of study that investigates the impact that individuals, groups, and structure have on behavior within an organization, and then it applies that knowledge to make organizations work more effectively. Specifically, OB focuses on how to improve productivity, reduce absenteeism and turnover, and increase employee citizenship and job satisfaction.

We all hold generalizations about the behavior of people. Some of our generalizations may provide valid insights into human behavior, but many are erroneous. Organizational behavior uses systematic study to improve predictions of behavior that would be made from intuition alone. But, because people are different, we need to look at OB in a contingency framework, using situational variables to moderate cause-and-effect relationships.

Organizational behavior offers both challenges and opportunities for managers. It recognizes differences and helps managers to see the value of workforce diversity and practices that may need to be changed when managing in different countries. It can help improve quality and employee productivity by showing managers how to empower their people as well as how to design and implement change programs. It offers specific insights to improve a manager's people skills. In times of rapid and ongoing change—what most managers face today—OB can help managers cope in a world of temporariness and learn ways to stimulate innovation. Finally, OB can offer managers guidance in creating an ethically healthy work climate.

EXHIBIT

1-7

Basic OB Model, Stage II

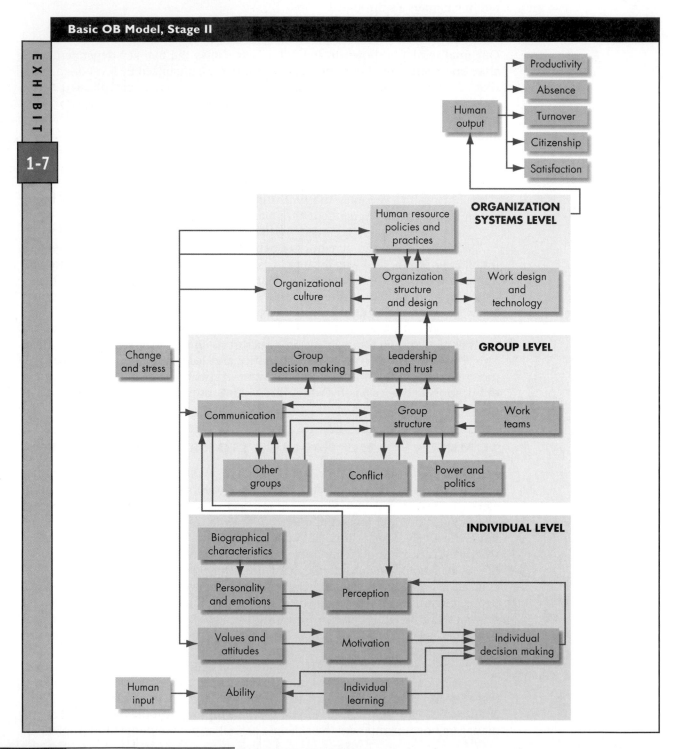

Successful Organizations Put People First

I ntel does it. So does Microsoft, Motorola, W. L. Gore & Associates, Southwest Airlines, Ben & Jerry's Homemade, Hewlett-Packard, Lincoln Electric, and Starbucks. What is *it*? These companies pursue "people-first" strategies.

There is an increasing amount of evidence that successful organizations put people first. Why? Astute managers have come to learn that their organization's employees are its only true competitive advantage. Competitors can match most organizations' products, processes, locations, distribution channels, and the like. What's far more difficult to emulate is a workforce made up of highly knowledgeable and motivated people. The characteristic that differentiates successful companies from their less successful counterparts in almost every industry is the quality of the people they're able to get and keep.

What kind of practices differentiate people-first organizations? We can list at least four: (1) They value cultural diversity. They actively seek a diverse workforce based on age, gender, and race. (2) They are family friendly. They help employees balance work and personal responsibilities through programs such as flexible work schedules and on-site child care facilities. (3) They invest in employee training. These organizations spend heavily to make sure employee skill levels are kept current. This not only ensures that employees can handle the latest technologies and processes for the organization but that employees will be marketable to other employers. (4) People-first organizations empower their employees. They push authority and responsibility down to the lowest levels.

Organizations that put people first have a more dedicated and committed workforce. This, in turn, translates into higher employee productivity and satisfaction. These employees are willing to put forth the extra effort—to do whatever is necessary to see that their jobs are done properly and completely. People-first strategies also lead to organizations being able to recruit smarter, more conscientious, and more loyal employees.

P utting "people first" is easy to say. And it's currently politically correct. What manager, in his or her right mind, is going to admit publicly that employees take a backseat to cost cutting or profitability? It's important, however, not to confuse talk with action.

Putting people first is not necessarily consistent with long-term competitiveness. Managers recognize this fact and are increasingly acting on it. Today's organizations are more typically pursuing a "labor-cost minimization" strategy rather than a people-first strategy.

When you look beyond what managers say, you find most business firms place profits over people. To stay competitive in a global economy, they look for cost-cutting measures. They reengineer processes and cut the size of their permanent workforce. And they substitute temporary workers for full-time permanent staff.

Organizations with problems typically look to staffing cuts as a first response. And organizations *without* problems are regularly reviewing their staffing needs to identify redundancies and overstaffing. Their goal is to keep themselves "lean and mean." In today's competitive environment, few organizations have the luxury to be able to provide workers with implied "permanent employment" or to offer anything more than minimal job security.

For almost all organizations today, employees are a variable cost. Staffing levels are kept to a minimum and employees are continually added or deleted as needed.

Interestingly, the labor-cost-minimization strategy appears to be spreading worldwide. It began in the United States in the early 1990s. Now it has become the model for companies in countries such as Japan, South Korea, and Thailand—places that historically protected their employees in good times and bad. Many firms in these countries have abandoned their permanent-employment, people-first policies. Why? Because such policies are inconsistent with aggressive, low-cost, global competition.

1. How are OB concepts addressed in management functions, roles, and skills?

2. Define *organizational behavior*. Relate it to *management*.

3. What is an organization? Is the family unit an organization? Explain.

4. Identify and contrast the three general management roles.

5. What is TQM? How is it related to OB?

6. What is reengineering? How is it related to OB?

7. "Behavior is generally predictable, so there is no need to formally study OB." Why is this statement incorrect?

8. What are the three levels of analysis in our OB model? Are they related? If so, how?

9. If job satisfaction is not a behavior, why is it considered an important dependent variable?

10. What are *effectiveness* and *efficiency*, and how are they related to organizational behavior?

Questions for Critical Thinking

1. Contrast the research comparing effective managers with successful managers. What are the implications from the research for practicing managers?

2. "The best way to view OB is through a contingency approach." Build an argument to support that statement.

3. Why do you think the subject of OB might be criticized as being "only common sense," when one would rarely hear such a criticism of a course in physics or statistics?

4. Millions of workers have lost their jobs due to downsizing. At the same time, many organizations are complaining that they can't find qualified people to fill vacancies. How do you explain this apparent contradiction?

5. On a 1 to 10 scale measuring the sophistication of a scientific discipline in predicting phenomena, mathematical physics would probably be a 10. Where do you think OB would fall on the scale? Why?

Team Exercise | Workforce Diversity

Purpose To learn about the different needs of a diverse workforce.

Time required Approximately 40 minutes.

Participants and roles Divide the class into six groups of approximately equal size. Each group is assigned one of the following roles:

Nancy is 28 years old. She is a divorced mother of three children, aged 3, 5, and 7. She is the department head. She earns $37,000 a year on her job and receives another $3,600 a year in child support from her ex-husband.

Ethel is a 72-year-old widow. She works 25 hours a week to supplement her $8,000 annual pension. Including her hourly wage of $7.50, she earns $17,750 a year.

John is a 34-year-old black male born in Trinidad who is now a U.S. resident. He is married and the father of two small children. John attends college at night and is within a year of earning his bachelor's degree. His salary is $24,000 a year. His wife is an attorney and earns approximately $44,000 a year.

Lu is a 26-year-old physically impaired male Asian American. He is single and has a master's degree in education. Lu is paralyzed and confined to a wheelchair as a result of an auto accident. He earns $29,000 a year.

Maria is a single 22-year-old Hispanic. Born and raised in Mexico, she came to the United States only three months ago. Maria's English needs considerable improvement. She earns $18,000 a year.

Mike is a 16-year-old white male high school sophomore who works 15 hours a week after school and during vacations. He earns $6.75 an hour, or approximately $5,200 a year.

The members of each group are to assume the character consistent with their assigned role.

Background

Our six participants work for a company that has recently installed a flexible benefits program. Instead of the traditional "one benefit package fits all," the company is allocating an additional 25 percent of each employee's annual pay to be used for discretionary benefits. Those benefits and their annual cost follow.

Supplementary health care for employee:

>   Plan A (No deductible and pays 90%) = $3,000

>   Plan B ($200 deductible and pays 80%) = $2,000

>   Plan C ($1,000 deductible and pays 70%) = $500

Supplementary health care for dependents (same deductibles and percentages as for employees):

>   Plan A = $2,000

>   Plan B = $1,500

>   Plan C = $500

Supplementary dental plan = $500

Life insurance:

>   Plan A ($25,000 coverage) = $500

>   Plan B ($50,000 coverage) = $1,000

>   Plan C ($100,000 coverage) = $2,000

>   Plan D ($250,000 coverage) = $3,000

Mental health plan = $500
Prepaid legal assistance = $300
Vacation = 2% of annual pay for each week, up to six weeks a year
Pension at retirement equal to approximately 50% of final annual earnings = $1,500
Four-day workweek during the three summer months (available only to full-time employees) = 4% of annual pay
Day care services (after company contribution) = $2,000 for all of an employee's children, regardless of number
Company-provided transportation to and from work = $750
College tuition reimbursement = $1,000
Language class tuition reimbursement = $500

The Task

1. Each group has 15 minutes to develop a flexible benefits package that consumes 25 percent (and no more!) of their character's pay.

2. After completing step 1, each group appoints a spokesperson who describes to the entire class the benefits package they have arrived at for their character.

3. The entire class then discusses the results. How did the needs, concerns, and problems of each participant influence the group's decision? What do the results suggest for trying to motivate a diverse workforce?

Source: Special thanks to Professor Penny Wright (San Diego State University) for her suggestions during the development of this exercise.

1. Find five organizations that purport to promote diversity through family-friendly policies. What are their policies? How do these policies attract and keep people?

2. Find an organization that directly addresses the cost of absenteeism or turnover on its Internet site.

What, if anything, is that organization doing to reduce those costs? What did your search tell you in terms of the importance or unimportance of these costs to organizations?

PHLIP Companion Web Site

We invite you to visit the Robbins homepage on the Prentice Hall Web site at **www.prenhall.com/robbins** for our on-line study guide, current events, links to related Web sites, and more.

Case Incident | Thanks for 24 Years of Service. Now Here's the Door!

Russ McDonald graduated from the University of Michigan with his M.B.A. in 1971. He had numerous job offers but chose General Motors for several reasons. The automobile industry offered terrific career opportunities, and GM was the world's number one car manufacturer. Salaries at GM were among the highest in corporate America, and a job at GM provided unparalleled security. A white-collar job with GM was the closest anybody could come to permanent employment, outside of working for the federal government.

Russ began his career at GM as a cost analyst at the company's Fisher Body division in Detroit. From there he proceeded through a long sequence of increased job responsibilities. By his twentieth anniversary with the company he had risen to the position of assistant vice president of finance in the corporate treasury department. His salary was $134,000 a year, and, in a good year, he could expect a bonus of anywhere from $10,000 to $25,000. But those bonuses had become increasingly rare because GM's profitability had declined throughout the 1980s. Increased foreign competition, aggressive action by Ford and Chrysler, and GM's slow response to change had resulted in a serious erosion in the company's market position. When Russ joined the company, nearly one out of every two new cars sold in the United States was a GM product. By the early 1990s, that number was down to one in four. As a result, GM's management was taking drastic action to try to stop its decline in market share. It was closing inefficient plants, reorganizing divisions, introducing new production

technologies, and making huge cuts in its staff. Tens of thousands of white-collar positions were eliminated. One of those was Russ McDonald's job. In the summer of 1995, less than a year short of his twenty-fifth anniversary with GM, he was given the opportunity to take early retirement. Russ saw the handwriting on the wall. If he didn't take early retirement, it would only be a matter of time—maybe a year or two at best—and he would be pushed out, and with a less attractive severance package. So he took the company's offer: nine months' pay plus lifetime health benefits for him and his family. Russ tried to put a positive spin on the situation. Maybe this was a blessing in disguise. He was only 49 years old. He had 24 years of experience with one of the world's foremost corporations. He would land on his feet with a company that was growing and offered opportunities that no longer existed at GM.

Russ's optimism had pretty well faded by New Year's Day 1998. He had been out of work for nearly 30 months. He had responded to dozens of employment ads. He had sent out more than 200 résumés. He had talked with several executive recruiting firms, and he had spent more than $7,000 on employment counseling. All for naught. What he kept hearing was that his experience wasn't relevant to today's workplace; there were no opportunities in large companies; small companies wanted people who were flexible, and they considered corporate types like Russ as "mentally rigid." Even if there was a job for which Russ was qualified, he would have to take at least a 50 percent cut in pay, and employers were very uncomfortable offering someone such a relatively low salary; they figured Russ would be demotivated and likely to "jump ship" at the first opportunity.

Questions

1. How valid do you think the comments are that Russ is hearing?

2. If you were a small business executive in need of someone with extensive financial experience, would you consider Russ? Explain your position.

3. What suggestions might you make to Russ to help him find suitable employment?

End Notes

1. D. Milbank, "Managers Are Sent to 'Charm Schools' to Discover How to Polish Up Their Acts," *Wall Street Journal*, December 14, 1990, p. B1.
2. M. Boardman "'Worker Dearth' in the 21st Century," *HR Magazine*, June 1999, p. 304; and R. W. Judy, "Labor Forecast: Gray Skies, Worker Drought Continues," *HR Magazine*, October 1999, pp. 18–26.
3. *The 1997 National Study of the Changing Workforce* (New York: Families and Work Institute, 1997).
4. Cited in A. Fisher, "Don't Blow Your New Job," *Fortune*, June 22, 1998, p. 159.
5. Ibid. p. 160.
6. S. A. Waddock, "Educating Tomorrow's Managers," *Journal of Management Education*, February 1991, pp. 69–96; and K. F. Kane, "MBAs: A Recruiter's-Eye View," *Business Horizons*, January–February 1993, pp. 65–71.
7. H. Fayol, *Industrial and General Administration* (Paris: Dunod, 1916).
8. H. Mintzberg, *The Nature of Managerial Work* (New York: Harper & Row, 1973).
9. R. L. Katz, "Skills of an Effective Administrator," *Harvard Business Review*, September–October 1974, pp. 90–102.
10. F. Luthans, "Successful vs. Effective Real Managers," *Academy of Management Executive*, May 1988, pp. 127–32; and F. Luthans, R. M. Hodgetts, and S. A. Rosenkrantz, *Real Managers* (Cambridge, MA: Ballinger, 1988).
11. See, for instance, J. E. Garcia and K. S. Keleman, "What Is Organizational Behavior Anyhow?" paper presented at the 16th Annual Organizational Behavior Teaching Conference, Columbia, MO, June 1989.
12. E. E. Lawler III and J.G. Rhode, *Information and Control in Organizations* (Pacific Palisades, CA: Goodyear, 1976), p. 22.
13. The general idea for this box theme was derived from S. F. Davis and J. J. Palladino, *Psychology*, 2nd ed. (Upper Saddle River, NJ: Prentice Hall, 1997).
14. R. R. Thomas Jr., "From Affirmative Action to Affirming Diversity," *Harvard Business Review*, March–April 1990, pp. 107–17.
15. H. N. Fullerton, "The 2005 Labor Force: Growing, But Slowly," *Monthly Labor Review*, November 1995, p. 41.
16. J. Dreyfuss, "Get Ready for the New Work Force," *Fortune*, April 23, 1990, p. 168.
17. See, for instance, E. E. Kossek and S. A. Lobel (eds.), *Managing Diversity* (Cambridge, MA: Blackwell, 1996); J. A. Segal, "Diversify for Dollars," *HR Magazine*, April 1997, pp.

134–40; and "Strength Through Diversity for Bottom-Line Success," *Working Women*, March 1999, pp. 67–77.
18. J. Teresko, "Alcatel Network Systems Inc.," *Industry Week*, October 20, 1997, pp. 24–30.
19. See, for instance, M. Sashkin and K. J. Kiser, *Putting Total Quality Management to Work* (San Francisco: Berrett-Koehler, 1993); and J. R. Hackman and R. Wageman, "Total Quality Management: Empirical, Conceptual, and Practical Issues," *Administrative Science Quarterly*, June 1995, pp. 309–42.
20. M. Hammer and J. Champy, *Reengineering the Corporation: A Manifesto for Business Revolution* (New York: HarperBusiness, 1993); and J. Champy, *Reengineering Management* (New York: HarperBusiness, 1995).
21. B. Dumaine, "The New Non-Manager Managers," *Fortune*, February 22, 1993, pp. 80–84.
22. M. Kaeter, "The Age of the Specialized Generalist," *Training*, December 1993, pp. 48–53; and N. Templin, "Auto Plants, Hiring Again, Are Demanding Higher-Skilled Labor," *Wall Street Journal*, March 11, 1994, p. A1.
23. See, for example, R. J. Grossman, "Short-Term Workers Raise Long-Term Issues," *HRMagazine*, April 1998, pp. 81–89.
24. E. J. Ottensmeyer and G. McCarthy, *Ethics in the Workplace* (New York: McGraw Hill, 1996).
25. G. R. Weaver, L. K. Trevino, and P. L. Cochran, "Corporate Ethics Practices in the Mid-1990's: An Empirical Study of the Fortune 1000," *Journal of Business Ethics*, February 1999, pp. 283–94.
26. S. R. Rhodes and R. M. Steers, *Managing Employee Absenteeism* (Reading, MA: Addison-Wesley, 1990). For a full review of the direct and indirect costs of absenteeism, see D. A. Harrison and J. J. Martocchio, "Time for Absenteeism: A 20-Year Review of Origins, Offshoots, and Outcomes," *Journal of Management*, Vol. 24, No. 3, 1998, pp. 305–50.
27. Cited in J. Schmid, "'Sick' German Workers Get Corporate Medicine," *International Herald Tribune*, September 28–29, 1996, p. 1.
28. Cited in "Expensive Absenteeism," *Wall Street Journal*, July 29, 1986, p. 1.
29. M. Mercer, "Turnover: Reducing the Costs," *Personnel*, December 1988, pp. 36–42; and R. Darmon, "Identifying Sources of Turnover Cost," *Journal of Marketing*, April 1990, pp. 46–56; and "The Cost of Employee Turnover," *AARP Working Age*, May/June 1999, pp.1–3.
30. See, for example, D. R. Dalton and W. D. Todor, "Func-

tional Turnover: An Empirical Assessment," *Journal of Applied Psychology*, December 1981, pp. 716–21; G. M. McEvoy and W. F. Cascio, "Do Good or Poor Performers Leave? A Meta-Analysis of the Relationship between Performance and Turnover," *Academy of Management Journal*, December 1987, pp. 744–62; and D. Gilbertson, "Why Do People Quit Their Jobs? Because They Can," *New York Times*, February 1, 1998, p. BU 12.

31. Cited in "You Often Lose the Ones You Love," *Industry Week*, November 21, 1988, p. 5.

32. D. W. Organ, *Organizational Citizenship Behavior: The Good Soldier Syndrome* (Lexington, MA: Lexington Books, 1988), p. 4.

33. See, for example, P. M. Podsakoff and S. B. MacKenzie, "Organizational Citizenship Behavior and Sales Unit Effectiveness," *Journal of Marketing Research*, August 1994, pp. 351–63; and P. M. Podsakoff, M. Ahearne, and S. B. MacKenzie, "Organizational Citizenship Behavior and the Quantity and Quality of Work Group Performance," *Journal of Applied Psychology*, April 1997, pp. 262–70.

34. H. J. Leavitt, *Managerial Psychology*, rev. ed. (Chicago: University of Chicago Press, 1964), p. 3.

PART ONE: Introduction

Starbucks as "The Front Porch": Corporate Culture Shapes Commitment to Quality

How do you design a store that reflects and welcomes all the diversity of customers you can reach in the United States?" The answer to that question illustrates an important point about how this book's organizational behavior themes carry over into the workplace, and specifically to a firm such as Starbucks.

Starbucks' planners decided on an eclectic approach to the design of the growing chain of coffee stores, so that each new store would suit the neighborhood and people it was meant to serve. They believed this approach would best convey the way senior management envisioned the Seattle-based firm: as their own front porch, their living room, a gathering place. As Howard Behar, president of Starbucks International, puts it, "Each city, each country has to interpret Starbucks for itself and has to make it theirs, otherwise it won't be successful." Many of their customers agreed with that approach, and the chain continues to flourish.

Starbucks now has over 2,400 stores at home and abroad and has opened a new one approximately every business day for the last three years.[1] It employs about 31,000 people, called partners, worldwide, and its 1998 revenues topped $1.3 billion.[2] In addition to its familiar storefront cafes, the firm has outlets in casinos, airports, hospitals, and hotels and even one in a library in Stamford, Connecticut.[3]

The eclecticism in Starbucks' design and architecture and the stylish but friendly atmosphere of its stores are an outgrowth of the firm's corporate culture of creativity, energy, and freedom to get the job done in the best possible way. CEO Howard Schultz knows that the firm's commitment to quality and its dedication to its people are linked. He says, "Our competitive advantage over the big coffee brands turned out to be our people . . . in a Starbucks store, you encounter real people who are informed and excited about the coffee, and enthusiastic about the brand."[4]

Study Questions

As you watch the Starbucks video segment, look for more evidence that successful management of organizational behavior, the "people skills" described in this chapter, lead directly to the company's principles and values. Specifically, answer the following questions:

1. How does management at Starbucks exemplify the core OB topics of motivation, leadership, communication, learning, and attitude development?

2. Cite some evidence from the video that indicates to you whether or not Starbucks managers accept that behavior in the workplace is directed toward a goal that the individual believes is in his or her best interest.

3. Howard Behar has said that one distinctive thing about Starbucks is its "diversity of thought," which comes from hiring a wide diversity of people. What do you think are some of the motivations for Starbucks' commitment to diversity in hiring? What advantages does the company gain from this value?

4. Choose one of OB's dependent variables. How does Starbucks manage this variable? Do you think it could do a better job? If so, how?

Source: [1]Mike Allen, "In Stamford, Just Call It Starbooks," *New York Times*, August 4, 1999, p. B1. [2]Information provided by Starbucks. [3]Allen, op. cit. [4]Howard Schultz and Dori Jones Yang, *Pour Your Heart Into It* (New York: Hyperion, 1997), p. 247.

As a rule, the person who can do all things equally well is a very mediocre individual.

—E. Hubbard

THE INDIVIDUAL

Microsoft receives more than 120,000 résumés a year at its Seattle headquarters from prospective job applicants. Out of that number, maybe a couple thousand of these applicants will get an interview. But interviews for a job at Microsoft are different than at most organizations. Those who get to the interview stage will find themselves trying to answer a number of strange questions such as: Why are manhole covers round? How many gas stations are there in the United States? How much water flows through the Mississippi daily?

Ironically, Microsoft interviewers don't expect job candidates to know the specific answers to these questions. What they're trying to learn is how the candidate thinks and how he or she verbalizes ideas. Microsoft interviewers are trying to find out how smart each candidate is.

In contrast to most organizations, where the selection process focuses on experience, Microsoft gives extraordinary attention to one single factor—intelligence![1] Employees at Microsoft are a diverse group. They come in all sizes and colors. But their one common denominator is that they're all very smart. Bill Gates, Microsoft's CEO, makes no apologies for his quest to find the smartest people to join his company. "There is no way of getting around [the fact] that, in terms of IQ, you've got to be very elitist in picking the people who deserve to write software." Gates argues that IQ is more important than experience—"you can teach smart people anything." The photo on your left shows some of those "smart people" that Microsoft hired.

Foundations of Individual Behavior

Microsoft believes its greatest asset is the collective intellectual resources of its employees. And to achieve this status, Gates and his recruiters have consistently sought out and hired the smartest individuals they can find. This deliberate effort of seeking out and holding on to smart people has been described as the single most important aspect of Microsoft's success.

ntelligence is but one characteristic that people bring with them when they join an organization. In this chapter, we look at how biographical characteristics (such as gender and age) and ability (which includes intelligence) affect employee performance and satisfaction. Then we show how people learn behaviors and what management can do to shape those behaviors.

BIOGRAPHICAL CHARACTERISTICS

As discussed in the previous chapter, this text is essentially concerned with finding and analyzing the variables that have an impact on employee productivity, absence, turnover, citizenship and satisfaction. The list of those variables—as shown in Exhibit 1-7 on page 24—is long and contains some complicated concepts. Many of the concepts—motivation, say, or power and politics or organizational culture—are hard to assess. It might be valuable, then, to begin by looking at factors that are easily definable and readily available; data that can be obtained, for the most part, simply from information available in an employee's personnel file. What factors would these be? Obvious characteristics would be an employee's age, gender,

AFTER READING THIS CHAPTER, YOU SHOULD BE ABLE TO

1. Define the key biographical characteristics
2. Identify two types of ability
3. Shape the behavior of others
4. Distinguish between the four schedules of reinforcement
5. Clarify the role of punishment in learning
6. Practice self-management
7. Exhibit effective discipline skills

biographical characteristics

Personal characteristics—such as age, gender, and marital status—that are objective and easily obtained from personnel records.

marital status, and length of service with an organization. Fortunately, there is a sizable amount of research that has specifically analyzed many of these **biographical characteristics**.

AGE

The relationship between age and job performance is likely to be an issue of increasing importance during the next decade. Why? There are at least three reasons. First, there is a widespread belief that job performance declines with increasing age. Regardless of whether it's true or not, a lot of people believe it and act on it. Second is the reality that the workforce is aging. For instance, workers 55 and older are the fastest-growing sector of the labor force; between 1994 and 2005, their ranks are expected to jump 36 percent.[2] The third reason is recent U.S. legislation that, for all intents and purposes, outlaws mandatory retirement. Most U.S. workers today no longer have to retire at the age of 70.

What is the perception of older workers? Evidence indicates that employers hold mixed feelings.[3] They see a number of positive qualities that older workers bring to their jobs: specifically, experience, judgment, a strong work ethic, and commitment to quality. But older workers are also perceived as lacking flexibility and as being resistant to new technology. And in a time when organizations strongly seek individuals who are adaptable and open to change, the negative perceptions associated with age clearly hinder the initial hiring of older workers and increase the likelihood that they will be let go during downsizing. Now let's take a look at the evidence. What effect does age *actually* have on turnover, absenteeism, productivity, and satisfaction?

The older you get, the less likely you are to quit your job. That conclusion is based on studies of the age–turnover relationship.[4] Of course, it should not be too surprising. As workers get older, they have fewer alternative job opportunities. In addition, older workers are less likely to resign than are younger workers because their long tenure tends to provide them with higher wage rates, longer paid vacations, and more attractive pension benefits.

It's tempting to assume that age is also inversely related to absenteeism. After all, if older workers are less likely to quit, won't they also demonstrate higher stability by coming to work more regularly? Not necessarily! Most studies do show an inverse relationship, but close examination finds that the age–absence relationship is partially a function of whether the absence is avoidable or unavoidable.[5] In general, older employees have lower rates of avoidable absence than do younger employees. However, they have higher rates of unavoidable absence, probably due to the poorer health associated with aging and the longer recovery period that older workers need when injured.

How does age affect productivity? There is a widespread belief that productivity declines with age. It is often assumed that an individual's skills—particularly speed, agility, strength, and coordination—decay over time and that prolonged job boredom and lack of intellectual stimulation all contribute to reduced productivity. The evidence, however, contradicts that belief and those assumptions. For instance, during a three-year period, a large hardware chain staffed one of its stores solely with employees over 50 and compared its results with those of five stores with younger employees. The store staffed by the over-50 employees was significantly more productive (measured in terms of sales generated against labor costs) than two of the other stores and held its own with the other three.[6] Other reviews of the research find

Lee Liput (left) is proof that age does not affect productivity. In her sixties, she was hired by Janice Grossman, who owns JanCo, a garment manufacturer, to perform a variety of jobs. Liput operates the firm's computer, answers phones, keeps the books, pays the bills, and deals with customers and suppliers. Grossman is more than satisfied with Liput's computer skills, work ethic, dependability, and flexibility in handling many different tasks.

that age and job performance are unrelated.[7] Moreover, this finding seems to be true for almost all types of jobs, professional and nonprofessional. The natural conclusion is that the demands of most jobs, even those with heavy manual labor requirements, are not extreme enough for any declines in physical skills due to age to have an impact on productivity; or, if there is some decay due to age, it is offset by gains due to experience.[8]

Our final concern is the relationship between age and job satisfaction. On this issue, the evidence is mixed. Most studies indicate a positive association between age and satisfaction, at least up to age 60.[9] Other studies, however, have found a U-shaped relationship.[10] Several explanations could clear up these results, the most plausible being that these studies are intermixing professional and nonprofessional employees. When the two types are separated, satisfaction tends to continually increase among professionals as they age, whereas it falls among nonprofessionals during middle age and then rises again in the later years.

GENDER

Few issues initiate more debates, misconceptions, and unsupported opinions than whether women perform as well on jobs as men do. In this section, we review the research on that issue.

The evidence suggests that the best place to begin is with the recognition that there are few, if any, important differences between men and women that will affect their job performance. There are, for instance, no consistent male-female differences in problem-solving ability, analytical skills, competitive drive, motivation, sociability, or learning ability.[11] Psychological studies have found that women are more willing to conform to authority and that men are more aggressive and more likely than women to have expectations of success, but those differences are minor. Given the significant changes that have taken place in the last 25 years in terms of increasing female participation rates in the workforce and rethinking what constitutes male and female roles, you should operate on the assumption that there is no significant difference in job productivity between men and women. Similarly, there is no evidence indicating that an employee's gender affects job satisfaction.[12]

One issue that does seem to differ between genders, especially where the employee has preschool children, is preference for work schedules.[13] Working mothers are more likely to prefer part-time work, flexible work schedules, and telecommuting in order to accommodate their family responsibilities.

But what about absence and turnover rates? Are women less stable employees than men? First, on the question of turnover, the evidence is mixed.[14] Some studies have found that women have higher turnover rates; others have found no difference. There doesn't appear to be enough information from which to draw meaningful conclusions. The research on absence, however, is a different story. The evidence consistently indicates that women have higher rates of absenteeism than men do.[15] The most logical explanation for this finding is that the research was conducted in North America, and North American culture has historically placed home and family responsibilities on the woman. When a child is ill or someone needs to stay home to wait for the plumber, it has been the woman who has traditionally taken time off from work. However, this research is undoubtedly time-bound.[16] The historical role of the woman in caring for children and as secondary breadwinner has definitely changed in the last generation, and a large proportion of men nowadays are as interested in day care and the problems associated with child care in general as are women.

MARITAL STATUS

There are not enough studies to draw any conclusions about the effect of marital status on productivity. But research consistently indicates that married employees have fewer absences, undergo less turnover, and are more satisfied with their jobs than are their unmarried co-workers.[17]

Marriage imposes increased responsibilities that may make a steady job more valuable and important. But the question of causation is not clear. It may very well be that conscientious and satisfied employees are more likely to be married. Another offshoot of this issue is that research has not pursued other statuses besides single or married. Does being divorced or widowed have an impact on an employee's performance and satisfaction? What about couples who live together without being married? These are questions in need of investigation.

TENURE

The last biographical characteristic we'll look at is tenure. With the exception of the issue of male-female differences, probably no issue is more subject to misconceptions and speculations than the impact of seniority on job performance.

Extensive reviews of the seniority–productivity relationship have been conducted.[18] If we define seniority as time on a particular job, we can say that the most recent evidence demonstrates a positive relationship between seniority and job productivity. So tenure, expressed as work experience, appears to be a good predictor of employee productivity.

The research relating tenure to absence is quite straightforward. Studies consistently demonstrate seniority to be negatively related to absenteeism.[19] In fact, in terms of both frequency of absence and total days lost at work, tenure is the single most important explanatory variable.[20]

> "Tenure has consistently been found to be negatively related to turnover and has been suggested as one of the single best predictors of turnover."

Tenure is also a potent variable in explaining turnover. "Tenure has consistently been found to be negatively related to turnover and has been suggested as one of the single best predictors of turnover."[21] Moreover, consistent with research that suggests that past behavior is the best predictor of future behavior,[22] evidence indicates that tenure on an employee's previous job is a powerful predictor of that employee's future turnover.[23]

The evidence indicates that tenure and satisfaction are positively related.[24] In fact, when age and tenure are treated separately, tenure appears to be a more consistent and stable predictor of job satisfaction than is chronological age.

ABILITY

Contrary to what we are taught in grade school, we aren't all created equal. Most of us are to the left of the median on some normally distributed ability curve. Regardless of how motivated you are, it is unlikely that you can act as well as Meryl Streep, run as fast as Michael Johnson, write horror stories as well as Stephen King, or sing as well as Whitney Houston. Of course, just because we aren't all equal in abilities does not imply that some individuals are inherently inferior to others. What we are acknowledging is that everyone has strengths and weaknesses in terms of ability that make him or her relatively superior or inferior to others in performing certain tasks or activities.[25] From management's standpoint, the issue is not whether people differ in terms of their abilities. They do! The issue is knowing how people differ in abilities and using that knowledge to increase the likelihood that an employee will perform his or her job well.

What does *ability* mean? As we will use the term, **ability** refers to an individual's capacity to perform the various tasks in a job. It is a current assessment of what one can do. An individual's overall abilities are essentially made up of two sets of factors: intellectual and physical abilities.

INTELLECTUAL ABILITIES

Intellectual abilities are those needed to perform mental activities. Intelligence quotient (IQ) tests, for example, are designed to ascertain one's general intellectual abilities. So, too, are popular college admission tests such as the SAT and ACT and graduate admission tests in business (GMAT), law (LSAT), and medicine (MCAT). The seven most frequently cited dimensions making up intellectual abilities are number aptitude, verbal comprehension, perceptual speed, inductive reasoning, deductive reasoning, spatial visualization, and memory.[26] Exhibit 2-1 describes those dimensions.

Jobs differ in the demands they place on incumbents to use their intellectual abilities. Generally speaking, the more information-processing demands that exist in a job, the more general intelligence and verbal abilities will be necessary to perform the job successfully.[27] Of course, a high IQ is not a prerequisite for all jobs. In fact, for many jobs—in which employee behavior is highly routine and there are little or no opportunities to exercise discretion—a high IQ may be unrelated to performance. On the other hand, a careful review of the evidence demonstrates that tests that assess verbal, numerical, spatial, and perceptual abilities are valid predictors of job proficiency at all levels of jobs.[28] Therefore, tests that measure specific dimensions of intelligence have been found to be strong predictors of future job performance. So Microsoft's practice of hiring on the

ability

An individual's capacity to perform the various tasks in a job.

intellectual ability

That required to do mental activities.

Dimensions of Intellectual Ability

Dimension	Description	Job Example
Number aptitude	Ability to do speedy and accurate arithmetic	Accountant: Computing the sales tax on a set of items
Verbal comprehension	Ability to understand what is read or heard and the relationship of words to each other	Plant manager: Following corporate policies
Perceptual speed	Ability to identify visual similarities and differences quickly and accurately	Fire investigator: Identifying clues to support a charge of arson
Inductive reasoning	Ability to identify a logical sequence in a problem and then solve the problem	Market researcher: Forecasting demand for a product in the next time period
Deductive reasoning	Ability to use logic and assess the implications of an argument	Supervisor: Choosing between two different suggestions offered by employees
Spatial visualization	Ability to imagine how an object would look if its position in space were changed	Interior decorator: Redecorating an office
Memory	Ability to retain and recall past experiences	Salesperson: Remembering the names of customers

EXHIBIT

2-1

basis of general intelligence, described at the beginning of this chapter, may be a valid competitive strategy.

The major dilemma faced by employers who use mental ability tests for selection, promotion, training, and similar personnel decisions is that they may have a negative impact on racial and ethnic groups.[29] The evidence indicates that some minority groups score, on the average, as much as one standard deviation lower than whites on verbal, numerical, and spatial ability tests.

PHYSICAL ABILITIES

physical ability

That required to do tasks demanding stamina, dexterity, strength, and similar characteristics.

To the same degree that intellectual abilities play a larger role in complex jobs with demanding information-processing requirements, specific **physical abilities** gain importance for successfully doing less skilled and more standardized jobs. For example, jobs in which success demands stamina, manual dexterity, leg strength, or similar talents require management to identify an employee's physical capabilities.

Research on the requirements needed in hundreds of jobs has identified nine basic abilities involved in the performance of physical tasks.[30] These are described in Exhibit 2-2. Individuals differ in the extent to which they have each of these abilities. Not surprisingly, there is also little relationship between them: A high score on one is no assurance of a high score on others. High employee performance is likely to be achieved when management has ascertained the extent to which a job requires each of the nine abilities and then ensures that employees in that job have those abilities.

THE ABILITY–JOB FIT

Our concern is with explaining and predicting the behavior of people at work. In this section, we have demonstrated that jobs make differing demands on people and that people differ in the abilities they possess. Employee performance, therefore, is enhanced when there is a high ability–job fit.

EXHIBIT 2-2

Nine Basic Physical Abilities	
Strength Factors	
1. Dynamic strength	Ability to exert muscular force repeatedly or continuously over time
2. Trunk strength	Ability to exert muscular strength using the trunk (particularly abdominal) muscles
3. Static strength	Ability to exert force against external objects
4. Explosive strength	Ability to expend a maximum of energy in one or a series of explosive acts
Flexibility Factors	
5. Extent flexibility	Ablity to move the trunk and back muscles as far as possible
6. Dynamic flexibility	Ability to make rapid, repeated flexing movements
Other Factors	
7. Body coordination	Ability to coordinate the simultaneous actions of different parts of the body
8. Balance	Ability to maintain equilibrium despite forces pulling off balance
9. Stamina	Ability to continue maximum effort requiring prolonged effort over time

Source: Reprinted with permission of *HRMagazine* published by the Society for Human Resource Management, Alexandria, VA.

The specific intellectual or physical abilities required for adequate job performance depend on the ability requirements of the job. So, for example, airline pilots need strong spatial-visualization abilities; beach lifeguards need both strong spatial-visualization abilities and body coordination; senior executives need verbal abilities; high-rise construction workers need balance; and journalists with weak reasoning abilities would likely have difficulty meeting minimum job-performance standards. Directing attention at only the employee's abilities or only the ability requirements of the job ignores the fact that employee performance depends on the interaction of the two.

What predictions can we make when the fit is poor? As alluded to previously, if employees lack the required abilities, they are likely to fail. If you are hired as a word processor and you cannot meet the job's basic keyboard typing requirements, your performance is going to be poor irrespective of your positive attitude or your high level of motivation. When the ability–job fit is out of sync because the employee has abilities that far exceed the requirements of the job, our predictions would be very different. Job performance is likely to be adequate, but there will be organizational inefficiencies and possible declines in employee satisfaction. Given that pay tends to reflect the highest skill level that employees possess, if an employee's abilities far exceed those necessary to do the job, management will be paying more than it needs to. Abilities significantly above those required can also reduce the employee's job satisfaction when the employee's desire to use his or her abilities is particularly strong and is frustrated by the limitations of the job.

A high ability–job fit at Specialized Bicycles, the Morgan Hill, California firm that introduced mountain bikes, requires that its product designers have physical abilities such as stamina and strength as well as intellectual abilities. To keep their company competitive, product developers design innovative bikes and bicycle gear and then test their innovations on challenging California terrain.

LEARNING

All complex behavior is learned. If we want to explain and predict behavior, we need to understand how people learn. In this section, we define learning, present three popular learning theories, and describe how managers can facilitate employee learning.

A DEFINITION OF LEARNING

What is **learning**? A psychologist's definition is considerably broader than the layperson's view that "it's what we did when we went to school." In actuality, each of us is continuously going "to school." Learning occurs all of the time. A generally accepted definition of learning is, therefore, *any relatively permanent change in behavior that occurs as a result of experience*.[31] Ironically, we can say that changes in behavior indicate that learning has taken place and that learning is a change in behavior.

Obviously, the foregoing definition suggests that we shall never see someone "learning." We can see changes taking place but not the learning itself. The concept is theoretical and, hence, not directly observable:

learning

Any relatively permanent change in behavior that occurs as a result of experience.

You have seen people in the process of learning, you have seen people who behave in a particular way as a result of learning and some of you (in fact, I guess the majority of you) have "learned" at some time in your life. In other words, we infer that learning has taken place if an individual behaves, reacts, responds as a result of experience in a manner different from the way he formerly behaved.[32]

Our definition has several components that deserve clarification. First, learning involves change. Change may be good or bad from an organizational point of view. People can learn unfavorable behaviors—to hold prejudices or to restrict their output, for example—as well as favorable behaviors. Second, the change must be relatively permanent. Temporary changes may be only reflexive and fail to represent any learning. Therefore, the requirement that learning must be relatively permanent rules out behavioral changes caused by fatigue or temporary adaptations. Third, our definition is concerned with behavior. Learning takes place when there is a change in actions. A change in an individual's thought processes or attitudes, if accompanied by no change in behavior, would not be learning. Finally, some form of experience is necessary for learning. Experience may be acquired directly through observation or practice, or it may be acquired indirectly, as through reading. The crucial test still remains: Does this experience result in a relatively permanent change in behavior? If the answer is Yes, we can say that learning has taken place.

[*Learning involves change.*]

THEORIES OF LEARNING

How do we learn? Three theories have been offered to explain the process by which we acquire patterns of behavior. These are classical conditioning, operant conditioning, and social learning.

classical conditioning

A type of conditioning in which an individual responds to some stimulus that would not ordinarily produce such a response.

Classical Conditioning **Classical conditioning** grew out of experiments to teach dogs to salivate in response to the ringing of a bell, conducted at the turn of the twentieth century by a Russian physiologist, Ivan Pavlov.[33] A simple surgical procedure allowed Pavlov to measure accurately the amount of saliva secreted by a dog. When Pavlov presented the dog with a piece of meat, the dog exhibited a noticeable increase in salivation. When Pavlov withheld the presentation of meat and merely rang a bell, the dog did not salivate. Then Pavlov proceeded to link the meat and the ringing of the bell. After repeatedly hearing the bell before getting the food, the dog began to salivate as soon as the bell rang. After a while, the dog would salivate merely at the sound of the bell, even if no food was offered. In effect, the dog had learned to respond—that is, to salivate—to the bell. Let's review this experiment to introduce the key concepts in classical conditioning.

The meat was an *unconditioned stimulus*; it invariably caused the dog to react in a specific way. The reaction that took place whenever the unconditioned stimulus occurred was called the *unconditioned response* (or the noticeable increase in salivation, in this case). The bell was an artificial stimulus, or what we call the *conditioned stimulus*. Although it was originally neutral, after the bell was paired with the meat (an unconditioned stimulus), it eventually produced a response when presented alone. The last key concept is the *conditioned response*. This describes the behavior of the dog; it salivated in reaction to the bell alone.

Using these concepts, we can summarize classical conditioning. Essentially, learning a conditioned response involves building up an association between a conditioned stimulus and an unconditioned stimulus. When the stimuli, one compelling and the other one neutral, are paired, the neutral one becomes a conditioned stimulus and, hence, takes on the properties of the unconditioned stimulus.

Classical conditioning can be used to explain why Christmas carols often bring back pleasant memories of childhood; the songs are associated with the festive Christmas spirit and evoke fond memories and feelings of euphoria. In an organizational setting, we can also see classical conditioning operating. For example, at one manufacturing plant, every time the top executives from the head office were scheduled to make a visit, the plant management would clean up the administrative offices and wash the windows. This went on for years. Eventually, employees would turn on their best behavior and look prim and proper whenever the windows were cleaned—even in those occasional instances when the cleaning was not paired with the visit from the top brass. People had learned to associate the cleaning of the windows with a visit from the head office.

Classical conditioning is passive. Something happens and we react in a specific way. It is elicited in response to a specific, identifiable event. As such, it can explain simple reflexive behaviors. But most behavior—particularly the complex behavior of individuals in organizations—is emitted rather than elicited. It is voluntary rather than reflexive. For example, employees choose to arrive at work on time, ask their

Source: THE FAR SIDE copyright 1990 & 1991 FARWORKS, INC./Dist. by UNIVERSAL PRESS SYNDICATE. Reprinted with permission. All rights reserved.

boss for help with problems, or "goof off" when no one is watching. The learning of those behaviors is better understood by looking at operant conditioning.

operant conditioning

A type of conditioning in which desired voluntary behavior leads to a reward or prevents a punishment.

Operant Conditioning **Operant conditioning** argues that behavior is a function of its consequences. People learn to behave to get something they want or to avoid something they don't want. Operant behavior means voluntary or learned behavior in contrast to reflexive or unlearned behavior. The tendency to repeat such behavior is influenced by the reinforcement or lack of reinforcement brought about by the consequences of the behavior. Reinforcement, therefore, strengthens a behavior and increases the likelihood that it will be repeated.

What Pavlov did for classical conditioning, the Harvard psychologist B. F. Skinner did for operant conditioning.[34] Building on earlier work in the field, Skinner's research extensively expanded our knowledge of operant conditioning. Even his staunchest critics, who represent a sizable group, admit that his operant concepts work.

Behavior is assumed to be determined from without—that is, learned—rather than from within—reflexive or unlearned. Skinner argued that creating pleasing consequences to follow specific forms of behavior would increase the frequency of that behavior. People will most likely engage in desired behaviors if they are positively reinforced for doing so. Rewards are most effective if they immediately follow the desired response. In addition, behavior that is not rewarded, or is punished, is less likely to be repeated.

You see illustrations of operant conditioning everywhere. For example, any situation in which it is either explicitly stated or implicitly suggested that reinforcements are contingent on some action on your part involves the use of operant learning. Your instructor says that if you want a high grade in the course you must supply correct answers on the test. A commissioned salesperson wanting to earn a sizable income finds that doing so is contingent on generating high sales in her territory. Of course, the linkage can also work to teach the individual to engage in behaviors that work against the best interests of the organization. Assume that your boss tells you that if you will work overtime during the next three-week busy season, you will be compensated for it at the next performance appraisal. However, when performance appraisal time comes, you find that you are given no positive reinforcement for your overtime work. The next time your boss asks you to work overtime, what will you do? You'll probably decline! Your behavior can be explained by operant conditioning: If a behavior fails to be positively reinforced, the probability that the behavior will be repeated declines.

social-learning theory

People can learn through observation and direct experience.

Social Learning Individuals can also learn by observing what happens to other people and just by being told about something, as well as by direct experiences. So, for example, much of what we have learned comes from watching models—parents, teachers, peers, motion picture and television performers, bosses, and so forth. This view that we can learn through both observation and direct experience has been called **social-learning theory**.[35]

Although social-learning theory is an extension of operant conditioning—that is, it assumes that behavior is a function of consequences—it also acknowledges the existence of observational learning and the importance of perception in learning. People respond to how they perceive and define consequences, not to the objective consequences themselves.

The influence of models is central to the social-learning viewpoint. Four processes have been found to determine the influence that a model will have on an individual. As we will show later in this chapter, the inclusion of the following processes when management sets up employee training programs will significantly improve the likelihood that the programs will be successful:

1. *Attentional processes*. People learn from a model only when they recognize and pay attention to its critical features. We tend to be most influenced by models that are attractive, repeatedly available, important to us, or similar to us in our estimation.
2. *Retention processes*. A model's influence will depend on how well the individual remembers the model's action after the model is no longer readily available.
3. *Motor reproduction processes*. After a person has seen a new behavior by observing the model, the watching must be converted to doing. This process then demonstrates that the individual can perform the modeled activities.
4. *Reinforcement processes*. Individuals will be motivated to exhibit the modeled behavior if positive incentives or rewards are provided. Behaviors that are positively reinforced will be given more attention, learned better, and performed more often.

Physician Sales & Service, a distributor of medical supplies to physicians' offices, applies social learning in training its sales representatives. After a one-week orientation program, newly hired employees spend 12 weeks in the field with veteran sales reps to learn about the job and what is expected of them. After the field training, they attend PSS University, shown here, to develop the skills they observed in working with their professional sales models.

SHAPING: A MANAGERIAL TOOL

Because learning takes place on the job as well as prior to it, managers will be concerned with how they can teach employees to behave in ways that most benefit the organization. When we attempt to mold individuals by guiding their learning in graduated steps, we are **shaping behavior**.

Consider the situation in which an employee's behavior is significantly different from that sought by management. If management rewarded the individual only when he or she showed desirable responses, there might be very little reinforcement taking place. In such a case, shaping offers a logical approach toward achieving the desired behavior.

We *shape* behavior by systematically reinforcing each successive step that moves the individual closer to the desired response. If an employee who has chronically been a half-hour late for work comes in only 20 minutes late, we can reinforce that improvement. Reinforcement would increase as responses more closely approximated the desired behavior.

shaping behavior
Systematically reinforcing each successive step that moves an individual closer to the desired response.

Methods of Shaping Behavior   There are four ways in which to shape behavior: through positive reinforcement, negative reinforcement, punishment, and extinction.

Following a response with something pleasant is called *positive reinforcement*. This would describe, for instance, the boss who praises an employee for a job well done. Following a response by the termination or withdrawal of something unpleasant is called *negative reinforcement*. If your college instructor asks a question and you don't know the answer, looking through your lecture notes is likely to preclude your being called on. This is a negative reinforcement because you have learned that looking busily through your notes prevents the instructor from calling on you. *Punishment* is causing an unpleasant condition in an attempt to eliminate an undesirable behavior. Giving an employee a two-day suspension from work without pay for showing up drunk is an example of punishment. Eliminating any reinforcement that is maintaining a behavior is called *extinction*. When the behavior is not reinforced, it tends to gradually be extinguished. College instructors who wish to discourage students from asking questions in class can eliminate this behavior in their students by ignoring those who raise their hands to ask questions. Hand-raising will become extinct when it is invariably met with an absence of reinforcement.

Both positive and negative reinforcement result in learning. They strengthen a response and increase the probability of repetition. In the preceding illustrations, praise strengthens and increases the behavior of doing a good job because praise is desired. The behavior of "looking busy" is similarly strengthened and increased by its terminating the undesirable consequence of being called on by the teacher. Both punishment and extinction, however, weaken behavior and tend to decrease its subsequent frequency.

Reinforcement, whether it is positive or negative, has an impressive record as a shaping tool. Our interest, therefore, is in reinforcement rather than in punishment or extinction. A review of research findings on the impact of reinforcement upon behavior in organizations concluded that

continuous reinforcement

A desired behavior is reinforced each and every time it is demonstrated.

1. Some type of reinforcement is necessary to produce a change in behavior.
2. Some types of rewards are more effective for use in organizations than others.
3. The speed with which learning takes place and the permanence of its effects will be determined by the timing of reinforcement.[36]

Point 3 is extremely important and deserves considerable elaboration.

At Transitions for Health, a firm that sells health products for women, CEO Sharon MacFarland (seated) uses positive reinforcement to shape behavior. She rewards employees with prizes like gift certificates and praise when they reach personal achievement goals that are tied to company core values. Employees shown here pose with props they used in a variety of volunteer tasks they completed in support of the firm's value of community service.

Schedules of Reinforcement The two major types of reinforcement schedules are *continuous* and *intermittent*. A **continuous reinforcement** schedule reinforces the desired behavior each and every time it is demonstrated. Take, for example, the case of someone who has historically had trouble arriving at work on time. Every time he is not tardy his manager might compliment him on his desirable behavior. In an intermittent schedule, on the other hand, not every instance of the desirable behavior is reinforced, but reinforcement is given often enough to make the behavior worth repeating. This latter schedule can be compared to the workings of a slot machine, which people will continue to play even when they know that it is adjusted to give a considerable return to the gambling house. The intermittent payoffs occur just often enough to reinforce the behavior of slipping in coins and pulling the handle. Evidence indicates that the intermittent, or varied, form of reinforcement tends to promote more resistance to extinction than does the continuous form.[37]

An **intermittent rein-forcement** can be of a ratio or interval type. *Ratio schedules* depend upon how many responses the subject makes. The individual is reinforced after giving a certain number of specific types of behavior. *Interval schedules* depend upon how much time has passed since the last reinforcement. With interval schedules, the

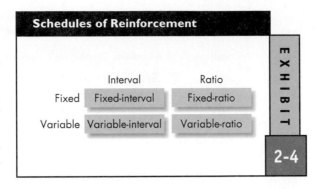

individual is reinforced on the first appropriate behavior after a particular time has elapsed. A reinforcement can also be classified as fixed or variable. Intermittent techniques for administering rewards can, therefore, be placed into four categories, as shown in Exhibit 2-4.

When rewards are spaced at uniform time intervals, the reinforcement schedule is of the **fixed-interval** type. The critical variable is time, and it is held constant. This is the predominant schedule for most salaried workers in North America. When you get your paycheck on a weekly, semimonthly, monthly, or other predetermined time basis, you are rewarded on a fixed-interval reinforcement schedule.

If rewards are distributed in time so that reinforcements are unpredictable, the schedule is of the **variable-interval** type. When an instructor advises her class that pop quizzes will be given during the term (the exact number of which is unknown to the students) and the quizzes will account for twenty percent of the term grade, she is using a variable-interval schedule. Similarly, a series of randomly timed unannounced visits to a company office by the corporate audit staff is an example of a variable-interval schedule.

In a **fixed-ratio** schedule, after a fixed or constant number of responses are given, a reward is initiated. For example, a piece-rate incentive plan is a fixed-ratio schedule; the employee receives a reward based on the number of work pieces generated. If the piece rate for a zipper installer in a dressmaking factory is $5.00 a dozen, the reinforcement (money in this case) is fixed to the number of zippers sewn into garments. After every dozen is sewn in, the installer has earned another $5.00.

When the reward varies relative to the behavior of the individual, he or she is said to be reinforced on a **variable-ratio** schedule. Salespeople on commission are examples of individuals on such a reinforcement schedule. On some occasions, they may make a sale after only two calls on a potential customer. On other occasions, they might need to make 20 or more calls to secure a sale. The reward, then, is variable in relation to the number of calls the salesperson makes. Exhibit 2-5 depicts the four categories of intermittent schedules.

Reinforcement Schedules and Behavior   Continuous reinforcement schedules can lead to early satiation, and under this schedule behavior tends to weaken rapidly when reinforcers are withheld. However, continuous reinforcers are appropriate for newly emitted, unstable, or low-frequency responses. In contrast, intermittent reinforcers preclude early satiation because they don't follow every response. They are appropriate for stable or high-frequency responses.

In general, variable schedules tend to lead to higher performance than fixed schedules. For example, as noted previously, most employees in organizations are paid on fixed-interval schedules. But such a schedule does not clearly link performance and rewards. The reward is given for time spent on the job rather than for

intermittent reinforcement

A desired behavior is reinforced often enough to make the behavior worth repeating but not every time it is demonstrated.

fixed-interval schedule

Rewards are spaced at uniform time intervals.

variable-interval schedule

Rewards are distributed in time so that reinforcements are unpredictable.

fixed-ratio schedule

Rewards are initiated after a fixed or constant number of responses.

variable-ratio schedule

The reward varies relative to the behavior of the individual.

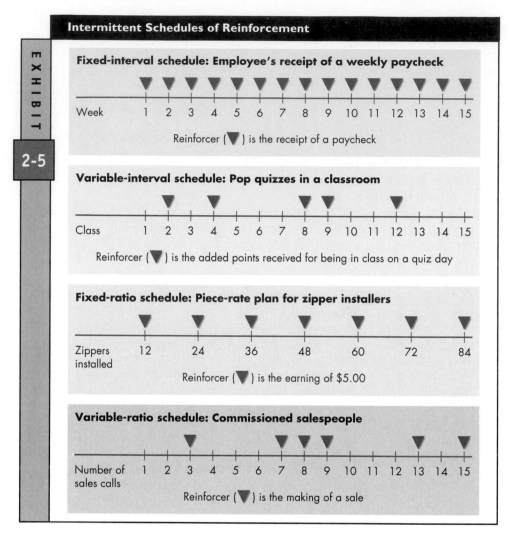

Intermittent Schedules of Reinforcement

EXHIBIT 2-5

Fixed-interval schedule: Employee's receipt of a weekly paycheck

Week   1 2 3 4 5 6 7 8 9 10 11 12 13 14 15

Reinforcer (▼) is the receipt of a paycheck

Variable-interval schedule: Pop quizzes in a classroom

Class   1 2 3 4 5 6 7 8 9 10 11 12 13 14 15

Reinforcer (▼) is the added points received for being in class on a quiz day

Fixed-ratio schedule: Piece-rate plan for zipper installers

Zippers installed   12   24   36   48   60   72   84

Reinforcer (▼) is the earning of $5.00

Variable-ratio schedule: Commissioned salespeople

Number of sales calls   1 2 3 4 5 6 7 8 9 10 11 12 13 14 15

Reinforcer (▼) is the making of a sale

a specific response (performance). In contrast, variable-interval schedules generate high rates of response and more stable and consistent behavior because of a high correlation between performance and reward and because of the uncertainty involved—the employee tends to be more alert since there is a surprise factor.

Behavior Modification   There is a classic study that took place a number of years ago with freight packers at Emery Air Freight (now part of CNF Transportation, Inc.).[38] Emery's management wanted packers to use freight containers for shipments whenever possible because of specific economic savings. When packers were asked as to the percentage of shipments containerized, the standard reply was 90 percent. An analysis by Emery found, however, that the actual container utilization rate was 45 percent. In order to encourage employees to use containers, management established a program of feedback and positive reinforcements. Each packer was instructed to keep a checklist of his or her daily packings, both containerized and noncontainerized. At the end of each day, the packer computed his or her container utilization rate. Almost unbelievably, container utilization jumped to more than 90 percent on the first day of the program and held to that level. Emery reported that this simple program of feedback and positive reinforcements saved the company $2 million over a three-year period.

"You Can't Teach an Old Dog New Tricks!"

This statement is false. It reflects the widely held stereotype that older workers have difficulties in adapting to new methods and techniques. Studies consistently demonstrate that older employees are *perceived* as being relatively inflexible, resistant to change, and less trainable than their younger counterparts, particularly with respect to information technology skills.[39] But these perceptions are wrong.

The evidence indicates that older workers (typically defined as people aged 50 and over) want to learn and are just as capable of learning as any other employee group. Older workers do seem to be somewhat less efficient in acquiring complex or de-manding skills. That is, they may take longer to train. But once trained, they perform at comparable levels to younger workers.[40]

The ability to acquire the skills, knowledge, or behavior necessary to perform a job at a given level—that is, trainability—has been the subject of much research. And the evidence indicates that there are differences between people in their train-ability. A number of individual-difference factors (such as ability, motivational level, and personality) have been found to significantly influence learning and training outcomes.[41] Age, however, has not been found to influence these outcomes.

This program at Emery Air Freight illustrates the use of behavior modification, or what has become more popularly called **OB Mod**.[42] It represents the application of reinforcement concepts to individuals in the work setting.

The typical OB Mod program follows a five-step problem-solving model: (1) identifying critical behaviors; (2) developing baseline data; (3) identifying behavioral consequences; (4) developing and implementing an intervention strategy; and (5) evaluating performance improvement.[43]

Everything an employee does on his or her job is not equally important in terms of performance outcomes. The first step in OB Mod, therefore, is to identify the critical behaviors that make a significant impact on the employee's job performance. These are those 5 to 10 percent of behaviors that may account for up to 70 or 80 percent of each employee's performance. Using containers whenever possible by freight packers at Emery Air Freight is an example of a critical behavior.

The second step requires the manager to develop some baseline performance data. This is obtained by determining the number of times the identified behavior is occurring under present conditions. In our freight packing example at Emery, this would have revealed that 45 percent of all shipments were containerized.

The third step is to perform a functional analysis to identify the behavioral contingencies or consequences of performance. This tells the manager the antecedent cues that emit the behavior and the consequences that are currently maintaining it. At Emery Air Freight, social norms and the greater difficulty in packing containers were the antecedent cues. This encouraged the practice of packing items separately. Moreover, the consequences for continuing the behavior, prior to the OB Mod intervention, were social acceptance and escaping more demanding work.

Once the functional analysis is complete, the manager is ready to develop and implement an intervention strategy to strengthen desirable performance behaviors and weaken undesirable behaviors. The appropriate strategy will entail changing some elements of the performance–reward linkage—structure, processes, technology, groups, or the task—with the goal of making high-level performance more rewarding. In the Emery example, the work technology was altered to require the keeping of a checklist. The checklist plus the computation,

OB Mod

The application of reinforcement cncepts to individuals in the work setting.

at the end of the day, of a container utilization rate acted to reinforce the desirable behavior of using containers.

The final step in OB Mod is to evaluate performance improvement. In the Emery intervention, the immediate improvement in the container utilization rate demonstrated that behavioral change took place. That it rose to 90 percent and held at that level further indicates that learning took place. That is, the employees underwent a relatively permanent change in behavior.

OB Mod has been used by a number of organizations to improve employee productivity and to reduce errors, absenteeism, tardiness, accident rates, and improve friendliness toward customers.[44] For instance, a clothing manufacturer saved $60,000 in one year from fewer absences. A packing firm improved productivity 16 percent, cut errors by 40 percent, and reduced accidents by more than 43 percent—resulting in savings of over $1 million. A bank successfully used OB Mod to increase the friendliness of its tellers, which led to a demonstrative improvement in customer satisfaction.

SOME SPECIFIC ORGANIZATIONAL APPLICATIONS

We have alluded to a number of situations in which learning theory could be helpful to managers. In this section, we will briefly look at six specific applications: using lotteries to reduce absenteeism, substituting well pay for sick pay, disciplining problem employees, developing effective employee training programs, creating mentoring programs for new employees, and applying learning theory to self-management.

Neopost, a postage-meter manufacturer, used OB Mod to improve employee productivity and overcome resistance to change. It invested millions of dollars in laptop computers and software for CD-ROM presentations and virtual product demonstrations. Mary McGaughan Perry (left), Neopost's national sales training manager, learned that salespeople weren't using their laptops. To increase computer use, Perry trained salespeople inexperienced in using computers so they could learn how computers could increase sales and ran a contest that rewarded salespeople with $10 each time they used their computer in selling. Her efforts resulted in a huge jump in sales.

Using Lotteries to Reduce Absenteeism Management can use learning theory to design programs to reduce absenteeism. For example, Continental Airlines has created a lottery that rewards its 40,000 employees for attendance.[45] Twice a year, Continental holds a raffle in which it gives away eight new sport utility vehicles. But only employees who have not missed a day of work during the previous six months are eligible. This lottery follows a variable-ratio schedule. A good attendance record increases an employee's probability of winning, yet having perfect attendance is no assurance that an employee will be rewarded with a new SUV. Consistent with the research on reinforcement schedules, management credits the lottery with significantly reducing the company's absence rate.

Well Pay vs. Sick Pay Most organizations provide their salaried employees with paid sick leave as part of the employee's fringe benefit program. But, ironically, organizations with paid sick leave programs experience almost twice the absenteeism of organizations without such programs.[46] The reality is that sick leave programs reinforce the wrong behavior—absence from work. When employees receive 10 paid sick days a year, it's the unusual employee who isn't sure to use them all up, regardless of whether he or she is sick. Organizations should reward *attendance,* not *absence*.

As a case in point, one Midwest organization implemented a well-pay program that paid a bonus to employees who had no absence for any given four-week period and then paid for sick leave only after the first eight hours of absence.[47] Evaluation of the well-pay program found that it produced increased savings to the organization, reduced absenteeism, increased productivity, and improved employee satisfaction.

Forbes magazine used the same approach to cut its health care costs.[48] It rewarded employees who stayed healthy and didn't file medical claims by paying

OB Mod at Turner Bros. Trucking

Turner Bros. Trucking, Inc., based in Oklahoma City, provides transportation and drilling-related services to petroleum and refining firms in Oklahoma, Texas, and Colorado. It has about 300 employees.

Since 1992, the company has been using OB Mod concepts to get employees to focus on safety. The company used its pre-1992 accident data as a benchmark. It determined the average historical losses at each team location, then lowered those by 30 percent to set a new achieveable standard. Successful achievement of the new goal rewarded each team member with one dozen work gloves, worth about $30 a month, because employees didn't have to spend their own money for gloves. Then the benchmark was reduced another 30 percent and coveralls were awarded for success. This part of the program put an additional $70 in each person's pocket—money they would have otherwise had to spend on providing their own work clothes. The gloves and coveralls worked so well that the company added a direct monetary incentive. If losses remained under $300 per month per team, each team member received a monthly incentive check for $50. After three consecutive months, the $50 was doubled. Other features of the safety program included behavioral observation of one another by workers, with feedback, and measurement and feedback on learning in defensive driving courses. Employees have been kept informed monthly on how their teams are doing by way of large colored graphs posted for all to see.

The program has provided impressive results. For several years prior to 1992, insurance premiums and self-funded losses were more than 12 percent of gross revenues. Six years later, it was down to 4 percent, including the cost of providing the safety incentives. In Texas alone, injury losses were reduced by 99 percent. Not only did the program create significant savings for the company in terms of lower insurance premiums and less money to adjusters and attorneys, the program's incentives added 3 to 11 percent to employee pay.

Source: G. M. Ritzky, "Turner Bros. Wins Safety Game with Behavioral Incentives," *HRMagazine*, June 1998, pp. 79–83.

them the difference between $500 and their medical claims, then doubling the amount. So if someone submitted no claims in a given year, he or she would receive $1,000 ($500 × 2). By rewarding employees for good health, *Forbes* cut its major medical and dental claims by over 30 percent.

Employee Discipline Every manager will, at some time, have to deal with an employee who drinks on the job, is insubordinate, steals company property, arrives consistently late for work, or engages in similar problem behaviors. Managers will respond with disciplinary actions such as oral reprimands, written warnings, and temporary suspensions. But our knowledge about punishment's effect on behavior indicates that the use of discipline carries costs. It may provide only a short-term solution and result in serious side effects.

Disciplining employees for undesirable behaviors only tells them what *not* to do. It doesn't tell them what alternative behaviors are preferred. The result is that this form of punishment frequently leads to only short-term suppression of the undesirable behavior rather than its elimination. Continued use of punishment, rather than positive reinforcement, also tends to produce a fear of the manager. As the punishing agent, the manager becomes associated in the employee's mind with adverse consequences. Employees respond by "hiding" from their boss. Hence, the use of punishment can undermine manager–employee relations.

Discipline does have a place in organizations. In practice, it tends to be popular because of its ability to produce fast results in the short run. Moreover, managers are reinforced for using discipline because it produces an immediate change in the employee's behavior. The suggestions offered in the "From Concepts to Skills" box can help you to more effectively implement disciplinary action.

Effective Discipline Skills

he essence of effective disciplining can be summarized by the following eight behaviors.[49]

1. *Respond immediately.* The more quickly a disciplinary action follows an offense, the more likely it is that the employee will associate the discipline with the offense rather than with you as the dispenser of the discipline. It's best to begin the disciplinary process as soon as possible after you notice a violation.

2. *Provide a warning.* You have an obligation to give warning before initiating disciplinary action. This means that the employee must be aware of the organization's rules and accept its standards of behavior. Disciplinary action is more likely to be interpreted by employees as fair when they have received clear warning that a given violation will lead to discipline and when they know what that discipline will be.

3. *State the problem specifically.* Give the date, time, place, individuals involved, and any mitigating circumstances surrounding the violation. Be sure to define the violation in exact terms instead of just reciting company regulations or terms from a union contract. It's not the violation of the rules per se that you want to convey concern about. It's the effect that the rule violation has on the work unit's performance. Explain why the behavior can't be continued by showing how it specifically affects the employee's job performance, the unit's effectiveness, and the employee's colleagues.

4. *Allow the employee to explain his or her position.* Regardless of what facts you have uncovered, due process demands that you give the employee the opportunity to explain his or her position. From the employee's perspective, what happened? Why did it happen? What was his or her perception of the rules, regulations, and circumstances?

5. *Keep discussion impersonal.* Penalties should be connected with a given violation, not with the personality of the individual violator. That is, discipline should be directed at what the employee has done, not at the employee.

6. *Be consistent.* Fair treatment of employees demands that disciplinary action be consistent. If you enforce rule violations in an inconsistent manner, the rules will lose their impact, morale will decline, and employees will likely question your competence. Consistency, however, need not result in treating everyone exactly alike; doing that would ignore mitigating circumstances. It's reasonable to modify the severity of penalties to reflect the employee's past history, job performance record, and the like. But the responsibility is yours to clearly justify disciplinary actions that might appear inconsistent to employees.

7. *Take progressive action.* Choose a punishment that's appropriate to the crime. Penalties should get progressively stronger if, or when, an offense is repeated. Typically, progressive disciplinary action begins with a verbal warning and then proceeds through a written reprimand, suspension, a demotion or pay cut, and finally, in the most serious cases, dismissal.

8. *Obtain agreement on change.* Disciplining should include guidance and direction for correcting the problem. Let the employee state what he or she plans to do in the future to ensure that the violation won't be repeated.

Developing Training Programs   Most organizations have some type of systematic training program. More specifically, U.S. corporations with 100 or more employees spent in excess of $62 billion in one recent year on formal training for 47.3 million workers.[50] Can these organizations draw from our discussion of learning in order to improve the effectiveness of their training programs? Certainly.

Social-learning theory offers such a guide. It tells us that training should offer a model to grab the trainee's attention; provide motivational properties; help the trainee to file away what he or she has learned for later use; provide opportunities to practice new behaviors; offer positive rewards for accomplishments; and, if the training has taken place off the job, allow the trainee some opportunity to transfer what he or she has learned to the job.[51]

Creating Mentoring Programs It's the unusual senior manager who, early in his or her career, didn't have an older, more experienced mentor higher up in the organization. This mentor took the protégé under his or her wing and provided advice and guidance on how to survive and get ahead in the organization. Mentoring, of course, is not limited to the managerial ranks. Union apprenticeship programs, for example, do the same thing by preparing individuals to move from unskilled apprentice status to that of skilled journeymen. A young electrician apprentice typically works under an experienced electrician for several years to develop the full range of skills necessary to effectively execute his or her job.

A successful mentoring program will be built on modeling concepts from social-learning theory. That is, a mentor's impact comes from more than merely what he or she explicitly tells a protégé. Mentors are role models. Protégés learn to convey the attitudes and behaviors that the organization wants by emulating the traits and actions of their mentors. They observe and then imitate. Top managers who are concerned with developing employees who will fit into the organization and with preparing young managerial talent for greater responsibilities should give careful attention to who takes on mentoring roles. The creating of formal mentoring programs—in which individuals are officially assigned a mentor—allows senior executives to manage the process and increases the likelihood that protégés will be molded the way top management desires.

Dori Thornhill (left) realized she needed help in managing her own behavior, not the behavior of her employees. Owner and president of a marketing consulting firm, Thornhill wanted to eliminate her bad business habit of spending too much time trying to help clients who had inadequate budgets. She hired a personal coach, Kathie Bolles (right), to improve her time-management and decision-making skills. Self-management is helping Thornhill reduce her frustration in wasting time and energy on unprofitable customers and focus more on profitable accounts.

Self-Management Organizational applications of learning concepts are not restricted to managing the behavior of others. These concepts can also be used to allow individuals to manage their own behavior and, in so doing, reduce the need for managerial control. This is called **self-management**.[52]

Self-management requires an individual to deliberately manipulate stimuli, internal processes, and responses to achieve personal behavioral outcomes. The basic processes involve observing one's own behavior, comparing the behavior with a standard, and rewarding oneself if the behavior meets the standard.

So how might self-management be applied? Here's an illustration. A group of state government blue-collar employees received eight hours of training in which they were taught self-management skills.[53] They were then shown how the skills could be used for improving job attendance. They were instructed on how to set specific goals for job attendance, both short term and intermediate term. They learned how to write a behavioral contract with themselves and identify self-chosen reinforcers. Finally, they learned the importance of self-monitoring their attendance behavior and administering incentives when they achieved their goals. The net result for these participants was a significant improvement in job attendance.

self-management

Learning techniques that allow individuals to manage their own behavior so that less external management control is necessary.

SUMMARY AND IMPLICATIONS FOR MANAGERS

This chapter looked at three individual variables—biographical characteristics, ability, and learning. Let's now try to summarize what we found and consider their importance for the manager who is trying to understand organizational behavior.

BIOGRAPHICAL CHARACTERISTICS

Biographical characteristics are readily available to managers. For the most part, they include data that are contained in almost every employee's personnel file. The most important conclusions we can draw after our review of the evidence are that age seems to have no relationship to productivity; older workers and those with longer tenure are less likely to resign; and married employees have fewer absences, less turnover, and report higher job satisfaction than do unmarried employees. But what value can this information have for managers? The obvious answer is that it can help in making choices among job applicants.

ABILITY

Ability directly influences an employee's level of performance and satisfaction through the ability–job fit. Given management's desire to get a compatible fit, what can be done?

First, an effective selection process will improve the fit. A job analysis will provide information about jobs currently being done and the abilities that individuals need to perform the jobs adequately. Applicants can then be tested, interviewed, and evaluated on the degree to which they possess the necessary abilities.

Second, promotion and transfer decisions affecting individuals already in the organization's employ should reflect the abilities of candidates. As with new employees, care should be taken to assess critical abilities that incumbents will need in the job and to match those requirements with the organization's human resources.

> *Ability directly influences an employees's level of performance and satisfaction through the ability–job fit.*

Third, the fit can be improved by fine-tuning the job to better match an incumbent's abilities. Often modifications can be made in the job that, while not having a significant impact on the job's basic activities, better adapts it to the specific talents of a given employee. Examples would be to change some of the equipment used or to reorganize tasks within a group of employees.

A final alternative is to provide training for employees. This is applicable to both new workers and present job incumbents. Training can keep the abilities of incumbents current or provide new skills as times and conditions change.

LEARNING

Any observable change in behavior is prima facie evidence that learning has taken place. What we want to do, of course, is to ascertain if learning concepts provide us with any insights that would allow us to explain and predict behavior.

Positive reinforcement is a powerful tool for modifying behavior. By identifying and rewarding performance-enhancing behaviors, management increases the likelihood that they will be repeated.

Our knowledge about learning further suggests that reinforcement is a more effective tool than punishment. Although punishment eliminates undesired behavior more quickly than negative reinforcement does, punished behavior tends to be only temporarily suppressed rather than permanently changed. And punishment may produce unpleasant side effects such as lower morale and higher absenteeism or turnover. In addition, the recipients of punishment tend to become resentful of the punisher. Managers, therefore, are advised to use reinforcement rather than punishment.

Finally, managers should expect that employees will look to them as models. Managers who are constantly late to work, or take two hours for lunch, or help themselves to company office supplies for personal use should expect employees to read the message they are sending and model their behavior accordingly.

Individual Differences Explain Organizational Behavior

The concept of an "organization" is an artificial notion.[1] The physical properties of organizations—such as building and equipment—tend to obscure the fact that organizations are really nothing other than aggregates of individuals. So to understand organizational behavior, you need to focus on individuals.

Casual observation leads all of us to the obvious conclusion that no two people in the same job behave in exactly the same way. Even in highly programmed jobs, such as assembly-line work in an automobile factory or processing claims in an insurance company, employee behavior varies. Why? Individual differences. College students certainly understand and act on this reality when they choose classes. If three instructors are all teaching Accounting 101 at the same time of day, most students will seek out information to find out the differences between the instructors. Even though they teach the same course as described in the college catalog, the instructors enjoy a considerable degree of freedom in how they meet their course objectives. Students know that, and they try to acquire accurate information that will allow them to select among the three. That is, they seek information on individual differences.

People go about doing their jobs in different ways. They differ in their interactions with their bosses and coworkers. They vary in terms of work habits—promptness in completing tasks, conscientiousness in doing quality work, cooperation with co-workers, and the like. They vary by degree of effort they are willing to exert on their job. And they vary in terms of the importance they place on factors such as security, recognition, or social support. What explains the variations? Individual difference variables such as values, attitudes, perceptions, motives, and personalities.

If you want to be able to explain employee behavior, you have to recognize the overwhelming influence that individual differences play.

If you want to understand the behavior of people at work, you need to focus on social structure—not individual differences.[2] Why? Because human beings are social animals.

Far too much emphasis in OB is placed on studying individual differences. It's not that values, attitudes, personalities, and similar personal characteristics are irrelevant to understanding organizational behavior. Rather, organizations come with a host of formal and informal control mechanisms that, in effect, largely shape, direct, and constrain members' behavior. That is, structure tends to override individual differences. Let's look at a couple of examples.

Almost all organizations have policies, procedures, rules, and other formal documentation that limit and shape behavior. This formal documentation sets standards of acceptable and unacceptable behavior, and allows us to predict a good deal of an employee's on-the-job behavior.

Almost all organizations differentiate roles horizontally, creating unique jobs and departments. The structure of these jobs allows others to predict behavior in those roles. Similarly, organizations also differentiate roles vertically by creating levels of management. In so doing, they create boss–employee relationships that constrain employee behavior.

When you join an organization, you are expected to adapt to its norms of acceptable behavior. These norms are unwritten rules but, nevertheless, they're powerful and controlling. An organization, for instance, may not have a formal dress code, but employees are expected to "dress appropriately"—which means adapting to the implied dress norms.

Our point here is that you shouldn't forget the *organizational* part of organizational behavior. It doesn't sound very nice, but organizations are instruments of domination. They put people into job "boxes" that constrain what they can do and with whom they can interact. To the degree that employees accept their organization's rules, roles, and norms, the latter become constraints on behavioral choices.

---

[1]Some points in this argument are based on B. M. Staw, "Dressing Up Like an Organization: When Psychological Actions Can Explain Organizational Action," *Journal of Management*, December 1991, pp. 805–19.

[2]Some points in this argument are based on J. Pfeffer, "Organization Theory and Structural Perspectives on Management," *Journal of Management*, December 1991, pp. 789–803.

1. Which biographical characteristics best predict productivity? Absenteeism? Turnover? Satisfaction?

2. Assess the validity of using intelligence scores for selecting new employees.

3. Describe the specific steps you would take to ensure that an individual has the appropriate abilities to satisfactorily do a given job.

4. Explain classical conditioning.

5. Contrast classical conditioning, operant conditioning, and social learning.

6. How might employees actually learn unethical behavior on their jobs?

7. Describe the four types of intermittent reinforcers.

8. What are the five steps in behavior modification?

9. If you had to take disciplinary action against an employee, how, specifically, would you do it?

10. Describe the four processes in successful social learning.

Questions for Critical Thinking

1. "All organizations would benefit from hiring the smartest people they can get." Do you agree or disagree with this statement? Support your answer.

2. What influences do you think an employee's age, experience, and physical abilities have on his or her job performance?

3. Besides past work history and an employee's job performance, what other mitigating factors do you think a manager should use in applying discipline? And doesn't the mere attempt to use mitigating circumstances turn disciplinary action into a political process?

4. Learning theory can be used to explain behavior and to control behavior. Can you distinguish between the two objectives? Can you give any ethical or moral arguments why managers should not seek control over others' behavior? How valid do you think these arguments are?

5. What have you learned about "learning" that could help you to explain the behavior of students in a classroom if: (a) The instructor gives only one test—a final examination at the end of the course? (b) The instructor gives four exams during the term, all of which are announced on the first day of class? (c) The student's grade is based on the results of numerous exams, none of which are announced by the instructor ahead of time?

Team Exercise | Positive and Negative Reinforcement

Exercise Overview (Steps 1–4)

This 10-step exercise takes approximately 20 minutes.

1. Two volunteers are selected to receive reinforcement from the class while performing a particular task. The volunteers leave the room.

2. The instructor identifies an object for the student volunteers to locate when they return to the room. (The object should be unobstructive but clearly visible to the class. Examples that have worked well include a small triangular piece of paper that was left behind when a notice was torn off a classroom bulletin board, a smudge on the chalkboard, and a chip in the plaster of a classroom wall.)

3. The instructor specifies the reinforcement contingencies that will be in effect when the volunteers return to the room. For negative reinforcement, students should hiss or boo when the first volunteer is moving away from the object. For

positive reinforcement, they should cheer and applaud when the second volunteer is getting closer to the object.

4. The instructor should assign a student to keep a record of the time it takes each of the volunteers to locate the object.

Volunteer 1 (Steps 5 and 6)

5. Volunteer 1 is brought back into the room and is told, "Your task is to locate and touch a particular object in the room and the class has agreed to help you. You can't use words or ask questions. Begin."

6. Volunteer 1 continues to look for the object until it is found, while the class assists by giving negative reinforcement.

Volunteer 2 (Steps 7 and 8)

7. Volunteer 2 is brought back into the room and is told, "Your task is to locate and touch a particu-

lar object in the room and the class has agreed to help you. You can't use words or ask questions. Begin."

8. Volunteer 2 continues to look for the object until it is found, while the class assists by giving positive reinforcement.

Class Review (Steps 9 and 10)

9. The timekeeper will present the results on how long it took each volunteer to find the object.

10. The class will discuss:

a. What was the difference in behavior of the two volunteers?

b. What are the implications of this exercise to reinforcement schedules in organizations?

Source: Adapted from an exercise developed by Larry Michaelson of the University of Oklahoma. With permission.

Internet Search Exercises

1. Find three reviews of R. Herrnstein and C. Murray's, *The Bell Curve* (Free Press, 1994). Summarize their position; then critique it.

2. Find three organizations that have been involved in age discrimination suits. What were the specific issues involved? If resolved, what was the outcome?

PHLIP Companion Web Site

We invite you to visit the Robbins homepage on the Prentice Hall Web site at **www.prenhall.com/robbins** for our on-line study guide, current events, links to related Web sites, and more.

Case Incident | Predicting Performance

Alix Maher is the new admissions director at a small, highly selective New England college. She has a bachelor's degree in education and a recent master's degree in educational administration. But she has no prior experience in college admissions.

Alix's predecessor, in conjunction with the college's admissions committee (made up of five faculty members), had given the following weights to student selection criteria: high school grades (40 percent); Scholastic Aptitude Test (SAT) scores (40 percent); extracurricular activities and achievements (10 percent); and the quality and creativity of a written theme submitted with the application (10 percent).

Alix has serious reservations about using SAT scores. In their defense, she recognizes that the quality of high schools varies greatly, so that the level of student performance that receives an A in American history at one school might earn only a C at a far more demanding school. Alix is also aware that the people who design the SATs, the Educational Testing Service, argue forcefully that these test scores are valid predictors of how well a person will do in college. Yet Alix has several concerns:

1. The pressure of the SAT exam is very great, and many students suffer from test anxiety. The results, therefore, may not truly reflect what a student knows.

2. There is evidence that coaching improves scores by between 40 and 150 points. Test scores, therefore, may adversely affect the chances of acceptance for students who cannot afford the $600 or $700 to take test-coaching courses.

3. Are SATs valid, or do they discriminate against minorities, the poor, and those who have had limited access to cultural growth experiences?

As Alix ponders whether she wants to recommend changing the college's selection criteria and weights, she is reminded of a recent conversation she had with a friend who is an industrial psychologist with a *Fortune* 100 company. He told her that his company regularly uses intelligence tests to help select from among job applicants. For instance, after the company's recruiters interview graduating seniors on college campuses and identify possible hires, they give the applicants a standardized intelligence test. Those who fail to score at least in the 80th percentile are eliminated from the applicant pool.

Alix thinks that if intelligence tests are used by billion-dollar corporations to screen job applicants, why shouldn't colleges use them? Moreover, since one of the objectives of a college should be to get its graduates placed in good jobs, maybe SAT scores should be given even higher weight than 40 percent in the selection decision. After all, if SATs tap intelligence and employers want intelligent job applicants, why not make college selection decisions predominantly on the basis of SAT scores? Or should her college replace the SAT with a pure intelligence test such as the Wechsler Adult Intelligence Scale?

Questions

1. What do you think SATs measure: aptitude, innate ability, achievement potential, intelligence, ability to take tests, or something else?

2. If the best predictor of future behavior is past behavior, what should admissions directors use to identify the best-qualified applicants?

3. If you were Alix, what would you do? Why?

End Notes

1. Based on R. E. Stross, "Microsoft's Big Advantage—Hiring Only the Supersmart," *Fortune,* November 25, 1996, pp. 159–62; and N. Munk and S. Oliver, "Think Fast!" *Forbes,* March 24, 1997, pp. 146–51.

2. R. W. Judy and C. D'Amico, *Workforce 2020* (Indianapolis: Hudson Institute, 1997).

3. "American Business and Older Workers: A Road Map to the 21st Century," a report prepared for the American Association of Retired Persons by DYG, Inc., 1995; and "Valuing Older Workers: A Study of Costs and Productivity," a report prepared for the American Association of Retired Persons by ICF Inc., 1995.

4. S. R. Rhodes, "Age-Related Differences in Work Attitudes and Behavior: A Review and Conceptual Analysis," *Psychological Bulletin,* March 1983, pp. 328–67; J. L. Cotton and J. M. Tuttle, "Employee Turnover: A Meta-Analysis and Review with Implications for Research," *Academy of Management Review,* January 1986, pp. 55–70; and D. R. Davies, G. Matthews, and C. S. K. Wong, "Ageing and Work," in C. L. Cooper and I. T. Robertson (eds.), *International Review of Industrial and Organizational Psychology*, vol. 6 (Chichester, England: Wiley, 1991), pp. 183–87.

5. Rhodes, "Age-Related Differences in Work Attitudes and Behavior," pp. 347–49; R. D. Hackett, "Age, Tenure, and Employee Absenteeism," *Human Relations*, July 1990, pp. 601–19; and Davies, Matthews, and Wong, "Ageing and Work," pp. 183–87.

6. Cited in K. Labich, "The New Unemployed," *Fortune,* March 8, 1993, p. 43.

7. See G. M. McEvoy and W. F. Cascio, "Cumulative Evidence of the Relationship between Employee Age and Job Performance," *Journal of Applied Psychology*, February 1989, pp. 11–17; and F. L. Schmidt and J. E. Hunter, "The Validity and Utility of Selection Methods in Personnel Psychology: Practical and Theoretical Implications of 85 Years of Research Findings," *Psychological Bulletin*, September 1998, pp. 262–74.

8. See, for instance, F. J. Landy, et al., *Alternatives to Chronological Age in Determining Standards of Suitability for Public Safety Jobs*. University Park: Center for Applied Behavioral Sciences, Pennsylvania State University, 1992.

9. A. L. Kalleberg and K. A. Loscocco, "Aging, Values, and Rewards: Explaining Age Differences in Job Satisfaction," *American Sociological Review*, February 1983, pp. 78–90; R. Lee and E. R. Wilbur, "Age, Education, Job Tenure, Salary, Job Characteristics, and Job Satisfaction: A Multivariate Analysis," *Human Relations*, August 1985, pp. 781–91; and Davies, Matthews, and Wong, "Ageing and Work," pp. 176–83.

10. K. M. Kacmar and G. R. Ferris, "Theoretical and Methodological Considerations in the Age–Job Satisfaction Relationship," *Journal of Applied Psychology*, April 1989, pp. 201–07; and G. Zeitz, "Age and Work Satisfaction in a Government Agency: A Situational Perspective," *Human Relations*, May 1990, pp. 419–38.

11. See, for example, A. H. Eagly and L. L. Carli, "Sex Researchers and Sex-Typed Communications as Determinants of Sex Differences in Influenceability: A Meta-Analysis of Social Influence Studies," *Psychological Bulletin*, August 1981, pp. 1–20; J. S. Hyde, "How Large Are Cognitive Gender Differences?" *American Psychologist*, October 1981, pp. 892–901; and P. Chance, "Biology, Destiny, and All That," *Across the Board*, July–August 1988, pp. 19–23.

12. R. P. Quinn, G. L. Staines, and M. R. McCullough, Job Satisfaction: Is There a Trend? Document 2900-00195 (Washington, DC: U.S. Government Printing Office, 1974).

13. See, for example, B. Kantrowitz, P. Wingert, and K. Robins, "Advocating a 'Mommy Track'," *Newsweek*, March 13, 1989, p. 45, and S. Shellenbarger, "More Job Seekers Put Family Needs First," *Wall Street Journal*, November 15, 1991, p. B1.

14. T. W. Mangione, "Turnover—Some Psychological and Demographic Correlates," in R. P. Quinn and T. W. Mangione (eds.), *The 1969–70 Survey of Working Conditions* (Ann Arbor: University of Michigan, Survey Research Center, 1973); and R. Marsh and H. Mannari, "Organizational Commitment and Turnover: A Predictive Study," *Administrative Science Quarterly*, March 1977, pp. 57–75.

15. See, for instance, J. P. Leigh, "Sex Differences in Absenteeism," *Industrial Relations*, Fall 1983, pp. 349–61; K. D. Scott and E. L. McClellan, "Gender Differences in Absenteeism," *Public Personnel Management*, Summer 1990, pp. 229–53; and A. VandenHeuvel and M. Wooden, "Do Explanations of Absenteeism Differ for Men and Women?" *Human Relations*, November 1995, pp. 1309–29.

16. See, for instance, M. Tait, M. Y. Padgett, and T. T. Baldwin, "Job and Life Satisfaction: A Reevaluation of the Strength of the Relationship and Gender Effects as a Function of the Date of the Study," *Journal of Applied Psychology*, June 1989, pp. 502–07; and R. A. Douthitt, "The Division of Labor within the Home: Have Gender Roles Changed?" *Sex Roles*, June 1989, pp. 693–704.

17. Garrison and Muchinsky, "Attitudinal and Biographical Predictors of Incidental Absenteeism"; C. J. Watson, "An Evaluation and Some Aspects of the Steers and Rhodes Model of Employee Attendance," *Journal of Applied Psychology*, June 1981, pp. 385–89; R. T. Keller, "Predicting Absenteeism from Prior Absenteeism, Attitudinal Factors, and Nonattitudinal Factors," *Journal of Applied Psychology*, August 1983, pp. 536–40; J. M. Federico, P. Federico, and G. W. Lundquist, "Predicting Women's Turnover as a Function of Extent of Met Salary Expectations and Biodemographic Data," *Personnel Psychology*, Winter 1976, pp. 559–66; Marsh and Mannari, "Organizational Commitment and Turnover"; and D. R. Austrom, T. Baldwin, and G. J. Macy, "The Single Worker: An Empirical Exploration of Attitudes, Behavior, and Well-Being," *Canadian Journal of Administrative Sciences*, December 1988, pp. 22–29.

18. M. E. Gordon and W. J. Fitzgibbons, "Empirical Test of the Validity of Seniority as a Factor in Staffing Decisions," *Journal of Applied Psychology*, June 1982, pp. 311–19; M. E. Gordon and W. A. Johnson, "Seniority: A Review of Its Legal and Scientific Standing," *Personnel Psychology*, Summer 1982, pp. 255–80; M. A. McDaniel, F. L. Schmidt, and J. E. Hunter, "Job Experience Correlates of Job Performance," *Journal of Applied Psychology*, May 1988, pp. 327–30; and M. A. Quinones, J. K. Ford, and M. S. Teachout, "The Relationship between Work Experience and Job Performance: A Conceptual and Meta-Analytic Review," *Personnel Psychology*, Winter 1995, pp. 887–910.

19. Garrison and Muchinsky, "Attitudinal and Biographical Predictors of Incidental Absenteeism", N. Nicholson, C. A. Brown, and J. K. Chadwick-Jones, "Absence from Work and Personal Characteristics," *Journal of Applied Psychology*, June 1977, pp. 319–27; and R. T. Keller, "Predicting Absenteeism from Prior Absenteeism, Attitudinal Factors, and Nonattitudinal Factors," *Journal of Applied Psychology*, August 1983, pp. 536–40.

20. P. O. Popp and J. A. Belohlav, "Absenteeism in a Low Status Work Environment," *Academy of Management Journal*, September 1982, p. 681.

21. H. J. Arnold and D. C. Feldman, "A Multivariate Analysis of the Determinants of Job Turnover," *Journal of Applied Psychology*, June 1982, p. 352.

22. R. D. Gatewood and H. S. Field, *Human Resource Selection* (Chicago: Dryden Press, 1987).

23. J. A. Breaugh and D. L. Dossett, "The Effectiveness of Biodata for Predicting Turnover," paper presented at the National Academy of Management Conference, New Orleans, August 1987.

24. A. G. Bedeian, G. R. Ferris, and K. M. Kacmar, "Age, Tenure, and Job Satisfaction: A Tale of Two Perspectives," *Journal of Vocational Behavior*, February 1992, pp. 33–48.

25. L. E. Tyler, *Individual Differences: Abilities and Motivational Directions* (Englewood Cliffs, NJ: Prentice Hall, 1974).

26. M. D. Dunnette, "Aptitudes, Abilities, and Skills," in M. D. Dunnette (ed.), *Handbook of Industrial and Organizational Psychology* (Chicago, IL: Rand McNally, 1976), pp. 478–83.

27. D. Lubinski and R. V. Dawis, "Aptitudes, Skills, and Proficiencies," in M. D. Dunnette and L. M. Hough (eds.), *Handbook of Industrial & Organizational Psychology*, vol. 3, 2nd ed. (Palo Alto, CA: Consulting Psychologists Press, 1992), pp. 30–33.

28. See, for instance, J. E. Hunter and R. F. Hunter, "Validity and Utility of Alternative Predictors of Job Performance," *Psychological Bulletin*, January 1984, pp. 72–98; J. E. Hunter, "Cognitive Ability, Cognitive Aptitudes, Job Knowledge, and Job Performance," *Journal of Vocational Behavior*, December 1986, pp. 340–62; W. M. Coward and P. R. Sackett, "Linearity of Ability–Performance Relationships: A Reconfirmation," *Journal of Applied Psychology*, June 1990, pp. 297–300; M. J. Ree, J. A. Earles, and M. S. Teachout, "Predicting Job Performance: Not Much More Than *g*," *Journal of Applied Psychology*, August 1994, pp. 518–24; F. L. Schmidt and J. E. Hunter, "The Validity and Utility of Selection Methods in Personnel Psychology;" L. S. Gottfredson, "Why g Matters: The Complexity of Everyday Life," *Intelligence*, January–February 1997, pp. 79–132; and A. R. Jensen, *The g Factor: The Science of Mental Ability*, (Westport, CT: Praeger, 1998).

29. Hunter and Hunter, "Validity and Utility of Alternative Predictors of Job Performance," pp. 73–74.

30. E. A. Fleishman, "Evaluating Physical Abilities Required by Jobs," *Personnel Administrator*, June 1979, pp. 82–92.

31. See, for instance, H. M. Weiss, "Learning Theory and Industrial and Organizational Psychology," in M. D. Dunnette and L. M. Hough (eds.) *Handbook of Industrial & Organizational Psychology*, 2nd ed., vol. 1 (Palo Alto: Consulting Psychologists Press, 1990), pp. 172–73.

32. W. McGehee, "Are We Using What We Know about Training?—Learning Theory and Training," *Personnel Psychology*, Spring 1958, p. 2.

33. I. P. Pavlov, *The Work of the Digestive Glands*, trans. W. H. Thompson (London: Charles Griffin, 1902). See also the special issue of *American Psychologist* (September 1997, pp. 933–72) commemorating Pavlov's work.

34. B. F. Skinner, *Contingencies of Reinforcement* (East Norwalk, CT: Appleton-Century-Crofts, 1971).

35. A. Bandura, *Social Learning Theory* (Upper Saddle River, NJ: Prentice Hall, 1977).

36. T. W. Costello and S. S. Zalkind, *Psychology in Administration* (Upper Saddle River, NJ: Prentice Hall, 1963), p. 193.

37. F. Luthans and R. Kreitner, *Organizational Behavior Modification and Beyond*, 2nd ed. (Glenview, IL: Scott, Foresman, 1985); and A. D. Stajkovic and F. Luthans, "A Meta-Analysis of the Effects of Organizational Behavior Modification on Task Performance, 1975–95," *Academy of Management Journal*, October 1997, pp. 1122–49.

38. "At Emery Air Freight: Positive Reinforcement Boosts Performance," *Organizational Dynamics*, Winter 1973, pp. 41–50.

39. See literature review in D. R. Davies, G. Matthews, and C. S. K. Wong, "Ageing and Work," in C. L. Cooper and I. T. Robertson (eds.), *International Review of Industrial and Organizational Psychology*, vol. 6 (Chichester, England: Wiley, 1991), pp. 159–60.

40. Ibid, p. 165.

41. M. E. Gordon and S. L. Cohen, "Training Behavior as a Predictor of Trainability," *Personnel Psychology*, Summer 1973, pp. 261–72; and I. Robertson and S. Downs, "Learning and the Prediction of Performance: Development of Trainability Testing in the United Kingdom," *Journal of Applied Psychology*, February 1979, pp. 42–50.

42. F. Luthans and R. Kreitner, *Organizational Behavior Modification and Beyond: An Operant and Social Learning Approach* (Glenview, IL: Scott, Foresman, 1985); and A. D. Stajkovic and F. Luthans, "A Meta-Analysis of the Effects of Organizational Behavior Modification on Task Performance, 1975–95," *Academy of Management Journal*, October 1997, pp. 1122–49.

43. A. D. Stajkovic and F. Luthans, "A Meta-Analysis of the Effects of Organizational Behavior Modification on Task Performance," p. 1123.

44. See, for instance, L. W. Frederiksen, *Handbook of Organizational Behavior Management* (New York: Wiley, 1982); B. Sulzer-Azarof, B. Loafman, R. J. Merante, and A. C. Hlavacek, "Improving Occupational Safety in a Large Industrial Plant: A Systematic Replication," *Journal of Organizational Behavior Management*, vol. 11, no. 1, 1990, pp. 99–120; J. C. Landau, "The Impact of a Change in an Attendance Control System on Absenteeism and Tardiness," *Journal of Organizational Behavior Management*, vol. 13, no. 2, 1993, pp. 51–70; C. S. Brown and B. Sulzer-Azaroff, "An Assessment of the Relationship between Customer Satisfaction and Service Friendliness," *Journal of Organizational Behavior Management*, vol. 14, no. 2, 1994, pp. 55–75; and F. Luthans and A. D. Stajkovic, "Reinforce for Performance: The Need to Go Beyond Pay and Even Rewards," *Academy of Management Executive*, May 1999, pp. 49–57.

45. S. J. Wells, "A Plan for Unplanned Absences," *New York Times*, July 5, 1998, p. BU-8.

46. D. Willings, "The Absentee Worker," *Personnel and Training Management*, December 1968, pp. 10–12.

47. B. H. Harvey, J. F. Rogers, and J. A. Schultz, "Sick Pay vs. Well Pay: An Analysis of the Impact of Rewarding Employees for Being on the Job," *Public Personnel Management Journal*, Summer 1983, pp. 218–24.

48. M. S. Forbes Jr., "There's a Better Way," *Forbes*, April 26, 1993, p. 23.

49. From A. Belohlav, *The Art of Disciplining Your Employees* (Upper Saddle River, NJ: Prentice Hall, 1985); R. H. Lussier, "A Discipline Model for Increasing Performance," *Supervisory Management*, August 1990, pp. 6–7; and J. J. Martocchio and T. A. Judge, "When We Don't See Eye to Eye: Discrepancies Between Supervisors and Subordinates in Absence Disciplinary Decisions," *Journal of Management*, vol. 21, no. 5, 1995, pp. 251–78.

50. Cited in *Training*, October 1999, p. 40.

51. See, for instance, S. J. Simon and J. M. Werner, "Computer Training Through Behavior Modeling, Self-Paced, and Instructional Approaches: A Field Experiment," *Journal of Applied Psychology*, December 1996, pp. 648–59; and D. Stamps, "Learning Is Social. Training Is Irrelevant?" *Training*, February 1997, pp. 34–42.

52. See, for instance, C. C. Manz and H. P. Sims, "Self-Management as a Substitute for Leadership: A Social Learning Theory Perspective," *Academy of Management Review*, July 1980, pp. 361–67; and S. E. Markham and I. S. Markham, "Self-Management and Self-Leadership Reexamined: A Levels-of-Analysis Perspective," *Leadership Quarterly*, Fall 1995, pp. 343–60.

53. G. P. Latham and C. A. Frayne, "Self-Management Training for Increasing Job Attendance: A Follow-Up and a Replication," *Journal of Applied Psychology*, June 1989, pp. 411–16.

How can I know what I think til I see what I say?

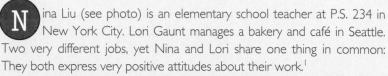

—E. M. Forster

part two

THE INDIVIDUAL

ina Liu (see photo) is an elementary school teacher at P.S. 234 in New York City. Lori Gaunt manages a bakery and café in Seattle. Two very different jobs, yet Nina and Lori share one thing in common: They both express very positive attitudes about their work.[1]

"I work in a terrific school," says Nina. "Collaboration is encouraged, and we're given the time to sit together and bounce ideas off one another—to be a think tank. There's a lot of debate and a sense of encouragement and support." Lori Gaunt's comments sound very similar, "I feel as if my opinions count a lot, and I've been instrumental in making changes. The owner isn't hands-off, but she loves what I do and tells me to run with it. It's neat to have that much freedom."

Are Nina's and Lori's attitudes toward work unusual nowadays? In a world where constant change has become a way of life and we read regularly about increased stress levels in the workplace, are Nina and Lori exceptions? Or do the majority of workers feel positive about their jobs? You might be surprised by the answers.

A recent Gallup poll surveyed Americans nationwide to find out their attitudes toward their jobs and their workplaces.[2] In spite of all the negative stories you may have read in the media, on a scale from 1 to 5, with 5 representing "extremely satisfied," 72 percent of the respondents rated their level of satisfaction with their place of employment at 4 or 5. Closer analysis indicated that a large part of these positive findings could be explained by the fact that jobs were generally meeting the primary needs of workers. They considered the following factors critical to their satisfaction and job performance: the opportunity to do what they do best; having their opinions count; and getting the opportunity to learn and grow. Eighty-two percent of the respondents indicated they had the opportunity to do what they do best every day; and 84 percent said they had the opportunity to learn and grow on the job.

Values, Attitudes, and Job Satisfaction

These positive attitudes toward work are not an aberration. Studies consistently show that workers are satisfied with their jobs. This is applicable over time as well as across national boundaries. Regardless of which studies you choose to look at, when American workers are asked if they are satisfied with their jobs, the results tend to be very similar: Between 70 and 80 percent report they're satisfied with their jobs.[3] These numbers do tend to vary with age—with older workers reporting the highest satisfaction. Ninety-three percent of workers over 55 say they're satisfied at work; yet even among those under 35, the majority (58 percent) say they're satisfied.[4]

Although there was some concern in the late 1970s that satisfaction was declining across almost all occupational groups,[5] recent reinterpretations of these data and additional longitudinal studies indicate that job satisfaction levels have held steady for decades—through economic recessions as well as prosperous times.[6] Moreover, these results are generally applicable to other developed countries. For instance, comparable studies among workers in Canada, the United Kingdom, Switzerland, Germany, and Mexico indicate more positive than negative results.[7]

How does one explain these findings? One answer is that whatever it is people want from their jobs, they seem to be getting it. But two additional points should be added.

First, people don't select jobs randomly. They tend to gravitate toward jobs that are compatible with their interests, values, and abilities.[8] Because people are likely to seek jobs that provide a good person–job fit, reports of high satisfaction shouldn't be totally surprising. Second, based on our knowledge of cognitive dissonance theory (discussed in this chapter), we might expect employees to resolve inconsistencies between dissatisfaction with their jobs and their staying with those jobs by not reporting the dissatisfaction. So these positive findings might be tainted by efforts to reduce dissonance.

LEARNING OBJECTIVES

AFTER READING THIS CHAPTER, YOU SHOULD BE ABLE TO

1. Contrast terminal and instrumental values

2. List the dominant values in today's workforce

3. Identify the five value dimensions of national culture

4. Contrast the three components of an attitude

5. Summarize the relationship between attitudes and behavior

6. Identify the role consistency plays in attitudes

7. State the relationship between job satisfaction and behavior

8. Identify four employee responses to dissatisfaction

n this chapter, we look more carefully at the concept of job satisfaction. First, however, we consider how values influence employee behavior.

VALUES

Is capital punishment right or wrong? How about racial quotas in hiring—are they right or wrong? If a person likes power, is that good or bad? The answers to these questions are value laden. Some might argue, for example, that capital punishment is right because it is an appropriate retribution for crimes such as murder and treason. However, others might argue, just as strongly, that no government has the right to take anyone's life.

values

Basic convictions that a specific mode of conduct or end-state of existence is personally or socially preferable to an opposite or converse mode of conduct or end-state of existence.

value system

A hierarchy based on a ranking of an individual's values in terms of their intensity.

Values represent basic convictions that "a specific mode of conduct or end-state of existence is personally or socially preferable to an opposite or converse mode of conduct or end-state of existence."[9] They contain a judgmental element in that they carry an individual's ideas as to what is right, good, or desirable. Values have both content and intensity attributes. The content attribute says that a mode of conduct or end-state of existence is *important*. The intensity attribute specifies *how important* it is. When we rank an individual's values in terms of their intensity, we obtain that person's **value system**. All of us have a hierarchy of values that forms our value system. This system is identified by the relative importance we assign to such values as freedom, pleasure, self-respect, honesty, obedience, and equality.

Are values fluid and flexible? Generally speaking, No! Values tend to be relatively stable and enduring.[10] A significant portion of the values we hold is established in our early years—from parents, teachers, friends, and others. As children,

[*Values tend to be relatively stable and enduring.*]

we are told that certain behaviors or outcomes are always desirable or always undesirable. There were few gray areas. You were told, for example, that you should be honest and responsible. You were never taught to be just a little bit honest or a little bit responsible. It is this absolute or "black-or-white" learning of values that more or less assures their stability and endurance. The process of questioning our values, of course, may result in a change. We may decide that our underlying convictions are no longer acceptable. More often, our questioning merely acts to reinforce those values we hold.

IMPORTANCE OF VALUES

Values are important to the study of organizational behavior because they lay the foundation for the understanding of attitudes and motivation and because they influence our perceptions. Individuals enter an organization with preconceived notions of what "ought" and what "ought not" to be. Of course, these notions are not value free. On the contrary, they contain interpretations of right and wrong. Furthermore, they imply that certain behaviors or outcomes are preferred over others. As a result, values cloud objectivity and rationality.

Values generally influence attitudes and behavior.[11] Suppose that you enter an organization with the view that allocating pay on the basis of performance is right, while allocating pay on the basis of seniority is wrong or inferior. How are you going to react if you find that the organization you have just joined rewards seniority and not performance? You're likely to be disappointed—and this can lead to job dissatisfaction and the decision not to exert a high level of effort since "it's probably not going to lead to more money, anyway." Would your attitudes and behavior be different if your values aligned with the organization's pay policies? Most likely.

TYPES OF VALUES

Can we classify values? The answer is: Yes! In this section, we review two approaches to developing value typologies.

Rokeach Value Survey Milton Rokeach created the Rokeach Value Survey (RVS).[12] The RVS consists of two sets of values, with each set containing 18 individual value items. One set, called **terminal values**, refers to desirable end-states of existence. These are the goals that a person would like to achieve during his or her lifetime. The other set, called **instrumental values**, refers to preferable modes of behavior, or means of achieving the terminal values. Exhibit 3-1 gives common examples for each of these sets.

Several studies confirm that the RVS values vary among groups.[13] People in the same occupations or categories (e.g., corporate managers, union members, parents, students) tend to hold similar values. For instance, one study compared corporate executives, members of the steelworkers' union, and members of a community activist group. Although a good deal of overlap was found among the three groups,[14] there were also some very significant differences. (See Exhibit 3-2.) The activists had value preferences that were quite different from those of the other two groups. They ranked "equality" as their most important terminal value; executives and union members ranked this value 12 and 13, respectively. Activists ranked "helpful" as their second-highest instrumental value. The other two groups both ranked it 14. These differences are important, since executives, union members, and activists all have a vested interest in what corporations do. "When corporations and critical stakeholder groups such as these [other] two come together in negotiations or contend with one another over economic and

terminal values

Desirable end-states of existence; the goals that a person would like to achieve during his or her lifetime.

instrumental values

Preferable modes of behavior or means of achieving one's terminal values.

Terminal and Instrumental Values in Rokeach Value Survey

Terminal Values	Instrumental Values
A comfortable life (a prosperous life)	Ambitious (hardworking, aspiring)
An exciting life (a stimulating, active life)	Broad-minded (open-minded)
A sense of accomplishment (lasting contribution)	Capable (competent, effective)
A world at peace (free of war and conflict)	Cheerful (lighthearted, joyful)
A world of beauty (beauty of nature and the arts)	Clean (neat, tidy)
Equality (brotherhood, equal opportunity for all)	Courageous (standing up for your beliefs)
Family security (taking care of loved ones)	Forgiving (willing to pardon others)
Freedom (independence, free choice)	Helpful (working for the welfare of others)
Happiness (contentedness)	Honest (sincere, truthful)
Inner harmony (freedom from inner conflict)	Imaginative (daring, creative)
Mature love (sexual and spiritual intimacy)	Independent (self-reliant, self-sufficient)
National security (protection from attack)	Intellectual (intelligent, reflective)
Pleasure (an enjoyable, leisurely life)	Logical (consistent, rational)
Salvation (saved, eternal life)	Loving (affectionate, tender)
Self-respect (self-esteem)	Obedient (dutiful, respectful)
Social recognition (respect, admiration)	Polite (courteous, well-mannered)
True friendship (close companionship)	Responsible (dependable, reliable)
Wisdom (a mature understanding of life)	Self-controlled (restrained, self-disciplined)

EXHIBIT 3-1

Source: M. Rokeach, *The Nature of Human Values* (New York: The Free Press, 1973).

EXHIBIT 3-2

Mean Value Ranking of Executives, Union Members, and Activists (Top Five Only)

Executives		Union Members		Activists	
Terminal	**Instrumental**	**Terminal**	**Instrumental**	**Terminal**	**Instrumental**
1. Self-respect	1. Honest	1. Family security	1. Responsible	1. Equality	1. Honest
2. Family security	2. Responsible	2. Freedom	2. Honest	2. A world of peace	2. Helpful
3. Freedom	3. Capable	3. Happiness	3. Courageous	3. Family security	3. Courageous
4. A sense of accomplishment	4. Ambitious	4. Self-respect	4. Independent	4. Self-respect	4. Responsible
5. Happiness	5. Independent	5. Mature love	5. Capable	5. Freedom	5. Capable

Source: Based on W. C. Frederick and J. Weber, "The Values of Corporate Managers and Their Critics: An Empirical Description and Normative Implications," in W. C. Frederick and L. E. Preston (eds.), *Business Ethics: Research Issues and Empirical Studies* (Greenwich, CT: JAI Press, 1990), pp. 123–44.

social policies, they are likely to begin with these built-in differences in personal value preferences. . . . Reaching agreement on any specific issue or policy where these personal values are importantly implicated might prove to be quite difficult."[15]

Contemporary Work Cohorts Your author has integrated a number of recent analyses of work values into a four-stage model that attempts to capture the unique values of different cohorts or generations in the U.S. workforce.[16] (No assumption is made that this framework would universally apply across all cultures.)[17] Exhibit 3-3 proposes that employees can be segmented by the era in which they entered the workforce. Because most people start work between the ages of 18 and 23, the eras also correlate closely with the chronological age of employees.

Workers who grew up influenced by the Great Depression, World War II, U.S. leadership in world manufacturing, the Andrews Sisters, and the Berlin blockade entered the workforce from the early 1940s through the early 1960s believing in the Protestant work ethic. Once hired, they tended to be loyal to their employer.

EXHIBIT 3-3

Dominant Work Values in Today's Workforce

Stage	Year Born	Entered the Workforce	Approximate Current Age	Dominant Work Values
I. Protestant work ethic	1925–1945	Early 1940s to early 1960s	55–75	Hard work, conservative; loyalty to the organization
II. Existential	1945–1955	1960s to mid-1970s	45–55	Quality of life, nonconforming, seeks autonomy; loyalty to self
III. Pragmatic	1955–1965	Mid-1970s to late 1980s	35–45	Success, achievement, ambition, hard work; loyalty to career
IV. Generation X	1965–1981	Late 1980s to present	Under 35	Flexibility, job satisfaction, balanced lifestyle; loyalty to relationships

In terms of the terminal values on the RVS, these employees are likely to place the greatest importance on a comfortable life and family security.

Employees who entered the workforce during the 1960s through the mid-1970s were influenced heavily by John F. Kennedy, the civil rights movement, the Beatles, the Vietnam war, and baby boom competition. They brought with them a large measure of the "hippie ethic" and existential philosophy. They are more concerned with the quality of their lives than with the amount of money and possessions they can accumulate. Their desire for autonomy has directed their loyalty toward themselves rather than toward the organization that employs them. In terms of the RVS, freedom and equality are rated highly.

Individuals who entered the workforce from the mid-1970s through the late 1980s reflect the society's return to more traditional values, but with far greater emphasis on achievement and material success. As a generation, they were strongly influenced by Reagan conservatism, the defense buildup, dual-career households, and $150,000 starter homes. Born toward the end of the baby boom period, these workers are pragmatists who believe that ends can justify means. They see the organizations that employ them merely as vehicles for their careers. Terminal values such as a sense of accomplishment and social recognition rank high with them.

Our final category encompasses what has become known as generation X. Their lives have been shaped by globalization, the fall of communism, MTV, AIDS, and computers. They value flexibility, a balanced lifestyle, and the achievement of job satisfaction. Family and relationships are very important to this cohort. Money is important as an indicator of career performance, but they are willing to trade off salary increases, titles, security, and promotions for increased leisure time and expanded lifestyle options. In search of balance in their lives, these more recent entrants into the workforce are less willing to make personal sacrifices for the sake of their employer than previous generations were. On the RVS, they rate high on true friendship, happiness, and pleasure.

An understanding that individuals' values differ but tend to reflect the societal values of the period in which they grew up can be a valuable aid in explaining and predicting behavior. Employees in their late thirties and sixties, for instance, are more likely to be conservative and accepting of authority than their existential co-workers in their early fifties. And workers under 35 are more likely than the other groups to balk at having to work overtime or weekends and more prone to leave a job in mid-career to pursue another that provides more leisure time.

Greg Matusky (center), president of Gregory Communications, understands the values of his Generation X employees. A baby boomer, Matusky has learned that his values differ from those of his young employees who work for his public relations firm in Ardmore, Pennsylvania. "The times I've tried to create competitive situations, it's failed," he says. "But when I've said, 'I need your help,' they've responded. . . . They'll give you their all if you make them part of the mission." Matusky says, "working evenings and weekends is off-limits," and that his employees want flexible work schedules.

VALUES, LOYALTY, AND ETHICAL BEHAVIOR

Did a decline in business ethics set in sometime in the late 1970s? The issue is debatable.[18] Nevertheless, a lot of people think so. If there has been a decline in ethical standards, perhaps we should look to our four-stage model of work cohort values (see Exhibit 3-3) for a possible explanation. After all, managers consistently report that the actions of their bosses are the most important factor influencing ethical behavior in their organizations.[19] Given this fact, the values of those in middle and upper management should have a significant bearing on the entire ethical climate within an organization.

Through the mid-1970s, the managerial ranks were dominated by Protestant-work-ethic types (Stage I) whose loyalties were to their employer. When faced with ethical dilemmas, their decisions were made in terms of what was best for their organization. Beginning in the late 1970s, individuals with existential values began to rise into the upper levels of management. They were soon followed by pragmatic types. By the late 1980s, a large portion of middle- and top-management positions in business organizations were held by people from Stages II and III.

The loyalty of existentials and pragmatics is to self and careers, respectively. Their focus is inward and their primary concern is with "looking out for number one." Such self-centered values would be consistent with a decline in ethical standards. Could this help explain the alleged decline in business ethics beginning in the late 1970s?

The potentially good news in this analysis is that recent entrants to the workforce, and tomorrow's senior managers, appear to be less self-centered. Since their loyalty is to relationships, they are more likely to consider the ethical implications of their actions on others around them. The result? We might look forward to an uplifting of ethical standards in business over the next decade or two merely as a result of changing values within the managerial ranks.

VALUES ACROSS CULTURES

In Chapter 1, we described the new global village and said "managers have to become capable of working with people from different cultures." Because values differ across cultures, an understanding of these differences should be helpful in explaining and predicting behavior of employees from different countries.

A Framework for Assessing Cultures   One of the most widely referenced approaches for analyzing variations among cultures has been done by Geert Hofstede.[20] He surveyed more than 116,000 IBM employees in 40 countries about their work-related values. He found that managers and employees vary on five value dimensions of national culture. They are listed and defined as follows:

- **Power distance.** The degree to which people in a country accept that power in institutions and organizations is distributed unequally. Ranges from relatively equal (low power distance) to extremely unequal (high power distance).
- **Individualism** versus **collectivism.** Individualism is the degree to which people in a country prefer to act as individuals rather than as members of groups. Collectivism is the equivalent of low individualism.
- **Quantity of life** versus **quality of life.** Quantity of life is the degree to which values such as assertiveness, the acquisition of money and material goods, and competition prevail. Quality of life is the degree to which people value relationships, and show sensitivity and concern for the welfare of others.[21]
- **Uncertainty avoidance.** The degree to which people in a country prefer structured over unstructured situations. In countries that score high on uncertainty avoidance, people have an increased level of anxiety, which manifests itself in greater nervousness, stress, and aggressiveness.
- **Long-term** versus **short-term orientation.** People in cultures with long-term orientations look to the future and value thrift and persistence. A short-term orientation values the past and present, and emphasizes respect for tradition and fulfilling social obligations.

Exhibit 3-4 provides a summary of how a number of countries rate on these five dimensions. For instance, not surprisingly, most Asian countries are more collectivist than individualistic. On the other hand, the United States ranked highest among all countries surveyed on individualism.

power distance

A national culture attribute describing the extent to which a society accepts that power in institutions and organizations is distributed unequally.

individualism

A national culture attribute describing the degree to which people prefer to act as individuals rather than a member of groups.

collectivism

A national culture attribute that describes a tight social framework in which people expect others in groups of which they are a part to look after them and protect them.

quantity of life

A national culture attribute describing the extent to which societal values are characterized by assertiveness and materialism.

quality of life

A national culture attribute that emphasizes relationships and concern for others.

uncertainty avoidance

A national culture attribute describing the extent to which a society feels threatened by uncertain and ambiguous situations and tries to avoid them.

long-term orientation

A national culture attribute that emphasizes the future, thrift, and persistence.

short-term orientation

A national culture attribute that emphasizes the past and present, respect for tradition, and fulfilling social obligation.

EXHIBIT

3-4

Examples of Cultural Dimensions

Country	Power Distance	Individualism*	Quantity of Life**	Uncertainty Avoidance	Long-Term Orientation***
China	High	Low	Moderate	Moderate	High
France	High	High	Moderate	High	Low
Germany	Low	High	High	Moderate	Moderate
Hong Kong	High	Low	High	Low	High
Indonesia	High	Low	Moderate	Low	Low
Japan	Moderate	Moderate	High	Moderate	Moderate
Netherlands	Low	High	Low	Moderate	Moderate
Russia	High	Moderate	Low	High	Low
United States	Low	High	High	Low	Low
West Africa	High	Low	Moderate	Moderate	Low

*A low score is synonymous with collectivism. **A low score is synonymous with high quality of life. ***A low score is synonymous with a short-term orientation.

Source: Adapted from G. Hofstede, "Cultural Constraints in Management Theories," *Academy of Management Executive*, February 1993, p. 91.

While cultural values change slowly, they *do* change. So it's important that you treat the ratings in Exhibit 3-4 as general guidelines that need to be modified over time to reflect major political, social, and economic shifts within a country. Hofstede's findings are based on research that is nearly three decades old. Since his original work, the world has changed. Some examples: Communism has fallen in Eastern Europe, China has become significantly more open; Hong Kong is run by the Chinese rather than British; Germany has become unified; South Africa has ended apartheid, Mexico has undergone significant economic development; and there has been a dramatic increase in the proportion of U.S. women in the labor force and in management positions. A recent follow-up to Hofstede's study confirmed much of the original findings but also found that transformational changes have made their way into various cultural values.[22] For instance, Mexico has moved in 30 years from an emphasis on collectivism to individualism. This is consistent with Mexico's economic development and the growth of capitalistic values. Similarly, U.S. values have shifted from quantity of life to quality, which undoubtedly reflects the influence of women and younger entrants to the workforce. Our point here is that even though cultural values are generally stable and enduring, you need to modify Hofstede's classifications to include transformational changes within countries.

Implications for OB Most of the concepts that currently make up the body of knowledge we call *organizational behavior* have been developed by Americans using

Dell Computer learned that Chinese work values differ from U.S. work values when it opened a computer factory in Xiamen, China. Chinese workers view the concept of a job for life. They expect to drink tea and read the papers on the job—and still keep their jobs. Dell China executives had to train employees so they understood that their jobs depended on their performance. To instill workers with a sense of ownership, managers gave employees stock options and explained to them how their increased productivity would result in higher pay.

American subjects within domestic contexts. A comprehensive study, for instance, of more than 11,000 articles published in 24 management and organizational behavior journals over a 10-year period revealed that approximately 80 percent of the studies were done in the United States and had been conducted by Americans.[23] Follow-up studies continue to confirm the lack of cross-cultural considerations in management and OB research,[24] although the last decade has seen some improvement. What this means is that (1) not all OB theories and concepts are universally applicable to managing people around the world, especially in countries where work values are considerably different from those in the United States; and (2) you should take into consideration cultural values when trying to understand the behavior of people in different countries. To help you with this second point, we'll regularly stop to consider the generalizability of theories and concepts presented in this book to different cultures.

ATTITUDES

attitudes

Evaluative statements or judgments concerning objects, people, or events.

cognitive component of an attitude

The opinion or belief segment of an attitude.

affective component of an attitude

The emotional or feeling segment of an attitude.

behavioral component of an attitude

An intention to behave in a certain way toward someone or something.

Attitudes are evaluative statements—either favorable or unfavorable—concerning objects, people, or events. They reflect how one feels about something. When I say "I like my job," I am expressing my attitude about work.

Attitudes are not the same as values, but the two are interrelated. You can see this by looking at the three components of an attitude: cognition, affect, and behavior.[25]

The belief that "discrimination is wrong" is a value statement. Such an opinion is the **cognitive component** of an attitude. It sets the stage for the more critical part of an attitude—its **affective component**. Affect is the emotional or feeling segment of an attitude and is reflected in the statement "I don't like Jon because he discriminates against minorities." Finally, and we'll discuss this issue at considerable length later in this section, affect can lead to behavioral outcomes. The **behavioral component** of an attitude refers to an intention to behave in a certain way toward someone or something. So, to continue our example, I might choose to avoid Jon because of my feeling about him.

Viewing attitudes as made up of three components—cognition, affect, and behavior—is helpful toward understanding their complexity and the potential relationship between attitudes and behavior. But for clarity's sake, keep in mind that the term *attitude* essentially refers to the affective part of the three components.

Also keep in mind that, in contrast to values, your attitudes are less stable. Advertising messages, for example, attempt to alter your attitudes toward a certain product or service: If the people at Ford can get you to hold a favorable feeling toward their cars, that attitude may lead to a desirable behavior (for them)—your purchase of a Ford product.

In organizations, attitudes are important because they affect job behavior. If workers believe, for example, that supervisors, auditors, bosses, and time-and-motion engineers are all in conspiracy to make employees work harder for the same or less money, then it makes sense to try to understand how these attitudes were formed, their relationship to actual job behavior, and how they might be changed.

TYPES OF ATTITUDES

A person can have thousands of attitudes, but OB focuses our attention on a very limited number of job-related attitudes. These job-related attitudes tap positive or negative evaluations that employees hold about aspects of their work environment. Most of the research in OB has been concerned with three attitudes: job satisfaction, job involvement, and organizational commitment.[26]

Job Satisfaction   The term *job satisfaction* refers to an individual's general attitude toward his or her job. A person with a high level of job satisfaction holds positive attitudes toward the job, while a person who is dissatisfied with his or her job holds negative attitudes about the job. When people speak of employee attitudes, more often than not they mean job satisfaction. In fact, the two are frequently used interchangeably. Because of the high importance OB researchers have given to job satisfaction, we'll review this attitude in considerable detail later in this chapter.

> *When people speak of employee attitudes, more often than not they mean job satisfaction.*

Job Involvement   The term **job involvement** is a more recent addition to the OB literature.[27] While there isn't complete agreement over what the term means, a workable definition states that job involvement measures the degree to which a person identifies psychologically with his or her job and considers his or her perceived performance level important to self-worth.[28] Employees with a high level of job involvement strongly identify with and really care about the kind of work they do.

High levels of job involvement have been found to be related to fewer absences and lower resignation rates.[29] However, it seems to more consistently predict turnover than absenteeism, accounting for as much as 16 percent of the variance in the former.[30]

job involvement

The degree to which a person identifies with his or her job, actively participates in it, and considers his or her performance important to self-worth.

Organizational Commitment   The third job attitude we shall discuss is **organizational commitment**, which is defined as a state in which an employee identifies with a particular organization and its goals, and wishes to maintain membership in the organization.[31] So, high job involvement means identifying with one's specific job, while high organizational commitment means identifying with one's employing organization.

As with job involvement, the research evidence demonstrates negative relationships between organizational commitment and both absenteeism and turnover.[32] In fact, studies demonstrate that an individual's level of organizational commitment is a better indicator of turnover than the far more frequently used job satisfaction predictor, explaining as much as 34 percent of the variance.[33] Organizational commitment is probably a better predictor because it is a more global and enduring response to the organization as a whole than is job satisfaction.[34] An employee may be dissatisfied with his or her particular job and consider it a temporary condition, yet not be dissatisfied with the organization as a whole. But when dissatisfaction spreads to the organization itself, individuals are more likely to consider resigning.

The foregoing evidence, most of which was drawn more than two decades ago, needs to be qualified to reflect the changing employee–employer relationship. The unwritten loyalty contract that existed 20 years ago between employees and employers has been seriously damaged; and the notion of an employee staying with a single organization for most of his or her career has become increasingly obsolete. As such, "measures of employee–firm attachment, such as commitment, are problematic for new employment relations."[35] This suggests that *organizational* commitment is probably less important as a job-related attitude than it once was. In its place we might expect something akin to *occupational* commitment to become a more relevant variable because it better reflects today's fluid workforce.[36]

organizational commitment

The degree to which an employee identifies with a particular organization and its goals and wishes to maintain membership in the organization.

ATTITUDES AND CONSISTENCY

Did you ever notice how people change what they say so it doesn't contradict what they do? Perhaps a friend of yours has consistently argued that the quality of American cars isn't up to that of the imports and that he'd never own anything but a foreign import. But his dad gives him a late-model American-made car, and suddenly they're not so bad. Or, when going through sorority rush, a new freshman believes that sororities are good and that pledging a sorority is important. If she fails to make a sorority, however, she may say, "I recognized that sorority life isn't all it's cracked up to be, anyway!"

Research has generally concluded that people seek consistency among their attitudes and between their attitudes and their behavior.[37] This means that individuals seek to reconcile divergent attitudes and align their attitudes and behavior so they appear rational and consistent. When there is an inconsistency, forces are initiated to return the individual to an equilibrium state in which attitudes and behavior are again consistent. This can be done by altering either the attitudes or the behavior, or by developing a rationalization for the discrepancy. Tobacco executives provide an example.[38] How, you might wonder, do these people cope with the ongoing barrage of data linking cigarette smoking and negative health outcomes? They can deny that any clear causation between smoking and cancer, for instance, has been established. They can brainwash themselves by continually articulating the benefits of tobacco. They can acknowledge the negative consequences of smoking but rationalize that people are going to smoke and that tobacco

Tobacco executives have changed their attitudes about smoking. For years they argued that tobacco is not addictive, and they challenged scientific evidence of the health risks of smoking. But in lawsuits against tobacco firms, damaging documents emerged showing that the firms knew of the risks and intentionally marketed to minors. Tobacco firm executives shown here testified before Congress and admitted that smoking plays a role in causing cancer and that their marketing included studies of teenage smokers. One executive said, "It is immoral, it is unethical, as well as illegal to market to people under age."

companies merely promote freedom of choice. They can accept the research evidence and begin actively working to make more healthy cigarettes or at least reduce their availability to more vulnerable groups, such as teenagers. Or they can quit their job because the dissonance is too great.

COGNITIVE DISSONANCE THEORY

Can we also assume from this consistency principle that an individual's behavior can always be predicted if we know his or her attitude on a subject? If Mr. Jones views the company's pay level as too low, will a substantial increase in his pay change his behavior, that is, make him work harder? The answer to this question is, unfortunately, more complex than merely a Yes or No.

Leon Festinger, in the late 1950s, proposed the theory of **cognitive dissonance**.[39] This theory sought to explain the linkage between attitudes and behavior. Dissonance means an inconsistency. Cognitive dissonance refers to any incompatibility that an individual might perceive between two or more of his or her attitudes, or between his or her behavior and attitudes. Festinger argued that any form of inconsistency is uncomfortable and that individuals will attempt to reduce the dissonance and, hence, the discomfort. Therefore, individuals will seek a stable state in which there is a minimum of dissonance.

Of course, no individual can completely avoid dissonance. You know that cheating on your income tax is wrong, but you "fudge" the numbers a bit every year, and hope you're not audited. Or you tell your children to brush after every meal, but *you* don't. So how do people cope? Festinger would propose that the desire to reduce dissonance would be determined by the *importance* of the elements creating the dissonance, the degree of *influence* the individual believes he or she has over the elements, and the *rewards* that may be involved in dissonance.

If the elements creating the dissonance are relatively unimportant, the pressure to correct this imbalance will be low. However, say that a corporate manager—Mrs. Smith—believes strongly that no company should pollute the air or water. Unfortunately, Mrs. Smith, because of the requirements of her job, is placed in the position of having to make decisions that would trade off her company's profitability against her attitudes on pollution. She knows that dumping the company's sewage into the local river (which we shall assume is legal) is in the best economic interest of her firm. What will she do? Clearly, Mrs. Smith is experiencing a high degree of cognitive dissonance. Because of the importance of the elements in this example, we cannot expect Mrs. Smith to ignore the inconsistency. There are several paths that she can follow to deal with her dilemma. She can change her behavior (stop polluting the river). Or she can reduce dissonance by concluding that the dissonant behavior is not so important after all ("I've got to make a living, and in my role as a corporate decision maker, I often have to place the good of my company above that of the environment or society"). A third alternative would be for Mrs. Smith to change her attitude ("There is nothing wrong in polluting the river"). Still another choice would be to seek out more consonant elements to outweigh the dissonant ones ("The benefits to society from manufacturing our products more than offset the cost to society of the resulting water pollution").

The degree of influence that individuals believe they have over the elements will have an impact on how they will react to the dissonance. If they perceive the dissonance to be an uncontrollable result—something over which they have no choice—they are less likely to be receptive to attitude change. If, for example, the dissonance-producing behavior is required as a result of the boss's directive, the pressure to reduce dissonance would be less than if the behavior was performed voluntarily. While dissonance exists, it can be rationalized and justified.

Rewards also influence the degree to which individuals are motivated to reduce dissonance. High rewards accompanying high dissonance tend to reduce the tension inherent in the dissonance. The rewards act to reduce dissonance by increasing the consistency side of the individual's balance sheet.

> *High rewards accompanying high dissonance tend to reduce the tension inherent in the dissonance.*

These moderating factors suggest that just because individuals experience dissonance they will not necessarily move directly toward consistency, that is, toward reduction of this dissonance. If the issues underlying the dissonance are of minimal importance, if an individual perceives that the dissonance is externally imposed and is substantially uncontrollable by him or her, or if rewards are significant enough to offset the dissonance, the individual will not be under great tension to reduce the dissonance.

What are the organizational implications of the theory of cognitive dissonance? It can help to predict the propensity to engage in attitude and behavioral change. If individuals are required, for example, by the demands of their job to say or do things that contradict their personal attitude, they will tend to modify their attitude in order to make it compatible with the cognition of what they have said or done. Additionally, the greater the dissonance—after it has been moderated by importance, choice, and reward factors—the greater the pressures to reduce it.

MEASURING THE A–B RELATIONSHIP

We have maintained throughout this chapter that attitudes affect behavior. The early research work on attitudes assumed that they were causally related to behavior; that is, the attitudes that people hold determine what they do. Common sense, too, suggests a relationship. Is it not logical that people watch television programs that they say they like or that employees try to avoid assignments they find distasteful?

However, in the late 1960s, this assumed relationship between attitudes and behavior (A–B) was challenged by a review of the research.[40] Based on an evaluation of a number of studies that investigated the A–B relationship, the reviewer concluded that attitudes were unrelated to behavior or, at best, only slightly related.[41] More recent research has demonstrated that attitudes significantly predict future behavior and confirmed Festinger's original belief that the relationship can be enhanced by taking moderating variables into account.[42]

Moderating Variables The most powerful moderators have been found to be the *importance* of the attitude, its *specificity*, its *accessibility*, whether *social pressures* exist, and whether a person has *direct experience* with the attitude.[43]

Important attitudes are ones that reflect fundamental values, self-interest, or identification with individuals or groups that a person values. Attitudes that individuals consider important tend to show a strong relationship to behavior.

The more specific the attitude and the more specific the behavior, the stronger the link between the two. For instance, asking someone specifically about her intention to stay with the organization for the next six months is likely to better predict turnover for that person than if you asked her how satisfied she was with her pay.

Attitudes that are easily remembered are more likely to predict behavior than attitudes that are not accessible in memory. Interestingly, you're more likely to remember attitudes that are frequently expressed. So the more you talk about your attitude on a subject, the more you're likely to remember it, and the more likely it is to shape your behavior.

Discrepancies between attitudes and behavior are more likely to occur when social pressures to behave in certain ways hold exceptional power. This tends to characterize behavior in organizations. This may explain why an employee who holds strong antiunion attitudes attends prounion organizing meetings; or why tobacco executives, who are not smokers themselves and who tend to believe the research linking smoking and cancer, don't actively discourage others from smoking in their offices!

Finally, the atttitude–behavior relationship is likely to be much stronger if an attitude refers to something with which the individual has direct personal experience. Asking college students with no significant work experience how they would respond to working for an authoritarian supervisor is far less likely to predict actual behavior than asking that same question of employees who have worked for such an individual.

Self-Perception Theory Although most A–B studies yield positive results, researchers have achieved still higher correlations by pursuing another direction— looking at whether or not behavior influences attitudes. This view, called **self-perception theory**, has generated some encouraging findings. Let's briefly review the theory.[44]

self-perception theory

Attitudes are used after the fact to make sense out of an action that has already occurred.

When asked about an attitude toward some object, individuals recall their behavior relevant to that object and then infer their attitude from their past behavior. So if an employee were asked about her feelings about being a training specialist at U.S. West, she would likely think, "I've had this same job at U.S. West as a trainer for 10 years. Nobody forced me to stay on this job. So I must like it!" Self-perception theory, therefore, argues that attitudes are used, after the fact, to make sense out of an action that has already occurred rather than as devices that precede and guide action. And contrary to cognitive dissonance theory, attitudes are just casual verbal statements. When people are asked about their attitudes, and they don't have strong convictions or feelings, self-perception theory says they tend to create plausible answers.

Self-perception theory has been well supported.[45] While the traditional attitude–behavior relationship is generally positive, the behavior–attitude relationship is stronger. This is particularly true when attitudes are vague and ambiguous. When you have had few experiences regarding an attitude issue or given little previous thought to it, you'll tend to infer your attitudes from your behavior. However, when your attitudes have been established for a while and are well defined, those attitudes are likely to guide your behavior.

Timberland, a footwear and apparel-maker, uses self-perception theory to develop positive attitudes toward community service among its employees. Because giving to the community is an important company value, Timberland pays each employee for 40 hours of volunteer work each year. Timberland employees shown here are volunteering at a New Hampshire food bank. Volunteer work can be a powerful force in shaping attitudes. One employee described her volunteering experience as a "religious experience."

AN APPLICATION: ATTITUDE SURVEYS

attitude surveys

Eliciting responses from employees through questionnaires about how they feel about their jobs, work groups, supervisors, and the organization.

The preceding review indicates that a knowledge of employee attitudes can be helpful to managers in attempting to predict employee behavior. But how does management get information about employee attitudes? The most popular method is through the use of **attitude surveys**.[46]

Exhibit 3-5 illustrates what an attitude survey might look like. Typically, attitude surveys present the employee with a set of statements or questions. Ideally, the items are tailored to obtain the specific information that management desires. An attitude score is achieved by summing up responses to individual questionnaire items. These scores can then be averaged for job groups, departments, divisions, or the organization as a whole.

Results from attitude surveys can frequently surprise management. For instance, managers at the Heavy-Duty Division of Springfield Remanufacturing thought everything was great.[47] Since employees were actively involved in division decisions and profitability was high within the entire company, management assumed morale was high. To confirm their beliefs, they conducted a short attitude survey. Employees were asked if they agreed or disagreed with the following statements: (1) At work, your opinions count; (2) those of you who want to be a leader in this company have the opportunity to become one; and (3) in the past six months someone has talked to you about your personal development. In the survey, 43 percent disagreed with the first statement, 48 percent with the second, and 62 percent with the third. Management was astounded. How could this be? The division had been holding shop floor meetings to review the numbers every week for more than 12 years. And most of the managers had come up through the ranks. Management responded by creating a committee made up of representatives from every department in the division and all three shifts. The committee quickly found that there were lots of little things the division was doing that was alienating employees. Out of this committee came a large number of suggestions that, after implementation, significantly improved

---

EXHIBIT 3-5

Sample Attitude Survey

Please answer each of the following statements using the following rating scale:

- 5 = Strongly agree
- 4 = Agree
- 3 = Undecided
- 2 = Disagree
- 1 = Strongly disagree

Statement	Rating
1. This company is a pretty good place to work.	_____
2. I can get ahead in this company if I make the effort.	_____
3. This company's wage rates are competitive with those of other companies.	_____
4. Employee promotion decisions are handled fairly.	_____
5. I understand the various fringe benefits the company offers.	_____
6. My job makes the best use of my abilities.	_____
7. My workload is challenging but not burdensome.	_____
8. I have trust and confidence in my boss.	_____
9. I feel free to tell my boss what I think.	_____
10. I know what my boss expects of me.	_____

---

employees' perception of their decision-making influence and their career opportunities in the division.

Using attitude surveys on a regular basis provides managers with valuable feedback on how employees perceive their working conditions. Policies and practices that management views as objective and fair may be seen as inequitable by employees in general or by certain groups of employees. That these distorted perceptions have led to negative attitudes about the job and organization should be important to management. This is because employee behaviors are based on perceptions, not reality. Remember, the employee who quits because she believes she is underpaid—when, in fact, management has objective data to support that her salary is highly competitive—is just as gone as if she had actually been underpaid. The use of regular attitude surveys can alert management to potential problems and employees' intentions early so that action can be taken to prevent repercussions.[48]

ATTITUDES AND WORKFORCE DIVERSITY

Managers are increasingly concerned with changing employee attitudes to reflect shifting perspectives on racial, gender, and other diversity issues. A comment to a co-worker of the opposite sex, which 20 years ago might have been taken as a compliment, can today become a career-limiting episode.[49] As such, organizations are investing in training to help reshape attitudes of employees.

A survey of U.S. organizations with 100 or more employees found that 47 percent of them sponsored some sort of diversity training.[50] Some examples: Police officers in Escondido, California, receive 36 hours of diversity training each

---

FROM CONCEPTS TO SKILLS

Changing Attitudes

Can you change unfavorable employee attitudes? Sometimes! It depends on who you are, the strength of the employee's attitude, the magnitude of the change, and the technique you choose to try to change the attitude.[51]

Employees are most likely to respond to change efforts made by someone who is liked, credible, and convincing. If people like you, they're more apt to identify and adopt your message. Credibility implies trust, expertise, and objectivity. So you're more likely to change an employee's attitude if that employee sees you as believable, knowledgeable, and unbiased in your presentation. Finally, successful attitude change is enhanced when you present your arguments clearly and persuasively.

It's easier to change an employee's attitude if he or she isn't strongly committed to it. Conversely, the stronger the belief about the attitude, the harder it is to change it. In addition, attitudes that have been expressed publicly are more difficult to change because it requires one to admit he or she has made a mistake.

It's easier to change attitudes when that change isn't very significant. To get an employee to accept a new attitude that varies greatly from his or her current position requires more effort. It may also threaten other deeply held attitudes and create increased dissonance.

All attitude-change techniques are not equally effective across situations. Oral persuasion techniques are most effective when you use a positive, tactful tone; present strong evidence to support your position; tailor your argument to the listener; use logic; and support your evidence by appealing to the employee's fears, frustrations, and other emotions. But people are more likely to embrace change when they can experience it. The use of training sessions in which employees share and personalize experiences and practice new behaviors can be powerful stimulants for change. Consistent with self-perception theory, changes in behavior can lead to changes in attitudes.

---

year. Pacific Gas & Electric Co. requires a minimum of four hours of training for its 12,000 employees. The Federal Aviation Administration sponsors a mandatory eight-hour diversity seminar for employees of its Western Pacific region.

What do these diversity programs look like and how do they address attitude change?[52] They almost all include a self-evaluation phase. People are pressed to examine themselves and to confront ethnic and cultural stereotypes they might hold. Then participants typically take part in group discussions or panels with representatives from diverse groups. So, for instance, a Hmong man might describe his family's life in Southeast Asia, and explain why they resettled in California; or a lesbian might describe how she discovered her sexual identity, and the reaction of her friends and family when she came out.

Additional activities designed to change attitudes include arranging for people to do volunteer work in community or social service centers in order to meet face-to-face with individuals and groups from diverse backgrounds and using exercises that let participants feel what it's like to be different. For example, when participants see the film *Eye of the Beholder*, in which people are segregated and stereotyped according to their eye color, participants see what it's like to be judged by something over which they have no control.

JOB SATISFACTION

We have already discussed job satisfaction briefly—earlier in this chapter as well as in Chapter 1. In this section, we want to dissect the concept more carefully. How do we measure job satisfaction? What is its effect on employee productivity, absenteeism, and turnover rates?

MEASURING JOB SATISFACTION

We've previously defined job satisfaction as an individual's general attitude toward his or her job. This definition is clearly a very broad one.[53] Yet this is inherent in the concept. Remember, a person's job is more than just the obvious activities of shuffling papers, waiting on customers, or driving a truck. Jobs require interaction with co-workers and bosses, following organizational rules and policies, meeting performance standards, living with working conditions that are often less than ideal, and the like.[54] This means that an employee's assessment of how satisfied or dissatisfied he or she is with his or her job is a complex summation of a number of discrete job elements. How, then, do we measure the concept?

The two most widely used approaches are a *single global rating* and a *summation score* made up of a number of job facets. The single global rating method is nothing more than asking individuals to respond to one question, such as "All things considered, how satisfied are you with your job?" Respondents then reply by circling a number between 1 and 5 that corresponds to answers from "highly satisfied" to "highly dissatisfied." The other approach—a summation of job facets—is more sophisticated. It identifies key elements in a job and asks for the employee's feelings about each. Typical factors that would be included are the nature of the work, supervision, present pay, promotion opportunities, and relations with co-workers.[55] These factors are rated on a standardized scale and then added up to create an overall job satisfaction score.

Is one of the foregoing approaches superior to the other? Intuitively, it would seem that summing up responses to a number of job factors would achieve a more accurate evaluation of job satisfaction. The research, however, doesn't support this intuition.[56] This is one of those rare instances in which simplicity

"Happy Workers Are Productive Workers"

This statement is false. The myth that "happy workers are productive workers" developed in the 1930s and 1940s, largely as a result of findings drawn by researchers conducting the Hawthorne studies at Western Electric. Based on those conclusions, managers began efforts to make their employees happier by such practices as engaging in laissez-faire leadership, improving working conditions, expanding health and family benefits such as insurance and college tuition reimbursement, providing company picnics and other informal get-togethers, and offering counseling services for employees.

But these paternalistic practices were based on questionable findings. A careful review of the research indicates that, if there is a positive relationship between happiness (i.e., satisfaction) and pro-ductivity, the correlations are low—in the vicinity of +0.14. This means that no more than 2 percent of the variance in output can be accounted for by employee satisfaction.[57]

Based on the evidence, a more accurate conclusion is actually the reverse—productive workers are likely to be happy workers. That is, productivity leads to satisfaction rather than the other way around.[58] If you do a good job, you intrinsically feel good about it. Additionally, assuming that the organization rewards productivity, your higher productivity should increase verbal recognition, your pay level, and probabilities for promotion. These rewards, in turn, increase your level of satisfaction with the job.

seems to work as well as complexity. Comparisons of one-question global ratings with the more lengthy summation-of-job-factors method indicate that the former is essentially as valid as the latter. The best explanation for this outcome is that the concept of job satisfaction is inherently so broad that the single question captures its essence.

THE EFFECT OF JOB SATISFACTION ON EMPLOYEE PERFORMANCE

Managers' interest in job satisfaction tends to center on its effect on employee performance. Researchers have recognized this interest, so we find a large number of studies that have been designed to assess the impact of job satisfaction on employee productivity, absenteeism, and turnover. Let's look at the current state of our knowledge.

Satisfaction and Productivity As the "Myth or Science?" box concludes, happy workers aren't necessarily productive workers. At the individual level, the evidence suggests the reverse to be more accurate—that productivity is likely to lead to satisfaction.

Interestingly, if we move from the individual level to that of the organization, there is renewed support for the original satisfaction–performance relationship.[59] When satisfaction and productivity data are gathered for the organization as a whole, rather than at the individual level, we find that organizations with more satisfied employees tend to be more effective than organizations with less satisfied employees. It may well be that the reason we haven't gotten strong support for the satisfaction-causes-productivity thesis is that studies have focused on individuals rather than the organization and that individual-level measures of productivity don't take into consideration all the interactions and complexities in the work process. So while we might not be able to say that a happy *worker* is more productive, it might be true that happy *organizations* are more productive.

Satisfaction and Absenteeism We find a consistent negative relationship between satisfaction and absenteeism, but the correlation is moderate—usually less than +0.40.[60] While it certainly makes sense that dissatisfied employees are more likely to miss work, other factors have an impact on the relationship and reduce the correlation coefficient. For example, remember our discussion of sick pay versus well pay in Chapter 2. Organizations that provide liberal sick leave benefits are encouraging all their employees—including those who are highly satisfied—to take days off. Assuming that you have a reasonable number of varied interests, you can find work satisfying and yet still take off work to enjoy a three-day weekend or tan yourself on a warm summer day if those days come free with no penalties.

An excellent illustration of how satisfaction directly leads to attendance, where there is a minimum impact from other factors, is a study done at Sears, Roebuck.[61] Satisfaction data were available on employees at Sears's two headquarters in Chicago and New York. Additionally, it is important to note that Sears's policy was not to permit employees to be absent from work for avoidable reasons without penalty. The occurrence of a freak April 2 snowstorm in Chicago created the opportunity to compare employee attendance at the Chicago office with attendance in New York, where the weather was quite nice. The interesting dimension in this study is that the snowstorm gave the Chicago employees a built-in excuse not to come to work. The storm crippled the city's transportation, and individuals knew they could miss work this day with no penalty. This natural experiment permitted the comparison of attendance records for satisfied and dissatisfied employees at two locations—one where you were expected to be at work (with normal pressures for attendance) and the other where you were free to choose with no penalty involved. If satisfaction leads to attendance, where there is an absence of outside factors, the more satisfied employees should have come to work in Chicago, while dissatisfied employees should have stayed home. The study found that on this particular April 2 absenteeism rates in New York were just as high for satisfied groups of workers as for dissatisfied groups. But in Chicago, the workers with high satisfaction scores had much higher attendance than did those with lower satisfaction levels. These findings are exactly what we would have expected if satisfaction is negatively correlated with absenteeism.

High employee turnover concerned Julie McHenry, chief executive of Wilson McHenry, a strategic business communications firm in Foster City, California. She hired a consultant to conduct an employee attitude survey and learned that her employees hated her mandatory training program because it did not satisfy their individual needs. McHenry let her employees design a voluntary training program, which helped reduce turnover. She says, "Employees are happier, bottom line. Especially here in Silicon Valley, where it's so competitive with employers, we need to keep them engaged."

Satisfaction and Turnover Satisfaction is also negatively related to turnover, but the correlation is stronger than what we found for absenteeism.[62] Yet, again, other factors such as labor market conditions, expectations about alternative job opportunities, and length of tenure with the organization are important constraints on the actual decision to leave one's current job.[63]

Evidence indicates that an important moderator of the satisfaction–turnover relationship is the employee's level of performance.[64] Specifically, level of satisfaction is less important in predicting turnover for superior performers. Why? The organization typically makes considerable efforts to keep these people. They get pay raises, praise, recognition, increased promotional opportunities, and so forth. Just the opposite tends to apply to poor performers. Few attempts are made by the organization to retain them. There may even be subtle pressures to encourage them to quit. We would expect, therefore, that job satisfaction is more important in influencing poor performers to stay than superior performers. Regardless of level of satisfaction, the latter are more likely to remain with the organization because the receipt of recognition, praise, and other rewards gives them more reasons for staying.

HOW EMPLOYEES CAN EXPRESS DISSATISFACTION

Employee dissatisfaction can be expressed in a number of ways.[65] For example, rather than quit, employees can complain, be insubordinate, steal organizational property, or shirk a part of their work responsibilities. Exhibit 3-6 offers four responses that differ from one another along two dimensions: constructiveness/destructiveness and activity/passivity. They are defined as follows:[66]

- **Exit:** Behavior directed toward leaving the organization, including looking for a new position as well as resigning.
- **Voice:** Actively and constructively attempting to improve conditions, including suggesting improvements, discussing problems with superiors, and some forms of union activity.
- **Loyalty:** Passively but optimistically waiting for conditions to improve, including speaking up for the organization in the face of external criticism and trusting the organization and its management to "do the right thing."
- **Neglect:** Passively allowing conditions to worsen, including chronic absenteeism or lateness, reduced effort, and increased error rate.

Exit and neglect behaviors encompass our performance variables—productivity, absenteeism, and turnover. But this model expands employee response to include voice and loyalty—constructive behaviors that allow individuals to tolerate unpleasant situations or to revive satisfactory working conditions. It helps us to understand situations, such as those sometimes found among unionized workers, in which low job satisfaction is coupled with low turnover.[67] Union members often express dissatisfaction through the grievance procedure or through formal contract negotiations. These voice mechanisms allow the union members to continue in their jobs while convincing themselves that they are acting to improve the situation.

exit
Dissatisfaction expressed through behavior directed toward leaving the organization.

voice
Dissatisfaction expressed through active and constructive attempts to improve conditions.

loyalty
Dissatisfaction expressed by passively waiting for conditions to improve.

neglect
Dissatisfaction expressed through allowing conditions to worsen.

Responses to Job Dissatisfaction

EXHIBIT 3-6

Source: C. Rusbult and D. Lowery, "When Bureaucrats Get the Blues," *Journal of Applied Social Psychology*, Vol. 15, No. 1 (1985), p. 83. With permission.

JOB SATISFACTION AND OCB

It seems logical to assume that job satisfaction should be a major determinant of an employee's organizational citizenship behavior (OCB).[68] Satisfied employees would seem more likely to talk positively about the organization, help others, and go beyond the normal expectations in their job. Moreover, satisfied employees might be more prone to go beyond the call of duty because they want to reciprocate their positive experiences. Consistent with this thinking, early discussions of OCB assumed that it was closely linked with satisfaction.[69] More recent evidence, however, suggests that satisfaction influences OCB, but through perceptions of fairness.

There is a modest overall relationship between job satisfaction and OCB.[70] But when fairness is controlled for, satisfaction is unrelated to OCB.[71] What does this mean? Basically, job satisfaction comes down to conceptions of fair outcomes, treatment, and procedures.[72] If you don't feel that your supervisor, the organization's procedures, or pay policies are fair, your job satisfaction is likely to suffer signficantly. However, when you perceive organizational processes and outcomes to be fair, trust is developed. And when you trust your employer, you're more willing to voluntarily engage in behaviors that go beyond your formal job requirements.

Union members often use their union convention to voice their opinions about work conditions. At the United Auto Workers convention shown here, union members express their demands in planning for their contract negotiations with the Big Three auto makers. These UAW members are particularly vocal in complaining about the practice of auto makers increasingly shifting more work to nonunion parts suppliers that pay lower wages.

SUMMARY AND IMPLICATIONS FOR MANAGERS

Why is it important to know an individual's values? Although they don't have a direct impact on behavior, values strongly influence a person's attitudes. So knowledge of an individual's value system can provide insight into his or her attitudes.

Given that people's values differ, managers can use the Rokeach Value Survey to assess potential employees and determine if their values align with the dominant values of the organization. An employee's performance and satisfaction are likely to be higher if his or her values fit well with the organization. For instance, the person who places high importance on imagination, independence, and freedom is likely to be poorly matched with an organization that seeks conformity from its employees. Managers are more likely to appreciate, evaluate positively, and allocate rewards to employees who "fit in," and employees are more likely to be satisfied if they perceive that they do fit in. This argues for management to strive during the selection of new employees to find job candidates who not only have the ability, experience, and motivation to perform but also have a value system that is compatible with the organization's.

Managers should be interested in their employees' attitudes because attitudes give warnings of potential problems and because they influence behavior.

Satisfied and committed employees, for instance, have lower rates of turnover and absenteeism. Given that managers want to keep resignations and absences down—especially among their more productive employees—they will want to do those things that will generate positive job attitudes.

Managers should also be aware that employees will try to reduce cognitive dissonance. More important, dissonance can be managed. If employees are required to engage in activities that appear inconsistent to them or that are at odds with their attitudes, the pressures to reduce the resulting dissonance are lessened when the employee perceives that the dissonance is externally imposed and is beyond his or her control or if the rewards are significant enough to offset the dissonance.

Managers Can Create Satisfied Employees

A review of the evidence has identified four factors conducive to high levels of employee job satisfaction: mentally challenging work, equitable rewards, supportive working conditions, and supportive colleagues.[1] Importantly, each of these factors is controllable by management.

Mentally challenging work. People prefer jobs that give them opportunities to use their skills and abilities and offer a variety of tasks, freedom, and feedback on how well they're doing. These characteristics make work mentally challenging.

Equitable rewards. Employees want pay systems and promotion policies that they perceive as being just, unambiguous, and in line with their expectations. When pay is seen as fair based on job demands, individual skill level, and community pay standards, satisfaction is likely to result. Similarly, employees seek fair promotion policies and practices. Promotions provide opportunities for personal growth, more responsibilities, and increased social status. Individuals who perceive that promotion decisions are made in a fair and just manner, therefore, are likely to experience satisfaction from their jobs.

Supportive working conditions. Employees are concerned with their work environment for both personal comfort and facilitating doing a good job. Studies demonstrate that employees prefer physical surroundings that are not dangerous or uncomfortable. Additionally, most employees prefer working close to home, in clean and relatively modern facilities, and with adequate tools and equipment.

Supportive colleagues. People get more out of work than merely money or tangible achievements. For most employees, work also fills the need for social interaction. Not surprisingly, therefore, having friendly and supportive co-workers leads to increased job satisfaction. The behavior of one's boss also is a major determinant of satisfaction. Studies generally find that employee satisfaction is increased when the immediate supervisor is understanding and friendly, offers praise for good performance, listens to employees' opinions, and shows a personal interest in them.

T he notion that managers and organizations can control the level of employee job satisfaction is inherently attractive. It fits nicely with the view that managers directly influence organizational processes and outcomes. Unfortunately, there is a growing body of evidence that challenges the notion that managers control the factors that influence employee job satisfaction. The most recent findings indicate that employee job satisfaction is largely genetically determined.[2]

Whether a person is happy or not is essentially determined by his or her gene structure. You either have happy genes or you don't. Approximately 80 percent of people's differences in happiness, or subjective well-being, has been found to be attributable to their genes.

Analysis of satisfaction data for a selected sample of individuals over a 50-year period found that individual results were consistently stable over time, even when these people changed employers and occupations. This analysis and other research suggest that an individual's disposition toward life—positive or negative—is established by his or her genetic makeup, holds over time, and carries over into his or her disposition toward work.

Given these findings, there is probably little that most managers can do to influence employee satisfaction. In spite of the fact that managers and organizations go to extensive lengths to try to improve employee job satisfaction through actions such as manipulating job characteristics, working conditions, and rewards, these actions are likely to have little effect. The only area in which managers will have any significant influence will be through their control of the selection process. If managers want satisfied workers, they need to make sure their selection process screens out the negative, maladjusted, trouble-making fault-finders who derive little satisfaction in anything about their jobs. This is probably best achieved through personality testing, in-depth interviewing, and careful checking of applicants' previous work records.

---

[1] E. A. Locke, "The Nature and Causes of Job Satisfaction," in M. D. Dunnette (ed.), *Handbook of Industrial and Organizational Psychology* (Chicago: Rand McNally), 1976, pp. 1319–28.

[2] See, for instance, T. A. Judge and S. Watanabe, "Another Look at the Job Satisfaction–Life Satisfaction Relationship," *Journal of Applied Psychology*, December 1993, pp. 939–48; R. D. Arvey, B. P. McCall, T. J. Bouchard Jr., and P. Taubman, "Genetic Influences on Job Satisfaction and Work Values," *Personality and Individual Differences*, July 1994, pp. 21–33; and D. Lykken and A. Tellegen, "Happiness Is a Stochastic Phenomenon," *Psychological Science*, May 1996, pp. 186–89.

1. Contrast the Protestant work ethic, existential, pragmatic, and generation X typologies with the terminal values identified in the Rokeach Value Survey.

2. Contrast the cognitive and affective components of an attitude.

3. What is cognitive dissonance and how is it related to attitudes?

4. What is self-perception theory? How does it increase our ability to predict behavior?

5. What contingency factors can improve the statistical relationship between attitudes and behavior?

6. Are most people satisfied with their jobs? Explain.

7. Are happy workers productive workers?

8. What is the relationship between job satisfaction and absenteeism? Turnover? Which is the stronger relationship?

9. How can managers get employees to more readily accept working with colleagues who are different from themselves?

10. Contrast exit, voice, loyalty, and neglect as employee responses to job dissatisfaction.

Questions for Critical Thinking

1. "Thirty-five years ago, young employees we hired were ambitious, conscientious, hardworking, and honest. Today's young workers don't have the same values." Do you agree or disagree with this manager's comments? Support your position.

2. Do you think there might be any positive and significant relationship between the possession of certain personal values and successful career progression in organizations such as Merrill Lynch, the AFL-CIO, and the city of Cleveland's police department? Discuss.

3. "Managers should do everything they can to enhance the job satisfaction of their employees." Do you agree or disagree? Support your position.

4. Discuss the advantages and disadvantages of using regular attitude surveys to monitor employee job satisfaction.

5. When employees are asked whether they would again choose the same work or whether they would want their children to follow in their footsteps, typically less than half answer in the affirmative. What, if anything, do you think this implies about employee job satisfaction?

Team Exercise	Assessing Work Attitudes

Objective   To compare attitudes about the workforce.

Time   Approximately 30 minutes.

Procedure   Answer the following five questions:

1. *Generally,* American workers (pick one)
   - _____ **a.** are highly motivated and hardworking
   - _____ **b.** try to give a fair day's effort
   - _____ **c.** will put forth effort if you make it worthwhile
   - _____ **d.** try to get by with a low level of effort
   - _____ **e.** are lazy and/or poorly motivated

2. The people *I have worked with* (pick one)
   - _____ **a.** are highly motivated and hardworking
   - _____ **b.** try to give a fair day's effort
   - _____ **c.** will put forth effort if you make it worthwhile
   - _____ **d.** try to get by with a low level of effort
   - _____ **e.** are lazy and/or poorly motivated

3. *Compared to foreign workers,* American workers are (pick one)
   _____ **a.** more productive
   _____ **b.** equally productive
   _____ **c.** less productive

4. *Over the past 20 years,* American workers have (pick one)
   _____ **a.** improved in overall quality of job performance
   _____ **b.** remained about the same in overall quality of job performance
   _____ **c.** deteriorated in overall quality of job performance

5. If you have a low opinion of the U.S. workforce, give the one step (or action) that could be taken that would lead to the most improvement.

Group Discussion

a. Break into groups of three to five members each. Compare your answers to the five questions.

b. For each question where one or more members disagree, discuss *why* each member chose his or her answer.

c. After this discussion, members are free to change their original answer. Did any in your group do so?

d. Your instructor will provide data from other student attitude responses to these questions and then lead the class in discussing the implications or accuracy of these attitudes.

Source: Based on D. R. Brown, "Dealing with Student Conceptions and Misconceptions about Worker Attitudes and Productivity," *Journal of Management Education,* May 1991, pp. 259–64.

Internet Search Exercises

1. Find the best and latest data you can that describe the level of job satisfaction in (a) the United States, (b) Canada, and (c) Japan. What conclusions are you able to draw from these data?

2. Find the results from three different attitude surveys dealing with organizational attitudes such as job satisfaction, job involvement, or organizational commitment. What, if anything, did these surveys and/or their results have in common?

PHLIP Companion Web Site

We invite you to visit the Robbins homepage on the Prentice Hall Web site at **www.prenhall.com/robbins** for our on-line study guide, current events, links to related Web sites, and more.

Case Incident   Will Volvo's Perks Give Ford Sticker Shock?

Ford Motor Company's purchase of Volvo in 1999 is likely to change the life of Volvo employees. And the employees aren't too excited about giving up the status quo.

Volvo's employees at the company's flagship plant in Gothenburg, Sweden, enjoy a wealth of benefits. For instance, they get to use the company gym, Olympic-size swimming pool, badminton and tennis courts, and outdoor track and tanning beds. There is also a hot-water pool, where workers go for physical therapy

sessions after a hard day on the assembly line. This is all made available to employees for $1.50 a day. Similar facilities exist at other Volvo plants. In contrast, although employees at U.S. Ford plants usually have a free-of-charge fitness center, the facilities are nothing like the health club at Volvo.

Volvo employees are worried. Will they lose their health club? Will Ford's goal to turn Volvo into a "volume car" change the way they work? That could mean a three-shift, round-the-clock production schedule, just like in the United States. Volvo employees currently work only two shifts. Will Volvo employees' job security be threatened? Will the quality of their work life change? Forty-year-old Jari Saarelainen, a Volvo night-shift worker, is concerned. He now works less than 30 hours a week but gets paid as if he worked 40 hours on the day shift. The shorter hours allow him to spend lots of time with his wife and four children. "It's a human way of work," he says. Saarelainen knows he has it good but argues that his relatively undemanding workload helps the company because productivity and morale are higher than they would be under a more conventional employer. "We hope that Ford can grasp that this system is better for the company and the workers," he says.

What is Ford's position? The company's CEO only says, "I respect the Swedish heritage." But he adds, "nothing is safe in this world; there are no guarantees."

Questions

1. Is there any way Ford can take away employee benefits at Volvo without hurting job satisfaction? Discuss.

2. If Volvo benefits are kept intact, what influence will it have on Ford employees in the United States?

3. Do you think concern about work and family conflicts is greater in Sweden than in the United States? Discuss.

4. What are the implications of this case for mergers and acquisitions?

Source: Based on A. Latour, "Detroit Meets a 'Worker Paradise,'" *Wall Street Journal*, March 3, 1999, p. B1.

| Video Case | Madison Park Greeting Card Company |

Attitudes have a lot to do with the way people look at and live their lives. Attitudes are not fixed, meaning they can change, but they generally are treated as being relatively stable. We can learn about how people approach work by understanding their attitudes.

Judy Jacobsen, the founder of Madison Park Greeting Card Company, has "a great attitude." What does this mean? Judy comes across as having a very positive outlook on life. This carries over into her attitudes and approaches to work. Although Judy worries about the bottom line, we get the idea that she is willing to forgo some profit to ensure that she, and others, have a chance to feel good about what they are doing. Judy does appreciate the need to run a strong and financially healthy company. At the same time, she is committed to having a happy, positive, and attitudinally healthy company, too!

In this video, you get the idea that at Madison Park Greeting, its people are its greatest asset. Nobody is forced to expose a lot about themselves or to "buy into" things with which they don't agree, but there is an opportunity to be part of a family—as much as to be part of a company—if one chooses to be. The staff meets daily (yes, daily) for brief status updates on key projects. These meetings give Jacobsen a chance to check up on how people are doing, too. It seems like Judy plays a bit of a motherly role.

The environment at Madison Park Greeting Card Company might seem a bit odd to you. It certainly is not what you would expect to find if you are finishing school and going to work for a large, *Fortune* 100 corporation. It is probably not even what you would expect if you were going to work for many smaller companies. The point is, this approach may not be for everyone. On the other hand, if this is the type of organization within which someone feels comfortable, it could be great for both the company and the individual. Working in a place that makes you feel good and that allows you to be yourself probably influences how well you work and how committed you are to the company. There are mixed opinions about how much to worry about employee turnover, but good employees are a valuable asset. If we accept that there is a relationship between a feeling of "belongingness" and good work, Judy Jacobsen might be on to something.

Questions

1. You have met Judy Jacobsen and learned a bit about how she started and evolved her business. Consider what she says about how she has grown as a business owner and the work environment she has established. How would you describe her attitudes about work?

2. What types of organizational commitment issues might exist among various employees at Madison Park Greeting Card Co.? Do you think everybody feels the same way about the company and their job as Judy does?

3. We learned two interesting things about Judy's approach to employing family. She believes that

there can be only one leader and has selected one of three children working with her to be the company president. And she required her children to work somewhere else before coming to work in the company. What do you think about these decisions? Do you agree with what Judy did? Why or why not?

4. We were introduced to various employment programs for people of various abilities and cultural backgrounds. This small company even has a program to help high school students earn money toward a college education. Do you think programs like these are necessary? Why do you think they have them?

End Notes

1. Based on J. L. Seglin, "The Happiest Workers in the World," *INC.: The State of Small Business 1996*, May 1996, pp. 62–76.
2. J. L. Seglin, "Americans @ Work," *INC.*, June 1998, pp. 91–94.
3. See, for instance, studies cited in A. F. Chelte, J. Wright, and C. Tausky, "Did Job Satisfaction Really Drop During the 1970s?" *Monthly Labor Review*, November 1982, pp. 33–36; "Job Satisfaction High in America, Says Conference Board Study," *Monthly Labor Review*, February 1985, p. 52; C. Hartman and S. Pearlstein, "The Joy of Working," *INC.*, November 1987, pp. 61–66; and E. Graham, "Work May Be a Rat Race, But It's Not a Daily Grind," *Wall Street Journal*, September 19, 1997, p. R1.
4. See "Employee Satisfaction Linked to Age," *Training*, June 1998, p. 16.
5. G. L. Staines and R. P. Quinn, "American Workers Evaluate the Quality of Their Jobs," *Monthly Labor Review*, January 1979, pp. 3–12.
6. Chelte, Wright, Tausky, "Did Job Satisfaction Really Drop?"; and B. M. Staw, N. E. Bell, and J. A. Clausen, "The Dispositional Approach to Job Attitudes: A Lifetime Longitudinal Test," *Administrative Science Quarterly*, March 1986, pp. 56–77.
7. Cited in L. Grant, "Unhappy in Japan," *Fortune*, January 13, 1997, p. 142; and "Survey Finds Satisfied Workers in Canada," *Manpower Argus*, January 1997, p. 6.
8. S. L. Wilk, L. B. Desmarais, and P. R. Sackett, "Gravitation to Jobs Commensurate with Ability: Longitudinal and Cross-Sectional Tests," *Journal of Applied Psychology*, February 1995, pp. 79–85.
9. M. Rokeach, *The Nature of Human Values* (New York: Free Press, 1973), p. 5.
10. M. Rokeach and S. J. Ball-Rokeach, "Stability and Change in American Value Priorities, 1968–1981," *American Psychologist*, May 1989, pp. 775–84.
11. See, for instance, B. M. Meglino and E. C. Ravlin, "Individual Values in Organizations: Concepts, Controversies, and Research," *Journal of Management*, vol. 24, no. 3, 1998, pp. 351–89.
12. M. Rokeach, *The Nature of Human Values*, p. 6.
13. J. M. Munson and B. Z. Posner, "The Factorial Validity of a Modified Rokeach Value Survey for Four Diverse Samples," *Educational and Psychological Measurement*, Winter 1980, pp. 1073–79; and W. C. Frederick and J. Weber, "The Values of Corporate Managers and Their Critics: An Empirical Description and Normative Implications," in W. C. Frederick and L. E. Preston (eds.), *Business Ethics: Research Issues and Empirical Studies* (Greenwich, CT: JAI Press, 1990), pp. 123–44.
14. Frederick and Weber, "The Values of Corporate Managers and Their Critics."
15. Ibid., p. 132.
16. See, for example R. Maynard, "A Less-Stressed Work Force," *Nation's Business*, November 1996, pp. 50–52; "Generation Xers Press Work/Life Issues," *Manpower Argus*, December 1997, p. 10; J. A. Conger, "How Generational Shifts Will Transform Organizational Life," in F. Hesselbein, M. Goldsmith, and R. Beckhard (eds.), *The Organization of the Future* (San Francisco: Jossey-Bass, 1997), pp. 17–24; and N. H. Woodward, "The Coming of the Managers," *HRMagazine*, March 1999, pp. 74–80.
17. As noted to your author by R. Volkema and R. L. Neal Jr., of American University, this model may also be limited in its application to minority populations and recent immigrants to North America.
18. R. E. Hattwick, Y. Kathawala, M. Monipullil, and L. Wall, "On the Alleged Decline in Business Ethics," *Journal of Behavioral Economics*, Summer 1989, pp. 129–43.
19. B. Z. Posner and W. H. Schmidt, "Values and the American Manager: An Update Updated," *California Management Review*, Spring 1992, p. 86.
20. G. Hofstede, *Culture's Consequences: International Differences in Work Related Values* (Beverly Hills, CA: Sage, 1980); G. Hofstede, *Cultures and Organizations: Software of the Mind* (London: McGraw-Hill, 1991); and G. Hofstede, "Cultural Constraints in Management Theories," *Academy of Management Executive*, February 1993, pp. 81–94.
21. Hofstede called this dimension masculinity versus femininity, but we've changed his terms because of their strong sexist connotation.
22. D. Fernandez, D. S. Carlson, L. P. Stepina, and J. D. Nicholson, "Hofstede's Country Classification 25 Years Later," *Journal of Social Psychology*, February 1997, pp. 43–54.
23. N. J. Adler, "Cross-Cultural Management Research: The Ostrich and the Trend," *Academy of Management Review*, April 1983, pp. 226–32.
24. L. Godkin, C. E. Braye, and C. L. Caunch, "U.S.-Based Cross Cultural Management Research in the Eighties," *Journal of Business and Economic Perspectives*, vol. 15 (1989), pp. 37–45; and T. K. Peng, M. F. Peterson, and

Y. P. Shyi, "Quantitative Methods in Cross-National Management Research: Trends and Equivalence Issues," *Journal of Organizational Behavior*, vol. 12 (1991), pp. 87–107.

25. S. J. Breckler, "Empirical Validation of Affect, Behavior, and Cognition as Distinct Components of Attitude," *Journal of Personality and Social Psychology*, May 1984, pp. 1191–1205; and S. L. Crites Jr., L. R. Fabrigar, and R. E. Petty, "Measuring the Affective and Cognitive Properties of Attitudes: Conceptual and Methodological Issues," *Personality and Social Psychology Bulletin*, December 1994, pp. 619–34.

26. P. P. Brooke Jr., D. W. Russell, and J. L. Price, "Discriminant Validation of Measures of Job Satisfaction, Job Involvement, and Organizational Commitment," *Journal of Applied Psychology*, May 1988, pp. 139–45; and R. T. Keller, "Job Involvement and Organizational Commitment as Longitudinal Predictors of Job Performance: A Study of Scientists and Engineers," *Journal of Applied Psychology*, August 1997, pp. 539–45.

27. See, for example, S. Rabinowitz and D. T. Hall, "Organizational Research in Job Involvement," *Psychological Bulletin*, March 1977, pp. 265–88; G. J. Blau, "A Multiple Study Investigation of the Dimensionality of Job Involvement," *Journal of Vocational Behavior*, August 1985, pp. 19–36; and N. A. Jans, "Organizational Factors and Work Involvement," *Organizational Behavior and Human Decision Processes*, June 1985, pp. 382–96.

28. Based on G. J. Blau and K. R. Boal, "Conceptualizing How Job Involvement and Organizational Commitment Affect Turnover and Absenteeism," *Academy of Management Review*, April 1987, p. 290.

29. G. J. Blau, "Job Involvement and Organizational Commitment as Interactive Predictors of Tardiness and Absenteeism," *Journal of Management*, Winter 1986, pp. 577–84; and K. Boal and R. Cidambi, "Attitudinal Correlates of Turnover and Absenteeism: A Meta Analysis," paper presented at the meeting of the American Psychological Association, Toronto, Canada, 1984.

30. G. Farris, "A Predictive Study of Turnover," *Personnel Psychology*, Summer 1971, pp. 311–28.

31. Blau and Boal, "Conceptualizing," p. 290.

32. See, for instance, P. W. Hom, R. Katerberg, and C. L. Hulin, "Comparative Examination of Three Approaches to the Prediction of Turnover," *Journal of Applied Psychology*, June 1979, pp. 280–90; H. Angle and J. Perry, "Organizational Commitment: Individual and Organizational Influence," *Work and Occupations*, May 1983, pp. 123–46; and J. L. Pierce and R. B. Dunham, "Organizational Commitment: Pre-Employment Propensity and Initial Work Experiences," *Journal of Management*, Spring 1987, pp. 163–78.

33. Hom, Katerberg, and Hulin, "Comparative Examination"; and R. T. Mowday, L. W. Porter, and R. M. Steers, *Employee Organization Linkages: The Psychology of Commitment, Absenteeism, and Turnover* (New York: Academic Press, 1982).

34. L. W. Porter, R. M. Steers, R. T. Mowday, and P. V. Boulian, "Organizational Commitment, Job Satisfaction, and Turnover Among Psychiatric Technicians," *Journal of Applied Psychology*, October 1974, pp. 603–09.

35. D. M. Rousseau, "Organizational Behavior in the New Organizational Era," in J. T. Spence, J. M. Darley, and D. J. Foss (eds.), *Annual Review of Psychology*, vol. 48 (Palo Alto, CA: Annual Reviews, 1997), p. 523.

36. Ibid.

37. See, for instance, A. J. Elliot and P. G. Devine, "On the Motivational Nature of Cognitive Dissonance: Dissonance as Psychological Discomfort," *Journal of Personality and Social Psychology*, September 1994, pp. 382–94.

38. See R. Rosenblatt, "How Do Tobacco Executives Live with Themselves?" *The New York Times Magazine*, March 20, 1994, pp. 34–41.

39. L. Festinger, *A Theory of Cognitive Dissonance* (Stanford, CA: Stanford University Press, 1957).

40. A. W. Wicker, "Attitude versus Action: The Relationship of Verbal and Overt Behavioral Responses to Attitude Objects," *Journal of Social Issues*, Autumn 1969, pp. 41–78.

41. Ibid., p. 65.

42. S. J. Kraus, "Attitudes and the Prediction of Behavior: A Meta-Analysis of the Empirical Literature," *Personality and Social Psychology Bulletin*, January 1995, pp. 58–75.

43. Ibid.

44. D. J. Bem, "Self-Perception Theory," in L. Berkowitz (ed.), *Advances in Experimental Social Psychology*, vol. 6 (New York: Academic Press, 1972), pp. 1–62.

45. See C. A. Kiesler, R. E. Nisbett, and M. P. Zanna, "On Inferring One's Belief from One's Behavior," *Journal of Personality and Social Psychology*, April 1969, pp. 321–27; S. E. Taylor, "On Inferring One's Attitudes from One's Behavior: Some Delimiting Conditions," *Journal of Personality and Social Psychology*, January 1975, pp. 126–31; and A. M. Tybout and C. A. Scott, "Availability of Well-Defined Internal Knowledge and the Attitude Formation Process: Information Aggregation Versus Self-Perception," *Journal of Personality and Social Psychology*, March 1983, pp. 474–91.

46. See, for example, B. Fishel, "A New Perspective: How to Get the Real Story from Attitude Surveys," *Training*, February 1998, pp. 91–94.

47. J. Stack, "Measuring Morale," *INC.*, January 1997, pp. 29–30.

48. See T. Lammers, "The Essential Employee Survey," *INC.*, December 1992, pp. 159–61; and S. Shellenbarger, "Companies Are Finding It Really Pays to Be Nice to Employees," *Wall Street Journal*, July 22, 1998, p. B1.

49. M. Crawford, "The New Office Etiquette," *Canadian Business*, May 1993, pp. 22–31.

50. Cited in A. Rossett and T. Bickham, "Diversity Training: Hope, Faith and Cynicism," *Training*, January 1994, p. 40.

51. This box is based on A. Bednar and W. H. Levie, "Attitude-Change Principles," in C. Fleming and W. H. Levie, *Instructional Message Design: Principles from the Behavioral and Cognitive Sciences*, 2nd ed. (Upper Saddle River, NJ: Educational Technology Publications, 1993); and R. E. Petty, D. T. Wegener, and L. R. Fabrigar, "Attitudes and Attitude Change," in J. T. Spence, J. M. Darley, and D. J. Foss (eds.), *Annual Review of Psychology*, vol. 48 (Palo Alto, CA: Annual Reviews Inc., 1997), pp. 609–47.

52. This section is based on A. Rossett and T. Bickham, "Diversity Training," pp. 40–46.

53. For problems with the concept of job satisfaction, see R. Hodson, "Workplace Behaviors," *Work and Occupations*, August 1991, pp. 271–90; and H. M. Weiss and R. Cropanzano, "Affective Events Theory: A Theoretical Discussion of the Structure, Causes and Consequences of Affective Experiences at Work," in B. M. Staw and L. L. Cummings (eds.), *Research in Organizational Behavior*, vol. 18 (Greenwich, CT: JAI Press, 1996), pp. 1–3.

54. The Wyatt Company's 1989 national WorkAmerica study identified 12 dimensions of satisfaction: work organization, working conditions, communications, job performance and performance review, co-workers, supervision, company management, pay, benefits, career development and training, job content and satisfaction, and company image and change.

55. See P. E. Spector, *Job Satisfaction: Application, Assessment, Causes, and Consequences* (Thousand Oaks, CA: Sage, 1997), p. 3.

56. J. P. Wanous, A. E. Reichers, and M. J. Hudy, "Overall Job Satisfaction: How Good Are Single-Item Measures?" *Journal of Applied Psychology*, April 1997, pp. 247–52.

57. V. H. Vroom, *Work and Motivation* (New York: Wiley, 1964); and M. T. Iaffaldano and P. M. Muchinsky, "Job Satisfaction and Job Performance: A Meta-Analysis," *Psychological Bulletin*, March 1985, pp. 251–73.

58. C. N. Greene, "The Satisfaction–Performance Controversy," *Business Horizons*, February 1972, pp. 31–41; E. E. Lawler III, *Motivation in Organizations* (Monterey, CA: Brooks/Cole, 1973); and M. M. Petty, G. W. McGee, and J. W. Cavender, "A Meta-Analysis of the Relationship Between Individual Job Satisfaction and Individual Performance," *Academy of Management Review*, October 1984, pp. 712–21.

59. C. Ostroff, "The Relationship Between Satisfaction, Attitudes, and Performance: An Organizational Level Analysis," *Journal of Applied Psychology*, December 1992, pp. 963–74; and A. M. Ryan, M. J. Schmit, and R. Johnson, "Attitudes and Effectiveness: Examining Relations at an Organizational Level," *Personnel Psychology*, Winter 1996, pp. 853–82.

60. E. A. Locke, "The Nature and Causes of Job Satisfaction," in M. D. Dunnette (ed.), *Handbook of Industrial and Organizational Psychology* (Chicago: Rand McNally, 1976), p. 1331; S. L. McShane, "Job Satisfaction and Absenteeism: A Meta-Analytic Re-Examination," *Canadian Journal of Administrative Science*, June 1984, pp. 61–77; R. D. Hackett and R. M. Guion, "A Reevaluation of the Absenteeism–Job Satisfaction Relationship," *Organizational Behavior and Human Decision Processes*, June 1985, p. 340–81; K. D. Scott and G. S. Taylor, "An Examination of Conflicting Findings on the Relationship Between Job Satisfaction and Absenteeism: A Meta-Analysis," *Academy of Management Journal*, September 1985, pp. 599–612; R. D. Hackett, "Work Attitudes and Employee Absenteeism: A Synthesis of the Literature," paper presented at 1988 National Academy of Management Conference, Anaheim, CA, August 1988; and R. P. Steel and J. R. Rentsch, "Influence of Cumulation Strategies on the Long-Range Prediction of Absenteeism," *Academy of Management Journal*, December 1995, pp. 1616–34.

61. F. J. Smith, "Work Attitudes as Predictors of Attendance on a Specific Day," *Journal of Applied Psychology*, February 1977, pp. 16–19.

62. Brayfield and Crockett, "Employee Attitudes"; Vroom, *Work and Motivation;* J. Price, *The Study of Turnover* (Ames: Iowa State University Press, 1977); and W. H. Mobley, R. W. Griffeth, H. H. Hand, and B. M. Meglino, "Review and Conceptual Analysis of the Employee Turnover Process," *Psychological Bulletin*, May 1979, pp. 493–522.

63. See, for example, C. L. Hulin, M. Roznowski, and D. Hachiya, "Alternative Opportunities and Withdrawal Decisions: Empirical and Theoretical Discrepancies and an Integration," *Psychological Bulletin*, July 1985, pp. 233–50; and J. M. Carsten and P. E. Spector, "Unemployment, Job Satisfaction, and Employee Turnover: A Meta-Analytic Test of the Muchinsky Model," *Journal of Applied Psychology*, August 1987, pp. 374–81.

64. D. G. Spencer and R. M. Steers, "Performance as a Moderator of the Job Satisfaction-Turnover Relationship," *Journal of Applied Psychology*, August 1981, pp. 511–14.

65. S. M. Puffer, "Prosocial Behavior, Noncompliant Behavior, and Work Performance Among Commission Salespeople," *Journal of Applied Psychology*, November 1987, pp. 615–21; J. Hogan and R. Hogan, "How to Measure Employee Reliability," *Journal of Applied Psychology*, May 1989, pp. 273–79; and C. D. Fisher and E. A. Locke, "The New Look in Job Satisfaction Research and Theory," in C. J. Cranny, P. C. Smith, and E. F. Stone (eds.), *Job Satisfaction*, (N.Y.: Lexington Books, 1992), pp. 165–94.

66. See D. Farrell, "Exit, Voice, Loyalty, and Neglect as Responses to Job Dissatisfaction: A Multidimensional Scaling Study," *Academy of Management Journal*, December 1983, pp. 596–606; C. E. Rusbult, D. Farrell, G. Rogers, and A. G. Mainous III, "Impact of Exchange Variables on Exit, Voice, Loyalty, and Neglect: An Integrative Model of Responses to Declining Job Satisfaction," *Academy of Management Journal*, September 1988, pp. 599–627; M. J. Withey and W. H. Cooper, "Predicting Exit, Voice, Loyalty, and Neglect," *Administrative Science Quarterly*, December 1989, pp. 521–39; and W. H. Turnley and D. C. Feldman, "The Impact of Psychological Contract Violations on Exit, Voice, Loyalty, and Neglect," *Human Relations*, July, 1999, pp. 895–922.

67. R. B. Freeman, "Job Satisfaction as an Economic Variable," *American Economic Review*, January 1978, pp. 135–41.

68. P. E. Spector, *Job Satisfaction*, pp. 57–58.

69. See T. S. Bateman and D. W. Organ, "Job Satisfaction and the Good Soldier: The Relationship Between Affect and Employee 'Citizenship,'" *Academy of Management Journal*, December 1983, pp. 587–95; C. A. Smith, D. W. Organ, and J. P. Near, "Organizational Citizenship Behavior: Its Nature and Antecedents," *Journal of Applied Psychology*, October 1983, pp. 653–63; and A. P. Brief, *Attitudes In and Around Organizations* (Thousand Oaks, CA: Sage, 1998), pp. 44–45.

70. D. W. Organ and K. Ryan, "A Meta-Analytic Review of Attitudinal and Dispositional Predictors of Organizational Citizenship Behavior," *Personnel Psychology*, Winter 1995, p. 791.

71. J. Fahr, P. M. Podsakoff, and D. W. Organ, "Accounting for Organizational Citizenship Behavior: Leader Fairness and Task Scope Versus Satisfaction," *Journal of Management*, December 1990, pp. 705–22; R. H. Moorman, "Relationship Between Organization Justice and Organizational Citizenship Behaviors: Do Fairness Perceptions Influence Employee Citizenship?" *Journal of Applied Psychology*, December 1991, pp. 845–55; and M. A. Konovsky and D. W. Organ, "Dispositional and Contextual Determinants of Organizational Citizenship Behavior," *Journal of Organizational Behavior*, May 1996, pp. 253–66.

72. D. W. Organ, "Personality and Organizational Citizenship Behavior," *Journal of Management*, Summer 1994, p. 466.

"Be yourself" is the worst advice you can give some people.

—T. Masson

When colleagues describe the personality of Jill Barad, CEO at toy giant, Mattel Inc., they use terms such as *competitive, combative, intense, energetic,* and *ambitious.*[1] Barad provides an excellent illustration of how an individual's personality shapes behavior and the importance of properly matching personalities with jobs.

Jill Barad (shown here with children of Mattel's employees from the firm's day care center) was born in 1951 and grew up in Queens, New York. Her early interests focused on show business. She loved to dress up and play entertainer. Her sister fondly remembers trying to sleep while Jill stood on her bed belting out songs from *Oklahoma!* and *Sound of Music.* This early interest in show biz undoubtedly reflected the influence of her dad, who was a technical director for NBC and later a TV director and producer. Jill's mother also had a role in shaping her aspirations. Jill's mother encouraged her. She told Jill that she could overcome obstacles and achieve her dreams. "My mother gave me a bumblebee pin when I started work," recalls Barad. "She said, 'Aerodynamically, bees shouldn't be able to fly. But they do.' " Barad's mother had successfully imparted in her daughter the belief that anything was possible.

Barad joined Mattel in 1981 as a product manager. In 1983, she was given the job of trying to revive the slumping sales of Barbie, Mattel's most valuable franchise. Unafraid to ruffle feathers, she used her intelligence, marketing sense, energy, and intense competitiveness to bring about one of the most dramatic turnarounds in corporate history.

Personality and Emotions

Barbie sales went from $200 million, when she took over in 1983, to $1.9 billion in 1997.

Barad thrived in Mattel's competitive culture. Unafraid to speak her mind, she forcefully pushed for greater responsibilities and promotions. "I always fought for my point of view." And she never camouflaged her ambition, "I just always wanted the next job," she says. "She was never afraid to go in and ask for a raise," adds a former colleague.

As one of the few women heading up a major American company, Jill Barad is still "dressing up and putting on shows." Glamorous and radiant, she seems more Hollywood than corporate. Barad's personality has certainly played a role in shaping her career, as did her decision to work for a company that valued and rewarded her assertive and competitive personality traits.

J ill Barad isn't unique. *All* our behavior is somewhat shaped by our personalities. In the first half of this chapter, we review the research on personality and its relationship to behavior. In the latter half, we look at how emotions shape many of our work-related behaviors.

PERSONALITY

Why are some people quiet and passive, while others are loud and aggressive? Are certain personality types better adapted to certain job types? Before we can answer these questions, we need to address a more basic one: What is personality?

LEARNING OBJECTIVES

AFTER READING THIS CHAPTER, YOU SHOULD BE ABLE TO

1. Explain the factors that determine an individual's personality

2. Describe the MBTI personality framework

3. Identify the key traits in the Big Five personality model

4. Explain the impact of job typology on the personality–job performance relationship

5. Differentiate emotions from moods

6. Contrast *felt* versus *displayed* emotions

7. Read emotions

8. Explain any gender differences in emotions

9. Describe external constraints on emotions

10. Apply concepts on emotions to OB issues

WHAT IS PERSONALITY?

When we talk of personality, we don't mean that a person has charm, a positive attitude toward life, a smiling face, or is a finalist for "Happiest and Friendliest" in this year's Miss America contest. When psychologists talk of personality, they mean a dynamic concept describing the growth and development of a person's whole psychological system. Rather than looking at parts of the person, personality looks at some aggregate whole that is greater than the sum of the parts.

The most frequently used definition of personality was produced by Gordon Allport more than 60 years ago. He said personality is "the dynamic organization within the individual of those psychophysical systems that determine his unique adjustments to his environment."[2] For our purposes, you should think of **personality** as the sum total of ways in which an individual reacts to and interacts with others. It is most often described in terms of measurable traits that a person exhibits.

personality

The sum total of ways in which an individual reacts and interacts with others.

PERSONALITY DETERMINANTS

An early argument in personality research was whether an individual's personality was the result of heredity or of environment. Was the personality predetermined at birth, or was it the result of the individual's interaction with his or her environment? Clearly, there is no simple answer. Personality appears to be a result of both influences. In addition, today we recognize a third factor—the situation. Thus, an adult's personality is now generally considered to be made up of both hereditary and environmental factors, moderated by situational conditions.

Heredity   Heredity refers to those factors that were determined at conception. Physical stature, facial attractiveness, gender, temperament, muscle composition and reflexes, energy level, and biological rhythms are characteristics that are generally considered to be either completely or substantially influenced by who your parents were, that is, by their biological, physiological, and inherent psychological makeup. The heredity approach argues that the ultimate explanation of an individual's personality is the molecular structure of the genes, located in the chromosomes.

Three different streams of research lend some credibility to the argument that heredity plays an important part in determining an individual's personality. The first looks at the genetic underpinnings of human behavior and temperament among young children. The second addresses the study of twins who were separated at birth. The third examines the consistency in job satisfaction over time and across situations.

Recent studies of young children lend strong support to the power of heredity.[3] Evidence demonstrates that traits such as shyness, fear, and distress are most likely caused by inherited genetic characteristics. This finding suggests that some personality traits may be built into the same genetic code that affects factors such as height and hair color.

Researchers have studied more than 100 sets of identical twins who were separated at birth and raised separately.[4] If heredity played little or no part in determining personality, you would expect to find few similarities between the separated twins. But the researchers found a lot in common. For almost every behavioral trait, a significant part of the variation between the twins turned out to be associated with genetic factors. For instance, one set of twins who had been separated for 39 years and raised 45 miles apart were found to drive the same model and color car, chain-smoked the same brand of cigarette, owned dogs with the same name, and regularly vacationed within three blocks of each other in a beach community 1,500 miles away. Researchers have found that genetics accounts for about 50 percent of the personality differences and more than 30 percent of the variation in occupational and leisure interests.

Further support for the importance of heredity can be found in studies of individual job satisfaction, which we discussed in the previous chapter. Individual job satisfaction is found to be remarkably stable over time. This result is consistent with what you would expect if satisfaction is determined by something inherent in the person rather than by external environmental factors.

If personality characteristics were *completely* dictated by heredity, they would be fixed at birth and no amount of experience could alter them. If you were relaxed and easygoing as a child, for example, that would be the result of your genes, and it would not be possible for you to change those characteristics. But personality characteristics are not completely dictated by heredity.

Environment Among the factors that exert pressures on our personality formation are the culture in which we are raised, our early conditioning, the norms among our family, friends, and social groups, and other influences that we experience. The environment to which we are exposed plays a substantial role in shaping our personalities.

For example, culture establishes the norms, attitudes, and values that are passed along from one generation to the next and create consistencies over time. An ideology that is intensely fostered in one culture may have only moderate influence in another. For instance, North Americans have had the themes of industriousness, success, competition, independence, and the Protestant work ethic constantly instilled in them through books, the school system, family, and friends. North Americans, as a result, tend to be ambitious and aggressive relative to individuals raised in cultures that have emphasized getting along with others, cooperation, and the priority of family over work and career.

Careful consideration of the arguments favoring either heredity or environment as the primary determinant of personality forces the conclusion that both are important. Heredity sets the parameters or outer limits, but an individual's full potential will be determined by how well he or she adjusts to the demands and requirements of the environment.

Situation A third factor, the situation, influences the effects of heredity and environment on personality. An individual's personality, although generally stable and consistent, does change in different situations. The varying demands of different situations call forth different aspects of one's personality. We should not, therefore, look at personality patterns in isolation.[5]

It seems only logical to suppose that situations will influence an individual's personality, but a neat classification scheme that would tell us the impact of various types of situations has so far eluded us. "Apparently we are not yet close to developing a system for clarifying situations so that they might be systematically studied."[6] However, we do know that certain situations are more relevant than others in influencing personality.

What is of interest taxonomically is that situations seem to differ substantially in the constraints they impose on behavior. Some situations (e.g., church, an employment interview) constrain many behaviors; other situations (e.g., a picnic in a public park) constrain relatively few.[7]

Furthermore, although certain generalizations can be made about personality, there are significant individual differences. As we shall see, the study of individual differences has come to receive greater emphasis in personality research, which originally sought out more general, universal patterns.

Environment played a significant role in shaping the personality of Rick Belluzzo, CEO of Silicon Graphics. He puts in 17-hour workdays and has few pastimes other than running and working out. Belluzzo credits his hard work ethic to his blue-collar roots. "I had immigrant parents who worked hard," Belluzzo says, "I was just brought up that way, to carry your weight." To help support his family, Belluzzo started working at age 11 doing jobs like picking prunes at orchards and sweeping floors at doctors' offices.

Source: PEANUTS reprinted by permission of United Features Syndicate, Inc.

PERSONALITY TRAITS

The early work in the structure of personality revolved around attempts to identify and label enduring characteristics that describe an individual's behavior. Popular characteristics include shyness, aggressiveness, submissiveness, laziness, ambition, loyalty, and timidity. These characteristics, when they are exhibited in a large number of situations, are called **personality traits**.[8] The more consistent the characteristic and the more frequently it occurs in diverse situations, the more important that trait is in describing the individual.

personality traits

Enduring characteristics that describe an individual's behavior.

Early Search for Primary Traits   Efforts to isolate traits have been hindered because there are so many of them. In one study, 17,953 individual traits were identified.[9] It is virtually impossible to predict behavior when such a large number of traits must be taken into account. As a result, attention has been directed toward reducing these thousands to a more manageable number.

One researcher isolated 171 traits but concluded that they were superficial and lacking in descriptive power.[10] What he sought was a reduced set of traits that would identify underlying patterns. The result was the identification of 16 personality factors, which he called the *source*, or *primary*, *traits*. They are shown in Exhibit 4-2. These 16 traits have been found to be generally steady and constant sources of behavior, allowing prediction of an individual's behavior in specific situations by weighing the characteristics for their situational relevance.

Sixteen Primary Traits		
1. Reserved	vs.	Outgoing
2. Less intelligent	vs.	More intelligent
3. Affected by feelings	vs.	Emotionally stable
4. Submissive	vs.	Dominant
5. Serious	vs.	Happy-go-lucky
6. Expedient	vs.	Conscientious
7. Timid	vs.	Venturesome
8. Tough-minded	vs.	Sensitive
9. Trusting	vs.	Suspicious
10. Practical	vs.	Imaginative
11. Forthright	vs.	Shrewd
12. Self-assured	vs.	Apprehensive
13. Conservative	vs.	Experimenting
14. Group dependent	vs.	Self-sufficient
15. Uncontrolled	vs.	Controlled
16. Relaxed	vs.	Tense

The Myers-Briggs Type Indicator One of the most widely used personality frameworks is called the **Myers-Briggs Type Indicator (MBTI)**.[11] It is essentially a 100-question personality test that asks people how they usually feel or act in particular situations.

On the basis of the answers individuals give to the test, they are classified as extroverted or introverted (E or I), sensing or intuitive (S or N), thinking or feeling (T or F), and perceiving or judging (P or J). These classifications are then combined into 16 personality types. (These types are different from the 16 primary traits in Exhibit 4-2.) To illustrate, let's take several examples. INTJs are visionaries. They usually have original minds and great drive for their own ideas and purposes. They are characterized as skeptical, critical, independent, determined, and often stubborn. ESTJs are organizers. They are realistic, logical, analytical, decisive, and have a natural head for business or mechanics. They like to organize and run activities. The ENTP type is a conceptualizer. He or she is innovative, individualistic, versatile, and attracted to entrepreneurial ideas. This person tends to be resourceful in solving challenging problems but may neglect routine assignments. A recent book that profiled 13 contemporary businesspeople who created supersuccessful firms including Apple Computer, Federal Express, Honda Motors, Microsoft, Price Club, and Sony found that all 13 are intuitive thinkers (NTs).[12] This result is particularly interesting because intuitive thinkers represent only about 5 percent of the population.

More than 2 million people a year take the MBTI in the United States alone. Organizations using the MBTI include Apple Computer, AT&T, Citicorp, Exxon, GE, 3M Co., plus many hospitals, educational institutions, and even the U.S. Armed Forces.

Ironically, there is no hard evidence that the MBTI is a valid measure of personality. But lack of evidence doesn't seem to deter its use in a wide range of organizations.

The Big Five Model MBTI may lack valid supporting evidence, but that can't be said for the five-factor model of personality—more typically called the Big Five.[13] In recent years, an impressive body of research supports that five basic dimensions underlie all others and encompass most of the significant variation in human personality. The Big Five factors are:

- **Extraversion.** This dimension captures one's comfort level with relationships. Extraverts tend to be gregarious, assertive, and sociable. Introverts tend to be reserved, timid, and quiet.
- **Agreeableness.** This dimension refers to an individual's propensity to defer to others. Highly agreeable people are cooperative, warm, and trusting. People who score low on agreeableness are cold, disagreeable, and antagonistic.
- **Conscientiousness.** This dimension is a measure of reliability. A highly conscientious person is responsible, organized, dependable, and persistent. Those who score low on this dimension are easily distracted, disorganized, and unreliable.
- **Emotional stability.** This dimension taps a person's ability to withstand stress. People with positive emotional stability tend to be calm, self-confident, and secure. Those with highly negative scores tend to be nervous, anxious, depressed, and insecure.
- **Openness to experience.** The final dimension addresses an individual's range of interests and fascination with novelty. Extremely open people are creative, curious, and artistically sensitive. Those at the other end of the openness category are conventional and find comfort in the familiar.

Myers-Briggs Type Indicator (MBTI)

A personality test that taps four characteristics and classifies people into one of 16 personality types.

extraversion

A personality dimension describing someone who is sociable, gregarious, and assertive.

agreeableness

A personality dimension that describes someone who is good-natured, cooperative, and trusting.

conscientiousness

A personality dimension that describes someone who is responsible, dependable, persistent, and organized.

emotional stability

A personality dimension that characterizes someone as calm, self-confident, secure (positive) versus nervous, depressed, and insecure (negative).

openness to experience

A personality dimension that characterizes someone in terms of imaginativeness, artistic, sensitivity, and intellectualism.

Bill Gates, co-founder and chairman of Microsoft, would score high on the conscientiousness dimension of the Big Five model. His success stems from his personality—an intense drive to succeed, persistence, personal intensity, brilliant intellect, and competitiveness. Gates's personality has influenced the culture—and success—of Microsoft and made him the most famous business celebrity in the world.

In addition to providing a unifying personality framework, research on the Big Five also has found important relationships between these personality dimensions and job performance.[14] A broad spectrum of occupations was examined: professionals (including engineers, architects, accountants, attorneys), police, managers, salespeople, and semiskilled and skilled employees. Job performance was defined in terms of performance ratings, training proficiency (performance during training programs), and personnel data such as salary level. The results showed that conscientiousness predicted job performance for all occupational groups. "The preponderance of evidence shows that individuals who are dependable, reliable, careful, thorough, able to plan, organized, hardworking, persistent, and achievement-oriented tend to have higher job performance in most if not all occupations."[15] In addition, employees who score more highly in conscientiousness develop higher levels of job knowledge, probably because highly conscientious people exert greater levels of effort on their job. The higher levels of job knowledge then contribute to higher levels of job performance. Consistent with these findings, evidence also finds a relatively strong and consistent relationship between conscientiousness and organizational citizenship behavior.[16] This, however, seems to be the only personality dimension that predicts OCB.

For the other personality dimensions, predictability depended upon both the performance criterion and the occupational group. For instance, extraversion predicted performance in managerial and sales positions. This finding makes sense since these occupations involve high social interaction. Similarly, openness to experience was found to be important in predicting training proficiency, which, too, seems logical. What wasn't so clear was why positive emotional stability wasn't related to job performance. Intuitively, it would seem that people who are calm and secure would do better on almost all jobs than people who are anxious and insecure. The researchers suggested that the answer might be that only people who have fairly high scores on emotional stability retain their jobs. So the range among those people studied, all of whom were employed, would tend to be quite small.

MAJOR PERSONALITY ATTRIBUTES INFLUENCING OB

In this section, we want to evaluate more carefully specific personality attributes that have been found to be powerful predictors of behavior in organizations. The first is related to where a person perceives the locus of control to be in his or her life. The others are Machiavellianism, self-esteem, self-monitoring, propensity for risk taking, and Type A personality. In this section, we shall briefly introduce these attributes and summarize what we know about their ability to explain and predict employee behavior.

internals

Individuals who believe that they control what happens to them.

externals

Individuals who believe that what happens to them is controlled by outside forces such as luck or chance.

locus of control

The degree to which people believe they are masters of their own fate.

Locus of Control Some people believe that they are masters of their own fate. Other people see themselves as pawns of fate, believing that what happens to them in their lives is due to luck or chance. The first type, those who believe that they control their destinies, have been labeled **internals**, whereas the latter, who see their lives as being controlled by outside forces, have been called **externals**.[17] A person's perception of the source of his or her fate is termed **locus of control**.

A large amount of research comparing internals with externals has consistently shown that individuals who have high scores in externality are less satisfied with their jobs, have higher absenteeism rates, are more alienated from the work setting, and are less involved on their jobs than are internals.[18]

Why are externals more dissatisfied? The answer is probably because they perceive themselves as having little control over those organizational outcomes that are important to them. Internals, facing the same situation, attribute organizational outcomes to their own actions. If the situation is unattractive, they believe that they have no one else to blame but themselves. Also, the dissatisfied internal is more likely to quit a dissatisfying job.

The impact of locus of control on absence is an interesting one. Internals believe that health is substantially under their own control through proper habits, so they take more responsibility for their health and have better health habits. Consequently, their incidences of sickness and, hence, of absenteeism are lower.[19]

We shouldn't expect any clear relationship between locus of control and turnover because there are opposing forces at work. "On the one hand, internals tend to take action and thus might be expected to quit jobs more readily. On the other hand, they tend to be more successful on the job and more satisfied, factors associated with less individual turnover."[20]

The overall evidence indicates that internals generally perform better on their jobs, but that conclusion should be moderated to reflect differences in jobs. Internals search more actively for information before making a decision, are more motivated to achieve, and make a greater attempt to control their environment. Externals, however, are more compliant and willing to follow directions. Therefore, internals do well on sophisticated tasks—which include most managerial and professional jobs—that require complex information processing and learning. In addition, internals are more suited to jobs that require initiative and independence of action. Almost all successful salespeople, for instance, are internals. Why? Because it's pretty difficult to succeed in sales if you don't believe you can effectively influence outcomes. In contrast, externals should do well on jobs that are well structured and routine and in which success depends heavily on complying with the direction of others.

> Almost all successful salespeople are internals. It's pretty difficult to succeed in sales if you don't believe you can effectively influence outcomes.

Machiavellianism   The personality characteristic of **Machiavellianism** (Mach) is named after Niccolò Machiavelli, who wrote in the sixteenth century on how to gain and use power. An individual high in Machiavellianism is pragmatic, maintains emotional distance, and believes that ends can justify means. "If it works, use it" is consistent with a high-Mach perspective.

A considerable amount of research has been directed toward relating high- and low-Mach personalities to certain behavioral outcomes.[21] High Machs manipulate more, win more, are persuaded less, and persuade others more than do low Machs.[22] Yet these high-Mach outcomes are moderated by situational factors. It has been found that high Machs flourish (1) when they interact face-to-face with others rather than indirectly; (2) when the situation has a minimum number of rules and regulations, thus allowing latitude for improvisation; and (3) when emotional involvements with details irrelevant to winning distract low Machs.[23]

Should we conclude that high Machs make good employees? That answer depends on the type of job and whether you consider ethical implications in evaluating performance. In jobs that require bargaining skills (such as labor negotiation) or that offer substantial rewards for winning (as in commissioned sales), high Machs will be productive. But if ends can't justify the means, if there are absolute standards of behavior, or if the three situational factors noted in the preceding paragraph are not in evidence, our ability to predict a high Mach's performance will be severely curtailed.

Machiavellianism

Degree to which an individual is pragmatic, maintains emotional distance, and believes that ends can justify means.

self-esteem

Individuals' degree of liking or disliking of themselves.

Self-Esteem People differ in the degree to which they like or dislike themselves. This trait is called **self-esteem**.[24] The research on self-esteem (SE) offers some interesting insights into organizational behavior. For example, self-esteem is directly related to expectations for success. High SEs believe that they possess the ability they need in order to succeed at work.

Individuals with high self-esteem will take more risks in job selection and are more likely to choose unconventional jobs than people with low self-esteem.

The most generalizable finding on self-esteem is that low SEs are more susceptible to external influence than are high SEs. Low SEs depend on the receipt of positive evaluations from others. As a result, they are more likely to seek approval from others and more prone to conform to the beliefs and behaviors of those they respect than are high SEs. In managerial positions, low SEs will tend to be concerned with pleasing others and, therefore, are less likely to take unpopular stands than are high SEs.

Not surprisingly, self-esteem has also been found to be related to job satisfaction. A number of studies confirm that high SEs are more satisfied with their jobs than are low SEs.

self-monitoring

A personality trait that measures an individual's ability to adjust his or her behavior to external, situational factors.

Self-Monitoring A personality trait that has recently received increased attention is called **self-monitoring**.[25] It refers to an individual's ability to adjust his or her behavior to external, situational factors.

Individuals high in self-monitoring show considerable adaptability in adjusting their behavior to external situational factors. They are highly sensitive to external cues and can behave differently in different situations. High self-monitors are capable of presenting striking contradictions between their public persona and their private self. Low self-monitors can't disguise themselves in that way. They tend to display their true dispositions and attitudes in every situation; hence, there is high behavioral consistency between who they are and what they do.

The research on self-monitoring is in its infancy, so predictions must be guarded. However, preliminary evidence suggests that high self-monitors tend to pay closer attention to the behavior of others and are more capable of conforming than are low self-monitors.[26] In addition, high self-monitoring managers tend to be more mobile in their careers and receive more promotions (both internal and cross-organizational).[27] We might also hypothesize that high self-monitors will be more successful in managerial positions in which individuals are required to play multiple, and even contradicting, roles. The high self-monitor is capable of putting on different "faces" for different audiences.

Risk Taking Donald Trump stands out for his willingness to take risks. He started with almost nothing in the 1960s. By the mid-1980s, he had made a fortune by betting on a resurgent New York City real estate market. Then, trying to capitalize on his previous successes, Trump overextended himself. By 1994, he had a *negative* net worth of $850 million. Never fearful of taking chances, "The Donald" leveraged the few assets he had left on several New York, New Jersey, and Caribbean real estate ventures. He hit it big again. By 1999, *Forbes* estimated his net worth at over $2 billion.

People differ in their willingness to take chances. This propensity to assume or avoid risk has been shown to have an impact on how long it takes managers to make a decision and how much information they require before making their choice. For instance, 79 managers worked on simulated personnel exercises that required them to make hiring decisions.[28] High risk-taking managers made more rapid decisions and used less information in making their choices than did the low risk-taking managers. Interestingly, the decision accuracy was the same for both groups.

While it is generally correct to conclude that managers in organizations are risk aversive,[29] there are still individual differences on this dimension.[30] As a result, it makes sense to recognize these differences and even to consider aligning risk-taking propensity with specific job demands. For instance, a high risk-taking propensity may lead to more effective performance for a stock trader in a brokerage firm because that type of job demands rapid decision making. On the other hand, a willingness to take risks might prove a major obstacle to an accountant who performs auditing activities. The latter job might be better filled by someone with a low risk-taking propensity.

Type A Personality   Do you know any people who are excessively competitive and always seem to be experiencing a chronic sense of time urgency? If you do, it's a good bet that those people have a **Type A personality**. A person with a Type A personality is "aggressively involved in a chronic, incessant struggle to achieve more and more in less and less time, and, if required to do so, against the opposing efforts of other things or other persons."[31] In the North American culture, such characteristics tend to be highly prized and positively associated with ambition and the successful acquisition of material goods.

Type A's
1. are always moving, walking, and eating rapidly;
2. feel impatient with the rate at which most events take place;
3. strive to think or do two or more things at once;
4. cannot cope with leisure time;
5. are obsessed with numbers, measuring their success in terms of how many or how much of everything they acquire.

In contrast to the Type A personality is the Type B, who is exactly the opposite. Type B's are "rarely harried by the desire to obtain a wildly increasing number of things or participate in an endless growing series of events in an ever-decreasing amount of time."[32]

Type B's
1. never suffer from a sense of time urgency with its accompanying impatience;
2. feel no need to display or discuss either their achievements or accomplishments unless such exposure is demanded by the situation;
3. play for fun and relaxation rather than to exhibit their superiority at any cost;
4. can relax without guilt.

Type A's operate under moderate to high levels of stress. They subject themselves to more or less continuous time pressure, creating for themselves a life of deadlines. These characteristics result in some rather specific behavioral outcomes. For example, Type A's are fast workers because they emphasize quantity over quality. In managerial positions, Type A's demonstrate their competitiveness by working long hours and, not infrequently, making poor decisions because they make them too fast. Type A's are also rarely creative. Because of their concern with quantity and speed, they rely on past experiences when faced with problems.

type A personality

Aggressive involvement in a chronic, incessant struggle to achieve more and more in less and less time and, if necessary, against the opposing efforts of other things or other people.

Richard Branson's propensity to take risks aligns with his job demands of being an entrepreneur. Branson, founder and chairman of a London-based Virgin Group, started risky ventures that compete against industry giants. His Virgin Atlantic airline, for example, has taken market share from British Airways and has earned the reputation as one of the financially healthiest airlines in the world. Branson's risk-taking personality extends to his leisure activities of speedboat racing, sky diving, and ballooning. Shown here, Branson prepares for an around-the-world balloon excursion.

They will not allocate the time that is necessary to develop unique solutions to new problems. They rarely vary in their responses to specific challenges in their milieu; hence, their behavior is easier to predict than that of Type B's.

Are Type A's or Type B's more successful in organizations? Despite the Type A's hard work, the Type B's are the ones who appear to make it to the top. Great salespersons are usually Type A's; senior executives are usually Type B's. Why? The answer lies in the tendency of Type A's to trade off quality of effort for quantity. Promotions in corporate and professional organizations "usually go to those who are wise rather than to those who are merely hasty, to those who are tactful rather than to those who are hostile, and to those who are creative rather than to those who are merely agile in competitive strife."[33]

PERSONALITY AND NATIONAL CULTURE

Do personality frameworks, such as the Big Five model, transfer across cultures? Are dimensions such as locus of control and the Type A personality relevant in all cultures? Let's try to answer these questions.

The five personality factors identified in the Big Five model appear in almost all cross-cultural studies.[34] This includes a wide variety of diverse cultures, such as China, Israel, Germany, Japan, Spain, Nigeria, Norway, Pakistan, and the United States. Differences tend to surface by the emphasis on dimensions. Chinese, for example, use the category of conscientiousness more often and use the category of agreeableness less often than do Americans. But there is a surprisingly high amount of agreement, especially among individuals from developed countries. As a case in point, a comprehensive review of studies covering people from the 15-nation European Community found that conscientiousness was a valid predictor of performance across jobs and occupational groups.[35] This is exactly what U.S. studies have found.

There are no common personality types for a given country. You can, for instance, find high and low risk takers in almost any culture. Yet a country's culture influences the dominant personality characteristics of its population. We can see this by looking at locus of control and the Type A personality.

There is evidence that cultures differ in terms of people's relationships to their environment.[37] In some cultures, such as those in North America, people believe that they can dominate their environment. People in other societies, such as Middle Eastern countries, believe that life is essentially preordained. Notice the close parallel to internal and external locus of control.[38] We should expect, therefore, a larger proportion of internals in the American and Canadian workforce than in the Saudi Arabian or Iranian workforce.

The prevalence of Type A personalities will be somewhat influenced by the culture in which a person grows up. There are Type A's in every country, but there will be more in capitalistic countries, where achievement and material success are highly valued. For instance, it is estimated that about 50 percent of the North American population is Type A.[39] This percentage shouldn't be too surprising. The United States and Canada both have a high emphasis on time management and efficiency. Both have cultures that stress accomplishments and acquisition of money and material goods. In cultures such as Sweden and France, where materialism is less revered, we would predict a smaller proportion of Type A personalities.

ACHIEVING PERSONALITY FIT

Twenty years ago, organizations were concerned with personality primarily because they wanted to match individuals to specific jobs. That concern still exists. But, in recent years, interest has expanded to include the individual-organization fit. Why? Because managers today are less interested in an applicant's ability to perform a *specific* job than with his or her *flexibility* to meet changing situations.

The Person-Job Fit In the discussion of personality attributes, our conclusions were often qualified to recognize that the requirements of the job moderated the relationship between possession of the personality characteristic and job performance. This concern with matching the job requirements with personality characteristics is best articulated in John Holland's **personality–job fit theory**.[40] The theory is based on the notion of fit between an individual's personality characteristics and his or her occupational environment. Holland presents six personality types and proposes that satisfaction and the propensity to leave a job depend on the degree to which individuals successfully match their personalities to an occupational environment.

Each one of the six personality types has a congruent occupational environment. Exhibit 4-3 describes the six types and their personality characteristics and gives examples of congruent occupations.

Holland has developed a Vocational Preference Inventory questionnaire that contains 160 occupational titles. Respondents indicate which of these occupations they like or dislike, and their answers are used to form personality profiles. Using this procedure, research strongly supports the hexagonal diagram in Exhibit 4-4.[41] This figure shows that the closer two fields or orientations are in the hexagon, the more compatible they are. Adjacent categories are quite similar, whereas those diagonally opposite are highly dissimilar.

What does all this mean? The theory argues that satisfaction is highest and turnover lowest when personality and occupation are in agreement. Social individuals should be in social jobs, conventional people in conventional jobs, and so forth. A realistic person in a realistic job is in a more congruent situation than is a realistic person in an investigative job. A realistic person in a social job is in

personality–job fit theory

Identifies six personality types and proposes that the fit between personality type and occupational environment determines satisfaction and turnover.

Holland's Typology of Personality and Congruent Occupations

EXHIBIT 4-3

Type	Personality Characteristics	Congruent Occupation
Realistic: Prefers physical activities that require skill, strength, and coordination	Shy, genuine, persistent, stable, conforming, practical	Mechanic, drill press operator, assembly-line worker, farmer
Investigative: Prefers activities that involve thinking, organizing, and understanding	Analytical, original, curious, independent	Biologist, economist, mathematician, news reporter
Social: Prefers activities that involve helping and developing others	Sociable, friendly, cooperative, understanding	Social worker, teacher, counselor, clinical psychologist
Conventional: Prefers rule-regulated, orderly, and unambiguous activities	Conforming, efficient, practical, unimaginative, inflexible	Accountant, corporate manager, bank teller, file clerk
Enterprising: Prefers verbal activities in which there are opportunities to influence others and attain power	Self-confident, ambitious, energetic, domineering	Lawyer, real estate agent, public relations specialist, small business manager
Artistic: Prefers ambiguous and unsystematic activities that allow creative expression	Imaginative, disorderly, idealistic, emotional, impractical	Painter, musician, writer, interior decorator

the most incongruent situation possible. The key points of this model are that (1) there do appear to be intrinsic differences in personality among individuals, (2) there are different types of jobs, and (3) people in job environments congruent with their personality types should be more satisfied and less likely to voluntarily resign than should people in incongruent jobs.

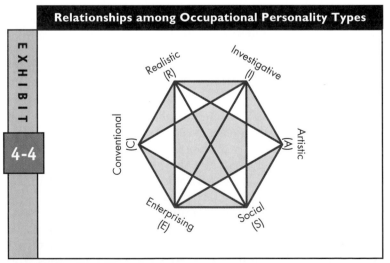

Relationships among Occupational Personality Types

EXHIBIT 4-4

Source: Reprinted by special permission of the publisher, Psychological Assessment Resources, Inc., from *Making Vocational Choices*, Copyright 1973, 1985, 1992 by Psychological Assessment Resources, Inc. All rights reserved.

The Person–Organization Fit As previously noted, attention in recent years has expanded to include matching people to *organizations* as well as *jobs*. To the degree that an organization faces a dynamic and changing environment and requires employees who are able to readily change tasks and move fluidly between teams, it's probably more important that employees' personalities fit with the overall organization's culture than with the characteristics of any specific job.

The person–organization fit essentially argues that people leave jobs that are not compatible with their personalities.[42] Using the Big Five terminology, for instance, we could expect that people high on extraversion fit better with aggressive and team-oriented cultures; people high on agreeableness will match up better with a supportive organizational climate than one that focuses on aggressiveness; and that people high on openness to experience fit better into organizations that emphasize innovation rather than standardization.[43] Following these guidelines at the time of hiring should lead to selecting new employees who fit better with the organization's culture, which, in turn, should result in higher employee satisfaction and reduced turnover.

"People work hard, but they have a good time. We are allowed to let our personalities show," says Mary Ann Adams, project director at Southwest Airlines. Southwest uses the person-organization fit during its selective hiring process. During interviews, applicants must prove that they have a sense of humor. It's a job requirement because it fits with the airline's fun-loving culture. During her job interview at Southwest, Adams recounted a practical joke she pulled when she turned an unflattering photo of a former boss into a computer screensaver for her department.

EMOTIONS

On one recent Friday, a 37-year-old U.S. postal worker in Milwaukee walked into his place of work. He pulled out a gun and shot and killed a co-worker with whom he had argued, wounded a supervisor who had scolded him, and injured another worker. He then killed himself.[44] For this worker, anger had led to violence.

Going on a shooting rampage at work is an extreme example but it does dramatically illustrate the theme of this section: Emotions are a critical factor in employee behavior.

Given the obvious role that emotions play in our everyday life, it might surprise you to learn that, until very recently, the topic of emotions had been given little or no attention within the field of OB. How could this be? We can offer two possible explanations. The first is the *myth of rationality*.[45] Since the late nineteenth century and the rise of scientific management, organizations have been specifically designed with the objective of trying to control emotions. A well-run organization was one that successfully eliminated frustration, fear, anger, love, hate, joy, grief, and similar feelings. Such emotions were the antithesis of rationality. So while researchers and managers knew that emotions were an inseparable part of everyday life, they tried to create organizations that were emotion free. That, of course, was not possible. The second factor that acted to keep emotions out of OB was the belief that *emotions of any kind were disruptive*.[46] When emotions were considered, the discussion focused on strong negative emotions—especially anger—that interfered with an employee's ability to do his or her job effectively. Emotions were rarely viewed as being constructive or able to stimulate performance-enhancing behaviors.

Certainly some emotions, particularly when exhibited at the wrong time, can reduce employee performance. But this doesn't change the reality that employees bring an emotional component with them to work every day and that no study of OB could be comprehensive without considering the role of emotions in workplace behavior.

WHAT ARE EMOTIONS?

affect

A broad range of feelings that people experience.

emotions

Intense feelings that are directed at someone or something.

moods

Feelings that tend to be less intense than emotions and that lack a contextual stimulus.

Although we don't want to obsess on definitions, before we can proceed with our analysis, we need to clarify three terms that are closely intertwined. These are *affect*, *emotions*, and *moods*.

Affect is a generic term that covers a broad range of feelings that people experience. It's an umbrella concept that encompasses both emotions and moods.[47] **Emotions** are intense feelings that are directed at someone or something.[48] Finally, **moods** are feelings that tend to be less intense than emotions and that lack a contextual stimulus.[49]

Emotions are reactions to an object, not a trait. They're object specific. You show your emotions when you're "happy about something, angry at someone, afraid of something."[50] Moods, on the other hand, aren't directed at an object. Emotions can turn into moods when you lose focus on the contextual object. So when a work colleague criticizes you for the way you spoke to a client, you might become angry at him. That is, you show emotion (anger) toward a specific object (your colleague). But later in the day, you might find yourself just generally dispirited. You can't attribute this feeling to any single event; you're just not your normal, upbeat self. This affective state describes a mood.

A related term that is gaining increasing importance in organizational behavior is *emotional labor*. Every employee expends physical and mental labor when they put their bodies and cognitive capabilities, respectively, into their job. But most jobs also require **emotional labor**. This is when an employee expresses organizationally desired emotions during interpersonal transactions.[51] The concept of emotional labor originally developed in relation to service jobs. Airline flight attendants, for instance, are expected to be cheerful, funeral counselors sad, and doctors emotionally neutral. But today the concept of emotional labor seems relevant to almost every job. You're expected, for example, to be courteous and not hostile in interactions with co-workers. And leaders are expected to draw on emotional labor to "charge the troops." Almost every great speech, for instance, contains a strong emotional component that stirs feelings in others. As we proceed in this section, you'll see that it's because of the increasing importance of emotional labor as a key component of effective job performance that an understanding of emotion has gained heightened relevance within the field of OB.

Emotional labor is an important component of effective job performance at the Happy Beauty Salon in Long Island, New York. Owner Happy Nomikos, shown here serving customers strawberries and grapes, requires that her nail technicians and hair stylists build customer loyalty by being courteous and cheerful. In interacting with her employees and customers, Nomikos says "I have to keep everyone happy." She hugs loyal customers, jokes with her staff, and offers customers pizza and cake in celebration of employees' birthdays.

FELT VERSUS DISPLAYED EMOTIONS

Emotional labor creates dilemmas for employees when their job requires them to exhibit emotions that are incongruous with their actual feelings. Not surprisingly, this is a frequent occurrence. There are people at work with whom you find it very difficult to be friendly. Maybe you consider their personality abrasive. Maybe you know they've said negative things about you behind your back. Regardless, your job requires you to interact with these people on a regular basis. So you're forced to feign friendliness.

It can help you to better understand emotions if you separate them into *felt* versus *displayed*.[52] **Felt emotions** are an individual's actual emotions. In contrast, **displayed emotions** are those that are organizationally required and considered appropriate in a given job. They're not innate; they're learned. "The ritual look of delight on the face of the first runner-up as the new Miss America is announced is a product of the display rule that losers should mask their sadness with an expression of joy for the winner."[53] Similarly, most of us know that we're expected to act sad at funerals regardless of whether we consider the person's death to be a loss; and to pretend to be happy at weddings even if we don't feel like celebrating.[54] Effective managers have learned to be serious when giving an employee a negative performance evaluation and to cover up their anger when they've been passed over for promotion. And the salesperson who hasn't learned to smile and appear friendly, regardless of his or her true feelings at the moment, isn't typically going to last long on most sales jobs.

The key point here is that felt and displayed emotions are often different. In fact, many people have problems working with others simply because they naively assume that the emotions they see others display is what those others actually feel. This is particularly true in organizations, where role demands and situations often require people to exhibit emotional behaviors that mask their true feelings.

EMOTION DIMENSIONS

How many emotions are there? In what ways do they vary? We'll answer these questions in this section.

Variety   There have been numerous efforts to limit and define the fundamental or basic set of emotions.[55] Research has identifed six universal emotions: anger, fear, sadness, happiness, disgust, and surprise.[56]

One factor that has strongly shaped what is and isn't listed in this basic set is the manner in which emotions were identified. Researchers tended to look for universally identified facial expressions and then convert them into categories (see Exhibit 4-5). Emotions that couldn't be readily identified by others through facial expressions, or which were considered a subset of one of the basic six, were not selected.

Exhibit 4-6 illustrates that the six emotions can be conceptualized as existing along a continuum.[57] The closer any two emotions are to each other on this continuum, the more people are likely to confuse them. For instance, happiness and surprise are frequently mistaken for each other, while happiness and disgust are rarely confused. In addition, as we'll elaborate on later in this section, cultural factors can also influence interpretations.

emotional labor

When an employee expresses organizationally desired emotions during interpersonal transactions.

felt emotions

An individual's actual emotions

displayed emotions

Emotions that are organizationally required and considered appropriate in a given job.

Facial Expressions Convey Emotions

Each picture portrays a different emotion. Try to identify them before looking at the answers. (Top, left to right: neutral, surprise, happiness. Bottom: fear, sadness, anger.)

EXHIBIT 4-5

Source: S. E. Taylor, L. A. Peplan, and D. O. Sears, *Social Psychology*, 9th ed. (Upper Saddle River, NJ: Prentice Hall, 1997), p. 98; photographs by Paul Ekman, Ph.D. Used with permission.

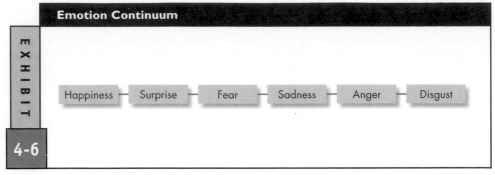

Do these six basic emotions surface in the workplace? Absolutely. I get *angry* after receiving a poor performance appraisal. I *fear* that I could be laid off as a result of a company cutback. I'm *sad* about one of my co-workers leaving to take a new job in another city. I'm *happy* after being selected as employee-of-the-month. I'm *disgusted* with the way my supervisor treats the women on our team. And I'm *surprised* to find out that management plans a complete restructuring of the company's retirement program.

Intensity   People give different responses to identical emotion-provoking stimuli. In some cases this can be attributed to the individual's personality. Other times it is a result of the job requirements.

People vary in their inherent ability to express intensity. You undoubtedly know individuals who almost never show their feelings. They rarely get angry. They never show rage. In contrast, you probably also know people who seem to be on an emotional roller coaster. When they're happy, their ecstatic. When they're sad, they're deeply depressed. And two people can be in the exact same situation—with one showing excitement and joy, while the other is calm and collected.

Jobs make different intensity demands in terms of emotional labor. For instance, air traffic controllers and trial judges are expected to be calm and controlled, even in stressful situations. Conversely, the effectiveness of television evangelists, public-address announcers at sporting events, and lawyers can depend on their ability to alter their displayed emotional intensity as the need arises.

Frequency and Duration   How often does an emotion need to be exhibited? And for how long?

Sean Wolfson is basically a quiet and reserved person. He loves his job as a financial planner. He doesn't enjoy, however, having to give occasional speeches in order to increase his visibility and to promote his programs. "If I had to speak to large audiences every day, I'd quit this business," he says. "I think this works for me because I can fake excitement and enthusiasm for an hour, a couple of times a month."

Emotional labor that requires high frequency or long durations is more demanding and requires more exertion by employees. So whether an employee can successfully meet the emotional demands of a given job depends not only on which emotions need to be displayed and their intensity, but also how frequently and for how long the effort has to be made.

CAN PEOPLE BE EMOTION*LESS*?

Are people who seem outwardly calm or apathetic in situations, in which others are clearly emotionally charged, without feeling? Can people be emotion*less*?

Some people have severe difficulty in expressing their emotions and understanding the emotions of others. Psychologists call this *alexithymia* (which is Greek for "lack of emotion").[58] People who suffer from alexithymia rarely cry and are often seen by others as bland and cold. Their own feelings make them uncomfortable, and they're not able to discriminate among their different emotions. Additionally, they're often at a complete loss to understand what others around them feel.

Does this inability to express emotions and read others mean that people who suffer from alexithymia are poor work performers? Not necessrily. Consistent with our discussion on matching personality types with appropriate jobs, people who lack emotion need to be in jobs that require little or no emotional labor. These people are not well suited to sales and managerial positions. But they might very well be effective performers, for instance, in a job writing program code or in any work that is confined exclusively to computer interaction.

GENDER AND EMOTIONS

It's widely assumed that women are more "in touch" with their feelings than men—that they react more emotionally and are better able to read emotions in others. Is there any truth to these assumptions?

The evidence does confirm differences between men and women when it comes to emotional reactions and ability to read others. In contrasting the genders, women show greater emotional expression than men;[59] they experience emotions more intensely; and they display more frequent expressions of both positive and negative emotions, except anger.[60] In contrast to men, women also

---

Reading Emotions

Understanding another person's felt emotions is a very difficult task. But we can learn to read others' displayed emotions. We do this by focusing on verbal, nonverbal, and paralinguistic cues.[61]

The easiest way to find out what someone is feeling is to ask them. Saying something as simple as "Are you OK? What's the problem?" can frequently provide you with the information to assess an individual's emotional state. But relying on a *verbal* response has two drawbacks. First, almost all of us conceal our emotions to some extent for privacy and to reflect social expectations. So we might be unwilling to share our true feelings. Second, even if we want to verbally convey our feelings, we may be unable to do so. As we've noted previously, some people have difficulty understanding their own emotions and, hence, are unable to verbally express them. So, at best, verbal responses provide only partial information.

You're talking with a co-worker. Does the fact that his back is rigid, his teeth clenched, and his facial muscles tight tell you something about his emotional state? It probably should. Facial expressions, gestures, body movements, and physical distance are *nonverbal* cues that can provide additional insights into what a person is feeling. The facial expressions shown in Exhibit 4–5, for instance, are a window into a person's feelings. Notice the difference in facial features: the height of the cheeks, the raising or lowering of the brow, the turn of the mouth, the positioning of the lips, and the configuration of the muscles around the eyes. Even something as subtle as the distance someone chooses to position himself or herself from you can convey their feelings, or lack thereof, of intimacy, aggressiveness, repugnance, or withdrawal.

As Janet and I talked, I noticed a sharp change in the tone of her voice and the speed at which she spoke. I was tapping into the third source of information on a person's emotions—*paralanguage*. This is communication that goes beyond the specific spoken words. It includes pitch, amplitude, rate, and voice quality of speech. Paralanguage reminds us that people convey their feelings not only in *what* they say but also in *how* they say it.

report more comfort in expressing emotions. Finally, women are better at reading nonverbal and paralinguistic cues than are men.[62]

What explains these differences? Three possible answers have been suggested. One explanation is the different ways men and women have been socialized.[63]

> *Women show greater emotional expression than men and experience emotions more intensely.*

Men are taught to be tough and brave; and showing emotion is inconsistent with this image. Women, on the other hand, are socialized to be nurturing. This may account for the perception that women are generally warmer and friendlier than men. For instance, women are expected to express more positive emotions on the job (shown by smiling) than men, and they do.[64] A second explanation is that women may have more innate ability to read others and present their emotions than do men.[65] Third, women may have a greater need for social approval and, thus, a higher propensity to show positive emotions such as happiness.

EXTERNAL CONSTRAINTS ON EMOTIONS

An emotion that is acceptable on the athletic playing field may be totally unacceptable when exhibited at the workplace. Similarly, what's appropriate in one country is often inappropriate in another. These facts illustrate the role that external constraints play in shaping displayed emotions.

Every organization defines boundaries that identify what emotions are acceptable and the degree to which they can be expressed. The same applies in different cultures. In this section, we look at organizational and cultural influences on emotions.

Organizational Influences If you can't smile and appear happy, you're unlikely to have much of a career working at a Disney amusement park. And a manual produced by McDonald's states that its counter personnel "must display traits such as sincerity, enthusiasm, confidence, and a sense of humor."[66]

There is no single emotional "set" sought by all organizations. However, at least in the United States, the evidence indicates that there's a bias against negative and intense emotions. Expressions of negative emotions such as fear, anxiety, and anger tend to be unacceptable except under fairly specific conditions.[67] For instance, one such condition might be a high-status member of a group conveying impatience with a low-status member.[68] Moreover, expressions of intense emotion, whether negative or positive, tend to be typically unacceptable because they're seen as undermining routine task performance.[69] Again, there are exceptional conditions in which this isn't true—for example, a brief grieving over the sudden death of a company's CEO or the celebration of a record year of profits. But for the most part, consistent with the myth of rationality, well-managed organizations are expected to be essentially emotion free.

Cultural Influences Cultural norms in the United States dictate that employees in service organizations should smile and act friendly when interacting with customers.[70] But this norm doesn't apply worldwide. In Israel, smiling by supermarket cashiers is seen as a sign of inexperience, so cashiers are encouraged to look somber.[71] In Moslem cultures, smiling is frequently taken as a sign of sexual attraction, so women are socialized not to smile at men.[72]

The foregoing examples illustrate the need to consider cultural factors as influencing what is or isn't considered as emotionally appropriate.[73] What's acceptable in one culture may seem extremely unusual or even dysfunctional in another. And cultures differ in terms of the interpretation they give to emotions.

There tends to be high agreement on what emotions mean *within* cultures but not between. For instance, one study asked Americans to match facial expressions with the six basic emotions.[74] The range of agreement was between 86 and 98 percent. When a group of Japanese was given the same task, they correctly labeled only surprise (with 97 percent agreement). On the other five emotions, their accuracy ranged from only 27 to 70 percent. In addition, studies indicate that some cultures lack words for such standard emotions as *anxiety*, *depression*, or *guilt*. Tahitians, as a case in point, don't have a word directly equivalent to *sadness*. When Tahitians are sad, their peers typically attribute their state to a physical illness.[75]

OB APPLICATIONS

We conclude our discussion of emotions by considering their application to several topics in OB. In this section, we assess how a knowledge of emotions can help you to better understand the selection process in organizations, decision making, motivation, leadership, interpersonal conflict, and deviant workplace behaviors.

Ability and Selection   People who know their own emotions and are good at reading others' emotions may be more effective in their jobs. That, in essence, is the theme underlying recent research on *emotional intelligence*.[76]

Emotional intelligence (EI) refers to an assortment of noncognitive skills, capabilities, and competencies that influence a person's ability to succeed in coping with environmental demands and pressures. It's composed of five dimensions:

> *Self-awareness*. The ability to be aware of what you're feeling.
> *Self-management*. The ability to manage one's own emotions and impulses.
> *Self-motivation*. The ability to persist in the face of setbacks and failures.
> *Empathy*. The ability to sense how others are feeling.
> *Social skills*. The ability to handle the emotions of others.

emotional intelligence

An assortment of noncognitive skills, capabilities, and competencies that influence a person's ability to succeed in coping with environmental demands and pressures.

Several studies suggest EI may play an important role in job performance. For instance, one study looked at the characteristics of Bell Lab engineers who were rated as stars by their peers. The scientists concluded that stars were better at relating to others. That is, it was EI, not academic IQ, that characterized high performers. A second study of Air Force recruiters generated similar findings. Top-performing recruiters exhibited high levels of EI. Using these findings, the Air Force revamped its selection critieria. A follow-up investigation found that future hires who had high EI scores were 2.6 times more successful than those who didn't. A recent poll of human resource managers asked: How important is it for your workers to demonstrate EI to move up the corporate ladder? Forty percent replied "very important." Another 16 percent said "moderately important."

The implications from the initial evidence on EI is that employers should consider it as a factor in selection, especially in jobs that demand a high degree of social interaction.

Decision Making   As you'll see in Chapter 5, traditional approaches to the study of decision making in organizations have emphasized rationality. They have downplayed, or even ignored, the role of anxiety, fear, frustration, doubt, happiness, excitement, and similar emotions. Yet it's naive to assume that decision choices aren't influenced by one's feelings at a particular moment. Given the same objective data, we should expect that people may make different

Hiring for Emotional Intelligence at the Men's Wearhouse

The Men's Wearhouse is now the leading discount retailer of men's clothing in the United States. It has more than 400 stores, 6,000 employees, and annual revenues of $630 million. The firm is growing rapidly—adding an average of one new store per week.

The Men's Wearhouse founder and CEO, George Zimmer (see photo), has built his business by trying to reinvent the shopping experience. "Most business practices repress our natural tendency to have fun and to socialize," says Zimmer. "The idea seems to be that in order to succeed, you have to suffer. But I believe that you do your best work when you are feeling enthusiastic about things. Our business is

based on faith in the value of human potential."

Hiring at the Men's Wearhouse reflects Zimmer's philosophy. In selecting and training new salespeople, for instance, management believes success has more to do with the ability to understand people than it does about understanding how to sell suits. "We don't look for people with specific levels of education and experience," says the company's vice president of training, Shlomo Maor. "We look for one criterion for hiring: optimism. We look for passion, excitement, energy. We want people who enjoy life."

What does optimism have to do with selling suits? *Everything*, argues Maor. "Optimistic people do not prejudge or pressure customers," he says. "You have to sell the right product to the right customer for the right reason—which often means delaying gratification and taking rejection in stride. That's emotional intelligence, and it's what makes great salespeople great."

Source: Adapted from E. Ransdell, "They Sell Suits with Soul," *Fast Company*, October 1998, pp. 66–68.

choices when they're angry and stressed out than when they're calm and collected.

Negative emotions can result in a limited search for new alternatives and a less vigilant use of information. On the other hand, positive emotions can increase problem solving and facilitate the integration of information.[77]

You can improve your understanding of decision making by considering "the heart" as well as "the head." People use emotions as well as rational and intuitive processes in making decisions. Failure to incorporate emotions into the study of decision processes will result in an incomplete (and often inaccurate) view of the process.

Motivation   We'll discuss motivation thoroughly in Chapters 6 and 7. At this point, we want to merely introduce the idea that, like decision making, the dominant approaches to the study of motivation reflect an overrationalized view of individuals.[78]

Motivation theories basically propose that individuals "are motivated to the extent that their behavior is expected to lead to desired outcomes. The image is that of rational exchange: the employee essentially trades effort for pay, security, promotions, and so forth."[79] But people aren't cold, unfeeling machines. Their perceptions and calculations of situations are filled with emotional content that significantly influences how much effort they exert. Moreover, when you see people who are highly motivated in their jobs, they're emotionally committed. People who are engaged in their work "become physically, cognitively, *and* emotionally immersed in the experience of activity, in the pursuit of a goal."[80]

Are all people emotionally engaged in their work? No! But many are. And if we focus only on rational calculations of inducements and contributions, we fail to be able to explain behaviors such as the individual who forgets to have dinner and works late into the night, lost in the thrill of her work.[81]

Leadership The ability to lead others is a fundamental quality sought by organizations. We'll discuss the topic of leadership in depth in Chapter 11. Here, however, we briefly introduce how emotions can be an integral part of leadership.

Effective leaders almost all rely on the expression of feelings to help convey their messages. In fact, the expression of emotions in speeches is often the critical element that results in individuals accepting or rejecting a leader's message. "When leaders feel excited, enthusiastic, and active, they may be more likely to energize their subordinates and convey a sense of efficacy, competence, optimism, and enjoyment."[82] Politicians, as a case in point, have learned to show enthusiasm when talking about their chances for winning an election, even when polls suggest otherwise.

Corporate executives know that emotional content is critical if employees are to buy into their vision of their company's future and accept change. When new visions are offered, especially when they contain distant or vague goals, change is often difficult to accept. So when effective leaders want to implement significant changes, they rely on "the evocation, framing, and mobilization of *emotions*."[83] By arousing emotions and linking them to an appealing vision, leaders increase the likelihood that managers and employees alike will accept change.

Interpersonal Conflict Few issues are more intertwined with emotions than the topic of interpersonal conflict. Whenever conflicts arise, you can be fairly certain that emotions are also surfacing. A manager's success in trying to resolve conflicts, in fact, is often largely due to his or her ability to identify the emotional elements in the conflict and to get the conflicting parties to work through their emotions. And the manager who ignores the emotional elements in conflicts, focusing singularly on rational and task concerns, is unlikely to be very effective in resolving those conflicts.

Deviant Workplace Behaviors Negative emotions can lead to a number of deviant workplace behaviors.

Anyone who has spent much time in an organization realizes that people often engage in voluntary actions that violate established norms and that threaten the organization, its members, or both. These actions are called **employee deviance**.[84] They fall into categories such as production (e.g., leaving early, intentionally working slowly); property (e.g., stealing, sabotage); political (e.g., gossiping, blaming co-workers); and personal aggression (e.g., sexual harassment, verbal abuse).[85] Many of these deviant behaviors can be traced to negative emotions.

For instance, envy is an emotion that occurs when you resent someone for having something that you don't, which you strongly desire.[86] It can lead to malicious deviant behaviors. Envy, for example, has been found to be associated with hostility, "backstabbing" and other forms of political behavior, negatively distorting others' successes, and positively distorting one's own accomplishments.[87]

employee deviance

Voluntary actions that violate established norms and that threaten the organization, its members, or both.

SUMMARY AND IMPLICATIONS FOR MANAGERS

PERSONALITY

A review of the personality literature offers general guidelines that can lead to effective job performance. As such, it can improve hiring, transfer, and promotion decisions. Because personality characteristics create the parameters for people's behavior, they give us a framework for predicting behavior. For example, individuals who are shy, introverted, and uncomfortable in social situations would probably be ill-suited as salespeople. Individuals who are submissive and conforming might not be effective as advertising "idea" people.

Can we predict which people will be high performers in sales, research, or assembly-line work on the basis of their personality characteristics alone? The answer is No. Personality assessment should be used in conjunction with other information such as skills, abilities, and experience.[88] But a knowledge of an individual's personality can aid in reducing mismatches, which, in turn, can lead to reduced turnover and higher job satisfaction.

We can look at certain personality characteristics that tend to be related to job success, test for those traits, and use the data to make selection more effective. A person who accepts rules, conformity, and dependence and rates high on authoritarianism is likely to feel more comfortable in, say, a structured assembly-line job, as an admittance clerk in a hospital, or as an administrator in a large public agency than as a researcher or an employee whose job requires a high degree of creativity.

EMOTIONS

Can managers control the emotions of their colleagues and employees? No. Emotions are a natural part of an individual's makeup. Managers err if they ignore the emotional elements in organizational behavior and assess individual behavior as if it were completely rational. As one consultant aptly put it, "You can't divorce emotions from the workplace because you can't divorce emotions from people."[89] Managers who understand the role of emotions will significantly improve their ability to explain and predict individual behavior.

Do emotions affect job performance? Yes. They can *hinder* performance, especially negative emotions. That's probably why organizations, for the most part, try to extract emotions out of the workplace. But emotions can also *enhance* performance. How? Two ways.[90] First, emotions can increase arousal levels, thus acting as motivators to higher performance. Second, emotional labor recognizes that feelings can be part of a job's required behavior. So, for instance, the ability to effectively manage emotions in leadership and sales positions may be critical to success in those positions.

What differentiates functional from dysfunctional emotions at work? While there is no precise answer to this, it's been suggested that the critical moderating variable is the complexity of the individual's task.[91] The more complex a task, the lower the level of arousal that can be tolerated without interfering with performance. While a certain minimal level of arousal is probably necessary for good performance, very high levels interfere with the ability to function, especially if the job requires calculative and detailed cognitive processes. Given that the trend is toward jobs becoming more complex, you can see why organizations are likely to go to considerable efforts to discourage the overt display of emotions—especially intense ones—in the workplace.

Traits are Powerful Predictors of Behavior

The essence of trait approaches in OB is that employees possess stable personality characteristics that significantly influence their attitudes toward, and behavioral reactions to, organizational settings. People with particular traits tend to be relatively consistent in their attitudes and behavior over time and across situations.[1]

Of course, trait theorists recognize that all traits are not equally powerful. They tend to put them into one of three categories. *Cardinal traits* are those so strong and generalized that they influence every act a person performs. *Primary traits* are generally consistent influences on behavior, but they may not show up in all situations. Finally, *secondary traits* are attributes that do not form a vital part of the personality but come into play only in particular situations. For the most part, trait theories have focused on the power of primary traits to predict employee behavior.

Trait theorists do a fairly good job of meeting the average person's face-validity test. Think of friends, relatives, and acquaintances you have known for a number of years. Do they have traits that have remained essentially stable over time? Most of us would answer that question in the affirmative. If Cousin Anne was shy and nervous when we last saw her 10 years ago, we would be surprised to find her outgoing and relaxed now.

Managers seem to have a strong belief in the power of traits to predict behavior. If managers believed that situations determined behavior, they would hire people almost at random and structure the situation properly. But the employee selection process in most organizations places a great deal of emphasis on how applicants perform in interviews and on tests. Assume you're an interviewer and ask yourself: What am I looking for in job candidates? If you answered with terms such as *conscientious, hardworking, persistent, confident,* and *dependable,* you're a trait theorist!

---

[1]Some of the points in this argument are from R. J. House, S. A. Shane, and D. M. Herold, "Rumors of the Death of Dispositional Research Are Vastly Exaggerated," *Academy of Management Review,* January 1996, pp. 203–24.

Few people would dispute that there are some stable individual attributes that affect reactions to the workplace. But trait theorists go beyond that generality and argue that individual behavior consistencies are widespread and account for much of the differences in behavior among people.[2]

There are two important problems with using traits to explain a large proportion of behavior in organizations. First, organizational settings are strong situations that have a large impact on employee behavior. Second, individuals are highly adaptive and personality traits change in response to organizational situations.

It has been well known for some time that the effects of traits are likely to be strongest in relatively weak situations and weakest in relatively strong situations. Organizational settings tend to be strong situations because they have rules and other formal regulations that define acceptable behavior and punish deviant behavior; and they have informal norms that dictate appropriate behaviors. These formal and informal constraints minimize the effects of personality traits.

By arguing that employees possess stable traits that lead to cross-situational consistencies in behaviors, trait theorists are implying that individuals don't really adapt to different situations. But there is a growing body of evidence that an individual's traits are changed by the organizations in which that individual participates. If the individual's personality changes as a result of exposure to organizational settings, in what sense can that individual be said to have traits that persistently and consistently affect his or her reactions to those very settings? Moreover, people typically belong to multiple organizations that often include very different kinds of members, and they adapt to those different situations. Instead of being the prisoners of a rigid and stable personality framework, as trait theorists propose, people regularly adjust their behavior to reflect the requirements of various situations.

---

[2]Based on A. Davis-Blake and J. Pfeffer, "Just a Mirage: The Search for Dispositional Effects in Organizational Research," *Academy of Management Review,* July 1989, pp. 385–400.

1. What is *personality*?

2. What constrains the power of personality traits to precisely predict behavior?

3. What behavioral predictions might you make if you knew that an employee had (a) an external locus of control? (b) a low Mach score? (c) low self-esteem? (d) a Type A personality?

4. What is the Myers-Briggs Type Indicator?

5. What were the six personality types identified by Holland?

6. Do people from the same country have a common personality type? Explain.

7. Why might managers today pay more attention to the person–organization fit than the person–job fit?

8. What's *emotional labor* and why is it important to understanding OB?

9. How does national culture influence expressed emotions?

10. What's *emotional intelligence* and why is it important?

Questions for Critical Thinking

1. "Heredity determines personality." (a) Build an argument to support this statement. (b) Build an argument against this statement.

2. "The type of job an employee does moderates the relationship between personality and job productivity." Do you agree or disagree with this statement? Discuss.

3. One day your boss comes in and he's nervous, edgy, and argumentative. The next day he is calm and relaxed. Does this behavior suggest that personality traits aren't consistent from day to day?

4. What, if anything, can managers do to *manage* emotions?

5. Give some examples of situations in which the overt expression of emotions might enhance job performance.

Team Exercise   "What Is a Team Personality?"

It's the unusual organization today that isn't using work teams. But not everybody is a good team player. This prompts the questions: What individual personality characteristics enhance a team's performance? And what characteristics might hinder team performance?

Break into groups of five or six. Based on the research presented in this chapter, each group should (a) identify personality characteristics that are associated with high-performance teams and justify these choices, (b) identify personality characteristics that hinder high-performance teams and justify these choices, and (c) resolve whether it is better to have teams composed of individuals with similar or dissimilar traits.

Each group should select an individual who will present his or her group's findings to the class.

Internet Search Exercises

1. Search for the most popular personality tests used in business firms for selection, placement, and promotion decisions. How were you able to conclude that these were the most popular?

2. Find five recent articles (published within the past 12 months) on emotional intelligence. Summarize these articles. What, if any, criticism of the concept surfaced in your search?

We invite you to visit the Robbins homepage on the Prentice Hall Web site at **www.prenhall.com/robbins** for our on-line study guide, current events, links to related Web sites, and more.

Case Incident | Using the Predictive Index

Should a personality test be the impetus for overthrowing a company? Laura McCann thought so.

Laura McCann was CEO of a New York City–based, private-label clothing manufacturer. She and her partner had owned the company for seven years. The firm made money, but it also was a source of aggravation for her as well as many of her managers. McCann had been concerned that a number of her staff members were unhappy with their jobs, including some of her highest-ranking managers. Moreover, she and her partner were constantly at each other's throats.

In late 1997, McCann stumbled upon a personality test, the Predictive Index, which changed the way she looked at her business and led to her decision to reinvent the company.

McCann had met a consultant in psychometric testing. He was a strong advocate of the Predictive Index—a simple checklist of 86 adjectives. The test takes about five minutes to complete. Respondents go through the 86 adjectives twice, once checking those terms that they feel describe "the way you are expected to act by others"; and the second time checking those that "you yourself believe really describe you." Examples of adjectives? *Fussy, selfish, fearful, conscientious, tolerant, loyal.* Once scored, the Predictive Index identifies four scales that purport to characterize any personality: dominance, extroversion, patience, and precision.

McCann had her partner and all the managers in her company take the Predictive Index test. The results, according to the test consultant, indicated that

the cause of all the trouble was that nearly half of those on the company's management team had personalities that didn't fit their job descriptions. What's more, McCann and her partner couldn't have been more poorly matched.

Within a month of seeing these results, McCann took action. "The test helped me realize that all this difficulty we were having wasn't a personal thing. It just wasn't meant to be." McCann bought out her partner; restructured her management team, keeping just a well-chosen few; and started a totally new business with new partners and a largely different staff.

Questions

1. Contrast the Predictive Index to the Big Five framework. How is it similar? Different?

2. "Anyone with half-a-brain can fake a personality test. I can be anything an employer wants me to be." Do you agree or disagree with this statement? Support your position.

3. Could a test of emotional intelligence have been more effective than the Predictive Index in helping Laura McCann make her decision? Explain your position.

4. Do you think Laura McCann's actions were justified based on the results of a five-minute personality test? Explain.

Source: Based on C. Caggiano, "Psycho Path," *INC.*, July 1998, pp. 77–85.

End Notes

1. K. Morris, "The Rise of Jill Barad," *Business Week*, May 25, 1998, pp. 112–19; and "Trouble in Toyland," *Business Week*, March 15, 1999, p. 40.
2. G. W. Allport, *Personality: A Psychological Interpretation* (New York: Holt, Rinehart & Winston, 1937), p. 48.

3. Reported in R. L. Hotz, "Genetics, Not Parenting, Key to Temperament, Studies Say," *Los Angeles Times*, February 20, 1994, p. A1.
4. See D. T. Lykken, T. J. Bouchard Jr., M. McGue, and A. Tellegen, "Heritability of Interests: A Twin Study," *Journal*

of *Applied Psychology*, August 1993, pp. 649–61; R. D. Arvey and T. J. Bouchard Jr., "Genetics, Twins, and Organizational Behavior," in B. M. Staw and L. L. Cummings (eds.), *Research in Organizational Behavior*, vol. 16 (Greenwich, CT: JAI Press, 1994), pp. 65–66; D. Lykken and A. Tellegen, "Happiness Is a Stochastic Phenomenon," *Psychological Science*, May 1996, pp. 186–89; and W. Wright, *Born That Way: Genes, Behavior, Personality* (New York: Knopf, 1998).

5. R. C. Carson, "Personality," in M. R. Rosenzweig and L. W. Porter (eds.), *Annual Review of Psychology*, vol. 40 (Palo Alto, CA: Annual Reviews, 1989), pp. 228–29.

6. L. Sechrest, "Personality," in M. R. Rosenzweig and L. W. Porter (eds.), *Annual Review of Psychology*, vol. 27 (Palo Alto, CA: Annual Reviews, 1976), p. 10.

7. W. Mischel, "The Interaction of Person and Situation," in D. Magnusson and N. S. Endler (eds.), *Personality at the Crossroads: Current Issues in Interactional Psychology* (Hillsdale, NJ: Erlbaum, 1977), pp. 166–207.

8. See A. H. Buss, "Personality as Traits," *American Psychologist*, November 1989, pp. 1378–88; and D. G. Winter, O. P. John, A. J. Stewart, E. C. Klohnen, and L. E. Duncan, "Traits and Motives: Toward an Integration of Two Traditions in Personality Research," *Psychological Review*, April 1998, pp. 230–50.

9. G. W. Allport and H. S. Odbert, "Trait Names, A Psycholexical Study," *Psychological Monographs*, no. 47 (1936).

10. R. B. Cattell, "Personality Pinned Down," *Psychology Today*, July 1973, pp. 40–46.

11. See R. R. McCrae and P. T. Costa Jr., "Reinterpreting the Myers-Briggs Type Indicator from the Perspective of the Five Factor Model of Personality," *Journal of Personality*, March 1989, pp. 17–40; and C. Fitzgerald and L. K. Kirby (eds.), *Developing Leaders: Research and Applications in Psychological Type and Leadership Development* (Palo Alto, CA: Davies-Black Publishing, 1997).

12. G. N. Landrum, *Profiles of Genius* (New York: Prometheus, 1993).

13. See, for example, J. M. Digman, "Personality Structure: Emergence of the Five-Factor Model," in M. R. Rosenzweig and L. W. Porter (eds.), *Annual Review of Psychology*, vol. 41 (Palo Alto, CA: Annual Reviews, 1990), pp. 417–40; R. R. McCrae, "Special Issue: The Five-Factor Model: Issues and Applications," *Journal of Personality*, June 1992; L. R. Goldberg, "The Structure of Phenotypic Personality Traits," *American Psychologist*, January 1993, pp. 26–34; and P. H. Raymark, M. J. Schmit, and R. M. Guion, "Identifying Potentially Useful Personality Constructs for Employee Selection," *Personnel Psychology*, Autumn 1997, pp. 723–36.

14. See, for instance, M. R. Barrick and M. K. Mount, "The Big Five Personality Dimensions and Job Performance: A Meta-Analysis," *Personnel Psychology* 44 (1991), pp. 1–26; R. P. Tett, D. N. Jackson, and M. Rothstein, "Personality Measures as Predictors of Job Performance: A Meta-Analytic Review," *Personnel Psychology*, Winter 1991, pp. 703–42; T. A. Judge, J. J. Martocchio, and C. J. Thoresen, "Five-Factor Model of Personality and Employee Absence," *Journal of Applied Psychology*, October 1997, pp. 745–55; and O. Behling, "Employee Selection: Will Intelligence and Conscientiousness Do the Job?"

Academy of Management Executive, February 1998, pp. 77–86; and F. S. Switzer III and P. L. Roth, "A Meta-Analytic Review of Predictors of Job Performance for Salespeople," *Journal of Applied Psychology*, August 1998, pp. 586–97.

15. M. K. Mount, M. R. Barrick, and J. P. Strauss, "Validity of Observer Ratings of the Big Five Personality Factors," *Journal of Applied Psychology*, April 1994, p. 272.

16. D. W. Organ, "Personality and Organizational Citizenship Behavior," *Journal of Management*, Summer 1994, pp. 465–78; D. W. Organ and K. Ryan, "A Meta-Analytic Review of Attitudinal and Dispositional Predictors of Organizational Citizenship Behavior," *Personnel Psychology*, Winter 1995, pp. 775–802; and M. A. Konovsky and D. W. Organ, "Dispositional and Contextual Determinants of Organizational Citizenship Behavior," *Journal of Organizational Behavior*, May 1996, pp. 253–66.

17. J. B. Rotter, "Generalized Expectancies for Internal versus External Control of Reinforcement," *Psychological Monographs* 80, no. 609 (1966).

18. See P. E. Spector, "Behavior in Organizations as a Function of Employee's Locus of Control," *Psychological Bulletin*, May 1982, pp. 482–97; and G. J. Blau, "Locus of Control as a Potential Moderator of the Turnover Process," *Journal of Occupational Psychology*, Fall 1987, pp. 21–29.

19. R. T. Keller, "Predicting Absenteeism from Prior Absenteeism, Attitudinal Factors, and Nonattitudinal Factors," *Journal of Applied Psychology*, August 1983, pp. 536–40.

20. Spector, "Behavior in Organizations as a Function of Employee's Locus of Control," p. 493.

21. R. G. Vleeming, "Machiavellianism: A Preliminary Review," *Psychological Reports*, February 1979, pp. 295–310.

22. R. Christie and F. L. Geis, *Studies in Machiavellianism* (New York: Academic Press, 1970), p. 312; and N. V. Ramanaiah, A. Byravan, and F. R. J. Detwiler, "Revised Neo Personality Inventory Profiles of Machiavellian and Non-Machiavellian People," *Psychological Reports*, October 1994, pp. 937–38.

23. Christie and Geis, *Studies in Machiavellianism*.

24. See J. Brockner, *Self-Esteem at Work* (Lexington, MA: Lexington Books, 1988); and N. Branden, *Self-Esteem at Work* (San Francisco: Jossey-Bass, 1998).

25. See M. Snyder, *Public Appearances/Private Realities: The Psychology of Self-Monitoring* (New York: W. H. Freeman, 1987).

26. Ibid.

27. M. Kilduff and D. V. Day, "Do Chameleons Get Ahead? The Effects of Self-Monitoring on Managerial Careers," *Academy of Management Journal*, August 1994, pp. 1047–60.

28. R. N. Taylor and M. D. Dunnette, "Influence of Dogmatism, Risk-Taking Propensity, and Intelligence on Decision-Making Strategies for a Sample of Industrial Managers," *Journal of Applied Psychology*, August 1974, pp. 420–23.

29. I. L. Janis and L. Mann, *Decision Making: A Psychological Analysis of Conflict, Choice, and Commitment* (New York: Free Press, 1977).

30. N. Kogan and M. A. Wallach, "Group Risk Taking as a Function of Members' Anxiety and Defensiveness," *Journal of Personality*, March 1967, pp. 50–63.

31. M. Friedman and R. H. Rosenman, *Type A Behavior and Your Heart* (New York: Alfred A. Knopf, 1974), p. 84 (emphasis in original).

32. Ibid., pp. 84–85.

33. Ibid, p. 86.

34. See, for instance, G. W. M. Ip and M. H. Bond, "Culture, Values, and the Spontaneous Self-Concept," *Asian Journal of Psychology*, vol. 1, 1995, pp. 30–36; J. E. Williams, J. L. Saiz, D. L. FormyDuval, M. L. Munick, E. E. Fogle, A. Adom, A. Haque, F. Neto, and J. Yu, "Cross-Cultural Variation in the Importance of Psychological Characteristics: A Seven-Country Study," *International Journal of Psychology*, October 1995, pp. 529–50; and V. Benet and N. G. Waller, "The Big Seven Factor Model of Personality Description: Evidence for Its Cross-Cultural Generalizability in a Spanish Sample," *Journal of Personality and Social Psychology*, October 1995, pp. 701–18.

35. J. F. Salgado, "The Five Factor Model of Personality and Job Performance in the European Community," *Journal of Applied Psychology*, February 1997, pp. 30–43.

36. P. L. Ackerman and L. G. Humphreys, "Individual Differences Theory in Industrial and Organizational Psychology," in M. D. Dunnette and L. M. Hough (eds.), *Handbook of Industrial & Organizational Psychology*, 2nd ed., vol. 1 (Palo Alto: Consulting Psychologists, 1990), pp. 223–82.

37. F. Kluckhohn and F. L. Strodtbeck, *Variations in Value Orientations* (Evanston, IL: Row Peterson, 1961).

38. P. B. Smith, F. Trompenaars, and S. Dugan, "The Rotter Locus of Control Scale in 43 Countries: A Test of Cultural Relativity, " *International Journal of Psychology*, June 1995, pp. 377–400.

39. Friedman and Rosenman, *Type A Behavior and Your Heart*, p. 86.

40. J. L. Holland, *Making Vocational Choices: A Theory of Vocational Personalities and Work Environments*, 2nd ed. (Englewood Cliffs, NJ: Prentice Hall, 1985). See also R. Hogan and R. J. Blake, "Vocational Interests: Matching Self-Concept with the Work Environment," in K. R. Murphy (ed.), *Individual Differences and Behavior in Organizations* (San Francisco: Jossey-Bass, 1996), pp. 89–144.

41. See, for example, A. R. Spokane, "A Review of Research on Person–Environment Congruence in Holland's Theory of Careers," *Journal of Vocational Behavior*, June 1985, pp. 306–43; D. Brown, "The Status of Holland's Theory of Career Choice," *Career Development Journal*, September 1987, pp. 13–23; J. L. Holland and G. D. Gottfredson, "Studies of the Hexagonal Model: An Evaluation (or, The Perils of Stalking the Perfect Hexagon)," *Journal of Vocational Behavior*, April 1992, pp. 158–70; and T. J. Tracey and J. Rounds, "Evaluating Holland's and Gati's Vocational-Interest Models: A Structural Meta-Analysis," *Psychological Bulletin*, March 1993, pp. 229–46.

42. See B. Schneider, "The People Make the Place," *Personnel Psychology*, Autumn 1987, pp. 437–53; D. E. Bowen, G. E. Ledford, Jr., and B. R. Nathan, "Hiring for the Organization, Not the Job," *Academy of Management Executive*,

November 1991, pp. 35–51; B. Schneider, H. W. Goldstein, and D. B. Smith, "The ASA Framework: An Update," *Personnel Psychology*, Winter 1995, pp. 747–73; A. L. Kristof, "Person-Organization Fit: An Integrative Review of Its Conceptualizations, Measurement, and Implications," *Personnel Psychology*, Spring 1996, pp. 1–49; and J. Schaubroeck, D. C. Ganster, and J. R. Jones, "Organization and Occupation Influences in the Attraction-Selection-Attrition Process," *Journal of Applied Psychology*, December 1998, pp. 869–91.

43. Based on T. A. Judge and D. M. Cable, "Applicant Personality, Organizational Culture, and Organization Attraction," *Personnel Psychology*, Summer 1997, pp. 359–94.

44. Cited in the *Los Angeles Times*, January 3, 1998, p. A3.

45. See, for example, L. L. Putnam and D. K. Mumby, "Organizations, Emotion and the Myth of Rationality," in S. Fineman (ed.), *Emotion in Organizations* (Thousand Oaks: Sage, 1993), pp. 36–57; J. Martin, K. Knopoff, and C. Beckman, "An Alternative to Bureaucratic Impersonality and Emotional Labor: Bounded Emotionality at the Body Shop," *Administrative Science Quarterly*, June 1998, pp. 429–69; and T. A. Domagalski, "Emotion in Organizations: Main Currents," *Human Relations*, June 1999, pp. 833–52.

46. B. E. Ashforth and R. H. Humphrey, "Emotion in the Workplace: A Reappraisal," *Human Relations*, February 1995, pp. 97–125.

47. J. M. George, "Trait and State Affect," in K. R. Murphy (ed.), *Individual Differences and Behavior in Organizations* (San Francisco: Jossey-Bass, 1996), p. 145.

48. See N. H. Frijda, "Moods, Emotion Episodes and Emotions," in M. Lewis and J. M. Haviland (eds.), *Handbook of Emotions* (New York: Guilford Press, 1993), pp. 381–403.

49. H. M. Weiss and R. Cropanzano, "Affective Events Theory," in B. M. Staw and L. L. Cummings (eds.), *Research in Organizational Behavior*, vol. 18 (Greenwich, CT: JAI Press, 1996), pp. 17–19.

50. N. H. Frijda, "Moods, Emotion Episodes and Emotions," p. 381.

51. See J. A. Morris and D. C. Feldman, "The Dimensions, Antecedents, and Consequences of Emotional Labor," *Academy of Management Review*, October 1996, pp. 986–1010; and C. S. Hunt, "Although I Might Be Laughing Loud and Hearty, Deep Inside I'm Blue: Individual Perceptions Regarding Feeling and Displaying Emotions at Work," paper presented at the Academy of Management National Conference; Cincinnati, OH, August 1996.

52. A. R. Hochschild, "Emotion Work, Feeling Rules, and Social Structure," *American Journal of Sociology*, November 1979, pp. 551–75.

53. B. M. DePaulo, "Nonverbal Behavior and Self-Presentation," *Psychological Bulletin*, March 1992, pp. 203–43.

54. C. S. Hunt, "Although I Might Be Laughing Loud and Hearty," p. 3.

55. See, for example, P. Shaver, J. Schwartz, D. Kirson, and C. O'Connor, "Emotion Knowledge: Further Exploration of a Prototype Approach," *Journal of Personality and Social Psychology*, June 1987, pp. 1061–86; P. Ekman, "An Argument for Basic Emotions," *Cognition*

and *Emotion*, May/July 1992, pp. 169–200; C. E. Izard, "Basic Emotions, Relations Among Emotions, and Emotion-Cognition Relations," *Psychological Bulletin*, November 1992, pp. 561–65; and R. Plutchik, *The Psychology and Biology of Emotion* (New York: HarperCollins, 1994).

56. H. M. Weiss and R. Cropanzano, "Affective Events Theory," pp. 20–22.

57. Cited in R. D. Woodworth, *Experimental Psychology* (New York: Holt, 1938).

58. See J. K. Salminen, S. Saarijanvi, E. Aairela, and T. Tamminen, "Alexithymia: State or Trait? One-Year Follow-Up Study of General Hospital Psychiatric Consultation Outpatients," *Journal of Psychosomatic Research*, July 1994, pp. 681–85.

59. K. Deaux, "Sex Differences," in M. R. Rosenzweig and L. W. Porter (eds.), *Annual Review of Psychology*, vol. 26 (Palo Alto, CA: Annual Reviews, 1985), pp. 48–82; M. LaFrance and M. Banaji, "Toward a Reconsideration of the Gender–Emotion Relationship," in M. Clark (ed.), *Review of Personality and Social Psychology*, vol. 14 (Newbury Park, CA: Sage, 1992), pp. 178–97; and A. M. Kring and A. H. Gordon, "Sex Differences in Emotion: Expression, Experience, and Physiology," *Journal of Personality and Social Psychology*, March 1998, pp. 686–703.

60. L. R. Brody and J. A. Hall, "Gender and Emotion," in M. Lewis and J. M. Haviland (eds.), *Handbook of Emotions* (New York: Guilford Press, 1993), pp. 447–60; and M. Grossman and W. Wood, "Sex Differences in Intensity of Emotional Experience: A Social Role Interpretation," *Journal of Personality and Social Psychology*, November 1993, pp. 1010–22.

61. V. P. Richmond, J. C. McCroskey, and S. K. Payne, *Nonverbal Behavior in Interpersonal Relations*, 2nd ed. (Englewood Cliffs, NJ: Prentice Hall, 1991), pp. 117–138; and L. A. King, "Ambivalence Over Emotional Expression and Reading Emotions in Situations and Faces," *Journal of Personality and Social Psychology*, March 1998, pp. 753–62.

62. J. A. Hall, *Nonverbal Sex Differences: Communication Accuracy and Expressive Style* (Baltimore: Johns Hopkins Press, 1984).

63. N. James, "Emotional Labour: Skill and Work in the Social Regulations of Feelings," *Sociological Review*, February 1989, pp. 15–42; A. Hochschild, *The Second Shift* (New York: Viking, 1989); and F. M. Deutsch, "Status, Sex, and Smiling: The Effect of Role on Smiling in Men and Women," *Personality and Social Psychology Bulletin*, September 1990, pp. 531–40.

64. A. Rafaeli, "When Clerks Meet Customers: A Test of Variables Related to Emotional Expression on the Job," *Journal of Applied Psychology*, June 1989, pp. 385–93; and M. LaFrance and M. Banaji, "Toward a Reconsideration of the Gender–Emotion Relationship."

65. L. W. Hoffman, "Early Childhood Experiences and Women's Achievement Motives," *Journal of Social Issues*, vol. 28, no. 2, 1972, pp. 129–55.

66. M. Boas and S. Chain, *Big Mac: The Unauthorized Story of McDonald's* (New York: Dutton, 1976), p. 84.

67. B. E. Ashforth and R. H. Humphrey, "Emotion in the Workplace," p. 104.

68. G. L. Flett, K. R. Blankstein, P. Pliner, and C. Bator, "Impression-Management and Self-Deception Components of Appraised Emotional Experience," *British Journal of Social Psychology*, January 1988, pp. 67–77.

69. B. E. Ashforth and R. H. Humphrey, "Emotion in the Workplace," p. 104.

70. A. Rafaeli and R. I. Sutton, "The Expression of Emotion in Organizational Life," in L. L. Cummings and B. M. Staw (eds.), *Research in Organizational Behavior*, vol. 11 (Greenwich, CT: JAI Press, 1989), p. 8.

71. A. Rafaeli, "When Cashiers Meet Customers: An Analysis of Supermarket Cashiers," *Academy of Management Journal*, June 1989, pp. 245–73.

72. Ibid.

73. B. Mesquita and N. H. Frijda, "Cultural Variations in Emotions: A Review," *Psychological Bulletin*, September 1992, pp. 179–204.

74. Described in S. Emmons, "Emotions at Face Value," *Los Angeles Times*, January 9, 1998, p. E1.

75. R. I. Levy, *Tahitians: Mind and Experience in the Society Islands* (Chicago: University of Chicago Press, 1973).

76. This section is based on Daniel Goleman, *Emotional Intelligence* (New York: Bantam, 1995); J. D. Mayer and G. Geher, "Emotional Intelligence and the Identification of Emotion," *Intelligence*, March–April 1996, pp. 89–113; J. Stuller, "EQ: Edging Toward Respectability," *Training*, June 1997, pp. 43–48; R. K. Cooper, "Applying Emotional Intelligence in the Workplace," *Training & Development*, December 1997, pp. 31–38; "HR Pulse: Emotional Intelligence," *HRMagazine*, January 1998, p. 19; M. Davies, L. Stankov, and R. D. Roberts, "Emotional Intelligence: In Search of an Elusive Construct," *Journal of Personality and Social Psychology*, October 1998, pp. 989–1015; and D. Goleman, *Working with Emotional Intelligence* (New York: Bantam, 1999).

77. See, for example, K. Fiedler, "Emotional Mood, Cognitive Style, and Behavioral Regulation," in K. Fiedler and J. Forgas (eds.), *Affect, Cognition, and Social Behavior* (Toronto: Hogrefe International, 1988), pp. 100–19; A. M. Isen, "Positive Affect and Decision Making," in M. Lewis and J. M. Haviland (eds.), *Handbook of Emotions* (New York: Guilford, 1993), pp. 261–77; and M. Luce, J. Bettman, and J. W. Payne, "Choice Processing in Difficult Decisions," *Journal of Experimental Psychology: Learning, Memory, and Cognition*, vol. 23, 1997, pp. 384–405.

78. B. E. Ashforth and R. H. Humphrey, "Emotion in the Workplace," p. 109.

79. Ibid.

80. Ibid., p. 110.

81. Ibid.

82. J. M. George, "Trait and State Affect," p. 162.

83. B. E. Ashforth and R. H. Humphrey, "Emotion in the Workplace," p. 116.

84. S. L. Robinson and R. J. Bennett, "A Typology of Deviant Workplace Behaviors: A Multidimensional Scaling Study," *Academy of Management Journal*, April 1995, p. 556.

85. Ibid., pp. 555–72.

86. Based on A. G. Bedeian, "Workplace Envy," *Organizational Dynamics*, Spring 1995, p. 50.

87. Ibid., p. 54.
88. R. Hogan, J. Hogan, and B. W. Roberts, "Personality Measurement and Employment Decisions," *American Psychologist*, May 1996, p. 475.
89. S. Nelton, "Emotions in the Workplace," *Nation's Business*, February 1996, p. 25.
90. H. M. Weiss and R. Cropanzano, "Affective Events Theory," p. 55.
91. See the Yerkes-Dodson law cited in D. O. Hebb, "Drives and the CNS (Conceptual Nervous System)," *Psychological Review*, July 1955, pp. 243–54.

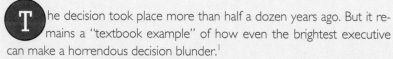

First umpire: "Some's balls and some's strikes and I calls 'em as they is."
Second umpire: "Some's balls and some's strikes and I calls 'em as I sees 'em."
Third umpire: "Some's balls and some's strikes but they ain't nothin' till I calls 'em."

—H. Cantril

The decision took place more than half a dozen years ago. But it remains a "textbook example" of how even the brightest executive can make a horrendous decision blunder.[1]

It was autumn 1994. The organization was Intel, the world's largest computer chip maker. And the executive in question was its co-founder and CEO at the time, Andrew Grove (see photo). A year earlier, Intel had introduced the powerful Pentium chip. It had quickly become the brains in more than 4 million personal computers.

In late October 1994, a professor in Virginia discovered a flaw in the Pentium chip. In division problems involving very large numbers, the solution was incorrect. When a trade publication wrote an article on the chip's flaw on November 7, Intel admitted that it had found the flaw four months earlier and had corrected it. A small but vocal group of customers and computer industry advocates was not happy with that response. They wanted Intel to replace all the flawed chips. Grove and his executive team approached the issue the way they attacked all large challenges—as an engineering problem. They broke it down into smaller parts, analyzed it rationally, and came to a conclusion. The company announced on November 14 that it had decided it would refuse to guarantee replacement chips for all customers. It would replace faulty Pentium chips, but only if computer owners could demonstrate that they really needed an extra margin of accuracy. The company argued that most users would encounter an inaccurate answer just once in 27,000 years. Grove considered the issue closed.

But consumers were angry. They didn't want a flawed product. Tens of thousands of people who had bought computers with the Pentium chip wanted a replacement regardless of whether they did complex calculations. Under pressure, Grove again met with his senior executive group to analyze the problem. After round-the-clock meetings, they decided to hold their ground. They described the flaw as "minor." Grove insisted that the odds were 9 billion to 1 against the Pentium chips causing a mathematical

Perception and Individual Decision Making

error. But Intel's stance only escalated criticism. Finally, after Intel's marketing director spent the better part of a Sunday afternoon hammering into Grove's head that his decision was wrong, Grove changed his mind. On December 21, 1994, Intel abruptly announced that it would replace all flawed Pentium chips for free, no questions asked. The company spent $475 million replacing those faulty chips. The damage to the company's reputation was undoubtedly a lot greater. Looking back, Grove describes his decision not to replace the flawed chips as "an enormous mistake."

How could Grove have made such a blunder? The answer is that he responded to the problem like the engineer he is. He treated the flaw as a technical problem, not a consumer problem. From a technical standpoint, logic and reason would argue that there was no need to replace all flawed chips since the flaw affected so few users. What Grove failed to grasp was that people who bought the flawed chip felt taken advantage of. They had paid for a perfect chip and didn't get one. Grove's position came across as condescending and arrogant. In this instance, the engineering mentality that Grove so successfully brought to technical problems did him in.

AFTER READING THIS CHAPTER, YOU SHOULD BE ABLE TO

1. Explain how two people can see the same thing and interpret it differently

2. List the three determinants of attribution

3. Describe how shortcuts can assist in or distort our judgment of others

4. Explain how perception affects the decision-making process

5. Outline the six steps in the rational decision-making model

6. Describe the actions of the boundedly rational decision maker

7. Identify the conditions in which individuals are most likely to use intuition in decision making

8. Describe four styles of decision making

9. Define heuristics and explain how they bias decisions

10. Contrast the three ethical decision criteria

LEARNING OBJECTIVES

M aking decisions is a critical element of organizational life. In this chapter, we'll describe how decisions in organizations are made. But first, we discuss perceptual processes and show how they are linked to individual decision making.

WHAT IS PERCEPTION, AND WHY IS IT IMPORTANT?

Perception can be defined as a process by which individuals organize and interpret their sensory impressions in order to give meaning to their environment. However, what one perceives can

perception

A process by which individuals organize and interpret their sensory impressions in order to give meaning to their environment.

be substantially different from objective reality. It need not be, but there is often disagreement. For example, it's possible that all employees in a firm may view it as a great place to work—favorable working conditions, interesting job assignments, good pay, an understanding and responsible management—but, as most of us know, it's very unusual to find such agreement.

Why is perception important in the study of OB? Simply because people's behavior is based on their perception of what reality is, not on reality itself. *The world as it is perceived is the world that is behaviorally important.*

FACTORS INFLUENCING PERCEPTION

How do we explain that individuals may look at the same thing, yet perceive it differently? A number of factors operate to shape and sometimes distort perception. These factors can reside in the *perceiver*, in the object or *target* being perceived, or in the context of the *situation* in which the perception is made.

THE PERCEIVER

When an individual looks at a target and attempts to interpret what he or she sees, that interpretation is heavily influenced by personal characteristics of the individual perceiver. Have you ever bought a new car and then suddenly noticed a large number of cars like yours on the road? It's unlikely that the number of such cars suddenly expanded. Rather, your own purchase has influenced your perception so that you are now more likely to notice them. This is an example of how factors related to the perceiver influence what he or she perceives. Among the more relevant personal characteristics affecting perception are attitudes, motives, interests, past experiences, and expectations.

Teri likes small classes because she enjoys asking a lot of questions of her teachers. Scott, on the other hand, prefers the anonymity of large lectures. On the first day of classes this term, Teri and Scott find themselves walking into the university auditorium for their introductory course in psychology. They both recognize that they will be among some 800 students in this class. But given the different *attitudes* held by Teri and Scott, it shouldn't surprise you to find that they interpret what they see differently. Teri sulks, while Scott's smile does little to hide his relief in being able to blend unnoticed into the large crowd. They both see the same thing, but they interpret it differently.

Unsatisfied needs or *motives* stimulate individuals and may exert a strong influence on their perceptions. This fact was dramatically demonstrated in research on hunger.[2] Individuals in the study had not eaten for varying numbers of hours. Some had eaten an hour earlier; others had gone as long as 16 hours without food. These subjects were shown blurred pictures, and the results indicated that the extent of hunger influenced the interpretation of the blurred pictures. Those who had not eaten for 16 hours perceived the blurred images as pictures of food far more frequently than did those subjects who had eaten only a short time earlier.

It should not surprise you that a plastic surgeon is more likely to notice an imperfect nose than a plumber is. The supervisor who has just been reprimanded by her boss for the high level of lateness among her staff is more likely to notice lateness by an employee tomorrow than she was last week. If you are preoccupied with a personal problem, you may find it hard to be attentive in class. These examples illustrate that the

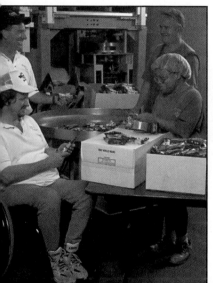

Philip Kosak (standing at left), president of Carolina Fine Snacks, admits his attitude about hiring workers with disabilities influenced his perception of their on-the-job performance. Faced with high employee turnover, absenteeism, and a plant that operated at only 60% of its capacity, Kosak decided to hire disabled workers, thinking, "What do I have to lose?" But, he says, "What I didn't realize was what I was about to gain." Disabled workers are performing far beyond Kosak's expectations, helping him to improve attendance and productivity and operate at 100% capacity. Kosak says his experience with disabled workers "has changed my perspective on life."

focus of our attention appears to be influenced by our *interests*. Because our individual interests differ considerably, what one person notices in a situation can differ from what others perceive.

Just as interests narrow one's focus, so do one's *past experiences*. You perceive those things to which you can relate. However, in many instances, your past experiences will act to nullify an object's interest.

Objects or events that have never been experienced before are more noticeable than those that have been experienced in the past. You are more likely to notice the operations along an assembly line if this is the first time you have seen an assembly line. In the late 1960s and early 1970s, women and minorities in managerial positions were highly visible because, historically, those positions were the province of white males. Today, women and minorities are more widely represented in the managerial ranks, so we are less likely to take notice that a manager is female, African American, Asian American, or Latino.

Finally, *expectations* can distort your perceptions in that you will see what you expect to see. If you expect police officers to be authoritative, young people to be unambitious, personnel directors to "like people," or individuals holding public office to be unscrupulous, you may perceive them as such regardless of their actual traits.

THE TARGET

Characteristics of the target that is being observed can affect what is perceived. Loud people are more likely to be noticed in a group than are quiet ones. So, too, are extremely attractive or unattractive individuals. Motion, sounds, size, and other attributes of a target shape the way we see it.

Because targets are not looked at in isolation, the relationship of a target to its background influences perception, as does our tendency to group close things and similar things together.

What we see depends on how we separate a figure from its general *background*. For instance, what you see as you read this sentence is black letters on a white page. You do not see funny-shaped patches of black and white because you recognize these shapes and organize the black shapes against the white background. Exhibit 5-1 dramatizes this effect. The object on the left may at first look like a white vase. However, if white is taken as the background, we see two green profiles. At first observation, the group of objects on the right appears to be some green modular figures against a white background. Closer inspection will reveal the word *FLY* once the background is defined as green.

Objects that are close to each other will tend to be perceived together rather than separately. As a result of physical or time proximity, we often put together

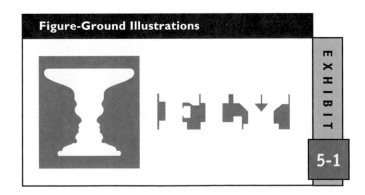

Figure-Ground Illustrations

EXHIBIT 5-1

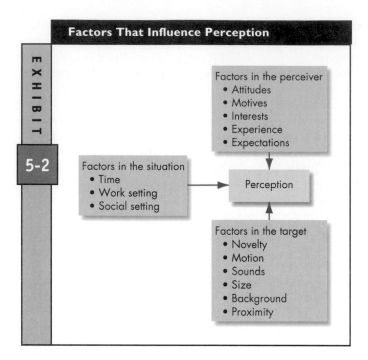

Factors That Influence Perception

EXHIBIT 5-2

Factors in the situation
• Time
• Work setting
• Social setting

Factors in the perceiver
• Attitudes
• Motives
• Interests
• Experience
• Expectations

Perception

Factors in the target
• Novelty
• Motion
• Sounds
• Size
• Background
• Proximity

objects or events that are unrelated. Celebrities Michael Kennedy and Sonny Bono died in similar ski accidents within a week of each other. Suddenly, many people concluded that skiing was a dangerous sport. Although the two incidents were totally unrelated, their proximity in time led many to perceive the risk from skiing in a new light.

Persons, objects, or events that are similar to each other also tend to be grouped together. The greater the similarity, the greater the probability that we will tend to perceive them as a common group. Women, blacks, or members of any other group that has clearly distinguishable characteristics in terms of features or color will tend to be perceived as alike in other, unrelated characteristics as well.

THE SITUATION

The context in which we see objects or events is important. Elements in the surrounding environment influence our perceptions. I may not notice a 25-year-old female in an evening gown and heavy makeup at a nightclub on Saturday night. Yet that same woman so attired for my Monday morning management class would certainly catch my attention (and that of the rest of the class). Neither the perceiver nor the target changed between Saturday night and Monday morning, but the situation is different. Similarly, you are more likely to notice your employees goofing off if your boss from the head office happens to be in town. Again, the situation affects your perception. The time at which an object or event is seen can influence attention, as can location, light, heat, or any number of situational factors. Exhibit 5-2 summarizes the factors influencing perception.

PERSON PERCEPTION: MAKING JUDGMENTS ABOUT OTHERS

Now we turn to the most relevant application of perception concepts to OB. This is the issue of *person perception*.

ATTRIBUTION THEORY

Our perceptions of people differ from our perceptions of inanimate objects such as desks, machines, or buildings because we make inferences about the actions of people that we don't make about inanimate objects. Nonliving objects are subject to the laws of nature, but they have no beliefs, motives, or intentions. People do. The result is that when we observe people, we attempt to develop explanations of why they behave in certain ways. Our perception and judgment of a person's actions, therefore, will be significantly influenced by the assumptions we make about that person's internal state.

Attribution theory has been proposed to develop explanations of the ways in which we judge people differently, depending on what meaning we attribute to a given behavior.[3] Basically, the theory suggests that when we observe an individual's behavior, we attempt to determine whether it was internally or externally caused. That determination, however, depends largely on three factors: (1) distinctiveness, (2) consensus, and (3) consistency. First, let's clarify the differences between internal and external causation and then we will elaborate on each of the three determining factors.

Internally caused behaviors are those that are believed to be under the personal control of the individual. *Externally* caused behavior is seen as resulting from outside causes; that is, the person is seen as having been forced into the behavior by the situation. If one of your employees is late for work, you might attribute his lateness to his partying into the wee hours of the morning and then oversleeping. This would be an internal attribution. But if you attribute his arriving late to a major automobile accident that tied up traffic on the road that this employee regularly uses, then you would be making an external attribution.

Distinctiveness refers to whether an individual displays different behaviors in different situations. Is the employee who arrives late today also the source of complaints by co-workers for being a "goof off"? What we want to know is whether this behavior is unusual. If it is, the observer is likely to give the behavior an external attribution. If this action is not unusual, it will probably be judged as internal.

If everyone who is faced with a similar situation responds in the same way, we can say the behavior shows *consensus*. Our late employee's behavior would meet this criterion if all employees who took the same route to work were also late. From an attribution perspective, if consensus is high, you would be expected to give an external attribution to the employee's tardiness, whereas if other employees who took the same route made it to work on time, your conclusion as to causation would be internal.

Finally, an observer looks for *consistency* in a person's actions. Does the person respond the same way over time? Coming in 10 minutes late for work is not perceived in the same way for the employee for whom it is an unusual case (she hasn't been late for several months) as it is for the employee for whom it is part of a routine pattern (she is regularly late two or three times a week). The more consistent the behavior, the more the observer is inclined to attribute it to internal causes.

Exhibit 5-3 summarizes the key elements in attribution theory. It would tell us, for instance, that if your employee—Kim Randolph—generally performs at about the same level on other related tasks as she does on her current task (low distinctiveness), if other employees frequently perform differently—better or worse—than Kim does on that current task (low consensus), and if Kim's performance on this current task is consistent over time (high consistency), you or

attribution theory

When individuals observe behavior, they attempt to determine whether it is internally or externally caused.

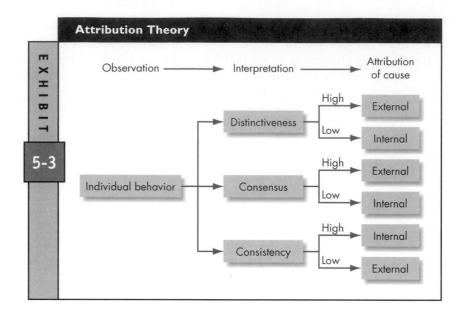

EXHIBIT 5-3

Attribution Theory

Observation → Interpretation → Attribution of cause

Individual behavior
- Distinctiveness
  - High → External
  - Low → Internal
- Consensus
  - High → External
  - Low → Internal
- Consistency
  - High → Internal
  - Low → External

anyone else who is judging Kim's work is likely to hold her primarily responsible for her task performance (internal attribution).

One of the more interesting findings from attribution theory is that there are errors or biases that distort attributions. For instance, there is substantial evidence that when we make judgments about the behavior of other people, we have a tendency to underestimate the influence of external factors and overestimate the influence of internal or personal factors.[4] This is called the **fundamental attribution error** and can explain why a sales manager is prone to attribute the poor performance of her sales agents to laziness rather than to the innovative product line introduced by a competitor. There is also a tendency for individuals to attribute their own successes to internal factors such as ability or effort while putting the blame for failure on external factors such as luck. This is called the **self-serving bias** and suggests that feedback provided to employees in performance reviews will be predictably distorted by recipients depending on whether it is positive or negative.

Are these errors or biases that distort attributions universal across different cultures? We can't answer that question definitively, but there is some preliminary evidence that indicates cultural differences.[5] For instance, a study of Korean managers found that, contrary to the self-serving bias, they tended to accept responsibility for group failure "because I was not a capable leader" instead of attributing it to group members.[6] Attribution theory was developed largely based on experiments with Americans and Western Europeans. But the Korean study suggests caution in making attribution theory predictions in non-Western societies, especially in countries with strong collectivist traditions.

FREQUENTLY USED SHORTCUTS IN JUDGING OTHERS

We use a number of shortcuts when we judge others. Perceiving and interpreting what others do is burdensome. As a result, individuals develop techniques for making the task more manageable. These techniques are frequently valuable—they allow us to make accurate perceptions rapidly and provide valid data for making predictions. However, they are not foolproof. They can and do get us into trouble. An understanding of these shortcuts can be helpful toward recognizing when they can result in significant distortions.

fundamental attribution error

The tendency to underestimate the influence of external factors and overestimate the influence of internal factors when making judgments about the behavior of others.

self-serving bias

The tendency for individuals to attribute their own successes to internal factors while putting the blame for failures on external factors.

Selective Perception   Any characteristic that makes a person, object, or event stand out will increase the probability that it will be perceived. Why? Because it is impossible for us to assimilate everything we see—only certain stimuli can be taken in. This tendency explains why, as we noted earlier, you are more likely to notice cars like your own or why some people may be reprimanded by their boss for doing something that, when done by another employee, goes unnoticed. Since we can't observe everything going on about us, we engage in **selective perception**. A classic example shows how vested interests can significantly influence which problems we see.

Dearborn and Simon performed a perceptual study in which 23 business executives read a comprehensive case describing the organization and activities of a steel company.[7] Six of the 23 executives were in the sales function, five in production, four in accounting, and eight in miscellaneous functions. Each manager was asked to write down the most important problem he found in the case. Eighty-three percent of the sales executives rated sales important; only 29 percent of the others did so. This, along with other results of the study, led the researchers to conclude that the participants perceived aspects of a situation that were specifically related to the activities and goals of the unit to which they were attached. A group's perception of organizational activities is selectively altered to align with the vested interests they represent. In other words, when the stimuli are ambiguous, as in the steel company case, perception tends to be influenced more by an individual's base of interpretation (i.e., attitudes, interests, and background) than by the stimulus itself.

But how does selectivity work as a shortcut in judging other people? Since we cannot assimilate all that we observe, we take in bits and pieces. But those bits and pieces are not chosen randomly; rather, they are selectively chosen according to our interests, background, experience, and attitudes. Selective perception allows us to "speed-read" others, but not without the risk of drawing an inaccurate picture. Because we see what we want to see, we can draw unwarranted conclusions from an ambiguous situation. If there is a rumor going around the office that your company's sales are down and that large layoffs may be coming, a routine visit by a senior executive from headquarters might be interpreted as the first step in management's identification of people to be fired, when in reality such an action may be the furthest thing from the mind of the senior executive.

Halo Effect   When we draw a general impression about an individual on the basis of a single characteristic, such as intelligence, sociability, or appearance, a **halo effect** is operating.[8] This phenomenon frequently occurs when students appraise their classroom instructor. Students may give prominence to a single trait such as enthusiasm and allow their entire evaluation to be tainted by how they judge the instructor on that one trait. Thus, an instructor may be quiet, assured, knowledgeable, and highly qualified, but if his style lacks zeal, those students would probably give him a low rating.

The reality of the halo effect was confirmed in a classic study in which subjects were given a list of traits such as intelligent, skillful, practical, industrious, determined, and warm and were asked to evaluate the person to whom those traits applied.[9] When those traits were used, the person was judged to be wise, humorous, popular, and imaginative. When the same list was modified—cold was substituted for warm—a

selective perception

People selectively interpret what they see on the basis of their interests, background, experience, and attitudes.

halo effect

Drawing a general impression about an individual on the basis of a single characteristic.

From Jaron Lanier's dreadlocks and overall appearance, you might decide that he is a rap artist or member of a rock band. Actually, Lanier was the pioneer of virtual reality and developed software that made virtual reality commercially viable. He's also in big demand as a corporate consultant and speaker on the future of technology for clients that include Xerox, the U.S. Department of Defense, Kodak, American Express, and Glaxo Wellcome.

completely different set of perceptions was obtained. Clearly, the subjects were allowing a single trait to influence their overall impression of the person being judged.

The propensity for the halo effect to operate is not random. Research suggests that it is likely to be most extreme when the traits to be perceived are ambiguous in behavioral terms, when the traits have moral overtones, and when the perceiver is judging traits with which he or she has had limited experience.[10]

Contrast Effects   There's an old adage among entertainers who perform in variety shows: Never follow an act that has kids or animals in it. Why? The common belief is that audiences love children and animals so much that you'll look bad in comparison. This example demonstrates how **contrast effects** can distort perceptions. We don't evaluate a person in isolation. Our reaction to one person is influenced by other persons we have recently encountered.

An illustration of how contrast effects operate is an interview situation in which one sees a pool of job applicants. Distortions in any given candidate's evaluation can occur as a result of his or her place in the interview schedule. The candidate is likely to receive a more favorable evaluation if preceded by mediocre applicants and a less favorable evaluation if preceded by strong applicants.

Projection   It's easy to judge others if we assume that they're similar to us. For instance, if you want challenge and responsibility in your job, you assume that others want the same. Or, you're honest and trustworthy, so you take it for granted that other people are equally honest and trustworthy. This tendency to attribute one's own characteristics to other people—which is called **projection**—can distort perceptions made about others.

People who engage in projection tend to perceive others according to what they themselves are like rather than according to what the person being observed is really like. When observing others who actually are like them, these observers are quite accurate—not because they are perceptive but because they always judge people as being similar to themselves. So when they finally do find someone who is like them, they are naturally correct. When managers engage in projection, they compromise their ability to respond to individual differences. They tend to see people as more homogeneous than they really are.

Stereotyping   When we judge someone on the basis of our perception of the group to which he or she belongs, we are using the shortcut called **stereotyping**.[11] F. Scott Fitzgerald engaged in stereotyping in his reported conversation with Ernest Hemingway when he said, "The very rich are different from you and me." Hemingway's reply, "Yes, they have more money," indicated that he refused to generalize characteristics about people on the basis of their wealth.

Generalization, of course, is not without advantages. It's a means of simplifying a complex world, and it permits us to maintain consistency. It's less difficult to deal with an unmanageable number of stimuli if we use stereotypes. As an example, assume you're a sales manager looking to fill a sales position in your territory. You want to hire someone who is ambitious and hardworking and who can deal well with adversity. You've had good success in the past by hiring individuals who participated in athletics during college. So you focus your search by looking for candidates who participated in collegiate athletics. In so doing, you have cut down considerably on your search time. Furthermore, to the

contrast effects

Evaluations of a person's characteristics that are affected by comparisons with other people recently encountered who rank higher or lower on the same characteristics.

projection

Attributing one's own characteristics to other people.

stereotyping

Judging someone on the basis of one's perception of the group to which that person belongs.

[
Generalization is not without advantages. It's a means of simplifying a complex world, and it permits us to maintain consistency.
]

extent that athletes are ambitious, hardworking, and able to deal with adversity, the use of this stereotype can improve your decision making. The problem, of course, is when we inaccurately stereotype.[12] All college athletes are *not necessarily* ambitious, hardworking, or good at dealing with adversity.

In organizations, we frequently hear comments that represent stereotypes based on gender, age, race, ethnicity, and even weight[13]: "Women won't relocate for a promotion"; "men aren't interested in child care"; "older workers can't learn new skills"; "Asian immigrants are hardworking and conscientious"; "overweight people lack discipline." From a perceptual standpoint, if people expect to see these stereotypes, that is what they will perceive, whether they are accurate or not.

Obviously, one of the problems of stereotypes is that they are widespread, despite the fact that they may not contain a shred of truth or that they may be irrelevant. Their being widespread may mean only that many people are making the same inaccurate perception on the basis of a false premise about a group.

SPECIFIC APPLICATIONS IN ORGANIZATIONS

People in organizations are always judging each other. Managers must appraise their employees' performances. We evaluate how much effort our co-workers are putting into their jobs. When a new person joins a work team, he or she is immediately "sized up" by the other team members. In many cases, these judgments have important consequences for the organization. Let's briefly look at a few of the more obvious applications.

Employment Interview   A major input into who is hired and who is rejected in any organization is the employment interview. It's fair to say that few people are hired without an interview. But the evidence indicates that interviewers make perceptual judgments that are often inaccurate. In addition, agreement among interviewers is often poor; that is, different interviewers see different things in the same candidate and thus arrive at different conclusions about the applicant.

Interviewers generally draw early impressions that become very quickly entrenched. If negative information is exposed early in the interview, it tends to be more heavily weighted than if that same information comes out later.[14] Studies indicate that most interviewers' decisions change very little after the first four or five minutes of the interview. As a result, information elicited early in the interview carries greater weight than does information elicited later, and a "good applicant" is probably characterized more by the absence of unfavorable characteristics than by the presence of favorable characteristics.

> The evidence indicates that interviewers make perceptual judgments that are often inaccurate.

Importantly, who you think is a good candidate and who I think is one may differ markedly. Because interviews usually have so little consistent structure and interviewers vary in terms of what they are looking for in a candidate, judgments of the same candidate can vary widely. If the employment interview is an important input into the hiring decision—and it usually is—you should recognize that perceptual factors influence who is hired and eventually the quality of an organization's labor force.

Performance Expectations   There is an impressive amount of evidence that demonstrates that people will attempt to validate their perceptions of reality, even when those perceptions are faulty.[15] This characteristic is particularly relevant when we consider performance expectations on the job.

self-fulfilling prophecy

When one person inaccurately perceives a second person and the resulting expectations cause the second person to behave in ways consistent with the original perception.

The terms **self-fulfilling prophecy** or *Pygmalion effect* have evolved to characterize the fact that people's expectations determine their behavior. In other words, if a manager expects big things from his people, they're not likely to let him down. Similarly, if a manager expects people to perform minimally, they'll tend to behave so as to meet those low expectations. The result then is that the expectations become reality.

An interesting illustration of the self-fulfilling prophecy is a study undertaken with 105 soldiers in the Israeli Defense Forces who were taking a 15-week combat command course.[16] The four course instructors were told that one-third of the specific incoming trainees had high potential, one-third had normal potential, and the potential of the rest was unknown. In reality, the trainees were randomly placed into those categories by the researchers. The results confirmed the existence of a self-fulfilling prophecy. Those trainees whom instructors were told had high potential scored significantly higher on objective achievement tests, exhibited more positive attitudes, and held their leaders in higher regard than did the other two groups. The instructors of the supposedly high-potential trainees got better results from them because the instructors expected it!

Performance Evaluation   Although the impact of performance evaluations on behavior will be discussed fully in Chapter 16, it should be pointed out here that an employee's performance appraisal is very much dependent on the perceptual process.[17] An employee's future is closely tied to his or her appraisal—promotions, pay raises, and continuation of employment are among the most obvious outcomes. The performance appraisal represents an assessment of an employee's work. Although the appraisal can be objective (e.g., a salesperson is appraised on how many dollars of sales she generates in her territory), many jobs are evaluated in subjective terms. Subjective measures are easier to implement, they provide managers with greater discretion, and many jobs do not readily lend themselves to objective measures. But subjective measures are, by definition, judgmental. The evaluator forms a general impression of an employee's work. To the degree that managers use subjective measures in appraising employees, what the evaluator perceives to be good or bad employee characteristics or behaviors will significantly influence the outcome of the appraisal.

Employee Effort   An individual's future in an organization is usually not dependent on performance alone. In many organizations, the level of an employee's effort is given high importance. Just as teachers frequently consider how hard you try in a course as well as how you perform on examinations, so often do managers. An assessment of an individual's effort is a subjective judgment susceptible to perceptual distortions and bias. If it is true, as some claim, that "more workers are fired for poor attitudes and lack of discipline than for lack of ability,"[18] then appraisal of an employee's effort may be a primary influence on his or her future in the organization.

> *Just as teachers frequently consider how hard you try in a course as well as how you perform on examinations, so often do managers.*

Employee Loyalty   Another important judgment that managers make about employees is whether or not they are loyal to the organization. Despite the general decline in employee loyalty noted in Chapter 1, few organizations appreciate it when employees, especially those in the managerial ranks, openly disparage the firm. Furthermore, in some organizations, if the word gets around that an employee is looking at other employment opportunities outside the firm, that employee may be labeled as disloyal and so may be cut off from all future advancement opportunities. The issue is not whether organizations are right in demanding loyalty. The issue is that many do, and that assessment of an employee's loyalty or commitment is highly judgmental. What is perceived as loyalty by one decision maker may be seen as excessive conformity by another. An employee who questions a top-management decision may be seen as disloyal by some, yet caring and concerned by others. As a case in point, **whistle-blowers**—individuals who report unethical practices by their employer to outsiders—typically act out of loyalty to their organization but are perceived by management as troublemakers.[19]

whistle-blowers

Individuals who report unethical practices by their employer to outsiders.

THE LINK BETWEEN PERCEPTION AND INDIVIDUAL DECISION MAKING

Individuals in organizations make **decisions**. That is, they make choices from among two or more alternatives. Top managers, for instance, determine their organization's goals, what products or services to offer, how best to finance operations, or where to locate a new manufacturing plant. Middle- and lower-level managers determine production schedules, select new employees, and decide how pay raises are to be allocated. Of course, making decisions is not the sole province of managers. Nonmanagerial employees also make decisions that affect their jobs and the organizations for which they work. The more obvious of these decisions might include whether or not to come to work on any given day, how much effort to put forward once at work, and whether or not to comply with a request made by the boss. In addition, an increasing number of organizations in recent years have been empowering their nonmanagerial employees with job-related decision-making authority that historically was reserved for managers alone. Individual decision making, therefore, is an important part of organizational behavior. But how individuals in organizations make decisions and the quality of their final choices are largely influenced by their perceptions.

decisions

The choices made from among two or more alternatives.

problem

A discrepancy between some current state of affairs and some desired state.

Decision making occurs as a reaction to a **problem**. That is, there is a discrepancy between some current state of affairs and some desired state, requiring consideration of alternative courses of action. So if your car breaks down and you rely on it to get to school, you have a problem that requires a decision on your part. Unfortunately, most problems don't come neatly packaged with a label "problem" clearly displayed on them. One person's *problem* is another person's *satisfactory state of affairs*. One manager may view her division's 2 percent decline in quarterly sales to be a serious problem requiring immediate action on her part. In contrast, her counterpart in another division of the same company, who also had a 2 percent sales decrease, may consider that percentage quite acceptable. So the awareness that a problem exists and that a decision needs to be made is a perceptual issue.

Entrepreneurs often launch startups to solve a problem. Rachel Bell and Sara Sutton decided to start their own company when they had a problem finding a summer internship during college. They cofounded JobDirect, an Internet job service for entry-level positions. Bell and Sutton correctly perceived that other college students shared their problem. Their service now lists 80,000 resumes, and more than 100 companies use JobDirect to recruit employees.

Moreover, every decision requires interpretation and evaluation of information. Data are typically received from multiple sources and they need to be screened, processed, and interpreted. Which data, for instance, are relevant to the decision and which are not? The perceptions of the decision maker will answer that question. Alternatives will be developed, and the strengths and weaknesses of each will need to be evaluated. Again, because alternatives don't come with "red flags" identifying them as such or with their strengths and weaknesses clearly marked, the individual decision maker's perceptual process will have a large bearing on the final outcome.

HOW SHOULD DECISIONS BE MADE?

Let's begin by describing how individuals should behave in order to maximize or optimize a certain outcome. We call this the *rational decision-making process*.

THE RATIONAL DECISION-MAKING PROCESS

rational

Refers to choices that are consistent and value maximizing.

rational decision-making model

A decision-making model that describes how individuals should behave in order to maximize some outcome.

The optimizing decision maker is **rational**. That is, he or she makes consistent, value-maximizing choices within specified constraints.[20] These choices are made following a six-step **rational decision-making model**.[21] Moreover, specific assumptions underlie this model.

The Rational Model The six steps in the rational decision-making model are listed in Exhibit 5-4.

The model begins by *defining the problem*. As noted previously, a problem exists when there is a discrepancy between an existing and a desired state of affairs.[22] If you calculate your monthly expenses and find you're spending $50 more than you allocated in your budget, you have defined a problem. Many poor decisions can be traced to the decision maker overlooking a problem or defining the wrong problem.

Once a decision maker has defined the problem, he or she needs to *identify the decision criteria* that will be important in solving the problem. In this step, the decision maker determines what is relevant in making the decision. This step brings the decision maker's interests, values, and similar personal preferences into the process. Identifying criteria is important because what one person thinks is relevant another person may not. Also keep in mind that any factors not identified in this step are considered irrelevant to the decision maker.

The criteria identified are rarely all equal in importance. So the third step requires the decision maker to *weight the previously identified criteria* in order to give them the correct priority in the decision.

Steps in the Rational Decision-Making Model
1. Define the problem.
2. Identify the decision criteria.
3. Allocate weights to the criteria.
4. Develop the alternatives.
5. Evaluate the alternatives.
6. Select the best alternative.

EXHIBIT 5-4

The fourth step requires the decision maker to *generate possible alternatives* that could succeed in resolving the problem. No attempt is made in this step to appraise these alternatives, only to list them.

Once the alternatives have been generated, the decision maker must critically analyze and evaluate each one. This is done by *rating each alternative on each criterion*. The strengths and weaknesses of each alternative become evident as they are compared with the criteria and weights established in the second and third steps.

The final step in this model requires *computing the optimal decision*. This is done by evaluating each alternative against the weighted criteria and selecting the alternative with the highest total score.

Assumptions of the Model The rational decision-making model we just described contains a number of assumptions.[23] Let's briefly outline those assumptions.

1. *Problem clarity*. The problem is clear and unambiguous. The decision maker is assumed to have complete information regarding the decision situation.
2. *Known options*. It is assumed the decision maker can identify all the relevant criteria and can list all the viable alternatives. Furthermore, the decision maker is aware of all the possible consequences of each alternative.
3. *Clear preferences*. Rationality assumes that the criteria and alternatives can be ranked and weighted to reflect their importance.
4. *Constant preferences*. It's assumed that the specific decision criteria are constant and that the weights assigned to them are stable over time.
5. *No time or cost constraints*. The rational decision maker can obtain full information about criteria and alternatives because it's assumed that there are no time or cost constraints.
6. *Maximum payoff*. The rational decision maker will choose the alternative that yields the highest perceived value.

IMPROVING CREATIVITY IN DECISION MAKING

The rational decision maker needs **creativity**, that is, the ability to produce novel and useful ideas.[24] These are ideas that are different from what's been done before but that are also appropriate to the problem or opportunity presented. Why is creativity important to decision making? It allows the decision maker to more fully appraise and understand the problem, including seeing problems others can't see. However, creativity's most obvious value is in helping the decision maker identify all viable alternatives.

creativity
The ability to produce novel and useful ideas.

Creative Potential Most people have creative potential that they can use when confronted with a decision-making problem. But to unleash that potential, they have to get out of the psychological ruts most of us get into and learn how to think about a problem in divergent ways.

We can start with the obvious. People differ in their inherent creativity. Einstein, Edison, Picasso, and Mozart were individuals of exceptional creativity. Not surprisingly, exceptional creativity is scarce. A study of lifetime creativity of 461 men and women found that fewer than 1 percent were exceptionally creative.[25] But 10 percent were highly creative and about 60 percent were somewhat creative. This suggests that most of us have creative potential, if we can learn to unleash it.

Three-Component Model of Creativity   Given that most people have the capacity to be at least moderately creative, what can individuals and organizations do to stimulate employee creativity? The best answer to this question lies in the **three-component model of creativity**.[26] Based on an extensive body of research, this model proposes that individual creativity essentially requires expertise, creative-thinking skills, and intrinsic task motivation (see Exhibit 5-5). Studies confirm that the higher the level is of each of these three components, the higher the creativity is.

Expertise is the foundation for all creative work. Picasso's understanding of art and Einstein's knowledge of physics were necessary conditions for them to be able to make creative contributions to their fields. And you wouldn't expect someone with a minimal knowledge of programming to be very creative as a software engineer. The potential for creativity is enhanced when individuals have abilities, knowledge, proficiencies, and similar expertise in their fields of endeavor.

The second component is *creative-thinking skills*. This encompasses personality characteristics associated with creativity, the ability to use analogies, as well as the talent to see the familiar in a different light. For instance, the following individual traits have been found to be associated with the development of creative ideas: intelligence, independence, self-confidence, risk taking, an internal locus of control, tolerance for ambiguity, and perseverance in the face of frustration.[27] The effective use of analogies allows decision makers to apply an idea from one context to another. One of the most famous examples in which analogy resulted in a creative breakthrough was Alexander Graham Bell's observation that it might be possible to take concepts that operate in the ear and apply them to his "talking box." He noticed that the bones in the ear are operated by a delicate, thin membrane. He wondered why, then, a thicker and strong piece of membrane shouldn't be able to move a piece of steel. Out of that analogy, the telephone was conceived. Of course, some people have developed their skill at being able to see problems in a new way. They're able to make the strange familiar and the familiar strange.[28] For instance, most of us think of hens laying eggs. But how many of us have considered that a hen is only an egg's way of making another egg?

three-component model of creativity

Proposes that individual creativity requires expertise, creative-thinking skills, and intrinsic task motivation.

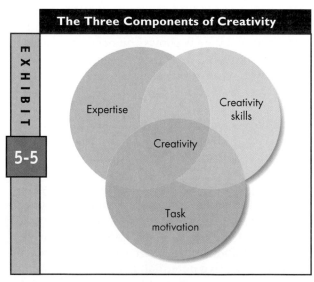

The Three Components of Creativity

EXHIBIT

5-5

Expertise

Creativity skills

Creativity

Task motivation

Source: T. M. Amabile, "Motivating Creativity in Organizations," *California Management Review*, Fall 1997, p. 43.

The final component in our model is *intrinsic task motivation*. This is the desire to work on something because it's interesting, involving, exciting, satisfying, or personally challenging. This motivational component is what turns creativity *potential* into *actual* creative ideas. It determines the extent to which individuals fully engage their expertise and creative skills. So creative people often love their work, to the point of seeming obsessed. Importantly, an individual's work environment can have a significant effect on intrinsic motivation. Specifically, five organizational factors have been found that can impede your creativity: (1) expected evaluation—focusing on how your work is going to be evaluated; (2) surveillance—being watched while you're working; (3) external motivators—emphasizing external, tangible rewards; (4) competition—facing win-lose situations with peers; and (5) constrained choice—being given limits on how you can do your work.[29]

The work environment at the headquarters of children's television channel Nickelodeon inspires creativity. It's designed as a fantasyland where employees can leave their adult inhibitions behind and immerse themselves in kid's culture. Meeting areas with overstuffed couches and lots of toys inspire creative brainstorming sessions.

HOW ARE DECISIONS ACTUALLY MADE IN ORGANIZATIONS?

Are decision makers in organizations rational? Do they carefully assess problems, identify all relevant criteria, use their creativity to identify all viable alternatives, and painstakingly evaluate every alternative to find an optimizing choice? When decision makers are faced with a simple problem having few alternative courses of action, and when the cost of searching out and evaluating alternatives is low, the rational model provides a fairly accurate description of the decision process.[30] But such situations are the exception. Most decisions in the real world don't follow the rational model. For instance, people are usually content to find an acceptable or reasonable solution to their problem rather than an optimizing one. As such, decision makers generally make limited use of their creativity. Choices tend to be confined to the neighborhood of the problem symptom and to the neighborhood of the current alternative. As one expert in decision making recently concluded: "Most significant decisions are made by judgment, rather than by a defined prescriptive model."[31]

The following reviews a large body of evidence to provide you with a more accurate description of how most decisions in organizations are actually made.[32]

BOUNDED RATIONALITY

When you considered which college to attend, did you look at *every* viable alternative? Did you carefully identify *all* the criteria that were important in your decision? Did you evaluate *each* alternative against the criteria in order to find the optimum college? I expect the answers to these questions is probably No. Well, don't feel badly. Few people made their college choice this way. Instead of optimizing, you probably satisficed.

When faced with a complex problem, most people respond by reducing the problem to a level at which it can be readily understood. This is because the limited information processing capability of human beings makes it impossible to assimilate and understand all the information necessary to optimize. So people *satisfice*; that is, they seek solutions that are satisfactory and sufficient.

Since the capacity of the human mind for formulating and solving complex problems is far too small to meet the requirements for full rationality, individuals operate within the confines of **bounded rationality**. They construct simplified models that extract the essential features from problems without capturing all their complexity.[33] Individuals can then behave rationally within the limits of the simple model.

How does bounded rationality work for the typical individual? Once a problem is identified, the search for criteria and alternatives begins. But the list of criteria is likely to be far from exhaustive. The decision maker will identify a limited list made up of the more conspicuous choices. These are the choices that are easy to find and that tend to be highly visible. In most cases, they will represent familiar criteria and previously tried-and-true solutions. Once this limited set of alternatives is identified, the decision maker will begin reviewing it. But the review will not be comprehensive—not all the alternatives will be carefully evaluated. Instead, the decision maker will begin with alternatives that differ only in a relatively small degree from the choice currently in effect. Following along familiar and well-worn paths, the decision maker proceeds to review alternatives only until he or she identifies an alternative that is "good enough"—one that meets an acceptable level of performance. The first alternative that meets the "good enough" criterion ends the search. So the final solution represents a satisficing choice rather than an optimum one.

One of the more interesting aspects of bounded rationality is that the order in which alternatives are considered is critical in determining which alternative is selected. Remember, in the fully rational decision-making model, all alternatives are eventually listed in a hierarchy of preferred order. Because all alternatives are considered, the initial order in which they are evaluated is irrelevant. Every potential solution would get a full and complete evaluation. But this isn't the case with bounded rationality. Assuming that a problem has more than one potential solution, the satisficing choice will be the first *acceptable* one the decision maker encounters. Since decision makers use simple and limited models, they typically begin by identifying alternatives that are obvious, ones with which they are familiar, and those not too far from the status quo. Those solutions that depart least from the status quo and meet the decision criteria are most likely to be selected. A unique and creative alternative may present an optimizing solution to the problem; however, it's unlikely to be chosen because an acceptable solution will be identified well before the decision maker is required to search very far beyond the status quo.

INTUITION

Joe Garcia has just committed his corporation to spend in excess of $40 million to build a new plant in Atlanta to manufacture electronic components for satellite communication equipment. As vice president of operations for his firm, Joe had before him a comprehensive analysis of five possible plant locations developed by a site location consulting firm he had hired. This report ranked the Atlanta location third among the five alternatives. After carefully reading the report and its conclusions, Joe decided against the consultant's recommendation. When asked to explain his decision, Joe said, "I looked the report over very carefully. But in spite of its recommendation, I felt that the numbers didn't tell the whole

bounded rationality

Individuals make decisions by constructing simplified models that extract the essential features from problems without capturing all their complexity.

[
In bounded rationality, the final solution represents a satisficing choice rather than an optimum one.
]

story. Intuitively, I just sensed that Atlanta would prove to be the best bet over the long run."

Intuitive decision making, like that used by Joe Garcia, has recently come out of the closet and into some respectability. Experts no longer automatically assume that using intuition to make decisions is irrational or ineffective.[34] There is growing recognition that rational analysis has been overemphasized and that, in certain instances, relying on intuition can improve decision making.

What do we mean by intuitive decision making? There are a number of ways to conceptualize intuition.[35] For instance, some consider it a form of extrasensory power or sixth sense, and some believe it is a personality trait that a limited number of people are born with. For our purposes, we define **intuitive decision making** as an unconscious process created out of distilled experience. It doesn't necessarily operate independently of rational analysis; rather, the two complement each other.

Research on chess playing provides an excellent example of how intuition works.[36] Novice chess players and grandmasters were shown an actual, but unfamiliar, chess game with about 25 pieces on the board. After five or ten seconds, the pieces were removed and each was asked to reconstruct the pieces by position. On average, the grandmaster could put 23 or 24 pieces in their correct squares, while the novice was able to replace only six. Then the exercise was changed. This time the pieces were placed randomly on the board. Again, the novice got only about six correct, but so did the grandmaster! The second exercise demonstrated that the grandmaster didn't have any better memory than the novice. What he did have was the ability, based on the experience of having played thousands of chess games, to recognize patterns and clusters of pieces that occur on chessboards in the course of games. Studies further show that chess professionals can play 50 or more games simultaneously, where decisions often must be made in only seconds, and exhibit only a moderately lower level of skill than when playing one game under tournament conditions, where decisions take half an hour or longer. The expert's experience allows him or her to recognize the pattern in a situation and draw upon previously learned information associated with that pattern to quickly arrive at a decision choice. The result is that the intuitive decision maker can decide rapidly with what appears to be very limited information.

When are people most likely to use intuitive decision making? Eight conditions have been identified: (1) when a high level of uncertainty exists; (2) when there is little precedent to draw on; (3) when variables are less scientifically predictable; (4) when "facts" are limited; (5) when facts don't clearly point the way to go; (6) when analytical data are of little use; (7) when there are several plausible alternative solutions from which to choose, with good arguments for each; and (8) when time is limited and there is pressure to come up with the right decision.[37]

Movie director and producer Steven Spielberg (left) is an intuitive decision maker. He describes his decision to make a movie this way: "The process for me is mostly intuitive. There are films that I feel I need to make, for a variety of reasons, for personal reasons, for reasons that I want to have fun, that the subject matter is cool, that I think my kids will like it. And sometimes I just think that it will make a lot of money, like the sequel to Jurassic Park." Spielberg's intuition works well. He is recognized as Hollywood's most successful director and producer. Spielberg is shown here directing Schindler's List, which won an Academy Award for Best Picture and Best Director.

Although intuitive decision making has gained in respectability, don't expect people—especially in North America, Great Britain, and other cultures in which rational analysis is the approved way of making decisions—to acknowledge they are using it. People with strong intuitive abilities don't usually tell their colleagues how they reached their conclusions. Since rational analysis is considered more socially desirable, intuitive ability is often disguised or hidden. As one top executive commented, "Sometimes one must dress up a gut decision in 'data clothes' to make it acceptable or palatable, but this fine-tuning is usually after the fact of the decision."[38]

PROBLEM IDENTIFICATION

As suggested earlier, problems don't come with flashing neon lights to identify themselves. And one person's *problem* is another person's *acceptable status quo*. So how do decision makers identify and select problems?

Problems that are visible tend to have a higher probability of being selected than ones that are important.[39] Why? We can offer at least two reasons. First, visible problems are more likely to catch a decision maker's attention. This explains why politicians are more likely to talk about the "crime problem" than the "illiteracy problem." Second, remember we're concerned with decision making in organizations. Decision makers want to appear competent and "on top of problems." This motivates them to focus attention on problems that are visible to others.

Don't ignore the decision maker's self-interest. If a decision maker faces a conflict between selecting a problem that is important to the organization and one that is important to the decision maker, self-interest tends to win out.[40] This also ties in with the issue of visibility. It's usually in a decision maker's best interest to attack high-profile problems. It conveys to others that things are under control. Moreover, when the decision maker's performance is later reviewed, the evaluator is more likely to give a high rating to someone who has been aggressively attacking visible problems than to someone whose actions have been less obvious.

ALTERNATIVE DEVELOPMENT

Since decision makers rarely seek an optimum solution, but rather a satisficing one, we should expect to find a minimal use of creativity in the search for alternatives. And that expectation is generally on target.

Efforts will be made to try to keep the search process simple. It will tend to be confined to the neighborhood of the current alternative. More complex search behavior, which includes the development of creative alternatives, will be resorted to only when a simple search fails to uncover a satisfactory alternative.

Rather than formulating new and unique problem definitions and alternatives, with frequent journeys into unfamiliar territory, the evidence indicates that decision making is incremental rather than comprehensive.[41] This means decision makers avoid the difficult task of considering all the important factors, weighing their relative merits and drawbacks, and calculating the value for each alternative. Instead, they make successive limited comparisons. This simplifies decision choices by comparing only those alternatives that differ in relatively small degrees from the choice currently in effect.

The picture that emerges is one of a decision maker who takes small steps toward his or her objective. Acknowledging the noncomprehensive nature of choice selection, decision makers make successive comparisons because decisions are never made forever and written in stone, but rather decisions are made and remade endlessly in small comparisons between narrow choices.

MAKING CHOICES

In order to avoid information overload, decision makers rely on **heuristics** or judgmental shortcuts in decision making.[42] There are two common categories of heuristics—availability and representativeness. Each creates biases in judgment. Another bias that decision makers often have is the tendency to escalate commitment to a failing course of action.

heuristics
Judgmental shortcuts in decision making.

Availability Heuristic Many more people suffer from fear of flying than fear of driving in a car. The reason is that many people think flying is more dangerous. It isn't, of course. With apologies ahead of time for this graphic example, if flying on a commercial airline was as dangerous as driving, the equivalent of two 747s filled to capacity would have to crash every week, killing all aboard, to match the risk of being killed in a car accident. But the media give a lot more attention to air accidents, so we tend to overstate the risk in flying and understate the risk in driving.

This illustrates an example of the **availability heuristic**, which is the tendency for people to base their judgments on information that is readily available to them. Events that evoke emotions, that are particularly vivid, or that have occurred more recently tend to be more available in our memory. As a result, we tend to be prone to overestimating unlikely events such as an airplane crash. The availability heuristic can also explain why managers, when doing annual performance appraisals, tend to give more weight to recent behaviors of an employee than those behaviors of six or nine months ago.

availability heuristic
The tendency for people to base their judgments on information that is readily available to them.

Representative Heuristic Literally millions of inner-city, African American boys in the United States talk about the goal of playing basketball in the NBA. In reality, they have a far better chance of becoming medical doctors than they do of

representative heuristic

Assessing the likelihood of an occurrence by drawing analogies and seeing identical situations in which they don't exist.

escalation of commitment

An increased commitment to a previous decision in spite of negative information.

playing in the NBA, but these kids are suffering from a **representative heuristic**. They tend to assess the likelihood of an occurrence by trying to match it with a preexisting category. They hear about a boy from their neighborhood 10 years ago who went on to play professional basketball. Or they watch NBA games on television and think that those players are like them. We all are guilty of using this heuristic at times. Managers, for example, frequently predict the performance of a new product by relating it to a previous product's success. Or if three graduates from the same college were hired and turned out to be poor performers, managers may predict that a current job applicant from the same college will not be a good employee.

Escalation of Commitment Another bias that creeps into decisions in practice is a tendency to escalate commitment when a decision stream represents a series of decisions.[43] **Escalation of commitment** is an increased commitment to a previous decision in spite of negative information. For example, a friend of mine had been dating a woman for about four years. Although he admitted that things weren't going too well in the relationship, he informed me that he was going to marry the woman. A bit surprised by his decision, I asked him why. He responded: "I have a lot invested in the relationship!"

It has been well documented that individuals escalate commitment to a failing course of action when they view themselves as responsible for the failure. That is, they "throw good money after bad" to demonstrate that their initial decision wasn't wrong and to avoid having to admit they made a mistake. Escalation of commitment is also congruent with evidence that people try to appear consistent in what they say and do. Increasing commitment to previous actions conveys consistency.

Escalation of commitment has obvious implications for managerial decisions. Many an organization has suffered large losses because a manager was determined to prove his or her original decision was right by continuing to commit resources to what was a lost cause from the beginning. Additionally, consistency is a characteristic often associated with effective leaders. So managers, in an effort to appear effective, may be motivated to be consistent when switching to another course of action may be preferable. In actuality, effective managers are those who are able to differentiate between situations in which persistence will pay off and situations in which it will not.

INDIVIDUAL DIFFERENCES: DECISION-MAKING STYLES

Put Chad and Sean into the same decision situation and Chad almost always seems to take longer to come to a solution. Chad's final choices aren't necessarily always better than Sean's, he's just slower in processing information. Additionally, if there's an obvious risk dimension in the decision, Sean seems to consistently prefer a riskier option than does Chad. What this illustrates is that all of us bring our individual style to the decisions we make.

Research on decision styles has identified four different individual approaches to making decisions.[44] This model was designed to be used by managers and aspiring managers, but its general framework can be used by any individual decision maker.

The basic foundation of the model is the recognition that people differ along two dimensions. The first is their way of *thinking*. Some people are logical and rational. They process information serially. In contrast, some people are intuitive and creative. They perceive things as a whole. Note that these differences are above and beyond general human limitations such as we described regarding bounded rationality. The other dimension addresses a person's *tolerance for ambiguity*. Some people have a high need to structure information in ways that minimize ambiguity, while others are able to process many thoughts at the same time. When these two dimensions are diagrammed, they form four styles of decision making (see Exhibit 5-6). These are directive, analytic, conceptual, and behavioral.

People using the *directive* style have low tolerance for ambiguity and seek rationality. They are efficient and logical, but their efficiency concerns result in decisions made with minimal information and with few alternatives assessed. Directive types make decisions fast and they focus on the short run.

The *analytic* type has a much greater tolerance for ambiguity than do directive decision makers. This leads to the desire for more information and consideration of more alternatives than is true for directives. Analytic managers would be best characterized as careful decision makers with the ability to adapt to or cope with new situations.

Individuals with a *conceptual* style tend to be very broad in their outlook and consider many alternatives. Their focus is long range and they are very good at finding creative solutions to problems.

The final category—the *behavioral* style—characterizes decision makers who work well with others. They're concerned with the achievement of peers and those working for them and are receptive to suggestions from others, relying heavily on meetings for communicating. This type of manager tries to avoid conflict and seeks acceptance.

Although these four categories are distinct, most managers have characteristics that fall into more than one. It's probably best to think in terms of a manager's dominant style and his or her backup styles. Some managers rely almost exclusively on their dominant style; however, more flexible managers can make shifts depending on the situation.

Business students, lower-level managers, and top executives tend to score highest in the analytic style. That's not surprising given the emphasis that formal education, particularly business education, gives to developing rational thinking. For instance, courses in accounting, statistics, and finance all stress rational analysis.

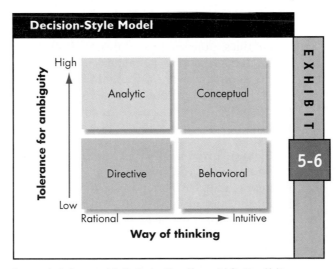

Decision-Style Model

Tolerance for ambiguity

High — Analytic | Conceptual

Low — Directive | Behavioral

Rational ⟶ Intuitive

Way of thinking

EXHIBIT

5-6

Source: A. J. Rowe and J. D. Boulgarides, *Managerial Decision Making*,
© 1992 Prentice Hall, Upper Saddle River, NJ, p. 29.

In addition to providing a framework for looking at individual differences, focusing on decision styles can be useful for helping you to understand how two equally intelligent people, with access to the same information, can differ in the ways they approach decisions and the final choices they make.

ORGANIZATIONAL CONSTRAINTS

The organization itself constrains decision makers. Managers, for instance, shape their decisions to reflect the organization's performance evaluation and reward system, to comply with the organization's formal regulations, and to meet organizationally imposed time constraints. Previous organizational decisions also act as precedents to constrain current decisions.

Performance Evaluation Managers are strongly influenced in their decision making by the criteria by which they are evaluated. If a division manager believes that the manufacturing plants under his responsibility are operating best when he hears nothing negative, we shouldn't be surprised to find his plant managers spending a good part of their time ensuring that negative information doesn't reach the division boss. Similarly, if a college dean believes that an instructor should never fail more than 10 percent of her students—to fail more reflects on the instructor's ability to teach—we should expect that new instructors, who want to receive favorable evaluations, will decide not to fail too many students.

Reward Systems The organization's reward system influences decision makers by suggesting to them what choices are preferable in terms of personal payoff. For example, if the organization rewards risk aversion, managers are more likely to make conservative decisions. From the 1930s through the mid-1980s, General Motors consistently gave out promotions and bonuses to those managers who kept a low profile, avoided controversy, and were good team players. The result was that GM managers became very adept at dodging tough issues and passing controversial decisions on to committees.

Formal Regulations David Gonzalez, a shift manager at a Taco Bell restaurant in San Antonio, Texas, describes constraints he faces on his job: "I've got rules and regulations covering almost every decision I make—from how to make a burrito to how often I need to clean the restrooms. My job doesn't come with much freedom of choice."

David's situation is not unique. All but the smallest of organizations create rules, policies, procedures, and other formalized regulations in order to standardize the behavior of their members. By programming decisions, organizations are able to get individuals to achieve high levels of performance without paying for the years of experience that would be necessary in the absence of regulations. And of course, in so doing, they limit the decision maker's choices.

System-Imposed Time Constraints Organizations impose deadlines on decisions. For instance, department budgets need to be completed by next Friday. Or the report on new-product development has to be ready for the executive committee to review by the first of the month. A host of decisions must be made quickly in order to stay ahead of the competition and keep customers satisfied. And almost all important decisions come with explicit deadlines. These conditions create time pressures on decision makers and often make it difficult, if not impossible, to gather all the information they might like to have before making a final choice.

BankAmerica has a legacy of racial and ethnic diversity. Its founder came to the United States from Italy and started the bank specifically to serve Italian, Chinese, Japanese, Swiss, and other immigrants. Today, BankAmerica continues its quest for diversity. Managers are evaluated according to how well they support the bank's diversity initiatives in making hiring and promotion decisions. Shown here is Hugh McColl, CEO of BankAmerica, greeting an employee.

Historical Precedents Decisions aren't made in a vacuum. They have a context. In fact, individual decisions are more accurately characterized as points in a stream of decisions.

Decisions made in the past are ghosts that continually haunt current choices. For instance, commitments made in the past constrain current options. To use a social situation as an example, the decision you might make after meeting "Mr. or Ms. Right" is more complicated if you're already married than if you're single. Prior commitments—in this case, having chosen to get married—constrain your options. Government budget decisions also offer an illustration of our point. It's common knowledge that the largest determining factor of the size of any given year's budget is last year's budget.[45] Choices made today, therefore, are largely a result of choices made over the years.

> *Decisions made in the past are ghosts that continually haunt current choices.*

CULTURAL DIFFERENCES

The rational model makes no acknowledgment of cultural differences. But Arabs, for instance, don't necessarily make decisions the same way that Canadians do. Therefore, we need to recognize that the cultural background of the decision maker can have significant influence on his or her selection of problems, depth of analysis, the importance placed on logic and rationality, or whether organizational decisions should be made autocratically by an individual manager or collectively in groups.[46]

Cultures, for example, differ in terms of time orientation, the importance of rationality, their belief in the ability of people to solve problems, and preference for collective decision making. Differences in time orientation help us understand why managers in Egypt will make decisions at a much slower and more deliberate pace than their American counterparts. While rationality is valued in North America, that's not true everywhere in the world. A North American manager might make an important decision intuitively, but he or she knows that it's important to appear to proceed in a rational fashion. This is because rationality is highly valued in the West. In countries such as Iran, where rationality is not deified, efforts to appear rational are not necessary.

Some cultures emphasize solving problems, while others focus on accepting situations as they are. The United States falls in the former category, while Thailand and Indonesia are examples of cultures that fall into the latter. Because problem-solving managers believe they can and should change situations to their benefit, American managers might identify a problem long before their Thai or Indonesian counterparts would choose to recognize it as such.

Decision making by Japanese managers is much more group oriented than in the United States. The Japanese value conformity and cooperation. So before Japanese CEOs make an important decision, they collect a large amount of information, which is then used in consensus-forming group decisions.

WHAT ABOUT ETHICS IN DECISION MAKING?

No contemporary discussion of decision making would be complete without inclusion of ethics because ethical considerations should be an important criterion in organizational decision making. In this final section, we present three different ways to ethically frame decisions and look at the factors that shape an individual's ethical decision-making behavior.

THREE ETHICAL DECISION CRITERIA

utilitarianism

Decisions are made so as to provide the greatest good for the greatest number.

An individual can use three different criteria in making ethical choices.[47] The first is the *utilitarian* criterion, in which decisions are made solely on the basis of their outcomes or consequences. The goal of **utilitarianism** is to provide the greatest good for the greatest number. This view tends to dominate business decision making. It is consistent with goals such as efficiency, productivity, and high profits. By maximizing profits, for instance, a business executive can argue he is securing the greatest good for the greatest number—as he hands out dismissal notices to 15 percent of his employees.

Another ethical criterion is to focus on *rights*. This calls on individuals to make decisions consistent with fundamental liberties and privileges as set forth in documents such as the Bill of Rights. An emphasis on rights in decision making means respecting and protecting the basic rights of individuals, such as the right to privacy, to free speech, and to due process. For instance, use of this criterion would protect whistle-blowers when they report unethical or illegal practices by their organization to the press or government agencies on the grounds of their right to free speech.

A third criterion is to focus on *justice*. This requires individuals to impose and enforce rules fairly and impartially so there is an equitable distribution of benefits and costs. Union members typically favor this view. It justifies paying people the same wage for a given job, regardless of performance differences, and using seniority as the primary determination in making layoff decisions.

Each of these three criteria has advantages and liabilities. A focus on utilitarianism promotes efficiency and productivity, but it can result in ignoring the rights of some individuals, particularly those with minority representation in the organization. The use of rights as a criterion protects individuals from injury and is consistent with freedom and privacy, but it can create an overly legalistic work environment that hinders productivity and efficiency. A focus on justice protects the interests of the underrepresented and less powerful, but it

MYTH OR SCIENCE?

"Ethical People Don't Do Unethical Things"

This statement is mostly true. People with high ethical standards are less likely to engage in unethical practices, even in organizations or situations in which there are strong pressures to conform.

The essential issue that this statement addresses is whether ethical behavior is more a function of the individual or the situational context. The evidence indicates that people with high ethical principles will follow them in spite of what others do or the dictates of organizational norms.[48] But when an individual's ethical and moral development is not at the highest level, he or she is more likely to be influenced by strong cultures. This is true even when those cultures encourage questionable practices.

Because ethical people essentially avoid unethical practices, managers should be encouraged to screen job candidates (through testing and background investigations) to determine their ethical standards. By seeking out people with integrity and strong ethical principles, the organization increases the likelihood that employees will act ethically. Of course, unethical practices can be further minimized by providing individuals with a supportive work climate.[49] This would include clear job descriptions, a written code of ethics, positive management role models, the evaluating and rewarding of means as well as ends, and a culture that encourages individuals to openly challenge questionable practices.

can encourage a sense of entitlement that reduces risk taking, innovation, and productivity.

Decision makers, particularly in for-profit organizations, tend to feel safe and comfortable when they use utilitarianism. A lot of questionable actions can be justified when framed as being in the best interests of "the organization" and stockholders. But many critics of business decision makers argue that this perspective needs to change.[50] Increased concern in society about individual rights and social justice suggests the need for managers to develop ethical standards based on nonutilitarian criteria. This presents a solid challenge to today's managers because making decisions using criteria such as individual rights and social justice involves far more ambiguities than using utilitarian criteria such as effects on efficiency and profits. This helps to explain why managers are increasingly criticized for their actions. Raising prices, selling products with questionable effects on consumer health, closing down plants, laying off large numbers of employees, moving production overseas to cut costs, and similar decisions can be justified in utilitarian terms. But that may no longer be the single criterion by which good decisions should be judged.

ETHICS AND NATIONAL CULTURE

What is seen as an ethical decision in China may not be seen as such in Canada. The reason is that there are no global ethical standards. Contrasts between Asia and the West provide an illustration.[51] Because bribery is commonplace in countries such as China, a Canadian working in China might face the dilemma: Should I pay a bribe to secure business if it is an accepted part of that country's culture? Or how about this for a shock? A manager of a large U.S. company operating in China caught an employee stealing. Following company policy, she fired him and turned him over to the local authorities. Later, she was horrified to learn that the employee had been summarily executed.[52]

While ethical standards may seem ambiguous in the West, criteria defining right and wrong are actually much clearer in the West than in Asia. Few issues are black and white there; most are gray. The need for global organizations to establish ethical principles for decision makers in countries such as India and China, and to modify them to reflect cultural norms, may be critical if high standards are to be upheld and if consistent practices are to be achieved.

SUMMARY AND IMPLICATIONS FOR MANAGERS

PERCEPTION

Individuals behave in a given manner based not on the way their external environment actually is but, rather, on what they see or believe it to be. An organization may spend millions of dollars to create a pleasant work environment for its employees. However, in spite of these expenditures, if an employee believes that his or her job is lousy, that employee will behave accordingly. It is the employee's perception of a situation that becomes the basis for his or her behavior. The employee who perceives his or her supervisor as a hurdle reducer who helps him or her do a better job and the employee who sees the same supervisor as "big brother, closely monitoring every motion, to ensure that I keep working" will differ in their behavioral responses to their supervisor. The difference has nothing to do with the reality of the supervisor's actions; the difference in employee behavior is due to different perceptions.

The evidence suggests that what individuals perceive from their work situation will influence their productivity more than will the situation itself. Whether or not a job is actually interesting or challenging is irrelevant. Whether or not a manager successfully plans and organizes the work of his or her employees and actually helps them to structure their work more efficiently and effectively is far less important than how employees perceive the manager's efforts. Similarly, issues such as fair pay for work performed, the validity of performance appraisals, and the adequacy of working conditions are not judged by employees in a way that assures common perceptions, nor can we be assured that individuals will interpret conditions about their jobs in a favorable light. Therefore, to be able to influence productivity, it is necessary to assess how workers perceive their jobs.

Absenteeism, turnover, and job satisfaction are also reactions to the individual's perceptions. Dissatisfaction with working conditions and the belief that there is a lack of promotion opportunities in the organization are judgments based on attempts to make some meaning out of one's job. The employee's conclusion that a job is good or bad is an interpretation. Managers must spend time understanding how each individual interprets reality and, where there is a significant difference between what is seen and what exists, try to eliminate the distortions. Failure to deal with the differences when individuals perceive the job in negative terms will result in increased absenteeism and turnover and lower job satisfaction.

INDIVIDUAL DECISION MAKING

Individuals think and reason before they act. It is because of this that an understanding of how people make decisions can be helpful for explaining and predicting their behavior.

Under some decision situations, people follow the rational decision-making model. But for most people, and most nonroutine decisions, this is probably more the exception than the rule. Few important decisions are simple or unambiguous enough for the rational model's assumptions to apply. So we find individuals looking for solutions that satisfice rather than optimize, injecting biases and prejudices into the decision process, and relying on intuition.

Given the evidence we've described on how decisions are actually made in organizations, what can managers do to improve their decision making? We offer five suggestions.

First, analyze the situation. Adjust your decision-making style to the national culture in which you're operating and to the criteria your organization evaluates and rewards. For instance, if you're in a country that doesn't value rationality, don't feel compelled to follow the rational decision-making model or even to try to make your decisions appear rational. Similarly, organizations differ in terms of the importance they place on risk, the use of groups, and the like. Adjust your decision style to ensure it's compatible with the organization's culture.

Second, be aware of biases. We all bring biases to the decisions we make. If you understand the biases influencing your judgment, you can begin to change the way you make decisions to reduce those biases.

Third, combine rational analysis with intuition. These are not conflicting approaches to decision making. By using both, you can actually improve your decision-making effectiveness. As you gain managerial experience, you should feel increasingly confident in imposing your intuitive processes on top of your rational analysis.

Fourth, don't assume that your specific decision style is appropriate for every job. Just as organizations differ, so too do jobs within organizations. And your effectiveness as a decision maker will increase if you match your decision style to the requirements of the job. For instance, if your decision-making style is directive, you'll be more effective working with people whose jobs require quick action. This style would match well with managing stockbrokers. An analytic style, on the other hand, would work well managing accountants, market researchers, or financial analysts.

Finally, try to enhance your creativity. Overtly look for novel solutions to problems, attempt to see problems in new ways, and use analogies. Additionally, try to remove work and organizational barriers that might impede your creativity.

When Hiring Employees: Emphasize the Positive

H iring new employees requires managers to become salespeople. They have to emphasize the positive, even if it means failing to mention the negative aspects in the job. While there is a real risk of setting unrealistic expectations about the organization and about the specific job, that's a risk managers have to take. As in dealing with any salesperson, it is the job applicant's responsibility to follow the dictum *caveat emptor*—let the buyer beware!

Why should managers emphasize the positive when discussing a job with a prospective candidate? They have no choice! First, there is a dwindling supply of qualified applicants for many job vacancies; and second, this approach is necessary to meet the competition.

The massive restructuring and downsizing of organizations that began in the late 1980s has drawn attention to corporate layoffs. What has often been overlooked in this process is the growing shortage of qualified applicants for literally millions of jobs. Through the foreseeable future, managers will find it increasingly difficult to get qualified people who can fill jobs such as legal secretary, nurse, accountant, salesperson, maintenance mechanic, computer-repair specialist, software programmer, social worker, physical therapist, environmental engineer, telecommunications specialist, and airline pilot. But managers will also find it harder to get qualified people to fill entry-level, minimum-wage jobs. There may be no shortage of physical bodies, but finding individuals who can read, write, perform basic mathematical calculations, and have the proper work habits to effectively perform these jobs isn't so easy. There is a growing gap between the skills workers have and the skills employers require. So managers need to *sell* jobs to the limited pool of applicants. And this means presenting the job and the organization in the most favorable light possible.

Another reason management is forced to emphasize the positive with job candidates is that this is what the competition is doing. Other employers also face a limited applicant pool. As a result, to get people to join their organizations, they are forced to put a positive "spin" on their descriptions of their organizations and the jobs they seek to fill. In this competitive environment, any employer who presents jobs realistically to applicants—that is, openly provides the negative aspects of a job along with the positive—risks losing most or all of the most desirable candidates.

R egardless of the changing labor market, managers who treat the recruiting and hiring of candidates as if the applicants must be sold on the job and exposed to only positive aspects set themselves up to have a workforce that is dissatisfied and prone to high turnover.[1]

Every applicant acquires, during the selection process, a set of expectations about the organization and about the specific job he or she hopes to be offered. When the information an applicant receives is excessively inflated, a number of things happen that have potentially negative effects on the organization. First, mismatched applicants who would probably become dissatisfied with the job and soon quit are less likely to select themselves out of the search process. Second, the absence of negative information builds unrealistic expectations. If hired, the new employee is likely to become quickly disappointed. And inaccurate perceptions lead to premature resignations. Third, new hires are prone to become disillusioned and less committed to the organization when they come face-to-face with the negatives in the job. Employees who feel they were tricked or misled during the hiring process are unlikely to be satisfied workers.

To increase job satisfaction among employees and reduce turnover, applicants should be given a realistic job preview—provided both unfavorable and favorable information—before an offer is made. For example, in addition to positive comments, the candidate might be told that there are limited opportunities to talk with co-workers during work hours, or that erratic fluctuations in workloads create considerable stress on employees during rush periods.

Research indicates that applicants who have been given a realistic job preview hold lower and more realistic expectations about the job they'll be doing and are better prepared for coping with the job and its frustrating elements. The result is fewer unexpected resignations by new employees. In a tight labor market, retaining people is as critical as hiring them in the first place. Presenting only the positive aspects of a job to a recruit may initially entice him or her to join the organization, but it may be a marriage that both parties will quickly regret.

[1] Information in this argument comes from J. A. Breaugh, "Realistic Job Previews: A Critical Appraisal and Future Research Directions," *Academy of Management Review*, October 1983, pp. 612–19; J. M. Phillips, "Effects of Realistic Job Previews on Multiple Organizational Outcomes: A Meta-Analyis," *Academy of Management Journal*, December 1998, pp. 673–90; and P. W. Hom, R. W. Griffeth, L. E. Palich, and J. S. Bracker, "Revisiting Met Expectations as a Reason Why Realistic Job Previews Work," *Personnel Psychology*, Spring 1999, pp. 97–112.

1. Define *perception*.

2. What is attribution theory? What are its implications for explaining organizational behavior?

3. How are our perceptions of our own actions different from our perceptions of the actions of others?

4. How does selectivity affect perception? Give an example of how selectivity can create perceptual distortion.

5. What is stereotyping? Give an example of how stereotyping can create perceptual distortion.

6. Give some positive results of using shortcuts when judging others.

7. What is the rational decision-making model? Under what conditions is it applicable?

8. Describe organizational factors that might constrain decision makers.

9. What role does intuition play in effective decision making?

10. Are unethical decisions more a function of the individual decision maker or the decision maker's work environment? Explain.

Questions for Critical Thinking

1. How might the differences in experiences of students and instructors affect their perceptions of students' written work and class comments?

2. An employee does an unsatisfactory job on an assigned project. Explain the attribution process that this person's manager will use to form judgments about this employee's job performance.

3. "For the most part, individual decision making in organizations is an irrational process." Do you agree or disagree? Discuss.

4. What factors do you think differentiate good decision makers from poor ones? Relate your answer to the six-step rational model.

5. Have you ever increased your commitment to a failed course of action? If so, analyze the follow-up decision to increase your commitment and explain why you behaved as you did.

Team Exercise | Biases in Decision Making

Step 1

Answer each of the following problems.

1. The following 10 corporations were ranked by *Fortune* magazine to be among the 500 largest U.S.-based firms according to sales volume for 1998:

   Group A: B. F. Goodrich, Hershey Foods, Mattel, Maytag, Quaker Oats

   Group B: Conagra, Enron, Ingram Micro, United Technologies, USX

   Which group of five organizations listed (A or B) had the larger total sales volume? By what percentage (10%, 50%, 100%, or ?) do you think the higher group's sales exceeded the lower group?

2. The best student in my introductory M.B.A class this past semester writes poetry and is rather shy and small in stature. Was the student's undergraduate major Chinese studies or psychology?

3. Which of the following causes more deaths in the United States each year?
   a. Stomach cancer
   b. Motor vehicle accidents

4. Which would you choose?
   a. A sure gain of $240
   b. A 25 percent chance of winning $1,000 and a 75 percent chance of winning nothing

5. Which would you choose?

   a. A sure loss of $750

   b. A 75 percent chance of losing $1,000 and a 25 percent chance of losing nothing

6. Which would you choose?

   a. A sure loss of $3,000

   b. An 80 percent chance of losing $4,000 and a 20 percent chance of losing nothing

Step 2   Break into groups of three to five. Compare your answers. Explain why you chose the answers that you did.

Step 3   Your instructor will give you the correct answers to each problem. Now discuss the accuracy of your decisions, the biases evident in the decisions you reached, and how you might improve your decision making to make it more accurate.

Source: These problems are based on examples provided in M. H. Bazerman, *Judgment in Managerial Decision Making*, 3rd ed. (New York: Wiley, 1994).

Ethical Dilemma | **Five Ethical Decisions: What Would You Do?**

Assume you're a middle manager in a company with about a thousand employees. How would you respond to each of the following situations?

1. You're negotiating a contract with a potentially very large customer whose representative has hinted that you could almost certainly be assured of getting his business if you gave him and his wife an all-expense-paid cruise to the Caribbean. You know the representative's employer wouldn't approve of such a "payoff," but you have the discretion to authorize such an expenditure. What would you do?

2. You have the opportunity to steal $100,000 from your company with absolute certainty that you would not be detected or caught. Would you do it?

3. Your company policy on reimbursement for meals while traveling on company business is that you will be repaid for your out-of-pocket costs, not to exceed $50 a day. You don't need receipts for these expenses—the company will take your word. When traveling, you tend to eat at fast-food places and rarely spend in excess of $15 a day. Most of your colleagues put in reimbursement requests in the range of $40 to $45 a day regardless of what their actual expenses are. How much would you request for your meal reimbursements?

4. You want to get feedback from people who are using one of your competitor's products. You believe you'll get much more honest responses from these people if you disguise the identity of your company. Your boss suggests you contact possible participants by using the fictitious name of the Consumer Marketing Research Corporation. What would you do?

5. You've discovered that one of your closest friends at work has stolen a large sum of money from the company. Would you do nothing? Go directly to an executive to report the incident before talking about it with the offender? Confront the individual before taking action? Make contact with the individual with the goal of persuading that person to return the money?

Source: Several of these scenarios are based on D. R. Altany, "Torn between Halo and Horns," *Industry Week*, March 15, 1993, pp. 15–20.

Internet Search Exercises

1. Find three articles or Web sites that describe ways to develop creative thinking skills. Do all of the techniques seem valid? How easy would it be for managers to help their employees develop creative thinking skills using these techniques?

2. Find comprehensive data that characterize the degree of ethical behavior exhibited by (a) college students and (b) employees at work. How do you interpret these findings?

We invite you to visit the Robbins homepage on the Prentice Hall Web site at **www.prenhall.com/robbins** for our on-line study guide, current events, links to related Web sites, and more.

Case Incident — Good Decisions That Went Bad?

Raymond Stubbs Jr. had driven Yellow Cabs in Boise, Idaho, for years. In 1995, he borrowed $151,000, and bought the Yellow Cab franchise. At the time, the company had about two dozen taxis, representing roughly half of Boise's total. Most were owned by drivers who paid Stubbs about $200 a week per vehicle for dispatch service.

Stubbs personally is a strong believer in customer service. He decided to make that a key element of his new business. "If you don't have the service, you aren't going to make it," he says. Stubbs urged his drivers to cultivate "personals"—regular customers who request the same driver each time. And responding to Stubbs's motto of treating passengers "as good as gold," his drivers bought their own cell phones to answer passengers' calls directly and distributed business cards listing their individual cell-phone numbers.

Meanwhile, to increase business, Stubbs was selling discounted vouchers to customers. Unfortunately, he failed to do the math. Both he and his drivers lost money on the voucher system. This created animosities toward Stubbs by the drivers.

The final blow came in April 1997. To cut costs, Stubbs ceased offering his dispatch service to those Yellow Cabs he didn't own. In response, exiled drivers went solo, joined rivals, or expanded their fleets and split off to create their own separate firms. And having followed Stubbs's dictate to build strong loyalties with their passengers, most customers went with the renegade drivers.

Facing greater competition and a decimated fleet, Stubbs now found it harder to deliver his first-rate service. "He ruined the customer relationship," said one knowledgeable observer. "The name Yellow Cab became a dirty name."

In October 1997, faced with high fixed costs and a decimated fleet, Stubbs dissolved the company and filed for bankruptcy.

Questions

1. How many decisions made by Stubbs can you find in this case? How would you rate each?

2. Which of the decisions do you think went wrong? Why?

3. How would you describe Stubbs's decision style? Explain your answer.

4. What did you learn from this case about decision making?

Source: Based on M. Hofman, "Taxi Company's Zeal for Service Backfires," *INC.*, December 1998, p. 29.

Video Case — The Fluker Cricket Farm

SMALL BUSINESS 2000

A company survives or fails based on the quality and outcome of decisions that are made by its employees and managers. Some people avoid jobs requiring a lot of decision making; others seek them out. Making sound business decisions is not easy, especially today when opportunities and markets often change very rapidly. Uncertainty may also complicate decision making for individuals and companies.

In this video segment, we trace the history of a business that faces all of the issues mentioned above and adds at least one additional twist. Richard Fluker has turned over the management of his business, the Fluker Cricket Farm, to his three children. You read the last sentence correctly; this case takes you on a tour of the Fluker Cricket Farm. You are probably wondering how hard it is to run a cricket farm—and why somebody would even want to. The answer is obvious when you consider the numbers—the Fluker Cricket Farm has annual sales in excess of $5 million, and they ship more than three million live crickets and worms around the world every week.

This company has not always been so successful. When Richard handed the company over to his children a few years ago, its annual sales were about $500,000. Since then, the Flukers have implemented many changes, most of them aimed at expanding their product lines and approaching markets that they had ignored in the past. As you might imagine, none of these initiatives happened on their own. The Flukers had to take action.

In this video case, you will learn about what it took to get the company to where it is today. You'll hear about some early decisions that influenced the formation of the original Fluker company and you'll also learn about decisions that are being made that will influence the company in the future. As you watch this case, be on the lookout for clues about why certain things were done. You may also want to think about what other options the Flukers may have had and why they didn't take them.

Questions

1. Richard Fluker talks about a decision he made in 1958 to turn his hobby as a fishing-bait farmer into a full-time job for himself. Its doubtful that this was an easy decision or one that was made without considerable thought. Discuss how Richard Fluker might have come to his decision and some of the choices he probably had to make.

2. Howard Fluker shares his ideas about decision making with us. In doing this he makes a distinction between the "big" things and the "little" things.

What do you think of his distinction between the two and of his thoughts on handling them?

3. David Fluker talks with us about attempts the company has made to expand their product line. One in particular, raising mice, didn't work out so well. What do you think about his attempt to enter this area; did he make sound decisions? Also, what do you think he meant when he said, "You've got to know when to say when"?

4. The Fluker Cricket Farm pays its employees above the industry average and provides benefits that similar businesses generally don't provide. Based on what you have learned about heuristics such as availability and representativeness, how might you explain the difference between the Fluker Cricket farm and other similar businesses? What do you think motivates the decision to provide above average compensation?

End Notes

1. Based on J. Markoff, "In About Face, Intel Will Swap Flawed Pentium Chip for Buyers," *New York Times*, December 21, 1994, p. A1; J. Carlton, "Humble Pie: Intel to Replace Its Pentium Chips," *Wall Street Journal*, December 21, 1994, p. B1; and A. Grove, "My Biggest Mistake," *INC.*, May 1998, p. 117.

2. D. C. McClelland and J. W. Atkinson, "The Projective Expression of Needs: The Effect of Different Intensities of the Hunger Drive on Perception," *Journal of Psychology*, vol. 25 (1948), pp. 205–22.

3. H. H. Kelley, "Attribution in Social Interaction," in E. Jones et al. (eds.), *Attribution: Perceiving the Causes of Behavior* (Morristown, NJ: General Learning Press, 1972).

4. See L. Ross, "The Intuitive Psychologist and His Shortcomings," in L. Berkowitz (ed.), *Advances in Experimental Social Psychology*, vol. 10 (Orlando, FL: Academic Press, 1977), pp. 174–220; and A. G. Miller and T. Lawson, "The Effect of an Informational Option on the Fundamental Attribution Error," *Personality and Social Psychology Bulletin*, June 1989, pp. 194–204.

5. See, for instance, G. R. Semin, "A Gloss on Attribution Theory," *British Journal of Social and Clinical Psychology*, November 1980, pp. 291–300; and M. W. Morris and K. Peng, "Culture and Cause: American and Chinese Attributions for Social and Physical Events," *Journal of Personality and Social Psychology*, December 1994, pp. 949–71.

6. S. Nam, "Cultural and Managerial Attributions for Group Performance," unpublished doctoral dissertation, University of Oregon, cited in R. M. Steers, S. J. Bischoff, and L. H. Higgins, "Cross-Cultural Management Research," *Journal of Management Inquiry*, December 1992, pp. 325–26.

7. D. C. Dearborn and H. A. Simon, "Selective Perception: A Note on the Departmental Identification of Executives," *Sociometry*, June 1958, pp. 140–44. Some of the conclusions in this classic study have recently been challenged in J. P. Walsh, "Selectivity and Selective Perception: An Investigation of Managers' Belief Structures and Information

Processing," *Academy of Management Journal*, December 1988, pp. 873–96; M. J. Waller, G. P. Huber, and W. H. Glick, "Functional Background as a Determinant of Executives' Selective Perception," *Academy of Management Journal*, August 1995, pp. 943–74; and J. M. Beyer, P. Chattopadhyay, E. George, W. H. Glick, dt Ogilvie, and D. Pugliese, "The Selective Perception of Managers Revisited," *Academy of Management Journal*, June 1997, pp. 716–37.

8. See K. R. Murphy and R. L. Anhalt, "Is Halo a Property of the Rater, the Ratees, or the Specific Behaviors Observed?" *Journal of Applied Psychology*, June 1992, pp. 494–500; and K. R. Murphy, R. A. Jako, and R. L. Anhalt, "Nature and Consequences of Halo Error: A Critical Analysis," *Journal of Applied Psychology*, April 1993, pp. 218–25.

9. S. E. Asch, "Forming Impressions of Personality," *Journal of Abnormal and Social Psychology*, July 1946, pp. 258–90.

10. J. S. Bruner and R. Tagiuri, "The Perception of People," in E. Lindzey (ed.), *Handbook of Social Psychology* (Reading, MA: Addison-Wesley, 1954), p. 641.

11. J. L. Hilton and W. von Hippel, "Stereotypes," in J. T. Spence, J. M. Darley, and D. J. Foss (eds.), *Annual Review of Psychology*, vol. 47 (Palo Alto, CA: Annual Reviews Inc., 1996), pp. 237–71.

12. See, for example, C. M. Judd and B. Park, "Definition and Assessment of Accuracy in Social Stereotypes," *Psychological Review*, January 1993, pp. 109–28.

13. See, for example, S. T. Fiske, D. N. Beroff, E. Borgida, K. Deaux, and M. E. Heilman, "Use of Sex Stereotyping Research in Price Waterhouse vs. Hopkins," *American Psychologist*, October 1991, pp. 1049–60; G. N. Powell, "The Good Manager: Business Students' Stereotypes of Japanese Managers versus Stereotypes of American Managers," *Group & Organizational Management*, March 1992, pp. 44–56; and K. J. Gibson, W. J. Zerbe, and R. E. Franken, "Job Search Strategies for Older Job Hunters: Addressing Employers' Perceptions," *Canadian Journal of Counseling*, July 1992, pp. 166–76.

14. See, for example, E. C. Webster, *Decision Making in the Employment Interview* (Montreal: McGill University, Industrial Relations Center, 1964).

15. See, for example, L. Jussim, "Self-Fulfilling Prophecies: A Theoretical and Integrative Review," *Psychological Review*, October 1986, pp. 429–45; D. Eden, *Pygmalion in Management* (Lexington, MA: Lexington, 1990); and D. Eden, "Leadership and Expectations: Pygmalion Effects and Other Self-Fulfilling Prophecies," *Leadership Quarterly*, Winter 1992, pp. 271–305.

16. D. Eden and A. B. Shani, "Pygmalion Goes to Boot Camp: Expectancy, Leadership, and Trainee Performance," *Journal of Applied Psychology*, April 1982, pp. 194–99.

17. See, for example, R. D. Bretz Jr., G. T. Milkovich, and W. Read, "The Current State of Performance Appraisal Research and Practice: Concerns, Directions, and Implications," *Journal of Management*, June 1992, pp. 323–24; and P. M. Swiercz, M. L. Icenogle, N. B. Bryan, and R. W. Renn, "Do Perceptions of Performance Appraisal Fairness Predict Employee Attitudes and Performance?" in D. P. Moore (ed.), *Proceedings of the Academy of Management* (Atlanta: Academy of Management, 1993), pp. 304–08.

18. D. Kipnis, *The Powerholders* (Chicago: University of Chicago Press, 1976).

19. See J. P. Near and M. P. Miceli, "Whistle-Blowers in Organizations: Dissidents or Reformers?" in L. L. Cummings and B. M. Staw (eds.), *Research in Organizational Behavior*, vol. 9 (Greenwich, CT: JAI Press, 1987), pp. 321–68.

20. See H. A. Simon, "Rationality in Psychology and Economics," *The Journal of Business*, October 1986, pp. 209–24; and A. Langley, "In Search of Rationality: The Purposes Behind the Use of Formal Analysis in Organizations," *Administrative Science Quarterly*, December 1989, pp. 598–631.

21. For a review of the rational model, see E. F. Harrison, *The Managerial Decision-Making Process*, 5th ed. (Boston: Houghton Mifflin, 1999), pp. 75–102.

22. W. Pounds, "The Process of Problem Finding," *Industrial Management Review*, Fall 1969, pp. 1–19; and I. Mitroff, *Smart Thinking for Crazy Times: The Art of Solving the Right Problems* (San Francisco: Berrett-Koehler, 1998).

23. J. G. March, *A Primer on Decision Making* (New York: Free Press, 1994), pp. 2–7.

24. T. M. Amabile, "A Model of Creativity and Innovation in Organizations," in B. M. Staw and L. L. Cummings (eds.), *Research in Organizational Behavior*, vol. 10 (Greenwich, CT: JAI Press, 1988), p. 126; and T. M. Amabile, "Motivating Creativity in Organizations," *California Management Review*, Fall 1997, p. 40.

25. Cited in C. G. Morris, *Psychology: An Introduction*, 9th ed. (Upper Saddle River, NJ: Prentice Hall, 1996), p. 344.

26. This section is based on T. M. Amabile, "Motivating Creativity in Organizations," pp. 42–52.

27. R. W. Woodman, J. E. Sawyer, and R. W. Griffin, "Toward a Theory of Organizational Creativity," *Academy of Management Review*, April 1993, p. 298.

28. W. J. J. Gordon, *Synectics* (New York: Harper & Row, 1961).

29. Cited in T. Stevens, "Creativity Killers," *Industry Week*, January 23, 1995, p. 63.

30. D. L. Rados, "Selection and Evaluation of Alternatives in Repetitive Decision Making," *Administrative Science Quarterly*, June 1972, pp. 196–206.

31. M. Bazerman, *Judgment in Managerial Decision Making*, 3rd ed. (New York: Wiley, 1994), p. 5.

32. See, for instance, L. R. Beach, *The Psychology of Decision Making* (Thousand Oaks: Sage, 1997).

33. See H. A. Simon, *Administrative Behavior*, 3rd ed. (New York: Free Press, 1976); and J. Forester, "Bounded Rationality and the Politics of Muddling Through," *Public Administration Review*, January–February 1984, pp. 23–31.

34. W. H. Agor (ed.), *Intuition in Organizations* (Newbury Park, CA: Sage Publications, 1989); O. Behling and N. L. Eckel, "Making Sense Out of Intuition," *Academy of Management Executive*, February 1991, pp. 46–47; G. Klein, *Sources of Power: How People Make Decisions* (Cambridge: MIT Press, 1998); P. E. Ross, "Flash of Genius," *Forbes*, November 16, 1998, pp. 98–104.

35. Behling and Eckel, "Making Sense Out of Intuition," pp. 46–54.

36. As described in H. A. Simon, "Making Management Decisions: The Role of Intuition and Emotion," *Academy of Management Executive*, February 1987, pp. 59–60.

37. Agor, "The Logic of Intuition," p. 9.

38. Ibid., p. 15.

39. See, for example, M. D. Cohen, J. G. March, and J. P. Olsen, "A Garbage Can Model of Organizational Choice," *Administrative Science Quarterly*, March 1972, pp. 1–25.

40. See J. G. Thompson, *Organizations in Action* (New York: McGraw-Hill, 1967), p. 123.

41. C. E. Lindholm, "The Science of 'Muddling Through,'" *Public Administration Review*, Spring 1959, pp. 79–88.

42. A. Tversky and K. Kahneman, "Judgment Under Uncertainty: Heuristics and Biases," *Science*, September 1974, pp. 1124–31; and J. S. Hammond, R. L. Keeney, and H. Raiffa, "The Hidden Traps in Decision Making," *Harvard Business Review*, September–October 1998, pp. 47–58.

43. See B. M. Staw, "The Escalation of Commitment to a Course of Action," *Academy of Management Review*, October 1981, pp. 577–87; and F. D. Schoorman and P. J. Holahan, "Psychological Antecedents of Escalation Behavior: Effects of Choice, Responsibility, and Decision Consequences," *Journal of Applied Psychology*, December 1996, pp. 786–94.

44. A. J. Rowe, J. D. Boulgarides, and M. R. McGrath, *Managerial Decision Making*, Modules in Management Series (Chicago: SRA, 1984), pp. 18–22.

45. A. Wildavsky, *The Politics of the Budgetary Process* (Boston: Little Brown & Co., 1964).

46. N. J. Adler, *International Dimensions of Organizational Behavior*, 3rd ed. (Cincinnati, OH: Southwestern, 1997), pp. 166–73.

47. G. F. Cavanagh, D. J. Moberg, and M. Valasquez, "The Ethics of Organizational Politics," *Academy of Management Journal*, June 1981, pp. 363–74.

48. L. Kohlberg, "Stage and Sequence: The Cognitive-Developmental Approach to Socialization," in D. A. Goslin (ed.), *Handbook of Socialization Theory and Research* (Chicago: Rand McNally, 1969), pp. 347–480.

49. B. Victor and J. B. Cullen, "The Organizational Bases of Ethical Work Climates," *Administrative Science Quarterly*, March 1988, pp. 101–25.

50. See, for example, T. Machan (ed.), *Commerce and Morality* (Totowa, NJ: Rowman and Littlefield, 1988).

51. W. Chow Hou, "To Bribe or Not to Bribe?" *Asia, Inc.*, October 1996, p. 104.

52. P. Digh, "Shades of Gray in the Global Marketplace," *HRMagazine*, April 1997, p. 91.

Set me anything to do as a task, and it is inconceivable the desire I have to do something else.

—G. B. Shaw

part two

THE INDIVIDUAL

T he chairman of BMC Software, Max Watson (front and center in photo), earned over $1 million in 1997. But two of his software developers made more![1]

BMC is a fast-growing, Houston-based producer of mainframe software products. Founded in 1988, the company already has a market capitalization in excess of $6 billion. Watson attributes a large part of BMC's success to its willingness to give its developers a piece of the action.

BMC relies on its software developers to both create new ideas for products and to produce them. So attracting and keeping top talent is a priority. To

motivate these valuable developers, BMC's management pays them an initial five percent of the revenue of each product they develop, working its way down to zero over five years. After that, designers can earn an additional two percent of revenues by updating the product. "We're not talkin' $40,000 year-end bonuses," Watson says. "We're talkin' money that'll make their grandkids happy!"

In addition to giving developers a percentage of any sales their products generate, BMC provides other rewards to top performers. For instance, at a recent awards ceremony, 93 software developers won free cruises. Three of them also earned special prizes of a Remington sculpture and a trip on the Orient Express because their products topped $25 million in sales.

BMC's incentive program seems to be working. Turnover remains low. Profit per employee is among the highest in the industry. And the company is introducing new products at a breathtaking pace.

Basic Motivation Concepts

Max Watson understands the value of motivating valuable employees with incentives. Unfortunately, many managers fail to understand the importance of motivation. In this chapter and the following chapter, we explain the basics of motivation and show you how to design effective motivation programs.

WHAT IS MOTIVATION?

Maybe the place to begin is to say what motivation isn't. Many people incorrectly view motivation as a personal trait—that is, some have it and others don't. In practice, inexperienced managers often label employees who seem to lack motivation as lazy. Such a label assumes that an individual is always lazy or is lacking in motivation. Our knowledge of motivation tells us that this just isn't true. What we know is that motivation is the result of the interaction of the individual and the situation. Certainly, individuals differ in their basic motivational drive. But the same student who finds it difficult to read a textbook for more than 20 minutes may devour a Stephen King novel in one afternoon. For this student, the change in motivation is driven by the situation. So as we analyze the concept of motivation, keep in mind that level of motivation varies both between individuals and within individuals at different times.

We'll define **motivation** as the processes that account for an individual's intensity, direction, and persistence of effort toward attaining a goal.[2] While general motivation is concerned with effort toward *any* goal, we'll narrow the focus to *organizational* goals in order to reflect our singular interest in work-related behavior.

The three key elements in our definition are intensity, direction, and persistence. *Intensity* is concerned with how hard a person

AFTER READING THIS CHAPTER, YOU SHOULD BE ABLE TO

1. Outline the motivation process
2. Describe Maslow's need hierarchy
3. Contrast Theory X and Theory Y
4. Differentiate motivators from hygiene factors
5. List the characteristics that high achievers prefer in a job
6. Summarize the types of goals that increase performance
7. State the impact of underrewarding employees
8. Clarify the key relationships in expectancy theory
9. Explain how the contemporary theories of motivation complement each other

motivation

The processes that account for an individual's intensity, direction, and persistence of effort toward attaining a goal.

tries. This is the element most of us focus on when we talk about motivation. However, high intensity is unlikely to lead to favorable job-performance outcomes unless the effort is channeled in a *direction* that benefits the organization. Therefore, we have to consider the quality of effort as well as its intensity. Effort that is directed toward, and consistent with, the organization's goals is the kind of effort that we should be seeking. Finally, motivation has a *persistence* dimension. This is a measure of how long a person can maintain his or her effort. Motivated individuals stay with a task long enough to achieve their goal.

EARLY THEORIES OF MOTIVATION

The 1950s were a fruitful period in the development of motivation concepts. Three specific theories were formulated during this period, which although heavily attacked and now questionable in terms of validity, are probably still the best-known explanations for employee motivation. These are the hierarchy of needs theory, Theories X and Y, and the two-factor theory. As you'll see later in this chapter, we have since developed more valid explanations of motivation, but you should know these early theories for at least two reasons: (1) They represent a foundation from which contemporary theories have grown, and (2) practicing managers still regularly use these theories and their terminology in explaining employee motivation.

HIERARCHY OF NEEDS THEORY

hierarchy of needs theory

There is a hierarchy of five needs—physiological, safety, social, esteem, and self-actualization—and as each need is substantially satisfied, the next need becomes dominant.

self-actualization

The drive to become what one is capable of becoming.

It's probably safe to say that the most well-known theory of motivation is Abraham Maslow's **hierarchy of needs**.[3] He hypothesized that within every human being there exists a hierarchy of five needs. These needs are:

1. *Physiological*: Includes hunger, thirst, shelter, sex, and other bodily needs
2. *Safety*: Includes security and protection from physical and emotional harm
3. *Social*: Includes affection, belongingness, acceptance, and friendship
4. *Esteem*: Includes internal esteem factors such as self-respect, autonomy, and achievement; and external esteem factors such as status, recognition, and attention
5. **Self-actualization**: The drive to become what one is capable of becoming; includes growth, achieving one's potential, and self-fulfillment

As each of these needs becomes substantially satisfied, the next need becomes dominant. In terms of Exhibit 6-1, the individual moves up the steps of the hierarchy. From the standpoint of motivation, the theory would say that although no need is ever fully gratified, a substantially satisfied need no longer mo-

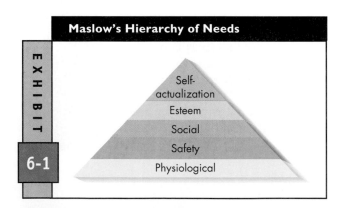

EXHIBIT 6-1

Maslow's Hierarchy of Needs

Self-actualization
Esteem
Social
Safety
Physiological

tivates. So if you want to motivate someone, according to Maslow, you need to understand what level of the hierarchy that person is currently on and focus on satisfying those needs at or above that level.

Maslow separated the five needs into higher and lower orders. Physiological and safety needs were described as **lower-order needs** and social, esteem, and self-actualization needs as **higher-order needs**. The differentiation between the two orders was made on the premise that higher-order needs are satisfied internally (within the person), whereas lower-order needs are predominantly satisfied externally (by such things as pay, union contracts, and tenure). In fact, the natural conclusion to be drawn from Maslow's classification is that in times of economic plenty, almost all permanently employed workers have their lower-order needs substantially met.

Maslow's need theory has received wide recognition, particularly among practicing managers. This can be attributed to the theory's intuitive logic and ease of understanding. Unfortunately, however, research does not generally validate the theory. Maslow provided no empirical substantiation, and several studies that sought to validate the theory found no support for it.[4]

Old theories, especially ones that are intuitively logical, apparently die hard. One researcher reviewed the evidence and concluded that "although of great societal popularity, need hierarchy as a theory continues to receive little empirical support."[5] Furthermore, the researcher stated that the "available research should certainly generate a reluctance to accept unconditionally the implication of Maslow's hierarchy."[6] Another review came to the same conclusion.[7] Little support was found for the prediction that need structures are organized along the dimensions proposed by Maslow, that unsatisfied needs motivate, or that a satisfied need activates movement to a new need level.

THEORY X AND THEORY Y

Douglas McGregor proposed two distinct views of human beings: one basically negative, labeled **Theory X**, and the other basically positive, labeled **Theory Y**.[8] After viewing the way in which managers dealt with employees, McGregor concluded that a manager's view of the nature of human beings is based on a certain grouping of assumptions and that he or she tends to mold his or her behavior toward employees according to these assumptions.

Under Theory X, the four assumptions held by managers are:

1. Employees inherently dislike work and, whenever possible, will attempt to avoid it.
2. Since employees dislike work, they must be coerced, controlled, or threatened with punishment to achieve goals.
3. Employees will avoid responsibilities and seek formal direction whenever possible.
4. Most workers place security above all other factors associated with work and will display little ambition.

In contrast to these negative views about the nature of human beings, McGregor listed the four positive assumptions that he called Theory Y:

1. Employees can view work as being as natural as rest or play.
2. People will exercise self-direction and self-control if they are committed to the objectives.
3. The average person can learn to accept, even seek, responsibility.
4. The ability to make innovative decisions is widely dispersed throughout the population and is not necessarily the sole province of those in management positions.

lower-order needs

Needs that are satisfied externally; physiological and safety needs.

higher-order needs

Needs that are satisfied internally; social, esteem, and self-actualization needs.

Theory X

The assumption that employees dislike work, are lazy, dislike responsibility, and must be coerced to perform.

Theory Y

The assumption that employees like work, are creative, seek responsibility, and can exercise self-direction.

"People Are Inherently Lazy"

This statement is false on two levels. *All* people are not inherently lazy; and "laziness" is more a function of the situation than an inherent individual characteristic.

If this statement is meant to imply that *all* people are inherently lazy, the evidence strongly indicates the contrary.[9] Many people today suffer from the opposite affliction—they're overly busy, overworked, and suffer from overexertion. Whether externally motivated or internally driven, a good portion of the labor force is anything *but* lazy.

Managers frequently draw the conclusion that people are lazy from watching some of their em-

ployees, who may be lazy at work. But these same employees are often quite industrious in one or more activities *off* the job. People's need structures differ.[10] Unfortunately for employers, work often ranks low in its ability to satisfy individual needs. So the same employee that shirks responsibility on the job may work obsessively on reconditioning an antique car, maintaining an award-winning garden, perfecting bowling skills, or selling Amway products on weekends. Very few people are perpetually lazy. They merely differ in terms of the activities they most enjoy doing. And because work isn't important to everyone, some may appear lazy.

What are the motivational implications if you accept McGregor's analysis? The answer is best expressed in the framework presented by Maslow. Theory X assumes that lower-order needs dominate individuals. Theory Y assumes that higher-order needs dominate individuals. McGregor himself held to the belief that Theory Y assumptions were more valid than Theory X. Therefore, he proposed such ideas as participative decision making, responsible and challenging jobs, and good group relations as approaches that would maximize an employee's job motivation.

Unfortunately, there is no evidence to confirm that either set of assumptions is valid or that accepting Theory Y assumptions and altering one's actions accordingly will lead to more motivated workers. As will become evident later in this chapter, either Theory X or Theory Y assumptions may be appropriate in a particular situation.

TWO-FACTOR THEORY

two-factor theory

Intrinsic factors are related to job satisfaction, while extrinsic factors are associated with dissatisfaction.

The **two-factor theory** (sometimes also called *motivation-hygiene theory*) was proposed by psychologist Frederick Herzberg.[11] In the belief that an individual's relation to work is basic and that one's attitude toward work can very well determine success or failure, Herzberg investigated the question, "What do people want from their jobs?" He asked people to describe, in detail, situations in which they felt exceptionally *good* or *bad* about their jobs. These responses were then tabulated and categorized.

From the categorized responses, Herzberg concluded that the replies people gave when they felt good about their jobs were significantly different from the replies given when they felt bad. As seen in Exhibit 6-2, certain characteristics tend to be consistently related to job satisfaction and others to job dissatisfaction. Intrinsic factors, such as the work itself, responsibility, and achievement, seem to be related to job satisfaction. Respondents who felt good about their work tended to attribute these factors to themselves. On the other hand, dissatisfied respondents tended to cite extrinsic factors, such as supervision, pay, company policies, and working conditions.

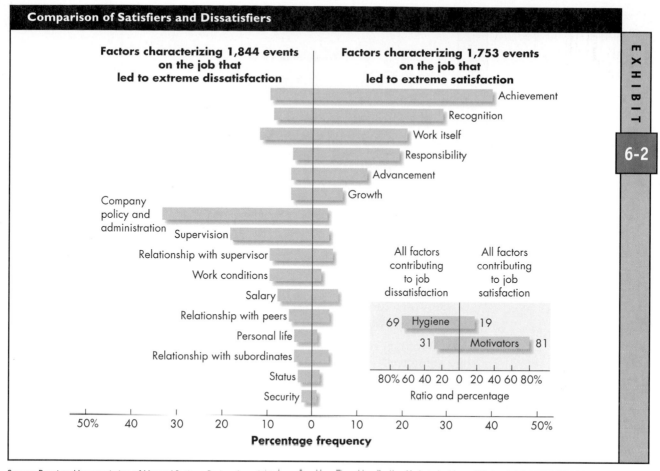

Comparison of Satisfiers and Dissatisfiers

Factors characterizing 1,844 events on the job that led to extreme dissatisfaction

Factors characterizing 1,753 events on the job that led to extreme satisfaction

Source: Reprinted by permission of *Harvard Business Review*. An exhibit from *One More Time: How Do You Motivate Employees?* By Frederick Herzberg, September/October 1987. Copyright © 1987 by the President and Fellows of Harvard College; all rights reserved.

The data suggest, said Herzberg, that the opposite of satisfaction is not dissatisfaction, as was traditionally believed. Removing dissatisfying characteristics from a job does not necessarily make the job satisfying. As illustrated in Exhibit 6-3, Herzberg proposed that his findings indicated the existence of a dual continuum: The opposite of "Satisfaction" is "No Satisfaction," and the opposite of "Dissatisfaction" is "No Dissatisfaction."

According to Herzberg, the factors leading to job satisfaction are separate and distinct from those that lead to job dissatisfaction. Therefore, managers who seek to eliminate factors that can create job dissatisfaction may bring about peace but not necessarily motivation. They will be placating their workforce rather than motivating them. As a result, conditions surrounding the job such as quality of supervision, pay, company policies, physical working conditions, relations with others, and job security were characterized by Herzberg as **hygiene factors**. When they're adequate, people will not be dissatisfied; neither will they be satisfied. If we want to motivate people on their jobs, Herzberg suggested emphasizing factors associated with the work itself or to outcomes directly derived from it, such as promotional opportunities, opportunities for personal growth, recognition, responsibility, and achievement. These are the characteristics that people find intrinsically rewarding.

hygiene factors

Those factors—such as company policy and administration, supervision, and salary—that, when adequate in a job, placate workers. When these factors are adequate, people will not be dissatisfied.

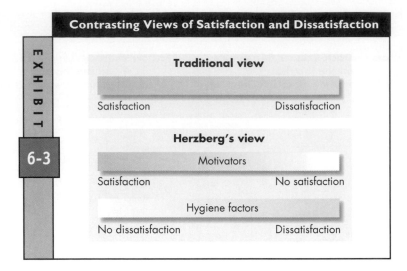

EXHIBIT 6-3

Contrasting Views of Satisfaction and Dissatisfaction

Traditional view

Satisfaction   Dissatisfaction

Herzberg's view

Motivators

Satisfaction   No satisfaction

Hygiene factors

No dissatisfaction   Dissatisfaction

The two-factor theory is not without detractors. The criticisms of the theory include the following:[12]

1. The procedure that Herzberg used is limited by its methodology. When things are going well, people tend to take credit themselves. Contrarily, they blame failure on the extrinsic environment.
2. The reliability of Herzberg's methodology is questioned. Raters have to make interpretations, so they may contaminate the findings by interpreting one response in one manner while treating a similar response differently.
3. No overall measure of satisfaction was utilized. A person may dislike part of his or her job yet still think the job is acceptable.
4. The theory is inconsistent with previous research. The two-factor theory ignores situational variables.
5. Herzberg assumed a relationship between satisfaction and productivity, but the research methodology he used looked only at satisfaction, not at productivity. To make such research relevant, one must assume a strong relationship between satisfaction and productivity.

Regardless of criticisms, Herzberg's theory has been widely read and few managers are unfamiliar with his recommendations. The popularity over the past 30 years of vertically expanding jobs to allow workers greater responsibility in planning and controlling their work can probably be attributed largely to Herzberg's findings and recommendations.

CONTEMPORARY THEORIES OF MOTIVATION

The previous theories are well known but, unfortunately, have not held up well under close examination. However, all is not lost. There are a number of contemporary theories that have one thing in common—each has a reasonable degree of valid supporting documentation. Of course, this doesn't mean that the theories we are about to introduce are unquestionably right. We call them "contemporary theories" not because they necessarily were developed recently but because they represent the current state of the art in explaining employee motivation.

ERG THEORY

Clayton Alderfer of Yale University has reworked Maslow's need hierarchy to align it more closely with the empirical research. His revised need hierarchy is labeled **ERG theory**.[13]

Alderfer argues that there are three groups of core needs—existence, relatedness, and growth—hence, the label: *ERG theory*. The *existence* group is concerned with providing our basic material existence requirements. They include the items that Maslow considered to be physiological and safety needs. The second group of needs are those of *relatedness*—the desire we have for maintaining important interpersonal relationships. These social and status desires require interaction with others if they are to be satisfied, and they align with Maslow's social need and the external component of Maslow's esteem classification. Finally, Alderfer isolates *growth* needs—an intrinsic desire for personal development. These include the intrinsic component from Maslow's esteem category and the characteristics included under self-actualization.

Besides substituting three needs for five, how does Alderfer's ERG theory differ from Maslow's? In contrast to the hierarchy of needs theory, the ERG theory demonstrates that (1) more than one need may be operative at the same time, and (2) if the gratification of a higher-level need is stifled, the desire to satisfy a lower-level need increases.

Maslow's need hierarchy follows a rigid, steplike progression. ERG theory does not assume that there exists a rigid hierarchy in which a lower-order need must be substantially gratified before one can move on. A person can, for instance, be working on growth even though existence or relatedness needs are unsatisfied; or all three need categories could be operating at the same time.

ERG theory also contains a frustration-regression dimension. Maslow, you'll remember, argued that an individual would stay at a certain need level until that need was satisfied. ERG theory counters by noting that when a higher order need level is frustrated, the individual's desire to increase a lower-level need takes place. Inability to satisfy a need for social interaction, for instance, might increase the desire for more money or better working conditions. So frustration can lead to a regression to a lower need.

In summary, ERG theory argues, like Maslow, that satisfied lower-order needs lead to the desire to satisfy higher-order needs; but multiple needs can be operating as motivators at the same time, and frustration in attempting to satisfy a higher-level need can result in regression to a lower-level need.

ERG theory is more consistent with our knowledge of individual differences among people. Variables such as education, family background, and cultural environment can alter the importance or driving force that a group of needs holds for a particular individual. The evidence demonstrating that people in other cultures rank the need categories differently—for instance, natives of Spain and

Netscape Communications offers employees many recreational opportunities that help satisfy their relatedness needs. For example, programmers who develop the firm's Internet software interact socially by playing hockey in the parking lot at Netscape's campus-like headquarters in Mountain View, California.

Japan place social needs before their physiological requirements[14]—would be consistent with ERG theory. Several studies have supported ERG theory,[15] but there is also evidence that it doesn't work in some organizations.[16] Overall, however, ERG theory represents a more valid version of the need hierarchy.

McCLELLAND'S THEORY OF NEEDS

You've got one beanbag and there are five targets set up in front of you. Each one is progressively farther away and, hence, more difficult to hit. Target A is a cinch. It sits almost within arm's reach of you. If you hit it, you get $2. Target B is a bit farther out, but about 80 percent of the people who try can hit it. It pays $4. Target C pays $8, and about half the people who try can hit it. Very few people can hit Target D, but the payoff is $16 if you do. Finally, Target E pays $32, but it's almost impossible to achieve. Which target would you try for? If you selected C, you're likely to be a high achiever. Why? Read on.

McClelland's theory of needs was developed by David McClelland and his associates.[17] The theory focuses on three needs: achievement, power, and affiliation. They are defined as follows:

- **Need for achievement**: The drive to excel, to achieve in relation to a set of standards, to strive to succeed
- **Need for power**: The need to make others behave in a way that they would not have behaved otherwise
- **Need for affiliation**: The desire for friendly and close interpersonal relationships

Some people have a compelling drive to succeed. They're striving for personal achievement rather than the rewards of success per se. They have a desire to do something better or more efficiently than it has been done before. This drive is the achievement need (*nAch*). From research into the achievement need, McClelland found that high achievers differentiate themselves from others by their desire to do things better.[18] They seek situations in which they can attain personal responsibility for finding solutions to problems, in which they can receive rapid feedback on their performance so they can tell easily whether they are improving or not, and in which they can set moderately challenging goals. High achievers are not gamblers; they dislike succeeding by chance. They prefer the challenge of working at a problem and accepting the personal responsibility for success or failure rather than leaving the outcome to chance or the actions of others. Importantly, they avoid what they perceive to be very easy or very difficult tasks. They want to overcome obstacles, but they want to feel that their success (or failure) is due to their own actions. This means they like tasks of intermediate difficulty.

High achievers perform best when they perceive their probability of success as being 0.5, that is, where they estimate that they have a 50–50 chance of success. They dislike gambling with high odds because they get no achievement satisfaction from happenstance success. Similarly, they dislike low odds (high probability of success) because then there is no challenge to their skills. They like to set goals that require stretching themselves a little. When there is an approximately equal chance of success or failure, there is the optimum opportunity to experience feelings of accomplishment and satisfaction from their efforts.

The need for power (*nPow*) is the desire to have impact, to be influential, and to control others. Individuals high in nPow enjoy being "in charge," strive for influence over others, prefer to be placed into competitive and status-oriented situations, and tend to be more concerned with prestige and gaining influence over others than with effective performance.

McClelland's theory of needs

Achievement, power, and affiliation are three important needs that help explain motivation.

achievement need

The drive to excel, to achieve in relation to a set of standards, to strive to succeed.

power need

The need to make others behave in a way that they could not have behaved otherwise.

affiliation need

The desire for friendly and close interpersonal relationships.

The third need isolated by McClelland is affiliation (*nAff*). This need has received the least attention from researchers. Affiliation can be likened to Dale Carnegie's goals—the desire to be liked and accepted by others. Individuals with a high affiliation motive strive for friendship, prefer cooperative situations rather than competitive ones, and desire relationships involving a high degree of mutual understanding.

How do you find out if someone is, for instance, a high achiever? There are questionnaires that tap this motive,[19] but most research uses a projective test in which subjects respond to pictures.[20] Each picture is briefly shown to the subject and then he or she writes a story based on the picture. As an example, the picture may show a male sitting at a desk in a pensive position, looking at a photograph of a woman and two children that sits at the corner of the desk. The subject will then be asked to write a story describing what is going on, what preceded this situation, what will happen in the future, and the like. The stories become, in effect, projective tests that measure unconscious motives. Each story is scored and a subject's rating on each of the three motives is obtained.

Relying on an extensive amount of research, some reasonably well-supported predictions can be made based on the relationship between achievement need and job performance. Although less research has been done on power and affiliation needs, there are consistent findings here, too.

First, as shown in Exhibit 6-4, individuals with a high need to achieve prefer job situations with personal responsibility, feedback, and an intermediate degree of risk. When these characteristics are prevalent, high achievers will be strongly motivated. The evidence consistently demonstrates, for instance, that high achievers are successful in entrepreneurial activities such as running their own businesses and managing a self-contained unit within a large organization.[21]

Second, a high need to achieve does not necessarily lead to being a good manager, especially in large organizations. People with a high achievement need are interested in how well they do personally and not in influencing others to do well. High-nAch salespeople do not necessarily make good sales managers, and the good general manager in a large organization does not typically have a high need to achieve.[22]

Third, the needs for affiliation and power tend to be closely related to managerial success. The best managers are high in their need for power and low in their need for affiliation.[23] In fact, a high power motive may be a requirement for managerial effectiveness.[24] Of course, what the cause is and what the effect is are arguable. It has been suggested that a high power need may occur simply as a function of one's level in a hierarchical organization.[25] The latter argument proposes that the higher the level an individual rises to in the organization, the

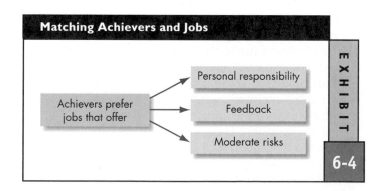

Matching Achievers and Jobs

Achievers prefer jobs that offer → Personal responsibility

Achievers prefer jobs that offer → Feedback

Achievers prefer jobs that offer → Moderate risks

EXHIBIT 6-4

greater is the incumbent's power motive. As a result, powerful positions would be the stimulus to a high power motive.

Finally, employees have been successfully trained to stimulate their achievement need. Trainers have been effective in teaching individuals to think in terms of accomplishments, winning, and success, and then helping them to learn how to *act* in a high achievement way by preferring situations in which they have personal responsibility, feedback, and moderate risks. So if the job calls for a high achiever, management can select a person with a high nAch or develop its own candidate through achievement training.[26]

Dell Computer seeks high achievers to sell its computers to small and mid-size firms. Marty Sedlacek, an account executive, is one of Dell's top performers. He has topped his sales quota for 22 consecutive months and was named the Account Executive of the Year. One year he brought Dell $37 million in new business. High achievers like Sedlacek have helped Dell Computer compete against well-entrenched firms like IBM, Toshiba, NEC, and Compaq Computers.

COGNITIVE EVALUATION THEORY

In the late 1960s, one researcher proposed that the introduction of extrinsic rewards such as pay for work effort that had been previously intrinsically rewarding due to the pleasure associated with the content of the work itself would tend to decrease the overall level of motivation.[27] This proposal—which has come to be called the **cognitive evaluation theory**—has been extensively researched, and a large number of studies have been supportive.[28] As we'll show, the major implications for this theory relate to the way in which people are paid in organizations.

cognitive evaluation theory

Allocating extrinsic rewards for behavior that had been previously intrinsically rewarding tends to decrease the overall level of motivation.

Historically, motivation theorists have generally assumed that intrinsic motivations such as achievement, responsibility, and competence are independent of extrinsic motivators such as high pay, promotions, good supervisor relations, and pleasant working conditions. That is, the stimulation of one would not affect the other. But the cognitive evaluation theory suggests otherwise. It argues that when extrinsic rewards are used by organizations as payoffs for superior performance, the intrinsic rewards, which are derived from individuals doing what they like, are reduced. In other words, when extrinsic rewards are given to someone for performing an interesting task, it causes intrinsic interest in the task itself to decline.

Why would such an outcome occur? The popular explanation is that the individual experiences a loss of control over his or her own behavior so that the previous intrinsic motivation diminishes. Furthermore, the elimination of extrinsic rewards can produce a shift—from an external to an internal explanation—in an individual's perception of causation of why he or she works on a task. If you're reading a novel a week because your English literature instructor requires you to, you can attribute your reading behavior to an external source. However, after the course is over, if you find yourself continuing to read a novel a week, your natural inclination is to say, "I must enjoy reading novels because I'm still reading one a week!"

If the cognitive evaluation theory is valid, it should have major implications for managerial practices. It has been a truism among compensation specialists for years that if pay or other extrinsic rewards are to be effective motivators, they should be made contingent on an individual's performance. But, cognitive evalu-

EXHIBIT

6-5

THE WALL STREET JOURNAL

"What do you *mean* money isn't everything? This is a bank!"

Source: From *The Wall Street Journal*, February 8, 1995. With permission of Cartoon Features Syndicate.

ation theorists would argue, this will only tend to decrease the internal satisfaction that the individual receives from doing the job. We have substituted an external stimulus for an internal stimulus. In fact, if cognitive evaluation theory is correct, it would make sense to make an individual's pay noncontingent on performance in order to avoid decreasing intrinsic motivation.

We noted earlier that the cognitive evaluation theory has been supported in a number of studies. Yet it has also met with attacks, specifically on the methodology used in these studies[29] and in the interpretation of the findings.[30] But where does this theory stand today? Can we say that when organizations use extrinsic motivators such as pay and promotions to stimulate workers' performance they do so at the expense of reducing intrinsic interest and motivation in the work being done? The answer is not a simple Yes or No.

Although further research is needed to clarify some of the current ambiguity, the evidence does lead us to conclude that the interdependence of extrinsic and intrinsic rewards is a real phenomenon.[31] However, its impact on employee motivation at work, in contrast to motivation in general, may be considerably less than originally thought. First, many of the studies testing the theory were done with students, not paid organizational employees. The researchers would observe what happens to a student's behavior when a reward that had been allocated is stopped. This is interesting, but it doesn't represent the typical work situation. In the real world, when extrinsic rewards are stopped, it usually means the individual is no longer part of the organization. Second, evidence indicates that very high intrinsic motivation levels are strongly resistant to the detrimental impacts of extrinsic rewards.[32] Even when a job is inherently interesting, there still exists a powerful norm for extrinsic payment.[33] At the other extreme, on dull tasks extrinsic rewards appear to increase intrinsic motivation.[34] Therefore, the theory may have limited applicability to work organizations because most low-level jobs are not inherently satisfying enough to foster high intrinsic interest and many managerial and professional positions offer intrinsic rewards. Cognitive evaluation theory may be relevant to that set of organizational jobs that falls in between—those that are neither extremely dull nor extremely interesting.

GOAL-SETTING THEORY

Gene Broadwater, coach of the Hamilton High School cross-country team, gave his squad these last words before they approached the line for the league championship race: "Each one of you is physically ready. Now, get out there and do your best. No one can ever ask more of you than that."

You've heard the phrase a number of times yourself: "Just do your best. That's all anyone can ask for." But what does "do your best" mean? Do we ever know if we've achieved that vague goal? Would the cross-country runners have recorded faster times if Coach Broadwater had given each a specific goal to shoot for? Might you have done better in your high school English class if your parents had said, "You should strive for 85 percent or higher on all your work in English" rather than telling you to "do your best"? The research on **goal-setting theory** addresses these issues, and the findings, as you will see, are impressive in terms of the effect that goal specificity, challenge, and feedback have on performance.

In the late 1960s, Edwin Locke proposed that intentions to work toward a goal are a major source of work motivation.[35] That is, goals tell an employee what needs to be done and how much effort will need to be expended.[36] The evidence strongly supports the value of goals. More to the point, we can say that specific goals increase performance; that difficult goals, when accepted, result in higher performance than do easy goals; and that feedback leads to higher performance than does nonfeedback.[37]

Specific hard goals produce a higher level of output than does the generalized goal of "do your best." The specificity of the goal itself acts as an internal stimulus. For instance, when a trucker commits to making 12 round-trip hauls between Toronto and Buffalo, New York, each week, this intention gives him a specific objective to try to attain. We can say that, all things being equal, the trucker with a specific goal will outperform his or her counterpart operating with no goals or the generalized goal of "do your best."

If factors such as ability and acceptance of the goals are held constant, we can also state that the more difficult the goal, the higher the level of performance. However, it's logical to assume that easier goals are more likely to be accepted. But once an employee accepts a hard task, he or she will exert a high level of effort until it is achieved, lowered, or abandoned.

People will do better when they get feedback on how well they are progressing toward their goals because feedback helps to identify discrepancies between what they have done and what they want to do; that is, feedback acts to guide behavior. But all feedback is not equally potent. Self-generated feedback—where the employee is able to monitor his or her own progress—has been shown to be a more powerful motivator than externally generated feedback.[38]

If employees have the opportunity to participate in the setting of their own goals, will they try harder? The evidence is mixed regarding the superiority of participative over assigned goals.[39] In some cases, participatively set goals elicited superior performance, while in other cases, individuals performed best when assigned goals by their boss. But a major advantage of participation may be in increasing acceptance of the goal itself as a desirable one toward which to work.[40] As we noted, resistance is greater when goals are difficult. If people participate in

goal-setting theory

The theory that specific and difficult goals, with goal/feedback, lead to higher performance.

goal setting, they are more likely to accept even a difficult goal than if they are arbitrarily assigned it by their boss. The reason is that individuals are more committed to choices in which they have a part. Thus, although participative goals may have no superiority over assigned goals when acceptance is taken as a given, participation does increase the probability that more difficult goals will be agreed to and acted upon.

Are there any contingencies in goal-setting theory or can we take it as a universal truth that difficult and specific goals will always lead to higher performance? In addition to feedback, four other factors have been found to influence the goals–performance relationship. These are goal commitment, adequate self-efficacy, task characteristics, and national culture. Goal-setting theory presupposes that an individual is committed to the goal, that is, is determined not to lower or abandon the goal. This is most likely to occur when goals are made public, when the individual has an internal locus of control, and when the goals are self-set rather than assigned.[41] **Self-efficacy** refers to an individual's belief that he or she is capable of performing a task.[42] The higher your self-efficacy, the more confidence you have in your ability to succeed in a task. So, in difficult situations, we find that people with low self-efficacy are more likely to lessen their effort or give up altogether, while those with high self-efficacy will try harder to master the challenge.[43] In addition, individuals high in self-efficacy seem to respond to negative feedback with increased effort and motivation, whereas those low in self-efficacy are likely to lessen their effort when given negative feedback.[44] Research indicates that individual goal setting doesn't work equally well on all tasks. The evidence suggests that goals seem to have a more substantial effect on performance when tasks are simple rather than complex, well learned rather than novel, and independent rather than interdependent.[45] On interdependent tasks, group goals are preferrable. Finally, goal-setting theory is culture bound. It's well adapted to countries such as the United States and Canada because its key components align reasonably well with North American cultures. It assumes that employees will be reasonably independent (not too high a score on power distance), that managers and employees will seek challenging goals (low in uncertainty avoidance), and that performance is considered important by both (high in quantity of life). So don't expect goal setting to necessarily lead to higher employee performance in countries such as Portugal or Chile, where the opposite conditions exist.

Our overall conclusion is that intentions—as articulated in terms of hard and specific goals—are a potent motivating force. Under the proper conditions, they can lead to higher performance. However, there is no evidence that such goals are associated with increased job satisfaction.[46]

Scott Grocki, president, and Jennifer Brown, business manager, believe that setting goals is the key to expanding their magic show business, Grocki Magic Studios. Grocki and Brown set weekly, monthly, six-month, yearly, and long-term goals. They paint long-term goals like "Broadway" and "Television" on their office walls to constantly remind them that they want to appear on national television, create a Broadway show, and open their own theatre. "When you set a goal, you create something and it becomes real," says Grocki. "You write it down. You focus on it. You aspire to it, and that's your motivation."

REINFORCEMENT THEORY

A counterpoint to goal-setting theory is **reinforcement theory**. The former is a cognitive approach, proposing that an individual's purposes direct his or her action. In reinforcement theory, we have a behavioristic approach, which argues that reinforcement conditions behavior. The two are clearly at odds philosophically. Reinforcement theorists see behavior as being environmentally caused. You need not be concerned, they would argue, with internal cognitive events; what controls behavior are reinforcers—any consequence that, when immediately following a response, increases the probability that the behavior will be repeated.

self-efficacy
The individual's belief that he or she is capable of performing a task.

reinforcement theory
Behavior is a function of its consequences.

Reinforcement theory ignores the inner state of the individual and concentrates solely on what happens to a person when he or she takes some action. Because it does not concern itself with what initiates behavior, it is not, strictly speaking, a theory of motivation. But it does provide a powerful means of analysis of what controls behavior, and it is for this reason that it is typically considered in discussions of motivation.[47]

We discussed the reinforcement process in detail in Chapter 2. We showed how using reinforcers to condition behavior gives us considerable insight into how people learn. Yet we cannot ignore the fact that reinforcement has a wide following as a motivational device. In its pure form, however, reinforcement theory ignores feelings, attitudes, expectations, and other cognitive variables that are known to impact behavior. In fact, some researchers look at the same experiments that reinforcement theorists use to support their position and interpret the findings in a cognitive framework.[48]

Reinforcement is undoubtedly an important influence on behavior, but few scholars are prepared to argue that it is the only influence. The behaviors you engage in at work and the amount of effort you allocate to each task are affected by the consequences that follow from your behavior. For instance, if you are consistently reprimanded for outproducing your colleagues, you will likely reduce your productivity. But your lower productivity may also be explained in terms of goals, inequity, or expectancies.

EQUITY THEORY

Jane Pearson graduated last year from the State University with a degree in accounting. After interviews with a number of organizations on campus, she accepted a position with one of the nation's largest public accounting firms and was assigned to its Boston office. Jane was very pleased with the offer she received: challenging work with a prestigious firm, an excellent opportunity to gain valuable experience, and the highest salary any accounting major at State was offered last year—$3,250 a month. But Jane was the top student in her class; she was ambitious and articulate and fully expected to receive a commensurate salary.

Twelve months have passed since Jane joined her employer. The work has proved to be as challenging and satisfying as she had hoped. Her employer is extremely pleased with her performance; in fact, she recently received a $200-a-month raise. However, Jane's motivational level has dropped dramatically in the past few weeks. Why? Her employer has just hired a fresh college graduate out of State University, who lacks the one-year experience Jane has gained, for $3,500 a month—$50 more than Jane now makes! It would be an understatement to describe Jane in any other terms than irate. Jane is even talking about looking for another job.

Jane's situation illustrates the role that equity plays in motivation. Employees make comparisons of their job inputs (i.e., effort, experience, education, competence) and outcomes (i.e., salary levels, raises, recognition) relative to those of others. We perceive what we get from a job situation (outcomes) in relation to what we put into it (inputs), and then we compare our outcome–input ratio with the outcome–input ratio of relevant others. This is shown in Exhibit 6-6. If we perceive our ratio to be equal to that of the relevant others with whom we compare ourselves, a state of equity is said to exist. We perceive our situation as fair—that justice prevails. When we see the ratio as unequal, we experience equity tension. J. Stacy Adams has proposed that this negative tension state provides the motivation to do something to correct it.[49]

EXHIBIT 6-6

Equity Theory

Ratio Comparisons*	Perception
$O/I_A < O/I_B$	Inequity due to being underrewarded
$O/I_A = O/I_B$	Equity
$O/I_A > O/I_B$	Inequity due to being overrewarded

*Where O/I_A represents the employee; and O/I_B represents relevant others.

The referent that an employee selects adds to the complexity of **equity theory**. Evidence indicates that the referent chosen is an important variable in equity theory.[50] There are four referent comparisons that an employee can use:

1. *Self-inside*: An employee's experiences in a different position inside his or her current organization
2. *Self-outside*: An employee's experiences in a situation or position outside his or her current organization
3. *Other-inside*: Another individual or group of individuals inside the employee's organization
4. *Other-outside*: Another individual or group of individuals outside the employee's organization

Employees might compare themselves to friends, neighbors, co-workers, colleagues in other organizations, or past jobs they themselves have had. Which referent an employee chooses will be influenced by the information the employee holds about referents as well as by the attractiveness of the referent. This has led to focusing on four moderating variables—gender, length of tenure, level in the organization, and amount of education or professionalism.[51] Research shows that both men and women prefer same-sex comparisons. The research also demonstrates that women are typically paid less than men in comparable jobs and have lower pay expectations than men for the same work. So a female that uses another female as a referent tends to result in a lower comparative standard. This leads us to conclude that employees in jobs that are not sex segregated will make more cross-sex comparisons than those in jobs that are either male or female dominated. This also suggests that if women are tolerant of lower pay, it may be due to the comparative standard they use.

Employees with short tenure in their current organizations tend to have little information about others inside the organization, so they rely on their own personal experiences. On the other hand, employees with long tenure rely more heavily on co-workers for comparison. Upper-level employees, those in the professional ranks, and those with higher amounts of education tend to be more cosmopolitan and have better information about people in other organizations. Therefore, these types of employees will make more other-outside comparisons.

Based on equity theory, when employees perceive an inequity, they can be predicted to make one of six choices:[52]

1. Change their inputs (e.g., don't exert as much effort)
2. Change their outcomes (e.g., individuals paid on a piece-rate basis can increase their pay by producing a higher quantity of units of lower quality)

equity theory

Individuals compare their job inputs and outcomes with those of others and then respond so as to eliminate any inequities.

Because of the financial crisis in Russia, many firms do not have money to pay their employees. Instead of receiving a salary, employees get paid in goods the factories produce. Velta Company, a bicycle maker in Russia, gives workers one bicycle a month instead of a paycheck. Workers then have to sell their bike for cash or barter it for food. Some workers deal with the inequity of not getting a salary by using a different referent. "We are luckier than people over at the chemical plant," says one Velta employee. "At least our factory gives us something we can sell."

3. Distort perceptions of self (e.g., "I used to think I worked at a moderate pace but now I realize that I work a lot harder than everyone else.")
4. Distort perceptions of others (e.g., "Mike's job isn't as desirable as I previously thought it was.")
5. Choose a different referent (e.g., "I may not make as much as my brother-in-law, but I'm doing a lot better than my Dad did when he was my age.")
6. Leave the field (e.g., quit the job)

The theory establishes the following propositions relating to inequitable pay:

1. *Given payment by time, overrewarded employees will produce more than will equitably paid employees.* Hourly and salaried employees will generate high quantity or quality of production in order to increase the input side of the ratio and bring about equity.
2. *Given payment by quantity of production, overrewarded employees will produce fewer, but higher-quality, units than will equitably paid employees.* Individuals paid on a piece-rate basis will increase their effort to achieve equity, which can result in greater quality or quantity. However, increases in quantity will only increase inequity, since every unit produced results in further overpayment. Therefore, effort is directed toward increasing quality rather than increasing quantity.
3. *Given payment by time, underrewarded employees will produce less or poorer-quality output.* Effort will be decreased, which will bring about lower productivity or poorer-quality output than equitably paid subjects.
4. *Given payment by quantity of production, underrewarded employees will produce a large number of low-quality units in comparison with equitably paid employees.* Employees on piece-rate pay plans can bring about equity because trading off quality of output for quantity will result in an increase in rewards with little or no increase in contributions.

These propositions have generally been supported, with a few minor qualifications.[53] First, inequities created by overpayment do not seem to have a very significant impact on behavior in most work situations. Apparently, people have a great deal more tolerance of overpayment inequities than of underpayment inequities, or are better able to rationalize them. Second, not all people are equity sensitive.[54] For example, there is a small part of the working population who actually prefer that their outcome–input ratio be less than the referent comparison. Predictions from equity theory are not likely to be very accurate with these "benevolent types."

It's also important to note that while most research on equity theory has focused on pay, employees seem to look for equity in the distribution of other organizational rewards. For instance, it's been shown that the use of high-status job titles as well as large and lavishly furnished offices may function as outcomes for some employees in their equity equation.[55]

Finally, recent research has been directed at expanding what is meant by equity or fairness.[56] Historically, equity theory focused on **distributive justice** or the perceived fairness of the *amount and allocation* of rewards among individuals. But equity should also consider **procedural justice**—the perceived fairness of the *process* used to determine the distribution of rewards. The evidence indicates that distributive justice has a greater influence on employee satisfaction than procedural justice, while procedural justice tends to affect an employee's organizational commitment, trust in his or her boss, and intention to quit.[57] As a result, managers should consider openly sharing information on how allocation decisions are made, following consistent and unbiased procedures, and engaging in

distributive justice

Perceived fairness of the amount and allocation of rewards among individuals.

procedural justice

The perceived fairness of the process used to determine the distribution of rewards.

similar practices to increase the perception of procedural justice. By increasing the perception of procedural fairness, employees are likely to view their bosses and the organization as positive even if they're dissatisfied with pay, promotions, and other personal outcomes. Moreover, as noted in Chapter 3, organizational citizenship behavior is significantly influenced by perceptions of fairness. Specifically, evidence indicates that although distributive justice issues such as pay are important, perceptions of procedural justice are particularly relevant to OCB.[58] So another plus from employees' perceptions of fair treatment is that they'll be more satisfied and reciprocate by volunteering for extra job activities, helping others, and engaging in similar positive behaviors.

In conclusion, equity theory demonstrates that, for most employees, motivation is influenced significantly by relative rewards as well as by absolute rewards, but some key issues are still unclear.[59] For instance, how do employees handle conflicting equity signals, such as when unions point to other employee groups who are substantially *better off*, while management argues how much things have *improved*? How do employees define inputs and outcomes? How do they combine and weigh their inputs and outcomes to arrive at totals? When and how do the factors change over time? Yet, regardless of these problems, equity theory continues to offer us some important insights into employee motivation.

EXPECTANCY THEORY

Currently, one of the most widely accepted explanations of motivation is Victor Vroom's **expectancy theory**.[60] Although it has its critics,[61] most of the research evidence is supportive of the theory.[62]

Expectancy theory argues that the strength of a tendency to act in a certain way depends on the strength of an expectation that the act will be followed by a given outcome and on the attractiveness of that outcome to the individual. In more practical terms, expectancy theory says that an employee will be motivated to exert a high level of effort when he or she believes that effort will lead to a good performance appraisal; that a good appraisal will lead to organizational rewards such as a bonus, a salary increase, or a promotion; and that the rewards will satisfy the employee's personal goals. The theory, therefore, focuses on three relationships (see Exhibit 6-7).

expectancy theory

The strength of a tendency to act in a certain way depends on the strength of an expectation that the act will be followed by a given outcome and on the attractiveness of that outcome to the individual.

1. *Effort–performance relationship*. The probability perceived by the individual that exerting a given amount of effort will lead to performance.
2. *Performance–reward relationship*. The degree to which the individual believes that performing at a particular level will lead to the attainment of a desired outcome.
3. *Rewards–personal goals relationship*. The degree to which organizational rewards satisfy an individual's personal goals or needs and the attractiveness of those potential rewards for the individual.[63]

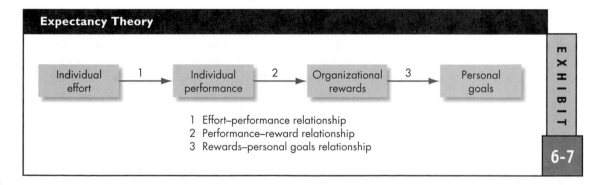

Expectancy Theory

Individual effort → 1 → Individual performance → 2 → Organizational rewards → 3 → Personal goals

1 Effort–performance relationship
2 Performance–reward relationship
3 Rewards–personal goals relationship

EXHIBIT 6-7

Expectancy theory helps explain why a lot of workers aren't motivated on their jobs and merely do the minimum necessary to get by. This is evident when we look at the theory's three relationships in a little more detail. We present them as questions employees need to answer in the affirmative if their motivation is to be maximized.

First, *if I give a maximum effort, will it be recognized in my performance appraisal*? For a lot of employees, the answer is No. Why? Their skill levels may be deficient, which means that no matter how hard they try, they're not likely to be high performers. The organization's performance appraisal system may be designed to assess nonperformance factors such as loyalty, initiative, or courage, which means more effort won't necessarily result in a higher evaluation. Still another possibility is that the employee, rightly or wrongly, perceives that her boss doesn't like her. As a result, she expects to get a poor appraisal regardless of her level of effort. These examples suggest that one possible source of low employee motivation is the belief, by the employee, that no matter how hard she works, the likelihood of getting a good performance appraisal is low.

> *Expectancy theory helps explain why a lot of workers aren't motivated on their jobs and merely do the minimum necessary to get by.*

Second, *if I get a good performance appraisal, will it lead to organizational rewards*? Many employees see the performance–reward relationship in their job as weak. The reason, as we elaborate upon in the next chapter, is that organizations reward a lot of things besides performance. For example, when pay is allocated to employees based on factors such as seniority, being cooperative, or for "kissing up" to the boss, employees are likely to see the performance–reward relationship as being weak and demotivating.

Finally, *if I'm rewarded, are the rewards ones that I find personally attractive*? The employee works hard in hope of getting a promotion but gets a pay raise instead. Or the employee wants a more interesting and challenging job but receives only a few words of praise. Or the employee puts in extra effort to be relocated to the company's Paris office but instead is transferred to Singapore. These examples illustrate the importance of the rewards being tailored to individual employee needs. Unfortunately, many managers are limited in the rewards they can distribute, which makes it difficult to individualize rewards. Moreover, some managers incorrectly assume that all employees want the same thing, thus overlooking the motivational effects of differentiating rewards. In either case, employee motivation is submaximized.

In summary, the key to expectancy theory is the understanding of an individual's goals and the linkage between effort and performance, between performance and rewards, and, finally, between the rewards and individual goal satisfaction. As a contingency model, expectancy theory recognizes that there is no universal principle for explaining everyone's motivations. Additionally, just because we understand what needs a person seeks to satisfy does not ensure that the individual perceives high performance as necessarily leading to the satisfaction of these needs.

Does expectancy theory work? Attempts to validate the theory have been complicated by methodological, criterion, and measurement problems. As a result, many published studies that purport to support or negate the theory must be viewed with caution. Importantly, most studies have failed to replicate the methodology as it was originally proposed. For example, the theory proposes to explain different levels of effort from the same person under different circumstances, but almost all replication studies have looked at different people. Correcting for this flaw has greatly improved support for the validity of expectancy theory.[64] Some critics suggest that the theory has only limited use, arguing that it tends to be a more valid predictor in situations in which effort–performance and performance–reward linkages are clearly perceived by the individual.[65] Since few individuals perceive a high correlation between performance and rewards in their jobs, the theory tends to be idealistic. If organizations actually rewarded individuals for performance rather than according to such criteria as seniority, effort, skill level, and job difficulty, then the theory's validity might be considerably greater. However, rather than invalidating expectancy theory, this criticism can be used in support of the theory, for it explains why a significant segment of the workforce exerts low levels of effort in carrying out job responsibilities.

DON'T FORGET ABILITY AND OPPORTUNITY

Robin and Chris both graduated from college a couple of years ago with degrees in elementary education. They each took jobs as first grade teachers but in different school districts. Robin immediately confronted a number of obstacles on the job: a large class (42 students), a small and dingy classroom, and inadequate supplies. Chris's situation couldn't have been more different. He had only 15 students in his class, plus a teaching aide for 15 hours each week, a modern and well-lighted room, a well-stocked supply cabinet, six iMac computers for students to use, and a highly supportive principal. Not surprisingly, at the end of their first school year, Chris had been considerably more effective as a teacher than had Robin.

The preceding episode illustrates an obvious but often overlooked fact. Success on a job is facilitated or hindered by the existence or absence of support resources.

A popular, although arguably simplistic, way of thinking about employee performance is as a function of the interaction of ability and motivation; that is, performance = $f(A \times M)$. If either is inadequate, performance will be negatively affected. This helps to explain, for instance, the hardworking athlete or student with modest abilities who consistently outperforms his or her more gifted, but lazy, rival. So, as we noted in Chapter 2, an individual's intelligence and skills (subsumed under the label *ability*) must be considered in addition to motivation if we are to be able to accurately explain and predict employee performance. But a piece of the puzzle is still missing. We need to add **opportunity to perform** to our equation—performance = $f(A \times M \times O)$.[66] Even though an individual may be willing and able, there may be obstacles that constrain performance. This is shown in Exhibit 6-8.

opportunity to perform
High levels of performance are partially a function of an absence of obstacles that constrain the employee.

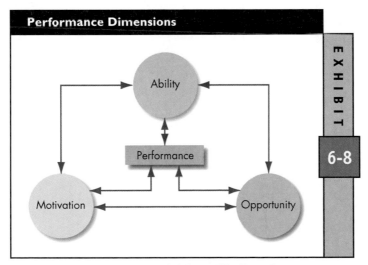

Performance Dimensions

EXHIBIT 6-8

Source: Adapted from M. Blumberg and C. D. Pringle, "The Missing Opportunity in Organizational Research: Some Implications for a Theory of Work Performance," *Academy of Management Review* (October 1982), p. 565.

When you attempt to assess why an employee may not be performing to the level that you believe he or she is capable of, take a look at the work environment to see if it's supportive. Does the employee have adequate tools, equipment, materials, and supplies? Does the employee have favorable working conditions, helpful co-workers, supportive work rules and procedures, sufficient information to make job-related decisions, adequate time to do a good job, and the like? If not, performance will suffer.

INTEGRATING CONTEMPORARY THEORIES OF MOTIVATION

We've looked at a lot of motivation theories in this chapter. The fact that a number of these theories have been supported only complicates the matter. How simple it would have been if, after presenting several theories, only one was found valid. But these theories are not all in competition with one another! Because one is valid doesn't automatically make the others invalid. In fact, many of the theories presented in this chapter are complementary. The challenge is now to tie these theories together to help you understand their interrelationships.[67]

Exhibit 6-9 presents a model that integrates much of what we know about motivation. Its basic foundation is the expectancy model shown in Exhibit 6-7. Let's work through Exhibit 6-9.

We begin by explicitly recognizing that opportunities can aid or hinder individual effort. The individual effort box also has another arrow leading into it.

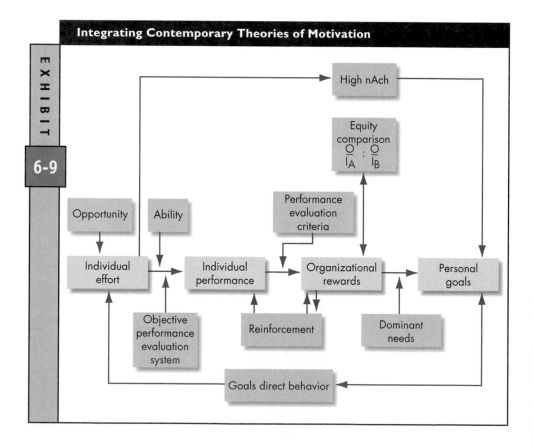

EXHIBIT 6-9

Integrating Contemporary Theories of Motivation

This arrow flows out of the person's goals. Consistent with goal-setting theory, this goals–effort loop is meant to remind us that goals direct behavior.

Expectancy theory predicts that an employee will exert a high level of effort if he or she perceives that there is a strong relationship between effort and performance, performance and rewards, and rewards and satisfaction of personal goals. Each of these relationships, in turn, is influenced by certain factors. For effort to lead to good performance, the individual must have the requisite ability to perform, and the performance appraisal system that measures the individual's performance must be perceived as being fair and objective. The performance–reward relationship will be strong if the individual perceives that it is performance (rather than seniority, personal favorites, or other criteria) that is rewarded. If cognitive evaluation theory were fully valid in the actual workplace, we would predict here that basing rewards on performance should decrease the individual's intrinsic motivation. The final link in expectancy theory is the rewards–goals relationship. ERG theory would come into play at this point. Motivation would be high to the degree that the rewards an individual received for his or her high performance satisfied the dominant needs consistent with his or her individual goals.

A closer look at Exhibit 6-9 will also reveal that the model considers the achievement need and reinforcement and equity theories. The high achiever is not motivated by the organization's assessment of his or her performance or organizational rewards, hence, the jump from effort to personal goals for those with a high nAch. Remember, high achievers are internally driven as long as the jobs they are doing provide them with personal responsibility, feedback, and moderate risks. They are not concerned with the effort–performance, performance–rewards, or rewards–goal linkages.

Reinforcement theory enters our model by recognizing that the organization's rewards reinforce the individual's performance. If management has designed a reward system that is seen by employees as "paying off" for good performance, the rewards will reinforce and encourage continued good performance. Rewards also play the key part in equity theory. Individuals will compare the rewards (outcomes) they receive from the inputs they make with the outcome–input ratio of relevant others ($O/I_A : O/I_B$), and inequities may influence the effort expended.

CAVEAT EMPTOR: MOTIVATION THEORIES ARE CULTURE BOUND

In our discussion of goal setting, we said that care needs to be taken in applying this theory because it assumes cultural characteristics that are not universal. This is true for many of the theories presented in this chapter. Most current motivation theories were developed in the United States by Americans and about Americans.[68] Maybe the most blatant pro-American characteristic inherent in these theories is the strong emphasis on what we defined in Chapter 3 as individualism and quantity of life. For instance, both goal-setting and expectancy theories emphasize goal accomplishment as well as rational and individual thought. Let's take a look at several motivation theories and consider their cross-cultural transferability.

Maslow's need hierarchy argues that people start at the physiological level and then move progressively up the hierarchy in this order: physiological, safety, social, esteem, and self-actualization. This hierarchy, if it has any application at

Satisfying social needs ranks high among employees in Finland. Far from the world's busy high-tech centers, these employees of Nokia, a cellular phone maker headquartered in Helsinki, Finland, enjoy a leisurely ride home from work. Jorma Ollila, Nokia's CEO, says Nokia draws strength from its collegial environment, which he likens to the Finnish character. "We don't snap our suspenders," he says.

all, aligns with American culture. In countries such as Japan, Greece, and Mexico, where uncertainty avoidance characteristics are strong, security needs would be on top of the need hierarchy. Countries that score high on quality-of-life characteristics—Denmark, Sweden, Norway, the Netherlands, and Finland—would have social needs on top.[69] We would predict, for instance, that group work will motivate employees more when the country's culture scores high on the quality criterion.

Another motivation concept that clearly has an American bias is the achievement need. The view that a high achievement need acts as an internal motivator presupposes two cultural characteristics—a willingness to accept a moderate degree of risk (which excludes countries with strong uncertainty avoidance characteristics) and a concern with performance (which applies almost singularly to countries with strong quantity-of-life characteristics). This combination is found in Anglo-American countries such as the United States, Canada, and Great Britain.[70] On the other hand, these characteristics are relatively absent in countries such as Chile and Portugal.

Equity theory has gained a relatively strong following in the United States. That's not surprising since U.S.-style reward systems are based on the assumption that workers are highly sensitive to equity in reward allocations. And in the United States, equity is meant to closely tie pay to performance. However, recent evidence suggests that in collectivist cultures, especially in the former socialist countries of Central and Eastern Europe, employees expect rewards to reflect their individual needs as well as their performance.[71] Moreover, consistent with a legacy of communism and centrally planned economies, employees exhibited an entitlement attitude—that is, they expected outcomes to be *greater* than their inputs.[72] These findings suggest that U.S.-style pay practices may need modification, especially in Russia and former communist countries, in order to be perceived as fair by employees.

But don't assume there aren't *any* cross-cultural consistencies. For instance, the desire for interesting work seems important to almost all workers, regardless of their national culture. In a study of seven countries, employees in Belgium, Britain, Israel, and the United States ranked "interesting work" number one among 11 work goals. And this factor was ranked either second or third in Japan, the Netherlands, and Germany.[73] Similarly, in a study comparing job-preference outcomes among graduate students in the United States, Canada, Australia, and Singapore, growth, achievement, and responsibility were rated the top three and had identical rankings.[74] Both of these studies suggest some universality to the importance of intrinsic factors in the two-factor theory.

SUMMARY AND IMPLICATIONS FOR MANAGERS

The theories we've discussed in this chapter address different outcome variables. Some, for instance, are directed at explaining turnover, while others emphasize productivity. The theories also differ in their predictive strength. In this section, we (1) review the key motivation theories to determine their relevance in explaining our dependent variables, and (2) assess the predictive power of each.[75]

Need Theories   We introduced four theories that focused on needs. These were Maslow's hierarchy, two-factor, ERG, and McClelland's needs theories. The strongest of these is probably the last, particularly regarding the relationship between achievement and productivity. If the other three have any value at all, that value relates to explaining and predicting job satisfaction.

Goal-Setting Theory   There is little dispute that clear and difficult goals lead to higher levels of employee productivity. This evidence leads us to conclude that goal-setting theory provides one of the more powerful explanations of this dependent variable. The theory, however, does not address absenteeism, turnover, or satisfaction.

Reinforcement Theory   This theory has an impressive record for predicting factors such as quality and quantity of work, persistence of effort, absenteeism, tardiness, and accident rates. It does not offer much insight into employee satisfaction or the decision to quit.

Equity Theory   Equity theory deals with all four dependent variables. However, it is strongest when predicting absence and turnover behaviors and weak when predicting differences in employee productivity.

Expectancy Theory   Our final theory focused on performance variables. It has proved to offer a relatively powerful explanation of employee productivity, absenteeism, and turnover. But expectancy theory assumes that employees have few constraints on their decision discretion. It makes many of the same assumptions that the rational model makes about individual decision making (see Chapter 5). This acts to restrict its applicability.

For major decisions, such as accepting or resigning from a job, expectancy theory works well because people don't rush into decisions of this nature. They're more prone to take the time to carefully consider the costs and benefits of all the alternatives. However, expectancy theory is not a very good explanation for more typical types of work behavior, especially for individuals in lower-level jobs, because such jobs come with considerable limitations imposed by work methods, supervisors, and company policies. We would conclude, therefore, that expectancy theory's power in explaining employee productivity increases where the jobs being performed are more complex and higher in the organization (where discretion is greater).

A Guide Through The Maze   Exhibit 6-10 summarizes what we know about the power of the more well-known motivation theories to explain and predict four of our dependent variables. While based on a wealth of research, it also includes some subjective judgments. However, it does provide a reasonable guide through the motivation theory maze.

EXHIBIT 6-10

Power of Motivation Theories[a]

			THEORIES		
Variable	Need	Goal Setting	Reinforcement	Equity	Expectancy
Productivity	3[b]	5	3	3	4[c]
Absenteeism			4	4	4
Turnover				4	5
Satisfaction	2			2	

[a]Theories are rated on a scale of 1 to 5, 5 being highest.

[b]Applies to individuals with a high need to achieve.

[c]Limited value in jobs in which employees have little discretionary choice.

Source: Based on F. J. Landy and W. S. Becker, "Motivation Theory Reconsidered," in L. L. Cummings and B. M. Staw (eds.), *Research in Organizational Behavior*, vol. 9 (Greenwich, CT: JAI Press, 1987), p. 33.

Money Motivates!

Behavioral scientists tend to downplay money as a motivator. They prefer to emphasize the importance of challenging jobs, goals, participative decision making, feedback, cohesive work teams, and other nonmonetary factors. We argue otherwise here—that is, money is *the* critical incentive to work motivation.

Money is important to employees because it's a medium of exchange. People may not work *only* for money, but take the money away and how many people would come to work? A study of nearly 2,500 employees found that while these people disagreed over what was their number-one motivator, they unanimously chose money as their number two.[1]

As equity theory suggests, money has symbolic value in addition to its exchange value. We use pay as the primary outcome against which we compare our inputs to determine if we are being treated equitably. That an organization pays one executive $80,000 a year and another $95,000 means more than the latter's earning $15,000 a year more. It's a message, from the organization to both employees, of how much it values the contribution of each.

In addition to equity theory, both reinforcement and expectancy theories attest to the value of money as a motivator. In the former, if pay is contingent on performance, it will encourage workers to generate high levels of effort. Consistent with expectancy theory, money will motivate to the extent that it is seen as being able to satisfy an individual's personal goals and is perceived as being dependent upon performance criteria.

However, maybe the best case for money is a review of studies that looked at four methods of motivating employee performance: money, goal setting, participative decision making, and redesigning jobs to give workers more challenge and responsibility. The average improvement from money was consistently higher than with any of the other methods.[2]

Money can motivate *some* people under *some* conditions, so the issue isn't really whether or not money can motivate. The answer to that is: It can! The more relevant question is: Does money motivate most employees in the workforce today? The answer to this question, we'll argue, is No.

For money to motivate an individual's performance, certain conditions must be met. First, money must be important to the individual. But money isn't important to everybody. High achievers, for instance, are intrinsically motivated. Money would have little impact on these people.

Second, money must be perceived by the individual as being a direct reward for performance. Unfortunately, performance and pay are poorly linked in most organizations. Pay increases are far more often determined by nonperformance factors such as experience, community pay standards, or company profitability.

Third, the marginal amount of money offered for the performance must be perceived by the individual as being significant. Research indicates that merit raises must be at least 7 percent of base pay for employees to perceive them as motivating. Unfortunately, recent surveys find nonmanagerial employees average merit increases of only 4.9 percent.[3]

Finally, management must have the discretion to reward high performers with more money. But unions and organizational compensation policies constrain managerial discretion. Where unions exist, that discretion is almost zero. In nonunionized environments, traditional limited compensation grades create severe restrictions on pay increases. For example, in one organization, a Systems Analyst IV's pay grade ranges from $4,775 to $5,500 a month. No matter how good a job that analyst does, her boss cannot pay her more than $5,500 a month. Similarly, no matter how poorly she performs, she will not earn less than $4,775. So money might be theoretically capable of motivating employee performance, but most managers aren't given enough flexibility to do much about it.

---

[1]S. Caudron, "Motivation? Money's Only No. 2," *Industry Week*, November 15, 1993, p. 33.

[2]E. A. Locke et al., "The Relative Effectiveness of Four Methods of Motivating Employee Performance" in K. D. Duncan, M. M. Gruenberg, and D. Wallis (eds.), *Changes in Working Life*, (London: John Wiley Ltd., 1980), pp. 363–83.

[3]A. Mitra, N. Gupta, and G. D. Jenkins Jr., "The Case of the Invisible Merit Raise: How People See Their Pay Raises," *Compensation & Benefits Review*, May–June 1995, pp. 71–76.

1. Does motivation come from within a person or is it a result of the situation? Explain.

2. What are the implications of Theories X and Y for motivation practices?

3. Compare and contrast Maslow's hierarchy of needs theory with (a) Alderfer's ERG theory and (b) Herzberg's two-factor theory.

4. Describe the three needs isolated by McClelland. How are they related to worker behavior?

5. Explain cognitive evaluation theory. How applicable is it to management practice?

6. What's the role of self-efficacy in goal setting?

7. Contrast distributive and procedural justice. What implications might they have for designing pay systems in different countries?

8. Identify the variables in expectancy theory.

9. Explain the formula: Performance $= f(A \times M \times O)$ and give an example.

10. What consistencies among motivation concepts, if any, apply cross-culturally?

Questions for Critical Thinking

1. "The cognitive evaluation theory is contradictory to reinforcement and expectancy theories." Do you agree or disagree? Explain.

2. "Goal setting is part of both reinforcement and expectancy theories." Do you agree or disagree? Explain.

3. Analyze the application of Maslow's and Herzberg's theories to an African or Caribbean nation where more than a quarter of the population is unemployed.

4. Can an individual be too motivated, so that his or her performance declines as a result of excessive effort? Discuss.

5. Identify three activities you really enjoy (e.g., playing tennis, reading a novel, going shopping). Next, identify three activities you really dislike (e.g., going to the dentist, cleaning the house, staying on a restricted-calorie diet). Using the expectancy model, analyze each of your answers to assess why some activities stimulate your effort while others don't.

Team Exercise | What Do People Want from Their Jobs?

Each class member begins by completing the following questionnaire:

Rate the following 12 job factors according to how important each is to you. Place a number on a scale of 1 to 5 on the line before each factor.

Very important		Somewhat important		Not important
5	4	3	2	1

_____ 1. An interesting job
_____ 2. A good boss
_____ 3. Recognition and appreciation for the work I do
_____ 4. The opportunity for advancement
_____ 5. A satisfying personal life
_____ 6. A prestigious or status job
_____ 7. Job responsibility
_____ 8. Good working conditions

Very important		Somewhat important		Not important
5	4	3	2	1

_____ 9. Sensible company rules, regulations, procedures, and policies

_____ 10. The opportunity to grow through learning new things

_____ 11. A job I can do well and succeed at

_____ 12. Job security

This questionnaire taps the dimensions in Herzberg's two-factor theory. To determine if hygiene or motivating factors are important to you, place the numbers 1–5 that represent your answers below.

Hygiene factors score

2. _____
5. _____
6. _____
8. _____
9. _____
12. _____

Total points _____

Motivational factors score

1. _____
3. _____
4. _____
7. _____
10. _____
11. _____

Total points _____

Add up each column. Did you select hygiene or motivating factors as being more important to you?

Now break into groups of five or six and compare your questionnaire results. (a) How similar are your scores? (b) How close did your group's results come to those found by Herzberg? (c) What motivational implications did your group arrive at based on your analysis?

Source: This exercise is based on R. N. Lussier, *Human Relations in Organizations: A Skill Building Approach*, 2nd ed. (Homewood, IL. Richard D. Irwin, 1993). With permission.

Internet Search Exercises

1. Choose a professional sport (baseball, basketball, football, etc.) and contrast the pay of the highest paid professional athletes with their performance over the last year. Consider the implications of equity theory on your findings.

2. Contrast the pay of senior executives in the Federal government (president, vice president, etc.); your state, local, or provincial government; and CEOs of a *Fortune* 1000 firm that is headquartered, or operates in your community or region. What conclusions can you draw from your findings?

PHLIP Companion Web Site

We invite you to visit the Robbins homepage on the Prentice Hall Web site at **www.prenhall.com/robbins** for our on-line study guide, current events, links to related Web sites, and more.

Michael Ferro Jr. (photo right) believes that an occasional kick in the pants is good for employee motivation. Ferro is the 31-year-old founder and CEO of Click Interactive Inc., a Chicago-based software design firm. The company provides systems that enable 24-hour, worldwide electronic ordering, tracking, and communication between manufacturers and their distributors, suppliers, and customers over the Internet. Clients include Mitsubishi, Motorola, and Omron Electronics.

Ferro has created what he calls "the penalty box" for his programmers who are burned out or who act overly cocky. In actuality, this is a temporary assignment—from a few weeks to a few months—in the company's sales department. While those chosen may see such a stint as a penalty, Ferro focuses on the positive—it gives isolated programmers new experiences and broadens their responsibilities.

The *punishment* part of "the box" is that all salespeople, including programmers on temporary assignment, are required to wear professional business attire at all times. This is in contrast to the more typical

jeans and T-shirt worn by the programmers on the job. Among programmers, who value their informal dress and insulated lifestyle, wearing suits is somewhat humiliating. In addition, most programmers don't particularly like giving up the cloistered existence of working full-time on their computer.

Instead of writing software, the temporary sales assignment requires programmers to call on customers. This isn't easy for people who are used to spending all day in front of a computer and who have chosen this profession to a large degree because of the job's isolation and independence.

While there is a stigma attached to being temporarily assigned to sales, some of the programmers acknowledge the value of the assignment. Jim Heising (photo left), for example, admits he's gained some valuable insights into customers while forced to make sales calls. Now the company's chief technologist, Heising says that although sometimes customers' requests are far-fetched, other times they come up with great ideas that can actually be implemented.

While Click is only three years old, the company is growing rapidly. In a marketplace where it has to compete against monsterous corporations, such as IBM, Ferro believes that being different can pay big dividends.

Questions

1. If you were a Click programmer, what would you think about being assigned to the penalty box?

2. Would it be a motivator or punishment? Explain using the theories in this chapter.

3. At a time when most managers are encouraged to coddle their employees, would you counsel Ferro to change his "motivation" system? Explain your answer.

Source: Based on E. Brown, "Spare the Rod . . . ," *Forbes*, May 18, 1998, pp. 76–78.

SMALL BUSINESS 2000

People work for many reasons. For most of us, it has something to do with earning money. But money itself is often not reason enough to hold a particular job with a particular company. There is usually something more to it. The issue becomes even

more interesting when you consider why people often stay in the same job for a long time—and enjoy it.

The Harbor Marine Corporation might be a good place to look to get a better understanding of work motivation. One thing is clear: Everyone who works at Harbor Marine enjoys the water. As one worker put it,

"It's a lot of fun, and I get paid for doing what I like doing, working on the water." A love of the water is probably not the only thing that gets these people excited about coming to work.

Another place to look to better understand the excitement about this company is its owner, Ray DiSanto. Ray has been in the construction business for over 30 years and has owned Harbor Marine for about 17 years. DiSanto has owned his own business since he was 19 years old. There is an obvious pattern in how he has moved from his one-person operation to what he has today. Ray loves to work, and he loves the career he has built for himself. Importantly, Ray realizes that he has not reached his goals alone. He talks about the importance of what the company stands for in the eyes of its customer's. Interestingly, he seems as concerned—if not more concerned—about what the company stands for in the eyes of his employees.

As you watch this video, pay attention to what Ray says about why he is proud to own his own business. Consider those things that might help you better understand what makes Ray tick. Next, think about Ray's comments about running a company and his ideas about how to treat employees. You get to meet some employees of the Harbor Marine Corporation. As you listen to them talk, think about how what they are saying relates to what you have learned about motivation. Do these guys like their jobs at Harbor Marine?

Questions

1. You have learned a lot about the evolution of Ray DiSanto's career in the construction industry. He does not appear to be a guy who sits still. What do you think motivates Ray DiSanto to keep trying new things?

2. Do you think the excitement that DiSanto brings to the job does anything to motivate his employees? What do you think it is about DiSanto that is important to his employees?

3. You met a few employees of the Harbor Marine Corporation. Using Alderfer's ERG model, discuss how basic needs are addressed through employment at Harbor Marine.

4. Ray talks about the importance of keeping the equipment in good working order. He likes to keep things working smoothly. Do you think this approach affects the motivation of his employees? Why or why not?

End Notes

1. C. Palmeri, "Making the Grandkids Happy," *Forbes*, August 25, 1997, pp. 60–63.
2. See, for instance, T. R. Mitchell, "Matching Motivational Strategies with Organizational Contexts," in L. L. Cummings and B. M. Staw (eds.), *Research in Organizational Behavior*, vol. 19 (Greenwich, CT: JAI Press, 1997), pp. 60–62.
3. A. Maslow, *Motivation and Personality* (New York: Harper & Row, 1954).
4. See, for example, E. E. Lawler III and J. L. Suttle, "A Causal Correlation Test of the Need Hierarchy Concept," *Organizational Behavior and Human Performance*, April 1972, pp. 265–87; D. T. Hall and K. E. Nougaim, "An Examination of Maslow's Need Hierarchy in an Organizational Setting," *Organizational Behavior and Human Performance*, February 1968, pp. 12–35; and J. Rauschenberger, N. Schmitt, and J. E. Hunter, "A Test of the Need Hierarchy Concept by a Markov Model of Change in Need Strength," *Administrative Science Quarterly*, December 1980, pp. 654–70.
5. A. K. Korman, J. H. Greenhaus, and I. J. Badin, "Personnel Attitudes and Motivation," in M. R. Rosenzweig and L. W. Porter (eds.), *Annual Review of Psychology* (Palo Alto, CA: Annual Reviews, 1977), p. 178.
6. Ibid., p. 179.
7. M. A. Wahba and L. G. Bridwell, "Maslow Reconsidered: A Review of Research on the Need Hierarchy Theory," *Organizational Behavior and Human Performance*, April 1976, pp. 212–40.
8. D. McGregor, *The Human Side of Enterprise* (New York: McGraw-Hill, 1960). For an updated analysis of Theory X and Theory Y constructs, see R. J. Summers and S. F. Cronshaw, "A Study of McGregor's Theory X, Theory Y and the Influence of Theory X, Theory Y Assumptions on Causal Attributions for Instances of Worker Poor Performance," in S. L. McShane (ed.), Organizational Behavior, *ASAC 1988 Conference Proceedings*, vol. 9, Part 5. Halifax, Nova Scotia, 1988, pp. 115–23.
9. See, for example, E. E. Lawler III, *Motivation in Work Organizations* (Belmont, CA: Brooks/Cole, 1973); and B. Weiner, *Human Motivation* (New York: Holt, Rinehart, and Winston, 1980).
10. Ibid.
11. F. Herzberg, B. Mausner, and B. Snyderman, *The Motivation to Work* (New York: John Wiley, 1959).
12. R. J. House and L. A. Wigdor, "Herzberg's Dual-Factor Theory of Job Satisfaction and Motivations: A Review of the Evidence and Criticism," *Personnel Psychology*, Win-

ter 1967, pp. 369–89; D. P. Schwab and L. L. Cummings, "Theories of Performance and Satisfaction: A Review," *Industrial Relations*, October 1970, pp. 403–30; and R. J. Caston and R. Braito, "A Specification Issue in Job Satisfaction Research," *Sociological Perspectives*, April 1985, pp. 175–97.

13. C. P. Alderfer, "An Empirical Test of a New Theory of Human Needs," *Organizational Behavior and Human Performance*, May 1969, pp. 142–75.

14. M. Haire, E. E. Ghiselli, and L. W. Porter, "Cultural Patterns in the Role of the Manager," *Industrial Relations*, February 1963, pp. 95–117.

15. C. P. Schneider and C. P. Alderfer, "Three Studies of Measures of Need Satisfaction in Organizations," *Administrative Science Quarterly*, December 1973, pp. 489–505.

16. J. P. Wanous and A. Zwany, "A Cross-Sectional Test of Need Hierarchy Theory," *Organizational Behavior and Human Performance*, May 1977, pp. 78–97.

17. D. C. McClelland, *The Achieving Society* (New York: Van Nostrand Reinhold, 1961); J. W. Atkinson and J. O. Raynor, *Motivation and Achievement* (Washington, DC: Winston, 1974); D. C. McClelland, *Power: The Inner Experience* (New York: Irvington, 1975); and M. J. Stahl, *Managerial and Technical Motivation: Assessing Needs for Achievement, Power, and Affiliation* (New York: Praeger, 1986).

18. McClelland, *The Achieving Society*.

19. See, for example, A. Mehrabian, "Measures of Achieving Tendency," *Educational and Psychological Measurement*, Summer 1969, pp. 445–51; H. J. M. Hermans, "A Questionnaire Measure of Achievement Motivation," *Journal of Applied Psychology*, August 1970, pp. 353–63; and J. M. Smith, "A Quick Measure of Achievement Motivation," *British Journal of Social and Clinical Psychology*, June 1973, pp. 137–43.

20. See W. D. Spangler, "Validity of Questionnaire and TAT Measures of Need for Achievement: Two Meta-Analyses," *Psychological Bulletin*, July 1992, pp. 140–54.

21. D. C. McClelland and D. G. Winter, *Motivating Economic Achievement* (New York: Free Press, 1969).

22. McClelland, *Power*; D. C. McClelland and D. H. Burnham, "Power Is the Great Motivator," *Harvard Business Review*, March–April 1976, pp. 100–10; and R.E. Boyatzis, "The Need for Close Relationships and the Manager's Job," in D. A. Kolb, I. M. Rubin, and J. M. McIntyre, *Organizational Psychology: Readings on Human Behavior in Organizations*, 4th ed. (Upper Saddle River, NJ: Prentice Hall, 1984), pp. 81–86.

23. Ibid.

24. J. B. Miner, *Studies in Management Education* (New York: Springer, 1965).

25. D. Kipnis, "The Powerholder," in J. T. Tedeschi (ed.), *Perspectives in Social Power* (Chicago: Aldine, 1974), pp. 82–123.

26. D. McClelland, "Toward a Theory of Motive Acquisition," *American Psychologist*, May 1965, pp. 321–33; and D. Miron and D. C. McClelland, "The Impact of Achievement Motivation Training on Small Businesses," *California Management Review*, Summer 1979, pp. 13–28.

27. R. de Charms, *Personal Causation: The Internal Affective Determinants of Behavior* (New York: Academic Press, 1968).

28. E. L. Deci, *Intrinsic Motivation* (New York: Plenum, 1975); R. D. Pritchard, K. M. Campbell, and D. J. Campbell, "Effects of Extrinsic Financial Rewards on Intrinsic Motivation," *Journal of Applied Psychology*, February 1977, pp. 9–15; E. L. Deci, G. Betly, J. Kahle, L. Abrams, and J. Porac, "When Trying to Win: Competition and Intrinsic Motivation," *Personality and Social Psychology Bulletin*, March 1981, pp. 79–83; and P. C. Jordan, "Effects of an Extrinsic Reward on Intrinsic Motivation: A Field Experiment," *Academy of Management Journal*, June 1986, pp. 405–12. See also J. M. Schrof, "Tarnished Trophies," *U.S. News & World Report*, October 25, 1993, pp. 52–59.

29. W. E. Scott, "The Effects of Extrinsic Rewards on 'Intrinsic Motivation': A Critique," *Organizational Behavior and Human Performance*, February 1976, pp. 117–19; B. J. Calder and B. M. Staw, "Interaction of Intrinsic and Extrinsic Motivation: Some Methodological Notes," *Journal of Personality and Social Psychology*, January 1975, pp. 76–80; and K. B. Boal and L. L. Cummings, "Cognitive Evaluation Theory: An Experimental Test of Processes and Outcomes," *Organizational Behavior and Human Performance*, December 1981, pp. 289–310.

30. G. R. Salancik, "Interaction Effects of Performance and Money on Self-Perception of Intrinsic Motivation," *Organizational Behavior and Human Performance*, June 1975, pp. 339–51; and F. Luthans, M. Martinko, and T. Kess, "An Analysis of the Impact of Contingency Monetary Rewards on Intrinsic Motivation," *Proceedings of the Nineteenth Annual Midwest Academy of Management*, St. Louis, 1976, pp. 209–21.

31. J. B. Miner, *Theories of Organizational Behavior* (Hinsdale, IL: Dryden Press, 1980), p. 157.

32. H. J. Arnold, "Effects of Performance Feedback and Extrinsic Reward upon High Intrinsic Motivation," *Organizational Behavior and Human Performance*, December 1976, pp. 275–88.

33. B. M. Staw, "Motivation in Organizations: Toward Synthesis and Redirection," in B. M. Staw and G. R. Salancik (eds.), *New Directions in Organizational Behavior* (Chicago: St. Clair, 1977), p. 76.

34. B. J. Calder and B. M. Staw, "Self-Perception of Intrinsic and Extrinsic Motivation," *Journal of Personality and Social Psychology*, April 1975, pp. 599–605.

35. E. A. Locke, "Toward a Theory of Task Motivation and Incentives," *Organizational Behavior and Human Performance*, May 1968, pp. 157–89.

36. P. C. Earley, P. Wojnaroski, and W. Prest, "Task Planning and Energy Expended: Exploration of How Goals Influence Performance," *Journal of Applied Psychology*, February 1987, pp. 107–14.

37. G. P. Latham and G. A. Yukl, "A Review of Research on the Application of Goal Setting in Organizations," *Academy of Management Journal*, December 1975, pp. 824–45; E. A. Locke, K. N. Shaw, L. M. Saari, and G. P. Latham, "Goal Setting and Task Performance," *Psychological Bulletin*, January 1981, pp. 125–52; A. J. Mento,

R. P. Steel, and R. J. Karren, "A Meta-Analytic Study of the Effects of Goal Setting on Task Performance: 1966–1984," *Organizational Behavior and Human Decision Processes*, February 1987, pp. 52–83; M. E. Tubbs "Goal Setting: A Meta-Analytic Examination of the Empirical Evidence," *Journal of Applied Psychology*, August 1986, pp. 474–83; P. C. Earley, G. B. Northcraft, C. Lee, and T. R. Lituchy, "Impact of Process and Outcome Feedback on the Relation of Goal Setting to Task Performance," *Academy of Management Journal*, March 1990, pp. 87–105; and E. A. Locke and G. P. Latham, *A Theory of Goal Setting and Task Performance* (Englewood Cliffs, NJ: Prentice Hall, 1990).

38. J. M. Ivancevich and J. T. McMahon, "The Effects of Goal Setting, External Feedback, and Self-Generated Feedback on Outcome Variables: A Field Experiment," *Academy of Management Journal*, June 1982, pp. 359–72.

39. See, for example, G. P. Latham, M. Erez, and E. A. Locke, "Resolving Scientific Disputes by the Joint Design of Crucial Experiments by the Antagonists: Application to the Erez-Latham Dispute Regarding Participation in Goal Setting," *Journal of Applied Psychology*, November 1988, pp. 753–72; and T. D. Ludwig and E. S. Geller, "Assigned Versus Participative Goal Setting and Response Generalization: Managing Injury Control Among Professional Pizza Deliverers," *Journal of Applied Psychology*, April 1997, pp. 253–61.

40. M. Erez, P. C. Earley, and C. L. Hulin, "The Impact of Participation on Goal Acceptance and Performance: A Two-Step Model," *Academy of Management Journal*, March 1985, pp. 50–66.

41. J. R. Hollenbeck, C. R. Williams, and H. J. Klein, "An Empirical Examination of the Antecedents of Commitment to Difficult Goals," *Journal of Applied Psychology*, February 1989, pp. 18–23. See also J. C. Wofford, V. L. Goodwin, and S. Premack, "Meta-Analysis of the Antecedents of Personal Goal Level and of the Antecedents and Consequences of Goal Commitment," *Journal of Management*, September 1992, pp. 595–615; and M. E. Tubbs, "Commitment as a Moderator of the Goal-Performance Relation: A Case for Clearer Construct Definition," *Journal of Applied Psychology*, February 1993, pp. 86–97.

42. A. Bandura, *Self-Efficacy: The Exercise of Control* (New York: W. H. Freeman, 1997).

43. E. A. Locke, E. Frederick, C. Lee, and P. Bobko, "Effect of Self-Efficacy, Goals, and Task Strategies on Task Performance," *Journal of Applied Psychology*, May 1984, pp. 241–51; M. E. Gist and T. R. Mitchell, "Self-Efficacy: A Theoretical Analysis of Its Determinants and Malleability," *Academy of Management Review*, April 1992, pp. 183–211; and A. D. Stajkovic and F. Luthans, "Self-Efficacy and Work-Related Performance: A Meta-Analysis," *Psychological Bulletin*, September 1998, pp. 240–61.

44. A. Bandura and D. Cervone, "Differential Engagement in Self-Reactive Influences in Cognitively-Based Motivation," *Organizational Behavior and Human Decision Processes*, August 1986, pp. 92–113.

45. See R. E. Wood, A. J. Mento, and E. A. Locke, "Task Complexity as a Moderator of Goal Effects: A Meta-Analysis," *Journal of Applied Psychology*, August 1987, pp. 416–25; R. Kanfer and P. L. Ackerman, "Motivation and Cognitive Abilities: An Integrative/Aptitude-Treatment Interaction Approach to Skill Acquisition," *Journal of Applied Psychology (monograph)*, vol. 74, 1989, pp. 657–90; T. R. Mitchell and W. S. Silver, "Individual and Group Goals When Workers Are Interdependent: Effects on Task Strategies and Performance," *Journal of Applied Psychology*, April 1990, pp. 185–93; and A. M. O'Leary-Kelly, J. J. Martocchio, and D. D. Frink, "A Review of the Influence of Group Goals on Group Performance," *Academy of Management Journal*, October 1994, pp. 1285–1301.

46. See J. C. Anderson and C. A. O'Reilly, "Effects of an Organizational Control System on Managerial Satisfaction and Performance," *Human Relations*, June 1981, pp. 491–501; and J. P. Meyer, B. Schacht-Cole, and I. R. Gellatly, "An Examination of the Cognitive Mechanisms by Which Assigned Goals Affect Task Performance and Reactions to Performance," *Journal of Applied Social Psychology*, vol. 18, no. 5, 1988, pp. 390–408.

47. J. L. Komaki, T. Coombs, and S. Schepman, "Motivational Implications of Reinforcement Theory," in R. M. Steers, L. W. Porter, and G. Bigley (eds.), *Motivation and Work Behavior*, 6th ed. (New York: McGraw-Hill, 1996), pp. 87–107.

48. E. A. Locke, "Latham vs. Komaki: A Tale of Two Paradigms," *Journal of Applied Psychology*, February 1980, pp. 16–23.

49. J. S. Adams, "Inequity in Social Exchanges," in L. Berkowitz (ed.), *Advances in Experimental Social Psychology* (New York: Academic Press, 1965), pp. 267–300.

50. P. S. Goodman, "An Examination of Referents Used in the Evaluation of Pay," *Organizational Behavior and Human Performance*, October 1974, pp. 170–95; S. Ronen, "Equity Perception in Multiple Comparisons: A Field Study," *Human Relations*, April 1986, pp. 333–46; R. W. Scholl, E. A. Cooper, and J. F. McKenna, "Referent Selection in Determining Equity Perception: Differential Effects on Behavioral and Attitudinal Outcomes," *Personnel Psychology*, Spring 1987, pp. 113–27; and T. P. Summers and A. S. DeNisi, "In Search of Adams' Other: Reexamination of Referents Used in the Evaluation of Pay," *Human Relations*, June 1990, pp. 497–511.

51. C. T. Kulik and M. L. Ambrose, "Personal and Situational Determinants of Referent Choice," *Academy of Management Review*, April 1992, pp. 212–37.

52. See, for example, E. Walster, G. W. Walster, and W. G. Scott, *Equity: Theory and Research* (Boston: Allyn & Bacon, 1978); and J. Greenberg, "Cognitive Reevaluation of Outcomes in Response to Underpayment Inequity," *Academy of Management Journal*, March 1989, pp. 174–84.

53. P. S. Goodman and A. Friedman, "An Examination of Adams' Theory of Inequity," *Administrative Science Quarterly*, September 1971, pp. 271–88; R. P. Vecchio, "An

Individual-Differences Interpretation of the Conflicting Predictions Generated by Equity Theory and Expectancy Theory," *Journal of Applied Psychology*, August 1981, pp. 470–81; J. Greenberg, "Approaching Equity and Avoiding Inequity in Groups and Organizations," in J. Greenberg and R. L. Cohen (eds.), *Equity and Justice in Social Behavior* (New York: Academic Press, 1982), pp. 389–435; E. W. Miles, J. D. Hatfield, and R. C. Huseman, "The Equity Sensitive Construct: Potential Implications for Worker Performance," *Journal of Management*, December 1989, pp. 581–88; and R. T. Mowday, "Equity Theory Predictions of Behavior in Organizations," in R. Steers, L. W. Porter, and G. Bigley (eds.), *Motivation and Work Behavior*, 6th ed. (New York: McGraw-Hill, 1996), pp. 111–31.

54. See, for example, W. C. King, E. W. Miles, and D. D. Day, "A Test and Refinement of the Equity Sensitive Construct," *Journal of Organizational Behavior*, July 1993, pp. 301–17.

55. J. Greenberg and S. Ornstein, "High Status Job Title as Compensation for Underpayment: A Test of Equity Theory," *Journal of Applied Psychology*, May 1983, pp. 285–97; and J. Greenberg, "Equity and Workplace Status: A Field Experiment," *Journal of Applied Psychology*, November 1988, pp. 606–13.

56. J. Greenberg, The Quest for Justice on the Job (Thousand Oaks, CA: Sage, 1996); and R. Cropanzano and J. Greenberg, "Progress in Organizational Justice: Tunneling Through the Maze," in C. L. Cooper and I. T. Robertson (eds.), *International Review of Industrial and Organizational Psychology*, vol. 12 (New York: Wiley, 1997).

57. See, for example, R. C. Dailey and D. J. Kirk, "Distributive and Procedural Justice as Antecedents of Job Dissatisfaction and Intent to Turnover," *Human Relations*, March 1992, pp. 305–16; D. B. McFarlin and P. D. Sweeney, "Distributive and Procedural Justice as Predictors of Satisfaction with Personal and Organizational Outcomes," *Academy of Management Journal*, August 1992, pp. 626–37; and M. A. Korsgaard, D. M. Schweiger, and H. J. Sapienza, "Building Commitment, Attachment, and Trust in Strategic Decision-Making Teams: The Role of Procedural Justice," *Academy of Management Journal*, February 1995, pp. 60–84.

58. R. H. Moorman, "Relationship Between Justice and Organizational Citizenship Behaviors: Do Fairness Perceptions Influence Employee Citizenship?" *Journal of Applied Psychology*, December 1991, pp. 845–55.

59. P. S. Goodman, "Social Comparison Process in Organizations," in B. M. Staw and G. R. Salancik (eds.), *New Directions in Organizational Behavior* (Chicago: St. Clair, 1977), pp. 97–132; and J. Greenberg, "A Taxonomy of Organizational Justice Theories," *Academy of Management Review*, January 1987, pp. 9–22.

60. V. H. Vroom, *Work and Motivation* (New York: John Wiley, 1964).

61. See, for example, H. G. Heneman III and D. P. Schwab, "Evaluation of Research on Expectancy Theory Prediction of Employee Performance," *Psychological Bulletin*, July 1972, pp. 1–9; T. R. Mitchell, "Expectancy Models of Job Satisfaction, Occupational Preference and Effort: A Theoretical, Methodological and Empirical Appraisal," *Psychological Bulletin*, November 1974, pp. 1053–77; and L. Reinharth and M. A. Wahba, "Expectancy Theory as a Predictor of Work Motivation, Effort Expenditure, and Job Performance," *Academy of Management Journal*, September 1975, pp. 502–37.

62. See, for example, L. W. Porter and E. E. Lawler III, *Managerial Attitudes and Performance* (Homewood, IL: Richard D. Irwin, 1968); D. F. Parker and L. Dyer, "Expectancy Theory as a Within-Person Behavioral Choice Model: An Empirical Test of Some Conceptual and Methodological Refinements," *Organizational Behavior and Human Performance*, October 1976, pp. 97–117; H. J. Arnold, "A Test of the Multiplicative Hypothesis of Expectancy-Valence Theories of Work Motivation," *Academy of Management Journal*, April 1981, pp. 128–41; and W. Van Eerde and H. Thierry, "Vroom's Expectancy Models and Work-Related Criteria: A Meta-Analysis," *Journal of Applied Psychology*, October 1996, pp. 575–86.

63. Vroom refers to these three variables as expectancy, instrumentality, and valence, respectively.

64. P. M. Muchinsky, "A Comparison of Within- and Across-Subjects Analyses of the Expectancy-Valence Model for Predicting Effort," *Academy of Management Journal*, March 1977, pp. 154–58.

65. R. J. House, H. J. Shapiro, and M. A. Wahba, "Expectancy Theory as a Predictor of Work Behavior and Attitudes: A Re-evaluation of Empirical Evidence," *Decision Sciences*, January 1974, pp. 481–506.

66. L. H. Peters, E. J. O'Connor, and C. J. Rudolf, "The Behavioral and Affective Consequences of Performance-Relevant Situational Variables," *Organizational Behavior and Human Performance*, February 1980, pp. 79–96; M. Blumberg and C. D. Pringle, "The Missing Opportunity in Organizational Research: Some Implications for a Theory of Work Performance," *Academy of Management Review*, October 1982, pp. 560–69; D. A. Waldman and W. D. Spangler, "Putting Together the Pieces: A Closer Look at the Determinants of Job Performance," *Human Performance*, vol. 2, 1989, pp. 29–59; and J. Hall, "Americans Know How to Be Productive If Managers Will Let Them," *Organizational Dynamics*, Winter 1994, pp. 33–46.

67. For other examples of models that seek to integrate motivation theories, see H. J. Klein, "An Integrated Control Theory Model of Work Motivation," *Academy of Management Review*, April 1989, pp. 150–72; E. A. Locke, "The Motivation Sequence, the Motivation Hub, and the Motivation Core," *Organizational Behavior and Human Decision Processes*, December 1991, pp. 288–99; and T. R. Mitchell, "Matching Motivational Strategies with Organizational Contexts," in *Research in Organizational Behavior*.

68. N. J. Adler, *International Dimensions of Organizational Behavior*, 3rd ed. (Cincinnati, OH: Southwestern, 1997), p. 158.

69. G. Hofstede, "Motivation, Leadership, and Organization: Do American Theories Apply Abroad?" *Organizational Dynamics*, Summer 1980, p. 55.

70. Ibid.

71. J. K. Giacobbe-Miller, D. J. Miller, and V. I. Victorov, "A Comparison of Russian and U.S. Pay Allocation Decisions, Distributive Justice Judgments, and Productivity Under Different Payment Conditions," *Personnel Psychology*, Spring 1998, pp. 137–63.

72. S. L. Mueller and L. D. Clarke, "Political-Economic Context and Sensitivity to Equity: Differences Between the United States and the Transition Economies of Central and Eastern Europe," *Academy of Management Journal*, June 1998, pp. 319–29.

73. I. Harpaz, "The Importance of Work Goals: An International Perspective," *Journal of International Business Studies*, First Quarter 1990, pp. 75–93.

74. G. E. Popp, H. J. Davis, and T. T. Herbert, "An International Study of Intrinsic Motivation Composition," *Management International Review*, January 1986, pp. 28–35.

75. This section is based on F. J. Landy and W. S. Becker, "Motivation Theory Reconsidered," in L. L. Cummings and B. M. Staw (eds.), *Research in Organizational Behavior*, vol. 9 (Greenwich, CT: JAI Press, 1987), pp. 24–35.

part two

THE
INDIVIDUAL

Who says money doesn't motivate? Not Diane Warren (see photo).[1] Diane and her husband Steven own a 100-seat restaurant and delicatessen in Columbus, Ohio. When she began to see her food costs spiraling out of control, Diane turned to her employees for answers.

Diane decided on a pay-for-performance system—called gainsharing—as a means to motivate her employees to cut costs. "I said, 'You guys reduce food costs down below 35 percent [of total sales], and I'll split the [savings] with you.'" Her employees immediately began offering cost-cutting suggestions, including matching perishable orders more closely to expected sales. This saved money by reducing waste.

Gainsharing provided immediate benefits for both the restaurant and its employees. In the first month, food costs fell 1.7 percentage points—and employees took home about $40 each in bonus money. During its first year, monthly payouts were as high as $95. And employees received bonuses in 10 of those first 12 months. Says Diane, "We reduced food costs and got the employees to begin thinking about how the business functions." So gainsharing proved to be a win-win outcome for Diane's business and her employees. By cutting costs, she increased her profits. And at the same time, her employees became better educated about the business's cost structure, more involved in their jobs and the restaurant, and earned more money for themselves.

In this chapter, we want to focus on how to apply motivation concepts. We want to link theories to practices such as gainsharing. For it's one thing to be able to regurgitate motivation theories. It's often another to see how, as a manager, you could use them.

In the following pages, we review a number of motivation techniques and programs that have gained varying degrees of

Motivation: From Concept to Applications

acceptance in practice. And for each of the techniques and programs we review, we specifically address how they build on one or more of the motivation theories covered in the previous chapter.

MANAGEMENT BY OBJECTIVES

Goal-setting theory has an impressive base of research support. But as a manager, how do you make goal setting operational? The best answer to that question is: Install a management by objectives (MBO) program.

WHAT IS MBO?

Management by objectives emphasizes participatively set goals that are tangible, verifiable, and measurable. It's not a new idea. In fact, it was originally proposed more than 45 years ago as a means of using goals to motivate people rather than to control them.[2] Today, no introduction to basic management concepts would be complete without a discussion of MBO.

MBO's appeal undoubtedly lies in its emphasis on converting overall organizational objectives into specific objectives for organizational units and individual members. MBO operationalizes the concept of objectives by devising a process by which objectives cascade down through the organization. As depicted in Exhibit 7-1, the organization's overall objectives are translated into specific objectives for each succeeding level (i.e., divisional, departmental, individual) in the organization. But because lower-unit managers jointly participate in setting their own goals, MBO works from the "bottom up" as well as from the "top down." The result is a hierarchy of objectives that links objectives at one level to those at the next level. And for the individual employee, MBO provides specific personal performance objectives.

AFTER READING THIS CHAPTER, YOU SHOULD BE ABLE TO

1. Identify the four ingredients common to MBO programs

2. Explain why managers might want to use employee involvement programs

3. Contrast participative management with employee involvement

4. Define quality circles

5. Explain how ESOPs can increase employee motivation

6. Contrast gainsharing and profit sharing

7. Describe the link between skill-based pay plans and motivation theories

8. Explain how flexible benefits turn benefits into motivators

9. Contrast the challenges of motivating professional employees versus low-skilled employees

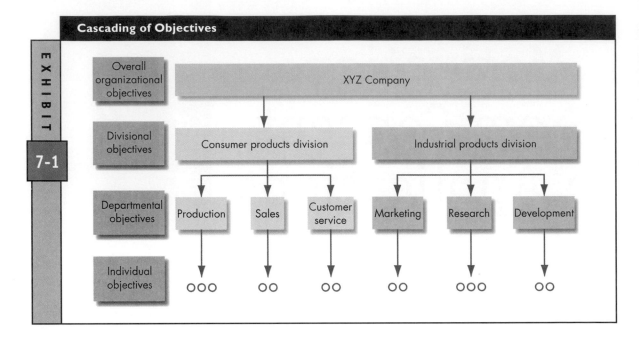

EXHIBIT 7-1

Cascading of Objectives

Overall organizational objectives	XYZ Company	
Divisional objectives	Consumer products division	Industrial products division
Departmental objectives	Production Sales Customer service	Marketing Research Development
Individual objectives	ooo oo oo	oo ooo oo

management by objectives (MBO)

A program that encompasses specific goals, participatively set, for an explicit time period, with feedback on goal progress.

There are four ingredients common to MBO programs. These are goal specificity, participative decision making, an explicit time period, and performance feedback.[3]

The objectives in MBO should be concise statements of expected accomplishments. It's not adequate, for example, to merely state a desire to cut costs, improve service, or increase quality. Such desires have to be converted into tangible objectives that can be measured and evaluated. To cut departmental costs *by 7 percent*, to improve service by ensuring that all telephone orders are processed *within 24 hours of receipt*, or to increase quality by keeping returns to *less than 1 percent of sales* are examples of specific objectives.

The objectives in MBO are not unilaterally set by the boss and then assigned to employees. MBO replaces imposed goals with participatively determined goals. The manager and employee jointly choose the goals and agree on how they will be measured.

Each objective has a specific time period in which it is to be completed. Typically the time period is three months, six months, or a year. So managers and employees have specific objectives and stipulated time periods in which to accomplish them.

The final ingredient in an MBO program is feedback on performance. MBO seeks to give continuous feedback on progress toward goals. Ideally, this is accomplished by giving ongoing feedback to individuals so they can monitor and correct their own actions. This is supplemented by periodic managerial evaluations, when progress is reviewed.

LINKING MBO AND GOAL-SETTING THEORY

Goal-setting theory demonstrates that hard goals result in a higher level of individual performance than do easy goals, that specific hard goals result in higher levels of performance than do no goals at all or the generalized goal of "do your best," and that feedback on one's performance leads to higher performance. Compare these findings with MBO.

MBO directly advocates specific goals and feedback. MBO implies, rather than explicitly states, that goals must be perceived as feasible. Consistent with goal setting, MBO would be most effective when the goals are difficult enough to require the person to do some stretching.

The only area of possible disagreement between MBO and goal-setting theory relates to the issue of participation—MBO strongly advocates it, while goal-setting theory demonstrates that assigning goals to subordinates frequently works just as well. The major benefit to using participation, however, is that it appears to induce individuals to establish more difficult goals.

MBO IN PRACTICE

How widely used is MBO? Reviews of studies that have sought to answer this question suggest that it's a popular technique. You'll find MBO programs in many business, health care, educational, government, and nonprofit organizations.[4]

MBO's popularity should not be construed to mean that it always works. There are a number of documented cases in which MBO had been implemented but failed to meet management's expectations.[5] A close look at these cases, however, indicates that the problems rarely lie with MBO's basic components. Rather, the culprits tend to be factors such as unrealistic expectations regarding results, lack of top-management commitment, and an inability or unwillingness by management to allocate rewards based on goal accomplishment. Nevertheless, MBO provides managers with the vehicle for implementing goal-setting theory.

EMPLOYEE RECOGNITION PROGRAMS

Laura Schendell only makes $6.50 an hour working at her fast-food job in Pensacola, Florida, and the job isn't very challenging or interesting. Yet Laura talks enthusiastically about her job, her boss, and the company that employs her. "What I like is the fact that Guy [her supervisor] appreciates the effort I make. He compliments me regularly in front of the other people on my shift, and I've been chosen 'Employee of the Month' twice in the past six months. Did you see my picture on that plaque on the wall?"

Organizations are increasingly recognizing what Laura Schendell is acknowledging: Recognition can be a potent motivator.

WHAT ARE EMPLOYEE RECOGNITION PROGRAMS?

Employee recognition programs can take numerous forms. The best ones use multiple sources and recognize both individual and group accomplishments. Convex Computer Corporation, a supercomputer manufacturer based in Texas that employs 1,200 people, provides an excellent illustration of a comprehensive recognition program.[6]

On a quarterly basis, Convex's vice president of operations recognizes individuals who have been nominated by their managers as having gone "above and beyond the call of duty." Annually, individuals may nominate their peers for the Customer Service Award, which recognizes such categories as risk taking, innovation, cost reduction, and overall customer service. And at the department level, recognition takes the form of team or department T-shirts, coffee mugs, banners, or pictures. Supervisors have used movie tickets, Friday afternoon bowling get-togethers, time off, and cash awards to acknowledge such achievements as three months of defect-free assembly, five years of perfect attendance, and completing a project early.

General Electric's chief executive Jack Welch recognizes the power of recognition. He motivates employees by personally handing out bonuses for good work. He constantly sends handwritten notes to managers and employees thanking them for a job well done, suggesting improvements, and expressing encouragement during family crises.

Source: S. Adams, *Share the Whales*, p. 66.

LINKING RECOGNITION PROGRAMS AND REINFORCEMENT THEORY

A few years ago, 1,500 employees were surveyed in a variety of work settings to find out what they considered to be the most powerful workplace motivator. Their response? Recognition, recognition, and more recognition![7]

Consistent with reinforcement theory, rewarding a behavior with recognition immediately following that behavior is likely to encourage its repetition. Recognition can take many forms. You can personally congratulate an employee in private for a good job. You can send a handwritten note or an e-mail message acknowledging something positive that the employee has done. For employees with a strong need for social acceptance, you can publicly recognize accomplishments. And to enhance group cohesiveness and motivation, you can celebrate team successes. You can use meetings to recognize the contributions and achievements of successful work teams.

EMPLOYEE RECOGNITION PROGRAMS IN PRACTICE

In today's highly competitive global economy, most organizations are under severe cost pressures. That makes recognition programs particularly attractive. In contrast to most other motivators, recognizing an employee's superior performance often costs little or no money. Maybe that's why a recent survey of 3,000 employers found that two-thirds use or plan to use special recognition awards.[8]

One of the most well-known and widely used recognition devices is the use of suggestion systems. Employees offer suggestions for improving processes or cutting costs and are recognized with small cash awards. The Japanese have been especially effective at making suggestion systems work. For instance, a typical high-performing Japanese plant in the auto components business generates 47 suggestions per employee a year and pays approximately the equivalent of U.S.$35 per suggestion. In contrast, a comparable Western factory generates about one suggestion per employee per year, but pays out $90 per suggestion.[9]

EMPLOYEE INVOLVEMENT PROGRAMS

The Donnelly Corporation, a major supplier of glass products to automobile manufacturers, uses committees of elected representatives to make all key decisions affecting Donnelly employees.[10] At a General Electric lighting plant in Ohio, work teams perform many tasks and assume many of the responsibilities once handled by their supervisors. In fact, when the plant was faced with a recent decline in the demand for the tubes it produces, the workers decided first to slow production and eventually to lay themselves off. Marketing people at USAA, a large insurance company, meet in a conference room for an hour every week to discuss ways in which they can improve the quality of their work and increase productivity. Management has implemented many of their suggestions. Childress Buick, an automobile dealer in Phoenix, allows its salespeople to negotiate and finalize deals with customers without any approval from management. The laws of Germany, France, Denmark, Sweden, and Austria require companies to have elected representatives from their employee groups as members of their boards of directors.[11]

The common theme throughout the preceding examples is that they all illustrate employee involvement programs. In this section, we clarify what we mean by employee involvement, describe some of the various forms that it takes, consider the motivational implications of these programs, and show some applications.

WHAT IS EMPLOYEE INVOLVEMENT?

Employee involvement has become a convenient catchall term to cover a variety of techniques.[12] For instance, it encompasses such popular ideas as employee participation or participative management, workplace democracy, empowerment, and employee ownership. Our position is, although each of these ideas has some unique characteristics, they all have a common core—that of employee involvement.

What specifically do we mean by **employee involvement**? We define it as a participative process that uses the entire capacity of employees and is designed to encourage increased commitment to the organization's success.[13] The underlying logic is that by involving workers in those decisions that affect them and by increasing their autonomy and control over their work lives, employees will become more motivated, more committed to the organization, more productive, and more satisfied with their jobs.[14]

Does that mean that participation and employee involvement are synonyms for each other? No. *Participation* is a more limited term. It's a subset within the larger framework of employee involvement. All of the employee involvement programs we describe include some form of employee participation but the term *participation*, per se, is too narrow and limiting.

employee involvement

A participative process that uses the entire capacity of employees and is designed to encourage increased commitment to the organization's success.

EXAMPLES OF EMPLOYEE INVOLVEMENT PROGRAMS

In this section we review four forms of employee involvement: participative management, representative participation, quality circles, and employee stock ownership plans.

Participative Management The distinct characteristic common to all **participative management** programs is the use of joint decision making. That is, subordinates actually share a significant degree of decision-making power with their immediate superiors.

Participative management has, at times, been promoted as a panacea for poor morale and low productivity. Some authors have even proposed that participative management is an ethical imperative.[15] But participative management is not appropriate for every organization or every work unit. For it to work, there must be adequate time to participate, the issues in which employees get involved must be relevant to their interests, employees must have the ability (intelligence, technical knowledge, communication skills) to participate, and the organization's culture must support employee involvement.[16]

Patricia Louko (right) practices participative management. The founder and president of Books Plus, a college bookstore in Lake Worth, Florida, Louko involves all her employees in making decisions. She prepares them for decision making by cross-training them in every job, including customer service, ordering, receiving, and book buyback. "Any employee is entitled to make any decision when working with customers," says Louko. Participative management is part of the bookstore's "total team approach" culture.

participative management

A process in which subordinates share a significant degree of decision-making power with their immediate superiors.

Why would management want to share its decision-making power with subordinates? There are a number of good reasons. As jobs have become more complex, managers often don't know everything their employees do. Thus, participation allows those who know the most to contribute. The result can be better decisions. The interdependence in tasks that employees often do today also requires consultation with people in other departments and work units. This increases the need for teams, committees, and group meetings to resolve issues that affect them jointly. Participation additionally increases commitment to decisions. People are less likely to undermine a decision at the time of its implementation if they shared in making that decision. Finally, participation provides intrinsic rewards for employees. It can make their jobs more interesting and meaningful.

Dozens of studies have been conducted on the participation-performance relationship. The findings, however, are mixed.[17] When the research is reviewed carefully, it appears that participation typically has only a modest influence on variables such as employee productivity, motivation, and job satisfaction. Of course, that doesn't mean that the use of participative management can't be beneficial under the right conditions. What it says, however, is that the use of participation is no sure means for improving employee performance.

representative participation

Workers participate in organizational decision making through a small group of representative employees.

Representative Participation Almost every country in Western Europe has some type of legislation requiring companies to practice **representative participation**. That is, rather than participate directly in decisions, workers are represented by a small group of employees who actually participate. Representative participation has been called "the most widely legislated form of employee involvement around the world."[18]

Representative participation has been called "the most widely legislated form of employee involvement around the world."

The goal of representative participation is to redistribute power within an organization, putting labor on a more equal footing with the interests of management and stockholders.

The two most common forms that representative participation takes are works councils and board representatives.[19] **Works councils** link employees with management. They are groups of nominated or elected employees who must be consulted when management makes decisions involving personnel. For example, in the Netherlands, if a Dutch company is taken over by another firm, the former's works council must be informed at an early stage, and if the council objects, it has 30 days to seek a court injunction to stop the takeover.[20] **Board representatives** are employees who sit on a company's board of directors and represent the interests of the firm's employees. In some countries, large companies may be legally required to make sure that employee representatives have the same number of board seats as stockholder representatives.

works councils

Groups of nominated or elected employees who must be consulted when management makes decisions involving personnel.

The overall influence of representative participation on working employees seems to be minimal.[21] For instance, the evidence suggests that works councils are dominated by management and have little impact on employees or the organization. And while this form of employee involvement might increase the motivation and satisfaction of those individuals who are doing the representing, there is little evidence that this trickles down to the operating employees whom they represent. Overall, "the greatest value of representative participation is symbolic. If one is interested in changing employee attitudes or in improving organizational performance, representative participation would be a poor choice."[22]

board representatives

A form of representative participation; employees sit on a company's board of directors and represent the interests of the firm's employees.

Quality Circles   "Probably the most widely discussed and undertaken formal style of employee involvement is the quality circle."[23] The quality circle concept is frequently mentioned as one of the techniques that Japanese firms utilize that has allowed them to make high-quality products at low costs. Originally begun in the United States and exported to Japan in the 1950s, the quality circle became quite popular in North America and Europe during the 1980s.[24]

What is a **quality circle**? It's a work group of eight to ten employees and supervisors who have a shared area of responsibility. They meet regularly—typically once a week, on company time and on company premises—to discuss their quality problems, investigate causes of the problems, recommend solutions, and take corrective actions. They take over the responsibility for solving quality problems, and they generate and evaluate their own feedback. But management typically retains control over the final decision regarding implementation of recommended solutions. Of course, it is not presumed that employees inherently have this ability to analyze and solve quality problems. Therefore, part of the quality circle concept includes teaching participating employees group communication skills, various quality strategies, and measurement and problem analysis techniques. Exhibit 7-3 describes a typical quality circle process.

quality circle

A work group of employees who meet regularly to discuss their quality problems, investigate causes, recommend solutions, and take corrective actions.

Do quality circles improve employee productivity and satisfaction? A review of the evidence indicates that they are much more likely to positively affect productivity. They tend to show little or no effect on employee satisfaction; and while

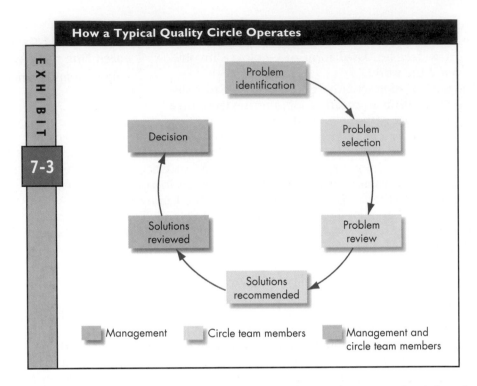

EXHIBIT 7-3

How a Typical Quality Circle Operates

Problem identification → Problem selection → Problem review → Solutions recommended → Solutions reviewed → Decision → (back to Problem identification)

■ Management   ■ Circle team members   ■ Management and circle team members

many studies report positive results from quality circles on productivity, these results are by no means guaranteed.[25] The failure of many quality circle programs to produce measurable benefits has also led to many of them being discontinued.

One author has gone as far as to say that while quality circles were the management fad of the 1980s, they've "become a flop."[26] He offers two possible explanations for their disappointing results. First is the little bit of time that actually deals with employee involvement. "At most, these programs operate for one hour per week, with the remaining 39 hours unchanged. Why should changes in 2.5 percent of a person's job have a major impact?"[27] Second, the ease of implementing quality circles often worked against them. They were seen as a simple device that could be added on to the organization with few changes required outside the program itself. In many cases, the only significant involvement by management was funding the program. So quality circles became an easy way for management to get on the employee involvement bandwagon. And, unfortunately, the lack of planning and top-management commitment often contributed to quality circle failures.

Employee Stock Ownership Plans The final employee involvement approach we'll discuss is **employee stock ownership plans (ESOPs)**.[28]

Employee ownership can mean any number of things from employees owning some stock in the company in which they work to the individuals working in the company owning and personally operating the firm. Employee stock ownership plans are company-established benefit plans in which employees acquire stock as part of their benefits. Approximately 20 percent of Polaroid, for example, is owned by its employees. Forty percent of Canadian-based Spruce Falls, Inc. is owned by its employees. Employees own 71 percent of Avis Corporation. And United Airlines and Weirton Steel are 100 percent owned by their employees.[29]

In the typical ESOP, an employee stock ownership trust is created. Companies contribute either stock or cash to buy stock for the trust and allocate the

employee stock ownership plans (ESOPs)

Company-established benefit plans in which employees acquire stock as part of their benefits.

stock to employees. While employees hold stock in their company, they usually cannot take physical possession of their shares or sell them as long as they're still employed at the company.

The research on ESOPs indicates that they increase employee satisfaction.[30] But their impact on performance is less clear. For instance, one study compared 45 ESOPs against 238 conventional companies.[31] The ESOPs outperformed the conventional firms both in terms of employment and sales growth. But other studies have shown disappointing results.[32]

ESOPs have the potential to increase employee job satisfaction and work motivation. But for this potential to be realized, employees need to psychologically experience ownership.[33] That is, in addition to merely having a financial stake in the company, employees need to be kept regularly informed on the status of the business and also have the opportunity to exercise influence over the business. The evidence consistently indicates that it takes ownership and a participative style of management to achieve significant improvements in an organization's performance.[34]

Employees own 75 percent of the stock at TDIndustries, a Dallas-based plumbing and air conditioning contractor. TDI keeps its employees informed about the financial status of the business by holding monthly information meetings. Stock ownership serves as a great motivator at TDI. "This company makes you feel like a human being again," says one employee.

LINKING EMPLOYEE INVOLVEMENT PROGRAMS AND MOTIVATION THEORIES

Employee involvement draws on a number of the motivation theories discussed in the previous chapter. For instance, Theory Y is consistent with participative management, while Theory X aligns with the more traditional autocratic style of managing people. In terms of two-factor theory, employee involvement programs could provide employees with intrinsic motivation by increasing opportunities for growth, responsibility, and involvement in the work itself. Similarly, the opportunity to make and implement decisions, and then seeing them work out, can help satisfy an employee's needs for responsibility, achievement, recognition, growth, and enhanced self-esteem. So employee involvement is compatible with ERG theory and efforts to stimulate the achievement need.

EMPLOYEE INVOLVEMENT PROGRAMS IN PRACTICE

Germany, France, Holland, and the Scandinavian countries have firmly established the principle of industrial democracy in Europe, and other nations, including Japan and Israel, have traditionally practiced some form of representative participation for decades. Participative management and representative participation were much slower to gain ground in North American organizations. But nowdays, employee involvement programs that stress participation have become the norm. While some managers continue to resist sharing decision-making power, the pressure is on managers to give up their autocratic decision-making style in favor of a more participative, supportive, coaching-like role.

What about quality circles? How popular are they in practice? The names of companies that have used quality circles read like a *Who's Who of Corporate*

America: Hewlett-Packard, General Electric, Texas Instruments, Inland Steel, Xerox, Eastman Kodak, Polaroid, Procter & Gamble, Control Data, General Motors, Ford, IBM, Motorola, American Airlines, and TRW.[35] But, as we noted, the success of quality circles has been far from overwhelming. They were popular in the 1980s, largely because they were easy to implement. In more recent years, many organizations have dropped their quality circles and replaced them with more comprehensive team-based structures (which we discuss in Chapter 9).

What about ESOPs? They have become the most popular form of employee ownership. They've grown from just a handful in 1974 to around 10,000 now, covering approximately 10 million employees. Many well-known companies, including Anheuser-Busch, Procter & Gamble, and Polaroid, have implemented ESOPs.[36] But so too have many smaller, not so well-known, companies. And that's likely to increase. A recent change in U.S. laws now allows S-corporations—which encompasses mostly small businesses—to establish ESOPs.[37]

VARIABLE PAY PROGRAMS

In order to make employees feel like owners in the company, Eastman Chemical recently introduced a top-to-bottom incentive-compensation program.[38] As part of that program, all 18,000 employees—from the lowest paid to the CEO—have to put at least 5 percent of their annual pay at risk. If the company doesn't achieve its annual performance target, the employees lose that pay. On the plus side, they can earn a bonus of up to 30 percent of their annual pay—5 percent in stock and 25 percent in cash—based on how much the company earns on its invested capital.

Safelite Glass Corp., of Columbus, Ohio, has scrapped its fixed hourly rate pay for glass installers and replaced it with a wage plan based on productivity.[39] Instead of earning $11 an hour, they receive $20 per unit installed. Installers now work faster and there are fewer absences. Under this new system, average productivity per worker has risen 20 percent.

Traders at Bayerische Vereinsbank, Germany's fourth largest bank, earn 75,000 marks (about $36,000) a year in base pay. They also can earn as much as a 50,000-mark bonus if they meet their individual performance goals.[40]

George Fisher, CEO of Eastman Kodak, took a $1.98 million "pay cut" in 1997.[41] That was the amount of bonus he received in 1996, but because of the company's poor performance, Fisher got no bonus in 1997.

The common thread in each of the previous examples is that they all illustrate variable-pay programs.

WHAT ARE VARIABLE-PAY PROGRAMS?

variable-pay programs

A portion of an employee's pay is based on some individual and/or organizational measure of performance.

Piece-rate plans, wage incentives, profit sharing, bonuses, and gainsharing are all forms of **variable-pay programs**. What differentiates these forms of compensation from more traditional programs is that instead of paying a person only for time on the job or seniority, a portion of an employee's pay is based on some individual and/or organizational measure of performance. Unlike more traditional base-pay programs, variable pay is not an annuity. There is no guarantee that just because you made $60,000 last year that you'll make the same amount this year. With variable pay, earnings fluctuate up and down with the measure of performance.[42]

It is precisely the fluctuation in variable pay that has made these programs attractive to management. It turns part of an organization's fixed labor costs into a variable cost, thus reducing expenses when performance declines. Additionally, by tying pay to performance, earnings recognize contribution rather than being a form of entitlement. Low performers find, over time, that their pay stagnates, while high performers enjoy pay increases commensurate with their contribution.

Four of the more widely used variable-pay programs are piece-rate wages, bonuses, profit sharing, and gainsharing.

Piece-rate wages have been around for nearly a century. They have long been popular as a means for compensating production workers. In **piece-rate pay plans** workers are paid a fixed sum for each unit of production completed. When an employee gets no base salary and is paid only for what he or she produces, this is a pure piece-rate plan. People who work ball parks selling peanuts and soda pop frequently are paid this way. They might get to keep 50 cents for every bag of peanuts they sell. If they sell 200 bags during a game, they make $100. If they sell only 40 bags, their take is only $20. The harder they work and the more peanuts they sell, the more they earn. Many organizations use a modified piece-rate plan, in which employees earn a base hourly wage plus a piece-rate differential. So a medical transcriber might be paid $7 an hour plus 20 cents per page. Such modified plans provide a floor under an employee's earnings, while still offering a productivity incentive.

piece-rate pay plans
Workers are paid a fixed sum for each unit of production completed.

Bonuses can be paid exclusively to executives or to all employees. For instance, annual bonuses in the millions of dollars are not uncommon in U.S. corporations. Banc One's CEO John B. McCoy, for example, received a $4 million "special recognition" bonus in 1997 for his success in restructuring the company.[43] Increasingly, bonus plans are taking on a larger net within organizations to include lower-ranking employees. One of the most ambitious bonus systems has recently been put in place by Levi Strauss.[44] If the company reaches cumulative cash flow of $7.6 billion for the next six years, each of the company's 37,500 employees in 60 countries, regardless of position, will get a full year's pay as a bonus. Levi Strauss estimates the potential cost of this bonus for the firm at about $750 million.

Profit-sharing plans are organizationwide programs that distribute compensation based on some established formula designed around a company's profitability. These can be direct cash outlays or, particularly in the case of top managers, allocated as stock options. When you read about executives such as Michael Eisner, the CEO at Disney, earning over $200 million in one year, almost all of this comes from cashing in stock options previously granted based on company profit performance.

profit sharing plans
Organizationwide programs that distribute compensation based on some established formula designed around a company's profitability.

The variable-pay program that has gotten the most attention in recent years is undoubtedly **gainsharing**.[45] This is a formula-based group incentive plan. Improvements in group productivity—from one period to another—determine the total amount of money that is to be allocated. The division of productivity savings can be split between the company and employees in any number of ways, but 50–50 is pretty typical.

gainsharing
An incentive plan in which improvements in group productivity determine the total amount of money that is allocated.

Isn't gainsharing the same as profit sharing? They're similar but not the same thing. By focusing on productivity gains rather than profits, gainsharing rewards specific behaviors that are less influenced by external factors. Employees in a gainsharing plan can receive incentive awards even when the organization isn't profitable.

Do variable-pay programs work? Do they increase motivation and productivity? The answer is a qualified Yes. For example, studies generally support that organizations with profit-sharing plans have higher levels of profitability than those without.[46] Similarly, gainsharing has been found to improve productivity in a majority of cases and often has a positive impact on employee attitudes.[47] An Ameri-

Bonus pay has tripled the income of Steve Scatino, a salesperson at the Scottsdale Plaza Resort in Arizona. In addition to a base salary, the resort offers two pay-for-performance bonus plans. First, salespeople get a monthly check for .5 percent of the business they book. Second, they receive a year-end bonus based on the resort's total revenue. The amount salespeople receive is based on the percentage of revenue they booked. The incentive pay has motivated Scatino to increase his productivity. He arrives at work at 6:30 A.M. and works until 6 P.M. and makes up to 70 sales calls per day.

can Management Association study of 83 companies that used gainsharing found, on average, that grievances dropped 83 percent, absences fell 84 percent, and lost-time accidents decreased by 69 percent.[48] The downside of variable pay, from an employee's perspective, is its unpredictability. With a straight base salary, employees know what they'll be earning. Adding in merit and cost-of-living increases, they can make fairly accurate predictions about what they'll be making next year and the year after. They can finance cars and homes based on reasonably solid assumptions. That's more difficult to do with variable pay. Your group's performance might slip this year or a recession might undermine your company's profits. Depending how your variable pay is determined, these can cut your income. Moreover, people begin to take repeated annual performance bonuses for granted. A 15 or 20 percent bonus, received three years in a row, begins to become expected in the fourth year. If it doesn't materialize, management may find itself with some disgruntled employees on its hands.

LINKING VARIABLE-PAY PROGRAMS AND EXPECTANCY THEORY

Variable pay is probably most compatible with expectancy theory predictions. Specifically, individuals should perceive a strong relationship between their performance and the rewards they receive if motivation is to be maximized. If rewards are allocated completely on nonperformance factors—such as seniority or job title—then employees are likely to reduce their effort.

The evidence supports the importance of this linkage, especially for operative employees working under piece-rate systems. For example, one study of 400 manufacturing firms found that those companies with wage incentive plans achieved 43 to 64 percent greater productivity than those without such plans.[49]

Group and organizationwide incentives reinforce and encourage employees to sublimate personal goals for the best interests of their department or the organization. Group-based performance incentives are also a natural extension for those organizations that are trying to build a strong team ethic. By linking rewards to team performance, employees are encouraged to make extra efforts to help their team succeed.

VARIABLE-PAY PROGRAMS IN PRACTICE

Variable pay is a concept that is rapidly replacing the annual cost-of-living raise. "There is a veritable explosion in variable-pay plans," says one consultant.[50] One reason, as cited earlier, is its motivational power—but don't ignore the cost implications. Bonuses, gainsharing, and other variable-based reward programs avoid the fixed expense of permanent salary boosts.

Pay for performance has been "in" for compensating managers for more than a decade. The new trend has been expanding this practice to nonmanagerial employees. IBM, Wal-Mart, Pizza Hut, Cigna Corp., and John Deere are just a few examples of companies using variable pay with rank-and-file employees.[51] In the late 1990s, 72 percent of large U.S. companies had some form of variable-pay plan for nonexecutives, up from 47 percent in 1990.[52]

Variable-pay plans that use bonuses are also becoming increasingly popular in Canada.[53] In 1992, typical senior executives in Canada could expect bonuses equal to 9.7 percent of their salaries. In 1996, that had almost doubled to 18.5 percent. And the growth in bonuses was even greater among hourly employees. The average bonus for an hourly worker during the same time period went from

1.1 percent of base pay to 5.8 percent. About 35 percent of Canadian companies now have companywide variable-pay incentive plans.

Even Japan is getting on the variable-pay "bandwagon." A recent survey found that 21.8 percent of Japanese companies now use such pay systems. The rate was less than 10 percent in the 1980s.[54]

Gainsharing's popularity seems to be narrowly focused among large, unionized manufacturing companies.[55] It is currently being used in about 2,000 companies including such major firms as Bell & Howell, American Safety Razor, Champion Spark Plug, Cincinnati Milacron, Eaton, Firestone Tire, Hooker Chemical, and Mead Paper.[56]

Among firms that haven't introduced performance-based compensation programs, common concerns tend to surface.[57] Managers fret over what should constitute performance and how it should be measured. They have to overcome the historical attachment to cost-of-living adjustments and the belief that they have an obligation to keep all employees' pay in step with inflation. Other barriers include salary scales keyed to what the competition is paying, traditional compensation systems that rely heavily on specific pay grades and relatively narrow pay ranges, and performance appraisal practices that produce inflated evaluations and expectations of full rewards. Of course, from the employees' standpoint, the major concern is a potential drop in earnings. Pay for performance often means employees have to share in the risks as well as the rewards of their employer's business.

SKILL-BASED PAY PLANS

Organizations hire people for their skills, then typically put them in jobs and pay them based on their job title or rank. For example, the director of corporate sales earns $120,000 a year, the regional sales managers make $75,000, and the district sales managers get $60,000. But if organizations hire people because of their competencies, why don't they pay them for those same competencies? Some organizations do.

Workers at American Steel & Wire can boost their annual salaries by up to $12,480 by acquiring as many as 10 skills. At AT&T's Universal Card service center in Jacksonville, Florida, the best-paid customer representatives have rotated through four to six trouble shooting assignments over two or three years, becoming adept at solving any billing, lost card, or other problem a credit card holder runs into. New employees at a Quaker Oats' pet food plant in Topeka, Kansas start at $8.75 an hour, but can reach a top rate of $14.50 when they master 10 to 12 skills such as operating lift trucks and factory computer controls. Salomon Brothers, a major brokerage firm, is using a skill-based pay system to turn narrowly trained and independent specialists into well-rounded product experts and to encourage them to be team players. Frito-Lay Corporation ties its compensation for managers to progress they make in developing their skills in leadership, group process facilitation, and communications.[58]

WHAT ARE SKILL-BASED PAY PLANS?

skill-based pay

Pay levels are based on how many skills employees have or how many jobs they can do.

Skill-based pay is an alternative to job-based pay. Rather than having an individual's job title define his or her pay category, **skill-based pay** (or also sometimes called *competency-based pay*) sets pay levels on the basis of how many skills employees have or how many jobs they can do.[59] For instance, at Polaroid Corporation, the highest pay you can earn as a machine operator is $14 an hour. However, because the company has a skill-based pay plan, if machine operators broaden their skills to include additional skills such as material accounting, maintenance of equipment, and quality inspection, they can earn up to a 10 percent premium. If they can learn some of their supervisor's skills, they can earn even more.[60]

What's the appeal of skill-based pay plans? From management's perspective, its appeal is its flexibility. Filling staffing needs is easier to do when employee skills are interchangeable. This is particularly true today, as many organizations cut the size of their workforce. Downsized organizations require more generalists and fewer specialists. While skill-based pay encourages employees to acquire a broader range of skills, there are also other benefits. It facilitates communication across the organization because people gain a better understanding of others' jobs. It lessens dysfunctional "protection of territory" behavior. Where skill-based pay exists, you're less likely to hear the phrase, "It's not my job!" Skill-based pay additionally helps meet the needs of ambitious employees who confront minimal advancement opportunities. These people can increase their earnings and knowledge without a promotion in job title. Finally, skill-based pay appears to lead to performance improvements. A broad-based survey of Fortune 1000 firms found that 60 percent of those with skill-based pay plans rated their plans as successful or very successful in increasing organizational performance, while only 6 percent considered them unsuccessful or very unsuccessful.[61]

What about the downside of skill-based pay? People can "top out"—learning all the skills the program calls for them to learn. This can frustrate employees after they've become challenged by an environment of learning, growth, and continual pay raises. Skills can become obsolete. When this happens, what should management do? Cut employee pay or continue to pay for skills that are no longer relevant? There is also the problem created by paying people for acquiring skills for which there may be no immediate need. This happened at IDS Financial Services.[62] The company found itself paying people more money even though there was little immediate use for their new skills. IDS eventually dropped its skill-based pay plan and replaced it with one that equally balances individual contribution and gains in work team productivity. Finally, skill-based plans don't address level of performance. They deal only with the issue of whether or not someone can perform the skill. For some skills, such as checking quality or leading a team, level of performance may be equivocal. While it's possible to assess how well employees perform each of the skills and combine that with a skill-based plan, that is not an inherent part of skill-based pay.

LINKING SKILL-BASED PAY PLANS TO MOTIVATION THEORIES

Skill-based pay plans are consistent with several motivation theories. Because they encourage employees to learn, expand their skills, and grow, they are consistent with ERG theory. Among employees whose lower-order needs are substantially satisfied, the opportunity to experience growth can be a motivator.

Paying people to expand their skill levels is also consistent with research on the achievement need. High achievers have a compelling drive to do things better or more efficiently. By learning new skills or improving the skills they already hold, high achievers will find their jobs more challenging.

There is also a link between reinforcement theory and skill-based pay. Skill-based pay encourages employees to develop their flexibility, to continue to learn, to cross-train, to be generalists rather than specialists, and to work cooperatively with others in the organization. To the degree that management wants employees to demonstrate such behaviors, skill-based pay should act as a reinforcer.

Skill-based pay may additionally have equity implications. When employees make their input–outcome comparisons, skills may provide a fairer input criterion for determining pay than factors such as seniority or education. To the degree that employees perceive skills as the critical variable in job performance, the use of skill-based pay may increase the perception of equity and help optimize employee motivation.

SKILL-BASED PAY IN PRACTICE

A number of studies have investigated the use and effectiveness of skill-based pay. The overall conclusion, based on these studies, is that skill-based pay is expanding and that it generally leads to higher employee performance and satisfaction.

For instance, between 1987 and 1993, the percentage of Fortune 1000 firms using some form of skill-based pay increased from 40 percent to 60 percent.[63]

A survey of 27 companies that pay employees for learning extra skills found 70 to 88 percent reported higher job satisfaction, product quality, or productivity. Some 70 to 75 percent cited lower operating costs or turnover.[64]

Additional research has discovered some other interesting trends. The increased use of skills as a basis for pay appears particularly strong among organizations facing aggressive foreign competition and those companies with shorter product life cycles and speed-to-market concerns.[65] Also, skill-based pay is moving from the shop floor to the white-collar workforce, and sometimes as far as the executive suite.[66]

> *Skill-based pay appears to be an idea whose time has come.*

Skill-based pay appears to be an idea whose time has come. As one expert noted, "Slowly, but surely, we're becoming a skill-based society where your market value is tied to what you can do and what your skill set is. In this new world where skills and knowledge are what really counts, it doesn't make sense to treat people as jobholders. It makes sense to treat them as people with specific skills and to pay them for those skills."[67]

FLEXIBLE BENEFITS

Todd Evans and Allison Murphy both work for PepsiCo, but they have very different needs in terms of fringe benefits. Todd is married, has three young children, and a wife who is at home full-time. Allison, too, is married, but her husband has a high-paying job with the federal government, and they have no children. Todd is concerned about having a good medical plan and enough life insurance to support his family if he weren't around. In contrast, Allison's husband already has her medical needs covered on his plan, and life insurance is a low priority for both her and her husband. Allison is more interested in extra vacation time and long-term financial benefits such as a tax-deferred savings plan.

WHAT ARE FLEXIBLE BENEFITS?

flexible benefits

Employees tailor their benefit program to meet their personal needs by picking and choosing from a menu of benefit options.

Flexible benefits allow employees to pick and choose from among a menu of benefit options. The idea is to allow each employee to choose a benefit package that is individually tailored to his or her own needs and situation. It replaces the traditional "one-benefit-plan-fits-all" programs that have dominated organizations for more than 50 years.[68]

The average organization provides fringe benefits worth approximately 40 percent of an employee's salary. Traditional benefit programs were designed for the typical employee of the 1950s—a male with a wife and two children at home. Less than 10 percent of employees now fit this stereotype. While 25 percent of today's employees are single, a third are part of two-income families without any children. As such, these traditional programs don't tend to meet the needs of today's more diverse workforce. Flexible benefits, however, do meet these diverse needs. An organization sets up a flexible spending account for each employee, usually based on some percentage of his or her salary, and then a price tag is put on each benefit. Options might include inexpensive medical plans with high deductibles; expensive medical plans with low or no deductibles; hearing, dental, and eye coverage; extended disability; a variety of savings and pension plans; life insurance; college tuition reimbursement plans; and extended vacation time. Employees then select benefit options until they have spent the dollar amount in their account.

LINKING FLEXIBLE BENEFITS AND EXPECTANCY THEORY

Giving all employees the same benefits assumes all employees have the same needs. Of course, we know this assumption is false. Thus, flexible benefits turn the benefits' expenditure into a motivator.

Consistent with expectancy theory's thesis that organizational rewards should be linked to each individual employee's goals, flexible benefits individualize rewards by allowing each employee to choose the compensation package that best satisfies his or her current needs. The fact that flexible benefits can turn the traditional homogeneous benefit program into a motivator was

Flexible benefits like on-site childcare for $250 a month motivate employees at software developer SAS Institute. SAS started its daycare facility because it didn't want to lose talented female employees. Employee turnover at SAS is just 4 percent compared to the industry average of 18 to 20 percent.

demonstrated at one company when 80 percent of the organization's employees changed their benefit packages when a flexible plan was put into effect.[69]

FLEXIBLE BENEFITS IN PRACTICE

In the mid-1990s, 12 percent of large- and medium-sized U.S. companies had flexible benefits programs. This included TRW Systems, Educational Testing Services, Chrysler, and Bell Atlantic.[70] Flexible benefits also appear to be increasingly available in companies with fewer than 50 employees.[71]

Now, let's look at the pluses and drawbacks. For employees, flexibility is attractive because they can tailor their benefits and levels of coverage to their own needs. The major drawback, from the employee's standpoint, is that the costs of individual benefits often go up, so fewer total benefits can be purchased.[72] For example, low-risk employees keep the cost of medical plans low for everyone. As they are allowed to drop out, the high-risk population occupies a larger segment and the costs of medical benefits go up. From the organization's standpoint, the good news is that flexible benefits often produce savings. Many organizations use the introduction of flexible benefits to raise deductibles and premiums. Moreover, once in place, costly increases in things such as health insurance premiums often have to be substantially absorbed by the employee. The bad news for the organization is that these plans are more cumbersome for management to oversee and administering the programs is often expensive.

> *In one company, 80 percent of the employees changed their benefit packages when a flexible plan was put into effect.*

SPECIAL ISSUES IN MOTIVATION

Various groups provide specific challenges in terms of motivation. In this section we look at some of the unique problems faced in trying to motivate professional employees, contingent workers, the diverse workforce, low-skilled service workers, and people doing highly repetitive tasks.

MOTIVATING PROFESSIONALS

In contrast to a generation ago, the typical employee today is more likely to be a highly trained professional with a college degree than a blue-collar factory worker. These professionals receive a great deal of intrinsic satisfaction from their work. They tend to be well paid. So what, if any, special concerns should you be aware of when trying to motivate a team of engineers at Intel, a software designer at Microsoft, or a group of CPAs at PricewaterhouseCoopers?

Professionals are typically different from nonprofessionals.[73] They have a strong and long-term commitment to their field of expertise. Their loyalty is more often to their profession than to their employer. To keep current in their field, they need to regularly update their knowledge, and their commitment to their profession means they rarely define their workweek in terms of 8 to 5 and five days a week.

What motivates professionals? Money and promotions typically are low on their priority list. Why? They tend to be well paid and they enjoy what they do. In contrast, job challenge tends to be ranked high. They like to tackle problems and find solutions. Their chief reward in their job is the work itself. Professionals also value support. They want others to think what they're working on is important. Although this may be true for all employees, because professionals tend to be more focused on their work as their central life interest, nonprofessionals typically have other interests outside of work that can compensate for needs not met on the job.

The foregoing description implies a few guidelines to keep in mind if you're trying to motivate professionals. Provide them with ongoing challenging projects. Give them autonomy to follow their interests and allow them to structure their work in ways that they find productive. Reward them with educational opportunities—training, workshops, attending conferences—that allow them to keep current in their field. Also reward them with recognition, and ask questions and engage in other actions that demonstrate to them you're sincerely interested in what they're doing.

An increasing number of companies are creating alternative career paths for their professional/technical people, allowing employees to earn more money and status, without assuming managerial responsibilities. At Merck & Co., IBM, and AT&T, the best scientists, engineers, and researchers gain titles such as fellow and senior scientist. Their pay and prestige are comparable to those of managers but without the corresponding authority or responsibility.

MOTIVATING CONTINGENT WORKERS

We noted in Chapter 1 that one of the more comprehensive changes taking place in organizations is the addition of temporary or contingent employees. As downsizing has eliminated millions of "permanent" jobs, an increasing number of new openings are for part-time, contract, and other forms of temporary workers. For instance, in 1995, approximately 6 million Americans, or 4.9 percent of those with jobs, considered themselves as part of the contingent workforce.[74] These contingent employees don't have the security or stability that permanent employees have. As such, they don't identify with the organization or display the commitment that other employees do. Temporary workers also are typically provided with little or no health care, pensions, or similar benefits.[75]

There is no simple solution for motivating temporary employees. For those who prefer the freedom of their temporary status—many students, working mothers, seniors, and professionals who don't want the demands of a permanent job—the lack of stability may not be an issue. Interestingly, this seems to be considerably more people than originally thought. Recent estimates on the percentage of contingent workers who have chosen this status voluntarily range from 33 to 77 percent.[76] The challenge, however, is in dealing with temporary employees who are in this status involuntarily.

What will motivate involuntarily temporary employees? An obvious answer is the opportunity for permanent status. In those cases in which permanent employees are selected from the pool of temporaries, temporaries will often work hard in hopes of becoming permanent. A less obvious answer is the opportunity for training. The ability of a temporary employee to find a new job largely depends on his or her skills. If the employee sees that the job he or she is doing for you can help develop salable skills, then motivation is increased. From an equity standpoint, you should also consider the repercussions of mixing permanent and temporary workers when pay differentials are significant.[77] When temps work alongside permanent employees who earn more, and get benefits too, for doing the same job, the performance of temps is likely to suffer. Separating such employees or converting all employees to a variable-pay or skill-based pay plan might help lessen this problem.

MOTIVATING THE DIVERSIFIED WORKFORCE

Not everyone is motivated by money. Not everyone wants a challenging job. The needs of women, singles, immigrants, the physically disabled, senior citizens, and others from diverse groups are not the same as a married, white American male with three dependents. A couple of examples can make this point clearer. Employees who are attending college typically place a high value on flexible work schedules. Such individuals may be attracted to organizations that offer flexible work hours, job sharing, or temporary assignments. Similarly, a father may prefer to work the midnight to 8 A.M. shift in order to spend time with his children during the day when his wife is at work.

If you're going to maximize your employees' motivation, you've got to understand and respond to this diversity. How? The key word to guide you should be *flexibility*. Be ready to design work schedules, compensation plans, benefits, physical work settings, and the like to reflect your employees' varied needs. This might include offering child and elder care, flexible work hours, and job sharing for employees with family responsibilities. It also might include offering flexible leave policies for immigrants who want occasionally to make extensive return trips to their homelands, or creating work teams for employees who come from countries with a strong collectivist orientation, or allowing employees who are going to school to vary their work schedules from semester to semester.

MOTIVATING LOW-SKILLED SERVICE WORKERS

One of the most challenging motivation problems in industries such as retailing and fast food is: How do you motivate individuals who are making very low wages and who have little opportunity to significantly increase their pay in either their current jobs or through promotions? These jobs are typically filled with people who have limited education and skills, and pay levels are little above minimum wage.

Traditional approaches for motivating these people have focused on providing more flexible work schedules and filling these jobs with teenagers and retirees whose financial needs are less. This has met with less than enthusiastic results. For instance, turnover rates of 200 percent or more are not uncommon for businesses such as McDonald's. Taco Bell has tried to make some of its service jobs more interesting and challenging but with limited results.[78] It has experimented with incentive pay and stock options for cashiers and cooks. These employees also have been given broader responsibility for inventory, scheduling, and hiring. But over a four-year period, this experiment has only reduced annual turnover from 223 percent to 160 percent.

What choices are left? Unless pay and benefits are significantly increased, high turnover probably has to be expected in these jobs. This can be somewhat offset by widening the recruiting net, making these jobs more appealing, and raising pay levels. You might also try some nontraditional approaches as well. As an example, Judy Wicks has found that celebrating employees' outside interests has dramatically cut turnover among waiters at her White Dog Café in Philadelphia.[79] For instance, to help create a close and family-like work climate, Wicks sets aside one night a year for employees to exhibit their art, read their poetry, explain their volunteer work, and introduce their new babies.

MOTIVATING PEOPLE DOING HIGHLY REPETITIVE TASKS

Our final category considers employees who do standardized and repetitive jobs. For instance, working on an assembly line or transcribing court reports are jobs that workers often find boring and even stressful.

Motivating individuals in these jobs can be made easier through careful selection. People vary in their tolerance for ambiguity. Many

Starbucks takes good care of its "partners," the part-time employees that comprise 83 percent of the company's workforce. Employees who work 20 hours a week receive full benefits plus a pound of free coffee each week. They also get stock options in Starbucks—a company whose stock price continues to grow as it opens new cafes throughout the world, such as the one shown here in Beijing, China.

individuals prefer jobs that have a minimal amount of discretion and variety. Such individuals are obviously a better match to standardized jobs than individuals with strong needs for growth and autonomy. Standardized jobs should also be the first considered for automation.

Many standardized jobs, especially in the manufacturing sector, pay well. This makes it relatively easy to fill vacancies. While high pay can ease recruitment problems and reduce turnover, it doesn't necessarily lead to highly motivated workers. And realistically, there are jobs that don't readily lend themselves to being made more challenging and interesting or to being redesigned. Some tasks, for instance, are just far more efficiently done on assembly lines than in teams. This leaves limited options. You may not be able to do much more than try to make a bad situation tolerable by creating a pleasant work climate. This might include providing clean and attractive work surroundings, ample work breaks, the opportunity to socialize with colleagues during these breaks, and empathetic supervisors.

SUMMARY AND IMPLICATIONS FOR MANAGERS

We've presented a number of motivation theories and applications in this and the previous chapter. While it's always dangerous to synthesize a large number of complex ideas into a few simple guidelines, the following suggestions summarize the essence of what we know about motivating employees in organizations.

Recognize Individual Differences Employees have different needs. Don't treat them all alike. Moreover, spend the time necessary to understand what's important to each employee. This will allow you to individualize goals, level of involvement, and rewards to align with individual needs.

Use Goals and Feedback Employees should have hard, specific goals, as well as feedback on how well they are faring in pursuit of those goals.

Allow Employees to Participate in Decisions That Affect Them Employees can contribute to a number of decisions that affect them: setting work goals, choosing their own benefits packages, solving productivity and quality problems, and the like. This can increase employee productivity, commitment to work goals, motivation, and job satisfaction.

Link Rewards to Performance Rewards should be contingent on performance. Importantly, employees must perceive a clear linkage. Regardless of how closely rewards are actually correlated to performance criteria, if individuals perceive this relationship to be low, the results will be low performance, a decrease in job satisfaction, and an increase in turnover and absenteeism statistics.

Check the System for Equity Rewards should also be perceived by employees as equating with the inputs they bring to the job. At a simplistic level, this should mean that experience, skills, abilities, effort, and other obvious inputs should explain differences in performance and, hence, pay, job assignments, and other obvious rewards.

The Power of Stock Options as a Motivator

S tock options are being used as incentives for booksellers at Borders, tellers at NationsBank, clerks at Wal-Mart, box packers at Pfizer, chemical-plant operators at Monstanto, baggage handlers at Delta Air Lines, and part-time espresso servers at Starbucks.[1]

In the last decade, an estimated 2,000 companies have instituted broad-based stock option plans. One study found that more than a third of all large U.S. companies now have stock option plans that cover all or a majority of employees—from the CEO down to operatives. And while plans vary, most are allocated as a percentage of annual income and allow employees to buy their employer's stock at a price below the fair market value.

Proponents of broad-based stock offer a long list of reasons to explain these plans' popularity: They help to create a companywide "ownership" culture by focusing employees' attention on the employer's financial performance; create a pay-for-performance climate; foster pride of ownership; raise morale; encourage retention of employees; help to attract new employees; and motivate front-line employees who interact with customers.

Starbucks's experience provides insights into the power of stock options as a motivator. Their program began in 1991. Each employee was awarded stock options worth 12 percent of his or her annual base pay. Every October since then, high profits have allowed Starbucks to raise the grant to 14 percent of base pay. By 1999, an employee making $20,000 a year in 1991 could have cashed in his or her 1991 options alone for more than $70,000.

Starbucks's management believes stock options allow employees to share both the ownership of the company and the rewards of financial success. And managment contends that it's working. The company's CEO says, "People started coming up with innovative ideas about how to cut costs, to increase sales, to create value. Most important, they could speak to our customers from the heart, as partners in the business."

B road-based stock options sound terrific in theory. Motivation increases because employees see themselves as owners rather than merely workers. And these options create the opportunity for moderately paid employees to accumulate substantial savings. What's wrong with the theory? Several things.[2]

First is the fact that options tend to be disportionately allocated to managers. Because options are typically distributed as a percentage of base pay, managers get more of them because they make more money. Senior executives also tend to get additional options based on company profitability or stock performance. This is how someone such as Sanford Weill, CEO of Travelers Group, can make $156 million in one year alone from his options. Such huge payoffs make the few thousand dollars a low-level Travelers' employee gets from his or her options seem like "chump change." This comparison is just as likely to anger or frustrate nonmanagerial employees as it is to motivate them.

Second, stock options are poor motivators because they offer a weak link between employee effort and rewards. How much impact can the average workers really have on the company's stock price? Very little!

Finally, stock options are great when a company is growing rapidly or during bull markets in stocks. Starbucks's plan proved very profitable for employees between 1991 and 1999 because the company grew rapidly and the stock market experienced an unprecedented rise. But all companies aren't growing nor do stock markets go up forever. When Wal-Mart stock tanked in 1994, so did employee morale. Stock options given all employees in 1989 at Houston-based Lyondell Petrochemical Co. were worthless seven years later because the company's stock never appreciated. Says Lyondell's CEO, "Employees may actually be de-motivated upon realizing that it [stock options] can be like a lottery."

[1]This is based on K. Capell, "Options for Everyone," *Business Week*, July 22, 1996, pp. 80–84; "Starbucks' Secret Weapon," *Fortune*, September 29, 1997, p. 268; "Stock Options for the Ranks," *Business Week*, September 7, 1998, p. 22; and J. Lardner, "OK, Here Are Your Options," *U.S. News & World Report*, March 1, 1999, pp. 44–46.

[2]This is based on K. Capell, "Options for Everyone," and J. Pitta and B. Upbin, "The Dark Side of Options," *Forbes*, May 17, 1999, pp. 211–13.

1. Relate goal-setting theory to the MBO process. How are they similar? Different?

2. What is an ESOP? How might it positively influence employee motivation?

3. Explain the roles of employees and management in quality circles.

4. What are the pluses of variable-pay programs from an employee's viewpoint? From management's viewpoint?

5. Contrast job-based and skill-based pay.

6. What is gainsharing? What explains its recent popularity?

7. What motivates professional employees?

8. What motivates contingent employees?

9. Is it possible to motivate low-skilled service workers? Discuss.

10. What can you do, as a manager, to increase the likelihood that your employees will exert a high level of effort?

Questions for Critical Thinking

1. Identify five different criteria by which organizations can compensate employees. Based on your knowledge and experience, do you think performance is the criterion most used in practice? Discuss.

2. "Recognition may be motivational for the moment but it doesn't have any staying power. It's an empty reinforcer. Why? Because they don't take recognition at the Safeway or Sears!" Do you agree or disagree? Discuss.

3. "Performance can't be measured, so any effort to link pay with performance is a fantasy. Differences in performance are often caused by the system, which means the organization ends up rewarding the circumstances. It's the same thing as rewarding the weather forecaster for a pleasant day." Do you agree or disagree with this statement? Support your position.

4. What drawbacks, if any, do you see in implementing flexible benefits? (Consider this question from the perspective of both the organization and the employee.)

5. Your text argues for recognizing individual differences. It also suggests paying attention to members of diversity groups. Is this contradictory? Discuss.

Team Exercise | Goal-Setting Task

Purpose

This exercise will help you learn how to write tangible, verifiable, measurable, and relevant goals as might evolve from an MBO program.

Time

Approximately 20 to 30 minutes.

Instructions

1. Break into groups of three to five.

2. Spend a few minutes discussing your class instructor's job. What does he or she do? What defines good performance? What behaviors will lead to good performance?

3. Each group is to develop a list of five goals that, although not established participatively with your instructor, you believe might be developed in an MBO program at your college. Try to select goals that seem most critical to the effective performance of your instructor's job.

4. Each group will select a leader who will share his or her group's goals with the entire class. For each group's goals, class discussion should focus on their (a) specificity, (b) ease of measurement, (c) importance, and (d) motivational properties.

Critics have described the astronomical pay packages given to American CEOs as "rampant greed." They note, for instance, that in recent years the average salary and bonus for a chief executive of a major U.S. corporation has been running at about 150 times the average factory worker's pay!

High levels of executive compensation seem to be widely spread in the United States. In 1998, for instance, Stephen M. Case of America Online took home $159.3 million; General Electric's Jack Welch was paid $84.5 million; and Coca-Cola's Douglas Ivester earned $57.5 million. These figures were for pay and exercised stock options only. They do *not* include potentially hundreds of millions more from appreciated value of unexercised stock options. Twenty years ago, an executive who earned a million dollars a year made headlines. Now it's "routine" for a senior executive at a large U.S. corporation to earn more than $1 million in compensation.

How do you explain these astronomical pay packages? Some say this represents a classic economic response to a situation in which the demand is great for high-quality, top-executive talent and the supply is low. Other arguments in favor of paying executives $1 million a year or more are the need to compensate people for the tremendous responsibilities and stress that go with such jobs, the motivating potential that seven- and eight-figure annual incomes provide to senior executives and those who might aspire to be, and the influence of senior executives on the company's bottom line.

Executive pay is considerably higher in the United States than in most other countries. In 1998, American CEOs of industrial companies with annual revenues of $250 million to $500 million made, on average, $1,072,000. Comparable figures for Britain, France, Canada, Mexico, and Japan were, respectively, $646,000, $520,000, $498,000, $457,000, and $421,000.

Critics of executive pay practices in the United States argue that CEOs choose board members whom they can count on to support ever-increasing pay (including lucrative bonus and stock option plans) for top management. If board members fail to "play along," they risk losing their positions, their fees, and the prestige and power inherent in board membership.

Is high compensation of U.S. executives a problem? If so, does the blame for the problem lie with CEOs or with the shareholders and boards that knowingly allow the practice? Are American CEOs greedy? Are these CEOs acting unethically? What do you think?

Source: J. M. Pennings, "Executive Reward Systems: A Cross-National Comparison," *Journal of Management Studies*, March 1993, pp. 261–80; A. Bryant, "American Pay Rattles Foreign Partners," *New York Times*, January 17, 1999, p. WK-1; and G. Strauss and D. Jones, "Wealth of Titans," *USA Today*, April 7, 1999, p. B1.

1. Find three Web sites detailing current trends in participative management. Is participative management becoming more, or less, popular? Why? What are the most common forms of participative management in the United States? What are the most common forms in Europe and Japan? What challenges do national differences in participative management systems have for multinational corporations?

2. Who are the top 20 paid CEO's in the United States? How do the salaries of the CEO's of U.S. based companies compare with those of CEO's from other nations including Germany, Japan, France and the U.K. in terms of base salary and total compensation received? From your research, how well does CEO compensation correlate with company performance?

We invite you to visit the Robbins homepage on the Prentice Hall Web site at **www.prenhall.com/robbins** for our on-line study guide, current events, links to related Web sites, and more.

The following memo was actually sent out three weeks before Christmas by the executive vice president of a re-gional financial brokerage firm. For obvious reasons, the identities of the firm and the executive are disguised.

December 4, 1999
To: LHI Retail Sales Group Employees
Re: Holiday Gifts for Nonexempt Employees

I have received a number of questions regarding the possibility of a holiday cash gift. This year, Larson Hughes Inc. will not be providing a holiday gift for nonexempt employees (employees through Level 8), which includes many sales assistants, operations staff, and administrative assistants in Retail Sales Group.

As you may know, we paid all nonexempt employees a holiday gift in December 1997 and 1998. The gift was not dependent upon individual performance. Rather, as we explained at the time, the gift was a reflection of the exceptional earnings recorded at the Corporate Financial Group level.

RSG is having a very successful year, and CFG revenues are expected to hit record levels in 1999. The contributions of RSG's nonexempt employees certainly have played a role in both. However, CFG's overall profitability—the ultimate barometer of our performance—has not exceeded expectations this year.

This decision is *not* a reflection of the overall performance of our nonexempt employees nor the importance of their contributions to Larson Hughes. We highly value the work of all of our employees; you are our most valuable asset and our competitive advantage.

I deeply appreciate everyone's contributions in 1999. Your efforts continue to be important to our success now and in the future.

Questions

1. Analyze this memo in terms of motivation concepts.

2. How would you respond if you received this memo?

3. What, if anything, would you have done differently if you were the executive vice president and a number of your nonexempt employees asked you questions regarding the possibility of a holiday cash gift?

End Notes

1. A. Livingston, "Gain-Sharing Encourages Productivity," *Nation's Business*, January 1998, pp. 21–22.
2. P. F. Drucker, *The Practice of Management* (New York: Harper & Row, 1954).
3. See, for instance, S. J. Carroll and H. L. Tosi, *Management by Objectives: Applications and Research* (New York: Macmillan, 1973); and R. Rodgers and J. E. Hunter, "Impact of Management by Objectives on Organizational Productivity," *Journal of Applied Psychology*, April 1991, pp. 322–36.
4. See, for instance, R. C. Ford, F. S. MacLaughlin, and J. Nixdorf, "Ten Questions About MBO," *California Management Review*, Winter 1980, p. 89; T. J. Collamore, "Making MBO Work in the Public Sector," *Bureaucrat*, Fall 1989, pp. 37–40; G. Dabbs, "Nonprofit Businesses in the 1990s: Models for Success," *Business Horizons*, September–October 1991, pp. 68–71; R. Rodgers and J. E. Hunter, "A Foundation of Good Management Practice in Government: Management by Objectives," *Public Administration Review*, January–February 1992, pp. 27–39; and T. H. Poister and G. Streib, "MBO in Municipal Government: Variations on a Traditional Management Tool," *Public Administration Review*, January/February 1995, pp. 48–56.
5. See, for instance, C. H. Ford, "MBO: An Idea Whose Time Has Gone?" *Business Horizons*, December 1979, p. 49; R. Rodgers and J. E. Hunter, "Impact of Management by Objectives on Organizational Productivity," *Journal of Ap-*

plied Psychology, April 1991, pp. 322–36; and R. Rodgers, J. E. Hunter, and D. L. Rogers, "Influence of Top Management Commitment on Management Program Success," *Journal of Applied Psychology*, February 1993, pp. 151–55.
6. S. Navarette, "Multiple Forms of Employee Recognition," *At Work*, July/August 1993, pp. 9–10.
7. Cited in S. Caudron, "The Top 20 Ways to Motivate Employees," *Industry Week*, April 3, 1995, pp. 15–16. See also B. Nelson, "Try Praise," *INC.*, September 1996, p. 115.
8. "Look, Movie Tickets: With Budgets Tight, Alternatives to Pay Increases Emerge," *Wall Street Journal*, September 27, 1994, p. A1.
9. Cited in *Asian Business*, December 1994, p. 3.
10. R. Levering and M. Moskowitz, "The Ten Best Companies to Work for in America," *Business and Society Review*, Spring 1993, p. 29
11. B. Saporito, "The Revolt Against 'Working Smarter,'" *Fortune*, July 21, 1986, pp. 58–65; "Quality Circles: Rounding Up Quality at USAA," *AIDE Magazine*, Fall 1983, p. 24; and J. Kerr, "The Informers," *INC.*, March 1995, pp. 50–61.
12. J. L. Cotton, *Employee Involvement* (Newbury Park, CA: Sage, 1993), pp. 3 and 14.
13. Ibid., p. 3.
14. See, for example, the increasing body of literature on empowerment such as R. C. Ford and M. D. Fottler, "Empowerment: A Matter of Degree," *The Academy of Manage-*

ment Executive, August 1995, pp. 21–31; and G. M. Spreitzer, "Psychological Empowerment in the Workplace: Dimensions, Measurement, and Validation," *Academy of Management Journal*, October 1995, pp. 1442–65.

15. See M. Sashkin, "Participative Management Is an Ethical Imperative," *Organizational Dynamics*, Spring 1984, pp. 5–22; and D. Collins, "The Ethical Superiority and Inevitability of Participatory Management as an Organizational System," *Organization Science*, September-October 1997, pp. 489–507.

16. R. Tannenbaum, I. R. Weschler, and F. Massarik, *Leadership and Organization: A Behavioral Science Approach* (New York: McGraw-Hill, 1961), pp. 88–100.

17. K. L. Miller and P. R. Monge, "Participation, Satisfaction, and Productivity: A Meta-Analytic Review," *Academy of Management Journal*, December 1986, pp. 727–53; J. A. Wagner III and R. Z. Gooding, "Shared Influence and Organizational Behavior: A Meta-Analysis of Situational Variables Expected to Moderate Participation-Outcome Relationships," *Academy of Management Journal*, September 1987, pp. 524–41; J. A. Wagner III, "Participation's Effects on Performance and Satisfaction: A Reconsideration of Research Evidence," *Academy of Management Review*, April 1994, pp. 312–30; C. Doucouliagos, "Worker Participation and Productivity in Labor-Managed and Participatory Capitalist Firms: A Meta-Analysis," *Industrial and Labor Relations Review*, October 1995, pp. 58–77; J. A. Wagner III, C. R. Leana, E. A. Locke, and D. M. Schweiger, "Cognitive and Motivational Frameworks in U.S. Research on Participation: A Meta-Analysis of Primary Effects," *Journal of Organizational Behavior*, vol. 18, 1997, pp. 49–65; J. S. Black and H. B. Gregersen, "Participative Decision-Making: An Integration of Multiple Dimensions," *Human Relations*, July 1997, pp. 859–78; and E. A. Locke, M. Alavi, and J. A. Wagner III, "Participation in Decision Making: An Information Exchange Perspective," in G. R. Ferris (ed.), *Research in Personnel and Human Resource Management*, vol. 15 (Greenwich, CT: JAI Press, 1997), pp. 293–331.

18. J. L. Cotton, *Employee Involvement*, p. 114.

19. See, for example, M. Poole, "Industrial Democracy: A Comparative Analysis," *Industrial Relations*, Fall 1979, pp. 262–72; IDE International Research Group, *European Industrial Relations* (Oxford, UK: Clarendon, 1981); E. M. Kassalow, "Employee Representation on U.S., German Boards," *Monthly Labor Review*, September 1989, pp. 39–42; T. H. Hammer, S. C. Currall, and R. N. Stern, "Worker Representation on Boards of Directors: A Study of Competing Roles," *Industrial and Labor Relations Review*, Winter 1991, pp. 661–80; and P. Kunst and J. Soeters, "Works Council Membership and Career Opportunities," *Organization Studies*, vol. 12, no. 1, 1991, pp. 75–93.

20. J. D. Kleyn and S. Perrick, "Netherlands," *International Financial Law Review*, February 1990, pp. 51–56.

21. J. L. Cotton, *Employee Involvement*, pp. 129–30 and 139–40.

22. Ibid., p. 140.

23. Ibid., p. 59.

24. See, for example, G. W. Meyer and R. G. Stott, "Quality Circles: Panacea or Pandora's Box?" *Organizational Dynamics*, Spring 1985, pp. 34–50; M. L. Marks, P. H. Mirvis, E. J. Hackett, and J. F. Grady, Jr., "Employee Participation in a Quality Circle Program: Impact on Quality of Work Life, Productivity, and Absenteeism," *Journal of Applied Psychology*, February 1986, pp. 61–69; E. E. Lawler III and S. A. Mohrman, "Quality Circles: After the Honeymoon," *Organizational Dynamics*, Spring 1987, pp. 42–54; R. P. Steel and R. F. Lloyd, "Cognitive, Affective, and Behavioral Outcomes of Participation in Quality Circles: Conceptual and Empirical Findings," *Journal of Applied Behavioral Science*, vol. 24, no. 1, 1988, pp. 1–17; T. R. Miller, "The Quality Circle Phenomenon: A Review and Appraisal," *SAM Advanced Management Journal*, Winter 1989, pp. 4–7; K. Buch and R. Spangler, "The Effects of Quality Circles on Performance and Promotions," *Human Relations*, June 1990, pp. 573–82; P. R. Liverpool, "Employee Participation in Decision-Making: An Analysis of the Perceptions of Members and Nonmembers of Quality Circles," *Journal of Business and Psychology*, Summer 1990, pp. 411–22, and E. E. Adams, Jr., "Quality Circle Performance," *Journal of Management*, March 1991, pp. 25–39.

25. J. L. Cotton, *Employee Involvement*, p. 76.

26. Ibid., p. 78.

27. Ibid., p. 87.

28. See K. M. Young (ed.), *The Expanding Role of ESOPs in Public Companies* (New York: Quorum, 1990); J. L. Pierce and C. A. Furo, "Employee Ownership: Implications for Management," *Organizational Dynamics*, Winter 1990, pp. 32–43; J. Blasi and D. L. Druse, *The New Owners: The Mass Emergence of Employee Ownership in Public Companies and What It Means to American Business* (Champaign, IL: Harper Business, 1991); F. T. Adams and G. B. Hansen, *Putting Democracy to Work: A Practical Guide for Starting and Managing Worker-Owned Businesses* (San Francisco: Berrett-Koehler, 1993); and A. A. Buchko, "The Effects of Employee Ownership on Employee Attitudes: An Integrated Causal Model and Path Analysis," *Journal of Management Studies*, July 1993, pp. 633–56.

29. J. L. Pierce and C. A. Furo, "Employee Ownership"; C. H. Farnsworth, "One Employee Buyout That Actually Worked," *New York Times*, February 5, 1995, p. F4; S. Chandler, "United We Own," *Business Week*, March 18, 1996, pp. 96–100; A. Bernstein, "Should Avis Try Harder—For Its Employees?" *Business Week*, August 12, 1996, pp. 68–69.

30. A. A. Buchko, "The Effects of Employee Ownership on Employee Attitudes."

31. C. M. Rosen and M. Quarrey, "How Well Is Employee Ownership Working?" *Harvard Business Review*, September–October 1987, pp. 126–32.

32. W. N. Davidson and D. L. Worrell, "ESOP's Fables: The Influence of Employee Stock Ownership Plans on Corporate Stock Prices and Subsequent Operating Performance," *Human Resource Planning*, January 1994, pp. 69–85.

33. J. L. Pierce and C. A. Furo, "Employee Ownership."

34. See data in D. Stamps, "A Piece of the Action," *Training*, March 1996, p. 66.

35. T. R. Miller, "The Quality Circle Phenomenon," p. 5.

36. J. L. Pierce and C. A. Furo, "Employee Ownership," p. 32; and S. Kaufman, "ESOPs' Appeal on the Increase," *Nation's Business*, June 1997, p. 43.

37. C. Farrell, "Now, More Can Join the ESOP Game," *Business Week*, May 25, 1998, pp. ENT20–22.

38. M. A. Verespej, "Top-to-Bottom Incentives," *Industry Week*, February 3, 1997, p. 30.

39. "Truly Tying Pay to Performance," *Business Week*, February 17, 1997, p. 25.

40. G. Steinmetz, "German Banks Note the Value of Bonuses," *Wall Street Journal*, May 9, 1995, p. A17.

41. J. S. Hirsch, "Kodak's Chairman Won't Receive a Bonus For 1997," *Wall Street Journal*, March 17, 1998, p. B10.

42. Based on J. R. Schuster and P. K. Zingheim, "The New Variable Pay: Key Design Issues," *Compensation & Benefits Review*, March–April 1993, p. 28; and K. S. Abosch, "Vari-

able Pay: Do We Have the Basics in Place?" *Compensation & Benefits Review*, July–August 1998, pp. 12–22.

43. M. Murray, "Banc One's McCoy Receives $4 Million in Special Award," *Wall Street Journal*, March 12, 1998, p. B8.

44. J. O'C. Hamilton, "Levi's Pot O' Gold," *Business Week*, June 24, 1996, p. 44.

45. See, for instance, S. C. Hanlon, D. G. Meyer, and R. R. Taylor, "Consequences of Gainsharing," *Group & Organization Management*, March 1994, pp. 87–111; J. G. Belcher, Jr., "Gainsharing and Variable Pay: The State of the Art," *Compensation & Benefits Review*, May–June 1994, pp. 50–60; and T. M. Welbourne and L. R. Gomez Mejia, "Gainsharing: A Critical Review and a Future Research Agenda," *Journal of Management*, vol. 21; no. 3, 1995, pp. 559–609.

46. C. G. Hanson and W. D. Bell, *Profit Sharing and Profitability: How Profit Sharing Promotes Business Success* (London: Kogan Page Ltd., 1987); and M. Magnan and S. St-Onge, "Profit-Sharing and Firm Performance: A Comparative and Longitudinal Analysis," paper presented at the 58th Annual Meeting of the Academy of Management (San Diego, CA, August 1998).

47. See E. M. Doherty, W. R. Nord, and J. L. McAdams, "Gainsharing and Organizational Development: A Productive Synergy," *Journal of Applied Behavioral Science*, August 1989, pp. 209–30; and T. C. McGrath, "How Three Screw Machine Companies Are Tapping Human Productivity Through Gainsharing," *Employment Relations Today*, vol. 20, no. 4, 1994, pp. 437–47.

48. See J. L. Cotton, *Employee Involvement*, pp. 89–113; and W. Imberman, "Boosting Plant Performance with Gainsharing," *Business Horizons*, November–December 1992, p. 79.

49. M. Fein, "Work Measurement and Wage Incentives," *Industrial Engineering*, September 1973, pp. 49–51. For an updated review of the effect of pay on performance, see G. D. Jenkins Jr., N. Gupta, A. Mitra, and J. D. Shaw, "Are Financial Incentives Related to Performance? A Meta-Analytic Review of Empirical Research," *Journal of Applied Psychology*, October 1998, pp. 777–87.

50. B. Wysocki, Jr., "Unstable Pay Becomes Ever More Common," *Wall Street Journal*, December 4, 1995, p. A1.

51. W. Zellner, "Trickle-Down Is Trickling Down at Work," *Business Week*, March 18, 1996, p. 34; and "Linking Pay to Performance Is Becoming a Norm in the Workplace," *Wall Street Journal*, April 6, 1999, p. A1.

52. Cited in D. L. McClain, "Tricks for Varying the Pay to Motivate the Ranks," *New York Times*, November 15, 1998, p. BU-5.

53. "Bonus Pay in Canada," *Manpower Argus*, September 1996, p. 5.

54. "More Than 20 Percent of Japanese Firms Use Pay Systems Based on Performance," *Manpower Argus*, May 1998, p. 7.

55. D. Beck, "Implementing a Gainsharing Plan: What Companies Need to Know," *Compensation & Benefits Review*, January–February 1992, p. 23.

56. W. Imberman, "Boosting Plant Performance with Gainsharing."

57. See, for example, R. Ganzel, "What's Wrong with Pay for Performance?" *Training*, December 1998, pp. 34–40.

58. These examples are cited in A. Gabor, "After the Pay Revolution, Job Titles Won't Matter," *New York Times*, May 17, 1992, p. F5; "Skill-Based Pay Boosts Worker Productivity and

Morale," *Wall Street Journal*, June 23, 1992, p. A1; L. Wiener, "No New Skills? No Raise," *U.S. News & World Report*, October 26, 1992, p. 78; and M. A. Verespej, "New Responsibilities? New Pay!" *Industry Week*, August 15, 1994, p. 14.

59. G. E. Ledford, Jr., "Paying for the Skills, Knowledge, and Competencies of Knowledge Workers," *Compensation & Benefits Review*, July–August 1995, pp. 55–62.

60. M. Rowland, "For Each New Skill, More Money," *New York Times*, June 13, 1993, p. F16.

61. E. E. Lawler III, G. E. Ledford, Jr., and L. Chang, "Who Uses Skill-Based Pay, and Why," *Compensation & Benefits Review*, March–April 1993, p. 22.

62. "Tensions of a New Pay Plan," *New York Times*, May 17, 1992, p. F5.

63. Cited in E. E. Lawler III, S. A. Mohrman, and G. E. Ledford, Jr., *Creating High Performance Organizations: Practices and Results in the Fortune 1000* (San Francisco: Jossey-Bass, 1995).

64. "Skill-Based Pay Boosts Worker Productivity and Morale," *Wall Street Journal*, June 23, 1992, p. A1.

65. E. E. Lawler III, G. E. Ledford, Jr., and L. Chang, "Who Uses Skill-Based Pay, and Why."

66. M. Rowland, "It's What You Can Do That Counts," *New York Times*, June 6, 1993, p. F17.

67. Ibid.

68. See, for instance, "When You Want to Contain Costs and Let Employees Pick Their Benefits: Cafeteria Plans," *INC.*, December 1989, p. 142; "More Benefits Bend with Workers' Needs," *Wall Street Journal*, January 9, 1990, p. B1; R. Thompson, "Switching to Flexible Benefits," *Nation's Business*, July 1991, pp. 16–23; and A. E. Barber, R. B. Dunham, and R. A. Formisano, "The Impact of Flexible Benefits on Employee Satisfaction: A Field Study," *Personnel Psychology*, Spring 1992, pp. 55–75.

69. E. E. Lawler III, "Reward Systems," in Hackman and Suttle (eds.), *Improving Life at Work*, p. 182.

70. U.S. Department of Labor, Bureau of Labor Statistics, 1995; and L. Alderman and S. Kim, "Get the Most from Your Company Benefits," *Money*, January 1996, pp. 102–06.

71. "When You Want to Contain Costs and Let Employees Pick Their Benefits."

72. H. Bernstein, "New Benefit Schemes Can Be Deceiving," *Los Angeles Times*, May 14, 1991, p. D3.

73. See, for instance, C. Meyer, "What Makes Workers Tick?" *INC.*, December 1997, pp. 74–81; N. Munk, "The New Organization Man," *Fortune*, March 16, 1998, pp. 62–74; and D. Levy, "Net Elite: 'It's Not About Money,'" *USA Today*, February 22, 1999, p. B1.

74. "Six Million Americans Say Jobs Are Temporary," *Manpower Argus*, November 1995, p. 2.

75. A. Penzias, "New Paths to Success," *Fortune*, June 12, 1995, pp. 90–94; and S. Greenhouse, "Equal Work, Less-Equal Perks," *New York Times*, March 30, 1998, p. C1.

76. See R. W. Judy and C. D'Amico, *Workforce 2020* (Indianapolis, IN: Hudson Institute, 1997), pp. 56–57; and "Majority of U.S. Part-Timers Choose That Type of Work," *Manpower Argus*, November 1997, p. 2.

77. B. Filipczak, "Managing a Mixed Work Force," *Training*, October 1997, pp. 96–103.

78. D. Hage and J. Impoco, "Jawboning the Jobs," *U.S. News & World Report*, August 9, 1993, p. 53.

79. M. P. Cronin, "One Life to Live," *INC.*, July 1993, pp. 56–60.

Being the Best at Doc Martens: Motivation and Values at a Company with Attitude

Dr. Martens makes shoes that say something about the wearer. Whether they are young or old, fans of the 40-year-old firm are proud to own distinctive footwear that speaks to the rebellious spirit in them and proclaims them as someone out of the ordinary. For its part, the family-owned British manufacturer wants to be "the number-one brown-shoe brand in the world," and it values its made-in-England tradition as much as the cutting-edge, anti-establishment image of its popular footwear products.

Dr. Martens employs over 3,000 people, most of them in England, and its management feels a strong responsibility to them and to their families. Benefits are generous, training is given top priority, and a sense of teamwork permeates the corporate culture, making it easy for anyone in the firm to be on a first-name basis with everyone else at every organizational level. While technology has been put to good use in distribution operations and is making an impact on manufacturing methods, each pair of shoes assembled in the noisy but well-ordered factory still undergoes many careful hand operations before it is packed for sale.

Howard Johnstone, Group Administration Director and Company Secretary, believes that developing employees is good for individuals *and* for the firm. Yet recruiting people with good technical skills is becoming more difficult. The footwear business is slowly shrinking in England, partly due to high labor costs, and lifetime or even long-term employment is a thing of the past. Dr. Martens faces problems finding and retaining skilled workers despite its willingness to train, motivate, and increase job satisfaction. Unwilling to outsource its manufacturing work abroad, the firm also hopes to shift the emphasis of its training from factory skills to management skills, and to find and retain the right management team to lead the company forward with its tradition of rebellion intact.

Study Questions

Dr. Martens faces several difficult issues. In spite of its counter-culture profile, its array of benefits, expanding training programs, and efforts to nurture a "caring" culture, it exists in a tight job market with workers who may feel little loyalty to any firm, and absenteeism is high. As you watch the video, try to identify ways in which the company might best use motivation and job satisfaction to retain its best employees. Specifically, answer the following questions:

1. Howard Johnstone talks about company benefit plans as a means of motivating employees, but he does not mention any ways in which the work itself might satisfy employees. What general aspects of their work would most people at Dr. Martens find motivating? If you gave different answers for factory workers than for management, explain why.

2. Do you agree with Howard Johnstone that younger people have different attitudes toward work than older people? Why or why not? How might that observation be related to his statement that "people are motivated by different things at different points in their career?"

3. Use what you've learned from the text to assess the problem of absenteeism at Dr. Martens.

4. What are some of the decision criteria used in hiring at Dr. Martens? (Some are mentioned in the film; you can infer others.) What are some of the external limitations on the choices its managers can make in hiring? If these were removed, how do you think the hiring decision would change?

part three

THE GROUP

Every Monday at 9:30 A.M., the 50 or so employees at The Phelps Group (see photo), a southern California marketing agency, get together for a short meeting.[1] Each week, these meetings move through the same agenda headings. First, the company's teams—advertising, direct marketing, production, and media—show off their new work. Second, the company's CEO announces important agency or client business. Third, each team delivers a one-minute mini-lesson, teaching everyone about some key piece of expertise or perhaps handing out and summarizing a helpful article. This exercise is meant to underscore the importance the agency places on brevity in communication. The final item on the agenda is the award presentation of a two-by-two-foot wooden plaque. The previous week's award winner selects the next recipient and passes on the plaque. The idea is to allow individual employees to recognize colleagues who have done an exemplary job during the prior week.

"It's great to have a group experience at the beginning of the week," says Phelps's CEO. He argues that it offers a counterbalance to the increasingly technology-enabled workplace, which fosters less and less face-to-face contact.

Like Phelps's CEO, more and more executives are coming to realize the value of groups. In this and the following chapter we'll show you the key elements necessary for creating effective groups and teams. Let's begin by defining groups and explaining why people join them.

216

Foundations of Group Behavior

DEFINING AND CLASSIFYING GROUPS

A **group** is defined as two or more individuals, interacting and interdependent, who have come together to achieve particular objectives. Groups can be either formal or informal. By **formal groups**, we mean those defined by the organization's structure, with designated work assignments establishing tasks. In formal groups, the behaviors that one should engage in are stipulated by and directed toward organizational goals. The six members making up an airline flight crew are an example of a formal group. In contrast, **informal groups** are alliances that are neither formally structured nor organizationally determined. These groups are natural formations in the work environment that appear in response to the need for social contact. Three employees from different departments who regularly eat lunch together are an example of an informal group.

It's possible to subclassify groups as command, task, interest, or friendship groups.[2] Command and task groups are dictated by the formal organization, whereas interest and friendship groups are informal alliances.

A **command group** is determined by the organization chart. It is composed of the individuals who report directly to a given manager. An elementary school principal and her 12 teachers form a command group, as do the director of postal audits and his five inspectors.

Task groups, also organizationally determined, represent those working together to complete a job task. However, a

AFTER READING THIS CHAPTER, YOU SHOULD BE ABLE TO

1. Differentiate between formal and informal groups

2. Compare two models of group development

3. Explain how group interaction can be analyzed

4. Identify the key factors in explaining group behavior

5. Explain how role requirements change in different situations

6. Describe how norms exert influence on an individual's behavior

7. Define social loafing and its effect on group performance

8. Identify the benefits and disadvantages of cohesive groups

9. List the strengths and weaknesses of group decision making

10. Contrast the effectiveness of interacting, brainstorming, nominal, and electronic meeting groups

group

Two or more individuals, interacting and interdependent, who have come together to achieve particular objectives.

formal group

A designated work group defined by the organization's structure.

informal group

A group that is neither formally structured nor organizationally determined; appears in response to the need for social contact.

command group

A manager and his or her immediate subordinates.

task group

Those working together to complete a job task.

interest group

Those working together to attain a specific objective with which each is concerned.

friendship group

Those brought together because they share one or more common characteristics.

task group's boundaries are not limited to its immediate hierarchical superior. It can cross command relationships. For instance, if a college student is accused of a campus crime, it may require communication and coordination among the dean of academic affairs, the dean of students, the registrar, the director of security, and the student's advisor. Such a formation would constitute a task group. It should be noted that all command groups are also task groups, but because task groups can cut across the organization, the reverse need not be true.

People who may or may not be aligned into common command or task groups may affiliate to attain a specific objective with which each is concerned. This is an **interest group**. Employees who band together to have their vacation schedules altered, to support a peer who has been fired, or to seek improved working conditions represent the formation of a united body to further their common interest.

Groups often develop because the individual members have one or more common characteristics. We call these formations **friendship groups**. Social alliances, which frequently extend outside the work situation, can be based on similar age or ethnic heritage, support for Notre Dame football, or the holding of similar political views, to name just a few such characteristics.

Informal groups provide a very important service by satisfying their members' social needs. Because of interactions that result from the close proximity of workstations or task interactions, we find workers playing golf together, commuting to work together, lunching together, and spending their breaks around the water cooler together. We must recognize that these types of interactions among individuals, even though informal, deeply affect their behavior and performance.

There is no single reason why individuals join groups. Because most people belong to a number of groups, it's obvious that different groups provide different benefits to their members. Exhibit 8-1 summarizes the most popular reasons people have for joining groups.

EXHIBIT 8-1

Why Do People Join Groups?

Security. By joining a group, individuals can reduce the insecurity of "standing alone." People feel stronger, have fewer self-doubts, and are more resistant to threats when they are part of a group.

Status. Inclusion in a group that is viewed as important by others provides recognition and status for its members.

Self-esteem. Groups can provide people with feelings of self-worth. That is, in addition to conveying status to those outside the group, membership can also give increased feelings of worth to the group members themselves.

Affiliation. Groups can fulfill social needs. People enjoy the regular interaction that comes with group membership. For many people, these on-the-job interactions are their primary source for fulfilling their needs for affiliation.

Power. What cannot be achieved individually often becomes possible through group action. There is power in numbers.

Goal Achievement. There are times when it takes more than one person to accomplish a particular task—there is a need to pool talents, knowledge, or power in order to complete a job. In such instances, management will rely on the use of a formal group.

STAGES OF GROUP DEVELOPMENT

Groups generally pass through a standardized sequence in their evolution. We call this sequence the five-stage model of group development. Recent studies, however, indicate that temporary groups with task-specific deadlines follow a very different pattern. In this section, we describe the five-stage general model and an alternative model for temporary groups with deadlines.

THE FIVE-STAGE MODEL

As shown in Exhibit 8-2, the **five-stage group-development model** characterizes groups as proceeding through five distinct stages: forming, storming, norming, performing, and adjourning.[3]

The first stage, **forming**, is characterized by a great deal of uncertainty about the group's purpose, structure, and leadership. Members are "testing the waters" to determine what types of behavior are acceptable. This stage is complete when members have begun to think of themselves as part of a group.

The **storming** stage is one of intragroup conflict. Members accept the existence of the group, but there is resistance to the constraints that the group imposes on individuality. Furthermore, there is conflict over who will control the group. When this stage is complete, there will be a relatively clear hierarchy of leadership within the group.

The third stage is one in which close relationships develop and the group demonstrates cohesiveness. There is now a strong sense of group identity and camaraderie. This **norming** stage is complete when the group structure solidifies and the group has assimilated a common set of expectations of what defines correct member behavior.

The fourth stage is **performing**. The structure at this point is fully functional and accepted. Group energy has moved from getting to know and understand each other to performing the task at hand.

For permanent work groups, performing is the last stage in their development. However, for temporary committees, teams, task forces, and similar groups that have a limited task to perform, there is an **adjourning** stage. In this stage, the group prepares for its disbandment. High task performance is no longer the group's top priority. Instead, attention is directed toward wrapping up activities. Responses of group members vary in this stage. Some are upbeat, basking in the group's accomplishments. Others may be depressed over the loss of camaraderie and friendships gained during the work group's life.

Many interpreters of the five-stage model have assumed that a group becomes more effective as it progresses through the first four stages. While this

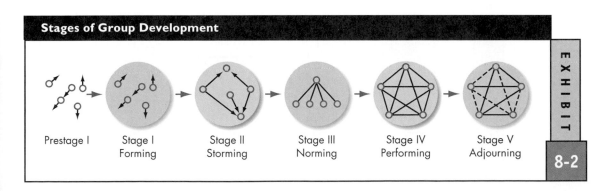

Stages of Group Development

| Prestage I | Stage I Forming | Stage II Storming | Stage III Norming | Stage IV Performing | Stage V Adjourning |

EXHIBIT 8-2

assumption may be generally true, what makes a group effective is more complex than this model acknowledges. Under some conditions, high levels of conflict are conducive to high group performance. So we might expect to find situations in which groups in Stage II outperform those in Stages III or IV. Similarly, groups do not always proceed clearly from one stage to the next. Sometimes, in fact, several stages go on simultaneously, as when groups are storming and performing at the same time. Groups even occasionally regress to previous stages. Therefore, even the strongest proponents of this model do not assume that all groups follow its five-stage process precisely or that Stage IV is always the most preferable.

Another problem with the five-stage model, in terms of understanding work-related behavior, is that it ignores organizational context.[4] For instance, a study of a cockpit crew in an airliner found that, within 10 minutes, three strangers assigned to fly together for the first time had become a high-performing group. What allowed for this speedy group development was the strong organizational context surrounding the tasks of the cockpit crew. This context provided the rules, task definitions, information, and resources needed for the group to perform. They didn't need to develop plans, assign roles, determine and allocate resources, resolve conflicts, and set norms the way the five-stage model predicts.

AN ALTERNATIVE MODEL: FOR TEMPORARY GROUPS WITH DEADLINES

Temporary groups with deadlines don't seem to follow the previous model. Studies indicate that they have their own unique sequencing of actions (or inaction): (1) Their first meeting sets the group's direction; (2) this first phase of group activity is one of inertia; (3) a transition takes place at the end of this first phase, which occurs exactly when the group has used up half its allotted time; (4) a transition initiates major changes; (5) a second phase of inertia follows the transition; and (6) the group's last meeting is characterized by markedly accelerated activity.[5] This pattern is called the **punctuated equilibruim model** and is shown in Exhibit 8-3.

The first meeting sets the group's direction. A framework of behavioral patterns and assumptions through which the group will approach its project emerges in this first meeting. These lasting patterns can appear as early as the first few seconds of the group's life.

Once set, the group's direction becomes "written in stone" and is unlikely to be reexamined throughout the first half of the group's life. This is a period of in-

punctuated-equilibrium model

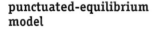

Temporary groups go through transitions between inertia and activity.

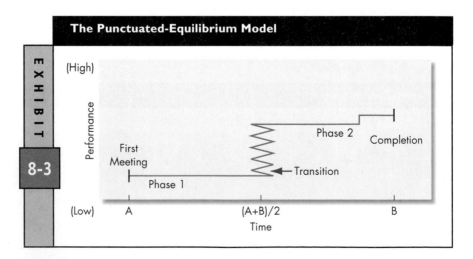

ertia—that is, the group tends to stand still or become locked into a fixed course of action. Even if it gains new insights that challenge initial patterns and assumptions, the group is incapable of acting on these new insights in Phase 1.

One of the more interesting discoveries made in these studies was that each group experienced its transition at the same point in its calendar—precisely halfway between its first meeting and its official deadline—despite the fact that some groups spent as little as an hour on their project while others spent six months. It was as if the groups universally experienced a midlife crisis at this point. The midpoint appears to work like an alarm clock, heightening members' awareness that their time is limited and that they need to "get moving."

This transition ends Phase 1 and is characterized by a concentrated burst of changes in which old patterns are dropped and new perspectives are adopted. The transition sets a revised direction for Phase 2.

Phase 2 is a new equilibrium or period of inertia. In this phase, the group executes plans created during the transition period.

The group's last meeting is characterized by a final burst of activity to finish its work.

In summary, the punctuated-equilibrium model characterizes groups as exhibiting long periods of inertia interspersed with brief revolutionary changes triggered primarily by their members' awareness of time and deadlines. Keep in mind, however, that this model doesn't apply to all groups. It's essentially limited to temporary task groups that are working under a time-constrained completion deadline.[6]

SOCIOMETRY: ANALYZING GROUP INTERACTION

Shirley Goldman knew the formal work groups in the branch bank she managed. The tellers made up one group, the loan processors another, administrative support personnel still another, and the task force she had created for suggesting ways to improve customer service was a fourth. What Shirley didn't feel as confident about were the informal groups in her branch. Who were in these groups? Who were their informal leaders? How might these groups be affecting communication in the bank or creating potential conflicts? To get answers to these questions, Shirley decided to use a technique she learned in business school. It's called **sociometry** (or sometimes also called *social network mapping* or *organizational network analysis*) and it's an analytical tool for studying group interactions.[7]

Sociometry seeks to find out who people like or dislike and with whom they would or would not wish to work. How do you get that information? Through the use of interviews or questionnaires. For instance, employees might be asked: (1) With whom in your organization would you like to associate in the process of carrying out your job? or (2) Name several organization members with whom you would like to spend some of your free time.

This information can then be used to create a **sociogram**. This is a diagram that graphically maps the preferred social interactions obtained from the interviews or questionnaires. Before we actually work through an example, let's define some key terms that you need to know when discussing and analyzing a sociogram:[8]

- **Social networks**. Specific sets of linkages among a defined set of individuals.
- **Clusters**. Groups that exist within social networks.
- **Prescribed clusters**. Formal groups such as departments, work teams, task forces, crews, or committees.

sociometry
An analytical technique for studying group interactions.

sociogram
A diagram that graphically maps the preferred social interactions obtained from interviews or questionnaires.

social networks
A specific set of linkages among a defined set of individuals.

clusters
Groups that exist within social networks.

prescribed clusters
Formal groups such as departments, work teams, task forces, or committees.

- **Emergent clusters**. Informal, unofficial groups.
- **Coalitions**. Clusters of individuals who temporarily come together to achieve a specific purpose.
- **Cliques**. Relatively permanent informal groupings that involve friendship.
- **Stars**. Individuals with the most linkages in a network.
- **Liaisons**. Individuals who connect two or more clusters but are not members of any cluster.
- **Bridges**. Individuals who serve as linking pins by belonging to two or more clusters.
- **Isolates**. Individuals who are not connected to a social network.

Shirley Goldman has just completed a sociometric survey of the 11 people who work in her Bank of America branch in Sacramento, California. She has had each employee fill out a questionnaire identifying with whom they would like to spend more time. Now Shirley has translated those preferences into the simplified sociogram shown in Exhibit 8-4. Each employee is shown as a letter. The arrow from B to A means B chose A. The two-headed arrow connecting A and D means both chose each other.

What information can Shirley deduce from this sociogram? A is the star. F is an isolate. D is a bridge. There don't appear to be any liaisons. In addition to the four prescribed clusters, two emergent clusters seem to exist. And without more information, Shirley can't tell if these emergent clusters are coalitions or cliques.

So what, if anything, can Shirley do with this information? It can help her predict communication patterns. For instance, D is likely to act as an information

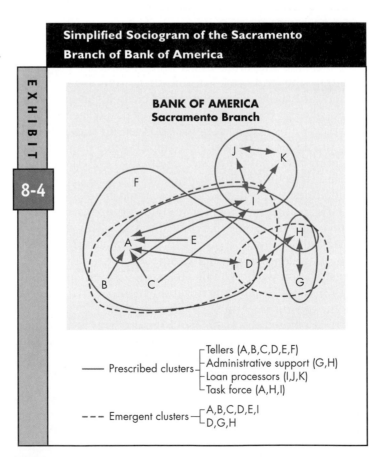

EXHIBIT 8-4

Simplified Sociogram of the Sacramento Branch of Bank of America

BANK OF AMERICA
Sacramento Branch

Prescribed clusters
- Tellers (A,B,C,D,E,F)
- Administrative support (G,H)
- Loan processors (I,J,K)
- Task force (A,H,I)

Emergent clusters
- A,B,C,D,E,I
- D,G,H

Using Sociometry to Help Build Submarines

Newport News Shipbuilding entered a joint venture with Electric Boat to build submarines for the U.S. Navy. But the two companies had different internal structures that could create problems. Electric Boat had moved to the use of teams. Newport News Shipbuilding was working toward a team-oriented approach but basically still operated with a traditional hierarchy. Success in this project would require people from both companies to communicate regularly. Where were the potential problems likely to be? To begin to answer that question, Joe LeClear, a systems engineering team leader at Newport News Shipbuilding, was given the task of mapping information exchange and communication paths at his company.

LeClear asked three basic questions of employees, who ranged in profession from welders to attorneys to purchasing agents: With whom do you interact to keep informed about developments within the company? From whom do you seek feedback and suggestions before making decisions? With whom do you interact to complete assignments? Employees were supplied with a roster of peers, subordinates, and managers and asked to rank their interaction with each as low, moderate, or high for each question.

The results identified to whom the employees believed they talked, to whom they actually talked, who actually heard them—and exactly where the gaps in communication were. Specifically, the sociometric analysis revealed that there were clusters of isolates who talked to each other but had limited communication outside their clusters. Knowing about the isolates and who they were, LeClear recommended actions to integrate the isolated clusters so they would better be able to contribute to the new joint venture.

Source: P. G. Doloff, "Beyond the Org Chart," *Across the Board*, February 1999, pp. 45–46.

conduit between the tellers and the administrative support group. Similarly, Shirley shouldn't be surprised that F is out of the gossip loop and tends to rely almost exclusively on formal communication to know what's happening in the branch. If Shirley was going on vacation and needed to pick someone to temporarily run the branch, a good choice might be A because this person seems to be well liked. When conflicts occur between the tellers and the administrative support group, a bridge like D might be the best person to help resolve them.

Before we leave the topic of sociometry, some research relating to turnover, conflict, and diversity should be briefly mentioned. First, turnover is likely to be linked to emergent clusters.[9] Employees who perceive themselves as members of common clusters tend to act in concert—they're likely to stay or quit as a group. Second, strong interpersonal relationships between members tend to be associated with lower conflict levels.[10] So since members of emergent clusters tend to interact more with each other, there should be less conflict among these members. Finally, women and minorities tend to form coalitions and cliques, and are less likely than their white male counterparts to become liaisons or bridges.[11]

TOWARD EXPLAINING WORK GROUP BEHAVIOR

Why are some group efforts more successful than others? The answer to that question is complex, but it includes variables such as the ability of the group's members, the size of the group, the level of conflict, and the internal pressures on members to conform to the group's norms. Exhibit 8-5 presents the major components that determine group performance and satisfaction.[12] The following discussions are based on this model.

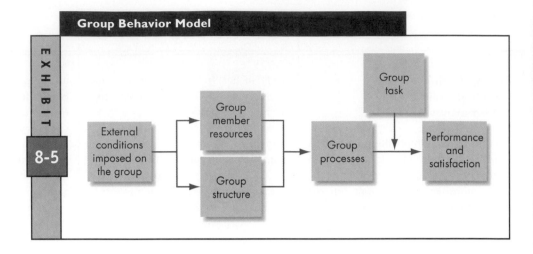

Group Behavior Model

EXHIBIT 8-5

EXTERNAL CONDITIONS IMPOSED ON THE GROUP

To begin understanding the behavior of a work group, you need to view it as a subsystem embedded in a larger system.[13] Work groups don't exist in isolation. They're part of a larger organization. A research team in Dow's plastic products division, for instance, must live within the rules and policies dictated from the division's headquarters and Dow's corporate offices. So every work group is influenced by external conditions imposed from outside it. These external conditions include the organization's overall strategy, its authority structures, formal regulations, resources, employee selection process, performance evaluation and reward systems, culture, and physical work setting.

An *organization's overall strategy*, typically put into place by top management, outlines the organization's goals and the means for attaining these goals. It might, for example, direct the organization toward reducing costs, improving quality, expanding market share, or shrinking the size of its overall operations. The strategy that an organization is pursuing, at any given time, will influence the power of various work groups, which, in turn, will determine the resources that the organization's top management is willing to allocate to them for performing their tasks. To illustrate, an organization that is retrenching through selling off or closing down major parts of its business is going to have work groups with a shrinking resource base, increased member anxiety, and the potential for heightened intragroup conflict.[14]

Organizations have *authority structures* that define who reports to whom, who makes decisions, and what decisions individuals or groups are empowered to make. This structure typically determines where a given work group is placed in the organization's hierarchy, the formal leader of the group, and formal relationships between groups. So while a work group might be led by someone who emerges informally from within the group, the formally designated leader—appointed by management—has authority that others in the group don't have.

Organizations create rules, procedures, policies, job descriptions, and other forms of *formal regulations* to standardize employee behavior. Because McDonald's has standard operating procedures for taking orders, cooking hamburgers, and filling soda containers, the discretion of work group members to set independent standards of behavior is severely limited. The more formal regulations that the organization imposes on all its employees, the more the behavior of work group members will be consistent and predictable.

Some organizations are large and profitable, with an abundance of resources. Their employees, for instance, will have modern, high-quality tools and equipment to do their jobs. Other organizations aren't as fortunate. When organizations have limited resources, so do their work groups. What a group actually accomplishes is, to a large degree, determined by what it is capable of accomplishing. The presence or absence of *resources* such as money, time, raw materials, and equipment—which are allocated to the group by the organization—have a large bearing on the group's behavior.

Members of any work group are, first, members of the organization of which the group is a part. Members of a cost-reduction task force at Boeing first had to be hired as employees of the company. So the criteria that an organization uses in its *selection process* will determine the kinds of people that will be in its work groups.

Another organizationwide variable that affects all employees is the *performance evaluation and reward system*.[15] Does the organization provide employees with challenging, specific performance objectives? Does the organization reward the accomplishment of individual or group objectives? Since work groups are part of the larger organizational system, group members' behavior will be influenced by how the organization evaluates performance and what behaviors are rewarded.

Every organization has an unwritten culture that defines standards of acceptable and unacceptable behavior for employees. After a few months, most employees understand their *organization's culture*. They know things like how to dress for work, whether or not rules are rigidly enforced, what kinds of questionable behaviors are sure to get them into trouble and which are likely to be overlooked, the importance of honesty and integrity, and the like. While many organizations have subcultures—often created around work groups—with an additional or modified set of standards, they still have a dominant culture that conveys to all employees those values the organization holds dearest. Members of work groups have to accept the standards implied in the organization's dominant culture if they are to remain in good standing.

Finally, the *physical work setting* that is imposed on the group by external parties has an important bearing on work group behavior.[16] Architects, industrial engineers, and office designers make decisions regarding the size and physical layout of an employee's work space, the arrangement of equipment, illumination levels, and the need for acoustics to cut down on noise distractions. These create both barriers and opportunities for work group interaction. It's obviously a lot easier for employees to talk or "goof off" if their work stations are close together, there are no physical barriers between them, and their supervisor is in an enclosed office 50 meters away.

The new headquarters of SEI Investments, a financial services firm, was designed to encourage group interaction. Al West, the firm's chief executive, asked architects to design a flexible work space in which employees could quickly and easily reconfigure their work areas to form groups. Coiled cables that drop from the ceiling contain telephone, computer, and electrical wiring. All office furniture is on wheels. By unplugging their cables and rolling their equipment to a new area, employees organize new work groups as their assignments change.

GROUP MEMBER RESOURCES

A group's potential level of performance depends, to a large extent, on the resources that its members individually bring to the group. In this section, we want to look at two general resources that have received the greatest amount of attention: knowledge, skills, and abilities; and personality characteristics.

KNOWLEDGE, SKILLS, AND ABILITIES

Part of a group's performance can be predicted by assessing the knowledge, skills, and abilities of its individual members. It's true that we occasionally read about the athletic team composed of mediocre players that, because of excellent coaching, determination, and precision teamwork, beats a far more talented group of players. But such cases make the news precisely because they represent an aberration. As the old saying goes, "The race doesn't always go to the swiftest nor the battle to the strongest, but that's the way to bet." A group's performance is not merely the summation of its individual members' abilities. However, these abilities set parameters for what members can do and how effectively they will perform in a group.

A review of the evidence has found that interpersonal skills consistently emerge as important for high work group performance.[17] These include conflict management and resolution, collaborative problem solving, and communication. For instance, members need to be able to recognize the type and source of conflict confronting the group and to implement an appropriate conflict resolution strategy; to identify situations requiring participative group problem solving and to utilize the proper degree and type of participation; and to listen nonevaluatively and to appropriately use active listening techniques.

PERSONALITY CHARACTERISTICS

There has been a great deal of research on the relationship between personality traits and group attitudes and behavior. The general conclusion is that attributes that tend to have a positive connotation in our culture tend to be positively related to group productivity, morale, and cohesiveness. These include traits such as sociability, initiative, openness, and flexibility. In contrast, negatively evaluated characteristics such as authoritarianism, dominance, and unconventionality tend to be negatively related to the dependent variables.[18] These personality traits affect group performance by strongly influencing how the individual will interact with other group members.

Is any one personality characteristic a good predictor of group behavior? The answer to that question is No. The magnitude of the effect of any single characteristic is small, but taking personality characteristics together, the consequences for group behavior are of major significance.

GROUP STRUCTURE

Work groups are not unorganized mobs. They have a structure that shapes the behavior of members and makes it possible to explain and predict a large portion of individual behavior within the group as well as the performance of the group itself. What are some of these structural variables? They include formal leadership, roles, norms, group status, group size, composition of the group, and the degree of group cohesiveness.

FORMAL LEADERSHIP

Almost every work group has a formal leader. He or she is typically identified by titles such as unit or department manager, supervisor, foreman, project leader, task force head, or committee chair. This leader can play an important part in the group's success—so much so, in fact, that we have devoted an entire chapter to the topic of leadership. In Chapter 11, we review the research on leadership and the effect that leaders have on individual and group performance variables.

ROLES

Shakespeare said, "All the world's a stage, and all the men and women merely players." Using the same metaphor, all group members are actors, each playing a **role**. By this term, we mean a set of expected behavior patterns attributed to someone occupying a given position in a social unit. The understanding of role behavior would be dramatically simplified if each of us chose one role and "played it out" regularly and consistently. Unfortunately, we are required to play a number of diverse roles, both on and off our jobs. As we shall see, one of the tasks in understanding behavior is grasping the role that a person is currently playing.

role

A set of expected behavior patterns attributed to someone occupying a given position in a social unit.

For example, Bill Patterson is a plant manager with Electrical Industries, a large electrical equipment manufacturer in Phoenix. He has a number of roles that he fulfills on that job—for instance, Electrical Industries employee, member of middle management, electrical engineer, and the primary company spokesperson in the community. Off the job, Bill Patterson finds himself in still more roles: husband, father, Catholic, Rotarian, tennis player, member of the Thunderbird Country Club, and president of his homeowners' association. Many of these roles are compatible; some create conflicts. For instance, how does his religious involvement influence his managerial decisions regarding layoffs, expense account padding, and providing accurate information to government agencies? A recent offer of promotion requires Bill to relocate, yet his family very much wants to stay in Phoenix. Can the role demands of his job be reconciled with the demands of his husband and father roles?

> People have the ability to shift roles rapidly when they recognize that the situation and its demands clearly require major changes.

The issue should be clear: Like Bill Patterson, we all are required to play a number of roles, and our behavior varies with the role we are playing. Bill's behavior when he attends church on Sunday morning is different from his behavior on the golf course later that same day. So different groups impose different role requirements on individuals.

Role Identity   There are certain attitudes and actual behaviors consistent with a role, and they create the **role identity**. People have the ability to shift roles rapidly when they recognize that the situation and its demands clearly require major changes. For instance, when union stewards were promoted to supervisory positions, it was found that their attitudes changed from prounion to promanagement within a few months of their promotion. When these promotions had to be rescinded later because of economic difficulties in the firm, it was found that the demoted supervisors had once again adopted their prounion attitudes.[19]

role identity

Certain attitudes and behaviors consistent with a role.

Role Perception   One's view of how one is supposed to act in a given situation is a **role perception**. Based on an interpretation of how we believe we are supposed to behave, we engage in certain types of behavior.

role perception

An individual's view of how he or she is supposed to act in a given situation.

Watching a veteran employee on the housekeeping staff helped Lisa Jackson (left) learn her entry-level job at a Marriott hotel. In addition to teaching on-the-job skills such as the proper way to make a bed, Jackson's apprenticeship training included observing how employees should react in stressful situations.

Where do we get these perceptions? We get them from stimuli all around us—friends, books, movies, television. Many current law enforcement officers learned their roles from reading Joseph Wambaugh novels, while many of tomorrow's lawyers will be influenced by watching the actions of attorneys in *Ally McBeal* or *The Practice*. Of course, the primary reason that apprenticeship programs exist in many trades and professions is to allow beginners to watch an "expert," so that they can learn to act as they are supposed to.

Role Expectations **Role expectations** are defined as how others believe you should act in a given situation. How you behave is determined to a large extent by the role defined in the context in which you are acting. The role of a U.S. federal judge is viewed as having propriety and dignity, whereas a football coach is seen as aggressive, dynamic, and inspiring to his players. In the same context, we might be surprised to learn that the neighborhood priest moonlights during the week as a bartender because our role expectations of priests and bartenders tend to be considerably different. When role expectations are concentrated into generalized categories, we have role stereotypes.

role expectations

How others believe a person should act in a given situation.

psychological contract

An unwritten agreement that sets out what management expects from the employee, and vice versa.

In the workplace, it can be helpful to look at the topic of role expectations through the perspective of the **psychological contract**. There is an unwritten agreement that exists between employees and their employer. This psychological contract sets out mutual expectations—what management expects from workers, and vice versa.[20] In effect, this contract defines the behavioral expectations that go with every role. Management is expected to treat employees justly, provide acceptable working conditions, clearly communicate what is a fair day's work, and give feedback on how well the employee is doing. Employees are expected to respond by demonstrating a good attitude, following directions, and showing loyalty to the organization.

What happens when role expectations as implied in the psychological contract are not met? If management is derelict in keeping up its part of the bargain, we can expect negative repercussions on employee performance and satisfaction. When employees fail to live up to expectations, the result is usually some form of disciplinary action up to and including firing.

The psychological contract should be recognized as a "powerful determiner of behavior in organizations."[21] It points out the importance of accurately communicating role expectations. In Chapter 17, we discuss how organizations socialize employees in order to get them to play out their roles in the way management desires.

role conflict

A situation in which an individual is confronted by divergent role expectations.

Role Conflict When an individual is confronted by divergent role expectations, the result is **role conflict**. It exists when an individual finds that compliance with one role requirement may make more difficult the compliance with another.[22] At the extreme, it would include situations in which two or more role expectations are mutually contradictory.

Our previous discussion of the many roles Bill Patterson had to deal with included several role conflicts—for instance, Bill's attempt to reconcile the expectations placed on him as a husband and father with those placed on him as an executive with Electrical Industries. The former, as you will remember, emphasizes stability and concern for the desire of his wife and children to remain in Phoenix. Electrical Industries, on the other hand, expects its employees to be responsive to the needs and requirements of the company. Although it might be in

Bill's financial and career interests to accept a relocation, the conflict comes down to choosing between family and career role expectations.

All of us have faced and will continue to face role conflicts. The critical issue, from our standpoint, is how conflicts imposed by divergent expectations within the organization impact on behavior. Certainly, they increase internal tension and frustration. There are a number of behavioral responses in which one may engage. For example, one can give a formalized bureaucratic response. The conflict is then resolved by relying on the rules, regulations, and procedures that govern organizational activities. For example, a worker faced with the conflicting requirements imposed by the corporate controller's office and his own plant manager decides in favor of his immediate boss—the plant manager. Other behavioral responses may include withdrawal, stalling, negotiation, or, as we found in our discussion of dissonance in Chapter 3, redefining the facts or the situation to make them appear congruent.

An Experiment: Zimbardo's Simulated Prison One of the more illuminating role experiments was done by Stanford University psychologist Philip Zimbardo and his associates.[23] They created a "prison" in the basement of the Stanford psychology building; hired at $15 a day two dozen emotionally stable, physically healthy, law-abiding students who scored "normal average" on extensive personality tests; randomly assigned them the role of either "guard" or "prisoner"; and established some basic rules.

To get the experiment off to a "realistic" start, Zimbardo got the cooperation of the City of Palo Alto Police Department. They went, unannounced, to each future prisoner's home, arrested and handcuffed them, put them in a squad car in front of friends and neighbors, and took them to police headquarters where they were booked and fingerprinted. From there, they were taken to the Stanford prison.

At the start of the planned two-week experiment, there were no measurable differences between those individuals assigned to be guards and those chosen to be prisoners. Additionally, the guards received no special training in how to be prison guards. They were told only to "maintain law and order" in the prison and not to take any nonsense from the prisoners: Physical violence was forbidden. To simulate further the realities of prison life, the prisoners were allowed visits from relatives and friends. And although the mock guards worked eight-hour shifts, the mock prisoners were kept in their cells around the clock and were allowed out only for meals, exercise, toilet privileges, head-count lineups, and work details.

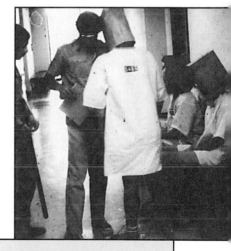

Students at Stanford University playing roles of "guard" and "prisoner" in a simulated prison experiment demonstrating how quickly individuals learn new roles different from their personalities and without any special training.

It took the "prisoners" little time to accept the authority positions of the guards, or the mock guards to adjust to their new authority roles. After the guards crushed a rebellion attempt on the second day, the prisoners became increasingly passive. Whatever the guards "dished out," the prisoners took. The prisoners actually began to believe and act as if they were, as the guards constantly reminded them, inferior and powerless. And every guard, at some time during the simulation, engaged in abusive, authoritative behavior. For example, one guard said, "I was surprised at myself . . . I made them call each other names and clean the toilets out with their bare hands. I practically considered the prisoners cattle, and I kept thinking: 'I have to watch out for them in case they try something.'" Another guard added, "I was tired of seeing the prisoners in their rags and smelling the strong odors of their bodies that filled the cells. I watched them tear at each other on orders given by us. They didn't see it as an experiment. It was real and they were fighting to keep their identity. But we were always there to show them who was boss." Surprisingly, during the entire experiment—even after days of abuse—not one prisoner said, "Stop this. I'm a student like you. This is just an experiment!"

The simulation actually proved too successful in demonstrating how quickly individuals learn new roles. The researchers had to stop the experiment after only six days because of the pathological reactions that the participants were demonstrating. And remember, these were individuals chosen precisely for their normalcy and emotional stability.

What should you conclude from this prison simulation? The participants in this experiment had, like the rest of us, learned stereotyped conceptions of guard and prisoner roles from the mass media and their own personal experiences in power and powerlessness relationships gained at home (parent–child), in school (teacher–student), and in other situations. This, then, allowed them easily and rapidly to assume roles that were very different from their inherent personalities. In this case, we saw that people with no prior personality pathology or training in their roles could execute extreme forms of behavior consistent with the roles they were playing.

NORMS

Did you ever notice that golfers don't speak while their partners are putting on the green or that employees don't criticize their bosses in public? Why? The answer is: 'Norms!'

norms

Acceptable standards of behavior within a group that are shared by the group's members.

All groups have established **norms**, that is, acceptable standards of behavior that are shared by the group's members. Norms tell members what they ought and ought not to do under certain circumstances. From an individual's standpoint, they tell what is expected of you in certain situations. When agreed to and accepted by the group, norms act as a means of influencing the behavior of group members with a minimum of external controls. Norms differ among groups, communities, and societies, but they all have them.[24]

Common Classes of Norms   A work group's norms are like an individual's fingerprints—each is unique. Yet there are still some common classes of norms that appear in most work groups.[25]

Probably the most common class of norms is *performance norms*. Work groups typically provide their members with explicit cues on how hard they should work, how to get the job done, their level of output, appropriate levels of tardiness, and the like.[26] These norms are extremely powerful in affecting an individual employee's performance—they are capable of significantly modifying a performance prediction that was based solely on the employee's ability and level of personal motivation.

A second category encompasses *appearance norms*. These include things such as appropriate dress, loyalty to the work group or organization, when to look busy, and when it's acceptable to goof off. Some organizations have formal dress codes. However, even in their absence, norms frequently develop to dictate the kind of clothing that should be worn to work. Similarly, presenting the appearance of loyalty is important, especially among professional employees and those in the executive ranks. So it's often considered inappropriate to be openly looking for another job.

Another category concerns *social arrangement norms*. These norms come from informal work groups and primarily regulate social interactions within the group. With whom group members eat lunch, friendships on and off the job, social games, and the like are influenced by these norms.

A final category relates to *allocation of resource norms*. These norms can originate in the group or in the organization and cover things such as pay, assignment of difficult jobs, and allocation of new tools and equipment.

Some Norms Are More Important Than Others Groups don't establish or enforce norms for every conceivable situation. The norms that the group will enforce tend to be those that are important to it.[27] But what makes a norm important? (1) *If it facilitates the group's survival*. Groups don't like to fail, so they look to enforce those norms that increase their chances for success. This means that they'll try to protect themselves from interference from other groups or individuals. (2) *If it increases the predictability of group members' behaviors*. Norms that increase predictability enable group members to anticipate each other's actions and to prepare appropriate responses. (3) *If it reduces embarrassing interpersonal problems for group members*. Norms are important if they ensure the satisfaction of their members and prevent as much interpersonal discomfort as possible. (4) *If it allows members to express the central values of the group and clarify what is distinctive about the group's identity*. Norms that encourage expression of the group's values and distinctive identity help to solidify and maintain the group.

Informality reigns at PeopleSoft, where "having fun" is an official corporate goal. Casual dress and playful behavior are norms at PeopleSoft, which sells enterprise resource planning software. It's not unusual to see employees like Mark Hoernemann (center) wearing a silly hat, shooting co-workers with a Nerf gun, or playing on a mini golf course that runs through the office. Industry analysts attribute PeopleSoft's financial success as much to the strength of the firm's fun-loving environment as to the high quality of its software.

Conformity As a member of a group, you desire acceptance by the group. Because of your desire for acceptance, you are susceptible to conforming to the group's norms. There is considerable evidence that groups can place strong pressures on individual members to change their attitudes and behaviors to conform to the group's standard.[28]

Do individuals conform to the pressures of all the groups to which they belong? Obviously not, because people belong to many groups and their norms vary. In some cases, they may even have contradictory norms. So what do people do? They conform to the important groups to which they belong or hope to belong. The important groups have been referred to as **reference groups** and are characterized as ones in which the person is aware of the others; the person defines himself or herself as a member, or would like to be a member; and the person feels that the group members are significant to him or her.[29] The implication, then, is that all groups do not impose equal conformity pressures on their members.

The impact that group pressures for **conformity** can have on an individual member's judgment and attitudes was demonstrated in the now classic studies by Solomon Asch.[30] Asch made up groups of seven or eight people, who sat in a classroom and were asked to compare two cards held by the experimenter. One card had one line, the other had three lines of varying length. As shown in Exhibit 8-6, one of the lines on the three-line card was identical to the line on the one-line card. Also as shown in Exhibit 8-6, the difference in line length was

reference groups

Important groups to which individuals belong or hope to belong and with whose norms individuals are likely to conform.

conformity

Adjusting one's behavior to align with the norms of the group.

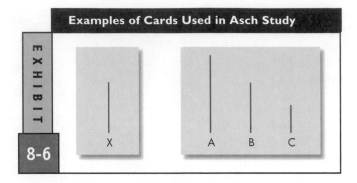

Examples of Cards Used in Asch Study

EXHIBIT

8-6

X   A   B   C

quite obvious; under ordinary conditions, subjects made fewer than 1 percent errors. The object was to announce aloud which of the three lines matched the single line. But what happens if the members in the group begin to give incorrect answers? Will the pressures to conform result in an unsuspecting subject (USS) altering his or her answer to align with the others? That was what Asch wanted to know. So he arranged the group so that only the USS was unaware that the experiment was "fixed." The seating was prearranged: The USS was placed so as to be the last to announce his or her decision.

The experiment began with several sets of matching exercises. All the subjects gave the right answers. On the third set, however, the first subject gave an obviously wrong answer—for example, saying "C" in Exhibit 8-6. The next subject gave the same wrong answer, and so did the others until it got to the unknowing subject. He knew "B" was the same as "X," yet everyone has said "C." The decision confronting the USS was this: Do you publicly state a perception that differs from the preannounced position of the others in your group? Or do you give an answer that you strongly believe is incorrect in order to have your response agree with that of the other group members?

The results obtained by Asch demonstrated that over many experiments and many trials, subjects conformed in about 35 percent of the trials; that is, the subjects gave answers that they knew were wrong but that were consistent with the replies of other group members. And what meaning can we draw from these results? They suggest that there are group norms that press us toward conformity. That is, we desire to be one of the group and avoid being visibly different.

The preceding conclusions are based on research that was conducted nearly 50 years ago. Has time altered their validity? And should we consider these findings generalizable across cultures? The evidence indicates that there have been changes in the level of conformity over time; and Asch's findings are culture bound.[31] Specifically, levels of conformity have steadily declined since Asch's studies in the early 1950s. In addition, conformity to social norms is higher in collectivist cultures than in individualistic cultures. Nevertheless, even in highly individualistic countries such as the United States, you should consider conformity to norms to still be a powerful force in groups.

STATUS

While teaching a college course on adolescence, the instructor asked the class to list things that contributed to status when they were in high school. The list was long and included being an athlete or a cheerleader and being able to cut class without getting caught. Then the instructor asked the students to list things that didn't contribute to status. Again, it was easy for the students to create a long list: getting straight A's, having your mother drive you to school, and so forth. Finally, the students were asked to develop a third list—those things that didn't matter one way or the other. There was a long silence. At last one student in the back row volunteered, "In high school, nothing didn't matter."[32]

Status—that is, a socially defined position or rank given to groups or group members by others—permeates society far beyond the walls of high school. It would not be extravagant to rephrase the preceding quotation to read, "In the status hierarchy of life, nothing doesn't matter." We live in a class-structured society. Despite all attempts to make it more egalitarian, we have made little progress toward a classless society. Even the smallest group will develop roles, rights, and rituals to differentiate its members. Status is an important factor in understanding human behavior because it is a significant motivator and has major behavioral consequences when individuals perceive a disparity between what they believe their status to be and what others perceive it to be.

status

A socially defined position or rank given to groups or group members by others.

Status and Norms   Status has been shown to have some interesting effects on the power of norms and pressures to conform. For instance, high-status members of groups often are given more freedom to deviate from norms than are other group members.[33] High-status people also are better able to resist conformity pressures than their lower-status peers. An individual who is highly valued by a group but who doesn't much need or care about the social rewards the group provides is particularly able to pay minimal attention to conformity norms.[34]

The previous findings explain why many star athletes, famous actors, top-performing salespeople, and outstanding academics seem oblivious to appearance or social norms that constrain their peers. As high-status individuals, they're given a wider range of discretion. But this is true only as long as the high-status person's activities aren't severely detrimental to group goal achievement.[35]

Status Equity   It is important for group members to believe that the status hierarchy is equitable. When inequity is perceived, it creates disequilibrium that results in various types of corrective behavior.[36]

The concept of equity presented in Chapter 6 applies to status. People expect rewards to be proportionate to costs incurred. If Dana and Anne are the two finalists for the head nurse position in a hospital, and it is clear that Dana has more seniority and better preparation for assuming the promotion, Anne will view the selection of Dana to be equitable. However, if Anne is chosen because she is the daughter-in-law of the hospital director, Dana will believe an injustice has been committed.

The trappings that go with formal positions are also important elements in maintaining equity. When we believe there is an inequity between the perceived ranking of an individual and the status accouterments that person is given by the organization, we are experiencing status incongruence. Examples of this kind of incongruence are the more desirable office location being held by a lower-ranking individual and paid country club membership being provided by the company for division managers but not for vice presidents. Pay incongruence has long been a problem in the insurance industry, where top sales agents often earn two to five times more than senior corporate executives. The result is that it is very hard for insurance companies to entice successful agents into management positions. Our point is that employees expect the things an individual has and receives to be congruent with his or her status.

Groups generally agree within themselves on status criteria and, hence, there is usually high concurrence in group rankings of individuals. However, individuals can find themselves in a conflict situation when they move between groups whose status criteria are different or when they join groups whose members have heterogeneous backgrounds. For instance, business executives may use personal income or the growth rate of their companies as determinants of status. Government bureaucrats may use the size of their budgets. Professional employees may use the degree of autonomy that comes with their job assignment. Blue-collar workers may use years of seniority. In groups made up of heterogeneous individuals or when heterogeneous groups are forced to be interdependent, status differences may initiate conflict as the group attempts to reconcile and align the differing hierarchies. As we'll see in the next chapter, this can be a particular problem when management creates teams made up of employees from across varied functions within the organization.

Status and Culture   Before we leave the topic of status, we should briefly address the issue of cross-culture transferability. Do cultural differences affect status? The answer is a resounding Yes.[37]

The importance of status does vary between cultures. The French, for example, are highly status conscious. Additionally, countries differ on the critieria that create status. For instance, status for Latin Americans and Asians tends to be derived from family position and formal roles held in organizations. In contrast, while status is still important in countries such as the United States and Australia, it tends to be less "in your face." And it tends to be bestowed more on accomplishments than on titles and family trees.

The message here is to make sure you understand who and what holds status when interacting with people from a culture different than your own. An American manager who doesn't understand that office size is no measure of a Japanese executive's position or who fails to grasp the importance that the British place on family geneology and social class is likely to unintentionally offend his Japanese or British counterpart and, in so doing, lessen his interpersonal effectiveness.

SIZE

Does the size of a group affect the group's overall behavior? The answer to this question is a definite Yes, but the effect depends on what dependent variables you consider.[38]

The evidence indicates, for instance, that smaller groups are faster at completing tasks than are larger ones. However, if the group is engaged in problem solving, large groups consistently get better marks than their smaller counterparts. Translating these results into specific numbers is a bit more hazardous, but we can offer some parameters. Large groups—with a dozen or more members—are good for gaining diverse input. So if the goal of the group is fact-finding, larger groups should be more effective. On the other hand, smaller groups are better at doing something productive with that input. Groups of approximately seven members tend to be more effective for taking action.

One of the most important findings related to the size of a group has been labeled **social loafing**. Social loafing is the tendency for individuals to expend less effort when working collectively than when working individually.[39] It directly challenges the logic that the productivity of the group as a whole should at least equal the sum of the productivity of each individual in that group.

A common stereotype about groups is that the sense of team spirit spurs individual effort and enhances the group's overall productivity. In the late 1920s, a German psychologist named Max Ringelmann compared the results of individual and group performance on a rope-pulling task.[40] He expected that the group's effort would be equal to the sum of the efforts of individuals within the group.

social loafing

The tendency for individuals to expend less effort when working collectively than when working individually.

That is, three people pulling together should exert three times as much pull on the rope as one person, and eight people should exert eight times as much pull. Ringelmann's results, however, didn't confirm his expectations. Groups of three people exerted a force only two-and-a-half times the average individual performance. Groups of eight collectively achieved less than four times the solo rate.

Replications of Ringelmann's research with similar tasks have generally supported his findings.[41] Increases in group size are inversely related to individual performance. More may be better in the sense that the total productivity of a group of four is greater than that of one or two people, but the individual productivity of each group member declines.

What causes this social loafing effect? It may be due to a belief that others in the group are not carrying their fair share. If you see others as lazy or inept, you can reestablish equity by reducing your effort. Another explanation is the dispersion of responsibility. Because the results of the group cannot be attributed to any single person, the relationship between an individual's input and the group's output is clouded. In such situations, individuals may be tempted to become "free riders" and coast on the group's efforts. In other words, there will be a reduction in efficiency when individuals think that their contribution cannot be measured.

The implications for OB of this effect on work groups are significant. When managers utilize collective work situations to enhance morale and teamwork, they must also provide means by which individual efforts can be identified. If this isn't done, management must weigh the potential losses in productivity from using groups against any possible gains in worker satisfaction.[42] However, this conclusion has a Western bias. It's consistent with individualistic cultures, such as the United States and Canada, that are dominated by self-interest. It is not consistent with collective societies in which individuals are motivated by in-group goals. For instance, in studies comparing employees from the United States with employees from the People's Republic of China and Israel (both collectivist societies), the Chinese and Israelis showed no propensity to engage in social loafing. In fact, the Chinese and Israelis actually performed better in a group than when working alone.[43]

The research on group size leads us to two additional conclusions: (1) Groups with an odd number of members tend to be preferable to those with an even number; and (2) groups made up of five or seven members do a pretty good job of exercising the best elements of both small and large groups.[44] Having an odd number of members eliminates the possibility of ties when votes are taken. And groups made up of five or seven members are large enough to form a majority and allow for diverse input, yet small enough to avoid the negative outcomes often associated with large groups, such as domination by a

> Groups made up of five or seven members do a pretty good job of exercising the best elements of both small and large groups.

few members, development of subgroups, inhibited participation by some members, and excessive time taken to reach a decision.

COMPOSITION

Most group activities require a variety of skills and knowledge. Given this requirement, it would be reasonable to conclude that heterogeneous groups—those composed of dissimilar individuals—would be more likely to have diverse abilities and information and should be more effective. Research studies generally substantiate this conclusion, especially on cognitive, creativity-demanding tasks.[45]

When a group is diverse in terms of personalities, gender, age, education, functional specialization, and experience, there is an increased probability that the group will possess the needed characteristics to complete its tasks effectively.[46] The group may be more conflict laden and less expedient as varied positions are introduced and assimilated, but the evidence generally supports the conclusion that heterogeneous groups perform more effectively than do those that are homogeneous. Essentially, diversity promotes conflict, which stimulates creativity and leads in turn to improved decision making.

But what about diversity created by racial or national differences? The evidence indicates that these elements of diversity interfere with group processes, at least in the short term.[47] Cultural diversity seems to be an asset on tasks that call for a variety of viewpoints. But culturally heterogeneous groups have more difficulty in learning to work with each other and in solving problems. The good news is that these difficulties seem to dissipate with time. While newly formed culturally diverse groups underperform newly formed culturally homogeneous groups, the differences disappear after about three months. The reason is that it takes diverse groups a while to learn how to work through disagreements and different approaches to solving problems.

An offshoot of the composition issue has recently received a great deal of attention by group researchers. This is the degree to which members of a group share a common demographic attribute, such as age, sex, race, educational level, or length of service in the organization, and the impact of this attribute on turnover. We call this variable **group demography**.

We discussed individual demographic factors in Chapter 2. Here we consider the same type of factors, but in a group context. That is, it's not whether a person is male or female or has been employed with the organization a year rather than 10 years that concerns us now, but rather the individual's attribute in relationship to the attributes of others with whom he or she works. Let's work through the logic of group demography, review the evidence, and then consider the implications.

Groups and organizations are composed of **cohorts**, which we define as individuals who hold a common attribute. For instance, everyone born in 1960 is of the same age. This means they also have shared common experiences. People born in 1970 have experienced the information revolution but not the Korean conflict. People born in 1945 shared the Vietnam War but not the Great Depression. Women in U.S. organizations today who were born before 1945 matured prior to the women's movement and have had substantially different experiences from women born after 1960. Group demography, therefore, suggests that such attributes as age or the date that someone joins a specific work group or organization should help us to predict turnover. Essentially, the logic goes like this: Turnover will be greater among those with dissimilar experiences because communication is more difficult. Conflict and power struggles are more likely and more severe when they occur. The increased conflict makes group membership less attractive, so employees

---

group demography

The degree to which members of a group share a common demographic attribute, such as age, sex, race, educational level, or length of service in the organization, and the impact of this attribute on turnover.

cohorts

Individuals who, as part of a group, hold a common attribute.

CNET employees share a common demographic attribute—they're young. The average age of CNET's 515 employees is 30 years old. CNET, an on-line media company, is banking on the enthusiasm and high-tech skills of its youthful cohorts to make it an Internet star and to differentiate it from more conservative media firms like Time Warner and Dow Jones.

are more likely to quit. Similarly, the losers in a power struggle are more apt to leave voluntarily or be forced out.

Several studies have sought to test this thesis, and the evidence is quite encouraging.[48] For example, in departments or separate work groups in which a large portion of members entered at the same time, there is considerably more turnover among those outside this cohort. Also, where there are large gaps between cohorts, turnover is higher. People who enter a group or an organization together, or at approximately the same time, are more likely to associate with one another, have a similar perspective on the group or organization, and, thus, be more likely to stay. On the other hand, discontinuities or bulges in the group's date-of-entry distribution are likely to result in a higher turnover rate within that group.

The implication of this line of inquiry is that the composition of a group may be an important predictor of turnover. Differences per se may not predict turnover. But large differences within a single group will lead to turnover. If everyone is moderately dissimilar from everyone else in a group, the feelings of being an outsider are reduced. So, it's the degree of dispersion on an attribute, rather than the level, that matters most.

We can speculate that variance within a group in respect to attributes other than date of entry, such as social background, gender differences, and levels of education, might similarly create discontinuities or bulges in the distribution that will encourage some members to leave. To extend this idea further, the fact that a group member is a female may, in itself, mean little in predicting turnover. In fact, if the work group is made up of nine women and one man, we'd be more likely to predict that the lone male would leave. In the executive ranks of organizations, however, where females are in the minority, we would predict that this minority status would increase the likelihood that female managers would quit.

COHESIVENESS

Groups differ in their **cohesiveness**, that is, the degree to which members are attracted to each other and are motivated to stay in the group.[49] For instance, some work groups are cohesive because the members have spent a great deal of time together, or the group's small size facilitates high interaction, or the group has experienced external threats that have brought members close together. Cohesiveness is important because it has been found to be related to the group's productivity.[50]

Studies consistently show that the relationship of cohesiveness and productivity depends on the performance-related norms established by the group. If performance-related norms are high (e.g., high output, quality work, cooperation with individuals outside the group), a cohesive group will be more productive than will a less cohesive group. But if cohesiveness is high and performance norms are low, productivity will be low. If cohesiveness is low and performance norms are high, productivity increases but less than in the high cohesiveness–high norms situation. Where cohesiveness and performance-related norms are both low, productivity will tend to fall into the low to moderate range. These conclusions are summarized in Exhibit 8-7.

What can you do to encourage group cohesiveness? You might try one or more of the following suggestions: (1) Make the group smaller. (2) Encourage agreement with group goals. (3) Increase the time members spend together. (4) Increase the status of the group and the perceived difficulty of attaining membership in the group. (5) Stimulate competition with other groups. (6) Give rewards to the group rather than to individual members. (7) Physically isolate the group.[51]

cohesiveness

Degree to which group members are attracted to each other and are motivated to stay in the group.

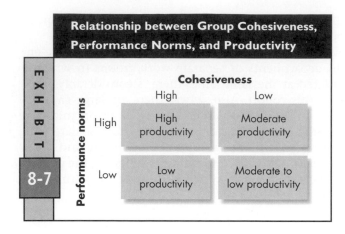

Relationship between Group Cohesiveness, Performance Norms, and Productivity

EXHIBIT 8-7

	Cohesiveness	
Performance norms	High	Low
High	High productivity	Moderate productivity
Low	Low productivity	Moderate to low productivity

GROUP PROCESSES

The next component of our group behavior model considers the processes that go on within a work group—the communication patterns used by members for information exchanges, group decision processes, leader behavior, power dynamics, conflict interactions, and the like. Chapters 10 through 13 elaborate on many of these processes.

Why are processes important to understanding work group behavior? One way to answer this question is to return to the topic of social loafing. We found that $1 + 1 + 1$ doesn't necessarily add up to 3. In group tasks in which each member's contribution is not clearly visible, there is a tendency for individuals to decrease their effort. Social loafing, in other words, illustrates a process loss as a result of using groups. But group processes can also produce positive results. That is, groups can create outputs greater than the sum of their inputs. The development of creative alternatives by a diverse group would be one such instance. Exhibit 8-8 illustrates how group processes can impact on a group's actual effectiveness.[52]

synergy

An action of two or more substances that results in an effect that is different from the individual summation of the substances.

Synergy is a term used in biology that refers to an action of two or more substances that results in an effect that is different from the individual summation of the substances. We can use the concept to better understand group processes.

Social loafing, for instance, represents negative synergy. The whole is less than the sum of its parts. On the other hand, research teams are often used in research laboratories because they can draw on the diverse skills of various individuals to produce more meaningful research as a group than could be generated by

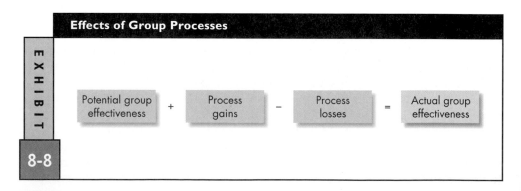

Effects of Group Processes

EXHIBIT 8-8

Potential group effectiveness + Process gains − Process losses = Actual group effectiveness

all of the researchers working independently. That is, they produce positive synergy. Their process gains exceed their process losses.

Another line of research that helps us to better understand group processes is the social facilitation effect.[53] Have you ever noticed that performing a task in front of others can have a positive or negative effect on your performance? For instance, you privately practice a complex springboard dive at your home pool for weeks. Then you do the dive in front of a group of friends and you do it better than ever. Or you practice a speech in private and finally get it down perfect, but you "bomb" when you have to give the speech in public.

The **social facilitation effect** refers to this tendency for performance to improve or decline in response to the presence of others. While this effect is not entirely a group phenomenon—people can work in the presence of others and not be members of a group—the group situation is more likely to provide the conditions for social facilitation to occur. The research on social facilitation tells us that the performance of simple, routine tasks tends to be speeded up and made more accurate by the presence of others. When the work is more complex, requiring closer attention, the presence of others is likely to have a negative effect on performance.[54] So what are the implications of this research in terms of managing process gains and losses? The implications relate to learning and training. People seem to perform better on a task in the presence of others if that task is very well learned but poorer if it is not well learned. So process gains will be maximized by training people for simple tasks in groups, while training people for complex tasks in individual private practice sessions.

social facilitation effect
The tendency for performance to improve or decline in response to the presence of others.

GROUP TASKS

Imagine, for a moment, that there are two groups at a major oil company. The job of the first is to consider possible location sites for a new refinery. The decision is going to affect people in many areas of the company—production, engineering, marketing, distribution, purchasing, real estate development, and the like—so key people from each of these areas will need to provide input into the decision. The job of the second group is to coordinate the building of the refinery after the site has been selected, the design finalized, and the financial arrangements completed. Research on group effectiveness tells us that management would be well advised to use a larger group for the first task than for the second.[55] The reason is that large groups facilitate pooling of information. The addition of a diverse perspective to a problem-solving committee typically results in a process gain. But when a group's task is coordinating and implementing a decision, the process loss created by each additional member's presence is likely to be greater than the process gain he or she makes. So the size–performance relationship is moderated by the group's task requirements.

The preceding conclusions can be extended: The impact of group processes on the group's performance and member satisfaction is also moderated by the tasks that the group is doing. The evidence indicates that the complexity and interdependence of tasks influence the group's effectiveness.[56]

Tasks can be generalized as either simple or complex. Complex tasks are ones that tend to be novel or nonroutine. Simple ones are routine and standardized. We would hypothesize that the more complex the task, the more the group will benefit from discussion among members on alternative work methods. If the task is simple, group members don't need to discuss such alternatives. They can rely on standardized operating procedures for doing the job. Similarly, if there is a high degree of interdependence among the tasks that group members must perform, they'll need to interact more. Effective communication and minimal levels of conflict, therefore, should be more relevant to group performance when tasks are interdependent.

These conclusions are consistent with what we know about information-processing capacity and uncertainty.[57] Tasks that have higher uncertainty—those that are complex and interdependent—require more information processing. This, in turn, puts more importance on group processes. So just because a group is characterized by poor communication, weak leadership, high levels of conflict, and the like, it doesn't necessarily mean that it will be low performing. If the group's tasks are simple and require little interdependence among members, the group still may be effective.

GROUP DECISION MAKING

The belief—characterized by juries—that two heads are better than one has long been accepted as a basic component of North American and many other countries' legal systems. This belief has expanded to the point that, today, many decisions in organizations are made by groups, teams, or committees. In this section, we want to review group decision making.

GROUPS VS. THE INDIVIDUAL

Decision-making groups may be widely used in organizations, but does that imply that group decisions are preferable to those made by an individual alone? The answer to this question depends on a number of factors. Let's begin by looking at the strengths and weaknesses of groups.[58]

Strengths of Group Decision Making Groups generate *more complete information and knowledge*. By aggregating the resources of several individuals, groups bring more input into the decision process. In addition to more input, groups can bring heterogeneity to the decision process. They offer *increased diversity of views*. This opens up the opportunity for more approaches and alternatives to be considered. The evidence indicates that a group will almost always outperform even the best individual. So groups generate *higher-quality decisions*. Finally, groups lead to increased *acceptance of a solution*. Many decisions fail after the final choice is made because people don't accept the solution. Group members who participated in making a decision are likely to enthusiastically support the decision and encourage others to accept it.

Weaknesses of Group Decision Making In spite of the pluses noted, group decisions have their drawbacks. They're *time consuming*. They typically take more time to reach a solution than would be the case if an individual were making the decision alone. There are *conformity pressures in groups*. The desire by group members to be accepted and considered an asset to the group can result in squashing any overt disagreement. Group discussion can be *dominated by one or a few members*. If this dominant coalition is composed of low- and medium-ability members, the group's overall effectiveness will suffer. Finally, group decisions suffer from *ambiguous responsibility*. In an individual decision, it's clear who is accountable for the final outcome. In a group decision, the responsibility of any single member is watered down.

United Asset Management uses group decision making in buying and selling stocks for its TJ Core Equity fund. The fund has eight co-managers who meet once a week to decide which stocks to buy or sell. Each manager, including the boss Tom Johnson (seated) gets one vote, and it takes five of the eight votes to make a buy or sell decision. Johnson believes that his group process works better than individual decision making. Each of his co-managers is an expert in a specific industry, such as in energy and communications. He believes the diversity of their views results in higher-quality decisions.

Effectiveness and Efficiency Whether groups are more effective than individuals depends on the criteria you use for defining effectiveness. In terms of *accuracy*, group decisions will tend to be more accurate. The evidence indicates that, on the average, groups make better-quality decisions than individuals.[59] However, if decision effectiveness is defined in terms of *speed*, individuals are superior. If *creativity* is important, groups tend to be more effective than individuals. And if effectiveness means the degree of *acceptance* the final solution achieves, the nod again goes to the group.[60]

But effectiveness cannot be considered without also assessing efficiency. In terms of efficiency, groups almost always stack up as a poor second to the individual decision maker. With few exceptions, group decision making consumes more work hours than if an individual were to tackle the same problem alone. The exceptions tend to be those instances in which to achieve comparable quantities of diverse input, the single decision maker must spend a great deal of time reviewing files and talking to people. Because groups can include members from diverse areas, the time spent searching for information can be reduced. However, as we noted, these advantages in efficiency tend to be the exception. Groups are generally less efficient than individuals. In deciding whether to use groups, then, consideration should be given to assessing whether increases in effectiveness are more than enough to offset the losses in efficiency.

Summary In summary, groups offer an excellent vehicle for performing many of the steps in the decision-making process. They are a source of both breadth and depth of input for information gathering. If the group is composed of individuals with diverse backgrounds, the alternatives generated should be more extensive and the analysis more critical. When the final solution is agreed upon, there are more people in a group decision to support and implement it. These pluses, however, can be more than offset by the time consumed by group decisions, the internal conflicts they create, and the pressures they generate toward conformity.

MYTH OR SCIENCE?

"Two Heads Are Better Than One"

This statement is mostly true if "better" means that two people will come up with more original and workable answers to a problem than one person working alone.

The evidence generally confirms the superiority of groups over individuals in terms of decision-making quality.[61] Groups usually produce more and better solutions to problems than do individuals working alone. And the choices groups make will be more accurate and creative. Why is this? Groups bring more complete information and knowledge to a decision, so they generate more ideas. In addition, the give-and-take that typically takes place in group decision processes provides diversity of opinion and increases the likelihood that weak alternatives will be identified and abandoned.

Research indicates that certain conditions favor groups over individuals.[62] These conditions include (1) diversity among members. The benefits of "two heads" require that they differ in relevant skills and abilities. (2) The group members must be able to communicate their ideas freely and openly. This requires an absence of hostility and intimidation. (3) The task being undertaken is complex. Relative to individuals, groups do better on complex rather than simple tasks.

GROUPTHINK AND GROUPSHIFT

Two by-products of group decision making have received a considerable amount of attention by researchers in OB. As we'll show, these two phenomena have the potential to affect the group's ability to appraise alternatives objectively and arrive at quality decision solutions.

The first phenomenon, called **groupthink**, is related to norms. It describes situations in which group pressures for conformity deter the group from critically appraising unusual, minority, or unpopular views. Groupthink is a disease that attacks many groups and can dramatically hinder their performance. The second phenomenon we shall review is called **groupshift**. It indicates that in discussing a given set of alternatives and arriving at a solution, group members tend to exaggerate the initial positions that they hold. In some situations, caution dominates, and there is a conservative shift. More often, however, the evidence indicates that groups tend toward a risky shift. Let's look at each of these phenomena in more detail.

groupthink

Phenomenon in which the norm for consensus overrides the realistic appraisal of alternative courses of action.

groupshift

A change in decision risk between the group's decision and the individual decision that members within the group would make; can be either toward conservatism or greater risk.

Groupthink   Have you ever felt like speaking up in a meeting, classroom, or informal group, but decided against it? One reason may have been shyness. On the other hand, you may have been a victim of groupthink, the phenomenon that occurs when group members become so enamored of seeking concurrence that the norm for consensus overrides the realistic appraisal of alternative courses of action and the full expression of deviant, minority, or unpopular views. It describes a deterioration in an individual's mental efficiency, reality testing, and moral judgment as a result of group pressures.[63]

We have all seen the symptoms of the groupthink phenomenon:

1. Group members rationalize any resistance to the assumptions they have made. No matter how strongly the evidence may contradict their basic assumptions, members behave so as to reinforce those assumptions continually.
2. Members apply direct pressures on those who momentarily express doubts about any of the group's shared views or who question the validity of arguments supporting the alternative favored by the majority.
3. Those members who have doubts or hold differing points of view seek to avoid deviating from what appears to be group consensus by keeping silent about misgivings and even minimizing to themselves the importance of their doubts.
4. There appears to be an illusion of unanimity. If someone doesn't speak, it's assumed that he or she is in full accord. In other words, abstention becomes viewed as a "Yes" vote.[64]

In studies of historic American foreign policy decisions, these symptoms were found to prevail when government policy-making groups failed—unpreparedness at Pearl Harbor in 1941, the U.S. invasion of North Korea, the Bay of Pigs fiasco, and the escalation of the Vietnam War.[65] More recently, the *Challenger* space shuttle disaster and the failure of the main mirror on the *Hubble* telescope have been linked to decision processes at NASA where groupthink symptoms were evident.[66]

Groupthink appears to be closely aligned with the conclusions Asch drew in his experiments with a lone dissenter. Individuals who hold a position that is different from that of the dominant majority are under pressure to suppress, withhold, or modify their true feelings and beliefs. As members of a group, we find it more pleasant to be in agreement—to be a positive part of the group—than to be a disruptive force, even if disruption is necessary to improve the effectiveness of the group's decisions.

Does groupthink attack all groups? No. It seems to occur most often where there is a clear group identity, where members hold a positive image of their group that they want to protect, and where the group perceives a collective threat to this positive image.[67] So groupthink is not a dissenter-suppression mechanism as much as it's a means for a group to protect its positive image. In the cases of the *Challenger* and *Hubble* fiascos, it was NASA's attempt to confirm it's identity as "the elite organization that could do no wrong."[68]

What can managers do to minimize groupthink?[69] One thing they can do is encourage group leaders to play an impartial role. Leaders should actively seek input from all members and avoid expressing their own opinions, especially in the early stages of deliberation. Another thing is to appoint one group member to play the role of devil's advocate. This member's role is to overtly challenge the majority position and offer divergent perspectives. Still another suggestion is to utilize exercises that stimulate active discussion of diverse alternatives without threatening the group and intensifying identity protection. One such exercise is to have group members talk about dangers or risks involved in a decision and delaying discussion of any potential gains. By requiring members to first focus on the negatives of a decision alternative, the group is less likely to stifle dissenting views and more likely to gain an objective evaluation.

Groupshift In comparing group decisions with the individual decisions of members within the group, evidence suggests that there are differences.[70] In some cases, the group decisions are more conservative than the individual decisions. More often, the shift is toward greater risk.[71]

What appears to happen in groups is that the discussion leads to a significant shift in the positions of members toward a more extreme position in the direction in which they were already leaning before the discussion. So conservative types become more cautious and the more aggressive types take on more risk. The group discussion tends to exaggerate the initial position of the group.

The groupshift can be viewed as actually a special case of groupthink. The decision of the group reflects the dominant decision-making norm that develops during the group's discussion. Whether the shift in the group's decision is toward greater caution or more risk depends on the dominant prediscussion norm.

The greater occurrence of the shift toward risk has generated several explanations for the phenomenon.[72] It's been argued, for instance, that the discussion creates familiarization among the members. As they become more comfortable with each other, they also become more bold and daring. Another argument is that most first-world societies value risk, that we admire individuals who are willing to take risks, and that group discussion motivates members to show that they are at least as willing as their peers to take risks. The most plausible explanation of the shift toward risk, however, seems to be that the group diffuses responsibility. Group decisions free any single member from accountability for the group's final choice. Greater risk can be taken because even if the decision fails, no one member can be held wholly responsible.

So how should you use the findings on groupshift? You should recognize that group decisions exaggerate the initial position of the individual members, that the shift has been shown more often to be toward greater risk, and that whether or not a group will shift toward greater risk or caution is a function of the members' prediscussion inclinations.

GROUP DECISION-MAKING TECHNIQUES

interacting groups

Typical groups in which members interact with each other face-to-face.

The most common form of group decision making takes place in **interacting groups**. In these groups, members meet face-to-face and rely on both verbal and nonverbal interaction to communicate with each other. But as our discussion of groupthink demonstrated, interacting groups often censor themselves and pressure individual members toward conformity of opinion. Brainstorming, the nominal group technique, and electronic meetings have been proposed as ways to reduce many of the problems inherent in the traditional interacting group.

brainstorming

An idea-generation process that specifically encourages any and all alternatives, while withholding any criticism of those alternatives.

Brainstorming is meant to overcome pressures for conformity in the interacting group that retard the development of creative alternatives.[73] It does this by utilizing an idea-generation process that specifically encourages any and all alternatives, while withholding any criticism of those alternatives.

EXHIBIT 8-9

Source: S. Adams, *Build a Better Life by Stealing Office Supplies* (Kansas City, MO, Andrews & McMeal, 1991), p. 31. DILBERT reprinted with permission of United Feature Syndicate, Inc.

In a typical brainstorming session, a half dozen to a dozen people sit around a table. The group leader states the problem in a clear manner so that it is understood by all participants. Members then "freewheel" as many alternatives as they can in a given length of time. No criticism is allowed, and all the alternatives are recorded for later discussion and analysis. That one idea stimulates others and that judgments of even the most bizarre suggestions are withheld until later encourage group members to "think the unusual." Brainstorming, however, is merely a process for generating ideas. The following two techniques go further by offering methods of actually arriving at a preferred solution.[74]

The **nominal group technique** restricts discussion or interpersonal communication during the decision-making process, hence, the term *nominal*. Group members are all physically present, as in a traditional committee meeting, but members operate independently. Specifically, a problem is presented and then the following steps take place:

1. Members meet as a group but, before any discussion takes place, each member independently writes down his or her ideas on the problem.
2. After this silent period, each member presents one idea to the group. Each member takes his or her turn, presenting a single idea until all ideas have been presented and recorded. No discussion takes place until all ideas have been recorded.
3. The group now discusses the ideas for clarity and evaluates them.
4. Each group member silently and independently rank-orders the ideas. The idea with the highest aggregate ranking determines the final decision.

The chief advantage of the nominal group technique is that it permits the group to meet formally but does not restrict independent thinking, as does the interacting group.

The most recent approach to group decision making blends the nominal group technique with sophisticated computer technology.[75] It's called the computer-assisted group or **electronic meeting**. Once the technology is in place, the concept is simple. Up to 50 people sit around a horseshoe shaped table, empty except for a series of computer terminals. Issues are presented to participants and they type their responses onto their computer screen. Individual comments, as well as aggregate votes, are displayed on a projection screen in the room.

The major advantages of electronic meetings are anonymity, honesty, and speed. Participants can anonymously type any message they want and it flashes on the screen for all to see at the push of a participant's keyboard. It also allows people to be brutally honest without penalty. And it's fast because chitchat is eliminated, discussions don't digress, and many participants can "talk" at once without stepping on one another's toes. The future of group meetings undoubtedly will include extensive use of this technology.

Each of these four group decision techniques has its own set of strengths and weaknesses. The choice of one technique over another will depend on what criteria you want to emphasize and the cost-benefit trade-off. For instance, as Exhibit 8-10 indicates, the interacting group is good for building group cohesiveness, brainstorming keeps social pressures to a minimum, the nominal group technique is an inexpensive means for generating a large number of ideas, and electronic meetings process ideas fast.

EXHIBIT 8-10

Evaluating Group Effectiveness

Effectiveness Criteria	Type of Group			
	Interacting	Brainstorming	Nominal	Electronic
Number of ideas	Low	Moderate	High	High
Quality of ideas	Low	Moderate	High	High
Social pressure	High	Low	Moderate	Low
Money costs	Low	Low	Low	High
Speed	Moderate	Moderate	Moderate	High
Task orientation	Low	High	High	High
Potential for interpersonal conflict	High	Low	Moderate	Low
Feelings of accomplishment	High to low	High	High	High
Commitment to solution	High	Not applicable	Moderate	Moderate
Development of group cohesiveness	High	High	Moderate	Low

Source: Based on J. K. Murnighan, "Group Decision Making: What Strategies Should You Use?" *Management Review*, February 1981, p. 61.

SUMMARY AND IMPLICATIONS FOR MANAGERS

We've covered a lot of territory in this chapter. Since we essentially organized our discussion around the group behavior model in Exhibit 8-5, let's use this model to summarize our findings regarding performance and satisfaction.

PERFORMANCE

Any predictions about a group's performance must begin by recognizing that work groups are part of a larger organization and that factors such as the organization's strategy, authority structure, selection procedures, and reward system can provide a favorable or unfavorable climate for the group to operate within. For example, if an organization is characterized by distrust between management and workers, it is more likely that work groups in that organization will develop norms to restrict effort and output than will work groups in an organization in which trust is high. So managers shouldn't look at any group in isolation. Rather, they should begin by assessing the degree of support external conditions provide the group. It is obviously a lot easier for any work group to be productive when the overall organization of which it is a part is growing and it has both top management's support and abundant resources. Similarly, a group is more likely to be productive when its members have the requisite skills to do the group's tasks and the personality characteristics that facilitate working well together.

A number of structural factors show a relationship to performance. Among the more prominent are role perception, norms, status inequities, the size of the group, its demographic makeup, the group's task, and cohesiveness.

There is a positive relationship between role perception and an employee's performance evaluation.[76] The degree of congruence that exists between an employee and his or her boss in the perception of the employee's job influences the degree to which that employee will be judged as an effective performer by the boss. To the extent that the employee's role perception fulfills the boss's role expectations, the employee will receive a higher performance evaluation.

Norms control group member behavior by establishing standards of right and wrong. If managers know the norms of a given group, it can help to explain the behaviors of its members. When norms support high output, managers can expect individual performance to be markedly higher than when group norms aim to restrict output. Similarly, acceptable standards of absenteeism will be dictated by the group norms.

Status inequities create frustration and can adversely influence productivity and the willingness to remain with an organization. Among those individuals who are equity sensitive, incongruence is likely to lead to reduced motivation and an increased search for ways to bring about fairness (i.e., taking another job).

The impact of size on a group's performance depends upon the type of task in which the group is engaged. Larger groups are more effective at fact-finding activities. Smaller groups are more effective at action-taking tasks. Our knowledge of social loafing suggests that if management uses larger groups, efforts should be made to provide measures of individual performance within the group.

We found the group's demographic composition to be a key determinant of individual turnover. Specifically, the evidence indicates that group members who share a common age or date of entry into the work group are less prone to resign.

We also found that cohesiveness can play an important function in influencing a group's level of productivity. Whether or not it does depends on the group's performance-related norms.

The primary contingency variable moderating the relationship between group processes and performance is the group's task. The more complex and interdependent the tasks, the more that inefficient processes will lead to reduced group performance.

SATISFACTION

As with the role perception–performance relationship, high congruence between a boss and employee, as to the perception of the employee's job, shows a significant association with high employee satisfaction.[77] Similarly, role conflict is associated with job-induced tension and job dissatisfaction.[78]

Most people prefer to communicate with others at their own status level or a higher one rather than with those below them.[79] As a result, we should expect satisfaction to be greater among employees whose job minimizes interaction with individuals who are lower in status than themselves.

The group size–satisfaction relationship is what one would intuitively expect: Larger groups are associated with lower satisfaction.[80] As size increases, opportunities for participation and social interaction decrease, as does the ability of members to identify with the group's accomplishments. At the same time, having more members also prompts dissension, conflict, and the formation of subgroups, which all act to make the group a less pleasant entity of which to be a part.

All Jobs Should Be Designed Around Groups

Groups, not individuals, are the ideal building blocks for an organization. There are at least six reasons for designing all jobs around groups.[1]

First, small groups are good for people. They can satisfy social needs and they can provide support for employees in times of stress and crisis.

Second, groups are good problem-solving tools. They are better than individuals in promoting creativity and innovation.

Third, in a wide variety of decision situations, groups make better decisions than individuals do.

Fourth, groups are very effective tools for implementation. Groups gain commitment from their members so that group decisions are likely to be willingly and more successfully carried out.

Fifth, groups can control and discipline individual members in ways that are often extremely difficult through impersonal, quasi-legal disciplinary systems. Group norms are powerful control devices.

Sixth, groups are a means by which large organizations can fend off many of the negative effects of increased size. Groups help to prevent communication lines from growing too long, the hierarchy from growing too steep, and the individual from getting lost in the crowd.

Given the preceding argument for the value of group-based job design, what would an organization look like that was truly designed around group functions? This might best be considered by merely taking the things that organizations do with individuals and applying them to groups. Instead of hiring individuals, they'd hire groups. Similarly, they'd train groups rather than individuals, pay groups rather than individuals, promote groups rather than individuals, fire groups rather than individuals, and so on.

The rapid growth of team-based organizations over the past decade suggests we may well be on our way toward the day when almost all jobs are designed around groups.

---

[1]Based on H. J. Leavitt, "Suppose We Took Groups Seriously," in E. L. Cass and F. G. Zimmer (eds.), *Man and Work in Society* (New York: Van Nostrand Reinhold, 1975), pp. 67–77.

Designing jobs around groups is consistent with socialistic doctrine. It might have worked well in the former Soviet Union or Eastern European countries. But capitalistic countries such as the United States, Canada, Australia, and the United Kingdom value the individual. Designing jobs around groups is inconsistent with the economic values of these countries. Moreover, as capitalism and entrepreneurship have spread throughout Eastern Europe, we should expect to see *less* emphasis on groups and *more* on the individual in workplaces throughout the world. Let's look at the United States to see how cultural and economic values shape employee attitudes toward groups.

America was built on the ethic of the individual. Americans strongly value individual achievement. They praise competition. Even in team sports, they want to identify individuals for recognition. Americans enjoy being part of a group in which they can maintain a strong individual identity. They don't enjoy sublimating their identity to that of the group.

The American worker likes a clear link between his or her individual effort and a visible outcome. It is not by chance that the United States, as a nation, has a considerably larger proportion of high achievers than exists in most of the world. America breeds achievers, and achievers seek personal responsibility. They would be frustrated in job situations in which their contribution is commingled and homogenized with the contributions of others.

Americans want to be hired, evaluated, and rewarded on their individual achievements. Americans believe in an authority and status hierarchy. They accept a system in which there are bosses and subordinates. They are not likely to accept a group's decision on such issues as their job assignments and wage increases. It's harder yet to imagine that they would be comfortable in a system in which the sole basis for their promotion or termination would be the performance of their group.

1. Compare and contrast command, task, interest, and friendship groups.

2. What might motivate you to join a group?

3. Describe the five-stage group-development model.

4. Define sociometry and explain its value to managers.

5. What is the relationship between a work group and the organization of which it is a part?

6. What are the implications of Zimbardo's prison experiment for OB?

7. Explain the implications of the Asch experiments.

8. How are status and norms related?

9. How can a group's demography help you to predict turnover?

10. What is groupthink? What is its effect on decision-making quality?

Questions for Critical Thinking

1. How could you use the punctuated-equilibrium model to better understand group behavior?

2. Identify five roles you play. What behaviors do they require? Are any of these roles in conflict? If so, in what way? How do you resolve these conflicts?

3. "High cohesiveness in a group leads to higher group productivity." Do you agree or disagree? Explain.

4. What effect, if any, do you expect that workforce diversity has on a group's performance and satisfaction?

5. If group decisions consistently achieve better-quality outcomes than those achieved by individuals, how did the phrase "a camel is a horse designed by a committee" become so popular and ingrained in the culture?

Team Exercise   Assessing Occupational Status

Rank the following 20 occupations from most prestigious (1) to least prestigious (20):

_____	Accountant	_____	Mayor of a large city
_____	Air traffic controller	_____	Minister
_____	Coach of a college football team	_____	Pharmacist
_____	Coach of a college women's basketball team	_____	Physician
_____	Criminal defense attorney	_____	Plumber
_____	Electrical engineer	_____	Real estate salesperson
_____	Environmental scientist	_____	Sports agent
_____	Freelance financial consultant	_____	Teacher in a public elementary school
_____	Manager of a British clothing manufacturer	_____	U.S. Army colonel
_____	Manager of a U.S. automobile plant	_____	Used car salesperson

Now form into groups of three to five students each. Answer the following questions:

a. How closely did your top five choices (1–5) match?

b. How closely did your bottom five choices (16–20) match?

c. What occupations were generally easiest to rate? Which were most difficult? Why?

d. What does this exercise tell you about criteria for assessing status?

e. What does this exercise tell you about stereotypes?

1. Find a situation in which there is substantive evidence that someone engaged in a behavior that was very much counter to his or her normal behavior and in which at least some of the explanation for this behavior was group pressure. Analyze your findings in terms of concepts described in this chapter.

2. Find data comparing Americans and Japanese in terms of their preference for group work. What do your findings suggest?

PHLIP Companion Web Site

We invite you to visit the Robbins homepage on the Prentice Hall Web site at **www.prenhall.com/robbins** for our on-line study guide, current events, links to related Web sites, and more.

Case Incident | The Law Offices of Dickinson, Stilwell, and Gardner (DSG)

James Dickinson and Richard Stilwell opened their El Paso, Texas, law office in 1966. It has since grown to employ two dozen people. Dickinson is now deceased and Stilwell is semiretired. The firm's senior managing partner is currently Charles Gardner. Gardner has been with the firm for more than 20 years.

Today, the law office of DSG has five partners and 12 full-time associates. Additionally, the firm employs an administrative manager (Linda Mendoza) and an assistant administrative manager, a receptionist, four secretaries, and two legal interns who work 20 hours a week doing research.

El Paso is a largely Hispanic community. For a variety of reasons, DSG has historically not done a very effective job of hiring and keeping Hispanic employees. Until very recently, none of the partners were Hispanic and only two of the associates were. Five months ago, the firm lured a prominent Hispanic lawyer, Francisco Jauregui, away from a competitor. Jauregui was brought in as a partner, at a base salary higher than any other DSG employee, with the exception of Charles Gardner.

The hiring of Jauregui has created a number of interpersonal issues at DSG. Many of the associates are unhappy. They feel the company hired Jauregui solely because he was one of the few big-name Hispanic lawyers in El Paso and could open doors for the firm into the Hispanic community. The associates were also concerned that the hiring of a new partner from the outside would lower the likelihood that they would make partner.

It was also clear that a clique was forming within the firm. It was made up of Jauregui, Mendoza, the two Hispanic associates, and one of the secretaries (all of whom are Hispanic by background). Morale has suffered in recent months. Privately, several employees have made complaints to Gardner such as "Linda gives favored treatment to Francisco and the Hispanic associates," "the Hispanic associates are suddenly working on the most visible and important cases within the firm," and "there's no future around here if you're not Hispanic."

Questions

1. Analyze this case using sociometric techniques.

2. What do you think you can learn from this case about diversity and group behavior?

3. What should Gardner do to deal with this dilemma?

SMALL BUSINESS 2000

Working with others is not always easy. Simply working in the same group or for the same company does not guarantee that people will be motivated to work together. Different individuals will have different work ethics, will be looking to satisfy different needs from work, and will have their own ways of doing things. There is no guarantee that a work group will function smoothly or cohesively.

Rick Presant learned about working with others when he joined his father's company, All Brand Appliance. Presant's case provides insight into a somewhat unique but not uncommon work situation. He was a family member breaking into a family-owned business. Being the boss's son or daughter probably has bad as well as good consequences. It sounds like Presant found this out. He eventually headed off to try his own thing. Presant may have struck out on his own for any number of reasons, but we get the idea that it had something to do with the way things were going between himself and others at All Brand.

An interesting outcome is that Presant eventually came back to All Brand. The difference this time, however, is that he did it on his own terms. Presant was returning to run the show and take the business over from his father. Also interesting is that, although Presant had issues related to the partnership structure the first time he was there, he came back to All Brand and established a new partnership. What was different this time? This time he was one of the partners. Second, he was taking over at a time when the company appeared to need an injection of new blood. Third, his partner was his brother.

Presant's story is an interesting one. As you watch this video think about how his work life has evolved from his first experience at All Brand to the way it is now. You might also want to think about some of the things Rick and his brother might be doing differently these days and the impact that it has had on the company's employees, most of whom have worked at All Brand for a long time.

Questions

1. Rick Presant talks about his decision to join his father's business after completing college. That didn't seem to satisfy him and he eventually left to start his own company. He mentions that part of his decision to try a store of his own was some issues between his father's partner and the partner's family. What types of things might have been going on there? What do you think of Presant's decision to leave the business? What else might he have done?

2. Presant eventually came back to All Brand Appliance and he and his brother are buying the business from their father. What is different for Presant this time around? What do you think the working relationship between Presant and his brother is like?

3. Rick and Jeff have several employees who have been working at the company for a long time. You saw some of these folks and heard about the way they approach their jobs. Do you think they are good organizational citizens? Why or why not?

4. The people at All Brand Appliance seem to work well together. What types of things do you see in the video that might contribute to the level of cooperation that exists at All Brand Appliance? Do you think cooperation is important? Why or why not?

End Notes

1. J. Grossman, "We've Got to Start Meeting Like This," *INC.*, April 1998, p. 72.
2. L. R. Sayles, "Work Group Behavior and the Larger Organization," in C. Arensburg et al. (eds.), *Research in Industrial Relations* (New York: Harper & Row, 1957), pp. 131–45.
3. B. W. Tuckman, "Developmental Sequences in Small Groups," *Psychological Bulletin*, June 1965, pp. 384–99; B. W. Tuckman and M. C. Jensen, "Stages of Small-Group Development Revisited," *Group and Organizational Studies*, December 1977, pp. 419–27; and M. F. Maples, "Group Development: Extending Tuckman's Theory," *Journal for Specialists in Group Work*, Fall 1988, pp. 17–23.
4. R. C. Ginnett, "The Airline Cockpit Crew," in J. R. Hackman (ed.), *Groups That Work (and Those That Don't)* (San Francisco: Jossey-Bass, 1990).
5. C. J. G. Gersick, "Time and Transition in Work Teams: Toward a New Model of Group Development," *Academy*

of Management Journal, March 1988, pp. 9–41; and C. J. G. Gersick, "Marking Time: Predictable Transitions in Task Groups," *Academy of Management Journal*, June 1989, pp. 274–309.

6. A. Seers and S. Woodruff, "Temporal Pacing in Task Forces: Group Development or Deadline Pressure?" *Journal of Management*, vol. 23, no. 2, 1997, pp. 169–87.

7. See J. L. Moreno, "Contributions of Sociometry to Research Methodology in Sociology," *American Sociological Review*, June 1947, pp. 287–92. Also J. W. Hart and R. Nath, "Sociometry in Business and Industry: New Developments in Historical Perspective," *Group Psychotherapy, Psychodrama and Sociometry*, vol. 32 (1979), pp. 128–49; D. Stamps, "Off the Charts," *Training*, October 1997, pp. 77–83; and K. A. Stephenson, "Network Management," *Focus*, no. 20, 1997, pp. 18–21; K. A. Stephenson, "Tracking Networks," *Anthropology Newsletter*, April 1997; and P. G. Doloff, "Beyond the Org Chart," *Across the Board*, February 1999, pp. 43–47.

8. N. M. Tichy, M. L. Tushman, and C. Fombrun, "Social Network Analysis for Organizations," *Academy of Management Review*, October 1979, pp. 507–19; and N. Tichy and C. Fombrun, "Network Analysis in Organizational Settings," *Human Relations*, November 1979, pp. 923–65.

9. D. Krackhardt and L. W. Porter, "The Snowball Effect: Turnover Embedded in Communication Networks," *Journal of Applied Psychology*, February 1986, pp. 50–55.

10. R. E. Nelson, "The Strength of Strong Ties: Social Networks and Intergroup Conflict in Organizations," *Academy of Management Journal*, June 1989, pp. 377–401.

11. H. Ibarra, "Personal Networks of Women and Minorities in Management: A Conceptual Framework," *Academy of Management Review*, January 1993, pp. 56–87.

12. This model is based on the work of P. S. Goodman, E. Ravlin, and M. Schminke, "Understanding Groups in Organizations," in L. L. Cummings and B. M. Staw (eds.), *Research in Organizational Behavior*, vol. 9 (Greenwich, CT: JAI Press, 1987), pp. 124–28; J. R. Hackman, "The Design of Work Teams," in J. W. Lorsch (ed.), *Handbook of Organizational Behavior* (Upper Saddle River, NJ: Prentice Hall, 1987), pp. 315–42; G. R. Bushe and A. L. Johnson, "Contextual and Internal Variables Affecting Task Group Outcomes in Organizations," *Group and Organization Studies*, December 1989, pp. 462–82; and M. A. Campion, G. J. Medsker, and A. C. Higgs, "Relations Between Work Group Characteristics and Effectiveness: Implications for Designing Effective Work Groups," *Personnel Psychology*, Winter 1993, pp. 823–50.

13. F. Friedlander, "The Ecology of Work Groups," in J. W. Lorsch (ed.) *Handbook of Organizational Behavior*, pp. 301–14; P. B. Paulus and D. Nagar, "Environmental Influences on Groups," in P. Paulus (ed.), *Psychology of Group Influence*, 2nd ed. (Hillsdale, NJ: Erlbaum, 1989); and E. Sundstrom and I. Altman, "Physical Environments and Work-Group Effectiveness," in L. L. Cummings and B. M. Staw (eds.), *Research in Organizational Behavior*, vol. 11 (Greenwich, CT: JAI Press, 1989), pp. 175–209.

14. See, for example, J. Krantz, "Group Processes Under Conditions of Organizational Decline," *The Journal of Applied Behavioral Science*, vol. 21, no. 1, 1985, pp. 1–17.

15. Hackman, "The Design of Work Teams," pp. 325–26.

16. See, for instance, G. R. Oldham and Y. Fried, "Employee Reactions to Workspace Characteristics," *Journal of Applied Psychology*, February 1987, pp. 75–80; and R. A. Baron, "The Physical Environment of Work Settings: Effects on Task Performance, Interpersonal Relations, and Job Satisfaction," in B. M. Staw and L. L. Cummings (eds.), *Research in Organizational Behavior*, vol. 16 (Greenwich, CT: JAI Press, 1994), pp. 1–46.

17. M. J. Stevens and M. A. Campion, "The Knowledge, Skill, and Ability Requirements for Teamwork: Implications for Human Resource Management," Journal of Management, Summer 1994, pp. 503–30.

18. M. E. Shaw, *Contemporary Topics in Social Psychology* (Morristown, NJ: General Learning Press, 1976); and D. C. Kinlaw, *Developing Superior Work Teams: Building Quality and the Competitive Edge* (San Diego, CA: Lexington, 1991).

19. S. Lieberman, "The Effects of Changes in Roles on the Attitudes of Role Occupants," *Human Relations*, November 1956, pp. 385–402.

20. See D. M. Rousseau, *Psychological Contracts in Organizations: Understanding Written and Unwritten Agreements* (Thousand Oaks, CA: Sage, 1995).

21. E. H. Schein, *Organizational Psychology*, 3rd ed. (Upper Saddle River, NJ: Prentice Hall, 1980), p. 24.

22. See M. F. Peterson et al., "Role Conflict, Ambiguity, and Overload: A 21-Nation Study," *Academy of Management Journal*, April 1995, pp. 429–52.

23. P. G. Zimbardo, C. Haney, W. C. Banks, and D. Jaffe, "The Mind Is a Formidable Jailer: A Pirandellian Prison," *New York Times*, April 8, 1973, pp. 38–60; and C. Haney and P. G. Zimbardo, "Social Roles and Role-Playing: Observations from the Stanford Prison Study," *Behavioral and Social Science Teacher*, January 1973, pp. 25–45.

24. For a recent review of the research on group norms, see J. R. Hackman, "Group Influences on Individuals in Organizations," in M. D. Dunnette and L. M. Hough (eds.), *Handbook of Industrial & Organizational Psychology*, 2nd ed., vol. 3 (Palo Alto, CA: Consulting Psychologists Press, 1992), pp. 235–50.

25. Adapted from Goodman, Ravlin, and Schminke, "Understanding Groups in Organizations," p. 159.

26. See, for instance, G. Blau, "Influence of Group Lateness on Individual Lateness: A Cross-Level Examination," *Academy of Management Journal*, October 1995, pp. 1483–96.

27. D. C. Feldman, "The Development and Enforcement of Group Norms," *Academy of Management Journal*, January 1984, pp. 47–53; and K. L. Bettenhausen and J. K. Murnighan, "The Development of an Intragroup Norm and the Effects of Interpersonal and Structural Challenges," *Administrative Science Quarterly*, March 1991, pp. 20–35.

28. C. A. Kiesler and S. B. Kiesler, *Conformity* (Reading, MA: Addison-Wesley, 1969).

29. Ibid, p. 27.

30. S. E. Asch, "Effects of Group Pressure upon the Modification and Distortion of Judgments," in H. Guetzkow (ed.), *Groups, Leadership and Men* (Pittsburgh: Carnegie Press, 1951), pp. 177–90.

31. R. Bond and P. B. Smith, "Culture and Conformity: A Meta-Analysis of Studies Using Asch's (1952, 1956) Line Judgment Task," *Psychological Bulletin*, January 1996, pp. 111–37.

32. R. Keyes, *Is There Life After High School?* (New York: Warner Books, 1976).

33. Cited in J. R. Hackman, "Group Influences on Individuals in Organizations," p. 236.

34. O.J. Harvey and C. Consalvi, "Status and Conformity to Pressures in Informal Groups," *Journal of Abnormal and Social Psychology*, Spring 1960, pp. 182–87.

35. J. A. Wiggins, F. Dill, and R. D. Schwartz, "On 'Status-Liability,'" *Sociometry*, April–May 1965, pp. 197–209.

36. J. Greenberg, "Equity and Workplace Status: A Field Experiment," *Journal of Applied Psychology*, November 1988, pp. 606–13.

37. This section is based on P. R. Harris and R. T. Moran, *Managing Cultural Differences*, 4th ed. (Houston: Gulf Publishing, 1996).

38. E. J. Thomas and C. F. Fink, "Effects of Group Size," *Psychological Bulletin*, July 1963, pp. 371–84; A. P. Hare, *Handbook of Small Group Research* (New York: Free Press, 1976); and M. E. Shaw, *Group Dynamics: The Psychology of Small Group Behavior*, 3rd ed. (New York: McGraw-Hill, 1981).

39. See D. R. Comer, "A Model of Social Loafing in Real Work Groups," *Human Relations*, June 1995, pp. 647–67.

40. W. Moede, "Die Richtlinien der Leistungs-Psychologie," *Industrielle Psychotechnik*, vol. 4 (1927), pp. 193–207. See also D. A. Kravitz and B. Martin, "Ringelmann Rediscovered: The Original Article," *Journal of Personality and Social Psychology*, May 1986, pp. 936–41.

41. See, for example, J. A. Shepperd, "Productivity Loss in Performance Groups: A Motivation Analysis," *Psychological Bulletin*, January 1993, pp. 67–81; and S. J. Karau and K. D. Williams, "Social Loafing: A Meta-Analytic Review and Theoretical Integration," *Journal of Personality and Social Psychology*, October 1993, pp. 681–706.

42. S. G. Harkins and K. Szymanski, "Social Loafing and Group Evaluation," *Journal of Personality and Social Psychology*, December 1989, pp. 934–41.

43. See P. C. Earley, "Social Loafing and Collectivism: A Comparison of the United States and the People's Republic of China," *Administrative Science Quarterly*, December 1989, pp. 565–81; and P. C. Earley, "East Meets West Meets Mideast: Further Explorations of Collectivistic and Individualistic Work Groups," *Academy of Management Journal*, April 1993, pp. 319–48.

44. Thomas and Fink, "Effects of Group Size"; Hare, *Handbook*; Shaw, *Group Dynamics*; and P. Yetton and P. Bottger, "The Relationships Among Group Size, Member Ability, Social Decision Schemes, and Performance," *Organizational Behavior and Human Performance*, October 1983, pp. 145–59.

45. See, for example, R. A. Guzzo and G. P. Shea, "Group Performance and Intergroup Relations in Organizations," in M. D. Dunnette and L. M. Hough, eds., *Handbook of Industrial & Organizational Psychology*, 2nd edition, vol. 3 (Palo Alto, CA: Consulting Psychologists Press, 1992), pp. 288–90; S. E. Jackson, K. E. May, and K. Whitney, "Understanding the Dynamics of Diversity in Decision-Making Teams," in R. A. Guzzo and E. Salas (eds.), *Team Effectiveness and Decision Making in Organizations* (San Francisco: Jossey-Bass, 1995), pp. 204–61; and K. Y. Williams and C. A. O'Reilly III, "Demography and Diversity in Organizations: A Review of 40 Years of Research," in B. M. Staw and L. L. Cummings (eds.), *Research in Organizational Behavior*, vol. 20 (Greenwich, CT: JAI Press, 1998), pp. 77–140.

46. Shaw, *Contemporary Topics*, p. 356.

47. W. E. Watson, K. Kumar, and L. K. Michaelsen, "Cultural Diversity's Impact on Interaction Process and Performance: Comparing Homogeneous and Diverse Task Groups," *Academy of Management Journal*, June 1993, pp. 590–602.

48. W. G. Wagner, J. Pfeffer, and C. A. O'Reilly III, "Organizational Demography and Turnover in Top-Management Groups," Administrative Science Quarterly, March 1984, pp. 74–92; J. Pfeffer and C. A. O'Reilly III, "Hospital Demography and Turnover Among Nurses," *Industrial Relations*, Spring 1987, pp. 158–73; C. A. O'Reilly III, D. F. Caldwell, and W. P. Barnett, "Work Group Demography, Social Integration, and Turnover," *Administrative Science Quarterly*, March 1989, pp. 21–37; S. E. Jackson, J. F. Brett, V. I. Sessa, D. M. Cooper, J. A. Julin, and K. Peyronnin, "Some Differences Make a Difference: Individual Dissimilarity and Group Heterogeneity as Correlates of Recruitment, Promotions, and Turnover," *Journal of Applied Psychology*, August 1991, pp. 675–89; M. F. Wiersema and A. Bird, "Organizational Demography in Japanese Firms: Group Heterogeneity, Individual Dissimilarity, and Top Management Team Turnover," *Academy of Management Journal*, October 1993, pp. 996–1025; F. J. Milliken and L. L. Martins, "Searching for Common Threads: Understanding the Multiple Effects of Diversity in Organizational Groups," *Academy of Management Review*, April 1996, pp. 402–33; and B. Lawrence, "The Black Box of Organizational Demography," *Organizational Science*, February 1997, pp. 1–22 .

49. For some of the controversy surrounding the definition of cohesion, see J. Keyton and J. Springston, "Redefining Cohesiveness in Groups," *Small Group Research*, May 1990, pp. 234–54.

50. C. R. Evans and K. L. Dion, "Group Cohesion and Performance: A Meta-Analysis," *Small Group Research*, May 1991, pp. 175–86; B. Mullen and C. Cooper, "The Relation Between Group Cohesiveness and Performance: An Integration," *Psychological Bulletin*, March 1994, pp. 210–27; and P. M. Podsakoff, S. B. MacKenzie, and M. Ahearne, "Moderating Effects of Goal Acceptance on the Relationship Between Group Cohesiveness and Productivity," *Journal of Applied Psychology*, December 1997, pp. 974–83.

51. Based on J. L. Gibson, J. M. Ivancevich, and J. H. Donnelly Jr., *Organizations*, 8th ed. (Burr Ridge, IL: Irwin, 1994), p. 323.

52. I. D. Steiner, *Group Process and Productivity* (New York: Academic Press, 1972).

53. R. B. Zajonc, "Social Facilitation," *Science*, March 1965, pp. 269–74.

54. C. F. Bond, Jr. and L.J. Titus, "Social Facilitation: A Meta-Analysis of 241 Studies," *Psychological Bulletin*, September 1983, pp. 265–92.

55. V. F. Nieva, E. A. Fleishman, and A. Rieck, "Team Dimensions: Their Identity, Their Measurement, and Their Relationships." Final Technical Report for Contract No. DAHC 19-C-0001. Washington, DC: Advanced Research Resources Organizations, 1978.

56. See, for example, J. R. Hackman and C. G. Morris, "Group Tasks, Group Interaction Process and Group Performance Effectiveness: A Review and Proposed Integration," in L. Berkowitz (ed.), *Advances in Experimental Social Psychology* (New York: Academic Press, 1975), pp. 45–99; and R. Saavedra, P. C. Earley, and L. Van Dyne, "Complex Interdependence in Task-Performing Groups," *Journal of Applied Psychology*, February 1993, pp. 61–72.

57. J. Galbraith, *Organizational Design* (Reading, MA: Addison-Wesley, 1977).

58. See N. R. F. Maier, "Assets and Liabilities in Group Problem Solving: The Need for an Integrative Function," *Psychological Review*, April 1967, pp. 239–49; G. W. Hill, "Group Versus Individual Performance: Are $N + 1$ Heads Better Than One?" *Psychological Bulletin*, May 1982, pp. 517–39; and A. E. Schwartz and J. Levin, "Better Group Decision Making," *Supervisory Management*, June 1990, p. 4.

59. See, for example, R. A. Cooke and J. A. Kernaghan, "Estimating the Difference Between Group versus Individual Performance on Problem-Solving Tasks," *Group & Organization Studies*, September 1987, pp. 319–42; and L. K. Michaelsen, W. E. Watson, and R. H. Black, "A Realistic Test of Individual versus Group Consensus Decision Making," *Journal of Applied Psychology*, October 1989, pp. 834–39.

60. See, for example, W. C. Swap and Associates, *Group Decision Making* (Newbury Park, CA: Sage, 1984).

61. See G. W. Hill, "Group Versus Individual Performance"; and L. K. Michaelsen, W. E. Watson, and R. H. Black, "A Realistic Test of Individual versus Group Consensus Decision Making."

62. J. H. Davis, *Group Performance* (Reading, MA: Addison-Wesley, 1969); J. P. Wanous and M. A. Youtz, "Solution Diversity and the Quality of Group Decisions," *Academy of Management Journal*, March 1986, pp. 149–59; and R. Libby, K. T. Trotman, and I. Zimmer, "Member Variation, Recognition of Expertise, and Group Performance," *Journal of Applied Psychology*, February 1987, pp. 81–87.

63. I. L. Janis, *Groupthink* (Boston: Houghton Mifflin, 1982); W. Park, "A Review of Research on Groupthink," *Journal of Behavioral Decision Making*, July 1990, pp. 229–45; C. P. Neck and G. Moorhead, "Groupthink Remodeled: The Importance of Leadership, Time Pressure, and Methodical Decision-Making Procedures," *Human Relations*, May 1995, pp. 537–58; and J. N. Choi and M. U. Kim, "The Organizational Application of Groupthink and Its Limits in Organizations," *Journal of Applied Psychology*, April 1999, pp. 297–306.

64. Janis, *Groupthink*.

65. Ibid.

66. G. Moorehead, R. Ference, and C. P. Neck, "Group Decision Fiascos Continue: Space Shuttle Challenger and a Revised Groupthink Framework," *Human Relations*, May 1991, pp. 539–50; and E. J. Chisson, *The Hubble Wars* (New York: HarperPerennial, 1994).

67. M. E. Turner and A. R. Pratkanis, "Mitigating Groupthink by Stimulating Constructive Conflict," in C. De Dreu and E. Van de Vliert (eds.), *Using Conflict in Organizations* (London: Sage, 1997), pp. 53–71.

68. Ibid., p. 68.

69. See N. R. F. Maier, *Principles of Human Relations* (New York: John Wiley & Sons, 1952); I. L. Janis, *Groupthink: Psychological Studies of Policy Decisions and Fiascoes*, 2nd ed. (Boston: Houghton Mifflin, 1982); and C. R. Leana, "A Partial Test of Janis' Groupthink Model: Effects of Group Cohesiveness and Leader Behavior on Defective Decision Making," *Journal of Management*, Spring 1985, pp. 5–17.

70. See D. J. Isenberg, "Group Polarization: A Critical Review and Meta-Analysis," *Journal of Personality and Social Psychology*, December 1986, pp. 1141–51; J. L. Hale and F. J. Boster, "Comparing Effect Coded Models of Choice Shifts," *Communication Research Reports*, April 1988, pp. 180–86; and P. W. Paese, M. Bieser, and M. E. Tubbs, "Framing Effects and Choice Shifts in Group Decision Making," *Organizational Behavior and Human Decision Processes*, October 1993, pp. 149–65.

71. See, for example, N. Kogan and M. A. Wallach, "Risk Taking as a Function of the Situation, the Person, and the Group," in *New Directions in Psychology*, vol. 3 (New York: Holt, Rinehart and Winston, 1967); and M. A. Wallach, N. Kogan, and D. J. Bem, "Group Influence on Individual Risk Taking," *Journal of Abnormal and Social Psychology*, vol. 65 (1962), pp. 75–86.

72. R. D. Clark III, "Group-Induced Shift Toward Risk: A Critical Appraisal," *Psychological Bulletin*, October 1971, pp. 251–70.

73. A. F. Osborn, *Applied Imagination: Principles and Procedures of Creative Thinking*, 3rd ed. (New York: Scribner, 1963). See also R. I. Sutton and A. Hargadon, "Brainstorming Groups in Context: Effectiveness in a Product Design Firm," *Administrative Science Quarterly*, December 1996, pp. 685–718.

74. See A. L. Delbecq, A. H. Van deVen, and D. H. Gustafson, *Group Techniques for Program Planning: A Guide to Nominal and Delphi Processes* (Glenview, IL: Scott, Foresman, 1975); and W. M. Fox, "Anonymity and Other Keys to Successful Problem-Solving Meetings," *National Productivity Review*, Spring 1989, pp. 145–56.

75. See, for instance, A. R. Dennis and J. S. Valacich, "Computer Brainstorms: More Heads Are Better Than One," *Journal of Applied Psychology*, August 1993, pp. 531–37; R. B. Gallupe and W. H. Cooper, "Brainstorming Electronically," *Sloan Management Review*, Fall 1993, pp. 27–36; and A. B. Hollingshead and J. E. McGrath, "Computer-Assisted Groups: A Critical Review of the Empirical

Research," in R. A. Guzzo and E. Salas (eds.), *Team Effectiveness and Decision Making in Organizations*, pp. 46–78.

76. T. P. Verney, "Role Perception Congruence, Performance, and Satisfaction," in D. J. Vredenburgh and R. S. Schuler (eds.), *Effective Management: Research and Application*, Proceedings of the 20th Annual Eastern Academy of Management, Pittsburgh, PA, May 1983, pp. 24–27.

77. Ibid.

78. M. Van Sell, A. P. Brief, and R. S. Schuler, "Role Conflict and Role Ambiguity: Integration of the Literature and Directions for Future Research," *Human Relations*, January 1981, pp. 43–71; and A. G. Bedeian and A. A. Armenakis, "A Path-Analytic Study of the Consequences of Role Conflict and Ambiguity," *Academy of Management Journal*, June 1981, pp. 417–24.

79. Shaw, *Group Dynamics*.

80. B. Mullen, C. Symons, L. Hu, and E. Salas, "Group Size, Leadership Behavior, and Subordinate Satisfaction," *Journal of General Psychology*, April 1989, pp. 155–70.

part three

THE GROUP

W. L. Gore & Associates is a billion-dollar-a-year business.[1] It's mostly known as the maker of Gore-Tex fabric, used in outerwear. In spite of its size, Gore stands out because it's organized completely around teams. Even though the company has more than 40 plants located around the world, none has more than 200 employees. This allows people to be organized into a manageable set of teams. It additionally allows everyone in a facility to know each other.

Gore is serious in its effort to organize all activities around teams. There are, for instance, no job titles, no bosses, and no chains of command. Everyone is an "associate" with equal authority (see photo). Plants and staff departments are headed by "leaders." "We don't have bosses, but we have leaders. People go to certain people as a matter of course," says Heidi

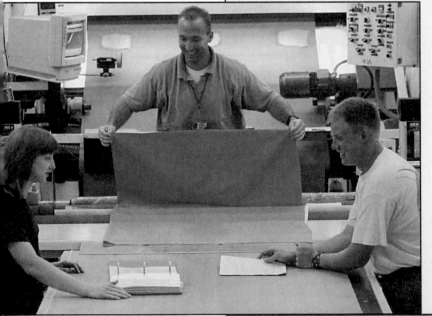

Cofran, who works in corporate communications at Gore. "It makes much more sense to let other people emerge as leaders, because others are much more likely to follow those people than people who are thrust upon them."

Gore's management tries to create a climate in which senior management empowers associates, and individual employees, as team members, to take responsibility for solving problems and achieving goals. The company articulates four principles that capture its management style: (1) Be fair. (2) Encourage, help, and allow other associates to learn and gain skills and responsibilities. (3) Allow associates to make commitments and keep them. (4) Consult with others before taking actions that can affect the company's health.

Understanding Work Teams

W hile few organizations go to the extremes that W. L. Gore does, Gore is at the cutting edge of a major trend. Teams are increasingly becoming the primary means for organizing work in contemporary business firms.

WHY HAVE TEAMS BECOME SO POPULAR?

Twenty years ago, when companies such as Gore, Volvo, and General Foods introduced teams into their production processes, it made news because no one else was doing it. Today, it's just the opposite. (See Exhibit 9-1.) It's the organization that *doesn't* use teams that has become newsworthy. Pick up almost any business periodical today and you'll read how teams have become an essential part of the way business is being done in companies such as General Electric, AT&T, Hewlett-Packard, Motorola, US Airways, Shiseido, Federal Express, DaimlerChrysler, Saab, 3M Co., John Deere, Texas Instruments, Australian Airlines, Johnson & Johnson, Shenandoah Life Insurance Co., Florida Power & Light, and Emerson Electric. Even the world-famous San Diego Zoo has restructured its native habitat zones around cross-departmental teams.

How do we explain the current popularity of teams? The evidence suggests that teams typically outperform individuals when the tasks being done require multiple skills, judgment, and experience.[2] As organizations have restructured themselves to compete more effectively and efficiently, they have turned to teams as a way to better utilize employee talents. Management has found that teams are more flexible and responsive to changing events than are traditional departments or other forms of permanent groupings. Teams have the capability to quickly assemble, deploy, refocus, and disband.

But don't overlook the motivational properties of teams. Consistent with our discussion in Chapter 7 of the role of employee involvement as a motivator, teams facilitate employee participation in operating decisions. For instance, some assembly-line workers at John Deere are part of sales teams that call on customers.[3] These workers know the products better than any traditional salesperson; and by traveling and speaking with farmers, these hourly workers develop new skills and become more involved in their jobs. So another explanation for the popularity of teams is that they are an effective means for management to democratize their organizations and increase employee motivation.

TEAMS VS. GROUPS: WHAT'S THE DIFFERENCE?

Groups and teams are not the same thing. In this section, we want to define and clarify the difference between a work group and a work team.[4]

In the last chapter, we defined a *group* as two or more individuals, interacting and interdependent, who have come together to achieve particular objectives. A **work group** is a group that interacts primarily to share information and to make decisions to help each member perform within his or her area of responsibility.

Work groups have no need or opportunity to engage in collective work that requires joint effort. So their performance is merely the summation of each group member's individual contribution. There is no positive synergy that would create an overall level of performance that is greater than the sum of the inputs.

A **work team** generates positive synergy through coordinated effort. Their individual efforts results in a level of performance that is greater than the sum of those individual inputs. Exhibit 9-2 highlights the differences between work groups and work teams.

These definitions help clarify why so many organizations have recently restructured work processes around teams. Management is looking for that positive synergy that will allow their organizations to increase performance. The exten-

work group

A group that interacts primarily to share information and to make decisions to help each group member perform within his or her area of responsibility.

work team

A group whose individual efforts result in a performance that is greater than the sum of the individual inputs.

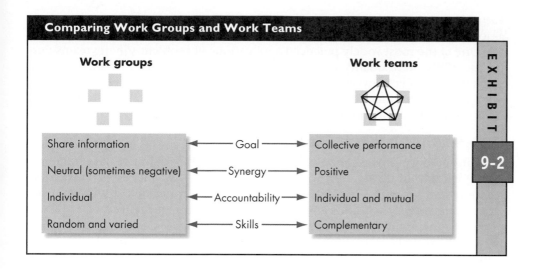

Comparing Work Groups and Work Teams

Work groups		Work teams
Share information	← Goal →	Collective performance
Neutral (sometimes negative)	← Synergy →	Positive
Individual	← Accountability →	Individual and mutual
Random and varied	← Skills →	Complementary

EXHIBIT 9-2

sive use of teams creates the *potential* for an organization to generate greater outputs with no increase in inputs. Notice, however, we said "potential." There is nothing inherently magical in the creation of teams that ensures the achievement of this positive synergy. Merely calling a *group* a *team* doesn't automatically increase its performance. As we show later in this chapter, effective teams have certain common characteristics. If management hopes to gain increases in organizational performance through the use of teams, it will need to ensure that its teams possess these characteristics.

TYPES OF TEAMS

The four most common forms of teams you're likely to find in an organization are *problem-solving teams, self-managed teams, cross-functional teams,* and *virtual teams* (see Exhibit 9-3).

PROBLEM-SOLVING TEAMS

If we look back 20 years or so, teams were just beginning to grow in popularity, and most of these teams took similar form. These were typically composed of 5 to 12 hourly employees from the same department who met for a few hours each week to discuss ways of improving quality, efficiency, and the work environment.[5] We call these **problem-solving teams**.

In problem-solving teams, members share ideas or offer suggestions on how work processes and methods can be improved. Rarely, however, are these

problem-solving teams

Groups of 5 to 12 employees from the same department who meet for a few hours each week to discuss ways of improving quality, efficiency, and the work environment.

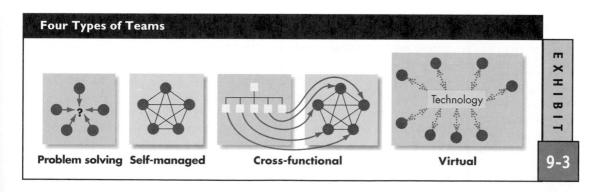

Four Types of Teams

Problem solving   Self-managed   Cross-functional   Virtual

Technology

EXHIBIT 9-3

teams given the authority to unilaterally implement any of their suggested actions.

One of the most widely practiced applications of problem-solving teams during the 1980s were quality circles.[6] As described in Chapter 7, these are work teams of 8 to 10 employees and supervisors who have a shared area of responsibility and meet regularly to discuss their quality problems, investigate causes of the problems, recommend solutions, and take corrective actions.

SELF-MANAGED WORK TEAMS

self-managed work teams

Groups of 10 to 15 people who take on responsibilities of their former supervisors.

Problem-solving teams were on the right track but they didn't go far enough in getting employees involved in work-related decisions and processes. This led to experimentations with truly autonomous teams that could not only solve problems but implement solutions and take full responsibility for outcomes.

Self-managed work teams are groups of employees (typically 10 to 15 in number) who perform highly related or interdependent jobs and take on many of the responsibilities of their former supervisors.[7] Typically, this includes planning and scheduling of work, assigning tasks to members, collective control over the pace of work, making operating decisions, and taking action on problems. Fully self-managed work teams even select their own members and have the members evaluate each other's performance. As a result, supervisory positions decrease in importance and may even be eliminated. At GE's locomotive-engine plant in Grove City, Pennsylvania, there are about 100 self-managed teams and they make most of the plant's decisions. They arrange the maintenance, schedule the work, and routinely authorize equipment purchases. One team spent $2 million and the plant manager never flinched. At the L-S Electrogalvanizing Co., in Cleveland, the entire plant is run by self-managed teams. They do their own scheduling, rotate jobs on their own, establish production targets, set pay scales that are linked to skills, fire co-workers, and do the hiring. "I never meet a new employee until his first day on the job," says the plant's general manager.[8]

Xerox, General Motors, Coors Brewing, PepsiCo, Hewlett-Packard, Honeywell, M&M/Mars, and Aetna Life are just a few familiar names that have implemented self-managed work teams. Overall, about 30 percent of U.S. employers now use this form of teams.[9]

Business periodicals have been chock full of articles describing successful applications of self-managed teams. Texas Instruments' defense group gives self-directed teams credit for helping it win the Malcolm Baldrige National Quality Award and for allowing it to achieve the same level of sales with 25 percent fewer employees.[10] Aid Association for Lutherans, one of the largest insurance and financial service companies in the United States, claims that self-managed teams were primarily responsible for helping to increase employee satisfaction and for allowing the company to increase business volume by 50 percent over a four-year period while cutting workforce staff by 15 percent.[11] Management at the Edy's Grand Ice Cream plant in Fort Wayne, Indiana, attributes the plant's recent 39 percent reduction in costs and 57 percent increase in productivity to self-managed teams.[12]

In spite of these impressive stories, a word of caution needs to be offered here. Some organizations have been disappointed with the results from self-managed teams. For instance, they don't seem to work well during organizational downsizing. Employees often view cooperating with the team concept as an exercise in assisting one's own execu-

At Unisys Corporation, a management information company, employees are given the responsibility of managing their work, training, and career development. Self-managed work teams at Unisys plants have helped the company double its product shipping schedules without doubling its workforce. Members of the Unisys Medium Speed Image Module Team shown here set their own production goals based on the plant's business plan. Some teams have developed their own business plan that requires a 10-hour-a-day, four-day workweek. The company is testing the new work schedule.

tioner.[13] The overall research on the effectiveness of self-managed work teams has not been uniformly positive.[14] Moreover, while individuals on these teams do tend to report higher levels of job satisfaction, they also sometimes have higher absenteeism and turnover rates. Inconsistency in findings suggests that the effectiveness of self-managed teams is situationally dependent.[15] In addition to downsizing, factors such as the strength and makeup of team norms, the type of tasks the team undertakes, and the reward structure can significantly influence how well the team performs.

CROSS-FUNCTIONAL TEAMS

US Airways Group used the latest application of the team concept to develop a low-fare airline for US Air. This application is called **cross-functional teams**. These are teams made up of employees from about the same hierarchical level, but from different work areas, who come together to accomplish a task.[16] At US Airways, the cross-functional team included flight crew, ramp personnel, mechanics, dispatchers, and reservation agents.[17]

Many organizations have used horizontal, boundary-spanning groups for years. For example, IBM created a large task force in the 1960s—made up of employees from across departments in the company—to develop the highly successful System 360. And a **task force** is really nothing other than a temporary cross-functional team. Similarly, **committees** composed of members from across departmental lines are another example of cross-functional teams.

But the popularity of cross-discipline work teams exploded in the late 1980s. All the major automobile manufacturers—including Toyota, Honda, Nissan, BMW, GM, Ford, and DaimlerChrysler—have turned to these forms of teams in order to coordinate complex projects. For example, Chrysler's Neon was developed completely by a cross-functional team. The model was delivered in a speedy 42 months and for a fraction of what any other manufacturer's small car has cost.[18]

Motorola's Iridium Project illustrates why so many companies have turned to cross-functional teams.[19] This project is developing a huge network that will contain 66 satellites. "We realized at the beginning that there was no way we could manage a project of this size and complexity in the traditional way and still get it done on time," says the project's general manager. For the first year and a half of the project, a cross-functional team of 20 Motorola people met every morning. This has since been expanded to include diverse expertise from people in dozens of other companies as well, such as Raytheon, Russia's Khrunichev Enterprise, Lockheed Martin, Scientific-Atlanta, and General Electric.

In summary, cross-functional teams are an effective means for allowing people from diverse areas within an organization (or even between organizations) to exchange information, develop new ideas and solve problems, and coordinate complex projects. Of course, cross-functional teams are no picnic to manage.[20] Their early stages of development are often very time consuming as members learn to work with diversity and complexity. It takes time to build trust and teamwork, especially among people from different backgrounds, with different experiences and perspectives.

VIRTUAL TEAMS

The previous types of teams do their work face-to-face. **Virtual teams** use computer technology to tie together physically dispersed members in order to achieve a common goal.[21] They allow people to collaborate on-line—using communication links such as wide area networks, video conferencing, or e-mail—whether they're only a room away or continents apart.

cross-functional teams

Employees from about the same hierarchical level, but from different work areas, who come together to accomplish a task.

task force

A temporary cross-functional team.

committees

Groups made up of members from across departmental lines.

virtual teams

Teams that use computer technology to tie together physically dispersed members in order to achieve a common goal.

OB *in the News*

Virtual Teams at VeriFone

A recent incident at VeriFone, a California-based manufacturer of in-store credit card authorization terminals, provides a glimpse of how virtual teams can work. A VeriFone sales representative in Greece knew he was in big trouble when he left the offices of an Athens bank at 4:30 P.M. A competitor had challenged VeriFone's ability to deliver a new payment-service technology. The sales rep knew his company was the main supplier of this technology in the United States and many other countries, but it was unproven in Greece. The rep needed to convince bank executives that this technology would work but he had no details on its effectiveness by users in other countries. His reaction was to create a virtual team. He found the nearest phone and hooked up his laptop to it. Then he sent an SOS e-mail to all VeriFone sales, marketing, and technical support staff worldwide.

In San Francisco, an international marketing staffer who was on duty to monitor such distress calls got the message at home when he checked his e-mail at 6:30 A.M. He organized a conference call with two other marketing staffers, one in Atlanta and one in Hong Kong, where it was 9:30 A.M. and 10:30 P.M., respectively. Together, they decided how to handle the data coming in from everyone who'd received the message. A few hours later, the two U.S. team members spoke on the phone again while they used the company's wide area network to fine-tune a sales presentation. Before leaving for the day, the leader passed the presentation on to the Hong Kong team member so he could add Asian information to the detailed account of experiences and references when he arrived at work.

The Greek sales rep awakened a few hours later. He retrieved the presentation from the network, got to the bank at 8 A.M., and showed the customer the data on his laptop. Impressed by the speedy and informative response, the customer's apprehensions about VeriFone's technology were alleviated. And the sales rep got the order.

Source: W. R. Pape, "Group Insurance," *INC. Technology*, July 1997, pp. 29–31.

Virtual teams can do all the things that other teams do—share information, make decisions, complete tasks. And they can include members from the same organization or link an organization's members with employees from other organizations (i.e., suppliers and joint partners). They can convene for a few days to solve a problem, a few months to complete a project, or exist permanently.[22]

The three primary factors that differentiate virtual teams from face-to-face teams are (1) the absence of paraverbal and nonverbal cues; (2) limited social context; and (3) the ability to overcome time and space constraints. In face-to-face conversation, people use paraverbal (tone of voice, inflection, voice volume) and nonverbal (eye movement, facial expression, hand gestures, and other body language) cues. These help clarify communication by providing increased meaning but aren't available in on-line interactions. Virtual teams often suffer from less social rapport and less direct interaction among members. They aren't able to duplicate the normal give-and-take of face-to-face discussion. Especially where members haven't personally met, virtual teams tend to be more task oriented and exchange less social-emotional information. Not surprisingly, virtual team members report less satisfaction with the group interaction process than do face-to-face teams. Finally, virtual teams are able to do their work even if members are thousands of miles apart and separated by a dozen or more time zones. It allows people to work together who might otherwise never be able to collaborate.

BEWARE! TEAMS AREN'T ALWAYS THE ANSWER

Teamwork takes more time and often more resources than individual work. Teams, for instance, have increased communication demands, conflicts to be managed, and meetings to be run. So the benefits of using teams have to exceed the costs. And that's not always the case. In the excitement to enjoy the benefits of teams, some managers have introduced them into situations in which the work is better done by individuals. So before you rush to implement teams, you should carefully assess whether the work requires or will benefit from a collective effort.

How do you know if the work of your group would be better done in teams? It's been suggested that three tests be applied to see if a team fits the situation.[23] First, can the work be done better by more than one person? A good indicator is the complexity of the work and the need for different perspectives. Simple tasks that don't require diverse input are probably better left to individuals. Second, does the work create a common purpose or set of goals for the people in the group that is more than the aggregate of individual goals? For instance, many new-car dealer service departments have introduced teams that link customer service personnel, mechanics, parts specialists, and sales representatives. Such teams can better manage collective responsibility for ensuring that customer needs are properly met. The final test to assess whether teams fit the situation is: Are the members of the group interdependent? Teams make sense when there is interdependence between tasks; when the success of the whole depends on the success of each one *and* the success of each one depends on the success of the others. Soccer, for instance, is an obvious *team* sport. Success requires a great deal of coordination between interdependent players. Conversely, except possibly for relays, swim teams are not really teams. They're groups of individuals, performing individually, whose total performance is merely the aggregate summation of their individual performances.

CREATING EFFECTIVE TEAMS

There is no shortage of efforts at trying to identify factors related to team effectiveness.[24] However, recent studies have taken what was once a "veritable laundry list of characteristics"[25] and organized them into a relatively focused model.[26] Exhibit 9-4 summarizes what we currently know about what makes teams effective. As you'll see, it builds on many of the group concepts introduced in the previous chapter.

The following discussion is based on the model in Exhibit 9-4. Keep in mind two caveats before we proceed. First, teams differ in form and structure. Since the model we present attempts to generalize across all varieties of teams, you need to be careful not to rigidly apply the model's predictions to all teams. The model should be used as a guide, not as an inflexible prescription. Second, the model assumes that it's already been determined that teamwork is preferable over individual work. Creating "effective" teams in situations in which individuals can do the job better is equivalent to solving the wrong problem perfectly!

The key components making up effective teams can be subsumed into four general categories. The first category is *work design*. The second relates to the team's *composition*. Third is the resources and other *contextual* influences that make teams effective. Finally, *process* variables reflect the things that go on in the team that influence effectiveness.

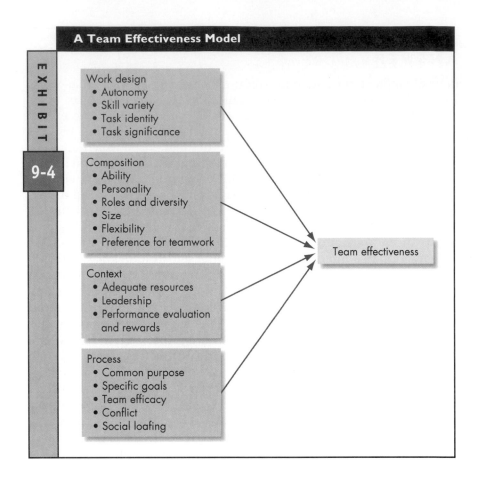

A Team Effectiveness Model

EXHIBIT 9-4

Work design
- Autonomy
- Skill variety
- Task identity
- Task significance

Composition
- Ability
- Personality
- Roles and diversity
- Size
- Flexibility
- Preference for teamwork

Context
- Adequate resources
- Leadership
- Performance evaluation and rewards

Process
- Common purpose
- Specific goals
- Team efficacy
- Conflict
- Social loafing

Team effectiveness

What does *team effectiveness* mean in this model? Typically this has included objective measures of the team's productivity, managers' ratings of the team's performance, and aggregate measures of member satisfaction.

WORK DESIGN

Effective teams need to work together and take collective responsibility to complete significant tasks. They must be more than a "team-in-name-only."[27] The work design category includes variables such as freedom and autonomy, the opportunity to utilize different skills and talents, the ability to complete a whole and identifiable task or product, and working on a task or project that has a substantial impact on others. The evidence indicates that these characteristics enhance member motivation and increase team effectiveness.[28] These work design characteristics motivate because they increase members' sense of responsibility and ownership over the work and because they make the work more interesting to perform.[29]

COMPOSITION

This category includes variables that relate to how teams should be staffed. In this section, we'll address the ability and personality of team members, allocating roles and diversity, size of the team, member flexibility, and members' preference for teamwork.

Abilities of Members To perform effectively, a team requires three different types of skills. First, it needs people with *technical expertise*. Second, it needs people with the *problem-solving and decision-making skills* to be able to identify problems, generate alternatives, evaluate those alternatives, and make competent choices. Finally, teams need people with good listening, feedback, conflict resolution, and other *interpersonal skills*.[30]

No team can achieve its performance potential without developing all three types of skills. The right mix is crucial. Too much of one at the expense of others will result in lower team performance. But teams don't need to have all the complementary skills in place at their beginning. It's not uncommon for one or more members to take responsibility to learn the skills in which the group is deficient, thereby allowing the team to reach its full potential.

Personality We demonstrated in Chapter 4 that personality has a significant influence on individual employee behavior. This can also be extended to team behavior. Many of the dimensions identified in the Big Five personality model have been shown to be relevant to team effectiveness. Specifically, teams that are rated more highly in mean levels of extraversion, agreeableness, conscientiousness, and emotional stability tend to receive higher managerial ratings for team performance.[31]

Each astronaut serving as a crew member aboard the Discovery space mission had specific skills that were needed for the mission's success. For example, Spain's astronaut Pedro Duque (right) contributed his problem-solving skills. He was the mission's troubleshooter for the 19 laptop computers used to run the shuttle's systems and experiments. Duque was also one of two crew members trained to work outside the orbiter in the event of an emergency. Duque is shown here with fellow astronauts Chiaki Mukia of Japan and Steve Lindsay of the United States.

Very interestingly, the evidence indicates that the variance in personality characteristics may be more important than the mean.[32] So, for example, while higher mean levels of conscientiousness on a team are desirable, mixing both conscientious and not-so-conscientious members tends to lower performance. "This may be because, in such teams, members who are highly conscientious not only must perform their own tasks but also must perform or re-do the tasks of low-conscientious members. It may also be because such diversity leads to feelings of contribution inequity."[33] Another interesting finding related to personality is that "one bad apple can spoil the barrel." A single team member who lacks a minimal level of, say, agreeableness, can negatively affect the whole team's performance. So including just one person who is low on agreeableness, conscientiousness, or extraversion can result in strained internal processes and decreased overall performance.[34]

Allocating Roles and Diversity Teams have different needs, and people should be selected for a team to ensure that there is diversity and that all various roles are filled.

We can identify nine potential team roles (see Exhibit 9-5). Successful work teams have people to fill all these roles and have selected people to play in these roles based on their skills and preferences.[35] (On many teams, individuals will play multiple roles.) Managers need to understand the individual strengths that each person can bring to a team, select members with their strengths in mind, and allocate work assignments that fit with members' preferred styles. By

EXHIBIT 9-5

Key Roles on Teams

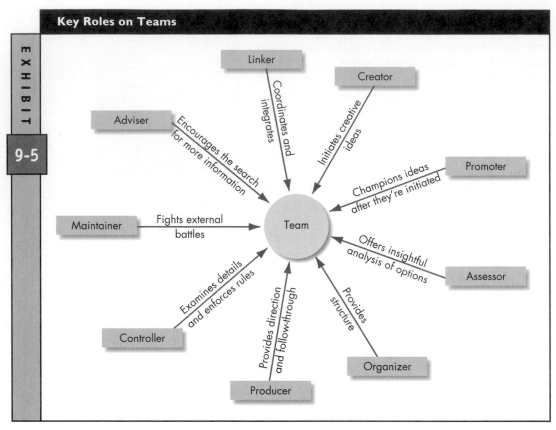

Source: Based on C. Margerison and D. McCann, *Team Management: Practical New Approaches* (London: Mercury Books, 1990).

matching individual preferences with team role demands, managers increase the likelihood that the team members will work well together.

Size of Teams   The most effective teams are neither very small (under four or five members) or very large (over a dozen).[36] Very small teams are likely to lack diversity of views. But when teams have more than about 10 to 12 members, it becomes difficult to get much done. Group members have trouble interacting constructively and agreeing, and large numbers of people usually can't develop the cohesiveness, commitment, and mutual accountability necessary to achieve high performance. So in designing effective teams, managers should keep them in the range of 5 to 12 people. If a natural working unit is larger and you want a team effort, consider breaking the group into subteams.

Member Flexibility   Teams made up of flexible individuals have members who can complete each other's tasks. This is an obvious plus to a team because it greatly improves its adaptability and makes it less reliant on any single member.[37] Selecting members who value flexibility and then cross-training them to be able to do each other's jobs should lead to higher team performance over time.

Member Preferences   Not every employee is a team player. Given the option, many employees will select themselves *out* of team participation. When people who would prefer to work alone are required to team up, there is a direct threat to the team's morale.[38] This suggests that, when selecting team members, individual preferences should be considered as well as abilities, personalities, and skills. High-performing teams are likely to be composed of people who prefer working as part of a group.

CONTEXT

The three contextual factors that appear to be most significantly related to team performance are the presence of adequate resources, effective leadership, and a performance evaluation and reward system that reflects team contributions.

Adequate Resources   In our work group model in the previous chapter, we acknowledged that a work group is part of a larger organization system. As such, all work teams rely on resources outside the group to sustain it. And a scarcity of resources directly reduces the ability of the team to perform its job effectively. As one set of researchers concluded, after looking at 13 factors potentially related to group performance, "perhaps one of the most important characteristics of an effective work group is the support the group receives from the organization."[39] This includes support such as timely information, technology, adequate staffing, encouragement, and administrative assistance. Teams must receive the necessary support from management and the larger organization if they are going to succeed in achieving their goals.

Leadership and Structure   Team members must agree on who is to do what and ensure that all members contribute equally in sharing the workload. Additionally, the team needs to determine how schedules will be set, what skills need to be developed, how the group will resolve conflicts, and how the group will make and modify decisions. Agreeing on the specifics of work and how they fit together to integrate individual skills requires team leadership and structure. This, incidentally, can be provided directly by management or by the team members themselves as they fulfill promoter, organizer, producer, maintainer, and linker roles (refer to Exhibit 9-5).

Leadership, of course, isn't always needed. For instance, the evidence indicates that self-managed work teams often perform better than teams with formally appointed leaders.[40] And leaders can obstruct high performance when they interfere with self-managing teams.[41] On self-managed teams, team members absorb many of the duties typically assumed by managers.

On traditionally managed teams, we find that two factors seem to be important in influencing team performance—the leader's expectations and his or her mood. Leaders who expect good things from their team are more likely to get them! For instance, military platoons under leaders who held high expectations performed significantly better in training than control platoons.[42] Additionally, studies have found that leaders who exhibit a positive mood get better team performance and lower turnover.[43]

Performance Evaluation and Reward Systems   How do you get team members to be both individually and jointly accountable? The traditional, individually oriented evaluation and reward system must be modified to reflect team performance.[44]

Individual performance evaluations, fixed hourly wages, individual incentives, and the like are not consistent with the development of high-performance teams. So in addition to evaluating and rewarding employees for their individual contributions, management should consider group-based appraisals, profit sharing, gainsharing, small-group incentives, and other system modifications that will reinforce team effort and commitment.

PROCESS

The final category related to team effectiveness is process variables. These include member commitment to a common purpose, establishment of specific team goals, team efficacy, a managed level of conflict, and the reduction of social loafing.

A Common Purpose Effective teams have a common and meaningful purpose that provides direction, momentum, and commitment for members.[45] This purpose is a vision. It's broader than specific goals.

Members of successful teams put a tremendous amount of time and effort into discussing, shaping, and agreeing upon a purpose that belongs to them both collectively and individually. This common purpose, when accepted by the team, becomes the equivalent of what celestial navigation is to a ship captain—it provides direction and guidance under any and all conditions.

Goals are important for high team performance. This team from a Motorola plant in Tianjin, China, won the grand prize award at the Motorola employee's total customer satisfaction team competition. The team was recognized for its success at achieving three supplier-related goals: providing increased support for existing suppliers, relocating high-tech support to China, and developing new local suppliers.

Specific Goals Successful teams translate their common purpose into specific, measurable, and realistic performance goals. Just as we demonstrated in Chapter 6 how goals lead individuals to higher performance, goals also energize teams. These specific goals facilitate clear communication. They also help teams maintain their focus on getting results.

Also, consistent with the research on individual goals, team goals should be challenging. Difficult goals have been found to raise team performance on those criteria for which they're set. So, for instance, goals for quantity tend to raise quantity, goals for speed tend to raise speed, goals for accuracy raise accuracy, and so on.[46]

Team Efficacy Effective teams have confidence in themselves. They believe they can succeed. We call this *team efficacy*.[47]

Success breeds success. Teams that have been successful raise their beliefs about future success. This, in turn, motivates them to work harder.

What, if anything, can management do to increase team efficacy? Two possible options are helping the team to achieve small successes and providing skill training. Small successes build team confidence. As a team develops an increasingly stronger performance record, it also increases the collective belief that future efforts will lead to success. In addition, managers should consider providing training to improve members' technical and interpersonal skills. The greater the abilities of team members, the greater the likelihood that the team will develop confidence and the capability to deliver on that confidence.

Conflict Levels Conflict on a team isn't necessarily bad. As we'll elaborate in Chapter 13, teams that are completely void of conflict are likely to become apathetic and stagnant. So conflict can actually improve team effectiveness.[48] But not all types of conflict. Relationship conflicts—those based on interpersonal incompatibilities, tension, and animosity toward others—are almost always dysfunctional. However, for teams performing nonroutine activities, disagreement among members about task content (called task conflicts) is not detrimental. In fact, it is often beneficial because it lessens the likelihood of groupthink. Task conflicts stimulate discussion, promote critical assessement of problems and options, and can lead to better team decisions. So effective teams will be characterized by an appropriate level of conflict.

Social Loafing We learned in the previous chapter that individuals can hide inside a group. They can engage in social loafing and coast on the group's effort because their individual contributions can't be identified. Effective teams undermine this tendency by holding themselves accountable at both the individual and team levels.

Successful teams make members individually and jointly accountable for the team's purpose, goals, and approach.[49] They are clear on what they are individually responsible for and what they are jointly responsible for.

TURNING INDIVIDUALS INTO TEAM PLAYERS

To this point, we've made a strong case for the value and growing popularity of teams. But many people are not inherently team players. They're loners or people who want to be recognized for their individual achievements. There are also a great many organizations that have historically nurtured individual accomplishments. They have created competitive work environments where only the strong survive. If these organizations adopt teams, what do they do about the selfish, "I-got-to-look-out-for-me" employees that they've created? Finally, as we discussed in Chapter 3, countries differ in terms of how they rate on individualism and collectivism. Teams fit well in countries that score high on collectivism.[50] But what if an organization wants to introduce teams into a work population that is made up largely of individuals born and raised in a highly individualistic society? As one writer so aptly put it, in describing the role of teams in the United States: "Americans don't grow up learning how to function in teams. In school we never receive a team report card or learn the names of the team of sailors who traveled with Columbus to America."[51] This limitation would obviously be just as true of Canadians, British, Australians, and others from highly individualistic societies.

THE CHALLENGE

The previous points are meant to dramatize that one substantial barrier to using work teams is individual resistance. An employee's success is no longer defined in terms of individual performance. To perform well as team members, individuals must be able to communicate openly and honestly, to confront differences and resolve conflicts, and to sublimate personal goals for the good of the team. For many employees, this is a difficult—sometimes impossible—task. The challenge of creating team players will be greatest where (1) the national culture is highly individualistic and (2) the teams are being introduced into an established organization that has historically valued individual achievement. This describes, for instance, what faced managers at AT&T, Ford, Motorola, and other large U.S.-based companies. These firms prospered by hiring and rewarding corporate stars, and they bred a competitive climate that encouraged individual achievement and recognition. Employees in these types of firms can be jolted by this sudden shift to the importance of team play.[52] A veteran employee of a large company, who had done well working alone, described the experience of joining a team: "I'm learning my lesson. I just had my first negative performance appraisal in 20 years."[53]

On the other hand, the challenge for management is less demanding when teams are introduced into cultures in which employees have strong collectivist values—such as in Japan or Mexico—or in new organizations that use teams as their initial form for structuring work. Saturn Corp., for instance, is an American organization owned by General Motors. The company was designed around teams from its inception. Everyone at Saturn was hired with the knowledge that they would be working in teams. The ability to be a good team player was a basic hiring qualification that all new employees had to meet.

SHAPING TEAM PLAYERS

The following summarizes the primary options managers have for trying to turn individuals into team players.

Selection Some people already possess the interpersonal skills to be effective team players. When hiring team members, in addition to the technical skills required to fill the job, care should be taken to ensure that candidates can fulfill their team roles as well as technical requirements.[54]

Many job candidates don't have team skills. This is especially true for those socialized around individual contributions. When faced with such candidates, managers basically have three options. The candidates can undergo training to make them into team players. If this isn't possible or doesn't work, the other two options are to transfer the individual to another unit within the organization without teams (if this possibility exists); or don't hire the candidate. In established organizations that decide to redesign jobs around teams, it should be expected that some employees will resist being team players and may be untrainable. Unfortunately, such people typically become casualties of the team approach.

Training On a more optimistic note, a large proportion of people raised on the importance of individual accomplishment can be trained to become team players. Training specialists conduct exercises that allow employees to experience the satisfaction that teamwork can provide. They typically offer workshops to help employees improve their problem-solving, communication, negotiation, conflict-management, and coaching skills. Employees also learn the five-stage group-development model described in Chapter 8. At Bell Atlantic, for example, trainers focus on how a team goes through various stages before it finally gels. And employees are reminded of the importance of patience—because teams take longer to make decisions than employees acting alone.[55]

Domino's Pizza sends its managers to Leading Concept Boot Camp to learn team-building skills. At the simulated military boot camp, managers develop teamwork and communication skills by forming a platoon that must survive in combat. The training helps managers become better team players and more willing to be judged as part of a team instead of as individuals.

Emerson Electric's Speciality Motor Division in Missouri, for instance, has achieved remarkable success in getting its 650-member workforce not only to accept, but to welcome, team training.[56] Outside consultants were brought in to give workers practical skills for working in teams. After less than a year, employees have enthusiastically accepted the value of teamwork.

Rewards   The reward system needs to be reworked to encourage cooperative efforts rather than competitive ones.[57] For instance, Hallmark Cards, Inc. added an annual bonus based on achievement of team goals to its basic individual incentive system. Trigon Blue Cross Blue Shield changed its system to reward an even split between individual goals and teamlike behaviors.[58]

Promotions, pay raises, and other forms of recognition should be given to individuals for how effective they are as collaborative team members. This doesn't mean individual contribution is ignored; rather, it is balanced with selfless contributions to the team. Examples of behaviors that should be rewarded include training new colleagues, sharing information with teammates, helping to resolve team conflicts, and mastering new skills that the team needs but in which it is deficient.

Lastly, don't forget the intrinsic rewards that employees can receive from teamwork. Teams provide camaraderie. It's exciting and satisfying to be an integral part of a successful team. The opportunity to engage in personal development and to help teammates grow can be a very satisfying and rewarding experience for employees.

CONTEMPORARY ISSUES IN MANAGING TEAMS

In this section, we address three issues related to managing teams: (1) How do teams facilitate the adoption of total quality management? (2) What are the implications of workforce diversity on team performance? (3) How does management reenergize stagnant teams?

TEAMS AND TOTAL QUALITY MANAGEMENT

One of the central characteristics of total quality management (TQM) is the use of teams. But why are teams an essential part of TQM?

The essence of TQM is process improvement, and employee involvement is the linchpin of process improvement. In other words, TQM requires management to give employees the encouragement to share ideas and act on what they suggest. As one author put it, "None of the various TQM processes and techniques will catch on and be applied except in work teams. All such techniques and processes require high levels of communication and contact, response and adaptation, and coordination and sequencing. They require, in short, the environment that can be supplied only by superior work teams."[59]

Teams provide the natural vehicle for employees to share ideas and to implement improvements. As stated by Gil Mosard, a TQM specialist at Boeing-McDonnell Douglas: "When your measurement system tells you your process is out of control, you need teamwork for structured problem solving. Not everyone needs to know how to do all kinds of fancy control charts for performance tracking, but everybody does need to know where their process stands so they can judge if it is improving."[60] Examples from Ford Motor Co. and Amana Refrigeration, Inc. illustrate how teams are being used in TQM programs.[61]

Ford began its TQM efforts in the early 1980s with teams as the primary organizing mechanism. "Because this business is so complex, you can't make an impact on it without a team approach," noted one Ford manager. In designing its quality problem-solving teams, Ford's management identified five goals. The teams should (1) be small enough to be efficient and effective; (2) be properly trained in the skills their members will need; (3) be allocated enough time to work on the problems they plan to address; (4) be given the authority to resolve the problems and implement corrective action; and (5) each have a designated "champion" whose job it is to help the team get around roadblocks that arise.

At Amana, cross-functional task forces made up of people from different levels within the company are used to deal with quality problems that cut across departmental lines. The various task forces each have a unique area of problem-solving responsibility. For instance, one handles in-plant products, another deals with items that arise outside the production facility, and still another focuses its attention specifically on supplier problems. Amana claims the use of these teams has improved vertical and horizontal communication within the company and substantially reduced both the number of units that don't meet company specifications and the number of service problems in the field.

TEAMS AND WORKFORCE DIVERSITY

Managing diversity on teams is a balancing act (see Exhibit 9-6). Diversity typically provides fresh perspectives on issues, but it makes it more difficult to unify the team and reach agreements.

The strongest case for diversity on work teams is when these teams are engaged in problem-solving and decision-making tasks.[62] Heterogeneous teams bring multiple perspectives to the discussion, thus increasing the likelihood that the team will identify creative or unique solutions. Additionally, the lack of a common perspective usually means diverse teams spend more time discussing issues, which decreases the chances that a weak alternative will be chosen. However, keep in mind that the positive contribution that diversity makes to decision-making teams undoubtedly declines over time. As we pointed out in the previous chapter, diverse groups have more difficulty working together and solving problems, *but this dissipates with time.* Expect the value-added component of diverse teams to decrease as members become more familiar with each other and the team becomes more cohesive.

Studies tell us that members of cohesive teams have greater satisfaction, lower absenteeism, and lower attrition from the group.[63] Yet cohesiveness is likely to be lower on diverse teams.[64] So here is a potential negative of diversity: It is detrimental to group cohesiveness. But again, referring to the last chapter,

Advantages and Disadvantages of Diversity	
Advantages	**Disadvantages**
Multiple perspectives	Ambiguity
Greater openness to new ideas	Complexity
Multiple interpretations	Confusion
Increased creativity	Miscommunication
Increased flexibility	Difficulty in reaching a single agreement
Increased problem-solving skills	Difficulty in agreeing on specific actions

EXHIBIT 9-6

Source: N. J. Adler (ed.), *International Dimensions of Organizational Behavior*, 3rd ed. (Cincinnati, OH: South-Western College Publishing, 1997), p. 100. With permission of South-Western College Publishing, a division of International Thomson Publishing, Inc.

we found that the relationship between cohesiveness and group productivity was moderated by performance-related norms. We suggest that if the norms of the team are supportive of diversity, then a team can maximize the value of heterogeneity while, at the same time, achieving the benefits of high cohesiveness.[65] This makes a strong case for team members to participate in diversity training.

REINVIGORATING MATURE TEAMS

Just because a team is performing well at a given point in time is no assurance that it will continue to do so.[66] Effective teams can become stagnant. Initial enthusiasm can give way to apathy. Time can diminish the positive value from diverse perspectives as cohesiveness increases.

In terms of the five-stage development model introduced in the previous chapter, teams don't automatically stay at the "performing stage." Familiarity breeds apathy. Success can lead to complacency. And maturity brings less openness to novel ideas and innovation.

Mature teams are particularly prone to suffer from groupthink. Members begin to believe they can read everyone's mind so they assume they know what everyone is thinking. As a result, team members become reluctant to express their thoughts and less likely to challenge each other.

Another source of problems for mature teams is that their early successes are often due to having taken on easy tasks. It's normal for new teams to begin by taking on those issues and problems that they can handle most easily. But as time passes, the easy problems become solved and the team has to begin to confront more difficult issues. At this point, the team has typically developed entrenched processes and routines, and members are reluctant to change the "perfect" system they've already worked out. The results can often be disasterous. Internal team processes no longer work smoothly. Communication bogs down. Conflicts increase because problems are less likely to have obvious solutions. And team performance can drop dramatically.

What can be done to reinvigorate mature teams? We offer four suggestions: (1) *Prepare members to deal with the problems of maturity*. Remind team members that they're not unique—all successful teams have to confront maturity issues. They shouldn't feel let down or lose their confidence in the team concept when the initial euphoria subsides and conflicts surface. (2) *Offer refresher training*. When teams get into ruts, it may help to provide them with refresher training in communication, conflict resolution, team processes, and similar skills. This can help members regain confidence and trust in one another. (3) *Offer advanced training*. The skills that worked with easy problems may be insufficient for more difficult ones. So mature teams can often benefit from advanced training to help members develop stronger problem-solving, interpersonal, and technical skills. (4) *Encourage teams to treat their development as a constant learning experience*. Like TQM, teams should approach their own development as part of a search for continuous improvement. Teams should look for ways to improve, to confront member fears and frustrations, and to use conflict as a learning opportunity.

SUMMARY AND IMPLICATIONS FOR MANAGERS

Few trends have influenced employee jobs as much as the massive movement to introduce teams into the workplace. The shift from working alone to working on teams requires employees to cooperate with others, share information, confront differences, and sublimate personal interests for the greater good of the team.

Effective teams have been found to have common characteristics. The work that members do should provide freedom and autonomy, the opportunity to utilize different skills and talents, the ability to complete a whole and identifiable task or product, and doing work that has a substantial impact on others. The teams require individuals with technical expertise, as well as problem-solving, decision-making, and interpersonal skills, and high scores on the personality characteristics of extraversion, agreeableness, conscientiousness, and emotional stability. Effective teams are neither too large or too small—typically they range in size from 5 to 12 people. They have members who fill role demands, are flexible, and who prefer to be part of a group. They also have adequate resources, effective leadership, and a performance evaluation and reward system that reflects team contributions. Finally, effective teams have members committed to a common purpose, specific team goals, members who believe in the team's capabilities, a manageable level of conflict, and a minimal degree of social loafing.

Because individualistic organizations and societies attract and reward individual accomplishment, it is more difficult to create team players in these environments. To make the conversion, management should try to select individuals with the interpersonal skills to be effective team players, provide training to develop teamwork skills, and reward individuals for cooperative efforts.

Once teams are mature and performing effectively, management's job isn't over. This is because mature teams can become stagnant and complacent. Managers need to support mature teams with advice, guidance, and training if these teams are to continue to improve.

Teams Benefit Both Employees and the Organization

The value of teams is now well known. Let's summarize the primary benefits that experts agree can result from the introduction of work teams.

Increased employee motivation. Work teams enhance employee involvement. They typically make jobs more interesting. They help employees meet their social needs. They also create social pressures on slackers to exert higher levels of effort in order to remain in the team's good graces.

Higher levels of productivity. Teams have the potential to create positive synergy. In recent years, the introduction of teams in most organizations has been associated with cuts in staff. What management has done is to use the positive synergy to get the same or greater output from fewer people.

Increased employee satisfaction. Employees have a need for affiliation. Working in teams can help meet this need by increasing worker interactions and creating camaraderie among team members.

Common commitment to goals. Teams encourage individuals to sublimate their individual goals for those of the group.

Expanded job skills. The implementation of teams almost always comes with expanded job training. Through this training, employees build their technical, decision-making, and interpersonal skills.

Organizational flexibility. Teams focus on processes rather than functions. They encourage cross-training, so members can do each other's jobs, and expansion of skills. This expansion of skills increases organizational flexibility. Work can be reorganized and workers allocated, as needed, to meet changing conditions.

Teams are no panacea. Let's take a critical look at three of the assumptions that seem to underlie the team ideology.

Mature teams are task oriented and have successfully minimized the negative influences of other group forces. Task-oriented teams still experience antitask behavior, and indeed have much in common with other types of groups. For instance, they often suffer from infighting over assignments and decision outcomes, low participation rates, and member apathy.

Individual, group, and organizational goals can all be integrated into common team goals. Contrary to what team advocates assume, people are not so simply motivated by the sociability and self-actualization supposedly offered by work teams. These teams suffer from competitiveness, conflict, and hostility. Contrary to the notion that teams increase job satisfaction, the evidence suggests that individuals experience substantial and continuing stress as team members.

The team environment drives out the subversive forces of politics, power, and conflict that divert groups from efficiently doing their work. Recipes for effective teams rate them on the quality of decision making, communication, cohesion, clarity and acceptance of goals, acceptance of minority views, and other criteria. Such recipes betray the fact that teams are made up of people with self-interests who are prepared to make deals, reward favorites, punish enemies, and engage in similar behaviors to further those self-interests.

The argument here has been that the team ideology, under the banner of benefits for all, ignores that teams are frequently used to camouflage coercion under the pretense of maintaining cohesion; conceal conflict under the guise of consensus; convert conformity into a semblance of creativity; delay action in the supposed interests of consultation; legitimize lack of leadership; and disguise expedient arguments and personal agendas. Teams do not necessarily provide fulfillment of individual needs, nor do they necessarily contribute to individual satisfaction and performance or organizational effectiveness. On the contrary, it's likely that the infatuation with teams and making every employee part of a team results in organizations not getting the best performance from many of their members.

Source: Based on A. Sinclair, "The Tyranny of a Team Ideology," *Organization Studies*, vol. 13, no. 4 (1992), pp. 611–26.

1. Contrast self-managed and cross-functional teams.

2. Contrast virtual and face-to-face teams.

3. List and describe nine team roles.

4. How do effective teams minimize social loafing?

5. How do effective teams minimize groupthink?

6. List and describe the process variables associated with effective team performance.

7. Under what conditions will the challenge of creating team players be greatest?

8. What role do teams play in TQM?

9. Contrast the pros and cons of having diverse teams.

10. How can management invigorate stagnant teams?

Questions for Critical Thinking

1. Don't teams create conflict? Isn't conflict bad? Why, then, would management support the concept of teams?

2. Are there factors in the Japanese society that make teams more acceptable in the workplace than in the United States or Canada? Explain.

3. What problems might surface in teams at each stage in the five-stage group-development model?

4. How do you think member expectations might affect team performance?

5. Would you prefer to work alone or as part of a team? Why? How do you think your answer compares with others in your class?

Team Exercise | Building Effective Work Teams

Objective

This exercise is designed to allow class members to (a) experience working together as a team on a specific task and (b) analyze this experience.

Time

Teams will have 90 minutes to engage in steps 2 and 3 that follow. Another 45–60 minutes will be used in class to critique and evaluate the exercise.

Procedure

1. Class members are assigned to teams of about six people.

2. Each team is required to:
   a. Determine a team name
   b. Compose a team song

3. Each team is to try to find the following items on its scavenger hunt:
   a. A picture of a team
   b. A newspaper article about a group or team
   c. A piece of apparel with the college name or logo
   d. A set of chopsticks
   e. A ball of cotton
   f. A piece of stationery from a college department
   g. A bottle of Liquid Paper
   h. A floppy disk
   i. A cup from McDonald's
   j. A dog leash
   k. A utility bill
   l. A calendar from last year
   m. A book by Ernest Hemingway
   n. An ad brochure for a Ford product

    o. A test tube
    p. A pack of gum
    q. An ear of corn
    r. A Garth Brooks tape or CD

4. After 90 minutes, all teams are to be back in the classroom. (A penalty, determined by the instructor, will be imposed on late teams.) The team with the most items on the list will be declared the winner. The class and instructor will determine whether or not the items meet the requirements of the exercise.

5. Debriefing of the exercise will begin by having each team engage in self-evaluation. Specifically, it should answer the following:

    a. What was the team's strategy?
    b. What roles did individual members perform?
    c. How effective was the team?
    d. What could the team have done to be more effective?

6. Full class discussion will focus on issues such as:

    a. What differentiated the more effective teams from the less effective teams?
    b. What did you learn from this experience that is relevant to the design of effective teams?

Source: Adapted from M. R. Manning and P. J. Schmidt, "Building Effective Work Teams: A Quick Exercise Based on a Scavenger Hunt," *Journal of Management Education*, August 1995, pp. 392–98. With permission.

Internet Search Exercises

1. Identify three new and/or current trends in terms of team building, team facilitation, and/or team development. Why have these trends emerged? What are the benefits of the tools on which these trends are based? How easy would it be for managers to implement these new tools?

2. Find three organizations that are using virtual teams. Describe how they are using these teams and any evidence on their effectiveness.

PHLIP Companion Web Site

We invite you to visit the Robbins homepage on the Prentice Hall Web site at **www.prenhall.com/robbins** for our on-line study guide, current events, links to related Web sites, and more.

Case Incident   Tape Resources, Inc.

Tape Resources, Inc. is a small company. It employs only a dozen people and has annual sales of $4.7 million. And it's growing fast. In the most recent year, sales increased 70 percent. Headquartered in Virginia Beach, Virginia, Tape Resources sells blank videotapes and audiotapes to businesses such as television stations and production companies. Its most popular tapes—from manufacturers such as Sony, BASF, and Panasonic—carry price tags ranging from $10 to $25. The company doesn't try to compete on price. Rather, it seeks to offer superior services to its customers. These include a guaranteed in-stock program and speedy delivery.

The company's owner, Seph Barnard, recently decided to energize his six-person sales staff. He added a commission incentive on top of the sales staff's salaries. These salespeople fill orders from repeat customers as well as from new ones corralled from direct-mail campaigns and trade-magazine advertising. The program immediately sparked resentment among the

rest of his employees. "Tensions appeared in the office that we'd never had before," says Barnard. These salespeople did their work in the same offices as everyone else—working over the phone. But the salespeople now had an opportunity to make considerably more money than people in shipping and other areas. And those excluded felt resentful.

The commission system also caused problems among the sales staff. Salespeople who once cooperated with one another became reluctant to spend time away from the phones, helping out on other tasks. They didn't like it when a colleague serviced a customer they had helped earlier—thereby taking the commission. Suddenly everyone had become territorial and began looking out for number one.

Within six months, Barnard began to think he had made a mistake. All he wanted to do was increase sales. Instead, he had undermined morale and increased divisions among people and departments. Yet something happened concurrently with the implementation of the new sales commission program that made Barnard think that maybe the problem wasn't with incentives. Over a three-month period, the entire sales team worked together to win a sales contest sponsored by BASF. The award was a trip to Cancun. Ironically, the entire sales staff rallied around that goal.

Questions

1. Does Tape Resources have groups or teams? Explain.

2. Why do you think the new incentive system failed?

3. Why did the BASF promotion work?

4. If you were Barnard, what would you do now?

5. What lesson(s) do you think Barnard learned as a result of this experience?

Source: Based on "Now That We're Not a Start-Up, How Do I Promote Teamwork?" *INC.*, October 20, 1998, pp. 154–56.

| Video Case | Jim Morris Environmental Tee Shirt Company |

People generally do things, at least important things, for a reason. They may be motivated by something that they believe in, they may be motivated by a perceived opportunity, or they may be motivated by a particular need. Whatever the case, we tend to make significant personal investments in things that we believe in. Jim Morris and the employees of the Jim Morris Environmental T-Shirt Company are people on a mission. Although they all earn a living and the company seems to be profitable, running a good business does not seem to be the only thing that makes these people tick. They appear to be running a good venture, but something else is going on in this company too.

Morris trained academically as a mathematician. But when it came to earning a living, he turned to something else. He is passionate and committed to doing his part to preserve our natural environment and to protect the animals that live in it. Interestingly, he has used his talents and interests to provide a comfortable workplace for himself and others.

At first glance, you might think that this company evolves totally around Jim Morris and his commitment to protecting the environment. On closer observation, however, we find a company made up of several individuals, all of whom share some common interests. Everyone at the company is not exactly like Morris, but each, in his or her own way, is concerned about the environment.

As you watch this video segment, you will see how a personal interest turned into a job for one man, and eventually a company. Although you will see many automated processes within the company, there is more to it than just Morris and a bunch of machines and computers. Morris employs about 20 people. Some people work together, others in departments of one. Pay attention to how individuals interact, how they feel about the company, and how Jim Morris, the company's founder, talks about his staff.

Questions

1. From what you have learned about Jim Morris, identify a group outside of his company to which you think he belongs. Support your answer with information from the video segment and your knowledge of groups.

2. Identify some teams that you believe exist within the Jim Morris Environmental T-Shirt Company.

Considering what you have learned about effective teams, select a team and briefly analyze it using as many of the components of the model in Exhibit 9-4 as possible.

3. It is obvious that the people who work at the Jim Morris Environmental T-Shirt Company share many ideals and values. This is a good step toward establishing a good working team. If you were a consultant to Jim Morris, what might you suggest that he pay attention to, so he can retain a strong and efficient team?

End Notes

1. A. Dominguez, "No Bosses in Corporate Fabric," *Seattle Post-Intelligencer*, July 1, 1998, p. D1.

2. See, for example, D. Tjosvold, *Team Organization: An Enduring Competitive Advantage* (Chichester, England: Wiley, 1991); J. Lipnack and J. Stamps, *The TeamNet Factor* (Essex Junction, VT: Oliver Wight, 1993); J. R. Katzenbach and D. K. Smith, *The Wisdom of Teams* (Boston: Harvard Business School Press, 1993); and S. A. Mohrman, S. G. Cohen, and A. M. Mohrman, Jr., *Designing Team-Based Organizations* (San Francisco: Jossey-Bass, 1995).

3. K. Kelly, "The New Soul of John Deere," *Business Week*, January 31, 1994, pp. 64–66.

4. This section is based on J. R. Katzenbach and D. K. Smith, *The Wisdom of Teams*, pp. 21, 45, and 85; and D. C. Kinlaw, *Developing Superior Work Teams* (Lexington, MA: Lexington Books, 1991), pp. 3–21.

5. J. H. Shonk, *Team-Based Organizations* (Homewood, IL: Business One Irwin, 1992); and M. A. Verespej, "When Workers Get New Roles," *Industry Week*, February 3, 1992, p. 11.

6. M. L. Marks, P. H. Mirvis, E. J. Hackett, and J. F. Grady, Jr., "Employee Participation in a Quality Circle Program: Impact on Quality of Work Life, Productivity, and Absenteeism," *Journal of Applied Psychology*, February 1986, pp. 61–69; T. R. Miller, "The Quality Circle Phenomenon: A Review and Appraisal," *SAM Advanced Management Journal*, Winter 1989, pp. 4–7; and E. E. Adams, Jr., "Quality Circle Performance," *Journal of Management*, March 1991, pp. 25–39.

7. See, for example, S. G. Cohen, G. E. Ledford, Jr., and G. M. Spreitzer, "A Predictive Model of Self-Managing Work Team Effectiveness," *Human Relations*, May 1996, pp. 643–76; R. A. Guzzo and M. W. Dickson, "Teams in Organizations," in J. T. Spence, J. M. Darley, and D. J. Foss, *Annual Review of Psychology*, vol. 47 (Palo Alto, CA: Annual Reviews, 1996), pp. 324–26; D. E. Yeats and C. Hyten, *High-Performing Self-Managed Work Teams: A Comparison of Theory to Practice* (Thousand Oaks, CA: Sage, 1998); and B. L. Kirkman and B. Rosen, "Beyond Self-Management: Antecedents and Consequences of Team Empowerment," *Academy of Management Journal*, February 1999, pp. 58–74.

8. J. Hillkirk, "Self-Directed Work Teams Give TI Lift," *USA Today*, December 20, 1993, p. 8B; and M. A. Verespej,

"Worker-Managers," *Industry Week*, May 16, 1994, p. 30.

9. "Teams," *Training*, October 1996, p. 69.

10. J. Hillkirk, "Self-Directed Work Teams."

11. "A Conversation with Charles Dull," *Organizational Dynamics*, Summer 1993, pp. 57–70.

12. T. B. Kirker, "Edy's Grand Ice Cream," *Industry Week*, October 18, 1993, pp. 29–32.

13. R. Zemke, "Rethinking the Rush to Team Up," *Training*, November 1993, pp. 55–61.

14. See, for instance, T. D. Wall, N. J. Kemp, P. R. Jackson, and C. W. Clegg, "Outcomes of Autonomous Workgroups: A Long-Term Field Experiment," *Academy of Management Journal*, June 1986, pp. 280–304; and J. L. Cordery, W.S. Mueller, and L. M. Smith, "Attitudinal and Behavioral Effects of Autonomous Group Working: A Longitudinal Field Study," *Academy of Management Journal*, June 1991, pp. 464–76.

15. J. R. Barker, "Tightening the Iron Cage: Concertive Control in Self-Managing Teams," *Administrative Science Quarterly*, September 1993, pp. 408–37; S. G. Cohen and G. E. Ledford Jr., "The Effectiveness of Self-Managing Teams: A Field Experiment, *Human Relations*, January 1994, pp. 13–43; and C. Smith and D. Comer, "Self-Organization in Small Groups: A Study of Group Effectiveness Within Non-Equilibrium Conditions," *Human Relations*, May 1994, pp. 553–81.

16. See J. Lipnack and J. Stamps, *The TeamNet Factor*, pp. 14–17; G. Taninecz, "Team Players," *Industry Week*, July 15, 1996, pp. 28–32; and D. R. Denison, S. L. Hart, and J. A. Kahn, "From Chimneys to Cross-Functional Teams: Developing and Validating a Diagnostic Model," *Academy of Management Journal*, August 1996, pp. 1005–23.

17. S. Carey, "US Air 'Peon' Team Pilots Start-Up of Low-Fare Airline," *Wall Street Journal*, March 24, 1998, p. B1.

18. D. Woodruff, "Chrysler's Neon: Is This the Small Car Detroit Couldn't Build?" *Business Week*, May 3, 1993, pp. 116–26.

19. T. B. Kinni, "Boundary-Busting Teamwork," *Industry Week*, March 21, 1994, pp. 72–78.

20. "Cross-Functional Obstacles," *Training*, May 1994, pp. 125–26.

21. See, for example, M. E. Warkentin, L. Sayeed, and R. Hightower, "Virtual Teams Versus Face-to-Face Teams: An Ex-

ploratory Study of a Web-Based Conference System," *Decision Sciences*, Fall 1997, pp. 975–93; A. M. Townsend, S. M. DeMarie, and A. R. Hendrickson, "Virtual Teams: Technology and the Workplace of the Future," *Academy of Management Executive*, August 1998, pp. 17–29; and D. Duarte and N. T. Snyder, *Mastering Virtual Teams: Strategies, Tools, and Techniques* (San Francisco: Jossey-Bass, 1999).

22. K. Kiser, "Working on World Time," *Training*, March 1999, p. 30.

23. A. B. Drexler and R. Forrester, "Teamwork—Not Necessarily the Answer," *HRMagazine*, January 1998, pp. 55–58.

24. See, for instance, D. L. Gladstein, "Groups in Context: A Model of Task Group Effectiveness," *Administrative Science Quarterly*, December 1984, pp. 499–517; J. R. Hackman, "The Design of Work Teams," in J. W. Lorsch (ed.), *Handbook of Organizational Behavior* (Upper Saddle River, NJ: Prentice Hall, 1987), pp. 315–42; M. A. Campion, G. J. Medsker, and C. A. Higgs, "Relations Between Work Group Characteristics and Effectiveness: Implications for Designing Effective Work Groups," *Personnel Psychology*, Winter 1993, pp. 823–50; and R. A. Guzzo and M. W. Dickson, "Teams in Organizations: Recent Research on Performance and Effectiveness," in J. T. Spence, J. M. Darley, and D. J. Foss, *Annual Review of Psychology*, vol. 47, pp. 307–38.

25. D. E. Hyatt and T. M. Ruddy, "An Examination of the Relationship Between Work Group Characteristics and Performance: Once More into the Breech," *Personnel Psychology*, Autumn 1997, p. 555.

26. This model is based on M. A. Campion, E. M. Papper, and G. J. Medsker, "Relations Between Work Team Characteristics and Effectiveness: A Replication and Extension," *Personnel Psychology*, Summer 1996, pp. 429–52; D. E. Hyatt and T. M. Ruddy, "An Examination of the Relationship Between Work Group Characteristics and Performance," pp. 553–85; and S. G. Cohen and D. E. Bailey, "What Makes Teams Work: Group Effectiveness Research from the Shop Floor to the Executive Suite," *Journal of Management*, vol. 23, no. 3 (1997), pp. 239–90.

27. R. Wageman, "Critical Success Factors for Creating Superb Self-Managing Teams," *Organizational Dynamics*, Summer 1997, p. 55.

28. M. A. Campion, E. M. Papper, and G. J. Medsker, "Relations Between Work Team Characteristics and Effectiveness," p. 430.

29. Ibid.

30. For a more detailed breakdown on team skills, see M. J. Stevens and M. A. Campion, "The Knowledge, Skill, and Ability Requirements for Teamwork: Implications for Human Resource Management," *Journal of Management*, Summer 1994, pp. 503–30.

31. M. R. Barrick, G. L. Stewart, M. J. Neubert, and M. K. Mount, "Relating Member Ability and Personality to Work-Team Processes and Team Effectiveness," *Journal of Applied Psychology*, June 1998, pp. 377–91.

32. Ibid.

33. Ibid., p. 388.

34. Ibid.

35. C. Margerison and D. McCann, *Team Management: Practical New Approaches* (London: Mercury Books, 1990).

36. V. F. Nieva, E. A. Fleishman, and A. Reick, *Team Dimensions: Their Identity, Their Measurement, and Their Relationships* (Research Note 85-12). Washington, D.C: U.S.

Army, Research Institute for the Behavioral and Social Sciences, 1985.

37. E. Sundstrom, K. P. Meuse, and D. Futrell, "Work Teams: Applications and Effectiveness," *American Psychologist*, February 1990, pp. 120–33.

38. D. E. Hyatt and T. M. Ruddy, "An Examination of the Relationship Between Work Group Characteristics and Performance."

39. Ibid., p. 577.

40. R. I. Beekun, "Assessing the Effectiveness of Sociotechnical Interventions: Antidote or Fad?" *Human Relations*, August 1989, pp. 877–97.

41. S. G. Cohen, G. E. Ledford, and G. M. Spreitzer, "A Predictive Model of Self-Managing Work Team Effectiveness."

42. D. Eden, "Pygmalion Without Interpersonal Contrast Effects: Whole Groups Gain From Raising Manager Expectations," *Journal of Applied Psychology*, August 1990, pp. 394–98.

43. J. M. George and K. Bettenhausen, "Understanding Prosocial Behavior, Sales, Performance, and Turnover: A Group-Level Analysis in a Service Context," *Journal of Applied Psychology*, October 1990, pp. 698–709; and J. M. George, "Leader Positive Mood and Group Performance: The Case of Customer Service," *Journal of Applied Social Psychology*, December 1995, pp. 778–94.

44. See S. T. Johnson, "Work Teams: What's Ahead in Work Design and Rewards Management," *Compensation & Benefits Review*, March–April 1993, pp. 35–41; A. M. Saunier and E. J. Hawk, "Realizing the Potential of Teams Through Team-Based Rewards," *Compensation & Benefits Review*, July–August 1994, pp. 24–33; and R. Wageman, "Interdependence and Group Effectiveness," *Administrative Science Quarterly*, March 1995, pp. 145–80.

45. K. Hess, *Creating the High-Performance Team* (New York: Wiley, 1987); J. R. Katzenbach and D. K. Smith, *The Wisdom of Teams*, pp. 43–64; and K. D. Scott and A. Townsend, "Teams: Why Some Succeed and Others Fail," *HRMagazine*, August 1994, pp. 62–67.

46. E. Weldon and L. R. Weingart, "Group Goals and Group Performance," *British Journal of Social Psychology*, Spring 1993, pp. 307–34.

47. R. A. Guzzo, P. R. Yost, R. J. Campbell, and G. P. Shea, "Potency in Groups: Articulating a Construct," *British Journal of Social Psychology*, March 1993, pp. 87–106; S. J. Zaccaro, V. Blair, C. Peterson, and M. Zazanis, "Collective Efficacy," in J. E. Maddux (ed.), *Self-Efficacy, Adaptation and Adjustment: Theory, Research and Application* (New York: Plenum, 1995), pp. 308–30; and D. L. Feltz and C. D. Lirgg, "Perceived Team and Player Efficacy in Hockey," *Journal of Applied Psychology*, August 1998, pp. 557–64.

48. K. Jehn, "A Multimethod Examination of the Benefits and Detriments of Intragroup Conflict," *Administrative Science Quarterly*, June 1995, pp. 256–82.

49. K. Hess, *Creating the High-Performance Team*.

50. See, for instance, B. L. Kirkman and D. L. Shapiro, "The Impact of Cultural Values on Employee Resistance to Teams: Toward a Model of Globalized Self-Managing Work Team Effectiveness," *Academy of Management Review*, July 1997, pp. 730–57.

51. D. Harrington-Mackin, *The Team Building Tool Kit* (New York: AMACOM, 1994), p. 53.

52. T. D. Schellhardt, "To Be a Star Among Equals, Be a Team Player," *Wall Street Journal*, April 20, 1994, p. B1.

53. Ibid.

54. See, for instance, J. Prieto, "The Team Perspective in Selection and Assessment," in H. Schuler, J. L. Farr, and M. Smith (eds.), *Personnel Selection and Assessment: Industrial and Organizational Perspectives* (Hillsdale, NJ: Erlbaum, 1994); and R. Klimoski and R. G. Jones, "Staffing for Effective Group Decision Making: Key Issues in Matching People and Teams," in R. A. Guzzo and E. Salas (eds.), *Team Effectiveness and Decision Making in Organizations* (San Francisco: Jossey-Bass, 1995), pp. 307–26.

55. T. D. Schellhardt, "To Be a Star Among Equals, Be a Team Player."

56. "Teaming Up for Success," *Training*, January 1994, p. S41.

57. J. S. DeMatteo, L. T. Eby, and E. Sundstrom, "Team-Based Rewards: Current Empirical Evidence and Directions for Future Research," in B. M. Staw and L. L. Cummings (eds.), *Research in Organizational Behavior*, vol. 20 (Greenwich, CT: JAI Press, 1998), pp. 141–83.

58. B. Geber, "The Bugaboo of Team Pay," *Training*, August 1995, pp. 27 and 34.

59. D. C. Kinlaw, *Developing Superior Work Teams*, p. 43.

60. B. Krone, "Total Quality Management: An American Odyssey," *The Bureaucrat*, Fall 1990, p. 37.

61. *Profiles in Quality: Blueprints for Action from 50 Leading Companies* (Boston: Allyn & Bacon, 1991), pp. 71–72 and 76–77.

62. See the review of the literature in S. E. Jackson, V. K. Stone, and E. B. Alvarez, "Socialization Amidst Diversity: The Impact of Demographics on Work Team Oldtimers and Newcomers," in L. L. Cummings and B. M. Staw (eds.), *Research in Organizational Behavior*, vol. 15 (Greenwich, CT: JAI Press, 1993), p. 64.

63. R. M. Stogdill, "Group Productivity, Drive, and Cohesiveness," *Organizational Behavior and Human Performance*, February 1972, pp. 36–43. See also M. Mayo, J. C. Pastor, and J. R. Meindl, "The Effects of Group Heterogeneity on the Self-Perceived Efficacy of Group Leaders," *Leadership Quarterly*, Summer 1996, pp. 265–84.

64. J. E. McGrath, *Groups: Interaction and Performance* (Upper Saddle River, NJ: Prentice Hall, 1984).

65. This idea is proposed in S. E. Jackson, V. K. Stone, and E. B. Alvarez, "Socialization Amidst Diversity," p. 68.

66. This section is based on M. Kaeter, "Replotting Mature Work Teams," *Training*, April 1994 (Supplement), pp. 4–6.

*I didn't say that I didn't say it.
I said that I didn't say that I said it.
I want to make that very clear.*

—**G. Romney**

Can the misunderstanding of a few words literally mean the difference between life and death? They can in the airline business. A number of aviation disasters have been largely attributed to problems in communication.[1] Consider the following:

History's worst aviation disaster occurred in 1977 at foggy Tenerife in the Canary Islands. The captain of a KLM flight thought the air traffic controller had cleared him to take off. But the controller intended only to give departure instructions. Although the language spoken between the Dutch KLM captain and the Spanish controller was English, confusion was created by heavy accents and improper terminology. The KLM Boeing 747 hit a Pan Am 747 at full throttle on the runway, killing 583 people.

In 1990, Colombian Avianca pilots, after several holding patterns caused by bad weather, told controllers as they neared New York Kennedy Airport that their Boeing 707 was "running low on fuel." Controllers hear those words all the time, so they took no special action. While the pilots knew there was a serious problem, they failed to use a key phrase—"fuel emergency"—which would have obligated controllers to direct the Avianca flight ahead of all others and clear it to land as soon as possible. The people at Kennedy never understood the true nature of the pilots' problem. The jet ran out of fuel and crashed 16 miles from Kennedy. Seventy-three people died.

In 1993, Chinese pilots flying a U.S.-built MD-80 tried to land in heavy fog at Urumqi, in northwest China. They were baffled by an audio alarm from the jet's ground proximity warning system. Just before impact, the cockpit recorder picked up one crew member saying to the other

Communication

in Chinese: "What does 'pull up' mean?" The plane hit power lines and crashed, killing 12.

On December 20, 1995, American Airlines Flight 965 was approaching the Cali, Colombia, airport. The pilot expected to hear either the words "cleared as filed" (meaning follow the flight plan filed before leaving Miami) or "cleared direct" (meaning fly straight from where you are to Cali, a slightly different route from the flight plan). But the pilot heard neither. The controller intended to clear him "as filed" but said "cleared to Cali." The pilot interpreted that as a direct clearance. When he checked back, the controller said "affirmative." Both were obviously confused. The plane crashed, killing 160 people.

In November 1996, there was a mid-air collision near New Delhi of a Saudia 747 and a Kazakhstan Airlines cargo plane. Investigators placed blame for the collision on poor communications between the Kazakh pilot and the Indian air-traffic controller. The crash killed 349 people.

In September 1997, a Garuda Airlines jetliner crashed into a jungle, just 20 miles south of the Medan Airport on the island of Sumatra. All 234 aboard were killed. The cause of this disaster was the pilot and the air traffic controller confusing the words "left" and "right" as the plane approached the airport under poor visibility conditions.

AFTER READING THIS CHAPTER, YOU SHOULD BE ABLE TO

1. Describe the communication process

2. List common barriers to effective communication

3. Identify factors affecting the use of the grapevine

4. Contrast the meaning of talk for men versus women

5. Discuss how technology is changing organizational communication

6. Describe potential problems in cross-cultural communication

7. List behaviors related to effective active listening

The preceding examples tragically illustrate how miscommunication can have deadly consequences. In this chapter, we'll show (obviously not in as dramatic a fashion) that good communication is essential to any group's or organization's effectiveness.

Research indicates that poor communication is probably the most frequently cited source of interpersonal conflict.[2] Because individuals spend nearly 70 percent of their waking hours com-

HELLO...? Companies claim they are improving communications with employees in this jittery era of downsizings. But a recent survey shows that they're not doing such a great job.

EMPLOYEES POLLED SAY THEY:

DON'T BELIEVE WHAT MANAGEMENT SAYS	AREN'T WELL-INFORMED OF COMPANY PLANS	DON'T GET DECISIONS EXPLAINED WELL
64%	61%	54%

DATA: COUNCIL OF COMMUNICATION MANAGEMENT: SURVEY OF 705 EMPLOYEES AT 70 COMPANIES

Source: *Business Week*, May 16, 1994, p. 8. Reprinted by special permission. Copyright © 1994 by McGraw-Hill, Inc.

municating—writing, reading, speaking, listening—it seems reasonable to conclude that one of the most inhibiting forces to successful group performance is a lack of effective communication. (See Exhibit 10-1.)

No group can exist without communication: the transference of meaning among its members. It is only through transmitting meaning from one person to another that information and ideas can be conveyed. Communication, however, is more than merely imparting meaning. It must also be understood. In a group in which one member speaks only German and the others do not know German, the individual speaking German will not be fully understood. Therefore, **communication** must include both the *transference and the understanding of meaning*.

An idea, no matter how great, is useless until it is transmitted and understood by others. Perfect communication, if there were such a thing, would exist when a thought or an idea was transmitted so that the mental picture perceived by the receiver was exactly the same as that envisioned by the sender. Although elementary in theory, perfect communication is never achieved in practice, for reasons we shall expand upon later.

Before making too many generalizations concerning communication and problems in communicating effectively, we need to review briefly the functions that communication performs and describe the communication process.

communication

The transference and understanding of meaning.

FUNCTIONS OF COMMUNICATION

Communication serves four major functions within a group or organization: control, motivation, emotional expression, and information.[3]

Communication acts to *control* member behavior in several ways. Organizations have authority hierarchies and formal guidelines that employees are required to follow. When employees, for instance, are required to first communicate any job-related grievance to their immediate boss, to follow their job description, or to comply with company policies, communication is performing a control function. But informal communication also controls behavior. When work groups tease or harass a member who produces too much (and makes the rest of the group look bad), they are informally communicating with, and controlling, the member's behavior.

Communication fosters *motivation* by clarifying to employees what is to be done, how well they are doing, and what can be done to improve performance if it's subpar. We saw this operating in our review of goal-setting and reinforcement theories in Chapter 6. The formation of specific goals, feedback on progress toward the goals, and reinforcement of desired behavior all stimulate motivation and require communication.

For many employees, their work group is a primary source for social interaction. The communication that takes place within the group is a fundamental mechanism by which members show their frustrations and feelings of satisfaction. Communication, therefore, provides a release for the *emotional expression* of feelings and for fulfillment of social needs.

The final function that communication performs relates to its role in facilitating decision making. It provides the *information* that individuals and groups need to make decisions by transmitting the data to identify and evaluate alternative choices.

No one of these four functions should be seen as being more important than the others. For groups to perform effectively, they need to maintain some form of control over members, stimulate members to perform, provide a means for emotional expression, and make decision choices. You can assume that almost every communication interaction that takes place in a group or organization performs one or more of these four functions.

THE COMMUNICATION PROCESS

Communication can be thought of as a process or flow. Communication problems occur when there are deviations or blockages in that flow. In this section, we describe the process in terms of a communication model, consider how distortions can disrupt the process, and introduce the concept of communication apprehension as another potential disruption.

A COMMUNICATION MODEL

Before communication can take place, a purpose, expressed as a message to be conveyed, is needed. It passes between a source (the sender) and a receiver. The message is encoded (converted to symbolic form) and is passed by way of some medium (channel) to the receiver, who retranslates (decodes) the message initiated by the sender. The result is a transference of meaning from one person to another.[4]

Exhibit 10-2 depicts the **communication process**. This model is made up of seven parts: (1) the communication source, (2) encoding, (3) the message, (4) the channel, (5) decoding, (6) the receiver, and (7) feedback.

The source initiates a message by **encoding** a thought. Four conditions have been described that affect the encoded message: skill, attitudes, knowledge, and the social-cultural system.

communication process
The steps between a source and a receiver that result in the transference and understanding of meaning.

encoding
Converting a communication message to symbolic form.

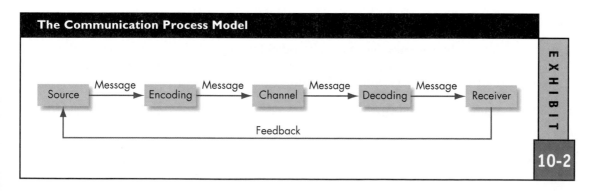

The Communication Process Model

EXHIBIT 10-2

Source → Message → Encoding → Message → Channel → Message → Decoding → Message → Receiver

Feedback

My success in communicating to you depends on my writing skills; if the authors of textbooks are without the requisite writing skills, their messages will not reach students in the form desired. One's total communicative success includes speaking, reading, listening, and reasoning skills as well. As we discussed in Chapter 3, our attitudes influence our behavior. We hold predisposed ideas on numerous topics, and our communications are affected by these attitudes. Furthermore, we are restricted in our communicative activity by the extent of our knowledge of the particular topic. We cannot communicate what we don't know, and should our knowledge be too extensive, it's possible that our receiver will not understand our message. Clearly, the amount of knowledge the source holds about his or her subject will affect the message he or she seeks to transfer. And, finally, just as attitudes influence our behavior, so does our position in the social-cultural system in which we exist. Your beliefs and values, all part of your culture, act to influence you as a communicative source.

message

What is communicated.

The **message** is the actual physical product from the source encoding. "When we speak, the speech is the message. When we write, the writing is the message. When we paint, the picture is the message. When we gesture, the movements of our arms, the expressions on our face are the message."[5] Our message is affected by the code or group of symbols we use to transfer meaning, the content of the message itself, and the decisions that we make in selecting and arranging both codes and content.

channel

The medium through which a communication message travels.

The **channel** is the medium through which the message travels. It is selected by the source, who must determine which channel is formal and which one is informal. Formal channels are established by the organization and transmit messages that pertain to the job-related activities of members. They traditionally follow the authority network within the organization. Other forms of messages, such as personal or social, follow the informal channels in the organization.

decoding

Retranslating a sender's communication message.

The receiver is the object to whom the message is directed. But before the message can be received, the symbols in it must be translated into a form that can be understood by the receiver. This is the **decoding** of the message. Just as the encoder was limited by his or her skills, attitudes, knowledge, and social-cultural system, the receiver is equally restricted. Just as the source must be skillful in writing or speaking, the receiver must be skillful in reading or listening, and both must be able to reason. One's knowledge, attitudes, and cultural background influence one's ability to receive, just as they do the ability to send.

feedback loop

The final link in the communication process; puts the message back into the system as a check against misunderstandings.

The final link in the communication process is a **feedback loop**. "If a communication source decodes the message that he encodes, if the message is put back into his system, we have feedback."[6] Feedback is the check on how successful we have been in transferring our messages as originally intended. It determines whether or not understanding has been achieved.

BARRIERS TO EFFECTIVE COMMUNICATION

There are a number of interpersonal and intrapersonal barriers that help to explain why the message that is decoded by a receiver is often different than that which the sender intended. The following reviews some of the more prominent barriers to effective communication.

filtering

A sender's manipulation of information so that it will be seen more favorably by the receiver.

Filtering **Filtering** refers to a sender manipulating information so that it will be seen more favorably by the receiver. For example, when a manager tells his boss what he feels his boss wants to hear, he is filtering information. Does this happen much in organizations? Sure! As information is passed up to senior executives, it has to be condensed and synthesized by underlings so those on top don't become overloaded with information. The personal interests and perceptions of what is important by those doing the synthesizing are going to result in filtering. As a former group vice president of General Motors described it, the filtering of communications through levels at GM made it impossible for senior managers to get objective information because "lower-level specialists provided information in such a way that they would get the answer they wanted. I know. I used to be down below and do it."[7]

Filtering is most likely to occur in organizations in which there is emphasis on status differences and among employees with strong career mobility aspirations.[8] Additionally, large organizations, because they typically have more vertical levels, create more opportunities for filtering to occur. So expect to see more filtering taking place in large corporations than in small business firms.

Selective Perception   We have mentioned selective perception before in this book. It appears again because the receivers in the communication process selectively see and hear based on their needs, motivations, experience, background, and other personal characteristics. Receivers also project their interests and expectations into communications as they decode them. The employment interviewer who expects a female job applicant to put her family ahead of her career is likely to see that in female applicants, regardless of whether the applicants feel that way or not. As we said in Chapter 5, we don't see reality; rather, we interpret what we see and call it reality.

Information Overload   Individuals have a finite capacity for processing data. For instance, research indicates that most of us have difficulty working with more than about seven pieces of information.[9] When the information we have to work with exceeds our processing capacity, the result is **information overload**.

Today's typical executive frequently complains of information overload. The demands of keeping up with e-mail, phone calls, faxes, meetings, and professional reading create an onslaught of data that is nearly impossible to process and assimilate.

What happens when individuals have more information than they can sort out and use? They tend to select out, ignore, pass over, or forget information. Or they may put off further processing until the overload situation is over. Regardless, the result is lost information and less effective communication.

Defensiveness   When people feel that they're being threatened, they tend to react in ways that reduce their ability to achieve mutual understanding. That is, they become defensive—engaging in behaviors such as verbally attacking others, making sarcastic remarks, being overly judgmental, and questioning others' motives.[10] So when individuals interpret another's message as threatening, they often respond in ways that retard effective communication.

Language   Words mean different things to different people. "The meanings of words are not in the words; they are in us."[11] Age, education, and cultural background are three of the more obvious variables that influence the language a person uses and the definitions he or she gives to words. Rap-artist Snoop Doggy Dogg and columnist George F. Will both speak English. But the language each uses is vastly different from the other. In fact, the typical "person on the street"

Selective perception worked against C. Richard Cowan (in photo), founder and president of Power Lift, a distributor of fork lift trucks. After a year in business, Cowan bought a competitor, where most employees had worked at least 15 years. Perceiving their new boss as young and inexperienced, 40 of the 200 employees quit their jobs, which caused rumors that Power Lift had financial problems. Cowan blamed the situation on poor communication, admitting that he should have met with his new employees to reassure them of the importance of their roles at Power Lift and of the firm's financial soundness. Now Cowan has made communication his top priority, talking personally with each employee to learn about his or her concerns.

information overload

A condition when information inflow exceeds an individual's processing capacity.

might have difficulty understanding both of these individuals' vocabulary. As a case in point, do you have any idea what George Will meant when he recently described Thomas Jefferson's defense of the French Revolution as: "It is meretricious to treat an epistolary extravagance as an index of implacable conviction"?[12]

In an organization, employees usually come from diverse backgrounds and, therefore, have different patterns of speech. Additionally, the grouping of employees into departments creates specialists who develop their own **jargon** or technical language. In large organizations, members are also frequently widely dispersed geographically—even operating in different countries—and individuals in each locale will use terms and phrases that are unique to their area. And the existence of vertical levels can also cause language problems. The language of senior executives, for instance, can be mystifying to operative employees not familiar with management jargon.

The point is that while you and I speak a common language—English—our usage of that language is far from uniform. If we knew how each of us modified the language, communication difficulties would be minimized. The problem is that members in an organization usually don't know how others with whom they interact have modified the language. Senders tend to assume that the words and terms they use mean the same to the receiver as they do to them. This, of course, is often incorrect, thus creating communication difficulties.

COMMUNICATION APPREHENSION

Another major roadblock to effective communication is that some people—an estimated 5 to 20 percent of the population[13]—suffer from debilitating **communication apprehension** or anxiety. Although lots of people dread speaking in front of a group, communication apprehension is a more serious problem because it affects a whole category of communication techniques. People who suffer from it experience undue tension and anxiety in oral communication, written communication, or both.[14] For example, oral apprehensives may find it extremely difficult to talk with others face-to-face or become extremely anxious when they have

jargon

Specialized terminology or technical language that members of a group use to aid communication among themselves.

communication apprehension

Undue tension and anxiety about oral communication, written communication, or both.

"It's Not What You *Say*, It's What You *Do*"

This statement is mostly true. Actions DO speak louder than words.[15] When faced with inconsistencies between words and actions, people tend to give greater credence to actions. It's behavior that counts! The implications of this is that managers and leaders are role models. Employees will imitate their behaviors and attitudes. They will, for example, watch what their boss does and then imitate or adapt what they do. This conclusion doesn't mean that words fall on deaf ears. Words can influence others.[16] But when words and actions diverge, people focus most on what they see in terms of behavior.

There is an obvious exception to the previous conclusion. An increasing number of leaders (and

their associates) have developed the skill of shaping words and putting the proper "spin" on situations so that others focus on the leader's words rather than the behavior. Successful politicians seem particularly adept at this skill. Why people believe these spins when faced with conflicting behavioral evidence is not clear. Do we want to believe that our leaders would not lie to us? Do we want to believe what politicians say, especially when we hold them in high regard? Do we give high-status people, for whom we've previously given our vote, the benefit of the doubt when confronted with their negative behavior? Additional research is necessary to clarify these questions.

---

to use the telephone. As a result, they may rely on memos or faxes to convey messages when a phone call would not only be faster but more appropriate.

Studies demonstrate that oral-communication apprehensives avoid situations that require them to engage in oral communication.[17] We should expect to find some self-selection in jobs so that such individuals don't take positions, such as teacher, in which oral communication is a dominant requirement.[18] But almost all jobs require some oral communication. And of greater concern is the evidence that high-oral-communication apprehensives distort the communication demands of their jobs in order to minimize the need for communication.[19] So we need to be aware that there is a set of people in organizations who severely limit their oral communication and rationalize this practice by telling themselves that more communication isn't necessary for them to do their job effectively.

COMMUNICATION FUNDAMENTALS

A working knowledge of communication requires a basic understanding of some fundamental concepts. In this section, we review those concepts. Specifically, we look at the flow patterns of communication, compare formal and informal communication networks, describe the importance of nonverbal communication, and consider how individuals select communication channels.

DIRECTION OF COMMUNICATION

Communication can flow vertically or laterally. The vertical dimension can be further divided into downward and upward directions.[20]

Downward Communication that flows from one level of a group or organization to a lower level is a downward communication.

When we think of managers communicating with employees, the downward pattern is the one we usually think of. It is used by group leaders and managers to assign goals, provide job instructions, inform underlings of policies and procedures, point out problems that need attention, and offer feedback about performance. But downward communication doesn't have to be oral or face-to-face contact. When management sends letters to employees' homes to advise them of the organization's new sick leave policy, it is using downward communication.

Upward Upward communication flows to a higher level in the group or organization. It is used to provide feedback to higher-ups, inform them of progress toward goals, and relay current problems. Upward communication keeps managers aware of how employees feel about their jobs, co-workers, and the organization in general. Managers also rely on upward communication for ideas on how things can be improved.

After G. Richard Thoman became the new chief executive of Xerox, he filmed an in-house video to communicate his vision to the company's 87,000 employees. Thoman's downward communication informed employees about his plans and strategies for accelerating the company's transition to digital technology.

Some organizational examples of upward communication are performance reports prepared by lower management for review by middle and top management, suggestion boxes, employee attitude surveys, grievance procedures, manager–employee discussions, and informal "gripe" sessions in which employees have the opportunity to identify and discuss problems with their boss or representatives of higher management.

For example, at the 3M Co., all employees complete a communication survey at least once a year. They are asked if they are receiving the information needed, and they rate the quality of communication from management.[21]

Lateral When communication takes place among members of the same work group, among members of work groups at the same level, among managers at the same level, or among any horizontally equivalent personnel, we describe it as lateral communications.

Why would there be a need for horizontal communications if a group or organization's vertical communications are effective? The answer is that horizontal communications are often necessary to save time and facilitate coordination. In some cases, these lateral relationships are formally sanctioned. Often, they are informally created to short-circuit the vertical hierarchy and expedite action. So lateral communications can, from management's viewpoint, be good or bad. Since strict adherence to the formal vertical structure for all communications can impede the efficient and accurate transfer of information, lateral communications can be beneficial. In such cases, they occur with the knowledge and support of superiors. But they can create dysfunctional conflicts when the formal vertical channels are breached, when members go above or around their superiors to get things done, or when bosses find out that actions have been taken or decisions made without their knowledge.

Canon, a Japanese manufacturer of office equipment and cameras, relies on lateral communication to train employees. Canon has production workers from its "mother plants" in Japan train other production workers at Canon's plants outside of Japan. At Canon's factory in Oita, Japan, assembly workers teach employees from the firm's manufacturing subsidiary in Malaysia how to assemble the Canon Elph, a new compact camera. After six weeks of training, the Malaysian women returned to their country and taught what they learned to their co-workers at Canon's Malaysian plant.

FORMAL VS. INFORMAL NETWORKS

communication networks

Channels by which information flows.

formal networks

Task-related communications that follow the authority chain.

informal network

The communication grapevine.

Communication networks define the channels by which information flows. These channels are one of two varieties—either formal or informal. **Formal networks** are typically vertical, follow the authority chain, and are limited to task-related communications. In contrast, the **informal network**—usually better known as the grapevine—is free to move in any direction, skip authority levels, and is as likely to satisfy group members' social needs as it is to facilitate task accomplishments.

Formal Small-Group Networks Exhibit 10-3 illustrates three common small-group networks. These are the chain, wheel, and all channel. The chain rigidly follows the formal chain of command. The wheel relies on the leader to act as the central conduit for all the group's communication. The all-channel network permits all group members to actively communicate with each other.

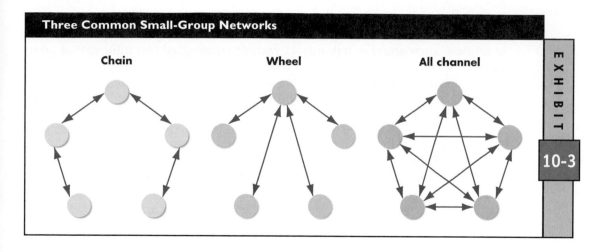

Three Common Small-Group Networks

Chain   Wheel   All channel

EXHIBIT 10-3

As Exhibit 10–4 demonstrates, the effectiveness of each network depends on the dependent variable you are concerned about. For instance, the structure of the wheel facilitates the emergence of a leader, the all-channel network is best if you are concerned with having high member satisfaction, and the chain is best if accuracy is most important. Exhibit 10-4 leads us to the conclusion that no single network will be best for all occasions.

The Informal Network   The previous discussion of networks emphasized formal communication patterns, but the formal system is not the only communication system in a group or between groups. Now let's turn our attention to the **grapevine**—the organization's *informal* communication network.

Is the grapevine important as a source for information? Absolutely. For instance, a recent survey found that 75 percent of employees hear about matters first through rumors on the grapevine.[22]

The grapevine has three main characteristics.[23] First, it is not controlled by management. Second, it is perceived by most employees as being more believable and reliable than formal communiques issued by top management. Third, it is largely used to serve the self-interests of those people within it.

One of the most famous studies of the grapevine investigated the communication pattern among 67 managerial personnel in a small manufacturing firm.[24] The basic approach used was to learn from each communication recipient how he or she first received a given piece of information and then trace it back to its source. It was found that, while the grapevine was an important source of information, only 10 percent of the executives acted as liaison individuals, that is,

grapevine

The organization's informal communication network.

Small-Group Networks and Effectiveness Criteria

	Networks		
Criteria	Chain	Wheel	All Channel
Speed	Moderate	Fast	Fast
Accuracy	High	High	Moderate
Emergence of a leader	Moderate	High	None
Member satisfaction	Moderate	Low	High

EXHIBIT 10-4

passed the information on to more than one other person. For example, when one executive decided to resign to enter the insurance business, 81 percent of the executives knew about it, but only 11 percent transmitted this information on to others.

Two other conclusions from this study are also worth noting. Information on events of general interest tended to flow between the major functional groups (e.g. production, sales) rather than within them. Also, no evidence surfaced to suggest that members of any one group consistently acted as liaisons; rather, different types of information passed through different liaison persons.

An attempt to replicate this study among employees in a small state government office also found that only a small percentage (10 percent) acted as liaison individuals.[25] This is interesting, since the replication contained a wider spectrum of employees—including rank-and-file as well as managerial personnel. However, the flow of information in the government office took place within, rather than between, functional groups. It was proposed that this discrepancy might be due to comparing an executive-only sample against one that also included rank-and-file workers. Managers, for example, might feel greater pressure to stay informed and, thus, cultivate others outside their immediate functional group. Also, in contrast to the findings of the original study, the replication found that a consistent group of individuals acted as liaisons by transmitting information in the government office.

Is the information that flows along the grapevine accurate? The evidence indicates that about 75 percent of what is carried is accurate.[26] But what conditions foster an active grapevine? What gets the rumor mill rolling?

It is frequently assumed that rumors start because they make titillating gossip. Such is rarely the case. Rumors have at least four purposes: to structure and reduce anxiety; to make sense of limited or fragmented information; to serve as a vehicle to organize group members, and possibly outsiders, into coalitions; and to signal a sender's status ("I'm an insider and, with respect to this rumor, you're an outsider") or power ("I have the power to make you into an insider").[27] Research indicates that rumors emerge as a response to situations that are important to us, in which there is ambiguity, and under conditions that arouse anxiety.[28] Work situations frequently contain these three elements, which explains why rumors flourish in organizations. The secrecy and competition that typically prevail in large organizations—around such issues as the appointment of new bosses, the relocation of offices, and the realignment of work assignments—create conditions that encourage and sustain rumors on the grapevine. A rumor will persist either until the wants and expectations creating the uncertainty underlying the rumor are fulfilled or until the anxiety is reduced.

What can we conclude from this discussion? Certainly, the grapevine is an important part of any group or organization's communication network and well worth understanding.[29] It identifies for managers those confusing issues that employees consider important and anxiety provoking. It acts, therefore, as both a filter and a feedback mechanism, picking up the issues that employees consider relevant. Perhaps more important, again from a managerial point of view, it seems possible to analyze grapevine information and to predict its flow, given that only a small set of individuals (around 10 percent) actively passes on information to more than one other person. By assessing which liaison individuals will consider a given piece of information to be relevant, we can improve our ability to explain and predict the pattern of the grapevine.

Can management entirely eliminate rumors? No! What management should do, however, is minimize the negative consequences of rumors by limiting their

Source: Adapted from L. Hirschhorn, "Managing Rumors," in L. Hirschhorn (ed.), *Cutting Back* (San Francisco: Jossey-Bass, 1983), pp. 54–56. With permission.

range and impact. Exhibit 10-5 offers a few suggestions for minimizing those negative consequences.

NONVERBAL COMMUNICATIONS

Anyone who has ever paid a visit to a singles bar or a nightclub is aware that communication need not be verbal in order to convey a message. A glance, a stare, a smile, a frown, a provocative body movement—they all convey meaning. This example illustrates that no discussion of communication would be complete without a discussion of **nonverbal communications**. This includes body language and paralinguistics. Since this topic surfaced in Chapter 4, in our discussion of emotions, we'll just briefly review it here.

Body language, expressed through body motions and facial expressions, is a significant part of any face-to-face communication. It's been argued, for example, that every body movement has a meaning and that no movement is accidental.[30] Through body language,

> We say, "Help me, I'm lonely. Take me, I'm available. Leave me alone, I'm depressed." And rarely do we send our messages consciously. We act out our state of being with nonverbal body language. We lift one eyebrow for disbelief. We rub our noses for puzzlement. We clasp our arms to isolate ourselves or to protect ourselves. We shrug our shoulders for indifference, wink one eye for intimacy, tap our fingers for impatience, slap our forehead for forgetfulness.[31]

The two most important messages that body language conveys are (1) the extent to which an individual likes another and is interested in his or her views and (2) the relative perceived status between a sender and receiver.[32] For instance, we're more likely to position ourselves closer to people we like

nonverbal communications

Messages conveyed through body movements, the intonations or emphasis we give to words, facial expressions, and the physical distance between the sender and receiver.

You can tell from his body language that David Weinberg likes his employees. Rather than talking down to them, he crouches to talk face-to-face with them. His smile is genuine. Weinberg is co-chairman of Fel-Pro, a Skokie, Illinois, manufacturer of auto parts. Fel-Pro is well known in the business world as a company that treats its employees exceptionally well. It gives employees profit sharing, above-market wages, $1,000 Treasury bonds when they have a new baby, and $3,500-a-year scholarship for children's college tuition. Weinberg's nonverbal messages are in sync with his verbal messages. Both express his sincere concern for employees.

and touch them more often. Similarly, if you feel that you're higher status than another, you're more likely to display body movements—such as crossed legs or a slouched seating position—that reflect a casual and relaxed manner.

While the specific meaning of any single body movement may be unclear, body language adds to and often complicates verbal communication. A body position or movement does not by itself have a precise or universal meaning, but when it's linked with spoken language, it gives fuller meaning to a sender's message. Keep in mind, of course, that body language differs between cultures. What is considered proper physical spacing in a face-to-face conversation is largely influenced by cultural norms. For example, what is businesslike distance in some European countries would be viewed as intimate in many parts of North America. If someone stands closer to you than is considered appropriate, it may indicate aggressiveness or sexual interest. If farther away than usual, it may mean disinterest or displeasure with what is being said.

If you read the verbatim minutes of a meeting, you could not grasp the impact of what was said in the same way you could if you had been there or saw the meeting on video. Why? The intonation or emphasis given to words or phrases is missing. *Paralinguistics* describes the nonverbal aspects of communication that encompass tone of voice, pacing, pitch, and similar aspects that go beyond the spoken word. Paralinguistics reminds us that we extract meaning from both the words that are used and how those words are expressed.

It's important for the receiver to be alert to these nonverbal aspects of communication. You should look for nonverbal cues as well as listen to the literal meaning of a sender's words. You should particularly be aware of contradictions between the messages. The boss may say that she is free to talk to you about that raise you have been seeking, but you may see nonverbal signals that suggest that this is not the time to discuss the subject. Regardless of what is being said, an individual who frequently glances at her wristwatch is giving the message that she would prefer to terminate the conversation. We misinform others when we express one belief verbally, such as trust, but nonverbally communicate a contradictory message that reads, "I don't have confidence in you."

CHOICE OF COMMUNICATION CHANNEL

Bucknell University, a 3,600-student campus in central Pennsylvania, regularly uses e-mail to convey career-center, athletics-department, and general-interest announcements to students. But the administration was widely criticized a few years back for insensitivity by using this communication channel to transmit the news that a fellow student had apparently committed suicide. "We enjoy a close-knit, friendly atmosphere at Bucknell, and it hurts everyone when a tragedy occurs," said the school paper's editor in an editorial. "In these situations, only a sympathetic method of conveying information can soften the blow of bad news."[33] The school's administration had erred by selecting the wrong channel for its message.

Why do people choose one channel of communication over another—for instance, a phone call instead of a face-to-face talk? One answer might be: Anxiety! As you will remember, some people are apprehensive about certain kinds of communication. What about the 80 to 95 percent of the population who don't suffer from this problem? Is there any general insight we might be able to provide regarding choice of communication channel? The answer is a qualified Yes. A model of media richness has been developed to explain channel selection among managers.[34]

Recent research has found that channels differ in their capacity to convey information. Some are rich in that they have the ability to (1) handle multiple cues simultaneously, (2) facilitate rapid feedback, and (3) be very personal. Others are lean in that they score low on these three factors. As Exhibit 10-6 illustrates, face-to-face talk scores highest in terms of **channel richness** because it provides for the maximum amount of information to be transmitted during a communication episode. That is, it offers multiple information cues (words, postures, facial expressions, gestures, intonations), immediate feedback (both verbal and nonverbal), and the personal touch of "being there." Impersonal written media such as bulletins and general reports rate lowest in richness.

channel richness

The amount of information that can be transmitted during a communication episode.

The choice of one channel over another depends on whether the message is routine or nonroutine. The former types of messages tend to be straightforward and have a minimum of ambiguity. The latter are likely to be complicated and have the potential for misunderstanding. Managers can communicate routine messages efficiently through channels that are lower in richness. However, they can communicate nonroutine messages effectively only by selecting rich channels. Referring to our example at Bucknell University, it appears that the administration's problem was using a channel relatively low in richness (e-mail) to convey a message that, because of its nonroutine nature and complexity, should have been conveyed using a rich communication medium.

Evidence indicates that high-performing managers tend to be more media sensitive than low-performing managers.[35] That is, they're better able to match appropriate media richness with the ambiguity involved in the communication.

The media richness model is consistent with organizational trends and practices during the past decade. It is not just coincidence that more and more senior managers have been using meetings to facilitate communication and regularly leaving the isolated sanctuary of their executive offices to "manage by walking around." These executives are relying on richer channels of communication to transmit the more ambiguous messages they need to convey. The past decade has been characterized by organizations closing facilities, imposing large layoffs, restructuring, merging, consolidating, and introducing new products and services at an accelerated pace—all nonroutine messages high in ambiguity and requiring the use of channels that can convey a large amount of information. It is not surprising, therefore, to see the most effective managers expanding their use of rich channels.

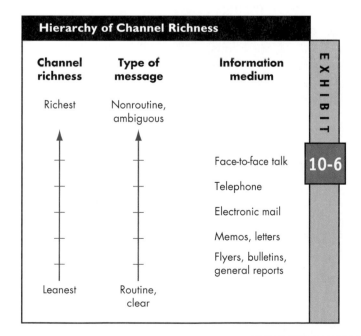

Hierarchy of Channel Richness

Channel richness	Type of message	Information medium	
Richest	Nonroutine, ambiguous		
		Face-to-face talk	
		Telephone	
		Electronic mail	
		Memos, letters	
		Flyers, bulletins, general reports	
Leanest	Routine, clear		

EXHIBIT 10-6

CURRENT ISSUES IN COMMUNICATION

In this section, we discuss four current issues related to communication in organizations: Why do men and women often have difficulty communicating with each other? What are the implications of the "politically correct" movement on communications in organizations? How can individuals improve their cross-cultural communications? And how is electronics changing the way people communicate with each other in organizations?

COMMUNICATION BARRIERS BETWEEN WOMEN AND MEN

Research by Deborah Tannen provides us with some important insights into the differences between men and women in terms of their conversational styles.[36] In particular, she has been able to explain why gender often creates oral communication barriers.

The essence of Tannen's research is that men use talk to emphasize status, while women use it to create connection. Her conclusion, of course, doesn't apply to *every* man or *every* woman. As she puts it, her generalization means "a larger percentage of women or men *as a group* talk in a particular way, or individual women and men *are more likely* to talk one way or the other."[37]

Tannen states that communication is a continual balancing act, juggling the conflicting needs for intimacy and independence. Intimacy emphasizes closeness and commonalities. Independence emphasizes separateness and differences. But here's the kick: Women speak and hear a language of connection and intimacy; men speak and hear a language of status, power, and independence. So, for many men, conversations are primarily a means to preserve independence and maintain status in a hierarchical social order. For many women, conversations are negotiations for closeness in which people try to seek and give confirmation and support. The following examples will illustrate Tannen's thesis.

Men frequently complain that women talk on and on about their problems. Women criticize men for not listening. What's happening is that when men hear a problem, they frequently assert their desire for independence and control by offering solutions. Many women, on the other hand, view telling a problem as a means to promote closeness. The women present the problem to gain support and connection, not to get the male's advice. Mutual understanding is symmetrical. But giving advice is asymmetrical—it sets the advice giver up as more knowledgeable, more reasonable, and more in control. This contributes to distancing men and women in their efforts to communicate.

Men are often more direct than women in conversation. A man might say, "I think you're wrong on that point." A woman might say, "Have you looked at the marketing department's research report on that point?" (the implication being that the re-

Michele Wong (right) supports Tannen's thesis that women speak and hear a language of connection and intimacy. Wong, president of software firm Synergex, fosters open communication. She shares the company's monthly financial statements with employees and holds biweekly open forums where employees can inform, thank, and question one another. She sponsors learning-at-lunch programs where employees share what they do with workers from other departments. Wong also publishes a newsletter on the company's intranet that keeps employees informed about Synergex products and people.

port will show the error). Men frequently see female indirectness as "covert" or "sneaky," but women are not as concerned as men with the status and one-upmanship that directness often creates.

Women tend to be less boastful than men. They often downplay their authority or accomplishments to avoid appearing as braggarts and to take the other person's feelings into account. However, men can frequently misinterpret this and incorrectly conclude that a woman is less confident and competent than she really is.

Finally, men often criticize women for seeming to apologize all the time. Men tend to see the phrase "I'm sorry" as a weakness because they interpret the phrase to mean the woman is accepting blame, when he knows she's not to blame. The woman also knows she's not to blame. The problem is that women frequently use "I'm sorry" to express regret and restore balance to a conversation: "I know you must feel badly about this; I do, too." For many women, "I'm sorry" is an expression of understanding and caring about the other person's feelings rather than an apology.

"POLITICALLY CORRECT" COMMUNICATION

What words do you use to describe a colleague who is wheelchair bound? What terms do you use in addressing a female customer? How do you communicate with a brand-new client who is not like you? The right answers can mean the dif-

EXHIBIT 10-7

THE FAR SIDE   By GARY LARSON

"Well, actually, Doreen, I rather resent being called a 'swamp thing.' ...I prefer the term 'wetlands-challenged mutant.'"

ference between losing a client, an employee, a lawsuit, a harassment claim, or a job.[38]

Most of us are acutely aware of how our vocabulary has been modified to reflect political correctness. For instance, most of us have cleansed the words *handicapped*, *blind*, and *elderly* from our vocabulary—and replaced them with terms such as *physically challenged*, *visually impaired*, and *senior*. The *Los Angeles Times*, for instance, allows its journalists to use the term *old age* but cautions that the onset of old age varies from "person to person," so a group of 75-year-olds aren't necessarily all old.[39]

We must be sensitive to others' feelings. Certain words can and do stereotype, intimidate, and insult individuals. In an increasingly diverse workforce, we must be sensitive to how words might offend others. But there's a downside to political correctness. It's shrinking our vocabulary and making it more difficult for people to communicate. To illustrate, you probably know what these four terms mean: *death*, *garbage*, *quotas*, and *women*. But each of these words also has been found to offend one or more groups. They've been replaced with terms such as *negative-patient outcome*, *postconsumer waste materials*, *educational equity*, and *people of gender*. The problem is that this latter group of terms is much less likely to convey a uniform message than the words they replaced. You know what death means; I know what death means; but can you be sure that "negative-patient outcome" will be consistently defined as synonymous with death? No! For instance, the phrase could also mean a longer stay than expected in the hospital or notification that your insurance company won't pay your hospital bill.

Some critics, for humor's sake, enjoy carrying political correctness to the extreme. Even those of us with thinning scalps, who aren't too thrilled at being labeled "bald," have to smirk when we're referred to as "follically challenged." But our concern here is with how politically correct language is contributing a new barrier to effective communication.

Words are the primary means by which people communicate. When we eliminate words from usage because they're politically incorrect, we reduce our options for conveying messages in the clearest and most accurate form. For the most part, the larger the vocabulary used by a sender and a receiver, the greater the opportunity to accurately transmit messages. By removing certain words from our vocabulary, we make it harder to communicate accurately. When we further replace these words with new terms whose meanings are less well understood, we have reduced the likelihood that our messages will be received as we had intended them.

We must be sensitive to how our choice of words might offend others. But we also have to be careful not to sanitize our language to the point where it clearly restricts clarity of communication. There is no simple solution to this dilemma. However, you should be aware of the trade-offs and the need to find a proper balance.

CROSS-CULTURAL COMMUNICATION

Effective communication is difficult under the best of conditions. Cross-cultural factors clearly create the potential for increased communication problems. This is illustrated in Exhibit 10-8. A gesture that is well understood and acceptable in one culture can be meaningless or lewd in another.[40]

Cultural Barriers   One author has identified four specific problems related to language difficulties in cross-cultural communications.[41]

Hand Gestures Mean Different Things in Different Countries

EXHIBIT

10-8

The A-OK Sign

In the United States, this is just a friendly sign for "All right!" or "Good going." In Australia and Islamic countries, it is equivalent to what generations of high school students know as "flipping the bird."

The "Hook'em Horns" Sign

This sign encourages University of Texas athletes, and it's a good luck gesture in Brazil and Venezuela. In parts of Africa it is a curse. In Italy, it is signaling to another that "your spouse is being unfaithful."

"V" for Victory Sign

In many parts of the world, this means "victory" or "peace." In England, if the palm and fingers face inward, it means "Up yours!" especially if executed with an upward jerk of the fingers.

Finger-Beckoning Sign

This sign means "come here" in the United States. In Malaysia, it is used only for calling animals. In Indonesia and Australia, it is used for beckoning "ladies of the night."

Source: "What's A-O.K. in the U.S.A. Is Lewd and Worthless Beyond," *New York Times*, August 19, 1996, p. F7. From Roger E. Axtell, GESTURES: The Do's and Taboos of Body Language Around the World. Copyright © 1991. This material is used by permission of John Wiley & Sons, Inc.

First, there are *barriers caused by semantics*. As we've noted previously, words mean different things to different people. This is particularly true for people from different national cultures. Some words, for instance, don't translate between cultures. Understanding the word *sisu* will help you in communicating with people from Finland, but this word is untranslatable into English. It means something akin to "guts" or "dogged persistence." Similarly, the new capitalists in Russia may have difficulty communicating with their British or Canadian counterparts because English terms such as *efficiency*, *free market*, and *regulation* are not directly translatable into Russian.

Second, there are *barriers caused by word connotations*. Words imply different things in different languages. Negotiations between Americans and Japanese executives, for instance, are made more difficult because the Japanese word *hai* translates as "yes," but its connotation may be "yes, I'm listening," rather than "yes, I agree."

Third are *barriers caused by tone differences*. In some cultures, language is formal, in others it's informal. In some cultures, the tone changes depending on the context: people speaking differently at home, in social situations, and at work. Using a personal, informal style in a situation in which a more formal style is expected can be embarrassing and off-putting.

Fourth, there are *barriers caused by differences among perceptions*. People who speak different languages actually view the world in different ways. Eskimos perceive snow differently because they have many words for it. Thais perceive "no" differently than Americans because the former have no such word in their vocabulary.

Cultural Context   A better understanding of these cultural barriers and their implications for communicating across cultures can be achieved by considering the concepts of high- and low-context cultures.[42]

Cultures tend to differ in the importance to which context influences the meaning that individuals take from what is actually said or written versus who the other person is. Countries such as China, Vietnam, and Saudi Arabia are **high-context cultures**. They rely heavily on nonverbal and subtle situational cues when communicating with others. What is *not* said may be more significant than what is said. A person's official status, place in society, and reputation carry considerable weight in communications. In contrast, people from Europe and North America reflect their **low-context cultures**. They rely essentially on words to convey meaning. Body language or formal titles are secondary to spoken and written words (see Exhibit 10-9).

What do these contextual differences mean in terms of communication? Actually, quite a lot! Communication in high-context cultures implies considerably more trust by both parties. What may appear, to an outsider, as a casual and insignificant conversation is important because it reflects the desire to build a relationship and create trust. Oral agreements imply strong commitments in high-context cultures. And who you are—your age, seniority, rank in the organization—are highly valued and heavily influence your credibility. But in low-context cultures, enforceable contracts will tend to be in writing, precisely worded, and highly legalistic. Similarly, low-context cultures value directness. Managers are expected to be explicit and precise in conveying intended meaning. It's quite different in high-context cultures, where managers tend to "make suggestions" rather than give orders.

high-context cultures

Cultures that rely heavily on nonverbal and subtle situational cues in communication.

low-context cultures

Cultures that rely heavily on words to convey meaning in communication.

EXHIBIT 10-9

High- vs. Low-Context Cultures

High context

Chinese
Korean
Japanese
Vietnamese
Arab
Greek
Spanish
Italian
English
North American
Scandinavian
Swiss
German

Low context

Source: Based on the work of E. T. Hall. From R. E. Duleck, J. S. Fielden, and J. S. Hill, "International Communication: An Executive Primer," *Business Horizons*, January–February 1991, p. 21.

A Cultural Guide   When communicating with people from a different culture, what can you do to reduce misperceptions, misinterpretations, and misevaluations? You can begin by trying to assess the cultural context. You're likely to have fewer difficulties if these people come from a cultural context similar to yours. In addition, the following four rules can be helpful:[43]

1. *Assume differences until similarity is proven*. Most of us assume that others are more similar to us than they actually are. But people from different countries often are very different from us. So you are far less likely to make an error if you assume others are different from you rather than assuming similarity until difference is proven.

2. *Emphasize description rather than interpretation or evaluation.* Interpreting or evaluating what someone has said or done, in contrast to description, is based more on the observer's culture and background than on the observed situation. As a result, delay judgment until you've had sufficient time to observe and interpret the situation from the differing perspectives of all the cultures involved.

3. *Practice empathy.* Before sending a message, put yourself in the recipient's shoes. What are his or her values, experiences, and frames of reference? What do you know about his or her education, upbringing, and background that can give you added insight? Try to see the other person as he or she really is.

4. *Treat your interpretations as a working hypothesis.* Once you've developed an explanation for a new situation or think you empathize with someone from a foreign culture, treat your interpretation as a hypothesis that needs further testing rather than as a certainty. Carefully assess the feedback provided by recipients to see if it confirms your hypothesis. For important decisions or communiqués, you can also check with other foreign and home-country colleagues to make sure that your interpretations are on target.

ELECTRONIC COMMUNICATIONS

Until the last 15 or 20 years, there were very few technological breakthroughs that significantly affected organizational communications. Early in this century, the telephone dramatically reduced personal, face-to-face communication. The popularization of the photocopy machine in the late 1960s was the death bell for carbon paper and made the copying of documents faster and easier. But beginning in the early 1980s, we've been subjected to an onslaught of new electronic technologies that are largely reshaping the way we communicate in organizations.[44] These include pagers, facsimile machines, video conferencing, electronic meetings, e-mail, cellular phones, voice messaging, and palm-sized personal communicators.

Electronic communications no longer make it necessary for you to be at your work station or desk to be "available." Pagers, cellular phones, and personal communicators allow you to be reached when you're in a meeting, during your lunch break, while visiting in a customer's office across town, or during a golf game on Saturday morning. The line between an employee's work and nonwork life is no longer distinct. In the electronic age, all employees can theoretically be "on call" 24 hours a day.

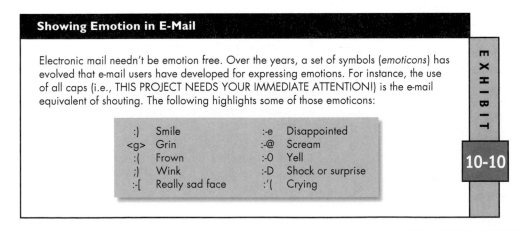

Showing Emotion in E-Mail

EXHIBIT 10-10

Electronic mail needn't be emotion free. Over the years, a set of symbols (*emoticons*) has evolved that e-mail users have developed for expressing emotions. For instance, the use of all caps (i.e., THIS PROJECT NEEDS YOUR IMMEDIATE ATTENTION!) is the e-mail equivalent of shouting. The following highlights some of those emoticons:

:)	Smile	:-e	Disappointed
<g>	Grin	:-@	Scream
:(	Frown	:-0	Yell
;)	Wink	:-D	Shock or surprise
:-[	Really sad face	:'(	Crying

Organizational boundaries become less relevant as a result of electronic communications. Why? Because networked computers—that is, computers that are interlinked to communicate with each other—allow employees to jump vertical levels within the organization, work full time at home or someplace other than an organizationally operated facility, and conduct ongoing communications with people in other organizations. The market researcher who wants to discuss an issue with the vice president of marketing (who is three levels up in the hierarchy) can by-pass the people in between and send an e-mail message directly. And in so doing, the traditional status hierarchy, largely determined by level and access, becomes essentially negated. Or that same market researcher may choose to live in the Cayman Islands and work at home via telecommuting rather than do his or her job in the company's Chicago office. And when an employee's computer is linked to suppliers' and customers' computers, the boundaries separating organizations become further blurred. Hundreds of suppliers, for instance, are linked into Wal-Mart's computers. This allows people at companies such as Levi Strauss to be able to monitor Wal-Mart's inventory of Levi jeans and to replace merchandise as needed, clouding the distinction between Levi and Wal-Mart employees.

Although the telephone allowed people to transmit verbal messages instantly, it's only been very recently that this same speed became available for

FROM CONCEPTS *TO* SKILLS

Improving Your Communication Skills

The following provides a set of eight rules that can help you improve your communication skills. They represent a synthesis from a variety of sources.[45]

1. *Use multiple channels.* When you use multiple channels to convey a message, you improve the likelihood of clarity for two reasons. First, you stimulate a number of the receiver's senses. A letter and a phone call, for example, provide sight and sound. Repeating a message by using a different channel acts to reinforce it and decreases the likelihood of distortions. Second, people have different abilities to absorb information. Some understand best when a message is in writing. For instance, they can read and reread a memo or fax, at their own pace, to fully absorb the intention of the sender. Others, however, prefer oral communications. Such individuals tend to rely on nonverbal cues to provide them with enhanced insights that words, alone, don't convey.

2. *Tailor the message to the audience.* Different people in the organization have different information needs. What is important to supervisors may not be so to middle managers. What is interesting information to someone in product planning may be irrelevant to someone in accounting. Jargon used with one group may be confusing to others. And, of course, cultural backgrounds can result in vastly different interpretations of messages, so messages need to be modified to reflect cultural differences. Since individuals in organizations vary in the type of information they need to know, their preferred channel for receiving the information, and their understanding of language, you should make sure you tailor your message to the needs of your intended audience.

3. *Empathize with others.* In verbal communications, you need to empathize with your listeners. You need to put yourself in their shoes. You need to be sensitive to their needs, perceptions, attitudes, and emotions. How are they likely to decode the message? When you put yourself in the other person's position or situation, you're more likely to see things from the other's perspective—and then to choose the best communication channel and the proper words to use.

4. *Remember the value of face-to-face communication when dealing with change.* In times of uncertainty and change—which increasingly characterize today's work environment—employees have lots of fears and concerns. Is their job in jeopardy? Will recently announced restructuring efforts require them to learn new skills or change work groups? Consistent with our previous discussion of channel richness, messages conveying significant changes are nonroutine and ambiguous. Since the maximum amount of information can be transmitted through face-to-face conversation, this channel is preferred when messages convey information that is likely to be seen as ambiguous, threatening, or implying significant change.

5. *Practice active listening.* Too many people take listening skills for granted. They confuse hearing with listening. What's the difference? Hearing is merely picking up sound vibrations. Listening is making sense out of what we hear. That is, listening requires paying attention, interpreting, and remembering sound stimuli.

   The average person normally speaks at the rate of 125 to 200 words per minute. However, the average listener can comprehend up to 400 words per minute. This leaves a lot of time for idle mind-wandering while listening. For most people, it also means they've acquired a number of bad listening habits to fill in the "idle time."

   The following behaviors are associated with *active listening* skills. If you want to improve your listening abilities, look to these behaviors as guides:

   Make eye contact. We may listen with our ears, but others tend to judge whether we're really listening by looking at our eyes.

   Exhibit affirmative head nods and appropriate facial expressions. The effective listener shows interest in what is being said through nonverbal signals.

   Avoid distracting actions or gestures. When listening, don't look at your watch, shuffle papers, play with your pencil, or engage in similar distractions. They make the speaker feel that you're bored or uninterested.

   Ask questions. The critical listener analyzes what he or she hears and asks questions. This behavior provides clarification, ensures understanding, and assures the speaker that you're listening.

   Paraphrase. Paraphrasing means restating what the speaker has said in your own words. By rephrasing what the speaker has said in your own words and feeding it back to the speaker, you verify the accuracy of your understanding.

   Avoid interrupting the speaker. Let the speaker complete his or her thought before you try to respond. Don't try to second-guess where the speaker's thoughts are going.

   Don't overtalk. While talking may be more fun and silence may be uncomfortable, you can't talk and listen at the same time. The good listener recognizes this fact and doesn't overtalk.

6. *Match your words and actions.* As we've noted previously, actions speak louder than words. When nonverbal messages contradict official messages as conveyed in formal communications, people become confused and the official message loses its focus. Moreover, for managers, inconsistencies can undermine credibility. So make sure that your verbal and nonverbal messages are aligned. You may say to a colleague, for example, that your door is always open. But if you frequently glance at your wristwatch when that colleague does come to your office, you're conveying another message.

7. *Use the grapevine.* The grapevine is not going away. Astute employees and effective managers accept its existence and use it. Employees listen to grapevine messages to enhance formal messages issued by management. And effective managers use the grapevine for identifying issues that employees consider important and that are likely to create anxiety. The grapevine also can serve as both a filter and feedback mechanism by highlighting issues that employees consider relevant and by consciously planting messages that managers want employees to hear.

8. *Use feedback.* Effective communication is a two-way process between sender and receiver. However, too often, it's only one way. This is especially true in downward communications. A top-management directive, for instance, is issued in a formal memo. It's then assumed that everyone in the organization has read it and that it's fully understood. In such instances, there needs to be a mechanism that allows executives to know that the message has been received and understood.

For many managers, performance feedback is a problem. They enjoy providing feedback when it's positive. But because negative feedback often meets resistance from employees, managers frequently avoid it or do it poorly. The following four suggestions can help you, as a manager, be more effective when you have to give performance feedback.

Focus on specific behaviors. Feedback should be specific rather than general. For instance, the phrase "You have a bad attitude" is too general. This is better: "Mark, I'm concerned with your attitude toward your work. You were a half hour late to yesterday's staff meeting, and then told me you hadn't read the preliminary report we were discussing. Today you tell me you're taking off three hours early for a dental appointment." Specific feedback should tell the recipient *why* you are being complimentary or critical.

Keep it impersonal. Feedback, particularly the negative kind, should be descriptive rather than judgmental or evaluative. If you're providing critical feedback, remember that you're criticizing an action, not the person.

Make it well-timed. Feedback is most meaningful to a recipient when there is a short interval between his or her behavior and the receipt of feedback about that behavior.

If negative, make sure the behavior is controllable by the recipient. There's little value in reminding a person of some shortcoming over which he or she has no control. Negative feedback, therefore, should be directed toward the behavior the recipient can do something about. It's also a good idea to indicate specifically what can be done to improve the situation. This offers guidance to recipients who understand the problem but don't know how to resolve it.

the written word. In the mid-1960s, organizations were almost completely dependent on interoffice memos for internal, on-site messages, and on wire services and the post office for external messages. Then came overnight express delivery and fax machines. Today, with almost all organizations having introduced e-mail and an increasing number providing their employees with access to the Internet, written communications can be transmitted with all the speed of the telephone.

Electronic communications have revolutionized both the ability to access other people and to reach them almost instantaneously. Unfortunately, this access and speed have come with some costs. Electronic mail, for instance, doesn't provide the nonverbal communication component that the face-to-face meeting does. Nor does e-mail convey the emotions and nuances that come through from verbal intonations in telephone conversations,[46] although efforts have been made to create emotional icons (see Exhibit 10-10 on page 301). It's been noted that meetings have historically served two distinct purposes—fulfilling a need for group affiliation and serving as a forum for completing task work.[47] Video conferences and electronic meetings do a good job at supporting tasks but don't address affiliation needs. For people with a high need for social contact, a heavy reliance on electronic communications is likely to lead to lower job satisfaction.

SUMMARY AND IMPLICATIONS FOR MANAGERS

A careful review of this chapter finds a common theme regarding the relationship between communication and employee satisfaction: the less the uncertainty, the greater the satisfaction. Distortions, ambiguities, and incongruities all increase uncertainty and, hence, they have a negative impact on satisfaction.[48]

The less distortion that occurs in communication, the more that goals, feedback, and other management messages to employees will be received as they were intended.[49] This, in turn, should reduce ambiguities and clarify the group's task. Extensive use of vertical, lateral, and informal channels will increase communication flow, reduce uncertainty, and improve group performance and satisfaction. We should also expect incongruities between verbal and nonverbal communiqués to increase uncertainty and to reduce satisfaction.

Findings in the chapter further suggest that the goal of perfect communication is unattainable. Yet, there is evidence that demonstrates a positive relationship between effective communication (which includes factors such as perceived trust, perceived accuracy, desire for interaction, top-management receptiveness, and upward information requirements) and worker productivity.[50] Choosing the correct channel, being an effective listener, and utilizing feedback may, therefore, make for more effective communication. But the human factor generates distortions that can never be fully eliminated. The communication process represents an exchange of messages, but the outcome is meanings that may or may not approximate those that the sender intended. Whatever the sender's expectations, the decoded message in the mind of the receiver represents his or her reality. And it is this "reality" that will determine performance, along with the individual's level of motivation and his or her degree of satisfaction. The issue of motivation is critical, so we should briefly review how communication is central in determining an individual's degree of motivation.

You will remember from expectancy theory that the degree of effort an individual exerts depends on his or her perception of the effort–performance, performance–reward, and reward–goal satisfaction linkages. If individuals are not given the data necessary to make the perceived probability of these linkages high, motivation will suffer. If rewards are not made clear, if the criteria for determining and measuring performance are ambiguous, or if individuals are not relatively certain that their effort will lead to satisfactory performance, then effort will be reduced. So communication plays a significant role in determining the level of employee motivation.

A final implication from the communication literature relates to predicting turnover. The use of realistic job previews acts as a communication device for clarifying role expectations (see the "Counterpoint" in Chapter 5). Employees who have been exposed to a realistic job preview have more accurate information about that job. Comparisons of turnover rates between organizations that use the realistic job preview versus either no preview or only presentation of positive job information show that those not using the realistic preview have, on average, almost 29 percent higher turnover.[51] This makes a strong case for managers to convey honest and accurate information about a job to applicants during the recruiting and selection process.

Open-Book Management Improves the Bottom Line

O pen-book management (OBM) seeks to get every employee to think and behave like an owner.[1] It throws out the notion that bosses run things and employees do what they're told. In the open-book approach, employees are given the information that historically was strictly kept within the management ranks.

There are three key elements to any OBM program. First, management opens the company's books and shares detailed financial and operating information with employees. If employees don't know how the company makes money, how can they be expected to make the firm more successful? Second, employees need to be taught to understand the company's financial statements. This means management must provide employees with a "basic course" in how to read and interpret income statements, balance sheets, and cash flow statements. And third, management needs to show employees how their work influences financial results. Showing employees the impact of their jobs on the bottom line makes financial statement analysis relevant.

Who is using OBM? A growing list of firms, including Springfield Remanufacturing Corp., Allstate Insurance, Amoco Canada, Kacey Fine Furniture, Rhino Foods, and Sprint's Government Systems division.

Why should it work? Access to detailed financial information and the ability to understand that information makes employees think like owners. And this leads to them making decisions that are best for the organization, not just for themselves.

Does it work? Most firms that have introduced OBM offer evidence that it has significantly helped the business. For instance, Springfield Remanufacturing lost $61,000 on sales of $16 million. Management attributes much of the company's current success—profits of $6 million a year on sales of $100 million—to OBM. Similarly, Allstate's Business Insurance Group used OBM to boost return on equity from 2.9 percent to 16.5 percent in just three years.

---

[1]Based on J. Case, "The Open-Book Revolution," *INC.*, June 1995, pp. 26–50; and J. P. Schuster, J. Carpenter, and M. P. Kane, *The Power of Open-Book Management* (New York: John Wiley, 1996).

T he owners of Optics 1 Inc., an optical-engineering company in southern California, with 23 employees and sales of less than $10 million a year implemented an OBM program. After a short time, the program was discontinued. Said one of the co-owners, "Employees used the information against me. When we made a profit, they demanded bigger bonuses and new computers. When I used profits to finance a new product line, everybody said, 'That's nice, but what's in it for me?' . . . If your employees misinterpret financial information, it's more damaging than their not having access at all. I gave them general and administrative rates. Next thing I knew they were backing out everyone's salaries, and I'd hear, 'You're paying that guy $86,000? I contribute more.'"

As the preceding illustrates, part of the downside to OBM is that employees may misuse or misinterpret the information they get against management.[2] Another potential problem is the leaking of confidential information to competitors. In the hands of the competition, detailed information on the company's operations and financial position may undermine a firm's competitive advantage.

When OBM succeeds, two factors seem to exist. First, the organization or unit in which it's implemented tends to be small. It's a lot easier to introduce OBM in a small, start-up company than in a large, geographically dispersed company that has operated for years with closed books and little employee involvement. Second, there needs to be a mutually trusting relationship between management and workers. In organizational cultures in which management doesn't trust employees to act selflessly or in which managers and accountants have been trained to keep information under lock and key, OBM isn't likely to work. Nor will it succeed when employees believe any new change program is only likely to further manipulate or exploit them for management's advantage.

---

[2]Based on S. L. Gruner, "Why Open the Books?" *INC.*, November 1996, p. 95; and T. R. V. Davis, "Open-Book Management: Its Promise and Pitfalls," *Organizational Dynamics*, Winter 1997, pp. 7–20.

1. Describe the functions that communication provides within a group or organization. Give an example of each.

2. Contrast encoding and decoding.

3. Identify three common small-group networks and give the advantages of each.

4. What is nonverbal communication? Does it aid or hinder verbal communication?

5. What characterizes a communication that is rich in its capacity to convey information?

6. What conditions stimulate the emergence of rumors?

7. Describe how political correctness can hinder effective communication.

8. Contrast high- and low-context cultures.

9. What are the managerial implications from the research contrasting male and female communication styles?

10. What can managers do to improve their skills at providing performance feedback?

Questions for Critical Thinking

1. "Ineffective communication is the fault of the sender." Do you agree or disagree? Discuss.

2. What can you do to improve the likelihood that your communiqués will be received and understood as you intend?

3. How might managers use the grapevine for their benefit?

4. Using the concept of channel richness, give examples of messages best conveyed by e-mail, by face-to-face communication, and on the company bulletin board.

5. Why do you think so many people are poor listeners?

Team Exercise | The Impact of Attentive Listening Skills

The objective of this exercise is to show the importance of listening skills to interpersonal success.

Form groups by counting off by sixes. There should be a minimum of three students to a group and a maximum of seven per group.

Each group has 30 minutes to address the following four questions. The groups should begin by brainstorming answers and then narrowing their selection to the three most significant answers. Appoint one member of the group to transcribe answers on the board and another to tell the class why the group selected these answers.

1. How do you know when a person is listening to you?

2. Describe a situation in which you exhibited oustanding listening behavior. How did it influence the speaker's subsequent communication behaviors?

3. How do you know when a person is ignoring you?

4. Describe a situation in which you ignored someone. What impact did it have on that person's subsequent communication behaviors?

Source: Adapted from T. Clark, "Sharing the Importance of Attentive Listening Skills," *Journal of Mangement Education*, April 1999, pp. 216–23.

1. Find the best example of poor organizational communication you can find on a company's Web site. Why did you choose this to illustrate poor communication? How might it be improved?

2. Find five companies whose primary business is helping employees in organizations to improve their interpersonal communication skills. What common characteristics, if any, did you find in the programs these companies offer?

PHLIP Companion Web Site

We invite you to visit the Robbins homepage on the Prentice Hall Web site at **www.prenhall.com/robbins** for our on-line study guide, current events, links to related Web sites, and more.

Case Incident | Have We Got a Communication Problem Here?

"I don't want to hear your excuses. Just get those planes in the air," Jim Tuchman was screaming at his gate manager. As head of American Airlines' operations at the Mexico City airport, Tuchman has been consistently frustrated by the attitude displayed by his native employees. Transferred from Dallas to Mexico City only three months ago, Tuchman was having difficulty adjusting to the Mexican style of work. "Am I critical of these people? You bet I am! They don't listen when I talk. They think things are just fine and fight every change I suggest. And they have no appreciation for the importance of keeping on schedule."

If Tuchman is critical of his Mexico City staff, it's mutual. They universally dislike him. Here's a few anonymous comments made about their boss: "He's totally insensitive to our needs." "He thinks if he yells and screams, that things will improve. We don't see it that way." "I've been working here for four years. Be-

fore he came here, this was a good place to work. Not anymore. I'm constantly in fear of being chewed out. I feel stress all the time, even at home. My husband has started commenting on it a lot."

Tuchman was brought in specifically to tighten up the Mexico City operation. High on his list of goals is improving American's on-time record in Mexico City, increasing productivity, and improving customer service. When Tuchman was asked if he thought he had any problems with his staff, he replied, "Yep. We just can't seem to communicate."

Questions

1. Does Jim Tuchman have a communication problem? Explain.

2. What suggestions, if any, would you make to Jim to help him improve his managerial effectiveness?

Video Case | Community Insurance Company

To deliver a message, we must communicate. We communicate in many ways: through our actions, through our words, through our appearance, and even through the company that we keep. What is communicated and how it is communicated is important to relationships between individuals, be-

tween departments in a company, and between a company and its customers.

Milt Moses, the leader of the Community Insurance Company, understands the importance of good communication to the success or failure of a business. Moses talks to us about the importance of communication from various perspectives. In describing how he was motivated to enter the insurance field, we learn about an impression of the industry that he got from his own insurance agent. Moses was not actively recruited, in fact he sought out the job. Why did he pursue insurance? Through observation, he got the idea that insurance could be a lucrative business, and one that might present fewer barriers to him than other careers that he had considered. In his own agency, Moses uses many approaches to convey a good image to the community.

Moses also talks about communication within his agency. We hear about his style of communicating with his staff, his policy toward maintaining an open door, and his belief in the importance of providing top quality service. His employees do not learn these things about Moses and the company by chance. At the same time, everyone who works at Community Insurance does not necessarily get the same message, in the same way, or at the same time.

One of the challenges that any company faces is to communicate in a way that the general message gets across. Milt Moses shows us that this can be done in several ways. We see evidence of business planning, job assignment, and an openness to talk with employees. Perhaps, most importantly, we get the feeling that Milt Moses walks the talk; not only does he share his beliefs about business, he openly practices them.

Questions

1. It seems obvious that at the Community Insurance Company, Milt Moses sets the tone. What do you think Moses is trying to convey to his staff about how the company should operate? Do you think he is successful in conveying this message?

2. You learned an instance when Moses sent very interesting messages through his actions: the listening of music was banned but later allowed as long as employees used headsets. Why do you think Moses changed his mind and allowed something that he did not necessarily agree with? What message do you think this sent to Moses's staff?

3. Milt Moses emphasizes the need to provide superb customer service. In fact, he appears to believe that such service is the key to success in his industry. From what you have learned about the Community Insurance Company and Milt Moses, do you think he is successful in communicating his commitment to providing excellent service? Why or why not?

End Notes

1. This opening section is based on J. Ritter, "Poor Fluency in English Means Mixed Signals," *USA Today*, January 18, 1996, p. 1A; P. Garrison, "Can Culture Cause a Crash?" *Conde Nast Traveler*, July 1997, pp. 24–28; and A. Kotarumalos, "Pilot Confused Before Deadly Jetliner Crash," *Seattle Post-Intelligencer*, September 30, 1997, p. A2.
2. See, for example, K. W. Thomas and W. H. Schmidt, "A Survey of Managerial Interests with Respect to Conflict," *Academy of Management Journal*, June 1976, p. 317.
3. W. G. Scott and T. R. Mitchell, *Organization Theory: A Structural and Behavioral Analysis* (Homewood, IL: Richard D. Irwin, 1976).
4. D. K. Berlo, *The Process of Communication* (New York: Holt, Rinehart & Winston, 1960), pp. 30–32.
5. Ibid., p. 54.
6. Ibid., p. 103.
7. J. DeLorean, quoted in S. P. Robbins, *The Administrative Process* (Upper Saddle River, NJ: Prentice Hall, 1976), p. 404.
8. M. J. Glauser, "Upward Information Flow in Organizations: Review and Conceptual Analysis," *Human Relations*, June 1984, pp. 613–43.
9. G. A. Miller, "The Magical Number Seven, Plus or Minus Two: Some Limits on Our Capacity for Processing Information," *The Psychological Review*, March 1956, pp. 81–97.
10. See, for instance, J. R. Gibb, "Defensive Communication," *Journal of Communication*, Fall 1961, pp. 141–48.
11. S. I. Hayakawa, *Language in Thought and Action* (New York: Harcourt Brace Jovanovich, 1949), p. 292.
12. Cited in J. J. Kilpatrick, "Uncommon Word Usage Can Enrich and Muddle Writing," *Seattle Times*, March 15, 1998, p. L4.
13. J. C. McCroskey, J. A. Daly, and G. Sorenson, "Personality Correlates of Communication Apprehension," *Human Communication Research*, Spring 1976, pp. 376–80.
14. B. H. Spitzberg and M. L. Hecht, "A Competent Model of Relational Competence," *Human Communication Research*, Summer 1984, pp. 575–99.
15. A. Bandura, *Social Learning Theory* (Upper Saddle River, NJ: Prentice Hall, 1977).
16. An example is assigned goals. See E. A. Locke and G. P. Latham, *A Theory of Goal Setting and Task Performance* (Upper Saddle River, NJ: Prentice Hall, 1990).
17. See, for example, L. Stafford and J. A. Daly, "Conversational Memory: The Effects of Instructional Set and Recall Mode on Memory for Natural Conversations," *Human Communication Research*, Spring 1984, pp. 379–402.

18. J. A. Daly and J. C. McCrosky, "Occupational Choice and Desirability as a Function of Communication Apprehension," paper presented at the annual meeting of the International Communication Association, Chicago, 1975.

19. J. A. Daly and M. D. Miller, "The Empirical Development of an Instrument of Writing Apprehension," *Research in the Teaching of English*, Winter 1975, pp. 242–49.

20. R. L. Simpson, "Vertical and Horizontal Communication in Formal Organizations," *Administrative Science Quarterly*, September 1959, pp. 188–96; and B. Harriman, "Up and Down the Communications Ladder," *Harvard Business Review*, Steptember–October 1974, pp. 143–51.

21. Cited in L. Tabak, "Quality Controls," *Hemispheres*, September 1996, p. 34.

22. Cited in "Heard It Through the Grapevine," *Forbes*, February 10, 1997, p. 22.

23. See, for instance, J. W. Newstrom, R. E. Monczka, and W. E. Reif, "Perceptions of the Grapevine: Its Value and Influence," *Journal of Business Communication*, Spring 1974, pp. 12–20; and S. J. Modic, "Grapevine Rated Most Believable," *Industry Week*, May 15, 1989, p. 14.

24. K. Davis, "Management Communication and the Grapevine," *Harvard Business Review*, September–October 1953, pp. 43–49.

25. H. Sutton and L. W. Porter, "A Study of the Grapevine in a Governmental Organization," *Personnel Psychology*, Summer 1968, pp. 223–30.

26. K. Davis, cited in R. Rowan, "Where Did That Rumor Come From?" *Fortune*, August 13, 1979, p. 134.

27. L. Hirschhorn, "Managing Rumors," in L. Hirschhorn (ed.), *Cutting Back* (San Francisco: Jossey-Bass, 1983), pp. 49–52.

28. R. L. Rosnow and G. A. Fine, *Rumor and Gossip: The Social Psychology of Hearsay* (New York: Elsevier, 1976).

29. See, for instance, J. G. March and G. Sevon, "Gossip, Information and Decision Making" in J. G. March (ed.), *Decisions and Organizations* (Oxford: Blackwell, 1988), pp. 429–42; M. Noon and R. Delbridge, "News from Behind My Hand: Gossip in Organizations," *Organization Studies*, vol. 14, no. 1, 1993, pp. 23–36; and N. DiFonzo, P. Bordia, and R. L. Rosnow, "Reining in Rumors," *Organizational Dynamics*, Summer 1994, pp. 47–62.

30. R. L. Birdwhistell, *Introduction to Kinesics* (Louisville, KY: University of Louisville Press, 1952).

31. J. Fast, *Body Language* (Philadelphia: M. Evan, 1970), p. 7.

32. A. Mehrabian, *Nonverbal Communication* (Chicago: Aldine-Atherton, 1972).

33. Reported in "On Line," *The Chronicle of Higher Education*, October 27, 1995, p. A23.

34. See R. L. Daft and R. H. Lengel, "Information Richness: A New Approach to Managerial Behavior and Organization Design," in B. M. Staw and L. L. Cummings (eds.), *Research in Organizational Behavior*, vol. 6 (Greenwich, CT: JAI Press, 1984), pp. 191–233; R. E. Rice and D. E. Shook, "Relationships of Job Categories and Organizational Levels to Use of Communication Channels, Including Electronic Mail: A Meta-Analysis and Extension," *Journal of Management Studies*, March 1990, pp. 195–229; R. E. Rice, "Task Analyzability, Use of New Media, and Effectiveness," *Organization Science*, November 1992, pp. 475–500; S. G. Straus and J. E. McGrath, "Does the Medium Matter? The Interaction of Task Type and Technology on Group Performance and Member Reaction," *Journal of Applied Psychology*, February 1994, pp. 87–97; J. Webster and L. K. Trevino, "Rational and Social Theories as Complementary Explanations of Communication Media Choices: Two Policy-Capturing Studies," *Academy of Management Journal*, December 1995, pp. 1544–72.

35. R. L. Daft, R. H. Lengel, and L. K. Trevino, "Message Equivocality, Media Selection, and Manager Performance: Implications for Information Systems," *MIS Quarterly*, September 1987, pp. 355–68.

36. See D. Tannen, *You Just Don't Understand: Women and Men in Conversation* (New York: Ballentine Books, 1991); and D. Tannen, *Talking from 9 to 5* (New York: William Morrow, 1995).

37. D. Tannen, *Talking from 9 to 5*, p. 15.

38. M. L. LaGanga, "Are There Words That Neither Offend Nor Bore?" *Los Angeles Times*, May 18, 1994, p. II-27; and J. Leo, "Language in the Dumps," *U.S. News & World Report*, July 27, 1998, p. 16.

39. Cited in J. Leo, "Falling for Sensitivity," *U.S. News & World Report*, December 13, 1993, p. 27.

40. R. E. Axtell, *Gestures: The Do's and Taboos of Body Language Around the World* (New York: Wiley, 1991).

41. See M. Munter, "Cross-Cultural Communication for Managers," *Business Horizons*, May–June 1993, pp. 75–76.

42. See E. T. Hall, *Beyond Culture* (Garden City, NY: Anchor Press/Doubleday, 1976); E. T. Hall, "How Cultures Collide," *Psychology Today*, July 1976, pp. 67–74; E. T. Hall and M. R. Hall, *Understanding Cultural Differences* (Yarmouth, ME: Intercultural Press, 1990); and R. E. Dulek, J. S. Fielden, and J. S. Hill, "International Communication: An Executive Primer," *Business Horizons*, January–February 1991, pp. 20–25.

43. N. Adler, *International Dimensions of Organizational Behavior*, 3rd ed. (Cincinnati, OH: Southwestern, 1997), pp. 87–88.

44. See, for instance, R. Hotch, "Communication Revolution," *Nation's Business*, May 1993, pp. 20–28; G. Brockhouse, "I Have Seen the Future . . . ," *Canadian Business*, August 1993, pp. 43–45; R. Hotch, "In Touch Through Technology," *Nation's Business*, January 1994, pp. 33–35; and P. LaBarre, "The Other Network," *Industry Week*, September 19, 1994, pp. 33–36.

45. See, for instance, S. P. Robbins and P. L. Hunsaker, *Training in InterPersonal Skills*, 2nd ed. (Upper Saddle River, NJ: Prentice Hall, 1996); M. Young and J. E. Post, "Managing to Communicate, Communicating to Manage: How Leading Companies Communicate With Employees," *Organizational Dynamics*, Summer 1993, pp. 31–43; J. A. DeVito, *The Interpersonal Communication Book*, 6th ed. (New York: HarperCollins, 1992); and A. G. Athos and J. J. Gabarro, *Interpersonal Behavior* (Upper Saddle River, NJ: Prentice Hall, 1978).

46. J. Hunter and M. Allen, "Adaptation to Electronic Mail," *Journal of Applied Communication Research*, August 1992, pp. 254–74.

47. A. LaPlante, "TeleConfrontationing," *Forbes ASAP*, September 13, 1993, p. 117.

48. See, for example. R. S. Schuler, "A Role Perception Transactional Process Model for Organizational Communication-Outcome Relationships," *Organizational Behavior and Human Performance*, April 1979, pp. 268–91.

49. J. P. Walsh, S. J. Ashford, and T. E. Hill, "Feedback Obstruction: The Influence of the Information Environment on Employee Turnover Intentions," *Human Relations*, January 1985, pp. 23–46.

50. S. A. Hellweg and S. L. Phillips, "Communication and Productivity in Organizations: A State-of-the-Art Review," in *Proceedings of the 40th Annual Academy of Management Conference*, Detroit, 1980, pp. 188–92.

51. R. R. Reilly, B. Brown, M. R. Blood, and C. Z. Malatesta, "The Effects of Realistic Previews: A Study and Discussion of the Literature," *Personnel Psychology*, Winter 1981, pp. 823–34.

Lead, follow, or get out of the way!

—Anonymous

part three

THE GROUP

Can one person make a difference in an organization's performance? Jurgen Schrempp, the chairman at DaimlerChrysler, is proving one can.[1]

When Schrempp took over the top spot in 1995, at what then was Daimler-Benz, the German company was at a low point. Daimler, in fact, would lose nearly US$4 billion in 1995. Whatever the company was doing wasn't working. It's largest and historically most profitable division, Mercedez-Benz, was getting trounced in the luxury marketplace by BMW, Lexus, and others. Mercedes' cars had gotten too expensive, too bulky, and product lines had become blurred. New models showed little innovation. Schrempp responded by completely shaking up the company, especially its Mercedes division.

Schrempp began by refocusing the company. He sold off or liquidated software services and aerospace divisions that didn't fit with Daimler's basic strategy. He imposed ambitious and specific financial goals for all 23 business units. He eliminated a layer of top managers. And he challenged his people to take risks and innovate. The result has been nothing short of miraculous. Within three years, the company was introducing new models almost on a monthly basis. And designers developed several startling concepts for new vehicles such as a three-wheeled, two-passenger city car and a high-mileage, low-pollution car powered by liquid methanol.

In the summer of 1998, Schrempp pulled off his biggest accomplishment. He negotiated the purchase of Chrysler Corp. The addition of Chrysler would give Daimler one of the world's most innovative design groups, a largely expanded worldwide sales organization, a solid position in the light-truck market, and a significantly broader product line. Schrempp also expects to generate considerable cost savings by adapting many of Chrysler's low-cost manufacturing principles to Mercedes, integrating sales and marketing worldwide, and combining the two company's back-office operations.

Leadership and Trust

So far, Schrempp's changes are working. In four years, sales have grown from under $60 billion to more than $154 billion. And the company is now making record profits.

A s Jurgen Schrempp is demonstrating at DaimlerChrysler, leaders can make a difference. In this chapter, we want to look at the various studies on leadership to determine what makes an effective leader and what differentiates leaders from nonleaders. We'll also introduce the topic of *trust* and demonstrate its importance to effective leadership. But first let's clarify what we mean by the term *leadership*

WHAT IS LEADERSHIP?

Leadership and *management* are two terms that are often confused. What's the difference between them?

John Kotter of the Harvard Business School argues that management is about coping with complexity.[2] Good management brings about order and consistency by drawing up formal plans, designing rigid organization structures, and monitoring results against the plans. Leadership, in contrast, is about coping with change. Leaders establish direction by developing a vision of the future; then they align people by communicating this vision and inspiring them to overcome hurdles.

Robert House of the Wharton School at the University of Pennsylvania basically concurs when he says that managers use the authority inherent in their designated formal rank to obtain compliance from organizational members.[3] Management consists of implementing the vision and strategy provided by leaders, coordinating and staffing the organization, and handling day-to-day problems.

LEARNING OBJECTIVES

AFTER READING THIS CHAPTER, YOU SHOULD BE ABLE TO

1. Contrast leadership and management

2. Summarize the conclusions of trait theories

3. Identify the limitations of behavioral theories

4. Describe Fiedler's contingency model

5. Summarize the path-goal theory

6. Explain leader-member exchange theory

7. Differentiate between transactional and transformational leaders

8. Describe the skills that visionary leaders exhibit

9. Identify the five dimensions of trust

10. Summarize how leaders can build trust

Although Kotter and House provide separate definitions of the two terms, both researchers and practicing managers frequently make no such distinctions. So we need to present leadership in a way that can capture how it is used in theory and practice.

We define **leadership** as the ability to influence a group toward the achievement of goals. The source of this influence may be formal, such as that provided by the possession of managerial rank in an organization. Since management positions come with some degree of formally designated authority, a person may assume a leadership role simply because of the position he or she holds in the organization. But not all leaders are managers; nor, for that matter, are all managers leaders. Just because an organization provides its managers with certain formal rights is no assurance that they will be able to lead effectively. We find that nonsanctioned leadership—that is, the ability to influence that arises outside the formal structure of the organization—is often as important or more important than formal influence. In other words, leaders can emerge from within a group as well as by formal appointment.

One last comment before we move on: Organizations need strong leadership and strong management for optimum effectiveness. In today's dynamic world, we need leaders to challenge the status quo, to create visions of the future, and to inspire organizational members to want to achieve the visions. We also need managers to formulate detailed plans, create efficient organizational structures, and oversee day-to-day operations.

TRAIT THEORIES

When Margaret Thatcher was prime minister of Great Britain, she was regularly singled out for her leadership. She was described in terms such as *confident*, *iron-willed*, *determined*, and *decisive*. These terms are traits and, whether Thatcher's advocates and critics recognized it at the time, when they described her in such terms they became trait-theorist supporters.

The media have long been believers in **trait theories of leadership**. They identify people such as Margaret Thatcher, South Africa's Nelson Mandela, Virgin Group CEO Richard Branson, Apple co-founder Steve Jobs, New Jersey Governor Christine Todd Whitman, and American Express's president Ken Chenault as leaders and then describe them in terms such as *charismatic*, *enthusiastic*, and *courageous*. Well the media aren't alone. The search for personality, social, physical, or intellectual attributes that would describe leaders and differentiate them from nonleaders goes back to the 1930s.

Research efforts at isolating leadership traits resulted in a number of dead ends. For instance, a review of 20 different studies identified nearly 80 leadership traits, but only five of these traits were common to four or more of the investigations.[4] If the search was intended to identify a set of traits that would always differentiate leaders from followers and effective from ineffective leaders, the search failed. Perhaps it was a bit optimistic to believe that there could be consistent and unique traits that would apply universally to all effective leaders, no matter whether they were in charge of DaimlerChrysler, the Mormon Tabernacle Choir, Ted's Malibu Surf Shop, the Brazilian national soccer team, or Oxford University.

If, however, the search was intended to identify traits that were consistently associated with leadership, the results can be interpreted in a more impressive light. For example, six traits on which leaders tend to

Ken Chenault, president and chief operating officer of American Express, frequently has his leadership described in trait terms. Co-workers and business associates say he is brilliant, hard driving, charismatic, inspirational, self-composed, patient, and persistent. "Ken radiates such a depth of belief that people would do anything for him. He is a true leader," says Rochelle Lazarus, chairman of Ogilvy & Mather, American Express's lead advertising agency.

differ from nonleaders are ambition and energy, the desire to lead, honesty and integrity, self-confidence, intelligence, and job-relevant knowledge.[5] Additionally, recent research provides strong evidence that people who are high self-monitors—that is, are highly flexible in adjusting their behavior in different situations—are much more likely to emerge as leaders in groups than low self-monitors.[6] Overall, the cumulative findings from more than half a century of research lead us to conclude that some traits increase the likelihood of success as a leader, but none of the traits *guarantee* success.[7]

But the trait approach has at least four limitations. First, there are no universal traits that predict leadership in all situations. Rather, traits appear to predict leadership in *selective* situations.[8] Second, traits predict behavior more in "weak" situations than in "strong" situations.[9] Strong situations are those in which there are strong behavioral norms, strong incentives for specific types of behaviors, and clear expectations as to what behaviors are rewarded and punished. Such strong situations create less opportunity for leaders to express their inherent dispositional tendencies. Since highly formalized organizations and those with strong cultures fit the description of strong situations, the power of traits to predict leadership in many organizations is probably limited. Third, the evidence is unclear in separating cause from effect. For example, are leaders self-confident, or does success as a leader build self-confidence? Finally, traits do a better job at predicting the appearance of leadership than in actually distinguishing between *effective* and *ineffective* leaders.[10] The facts that an individual exhibits the traits and others consider that person to be a leader do not necessarily mean that the leader is successful at getting his or her group to achieve its goals.

These limitations have led researchers to look in other directions. Although there has been a resurgent interest in traits during the past 15 to 20 years, a major movement away from traits began as early as the 1940s. Leadership research from the late 1940s through the mid-1960s emphasized the preferred behavioral styles that leaders demonstrated.

BEHAVIORAL THEORIES

The inability to strike "gold" in the trait "mines" led researchers to look at the behaviors that specific leaders exhibited. They wondered if there was something unique in the way that effective leaders behave. For example, Times Mirror chairman Mark Willes and Titan International CEO Morry Taylor both have been very successful in leading their companies through difficult times.[11] And they both rely on a common leadership style—tough-talking, intense, autocratic. Does this suggest that autocratic behavior is a preferred style for all leaders? In this section, we look at four different **behavioral theories of leadership** in order to answer that question. First, however, let's consider the practical implications of the behavioral approach.

If the behavioral approach to leadership were successful, it would have implications quite different from those of the trait approach. If trait research had been successful, it would have provided a basis for *selecting* the "right" persons to assume formal positions in groups and organizations requiring leadership. In contrast, if behavioral studies were to turn up critical behavioral determinants of leadership, we could *train* people to be leaders. The difference between trait and behavioral theories, in terms of application, lies in their underlying assumptions. If trait theories were valid, then leadership is basically inborn: You either have it or you don't. On the other hand, if there were specific behaviors that identified leaders, then we could teach leadership—we could design programs that im-

behavioral theories of leadership

Theories proposing that specific behaviors differentiate leaders from nonleaders.

planted these behavioral patterns in individuals who desired to be effective leaders. This was surely a more exciting avenue, for it meant that the supply of leaders could be expanded. If training worked, we could have an infinite supply of effective leaders.

OHIO STATE STUDIES

The most comprehensive and replicated of the behavioral theories resulted from research that began at Ohio State University in the late 1940s.[12] These researchers sought to identify independent dimensions of leader behavior. Beginning with over a thousand dimensions, they eventually narrowed the list into two categories that substantially accounted for most of the leadership behavior described by employees. They called these two dimensions *initiating structure* and *consideration*.

initiating structure

The extent to which a leader is likely to define and structure his or her role and roles of subordinates in the search for goal attainment.

Initiating structure refers to the extent to which a leader is likely to define and structure his or her role and those of employees in the search for goal attainment. It includes behavior that attempts to organize work, work relationships, and goals. The leader characterized as high in initiating structure could be described as someone who "assigns group members to particular tasks," "expects workers to maintain definite standards of performance," and "emphasizes the meeting of deadlines." Mark Willes and Morry Taylor exhibit high initiating structure behavior.

consideration

The extent to which a leader is likely to have job relationships characterized by mutual trust, respect for subordinates' ideas, and regard for their feelings.

Consideration is described as the extent to which a person is likely to have job relationships that are characterized by mutual trust, respect for employees' ideas, and regard for their feelings. He or she shows concern for followers' comfort, well-being, status, and satisfaction. A leader high in consideration could be described as one who helps employees with personal problems, is friendly and approachable, and treats all employees as equals. The current chairman of Southwest Airlines, Herb Kelleher, rates high on consideration behavior. His leadership style is very people oriented, emphasizing friendliness and empowerment.

Extensive research, based on these definitions, found that leaders high in initiating structure and consideration (a "high-high" leader) tended to achieve high employee performance and satisfaction more frequently than those who rated low on either consideration, initiating structure, or both. However, the "high-high" style did not always result in positive consequences. For example, leader behavior characterized as high on initiating structure led to greater rates of grievances, absenteeism, and turnover and lower levels of job satisfaction for workers performing routine tasks. Other studies found that high consideration was negatively related to performance ratings of the leader by his or her superior. In conclusion, the Ohio State studies suggested that the "high-high" style generally resulted in positive outcomes, but enough exceptions were found to indicate that situational factors needed to be integrated into the theory.

UNIVERSITY OF MICHIGAN STUDIES

Leadership studies undertaken at the University of Michigan's Survey Research Center, at about the same time as those being done at Ohio State, had similar research objectives: to locate behavioral characteristics of leaders that appeared to be related to measures of performance effectiveness.

employee-oriented leader

One who emphasizes interpersonal relations.

production-oriented leader

One who emphasizes technical or task aspects of the job.

The Michigan group also came up with two dimensions of leadership behavior that they labeled **employee oriented** and **production oriented**.[13] Leaders who were employee oriented were described as emphasizing interpersonal relations; they took a personal interest in the needs of their employees and accepted individual differences among members. The production-oriented leaders, in contrast, tended to emphasize the technical or task aspects of the job—their main concern was in accomplishing their group's tasks, and the group members were a means to that end.

The conclusions arrived at by the Michigan researchers strongly favored the leaders who were employee oriented in their behavior. Employee-oriented leaders were associated with higher group productivity and higher job satisfaction. Production-oriented leaders tended to be associated with low group productivity and lower job satisfaction.

THE MANAGERIAL GRID

A graphic portrayal of a two-dimensional view of leadership style was developed by Blake and Mouton.[14] They proposed a **Managerial Grid** based on the styles of "concern for people" and "concern for production," which essentially represent the Ohio State dimensions of consideration and initiating structure or the Michigan dimensions of employee oriented and production oriented.

The grid, depicted in Exhibit 11-1, has nine possible positions along each axis, creating 81 different positions in which the leader's style may fall. The grid does not show results produced but, rather, the dominating factors in a leader's thinking in regard to getting results.

Based on the findings of Blake and Mouton, managers were found to perform best under a 9,9 style, as contrasted, for example, with a 9,1 (authority type) or 1,9 (lassiez-faire type) style.[15] Unfortunately, the grid offers a better framework for conceptualizing leadership style than for presenting any tangible new information in clarifying the leadership quandary, since there is little substantive evidence to support the conclusion that a 9,9 style is most effective in all situations.[16]

SCANDINAVIAN STUDIES

The three behavioral approaches we've just reviewed were essentially developed between the late 1940s and early 1960s. These approaches evolved during a time when the world was a far more stable and predictable place. In the belief that these studies fail to capture the more dynamic realities of today, researchers in

Managerial Grid

A nine-by-nine matrix outlining 81 different leadership styles.

The Managerial Grid

EXHIBIT 11-1

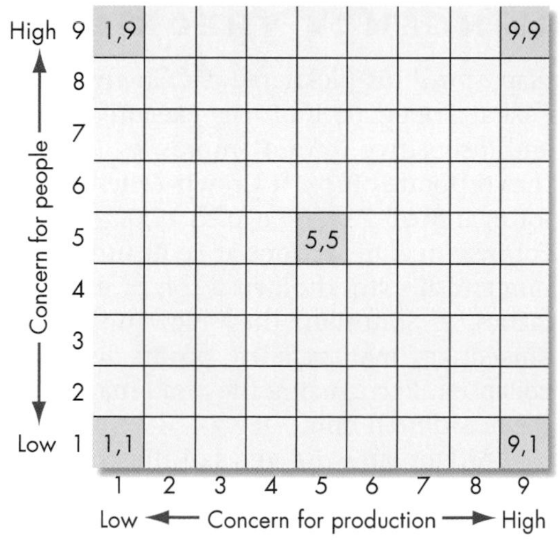

development-oriented leader

One who values experimentation, seeking new ideas, and generating and implementing change.

Finland and Sweden have been reassessing whether there are only two dimensions that capture the essence of leadership behavior.[17] Their basic premise is that in a changing world, effective leaders would exhibit **development-oriented** behavior. These are leaders who value experimentation, seek new ideas, and generate and implement change.

For instance, these Scandinavian researchers reviewed the original Ohio State data. They found that the Ohio State people included development items such as "pushes new ways of doing things," "originates new approaches to problems," and "encourages members to start new activities." But these items, at the time, didn't explain much toward effective leadership. It could be, the Scandinavian researchers proposed, that this was because developing new ideas and implementing change were not critical in those days. In today's dynamic environment, this may no longer be true. So the Scandinavian researchers have been conducting new studies to see if there is a third dimension—development orientation—that is related to leader effectiveness.

The early evidence is positive. Using samples of leaders in Finland and Sweden, the researchers have found strong support for development-oriented leader behavior as a separate and independent dimension. That is, the previous behavioral approaches that focused in on only two behaviors may not appropriately capture leadership in the twenty-first century. Moreover, while initial conclusions need to be guarded without more confirming evidence, it also appears that leaders who demonstrate development-oriented behavior have more satisfied employees and are seen as more competent by those employees.

SUMMARY OF BEHAVIORAL THEORIES

The behavioral theories have had modest success in identifying consistent relationships between leadership behavior and group performance. What seems to be missing is consideration of the situational factors that influence success or failure. For example, it seems unlikely that Martin Luther King, Jr. would have been a great civil rights leader during the early 1900s yet he was in the 1950s and 1960s. Would Ralph Nader have risen to lead a consumer activist group had he been born in 1834 rather than 1934, or in Costa Rica rather than Connecticut? It seems quite unlikely, yet the behavioral approaches we have described could not clarify these situational factors.

CONTINGENCY THEORIES

Al Dunlap *earned* his nickname of "Chainsaw Al." A West Point graduate and former paratrooper, he built his executive reputation on being tough, arrogant, and insensitive toward employees. At Lily Tulip he fired 50 percent of the corporate office; at Crown-Zellerbach, he cut 20 percent of the workforce; at Scott Paper, he axed 11,000 employees.[18] And this style worked. For instance, his actions at Scott turned the company around and made him and his stockholders a ton of money. But when Dunlap tried these tactics at Sunbeam, they blew up in his face. Employee motivation tanked, key managers left, profits disappeared, and the company's stock collapsed. Recognizing they had made a huge mistake in hiring Dunlap, the board fired him.

Al Dunlap's rise and fall illustrates what became increasingly clear to those studying the leadership phenomenon decades earlier: Predicting leadership success is more complex than isolating a few traits or

Al Dunlap's experiences demonstrate that leadership success reflects the situation. His solution of laying-off thousands of employess to cut costs worked at some firms, but it didn't guarantee success at Sunbeam. There his leadership style was ineffective and, because of that, he was fired.

preferable behaviors. What works at Scott Paper in 1996 doesn't necessarily work at Sunbeam in 1998. The failure by researchers to obtain consistent results led to a focus on situational influences. The relationship between leadership style and effectiveness suggested that under condition *a*, style *x* would be appropriate, while style *y* would be more suitable for condition *b*, and style *z* for condition *c*. But what were the conditions *a*, *b*, *c*, and so forth? It was one thing to say that leadership effectiveness depends on the situation and another to be able to isolate those situational conditions.

Several approaches to isolating key situational variables have proven more successful than others and, as a result, have gained wider recognition. We shall consider five of these: the Fiedler model, Hersey and Blanchard's situational theory, leader–member exchange theory, and the path-goal and leader-participation models.

FIEDLER MODEL

The first comprehensive contingency model for leadership was developed by Fred Fiedler.[19] The **Fiedler contingency model** proposes that effective group performance depends upon the proper match between the leader's style and the degree to which the situation gives control to the leader.

Identifying Leadership Style   Fiedler believes a key factor in leadership success is the individual's basic leadership style. So he begins by trying to find out what that basic style is. Fiedler created the **least preferred co-worker (LPC) questionnaire** for this purpose. It purports to measure whether a person is task or relationship oriented. The LPC questionnaire contains 16 contrasting adjectives (such as pleasant–unpleasant, efficient–inefficient, open–guarded, supportive–hostile). It asks respondents to think of all the co-workers they have ever had and to describe the one person they *least enjoyed* working with by rating him or her on a scale of 1 to 8 for each of the 16 sets of contrasting adjectives. Fiedler believes that based on the respondents' answers to this LPC questionnaire, he can determine their basic leadership style. If the least preferred co-worker is described in relatively positive terms (a high LPC score), then the respondent is primarily interested in good personal relations with this co-worker. That is, if you essentially describe the person you are least able to work with in favorable terms, Fiedler would label you *relationship oriented*. In contrast, if the least preferred co-worker is seen in relatively unfavorable terms (a low LPC score), the respondent is primarily interested in productivity and, thus, would be labeled *task oriented*. About 16 percent of respondents score in the middle range.[20] Such individuals cannot be classified as either relationship oriented or task oriented and, thus, fall outside the theory's predictions. The rest of our discussion, therefore, relates to the 84 percent who score in either the high or low range of the LPC.

Fiedler assumes that an individual's leadership style is fixed. As we'll show in a moment, this is important because it means that if a situation requires a task-oriented leader and the person in that leadership position is relationship oriented, either the situation has to be modified or the leader removed and replaced if optimum effectiveness is to be achieved.

Defining the Situation   After an individual's basic leadership style has been assessed through the LPC, it is necessary to match the leader with the situation. Fiedler has identified three contingency dimensions that, he argues, define the

Fiedler contingency model

The theory that effective groups depend upon a proper match between a leader's style of interacting with subordinates and the degree to which the situation gives control and influence to the leader.

least preferred co-worker (LPC) questionnaire

An instrument that purports to measure whether a person is task or relationship oriented.

key situational factors that determine leadership effectiveness. These are leader–member relations, task structure, and position power. They are defined as follows:

leader–member relations

The degree of confidence, trust, and respect subordinates have in their leader.

task structure

The degree to which job assignments are procedurized.

position power

Influence derived from one's formal structural position in the organization; includes power to hire, fire, discipline, promote, and give salary increases.

1. **Leader–member relations**: The degree of confidence, trust, and respect members have in their leader
2. **Task structure**: The degree to which the job assignments are procedurized (i. e., structured or unstructured)
3. **Position power**: The degree of influence a leader has over power variables such as hiring, firing, discipline, promotions, and salary increases

The next step in the Fiedler model is to evaluate the situation in terms of these three contingency variables. Leader–member relations are either good or poor, task structure is either high or low, and position power is either strong or weak.

Fiedler states the better the leader–member relations, the more highly structured the job, and the stronger the position power, the more control the leader has. For example, a very favorable situation (where the leader would have a great deal of control) might involve a payroll manager who is well respected and whose employees have confidence in her (good leader–member relations), where the activities to be done—such as wage computation, check writing, report filing—are specific and clear (high task structure), and the job provides considerable freedom for her to reward and punish her employees (strong position power). On the other hand, an unfavorable situation might be the disliked chairperson of a voluntary United Way fund-raising team. In this job, the leader has very little control. Altogether, by mixing the three contingency variables, there are potentially eight different situations or categories in which leaders could find themselves.

Matching Leaders and Situations With knowledge of an individual's LPC and an assessment of the three contingency variables, the Fiedler model proposes matching them up to achieve maximum leadership effectiveness.[21] Based on his research, Fiedler concluded that task-oriented leaders tend to perform better in situations that were very favorable to them and in situations that were very unfavorable (see Exhibit 11-2). So Fiedler would predict that when faced with a category I, II, III, VII, or VIII situation, task-oriented leaders perform better. Relationship-oriented leaders, however, perform better in moderately favorable situations—categories IV through VI. In recent years, Fiedler has condensed these eight situations down to three.[22] He now says that task-oriented leaders perform best in situations of high and low control, while relationship-oriented leaders perform best in moderate control situations.

Given Fiedler's findings, how would you apply them? You would seek to match leaders and situations. Individuals' LPC scores would determine the type of situation for which they were best suited. That "situation" would be defined by evaluating the three contingency factors of leader–member relations, task structure, and position power. But remember that Fiedler views an individual's leadership style as being fixed. Therefore, there are really only two ways in which to improve leader effectiveness.

First, you can change the leader to fit the situation—as in a baseball game, a manager can reach into the bullpen and put in a right-handed pitcher or a left-handed pitcher, depending on the situational characteristics of the hitter. So, for example, if a group situation rates as highly unfavorable but is currently led by a relationship-oriented manager, the group's performance could be improved by replacing that manager with one who is task oriented. The second alternative

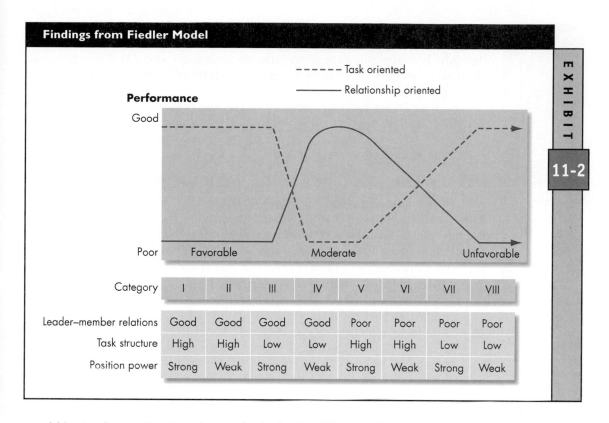

Findings from Fiedler Model

EXHIBIT

11-2

Task oriented
Relationship oriented

Performance

Good

Poor

	Favorable			Moderate			Unfavorable

Category	I	II	III	IV	V	VI	VII	VIII
Leader–member relations	Good	Good	Good	Good	Poor	Poor	Poor	Poor
Task structure	High	High	Low	Low	High	High	Low	Low
Position power	Strong	Weak	Strong	Weak	Strong	Weak	Strong	Weak

would be to change the situation to fit the leader. That could be done by restructuring tasks or increasing or decreasing the power that the leader has to control factors such as salary increases, promotions, and disciplinary actions.

Evaluation As a whole, reviews of the major studies that tested the overall validity of the Fiedler model lead to a generally positive conclusion. That is, there is considerable evidence to support at least substantial parts of the model.[23] If predictions from the model use only three categories rather than the original eight, there is ample evidence to support Fiedler's conclusions.[24] But there are problems with the LPC and the practical use of the model that need to be addressed. For instance, the logic underlying the LPC is not well understood and studies have shown that respondents' LPC scores are not stable.[25] Also, the contingency variables are complex and difficult for practitioners to assess. It's often difficult in practice to determine how good the leader–member relations are, how structured the task is, and how much position power the leader has.[26]

Cognitive Resource Theory More recently, Fiedler and an associate, Joe Garcia, reconceptualized the former's original theory.[27] Specifically, they've focused on the role of stress as a form of situational unfavorableness and how a leader's intelligence and experience influence his or her reaction to stress. They call this reconceptualization **cognitive resource theory**.

The essence of the new theory is that stress is the enemy of rationality. It's difficult for leaders (or anyone else, for that matter) to think logically and analytically when they're under stress. Moreover, the importance of a leader's intelligence and experience to his or her effectiveness differs under low- and high-stress situations. Basically, Fiedler and Garcia found that intelligence and experience interfere with each other. This has led to three conclusions: (1) Directive behavior

cognitive resource theory

A theory of leadership that states that stress unfavorably effects the situation, and intelligence and experience can lessen the influence of stress on the leader.

Cynthia Trudell's intelligence and leadership experience in manufacturing and labor relations has made her a top performer in the automotive industry. Trudell applied her Ph.D. in physcial chemistry in various engineering and manufacturing jobs at Ford and General Motors during the last 20 years. As president of a GM subsidiary in England, she demonstrated her labor-relations skills by working successfully with five labor unions. Trudell's accumulation of manufacturing expertise and her ability to form strong partnerships with unions won the confidence of GM executives in choosing her as president and chairman of Saturn Corp.

situational leadership theory (SLT)

A contingency theory that focuses on followers' readiness.

results in good performance only if linked with high intelligence in supportive, low-stress situations; (2) in high-stress situations, there is a positive relationship between job experience and performance; and (3) the intellectual abilities of leaders correlate with group performance in situations that the leader perceives as low in stress.

In spite of its newness, cognitive resource theory is developing a solid body of research support.[28] Most importantly, at this time, its major contribution seems to be to include stress as an important situational variable in the leadership equation.

HERSEY AND BLANCHARD'S SITUATIONAL THEORY

Paul Hersey and Ken Blanchard have developed a leadership model that has gained a strong following among management development specialists.[29] This model—called **situational leadership theory (SLT)**—has been incorporated into leadership training programs at over 400 of the Fortune 500 companies; and over 1 million managers a year from a wide variety of organizations are being taught its basic elements.[30]

Situational leadership is a contingency theory that focuses on the followers. Successful leadership is achieved by selecting the right leadership style, which Hersey and Blanchard argue is contingent on the level of the followers' readiness. Before we proceed, we should clarify two points: Why focus on the followers? What do they mean by the term *readiness*?

The emphasis on the followers in leadership effectiveness reflects the reality that it is the followers who accept or reject the leader. Regardless of what the leader does, effectiveness depends on the actions of his or her followers. This is an important dimension that has been overlooked or underemphasized in most leadership theories. The term *readiness*, as defined by Hersey and Blanchard, refers to the extent to which people have the ability and willingness to accomplish a specific task.

SLT essentially views the leader–follower relationship as analogous to that between a parent and child. Just as a parent needs to relinquish control as a child becomes more mature and responsible, so too should leaders. Hersey and Blanchard identify four specific leader behaviors—from highly directive to highly laissez-faire. The most effective behavior depends on followers' ability and motivation. So SLT says if followers are *unable* and *unwilling* to do a task, the leader needs to give clear and specific directions; if followers are *unable* and *willing*, the leader needs to display high task orientation to compensate for the followers' lack of ability and high relationship orientation to get followers to "buy into" the leader's desires. If followers are *able* and *unwilling*, the leader needs to use a supportive and participative style, and if employees are both *able* and *willing*, the leader doesn't need to do much.

SLT has an intuitive appeal. It acknowledges the importance of followers and builds on the logic that leaders can compensate for ability and motivational limitations in their followers. Yet research efforts to test and support the theory have generally been disappointing.[31] Why? Possible explanations include internal ambiguities and inconsistencies in the model itself as well as problems with research methodology in tests of the theory. So in spite of its intuitive appeal and wide popularity, at least at this point in time, any enthusiastic endorsement has to be cautioned against.

LEADER–MEMBER EXCHANGE THEORY

The leadership theories we've covered to this point have largely assumed that leaders treat all their followers in the same manner. But think about your experiences in groups. Did you notice that leaders often act very differently toward different people? Did the leader tend to have favorites who made up his or her "in-group"? If you answered Yes to both these questions, you're acknowledging the foundation of leader-member exchange theory.[32]

The **leader–member exchange (LMX) theory** argues that because of time pressures, leaders establish a special relationship with a small group of their followers. These individuals make up the in-group—they are trusted, get a disproportionate amount of the leader's attention, and are more likely to receive special privileges. Other followers fall into the out-group. They get less of the leader's time, fewer of the preferred rewards that the leader controls, and have leader–follower relations based on formal authority interactions.

The theory proposes that early in the history of the interaction between a leader and a given follower, the leader implicitly categorizes the follower as an "in" or an "out" and that relationship is relatively stable over time.[33] Just precisely how the leader chooses who falls into each category is unclear, but there is evidence that leaders tend to choose in-group members because they have attitude and personality characteristics that are similar to the leader's or a higher level of competence than out-group members.[34] (See Exhibit 11-3.) A key point to note here is that even though it is the leader who is doing the choosing, it is the follower's characteristics that are driving the leader's categorizing decision.

Research to test LMX theory has been generally supportive. More specifically, the theory and research surrounding it provide substantive evidence that leaders do differentiate among followers; that these disparities are far from random; and that followers with in-group status will have higher performance ratings, lower turnover intentions, greater satisfaction with their superiors, and higher overall satisfaction than will the out-group.[35] These positive findings for in-group members shouldn't be totally surprising given our knowledge of the self-fulfilling prophesy (see Chapter 5). Leaders invest their resources with those whom they expect to perform best. And "knowing" that in-group members are most competent, leaders treat them as such and unwittingly fulfill their prophesy.[36]

leader–member exchange (LMX) theory

Leaders create in-groups and out-groups, and subordinates with in-group status will have higher performance ratings, less turnover, and greater satisfaction with their superior.

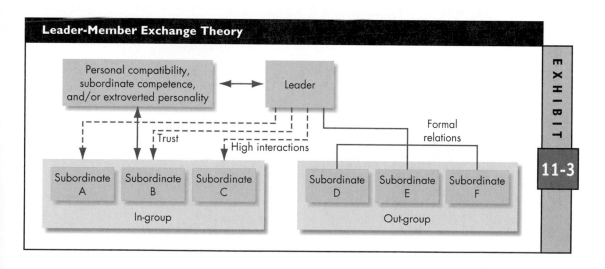

EXHIBIT 11-3

Leader-Member Exchange Theory

PATH-GOAL THEORY

Currently, one of the most respected approaches to leadership is the path-goal theory. Developed by Robert House, path-goal theory is a contingency model of leadership that extracts key elements from the Ohio State leadership research on initiating structure and consideration and the expectancy theory of motivation.[37]

path-goal theory

The theory that a leader's behavior is acceptable to subordinates insofar as they view it as a source of either immediate or future satisfaction.

The essence of the **path-goal theory** is that it's the leader's job to assist followers in attaining their goals and to provide the necessary direction and/or support to ensure that their goals are compatible with the overall objectives of the group or organization. The term *path-goal* is derived from the belief that effective leaders clarify the path to help their followers get from where they are to the achievement of their work goals and make the journey along the path easier by reducing roadblocks.

House identified four leadership behaviors. The *directive leader* lets followers know what is expected of them, schedules work to be done, and gives specific guidance as to how to accomplish tasks. The *supportive leader* is friendly and shows concern for the needs of followers. The *participative leader* consults with followers and uses their suggestions before making a decision. The *achievement-oriented leader* sets challenging goals and expects followers to perform at their highest level. In contrast to Fiedler, House assumes leaders are flexible and that the same leader can display any or all of these behaviors depending on the situation.

As Exhibit 11-4 illustrates, path-goal theory proposes two classes of situational or contingency variables that moderate the leadership behavior–outcome relationship—those in the environment that are outside the control of the employee (task structure, the formal authority system, and the work group) and those that are part of the personal characteristics of the employee (locus of control, experience, and perceived ability). Environmental factors determine the type of leader behavior required as a complement if follower outcomes are to be maximized, while personal characteristics of the employee determine how the environment and leader behavior are interpreted. So the theory proposes that leader behavior will be ineffective when it is redundant with sources of environmental structure or incongruent with employee charac-

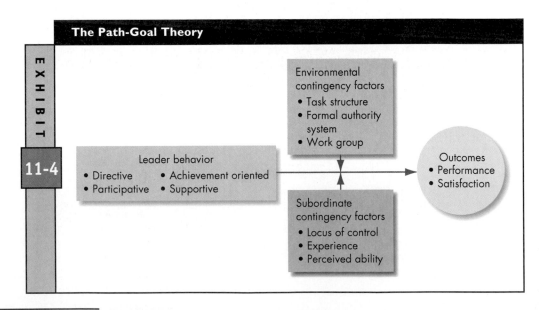

EXHIBIT 11-4

The Path-Goal Theory

Leader behavior
- Directive
- Participative
- Achievement oriented
- Supportive

Environmental contingency factors
- Task structure
- Formal authority system
- Work group

Subordinate contingency factors
- Locus of control
- Experience
- Perceived ability

Outcomes
- Performance
- Satisfaction

teristics. For example, the following are illustrations of predictions based on path-goal theory:

- Directive leadership leads to greater satisfaction when tasks are ambiguous or stressful than when they are highly structured and well laid out.
- Supportive leadership results in high employee performance and satisfaction when employees are performing structured tasks.
- Directive leadership is likely to be perceived as redundant among employees with high perceived ability or with considerable experience.
- Employees with an internal locus of control will be more satisfied with a participative style.
- Achievement-oriented leadership will increase employees' expectancies that effort will lead to high performance when tasks are ambiguously structured.

The research evidence generally supports the logic underlying the path-goal theory.[38] That is, employee performance and satisfaction are likely to be positively influenced when the leader compensates for things lacking in either the employee or the work setting. However, the leader who spends time explaining tasks when those tasks are already clear or when the employee has the ability and experience to handle them without interference is likely to be ineffective because the employee will see such directive behavior as redundant or even insulting.

LEADER-PARTICIPATION MODEL

In 1973, Victor Vroom and Phillip Yetton developed a **leader-participation model** that related leadership behavior and participation in decision making.[39] Recognizing that task structures have varying demands for routine and nonroutine activities, these researchers argued that leader behavior must adjust to reflect the task structure. Vroom and Yetton's model was normative—it provided a sequential set of rules that should be followed in determining the form and amount of participation in decision making, as determined by different types of situations. The model was a decision tree incorporating seven contingencies (whose relevance could be identified by making "yes" or "no" choices) and five alternative leadership styles.

More recent work by Vroom and Arthur Jago has resulted in a revision of this model.[40] The new model retains the same five alternative leadership styles—from the leader's making the decision completely by himself or herself to sharing the problem with the group and developing a consensus decision—but adds a set of problem types and expands the contingency variables to twelve. (See Exhibit 11-5.)

leader-participation model

A leadership theory that provides a set of rules to determine the form and amount of participative decision making in different situations.

Contingency Variables in the Revised Leader-Participation Model
1. Importance of the decision
2. Importance of obtaining subordinate commitment to the decision
3. Whether the leader has sufficient information to make a good decision
4. How well structured the problem is
5. Whether an autocratic decision would receive subordinate commitment
6. Whether subordinates "buy into" the organization's goals
7. Whether there is likely to be conflict among subordinates over solution alternatives
8. Whether subordinates have the necessary information to make a good decision
9. Time constraints on the leader that may limit subordinate involvement
10. Whether costs to bring geographically dispersed subordinates together are justified
11. Importance to the leader of minimizing the time it takes to make the decision
12. Importance of using participation as a tool for developing subordinate decision skills

EXHIBIT 11-5

Research testing both the original and revised leader-participation models has been encouraging.[41] Criticism has tended to focus on variables that have been omitted and on the model's overall complexity.[42] Other contingency theories demonstrate that stress, intelligence, and experience are important situational variables. Yet the leader-participation model fails to include them. But more important, at least from a practical point of view, is the fact that the model is far too complicated for the typical manager to use on a regular basis. While Vroom and Jago have developed a computer program to guide managers through all the decision branches in the revised model, it's not very realistic to expect practicing managers to consider twelve contingency variables, eight problem types, and five leadership styles in trying to select the appropriate decision process for a specific problem.

We obviously haven't done justice in this discussion to the model's sophistication. So what can you gain from this brief review? Additional insights into relevant contingency variables. Vroom and his associates have provided us with some specific, empirically supported contingency variables that you should consider when choosing your leadership style.

SOMETIMES LEADERSHIP IS IRRELEVANT!

In keeping with the contingency spirit, we conclude this section by offering this notion: The belief that some leadership style *will always* be effective *regardless* of the situation may not be true. Leadership may not always be important. Data from numerous studies collectively demonstrate that, in many situations, whatever actions leaders exhibit are irrelevant. Certain individual, job, and organizational variables can act as *substitutes* for leadership or *neutralize* the leader's effect to influence his or her followers.[43]

Neutralizers make it impossible for leader behavior to make any difference to follower outcomes. They negate the leader's influence. Substitutes, on the other hand, make a leader's influence not only impossible but also unnecessary. They act as a replacement for the leader's influence. For instance, characteristics of employees such as their experience, training, "professional" orientation, or indifference toward organizational rewards can substitute for, or neutralize the effect of, leadership. Experience and training, for instance, can replace the need for a leader's support or ability to create structure and reduce task ambiguity. Jobs that are inherently unambiguous and routine or that are intrinsically satisfying may place fewer demands on the leadership variable. Organizational characteristics such as explicit formalized goals, rigid rules and procedures, and cohesive work groups can replace formal leadership (see Exhibit 11-6).

This recent recognition that leaders don't always have an impact on follower outcomes should not be that surprising. After all, we have introduced a number of variables—attitudes, personality, ability, and group norms, to name but a few—that have been documented as having an effect on employee performance and satisfaction. Yet supporters of the leadership concept have tended to place an undue burden on this variable for explaining and predicting behavior. It is too simplistic to consider employees as guided to goal accomplishments solely by the actions of their leader. It is important, therefore, to recognize explicitly that leadership is merely another independent variable in our overall OB model. In some situations, it may contribute a lot to explaining employee productivity, absence, turnover, citizenship, and satisfaction, but in other situations, it may contribute little toward that end.

Substitutes and Neutralizers for Leadership			
Defining Characteristics	**Relationship-Oriented Leadership**	**Task-Oriented Leadership**	
Individual			
Experience/training	No effect on	Substitutes for	
Professionalism	Substitutes for	Substitutes for	
Indifference to rewards	Neutralizes	Neutralizes	
Job			
Highly structured task	No effect on	Substitutes for	
Provides its own feedback	No effect on	Substitutes for	
Intrinsically satisfying	Substitutes for	No effect on	
Organization			
Explicit formalized goals	No effect on	Substitutes for	
Rigid rules and procedures	No effect on	Substitutes for	
Cohesive work groups	Substitutes for	Substitutes for	

EXHIBIT 11-6

Source: Based on S. Kerr and J. M. Jermier, "Substitutes for Leadership: Their Meaning and Measurement," *Organizational Behavior and Human Performance*, December 1978, p. 378.

NEOCHARISMATIC THEORIES

The final set of leadership studies we'll review has been called **neocharismatic theories**.[44] These theories have three common themes. First, they stress symbolic and emotionally appealing leader behaviors. Second, they attempt to explain how certain leaders are able to achieve extraordinary levels of follower commitment. And third, they deemphasize theoretical complexity and look at leadership more the way the average "person on the street" today views the subject.

neocharismatic theories

Leadership theories that emphasize symbolism, emotional appeal, and extraordinary follower commitment.

CHARISMATIC LEADERSHIP

Charismatic leadership theory says that followers make attributions of heroic or extraordinary leadership abilities when they observe certain behaviors.[45] Studies on charismatic leadership have, for the most part, been directed at identifying those behaviors that differentiate charismatic leaders from their noncharismatic counterparts. Some examples of individuals frequently cited as being charismatic leaders include John F. Kennedy, Martin Luther King, Jr., Mary Kay Ash (founder of Mary Kay Cosmetics), Steve Jobs (co-founder of Apple Computer), Lee Iacocca (former chairman of Chrysler), and Herb Kelleher (CEO of Southwest Airlines).

There have been a number of studies that have attempted to identify personal characteristics of the charismatic leader.[46] The best-documented study has isolated five such characteristics—charismatic leaders have a vision, are willing to take risks to achieve that vision, are sensitive to both environmental constraints and follower needs, and exhibit behaviors that are out of the ordinary—that differentiate charismatic leaders from noncharismatic ones.[47] (See Exhibit 11-7.)

How do charismatic leaders actually influence followers? The evidence suggests a four-step process.[48] It begins by the leader articulating an appealing vision. This vision provides a sense of continuity for followers by linking the present with a better future for the organization. The leader then communicates

charismatic leadership

Followers make attributions of heroic or extraordinary leadership abilities when they observe certain behaviors.

EXHIBIT

11-7

1. *Vision and articulation.* They have a vision—expressed as an idealized goal—that proposes a future better than the status quo. They are able to clarify the importance of the vision in terms that are understandable to others.
2. *Personal risk.* Charismatic leaders are willing to take on high personal risk, incur high costs, and engage in self-sacrifice to achieve the vision.
3. *Environmental sensitivity.* They are able to make realistic assessments of the environmental constraints and resources needed to bring about change.
4. *Sensitivity to follower needs.* Charismatic leaders are perceptive of others' abilities and responsive to their needs and feelings.
5. *Unconventional behavior.* Those with charisma engage in behaviors that are perceived as novel and counter to norms.

Source: Based on J. A. Conger and R. N. Kanungo, *Charismatic Leadership in Organizations* (Thousand Oaks, CA: Sage, 1998), p. 94.

high performance expectations and expresses confidence that followers can attain them. This enhances follower self-esteem and self-confidence. Next, the leader conveys, through words and actions, a new set of values and, by his or her behavior, sets an example for followers to imitate. Finally, the charismatic leader makes self-sacrifices and engages in unconventional behavior to demonstrate courage and convictions about the vision.

What can we say about the charismatic leader's effect on his or her followers? There is an increasing body of research that shows impressive correlations between charismatic leadership and high performance and satisfaction among followers.[49] People working for charismatic leaders are motivated to exert extra work effort and, because they like and respect their leader, express greater satisfaction.

If charisma is desirable, can people learn to be charismatic leaders? Or are charismatic leaders born with their qualities? While a small minority still think charisma cannot be learned, most experts believe that individuals can be trained to exhibit charismatic behaviors and can, thus, enjoy the benefits that accrue to being labeled "a charismatic leader."[50] For instance, one set of authors proposes that a person can learn to become charismatic by following a three-step process.[51] First, an individual needs to develop the aura of charisma by maintaining an optimistic view; using passion as a catalyst for generating enthusiasm; and communicating with the whole body, not just with words. Second, an individual draws others in by creating a bond that inspires others to follow. And third, the individual brings out the potential in followers by tapping into their emotions. This approach seems to work as evidenced by researchers who've succeeded in actually scripting undergraduate business students to "play" charismatic.[52] The students were taught to articulate an overarching goal, communicate high performance expectations, exhibit confidence in the ability of followers to meet these expectations, and empathize with the needs of their followers; they learned to project a powerful, confident, and dynamic presence; and they practiced using a captivating and engaging voice tone. To further capture the dynamics and energy of charisma, the students were trained to evoke charismatic nonverbal characteristics: They alternated between pacing and sitting on the edges of their desks, leaned toward the subjects, maintained direct eye contact, and had relaxed postures and animated facial expressions. These researchers found that these students could learn how to project charisma. Moreover, followers of these student leaders had higher task performance, task adjustment, and adjustment to the leader and to the group than did followers who worked under groups led by non-charismatic leaders.

One last comment on this topic: Charismatic leadership may not always be needed to achieve high levels of employee performance. Charisma appears to be most appropriate when the follower's task has an ideological component or when the environment involves a high degree of stress and uncertainty.[53] This may explain why, when charismatic leaders surface, it's more likely to be in politics, religion, wartime; or when a business firm is in its infancy or facing a life-threatening crisis. In the 1930s, Franklin D. Roosevelt offered a vision to get Americans out of the Great Depression. In the early 1970s, when Chrysler Corp. was on the brink of bankruptcy, it needed a charismatic leader with unconventional ideas like Lee Iacocca to reinvent the company. In contrast, General Motors' failure to directly address its problems in the late 1990s—such as GM's inability to launch new vehicles on time, deep-seated aversion to change, and lackluster financial performance—were frequently attributed to CEO John Smith Jr. and his *lack* of charisma.[54]

TRANSFORMATIONAL LEADERSHIP

Another stream of research is the recent interest in differentiating transformational leaders from transactional leaders.[55] As you'll see, because transformational leaders are also charismatic, there is some overlap between this topic and our previous discussion of charismatic leadership.

Most of the leadership theories presented in this chapter—for instance, the Ohio State studies, Fiedler's model, path-goal theory, and the leader-participation model—have concerned **transactional leaders**. These kinds of leaders guide or motivate their followers in the direction of established goals by clarifying role and task requirements. There is also another type of leader who inspires followers to transcend their own self-interests for the good of the organization, and who is capable of having a profound and extraordinary effect on his or her followers. These are **transformational leaders** like Jack Welch at General Electric and Richard Branson of the Virgin Group. They pay attention to the concerns and developmental needs of individual followers; they change followers' awareness of issues by helping them to look at old problems in new ways; and they are able to excite, arouse, and inspire followers to put out extra effort to achieve group goals. Exhibit 11-8 briefly identifies and defines the four characteristics that differentiate these two types of leaders.

Transactional and transformational leadership shouldn't be viewed as opposing approaches to getting things done.[56] Transformational leadership is built *on top of* transactional leadership—it produces levels of follower effort and performance that go beyond what would occur with a transactional approach alone. Moreover, transformational leadership is more than charisma. "The purely charismatic [leader] may want followers to adopt the charismatic's world view and go no further; the transformational leader will attempt to instill in followers the ability to question not only established views but eventually those established by the leader."[57]

The evidence supporting the superiority of transformational leadership over the transactional variety is overwhelmingly impressive. For instance, a number of studies with U.S., Canadian, and German military officers found, at every level, that transformational leaders were evaluated as more effective than their transactional counterparts.[58] And managers at Federal Express who were rated by their followers as exhibiting more transformational leadership were evaluated by their

transactional leaders

Leaders who guide or motivate their followers in the direction of established goals by clarifying role and task requirements.

transformational leaders

Leaders who provide individualized consideration and intellectual stimulation, and who possess charisma.

Characteristics of Transactional and Transformational Leaders

Transactional Leader

Contingent Reward: Contracts exchange of rewards for effort, promises rewards for good performance, recognizes accomplishments.

Management by Exception (active): Watches and searches for deviations from rules and standards, takes corrective action.

Management by Exception (passive): Intervenes only if standards are not met.

Laissez-Faire: Abdicates responsibilities, avoids making decisions.

Transformational Leader

Charisma: Provides vision and sense of mission, instills pride, gains respect and trust.

Inspiration: Communicates high expectations, uses symbols to focus efforts, expresses important purposes in simple ways.

Intellectual Stimulation: Promotes intelligence, rationality, and careful problem solving.

Individualized Consideration: Gives personal attention, treats each employee individually, coaches, advises.

Source: B. M. Bass, "From Transactional to Transformational Leadership: Learning to Share the Vision," *Organizational Dynamics*, Winter 1990, p. 22. Reprinted by permission of the publisher. American Management Association, New York. All rights reserved.

immediate supervisors as higher performers and more promotable.[59] In summary, the overall evidence indicates that transformational leadership is more strongly correlated than transactional leadership with lower turnover rates, higher productivity, and higher employee satisfaction.[60]

VISIONARY LEADERSHIP

The term *vision* appeared in our previous discussion of charismatic leadership, but visionary leadership goes beyond charisma. In this section, we review recent revelations about the importance of visionary leadership.

visionary leadership

The ability to create and articulate a realistic, credible, attractive vision of the future for an organization or organizational unit that grows out of and improves upon the present.

Visionary leadership is the ability to create and articulate a realistic, credible, attractive vision of the future for an organization or organizational unit, which grows out of and improves upon the present.[61] This vision, if properly selected and implemented, is so energizing that it "in effect jump-starts the future by calling forth the skills, talents, and resources to make it happen."[62]

A review of various definitions finds that a vision differs from other forms of direction setting in several ways: "A vision has clear and compelling imagery that offers an innovative way to improve, which recognizes and draws on traditions, and connects to actions that people can take to realize change. Vision taps people's emotions and energy. Properly articulated, a vision creates the enthusiasm that people have for sporting events and other leisure-time acitivites, bringing this energy and commitment to the workplace."[63]

The key properties of a vision seem to be inspirational possibilities that are value centered, realizable, with superior imagery and articulation.[64] Visions should be able to create possibilities that are inspirational, unique, and offer a new order that can produce organizational distinction. A vision is likely to fail if it doesn't offer a view of the future that is clearly and demonstrably better for the organization and its members. Desirable visions fit the times and circumstances and reflect the uniqueness of the organization. People in the organization must also believe that the vision is attainable. It should be perceived as challenging yet doable. Visions that have clear articulation and powerful imagery are more easily grasped and accepted.

What are some examples of visions? Rupert Murdoch had a vision of the future of the communication industry by combining entertainment and media. Through his News Corporation, Murdoch has successfully integrated a broadcast network, TV stations, movie studio, publishing, and global satellite distribution. Mary Kay Ash's vision of women as entrepreneurs, selling products that improved their self-image, gave impetus to her cosmetics company. Michael Dell has created a vision of a business that allows Dell Computer to sell and deliver a finished PC directly to a customer in fewer than eight days.

What skills do visionary leaders exhibit? Once the vision is identified, these leaders appear to have three qualities that are related to effectiveness in their visionary roles.[65] First is the ability to explain the vision to others. The leader needs to make the vision clear in terms of required actions and aims through clear oral and written communication. Ronald Reagan—the so called "great communicator"—used his years of acting experience to help him articulate a simple vision for his presidency: a return to

Germany's Hasso Plattner (center) is hailed as a technical visionary. As a young engineer working for IBM in 1972, Plattner and several colleagues developed a computer program that could integrate several business functions, such as finance and production. Back then, software could handle only one function. When IBM passed on the idea, Plattner resigned and formed his own firm—SAP. Combining his enormous energy and enthusiasm with technical know-how, Plattner made his vision a reality. Today SAP is the fourth largest software firm in the world. Global giants like Amoco, Reebok, Bristol-Myers Squibb, and Volkswage use SAP software to integrate all their business functions on a worldwide basis.

"Men Make Better Leaders Than Women"

This statement is false. There is no evidence to support the myth that men make better leaders than women.

The evidence indicates that the similarities in leadership style between men and women tend to outweigh the differences. And the differences tend to favor women, not men![66]

Women tend to use a more democratic leadership style. They encourage participation, share power and information, and attempt to enhance followers' self-worth. They prefer to lead through inclusion and rely on their charisma, expertise, contacts, and interpersonal skills to influence others. Men, on the other hand, are more likely to use a directive command-and-control style. They rely on the formal authority of their managerial position for their influence base.

In today's organizations, flexibility, teamwork, trust, and information sharing are replacing rigid structures, competitive individualism, control, and secrecy. The best leaders listen, motivate, and provide support to their people. And many women seem to do those things better than men. As a specific example, the expanded use of cross-functional teams in organizations means that effective leaders must become skillful negotiators. The leadership styles women typically use can make them better at negotiating, as they tend to treat negotiations in the context of a continuing relationship—trying hard to make the other party a winner in its own and other's eyes.

a happier and more prosperous times through less government, lower taxes, and a strong military. Second is to be able to express the vision not just verbally but through the leader's behavior. This requires behaving in ways that continually convey and reinforce the vision. Herb Kelleher at Southwest Airlines lives and breathes his commitment to customer service. He's famous within the company for jumping in, when needed, to help check in passengers, load baggage, fill in for flight attendants, or do anything else to make the customer's experience more pleasant. The third skill is being able to extend the vision to different leadership contexts. This is the ability to sequence activities so the vision can be applied in a variety of situations. For instance, the vision has to be as meaningful to the people in accounting as to those in marketing, and to employees in Prague as well as in Pittsburgh.

CONTEMPORARY ISSUES IN LEADERSHIP

Is emotional intelligence an essential element of leadership? What unique demands do teams place on leaders? Is there a moral dimension to leadership? How does national culture affect the choice of leadership style? In this section, we briefly address these four contemporary issues in leadership.

EMOTIONAL INTELLIGENCE AND LEADERSHIP

We introduced emotional intelligence (EI) in our discussion of emotions in Chapter 4. We briefly revisit the topic here because of recent studies indicating that EI—more than IQ, expertise, or any other single factor—is the best predictor of who will emerge as a leader.[67]

As our trait research demonstrated, leaders need basic intelligence and job-relevant knowledge. But IQ and technical skills are "threshold capabilities." They're necessary but not sufficient requirements for leadership. It's the possession of the five components of emotional intelligence—self-awareness, self-management, self-motivation, empathy, and social skills—that allows an individual to become a star performer. Without EI, a person can have outstanding training, a highly analytical mind, a long-term vision, and an endless supply of terrific ideas but still not make a great leader. This is especially true as individuals move up in an organization. The evidence indicates that the higher the rank of a person considered to be a star performer, the more that EI capabilities surface as the reason for his or her effectiveness. Specifically, when star performers were compared with average ones in senior management positions, nearly 90 percent of the difference in their effectiveness was attributable to EI factors rather than basic intelligence.

EI has been shown to be positively related to job performance at all levels. But it appears to be especially relevant in jobs that demand a high degree of social interaction. And of course, that's what leadership is all about. Great leaders demonstrate their EI by exhibiting all five of its key components:

- *Self-awareness*: Exhibited by self-confidence, realistic self-assessment, and a self-deprecating sense of humor.
- *Self-management*: Exhibited by trustworthiness and integrity, comfort with ambiguity, and openness to change.
- *Self-motivation*: Exhibited by a strong drive to achieve, optimism, and high organizational commitment.
- *Empathy*: Exhibited by expertise in building and retaining talent, cross-cultural sensitivity, and service to clients and customers.

■ *Social skills*: Exhibited by the ability to lead change efforts, persuasiveness, and expertise in building and leading teams.

The recent evidence makes a strong case for concluding that EI is an essential element in leadership effectiveness. As such, it should probably be added to our earlier list of traits associated with leadership.

TEAM LEADERSHIP

Leadership is increasingly taking place within a team context. As teams grow in popularity, the role of the leader in guiding team members takes on heightened importance.[68] And the role of team leader is different from the traditional leadership role performed by first-line supervisors. J. D. Bryant, a supervisor at Texas Instruments' Forest Lane plant in Dallas, found that out.[69] One day he was happily overseeing a staff of 15 circuit-board assemblers. The next day he was informed that the company was moving to teams and that he was to become a "facilitator." "I'm supposed to teach the teams everything I know and then let them make their own decisions," he said. Confused about his new role, he admitted "there was no clear plan on what I was supposed to do." In this section, we consider the challenge of being a team leader, review the new roles that team leaders take on, and offer some tips on how to increase the likelihood that you can perform effectively in this position.

Many leaders are not equipped to handle the change to teams. As one prominent consultant noted, "even the most capable managers have trouble making the transition because all the command-and-control type things they were encouraged to do before are no longer appropriate. There's no reason to have any skill or sense of this."[70] This same consultant estimated that "probably 15 percent of managers are natural team leaders; another 15 percent could never lead a team because it runs counter to their personality, [They're unable to sublimate their dominating style for the good of the team.] Then there's that huge group in the middle: Team leadership doesn't come naturally to them, but they can learn it."[71]

The challenge for most managers, then, is to learn how to become an effective team leader. They have to learn skills such as the patience to share information, to trust others, to give up authority, and understanding when to intervene. Effective leaders have mastered the difficult balancing act of knowing when to leave their teams alone and when to intercede. New team leaders may try to retain too much control at a time when team members need more autonomy, or they may abandon their teams at times when the teams need support and help.[72]

A high degree of emotional intelligence helped Patricia Gallup launch and grow PC Connection, a $500 million mail-order computer firm in New Hampshire. "I knew from the start I'd be successful," says Gallup. With a degree in anthropology and no experience in high-tech, Gallup saw an opportunity in the early 1980s to sell computers by mail. And she would offer customers more support by telephone when they had problems than what they were getting at retail stores. Gallup's social skills sold small and mid-size business customers on her idea. Her ability to communicate her vision motivated employees to fulfill her vision. Today, Gallup communicates directly with most employees daily, either in person or through e-mail. She greets them by name and keeps her office door open for them to visit.

A study of 20 organizations that had reorganized themselves around teams found certain common responsibilities that all leaders had to assume. These included coaching, facilitating, handling disciplinary problems, reviewing team/individual performance, training, and communication.[73] Many of these responsibilities apply to managers in general. A more meaningful way to describe the team leader's job is to focus on two priorities: managing the team's external boundary and facilitating the team process.[74] We've broken these priorities down into four specific roles.

First, team leaders are *liaisons with external constituencies*. These include upper management, other internal teams, customers, and suppliers. The leader represents the team to other constituencies, secures needed resources, clarifies others' expectations of the team, gathers information from the outside, and shares this information with team members.

Second, team leaders are *troubleshooters*. When the team has problems and asks for assistance, team leaders sit in on meetings and help try to resolve the problems. This rarely relates to technical or operational issues because the team members typically know more about the tasks being done than does the team leader. Where the leader is most likely to contribute is by asking penetrating questions, helping the team talk through problems, and by getting needed resources from external constituencies. For instance, when a team in an aerospace firm found itself short-handed, its team leader took responsibility for getting more staff. He presented the team's case to upper management and got the approval through the company's human resources department.

Third, team leaders are *conflict managers*. When disagreements surface, they help process the conflict. What's the source of the conflict? Who is involved? What are the issues? What resolution options are available? What are the advantages and disadvantages of each? By getting team members to address questions such as these, the leader minimizes the disruptive aspects of intrateam conflicts.

Finally, team leaders are *coaches*. They clarify expectations and roles, teach, offer support, cheerlead, and whatever else is necessary to help team members improve their work performance.

MORAL LEADERSHIP

The topic of leadership and ethics has received surprisingly little attention. Only very recently have ethicists and leadership researchers begun to consider the ethical implications in leadership.[75] Why now? One reason may be the growing general interest in ethics throughout the field of management. Another reason may be the discovery by probing biographers that many of our past leaders—such as Martin Luther King, Jr., John F. Kennedy, and Franklin D. Roosevelt—suffered from ethical shortcomings. And certainly the recent impeachment of American president Bill Clinton on grounds of perjury and other charges has done nothing to lessen concern about ethical leadership.

Ethics touches on leadership at a number of junctures. Transformational leaders, for instance, have been described by one authority as fostering moral virtue when they try to change the attitudes and behaviors of followers.[76] Charisma, too, has an ethical component. Unethical leaders are more likely to use their charisma to enhance *power over* followers, directed toward self-serving ends. Ethical leaders are considered to use their charisma in a socially constructive way to serve others.[77] There is also the issue of abuse of power by leaders, for example, when they give themselves large salaries and bonuses while, at the same time, they seek to cut costs by laying off long-time employees. And, of course, the topic of trust explicitly deals with honesty and integrity in leadership.

Leadership effectiveness needs to address the *means* that a leader uses in trying to achieve goals as well as the content of those goals. GE's Jack Welch, for instance, is consistently described as a highly effective leader because he has succeeded in achieving outstanding returns for shareholders. But Welch is also widely regarded as one of the world's toughest managers. He is regularly listed high on *Fortune's* annual list of the most hated and reviled executives. Similarly, Bill Gates's success in leading Microsoft to domination of the world's software business has

Gerald Chamales (center), president of Omni Computer Products, provides a good example of moral leadership. A key part of his corporate strategy is giving hard-to-employ people an opportunity to succeed in the workplace. Chamales hires people with drug and alcohol addiction problems and uses the principles of recovery programs in managing them. Chamales's rehabilitating mission includes providing in-house mentors who counsel new employees on basic social and workplace skills. Tolerant of their personal struggles, he helps them handle legal, health, and family problems caused by their addiction. Chamales views his recovering employees as long-term investments who have helped him build his start-up firm into a $28 million company.

been achieved by means of an extremely demanding work culture. Microsoft's culture demands long work hours by employees and is intolerant of individuals who want to balance work and their personal life. Additionally, ethical leadership must address the content of a leader's goals. Are the changes that the leader seeks for the organization morally acceptable? Is a business leader effective if he or she builds an organization's success by selling products that damage the health of its users? This question might be asked of tobacco executives. Or is a military leader successful by winning a war that should not have been fought in the first place?

Leadership is not value free. Before we judge any leader to be effective, we should consider both the means used by the leader to achieve his or her goals and the moral content of those goals.

CROSS-CULTURAL LEADERSHIP

One general conclusion that surfaces from our discussion of leadership is that effective leaders don't use any single style. They adjust their style to the situation. While not mentioned explicitly in any of the theories we presented, certainly national culture is an important situational factor determining which leadership style will be most effective.[78] We propose that you consider it as another contingency variable. It can help explain, for instance, why executives at the highly successful Asia Department Store in central China blatantly brag about practicing "heartless" management, require new employees to undergo two to four weeks of military training with units of the People's Liberation Army in order to increase their obedience, and conduct the store's in-house training sessions in a public place where employees can openly suffer embarrassment from their mistakes.[79]

National culture affects leadership style by way of the follower. Leaders cannot choose their styles at will. They are constrained by the cultural conditions that their followers have come to expect. Consider the following: Korean leaders are expected to be paternalistic toward employees.[80] Arab leaders who show kindness or generosity without being asked to do so are seen by other Arabs as weak.[81] Japanese leaders are expected to be humble and speak infrequently.[82] And Scandinavian and Dutch leaders who single out individuals with public praise are likely to embarrass those individuals rather than energize them.[83]

Remember that most leadership theories were developed in the United States, using U.S. subjects, so they have an American bias. They emphasize follower responsibilities rather than rights; assume hedonism rather than commitment to duty or altruistic motivation; assume centrality of work and democratic value orientation; and stress rationality rather than spirituality, religion, or superstition.[84]

As a guide for adjusting your leadership style, you might consider the value dimensions of national culture presented in Chapter 3. For example, a manipulative or autocratic style is compatible with high power distance, and we find high power distance scores in Arab, Far Eastern, and Latin countries. Power distance rankings should also be good indicators of employee willingness to accept participative leadership. Participation is likely to be most effective in such low power distance cultures as exist in Norway, Finland, Denmark, and Sweden. Not incidentally, this may explain (1) why a number of leadership theories (the more obvious being ones such as the University of Michigan behavioral studies and the leader-participation model) implicitly favor the use of a participative or people-oriented style; (2) the emergence of development-oriented leader behavior found by Scandinavian researchers; and (3) the recent enthusiasm in North America with empowerment.

TRUST AND LEADERSHIP

Trust, or lack of trust, is an increasingly important issue in today's organizations. In this chapter, we define what trust is and provide you with some guidelines for helping build credibility and trust.

WHAT IS TRUST?

trust

A positive expectation that another will not act opportunistically.

Trust is a positive expectation that another will not—through words, actions, or decisions—act opportunistically.[85] The two most important elements implied in our definition are familiarity and risk.

The phrase *positive expectation* in our definition assumes knowledge and familiarity about the other party. Trust is a history-dependent process based on relevant but limited samples of experience.[86] It takes time to form, building incrementally and accumulating. Most of us find it hard, if not impossible, to trust someone immediately if we don't know anything about them. At the extreme, in the case of total ignorance, we can gamble but we can't trust.[87] But as we get to know someone, and the relationship matures, we gain confidence in our ability to make a positive expectation.

The term *opportunistically* refers to the inherent risk and vulnerability in any trusting relationship. Trust involves making oneself vulnerable as when, for example, we disclose intimate information or rely on another's promises.[88] By its very nature, trust provides the opportunity for disappointment or to be taken advantage of.[89] But trust is not taking risk per se; rather it is a *willingness* to take risk.[90] So when I trust someone, I expect that they will not take advantage of me. This willingness to take risks is common to all situations of trust.[91]

What are the key dimensions that underlie the concept of trust? Recent evidence has identified five: integrity, competence, consistency, loyalty, and openness.[92] (See Exhibit 11-9.)

Integrity refers to honesty and truthfulness. Of all five dimensions, this one seems to be most critical when someone assesses another's trustworthiness. "Without a perception of the other's 'moral character' and 'basic honesty,' other dimensions of trust [are] meaningless."[93]

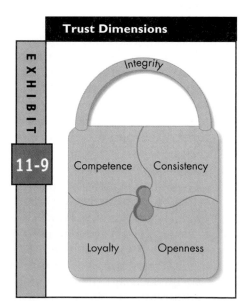

EXHIBIT 11-9

Trust Dimensions

Integrity

Competence   Consistency

Loyalty   Openness

Competence encompasses an individual's technical and interpersonal knowledge and skills. Does the person know what he or she is talking about? You're unlikely to listen to or depend upon someone whose abilities you don't respect. You need to believe that the person has the skills and abilities to carry out what he or she says they will do.

Consistency relates to an individual's reliability, predictability, and good judgment in handling situations. "Inconsistencies between words and action decrease trust."[94] This dimension is particularly relevant for managers. "Nothing is noticed more quickly ... than a discrepancy between what executives preach and what they expect their associates to practice."[95]

Loyalty is the willingness to protect and save face for another person. Trust requires that you can depend on someone not to act opportunistically.

The final dimension of trust is *openness*. Can you rely on the person to give you the full truth?

TRUST AS THE FOUNDATION OF LEADERSHIP

Trust appears to be a primary attribute associated with leadership. In fact, if you look back at our discussion of traits, honesty and integrity were among the six traits found to be consistently associated with leadership. It appears increasingly evident that it's impossible to lead people who don't trust you.

As one author noted: "Part of the leader's task has been, and continues to be, working with people to find and solve problems, but whether leaders gain access to the knowledge and creative thinking they need to solve problems depends on how much people trust them. Trust and trust-worthiness modulate the leader's access to knowledge and cooperation."[96]

OB *in the News*

Pamela Barefoot and the Blue Crab Bay Co.

Leadership is a challenge whether you're running a billion-dollar corporation or a small business. Pamela Barefoot (left, in photo) learned that developing leadership skills is as important for running her small business as it is for the Jurgen Schrempp and Bill Gates of the world.

Barefoot started Blue Crab Bay Co., a Virginia-based producer of specialty foods and gifts, in her home in 1985. Sales and profits grew, but she continued to be unsure of herself. "My lack of confidence in where we were going and how we were going to get there affected everybody ... I had to decide: Am I going to get on this horse and ride it, or am I just going to stand on the sidelines and let it run ahead?" So in the early 1990s, with the help of a consulting firm, Barefoot got serious about developing her skills in communication, creating accountability, and building trust.

Barefoot needed to improve her ability to communicate. "It seems as if every time we get upset here, or something goes wrong," she says, "it's because we're not communicating. Somebody will say something, and somebody else will hear it a different way." So Barefoot focused on developing a mission statement for her business, identifying clear goals, and explaining those goals to her staff. This helped clarify for employees, and herself, what the firm was all about.

Next, Barefoot focused on accountability. She needed to hold people accountable for how well they perform in trying to achieve those goals. Barefoot added a layer of management—not to separate herself from her employees, but to allow supervisors to make independent decisions. By delegating day-to-day tasks, Barefoot was able to concentrate her efforts on growing the business.

Finally, Barefoot learned she had to trust the people she had working for her. This would allow her more time to get away from the business and increase employee commitment to the business. Problems get resolved faster now. Says Barefoot, "When I leave here, they can run this business just as well as I can because they know the way I want it done."

Barefoot has proven to be a worthy student of leadership. Today her company employs two dozen people and was recently honored as a Blue Chip Enterprise—an award recognizing small businesses that have successfully weathered significant challenges.

Source: Based on M. Barrier, "Leadership Skills Employees Respect," *Nation's Business*, January 1999, pp. 28–30.

When followers trust a leader, they are willing to be vulnerable to the leader's actions—confident that their rights and interests will not be abused.[97] People are unlikely to look up to or follow someone who they perceive as dishonest or who is likely to take advantage of them. Honesty, for instance, consistently ranks at the top of most people's list of characteristics they admire in their leaders. "Honesty is absolutely essential to leadership. If people are going to follow someone willingly, whether it be into battle or into the boardroom, they first want to assure themselves that the person is worthy of their trust."[98]

Now, more than ever, managerial and leadership effectiveness depends on the ability to gain the trust of followers.[99] For instance, reengineering, downsizing, and the increased use of temporary employees have undermined a lot of employees' trust in management. A recent survey of employees by a firm in Chicago found 40 percent agreed with the statement: "I often don't believe what management says."[100] In times of change and instability, people turn to personal relationships for guidance; and the quality of these relationships are largely determined by level of trust. Moreover, contemporary management practices such as empowerment and the use of work teams require trust to be effective.

THREE TYPES OF TRUST

There are three types of trust in organizational relationships: *deterrrence* based, *knowledge* based, and *identification* based.[101]

deterrence-based trust

Trust based on fear of reprisal if the trust is violated.

Deterrence-Based Trust The most fragile relationships are contained in **deterrence-based trust**. One violation or inconsistency can destroy the relationship. This form of trust is based on fear of reprisal if the trust is violated. Individuals who are in this type of relationship do what they say because they fear the consequences from not following through on their obligations.

Deterrence-based trust will work only to the degree that punishment is possible, consequences are clear, and the punishment is actually imposed if the trust is violated. To be sustained, the potential loss of future interaction with the other party must outweigh the profit potential that comes from violating expectations. Moreover, the potentially harmed party must be willing to introduce harm (e.g., I have no qualms about speaking badly of you if you betray my trust) to the person acting distrustingly.

Most new relationships begin on a base of deterrence. Take, as an illustration, a situation in which you're selling your car to a friend of a friend. You don't know the buyer. You might be motivated to refrain from telling this buyer all the problems with the car that you know about. Such behavior would increase your chances of selling the car and securing the highest price. But you don't withhold information. You openly share the car's flaws. Why? Probably because of fear of reprisal. If the buyer later thinks you deceived him, he is likely to share this with your mutual friend. If you knew that the buyer would never say anything to the mutual friend, you might be tempted to take advantage of the opportunity. If it's clear that the buyer would tell and that your mutual friend would think considerably less of you for taking advantage of this buyer-friend, your honesty could be explained in deterrence terms.

Another example of deterrence-based trust is a new manager–employee relationship. As an employee, you typically trust a new boss even though there is little experience on which to base that trust. The bond that creates this trust lies in the authority held by the boss and the punishment he or she can impose if you fail to fulfill your job-related obligations.

Knowledge-Based Trust Most organizational relationships are rooted in **knowledge-based trust**. That is, trust is based on the behavioral predictability that comes from a history of interaction. It exists when you have adequate information about someone to understand them well enough to be able to accurately predict their likely behavior.

Knowledge-based trust relies on information rather than deterrence. Knowledge of the other party and predictability of his or her behavior replaces the contracts, penalties, and legal arrangements more typical of deterrence-based trust. This knowledge develops over time, largely as a function of experience that builds confidence of trustworthiness and predictability. The better you know someone, the more accurately you can predict what he or she will do. Predictability enhances trust—even if the other is predictably untrustworthy—because the ways that the other will violate the trust can be predicted! The more communication and regular interaction you have with someone else, the more this form of trust can be developed and depended upon.

Interestingly, at the knowledge-based level, trust is not necessarily broken by inconsistent behavior. If you believe you can adequately explain or understand another's apparent violation, you can accept it, forgive the person, and move on

knowledge-based trust

Trust based on behavioral predictability that comes from a history of interaction.

FROM CONCEPTS *TO* SKILLS

How Do You Build Trust?

Managers who have learned to build trusting relationships engage in certain common practices. The following summarizes what you can do to emulate these successful managers.[102]

Practice openness. Mistrust comes as much from what people don't know as from what they do know. Openness leads to confidence and trust. So keep people informed, make the critieria on how decisions are made overtly clear, explain the rationale for your decisions, be candid about problems, and fully disclose relevant information.

Be fair. Before making decisions or taking actions, consider how others will perceive them in terms of objectivity and fairness. Give credit where it's due, be objective and impartial in performance appraisals, and pay attention to equity perceptions in reward distributions.

Speak your feelings. Managers who convey only hard facts come across as cold and distant. If you share your feelings, others will see you as real and human. They will know who you are and their respect for you will increase.

Tell the truth. If integrity is critical to trust, you must be perceived as someone who tells the truth. People are generally more tolerant of learning something they "don't want to hear" than finding out that their manager lied to them.

Show consistency. People want predictability. Mistrust comes from not knowing what to expect. Take the time to think about your values and beliefs. Then let them consistently guide your decisions. When you know your central purpose, your actions will follow accordingly, and you will project a consistency that earns trust.

Fulfill your promises. Trust requires that people believe that you are dependable. So you need to ensure that you keep your word and commitments. Promises made must be promises kept.

Maintain confidences. You trust people who are discreet and upon whom you can rely. So if people make themselves vulnerable by telling you something in confidence, they need to feel assured that you will not discuss it with others or betray that confidence. If people perceive you as someone who leaks personal confidences or someone who can't be depended on, you won't be perceived as trustworthy.

Demonstrate competence. Develop the admiration and respect of others by demonstrating technical and professional ability. Pay particular attention to developing and displaying your communication, negotiation, and other interpersonal skills.

in the relationship. However, the same inconsistency at the deterrence level is likely to irrevocably break the trust.

In an organizational context, most manager–employee relationships are knowledge based. Both parties have enough experience working with each other so that they know what to expect. A long history of consistently open and honest interactions, for instance, is not likely to be permanently destroyed by a single violation.

Identification-Based Trust   The highest level of trust is achieved when there is an emotional connection between the parties. It allows one party to act as an agent for the other and substitute for that person in interpersonal transactions. This is called **identification-based trust**. Trust exists because the parties understand each other's intentions and appreciate the other's wants and desires. This mutual understanding is developed to the point that each can effectively act for the other.

Controls are minimal at this level. You don't need to monitor the other party because there exists unquestioned loyalty.

The best example of identification-based trust is a long-term, happily married couple. A husband comes to learn what's important to his wife and anticipates those actions. She, in turn, trusts that he will anticipate what's important to her without having to ask. Increased identification enables each to think like the other, feel like the other, and respond like the other.

You see identification-based trust occasionally in organizations among people who have worked together for long periods of time and have a depth of experience that allows them to know each other inside and out. This is also the type of trust that managers ideally seek in teams. Team members are so comfortable and trusting of each other that they can anticipate each other and freely act in each other's absence. Realistically, in the current work world, most large corporations have broken the bonds of identification-based trust they may have built with long-term employees. Broken promises have led to a breakdown in what was, at one time, a bond of unquestioned loyalty. It's likely to have been replaced with knowledge-based trust.

identification-based trust

Trust based on a mutual understanding of each other's intentions and appreciation of the other's wants and desires.

SUMMARY AND IMPLICATIONS FOR MANAGERS

Leadership plays a central part in understanding group behavior, for it's the leader who usually provides the direction toward goal attainment. Therefore, a more accurate predictive capability should be valuable in improving group performance.

The original search for a set of universal leadership traits failed. At best, we can say that individuals who are ambitious, have high energy, a desire to lead, self-confidence, intelligence, hold job-relevant knowledge, are perceived as honest and trustworthy, and are flexible are more likely to succeed as leaders than individuals without these traits.

The behavioral approach's major contribution was narrowing leadership into task-oriented and people-oriented styles. But no one style was found to be effective in all situations.

A major breakthrough in our understanding of leadership came when we recognized the need to develop contingency theories that included situational factors. At present, the evidence indicates relevant situational variables would include the task structure of the job; level of situational stress; level of group support; the leader's intelligence and experience; and follower characteristics such as personality, experience, ability, and motivation.

More recently, neocharismatic theories have gained increased acceptance. As we learn more about the personal characteristics that followers attribute to charismatic and transformational leaders, and about the conditions that facilitate their emergence, we should be better able to predict when followers will exhibit extraordinary commitment and loyalty to their leaders and to those leaders' goals.

Finally, we discussed the role that trust plays in leadership. Effective managers today must develop trusting relationships with those whom they seek to lead. Why? Because as organizations have become less stable and predictable, strong bonds of trust are likely to be replacing bureaucratic rules in defining expectations and relationships.

The Perils of Leadership Training

O rganizations spend billions of dollars on leadership training every year. They send managers and manager-wannabes to a wide range of leadership training activities—formal M.B.A. programs, leadership seminars, weekend retreats, and even outward-bound adventures. They appoint mentors. They establish "fast tracks" for high-potential individuals in order that they can gain a variety of the "right kinds of experience." We propose that much of this effort to train leaders is probably a waste of money. And we base our position by looking at two very basic assumptions that underlie leadership training.[1]

The first assumption is that we know what leadership is. We don't. Experts can't agree if it's a trait, a characteristic, a behavior, a role, a style, or an ability. They further can't even agree on whether leaders really make a difference in organizational outcomes. Some experts have persuasively argued that leadership is merely an attribution made to explain organizational successes and failures, which themselves occur by chance. Leaders are the people who get credit for successes and take the blame for failures, but they may actually have little influence over organizational outcomes.

The second basic assumption is that we can train people to lead. The evidence here is not very encouraging. We do seem to be able to teach individuals *about leadership*. Unfortunately, findings indicate we aren't so good at teaching people *to lead*. There are several possible explanations. To the degree that personality is a critical element in leadership effectiveness, some people may not have the right personality traits. A second explanation is that there is no evidence that individuals can substantially alter their basic leadership style.[2] A third possibility is that, even if certain theories could actually guide individuals in leadership situations and even if individuals could alter their style, the complexity of those theories makes it nearly impossible for any normal human being to assimilate all the variables and be capable of enacting the right behaviors in every situation.

L eadership training exists and is a multibillion-dollar industry because it works. Decision makers are, for the most part, rational. Would a company such as General Electric spend literally tens of millions of dollars each year on leadership training if it didn't expect a handsome return? We don't think so! And the ability to successfully lead is why corporations such as Disney willingly pay Michael Eisner $100 million a year or more. By his ability to lead, Eisner has increased the value of Disney stock by thirtyfold.

While there are certainly disagreements over the exact definition of leadership, most academics and businesspeople agree that leadership is a process of influence in which an individual, by his or her actions, facilitates the movement of a group of people toward the achievement of a common goal.

Do leaders affect organizational outcomes? Of course, they do. Successful leaders anticipate change, vigorously exploit opportunities, motivate their followers to higher levels of productivity, correct poor performance, and lead the organization toward its objectives. A review of the leadership literature, in fact, led two academics to conclude that the research shows "a consistent effect for leadership explaining 20 to 45 percent of the variance on relevant organizational outcomes."[3]

What about the effectiveness of leadership training programs? They vary. And well they should since the programs themselves are so diverse. Moreover, people learn in different ways. Since some leadership programs are better than others and because some people participate in programs that are poorly matched to their needs and learning style, we should expect leadership-training effectiveness to have a spotty record. So decision makers need to be careful in choosing leadership-training experiences for their managers. But they shouldn't conclude that all leadership training is a waste of money.

---

[3]D. V. Day and R. G. Lord, "Executive Leadership and Organizational Performance: Suggestions for a New Theory and Methodology," *Journal of Management*, Fall 1988, pp. 453–64.

---

[1]See R. A. Barker, "How Can We Train Leaders If We Do Not Know What Leadership Is?" *Human Relations*, April 1997, pp. 343–62.

[2]R. J. House and R. N. Aditya, "The Social Scientific Study of Leadership: Quo Vadis?" *Journal of Management*, vol. 23, no. 3, 1997, pp. 460–61.

1. Trace the development of leadership research.

2. Describe the strengths and weaknesses in the trait approach to leadership.

3. What is the Managerial Grid? Contrast its approach to leadership with the approaches of the Ohio State and Michigan groups.

4. What was the contribution of the Scandinavian studies to the behavioral theories?

5. Describe leader–member exchange theory. What are its implications for leadership practice?

6. When might leaders be irrelevant?

7. How is team leadership different from one-on-one leadership?

8. What is moral leadership?

9. How might leadership in Japan contrast with leadership in the United States or Canada?

10. Contrast the three types of trust. Relate them to your experience in personal relationships.

Questions for Critical Thinking

1. Develop an example in which you operationalize the Fiedler model.

2. Develop an example in which you operationalize path-goal theory.

3. What kind of activities could a full-time college student pursue that might lead to the perception that he or she is a charismatic leader? In pursuing those activities, what might the student do to enhance this perception of being charismatic?

4. Do you think trust evolves out of an individual's personal characteristics or out of specific situations? Explain.

5. What role do you think training plays in an individual's ability to trust? For instance, does the training of lawyers, accountants, law enforcement personnel, and social workers take different approaches toward trusting others? Explain.

Team Exercise | Practicing to Be Charismatic

People who are charismatic engage in the following behaviors:

1. *Project a powerful, confident, and dynamic presence.* This has both verbal and nonverbal components. Those with charisma use a captivating and engaging voice tone. They convey confidence. They also talk directly to people, maintaining direct eye contact, and holding their body posture in a way that says they're sure of themselves. They speak clearly, avoid stammering, and avoid sprinkling their sentences with noncontent phrases such as "ahhh" and "you know."

2. *Articulate an overarching goal.* They have a vision for the future, unconventional ways of achieving the vision, and the ability to communicate the vision to others.

   The vision is a clear statement of where they want to go and how they're going to get there. They are able to persuade others how the achievement of this vision is in the others' self-interest.

They look for fresh and radically different approaches to problems. The road to achieving their vision is novel but also appropriate to the context.

They not only have a vision but they're able to get others to buy into it. The real power of Martin Luther King, Jr. was not that he had a dream, but that he could articulate it in terms that made it accessible to millions.

3. *Communicate high performance expectations and confidence in others' ability to meet these expectations.* They demonstrate their confidence in people by stating ambitious goals for them individually and as a group. They convey absolute belief that they will achieve their expectations.

4. *Are sensitive to the needs of followers.* Charismatic leaders get to know their followers individually. They understand their individual needs and are able to develop intensely personal relationships with each. They do this through encouraging followers to express their points of view, being approachable, genuinely listening to and caring about their followers' concerns, and by asking

questions so they can learn what is really important to them.

Now that you know what charismatic leaders do, you get the opportunity to practice projecting charisma.

   a. The class should break into pairs.

   b. Student A's task is to "lead" Student B through a new-student orientation to your college. The orientation should last about 10 to 15 minutes. Assume Student B is new to your college and is unfamiliar with the campus. Remember, Student A should attempt to project himself or herself as charismatic.

   c. Roles now reverse and Student B's task is to "lead" Student A in a 10- to 15-minute program on how to study more effectively for college exams. Take a few minutes to think about what has worked well for you and assume that Student A is a new student interested in improving his or her study habits. Again remember that Student B should attempt to project himself or herself as charismatic.

   d. When both role plays are complete, each pair should assess how well they did in projecting charisma and how they might improve.

Source: This exercise is based on J. M. Howell and P. J. Frost, "A Laboratory Study of Charismatic Leadership," *Organizational Behavior and Human Decision Processes*, April 1989, pp. 243–69.

Internet Search Exercises

1. Find five companies whose CEOs have left for reasons other than normal retirement in the past 12 months. Assess their company's performance following their departure. Was the organization's stock price affected? Why might a CEOs departure affect company performance?

2. Find five retail or manufacturing companies that proclaim that trust is an important element in their interactions with customers and/or employees. Describe this proclamation. Can you find any substantiation for this claim or do you think it's merely saying what is politically correct?

PHLIP Companion Web Site

We invite you to visit the Robbins homepage on the Prentice Hall Web site at **www.prenhall.com/robbins** for our on-line study guide, current events, links to related Web sites, and more.

Case Incident   Jack Hartnett at D. L. Rogers Corp.

D. L. Rogers Corp., based in Bedford, Texas, primarily owns 54 franchises of Sonic Corp., a chain of fast-food drive-in restaurants. Jack Hartnett, Rogers's president, leads by combining ingredients from both the Stone Age and the New Age.

Hartnett prides himself on knowing everything about his employees—both at work and at home. If they've got marital problems or credit card debt, he wants to know. And he thinks nothing of using that information if he thinks he can help. For instance, how many executives do you know who counsel employees on their sex life? Hartnett does. When a wife of one of his managers called Hartnett to say her husband was impotent and didn't know what to do, Hartnett had an answer. He met with the couple in a motel room, where he prodded the fellow to confess to an affair and to beg for forgiveness.

Is Hartnett's style intrusive? Yes, but he doesn't consider it a problem. "There are no secrets here," he says. No subject is too delicate for his ears. And his defense? He's merely doing what any good friend might do. Also, he believes that the more he knows about his workers, the more he can help them stay focused at work and happy at home.

Hartnett plays golf with his managers, sends them personally signed birthday cards, and drops by their homes to take them to dinner. But if you think he's "Mr. Nice Guy," think again. He badmouths academic theories that propose that leaders need to persuade workers to "buy in" to the leader's vision. Hartnett instructs his employees to "do it the way we tell you to do it." He's perfectly comfortable using the authority in his position to make rules and dish out punishments. One of Hartnett's basic rules is "I will only tell you something once." Break one of his rules twice and he'll fire you.

The managers who work for Hartnett are well compensated for meeting his demanding requirements. His unit managers and regional managers earn an average of $60,000 and $125,000, respectively. This compares with industry averages of $30,000 and $52,700.

Does Hartnett seem inconsistent? Maybe. He believes in openness, integrity, and honesty. But he expects as much as he gives. It's not an option. So he's "your best friend" and, at the same time, he's rigid and autocratic. He admits to purposely keeping everybody slightly off balance "so they'll work harder."

Hartnett's approach to leadership seems to be effective. His per-store revenues are nearly 18 percent higher than the chain's average, and profits are 25 percent above the norm. Moreover, people seem to like working for him. In an industry known for high turnover, Hartnett's managers stay about nine years compared with an industry average of less than two.

Questions

1. Is Hartnett a transactional or transformational leader? Explain your answer in detail.

2. What situational variables do you think explain his success at Rogers?

3. Would you want to work for Hartnett? Why or why not?

Source: Based on M. Ballon, "Extreme Managing," *INC.*, July 1998, pp. 60–71.

| Video Case | Ironbound Supply Company |

SMALL BUSINESS 2000

You can probably easily think of some businesses that you know that have been around for a long time. You can probably think of others that have not lasted very long. Why do you think some survive while others don't make it? One thing you might consider is the leadership of the company. You might also think that if a company has survived for a long time, then it can survive forever. Although, at first this might make sense, think about it for a minute. Do you drive the same type of car that your parents did when they were your age? Is the PC you buy today the same as the one you might have brought even three years ago? The answer to these questions is probably no. Age alone does not guarantee success. It is the knowledge and experience that age can provide that contributes to a company's success.

In Newark, New Jersey, Howard Kent has been running a pipe and industrial valve company for more than 30 years. The basic products that he sells haven't changed much. But the way that the company runs sure has. Howard takes us on a trip down memory lane and discusses the evolution of his company. Some companies change because the technology or product that they sell changes. The Ironbound Supply Company changed—and still does—because of the approach Howard Kent has to running a business.

In addition to understanding how the business has evolved over 30 years, we learn at least two other things from Kent. First, we gain an understanding of the importance of working smart. Kent talks about efficiency and the importance of taking advantage of technology in running a company. Second, we learn about Kent's attitude toward the importance of the people that make up a company. Howard Kent is no pushover, but he is concerned about being fair with his employees. As you watch his video, try to imagine how this company has changed from the day Kent started it as a one-person operation to what it is today.

Questions

1. Howard Kent does not run the same company that he did 30 years ago. What do you think about Howard Kent as a leader; do you think he is a leader? Why or why not?

2. We met Scott Gross, an 18-year veteran at Ironbound Supply who has worked his way up from truck driver to vice president. Howard Kent talked about what he thought of Gross, and a little bit about why he has the job he does today. What do you think this says about Kent's approach to leadership?

3. Kent talked about "backing off and relinquishing some control." Do you think this is easy for him to do? What advise might you give him on how to handle mistakes that might be made as new managers grow into their new roles?

4. What do you think about Kent's attitude toward sharing the wealth and determining if raises should be given or not? Do you think this is a good attitude for him to have? Why or why not?

1. Based on A. Taylor III, "'Neutron Jurgen' Ignites a Revolution at Daimler-Benz," *Fortune*, November 10, 1997, pp. 144–52; G. L. White, "DaimlerChrysler Unveils Reshuffling of Its U.S. Manufacturing Executives," *Wall Street Journal*, December 15, 1998, p. B10; A. Taylor III, "The Germans Take Charge," *Fortune*, January 11, 1999, pp. 92–96; and M. Krebs, "DaimlerChrysler Has 23% Rise in Profits," *New York Times*, April 29, 1999, p. C5.

2. J. P. Kotter, "What Leaders Really Do," *Harvard Business Review*, May–June 1990, pp. 103–11; and J. P. Kotter, *A Force for Change: How Leadership Differs from Management* (New York: Free Press, 1990).

3. R. J. House and R. N. Aditya, "The Social Scientific Study of Leadership: Quo Vadis?" *Journal of Management*, vol. 23, no. 3, 1997, p. 445.

4. J. G. Geier, "A Trait Approach to the Study of Leadership in Small Groups," *Journal of Communication*, December 1967, pp. 316–23.

5. S. A. Kirkpatrick and E. A. Locke, "Leadership: Do Traits Matter?" *Academy of Management Executive*, May 1991, pp. 48–60.

6. G. H. Dobbins. W. S. Long, E. J. Dedrick, and T. C. Clemons, "The Role of Self-Monitoring and Gender on Leader Emergence: A Laboratory and Field Study," *Journal of Management*, September 1990, pp. 609–18; and S. J. Zaccaro, R. J. Foti, and D. A. Kenny, "Self-Monitoring and Trait-Based Variance in Leadership: An Investigation of Leader Flexibility Across Multiple Group Situations," *Journal of Applied Psychology*, April 1991, pp. 308–15.

7. G. Yukl and D. D. Van Fleet, "Theory and Research on Leadership in Organizations," in M. D. Dunnette and L. M. Hough (eds.), *Handbook of Industrial & Organizational Psychology*, 2nd ed., vol. 3 (Palo Alto, CA: Consulting Psychologists Press, 1992), p. 150.

8. B. Schneider, "Interactional Psychology and Organizational Behavior," in L. L. Cummings and B. M. Staw (eds.), *Research in Organizational Behavior*, vol. 5 (Greenwich, CT: JAI Press), pp. 1–31.

9. See W. Mischel, "Toward a Cognitive Social Learning Reconceptualization of Personality," *Psychological Review*, July 1973, pp. 252–83; and M. R. Barrick and M. K. Mount, "Autonomy as a Moderator of the Relationship Between the Big Five Personality Dimensions and Job Performance," *Journal of Applied Psychology*, February 1993, pp. 111–18.

10. R. G. Lord, C. L. DeVader, and G. M. Alliger, "A Meta-Analysis of the Relation Between Personality Traits and Leadership Perceptions: An Application of Validity Generalization Procedures," *Journal of Applied Psychology*, August 1986, pp. 402–10; and J. A. Smith and R. J. Foti, "A Pattern Approach to the Study of Leader Emergence," *Leadership Quarterly*, Summer 1998, pp. 147–60.

11. See A. Marsh, "Rewriting the Book on Journalism," *Forbes*, June 15, 1998, p. 47; C. Palmeri, "The Grizz Gets Grizzly," *Forbes*, November 16, 1998, p. 196; and R. LaFranco, "Tear Down Walls, or Hit Them?" *Forbes*, August 9, 1999, p. 56.

12. R. M. Stogdill and A. E. Coons (eds.), *Leader Behavior: Its Description and Measurement*, Research Monograph No. 88 (Columbus: Ohio State University, Bureau of Business Research, 1951). This research is updated in C. A. Schriesheim, C. C. Cogliser, and L. L. Neider, "Is It 'Trustworthy'? A Multiple-Levels-of-Analysis Reexamination of an Ohio State Leadership Study, with Implications for Future Research," *Leadership Quarterly*, Summer 1995, pp. 111–45.

13. R. Kahn and D. Katz, "Leadership Practices in Relation to Productivity and Morale," D. Cartwright and A. Zander (eds.), *Group Dynamics: Research and Theory*, 2nd ed. (Elmsford, NY: Row, Paterson, 1960).

14. R. R. Blake and J. S. Mouton, *The Managerial Grid* (Houston: Gulf, 1964).

15. See, for example, R. R. Blake and J. S. Mouton, "A Comparative Analysis of Situationalism and 9,9 Management by Principle," *Organizational Dynamics*, Spring 1982, pp. 20–43.

16. See, for example, L. L. Larson, J. G. Hunt, and R. N. Osborn, "The Great Hi-Hi Leader Behavior Myth: A Lesson from Occam's Razor," *Academy of Management Journal*, December 1976, pp. 628–41; and P. C. Nystrom, "Managers and the Hi-Hi Leader Myth," *Academy of Management Journal*, June 1978, pp. 325–31.

17. See G. Ekvall and J. Arvonen, "Change-Centered Leadership: An Extension of the Two-Dimensional Model," *Scandinavian Journal of Management*, vol. 7, no. 1, 1991, pp. 17–26; M. Lindell and G. Rosenqvist, "Is There a Third Management Style?" *The Finnish Journal of Business Economics*, vol. 3, 1992, pp. 171–98; and M. Lindell and G. Rosenqvist, "Management Behavior Dimensions and Development Orientation," *Leadership Quarterly*, Winter 1992, pp. 355–77.

18. J. Stein, "Bosses From Hell," *Time*, December 7, 1998, p. 181.

19. F. E. Fiedler, *A Theory of Leadership Effectiveness* (New York: McGraw-Hill, 1967).

20. S. Shiflett, "Is There a Problem with the LPC Score in LEADER MATCH?" *Personnel Psychology*, Winter 1981, pp. 765–69.

21. F. E. Fiedler, M. M. Chemers, and L. Mahar, *Improving Leadership Effectiveness: The Leader Match Concept* (New York: John Wiley & Sons, 1977).

22. Cited in House and Aditya, "The Social Scientific Study of Leadership," p. 422.

23. L. H. Peters, D. D. Hartke, and J. T. Pohlmann, "Fiedler's Contingency Theory of Leadership: An Application of the Meta-Analysis Procedures of Schmidt and Hunter," *Psychological Bulletin*, March 1985, pp. 274–85; C. A. Schriesheim, B. J. Tepper, and L. A. Tetrault, "Least Preferred Co-Worker Score, Situational Control, and Leadership Effectiveness: A Meta-Analysis of Contingency Model Performance Predictions," *Journal of Applied Psychology*, August 1994, pp. 561–73; and R. Ayman, M. M. Chemers, and F. Fiedler, "The Contingency Model of Leadership Effectiveness: Its Levels of Analysis," *Leadership Quarterly*, Summer 1995, pp. 147–67.

24. House and Aditya, "The Social Scientific Study of Leadership," p. 422.

25. See, for instance, R. W. Rice, "Psychometric Properties of the Esteem for the Least Preferred Coworker (LPC)

Scale," *Academy of Management Review*, January 1978, pp. 106–18; C. A. Schriesheim, B. D. Bannister, and W. H. Money, "Psychometric Properties of the LPC Scale: An Extension of Rice's Review," *Academy of Management Review*, April 1979, pp. 287–90; and J. K. Kennedy, J. M. Houston, M. A. Korgaard, and D. D. Gallo, "Construct Space of the Least Preferred Co-Worker (LPC) Scale," *Educational & Psychological Measurement*, Fall 1987, pp. 807–14.

26. See E. H. Schein, *Organizational Psychology*, 3rd ed. (Englewood Cliffs, NJ: Prentice Hall, 1980), pp. 116–17; and B. Kabanoff, "A Critique of Leader Match and Its Implications for Leadership Research," *Personnel Psychology*, Winter 1981, pp. 749–64.

27. F. E. Fiedler and J. E. Garcia, *New Approaches to Effective Leadership: Cognitive Resources and Organizational Performance* (New York: John Wiley & Sons, 1987).

28. See F. W. Gibson, F. E. Fiedler, and K. M. Barrett, "Stress, Babble, and the Utilization of the Leader's Intellectual Abilities," *Leadership Quarterly*, Summer 1993, pp. 189–208; and F. E. Fiedler, "Cognitive Resources and Leadership Performance," *Applied Psychology—An International Review*, January 1995, pp. 5–28.

29. P. Hersey and K. H. Blanchard, "So You Want to Know Your Leadership Style?" *Training and Development Journal*, February 1974, pp. 1–15; and P. Hersey and K. H. Blanchard, *Management of Organizational Behavior: Utilizing Human Resources*, 6th ed. (Englewood Cliffs, NJ: Prentice Hall, 1993).

30. Cited in C. F. Fernandez and R. P. Vecchio, "Situational Leadership Theory Revisited. A Test of an Across-Jobs Perspective," *Leadership Quarterly*, vol. 8, no. 1, 1997, p. 67.

31. See, for instance, ibid. pp. 67–84; and C. L. Graeff, "Evolution of Situational Leadership Theory: A Critical Review," *Leadership Quarterly*, vol. 8, no. 2, 1997, pp. 153–70.

32. R. M. Dienesch and R. C. Liden, "Leader–Member Exchange Model of Leadership: A Critique and Further Development," *Academy of Management Review*, July 1986, pp. 618–34; G. B. Graen and M. Uhl-Bien, "Relationship-Based Approach to Leadership: Development of Leader–Member Exchange (LMX) Theory of Leadership Over 25 Years: Applying a Multi-Domain Perspective," *Leadership Quarterly*, Summer 1995, pp. 219–47; and R. C. Liden, R. T. Sparrowe, and S. J. Wayne, "Leader–Member Exchange Theory: The Past and Potential for the Future," in G.R. Ferris (ed.), *Research in Personnel and Human Resource Management*, vol. 15 (Greenwich, CT: JAI Press, 1997), pp. 47–119.

33. R. Liden and G. Graen, "Generalizability of the Vertical Dyad Linkage Model of Leadership," *Academy of Management Journal*, September 1980, pp. 451–65; and R. C. Liden, S. J. Wayne, and D. Stilwell, "A Longitudinal Study of the Early Development of Leader–Member Exchanges," *Journal of Applied Psychology*, August 1993, pp. 662–74.

34. D. Duchon, S. G. Green, and T. D. Taber, "Vertical Dyad Linkage: A Longitudinal Assessment of Antecedents, Measures, and Consequences," *Journal of Applied Psychology*, February 1986, pp. 56–60; R. C. Liden, S. J. Wayne, and D. Stilwell, "A Longitudinal Study on the Early Development of Leader-Member Exchanges"; R. J. Deluga

and J. T. Perry, "The Role of Subordinate Performance and Ingratiation in Leader–Member Exchanges," *Group & Organization Management*, March 1994, pp. 67–86; T. N. Bauer and S. G. Green, "Development of Leader–Member Exchange: A Longitudinal Test," *Academy of Management Journal*, December 1996, pp. 1538–67; and S. J. Wayne, L. M. Shore, and R. C. Liden, "Perceived Organizational Support and Leader–Member Exchange: A Social Exchange Perspective," *Academy of Management Journal*, February 1997, pp. 82–111.

35. See C. R. Gerstner and D. V. Day, "Meta-Analytic Review of Leader–Member Exchange Theory: Correlates and Construct Issues," *Journal of Applied Psychology*, December 1997, pp. 827–44.

36. D. Eden, "Leadership and Expectations: Pygmalion Effects and Other Self-Fulfilling Prophecies in Organizations," *Leadership Quarterly*, Winter 1992, pp. 278–79.

37. R. J. House, "A Path-Goal Theory of Leader Effectiveness," *Administrative Science Quarterly*, September 1971, pp. 321–38; R. J. House and T. R. Mitchell, "Path-Goal Theory of Leadership," *Journal of Contemporary Business*, Autumn 1974, pp. 81–97; and R. J. House, "Path-Goal Theory of Leadership: Lessons, Legacy, and a Reformulated Theory," *Leadership Quarterly*, Fall 1996, pp. 323–52.

38. J. C. Wofford and L. Z. Liska, "Path-Goal Theories of Leadership: A Meta-Analysis," *Journal of Management*, Winter 1993, pp. 857–76.

39. V. H. Vroom and P. W. Yetton, *Leadership and Decision-Making* (Pittsburgh: University of Pittsburgh Press, 1973).

40. V. H. Vroom and A. G. Jago, *The New Leadership: Managing Participation in Organizations* (Englewood Cliffs, NJ: Prentice Hall, 1988). See also V. H. Vroom and A. G. Jago, "Situation Effects and Levels of Analysis in the Study of Leader Participation," *Leadership Quarterly*, Summer 1995, pp. 169–81.

41. See, for example, R. H. G. Field, "A Test of the Vroom-Yetton Normative Model of Leadership," *Journal of Applied Psychology*, October 1982, pp. 523–32; C. R. Leana, "Power Relinquishment versus Power Sharing: Theoretical Clarification and Empirical Comparison of Delegation and Participation," *Journal of Applied Psychology*, May 1987, pp. 228–33; J. T. Ettling and A. G. Jago, "Participation Under Conditions of Conflict: More on the Validity of the Vroom-Yetton Model," *Journal of Management Studies*, January 1988, pp. 73–83; and R. H. G. Field and R. J. House, "A Test of the Vroom-Yetton Model Using Manager and Subordinate Reports," *Journal of Applied Psychology*, June 1990, pp. 362–66.

42. House and Aditya, "The Social Scientific Study of Leadership," p. 428.

43. S. Kerr and J. M. Jermier, "Substitutes for Leadership: Their Meaning and Measurement," *Organizational Behavior and Human Performance*, December 1978, pp. 375–403; J. P. Howell and P. W. Dorfman, "Substitutes for Leadership: Test of a Construct," *Academy of Management Journal*, December 1981, pp. 714–28; P. M. Podsakoff, B. P. Niehoff, S. B. MacKenzie, and M. L. Williams, "Do Substitutes for Leadership Really Substitute for Leadership? An Empirical Examination of Kerr and Jermier's Situational Leadership Model," *Organizational Behavior and Human Decision Processes*, February 1993, pp. 1–44; P. M. Podsakoff and S. B. MacKenzie,

"An Examination of Substitutes for Leadership Within a Levels-of-Analysis Framework," *Leadership Quarterly*, Fall 1995, pp. 289–328; P. M. Podsakoff, S. B. MacKenzie, and W. H. Bommer, "Meta-Analysis of the Relationships Between Kerr and Jermier's Substitutes for Leadership and Employee Attitudes, Role Perceptions, and Performance," *Journal of Applied Psychology*, August 1996, pp. 380–99; and J. M. Jermier and S. Kerr, "'Substitutes for Leadership: Their Meaning and Measurement—Contextual Recollections and Current Observations," *Leadership Quarterly*, vol. 8, no. 2, 1997, pp. 95–101.

44. House and Aditya, "The Social Scientific Study of Leadership," p. 439.

45. J. A. Conger and R. N. Kanungo, "Behavioral Dimensions of Charismatic Leadership," in J. A. Conger, R. N. Kanungo and Associates, *Charismatic Leadership* (San Francisco: Jossey-Bass, 1988), p. 79.

46. See, for example, R. J. House, "A 1976 Theory of Charismatic Leadership," in J. G. Hunt and L. L. Larson (eds.), *Leadership: The Cutting Edge* (Carbondale: Southern Illinois University Press, 1977), pp. 189–207; W. Bennis, "The 4 Competencies of Leadership," *Training and Development Journal*, August 1984, pp. 15–19; and Conger and Kanungo, "Behavioral Dimensions of Charismatic Leadership," pp. 78–97.

47. J. A. Conger and R. N. Kanungo, *Charismatic Leadership in Organizations* (Thousand Oaks, CA: Sage, 1998).

48. B. Shamir, R. J. House, and M. B. Arthur, "The Motivational Effects of Charismatic Leadership: A Self-Concept Theory," *Organization Science*, November 1993, pp. 577–94.

49. R. J. House, J. Woycke, and E. M. Fodor, "Charismatic and Noncharismatic Leaders: Differences in Behavior and Effectiveness," in Conger and Kanungo, *Charismatic Leadership*, pp. 103–04; D. A. Waldman, B. M. Bass, and F. J. Yammarino, "Adding to Contingent-Reward Behavior: The Augmenting Effect of Charismatic Leadership," *Group & Organization Studies*, December 1990, pp. 381–94; S. A. Kirkpatrick and E. A. Locke, "Direct and Indirect Effects of Three Core Charismatic Leadership Components on Performance and Attitudes," *Journal of Applied Psychology*, February 1996, pp. 36–51; and J. A. Conger, R. N. Kanungo, and S. T. Menon, "Charismatic Leadership and Follower Outcome Effects," paper presented at the 58th Annual Academy of Management Meetings; San Diego, CA; August 1998.

50. J. A. Conger and R. N. Kanungo, "Training Charismatic Leadership: A Risky and Critical Task," in Conger and Kanungo, *Charismatic Leadership*, pp. 309–23; and S. Caudron, "Growing Charisma," *Industry Week*, May 4, 1998, pp. 54–55.

51. R. J. Richardson and S. K. Thayer, *The Charisma Factor: How to Develop Your Natural Leadership Ability* (Upper Saddle River, NJ: Prentice Hall, 1993).

52. J. M. Howell and P. J. Frost, "A Laboratory Study of Charismatic Leadership," *Organizational Behavior and Human Decision Processes*, April 1989, pp. 243–69.

53. House, "A 1976 Theory of Charismatic Leadership;" and House and Aditya, "The Social Scientific Study of Leadership," p. 441.

54. See A. Taylor III, "Is Jack Smith the Man to Fix GM?" *Fortune*, August 3, 1998, pp. 86–92.

55. See, for instance, B. M. Bass, *Leadership and Performance Beyond Expectations* (New York: Free Press, 1985); B. M. Bass, "From Transactional to Transformational Leadership: Learning to Share the Vision," *Organizational Dynamics*, Winter 1990, pp. 19–31; F. J. Yammarino, W. D. Spangler, and B. M. Bass, "Transformational Leadership and Performance: A Longitudinal Investigation," *Leadership Quarterly*, Spring 1993, pp. 81–102; and J. C. Wofford, V. L. Goodwin, and J. L. Whittington, "A Field Study of a Cognitive Approach to Understanding Transformational and Transactional Leadership," *Leadership Quarterly*, vol. 9, no. 1, 1998, pp. 55–84.

56. B. M. Bass, "Leadership: Good, Better, Best," *Organizational Dynamics*, Winter 1985, pp. 26–40; and J. Seltzer and B. M. Bass, "Transformational Leadership: Beyond Initiation and Consideration," *Journal of Management*, December 1990, pp. 693–703.

57. B. J. Avolio and B. M. Bass, "Transformational Leadership, Charisma and Beyond," working paper, School of Management, State University of New York, Binghamton, 1985, p. 14.

58. Cited in B. M. Bass and B. J. Avolio, "Developing Transformational Leadership: 1992 and Beyond," *Journal of European Industrial Training*, January 1990, p. 23.

59. J. J. Hater and B. M. Bass, "Supervisors' Evaluation and Subordinates' Perceptions of Transformational and Transactional Leadership," *Journal of Applied Psychology*, November 1988, pp. 695–702.

60. Bass and Avolio, "Developing Transformational Leadership;" and K. B. Lowe, K. G. Kroeck, and N. Sivasubramaniam, ""Effectiveness Correlates of Transformational and Transactional Leadership: A Meta-Analytic Review of the MLQ Literature," *Leadership Quarterly*, Fall 1996, pp. 385–425.

61. This definition is based on M. Sashkin, "The Visionary Leader," in Conger and Kanungo (eds.), *Charismatic Leadership*, pp. 124–25; B. Nanus, *Visionary Leadership* (New York: Free Press, 1992), p. 8; N. H. Snyder and M. Graves, "Leadership and Vision," *Business Horizons*, January-February 1994, p. 1; and J. R. Lucas, "Anatomy of a Vision Statement," *Management Review*, February 1998, pp. 22–26.

62. Nanus, *Visionary Leadership*, p. 8.

63. P. C. Nutt and R. W. Backoff, "Crafting Vision," *Journal of Management Inquiry*, December 1997, p. 309.

64. Ibid., pp. 312–14.

65. Based on Sashkin, "The Visionary Leader," pp. 128–30; and J. R. Baum, E. A. Locke, and S. A. Kirkpatrick, "A Longitudinal Study of the Relation of Vision and Vision Communication to Venture Growth in Entrepreneurial Firms," *Journal of Applied Psychology*, February 1998, pp. 43–54.

66. A. H. Eagly and B. T. Johnson, "Gender and Leadership Style: A Meta-Analysis," *Psychological Bulletin*, September 1990, pp. 233–56; S. Helgesen, *The Female Advantage: Women's Ways of Leadership* (New York: Doubleday, 1990); and J. B. Rosener, "Ways Women Lead," *Harvard Business Review*, November–December 1990, pp. 119–25.

67. This section is based on D. Goleman, *Working with Emotional Intelligence* (New York: Bantam, 1998); and D. Goleman, "What Makes a Leader?" *Harvard Business Review*, November–December 1998, pp. 93–102.

68. See, for instance, J. H. Zenger, E. Musselwhite, K. Hurson, and C. Perrin, *Leading Teams: Mastering the New Role* (Homewood, IL: Business One Irwin, 1994); and M. Frohman, "Nothing Kills Teams Like Ill-Prepared Leaders," *Industry Week*, October 2, 1995, pp. 72–76.

69. S. Caminiti, "What Team Leaders Need to Know," *Fortune*, February 20, 1995, pp. 93–100.

70. Ibid., p. 93.

71. Ibid., p. 100.

72. N. Steckler and N. Fondas, "Building Team Leader Effectiveness: A Diagnostic Tool," *Organizational Dynamics*, Winter 1995, p. 20.

73. R. S. Wellins, W. C. Byham, and G. R. Dixon, *Inside Teams* (San Francisco: Jossey-Bass, 1994), p. 318.

74. Steckler and Fondas, "Building Team Leader Effectiveness," p. 21.

75. This section is based on R. B. Morgan, "Self- and Co-Worker Perceptions of Ethics and Their Relationships to Leadership and Salary," *Academy of Management Journal*, February 1993, pp. 200–14; J. B. Ciulla, "Leadership Ethics: Mapping the Territory," *Business Ethics Quarterly*, January 1995, pp. 5–28; E. P. Hollander, "Ethical Challenges in the Leader–Follower Relationship," *Business Ethics Quarterly*, January 1995, pp. 55–65; J. C. Rost, "Leadership: A Discussion About Ethics," *Business Ethics Quarterly*, January 1995, pp. 129–42; and R. N. Kanungo and M. Mendonca, *Ethical Dimensions of Leadership* (Thousand Oaks, CA: Sage Publications, 1996).

76. J. M. Burns, *Leadership* (New York: Harper & Row, 1978).

77. J. M. Howell and B. J. Avolio, "The Ethics of Charismatic Leadership: Submission or Liberation?" *Academy of Management Executive*, May 1992, pp. 43–55.

78. For a review of the cross-cultural applicability of the leadership literature, see R. S. Bhagat, B. L. Kedia, S. E. Crawford, and M. R. Kaplan, "Cross-Cultural Issues in Organizational Psychology: Emergent Trends and Directions for Research in the 1990s," in C. L. Cooper and I. T. Robertson (eds.), *International Review of Industrial and Organizational Psychology*, vol. 5 (Chichester, England: John Wiley & Sons, 1990), pp. 79–89; and M. F. Peterson and J. G. Hunt, "International Perspectives on International Leadership," *Leadership Quarterly*, Fall 1997, pp. 203–31.

79. "Military-Style Management in China," *Asia Inc.*, March 1995, p. 70.

80. Cited in House and Aditya, "The Social Scientific Study of Leadership," p. 463.

81. R. J. House, "Leadership in the Twenty-First Century," in A. Howard (ed.), *The Changing Nature of Work* (San Francisco: Jossey-Bass, 1995), p. 442.

82. Ibid.

83. House and Aditya, "The Social Scientific Study of Leadership," p. 463.

84. House, "Leadership in the Twenty-First Century," p. 443.

85. Based on S. D. Boon and J. G. Holmes, "The Dynamics of Interpersonal Trust: Resolving Uncertainty in the Face of Risk," in R. A. Hinde and J. Groebel (eds.), *Cooperation and Prosocial Behavior* (Cambridge, UK: Cambridge University Press, 1991), p. 194; D. J. McAllister, "Affect- and Cognition-Based Trust as Foundations for Interpersonal Cooperation in Organizations," *Academy of Management Journal*, February 1995, p. 25; and D. M. Rousseau, S. B.

Sitkin, R. S. Burt, and C. Camerer, "Not So Different After All: A Cross-Discipline View of Trust," *Academy of Management Review*, July 1998, pp. 393–404.

86. J. B. Rotter, "Interpersonal Trust, Trustworthiness, and Gullibility," *American Psychologist*, January 1980, pp. 1–7.

87. J. D. Lewis and A. Weigert, "Trust as a Social Reality," *Social Forces*, June 1985, p. 970.

88. J. K. Rempel, J. G. Holmes, and M. P. Zanna, "Trust in Close Relationships," *Journal of Personality and Social Psychology*, July 1985, p. 96.

89. M. Granovetter, "Economic Action and Social Structure: The Problem of Embeddedness," *American Journal of Sociology*, November 1985, p. 491.

90. R. C. Mayer, J. H. Davis, and F. D. Schoorman, "An Integrative Model of Organizational Trust," *Academy of Management Review*, July 1995, p. 712.

91. C. Johnson-George and W. Swap, "Measurement of Specific Interpersonal Trust: Construction and Validation of a Scale to Assess Trust in a Specific Other," *Journal of Personality and Social Psychology*, September 1982, p. 1306.

92. P. L. Schindler and C. C. Thomas, "The Structure of Interpersonal Trust in the Workplace," *Psychological Reports*, October 1993, pp. 563–73.

93. J. K. Butler Jr. and R. S. Cantrell, "A Behavioral Decision Theory Approach to Modeling Dyadic Trust in Superiors and Subordinates," *Psychological Reports*, August 1984, pp. 19–28.

94. D. McGregor, *The Professional Manager* (New York: McGraw-Hill, 1967), p. 164.

95. B. Nanus, *The Leader's Edge: The Seven Keys to Leadership in a Turbulent World* (Chicago: Contemporary Books, 1989), p. 102.

96. D. E. Zand, *The Leadership Triad: Knowledge, Trust, and Power* (New York: Oxford Press, 1997), p. 89.

97. Based on L. T. Hosmer, "Trust: The Connecting Link between Organizational Theory and Philosophical Ethics," *Academy of Management Review*, April 1995, p. 393; and R. C. Mayer, J. H. Davis, and F. D. Schoorman, "An Integrative Model of Organizational Trust," *Academy of Management Review*, July 1995, p. 712.

98. J. M. Kouzes and B. Z. Posner, *Credibility: How Leaders Gain and Lose It, and Why People Demand It* (San Francisco: Jossey-Bass, 1993), p. 14.

99. J. Brockner, P. A. Siegel, J. P. Daly, T. Tyler, and C. Martin, "When Trust Matters: The Moderating Effect of Outcome Favorability," *Administrative Science Quarterly*, September 1997, p. 558.

100. Cited in C. Lee, "Trust Me," *Training*, January 1997, p. 32.

101. This section is based on D. Shapiro, B. H. Sheppard, and L. Cheraskin, "Business on a Handshake," *Negotiation Journal*, October 1992, pp. 365–77; and R. J. Lewicki and B. B. Bunker, "Developing and Maintaining Trust in Work Relationships," in R. M. Kramer and T. R. Tyler (eds.), *Trust in Organizations* (Thousand Oaks, CA: Sage, 1996), pp. 119–24.

102. This section is based on F. Bartolome, "Nobody Trusts the Boss Completely—Now What?" *Harvard Business Review*, March-April 1989, pp. 135–42; and J. K. Butler Jr., "Toward Understanding and Measuring Conditions of Trust: Evolution of a Condition of Trust Inventory," *Journal of Management*, September 1991, pp. 643–63.

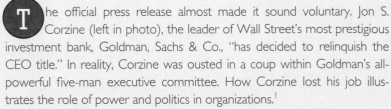

It's good to be the King!

—M. Brooks

The official press release almost made it sound voluntary. Jon S. Corzine (left in photo), the leader of Wall Street's most prestigious investment bank, Goldman, Sachs & Co., "has decided to relinquish the CEO title." In reality, Corzine was ousted in a coup within Goldman's all-powerful five-man executive committee. How Corzine lost his job illustrates the role of power and politics in organizations.[1]

Corzine was named chairman of Goldman in 1994. The firm, at the time, was struggling with trading losses and the sudden loss of a number of senior partners. Corzine took control, stablized the firm, and helped raise morale and profitability. But several incidences in 1998 undermined Corzine's power.

First, Goldman's partners had decided to take the company public. This would put tens of millions of dollars into each partner's pockets. But investors penalize firms that depend on proprietary trading because of its unpredictability. Trading produces huge profits one quarter and huge losses the next. Investment banks, on the other hand, sell at a higher price. They earn stable fees from commissions, mutual funds, and underwriting. Because Goldman performed both functions, the all-powerful five-man executive committee decided to pitch the firm to investors as an investment bank. The problem was that Corzine's roots were in the trading side of the business. A natural leader with a low-key, rumpled style, he was seen by people in the financial community as a trader. In contrast, Corzine's No. 2, Henry Paulson Jr., (right in photo) who just happened to also be a member of the executive committee, came from the investment banking side of the business. Reserved, polished, and highly organized, Paulson fit better with the image that the firm wanted to present to the financial community. Second, in August and September 1998, Goldman was hit with $500 million to a billion dollars in trading losses when the market took a nosedive. This was

chapter 12

Power and Politics

just months before the company was planning its public offering. This reinforced the problems with the trading side of the business and undermined Corzine's image in the firm. Third, one of Corzine's prime supporters, Vice-Chairman Roy Zuckerberg, retired from the executive committee in late November. Finally, Corzine and Paulson had never been close. Their backgrounds and styles were very different, creating a long and rocky relationship. With Corzine's support slipping and the perception that Paulson would make a better leader for taking the firm public, the time seemed right for Paulson to strike. And that's exactly what he did.

On January 11, 1999, the firm issued a press release saying that Corzine was stepping down, and that the executive committee would be dissolved and replaced by a 15-man management committee chaired by Paulson.

P ower has been described as the last dirty word. It is easier for most of us to talk about money than it is to talk about power. People who have it deny it, people who want it try not to appear to be seeking it, and those who are good at getting it are secretive about how they got it.[2] OB researchers have learned a lot in recent years about how people gain and use power in organizations. In this chapter, we present you with their findings.

A major theme throughout this chapter is that power is a natural process in any group or organization. As such, you need to know how it's acquired and exercised if you're going to fully understand organizational behavior. Although you may have heard the phrase that "power corrupts, and absolute power corrupts absolutely," power is not always bad. As one author has noted, most medicines can kill if taken in the wrong amount and

LEARNING OBJECTIVES

AFTER READING THIS CHAPTER, YOU SHOULD BE ABLE TO

1. Contrast leadership and power

2. Define the four bases of power

3. Clarify what creates dependency in power relationships

4. List seven power tactics and their contingencies

5. Explain how sexual harassment is about the abuse of power

6. Describe the importance of a political perspective

7. List those individual and organizational factors that stimulate political behavior

8. Identify seven techniques for managing the impression one makes on others

9. Explain how defensive behaviors can protect an individual's self-interest

10. List the three questions that can help determine if a political action is ethical

thousands die each year in automobile accidents, but we don't abandon chemicals or cars because of the dangers associated with them. Rather, we consider danger an incentive to get training and information that'll help us to use these forces productively.[3] The same applies to power. It's a reality of organizational life and it's not going to go away. Moreover, by learning how power works in organizations, you'll be better able to use your knowledge to help you be a more effective manager.

A DEFINITION OF POWER

power

A capacity that A has to influence the behavior of B so that B acts in accordance with A's wishes.

dependency

B's relationship to A when A possesses something that B requires.

Power refers to a capacity that A has to influence the behavior of B, so that B acts in accordance with A's wishes.[4] This definition implies a *potential* that need not be actualized to be effective and a *dependency* relationship.

Power may exist but not be used. It is, therefore, a capacity or potential. One can have power but not impose it.

Probably the most important aspect of power is that it is a function of **dependency**. The greater B's dependence on A, the greater is A's power in the relationship. Dependence, in turn, is based on alternatives that B perceives and the importance that B places on the alternative(s) that A controls. A person can have power over you only if he or she controls something you desire. If you want a college degree and have to pass a certain course to get it, and your current instructor is the only faculty member in the college who teaches that course, he or she has power over you. Your alternatives are highly limited and you place a high degree of importance on obtaining a passing grade. Similarly, if you're attending college on funds totally provided by your parents, you probably recognize the power that they hold over you. You're dependent on them for financial support. But once you're out of school, have a job, and are making a good income, your parents' power is reduced significantly. Who among us, though, has not known or heard of the rich relative who is able to control a large number of family members merely through the implicit or explicit threat of "writing them out of the will"?

CONTRASTING LEADERSHIP AND POWER

A careful comparison of our description of power with our description of leadership in the previous chapter reveals that the two concepts are closely intertwined. Leaders use power as a means of attaining group goals. Leaders achieve goals, and power is a means of facilitating their achievement.

What differences are there between the two terms? One difference relates to goal compatibility. Power does not require goal compatibility, merely dependence. Leadership, on the other hand, requires some congruence between the goals of the leader and those being led. A second difference relates to the direction of influence. Leadership focuses on the downward influence on one's followers. It minimizes the importance of lateral and upward influence patterns. Power does not. Still another difference deals with research emphasis. Leadership research, for the most part, emphasizes style. It seeks answers to such questions as: How supportive should a leader be? How much decision making should be shared with followers? In contrast, the research on power has tended to encompass a broader area and focus on tactics for gaining compliance. It has gone beyond the individual as exerciser because power can be used by groups as well as by individuals to control other individuals or groups.

BASES OF POWER

Where does power come from? What is it that gives an individual or a group influence over others? The answer to these questions is a five-category classification scheme identified by French and Raven.[5] They proposed that there are five bases or sources of power: coercive, reward, legitimate, expert, and referent (see Exhibit 12-1).

COERCIVE POWER

The **coercive power** base is defined by French and Raven as being dependent on fear. One reacts to this power out of fear of the negative results that might occur if one failed to comply. It rests on the application, or the threat of application, of physical sanctions such as the infliction of pain, the generation of frustration through restriction of movement, or the controlling by force of basic physiological or safety needs.

coercive power

Power that is based on fear.

> Of all the bases of power available to man, the power to hurt others is possibly most often used, most often condemned, and most difficult to control . . . the state relies on its military and legal resources to intimidate nations, or even its own citizens. Businesses rely upon the control of economic resources. Schools and universities rely upon their rights to deny students formal education, while the church threatens individuals with loss of grace. At the personal level, individuals exercise coercive power through a reliance upon physical strength, verbal facility, or the ability to grant or withhold emotional support from others. These bases provide the individual with the means to physically harm, bully, humiliate, or deny love to others.[6]

At the organizational level, A has coercive power over B if A can dismiss, suspend, or demote B, assuming that B values his or her job. Similarly, if A can assign B work activities that B finds unpleasant or treat B in a manner that B finds embarrassing, A possesses coercive power over B.

Measuring Bases of Power

Does a person have one or more of the five bases of power? Affirmative responses to the following questions can answer this question:

- The person can make things difficult for people, and you want to avoid getting him or her angry. [coercive power]
- The person is able to give special benefits or rewards to people, and you find it advantageous to trade favors with him or her. [reward power]
- The person has the right, considering his or her position and your job responsibilities, to expect you to comply with legitimate requests. [legitimate power]
- The person has the experience and knowledge to earn your respect, and you defer to his or her judgment in some matters. [expert power]
- You like the person and enjoy doing things for him or her. [referent power]

EXHIBIT 12-1

Source: G. Yukl and C. M. Falbe, "Importance of Different Power Sources in Downward and Lateral Relations," *Journal of Applied Psychology*, June 1991, p. 417. With permission.

REWARD POWER

reward power

Compliance achieved based on the ability to distribute rewards that others view as valuable.

The opposite of coercive power is **reward power**. People comply with the wishes or directives of another because doing so produces positive benefits; therefore, one who can distribute rewards that others view as valuable will have power over those others. These rewards can be anything that another person values. In an organizational context, we think of money, favorable performance appraisals, promotions, interesting work assignments, friendly colleagues, important information, and preferred work shifts or sales territories.

Coercive power and reward power are actually counterparts of each other. If you can remove something of positive value from another or inflict something of negative value upon him or her, you have coercive power over that person. If you can give someone something of positive value or remove something of negative value, you have reward power over that person. You don't need to be a manager to be able to exert influence through rewards. Rewards such as friendliness, acceptance, and praise are available to everyone in an organization. To the degree that an individual seeks such rewards, your ability to give or withhold them gives you power over that individual.

LEGITIMATE POWER

legitimate power

The power a person receives as a result of his or her position in the formal hierarchy of an organization.

In formal groups and organizations, probably the most frequent access to one or more of the power bases is one's structural position. This is called **legitimate power**. It represents the power a person receives as a result of his or her position in the formal hierarchy of an organization.

EXHIBIT 12-2

"I was just going to say 'Well, I don't make the rules.' But, of course, I _do_ make the rules."

Source: Drawing by Leo Cullum in *The New Yorker*. Copyright © 1986. The New Yorker Magazine. Reprinted by permission.

Positions of authority include coercive and reward powers. Legitimate power, however, is broader than the power to coerce and reward. Specifically, it includes acceptance by members of an organization of the authority of a position. When school principals, bank presidents, or army captains speak (assuming that their directives are viewed to be within the authority of their positions), teachers, tellers, and first lieutenants listen and usually comply.

EXPERT POWER

Expert power is influence wielded as a result of expertise, special skill, or knowledge. Expertise has become one of the most powerful sources of influence as the world has become more technologically oriented. As jobs become more specialized, we become increasingly dependent on experts to achieve goals. So, while it is generally acknowledged that physicians have expertise and, hence, expert power—most of us follow the advice that our doctor gives us—you should also recognize that computer specialists, tax accountants, economists, industrial psychologists, and other specialists are able to wield power as a result of their expertise.

REFERENT POWER

The last category of influence that French and Raven identified is **referent power**. Its base is identification with a person who has desirable resources or personal traits. If I admire and identify with you, you can exercise power over me because I want to please you.

Referent power develops out of admiration of another and a desire to be like that person. In a sense, then, it is a lot like charisma. If you admire someone to the point of modeling your behavior and attitudes after him or her, this person possesses referent power over you. Referent power explains why celebrities are paid millions of dollars to endorse products in commercials. Marketing research shows that people like Michael Jordan and Bill Cosby have the power to influence your choice of athletic shoes and desserts. With a little practice, you and I could probably deliver as smooth a sales pitch as these celebrities, but the buying public doesn't identify with you and me. In organizations, if you are articulate, domineering, physically imposing, or charismatic, you hold personal characteristics that may be used to get others to do what you want.

As chairman of Paramount Pictures' Motion Picture Group, Sherry Lansing is the most powerful woman in Hollywood. Lansing's power comes from her expertise in moviemaking. She's been an actress, a story editor at MGM, the head of production at Twentieth Century Fox, and an independent movie producer. Lansing's expertise draws top filmmakers to Paramount. Since she joined the studio in 1992, it's won three Best Picture Oscars. By creating blockbusters like *Titanic*, *Saving Private Ryan*, and *The Truman Show*, Lansing has rebuilt Paramount into Hollywood's top motion picture studio.

DEPENDENCY: THE KEY TO POWER

Earlier in this chapter it was said that probably the most important aspect of power is that it is a function of dependence. In this section, we show how an understanding of dependency is central to furthering your understanding of power itself.

THE GENERAL DEPENDENCY POSTULATE

Let's begin with a general postulate: *The greater B's dependency on A, the greater the power A has over B.* When you possess anything that others require but that you alone control, you make them dependent upon you and, therefore, you gain power over them.[7] Dependency, then, is inversely proportional to the alternative sources of supply. If something is plentiful, possession of it will not increase your power. If everyone is intelligent, intelligence gives no special advantage. Similarly, among the superrich, money is no longer power. But, as the old saying goes, "In the land of the blind, the one-eyed man is king!" If you can create a monopoly by controlling information, prestige, or anything that others crave, they become dependent on you. Conversely, the more that you can expand your options, the less power you place in the hands of others. This explains, for example, why most organizations develop multiple suppliers rather than give their business to only one. It also explains why so many of us aspire to financial independence. Financial independence reduces the power that others can have over us.

Steven Appleton provides an example of the role that dependency plays in a work group or organization.[8] Appleton became CEO of Boise-based chip maker Micron Technology in 1994 at age 34. After a number of run-ins with the company's overbearing board of directors, composed of six Idaho agribusiness tycoons, Appleton was abruptly fired in January 1996. But the board quickly realized that they needed Appleton back when their handpicked successor quit after just a couple of days. To make matters worse, more than 20 executives confronted the board and threatened to resign if Appleton wasn't reinstated. Meanwhile, Appleton wasn't sitting around fretting over his loss. He had taken off for Los Angeles, had begun growing a goatee, and started planning a biplane trip to Australia. The board pleaded with Appleton to come back. He did, but on his terms. His eight-day "retirement" came to an end when the board agreed to his demands—including an end to intrusions by the board, resignation of his primary board protagonist, and sweetened severance packages to protect managers who had voiced their frustrations.

WHAT CREATES DEPENDENCY?

Dependency is increased when the resource you control is important, scarce, and nonsubstitutable.[9]

Importance If nobody wants what you've got, it's not going to create dependency. To create dependency, therefore, the thing(s) you control must be perceived as being important. It's been found, for instance, that organizations actively seek to avoid uncertainty.[10] We should, therefore, expect that those individuals or groups who can absorb an organization's uncertainty will be perceived as controlling an important resource. For instance, a study of industrial organizations found that the marketing departments in these firms were consistently rated as the most powerful.[11] It was concluded by the researcher that the most critical uncertainty facing these firms was selling their products. This might suggest that during a labor strike, the organization's negotiating representatives have increased power, or that engineers, as a group, would be more powerful at Intel than at Procter & Gamble. These inferences appear to be generally valid. Labor negotiators do become more powerful within the human resources area and the organization as a whole during periods of labor strife. An organization such as Intel, which is heavily technologically oriented, is highly dependent on its engineers to maintain its products' technical advantages and quality. And, at Intel, engineers are clearly a powerful group. At Procter & Gamble, marketing is the name of the game, and marketers are the most powerful occupational group. These examples support not only the view that the ability to reduce uncertainty increases a group's importance and, hence, its power but also that what's important is situational. It varies between organizations and undoubtedly also varies over time within any given organization.

Scarcity As noted previously, if something is plentiful, possession of it will not increase your power. A resource needs to be perceived as scarce to create dependency.

This can help to explain how low-ranking members in an organization who have important knowledge not available to high-ranking members gain power over the high-ranking members. Possession of a scarce resource—in this case, important knowledge—makes the high-ranking member dependent on the low-ranking member. This also helps to make sense out of behaviors of low-ranking members that otherwise might seem illogical, such as destroying the procedure manuals that describe how a job is done, refusing to train people in their jobs or even to show others exactly what they do, creating specialized language and terminology that inhibit others from understanding their jobs, or operating in secrecy so an activity will appear more complex and difficult than it really is.

The scarcity–dependency relationship can further be seen in the power of occupational categories. Individuals in occupations in which the supply of personnel is low relative to demand can negotiate compensation and benefit packages that are far more attractive than can those in occupations in which there is an abundance of candidates. College administrators have no problem today finding English instructors. The market for computer-engineering teachers, in contrast, is extremely tight, with the demand high and the supply limited. The result is that the bargaining power of computer-engineering faculty allows them to negotiate higher salaries, lighter teaching loads, and other benefits.

Nonsubstitutability   The more that a resource has no viable substitutes, the more power that control over that resource provides. Higher education again provides an excellent example. In universities where there are strong pressures for the faculty to publish, we can say that a department head's power over a faculty member is inversely related to that member's publication record. The more recognition the faculty member receives through publication, the more mobile he or she is. That is, since other universities want faculty who are highly published and visible, there is an increased demand for his or her services. Although the concept of tenure can act to alter this relationship by restricting the department head's alternatives, those faculty members with little or no publications have the least mobility and are subject to the greatest influence from their superiors.

> *The more that a resource has no viable substitutes, the more power that control over that resource provides.*

IDENTIFYING WHERE THE POWER IS

Mike Cisco got a summer job, between his junior and senior years in college, working in the lab at Phoenix Lutheran Hospital. As a chemistry major, Mike had never taken any courses in management or organizational behavior, but he had seen pictures of organization charts before. So on that first day at work, when the assistant in the human resources department gave Mike his orientation and showed him where the lab fit on the hospital's organization chart, he felt pretty good. The lab ranked high up on the chart.

After about a week or so at the hospital, Mike noticed that the lab's manager didn't seem to have near the clout that the managers of marketing and finance had. And what puzzled Mike was that all three managers ranked at the same level on the hospital's organization chart.

Mike's first theory was that the marketing and finance managers were more aggressive individuals, but that clearly wasn't the case. It was obvious to almost

The location of power varies among organizations. At Walt Disney Co., enormous power is held by high-tech scientists in the research and development group of Disney Imagineering, a division created by Walt Disney in 1952 to create Disneyland. Today, the company is relying on Bran Ferren (upper left), who heads the R&D unit, and his highly skilled and creative staffers to develop cyberland fantasies like virtual-reality theme parks, Web sites for kids, and smart TV sets that learn viewers' programming preferences and automatically record programs they forget to watch.

everyone at the hospital that Mike's manager was smarter, more articulate, and more forceful than the other two managers. So Mike was at a loss to figure out why the marketing and finance managers seemed to be considered more important than his manager.

Mike got his answer over lunch during the second week. Traci Chou, a summer intern in the admissions office who was also working on her masters in business administration, clarified it for him. "The organization chart is deceptive. It doesn't tell you where the power is around here," Traci stated. "Ten years ago, the lab was equal to or maybe more important than finance or marketing, but not anymore. As competition has increased in the health care industry, hospitals have had to learn how to cut costs, do more with less, and develop new sources of revenue. This has resulted in expanding the power of departments like finance and marketing around here."

How do you determine where the power is in an organization at any given point in time? We can answer this question from both the departmental and individual manager levels.

At the department level, answers to the following questions will give you a good idea of how powerful that department is: What proportion of the organization's top-level managers came up through the department? Is the department represented on important interdepartmental teams and committees? How does the salary of the senior manager in the department compare with others at his or her level? Is the department located in the headquarters building? What's the average size of offices for people working in the department compared to offices in other departments? Has the department grown in number of employees relative to other departments? How does the promotion rate for people in the department compare to other units? Has the department's budget allocation been increasing relative to other departments?[12]

At the level of the individual manager, there are certain symbols you should be on the lookout for that suggest that a manager has power.[13] These include the ability to intercede favorably on behalf of someone in trouble in the organization, to get approval for expenditures beyond the budget, to get items on the agenda at major meetings, and to get fast access to top decision makers in the organization.

POWER TACTICS

power tactics

Ways in which individuals translate power bases into specific actions.

This section is a logical extension of our previous discussions. We've reviewed where power comes from. Now, we move to the topic of **power tactics** to learn how employees translate their power bases into specific actions. Recent research indicates that there are standardized ways by which powerholders attempt to get what they want.[14]

When 165 managers were asked to write essays describing an incident in which they influenced their bosses, co-workers, or employees, a total of 370 power tactics grouped into 14 categories were identified. These answers were condensed, rewritten into a 58-item questionnaire, and given to over 750 employees. These respondents were not only asked how they went about influencing others at work but also for the possible reasons for influencing the target person. The results, which are summarized here, give us considerable insight into power tactics—how managerial employees influence others and the conditions under which one tactic is chosen over another.[15]

The findings identified seven tactical dimensions or strategies:

- *Reason*: Use of facts and data to make a logical or rational presentation of ideas
- *Friendliness*: Use of flattery, creation of goodwill, acting humble, and being friendly prior to making a request
- *Coalition*: Getting the support of other people in the organization to back up the request
- *Bargaining*: Use of negotiation through the exchange of benefits or favors
- *Assertiveness*: Use of a direct and forceful approach such as demanding compliance with requests, repeating reminders, ordering individuals to do what is asked, and pointing out that rules require compliance
- *Higher authority*: Gaining the support of higher levels in the organization to back up requests
- *Sanctions*: Use of organizationally derived rewards and punishments such as preventing or promising a salary increase, threatening to give an unsatisfactory performance evaluation, or withholding a promotion

The researchers found that employees do not rely on the seven tactics equally. However, as shown in Exhibit 12-3, the most popular strategy was the use of reason, regardless of whether the influence was directed upward or downward. Additionally, the researchers uncovered four contingency variables that affect the selection of a power tactic: the manager's relative power, the manager's objectives for wanting to influence, the manager's expectation of the target person's willingness to comply, and the organization's culture.

A manager's relative power impacts the selection of tactics in two ways. First, managers who control resources that are valued by others, or who are perceived to be in positions of dominance, use a greater variety of tactics than do those with less power. Second, managers with power use assertiveness with greater frequency than do those with less power. Initially, we can expect that most managers will attempt to use simple requests and reason. Assertiveness is a backup strategy, used when the target of influence refuses or appears reluctant to comply with the request. Resistance leads to managers using more directive

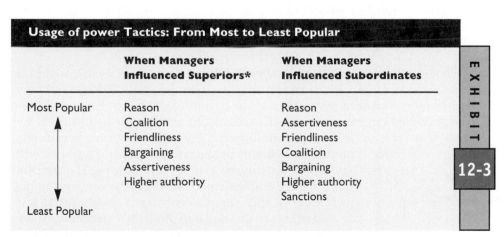

Usage of power Tactics: From Most to Least Popular

EXHIBIT 12-3

	When Managers Influenced Superiors*	When Managers Influenced Subordinates
Most Popular	Reason	Reason
↑	Coalition	Assertiveness
	Friendliness	Friendliness
	Bargaining	Coalition
	Assertiveness	Bargaining
	Higher authority	Higher authority
↓		Sanctions
Least Popular		

*The dimension of sanctions is omitted in the scale that measures upward influence.

Source: Reprinted, by permission of the publisher, from "Patterns of Managerial Influence: Shotgun Managers, Tacticians, and Bystanders," by D. Kipnis et al. *Organizational Dynamics*, Winter 1984, p. 62. © 1984 Periodicals Division, American Management Association, New York. All rights reserved.

strategies. Typically, they shift from using simple requests to insisting that their demands be met. But the manager with relatively little power is more likely to stop trying to influence others when he or she encounters resistance because he or she perceives the costs associated with assertiveness as unacceptable.

Managers vary their power tactics in relation to their objectives. When managers seek benefits from a superior, they tend to rely on kind words and the promotion of pleasant relationships; that is, they use friendliness. In comparison, managers attempting to persuade their superiors to accept new ideas usually rely on reason. This matching of tactics to objectives also holds true for downward influence. For example, managers use reason to sell ideas to employees and friendliness to obtain favors.

The manager's expectations of success guide his or her choice of tactics. When past experience indicates a high probability of success, managers use simple requests to gain compliance. Where success is less predictable, managers are more tempted to use assertiveness and sanctions to achieve their objectives.

Finally, we know that cultures within organizations differ markedly—for example, some are warm, relaxed, and supportive; others are formal and conservative. The organizational culture in which a manager works, therefore, will have a significant bearing on defining which tactics are considered appropriate. Some cultures encourage the use of friendliness, some encourage reason, and still others rely on sanctions and assertiveness. So the organization itself will influence which subset of power tactics is viewed as acceptable for use by managers.

POWER IN GROUPS: COALITIONS

coalition

An informal group bound together by the active pursuit of a single issue.

Those "out of power" and seeking to be "in" will first try to increase their power individually. Why share the spoils if one doesn't have to? But if this proves ineffective, the alternative is to form a **coalition**—an informal group bound together by the active pursuit of a single issue.[16] The logic of a coalition? There's strength in numbers.

The natural way to gain influence is to become a powerholder. Therefore, those who want power will attempt to build a personal power base. But, in many instances, this may be difficult, risky, costly, or impossible. In such cases, efforts will be made to form a coalition of two or more "outs" who, by joining together, can combine their resources to increase rewards for themselves.[17] Successful coalitions have been found to contain fluid membership and are able to form swiftly, achieve their target issue, and quickly disappear.[18]

What predictions can we make about coalition formation?[19] First, coalitions in organizations often seek to maximize their size. In political science theory, coalitions move the other way—they try to minimize their size. They tend to be just large enough to exert the power necessary to achieve their objectives. But

> *The logic of a coalition? There's strength in numbers.*

legislatures are different from organizations. Specifically, decision making in organizations does not end just with selection from among a set of alternatives. The decision must also be implemented. In organizations, the implementation of and commitment to the decision is at least as important as the decision itself. It's necessary, therefore, for coalitions in organizations to seek a broad constituency to support the coalition's objectives. This means expanding the coalition to encompass as many interests as possible. This coalition expansion to facilitate consensus building, of course, is more likely to occur in organizational cultures in which cooperation, commitment, and shared decision making are highly valued. In autocratic and hierarchically controlled organizations, this search for maximizing the coalition's size is less likely to be sought.

Another prediction about coalitions relates to the degree of interdependence within the organization. More coalitions will likely be created where there is a great deal of task and resource interdependence. In contrast, there will be less interdependence among subunits and less coalition formation activity when subunits are largely self-contained or resources are abundant.

Finally, coalition formation will be influenced by the actual tasks that workers do. The more routine the task of a group, the greater the likelihood that coalitions will form. The more that the work people do is routine, the greater their substitutability for each other and, thus, the greater their dependence. To offset this dependence, they can be expected to resort to a coalition.

SEXUAL HARASSMENT: UNEQUAL POWER IN THE WORKPLACE

The issue of sexual harassment got increasing attention by corporations and the media in the 1980s because of the growing ranks of female employees, especially in nontraditional work environments. But it was the congressional hearings in the fall of 1991 in which law professor Anita Hill graphically accused Supreme Court nominee Clarence Thomas of sexual harassment that challenged organizations to reassess their harassment policies and practices.[20]

Sexual harassment is defined as any unwanted activity of a sexual nature that affects an individual's employment. A 1993 Supreme Court decision helped to clarify this definition by adding that the key test for determining if sexual harassment has occurred is whether comments or behavior in a work environment "would reasonably be perceived, and is perceived, as hostile or abusive."[21] But there continues to be disagreement as to what *specifically* constitutes sexual harassment. Organizations have generally made considerable progress in the last few years toward limiting overt forms of sexual harassment of female employees. This includes unwanted physical touching, recurring requests for dates when it is made clear the woman isn't interested, and coercive threats that a woman will lose her job if she refuses a sexual proposition. The problems today are likely to surface around more subtle forms of sexual harassment—unwanted looks or comments, off-color jokes, sexual artifacts such as nude calendars in the workplace, or misinterpretations of where the line between "being friendly" ends and "harassment" begins.

Most studies confirm that the concept of power is central to understanding sexual harassment.[22] This seems to be true whether the harassment comes from a supervisor, a co-worker, or even an employee.

The supervisor–employee dyad best characterizes an unequal power relationship in which position power gives the su-

sexual harassment

Unwelcome advances, requests for sexual favors, and other verbal or physical conduct of a sexual nature.

Advocates against sexual harassment in the workplace marched outside the Supreme Court during a case brought by Kimberly Ellerth against her former employer, Burlington Industries. Ellerth sued Burlington because of constant verbal harassment from her supervisor, a sales manager. The Supreme Court ruled in favor of Ellerth, citing that firms are responsible for their supervisors' conduct, even when top management is unaware of an abusive work situation.

pervisor the capacity to reward and coerce. Supervisors give employees their assignments, evaluate their performance, make recommendations for salary adjustments and promotions, and even decide whether or not an employee retains his or her job. These decisions give a supervisor power. Since employees want favorable performance reviews, salary increases, and the like, it's clear supervisors control resources that most employees consider important and scarce. It's also worth noting that individuals who occupy high-status roles (such as management positions) sometimes believe that sexually harassing female employees is merely an extension of their right to make demands on lower-status individuals. Because of power inequities, sexual harassment by one's boss typically creates the greatest difficulty for those who are being harassed. If there are no witnesses, it is her word against his. Are there others this boss has harassed and, if so, will they come forward? Because of the supervisor's control over resources, many of those who are harassed are afraid of speaking out for fear of retaliation by the supervisor.

Although co-workers don't have position power, they can have influence and use it to sexually harass peers. In fact, although co-workers appear to engage in somewhat less severe forms of harassment than do supervisors, co-workers are the most frequent perpetrators of sexual harassment in organizations. How do co-workers exercise power? Most often it's by providing or withholding information, cooperation, and support. For example, the effective performance of most jobs requires interaction and support from co-workers. This is especially true nowadays as work is assigned to teams. By threatening to withhold or delay providing information that's necessary for the successful achievement of your work goals, co-workers can exert power over you.

Although it doesn't get nearly the attention that harassment by a supervisor does, women in positions of power can be subjected to sexual harassment from males who occupy less powerful positions within the organization. This is usually achieved by the employee devaluing the woman through highlighting traditional gender stereotypes (such as helplessness, passivity, lack of career commitment) that reflect negatively on the woman in power. An employee may engage in such practices to attempt to gain some power over the higher-ranking female or to minimize power differentials.

The topic of sexual harassment is about power. It's about an individual controlling or threatening another individual. It's wrong. Moreover, it's illegal. But you can understand how sexual harassment surfaces in organizations if you analyze it in power terms.

POLITICS: POWER IN ACTION

When people get together in groups, power will be exerted. People want to carve out a niche from which to exert influence, to earn awards, and to advance their careers.[23] When employees in organizations convert their power into action, we describe them as being engaged in politics. Those with good political skills have the ability to use their bases of power effectively.[24]

DEFINITION

political behavior

Those activities that are not required as part of one's formal role in the organization, but that influence, or attempt to influence, the distribution of advantages and disadvantages within the organization.

There has been no shortage of definitions for organizational politics. Essentially, however, they have focused on the use of power to affect decision making in the organization or on behaviors by members that are self-serving and organizationally nonsanctioned.[25] For our purposes, we shall define **political behavior** in organizations as *those activities that are not required as part of one's formal role in the* *organization, but that influence, or attempt to influence, the distribution of advantages and disadvantages within the organization.*[26]

This definition encompasses key elements from what most people mean when they talk about organizational politics. Political behavior is outside one's specified job requirements. The behavior requires some attempt to use one's power bases. Additionally, our definition encompasses efforts to influence the goals, criteria, or processes used for *decision making* when we state that politics is concerned with "the distribution of advantages and disadvantages within the organization." Our definition is broad enough to include such varied political behaviors as withholding key information from decision makers, whistle-blowing, spreading rumors, leaking confidential information about organizational activities to the media, exchanging favors with others in the organization for mutual benefit, and lobbying on behalf of or against a particular individual or decision alternative.

> When employees in organizations convert their power into action, we describe them as being engaged in politics.

A final comment relates to what has been referred to as the "legitimate–illegitimate" dimension in political behavior.[27] **Legitimate political behavior** refers to normal everyday politics—complaining to your supervisor, bypassing the chain of command, forming coalitions, obstructing organizational policies or decisions through inaction or excessive adherence to rules, and developing contacts outside the organization through your professional activities. On the other hand, there are also **illegitimate political behaviors** that violate the implied rules of the game. Those who pursue such extreme activities are often described as individuals who "play hardball." Illegitimate activities include sabotage, whistle-blowing, and symbolic protests such as wearing unorthodox dress or protest buttons, and groups of employees simultaneously calling in sick.

legitimate political behavior

Normal everyday politics.

illegitimate political behavior

Extreme political behavior that violates the implied rules of the game.

The vast majority of all organizational political actions are of the legitimate variety. The reasons are pragmatic: The extreme illegitimate forms of political behavior pose a very real risk of loss of organizational membership or extreme sanctions against those who use them and then fall short in having enough power to ensure that they work.

THE REALITY OF POLITICS

Politics is a fact of life in organizations. People who ignore this fact of life do so at their own peril. But why, you may wonder, must politics exist? Isn't it possible for an organization to be politics free? It's *possible*, but most unlikely.

Organizations are made up of individuals and groups with different values, goals, and interests.[28] This sets up the potential for conflict over resources. Departmental budgets, space allocations, project responsibilities, and salary adjustments are just a few examples of the resources about whose allocation organizational members will disagree.

Resources in organizations are also limited, which often turns potential conflict into real conflict.[29] If resources were abundant, then all the various constituencies within the organization could satisfy their goals. But because they are limited, not everyone's interests can be provided for. Furthermore, whether true or not, gains by one individual or group are often *perceived* as being at the expense of others within the organization. These forces create a competition among members for the organization's limited resources.

Maybe the most important factor leading to politics within organizations is the realization that most of the "facts" that are used to allocate the limited resources are open to interpretation. What, for instance, is *good* performance? What's an *adequate* improvement? What constitutes an *unsatisfactory* job? One person's view that an act is a "selfless effort to benefit the organization" is seen by another as a "blatant attempt to further one's interest."[30] The manager of any major league baseball team knows a .400 hitter is a high performer and a .125 hitter is a poor performer. You don't need to be a baseball genius to know you should play your .400 hitter and send the .125 hitter back to the minors. But what if you have to choose between players who hit .280 and .290? Then other factors—less objective ones—come into play: fielding expertise, attitude, potential, ability to perform in the clutch, loyalty to the team, and so on. More managerial decisions resemble choosing between a .280 and a .290 hitter than deciding between a .125 hitter and a .400 hitter. It is in this large and ambiguous middle ground of organizational life—where the facts *don't* speak for themselves—that politics flourish (see Exhibit 12-4).

Finally, because most decisions have to be made in a climate of ambiguity—where facts are rarely fully objective and, thus, are open to interpretation—people within organizations will use whatever influence they can to taint the facts to support their goals and interests. That, of course, creates the activities we call *politicking.*

Therefore, to answer the earlier question of whether or not it is possible for an organization to be politics free, we can say: Yes, if all members of that organization hold the same goals and interests, if organizational resources are not scarce, and if performance outcomes are completely clear and objective. But that doesn't describe the organizational world that most of us live in!

Politics Is in the Eye of the Beholder

EXHIBIT 12-4

A behavior that one person labels as "organizational politics" is very likely to be characterized as an instance of "effective management" by another. The fact is not that effective management is necessarily political, although in some cases it might be. Rather, a person's reference point determines what he or she classifies as organizational politics. Take a look at the following labels used to describe the same phenomenon. These suggest that politics, like beauty, is in the eye of the beholder.

"Political" Label	"Effective Management" Label
1. Blaming others	1. Fixing responsibility
2. "Kissing up"	2. Developing working relationships
3. Apple polishing	3. Demonstrating loyalty
4. Passing the buck	4. Delegating authority
5. Covering your rear	5. Documenting decisions
6. Creating conflict	6. Encouraging change and innovation
7. Forming coalitions	7. Facilitating teamwork
8. Whistle-blowing	8. Improving efficiency
9. Scheming	9. Planning ahead
10. Overachieving	10. Competent and capable
11. Ambitious	11. Career-minded
12. Opportunistic	12. Astute
13. Cunning	13. Practical-minded
14. Arrogant	14. Confident
15. Perfectionist	15. Attentive to detail

Source: This exhibit is based on T. C. Krell, M. E. Mendenhall, and J. Sendry, "Doing Research in the Conceptual Morass of Organizational Politics," paper presented at the Western Academy of Management Conference, Hollywood, CA, April 1987.

"It's Not *What* You Know, It's *Who* You Know"

This statement is somewhat true. While knowledge of *facts* is an increasingly important source of power in an information-based society, knowing the *right people* increases your chances of getting ahead.

Networking is the term usually used to refer to establishing effective relationships with key people inside and outside the organization. And networking has been found to be the most important activity performed by managers who were promoted the fastest.[31]

A study of general managers found that they fully understood the importance of networking.[32] They established a wide political network of key people from both inside and outside their organizations. This network provided these managers with information and established cooperative relationships that could enhance their careers. The man-agers did favors for these contacts, stressed the obligations of these contacts to them, and "called in" these obligations when support was needed.

Research also indicates that a person's location within an organization is an important determinant of his or her influence.[33] Being in the right place increases your ability to know "the right people." This would further support the importance of contacts over knowledge of facts in gaining influence.

The preceding evidence should not be interpreted as a rejection of job-relevant expertise. Rather, it indicates that "who you know" is an important *additional* factor in organizational life. And for people who want to get ahead or build their political power within an organization, they should spend time and effort in developing a network of contacts.

FACTORS CONTRIBUTING TO POLITICAL BEHAVIOR

Not all groups or organizations are equally political. In some organizations, for instance, politicking is overt and rampant, while in others, politics plays a small role in influencing outcomes. Why is there this variation? Recent research and observation have identified a number of factors that appear to encourage political behavior. Some are individual characteristics, derived from the unique qualities of the people the organization employs; others are a result of the organization's culture or internal environment. Exhibit 12-5 illustrates how both individual and organizational factors can increase political behavior and provide favorable outcomes (increased rewards and averted punishments) for both individuals and groups in the organization.

Individual Factors At the individual level, researchers have identified certain personality traits, needs, and other factors that are likely to be related to political behavior. In terms of traits, we find that employees who are high self-monitors, possess an internal locus of control, and have a high need for power are more likely to engage in political behavior.[34]

The high self-monitor is more sensitive to social cues, exhibits higher levels of social conformity, and is more likely to be skilled in political behavior than the low self-monitor. Individuals with an internal locus of control, because they believe they can control their environment, are more prone to take a proactive stance and attempt to manipulate situations in their favor. Not surprisingly, the Machiavellian personality—which is characterized by the will to manipulate and the desire for power—is comfortable using politics as a means to further his or her self-interest.

Additionally, an individual's investment in the organization, perceived alternatives, and expectations of success will influence the degree to which he or she will pursue illegitimate means of political action.[35] The more that a person

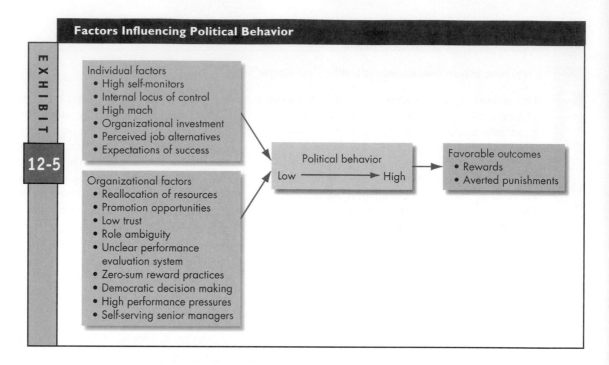

EXHIBIT 12-5

Factors Influencing Political Behavior

Individual factors
- High self-monitors
- Internal locus of control
- High mach
- Organizational investment
- Perceived job alternatives
- Expectations of success

Organizational factors
- Reallocation of resources
- Promotion opportunities
- Low trust
- Role ambiguity
- Unclear performance evaluation system
- Zero-sum reward practices
- Democratic decision making
- High performance pressures
- Self-serving senior managers

Political behavior
Low ————→ High

Favorable outcomes
- Rewards
- Averted punishments

has invested in the organization in terms of expectations of increased future benefits, the more a person has to lose if forced out and the less likely he or she is to use illegitimate means. The more alternative job opportunities an individual has—due to a favorable job market or the possession of scarce skills or knowledge, a prominent reputation, or influential contacts outside the organization—the more likely he or she is to risk illegitimate political actions. Finally, if an individual has a low expectation of success in using illegitimate means, it is unlikely that he or she will attempt to do so. High expectations of success in the use of illegitimate means are most likely to be the province of both experienced and powerful individuals with polished political skills and inexperienced and naive employees who misjudge their chances.

Organizational Factors   Political activity is probably more a function of the organization's characteristics than of individual difference variables. Why? Because many organizations have a large number of employees with the individual characteristics we listed, yet the extent of political behavior varies widely.

Although we acknowledge the role that individual differences can play in fostering politicking, the evidence more strongly supports that certain situations and cultures promote politics. More specifically, when an organization's resources are declining, when the existing pattern of resources is changing, and when there is opportunity for promotions, politics is more likely to surface.[36] In addition, cultures characterized by low trust, role ambiguity, unclear performance evaluation systems, zero-sum reward allocation practices, democratic decision making, high pressures for performance, and self-serving senior managers will create breeding grounds for politicking.[37]

When organizations downsize to improve efficiency, reductions in resources have to be made. Threatened with the loss of resources, people may engage in political actions to safeguard what they have. But any changes, especially those that imply significant reallocation of resources within the organization, are likely to stimulate conflict and increase politicking.

Promotion decisions have consistently been found to be one of the most political in organizations. The opportunity for promotions or advancement encourages people to compete for a limited resource and to try to positively influence the decision outcome.

The less trust there is within the organization, the higher the level of political behavior and the more likely that the political behavior will be of the illegitimate kind. So high trust should suppress the level of political behavior in general and inhibit illegitimate actions in particular.

Role ambiguity means that the prescribed behaviors of the employee are not clear. There are fewer limits, therefore, to the scope and functions of the employee's political actions. Since political activities are defined as those not required as part of one's formal role, the greater the role ambiguity, the more one can engage in political activity with little chance of it being visible.

The practice of performance evaluation is far from a perfected science. The more that organizations use subjective criteria in appraisal, emphasize a single outcome measure, or allow significant time to pass between the time of an action and its appraisal, the greater the likelihood that an employee can get away with politicking. Subjective performance criteria create ambiguity. The use of a single outcome measure encourages individuals to do whatever is necessary to "look good" on that measure, but this is often at the expense of performing well on other important parts of the job that are not being appraised. The amount of time that elapses between an action and its appraisal is also a relevant factor. The longer the time period, the more unlikely that the employee will be held accountable for his or her political behaviors.

Outraged employees stormed Hyundai's headquarters in Seoul, Korea, after the automaker announced plans for massive layoffs. The company hired riot police to protect its headquarters from the rage of employees who felt betrayed because their employer did not honor the social compact of lifetime employment that Korean workers rely on for their financial security.

The more that an organization's culture emphasizes the zero-sum or win-lose approach to reward allocations, the more employees will be motivated to engage in politicking. The zero-sum approach treats the reward "pie" as fixed so that any gain one person or group achieves has to come at the expense of another person or group. If I win, you must lose! If $10,000 in annual raises is to be distributed among five employees, then any employee who gets more than $2,000 takes money away from one or more of the others. Such a practice encourages making others look bad and increasing the visibility of what you do.

In the last 25 years, there has been a general move in North America and among most developed nations toward making organizations less autocratic. Managers in these organizations are being asked to behave more democratically. They're told that they should allow employees to advise them on decisions and that they should rely to a greater extent on group input into the decision process. Such moves toward democracy, however, are not necessarily embraced by all individual managers. Many managers sought their positions in order to have legitimate power so as to be able to make unilateral decisions. They fought hard and often paid high personal costs to achieve their influential positions. Sharing their power with others runs directly against their desires. The result is that managers, especially those who began their careers in the 1950s and 1960s, may use the required committees, conferences, and group meetings in a superficial way, as arenas for maneuvering and manipulating.

The more pressure that employees feel to perform well, the more likely they are to engage in politicking. When people are held strictly accountable for outcomes, this puts great pressure on them to "look good." If a person perceives that his or her entire career is riding on next quarter's sales figures or next month's plant productivity report, there is motivation to do whatever is necessary to make sure the numbers come out favorably.

Politicking

Forget, for a moment, the ethics of politicking and any negative impressions you may have of people who engage in organizational politics. If you wanted to be more politically adept in your organization, what could you do? The following eight suggestions are likely to improve your political effectiveness.[38]

1. *Frame arguments in terms of organizational goals.* Effective politicking requires camouflaging your self-interest. No matter that your objective is self-serving; all the arguments you marshal in support of it must be framed in terms of the benefits that will accrue to the organization. People whose actions appear to blatantly further their own interests at the expense of the organization are almost universally denounced, are likely to lose influence, and often suffer the ultimate penalty of being expelled from the organization.

2. *Develop the right image.* If you know your organization's culture, you understand what the organization wants and values from its employees—in terms of dress, associates to cultivate and those to avoid; whether to appear risk taking or risk aversive, the preferred leadership style, the importance placed on getting along well with others, and so forth. Then you are equipped to project the appropriate image. Because the assessment of your performance is not a fully objective process, style as well as substance must be attended to.

3. *Gain control of organizational resources.* The control of organizational resources that are scarce and important is a source of power. Knowledge and expertise are particularly effective resources to control. They make you more valuable to the organization and, therefore, more likely to gain security, advancement, and a receptive audience for your ideas.

4. *Make yourself appear indispensable.* Because we're dealing with appearances rather than objective facts, you can enhance your power by appearing to be indispensable. That is, you don't have to really be indispensable as long as key people in the organization believe that you are. If the organization's prime decision makers believe there is no ready substitute for what you are giving the organization, they are likely to go to great lengths to ensure that your desires are satisfied.

5. *Be visible.* Because performance evaluation has a substantial subjective component, it's important that your boss and those in power in the organization be made aware of your contribution. If you are fortunate enough to have a job that brings your accomplishments to the attention of others, it may not be necessary to take direct measures to increase your visibility. But your job may require you to handle activities that are low in visibility, or your specific contribution may be indistinguishable because you're part of a team endeavor. In such cases—without appearing to be tooting your own horn or creating the image of a braggart—you'll want to call attention to yourself by highlighting your successes in routine reports, having satisfied customers relay their appreciation to senior executives in your organization, being seen at social functions, being active in your professional associations, developing powerful allies who speak positively about your accomplishments, and similar tactics. Of course, the skilled politician actively and successfully lobbies to get those projects that will increase his or her visibility.

6. *Develop powerful allies.* It helps to have powerful people in your camp. Cultivate contacts with potentially influential people above you, at your own level, and in the lower ranks. They can provide you with important information that may not be available through normal channels. Additionally, there will be times when decisions will be made in favor of those with the greatest support. Having powerful allies can provide you with a coalition of support if and when you need it.

7. *Avoid "tainted" members.* In almost every organization, there are fringe members whose status is questionable. Their performance and/or loyalty is suspect. Keep your distance from such individuals. Given the reality that effectiveness has a large subjective component, your own effectiveness might be called into question if you're perceived as being too closely associated with tainted members.

8. *Support your boss.* Your immediate future is in the hands of your current boss. Since he or she evaluates your performance, you will typically want to do whatever is necessary to have your boss on your side. You should make every effort to help your boss succeed, make her look good, support her if she is under siege, and spend the time to find out what criteria she will be using to assess your effectiveness. Don't undermine your boss. And don't speak negatively of her to others.

Finally, when employees see the people on top engaging in political behavior, especially when they do so successfully and are rewarded for it, a climate is created that supports politicking. Politicking by top management, in a sense, gives permission to those lower in the organization to play politics by implying that such behavior is acceptable.

IMPRESSION MANAGEMENT

We know that people have an ongoing interest in how others perceive and evaluate them. For example, North Americans spend billions of dollars on diets, health club memberships, cosmetics, and plastic surgery—all intended to make them more attractive to others.[39] Being perceived positively by others should have benefits for people in organizations. It might, for instance, help them initially to get the jobs they want in an organization and, once hired, to get favorable evaluations, superior salary increases, and more rapid promotions. In a political context, it might help sway the distribution of advantages in their favor.

The process by which individuals attempt to control the impression others form of them is called **impression management**.[40] It's a subject that only quite recently has gained the attention of OB researchers.[41]

Is everyone concerned with impression management (IM)? No! Who, then, might we predict to engage in IM? No surprise here! It's our old friend, the high self-monitor.[42] Low self-monitors tend to present images of themselves that are consistent with their personalities, regardless of the beneficial or detrimental effects for them. In contrast, high self-monitors are good at reading situations and molding their appearances and behavior to fit each situation.

Given that you want to control the impression others form of you, what techniques could you use? Exhibit 12-6 summarizes some of the more popular IM techniques and provides an example of each.

Keep in mind that IM does not imply that the impressions people convey are necessarily false (although, of course, they sometimes are).[43] Excuses and acclamations, for instance, may be offered with sincerity. Referring to the examples used in Exhibit 12-6, you can *actually* believe that ads contribute little to sales in your region or that you are the key to the tripling of your division's sales. But misrepresentation can have a high cost. If the image claimed is false, you may be discredited.[44] If you "cry wolf" once too often, no one is likely to believe you when the wolf really comes. So the impression manager must be cautious not to be perceived as insincere or manipulative.[45]

Are there *situations* in which individuals are more likely to misrepresent themselves or more likely to get away with it? Yes—situations that are characterized by high uncertainty or ambiguity.[46] These situations provide relatively little information for challenging a fraudulent claim and reducing the risks associated with misrepresentation.

Only a limited number of studies have been undertaken to test the effectiveness of IM techniques, and these have been essentially limited to determining whether or not IM behavior is related to job interview success. Employment interviews make a particularly relevant area of study since applicants are clearly attempting to present positive images of themselves and there are relatively objective outcome measures (written assessments and typically a hire–don't hire recommendation).

The evidence is that IM behavior works.[47] In one study, for instance, interviewers felt that those applicants for a position as a customer service representative who used IM techniques performed better in the interview, and they seemed somewhat more inclined to hire these people.[48] Moreover, when the researchers

impression management

The process by which individuals attempt to control the impression others form of them.

Conformity

Agreeing with someone else's opinion in order to gain his or her approval.
Example: A manager tells his boss, "You're absolutely right on your reorganization plan for the western regional office. I couldn't agree with you more."

Excuses

Explanations of a predicament-creating event aimed at minimizing the apparent severity of the predicament.
Example: Sales manager to boss, "We failed to get the ad in the paper on time, but no one responds to those ads anyway."

Apologies

Admitting responsibility for an undesirable event and simultaneously seeking to get a pardon for the action.
Example: Employee to boss, "I'm sorry I made a mistake on the report. Please forgive me."

Acclamation

Explanation of favorable events to maximize the desirable implications for oneself.
Example: A salesperson informs a peer, "The sales in our division have nearly tripled since I was hired."

Flattery

Complimenting others about their virtues in an effort to make oneself appear perceptive and likable.
Example: New sales trainee to peer, "You handled that client's complaint so tactfully! I could never have handled that as well as you did."

Favors

Doing something nice for someone to gain that person's approval.
Example: Salesperson to prospective client, "I've got two tickets to the theater tonight that I can't use. Take them. Consider it a thank-you for taking the time to talk with me."

Association

Enhancing or protecting one's image by managing information about people and things with which one is associated.
Example: A job applicant says to an interviewer, "What a coincidence. Your boss and I were roommates in college."

Source: Based on B. R. Schlenker, *Impression Management* (Monterey, CA: Brooks/Cole, 1980); W. L. Gardner and M. J. Martinko, "Impression Management in Organizations," *Journal of Management*, June 1988, p. 332; and R. B. Cialdini, "Indirect Tactics of Image Management: Beyond Basking," in R. A. Giacalone and P. Rosenfeld (eds.), *Impression Management in the Organization* (Hillsdale, NJ: Lawrence Erlbaum Associates, 1989), pp. 45–71.

considered applicants' credentials, they concluded that it was the IM techniques alone that influenced the interviewers. That is, it didn't seem to matter if applicants were well or poorly qualified. If they used IM techniques, they did better in the interview.

Another employment interview study looked at whether certain IM techniques work better than others.[49] The researchers compared applicants who used IM techniques that focused the conversation on themselves (called a *controlling style*) to applicants who used techniques that focused on the interviewer (referred to as a *submissive style*). The researchers hypothesized that applicants who used the controlling style would be more effective because of the implicit expectations inherent in employment interviews. We tend to expect job applicants to use self-enhancement, self-promotion, and other active controlling techniques in an interview because they reflect self-confidence and initiative. The researchers predicted that these active controlling techniques would work better for applicants than submissive tactics such as conforming their opinions to those of the interviewer and offering favors to the interviewer. The results confirmed the researchers' predictions. Those applicants who used the controlling style were rated more highly by interviewers on factors such as motivation, enthusiasm, and even technical skills—and they received more job offers. A more recent study confirmed the value of a controlling style over a submissive one.[50] Specifically, recent college graduates that used more self-promotion tactics got higher evaluations by interviewers and more follow-up job site visits, even after adjusting for grade point average, gender, and job type.

DEFENSIVE BEHAVIORS

Organizational politics includes protection of self-interest as well as promotion. Individuals often engage in reactive and protective "defensive" behaviors to avoid action or blame.[51] This section discusses common varieties of **defensive behaviors**, classified by their objective.

Avoiding Action   Sometimes the best political strategy is to avoid action. That is, the best action is no action! However, role expectations typically dictate that one at least give the impression of doing something. Here are six popular ways to avoid action:

1. *Overconforming.* You strictly interpret your responsibility by saying things such as, "The rules clearly state . . . " or "This is the way we've always done it." Rigid adherence to rules, policies, and precedents avoids the need to consider the nuances of a particular case.
2. *Buck passing.* You transfer responsibility for the execution of a task or decision to someone else.
3. *Playing dumb.* This is a form of strategic helplessness. You avoid an unwanted task by falsely pleading ignorance or inability.
4. *Depersonalizing.* You treat other people as objects or numbers, distancing yourself from problems and avoiding having to consider the idiosyncrasies of particular people or the impact of events on them. Hospital physicians often refer to patients by their room number or disease in order to avoid becoming too personally involved with them.
5. *Stretching and smoothing.* Stretching refers to prolonging a task so that you appear to be occupied—for example, you turn a two-week task into a four-month job. Smoothing refers to covering up fluctuations in effort or output. Both of these practices are designed to make you appear continually busy and productive.
6. *Stalling.* This "foot-dragging" tactic requires you to appear more or less supportive publicly while doing little or nothing privately.

Impression management worked for these employees during their job interview at Lander International, an executive recruitment firm that specializes in placing information-technology auditors. Richard Tuck, Lander's CEO, is not interested in hiring experienced recruiters. He hires people who know what makes them happy. Tuck's goal during interviews is to identify how well applicants know themselves. He focuses the interview entirely on applicants, asking them to talk about their outside interests and what they've done that's unusual, passionate, or intense. The 28 employees who impressed Tuck during their interviews include a fish biologist, a driftwood artisan, a former concert bass trombonist, a Third World latrine builder, and a former American Express executive who designs golf putting greens on the side.

Avoiding Blame   What can you do to avoid blame for actual or anticipated negative outcomes? You can try one of the following tactics:

1. *Buffing.* This is a nice way to refer to "covering your rear." It describes the practice of rigorously documenting activity to project an image of competence and thoroughness. "I can't provide that information unless I get a formal written requisition from you," is an example.
2. *Playing safe.* This encompasses tactics designed to evade situations that may reflect unfavorably on you. It includes taking on only projects with a high probability of success, having risky decisions approved by superiors, qualifying expressions of judgment, and taking neutral positions in conflicts.

defensive behaviors
Reactive and protective behaviors to avoid action, blame, or change.

3. *Justifying*. This tactic includes developing explanations that lessen your responsibility for a negative outcome and/or apologizing to demonstrate remorse.
4. *Scapegoating*. This is the classic effort to place the blame for a negative outcome on external factors that are not entirely blameworthy. "I would have had the paper in on time but my computer went down—and I lost everything—the day before the deadline."
5. *Misrepresenting*. This tactic involves the manipulation of information by distortion, embellishment, deception, selective presentation, or obfuscation.

Effects of Defensive Behavior In the short run, extensive use of defensiveness may well promote an individual's self-interest. But in the long run, it more often than not becomes a liability. This is because defensive behavior frequently becomes chronic or even pathological over time. People who constantly rely on defensiveness find that, eventually, it is the only way they know how to behave. At that point, they lose the trust and support of their peers, bosses, employees, and clients. In moderation, however, defensive behavior can be an effective device for surviving and flourishing in an organization because it is often deliberately or unwittingly encouraged by management.

In terms of the organization, defensive behavior tends to reduce effectiveness. In the short run, defensiveness delays decisions, increases interpersonal and intergroup tensions, reduces risk taking, makes attributions and evaluations unreliable, and restricts change efforts. In the long term, defensiveness leads to organizational rigidity and stagnation, detachment from the organization's environment, an organizational culture that is highly politicized, and low employee morale.

THE ETHICS OF BEHAVING POLITICALLY

We conclude our discussion of politics by providing some ethical guidelines for political behavior. While there are no clear-cut ways to differentiate ethical from unethical politicking, there are some questions you should consider.

Exhibit 12-7 illustrates a decision tree to guide ethical actions.[52] This tree is built on the three ethical decision criteria—utilitarianism, rights, and justice—presented in Chapter 5. The first question you need to answer addresses self-interest versus organizational goals. Ethical actions are consistent with the organization's goals. Spreading untrue rumors about the safety of a new product in-

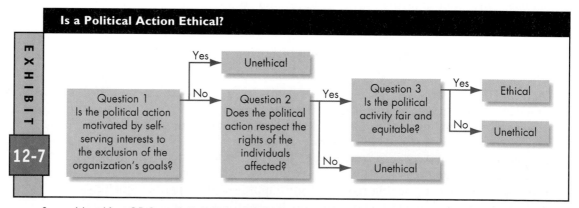

E X H I B I T 12-7

Is a Political Action Ethical?

Source: Adapted from G.F. Cavanagh, D. Moberg, and M. Valasquez, "The Ethic of Organizational Politics," *Academy of Management Review*, July 1981, p. 368. Reprinted with permission.

troduced by your company, in order to make that product's design team look bad, is unethical. However, there may be nothing unethical if a department head exchanges favors with her division's purchasing manager in order to get a critical contract processed quickly.

The second question concerns the rights of other parties. If the department head described in the previous paragraph went down to the mail room during her lunch hour and read through the mail directed to the purchasing manager—with the intent of "getting something on him" so he'll expedite the contract—she would be acting unethically. She would have violated the purchasing manager's right to privacy.

The final question that needs to be addressed relates to whether or not the political activity conforms to standards of equity and justice. The department head that inflates the performance evaluation of a favored employee and deflates the evaluation of a disfavored employee—then uses these evaluations to justify giving the former a big raise and nothing to the latter—has treated the disfavored employee unfairly.

Unfortunately, the answers to the questions in Exhibit 12-7 are often argued in ways to make unethical practices seem ethical. Powerful people, for example, can become very good at explaining self-serving behaviors in terms of the organization's best interests. Similarly, they can persuasively argue that unfair actions are really fair and just. Our point is that immoral people can justify almost any behavior. Those who are powerful, articulate, and persuasive are most vulnerable because they are likely to be able to get away with unethical practices successfully. When faced with an ethical dilemma regarding organizational politics, try to answer the questions in Exhibit 12-7 truthfully. If you have a strong power base, recognize the ability of power to corrupt. Remember, it's a lot easier for the powerless to act ethically, if for no other reason than they typically have very little political discretion to exploit.

SUMMARY AND IMPLICATIONS FOR MANAGERS

If you want to get things done in a group or organization, it helps to have power. As a manager who wants to maximize your power, you will want to increase others' dependence on you. You can, for instance, increase your power in relation to your boss by developing knowledge or a skill that he needs and for which he perceives no ready substitute. But power is a two-way street. You will not be alone in attempting to build your power bases. Others, particularly employees and peers, will be seeking to make you dependent on them. The result is a continual battle. While you seek to maximize others' dependence on you, you will be seeking to minimize your dependence on others. And, of course, others you work with will be trying to do the same.

Few employees relish being powerless in their job and organization. It's been argued, for instance, that when people in organizations are difficult, argumentative, and temperamental it may be because they are in positions of powerlessness in which the performance expectations placed on them exceed their resources and capabilities.[53]

There is evidence that people respond differently to the various power bases.[54] Expert and referent forms of power are derived from an individual's personal qualities. In contrast, coercion, reward, and legitimate forms of power are essentially organizationally derived. Since people are more likely to enthusiastically accept and commit to an individual whom they admire or whose knowledge they respect (rather than someone who relies on his or her position to reward or coerce them), the effective use of expert and referent power should lead to higher employee performance, commitment, and satisfaction.[55] Competence especially appears to offer wide appeal, and its use as a power base results in high performance by group members. The message for managers seems to be: Develop and use your expert power base!

The power of your boss may also play a role in determining your job satisfaction. "One of the reasons many of us like to work for and with people who are powerful is that they are generally more pleasant—not because it is their native disposition, but because the reputation and reality of being powerful permits them more discretion and more ability to delegate to others."[56]

The effective manager accepts the political nature of organizations. By assessing behavior in a political framework, you can better predict the actions of others and use this information to formulate political strategies that will gain advantages for you and your work unit.

We can only speculate at this time on whether or not organizational politics is positively related to *actual* performance. However, there seems to be ample evidence that good political skills are positively related to high performance evaluations and, hence, to salary increases and promotions.[57] We can comment more confidently on the relationship between politics and employee satisfaction. The more political that employees perceive an organization to be, the lower their satisfaction.[58] However, this conclusion needs to be moderated to reflect the employees' level in the organization.[59] Lower-ranking employees, who lack the power base and the means of influence needed to benefit from the political game, perceive organizational politics as a source of frustration and indicate lower satisfaction. But higher-ranking employees, who are in a better position to handle political behavior and benefit from it, don't tend to exhibit this negative attitude.

A final thought on organizational politics: Regardless of level in the organization, some people are just significantly more "politically astute" than are others. Although there is little evidence to support or negate the following conclusion, it seems reasonable that the politically naive or inept are likely to exhibit lower job satisfaction than their politically astute counterparts. The politically naive and inept tend to feel continually powerless to influence those decisions that most affect them. They look at actions around them and are perplexed at why they are regularly "shafted" by colleagues, bosses, and "the system."

Empowerment Improves Employee Productivity

The empowerment trend is sweeping organizations around the world. From Pittsburgh to Prague, companies are encouraging employees to share their ideas on how to run the business and they're providing skill training so employees can take on key job-related responsibilities. In the United States alone, empowerment programs have been adopted by more than 40 percent of manufacturers.[1]

The business press is filled with stories of how empowerment has led to dramatic increases in employee productivity. Empowerment, for instance, is a critical factor in Saturn Corporation's ability to efficiently produce cars whose quality experts continually rank right up there with the best of the Japanese and German automobile manufacturers. Executives at companies such as Colgate-Palmolive, Xerox, and Eastman Chemical credit empowerment with significantly improving employee and operating productivity.

Why has empowerment become so popular? There are at least three forces at work. First, the workforce has changed. Today's workers are far better educated and trained than their parents or grandparents. In fact, because of the complexity of many jobs, today's workers are often considerably more knowledgeable than their managers about how best to do their jobs. Second, global competitiveness demands that organizations be able to move fast. When the people who actually do the work are allowed to make their own job-related decisions, both the speed and quality of those decisions often improve. Finally, there is the effect of dismantling organizational hierarchies. The process of flattening structures has left many lower-level managers with a lot more people to supervise. A manager who had only six or eight employees to oversee could closely monitor each person's work and micromanage activities. Now that manager is likely to have 20 or 30 people to oversee and can't possibly know everything that is going on. So managers have been forced to let go of some of their authority.

No one can challenge the claim that employee empowerment is rapidly growing in popularity. But what is often being overlooked is that many of these programs are failing. There appear to be some common characteristics found among those empowerment efforts that haven't succeeded.[2]

First, many people aren't suited to the empowerment system. They may only want to put in their eight hours of work and go home. They don't want the responsibility or increased stress that comes with empowerment. Or they may be deficient in empowerment skills. Because empowerment typically revolves around teams, employees need to be group oriented and have solid interpersonal skills. These are qualities not possessed by all employees.

Second, empowerment doesn't mesh well with many organizational cultures. To succeed, the organization needs a high-trust, high-risk-taking, and participative culture. This requires that managers be willing to give up authority and let employees make mistakes. This does not exist at many large and established organizations.

Third, even when employees are willing and the culture is supportive, empowerment won't succeed unless management provides the training and commits the resources for employees to do a good job.

Finally, successful empowerment programs must be balanced with appropriate monitoring and control systems. Empowerment increases the risk that people will do things that could damage the business. Therefore, proper controls are needed.

The foregoing factors suggest that empowerment is likely to improve productivity only when employees are willing to accept increased responsibilities, are group oriented, and have good interpersonal skills; when the organization's culture is characterized by trust, risk taking, and employee participation; when employees have been trained in empowerment skills and given the necessary resources; and when management has put into place a comprehensive control system that monitors employee actions and alerts management quickly of major problems.

---

[1]Cited in T. Aeppel, "U.S. Workers Find Empowerment Can Be Daunting," *Wall Street Journal Europe*, September 11, 1997, p. 4.

[2]Ibid., and P. G. Foster-Fishman and C. B. Keys, "The Inverted Pyramid: How a Well Meaning Attempt to Initiate Employee Empowerment Ran Afoul of the Culture of a Public Bureaucracy," in D. P. Moore (ed.), *Academy of Management Best Paper Proceedings* (Vancouver, BC, 1995), pp. 364–68.

1. What is power? How do you get it?

2. Contrast power tactics with power bases. What are some of the key contingency variables that determine which tactic a powerholder is likely to use?

3. Which of the five power bases lie with the individual? Which are derived from the organization?

4. State the general dependency postulate. What does it mean?

5. What creates dependency? Give an applied example.

6. What is a coalition? When is it likely to develop?

7. How are power and politics related?

8. Define political behavior. Why is politics a fact of life in organizations?

9. What factors contribute to political activity?

10. What is impression management? What type of people are most likely to engage in IM?

1. Based on the information presented in this chapter, what would you do as a recent college graduate entering a new job to maximize your power and accelerate your career progress?

2. "Politics isn't inherently bad. It is merely a way to get things accomplished within organizations." Do you agree or disagree? Defend your position.

3. You're a sales representative for an international software company. After four excellent years, sales in your territory are off 30 percent this year. Describe three defensive responses you might use to reduce the potential negative consequences of this decline in sales.

4. "Sexual harassment should not be tolerated at the workplace." "Workplace romances are a natural occurrence in organizations." Are both of these statements true? Can they be reconciled?

5. Which impression management techniques have you used? What ethical implications are there, if any, in using impression management?

Team Exercise | Understanding Power Dynamics

1. Creation of groups

Students are to turn in a dollar bill (or similar value of currency) to the instructor and are divided into three groups based on criteria given by the instructor, assigned to their workplaces, and instructed to read the following rules and tasks. The money is divided into thirds, giving two-thirds of it to the top group, one-third to the middle group, and none to the bottom group.

2. Conduct exercise

Groups go to their assigned workplaces and have 30 minutes to complete their tasks.

Rules

a. Members of the top group are free to enter the space of either of the other groups and to communicate whatever they wish, whenever they wish. Members of the middle group may enter the space of the lower group when they wish but must request permission to enter the top group's space (which the top group can refuse). Members of the lower group may not disturb the top group in any way unless specifically invited by the top. The lower group does have the right to knock on the door of the middle group and request permission to communicate with them (which can also be refused).

b. The members of the top group have the authority to make any change in the rules that they wish, at any time, with or without notice.

Tasks

a. Top Group: To be responsible for the overall effectiveness and learning from the exercise, and to decide how to use its money.

b. Middle Group: To assist the top group in providing for the overall welfare of the organization, and to decide how to use its money.

c. Bottom Group: To identify its resources and to decide how best to provide for learning and the overall effectiveness of the organization.

3. Debriefing

Each of the three groups chooses two representatives to go to the front of the class and discuss the following questions:

a. Summarize what occurred within and among the three groups.

b. What are some of the differences between being in the top group versus being in the bottom group?

c. What can we learn about power from this experience?

d. How accurate do you think this exercise is to the reality of resource allocation decisions in large organizations?

Source: This exercise is adapted from L. Bolman and T. E. Deal, *Exchange*, vol. 3, no. 4, 1979, pp. 38–42. Reprinted by permission of Sage Publications, Inc.

Internet Search Exercises

1. Find the number of sexual harassment suits filed in the United States, or in your local state or province, in the last year. How does this compare with five years ago? Is there a trend? Explain.

2. Review the make-up of the board of directors in five firms among the current top 20 of the Fortune 500. What base(s) of power are available to board members? What percentage of the board members are women? Has this percentage increased or decreased over the last ten years? What does this say about women's power in organizations today?

PHLIP Companion Web Site

We invite you to visit the Robbins homepage on the Prentice Hall Web site at **www.prenhall.com/robbins** for our on-line study guide, current events, links to related Web sites, and more.

Case Incident   Damned If You Do; Damned If You Don't

Fran Gilson has spent 15 years with the Thompson Grocery Company.* Starting out as a part-time cashier while attending college, Fran has risen up through the ranks of this 50-store grocery store chain. Today, at the age of 34, she is a regional manager, overseeing seven stores and earning approximately $95,000 a year. Fran also thinks she's ready to take on more responsibility. About five weeks ago, she was contacted by an executive-search recruiter inquiring about her interest in the position of vice president and regional manager for a national drugstore chain. She would be responsible for more than 100 stores in five states. She agreed to meet with the recruiter. This led to two meetings with top executives at the drugstore chain. The recruiter called Fran two days ago to tell her she was one of the two finalists for the job.

The only person at Thompson who knows Fran is looking at this other job is her good friend and colleague, Ken Hamilton. Ken is director of finance for the grocery chain. "It's a dream job," Fran told Ken. "It's a lot more responsibility and it's a good company to work for. The regional office is just 20 miles from here so I wouldn't have to move, and the pay is first rate. With the performance bonus, I could make nearly $200,000 a year. But best of all, the job provides terrific visibility. I'd be their only female vice president. The job would allow me to be a more visible role model for young women and give me a bigger voice in opening up doors for women and ethnic minorities in retailing management."

Since Fran considered Ken a close friend and wanted to keep the fact that she was looking at another job secret, she asked Ken last week if she could use his name as a reference. Said Ken, "Of course. I'll give you a great recommendation. We'd hate to lose you here, but you've got a lot of talent. They'd be lucky to get someone with your experience and energy." Fran passed Ken's name on to the executive recruiter as her only reference at Thompson. She made it very clear to the recruiter that Ken was the only person at Thompson who knew she was considering another job. Thompson's top management is conservative and places a high value on loyalty. If anyone heard she was talking to another company, it might seriously jeopardize her chances for promotion. But she trusted Ken completely. It's against this backdrop that this morning's incident became more than just a question of sexual harrassment. It became a full-blown ethical and political dilemma for Fran.

Jennifer Chung has been a financial analyst in Ken's department for five months. Fran met Jennifer through Ken. The three have chatted together on a number of occasions in the coffee room. Fran's impression of Jennifer is quite positive. In many ways, Jennifer strikes Fran as a lot like she was 10 years ago. This morning, Fran came to work around 6:30 A.M., as she usually does. It allows her to get a lot accomplished before "the troops" roll in at 8 A.M. At about 6:45, Jennifer came into Fran's office. It was immediately evident that something was wrong. Jennifer was very nervous and uncomfortable, which was most unlike her. She asked Fran if they could talk. Fran sat her down and listened to her story.

What Fran heard was hard to believe, but she had no reason to think Jennifer was lying. Jennifer said

that Ken began making off-color comments to her when they were alone within a month after Jennifer joined Thompson. From there it got progressively worse. Ken would leer at her. He put his arm over her shoulder when they were reviewing reports. He patted her rear. Every time one of these occurrences happened, Jennifer would ask him to stop and not do it again, but it fell on deaf ears. Yesterday, Ken reminded Jennifer that her six-month probationary review was coming up. "He told me that if I didn't sleep with him that I couldn't expect a very favorable evaluation." She told Fran that all she could do was go to the ladies' room and cry.

Jennifer said that she had come to Fran because she didn't know what to do or to whom to turn. "I came to you, Fran, because you're a friend of Ken's and the highest-ranking woman here. Will you help me?" Fran had never heard anything like this about Ken before. About all she knew regarding his personal life was that he was in his late 30s, single, and involved in a long-term relationship.

Questions

1. Analyze Fran's situation in a purely legalistic sense. You might want to talk to friends or relatives who are in management or the legal profession for advice in this analysis.

2. Analyze Fran's dilemma in political terms.

3. Analyze Fran's situation in an ethical sense. What is the ethically right thing for her to do? Is that also the politically right thing to do?

4. If you were Fran, what would you do?

---

*The identity of this organization and the people described are disguised for obvious reasons.

Video Case	Cloud 9

SMALL BUSINESS 2000

If you were talking with a friend on a cellular phone and she told you that she was on "cloud nine," you'd probably think that she was in a great mood and very happy about something. If that friend was calling you from San Diego, she'd probably be telling you something completely different—that she was riding to the airport in a 12-passenger van. In San Diego, Cloud 9 stands for a company that has over 75 percent of the ground transportation market to and from the San Diego airport.

What makes Cloud 9 so interesting to us? There are several reasons but of particular interest is how its

leader took a bankrupt company with a weak image and mediocre employee moral and turned it into a market leader. John Hawkins will be the first one to tell you that he did not accomplish this feat alone. In John's words, "our most important asset is the people." He's not referring to his customers; he's talking about his employees.

Hawkins has done a lot to create and exploit an image for the company. For now though, let's focus on his relationship with his employees. Painting the vans with a new name and having employees wear a tie with the company logo on it is only a small part of the new mind-set that Hawkins wanted to create at Cloud

9. John Hawkins wanted a ride in a Cloud 9 van to be a fun experience; he also wanted working at Cloud 9 to be fun. To accomplish this, everyone needed to buy into the concept and get as excited about their jobs as John and his managers. As you watch this segment, think about what you would have done if you were in John Hawkins's shoes.

Questions

I. John Hawkins talks about what it was like to take over the Super Shuttle franchise in San Diego and transform it into what is now Cloud 9 Shuttle. Hawkins is the man in charge and seems to have been successful in bringing along some employees of the old company and gaining the support of new hires. What do you think Hawkins did to gain this support? On what foundation do you think Hawkins established his power base within the company?

2. Cloud 9 is a company that hit bottom and came out swinging. We can assume that many eyes were on this company when it emerged from bankruptcy. We can also assume the resources were limited. What types of political issues, within the organization, do you think the managers might have thought about? Do you think this was a stage of the company's development at which politics were an issue? Why or why not?

End Notes

1. Based on L. M. Spiro, "The Coup at Goldman," *Business Week*, January 25, 1999, pp. 84–90.
2. R. M. Kanter, "Power Failure in Management Circuits," *Harvard Business Review*, July–August 1979, p. 65.
3. J. Pfeffer, "Understanding Power in Organizations," *California Management Review*, Winter 1992, p. 35.
4. Based on B. M. Bass, *Bass & Stogdill's Handbook of Leadership*, 3rd ed. (New York: Free Press, 1990).
5. J. R. P. French, Jr. and B. Raven, "The Bases of Social Power," in D. Cartwright (ed.), *Studies in Social Power* (Ann Arbor: University of Michigan, Institute for Social Research, 1959), pp. 150–67. For an update on French and Raven's work, see D. E. Frost and A. J. Stahelski, "The Systematic Measurement of French and Raven's Bases of Social Power in Workgroups," *Journal of Applied Social Psychology*, April 1988, pp. 375–89; T. R. Hinkin and C. A. Schriesheim, "Development and Application of New Scales to Measure the French and Raven (1959) Bases of Social Power," *Journal of Applied Psychology*, August 1989, pp. 561–67; and G. E. Littlepage, J. L. Van Hein, K. M. Cohen, and L. L. Janiec, "Evaluation and Comparison of Three Instruments Designed to Measure Organizational Power and Influence Tactics," *Journal of Applied Social Psychology*, January 16–31, 1993, pp. 107–25.
6. D. Kipnis, *The Powerholders* (Chicago: University of Chicago Press, 1976), pp. 77–78.
7. R. E. Emerson, "Power-Dependence Relations," *American Sociological Review*, vol. 27 (1962), pp. 31–41.
8. P. Burrows, "Micron's Comeback Kid," *Business Week*, May 13, 1996, pp. 70–74.
9. H. Mintzberg, *Power In and Around Organizations* (Upper Saddle River, NJ: Prentice Hall, 1983), p. 24.
10. R. M. Cyert and J. G. March, *A Behavioral Theory of the Firm* (Englewood Cliffs, NJ: Prentice Hall, 1963).
11. C. Perrow, "Departmental Power and Perspective in Industrial Firms," in M. N. Zald (ed.), *Power in Organizations* (Nashville, TN: Vanderbilt University Press, 1970).
12. Adapted from J. Pfeffer, *Managing With Power* (Boston: Harvard Business School Press, 1992), pp. 63–64.
13. Adapted from R. M. Kanter, "Power Failure in Management Circuits," *Harvard Business Review*, July–August 1979, p. 67.
14. See, for example, D. Kipnis, S. M. Schmidt, C. Swaffin-Smith, and I. Wilkinson, "Patterns of Managerial Influence: Shotgun Managers, Tacticians, and Bystanders," *Organizational Dynamics*, Winter 1984, pp. 58–67; T. Case, L. Dosier, G. Murkison, and B. Keys, "How Managers Influence Superiors: A Study of Upward Influence Tactics," *Leadership and Organization Development Journal*, vol. 9, no. 4, 1988, pp. 25–31; D. Kipnis and S. M. Schmidt, "Upward-Influence Styles: Relationship with Performance Evaluations, Salary, and Stress," *Administrative Science Quarterly*, December 1988, pp. 528–42; G. Yukl and C. M. Falbe, "Influence Tactics and Objectives in Upward, Downward, and Lateral Influence Attempts," *Journal of Applied Psychology*, April 1990, pp. 132–40; G. Yukl, H. Kim, and C. M. Falbe, "Antecedents of Influence Outcomes," *Journal of Applied Psychology*, June 1996, pp. 309–17; K. E. Lauterbach and B. J. Weiner, "Dynamics of Upward Influence: How Male and Female Managers Get Their Way," *Leadership Quarterly*, Spring 1996, pp. 87–107; S. J. Wayne, R. C. Liden, I. K. Graf, and G. R. Ferris, "The Role of Upward Influence Tactics in Human Resource Decisions," *Personnel Psychology*, Winter 1997, pp. 979–1006.
15. This section is adapted from Kipnis, Schmidt, Swaffin-Smith, and Wilkinson, "Patterns of Managerial Influence."
16. Based on W. B. Stevenson, J. L. Pearce, and L. W. Porter, "The Concept of 'Coalition' in Organization Theory and Research," *Academy of Management Review*, April 1985, pp. 261–63.
17. P. P. Poole, "Coalitions: The Web of Power," in *Research and Application, Proceedings of the 20th Annual Eastern Academy Conference*. D. J. Vredenburgh and R. S. Schuler (eds.), *Effective Management: Academy of Management*, Pittsburgh, May 1983, pp. 79–82.
18. J. K. Murnighan and D. J. Brass, "Intraorganizational Coalitions," in M. H. Bazerman, R. J. Lewicki, and B. H. Sheppard (eds.), *Research on Negotiation in Organizations* (Greenwich, CT: JAI Press, 1991).

19. See J. Pfeffer, *Power in Organizations* (Marshfield, MA: Pitman, 1981), pp. 155–57.

20. For recent reviews of the literature, see L. F. Fitzgerald and S. L. Shullman, "Sexual Harassment: A Research Analysis and Agenda for the 1990s," *Journal of Vocational Behavior*, February 1993, pp. 5–27; and M. L. Lengnick-Hall, "Sexual Harassment Research: A Methodological Critique," *Personnel Psychology*, Winter 1995, pp. 841–64.

21. S. Silverstein and S. Christian, "Harassment Ruling Raises Free-Speech Issues," *Los Angeles Times*, November 11, 1993, p. D2.

22. The following section is based on J. N. Cleveland and M. E. Kerst, "Sexual Harassment and Perceptions of Power: An Under-Articulated Relationship," *Journal of Vocational Behavior*, February 1993, pp. 49–67.

23. S. A. Culbert and J. J. McDonough, *The Invisible War: Pursuing Self-Interest at Work* (New York: John Wiley, 1980), p. 6.

24. Mintzberg, *Power In and Around Organizations*, p. 26.

25. D. J. Vredenburgh and J. G. Maurer, "A Process Framework of Organizational Politics," *Human Relations*, January 1984, pp. 47–66.

26. D. Farrell and J. C. Petersen, "Patterns of Political Behavior in Organizations," *Academy of Management Review*, July 1982, p. 405. For analyses of the controversies underlying the definition of organizational politics, see A. Drory and T. Romm, "The Definition of Organizational Politics: A Review," *Human Relations*, November 1990, pp. 1133–54; and R. S. Cropanzano, K. M. Kacmar, and D. P. Bozeman, "Organizational Politics, Justice, and Support: Their Differences and Similarities," in R.S. Cropanzano and K. M. Kacmar (eds.), *Organizational Politics, Justice and Support: Managing Social Climate at Work* (Westport, CT: Quorum Books, 1995), pp. 1–18.

27. Farrell and Peterson, "Patterns of Political Behavior," pp. 406–07; and A. Drory, "Politics in Organization and Its Perception Within the Organization," *Organization Studies*, vol. 9, no. 2, 1988, pp. 165–79.

28. Pfeffer, *Power in Organizations*.

29. A. Drory and T. Romm, "The Definition of Organizational Politics."

30. K. K. Eastman, "In the Eyes of the Beholder: An Attributional Approach to Ingratiation and Organizational Citizenship Behavior," *Academy of Management Journal*, October 1994, pp. 1379–91; and M. C. Bolino, "Citizenship and Impression Management: Good Soldiers or Good Actors?" *Academy of Management Review*, January 1999, pp. 82–98.

31. F. Luthans, R. M. Hodgetts, and S. A. Rosenkrantz, *Real Managers* (Cambridge, MA: Allinger, 1988).

32. J. P. Kotter, *The General Managers* (New York: The Free Press, 1982).

33. D. J. Brass, "Being in the Right Place: A Structural Analysis of Individual Influence in an Organization," *Administrative Science Quarterly*, December 1984, pp. 518–39.

34. See, for example, G. Biberman, "Personality and Characteristic Work Attitudes of Persons with High, Moderate, and Low Political Tendencies," *Psychological Reports*, October 1985, pp. 1303–10; R. J. House, "Power and Personality in Complex Organizations," in B. M. Staw and L. L. Cummings, (eds.) *Research in Organizational Behavior*, vol. 10 (Greenwich, CT: JAI Press, 1988), pp. 305–57; and G. R. Ferris, G. S. Russ, and P. M. Fandt, "Politics in Organizations," in R. A. Giacalone and P. Rosenfeld (eds.), *Impression Management in the Organization* (Hillsdale, NJ: Lawrence Erlbaum Associates, 1989), pp. 155–56.

35. Farrell and Petersen, "Patterns of Political Behavior," p. 408.

36. S. C. Goh and A. R. Doucet, "Antecedent Situational Conditions of Organizational Politics: An Empirical Investigation," paper presented at the Annual Administrative Sciences Association of Canada Conference, Whistler, B. C., May 1986; C. Hardy, "The Contribution of Political Science to Organizational Behavior," in J. W. Lorsch (ed.), *Handbook of Organizational Behavior* (Upper Saddle River, NJ: Prentice Hall, 1987), p. 103; and G. R. Ferris and K. M. Kacmar, "Perceptions of Organizational Politics," *Journal of Management*, March 1992, pp. 93–116.

37. See, for example, Farrell and Petersen, "Patterns of Political Behavior," p. 409; P. M. Fandt and G. R. Ferris, "The Management of Information and Impressions: When Employees Behave Opportunistically," *Organizational Behavior and Human Decision Processes*, February 1990, pp. 140–58; and Ferris, Russ, and Fandt, "Politics in Organizations," p. 147.

38. S. P. Robbins and P. L. Hunsaker, *Training in InterPersonal Skills: TIPS for Managing People at Work*, 2nd ed. (Upper Saddle River, NJ: Prentice Hall, 1996), pp. 131–34.

39. M. R. Leary and R. M. Kowalski, "Impression Management: A Literature Review and Two-Component Model," *Psychological Bulletin*, January 1990, pp. 34–47.

40. Ibid., p. 34.

41. See, for instance, B. R. Schlenker, *Impression Management: The Self-Concept, Social Identity, and Interpersonal Relations* (Monterey, CA: Brooks/Cole, 1980); W. L. Gardner and M. J. Martinko, "Impression Management in Organizations," *Journal of Management*, June 1988, pp. 321–38; D. C. Gilmore and G. R. Ferris, "The Effects of Applicant Impression Management Tactics on Interviewer Judgments," *Journal of Management*, December 1989, pp. 557–64; Leary and Kowalski, "Impression Management: A Literature Review and Two-Component Model," pp. 34–47; P. R. Rosenfeld, R. A. Giacalone, and C. A. Riordan, *Impression Management in Organizations: Theory, Measurement, and Practice* (New York: Routledge, 1995); S. J. Wayne and R. C. Liden, "Effects of Impression Management on Performance Ratings: A Longitudinal Study," *Academy of Management Journal*, February 1995, pp. 232–60; and C. K. Stevens and A. L. Kristof, "Making the Right Impression: A Field Study of Applicant Impression Management During Job Interviews," *Journal of Applied Psychology*, October 1995, pp. 587–606.

42. M. Snyder and J. Copeland, "Self-Monitoring Processes in Organizational Settings," in Giacalone and Rosenfeld, *Impression Management in the Organization*, p. 11; E. D. Long and G. H. Dobbins, "Self-Monitoring, Impression Management, and Interview Ratings: A Field and Laboratory Study," in J. L. Wall and L. R. Jauch (eds.), *Proceedings of the 52nd Annual Academy of Management Conference*; Las Vegas, August 1992, pp. 274–78; and A. Montagliani and R. A. Giacalone, "Impression Management and Cross-

Cultural Adaption," *Journal of Social Psychology*, October 1998, pp. 598–608.

43. Leary and Kowalski, "Impression Management," p. 40.

44. Gardner and Martinko, "Impression Management in Organizations," p. 333.

45. R. A. Baron, "Impression Management by Applicants During Employment Interviews: The 'Too Much of a Good Thing' Effect," in R. W. Eder and G. R. Ferris (eds.), *The Employment Interview: Theory, Research, and Practice* (Newbury Park, CA: Sage Publishers, 1989), pp. 204–15.

46. Ferris, Russ, and Fandt, "Politics in Organizations."

47. Baron, "Impression Management by Applicants During Employment Interviews"; Gilmore and Ferris, "The Effects of Applicant Impression Management Tactics on Interviewer Judgments"; and Stevens and Kristof, "Making the Right Impression: A Field Study of Applicant Impression Management During Job Interviews."

48. Gilmore and Ferris, "The Effects of Applicant Impression Management Tactics on Interviewer Judgments."

49. K. M. Kacmar, J. E. Kelery, and G. R. Ferris, "Differential Effectiveness of Applicant IM Tactics on Employment Interview Decisions," *Journal of Applied Social Psychology*, August 16–31, 1992, pp. 1250–72.

50. Stevens and Kristof, "Making the Right Impression: A Field Study of Applicant Impression Management During Job Interviews."

51. This section is based on B. E. Ashforth and R. T. Lee, "Defensive Behavior in Organizations: A Preliminary Model," *Human Relations*, July 1990, pp. 621–48.

52. This figure is based on G. F. Cavanagh, D. J. Moberg, and M. Valasquez, "The Ethics of Organizational Politics," *Academy of Management Journal*, June 1981, pp. 363–74.

53. R. M. Kanter, *Men and Women of the Corporation* (New York: Basic Books, 1977).

54. See, for instance, C. M. Falbe and G. Yukl, "Consequences for Managers of Using Single Influence Tactics and Combinations of Tactics," *Academy of Management Journal*, August 1992, pp. 638–52.

55. See J. G. Bachman, D. G. Bowers, and P. M. Marcus, "Bases of Supervisory Power: A Comparative Study in Five Organizational Settings," in A. S. Tannenbaum (ed.), *Control in Organizations* (New York: McGraw-Hill, 1968), p. 236; M. A. Rahim, "Relationships of Leader Power to Compliance and Satisfaction with Supervision: Evidence from a National Sample of Managers," *Journal of Management*, December 1989, pp. 545–56; and P. A. Wilson, "The Effects of Politics and Power on the Organizational Commitment of Federal Executives," *Journal of Management*, Spring 1995, pp. 101–18.

56. J. Pfeffer, *Managing With Power*, p. 137.

57. See, for example, N. Gupta and G. D. Jenkins Jr., "The Politics of Pay," *Compensation & Benefits Review*, March/April 1996, pp. 23–30.

58. G. R. Ferris and K. M. Kacmar, "Perceptions of Organizational Politics."

59. A. Drory, "Perceived Political Climate and Job Attitudes," *Organization Studies*, vol. 14, no. 1, 1993, pp. 59–71.

part three

THE GROUP

In 1995, Anna Seaton Huntington was part of history. She was a member of America[3], the first women's team to enter the America's Cup yachting race. This team ultimately fell short of its goal to win the cup, but Huntington and her teammates learned a lot from the experience. As she relates, one of those lessons was that too much focus on building consensus can hinder success.[1]

"We spent a year training and racing 12 hours a day, six or seven days a week. But because we wanted teamwork to be the driving force behind the team, we decided to sail without a skipper. We thought that if we set things up so the leadership duties were shared, instead of having one person in charge, it would encourage working together as a team. We found out the hard way that traditions such as hierarchical leadership on boats exist for a good reason.

"For example, our tactician and our helmsperson, the two key decision makers during racing, did not always agree on the course of action. Neither could pull rank. Mistakes were made on the race course, then repeated. The pressure and tension grew as the races became more crucial during the three-month racing schedule.

"For our team, the premium was on harmony, or at least an appearance of harmony. We handled conflict by tolerating and avoiding disputes and sticky issues. Because we were told repeatedly to maintain a smooth facade, our conflicts festered instead of erupting, being resolved, and spurring us forward."

Conflict and Negotiation

Huntington and her America³ teammates naively assumed that good teamwork has no conflict. As we'll show in this chapter, the way to create effective teams is to accept the existence of conflict, resolve it when it hinders performance, and even encourage it at times.

Conflict can be a serious problem in an organization. It can create chaotic conditions that make it nearly impossible for employees to work together. On the other hand, as the America³ team found out too late, conflict also has a positive side. We'll explain the difference between negative and positive conflicts in this chapter and provide a guide to help you understand how conflicts develop. We'll also present a topic closely akin to conflict—negotiation. But first, let's clarify what we mean by conflict.

A DEFINITION OF CONFLICT

There has been no shortage of definitions of conflict.[²] Despite the divergent meanings the term has acquired, several common themes underlie most definitions. Conflict must be perceived by the parties to it; whether or not conflict exists is a perception issue. If no one is aware of a conflict, then it is generally agreed that no conflict exists. Additional commonalities in the definitions are opposition or incompatibility and some form of interaction.[3] These factors set the conditions that determine the beginning point of the conflict process.

We can define **conflict**, then, as a process that begins when one party perceives that another party has negatively af-

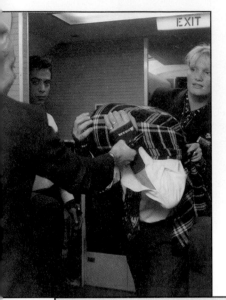

fected, or is about to negatively affect, something that the first party cares about.[4]

This definition is purposely broad. It describes that point in any ongoing activity when an interaction "crosses over" to become an interparty conflict. It encompasses the wide range of conflicts that people experience in organizations—incompatibility of goals, differences over interpretations of facts, disagreements based on behavioral expectations, and the like. Finally, our definition is flexible enough to cover the full range of conflict levels—from overt and violent acts to subtle forms of disagreement.

TRANSITIONS IN CONFLICT THOUGHT

It is entirely appropriate to say that there has been "conflict" over the role of conflict in groups and organizations. One school of thought has argued that conflict must be avoided—that it indicates a malfunctioning within the group. We call this the *traditional* view. Another school of thought, the *human relations* view, argues that conflict is a natural and inevitable outcome in any group and that it need not be evil, but rather has the potential to be a positive force in determining group performance. The third, and most recent, perspective proposes not only that conflict *can* be a positive force in a group but explicitly argues that some conflict is *absolutely necessary* for a group to perform effectively. We label this third school the *interactionist* approach. Let's take a closer look at each of these views.

THE TRADITIONAL VIEW

The early approach to conflict assumed that all conflict was bad. Conflict was viewed negatively, and it was used synonymously with such terms as *violence*, *destruction*, and *irrationality* to reinforce its negative connotation. Conflict, by definition, was harmful and was to be avoided. The America[3] syndicate's management and the yacht's team members essentially subscribed to this view of conflict.

The **traditional** view was consistent with the attitudes that prevailed about group behavior in the 1930s and 1940s. Conflict was seen as a dysfunctional outcome resulting from poor communication, a lack of openness and trust between people, and the failure of managers to be responsive to the needs and aspirations of their employees.

The view that all conflict is bad certainly offers a simple approach to looking at the behavior of people who create conflict. Since all conflict is to be avoided, we need merely direct our attention to the causes of conflict and correct these malfunctionings in order to improve group and organizational performance. Although research studies now provide strong evidence to dispute that this approach to conflict reduction results in high group performance, many of us still evaluate conflict situations utilizing this outmoded standard. So, too, do many senior executives and boards of directors.

THE HUMAN RELATIONS VIEW

The **human relations** position argued that conflict was a natural occurrence in all groups and organizations. Since conflict was inevitable, the human relations school advocated acceptance of conflict. Proponents rationalized its existence: It cannot be eliminated, and there are even times when conflict may benefit a group's performance. The human relations view dominated conflict theory from the late 1940s through the mid-1970s.

Conflict in the airline industry often stems from disagreements based on behavioral expectations of flight crews and passengers. Passenger interference, the biggest security problem facing airlines today, conflicts with airlines' top priority of travel safety. Airlines such as KLM and USAirways are dealing with the conflict by teaching their crew members how to handle aggressive passenger behavior.

conflict

A process that begins when one party perceives that another party has negatively affected, or is about to negatively affect, something that the first party cares about.

traditional view of conflict

The belief that all conflict is harmful and must be avoided.

human relations view of conflict

The belief that conflict is a natural and inevitable outcome in any group.

THE INTERACTIONIST VIEW

While the human relations approach accepted conflict, the **interactionist** approach encourages conflict on the grounds that a harmonious, peaceful, tranquil, and cooperative group is prone to becoming static, apathetic, and nonresponsive to needs for change and innovation.[5] The major contribution of the interactionist approach, therefore, is encouraging group leaders to maintain an ongoing minimum level of conflict—enough to keep the group viable, self-critical, and creative.

Given the interactionist view—and it is the one that we shall take in this chapter—it becomes evident that to say conflict is all good or bad is inappropriate and naive. Whether a conflict is good or bad depends on the type of conflict.

interactionist view of conflict

The belief that conflict is not only a positive force in a group but that it is absolutely necessary for a group to perform effectively.

FUNCTIONAL VS. DYSFUNCTIONAL CONFLICT

The interactionist view does not propose that all conflicts are good. Rather, some conflicts support the goals of the group and improve its performance; these are **functional**, constructive forms of conflict. Additionally, there are conflicts that hinder group performance; these are **dysfunctional** or destructive forms of conflict.

What differentiates functional from dysfunctional conflict? The evidence indicates that you need to look at the *type* of conflict.[6] Specifically, there are three types: task, relationship, and process.

Task conflict relates to the content and goals of the work. **Relationship conflict** focuses on interpersonal relationships. **Process conflict** relates to how the work gets done. Studies demonstrate that relationship conflicts are almost always dysfunctional. Why? It appears that the friction and interpersonal hostilities inherent in relationship conflicts increase personality clashes and decrease mutual understanding, thereby hindering the completion of organizational tasks. On the other hand, low levels of process conflict and low-to-moderate levels of task conflict are functional. For process conflict to be productive, it must be kept low. Intense arguments about who should do what become dysfunctional when they create uncertainty about task roles, increase the time to complete tasks, and lead to members working at cross-purposes. A low-to-moderate level of task conflict consistently demonstrates a positive effect on group performance because it stimulates discussion of ideas that help groups perform better. The America[3] yacht team illustrates a group whose performance suffered from a lack of functional conflict. Low levels of process and task conflicts could have enhanced the team's performance.

functional conflict

Conflict that supports the goals of the group and improves its performance.

dysfunctional conflict

Conflict that hinders group performance.

task conflict

Conflicts over content and goals of the work.

relationship conflict

Conflict based on interpersonal relationships.

process conflict

Conflict over how work gets done.

THE CONFLICT PROCESS

The **conflict process** can be seen as comprising five stages: potential opposition or incompatibility, cognition and personalization, intentions, behavior, and outcomes. The process is diagrammed in Exhibit 13-1.

STAGE I: POTENTIAL OPPOSITION OR INCOMPATIBILITY

The first step in the conflict process is the presence of conditions that create opportunities for conflict to arise. They *need not* lead directly to conflict, but one of these conditions is necessary if conflict is to arise. For simplicity's sake, these conditions (which also may be looked at as causes or sources of conflict) have been condensed into three general categories: communication, structure, and personal variables.[7]

conflict process

Five stages: potential opposition or incompatibility; cognition and personalization; intentions; behavior; and outcomes.

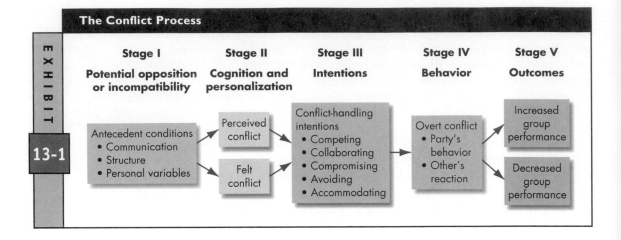

Exhibit 13-1

The Conflict Process

Stage I	Stage II	Stage III	Stage IV	Stage V
Potential opposition or incompatibility	Cognition and personalization	Intentions	Behavior	Outcomes

Antecedent conditions
• Communication
• Structure
• Personal variables

→ Perceived conflict

→ Felt conflict

→ Conflict-handling intentions
• Competing
• Collaborating
• Compromising
• Avoiding
• Accommodating

→ Overt conflict
• Party's behavior
• Other's reaction

→ Increased group performance

Decreased group performance

Communication Susan had worked in purchasing at Bristol-Myers Squibb for three years. She enjoyed her work in large part because her boss, Tim McGuire, was a great guy to work for. Then Tim got promoted six months ago and Chuck Benson took his place. Susan says her job is a lot more frustrating now. "Tim and I were on the same wavelength. It's not that way with Chuck. He tells me something and I do it. Then he tells me I did it wrong. I think he means one thing but says something else. It's been like this since the day he arrived. I don't think a day goes by when he isn't yelling at me for something. You know, there are some people you just find it easy to communicate with. Well, Chuck isn't one of those!"

Susan's comments illustrate that communication can be a source of conflict. It represents those opposing forces that arise from semantic difficulties, misunderstandings, and "noise" in the communication channels. Much of this discussion can be related back to our comments on communication in Chapter 10.

A review of the research suggests that differing word connotations, jargon, insufficient exchange of information, and noise in the communication channel are all barriers to communication and potential antecedent conditions to conflict. Evidence demonstrates that semantic difficulties arise as a result of differences in training, selective perception, and inadequate information about others. Research has further demonstrated a surprising finding: The potential for conflict increases when either too little or too much communication takes place. Apparently, an increase in communication is functional up to a point, whereupon it is possible to overcommunicate, with a resultant increase in the potential for conflict. Too much information as well as too little can lay the foundation for conflict. Furthermore, the channel chosen for communicating can have an influence on stimulating opposition. The filtering process that occurs as information is passed among members and the divergence of communications from formal or previously established channels offer potential opportunities for conflict to arise.

Structure Charlotte and Teri both work at the Portland Furniture Mart—a large discount furniture retailer. Charlotte is a salesperson on the floor; Teri is the company credit manager. The two women have known each other for years and have much in common—they live within two blocks of each other, and their oldest daughters attend the same middle school and are best friends. In reality, if Charlotte and Teri had different jobs they might be best friends themselves, but these two women are consistently fighting battles with each other. Charlotte's job is to sell furniture and she does a heck of a job. But most of her sales are made on credit. Because Teri's job is to make sure the company minimizes credit losses, she regularly has to turn down the credit application of a customer to whom Charlotte has just closed a sale. It's nothing personal between Charlotte and Teri—the requirements of their jobs just bring them into conflict.

The conflicts between Charlotte and Teri are structural in nature. The term *structure* is used, in this context, to include variables such as size, degree of specialization in the tasks assigned to group members, jurisdictional clarity, member–goal compatibility, leadership styles, reward systems, and the degree of dependence between groups.

Research indicates that size and specialization act as forces to stimulate conflict. The larger the group and the more specialized its activities, the greater the likelihood of conflict. Tenure and conflict have been found to be inversely related. The potential for conflict tends to be greatest when group members are younger and when turnover is high.

The greater the ambiguity in precisely defining where responsibility for actions lies, the greater the potential for conflict to emerge. Such jurisdictional ambiguities increase intergroup fighting for control of resources and territory.

Disney's Chairman Michael Eisner takes the interactionist view of conflict. At Disney, managers of the company's many divisions, such as theme parks and cable networks, are pitted against a centralized strategic planning unit. Strategic planners act as a check on the division managers' power. During company meetings Eisner listens to the ideas of both division managers and strategic planners. "His feeling is that you put a lot of smart people in a room and listen to them duke it out, and the best idea will pop out—and it does," says one industry observer.

Groups within organizations have diverse goals. For instance, purchasing is concerned with the timely acquisition of inputs at low prices, marketing's goals concentrate on disposing of outputs and increasing revenues, quality control's attention is focused on improving quality and ensuring that the organization's products meet standards, and production units seek efficiency of operations by maintaining a steady production flow. This diversity of goals among groups is a major source of conflict. When groups within an organization seek diverse ends, some of which—such as sales and credit at Portland Furniture Mart—are inherently at odds, there are increased opportunities for conflict.

There is some indication that a close style of leadership—tight and continuous observation with general control of others' behaviors—increases conflict potential, but the evidence is not particularly strong. Too much reliance on participation may also stimulate conflict. Research tends to confirm that participation and conflict are highly correlated, apparently because participation encourages the promotion of differences. Reward systems, too, are found to create conflict when one member's gain is at another's expense. Finally, if a group is dependent on another group (in contrast to the two being mutually independent) or if interdependence allows one group to gain at another's expense, opposing forces are stimulated.

Personal Variables   Did you ever meet individuals to whom you took an immediate disliking? Most of the opinions they expressed, you disagreed with. Even insignificant characteristics—the sound of their voice, the smirk when they smiled, their personality—annoyed you. We've all met people like that. When you have to work with such individuals, there is often the potential for conflict.

Our last category of potential sources of conflict is personal variables. As indicated, they include the individual value systems that each person has and the personality characteristics that account for individual idiosyncrasies and differences.

"The Source of Most Conflicts Is Lack of Communication"

This statement is probably false. A popular myth in organizations is that poor communication is the primary source of conflicts. And certainly problems in the communication process do act to retard collaboration, stimulate misunderstandings, and create conflicts. But a review of the literature suggests that within organizations, structural factors and individual value differences are probably greater sources of conflict.[8]

Conflicts in organizations are frequently structurally derived. For instance, conflicts between people in sales and credit are typically due to their different departmental goals. Sales seeks to sell as much as possible, regardless of creditworthiness. And the credit department's goal of minimizing credit losses impinges on sales' objective. When people have to work together but are pursuing diverse goals, conflicts ensue. Similarly, increased or-

ganizational size, routinization, work specialization, and zero-sum reward systems are all examples of structural factors that can lead to conflicts.

Many conflicts that are attributed to poor communication are, on closer examination, due to value differences. For instance, prejudice is a value-based source of conflict. When managers incorrectly treat a value-based conflict as a communication problem, the conflict is rarely eliminated. To the contrary, increased communication efforts are only likely to crystallize and reinforce differences. "Before this conversation, I thought you *might* be closed-minded. Now I *know* you are!"

Lack of communication *can* be a source of conflict. But managers should first look to structural or value-based explanations since they are more prevalent in organizations.

The evidence indicates that certain personality types—for example, individuals who are highly authoritarian and dogmatic, and who demonstrate low esteem—lead to potential conflict. Most important, and probably the most overlooked variable in the study of social conflict, is differing value systems. Value differences, for example, are the best explanation of such diverse issues as prejudice, disagreements over one's contribution to the group and the rewards one deserves, and assessments of whether this particular book is any good. That John dislikes African Americans and Dana believes John's position indicates his ignorance, that an employee thinks he is worth $45,000 a year but his boss believes him to be worth $40,000, and that Ann thinks this book is interesting to read while Jennifer views it as trash are all value judgments. And differences in value systems are important sources for creating the potential for conflict.

STAGE II: COGNITION AND PERSONALIZATION

If the conditions cited in Stage I negatively affect something that one party cares about, then the potential for opposition or incompatibility becomes actualized in the second stage. The antecedent conditions can only lead to conflict when one or more of the parties are affected by, and aware of, the conflict.

As we noted in our definition of conflict, perception is required. Therefore, one or more of the parties must be aware of the existence of the antecedent conditions. However, because a conflict is **perceived** does not mean that it is personalized. In other words, "A may be aware that B and A are in serious disagreement . . . but it may not make A tense or anxious, and it may have no effect whatsoever on A's affection toward B."[9] It is at the **felt** level, when individuals become emotionally involved, that parties experience anxiety, tension, frustration, or hostility.

perceived conflict

Awareness by one or more parties of the existence of conditions that create opportunities for conflict to arise.

felt conflict

Emotional involvement in a conflict creating anxiety, tenseness, frustration, or hostility.

Keep in mind two points. First, Stage II is important because it's where conflict issues tend to be defined. This is the place in the process where the parties decide what the conflict is about.[10] And, in turn, this "sense making" is critical because the way a conflict is defined goes a long way toward establishing the sort of outcomes that might settle it. For instance, if I define our salary disagreement as a zero-sum situation—that is, if you get the increase in pay you want, there will be just that amount less for me—I am going to be far less willing to compromise than if I frame the conflict as a potential win-win situation (i.e., the dollars in the salary pool might be increased so that both of us could get the added pay we want). So the definition of a conflict is important, for it typically delineates the set of possible settlements. Our second point is that emotions play a major role in shaping perceptions.[11] For example, negative emotions have been found to produce oversimplification of issues, reductions in trust, and negative interpretations of the other party's behavior.[12] In contrast, positive feelings have been found to increase the tendency to see potential relationships among the elements of a problem, to take a broader view of the situation, and to develop more innovative solutions.[13]

Positive emotions played a role in shaping perceptions when a new member joined the world-famous Tokyo String Quartet. The chemistry among the original members, all Japanese musicians, was incredibly strong, as they had practiced and performed together for decades. When one of the original violinists left the group, a Canadian took his place and, with an outsider's perspective, began questioning everything the ensemble did, from musical selections to tour destinations. Rather than perceiving the new violinist's ideas in a negative way, the other members framed the conflict as a potential win-win situation. They took a positive approach, viewing the situation as an opportunity to see themselves more objectively and as a challenge to make the group more creative and innovative.

STAGE III: INTENTIONS

Intentions intervene between people's perceptions and emotions and their overt behavior. These intentions are decisions to act in a given way.[14]

Why are intentions separated out as a distinct stage? You have to infer the other's intent in order to know how to respond to that other's behavior. A lot of conflicts are escalated merely by one party attributing the wrong intentions to the other party. Additionally, there is typically a great deal of slippage between intentions and behavior, so that behavior does not always accurately reflect a person's intentions.

Exhibit 13-2 represents one author's effort to identify the primary conflict-handling intentions. Using two dimensions—*cooperativeness* (the degree to which one party attempts to satisfy the other party's concerns) and *assertiveness* (the degree to which one party attempts to satisfy his or her own concerns)—five conflict-handling intentions can be identified: *competing* (assertive and uncooperative), *collaborating* (assertive and cooperative), *avoiding* (unassertive and uncooperative), *accommodating* (unassertive and cooperative), and *compromising* (midrange on both assertiveness and cooperativeness).[15]

Competing   When one person seeks to satisfy his or her own interests, regardless of the impact on the other parties to the conflict, he or she is **competing**.

intentions

Decisions to act in a given way in a conflict episode.

competing

A desire to satisfy one's interests, regardless of the impact on the other party to the conflict.

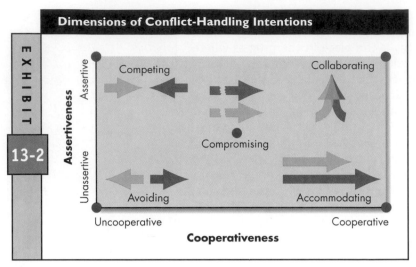

Dimensions of Conflict-Handling Intentions

Source: K. Thomas, "Conflict and Negotiation Processes in Organizations," in M. D. Dunnette and L. M. Hough (eds.), *Handbook of Industrial and Organizational Psychology*, 2nd ed., vol. 3 (Palo Alto, CA: Consulting Psychologists Press, 1992), p. 668. With permission.

Examples include intending to achieve your goal at the sacrifice of the other's goal, attempting to convince another that your conclusion is correct and his or hers is mistaken, and trying to make someone else accept blame for a problem.

Collaborating   When the parties to conflict each desire to fully satisfy the concerns of all parties, we have cooperation and the search for a mutually beneficial outcome. In **collaborating**, the intention of the parties is to solve the problem by clarifying differences rather than by accommodating various points of view. Examples include attempting to find a win-win solution that allows both parties' goals to be completely achieved and seeking a conclusion that incorporates the valid insights of both parties.

Avoiding   A person may recognize that a conflict exists and want to withdraw from it or suppress it. Examples of **avoiding** include trying to just ignore a conflict and avoiding others with whom you disagree.

Accommodating   When one party seeks to appease an opponent, that party may be willing to place the opponent's interests above his or her own. In other words, in order for the relationship to be maintained, one party is willing to be self-sacrificing. We refer to this intention as **accommodating**. Examples are a willingness to sacrifice your goal so the other party's goal can be attained, supporting someone else's opinion despite your reservations about it, and forgiving someone for an infraction and allowing subsequent ones.

Compromising   When each party to the conflict seeks to give up something, sharing occurs, resulting in a compromised outcome. In **compromising**, there is no clear winner or loser. Rather, there is a willingness to ration the object of the conflict and accept a solution that provides incomplete satisfaction of both parties' concerns. The distinguishing characteristic of compromising, therefore, is that each party intends to give up something. Examples might be willingness to accept a raise of $1 an hour rather than $2, to acknowledge partial agreement with a specific viewpoint, and to take partial blame for an infraction.

collaborating

A situation in which the parties to a conflict each desire to satisfy fully the concerns of all parties.

avoiding

The desire to withdraw from or suppress a conflict.

accommodating

The willingness of one party in a conflict to place the opponent's interests above his or her own.

compromising

A situation in which each party to a conflict is willing to give up something.

Intentions provide general guidelines for parties in a conflict situation. They define each party's purpose. Yet, people's intentions are not fixed. During the course of a conflict, they might change because of reconceptualization or because of an emotional reaction to the behavior of the other party. However, research indicates that people have an underlying disposition to handle conflicts in certain ways.[16] Specifically, individuals have preferences among the five conflict-handling intentions just described; these preferences tend to be relied upon quite consistently, and a person's intentions can be predicted rather well from a combination of intellectual and personality characteristics. So it may be more appropriate to view the five conflict-handling intentions as relatively fixed rather than as a set of options from which individuals choose to fit an appropriate situation. That is, when confronting a conflict situation, some people want to win it all at any cost, some want to find an optimum solution, some want to run away, others want to be obliging, and still others want to "split the difference."

STAGE IV: BEHAVIOR

When most people think of conflict situations, they tend to focus on Stage IV. Why? Because this is where conflicts become visible. The behavior stage includes the statements, actions, and reactions made by the conflicting parties.

These conflict behaviors are usually overt attempts to implement each party's intentions. But these behaviors have a stimulus quality that is separate from intentions. As a result of miscalculations or unskilled enactments, overt behaviors sometimes deviate from original intentions.[17]

It helps to think of Stage IV as a dynamic process of interaction. For example, you make a demand on me; I respond by arguing; you threaten me; I threaten you back; and so on. Exhibit 13-3 provides a way of visualizing conflict behavior. All conflicts exist somewhere along this continuum. At the lower part of the continuum, we have conflicts characterized by subtle, indirect, and highly controlled forms of tension. An illustration might be a student questioning in class a point the instructor has just made. Conflict intensities escalate as they move upward along the continuum until they become highly destructive. Strikes, riots, and wars clearly fall in this upper range. For the most part, you should assume that conflicts that reach the upper ranges of the continuum are almost always dysfunctional. Functional conflicts are typically confined to the lower range of the continuum.

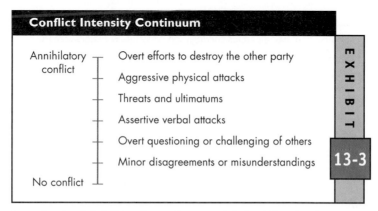

Conflict Intensity Continuum

Annihilatory conflict
— Overt efforts to destroy the other party
— Aggressive physical attacks
— Threats and ultimatums
— Assertive verbal attacks
— Overt questioning or challenging of others
— Minor disagreements or misunderstandings
No conflict

EXHIBIT
13-3

Source: Based on S. P. Robbins, *Managing Organizational Conflict: A Nontraditional Approach* (Upper Saddle River, NJ: Prentice Hall, 1974), pp. 93–97; and F. Glasl, "The Process of Conflict Escalation and the Roles of Third Parties," in G. B. J. Bomers and R. Peterson (eds.), *Conflict Management and Industrial Relations* (Boston: Kluwer-Nijhoff, 1982), pp. 119–40.

conflict management

The use of resolution and stimulation techniques to achieve the desired level of conflict.

If a conflict is dysfunctional, what can the parties do to deescalate it? Or, conversely, what options exist if conflict is too low and needs to be increased? This brings us to **conflict management** techniques. Exhibit 13-4 lists the major resolution and stimulation techniques that allow managers to control conflict levels. Notice that several of the resolution techniques were earlier described as conflict-handling intentions. This, of course, shouldn't be surprising. Under ideal conditions, a person's intentions should translate into comparable behaviors.

STAGE V: OUTCOMES

The action-reaction interplay between the conflicting parties results in consequences. As our model (see Exhibit 13-1) demonstrates, these outcomes may be functional in that the conflict results in an improvement in the group's performance, or dysfunctional in that it hinders group performance.

EXHIBIT 13-4

Conflict Management Techniques

Conflict Resolution Techniques

Problem solving	Face-to-face meeting of the conflicting parties for the purpose of identifying the problem and resolving it through open discussion.
Superordinate goals	Creating a shared goal that cannot be attained without the cooperation of each of the conflicting parties.
Expansion of resources	When a conflict is caused by the scarcity of a resource—say, money, promotion opportunities, office space—expansion of the resource can create a win-win solution.
Avoidance	Withdrawal from, or suppression of, the conflict.
Smoothing	Playing down differences while emphasizing common interests between the conflicting parties.
Compromise	Each party to the conflict gives up something of value.
Authoritative command	Management uses its formal authority to resolve the conflict and then communicates its desires to the parties involved.
Altering the human variable	Using behavioral change techniques such as human relations training to alter attitudes and behaviors that cause conflict.
Altering the structural variables	Changing the formal organization structure and the interaction patterns of conflicting parties through job redesign, transfers, creation of coordinating positions, and the like.

Conflict Stimulation Techniques

Communication	Using ambiguous or threatening messages to increase conflict levels.
Bringing in outsiders	Adding employees to a group whose backgrounds, values, attitudes, or managerial styles differ from those of present members.
Restructuring the organization	Realigning work groups, altering rules and regulations, increasing interdependence, and making similar structural changes to disrupt the status quo.
Appointing a devil's advocate	Designating a critic to purposely argue against the majority positions held by the group.

Source: Based on S. P. Robbins, *Managing Organizational Conflict: A Nontraditional Approach* (Upper Saddle River, NJ: Prentice Hall, 1974), pp. 59–89.

Functional Outcomes   How might conflict act as a force to increase group performance? It is hard to visualize a situation in which open or violent aggression could be functional. But there are a number of instances in which it is possible to envision how low or moderate levels of conflict could improve the effectiveness of a group. Because people often find it difficult to think of instances in which conflict can be constructive, let's consider some examples and then review the research evidence. Note how all these examples focus on task and process conflicts and exclude the relationship variety.

Conflict is constructive when it improves the quality of decisions, stimulates creativity and innovation, encourages interest and curiosity among group members, provides the medium through which problems can be aired and tensions released, and fosters an environment of self-evaluation and change. The evidence suggests that conflict can improve the quality of decision making by allowing all points, particularly the ones that are unusual or held by a minority, to be weighed in important decisions.[18] Conflict is an antidote for groupthink. It doesn't allow the group passively to "rubber-stamp" decisions that may be based on weak assumptions, inadequate consideration of relevant alternatives, or other debilities. Conflict challenges the status quo and, therefore, furthers the creation of new ideas, promotes reassessment of group goals and activities, and increases the probability that the group will respond to change.

For an example of a company that has suffered because it had too little functional conflict, you don't have to look further than automobile behemoth General Motors.[19] Many of GM's problems over the past three decades can be traced to a lack of functional conflict. It hired and promoted individuals who were "yes men," loyal to GM to the point of never questioning company actions. Managers were, for the most part, conservative white Anglo-Saxon males raised in the midwestern United States who resisted change—they preferred looking back to past successes rather than forward to new challenges. They were almost sanctimonious in their belief that what had worked in the past would continue to work in the future. Moreover, by sheltering executives in the company's Detroit offices and encouraging them to socialize with others inside the GM ranks, the company further insulated managers from conflicting perspectives.

Research studies in diverse settings confirm the functionality of conflict. Consider the following findings.

The comparison of six major decisions made during the administration of four different U.S. presidents found that conflict reduced the chance that groupthink would overpower policy decisions. The comparisons demonstrated that conformity among presidential advisors was related to poor decisions, while an atmosphere of constructive conflict and critical thinking surrounded the well-developed decisions.[20]

There is evidence indicating that conflict can also be positively related to productivity. For instance, it was demonstrated that, among established groups, performance tended to improve more when there was conflict among members than when there was fairly close agreement. The investigators observed that when groups analyzed decisions that had been made by the individual members of that group, the average improvement among the high-conflict groups was 73 percent greater than was that of those groups characterized by low-conflict conditions.[21] Others have found similar results: Groups composed of members with different interests tend to produce higher-quality solutions to a variety of problems than do homogeneous groups.[22]

The preceding leads us to predict that the increasing cultural diversity of the workforce should provide benefits to organizations. And that's what the evidence indicates. Research demonstrates that heterogeneity among group and organization members can increase creativity, improve the quality of decisions, and facilitate change by enhancing member flexibility.[23] For example, researchers compared decision-making groups composed of all Anglo individuals with groups that also contained members from Asian, Hispanic, and black ethnic groups. The ethnically diverse groups produced more effective and more feasible ideas and the unique ideas they generated tended to be of higher quality than the unique ideas produced by the all-Anglo group.

Similarly, studies of professionals—systems analysts and research and development scientists—support the constructive value of conflict. An investigation of 22 teams of systems analysts found that the more incompatible groups were likely to be more productive.[24] Research and development scientists have been found to be most productive when there is a certain amount of intellectual conflict.[25]

Religious conflicts between employees and employers are increasing as more immigrants enter the workforce. But Pizza Hut views religious diversity as good for business. A Pizza Hut restaurant in Aurora, Colorado, has been attracting more Muslim patrons since hiring waitress Threase-Mae Jacobs, who observes her religion by wearing a hijab—a Muslim head scarf. Pizza Hut executives say their company respects different religious traditions, noting that its employees include turbaned Sikhs, veiled Muslim women, and yarmulke-wearing Jews.

Dysfunctional Outcomes The destructive consequences of conflict upon a group or organization's performance are generally well known. A reasonable summary might state: Uncontrolled opposition breeds discontent, which acts to dissolve common ties, and eventually leads to the destruction of the group. And, of course, there is a substantial body of literature to document how conflict—the dysfunctional varieties—can reduce group effectiveness.[26] Among the more undesirable consequences are a retarding of communication, reductions in group cohesiveness, and subordination of group goals to the primacy of infighting between members. At the extreme, conflict can bring group functioning to a halt and potentially threaten the group's survival.

The demise of an organization as a result of too much conflict isn't as unusual as it might first appear. For instance, one of New York's best-known law firms, Shea & Gould, closed down solely because the 80 partners just couldn't get along.[27] As one legal consultant, familiar with the organization, said: "This was a a firm that had basic and principled differences among the partners that were basically irreconcilable." That same consultant also addressed the partners at their last meeting: "You don't have an economic problem," he said. "You have a personality problem. You hate each other!"

Creating Functional Conflict We briefly mentioned conflict stimulation as part of Stage IV of the conflict process. Since the topic of conflict stimulation is relatively new and somewhat controversial, you might be wondering: If managers accept the interactionist view toward conflict, what can they do to encourage functional conflict in their organizations?[28]

There seems to be general agreement that creating functional conflict is a tough job, particularly in large American corporations. As one consultant put it, "A high proportion of people who get to the top are conflict avoiders. They don't like hearing negatives, they don't like saying or thinking negative things. They frequently make it up the ladder in part because they don't irritate people on the way up." Another suggests that at least seven out of ten people in American business hush up when their opinions are at odds with those of their superiors, allowing bosses to make mistakes even when they know better.

Such anticonflict cultures may have been tolerable in the past but not in today's fiercely competitive global economy. Those organizations that don't encourage and support dissent may find their survival threatened. Let's look at a couple of approaches organizations are using to encourage their people to challenge the system and develop fresh ideas.

Hewlett-Packard rewards dissenters by recognizing go-against-the-grain types, or people who stay with the ideas they believe in even when those ideas are rejected by management. Herman Miller Inc., an office-furniture manufacturer, has a formal system in which employees evaluate and criticize their bosses. IBM also has a formal system that encourages dissension. Employees can question their boss with impunity. If the disagreement can't be resolved, the system provides a third party for counsel.

Royal Dutch Shell Group, General Electric, and Anheuser-Busch build devil's advocates into the decision process. For instance, when the policy committee at Anheuser-Busch considers a major move, such as getting into or out of a business or making a major capital expenditure, it often assigns teams to make the case for each side of the question. This process frequently results in decisions and alternatives that previously hadn't been considered.

One common ingredient in organizations that successfully create functional conflict is that they reward dissent and punish conflict avoiders. The president of Innovis Interactive Technologies, for instance, fired a top executive who refused to dissent. His explanation: "He was the ultimate yes-man. In this organization, I can't afford to pay someone to hear my own opinion." But the real challenge for managers is when they hear news that they don't want to hear. The news may make their blood boil or their hopes collapse, but they can't show it. They have to learn to take the bad news without flinching. No tirades, no tight-lipped sarcasm, no eyes rolling upward, no gritting of teeth. Rather, managers should ask calm, even-tempered questions: "Can you tell me more about what happened?" "What do you think we ought to do?" A sincere "Thank you for bringing this to my attention" will probably reduce the likelihood that managers will be cut off from similar communications in the future.

NEGOTIATION

Negotiation permeates the interactions of almost everyone in groups and organizations. There's the obvious: Labor bargains with management. There's the not so obvious: Managers negotiate with employees, peers, and bosses; salespeople negotiate with customers; purchasing agents negotiate with suppliers. And there's the subtle: A worker agrees to answer a colleague's phone for a few minutes in exchange for some past or future benefit. In today's team-based organizations, in which members are increasingly finding themselves having to work with colleagues over whom they have no direct authority and with whom they may not even share a common boss, negotiation skills become critical.

Behind the Labor Peace at Ford

General Motors has a long history of conflict with the United Auto Workers union. In 1998, for instance, it was paralyzed by a 54-day strike that cost GM $2 billion in after-tax profits. In contrast, Ford Motor Co. has excellent relations with the UAW and hasn't had a single strike in the United States since 1986. The difference? Many auto industry observers think it's Ford's vice chairman and chief labor negotiator, Peter J. Pestillo.

Most auto company labor negotiators are former factory managers, with M.B.A.s, who come from upper-class roots. Not Pestillo. The son of a union machinist, his first job after high school was in a ball bearing company where

he was a dues-paying member of the UAW. After graduating from Fairfield University, he worked his way through Georgetown University's law school. At the age of 38, having honed his negotiation skills at General Electric and B.F. Goodrich, Pestillo came to Ford to oversee its labor policy. Twenty-three years later, he's still doing it.

Pestillo stands out among auto executives because of his belief in cooperation with the unions. He encourages factory managers to work closely with workers and union leaders. And he's forced out factory managers who couldn't. "In the old days, they were happy to make loads of union grievances and disciplinary actions to prove how tough they were," he says. "Now we measure how effective they are." In no small part to Pestillo, Ford plants are now among

America's best. A recent survey found that Ford ran 4 of America's 10 most productive car factories and 7 of the 10 most productive light truck factories.

Pestillo has built close, personal ties with key UAW officials. He likes them and they like him. The current president of the UAW, for instance, considers Pestillo a friend, with whom he enjoys drinking and playing golf. This close relationship has benefited Ford. The UAW traditionally negotiates a three-year agreement with one automaker and uses that as a reference point when negotiating with the others. For most of the past 20 years, the union has gone to Ford first because of its cooperative relationship. Pestillo has then used this opportunity to negotiate deals that have cut Ford's costs and done little to help its rival, GM.

Source: Adapted from K. Bradsher, "Behind the Labor Peace at Ford," *New York Times*, March 21, 1999, p. BU-2.

---

negotiation

A process in which two or more parties exchange goods or services and attempt to agree upon the exchange rate for them.

We'll define **negotiation** as a process in which two or more parties exchange goods or services and attempt to agree upon the exchange rate for them.[29] Note that we use the terms *negotiation* and *bargaining* interchangeably.

In this section, we'll contrast two bargaining strategies, provide a model of the negotiation process, ascertain the role of personality traits on bargaining, review cultural differences in negotiation, and take a brief look at third-party negotiations.

BARGAINING STRATEGIES

There are two general approaches to negotiation—*distributive bargaining* and *integrative bargaining*.[30] These are compared in Exhibit 13-5.

distributive bargaining

Negotiation that seeks to divide up a fixed amount of resources; a win-lose situation.

Distributive Bargaining   You see a used car advertised for sale in the newspaper. It appears to be just what you've been looking for. You go out to see the car. It's great and you want it. The owner tells you the asking price. You don't want to pay that much. The two of you then negotiate over the price. The negotiating strategy you're engaging in is called **distributive bargaining**. Its most identifying feature is that it operates under zero-sum conditions. That is, any gain I make is at your expense, and vice versa. Referring back to the used-car example, every dollar you can get the seller to cut from the car's price is a dollar you save. Conversely, every dollar more the seller can get from you comes at your expense. So the essence of distributive bargaining is negotiating over who gets what share of a fixed pie.

Probably the most widely cited example of distributive bargaining is in labor–management negotiations over wages. Typically, labor's representatives

Distributive vs. Integrative Bargaining

Bargaining Characteristic	Distributive Characteristic	Integrative Characteristic
Available resources	Fixed amount of resources to be divided	Variable amount of resources to be divided
Primary motivations	I win, you lose	I win, you win
Primary interests	Opposed to each other	Convergent or congruent with each other
Focus of relationships	Short term	Long term

EXHIBIT 13-5

Source: Based on R. J. Lewicki and J. A. Litterer, *Negotiation* (Homewood, IL: Irwin, 1985), p. 280.

come to the bargaining table determined to get as much money as possible out of management. Since every cent more that labor negotiates increases management's costs, each party bargains aggressively and treats the other as an opponent who must be defeated.

The essence of distributive bargaining is depicted in Exhibit 13-6. Parties A and B represent two negotiators. Each has a *target point* that defines what he or she would like to achieve. Each also has a *resistance point*, which marks the lowest outcome that is acceptable—the point below which they would break off negotiations rather than accept a less favorable settlement. The area between these two points makes up each one's aspiration range. As long as there is some overlap between A and B's aspiration ranges, there exists a settlement range where each one's aspirations can be met.

When engaged in distributive bargaining, one's tactics focus on trying to get one's opponent to agree to one's specific target point or to get as close to it as possible. Examples of such tactics are persuading your opponent of the impossibility of getting to his or her target point and the advisability of accepting a settlement near yours; arguing that your target is fair, while your opponent's isn't; and attempting to get your opponent to feel emotionally generous toward you and, thus, accept an outcome close to your target point.

Integrative Bargaining A sales representative for a women's sportswear manufacturer has just closed a $15,000 order from a small clothing retailer. The sales rep calls in the order to her firm's credit department. She is told that the firm can't approve credit to this customer because of a past slow-pay record. The next

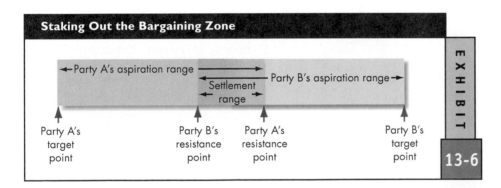

Staking Out the Bargaining Zone

Party A's aspiration range · Settlement range · Party B's aspiration range

Party A's target point · Party B's resistance point · Party A's resistance point · Party B's target point

EXHIBIT 13-6

day, the sales rep and the firm's credit manager meet to discuss the problem. The sales rep doesn't want to lose the business. Neither does the credit manager, but he also doesn't want to get stuck with an uncollectible debt. The two openly review their options. After considerable discussion, they agree on a solution that meets both their needs: The credit manager will approve the sale, but the clothing store's owner will provide a bank guarantee that will ensure payment if the bill isn't paid within 60 days.

integrative bargaining

Negotiation that seeks one or more settlements that can create a win-win solution.

This sales–credit negotiation is an example of **integrative bargaining**. In contrast to distributive bargaining, integrative problem solving operates under the assumption that there exists one or more settlements that can create a win-win solution.

In terms of intraorganizational behavior, all things being equal, integrative bargaining is preferable to distributive bargaining. Why? Because the former builds long-term relationships and facilitates working together in the future. It bonds negotiators and allows each to leave the bargaining table feeling that he or she has achieved a victory. Distributive bargaining, on the other hand, leaves one party a loser. It tends to build animosities and deepen divisions when people have to work together on an ongoing basis.

Why, then, don't we see more integrative bargaining in organizations? The answer lies in the conditions necessary for this type of negotiation to succeed. These include parties who are open with information and candid about their concerns, a sensitivity by both parties to the other's needs, the ability to trust one another, and a willingness by both parties to maintain flexibility.[31] Since these conditions often don't exist in organizations, it isn't surprising that negotiations often take on a win-at-any-cost dynamic.

THE NEGOTIATION PROCESS

Exhibit 13-7 provides a simplified model of the negotiation process. It views negotiation as made up of five steps: (1) preparation and planning; (2) definition of ground rules; (3) clarification and justification; (4) bargaining and problem solving; and (5) closure and implementation.[32]

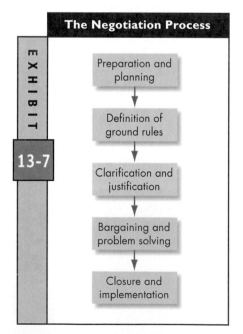

EXHIBIT 13-7

The Negotiation Process

Preparation and planning

↓

Definition of ground rules

↓

Clarification and justification

↓

Bargaining and problem solving

↓

Closure and implementation

Preparation and Planning Before you start negotiating, you need to do your homework. What's the nature of the conflict? What's the history leading up to this negotiation? Who's involved and what are their perceptions of the conflict?

What do you want from the negotiation? What are *your* goals? If you're a purchasing manager at Dell Computer, for instance, and your goal is to get a significant cost reduction from your supplier of keyboards, make sure that this goal stays paramount in your discussions and doesn't get overshadowed by other issues. It often helps to put your goals in writing and develop a range of outcomes—from "most hopeful" to "minimally acceptable"—to keep your attention focused.

You also want to prepare an assessment of what you think the other party to your negotiation's goals are. What is he or she likely to ask for? How entrenched is the other party likely to be in his or her position? What intangible or hidden interests may be important to the other party? What might he or she be willing to settle on? When you can anticipate your opponent's position, you are better equipped to counter his or her arguments with the facts and figures that support your position.

The importance of sizing up the other party is illustrated by the experience of Keith Rosenbaum, a partner in a major Los Angeles law firm. "Once when we were negotiating to buy a business, we found that the owner was going through a nasty divorce. We were on good terms with the wife's attorney and we learned the seller's net worth. California is a community property law state, so we knew he had to pay her half of everything. We knew his time frame. We knew what he was willing to part with and what he was not. We knew a lot more about him than he would have wanted us to know. We were able to twist him a little bit, and get a better price."[33]

Once you've gathered your information, use it to develop a strategy. Like expert chess players in a chess match, negotiators should have a strategy. They know ahead of time how they will respond to any given situation. As part of your strategy, you should determine yours and the other side's *Best Alternative To a Negotiated Agreement* (**BATNA**).[34] Your BATNA determines the lowest value acceptable to you for a negotiated agreement. Any offer you receive that is higher than your BATNA is better than an impasse. Conversely, you shouldn't expect success in your negotiation effort unless you're able to make the other side an offer it finds more attractive than its BATNA. If you go into your negotiation having a good idea of what the other party's BATNA is, even if you're not able to meet it, you might be able to get the other party to change it.

BATNA

The best alternative to a negotiated agreement; the lowest acceptable value to an individual for a negotiated agreement.

Definition of Ground Rules   Once you've done your planning and developed a strategy, you're ready to begin defining the ground rules and procedures with the other party over the negotiation itself. Who will do the negotiating? Where will it take place? What time constraints, if any, will apply? To what issues will negotiation be limited? Will there be a specific procedure to follow if an impasse is reached? During this phase, the parties will also exchange their initial proposals or demands.

Clarification and Justification   When initial positions have been exchanged, both you and the other party will explain, amplify, clarify, bolster, and justify your original demands. This needn't be confrontational. Rather, it is an opportunity for educating and informing each other on the issues, why they are important, and how each arrived at their initial demands. This is the point at which you might want to provide the other party with any documentation that helps support your position.

Bargaining and Problem Solving   The essence of the negotiation process is the actual give-and-take in trying to hash out an agreement. Concessions will undoubtedly need to be made by both parties. The "From Concepts to Skills" box on negotiating (see page 400) directly addresses some of the actions you should take to improve the likelihood that you can achieve a good agreement.

Closure and Implementation   The final step in the negotiation process is formalizing the agreement that has been worked out and developing any procedures that are necessary for implementation and monitoring. For major negotiations—which would include everything from labor–management negotiations, to bargaining over lease terms, to buying a piece of real estate, to negotiating a job

Negotiating

Once you've taken the time to assess your own goals, considered the other party's goals and interests, and developed a strategy, you're ready to begin actual negotiations. The following suggestions should improve your negotiating skills.[35]

Begin with a positive overture. Studies on negotiation show that concessions tend to be reciprocated and lead to agreements. As a result, begin bargaining with a positive overture—perhaps a small concession—and then reciprocate your opponent's concessions.

Address problems, not personalities. Concentrate on the negotiation issues, not on the personal characteristics of your opponent. When negotiations get tough, avoid the tendency to attack your opponent. It's your opponent's ideas or position that you disagree with, not him or her personally. Separate the people from the problem, and don't personalize differences.

Pay little attention to initial offers. Treat an initial offer as merely a point of departure. Everyone has to have an initial position. These initial offers tend to be extreme and idealistic. Treat them as such.

Emphasize win-win solutions. Inexperienced negotiators often assume that their gain must come at the expense of the other party. As noted with integrative bargaining, that needn't be the case. There are often win-win solutions. But assuming a zero-sum game means missed opportunities for trade-offs that could benefit both sides. So if conditions are supportive, look for an integrative solution. Frame options in terms of your opponent's interests and look for solutions that can allow your opponent, as well as yourself, to declare a victory.

Create an open and trusting climate. Skilled negotiators are better listeners, ask more questions, focus their arguments more directly, are less defensive, and have learned to avoid words and phrases that can irritate an opponent (i.e., "generous offer," "fair price," "reasonable arrangement"). In other words, they are better at creating the open and trusting climate necessary for reaching an integrative settlement.

offer for a senior-management position—this will require hammering out the specifics in a formal contract. For most cases, however, closure of the negotiation process is nothing more formal than a handshake.

ISSUES IN NEGOTIATION

We conclude our discussion of negotiation by reviewing four contemporary issues in negotiation: the role of personality traits, gender differences in negotiating, the effect of cultural differences on negotiating styles, and the use of third parties to help resolve differences.

The Role of Personality Traits in Negotiation   Can you predict an opponent's negotiating tactics if you know something about his or her personality? It's tempting to answer Yes to this question. For instance, you might assume that high risk takers would be more aggressive bargainers who make fewer concessions. Surprisingly, the evidence doesn't support this intuition.[36]

Overall assessments of the personality–negotiation relationship finds that personality traits have no significant direct effect on either the bargaining process or negotiation outcomes. This conclusion is important. It suggests that you should concentrate on the issues and the situational factors in each bargaining episode and not on your opponent's personality.

Gender Differences in Negotiations   Do men and women negotiate differently? The answer appears to be No.[37]

A popular stereotype held by many is that women are more cooperative, pleasant, and relationship oriented in negotiations than are men. The evidence doesn't support this belief. Comparisons between experienced male and female managers find women are neither worse nor better negotiators, neither more cooperative nor open to the other, and neither more nor less persuasive nor threatening than are men.

The belief that women are "nicer" than men in negotiations is probably due to confusing gender and the lack of power typically held by women in most large organizations. The research indicates that low-power managers, regardless of gender, attempt to placate their opponents and to use softly persuasive tactics rather than direct confrontation and threats. Where women and men have similar power bases, there shouldn't be any significant differences in their negotiation styles.

While gender may not be relevant in terms of negotiation outcomes, women's attitudes toward negotiation and toward themselves as negotiators appear to be quite different from men's. Managerial women demonstrate less confidence in anticipation of negotiating and are less satisfied with their performance after the process is complete, despite the fact that their performance and the outcomes they achieve are similar to men.

This latter conclusion suggests that women may unduly penalize themselves by failing to engage in negotiations when such action would be in their best interests.

Cultural Differences in Negotiations   Although there appears to be no significant direct relationship between an individual's personality and negotiation style, cultural background does seem to be relevant. Negotiating styles clearly vary across national cultures.[38]

The French like conflict. They frequently gain recognition and develop their reputations by thinking and acting against others. As a result, the French tend to take a long time in negotiating agreements and they aren't overly concerned about whether their opponents like or dislike them.[39] The Chinese also draw out negotiations but that's because they believe negotiations never end. Just when you think you've pinned down every detail and reached a final solution with a Chinese executive, that executive might smile and start the process all over again. Like the Japanese, the Chinese negotiate to develop a relationship and a commitment to work together rather than to tie up every loose end.[40] Americans are known around the world for their impatience and their desire to be liked.[41] Astute negotiators from other countries often turn these characteristics to their advantage by dragging out negotiations and making friendship conditional on the final settlement.

The cultural context of the negotiation significantly influences the amount and type of preparation for bargaining, the relative emphasis on task versus interpersonal relationships, the tactics used, and even where the negotiation should be conducted. To further illustrate some of these differences, let's look at two studies comparing the influence of culture on business negotiations.

The first study compared North Americans, Arabs, and Russians.[42] Among the factors considered were their negotiating style, how they responded to an opponent's arguments, their approach to making concessions, and how they handled negotiating deadlines. North Americans tried to persuade by relying on facts and appealing to logic. They countered opponents' arguments with objective facts. They made small concessions early in the negotiation to establish a relationship, and usually reciprocated opponent's concessions. North Americans treated deadlines as very important. The Arabs tried to persuade by appealing to emotion.

Ellen Aschendorf is evidence that men and women do not negotiate differently. As president of Egg Electric, a $15 million electrical subcontracting firm in New York, Aschendorf has built a successful business in the male-dominated construction industry. She spends most of her time negotiating contracts with high-profile clients like Shea Stadium, home of the New York Mets. Aschendorf's negotiating skills are based on her expertise in analyzing specifications and reengineering jobs to reduce costs and her knowledge of risk management, financial management, and environmental and construction regulations.

They countered opponent's arguments with subjective feelings. They made concessions throughout the bargaining process and almost always reciprocated opponents' concessions. Arabs approached deadlines very casually. The Russians based their arguments on asserted ideals. They made few, if any, concessions. Any concession offered by an opponent was viewed as a weakness and almost never reciprocated. Finally, the Russians tended to ignore deadlines.

The second study looked at verbal and nonverbal negotiation tactics exhibited by North Americans, Japanese, and Brazilians during half-hour bargaining sessions.[43] Some of the differences were particularly interesting. For instance, the Brazilians on average said No 83 times, compared to five times for the Japanese and nine times for the North Americans. The Japanese displayed more than five periods of silence lasting longer than 10 seconds during the 30-minute sessions. North Americans averaged 3.5 such periods; the Brazilians had none. The Japanese and North Americans interrupted their opponent about the same number of times, but the Brazilians interrupted 2.5 to 3 times more often than the North Americans and the Japanese. Finally, while the Japanese and the North Americans had no physical contact with their opponents during negotiations except for handshaking, the Brazilians touched each other almost five times every half-hour.

Third-Party Negotiations To this point, we've discussed bargaining in terms of direct negotiations. Occasionally, however, individuals or group representatives reach a stalemate and are unable to resolve their differences through direct negotiations. In such cases, they may turn to a third party to help them find a solution. There are four basic third-party roles: mediator, arbitrator, conciliator, and consultant.[44]

A **mediator** is a neutral third party who facilitates a negotiated solution by using reasoning and persuasion, suggesting alternatives, and the like. Mediators are widely used in labor–management negotiations and in civil court disputes.

The overall effectiveness of mediated negotiations is fairly impressive. The settlement rate is approximately 60 percent, with negotiator satisfaction at about 75 percent. But the situation is the key to whether or not mediation will succeed; the conflicting parties must be motivated to bargain and resolve their conflict. Additionally, conflict intensity can't be too high; mediation is most effective under moderate levels of conflict. Finally, perceptions of the mediator are important; to be effective, the mediator must be perceived as neutral and noncoercive.

An **arbitrator** is a third party with the authority to dictate an agreement. Arbitration can be voluntary (requested) or compulsory (forced on the parties by law or contract).

The authority of the arbitrator varies according to the rules set by the negotiators. For instance, the arbitrator might be limited to choosing one of the negotiator's last offers or to suggesting an agreement point that is nonbinding, or free to choose and make any judgment he or she wishes.

The big plus of arbitration over mediation is that it always results in a settlement. Whether or not there is a negative side depends on how "heavy-handed" the arbitrator appears. If one party is left feeling overwhelmingly defeated, that party is certain to be dissatisfied and unlikely to graciously accept the arbitrator's decision. Therefore, the conflict may resurface at a later time.

A **conciliator** is a trusted third party who provides an informal communication link between the negotiator and the opponent. This role was made famous by Robert Duval in the first *Godfather* film. As Don Corleone's adopted son and a lawyer by training, Duval acted as an intermediary between the Corleone family and the other Mafioso families.

mediator

A neutral third party who facilitates a negotiated solution by using reasoning, persuasion, and suggestions for alternatives.

arbitrator

A third party to a negotiation who has the authority to dictate an agreement.

conciliator

A trusted third party who provides an informal communication link between the negotiator and the opponent.

Conciliation is used extensively in international, labor, family, and community disputes. Comparing its effectiveness to mediation has proven difficult because the two overlap a great deal. In practice, conciliators typically act as more than mere communication conduits. They also engage in fact-finding, interpreting messages, and persuading disputants to develop agreements.

A **consultant** is a skilled and impartial third party who attempts to facilitate problem solving through communication and analysis, aided by his or her knowledge of conflict management. In contrast to the previous roles, the consultant's role is not to settle the issues but, rather, to improve relations between the conflicting parties so that they can reach a settlement themselves. Instead of putting forward specific solutions, the consultant tries to help the parties learn to understand and work with each other. Therefore, this approach has a longer-term focus: to build new and positive perceptions and attitudes between the conflicting parties.

consultant as negotiator

An impartial third party, skilled in conflict management, who attempts to facilitate creative problem solving through communication and analysis.

SUMMARY AND IMPLICATIONS FOR MANAGERS

Many people automatically assume that conflict is related to lower group and organizational performance. This chapter has demonstrated that this assumption is frequently incorrect. Conflict can be either constructive or destructive to the functioning of a group or unit. As shown in Exhibit 13-8, levels of conflict can be either too high or too low. Either extreme hinders performance. An optimal level is where there is enough conflict to prevent stagnation, stimulate creativity, allow tensions to be released, and initiate the seeds for change, yet not so much as to be disruptive or deter coordination of activities.

Inadequate or excessive levels of conflict can hinder the effectiveness of a group or an organization, resulting in reduced satisfaction of group members, increased absence and turnover rates, and, eventually, lower productivity. On the other hand, when conflict is at an optimal level, complacency and apathy should be minimized, motivation should be enhanced through the creation of a challenging and questioning environment with a vitality that makes work interesting, and there should be the amount of turnover needed to rid the organization of misfits and poor performers.

What advice can we give managers faced with excessive conflict and the need to reduce it? Don't assume there's one conflict-handling intention that will always be best! You should select an intention appropriate for the situation. The following provides some guidelines:[45]

Use *competition* when quick, decisive action is vital (in emergencies); on important issues, when unpopular actions need implementing (in cost cutting, enforcing unpopular rules, discipline); on issues vital to the organization's welfare when you know you're right; and against people who take advantage of noncompetitive behavior.

Use *collaboration* to find an integrative solution when both sets of concerns are too important to be compromised; when your objective is to learn; to merge insights from people with different perspectives; to gain commitment by incorporating concerns into a consensus; and to work through feelings that have interfered with a relationship.

Use *avoidance* when an issue is trivial, or more important issues are pressing; when you perceive no chance of satisfying your concerns; when potential disruption outweighs the benefits of resolution; to let people cool down and regain perspective; when gathering information supersedes immediate decision; when others can resolve the conflict more effectively; and when issues seem tangential or symptomatic of other issues.

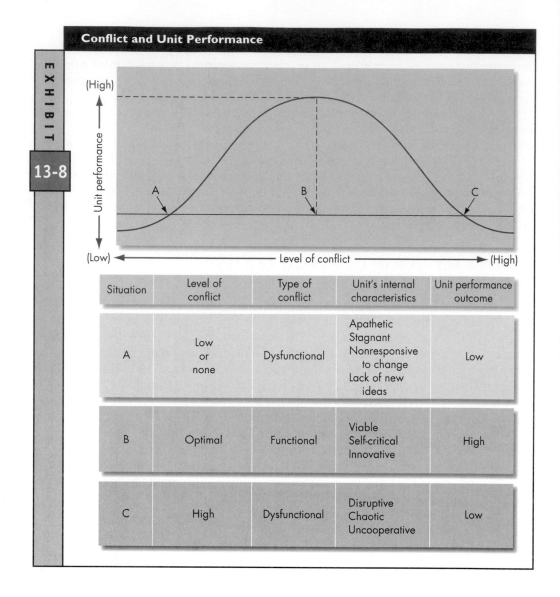

Conflict and Unit Performance

EXHIBIT 13-8

Situation	Level of conflict	Type of conflict	Unit's internal characteristics	Unit performance outcome
A	Low or none	Dysfunctional	Apathetic Stagnant Nonresponsive to change Lack of new ideas	Low
B	Optimal	Functional	Viable Self-critical Innovative	High
C	High	Dysfunctional	Disruptive Chaotic Uncooperative	Low

Use *accommodation* when you find you're wrong and to allow a better position to be heard, to learn, and to show your reasonableness; when issues are more important to others than yourself and to satisfy others and maintain cooperation; to build social credits for later issues; to minimize loss when you are outmatched and losing; when harmony and stability are especially important; and to allow employees to develop by learning from mistakes.

Use *compromise* when goals are important but not worth the effort of potential disruption of more assertive approaches; when opponents with equal power are committed to mutually exclusive goals; to achieve temporary settlements to complex issues; to arrive at expedient solutions under time pressure; and as a backup when collaboration or competition is unsuccessful.

Negotiation was shown to be an ongoing activity in groups and organizations. Distributive bargaining can resolve disputes but it often negatively affects one or more negotiators' satisfaction because it is focused on the short term and because it is confrontational. Integrative bargaining, in contrast, tends to provide outcomes that satisfy all parties and that build lasting relationships.

Conflict Benefits Organizations

Let's briefly review how stimulating conflict can provide benefits to the organization.

Conflict is a means by which to bring about radical change. It's an effective device by which management can drastically change the existing power structure, current interaction patterns, and entrenched attitudes.

Conflict facilitates group cohesiveness. While conflict increases hostility between groups, external threats tend to cause a group to pull together as a unit. Intergroup conflicts raise the extent to which members identify with their own group and increase feelings of solidarity.

Conflict improves group and organizational effectiveness. The stimulation of conflict initiates the search for new means and goals and clears the way for innovation. The successful solution of a conflict leads to greater effectiveness, to more trust and openness, to greater attraction of members for each other, and to depersonalization of future conflicts.

Conflict brings about a slightly higher, more constructive level of tension. When the level of tension is very low, the parties are not sufficiently motivated to do something about a conflict.

Groups or organizations devoid of conflict are likely to suffer from apathy, stagnation, groupthink, and other debilitating diseases. In fact, more organizations probably fail because they have *too little* conflict, not because they have too much. Take a look at a list of large organizations that have failed or suffered serious financial setbacks over the past decade or two. You see names such as E.F. Hutton, General Motors, Western Union, Gimbel's, Kmart, Morrison Knudsen, Eastern Airlines, Greyhound, and Digital Computer. The common thread through these companies is that they stagnated. Their managements became complacent and unable or unwilling to facilitate change. These organizations could have benefited from functional conflict.

It may be true that conflict is an inherent part of any group or organization. It may not be possible to eliminate it completely. However, just because conflicts exist is no reason to deify them. All conflicts are dysfunctional, and it is one of management's major responsibilities to keep conflict intensity as low as humanly possible. A few points will support this case.

The negative consequences from conflict can be devastating. The list of negatives associated with conflict is awesome. The most obvious are increased turnover, decreased employee satisfaction, inefficiencies between work units, sabotage, labor grievances and strikes, and physical aggression.

Effective managers build teamwork. A good manager builds a coordinated team. Conflict works against such an objective. A successful work group is like a successful sports team; each member knows his or her role and supports his or her teammates. When a team works well, the whole becomes greater than the sum of the parts. Management creates teamwork by minimizing internal conflicts and facilitating internal coordination.

Managers who accept and stimulate conflict don't survive in organizations. The whole argument on the value of conflict may be moot as long as the majority of senior executives in organizations have a traditional view of conflict. In the traditional view, any conflict will be seen as bad. Since the evaluation of a manager's performance is made by higher-level executives, those managers who do not succeed in eliminating conflicts are likely to be appraised negatively. This, in turn, will reduce opportunities for advancement. Any manager who aspires to move up in such an environment will be wise to follow the traditional view and eliminate any outward signs of conflict. Failure to follow this advice might result in the premature departure of the manager.

Questions for Review

1. What are the disadvantages to conflict? What are its advantages?

2. What is the difference between functional and dysfunctional conflict? What determines functionality?

3. Under what conditions might conflict be beneficial to a group?

4. What are the components in the conflict process model? From your own experiences, give an example of how a conflict proceeded through the five stages.

5. How could a manager stimulate conflict in his or her department?

6. What defines the settlement range in distributive bargaining?

7. Why isn't integrative bargaining more widely practiced in organizations?

8. How do men and women differ, if at all, in their approaches to negotiation?

9. What problems might Americans have in negotiating with people from collectivist cultures such as China and Japan?

10. What can you do to improve your negotiating effectiveness?

Questions for Critical Thinking

1. Do you think competition and conflict are different? Explain.

2. "Participation is an excellent method for identifying differences and resolving conflicts." Do you agree or disagree? Discuss.

3. From your own experience, describe a situation you were involved in where the conflict was dysfunctional. Describe another example, from your experience, where the conflict was functional. Now analyze how other parties in both conflicts might have interpreted the situation in terms of whether the conflicts were functional or dysfunctional.

4. Assume a Canadian had to negotiate a contract with someone from Spain. What problems might he or she face? What suggestions would you make to help facilitate a settlement?

5. General Motors seems to have too much conflict between itself and the UAW, yet too little conflict within its executive cadre. How could this be? What does this say about conflict levels, functional versus dyfunctional conflict, and managing conflict?

Team Exercise | A Negotiation Role Play

This role play is designed to help you develop your negotiating skills. The class is to break into pairs. One person will play the role of Alex, the department supervisor. The other person will play C.J., Alex's boss.

The Situation: Alex and C.J. work for Nike in Portland, Oregon. Alex supervises a research laboratory. C.J. is the manager of research and development. Alex and C.J. are former college runners who have worked for Nike for more than six years. C.J. has been Alex's boss for two years.

One of Alex's employees has greatly impressed Alex. This employee is Lisa Roland. Lisa was hired 11 months ago. She is 24 years old and holds a master's degree in mechanical engineering. Her entry-level salary was $37,500 a year. She was told by Terry that, in accordance with corporation policy, she would receive an initial performance evaluation at six months and a comprehensive review after one year. Based on her performance record, Lisa was told she could expect a salary adjustment at the time of the one-year evaluation.

Alex's evaluation of Lisa after six months was very positive. Alex commented on the long hours Lisa was putting in, her cooperative spirit, the fact that others in the lab enjoyed working with her, and that she was making an immediate positive impact on the project to which she had been assigned. Now that Lisa's first anniversary is coming up, Alex has again reviewed Lisa's performance. Alex thinks Lisa may be the best new person the R&D group has ever hired. After only a year, Alex has ranked Lisa as the number-three performer in a department of 11.

Salaries in the department vary greatly. Alex, for instance, has a basic salary of $67,000, plus eligibility for a bonus that might add another $5,000 to $8,000 a year. The salary range of the 11 department members is $30,400 to $56,350. The lowest salary is a recent hire with a bachelor's degree in physics. The two people that Alex has rated above Lisa earn base salaries of $52,700 and $56,350. They're both 27 years old and have been at Nike for three and four years, respectively. The median salary in Alex's department is $46,660.

Alex's Role: You want to give Lisa a big raise. Although she's young, she has proven to be an excellent addition to the department. You don't want to lose her. More importantly, she knows in general what other people in the department are earning and she thinks she's underpaid. The company typically gives one-year raises of 5 percent, although 10 percent is not unusual and 20 to 30 percent increases have been approved on occasion. You'd like to get Lisa as large an increase as C.J. will approve.

C.J.'s Role: All your supervisors typically try to squeeze you for as much money as they can for their people. You understand this because you did the same thing when you were a supervisor, but your boss wants to keep a lid on costs. He wants you to keep raises for recent hires generally in the 5 to 8 percent range. In fact, he's sent a memo to all managers and supervisors saying this. However, your boss is also very concerned with equity and paying people what they're worth. You feel assured that he will support any salary recommendation you make, as long as it can be justified. Your goal, consistent with cost reduction, is to keep salary increases as low as possible.

The Negotiation: Alex has a meeting scheduled with C.J. to discuss Lisa's performance review and salary adjustment. Take a couple of minutes to think through the facts in this exercise and to prepare a strategy. Then you have up to 15 minutes to conduct your negotiation. When your negotiation is complete, the class will compare the various strategies used and compare outcomes.

Internet Search Exercises

1. Find an American manufacturing firm, a German company, and a government agency (in any country) that have recently resolved a labor negotiation. What were the initial positions of management and the union? What were the final resolutions? Can you explain any significant differences you found among the three?

2. Find (a) an organization whose recent performance was in some way hindered as a result of having too much conflict and (b) an organization whose performance was hindered as a result of having too little conflict. Explain how you arrived at your assessment of each.

PHLIP Companion Web Site

We invite you to visit the Robbins homepage on the Prentice Hall Web site at **www.prenhall.com/robbins** for our on-line study guide, current events, links to related Web sites, and more.

Case Incident | Working at ThinkLink

Mallory Murray hadn't had much experience working as part of a team. A recent graduate of the University of Alabama, her business program had focused primarily on individual projects and accomplishments. What little exposure she had had to teams was in her organizational behavior, marketing research, and strategy formulation courses. When she interviewed with ThinkLink, an educational software firm out of

Gainesville, Florida, she didn't give much concern to the fact that ThinkLink made extensive use of cross-functional teams. During on-site interviews, she told interviewers and managers alike that she had limited experience on teams. But she did tell them she worked well with people and thought that she could be an effective team player. Unfortunately, Mallory Murray was mistaken.

Mallory joined ThinkLink as an assistant marketing manager for the company's high school core programs. These are essentially software programs designed to help students learn algebra and geometry. Mallory's boss is Lin Chen (marketing manager). Other members of the team she is currently working with include Todd Schlotsky (senior programmer), Laura Willow (advertising), Sean Traynor (vice president for strategic marketing), Joyce Rothman (co-founder of ThinkLink, who now only works part-time in the company; formerly a high school math teacher; the formal leader of this project), and Harlow Gray (educational consultant).

After her first week on the job, Mallory was seriously thinking about quitting. "I never imagined how difficult it would be working with people who are so opinionated and competitive. Every decision seems to be a power contest. Sean, Joyce, and Harlow are particularly troublesome. Sean thinks his rank entitles him to the last word. Joyce thinks her opinions should carry more weight because she was instrumental in creating the company. And Harlow views everyone as less knowledgeable than he is. Because he consults with a number of software firms and school districts, Harlow's a 'know-it-all.' To make things worse, Lin is passive and quiet. He rarely speaks up in meetings and appears to want to avoid any conflicts."

"What makes my job particularly difficult," Mallory went on, "is that I don't have any specific job responsibilities. It seems that someone else is always interfering with what I'm doing or telling me how to do it. Our team has seven members—six chiefs and me!"

The projects team that Mallory is working on has a deadline to meet that is only six weeks away. Currently the team is at least two weeks behind schedule. Everyone is aware that there's a problem but no one seems to be able to solve it. What is especially frustrating to Mallory is that neither Lin Chen nor Joyce Rothman is showing any leadership. Lin is preoccupied with a number of other projects, and Joyce can't seem to control Sean and Harlow's strong personalities.

Questions

1. Discuss cross-functional teams in terms of their propensity to create conflict.

2. What techniques or procedures might help reduce conflict on cross-functional teams?

3. If you were Mallory, is there anything you could do to lessen the conflict on the core project? Elaborate.

End Notes

1. A. Seaton Huntington, "A Ship With No Captain," *HRMagazine*, November 1997, pp. 94–99.
2. See, for instance, C. F. Fink, "Some Conceptual Difficulties in the Theory of Social Conflict," *Journal of Conflict Resolution*, December 1968, pp. 412–60. For an updated review of the conflict literature, see J. A. Wall, Jr. and R. R. Callister, "Conflict and Its Management," *Journal of Management*, vol. 21, no. 3, 1995, pp. 515–58.
3. L. L. Putnam and M. S. Poole, "Conflict and Negotiation," in F. M. Jablin, L. L. Putnam, K. H. Roberts, and L. W. Porter (eds.), *Handbook of Organizational Communication: An Interdisciplinary Perspective* (Newbury Park, CA: Sage, 1987), pp. 549–99.
4. K. W. Thomas, "Conflict and Negotiation Processes in Organizations," in M. D. Dunnette and L. M. Hough (eds.), *Handbook of Industrial and Organizational Psychology*, 2nd ed., vol. 3 (Palo Alto, CA: Consulting Psychologists Press, 1992), pp. 651–717.
5. For a comprehensive review of the interactionist approach, see C. De Dreu and E. Van de Vliert (eds.), *Using Conflict in Organizations* (London: Sage Publications, 1997).
6. See K. A. Jehn, "A Multimethod Examination of the Benefits and Detriments of Intragroup Conflict," *Administrative Science Quarterly*, June 1995, pp. 256–82; K. A. Jehn, "A Qualitative Analysis of Conflict Types and Dimensions in Organizational Groups," *Administrative Science Quarterly*, September 1997, pp. 530–57; and K. A. Jehn, "Affective and Cognitive Conflict in Work Groups: Increasing Performance Through Value-Based Intragroup Conflict," in C. DeDreu and E. Van deVliert (eds.), *Using Conflict in Organizations*, pp. 87–100.
7. See S. P. Robbins, *Managing Organizational Conflict: A Nontraditional Approach* (Upper Saddle River, NJ: Prentice Hall, 1974), pp. 31–55; and J. A. Wall, Jr. and R. R. Callister, "Conflict and Its Management," pp. 517–23.
8. S. P. Robbins, *Managing Organizational Conflict*.
9. L. R. Pondy, "Organizational Conflict: Concepts and Models," *Administrative Science Quarterly*, September 1967, p. 302.
10. See, for instance, R. L. Pinkley, "Dimensions of Conflict Frame: Disputant Interpretations of Conflict," *Journal of Applied Psychology*, April 1990, pp. 117–26; and R. L. Pinkley and G. B. Northcraft, "Conflict Frames of Reference: Implications for Dispute Processes and Outcomes," *Academy of Management Journal*, February 1994, pp. 193–205.
11. R. Kumar, "Affect, Cognition and Decision Making in Negotiations: A Conceptual Integration," in M. A. Rahim (ed.), *Managing Conflict: An Integrative Approach* (New York: Praeger, 1989), pp. 185–94.
12. Ibid.

13. P. J. D. Carnevale and A. M. Isen, "The Influence of Positive Affect and Visual Access on the Discovery of Integrative Solutions in Bilateral Negotiations," *Organizational Behavior and Human Decision Processes*, February 1986, pp. 1–13.

14. Thomas, "Conflict and Negotiation Processes in Organizations."

15. Ibid.

16. See R. J. Sternberg and L. J. Soriano, "Styles of Conflict Resolution," *Journal of Personality and Social Psychology*, July 1984, pp. 115–26; R. A. Baron, "Personality and Organizational Conflict: Effects of the Type A Behavior Pattern and Self-Monitoring," *Organizational Behavior and Human Decision Processes*, October 1989, pp. 281–96; and R. J. Volkema and T. J. Bergmann, "Conflict Styles as Indicators of Behavioral Patterns in Interpersonal Conflicts," *Journal of Social Psychology*, February 1995, pp. 5–15.

17. Thomas, "Conflict and Negotiation Processes in Organizations."

18. See, for instance, R. A. Cosier and C. R. Schwenk, "Agreement and Thinking Alike: Ingredients for Poor Decisions," *Academy of Management Executive*, February 1990, pp. 69–74; K. A. Jehn, "Enhancing Effectiveness: An Investigation of Advantages and Disadvantages of Value-Based Intragroup Conflict," *International Journal of Conflict Management*, July 1994, pp. 223–38; and R. L. Priem, D. A. Harrison, and N. K. Muir, "Structured Conflict and Consensus Outcomes in Group Decision Making," *Journal of Management*, vol. 21, no. 4, 1995, pp. 691–710.

19. See, for instance, C. J. Loomis, "Dinosaurs?" *Fortune*, May 3, 1993, pp. 36–42.

20. I. L. Janis, *Victims of Groupthink* (Boston: Houghton Mifflin, 1972).

21. J. Hall and M. S. Williams, "A Comparison of Decision-Making Performances in Established and Ad-Hoc Groups," *Journal of Personality and Social Psychology*, February 1966, p. 217.

22. R. L. Hoffman, "Homogeneity of Member Personality and Its Effect on Group Problem-Solving," *Journal of Abnormal and Social Psychology*, January 1959, pp. 27–32; and R. L. Hoffman and N. R. F. Maier, "Quality and Acceptance of Problem Solutions by Members of Homogeneous and Heterogeneous Groups," *Journal of Abnormal and Social Psychology*, March 1961, pp. 401–07.

23. See T. H. Cox and S. Blake, "Managing Cultural Diversity: Implications for Organizational Competitiveness," *Academy of Management Executive*, August 1991, pp. 45–56; T. H. Cox, S. A. Lobel, and P. L. McLeod, "Effects of Ethnic Group Cultural Differences on Cooperative Behavior on a Group Task," *Academy of Management Journal*, December 1991, pp. 827–47; P. L. McLeod and S. A. Lobel, "The Effects of Ethnic Diversity on Idea Generation in Small Groups," paper presented at the Annual Academy of Management Conference, Las Vegas, August 1992; C. Kirchmeyer and A. Cohen, "Multicultural Groups: Their Performance and Reactions with Constructive Conflict," *Group & Organization Management*, June 1992, pp. 153–70; D. E. Thompson and L. E. Gooler, "Capitalizing on the Benefits of Diversity Through Workteams," in E. E. Kossek and S. A. Lobel (eds.), *Managing Diversity: Human Resource Strategies for Transforming the Workplace* (Cambridge, MA: Blackwell, 1996), pp. 392–437; and L. H. Pelled, K. M. Eisenhardt, and K. R. Xin, "Exploring the Black Box: An Analysis of Work Group Diversity, Conflict, and Performance," *Administrative Science Quarterly*, March 1999, pp. 1–28.

24. R. E. Hill, "Interpersonal Compatibility and Work Group Performance Among Systems Analysts: An Empirical Study," *Proceedings of the Seventeenth Annual Midwest Academy of Management Conference*, Kent, OH, April 1974, pp. 97–110.

25. D. C. Pelz and F. Andrews, *Scientists in Organizations* (New York: John Wiley, 1966).

26. See J. A. Wall, Jr. and R. R. Callister, "Conflict and Its Management," pp. 523–26 for evidence supporting the argument that conflict is almost uniformly dysfunctional.

27. M. Geyelin and E. Felsenthal, "Irreconcilable Differences Force Shea & Gould Closure," *Wall Street Journal*, January 31, 1994, p. B1.

28. This section is based on F. Sommerfield, "Paying the Troops to Buck the System," *Business Month*, May 1990, pp. 77–79; W. Kiechel III, "How to Escape the Echo Chamber," *Fortune*, June 18, 1990, pp. 129–30; E. Van de Vliert and C. De Dreu, "Optimizing Performance by Stimulating Conflict," *International Journal of Conflict Management*, July 1994, pp. 211–22; E. Van de Vliert, "Enhancing Performance by Conflict-Stimulating Intervention," in C. De Dreu and E. Van de Vliert (eds.), *Using Conflict in Organizations*, pp. 208–22; and K. M. Eisenhardt, J. L. Kahwajy, and L. J. Bourgeois III, "How Management Teams Can Have a Good Fight," *Harvard Business Review*, July–August 1997, pp. 77–85.

29. J. A. Wall, Jr., *Negotiation: Theory and Practice* (Glenview, IL: Scott, Foresman, 1985).

30. R. E. Walton and R. B. McKersie, *A Behavioral Theory of Labor Negotiations: An Analysis of a Social Interaction System* (New York: McGraw-Hill, 1965).

31. Thomas, "Conflict and Negotiation Processes in Organizations."

32. This model is based on R. J. Lewicki, "Bargaining and Negotiation," *Exchange: The Organizational Behavior Teaching Journal*, vol. 6, no. 2, 1981, pp. 39–40; and B. S. Moskal, "The Art of the Deal," *Industry Week*, January 18, 1993, p. 23.

33. J. Lee, "The Negotiators," *Forbes*, January 11, 1999, pp. 22–24.

34. M. H. Bazerman and M. A. Neale, *Negotiating Rationally* (New York: Free Press, 1992), pp. 67–68.

35. These suggestions are based on J. A. Wall, Jr. and M. W. Blum, "Negotiations," *Journal of Management*, June 1991, pp. 278–82; and J.S. Pouliot, "Eight Steps to Success in Negotiating," *Nation's Business*, April 1999, pp. 40–42.

36. Ibid.

37. C. Watson and L. R. Hoffman, "Managers as Negotiators: A Test of Power versus Gender as Predictors of Feelings, Behavior, and Outcomes," *Leadership Quarterly*, Spring 1996, pp. 63–85.

38. See N. J. Adler, *International Dimensions of Organizational Behavior*, 3rd ed. (Cincinnati, OH: Southwestern, 1997), pp. 189–232; and J. M. Brett and T. Okumura, "Inter- and Intracultural Negotiation: U.S. and Japanese Negotiators,"

Academy of Management Journal, October 1998, pp. 495–510.

39. K. D. Schmidt, *Doing Business in France* (Menlo Park, CA: SRI International, 1987).

40. S. Lubman, "Round and Round," *Wall Street Journal*, December 10, 1993, p. R3.

41. P. R. Harris and R. T. Moran, *Managing Cultural Differences*, 4th ed. (Houston: Gulf Publishing, 1996), pp. 43–44.

42. E. S. Glenn, D. Witmeyer, and K. A. Stevenson, "Cultural Styles of Persuasion," *Journal of Intercultural Relations*, Fall 1977, pp. 52–66.

43. J. Graham, "The Influence of Culture on Business Negotiations," *Journal of International Business Studies*, Spring 1985, pp. 81–96.

44. J. A. Wall, Jr. and M. W. Blum, "Negotiations," pp. 283–87.

45. K. W. Thomas, "Toward Multidimensional Values in Teaching: The Example of Conflict Behaviors," *Academy of Management Review*, July 1977, p. 487.

A Coach for All Seasons: Effective Group Behavior Can Be Learned

Lois Frankel thrives on conflict. The co-founder and president of Corporate Coaching International (CCI), Frankel trains and counsels groups and teams at corporate workplaces around the U.S. in all aspects of teamwork and group behavior. Whether the problem is too much conflict or too little communication, she works with employees to identify the behaviors hampering their team operations and points them toward new behaviors designed to improve their interaction.

Putting organizational behavior principles into action is CCI's stock in trade. Frankel's extensive background in human resources, coaching, and psychology gives her an added advantage in working with teams. Her favorite icebreaker when beginning a new coaching session with a client's team is designed to demonstrate to team members that "we are all in this boat together." Participants are asked to draw a boat on a large piece of paper and then add each member of the group to the picture, not necessarily inside the boat. This exercise in establishing a common purpose often reveals problems with group cohesion or shared goals, as well as suggesting a potential imbalance of power.

Conflict is a potential part of every group interaction, says Frankel. Her goal is not to eradicate conflict but to show clients how to manage it so that it leads to increased creativity and productivity for the group. Effective management of conflict begins, she advises, with the recognition by all team and group members of the differing needs and strengths of everyone in the group.

Communication skills are paramount in successful group functioning. Frankel aims to have participants be themselves in their coaching sessions, in order for her to diagnose any miscommunications, gender or cultural differences, tendencies toward groupthink, or other barriers to effective communication, whether that communication is moving up, down, or across the organization.

In the video you will see her working with a group of senior staff members of the Museum of Natural History of Los Angeles. These professionals are about to embark on an extensive planning process leading up to the design and completion of a new museum building, while maintaining and operating the existing museum. They are looking for ways to strengthen their teamwork and their leadership skills to ensure the success of the two-part task they now face.

Study Questions

As you watch the video of Lois Frankel working with her clients, look for indications of the problems you think they might be having. Specifically, answer the following questions:

1. What elements of effective group behavior does Frankel use herself, and which does she advocate for the group? How will participants try to change their behavior as a result?

2. Do you think the group's body language conveys the same message as their words? If not, point out inconsistencies.

3. Is there a group leader (not Lois Frankel)? Who is it, and what is the basis of his or her leadership?

4. Can you discern any conflict within the group? What kind of conflict do you think it is? Do you think it can be turned into functional conflict? If so, how?

The dinosaur's eloquent lesson is that if some bigness is good, an overabundance of bigness is not necessarily better.

—E. A. Johnston

part four

THE ORGANIZATION SYSTEM

Marie and Claudette Trudeau are twins. Born and raised in the south of France, they went to college together in Marseille. After graduating in 1999 with degrees in accounting, they went to Paris to begin their work careers.

Marie joined the Credit Lyonnais Group. One of the largest banking firms in Europe, Credit Lyonnais employs more than 50,000 people. In contrast, Claudette chose to work for Valso, a small, specialty cosmetics firm employing less than 100. While the size of their organizations were very different, both womens' jobs drew heavily on their accounting skills. And their starting salaries were within 25 euros a month of each other.

The first six months on their jobs passed quickly. Because they had separate apartments and busy work schedules, they found they had little time to chat and socialize as they had in college. So it was Christmas 1999, as they gathered at their parents' home for the holidays, that the two women had their first lengthy discussion about their new work lives.

Claudette spoke passionately about Valso. She loved her boss, although she rarely saw him. After little more than a few days of indoctrination, the company basically set her free to work on three separate projects. When Claudette had questions, she went to her boss. But she was encouraged to take initiative and even make mistakes. "That's the way you learn," her boss said. Claudette enjoyed the diversity in her job tasks, the informal communication channels in the company, and the lack of rules. "In many ways, I feel like I'm my own boss."

Marie listened intently to her sister. "How is it possible," Marie asked, "that we could be in such different places?" Marie hated her boss, her boss's boss, the regimentation, and all the bureaucratic rules she had to deal with at Credit Lyonnais. "As soon as I arrived, they put me into a two-month training program. I met people from all the various departments. They spent days just going over every company regulation and policy. Then

Foundations of Organization Structure

they put me into this room with at least 30 other accountants and four supervisors. They watch us like hawks. If you make a mistake, they make a big deal out of it. They never let you forget your errors. And since my training ended, I haven't seen or talked to anyone outside my department. I'll tell you, Claudie, I can't take this much longer. I'm already looking in the paper for other jobs."

A s Marie and Claudette are finding out, organizations have different structures and these structures have a bearing on employee attitudes and behavior. That's the theme of this chapter. In the following pages, we define the key components that make up an organization's structure, present half a dozen or so structural design options from which managers can choose, identify the contingency factors that make certain structural designs preferable in varying situations, and conclude by considering the different effects that various organizational designs have on employee behavior.

WHAT IS ORGANIZATIONAL STRUCTURE?

An **organizational structure** defines how job tasks are formally divided, grouped, and coordinated. There are six key elements that managers need to address when they design their organization's structure. These are work specialization, departmentalization, chain of command, span of control, centralization and decentralization, and formalization.[1] Exhibit 14-1 presents each of these elements as answers to an important structural question. The following sections describe these six elements of structure.

AFTER READING THIS CHAPTER, YOU SHOULD BE ABLE TO

1. Identify the six key elements that define an organization's structure

2. Explain the characteristics of a bureaucracy

3. Describe a matrix organization

4. Explain the characteristics of a virtual organization

5. Summarize why managers want to create boundaryless organizations

6. Contrast mechanistic and organic structural models

7. List the factors that favor different organizational structures

8. Explain the behavioral implications of different organizational designs

	Six Key Questions That Managers Need to Answer in Designing the Proper Organizational Structure	
E X H I B I T	**The Key Question**	**The Answer Is Provided By**
14-1	1. To what degree are tasks subdivided into separate jobs?	Work specialization
	2. On what basis will jobs be grouped together?	Departmentalization
	3. To whom do individuals and groups report?	Chain of command
	4. How many individuals can a manager efficiently and effectively direct?	Span of control
	5. Where does decision-making authority lie?	Centralization and decentralization
	6. To what degree will there be rules and regulations to direct employees and managers?	Formalization

WORK SPECIALIZATION

organizational structure

How job tasks are formally divided, grouped, and coordinated.

Early in the twentieth century, Henry Ford became rich and famous by building automobiles on an assembly line. Every Ford worker was assigned a specific, repetitive task. For instance, one person would just put on the right-front wheel and someone else would install the right-front door. By breaking jobs up into small standardized tasks, which could be performed over and over again, Ford was able to produce cars at the rate of one every 10 seconds, while using employees who had relatively limited skills.

Ford demonstrated that work can be performed more efficiently if employees are allowed to specialize. Today we use the term **work specialization** or *division of labor* to describe the degree to which tasks in the organization are subdivided into separate jobs.

work specialization

The degree to which tasks in the organization are subdivided into separate jobs.

The essence of work specialization is that, rather than an entire job being done by one individual, it is broken down into a number of steps, each step being completed by a separate individual. In essence, individuals specialize in doing part of an activity rather than the entire activity.

By the late 1940s, most manufacturing jobs in industrialized countries were being done with high work specialization. Management saw this as a means to make the most efficient use of its employees' skills. In most organizations, some tasks require highly developed skills; others can be performed by the untrained. If all workers were engaged in each step of, say, an organization's manufacturing process, all would have to have the skills necessary to perform both the most demanding and the least demanding jobs. The result would be that, except when performing the most skilled or highly complex tasks, employees would be working below their skill levels. And since skilled workers are paid more than unskilled workers and their wages tend to reflect their highest level of skill, it represents an inefficient usage of organizational resources to pay highly skilled workers to do easy tasks.

Managers also looked for other efficiencies that could be achieved through work specialization. Employee skills at performing a task successfully increase through repetition. Less time is spent in changing tasks, in putting away one's

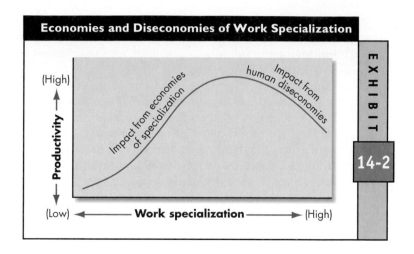

Economies and Diseconomies of Work Specialization

EXHIBIT 14-2

Impact from economies of specialization

Impact from human diseconomies

Productivity (High) → (Low)

(Low) ← Work specialization → (High)

tools and equipment from a prior step in the work process, and in getting ready for another. Equally important, training for specialization is more efficient from the organization's perspective. It is easier and less costly to find and train workers to do specific and repetitive tasks. This is especially true of highly sophisticated and complex operations. For example, could Cessna produce one Citation jet a year if one person had to build the entire plane alone? Not likely! Finally, work specialization increases efficiency and productivity by encouraging the creation of special inventions and machinery.

For much of the first half of the twentieth century, managers viewed work specialization as an unending source of increased productivity. And they were probably right. Because specialization was not widely practiced, its introduction almost always generated higher productivity. But by the 1960s, there became increasing evidence that a good thing can be carried too far. The point had been reached in some jobs in which the human diseconomies from specialization—which surfaced as boredom, fatigue, stress, low productivity, poor quality, increased absenteeism, and high turnover—more than offset the economic advantages (see Exhibit 14-2). In such cases, productivity could be increased by enlarging, rather than narrowing, the scope of job activities. Additionally, a number of companies found that by giving employees a variety of activities to do, allowing them to do a whole and complete job, and by putting them into teams with interchangeable skills, they often achieved significantly higher output with increased employee satisfaction.

Most managers today see work specialization as neither obsolete nor as an unending source of increased productivity. Rather, managers recognize the economies it provides in certain types of jobs and the problems it creates when it's carried too far. You'll find, for example, high work specialization being used by McDonald's to efficiently make and sell hamburgers and fries, and by medical specialists in most health maintenance organizations. On the other hand, companies such as Saturn Corporation have had success by broadening the scope of jobs and reducing specialization.

DEPARTMENTALIZATION

Once you've divided jobs up through work specialization, you need to group these jobs together so common tasks can be coordinated. The basis by which jobs are grouped together is called **departmentalization**.

departmentalization
The basis by which jobs are grouped together.

One of the most popular ways to group activities is by *functions* performed. A manufacturing manager might organize his or her plant by separating engineering, accounting, manufacturing, personnel, and purchasing specialists into common departments. Of course, departmentalization by function can be used in all types of organizations. Only the functions change to reflect the organization's objectives and activities. A hospital might have departments devoted to research, patient care, accounting, and so forth. A professional football franchise might have departments entitled player personnel, ticket sales, and travel and accommodations. The major advantage to this type of grouping is obtaining efficiencies from putting like specialists together. Functional departmentalization seeks to achieve economies of scale by placing people with common skills and orientations into common units.

Tasks can also be departmentalized by the type of *product* the organization produces. Procter & Gamble, for instance, recently reorganized along these lines. Each major product—such as Tide, Pampers, Charmin, and Pringles—will be placed under the authority of an executive who will have complete global responsibility for that product. The major advantage to this type of grouping is increased accountability for product performance, since all activities related to a specific product are under the direction of a single manager. If an organization's activities are service rather than product related, each service would be autonomously grouped. For instance, an accounting firm could have departments for tax, management consulting, auditing, and the like. Each would offer a common array of services under the direction of a product or service manager.

Another way to departmentalize is on the basis of *geography* or territory. The sales function, for instance, may have western, southern, midwestern, and eastern regions. Each of these regions is, in effect, a department organized around geography. If an organization's customers are scattered over a large geographic area and have similar needs based on their location, then this form of departmentalization can be valuable.

Healthcare facilities often use functional departmentalization in grouping work activities. Departments may include patient records, food service, admissions, accounting, radiology, pharmaceutical, and patient care. At River Hills West Hills Healthcare Center in Pewaukee, Wisconsin, information technology helps coordinate activities among departments. The nurse shown here uses an electronic notepad to write in the name, dose, and time medication was given to a patient. This information is stored and instantly updated for the recordkeeping department.

At a Reynolds Metals aluminum tubing plant in upstate New York, production is organized into five departments: casting; press; tubing; finishing; and inspecting, packing, and shipping. This is an example of *process* departmentalization because each department specializes in one specific phase in the production of aluminum tubing. The metal is cast in huge furnaces; sent to the press department, where it is extruded into aluminum pipe; transferred to the tube mill, where it is stretched into various sizes and shapes of tubing; moved to finishing, where it is cut and cleaned; and finally arrives in the inspecting, packing, and shipping department. Since each process requires different skills, this method offers a basis for the homogeneous categorizing of activities.

Process departmentalization can be used for processing customers as well as products. If you've ever been to a state motor vehicles office to get a driver's license, you probably went through several departments before receiving your license. In one state, applicants must go through three steps, each handled by a separate department: (1) validation by motor vehicles division; (2) processing by the licensing department; and (3) payment collection by the treasury department.

A final category of departmentalization is to use the particular type of *customer* the organization seeks to reach. Microsoft, for instance, recently reorganized around four customer markets: consumers, large corporations, software developers, and small businesses. The assumption underlying customer departmentalization is that customers in each department have a common set of problems and needs that can best be met by having specialists for each.

Large organizations may use all of the forms of departmentalization that we've described. A major Japanese electronics firm, for instance, organizes each of its divisions along functional lines and its manufacturing units around processes; it departmentalizes sales around seven geographic regions, and divides each sales region into four customer groupings. Across organizations of all sizes, one strong trend has developed over the past decade. Rigid, functional departmentalization is being increasingly complemented by teams that cross over traditional departmental lines. As we described in Chapter 9, as tasks have become more complex and more diverse skills are needed to accomplish those tasks, management has turned to cross-functional teams.

CHAIN OF COMMAND

Twenty-five years ago, the chain-of-command concept was a basic cornerstone in the design of organizations. As you'll see, it has far less importance today. But contemporary managers should still consider its implications when they decide how best to structure their organizations.

The **chain of command** is an unbroken line of authority that extends from the top of the organization to the lowest echelon and clarifies who reports to whom. It answers questions for employees such as "To whom do I go if I have a problem?" and "To whom am I responsible?"

You can't discuss the chain of command without discussing two complementary concepts: *authority* and *unity of command*. **Authority** refers to the rights inherent in a managerial position to give orders and expect the orders to be obeyed. To facilitate coordination, each managerial position is given a place in the chain of command, and each manager is given a degree of authority in order to meet his or her responsibilities. The **unity-of-command** principle helps preserve the concept of an unbroken line of authority. It states that a person should have one and only one superior to whom he or she is directly responsible. If the unity of command is broken, an employee might have to cope with conflicting demands or priorities from several superiors.

Times change and so do the basic tenets of organizational design. The concepts of chain of command, authority, and unity of command have substantially less relevance today because of advancements in computer technology and the trend toward empowering employees. Just how different things are today is illustrated in the following excerpt from an article in *Business Week*.

> Puzzled, Charles Chaser scanned the inventory reports from his company's distribution centers one Wednesday morning in mid-March. According to the computer printouts, stocks of Rose Awakening Cutex

chain of command

The unbroken line of authority that extends from the top of the organization to the lowest echelon and clarifies who reports to whom.

authority

The rights inherent in a managerial position to give orders and to expect the orders to be obeyed.

unity of command

A subordinate should have only one superior to whom he or she is directly responsible.

The Beverly Hills Hotel employs the chain of command concept to deliver exceptional service to hotel guests. In the hotel's dining room, the maitre'd has authority to give orders to the wait staff. Waiters report directly to their superior—the maitre'd. In this photo the maitre'd conducts an inspection of the waiters before they serve guests.

nail polish were down to three days' supply, well below the three-and-a-half week stock Chesebrough-Pond's Inc. tries to keep on hand. But Chaser knew his Jefferson City (Missouri) plant had shipped 346 dozen bottles of the polish just two days before. Rose Awakening must be flying off store shelves, he thought. So Chaser turned to his terminal next to the production line and typed in instructions to produce 400 dozen more bottles on Thursday morning.

All in a day's work for a scheduling manager, right? Except for one detail: Chaser isn't management. He's a line worker—officially a "line coordinator"—one of hundreds who routinely tap the plant's computer network to track shipments, schedule their own workloads, and generally perform functions that used to be the province of management.[2]

A low-level employee today can access information in seconds that 25 years ago was available only to top managers. Similarly, computer technology increasingly allows employees anywhere in an organization to communicate with anyone else without going through formal channels. Moreover, the concepts of authority and maintaining the chain of command are increasingly less relevant as operating employees are being empowered to make decisions that previously were reserved for management. Add to this the popularity of self-managed and cross-functional teams and the creation of new structural designs that include multiple bosses, and the unity-of-command concept takes on less relevance. There are, of course, still many organizations that find they can be most productive by enforcing the chain of command. There just seem to be fewer of them nowadays.

SPAN OF CONTROL

span of control

The number of subordinates a manager can efficiently and effectively direct.

How many employees can a manager efficiently and effectively direct? This question of **span of control** is important because, to a large degree, it determines the number of levels and managers an organization has. All things being equal, the wider or larger the span, the more efficient the organization. An example can illustrate the validity of this statement.

Assume that we have two organizations, both of which have approximately 4,100 operative-level employees. As Exhibit 14-3 illustrates, if one has a uniform span of four and the other a span of eight, the wider span would have two fewer levels and approximately 800 fewer managers. If the average manager made $40,000 a year, the wider span would save $32 million a year in management salaries! Obviously, wider spans are more efficient in terms of cost. However, at some point wider spans reduce effectiveness. That is, when the span becomes too large, employee performance suffers because supervisors no longer have the time to provide the necessary leadership and support.

Narrow or small spans have their advocates. By keeping the span of control to five or six employees, a manager can maintain close control.[3] But narrow spans have three major drawbacks. First, as already described, they're expensive because they add levels of management. Second, they make vertical communication in the organization more complex. The added levels of hierarchy slow down decision making and tend to isolate upper management. Third, narrow spans of control encourage overly tight supervision and discourage employee autonomy.

The trend in recent years has been toward wider spans of control.[4] They're consistent with recent efforts by companies to reduce costs, cut overhead, speed up

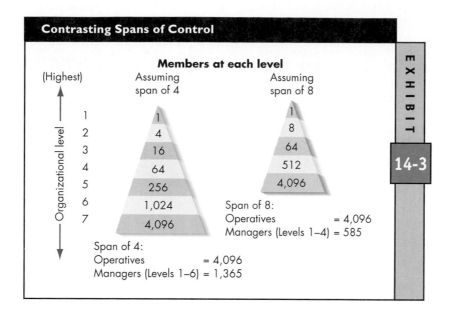

Contrasting Spans of Control

Members at each level

Organizational level (Highest → Lowest)

Level	Assuming span of 4	Assuming span of 8
1	1	1
2	4	8
3	16	64
4	64	512
5	256	4,096
6	1,024	
7	4,096	

Span of 4:
Operatives = 4,096
Managers (Levels 1–6) = 1,365

Span of 8:
Operatives = 4,096
Managers (Levels 1–4) = 585

EXHIBIT 14-3

decision making, increase flexibility, get closer to customers, and empower employees. However, to ensure that performance doesn't suffer because of these wider spans, organizations have been investing heavily in employee training. Managers recognize that they can handle a wider span when employees know their jobs inside and out or can turn to their co-workers when they have questions.

CENTRALIZATION AND DECENTRALIZATION

In some organizations, top managers make all the decisions. Lower level managers merely carry out top management's directives. At the other extreme, there are organizations in which decision making is pushed down to those managers who are closest to the action. The former organizations are highly centralized; the latter are decentralized.

The term **centralization** refers to the degree to which decision making is concentrated at a single point in the organization. The concept includes only formal authority, that is, the rights inherent in one's position. Typically, it's said that if top management makes the organization's key decisions with little or no input from lower-level personnel, then the organization is centralized. In contrast, the more that lower-level personnel provide input or are actually given the discretion to make decisions, the more **decentralization** there is.

An organization characterized by centralization is an inherently different structural animal from one that is decentralized. In a decentralized organization, action can be taken more quickly to solve problems, more people provide input into decisions, and employees are less likely to feel alienated from those who make the decisions that affect their work lives.

Consistent with recent management efforts to make organizations more flexible and responsive, there has been a marked trend toward decentralizing decision making. In large companies, lower-level managers are closer to "the action" and typically have more detailed knowledge about problems than do top managers. Big retailers such as Sears and JCPenney have given their store managers considerably more discretion in choosing what merchandise to stock. This allows those stores to compete more effectively against local merchants. Similarly, the Bank of Montreal grouped its 1,164 Canadian branches into 236 "com-

centralization

The degree to which decision making is concentrated at a single point in the organization.

decentralization

Decision discretion is pushed down to lower-level employees.

EXHIBIT

14-4

Source: S. Adams, *Dogbert's Big Book of Business*, DILBERT reprinted by permission of United Feature Syndicate, Inc.

munities," that is, a group of branches within a limited geographical area.[5] Each community is led by a community area manager, who typically works within a 20-minute drive of the other branches. These area managers can respond more quickly and more intelligently to problems in their communities than could some senior executive in Montreal. IBM Europe's chairperson Renato Riverso has similarly sliced the continent into some 200 autonomous business units, each with its own profit plan, employee incentives, and customer focus. "We used to manage from the top, like an army," said Riverso. "Now we're trying to create entities that drive themselves."[6]

FORMALIZATION

formalization

The degree to which jobs within the organization are standardized.

Formalization refers to the degree to which jobs within the organization are standardized. If a job is highly formalized, then the job incumbent has a minimum amount of discretion over what is to be done, when it is to be done, and how he or she should do it. Employees can be expected always to handle the same input in exactly the same way, resulting in a consistent and uniform output. There are explicit job descriptions, lots of organizational rules, and clearly

Delegating Authority

I f you're a manager and want to delegate some of your authority to someone else, how do you go about it? The following summarizes the primary steps you need to take.

1. *Clarify the assignment.* The place to begin is to determine what is to be delegated and to whom. You need to identify the person most capable of doing the task and then determine if he or she has the time and motivation to do the job.

   Assuming you have a willing and able individual, it is your responsibility to provide clear information on what is being delegated, the results you expect, and any time or performance expectations you hold.

2. *Specify the delegatee's range of discretion.* Every act of delegation comes with constraints. You're delegating authority to act on certain issues and, on those issues, within certain parameters. You need to specify what those parameters are so the individual knows, in no uncertain terms, the range of his or her discretion.

3. *Allow the delegatee to participate.* One of the best sources for determining how much authority will

be necessary to accomplish a task is the person who will be held accountable for that task. If you allow employees to participate in determining what is delegated, how much authority is needed to get the job done, and the standards by which they'll be judged, you increase employee motivation, satisfaction, and accountability for performance.

4. *Inform others that delegation has occurred.* Delegation should not take place in a vacuum. Not only do you and the delegatee need to know specifically what has been delegated and how much authority has been granted, but anyone else who may be affected by the delegation act also needs to be informed.

5. *Establish feedback controls.* The establishment of controls to monitor the employee's progress increases the likelihood that important problems will be identified early and that the task will be completed on time and to the desired specifications. For instance, agree on a specific time for completion of the task, and then set progress dates when the employee will report back on how well he or she is doing and any major problems that have surfaced.

---

defined procedures covering work processes in organizations in which there is high formalization. When formalization is low, job behaviors are relatively nonprogrammed and employees have a great deal of freedom to exercise discretion in their work. Since an individual's discretion on the job is inversely related to the amount of behavior in that job that is preprogrammed by the organization, the greater the standardization, the less input the employee has into how his or her work is to be done. Standardization not only eliminates the possibility of employees engaging in alternative behaviors, but it even removes the need for employees to consider alternatives.

The degree of formalization can vary widely between organizations and within organizations. Certain jobs, for instance, are well known to have little formalization. College book travelers—the representatives of publishers who call on professors to inform them of their company's new publications—have a great deal of freedom in their jobs. They have no standard

A low degree of formalization characterizes the profession of these traders on the Sao Paulo stock exchange. They have a great deal of discretion in making choices about when they buy and sell stocks.

sales "spiel," and the extent of rules and procedures governing their behavior may be little more than the requirement that they submit a weekly sales report and some suggestions on what to emphasize for the various new titles. At the other extreme, there are clerical and editorial positions in the same publishing houses where employees are required to "clock in" at their workstations by 8:00 A.M. or be docked a half-hour's pay and, once at that workstation, to follow a set of precise procedures dictated by management.

COMMON ORGANIZATIONAL DESIGNS

We now turn to describing three of the more common organizational designs found in use: the *simple structure*, the *bureaucracy*, and the *matrix structure*.

THE SIMPLE STRUCTURE

What do a small retail store, an electronics firm run by a hard-driving entrepreneur, a new Planned Parenthood office, and an airline in the midst of a company-wide pilot's strike have in common? They probably all utilize the **simple structure**.

The simple structure is said to be characterized most by what it is not rather than what it is. The simple structure is not elaborated.[7] It has a low degree of departmentalization, wide spans of control, authority centralized in a single person, and little formalization. The simple structure is a "flat" organization; it usually has only two or three vertical levels, a loose body of employees, and one individual in whom the decision-making authority is centralized.

The simple structure is most widely practiced in small businesses in which the manager and the owner are one and the same. This, for example, is illustrated in Exhibit 14-5, an organization chart for a retail men's store. Jack Gold owns and manages this store. Although Jack Gold employs five full-time salespeople, a cashier, and extra personnel for weekends and holidays, he "runs the show."

The strength of the simple structure lies in its simplicity. It's fast, flexible, inexpensive to maintain, and accountability is clear. One major weakness is that it's difficult to maintain in anything other than small organizations. It becomes increasingly inadequate as an organization grows because its low formalization and high centralization tend to create information overload at the top. As size increases, decision making typically becomes slower and can eventually come to a standstill as the single executive tries to continue making all the decisions. This often proves to be the undoing of many small businesses. When an organization begins to employ 50 or 100 people, it's very difficult for the owner-manager to make all the choices. If the structure isn't changed and made more elaborate, the

EXHIBIT 14-5

A Simple Structure (Jack Gold's Men's Store)

Jack Gold, owner-manager

Johnny Moore, salesperson | Edna Joiner, salesperson | Bob Munson, salesperson | Norma Sloman, salesperson | Jerry Plotkin, salesperson | Helen Wright, cashier

firm often loses momentum and can eventually fail. The simple structure's other weakness is that it's risky—everything depends on one person. One heart attack can literally destroy the organization's information and decision-making center.

The simple structure isn't strictly limited to small organizations, it's just harder to make it work effectively in larger firms. One large company that seems to have succeeded with the simple structure is Nucor Corp., a $4.2 billion steel company that operates minimills in Indiana and Arkansas.[8] Its headquarters in Charlotte, North Carolina employs just 25 people. And there are only four management levels between the company's CEO and front-line workers. The company has no corporate legal department, purchasing department, engineering department, public relations department, or marketing department. This lean structure has helped Nucor to become the fastest growing, and one of the most profitable, steelmakers in the United States. It is now the second-largest steelmaker in America, ahead of both Bethlehem Steel and LTV.

THE BUREAUCRACY

Standardization! That's the key concept that underlies all bureaucracies. Take a look at the bank where you keep your checking account, the department store where you buy your clothes, or the government offices that collect your taxes, enforce health regulations, or provide local fire protection. They all rely on standardized work processes for coordination and control.

The **bureaucracy** is characterized by highly routine operating tasks achieved through specialization, very formalized rules and regulations, tasks that are grouped into functional departments, centralized authority, narrow spans of control, and decision making that follows the chain of command.

The primary strength of the bureaucracy lies in its ability to perform standardized activities in a highly efficient manner. Putting like specialties together in functional departments results in economies of scale, minimum duplication of personnel and equipment, and employees who have the opportunity to talk "the same language" among their peers. Furthermore, bureaucracies can get by nicely with less talented—and, hence, less costly—middle- and lower-level managers. The pervasiveness of rules and regulations substitutes for managerial discretion. Standardized operations, coupled with high formalization, allow decision making to be centralized. There is little need, therefore, for innovative and experienced decision makers below the level of senior executives.

One of the major weaknesses of a bureaucracy is illustrated in the following dialogue between four executives in one company: "Ya know, nothing happens in this place until we *produce* something," said the production executive. "Wrong," commented the research and development manager, "nothing happens until we *design* something!" "What are you talking about?" asked the marketing executive. "Nothing happens here until we *sell* something!" Finally, the exasperated accounting manager responded, "It doesn't matter what you produce, design, or sell. No one knows what happens until we *tally up the results!*" This conversation points up the fact that specialization creates subunit conflicts. Functional unit goals can override the overall goals of the organization.

The other major weakness of a bureaucracy is something we've all experienced at one time or another when having to deal with people who work in these organizations: obsessive concern with following the rules. When cases arise that don't precisely fit the rules, there is no room for modification. The bureaucracy is efficient only as long as employees confront problems that they have previously encountered and for which programmed decision rules have already been established.

bureaucracy

A structure with highly routine operating tasks achieved through specialization, very formalized rules and regulations, tasks that are grouped into functional departments, centralized authority, narrow spans of control, and decision making that follows the chain of command.

THE MATRIX STRUCTURE

matrix structure

A structure that creates dual lines of authority; combines functional and product departmentalization.

Another popular organizational design option is the **matrix structure**. You'll find it being used in advertising agencies, aerospace firms, research and development laboratories, construction companies, hospitals, government agencies, universities, management consulting firms, and entertainment companies.[9] Essentially, the matrix combines two forms of departmentalization: functional and product.

The strength of functional departmentalization lies in putting like specialists together, which minimizes the number necessary, while it allows the pooling and sharing of specialized resources across products. Its major disadvantage is the difficulty of coordinating the tasks of diverse functional specialists so that their activities are completed on time and within budget. Product departmentalization, on the other hand, has exactly the opposite benefits and disadvantages. It facilitates coordination among specialties to achieve on-time completion and meet budget targets. Furthermore, it provides clear responsibility for all activities related to a product, but with duplication of activities and costs. The matrix attempts to gain the strengths of each, while avoiding their weaknesses.

The most obvious structural characteristic of the matrix is that it breaks the unity-of-command concept. Employees in the matrix have two bosses—their functional department managers and their product managers. Therefore, the matrix has a dual chain of command.

Exhibit 14-6 shows the matrix form as used in a college of business administration. The academic departments of accounting, economics, marketing, and so forth are functional units. Additionally, specific programs (i.e., products) are overlaid on the functions. In this way, members in a matrix structure have a dual assignment—to their functional department, and to their product groups. For instance, a professor of accounting who is teaching an undergraduate course reports to the director of undergraduate programs as well as to the chairperson of the accounting department.

The strength of the matrix lies in its ability to facilitate coordination when the organization has a multiplicity of complex and interdependent activities. As an organization gets larger, its information processing capacity can become over-

EXHIBIT 14-6

Matrix Structure for a College of Business Administration

Academic departments \ Programs	Undergraduate	Master's	Ph.D.	Research	Executive development	Community service
Accounting						
Administrative studies						
Finance						
Information and decision sciences						
Marketing						
Organizational behavior						
Quantitative methods						

loaded. In a bureaucracy, complexity results in increased formalization. The direct and frequent contact between different specialties in the matrix can make for better communication and more flexibility. Information permeates the organization and more quickly reaches those people who need to take account of it. Furthermore, the matrix reduces bureaupathologies. The dual lines of authority reduce tendencies of departmental members to become so busy protecting their little worlds that the organization's overall goals become secondary.

There is also another advantage to the matrix. It facilitates the efficient allocation of specialists. When individuals with highly specialized skills are lodged in one functional department or product group, their talents are monopolized and underutilized. The matrix achieves the advantages of economies of scale by providing the organization with both the best resources and an effective way of ensuring their efficient deployment.

The major disadvantages of the matrix lie in the confusion it creates, its propensity to foster power struggles, and the stress it places on individuals.[10] When you dispense with the unity-of-command concept, ambiguity is significantly increased and ambiguity often leads to conflict. For example, it's frequently unclear who reports to whom, and it is not unusual for product managers to fight over getting the best specialists assigned to their products. Confusion and ambiguity also create the seeds of power struggles. Bureaucracy reduces the potential for power grabs by defining the rules of the game. When those rules are "up for grabs," power struggles between functional and product managers result. For individuals who desire security and absence from ambiguity, this work climate can produce stress. Reporting to more than one boss introduces role conflict, and unclear expectations introduce role ambiguity. The comfort of bureaucracy's predictability is absent, replaced by insecurity and stress.

NEW DESIGN OPTIONS

Over the last decade or two, senior managers in a number of organizations have been working to develop new structural options that can better help their firms compete effectively. In this section, we'll describe three such structural designs: the *team structure*, the *virtual organization*, and the *boundaryless organization*.

THE TEAM STRUCTURE

As described in Chapter 9, teams have become an extremely popular means around which to organize work activities. When management uses teams as its central coordination device, you have a **team structure**.[11] The primary characteristics of the team structure are that it breaks down departmental barriers and decentralizes decision making to the level of the work team. Team structures also require employees to be generalists as well as specialists.[12]

team structure
The use of teams as the central device to coordinate work activities.

In smaller companies, the team structure can define the entire organization. For instance, Imedia, a 30-person marketing firm in New Jersey, is organized completely around teams that have full responsibility for most operational issues and client services.[13] Whole Foods Market, Inc., the largest natural-foods grocer in the United States, is structured entirely around teams.[14] Every one of Whole Foods' 43 stores is an autonomous profit center composed of an average of 10 self-managed teams, each with a designated team leader. The team leaders in each store are a team; store leaders in each region are a team; and the company's six regional presidents are a team.

More often, particularly among larger organizations, the team structure complements what is typically a bureaucracy. This allows the organization to achieve the efficiency of bureaucracy's standardization, while gaining the flexibility that teams provide. To improve productivity at the operating level, for instance, companies such as Chrysler, Saturn, Motorola, and Xerox have made extensive use of self-managed teams. On the other hand, when companies such as Boeing, Baxter International, and Hewlett-Packard need to design new products or coordinate major projects, they'll structure activities around cross-functional teams.

THE VIRTUAL ORGANIZATION

virtual organization

A small, core organization that outsources major business functions.

Why own when you can rent? That question captures the essence of the **virtual organization** (also sometimes called the *network* or *modular* organization), typically a small, core organization that outsources major business functions.[15] In structural terms, the virtual organization is highly centralized, with little or no departmentalization.

The prototype of the virtual structure is today's movie-making organization. In Hollywood's golden era, movies were made by huge, vertically integrated corporations. Studios such as MGM, Warner Brothers, and 20th-Century Fox owned large movie lots and employed thousands of full-time specialists—set designers, camera people, film editors, directors, and even actors. Nowadays, most movies are made by a collection of individuals and small companies who come together and make films project by project.[16] This structural form allows each project to be staffed with the talent most suited to its demands, rather than having to choose just from those people the studio employs. It minimizes bureaucratic overhead since there is no lasting organization to maintain. And it lessens long-term risks and their costs because there is no long term—a team is assembled for a finite period and then disbanded.

Wendy Rickard runs a virtual organization. She, her assistant, and one part-time employee produce a wide range of magazines and marketing materials, but Wendy's firm, Rickard Associates, is run out of an old house in Hopewell, New Jersey. This virtual firm contracts art from someone in Arizona; uses editors in Florida, Georgia, and Michigan; and employs dozens of freelancers from all over North America. Using the Internet and America Online, these people are able to work together as if they were in the same office.

When large organizations use the virtual structure, they frequently use it to outsource manufacturing. Companies such as Nike, Reebok, L. L. Bean, and Dell Computer are just a few of the thousands of companies that have found that they can do hundreds of millions of dollars in business without owning manufacturing facilities. Dell Com-

Bruce Brown (wearing hat) operates a virtual organization. He publishes an on-line newsletter, BugNet, that provides subscribers with solutions for fixing computer bugs. Brown and employees are shown here at the firm's headquarters in Sumas, Washington. But most functions are outsourced to people throughout the country and as far away as London. They're managed through an intranet that contains editorial guidelines, deadlines, contact information, and photos. Brown has never met most of these people, including a senior editor in Cleveland who he has worked with for five years.

puter, for instance, owns no plants and merely assembles computers from outsourced parts. But National Steel Corporation contracts out its mail-room operations; AT&T farms out its credit card processing; and Mobil Oil Corporation has turned over maintenance of its refineries to another firm.

What's going on here? A quest for maximum flexibility. These virtual organizations have created networks of relationships that allow them to contract out manufacturing, distribution, marketing, or any other business function when management feels that others can do it better or more cheaply.

The virtual organization stands in sharp contrast to the typical bureaucracy that has many vertical levels of management and where control is sought through ownership. In such organizations, research and development are done in-house, production occurs in company-owned plants, and sales and marketing are performed by the company's own employees. To support all this, management has to employ extra personnel including accountants, human resource specialists, and lawyers. The virtual organization, however, outsources many of these functions and concentrates on what it does best. For most U.S. firms, that means focusing on design or marketing.

Exhibit 14-7 shows a virtual organization in which management outsources all of the primary functions of the business. The core of the organization is a small group of executives, whose job is to oversee directly any activities that are done in-house and to coordinate relationships with the other organizations that manufacture, distribute, and perform other crucial functions for the virtual organization. The dotted lines in Exhibit 14-7 represent those relationships typically maintained under contracts. In essence, managers in virtual structures spend most of their time coordinating and controlling external relations, typically by way of computer-network links.

The major advantage to the virtual organization is its flexibility. For instance, it allowed someone with an innovative idea and little money, such as Michael Dell and his Dell Computer firm, to successfully compete against large companies such as IBM. The primary drawback to this structure is that it reduces management's control over key parts of its business.

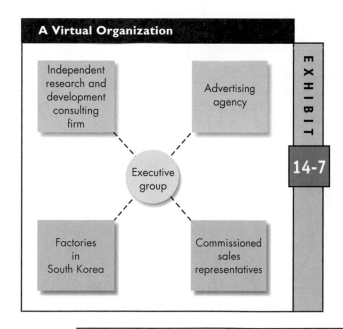

A Virtual Organization

Independent research and development consulting firm

Advertising agency

Executive group

Factories in South Korea

Commissioned sales representatives

EXHIBIT 14-7

THE BOUNDARYLESS ORGANIZATION

boundaryless organization

An organization that seeks to eliminate the chain of command, have limitless spans of control, and replace departments with empowered teams.

General Electric chairman, Jack Welch, coined the term **boundaryless organization** to describe his idea of what he wanted GE to become. Welch wanted to turn his company into a "$60 billion family grocery store."[17] That is, in spite of its monstrous size, he wanted to eliminate *vertical* and *horizontal* boundaries within GE and break down *external* barriers between the company and its customers and suppliers. The boundaryless organization seeks to eliminate the chain of command, have limitless spans of control, and replace departments with empowered teams. And because it relies so heavily on information technology, some have turned to calling this structure the *T-form* (or technology-based) organization.[18]

Although GE has not yet achieved this boundaryless state—and probably never will—it has made significant progress toward that end. So have other companies such as Hewlett-Packard, AT&T, Motorola, and Oticon A/S. Let's consider what a boundaryless organization would look like and what some firms are doing to try to make it a reality.[19]

By removing vertical boundaries, management flattens the hierarchy. Status and rank are minimized. Cross-hierarchical teams (which include top executives, middle managers, supervisors, and operative employees), participative decision-making practices, and the use of 360-degree performance appraisals (in which peers and others above and below the employee evaluate his or her performance) are examples of what GE is doing to break down vertical boundaries. At Oticon A/S, a $160-million-a-year Danish hearing aid manufacturer, all traces of hierarchy have disappeared. Everyone works at uniform mobile workstations. And project teams, not functions or departments, are used to coordinate work.

Functional departments create horizontal boundaries. And these boundaries stifle interaction between functions, product lines, and units. The way to reduce these barriers is to replace functional departments with cross-functional teams and to organize activities around processes. For instance, Xerox now develops new products through multidisciplinary teams that work in a single process instead of around narrow functional tasks. Similarly, some AT&T units are now doing annual budgets based not on functions or departments but on processes such as the maintenance of a worldwide telecommunications network. Another way management can cut through horizontal barriers is to use lateral transfers and rotate people into and out of different functional areas. This approach turns specialists into generalists.

When fully operational, the boundaryless organization also breaks down barriers to external constituencies (suppliers, customers, regulators, etc.) and barriers created by geography. Globalization, strategic alliances, customer–organization linkages, and telecommuting are all examples of

The automobile industry is moving toward the boundaryless organization, with automakers forming partnerships with suppliers to design, manufacture, and assemble the final product. Daimler-Benz's new Smart Car was designed by SMH Automotive, a Swiss firm that also designs Swatch watches. Suppliers that produce different parts of the car even help to assemble it. The Daimler-Benz plant in Hambach, France, shown here, consists of seven separate factories, each occupied by a different supplier that produces a different system for the car. Involving suppliers in assembling the Smart Car reduced the final assembly time to just four hours compared to the 20 hours it typically takes an automaker to assemble a vehicle.

practices that reduce external boundaries. Coca-Cola, for instance, sees itself as a global corporation, not as a U.S. or Atlanta company. Firms such as NEC Corp., Boeing, and Apple Computer each have strategic alliances or joint partnerships with dozens of companies. These alliances blur the distinction between one organization and another as employees work on joint projects. Companies such as AT&T and TWA are allowing customers to perform functions that previously were done by management. For instance, some AT&T units are receiving bonuses based on customer evaluations of the teams that serve them. TWA's Royal Ambassador frequent flyers get "Something Good" coupons to give to outstanding TWA employees. Recipients can turn the coupons in for prizes and will be featured in company ads. This practice, in essence, allows TWA's customers to participate in employee appraisals. Finally, we suggest that telecommuting is blurring organizational boundaries. The security analyst with Merrill Lynch who does his job from his ranch in Montana or the software designer who works for a San Francisco company but does her job in Boulder, Colorado, are just two examples of the millions of workers who are now doing their jobs outside the physical boundaries of their employers' premises.

The one common technological thread that makes the boundaryless organization possible is networked computers. They allow people to communicate across intraorganizational and interorganizational boundaries.[20] Electronic mail, for instance, enables hundreds of employees to share information simultaneously and allows rank-and-file workers to communicate directly with senior executives. Additionally, many large companies, including Federal Express, AT&T, and 3M, are developing private nets or "intranets." Using the infrastructure and standards of the Internet and the World Wide Web, these private nets are internal communication systems, protected from the public Internet by special software. And interorganizational networks now make it possible for Wal-Mart suppliers such as Procter & Gamble and Levi-Strauss to monitor inventory levels of laundry soap and jeans, respectively, because P&G and Levi's computer systems are networked to Wal-Mart's system.

WHY DO STRUCTURES DIFFER?

In the previous sections, we described a variety of organizational designs ranging from the highly structured and standardized bureaucracy to the loose and amorphous boundaryless organization. The other designs we discussed tend to exist somewhere between these two extremes.

Exhibit 14-8 reconceptualizes our previous discussions by presenting two extreme models of organizational design. One extreme we'll call the **mechanistic model**. It is generally synonymous with the bureaucracy in that it has extensive departmentalization, high formalization, a limited information network (mostly downward communication), and little participation by low-level members in decision making. At the other extreme is the **organic model**. This model looks a lot like the boundaryless organization. It's flat, uses cross-hierarchical and cross-functional teams, has low formalization, possesses a comprehensive information network (utilizing lateral and upward communication as well as downward), and it involves high participation in decision making.[21]

With these two models in mind, we're now prepared to address the question: Why are some organizations structured along more mechanistic lines while others follow organic characteristics? What are the forces that influence the design that is chosen? In the following pages, we present the major forces that have been identified as causes or determinants of an organization's structure.[22]

mechanistic model

A structure characterized by extensive departmentalization, high formalization, a limited information network, and centralization.

organic model

A structure that is flat, uses cross-hierarchical and cross-functional teams, has low formalization, possesses a comprehensive information network, and relies on participative decision making.

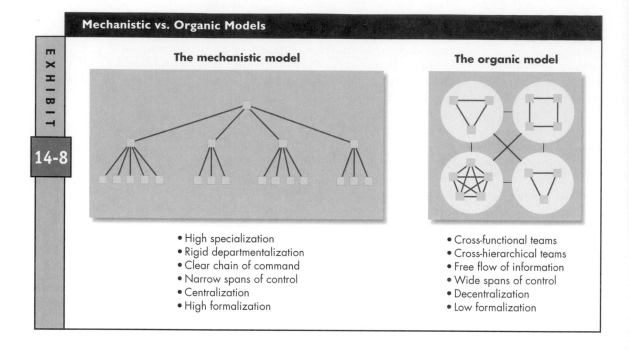

EXHIBIT

14-8

Mechanistic vs. Organic Models

The mechanistic model

- High specialization
- Rigid departmentalization
- Clear chain of command
- Narrow spans of control
- Centralization
- High formalization

The organic model

- Cross-functional teams
- Cross-hierarchical teams
- Free flow of information
- Wide spans of control
- Decentralization
- Low formalization

STRATEGY

An organization's structure is a means to help management achieve its objectives. Since objectives are derived from the organization's overall strategy, it is only logical that strategy and structure should be closely linked. More specifically, structure should follow strategy. If management makes a significant change in its organization's strategy, the structure will need to be modified to accommodate and support this change.[23]

Most current strategy frameworks focus on three strategy dimensions—innovation, cost minimization, and imitation—and the structural design that works best with each.[24]

To what degree does an organization introduce major new products or services? An **innovation strategy** does not mean a strategy merely for simple or cosmetic changes from previous offerings but rather one for meaningful and unique innovations. Obviously, not all firms pursue innovation. This strategy may appropriately characterize 3M Co., but it's not a strategy pursued by conservative retailer Marks & Spencer.

An organization that is pursuing a **cost-minimization strategy** tightly controls costs, refrains from incurring unnecessary innovation or marketing expenses, and cuts prices in selling a basic product. This would describe the strategy pursued by Wal-Mart or the sellers of generic grocery products.

Organizations following an **imitation strategy** try to capitalize on the best of both of the previous strategies. They seek to minimize risk and maximize opportunity for profit. Their strategy is to move into new products or new markets only after viability has been proven by innovators. They take the successful ideas of innovators and copy them. Manufacturers of mass-marketed fashion goods that are rip-offs of designer styles follow the imitation strategy. This label also probably characterizes such well-known firms as IBM and Caterpillar. They essentially follow their smaller and more innovative competitors

innovation strategy

A strategy that emphasizes the introduction of major new products and services.

cost-minimization strategy

A strategy that emphasizes tight cost controls, avoidance of unnecessary innovation or marketing expenses, and price cutting.

imitation strategy

A strategy that seeks to move into new products or new markets only after their viability has already been proven.

Strategy	Structural Option
Innovation	**Organic**: A loose structure; low specialization, low formalization, decentralization
Cost minimization	**Mechanistic**: Tight control; extensive work specialization, high formalization, high centralization
Imitation	**Mechanistic and organic**: Mix of loose with tight properties; tight controls over current activities and looser controls for new undertakings

EXHIBIT 14-9

with superior products, but only after their competitors have demonstrated that the market is there.

Exhibit 14-9 describes the structural option that best matches each strategy. Innovators need the flexibility of the organic structure, while cost minimizers seek the efficiency and stability of the mechanistic structure. Imitators combine the two structures. They use a mechanistic structure in order to maintain tight controls and low costs in their current activities, while at the same time they create organic subunits in which to pursue new undertakings.

ORGANIZATION SIZE

There is considerable evidence to support that an organization's size significantly affects its structure.[25] For instance, large organizations—those typically employing 2,000 or more people—tend to have more specialization, more departmentalization, more vertical levels, and more rules and regulations than do small organizations. However, the relationship isn't linear. Rather, size affects structure at a decreasing rate. The impact of size becomes less important as an organization expands. Why is this? Essentially, once an organization has around 2,000 employees, it's already fairly mechanistic. An additional 500 employees will not have much impact. On the other hand, adding 500 employees to an organization that has only 300 members is likely to result in a shift toward a more mechanistic structure.

TECHNOLOGY

The term **technology** refers to how an organization transfers its inputs into outputs. Every organization has at least one technology for converting financial, human, and physical resources into products or services. The Ford Motor Co., for instance, predominantly uses an assembly-line process to make its products. On the other hand, colleges may use a number of instruction technologies—the ever-popular formal lecture method, the case analysis method, the experiential exercise method, the programmed learning method, and so forth. In this section we want to show that organizational structures adapt to their technology.

Numerous studies have been carried out on the technology–structure relationship.[26] The details of those studies are quite complex, so we'll go straight to "the bottom line" and attempt to summarize what we know.

The common theme that differentiates technologies is their *degree of routineness*. By this we mean that technologies tend toward either routine or nonroutine

technology
How an organization transfers its inputs into outputs.

activities. The former are characterized by automated and standardized operations. Nonroutine activities are customized. They include such varied operations as furniture restoring, custom shoemaking, and genetic research.

What relationships have been found between technology and structure? Although the relationship is not overwhelmingly strong, we find that routine tasks are associated with taller and more departmentalized structures. The relationship between technology and formalization, however, is stronger. Studies consistently show routineness to be associated with the presence of rule manuals, job descriptions, and other formalized documentation. Finally, there has been found to be an interesting relationship between technology and centralization. It seems logical that routine technologies would be associated with a centralized structure, whereas nonroutine technologies, which rely more heavily on the knowledge of specialists, would be characterized by delegated decision authority. This position has met with some support. However, a more generalizable conclusion is that the technology–centralization relationship is moderated by the degree of formalization. Formal regulations and centralized decision making are both control mechanisms and management can substitute one for the other. Routine technologies should be associated with centralized control if there is a minimum of rules and regulations. However, if formalization is high, routine technology can be accompanied by decentralization. So, we would predict that routine technology would lead to centralization, but only if formalization is low.

ENVIRONMENT

environment

Those institutions or forces outside the organization that potentially affect the organization's performance.

An organization's **environment** is composed of those institutions or forces that are outside the organization and potentially affect the organization's performance. These typically include suppliers, customers, competitors, government regulatory agencies, public pressure groups, and the like.

Why should an organization's structure be affected by its environment? Because of environmental uncertainty. Some organizations face relatively static environments—few forces in their environment are changing. There are, for example, no new competitors, no new technological breakthroughs by current competitors, or little activity by public pressure groups to influence the organization. Other organizations face very dynamic environments—rapidly changing government regulations affecting their business, new competitors, difficulties in acquiring raw materials, continually changing product preferences by customers, and so on. Static environments create significantly less uncertainty for managers than do dynamic ones. And since uncertainty is a threat to an organization's effectiveness, management will try to minimize it. One way to reduce environmental uncertainty is through adjustments in the organization's structure.[27]

Recent research has helped clarify what is meant by environmental uncertainty. It's been found that there are three key dimensions to any organization's environment. They are capacity, volatility, and complexity.[28]

The *capacity* of an environment refers to the degree to which it can support growth. Rich and growing environments generate excess resources, which can buffer the organization in times of relative scarcity. Abundant capacity, for example, leaves room for an organization to make mistakes, while scarce capacity does not. In the year 2000, firms operating in the multimedia software business had relatively abundant environments, whereas those in the full-service brokerage business faced relative scarcity.

The degree of instability in an environment is captured in the *volatility* dimension. Where there is a high degree of unpredictable change, the environment is dynamic. This makes it difficult for management to predict accurately the probabilities associated with various decision alternatives. At the other extreme is a stable environment. The accelerated changes in Eastern Europe and the demise of the Cold War had dramatic effects on the U.S. defense industry in the 1990s. This moved the environment of major defense contractors such as Lockheed Martin, General Dynamics, and Northrop Grumman from relatively stable to dynamic.

Finally, the environment needs to be assessed in terms of *complexity*, that is, the degree of heterogeneity and concentration among environmental elements. Simple environments are homogeneous and concentrated. This might describe the tobacco industry, since there are relatively few players. It's easy for firms in this industry to keep a close eye on the competition. In contrast, environments characterized by heterogeneity and dispersion are called complex. This is essentially the current environment for firms competing in the Internet-connection business. Every day there seems to be another "new kid on the block" with whom current Internet access providers have to deal.

Exhibit 14-10 summarizes our definition of the environment along its three dimensions. The arrows in this figure are meant to indicate movement toward higher uncertainty. So organizations that operate in environments characterized as scarce, dynamic, and complex face the greatest degree of uncertainty. Why? Because they have little room for error, high unpredictability, and a diverse set of elements in the environment to monitor constantly.

Given this three-dimensional definition of environment, we can offer some general conclusions. There is evidence that relates the degrees of environmental uncertainty to different structural arrangements. Specifically, the more scarce, dynamic, and complex the environment, the more organic a structure should be. The more abundant, stable, and simple the environment, the more the mechanistic structure will be preferred.

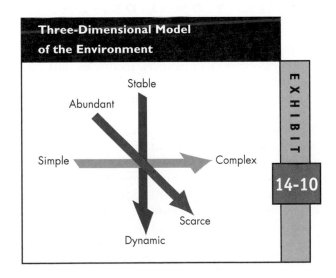

Three-Dimensional Model of the Environment

Stable

Abundant

Simple — Complex

Scarce

Dynamic

EXHIBIT

14-10

"Bureaucracy Is Dead"

This statement is false. Some bureaucratic characteristics are in decline. And bureaucracy is undoubtedly going through changes. But it's far from dead.

Bureaucracy is characterized by specialization, formalization, departmentalization, centralization, narrow spans of control, and adherence to a chain of command. Have these characteristics disappeared from today's modern organizations? No. In spite of the increased use of empowered teams and flattened structures, certain facts remain.[29] (1) Large size prevails. Organizations that succeed and survive tend to grow to large size, and bureaucracy is efficient with large size. Small organizations and their nonbureaucratic structures are more likely to fail, so over time, small organizations may come and go but large bureaucracies stay. Moreover, while the average business today has considerably fewer employees than 30 years ago, these smaller firms are increasingly part of a large, multilocation organization with the financial and technological resources to compete in a global marketplace. (2) Environmental turbulence can be largely managed. The impact of uncertainties in the environment on the organization are substantially reduced by management strategies such as environmental scanning, strategic

alliances, advertising, and lobbying. This allows organizations facing dynamic environments to maintain bureaucratic structures and still be efficient. (3) Bureaucracy's goal of standardization can be increasingly achieved through hiring people who have undergone extensive educational training. Rational discipline, rather than imposed by rules and regulations, is internalized by hiring professionals with college and university training. They come preprogrammed. Additionally, strong cultures help achieve standardization by substituting for high formalization. (4) Finally, technology maintains control. Networked computers allow management to closely monitor the actions of employees without centralization or narrow spans of control. Technology has merely replaced some previously bureaucratic characteristics but without any loss of management control.

In spite of some changes, bureaucracy is alive and well in many venues. It continues to be a dominant structural form in manufacturing, service firms, hospitals, schools and colleges, the military, and voluntary associations. Why? It's still the most efficient way to organize large-scale activities.

ORGANIZATIONAL DESIGNS AND EMPLOYEE BEHAVIOR

We opened this chapter by implying that an organization's structure can have significant effects on its members. In this section, we want to directly assess just what those effects might be.

A review of the evidence linking organizational structures to employee performance and satisfaction leads to a pretty clear conclusion—you can't generalize! Not everyone prefers the freedom and flexibility of organic structures. Some people are most productive and satisfied when work tasks are standardized and ambiguity is minimized—that is, in mechanistic structures. So any discussion of the effect of organizational design on employee behavior has to address individual differences. To illustrate this point, let's consider employee preferences for work specialization, span of control, and centralization.[30]

The evidence generally indicates that *work specialization* contributes to higher employee productivity but at the price of reduced job satisfaction. However, this statement ignores individual differences and the type of job tasks people do.

As we noted previously, work specialization is not an unending source of higher productivity. Problems start to surface, and productivity begins to suffer, when the human diseconomies of doing repetitive and narrow tasks overtake the economies of specialization. As the workforce has become more highly educated and desirous of jobs that are intrinsically rewarding, the point at which productivity begins to decline seems to be reached more quickly than in decades past.

While more people today are undoubtedly turned off by overly specialized jobs than were their parents or grandparents, it would be naive to ignore the reality that there is still a segment of the workforce that prefers the routine and repetitiveness of highly specialized jobs. Some individuals want work that makes minimal intellectual demands and provides the security of routine. For these people, high work specialization is a source of job satisfaction. The empirical question, of course, is whether this represents 2 percent of the workforce or 52 percent. Given that there is some self-selection operating in the choice of careers, we might conclude that negative behavioral outcomes from high specialization are most likely to surface in professional jobs occupied by individuals with high needs for personal growth and diversity.

A review of the research indicates that it is probably safe to say there is no evidence to support a relationship between *span of control* and employee performance. While it is intuitively attractive to argue that large spans might lead to higher employee performance because they provide more distant supervision and more opportunity for personal initiative, the research fails to support this notion. At this point it is impossible to state that any particular span of control is best for producing high performance or high satisfaction among employees. The reason is, again, probably individual differences. That is, some people like to be left alone, while others prefer the security of a boss who is quickly available at all times. Consistent with several of the contingency theories of leadership discussed in Chapter 11, we would expect factors such as employees' experiences and abilities and the degree of structure in their tasks to explain when wide or narrow spans of control are likely to contribute to their performance and job satisfaction. However, there is some evidence indicating that a manager's job satisfaction increases as the number of employees he or she supervises increases.

The tasks of workers on an assembly line at Swiss candy maker Nestle are highly standardized. Individual differences influence how these workers respond to their high work specialization. Many may enjoy the routine and repetitiveness of their highly specialized jobs, especially since working closely with other employees gives them the chance to socialize on the job.

We find fairly strong evidence linking *centralization* and job satisfaction. In general, organizations that are less centralized have a greater amount of participative decision making. And the evidence suggests that participative decision making is positively related to job satisfaction. But, again, individual differences surface. The decentralization–satisfaction relationship is strongest with employees who have low self-esteem. Because individuals with low self-esteem have less confidence in their abilities, they place a higher value on shared decision making, which means that they're not held solely responsible for decision outcomes.

Our conclusion: To maximize employee performance and satisfaction, individual differences, such as experience, personality, and the work task, should be taken into account. In addition, national culture influences preference for structure so it, too, needs to be considered.[31] Organizations operating with people from high power distance cultures, such as found in Greece, France, and most of Latin America, will find employees much more accepting of mechanistic structures than when employees come from low power distance countries. So you need to consider cultural differences along with individual differences when making predictions on how structure will affect employee performance and satisfaction.

One obvious insight needs to be made before we leave this topic. People don't select employers randomly. There is substantial evidence that individuals are attracted to, selected by, and stay with organizations that suit their personal characteristics.[32] Job candidates who prefer predictability, for instance, are likely to seek out and take employment in mechanistic structures, while those who want autonomy are more likely to end up in an organic structure. So the effect of structure on employee behavior is undoubtedly reduced when the selection process facilitates proper matching of individual characteristics with organizational characteristics.

SUMMARY AND IMPLICATIONS FOR MANAGERS

The theme of this chapter has been that an organization's internal structure contributes to explaining and predicting behavior. That is, in addition to individual and group factors, the structural relationships in which people work have a bearing on employee attitudes and behavior.

What's the basis for the argument that structure has an impact on both attitudes and behavior? To the degree that an organization's structure reduces ambiguity for employees and clarifies such concerns as "What am I supposed to do?" "How am I supposed to do it?" "To whom do I report?" and "To whom do I go if I have a problem?" it shapes their attitudes and facilitates and motivates them to higher levels of performance.

Of course, structure also constrains employees to the extent that it limits and controls what they do. For example, organizations structured around high levels of formalization and specialization, strict adherence to the chain of command, limited delegation of authority, and narrow spans of control give employees little autonomy. Controls in such organizations are tight and behavior will tend to vary within a narrow range. In contrast, organizations that are structured around limited specialization, low formalization, wide spans of control, and the like provide employees greater freedom and, thus, will be characterized by greater behavioral diversity.

Exhibit 14-11 visually summarizes what we've discussed in this chapter. Strategy, size, technology, and environment determine the type of structure an organization will have. For simplicity's sake, we can classify structural designs around one of two models: mechanistic or organic. The specific effect of structural designs on performance and satisfaction is moderated by employees' individual preferences and cultural norms.

One last point: Managers need to be reminded that structural variables such as work specialization, span of control, formalization, and centralization are objective characteristics that can be measured by organizational researchers. The findings and conclusions we've offered in this chapter, in fact, are directly a result of the work of these researchers. But employees don't objectively measure these structural characteristics! They observe things around them in an unscientific fashion and then form their own implicit models of what the organization's

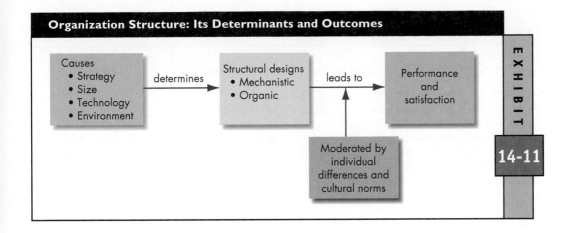

Organization Structure: Its Determinants and Outcomes

EXHIBIT 14-11

Causes
- Strategy
- Size
- Technology
- Environment

determines →

Structural designs
- Mechanistic
- Organic

leads to →

Performance and satisfaction

↑ Moderated by individual differences and cultural norms

structure is like. How many people did they have to interview with before they were offered their jobs? How many people work in their departments and buildings? Is there an organization policy manual? If so, is it readily available and do people follow it closely? How is the organization and its top management described in newspapers and periodicals? Answers to questions such as these, when combined with an employee's past experiences and comments made by peers, lead members to form an overall subjective image of what their organization's structure is like. This image, though, may in no way resemble the organization's actual objective structural characteristics.

The importance of these **implicit models of organizational structure** should not be overlooked. As we noted in Chapter 5, people respond to their perceptions rather than objective reality. The research, for instance, on the relationship between many structural variables and subsequent levels of performance or job satisfaction is far from consistent. We explained some of this as being attributable to individual differences. However, an additional contributing cause to these inconsistent findings might be diverse perceptions of the objective characteristics. Researchers typically focus on actual levels of the various structural components, but these may be irrelevant if people interpret similar components differently. The bottom line, therefore, is to understand how employees interpret their organization's structure. That should prove a more meaningful predictor of their behavior than the objective characteristics themselves.

implicit models of organizational structure

Perceptions that people hold regarding structural variables formed by observing things around them in an unscientific fashion.

The Case for Flexibility in Organization Design

In today's chaotic and uncertain world, there is essentially only one type of design that will work. That's an organic structure. Our reasoning goes like this: Uncertainty is a major determinant of an organization's structure. Today's organizations face uncertainty caused by constant change in the environment. They also face technological uncertainty as a result of their quest for innovation. This uncertainty requires that organizations be flexible. And what type of structure is most adaptive? The organic structure.

Organizations face uncertainty because factors such as market demand, competitors' actions, future technological breakthroughs, and employees' availability are not fully known or understood. Managers have never been all-seeing, all-knowing futurists. But in the past couple of decades, change has come with unprecedented speed. When managers could anticipate a competitor's new product three years in advance, flexibility wasn't that important. Three years provided plenty of lead time to respond. Nowdays, lead times are more likely weeks than years. And the competitor might be someone who didn't even exist a year ago. So the type of structure that worked in the 1960s or 1970s won't work today.

Flexibility is the degree to which an organization is able to absorb, cause, or respond to strategic changes.[1] Organizations that are flexible are able to reposition themselves in a market, change their game plans, or dismantle their current strategies. They are quick on their feet. They can rapidly reemploy their resources to take advantage of new opportunities and extricate themselves from past commitments.

It's true that high flexibility comes with a price. It trades off efficiency. The organic structure has redundant functions and wasteful slack. It lacks definitive regulations and clear lines of authority. Yet today's managers have little choice. They either build structures that are flexible, or they risk being defeated by their more adaptive competitors.

[1]O. Meilich, "The Flexibility-Efficiency Debate: Review and Theoretical Framework." Paper presented at the 1997 Academy of Management Conference, Boston, MA.

It's true that there is a trade-off between flexibility and efficiency. But don't be too quick to conclude that only the flexible survive. Efficiency is still a desirable attribute in organizations. As long as consumers assess the cost of a product or service before they buy it—and there is nothing to suggest that cost consciousness has gone out of fashion—there will be a concern with efficiency. And the mechanistic structure continues to be the most *efficient* way to organize work activities.

Flexibility requires an organization to possess slack resources. And these unused or underutilized resources reduce the organization's efficiency. This suggests that organizations can be *too* flexible. Because flexibility comes with high costs, organizations that are overadaptive jeopardize their existence through inefficiency. The PC maker, for instance, that is overly flexible will have higher costs than its more rigid and efficient competitors. Unless the highly flexible firm can continually generate more innovative products, consumers will not be able to justify the higher costs of its PCs.

Mechanistic structures can still thrive. Their high specialization, formalization, and rigid decision-making hierarchy make them efficiency machines. For completing routine tasks in relatively stable environments, they can consistently underprice and outperform their more flexible counterparts.

The case *for* the mechanistic structure and *against* flexibility is essentially this. The mechanistic structure maximizes efficiency. It allows firms to produce at lower costs and to pass those lower costs on in lower prices. As long as there are consumers who value low price over the latest innovation, the mechanistic structure will survive. Moreover, to the degree that management can insulate its organization against environmental uncertainty—through actions such as forecasting, competitive intelligence, stockpiling inventories, advertising, and lobbying—then it can continue to use the mechanistic structure and enjoy its efficiencies even under conditions of high uncertainty.

1. Why isn't work specialization an unending source of increased productivity?

2. All things being equal, which is more efficient, a wide or narrow span of control? Why?

3. In what ways can management departmentalize?

4. What is a matrix structure? When would management use it?

5. Contrast the virtual organization with the boundaryless organization.

6. What type of structure works best with an innovation strategy? A cost-minimization strategy? An imitation strategy?

7. Summarize the size–structure relationship.

8. Define and give an example of what is meant by the term *technology*.

9. Summarize the environment–structure relationship.

10. Explain the importance of the statement: "Employees form implicit models of organizational structure."

Questions for Critical Thinking

1. How is the typical large corporation of today organized in contrast to how that same organization was probably organized in the 1960s?

2. Do you think most employees prefer high formalization? Support your position.

3. If you were an employee in a matrix structure, what pluses do you think the structure would provide? What about minuses?

4. What behavioral predictions would you make about people who worked in a "pure" boundaryless organization (if such a structure were ever to exist)?

5. Daimler-Benz buys Chrysler. Travelers Group purchases Citicorp. Aetna Life & Casualty merges with U.S. Healthcare. Each of these are recent examples of large companies combining with other large companies. Does this imply that small isn't necessarily beautiful? Are mechanistic forms winning the "survival of the fittest" battle? What are the implications of this consolidation trend for organizational behavior?

Team Exercise | Authority Figures

Purpose   To learn about one's experiences with and feelings about authority.

Time   Approximately 75 minutes.

Procedure

1. Your instructor will separate class members into groups based on their birth order. Groups are formed consisting of "only children," "eldest," "middle," and "youngest," according to placement in families. Larger groups will be broken into smaller ones, with four or five members, to allow for freer conversation.

2. Each group member should talk about how he or she "typically reacts to the authority of others." Focus should be on specific situations that offer general information about how individuals deal with authority figures (e.g., bosses, teachers, parents, or coaches). The group has 25 minutes to develop a written list of how the group generally deals with others' authority. Be sure to separate tendencies that group members share and those they do not.

3. Repeat Step 2 except this time discuss how group members "typically act as authority figures." Again make a list of shared characteristics.

4. Each group will share its general conclusions with the entire class.

5. Class discussion will focus on questions such as:

   a. What patterned differences have surfaced between the groups?

   b. What may account for these differences?

   c. What hypotheses might explain the connection between how individuals react to the authority of others and how they act as authority figures?

Source: This exercise is adapted from W. A. Kahn, "An Exercise of Authority," *Organizational Behavior Teaching Review*, vol. XIV, Issue 2, 1989–90, pp. 28–42. Reprinted with permission.

Ethical Dilemma | Employee Monitoring: How Far Is Too Far?

When does management's effort to control the actions of others become an invasion of privacy? Consider three cases.[33]

Employees at General Electric's answering center handle telephone inquiries from customers all day long. Those conversations are taped by GE and occasionally reviewed by its management.

The Internal Revenue Service's internal audit group monitors a computer log that shows employee access to taxpayers' accounts. This monitoring activity allows management to check and see what employees are doing on their computers.

Versus Technology recently introduced a system that lets employers keep track of their workers' whereabouts. It deploys a series of sensors, each the size of a hockey puck, in office ceilings. They track infrared light pulses produced by personal ID tags. Workers' movements are then tracked on a Windows program, letting the boss tap in by laptop computer.

Are any of these cases—monitoring calls, computer activities, or locale—an invasion of privacy? When does management overstep the bounds of decency and privacy by silently (even covertly) scrutinizing the behavior of its employees or associates?

Managers at GE and the IRS defend their practice in terms of ensuring quality, productivity, and proper employee behavior. GE can point to U.S. government statistics estimating that as many as 26 million workers are being electronically monitored on their jobs. And silent surveillance of telephone calls can be used to help employees do their jobs better. One IRS audit of its southeastern regional offices found that 166 employees took unauthorized looks at the tax returns of friends, neighbors, or celebrities. A product manager at Versus says his company's system doesn't watch what you do, it just knows where you are. And this can help management better distribute employees and provide customers with better service.

There are laws and ethical guidelines aimed to curb employers' rights to use electronic monitoring. For example, the Privacy for Consumers and Workers Act requires that precise notification be given to U.S. employees of when they will be monitored. Similarly, industry groups in telemarketing have established guidelines that include a recommendation that employees be given the option to be informed when they are being monitored.

When does management's need for information about employee performance cross over the line and interfere with a worker's right to privacy? For instance, must employees be notified ahead of time that they will be monitored? Does management's right to protect its interests extend to electronic monitoring of every place a worker might be—bathrooms, locker rooms, and dressing rooms?

Internet Search Exercises

1. Find three companies (not mentioned in your text) that are in some way monitoring their employees via computer controls. Describe each.

2. Contrast the organizational structures of three companies—one each from (a) a manufacturer of pharmaceuticals; (b) a large retail chain; and (c) a large software developer. What contingency variables do you think best explain each one's structure?

PHLIP Companion Web Site

We invite you to visit the Robbins homepage on the Prentice Hall Web site at **www.prenhall.com/robbins** for our on-line study guide, current events, links to related Web sites, and more.

If ever there was an organization that exemplified the challenges of managing in rapidly changing times, it's Motorola Inc. In the mid-1980s, Motorola teams achieved technological breakthroughs in miniaturizing pagers and cellular phones—just before those markets took off. As recently as 1995, the company was the world leader in pagers and cell phones—and generating record-breaking growth rates in sales and earnings. By 1999, however, the company was struggling.

Motorola stumbled badly when it failed to anticipate the industry's switch to digital cell phones from the long-dominant analog devices. It then overestimated its capability to get digital equipment to market. A major player in Japan and Southeast Asia, Motorola has seen the collapse of consumer demand for its products as a result of the economic downturn in Asia. And it now has serious problems in marketing, timely delivery of products, and in the quality of its wireless networks. While it still holds on, although weakly, to its number-one spot in the U.S. market for wireless phones, its share has fallen about 30 percent between 1996 and 1999, to just above one-third of the industry's sales. Its worldwide share of wireless network systems has dropped sharply over the same period, to below one-third.

What was once hailed as one of Motorola's competitive advantages—its heavy reliance on teams and group sectors as an organizing device—is now seen by many as a negative. The original idea was to create tribes that would compete internally for funding and support from headquarters. This tribal approach would weed out weak ideas and identify the strongest products. Critics now blame the "warring tribes" for much of Motorola's problems. It has impeded the company's ability to work with outside partners to provide critical components that the company is unable to produce internally as well as creating internal conflicts. In one memorable incident, top managers visiting Hungary were shaken when a telecommunications minister flung Motorola business cards at them from a dozen different Motorola divisions. "Which of these people am I supposed to talk to?" the minister demanded.

The company's current CEO, Christopher Galvin, took over in January 1997. The grandson of Motorola's founder, he follows in the footsteps of his father who led the company in its glory days. Galvin, 48, knows the business. He grew up in it. But some wonder if he's up to the job. He'll need to replace many senior managers in the near future. Two-thirds of the company's top managers are currently 57 or older. Some critics suggest that Galvin may be too nice to run a company in crisis. For instance, he shows no willingness to hold his executives accountable. He recently announced an "amnesty" for "past mistakes and judgments so we can move forward." Still others criticize Galvin for his willingness to think big. He seems open to practically anything. He regularly holds executive meetings in which he and others brainstorm about the future. He talks, for instance, about going after markets for chip implants for human ears that could be hooked up to cell-phone networks and developing semiconductors that could be placed in trees to help timber firms monitor growth. Acknowledging that such ideas may sound silly, he points out that the company's early investment in transistors was also considered a long shot. "I don't know what the next business will be in 2003," he adds.

Questions

1. Is Motorola's problem one of poor leadership or inadequate structural design? Explain.

2. Analyze this case from a conflict-management perspective.

3. If you were a consultant advising Galvin, what would you suggest?

Source: Q. Hardy, "Motorola, Broadsided by the Digital Era, Struggles for a Footing," *Wall Street Journal*, April 22, 1998, p. A1; and W. J. Holstein, "A Motorola Coaster," *U.S. News & World Report*, June 21, 1999, pp. 42–44.

Video Case | **Urocor**

SMALL BUSINESS 2000

One way to learn something about a company is to look at its organizational chart. From an organizational chart, we can learn something about a company's size (by considering the number of people it employees), how it organizes its staff, how many locations it has, how it is structured, and how it divides the work that must get done. This may sound like a lot of information, but it is only the start of understanding how a company is organized. Another thing you might do is look at organizational charts for the same company that are a few years apart. Why would you want to do this? It might tell you something about how the company has changed, at least in the way it is organized. In turn, this might give you some hints about what is important to the firm you are studying.

Analyzing organizational charts is useful, but we have more work to do. We need to understand more about the options that are considered and the decisions that are made that result in the organizations that we observe. Bill Hagstrom, the CEO and president of Urocor, talks with us about how he helped to transform an R&D venture with a good product, but no market, into a 200–employee venture that has annual sales in excess of $25 million. Hagstrom discusses many aspects of the growth of Urocor, but he focuses on the importance of how firms organize and how sensitive people within an organization are to its growth, change, and development. This is likely to be particularly important to an early stage venture such as Urocor but can be equally important to an older, more established company, too. Think about how some large companies have had to reinvest themselves to adapt to major shifts in their operating environments.

Fortunately for us, Hagstrom lets us hear from some other key managers in his organization. Thus, we not only get Hagstrom's take on the organization, we find out what others value as well. As you watch this segment, think about what Hagstrom and his staff are telling us about the importance of planning, adaptation, synergy, and responsibility. You might also think about what Hagstrom has learned over the last five years and what he might be thinking about how Urocor should be organized for the next five years.

Questions

1. Bill Hagstrom took over a company of 12 and over the last five years has seen it turn into a $25 million operation with over 200 employees. Although success did not happen overnight, it did happen quickly. What kind of issues do you think Hagstrom might have experienced in building a staff that quickly?

2. What factors do you think best explain Urocor's current structure?

3. It seems like Urocor has carved out a niche for itself in a very specialized area of medical services. It is possible though that Urocor may want to grow into other areas. How might alternative structures be useful to Urocor if it decides to expand its operation?

End Notes

1. See, for instance, R. L. Daft, *Organization Theory and Design*, 6th ed. (Cincinnati, OH: Thomsen, 1998).
2. J. B. Treece, "Breaking the Chains of Command," *Business Week/The Information Revolution 1994*, p. 112.
3. See, for instance, L. Urwick, *The Elements of Administration* (New York: Harper & Row, 1944), pp. 52–53.
4. J. R. Brandt, "Middle Management: Where the Action Will Be," *Industry Week*, May 2, 1994, p. 31.
5. A. Ross, "BMO's Big Bang," *Canadian Business*, January 1994, pp. 58–63.
6. J. B. Levine, "For IBM Europe, 'This Is the Year of Truth,'" *Business Week*, April 19, 1993, p. 45.
7. H. Mintzberg, *Structure in Fives: Designing Effective Organizations* (Upper Saddle River, NJ: Prentice Hall, 1983), p. 157.
8. J. H. Sheridan, "Tale of a 'Maverick,'" *Industry Week*, June 8, 1998, pp. 22–28.
9. K. Knight, "Matrix Organization: A Review," *Journal of Management Studies*, May 1976, pp. 111–30; L. R. Burns and D. R. Wholey, "Adoption and Abandonment of Matrix Management Programs: Effects of Organizational Characteristics and Interorganizational Networks," *Academy of Management Journal*, February 1993, pp. 106–38; and R. E. Anderson, "Matrix Redux," *Business Horizons*, November–December 1994, pp. 6–10.
10. See, for instance, S. M. Davis and P. R. Lawrence, "Problems of Matrix Organization," *Harvard Business Review*, May–June 1978, pp. 131–42.
11. S. A. Mohrman, S. G. Cohen, and A. M. Mohrman Jr., *Designing Team-Based Organizations* (San Francisco: Jossey-Bass, 1995).
12. M. Kaeter, "The Age of the Specialized Generalist," *Training*, December 1993, pp. 48–53.
13. L. Brokaw, "Thinking Flat," *INC.*, October 1993, p. 88.
14. C. Fishman, "Whole Foods Is All Teams," *Fast Company*, Greatest Hits, vol. 1, 1997, pp. 102–13.
15. See, for instance, E. A. Gargan, "'Virtual' Companies Leave the Manufacturing to Others," *New York Times*, July 17, 1994, p. F5; D. W. Cravens, S. H. Shipp, and K. S. Cravens, "Reforming the Traditional Organization: The Mandate for Developing Networks," *Business Horizons*, July–August 1994, pp. 19–27; R. E. Miles and C. C. Snow, "The New Network Firm: A Spherical Structure Built on Human Investment Philosophy," *Organizational Dynamics*, Spring 1995, pp. 5–18; G. G. Dess, A. M. A. Rasheed, K. J. McLaughlin, and R. L. Priem, "The New Corporate Architecture," *Academy of Management Executive*, August 1995, pp. 7–20; D. Morse, "Where's the Company?" *Wall Street Journal*, May 21, 1998, p. R19; and G. Hamel and J. Sampler, "The e-Corporation," *Fortune*, December 7, 1998, pp. 80–92.
16. J. Bates, "Making Movies and Moving On," *Los Angeles Times*, January 19, 1998, p. A1.
17. "GE: Just Your Average Everyday $60 Billion Family Grocery Store," *Industry Week*, May 2, 1994, pp. 13–18.
18. H. C. Lucas Jr., *The T-Form Organization: Using Technology to Design Organizations for the 21st Century* (San Francisco: Jossey-Bass, 1996).
19. This section is based on L. Grant, "The Management Model That Jack Built," *Los Angeles Times Magazine*, May 9, 1993, pp. 20–22; P. LaBarre, "The Seamless Enterprise," *Industry Week*, June 19, 1995, pp. 22–34; D. D. Davis, "Form, Function and Strategy in Boundaryless Organizations," in A. Howard (ed.), *The Changing Nature of Work* (San Francisco: Jossey-Bass, 1995), pp. 112–38; R. Ashkenas, D. Ulrich, T. Jick, and S. Kerr, *The Boundaryless Organization: Breaking the Chains of Organizational Structure* (San Francisco: Jossey-Bass, 1995); and P. Roberts, "We Are One

Company, No Matter Where We Are. Time and Space Are Irrelevant," *Fast Company*, April/May 1998, pp. 122–28.

20. See J. Lipnack and J. Stamps, *The TeamNet Factor* (Essex Junction, VT: Oliver Wight Publications, 1993); J. Fulk and G. DeSanctis, "Electronic Communication and Changing Organizational Forms," *Organization Science*, July–August 1995, pp. 337–49; and A. Cortese, "Here Comes the Intranet," *Business Week*, February 26, 1996, pp. 76–84.

21. T. Burns and G. M. Stalker, *The Management of Innovation* (London: Tavistock, 1961); and J. A. Courtright, G. T. Fairhurst, and L. E. Rogers, "Interaction Patterns in Organic and Mechanistic Systems," *Academy of Management Journal*, December 1989, pp. 773–802.

22. This analysis is referred to as a contingency approach to organization design. See, for instance, J. M. Pennings, "Structural Contingency Theory: A Reappraisal," in B. M. Staw and L. L. Cummings (eds.), *Research in Organizational Behavior*, vol. 14 (Greenwich, CT: JAI Press, 1992), pp. 267–309.

23. The strategy–structure thesis was originally proposed in A. D. Chandler, Jr., *Strategy and Structure: Chapters in the History of the Industrial Enterprise* (Cambridge, MA: MIT Press, 1962). For an updated analysis, see T. L. Amburgey and T. Dacin, "As the Left Foot Follows the Right? The Dynamics of Strategic and Structural Change," *Academy of Management Journal*, December 1994, pp. 1427–52.

24. See R. E. Miles and C. C. Snow, *Organizational Strategy, Structure, and Process* (New York: McGraw-Hill, 1978); D. Miller, "The Structural and Environmental Correlates of Business Strategy," *Strategic Management Journal*, January–February 1987, pp. 55–76; and D. C. Galunic and K. M. Eisenhardt, "Renewing the Strategy-Structure-Performance Paradigm," in B. M. Staw and L. L. Cummings (eds.), *Research in Organizational Behavior*, vol. 16 (Greenwich, CT: JAI Press, 1994), pp. 215–55.

25. See, for instance, P. M. Blau and R. A. Schoenherr, *The Structure of Organizations* (New York: Basic Books, 1971); D. S. Pugh, "The Aston Program of Research: Retrospect and Prospect," in A. H. Van de Ven and W. F. Joyce (eds.), *Perspectives on Organization Design and Behavior* (New York: John Wiley, 1981), pp. 135–66; R. Z. Gooding and J. A. Wagner III, "A Meta-Analytic Review of the Relationship Between Size and Performance: The Productivity and Efficiency of Organizations and Their Subunits," *Administrative Science Quarterly*, December 1985, pp. 462–81; and A. C. Bluedorn, "Pilgrim's Progress: Trends and Convergence in Research on Organizational Size and Environments," *Journal of Management*, Summer 1993, pp. 163–92.

26. See J. Woodward, *Industrial Organization: Theory and Practice* (London: Oxford University Press, 1965); C. Perrow, "A Framework for the Comparative Analysis of Organizations," *American Sociological Review*, April 1967, pp. 194–208; J. D. Thompson, *Organizations in Action* (New York: McGraw-Hill, 1967); J. Hage and M. Aiken, "Routine Technology, Social Structure, and Organizational Goals," *Administrative Science Quarterly*, September 1969, pp. 366–77; and C. C. Miller, W. H. Glick, Y. Wang, and G. P. Huber, "Understanding Technology–Structure Relationships: Theory Development and Meta-Analytic Theory Testing," *Academy of Management Journal*, June 1991, pp. 370–99.

27. See F. E. Emery and E. Trist, "The Causal Texture of Organizational Environments," *Human Relations*, February 1965, pp. 21–32; P. Lawrence and J. W. Lorsch, *Organization and Environment: Managing Differentiation and Integration* (Boston: Harvard Business School, Division of Research, 1967); M. Yasai-Ardekani, "Structural Adaptations to Environments," *Academy of Management Review*, January 1986, pp. 9–21; and A. C. Bluedorn, "Pilgrim's Progress."

28. G. G. Dess and D. W. Beard, "Dimensions of Organizational Task Environments," *Administrative Science Quarterly*, March 1984, pp. 52–73; E. A. Gerloff, N. K. Muir, and W. D. Bodensteiner, "Three Components of Perceived Environmental Uncertainty: An Exploratory Analysis of the Effects of Aggregation," *Journal of Management*, December 1991, pp. 749–68; and O. Shenkar, N. Aranya, and T. Almor, "Construct Dimensions in the Contingency Model: An Analysis Comparing Metric and Non-Metric Multivariate Instruments," *Human Relations*, May 1995, pp. 559–80.

29. See S. P. Robbins, *Organization Theory: Structure, Design, and Applications*, 3rd ed. (Upper Saddle River, NJ: Prentice Hall, 1990), pp. 320–25; and B. Harrison, *Lean and Mean: The Changing Landscape of Corporate Power in the Age of Flexibility* (New York: Basic Books, 1994).

30. See, for instance, L. W. Porter and E. E. Lawler III, "Properties of Organization Structure in Relation to Job Attitudes and Job Behavior," *Psychological Bulletin*, July 1965, pp. 23–51; L. R. James and A. P. Jones, "Organization Structure: A Review of Structural Dimensions and Their Conceptual Relationships with Individual Attitudes and Behavior," *Organizational Behavior and Human Performance*, June 1976, pp. 74–113; D. R. Dalton, W. D. Todor, M. J. Spendolini, G. J. Fielding, and L. W. Porter, "Organization Structure and Performance: A Critical Review," *Academy of Management Review*, January 1980, pp. 49–64; W. Snizek and J. H. Bullard, "Perception of Bureaucracy and Changing Job Satisfaction: A Longitudinal Analysis," *Organizational Behavior and Human Performance*, October 1983, pp. 275–87; and D. B. Turban and T. L. Keon, "Organizational Attractiveness: An Interactionist Perspective," *Journal of Applied Psychology*, April 1994, pp. 184–93.

31. See, for example, P. R. Harris and R. T. Moran, *Managing Cultural Differences*, 4th ed. (Houston: Gulf Publishing, 1996).

32. See, for instance, B. Schneider, "The People Make the Place," *Personnel Psychology*, Autumn 1987, pp. 437–53; B. Schneider, H. W. Goldstein, and D. B. Smith, "The ASA Framework: An Update," *Personnel Psychology*, Winter 1995, pp. 747–73; and J. Schaubroeck, D. C. Ganster, and J. R. Jones, "Organization and Occupation Influences in the Attraction-Selection-Attrition Process," *Journal of Applied Psychology*, December 1998, pp. 869–91.

33. G. Bylinsky, "How Companies Spy on Employees," *Fortune*, November 4, 1991, pp. 131–40; D. Warner, "The Move to Curb Worker Monitoring," *Nation's Business*, December 1993, pp. 37–38; M. Picard, "Working Under an Electronic Thumb," *Training*, February 1994, pp. 47–51; J. M. Stanton and J. L. Barnes-Farrell, "Effects of Electronic Performance Monitoring on Personal Control, Task Satisfaction, and Task Performance," *Journal of Applied Psychology*, December 1996, pp. 738–45; and B. Pappas, "They Spy," *Forbes*, February 8, 1999, p. 47.

part four

THE
ORGANIZATION
SYSTEM

he chairman of Alcoa, Paul H. O'Neill, believes strongly that architecture influences behavior.[1] So much so that he personally helped design the company's new $67 million Pittsburgh headquarters to ensure it would convey to both employees and visitors that Alcoa was an open, responsive, and flexible company.

The new six-floor building replaces a 31-story office tower just across the Allegheny River. Built in the shape of a wave and made of aluminum and clear glass, the new headquarters snakes along the river, mimicking its form. The real change, however, is on the inside, where approximately 400 people work. "I've been collecting ideas for 40 years about people and what causes them to relate to each other and work together well." One of his most basic concerns was how traditional executive offices could intimidate people and limit communication. He was insistent that the offices in Alcoa's new headquarters would not be threatening and would bring people together.

To facilitate openness, O'Neill decided that there would be no hallways or private offices. He had kitchens installed on every floor because food draws people together. He wanted flexibility, so he asked for office configurations that could be changed in a day. He wanted inclusion, so he requested conference rooms of glass. And he insisted on escalators, because he wanted to make people visible and make it easier to interact. Most importantly, O'Neill was determined to break down traditional hierarchical barriers. There would be no grand mahogany suites for executives. So just like everyone else in the building, O'Neill and all his senior executives work in cubicles that measure 9 feet by 9 feet (see photo where O'Neill is at work in his "office").

Work Design and Technology

Not everyone is enthusiastic about the new office layout. Some executives complain about the loss of status. Others dislike the lack of privacy. Overall, however, O'Neill believes the new building is doing what he hoped. "I see more people now by accident than I ever did on purpose because it's a natural consequence of the way we have organized the flow." Employees, too, comment positively on how much more often they interact with colleagues and how much friendlier people are. The building's architect compares the new design to street life in a vital city. "It gives you a sense that you're in a place with dynamism. In traditional architecture, it would be an administrative assistant phoning another administrative assistant so people could get together. Now its' simply, "Do you have a moment?" Admitting that measuring the effectiveness of the new office design is difficult, O'Neill says the proof is in the profits. "We're beating the liver out of the competition."

Alcoa is among a growing number of companies that are redesigning their work spaces in order to improve collaboration and communication. In this chapter, we discuss work space design in detail and explain how it can affect employee work behavior. We also present several frameworks for analyzing jobs, demonstrate how technology is changing organizations and the jobs that people do, and conclude by showing how management can redesign jobs and work schedules in ways that can increase employee productivity and satisfaction.

CONCEPTUAL FRAMEWORKS FOR ANALYZING WORK TASKS

"Every day was the same thing," Frank Greer began. "Put the right passenger seat into Jeeps as they came down the assembly line, pop in four bolts locking the seat frame to the car body, then tighten

AFTER READING THIS CHAPTER, YOU SHOULD BE ABLE TO

1. Explain the job characteristics model

2. Contrast the social information processing model to the job characteristics model

3. Describe the role of the PDCA cycle in continuous improvement

4. Contrast reengineering and TQM

5. Describe the implications of flexible manufacturing systems on people who work within them

6. Identify who is affected by worker obsolescence

7. Explain how work space design might influence employee behavior

8. Describe how a job can be enriched

9. Contrast the benefits and drawbacks to telecommuting from the employee's point of view

the bolts with my electric wrench. Thirty cars and 120 bolts an hour, eight hours a day. I didn't care that they were paying me $22 an hour, I was going crazy. I did it for almost a year and a half. Finally, I just said to my wife that this isn't going to be the way I'm going to spend the rest of my life. My brain was turning to Jell-O on that job. So I quit. Now I work in a print shop and I make less than $15 an hour. But let me tell you, the work I do is really interesting. It challenges me! I look forward every morning to going to work again."

Frank Greer is acknowledging two facts we all know: (1) Jobs are different and (2) some are more interesting and challenging than others. These facts have not gone unnoticed by OB researchers. They have responded by developing a number of **task characteristics theories** that seek to identify task characteristics of jobs, how these characteristics are combined to form different jobs, and the relationship of these task characteristics to employee motivation, satisfaction, and performance.

There are at least seven different task characteristics theories.[2] Fortunately, there is a significant amount of overlap between them.[3] For instance, Herzberg's two-factor theory and the research on the achievement need (both discussed in Chapter 6) are essentially task characteristics theories. You'll remember that Herzberg argued that jobs that provided opportunities for achievement, recognition, responsibility, and the like would increase employee satisfaction. Similarly, McClelland demonstrated that high achievers performed best in jobs that offered personal responsibility, feedback, and moderate risks.

In this section, we review the three most important task characteristics theories—requisite task attributes theory, the job characteristics model, and the social information processing model.

REQUISITE TASK ATTRIBUTES THEORY

The task characteristics approach began with the pioneering work of Turner and Lawrence in the mid-1960s.[4] They developed a research study to assess the effect of different kinds of jobs on employee satisfaction and absenteeism. They predicted that employees would prefer jobs that were complex and challenging; that is, such jobs would increase satisfaction and result in lower absence rates. They defined job complexity in terms of six task characteristics: (1) variety; (2) autonomy; (3) responsibility; (4) knowledge and skill; (5) required social interaction; and (6) optional social interaction. The higher a job scored on these characteristics, according to Turner and Lawrence, the more complex it was.

Their findings confirmed their absenteeism prediction. Employees in high-complexity tasks had better attendance records. But they found no general correlation between task complexity and satisfaction—until they broke their data down by the background of employees. When individual differences in the form of urban-versus-rural background were taken into account, employees from urban settings were shown to be more satisfied with low-complexity jobs. Employees with rural backgrounds reported higher satisfaction in high-complexity jobs. Turner and Lawrence concluded that workers in larger communities had a variety of nonwork interests and, thus, were less involved and motivated by their work. In contrast, workers from smaller towns had fewer nonwork interests and were more receptive to the complex tasks of their jobs.

Turner and Lawrence's requisite task attributes theory was important for at least three reasons. First, they demonstrated that employees did respond differently to different types of jobs. Second, they provided a preliminary set of task attributes by which jobs could be assessed. And third, they focused attention on the need to consider the influence of individual differences on employees' reaction to jobs.

---

task characteristic theories

Seek to identify task characteristics of jobs, how these characteristics are combined to form different jobs, and their relationship to employee motivation, satisfaction, and performance.

THE JOB CHARACTERISTICS MODEL

Turner and Lawrence's requisite task attributes theory laid the foundation for what is today the dominant framework for defining task characteristics and understanding their relationship to employee motivation, performance, and satisfaction. That is Hackman and Oldham's **job characteristics model** (JCM).[5]

According to the JCM, any job can be described in terms of five core job dimensions, defined as follows:

1. **Skill variety**: The degree to which the job requires a variety of different activities so the worker can use a number of different skills and talent
2. **Task identity**: The degree to which the job requires completion of a whole and identifiable piece of work
3. **Task significance**: The degree to which the job has a substantial impact on the lives or work of other people
4. **Autonomy**: The degree to which the job provides substantial freedom, independence, and discretion to the individual in scheduling the work and in determining the procedures to be used in carrying it out
5. **Feedback**: The degree to which carrying out the work activities required by the job results in the individual obtaining direct and clear information about the effectiveness of his or her performance

Exhibit 15-1 offers examples of job activities that rate high and low for each characteristic.

job characteristics model

Identifies five job characteristics and their relationship to personal and work outcomes.

skill variety

The degree to which the job requires a variety of different activities.

task identity

The degree to which the job requires completion of a whole and identifiable piece of work.

task significance

The degree to which the job has a substantial impact on the lives or work of other people.

Examples of High and Low Job Characteristics

EXHIBIT 15-1

Skill Variety

| High variety | The owner-operator of a garage who does electrical repairs, rebuilds engines, does body work, and interacts with customers |
| Low variety | A body shop worker who sprays paint eight hours a day |

Task Identity

| High identity | A cabinetmaker who designs a piece of furniture, selects the wood, builds the object, and finishes it to perfection |
| Low identity | A worker in a furniture factory who operates a lathe solely to make table legs |

Task Significance

| High significance | Nursing the sick in a hospital intensive care unit |
| Low significance | Sweeping hospital floors |

Autonomy

| High autonomy | A telephone installer who schedules his or her own work for the day, makes visits without supervision, and decides on the most effective techniques for a particular installation |
| Low autonomy | A telephone operator who must handle calls as they come according to a routine, highly specified procedure |

Feedback

| High feedback | An electronics factory worker who assembles a radio and then tests it to determine if it operates properly |
| Low feedback | An electronics factory worker who assembles a radio and then routes it to a quality control inspector who tests it for proper operation and makes needed adjustments |

Source: Adapted from G. Johns, *Organizational Behavior: Understanding and Managing Life at Work*, 4th ed. Copyright © 1996 by HarperCollins College Publishers. Reprinted by permission of Addison-Wesley Educational Publishers, Inc.

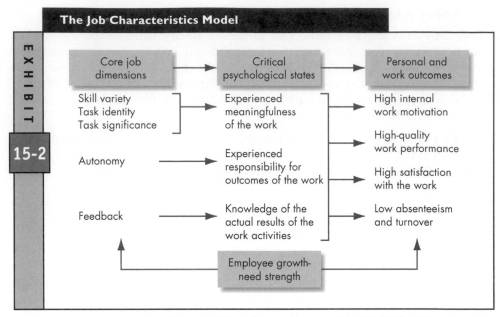

The Job Characteristics Model

EXHIBIT 15-2

| Core job dimensions | Critical psychological states | Personal and work outcomes |

Skill variety
Task identity
Task significance → Experienced meaningfulness of the work

Autonomy → Experienced responsibility for outcomes of the work

Feedback → Knowledge of the actual results of the work activities

High internal work motivation

High-quality work performance

High satisfaction with the work

Low absenteeism and turnover

Employee growth-need strength

Source: J. R. Hackman and G. R. Oldham, *Work Design* (excerpted from pages 78–80) © 1980 by Addison-Wesley Publishing Co., Inc. Reprinted by permission of Addison-Wesley Longman Inc.

autonomy

The degree to which the job provides substantial freedom and discretion to the individual in scheduling the work and in determining the procedures to be used in carrying it out.

feedback

The degree to which carrying out the work activities required by a job results in the individual obtaining direct and clear information about the effectiveness of his or her performance.

motivating potential score

A predictive index suggesting the motivating potential in a job.

Exhibit 15-2 presents the model. Notice how the first three dimensions—skill variety, task identity, and task significance—combine to create meaningful work. That is, if these three characteristics exist in a job, we can predict that the incumbent will view the job as being important, valuable, and worthwhile. Notice, too, that jobs that possess autonomy give job incumbents a feeling of personal responsibility for the results and that, if a job provides feedback, employees will know how effectively they are performing. From a motivational standpoint, the model says that internal rewards are obtained by individuals when they learn (knowledge of results) that they personally (experienced responsibility) have performed well on a task that they care about (experienced meaningfulness).[6] The more that these three psychological states are present, the greater will be employees' motivation, performance, and satisfaction, and the lower their absenteeism and likelihood of leaving the organization. As Exhibit 15-2 shows, the links between the job dimensions and the outcomes are moderated or adjusted by the strength of the individual's growth need, that is, by the employee's desire for self-esteem and self-actualization. This means that individuals with a high growth need are more likely to experience the psychological states when their jobs are enriched than are their counterparts with a low growth need. Moreover, they will respond more positively to the psychological states when they are present than will individuals with a low growth need.

The core dimensions can be combined into a single predictive index, called the **motivating potential score** (MPS). Its computation is shown in Exhibit 15-3.

Jobs that are high on motivating potential must be high on at least one of the three factors that lead to experienced meaningfulness, and they must be high on both autonomy and feedback. If jobs score high on motivating potential, the model predicts that motivation, performance, and satisfaction will be positively affected, while the likelihood of absence and turnover will be lessened.

The job characteristics model has been well researched. Most of the evidence supports the general framework of the theory—that is, there is a multiple set of

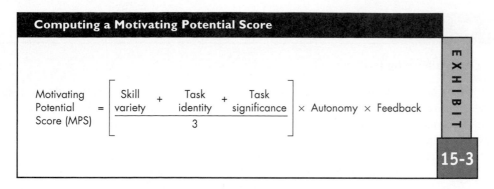

Computing a Motivating Potential Score

$$\text{Motivating Potential Score (MPS)} = \left[\frac{\text{Skill variety} + \text{Task identity} + \text{Task significance}}{3} \right] \times \text{Autonomy} \times \text{Feedback}$$

EXHIBIT

15-3

job characteristics and these characteristics impact behavioral outcomes.[7] But there is still considerable debate around the five specific core dimensions in the JCM, the multiplicative properties of the MPS, and the validity of growth-need strength as a moderating variable.

There is some question as to whether or not task identity adds to the model's predictive ability,[8] and there is evidence suggesting that skill variety may be redundant with autonomy.[9] Furthermore, a number of studies have found that by adding all the variables in the MPS, rather than adding some and multiplying by others, the MPS becomes a better predictor of work outcomes.[10] Finally, the strength of an individual's growth needs as a meaningful moderating variable has been called into question.[11] Other variables, such as the presence or absence of social cues, perceived equity with comparison groups, and propensity to assimilate work experience,[12] may be more valid in moderating the job characteristics–outcome relationship. Given the current state of research on moderating variables, one should be cautious in unequivocally accepting growth-need strength as originally included in the JCM.

Where does this leave us? Given the current state of evidence, we can make the following statements with relative confidence: (1) People who work on jobs with high-core job dimensions are generally more motivated, satisfied, and productive than are those who do not. (2) Job dimensions operate through the psychological states in influencing personal and work outcome variables rather than influencing them directly.[13]

SOCIAL INFORMATION PROCESSING MODEL

At the beginning of this section on task characteristics theories, do you remember Frank Greer complaining about his former job on the Jeep assembly line? Would it surprise you to know that one of Frank's best friends, Russ Wright, is still working at Jeep, doing the same job that Frank did, and that Russ thinks his job is perfectly fine? Probably not! Why? Because, consistent with our discussion of perception in Chapter 5, we recognize that people can look at the same job and evaluate it differently. The fact that people respond to their jobs as they perceive them rather than to the objective jobs themselves is the central thesis in our third task characteristics theory. It's called the **social information processing (SIP) model**.[14]

The SIP model argues that employees adopt attitudes and behaviors in response to the social cues provided by others with whom they have contact. These others can be co-workers, supervisors, friends, family members, or customers. For instance, Gary Ling got a summer job working in a British Columbia sawmill. Since jobs were scarce and this one paid particularly well, Gary arrived on his first day of work highly motivated. Two weeks later, however, his motivation was

social information processing (SIP) model

Employees adopt attitudes and behaviors in response to the social cues provided by others with whom they have contact.

"Everyone Wants a Challenging Job"

This statement is false. In spite of all the attention focused by the media, academicians, and social scientists on human potential and the needs of individuals, there is no evidence to support that the vast majority of workers want challenging jobs.[15] Some individuals prefer highly complex and challenging jobs; others prosper in simple, routinized work.

The individual-difference variable that seems to gain the greatest support for explaining who prefers a challenging job and who doesn't is the strength of an individual's higher-order needs.[16] Individuals with high growth needs are more responsive to challenging work. What percentage of rank-and-file workers actually desire higher-order need satisfactions and will respond positively to challenging jobs? No current data are available, but a study from the 1970s estimated the figure at about 15 percent.[17] Even after adjusting for changing work attitudes and the

growth in white-collar jobs, it seems unlikely that the number today exceeds 40 percent.

The strongest voice advocating challenging jobs has *not* been workers—it's been professors, social science researchers, and media personnel. Professors, researchers, and journalists undoubtedly made their career choices, to some degree, because they wanted jobs that gave them autonomy, identity, and challenge. That, of course, is their choice. But for them to project their needs onto the workforce in general is presumptuous.

Not every employee is looking for a challenging job. Many workers meet their higher-order needs *off* the job. There are 168 hours in every individual's week. Work rarely consumes more than 30 percent of this time. That leaves considerable opportunity, even for individuals with strong growth needs, to find higher-order need satisfaction outside the workplace.

quite low. What happened was that his co-workers consistently bad-mouthed their jobs. They said the work was boring, that having to clock in and out proved management didn't trust them, and that supervisors never listened to their opinions. The objective characteristics of Gary's job had not changed in the two-week period; rather, Gary had reconstructed reality based on messages he had received from others.

A number of studies generally confirm the validity of the SIP model.[18] For instance, it has been shown that employee motivation and satisfaction can be manipulated by such subtle actions as a co-worker or boss commenting on the existence or absence of job features such as difficulty, challenge, and autonomy. So managers should give as much (or more) attention to employees' perceptions of their jobs as to the actual characteristics of those jobs. They might spend more time telling employees how interesting and important their jobs are. And managers should also not be surprised that newly hired employees and people transferred or promoted to a new position are more likely to be receptive to social information than are those with greater seniority.

TECHNOLOGY AND NEW WORK DESIGNS

We introduced the term *technology* in the previous chapter's discussion of why structures differ. We said it was how an organization transfers its inputs into outputs. In recent years, the term has become widely used by economists, managers, consultants, and business analysts to describe machinery and equipment that utilize sophisticated electronics and computers to produce those outputs.

The common theme among new technologies in the workplace is that they substitute machinery for human labor in transforming inputs into outputs. This substitution of capital for labor has been going on essentially nonstop since the

THE WALL STREET JOURNAL

COCHRON!

"Cool! A keyboard that writes without a printer."

Source: *Wall Street Journal*, October 11, 1995, With permission from Cartoon Features Syndicate.

industrial revolution began in the mid-1800s. For instance, the introduction of electricity allowed textile factories to introduce mechanical looms that could produce cloth far faster and more cheaply than was previously possible when the looms were powered by individuals. But it's been the computerization of equipment and machinery in the last quarter-century that has been the prime mover in reshaping the contemporary workplace.

This book is concerned with the behavior of people at work. No coverage of this topic today would be complete without discussing how recent advances in technology are changing the workplace and affecting the work lives of employees. In this section, we'll look at four specific issues related to technology and work. These are TQM and continuous improvement processes, reengineering, flexible manufacturing systems, and worker obsolescence.

CONTINUOUS IMPROVEMENT PROCESSES

In Chapter 1, we described total quality management (TQM) as a philosophy of management that's driven by the constant attainment of customer satisfaction through the continuous improvement of all organizational processes. Managers in many organizations, especially in North America, have been criticized for accepting a level of performance that is below perfection. TQM, however, argues that *good* isn't *good enough!* To dramatize this point, it's easy to assume that 99.9 percent error-free performance represents the highest standards of excellence. Yet it doesn't look so impressive when you recognize that this standard would result in the U.S. Post Office losing 2,000 pieces of mail per hour, or U.S. doctors performing 500 incorrect surgical operations per week, or two plane crashes per day at O'Hare Airport in Chicago![19]

TQM programs seek to achieve continuous process improvements so that variability is constantly reduced. When you eliminate variations, you increase the uniformity of the product or service. This, in turn, results in lower costs and

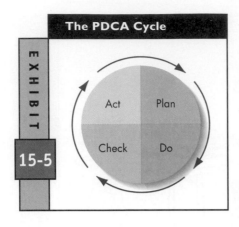

The PDCA Cycle

EXHIBIT

15-5

Act | Plan
Check | Do

higher quality. For instance, Advanced Filtration Systems Inc., of Champaign, Illinois, recently cut the number of product defects—as determined by a customer quality audit—from 26.5 per 1,000 units to zero over four years. And that occurred during a period when monthly unit production tripled and the number of workers declined by 20 percent.

Continuous improvement runs counter to the more historical American management approach of seeing work projects as being linear—with a beginning and an end. For example, American managers traditionally looked at cost cutting as a short-term project. They set a goal of cutting costs by 20 percent, achieved it, and then said: "Whew! Our cost cutting is over." The Japanese, on the other hand, have regarded cost control as something that never ends. The search for continual improvement creates a race without a finish line.

The search for never-ending improvement requires a circular approach rather than a linear one. This is illustrated in the Plan-Do-Check-Act (PDCA) cycle shown in Exhibit 15-5.[20] Management plans a change, does it, checks the results and, depending on the outcome, acts to standardize the change or begin the cycle of improvement again with new information. This cycle treats all organizational processes as being in a constant state of improvement.

As literally tens of thousands of organizations introduce TQM and continuous process improvement, what does it mean for employees and their jobs? It means they're no longer able to rest on their previous accomplishments and successes. So, for some people, they may experience increased stress from a work climate that no longer accepts complacency with the status quo. A race with no finish line means a race that's never over, which creates constant tension. While this tension may be positive for the organization (remember *functional conflict* from Chapter 13), the pressures from an unrelenting search for process improvements can create anxiety and stress in some employees. Probably the most significant implication for employees is that management will look to them as the prime source for improvement ideas. Employee involvement programs, therefore, are part and parcel of TQM. Empowered work teams who have hands-on involvement in process improvement, for instance, are widely used in those organizations that have introduced TQM.

REENGINEERING WORK PROCESSES

We also introduced reengineering in Chapter 1. We described it as considering how things would be done if you could start all over from scratch.

The term *reengineering* comes from the historical process of taking apart an electronics product and designing a better version. Michael Hammer coined the term for organizations. When he found companies using computers simply to automate outdated processes, rather than finding fundamentally better ways of doing things, he realized the same principles could be applied to business. So, as applied to organizations, reengineering means management should start with a clean sheet of paper—rethinking and redesigning those processes by which the organization creates value and does work, ridding itself of operations that have become antiquated in the computer age.[21]

Key Elements   Three key elements of reengineering are identifying an organization's distinctive competencies, assessing core processes, and reorganizing horizontally by process.

An organization's **distinctive competencies** define what it is that the organization is more superior at delivering than its competition. Examples might include superior store locations, a more efficient distribution system, higher-quality products, more knowledgeable sales personnel, or superior technical support. Dell Computer, for instance, differentiates itself from its competitors by emphasizing high-quality hardware, comprehensive service and technical support, and low prices. Why is identifying distinctive competencies so important? Because it guides decisions regarding what activities are crucial to the organization's success.

Management also needs to assess the core processes that clearly add value to the organization's distinctive competencies. These are the processes that transform materials, capital, information, and labor into products and services that the customer values. When the organization is viewed as a series of processes, ranging from strategic planning to after-sales customer support, management can determine to what degree each adds value. Not surprisingly, this **process value analysis** typically uncovers a whole lot of activities that add little or nothing of value and whose only justification is "we've always done it this way."

Reengineering requires management to reorganize around horizontal processes. This means cross-functional and self-managed teams. It means focusing on processes rather than functions. So, for instance, the vice president of marketing might become the "process owner of finding and keeping customers."[22] And it also means cutting out levels of middle management. As Hammer pointed out, "Managers are not value-added. A customer never buys a product because of the caliber of management. Management is, by definition, indirect. So if possible, less is better. One of the goals of reengineering is to minimize the necessary amount of management."[23]

One reengineering initiative at Goodyear Tire & Rubber focuses on the manufacturing process. A typical tire assembly line stretches about one-half mile and carries tires on hundreds of feet of conveyors that move products from one process to another. By installing an automated system, Goodyear expects to eliminate half the steps in the process, reduce factory floor space by 25 percent, and reduce labor costs by 35 percent. Goodyear plans to install the system at its 85 plants worldwide, including the plant shown here in Napinee, Ontario.

Reengineering vs. TQM   Is reengineering just another term for TQM? No! They do have some common characteristics.[24] They both, for instance, emphasize processes and satisfying the customer. After that, they diverge radically. This is evident in their goals and the means they use for achieving their goals.

TQM seeks incremental improvements, while reengineering looks for quantum leaps in performance. That is, the former is essentially about improving something that is basically okay; the latter is about taking something that is irrelevant, throwing it out, and starting over. And the means the two approaches use are totally different. TQM relies on bottom-up, participative decision making in both the planning of a TQM program and its execution. Reengineering, on the other hand, is initially driven by top management. When reengineering is complete, the workplace is largely self-managed. But getting there is a very autocratic, nondemocratic process. Reengineering's supporters argue that it has to be this way because the level of change that the process demands is highly threatening to people and they aren't likely to accept it voluntarily. When top management commits to reengineering, employees have no choice. As Hammer is fond of saying, "you either get on the train, or we'll run over you with the train."[25] Of course, autocratically imposed change is likely to face employee resistance. While there is no easy solution to

distinctive competencies

Defines what it is that the organization is more superior at delivering than its competition.

process value analysis

Determination to what degree each organizational process adds value to the organization's distinctive competencies.

the resistance that top-down change creates, some of the techniques presented in Chapter 18 in our discussion of overcoming resistance to change can be helpful.

Implications for Employees   Lots of people have lost, and will continue to lose, their jobs as a direct result of reengineering efforts. The specific number, however, is unclear. Undoubtedly much of the downsizing movement can be directly traced to reengineering efforts. But regardless of the number, the impact won't be uniform across the organization. Staff support jobs, especially middle managers, will be most vulnerable. So, too, will clerical jobs in service industries. Bank tellers' jobs, for example, are highly susceptible to elimination as their functions are replaced by ATMs and on-line banking.

Those employees that keep their jobs after reengineering will find that they aren't the same jobs any longer. These new jobs will typically require a wider range of skills, include more interaction with customers and suppliers, offer greater challenge, contain increased responsibilities, and provide higher pay. However, the three-to five-year period it takes to implement reengineering is usually tough on employees. They suffer from uncertainty and anxiety associated with taking on new tasks and having to discard long-established work practices and formal social networks.

FLEXIBLE MANUFACTURING SYSTEMS

When customers were willing to accept standardized products, fixed assembly lines made sense. But nowadays, flexible technologies are increasingly necessary to compete effectively.

flexible manufacturing system

Integration of computer-aided design, engineering, and manufacturing to produce low-volume products at mass-production costs.

The unique characteristic of **flexible manufacturing systems** is that by integrating computer-aided design, engineering, and manufacturing, they can produce low-volume products for customers at a cost comparable to what had been previously possible only through mass production.[26] Flexible manufacturing systems are, in effect, repealing the laws of economies of scale. Management no longer has to mass-produce thousands of identical products to achieve low per-unit production costs. With flexible manufacturing, when management wants to produce a new part, it doesn't change machines—it just changes the computer program. For instance, John Deere has a $1.5 billion automated factory that can turn out 10 basic tractor models with as many as 3,000 options without plant shutdowns for retooling. National Bicycle Industrial Co., which sells its bikes under the Panasonic brand, uses flexible manufacturing to produce any of 11,231,862 variations on 18 models of racing, road, and mountain bikes in 199 color patterns and an almost unlimited number of sizes. This allows Panasonic to provide almost customized bikes at mass-produced prices.[27]

What do flexible manufacturing systems mean for people who have to work within them? They require a different breed of industrial employee.[28] Workers in flexible manufacturing plants need more training and higher skills. This is because there are fewer employees, so each has to be able to do a greater variety of tasks. For instance, at a flexible Carrier plant in Arkansas, which makes compressors for air conditioners, all employees undergo six weeks of training before they start their jobs. This training includes learning to read blueprints, math such as fractions and metric calculations, statistical process-control methods, some computer skills, and solving the problems involved in dealing with fellow workers. In addition to higher skills, employees in flexible plants are typically organized into teams and given considerable decision-making discretion. Consistent with the objective of high flexibility, these plants tend to have organic structures. They decentralize authority into the hands of the operating teams.

WORKER OBSOLESCENCE

Changes in technology have cut the shelf life of most employees' skills. A factory worker or clerical employee in the 1950s could learn one job and be reasonably sure that his or her skills would be adequate to do that job for most of his or her work life. That certainly is no longer true. New technologies driven by computers, reengineering, TQM, and flexible manufacturing systems are changing the demands of jobs and the skills employees need to do them.

Repetitive tasks such as those traditionally performed on assembly lines and by low-skilled office clerks will continue to be automated. And a good number of jobs will be upgraded. For instance, as most managers and professionals take on the task of writing their own memos and reports using word processing software, the traditional secretary's job will be upgraded to become more of an administrative assistant. Those secretaries who aren't equipped to take on these expanded roles will be displaced.

Reengineering, as we previously noted, is producing significant increases in employee productivity. The redesign of work processes is achieving higher output with fewer workers. And these reengineered jobs require different skills. Employees who are computer illiterate, have poor interpersonal skills, or can't work autonomously will increasingly find themselves ill prepared for the demands of new technologies.

Keep in mind that the obsolescence phenomenon doesn't exclude managers. Those middle managers who merely acted as conduits in the chain of command between top management and the operating floor are being eliminated. And new skills—for example, coaching, negotiating, and building teams—are becoming absolute necessities for every manager.

Finally, software is changing the jobs of many professionals, including lawyers, doctors, accountants, financial planners, and librarians.[29] Software programs will allow laypeople to use specialized knowledge to solve routine problems themselves or opt for a software-armed paraprofessional. Particularly vulnerable are those professionals who do standardized jobs. A lot of legal work, for instance, consists of writing standard contracts and other routine activities. These tasks will be done inside law firms by computers and paralegals; they might even be done by clients themselves, using software designed to prepare wills, trusts, incorporations, and partnerships. Software packages, such as TurboTax, will continue to take a lot of work away from professional accountants. And hospitals are using software to help doctors make their diagnoses. Punch in a patient's age, sex, lab results, and symptoms; answer a set of structured questions; and a

Some jobs are becoming obsolete as professionals use technology to perform their own tasks. For example, Todd Bertsch (center), a floor broker on the New York Stock Exchange, uses his wireless hand-held computer to record and transmit securities transactions. In the past, Bertsch wrote details about his transactions on slips of paper and gave them to a "runner" who carried them to the trading booths. By using the wireless computer, Bertsch speeds up the process of buying and selling securities.

$995 program called Illiad will draw on its knowledge of nine subspecialties of internal medicine to diagnose the patient's problem. These examples demonstrate that even the knowledge of highly trained professionals can become obsolete. As the world changes, professionals will also need to change if they're to survive.

WORK SPACE DESIGN

As described at the opening of this chapter, Alcoa's CEO, Paul O'Neill, believes that physical work space influences employee behavior. And he acted on this belief by designing a new corporate headquarters that facilitated access and communication. Paul O'Neill and Alcoa aren't alone. Hundreds of companies—including Northern Telecom Ltd., Du Pont, Hewlett-Packard, 3Com, Sun Microsystems, Chiat/Day advertising, and the Greater Omaha Packing Company—have redesigned their buildings and workplaces with the intent of reshaping employee attitudes and behaviors.[30] In this section, we'll look specifically at how the amount of work space made available to employees, the arrangement or layout of that work space, and the degree of privacy it provides affect an employee's behavior.[31]

OB *in the News*

The Remaking of LLG

Lipschultz, Levin, and Gray (LLG) is a public accounting firm just outside Chicago. Started in 1947, the firm grew to a peak of 55 employees by the early 1990s. But to the disappointment of the firm's five partners, profitability was half of the industry norm. Part of the problem was that LLG followed the pattern of the big accounting firms. It had large plush offices, a pyramid hierarchy, and huge overhead. The place looked stuffy and conservative. And people responded by hiding away in their private offices and thinking like "bean counters." This was all about to change.

The firm's new managing partner, Steve Siegel, decided that the major problem at LLG was that the work space was limiting creativity and flexibility. His idea: Change the work space

and make it easier for people to communicate and work together, and good things would happen. He envisioned a firm that was smaller, more creative, offering clients extended services, and all within an environment that could attract the "best and brightest" job candidates. If open spaces could stimulate creativity in an ad agency, why not in an accounting firm?

After two years of preparation, LLG moved into its new facility in November 1997. Nearly 60 percent smaller than the previous space, it has no walls, cubicles, or offices. In their place is an open work environment, where people can all see each other and interact freely.

Today, LLG has 26 employees. It has recently added business development, Internet technology, financial, and recruiting consulting to its accounting, audit, and tax services. Profits are up solidly. And the firm is finding it's able to recruit candidates who never would have worked in the previous location. Says Siegel, "The old building was a huge impediment to sitting and meeting and talking about things. Just being next to each other and hearing what's going on, that's what allowed us to get those things going."

Source: N. K. Austin, "Tear Down the Walls," *INC.*, April 1999, pp. 66–76.

SIZE

Size is defined by the square feet per employee. Historically, the most important determinant of space provided to employees was status.[32] The higher an individual was in the organization's hierarchy, the larger office he or she typically got. That, however, no longer seems to be true. As organizations have sought to become more egalitarian, the trends have been toward reducing space dedicated to specific employees, lessening or eliminating space allocations based on hierarchical position, and making more space available for groups or teams to meet in.

It's been estimated that, over the past decade, the personal office space provided by organizations to administrative employees has shrunk 25 to 50 percent.[33] Part of this has been economically motivated. Space costs money and reducing space cuts costs. But a lot of this reduction can be traced to reengineering. As jobs have been redesigned and traditional hierarchies replaced with teamwork, the need for large offices has lessened.[34]

In the past, it was not unusual for organizations, especially large ones such as IBM and General Motors, to define square footage for each level in the hierarchy. Senior executives, for instance, may have been assigned 800 square feet plus 300 square feet for a private secretary's office. A section manager may have gotten 400 square feet, a unit manager 120, and supervisors only 80 square feet. Today, an increasing number of organizations are replacing closed offices with cubicles, making the cubicles constant in size, and acknowledging little or no differences due to managerial rank.[35]

When extra space is being allocated, rather than giving it to specific individuals, the trend today is toward setting it aside where people can meet and teams can work. These "public spaces" can be used for socializing, small group meetings, or as places where team members can work through problems.

ARRANGEMENT

While size measures the amount of space per employee, arrangement refers to the distance between people and facilities. As we'll show, the arrangement of one's workplace is important primarily because it significantly influences social interaction.

There is a sizeable amount of research that supports that you're more likely to interact with those individuals who are physically close.[36] An employee's work location, therefore, is likely to influence the information to which one is privy and one's inclusion or exclusion from organization events. Whether you are on a certain grapevine network or not, for instance, will be largely determined by where you are physically located in the organization.

One topic that has received a considerable amount of attention is furniture arrangements in traditional offices, specifically the placement of the desk and where the officeholder chooses to sit.[37] Unlike factory floors, individuals typically have some leeway in laying out their office furniture. And the arrangement of an office conveys nonverbal messages to visitors. For instance, a desk between two parties conveys formality and the authority of the officeholder, while setting chairs so individuals can sit at right angles to each other conveys a more natural and informal relationship.

PRIVACY

Privacy is in part a function of the amount of space per person and the arrangement of that space. But it also is influenced by walls, partitions, and other physical barriers. One of the most widespread work space design trends in recent years has been the phasing out of closed offices and replacing them with open office plans that have few, if any, walls or doors. Sometimes described as the cave versus cube debate, the former provides privacy while the latter facilitates open communication. It's estimated that 40 million Americans, or nearly 60 percent of the whole U.S. white-collar workforce, now work in cubes.[38]

Caves limit interaction. So organizations have sought to increase flexibility and employee collaboration by removing physical barriers such as high walls, closed offices, and doors. Yet, while the trend is clearly toward cubes, organizations are making exceptions for employees engaged in work that requires deep concentration.[39] Companies such as Microsoft, Apple Computer, and Adobe Systems, for example, continue to rely primarily on private offices for software programmers. People who write code need to cooperate with others at times, but theirs is essentially a lonely task requiring tremendous concentration. This is best achieved in a closed workplace, cut off from others.

A further extension of the open office concept is called **hoteling**.[40] Employees book reservations for space with the company concierge, get assigned a workplace, pull over a desk-on-wheels, plug their phone into a modem jack, and begin their work. The only space that employees can actually call their own is typically a bin or locker where they can stow their personal belongings. Employees "check out" each

Architects designed the new offices of Calyx & Corolla to satisfy the different needs of the firm's employees. Calyx & Corolla, which ships flowers directly from growers to customers, has two groups of employees: a marketing/executive group and an operating group. Marketers and executives have individual offices to accommodate their need for concentration, while the production team and call center staff work from cubicles, as shown here.

hoteling

Employees have no permanent work space; they are assigned space each day when they arrive and check out each day when they depart.

day when they depart. Used by organizations in management-consulting, financial, and high-tech sectors—by firms such as Andersen Consulting, KPMG Peat Marwick, and Cisco Systems—where employees spend a significant percentage of their work time outside the office or in team meetings, it provides maximum office space flexibility. However, hoteling has some serious downsides.[41] Employees often feel rootless and complain that hoteling restricts the informal socializing and learning that come from having a fixed workplace location.

What about individual differences? There is growing evidence that the desire for privacy is a strong one on the part of many people.[42] Yet the trend is clearly toward less privacy at the workplace. Further research is needed to determine whether or not organizational efforts to open work spaces and individual preferences for privacy are incompatible and result in lower employee performance and satisfaction.

WORK SPACE DESIGN AND PRODUCTIVITY

How does a redesigned work space positively affect employee productivity? Studies suggest that work space, in and of itself, doesn't have a substantial motivational impact on people.[43] Rather, it makes certain behaviors easier or harder to perform. In this way, employee effectiveness is enhanced or reduced. More specifically, evidence indicates that work space designs that increase employee access, comfort, and flexibility are likely to positively influence motivation and productivity.[44] For instance, Amoco Corp. in Denver reported a 25 percent decrease in product cycle time, a 75 percent decrease in formal meeting time, an 80 percent reduction in duplicated files, and a 44 percent reduction in overall space costs after offices were redesigned to facilitate teamwork.[45] Based on the evidence to date, we suggest an approach called "cognitive ergonomics," which means matching the office to the brain work.[46] Jobs that are complex and require high degrees of concentration are likely to be made more difficult by noise and constant interruptions. Such jobs are best done in closed offices. But most jobs don't require quiet and privacy. In fact, quite the contrary. Jobs today increasingly require regular interaction with others to achieve maximum productivity. This is probably best achieved in an open office setting.

WORK REDESIGN OPTIONS

What are some of the options managers have at their disposal if they want to redesign or change the makeup of employee jobs? The following discusses four options: job rotation, job enlargement, job enrichment, and team-based designs.

JOB ROTATION

If employees suffer from overroutinization of their work, one alternative is to use **job rotation** (or what many now call *cross-training*). When an activity is no longer challenging, the employee is rotated to another job, at the same level, that has similar skill requirements.[47]

G.S.I. Transcomm Data Systems Inc. in Pittsburgh uses job rotation to keep its staff of 110 people from getting bored.[48] Over one two-year period, nearly 20 percent of Transcomm's employees made lateral job switches. Management believes the job rotation program has been a major contributor to cutting employee turnover from 25 percent to less than 7 percent a year. Brazil's Semco SA makes extensive use of job rotation. "Practically no one," says Semco's president, "stays in the same position for more than two or three years. We try to motivate people to move their areas completely from time to time so they don't get stuck to the technical solutions, to ways of doing things in which they have become entrenched."[49] Mike Conway, CEO of America West Airlines, describes how his company fully cross-trains their customer service representatives. He says America West does it "to give the employees a better job, to give them more job variety. It's more challenging, and for those who are interested in upward mobility, it exposes them to about 16 different areas of the company versus the one they would be exposed to if we specialized."[50]

The strengths of job rotation are that it reduces boredom and increases motivation through diversifying the employee's activities. Of course, it can also have indirect benefits for the organization since employees with a wider range of skills give management more flexibility in scheduling work, adapting to changes, and filling vacancies. On the other hand, job rotation is not without its drawbacks. Training costs are increased, and productivity is reduced by moving a worker into a new position just when his or her efficiency at the prior job was creating organizational economies. Job rotation also creates disruptions. Members of the work group have to adjust to the new employee. The supervisor may also have to spend more time answering questions and monitoring the work of the recently rotated employee. Finally, job rotation can demotivate intelligent and ambitious trainees who seek specific responsibilities in their chosen specialty.

job rotation

The periodic shifting of a worker from one task to another.

Job rotation allowed Harry Cedarbaum (center) to balance the needs of his job, his wife and three children, and his parents. Cedarbaum, a management consultant at Booz, Allen & Hamilton in New York, signed up for the firm's job-rotation program after learning that his parents—who live in Europe—were suffering from poor health and needed help to close the family business. Cedarbaum took a less-demanding job as a recruiter at Columbia University, giving him time to take trips to Europe to help his parents. A grateful Cedarbaum says, "This loyalty is an incredible thing." Job rotation is one of many programs Booz Allen offers to win employee loyalty.

JOB ENLARGEMENT

job enlargement

The horizontal expansion of jobs.

More than 35 years ago, the idea of expanding jobs horizontally, or what we call **job enlargement**, grew in popularity. Increasing the number and variety of tasks that an individual performed resulted in jobs with more diversity. Instead of only sorting the incoming mail by department, for instance, a mail sorter's job could be enlarged to include physically delivering the mail to the various departments or running outgoing letters through the postage meter.

Efforts at job enlargement met with less than enthusiastic results.[51] As one employee who experienced such a redesign on his job remarked, "Before I had one lousy job. Now, through enlargement, I have three!" However, there have been some successful applications of job enlargement. For example, U.S. Shoe Co. created modular work areas to replace production lines in over half of its factories. In these work areas, workers perform two or three shoe-making steps instead of only one, as in traditional production lines. The result has been footwear produced more efficiently and with greater attention to quality.[52]

So, while job enlargement attacked the lack of diversity in overspecialized jobs, it did little to instill challenge or meaningfulness to a worker's activities. Job enrichment was introduced to deal with the shortcomings of enlargement.

JOB ENRICHMENT

job enrichment

The vertical expansion of jobs.

Job enrichment refers to the vertical expansion of jobs. It increases the degree to which the worker controls the planning, execution, and evaluation of his or her work. An enriched job organizes tasks so as to allow the worker to do a complete activity, increases the employee's freedom and independence, increases responsibility, and provides feedback, so an individual will be able to assess and correct his or her own performance.[53]

Lawrence Buettner enriched the jobs of employees in his international trade banking department at First Chicago Corporation.[54] His department's chief product is commercial letters of credit—essentially a bank guarantee to stand behind huge import and export transactions. When he took over the department of 300 employees, he found paperwork crawling along a document "assembly line," with errors creeping in at each handoff. And employees did little to hide the boredom they were experiencing in their jobs. Buettner replaced the narrow, specialized tasks that employees were doing with enriched jobs. Each clerk is now a trade expert who can handle a customer from start to finish. After 200 hours of training in finance and law, the clerks became full-service advisers who could turn around documents in a day while advising clients on such arcane matters as bank procedures in Turkey and U.S. munitions' export controls. And the results? Productivity has more than tripled, employee satisfaction has soared, and transaction volume has risen more than 10 percent a year. Additionally, increased skills have translated into higher pay for the employees who are performing the enriched jobs. These trade service representatives, some of whom had come to the bank directly out of high school, now earn from $25,000 to $50,000 a year.

The First Chicago example shouldn't be taken as a blanket endorsement of job enrichment. The overall evidence generally shows that job enrichment reduces absenteeism and turnover costs and increases satisfaction, but on the critical issue of productivity, the evidence is inconclusive.[55] In some situations, such as at First Chicago, job enrichment increases productivity; in others, it decreases it. However, even when productivity goes down, there does seem to be consistently more conscientious use of resources and a higher quality of product or service.

Designing Enriched Jobs

How does management enrich an employee's job? The following suggestions, based on the job characteristics model, specify the types of changes in jobs that are most likely to lead to improving their motivating potential.[56]

1. *Combine tasks.* Managers should seek to take existing and fractionalized tasks and put them back together to form a new and larger module of work. This increases skill variety and task identity.

2. *Create natural work units.* The creation of natural work units means that the tasks an employee does form an identifiable and meaningful whole. This increases employee "ownership" of the work and improves the likelihood that employees will view their work as meaningful and important rather than as irrelevant and boring.

3. *Establish client relationships.* The client is the user of the product or service that the employee works on (and may be an "internal customer" as well as someone outside the organization). Wherever possible, managers should try to establish direct relationships between workers and their clients. This increases skill variety, autonomy, and feedback for the employee.

4. *Expand jobs vertically.* Vertical expansion gives employees responsibilities and control that were formerly reserved to management. It seeks to partially close the gap between the "doing" and the "controlling" aspects of the job, and it increases employee autonomy.

5. *Open feedback channels.* By increasing feedback, employees not only learn how well they are performing their jobs, but also whether their performance is improving, deteriorating, or remaining at a constant level. Ideally, this feedback about performance should be received directly as the employee does the job, rather than from management on an occasional basis.

TEAM-BASED WORK DESIGNS REVISITED

Increasingly, people are doing work in groups and teams. What, if anything, can we say about the design of group-based work to try to improve employee performance in those groups? We know a lot more about individual-based work design than we do about design at the group level,[57] mostly because the wide popularity of teams—specifically assigning tasks to a group of individuals instead of to a single person—is a relatively recent phenomenon. That said, the best work in this area offers two sets of suggestions.[58]

First, the JCM recommendations seem to be as valid at the group level as they are at the individual level. Managers should expect a group to perform at a high level when (1) the group task requires members to use a variety of relatively high-level skills; (2) the group task is a whole and meaningful piece of work, with a visible outcome; (3) the outcomes of the group's work on the task have significant consequences for other people; (4) the task provides group members with substantial autonomy for deciding how they do the work; and (5) work on the task generates regular, trustworthy feedback about how well the group is performing.

Second, group composition is critical to the success of the work group. Consistent with findings described in Chapter 9, managers should try to ensure that the following four conditions are met: (1) Individual members have the necessary task-relevant expertise to do their work; (2) the group is large enough to perform the work; (3) members possess interpersonal as well as task skills; and (4) membership is moderately diverse in terms of talents and perspectives.

WORK SCHEDULE OPTIONS

Susan Ross is your classic "morning person." She rises each day at 5 A.M. sharp, full of energy. On the other hand, as she puts it, "I'm usually ready for bed right after the 7 P.M. news."

Susan's work schedule as a claims processor at Hartford Insurance is flexible. It allows her some degree of freedom as to when she comes to work and when she leaves. Her office opens at 6 A.M. and closes at 7 P.M. It's up to her how she schedules her eight-hour day within this 13-hour period. Because Susan is a morning person and also has a seven-year-old son who gets out of school at 3 P.M. every day, she opts to work from 6 A.M. to 3 P.M. "My work hours are perfect. I'm at the job when I'm mentally most alert, and I can be home to take care of Sean after he gets out of school."

Most people work an eight-hour day, five days a week. They start at a fixed time and leave at a fixed time. But a number of organizations have introduced alternative work schedule options. In this section, we review some of these alternatives. The common theme among these is that they all increase flexibility for employees. In a work world where employees are increasingly complaining about being pressed for time and the difficulty of balancing work and personal responsibilities, increasing work schedule options can be a way to improve employee motivation, productivity, and satisfaction.

COMPRESSED WORKWEEK

compressed workweek

A four-day week, with employees working 10 hours a day.

The most popular form of **compressed workweek** is four 10-hour days.[59] For instance, the 150 employees at a biotech plant of Baxter International in Round Lake, Illinois, are now in their fifth year of working four 10-hour days. They all take Friday off.[60]

The 4–40 program was conceived to allow workers more leisure time and shopping time, and to permit them to travel to and from work at non–rush-hour times. Supporters suggest that such a program can increase employee enthusiasm, morale, and commitment to the organization; increase productivity and reduce costs; reduce machine downtime in manufacturing; reduce overtime, turnover, and absenteeism; and make it easier for the organization to recruit employees.

Currently about 25 percent of major U.S. companies offer a four-day schedule for at least some of their workers.[61] This is double what it was in the late 1980s. And a recent national survey found that two-thirds of working adults would prefer a four-day workweek to the standard five-day schedule.[62]

Proponents argue that the compressed workweek may positively affect productivity in situations in which the work process requires significant start-up and shutdown periods.[63] When start-up and shutdown times are a major factor, productivity standards take these periods into consideration in determining the time required to generate a given output. Consequently, in such cases, the compressed workweek will increase productivity even though worker performance is not affected, simply because the improved work scheduling reduces nonproductive time.

The evidence on 4–40 program performance is generally positive.[64] While some employees complain of fatigue near the end of the day, and about the difficulty of coordinating their jobs with their personal lives—the latter a problem especially for working mothers—most like the 4–40 program. In one study, for instance, when employees were asked whether they wanted to continue their 4–40 program, which had been in place for six months, or go back to a traditional five-day week, 78 percent wanted to keep the compressed workweek.[65]

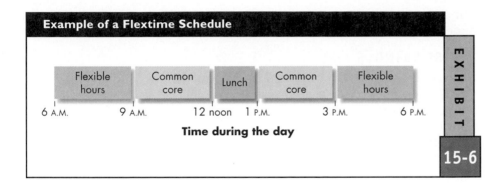

Example of a Flextime Schedule

| Flexible hours | Common core | Lunch | Common core | Flexible hours |

6 A.M.　9 A.M.　12 noon　1 P.M.　3 P.M.　6 P.M.

Time during the day

EXHIBIT 15-6

FLEXTIME

Flextime is a scheduling option that allows employees, within specific parameters, to decide when to go to work. Susan Ross's work schedule at Hartford Insurance is an example of flextime. But what specifically is flextime?

Flextime is short for flexible work hours. It allows employees some discretion over when they arrive at and leave work. Employees have to work a specific number of hours a week, but they are free to vary the hours of work within certain limits. As shown in Exhibit 15-6, each day consists of a common core, usually six hours, with a flexibility band surrounding the core. For example, exclusive of a one-hour lunch break, the core may be 9 A.M. to 3 P.M., with the office actually opening at 6 A.M. and closing at 6 P.M. All employees are required to be at their jobs during the common core period, but they are allowed to accumulate their other two hours before and/or after the core time. Some flextime programs allow extra hours to be accumulated and turned into a free day off each month.

Flextime has become an extremely popular scheduling option. The proportion of full-time U.S. employees on flextime almost doubled from 1991 to 1997. Approximately 25 million employees, or nearly 28 percent of the U.S. full-time workforce, now have flexibility in their daily arrival and departure times.[66] But flextime isn't available to all employees equally. While 42.4 percent of managers enjoy the freedom of flextime, only 23.3 percent of manufacturing workers are offered a flexible schedule.[67]

The benefits claimed for flextime are numerous. They include reduced absenteeism, increased productivity, reduced overtime expenses, a lessening in hostility toward management, reduced traffic congestion around work sites, elimination of tardiness, and increased autonomy and responsibility for employees that may increase employee job satisfaction.[68] But beyond the claims, what's flextime's record?

Most of the performance evidence stacks up favorably. Flextime tends to reduce absenteeism and frequently improves worker productivity,[69] probably for several reasons. Employees can schedule their work hours to align with personal demands, thus reducing tardiness and absences, and employees can adjust their work activities to those hours in which they are individually more productive.

Flextime's major drawback is that it's not applicable to every job. It works well with clerical tasks in which an employee's interaction with people outside his or her department is limited. It is not a viable option for receptionists, sales personnel in retail stores, or similar jobs in which

flextime

Employees work during a common core time period each day but have discretion in forming their total workday from a flexible set of hours outside the core.

Because her company offers flextime, Kelly Ramsey-Dolson can work full-time and still take care of her son Jeffrey. Ramsey-Dolson is an accountant with Ernst & Young, which has created an Office of Retention to develop ways to keep its valuable knowledge workers. When the accounting firm surveyed its employees about flexible scheduling, it learned that 65 percent of its workforce would have left the firm if it didn't offer flextime.

comprehensive service demands that people be at their workstations at predetermined times.

JOB SHARING

A recent work scheduling innovation is **job sharing**. It allows two or more individuals to split a traditional 40-hour-a-week job. So, for example, one person might perform the job from 8 A.M. to noon, while another performs the same job from 1 P.M. to 5 P.M.; or the two could work full, but alternate, days.

Approximately 36 percent of large organizations now offer their employees job sharing.[70] NOVA Corp. in Calgary, Canada, is one company that does. Kim Sarjeant and Loraine Champion, for instance, are staff lawyers at NOVA who divide one position in the company's human resources department.[71] Both have young children and wanted the flexibility that job sharing provides. Sarjeant works Monday through Wednesday, while Champion is on the job Wednesday to Friday. The arrangement allows them one day a week to work side by side, to share information, and to make joint decisions.

Job sharing allows the organization to draw upon the talents of more than one individual in a given job. A bank manager who oversees two job sharers describes it as an opportunity to get two heads, but "pay for one."[72] It also opens up the opportunity to acquire skilled workers—for instance, women with young children and retirees—who might not be available on a full-time basis.[73] From the employee's perspective, job sharing increases flexibility. As such, it can increase motivation and satisfaction for those to whom a 40-hour-a-week job is just not practical. On the other hand, the major drawback from management's perspective is finding compatible pairs of employees who can successfully coordinate the intricacies of one job.[74]

TELECOMMUTING

It might be close to the ideal job for many people. No commuting, flexible hours, freedom to dress as you please, and little or no interruptions from colleagues. It's called **telecommuting** and refers to employees who do their work at home at least two days a week on a computer that is linked to their office.[75] (A closely related term—*the virtual office*—is being increasingly used to describe employees who work out of their home on a relatively permanent basis). Currently, about 11.1 million people telecommute in the United States.[76] For instance, 20 percent or more of the employees at PeopleSoft, Erie Insurance, American Management Systems, Great Plains Software, Patagonia, and Xerox are telecommuting.[77] The U.S. Department of Transportation predicts that the number of U.S. telecommuters may reach 15 million, representing over 10 percent of the workforce, by 2002.[78] The concept is also catching on worldwide, although more slowly. In Great Britain and France, there are currently 563,000 and 215,000 telecommuters, respectively.[79]

What kinds of jobs lend themselves to telecommuting? Three categories have been identified as most appropriate: routine information-handling tasks, mobile activities, and professional and other knowledge-related tasks.[80] Writers, attorneys, analysts, and employees who spend the majority of their time on computers or the telephone are natural candidates for telecommuting. For instance, telemarketers, customer service representatives, reservation agents, and product support specialists spend most of their time on the phone. As telecommuters, they can access information on their computer screens at home as easily as the company screen in any office.

The extent to which the virtual office may someday permeate global organizations is illustrated in the experience of Liz Codling, a senior manager at Bank of Montreal in Toronto.[81] After running the bank's staff education center for four years and overseeing a team of eight people, she and her husband decided to return to their British homeland. But her bosses didn't want to lose her. So she became the bank's first transatlantic telecommuter. Although separated from her staff by five time zones and more than 3,000 miles, she is able to manage her team by relying on communication technology—phone, fax, computer, modem, e-mail, voice mail, videoconferencing, and the Internet. Some adjustments were needed. For instance, Ms. Codling has had to adjust her workday to align with Toronto hours and her colleagues have had to learn to schedule meetings in the mornings so she can be included. But after more than two years, this long-distance telecommute seems to be a success.

There are numerous other stories of telecommuting's success.[82] AT&T has 35,000 telecommuters and claims that it has saved the company as much as $500 million. And 75 percent of these AT&T telecommuters said they were more satisfied with their personal and family lives than before they started working at home. Cisco Systems claims that telecommuting has increased productivity 25 percent, has helped retain key employees who might otherwise have left, and saved the company about $1 million in overhead. As the cost of traditional office space has escalated and the cost of telecommunications equipment has plummeted, managers are increasingly motivated to introduce the virtual office as a way to increase employee flexibility and productivity, improve employee morale, and cut costs.

Source: S. Adams, *Dogbert's Big Book of Business* (Kansas City: Andrews & McMeel, 1991), p. 88.

Not all employees embrace the idea of telecommuting. After the massive Los Angeles earthquake in January 1994, many L.A. firms began offering telecommuting to their workers.[83] It was popular for a week or two, but that soon faded. Many workers complained they were missing out on important meetings and informal interactions that led to new policies and ideas. The vast majority were willing to put up with two- and three-hour commutes, while bridges and freeways were being rebuilt, in order to maintain their social contacts at work.

The long-term future of telecommuting depends on some questions for which we don't yet have definitive answers. For instance, will employees who do their work at home be at a disadvantage in office politics? Might they be less likely to be considered for salary increases and promotions? Is being out of sight equivalent to being out of mind? Will non–work-related distractions such as children, neighbors, and the close proximity of the refrigerator significantly reduce productivity for those without superior will power and discipline?

SUMMARY AND IMPLICATIONS FOR MANAGERS

An understanding of work design can help managers design jobs that positively affect employee motivation. For instance, jobs that score high in motivating potential increase an employee's control over key elements in his or her work. Therefore, jobs that offer autonomy, feedback, and similar complex task characteristics help to satisfy the individual goals of those employees who desire greater control over their work. Of course, consistent with the social information processing model, the perception that task characteristics are complex is probably more important in influencing an employee's motivation than the objective task characteristics themselves. The key, then, is to provide employees with cues that suggest that their jobs score high on factors such as skill variety, task identity, autonomy, and feedback.

Technology is changing people's jobs and their work behavior. TQM and its emphasis on continuous process improvement can increase employee stress as individuals find that performance expectations are constantly being increased. Reengineering is eliminating millions of jobs and completely reshaping the jobs of those who remain. Flexible manufacturing systems require employees to learn new skills and accept increased responsibilities. And technology is making many job skills obsolete and shortening the life span of almost all skills—technical, administrative, and managerial. Work space design variables such as size, arrangement, and privacy have implications for communication, status, socializing, satisfaction, and productivity. For instance, an enclosed office typically conveys more status than an open cubical. So employees with a high need for status might find an enclosed office increases their job satisfaction.

Alternative work schedule options such as the compressed workweek, flextime, job sharing, and telecommuting have grown in popularity in recent years. They have become an important strategic tool as organizations try to increase the flexibility their employees need in a changing workplace.

Jobs Are Becoming Obsolete

Prior to 1800, very few people had a job. People worked hard raising food or making things at home. They had no regular hours, no job descriptions, no bosses, and no employee benefits. Instead, they put in long hours on a shifting array of tasks, in a variety of locations, on a schedule set by the weather and needs of the day. It was the industrial revolution and the creation of large manufacturing companies that brought about the concept of what we have come to think of as *jobs*.[1]

But the conditions that have created "the job" are disappearing. Customized production is pushing out mass production; most workers now handle information, not physical products; and competitive conditions are demanding rapid response to changing markets. Media people like to talk about the disappearance of jobs in certain industries or countries. The reality is that *the job itself* is becoming obsolete.

In a fast-moving economy, jobs are rigid solutions to an elastic problem. When the work that needs doing changes constantly—which increasingly describes today's world—organizations can't afford the inflexibility that traditional jobs, with their limiting job descriptions, bring with them.

In the near future, very few people will have jobs as we have come to know them. In place of jobs, there will be part-time and temporary work situations. Organizations will be made up of "hired guns"—contingent employees (temporaries, part-timers, consultants, and contract workers) who join project teams created to complete a specific task. When that task is finished, the team disbands. People will work on more than one team at a time, keeping irregular hours, and relying heavily on networked computers to stay in contact with other team members. Few of these employees will be working nine to five at specific work spots, and they'll have little of the security that their grandfathers had.

[1]This argument is based on W. Bridges, *JobShift* (Reading, MA: Addison-Wesley, 1994).

The central core to any discussion of work or organizational behavior is the concept of a job. It is the aggregation of tasks that defines an individual's duties and responsibilities.

When an organization is created, managers have to determine what tasks need to be accomplished for the organization to achieve its goals and who will perform those tasks. These decisions precede the hiring of a workforce. Remember, it's the tasks that determine the need for people, not the other way around.

Can you conceive of an organization without jobs? No more than you can conceive of a car without an engine. There are no doubt changes taking place in organizations that are requiring managers to redefine what a job is. For instance, today's jobs often include extensive customer interaction as well as team responsibilities. In many cases, organizations are having to make job descriptions more flexible to reflect the more dynamic nature of work today. Because it's inefficient to rewrite job descriptions on a weekly basis, managers are rethinking what makes up a job and defining jobs in more fluid terms. But the concept of jobs continues to be at the core of any work design effort and a fundamental cornerstone to understanding formal work behavior in organizations.[2]

For those who believe that the concept of jobs is on the wane, all they need to do is look to the trade union movement and its determination to maintain clear job delineations. Labor unions have a vested interest in the status quo and will fight hard to protect the security and predictability that traditional jobs provide. Moreover, if it looked like the jobless society was to become a widespread reality, politicians would be under strong pressure to create legislation to outlaw it. Working people want the stability and predictability of jobs and, if need be, they will look to their elected representatives for protection.

[2]See J. Mays, "Why We Haven't Seen 'the End of Jobs' or the End of Pay Surveys," *Compensation & Benefits Review*, July–August 1997, pp. 25–29.

1. Describe three jobs that score high on the JCM. Describe three jobs that score low.

2. What are the implications of the social information processing model for predicting employee behavior?

3. What are the implications for employees of a continuous improvement program?

4. What are the implications for employees of a reengineering program?

5. What are flexible manufacturing systems?

6. How could you design an office so as to increase the opportunity for employees to be productive?

7. What can you do to improve employee performance on teams through work design?

8. What are the advantages of flextime from an employee's perspective? From management's perspective?

9. What are the advantages of job sharing from an employee's perspective? From management's perspective?

10. From an employee's perspective, what are the pros and cons to telecommuting?

Questions for Critical Thinking

1. Reengineering needs to be autocratically imposed in order to overcome employee resistance. This runs directly counter to the model of a contemporary manager who is a good listener, a coach, motivates through employee involvement, and who possesses strong team support skills. Can these two positions be reconciled?

2. How has technology changed the manager's job over the past 20 years?

3. Would you want a full-time job telecommuting? How do you think most of your friends would feel about such a job? Do you think telecommuting has a future?

4. What can management do to improve employees' perceptions that their jobs are interesting and challenging?

5. What are the implications of worker obsolescence on (a) society; (b) management practice; and (c) you, as an individual, planning a career?

Team Exercise | Analyzing and Redesigning Jobs

Break into groups of five to seven members each. Each student should describe the worst job he or she has ever had. Use any criteria you want to select one of these jobs for analysis by the group.

Members of the group will analyze the job selected by determining how well it scores on the job characteristics model. Use the following scale for your analysis of each job dimension:

7 = Very high
6 = High
5 = Somewhat high
4 = Moderate
3 = Somewhat low
2 = Low
1 = Very low

Following are sample questions that can guide the group in its analysis of the job in question:

- *Skill variety*: Describe the different identifiable skills required to do this job. What is the nature of the oral, written, and/or quantitative skills needed? Physical skills? Does the jobholder get the opportunity to use all of his or her skills?

- *Task identity*: What is the product that the jobholder creates? Is he or she involved in its production from beginning to end? If not, is he or she involved in a particular phase of its production from beginning to end?

- *Task significance*: How important is the product? How important is the jobholder's role in producing it? How important is the jobholder's contribution to the people with whom he or she works? If the jobholder's job were eliminated, how inferior would the product be?

- *Autonomy*: How much independence does the jobholder have? Does he or she have to follow a strict schedule? How closely is he or she supervised?
- *Feedback*: Does the jobholder get regular feedback from his or her supervisor? From peers? From those below? From customers? How about intrinsic performance feedback when doing the job?

Using the formula in Exhibit 15–3, calculate the job's motivating potential. Then using the suggestions offered in the chapter for redesigning jobs, describe specific actions management could take to increase this job's motivating potential.

Calculate the costs to management of redesigning the job in question. Do the benefits exceed the costs?

Conclude the exercise by having a representative of each group share his or her group's analysis and redesign suggestions with the entire class. Possible topics for class discussion might include similarities in the jobs chosen, problems in rating job dimensions, and the cost-benefit assessment of design changes.

———

Source: This exercise is based on W. P. Ferris, "Enlivening the Job Characteristics Model," in C. Harris and C. C. Lundberg, *Proceedings of the 29th Annual Eastern Academy of Management Meeting*; Baltimore, MD; May 1992, pp. 125–28.

Internet Search Exercises

1. Find the latest data and/or reputable opinions indicating the popularity of flextime and telecommuting.

2. Find three Web sites that discuss why process reengineering might fail to live up to expectations. What factors are detailed in these explanations? What can companies do to avoid these problems?

PHLIP Companion Web Site

We invite you to visit the Robbins homepage on the Prentice Hall Web site at **www.prenhall.com/robbins** for our on-line study guide, current events, links to related Web sites, and more.

Case Incident   One Man's Saturn Experience

Dave Steadman graduated from high school and joined the Coast Guard. Then he went to work at General Motors' Buick City plant in Flint, Michigan. He got laid off in the early 1980's. He'd been out of work for 10 years. Then Saturn started up and he moved to Tennessee to work in its plant just outside Nashville.

Along with three others, Dave is stationed around a huge rotating machine that injects foam into molds and makes dashboards. The machine is really a robot and Dave's job is to feed it. More specifically, Dave squirts some filler release into a hole, lifts a plastic mold and places it on a protruding lip of the machine, bangs a board with his knee to drop three locks to hold the mold in place, checks the locks, and pushes a black button to bring the lip down into the right position for the next guy. Then Dave waits for the machine to rotate and present him with a new lip. The whole process

takes 10 seconds. And Dave repeats this 360 times an hour, all day long.

"I've just turned 40," Dave said. "That means 17 years to go." Seventeen years more of this and he can retire. Even Dave realized how simple and repetitive his job is. But with bonuses, he makes about $55,000 a year. "Why do you think they pay me so well? They pay me to be bored."

Dave is quick to talk about the good points of his job. It doesn't demand anything intellectually. And there is lots of time to chat with the other team members who are feeding the same machine. Of course, there are also the pluses of working at Saturn. "It's fairly loose. We decide within the team when to take a break, determine our own vacations and schedules, do our own quality checks, swap jobs within the team. There are 14 of us and we get along well, but for all that, it's really just another job on the line."

When the topic of quality came up, Dave seemed able to rationalize the occasional defect. "Say there's a rattle or a loose wire. I'd think maybe the guy on the line was hung over that day, or maybe he had an argument with his wife or trouble with the kids. His mind was elsewhere. You see how it is: you can't keep your mind long on this kind of work. You'd be inhuman not to wander off. And that's when mistakes creep in."

When Dave was asked to what he attributed the higher quality in American cars nowadays, he replied, "We're afraid for our jobs. Back in the early 80's, it never occurred to us we could be laid off. You got a union card and the job was yours for life, so there was no reason to work hard or make sure quality was high. Now we know what can happen." Then, with a grin, Dave adds, "Plus, I've got a dozen team members who are going to get on my case if I don't do my job properly."

Questions

1. Dave Steadman says Saturn "pays me to be bored." Do you think that, in general, the lower a job rates on the JCM's motivating potential score, the more it pays? Explain.

2. What role, if any, do teams play in shaping Dave's attitudes and behavior?

3. Could Dave's job be enriched or reengineered to make him more productive and satisfied?

4. "Who cares if Dave is satisfied or not? He's not going anywhere. He'll just do his job for another 17 years." How do you respond to this assessment?

Source: Adapted from L. Hazelton, "Dave and Audrey Get Down to the Nuts and Bolts," *New York Times,* October 21, 1998, p. 24.

Video Case | **The King Company**

David Arnold, the founder of the King Company, tells us about a problem he was having and how he used technology to help solve it. David said that he was "selling a lot of watches, that wasn't the problem; we just weren't making any money at it." The King Company has found that properly managed and maintained information systems can be at the heart of a company's success. The King Company is the sole U.S. distributor for the Lorus line of Seiko watches. It employs about 60 people and has annual sales in excess of $50 million. King Company's customers include retailers as large as Wal-Mart and as small as your corner drug store.

How does information management fit into King Company's operation? Not only does the company use its information sytem to improve its own business performance, it uses it to interact electronically with most of its customers. Approximately 95 percent of all communication, from taking an order to final payment, is handled electronically—little or no human intervention is needed. In addition, because the company has a direct electronic interface with its customers, orders, inquiries, billing and even payment can be done without the generation of a single piece of paper. The King Company also uses its information as a marketing tool. The company not only tracks what it has sold to its customers, it also, in some cases, monitors its customers' sales on a daily basis. The knowledge from this activity supports short-term needs such as ordering and production planning, but it also has longer-range value. Over time, the company can track product trends and make product-line development decisions based on real market input.

Companies today must deal with many issues when it comes to information and information management. You might think that a simple solution is to collect everything you can and save it. On the surface this may make sense, but think about it for a minute. How useful is information if it is not organized, if it is not stored in an easy-to-retrieve manner, if it cannot be accessed in a timely manner, and if no one has a real use for it? Remember, having volumes of useless information is not nearly as valuable as having a small pile that actually means something.

Questions

1. David Arnold added staff to manage information and technology in the early stages of the King Company's relationship with Seiko. What are some advantages and disadvantages of adding computer and information management processes early on in a company's development?

2. King Company's operation was not always automated. How do you think David Arnold's employees feel about all of this automation? Try to use some examples from the video and be sure to consider both valuable and threatening aspects of automation in developing your answer.

3. The King Company collects information about its customers and the final purchasers of its products. Do you think there are any ethical issues in establishing such information transfers between vendors and customers? Why or why not?

1. T. Hall, "And the Walls Came Tumbling Down," *New York Times Magazine,* December 13, 1998, pp. 82–86.

2. R. M. Steers and R. T. Mowday, "The Motivational Properties of Tasks," *Academy of Management Review,* October 1977, pp. 645–58.

3. D. G. Gardner and L. L. Cummings, "Activation Theory and Job Design: Review and Reconceptualization," in B. M. Staw and L. L. Cummings (eds.), *Research in Organizational Behavior,* vol. 10 (Greenwich, CT: JAI Press, 1988), p. 100.

4. A. N. Turner and P. R. Lawrence, *Industrial Jobs and the Worker* (Boston: Harvard University Press, 1965).

5. J. R. Hackman and G. R. Oldham, "Motivation Through the Design of Work: Test of a Theory," *Organizational Behavior and Human Performance,* August 1976, pp. 250–79.

6. J. R. Hackman, "Work Design," in J. R. Hackman and J. L. Suttle (eds.), *Improving Life at Work* (Santa Monica, CA: Goodyear, 1977), p. 129.

7. See "Job Characteristics Theory of Work Redesign," in J. B. Miner, *Theories of Organizational Behavior* (Hinsdale, IL: Dryden Press, 1980), pp. 231–66; B. T. Loher, R. A. Noe, N. L. Moeller, and M. P. Fitzgerald, "A Meta-Analysis of the Relation of Job Characteristics to Job Satisfaction," *Journal of Applied Psychology,* May 1985, pp. 280–89; W. H. Glick, G. D. Jenkins, Jr., and N. Gupta, "Method versus Substance: How Strong Are Underlying Relationships Between Job Characteristics and Attitudinal Outcomes?" *Academy of Management Journal,* September 1986, pp. 441–64; Y. Fried and G. R. Ferris, "The Validity of the Job Characteristics Model: A Review and Meta-Analysis," *Personnel Psychology,* Summer 1987, pp. 287–322; S. J. Zaccaro and E. F. Stone, "Incremental Validity of an Empirically Based Measure of Job Characteristics," *Journal of Applied Psychology,* May 1988, pp. 245–52; and J. R. Rentsch and R. P. Steel, "Testing the Durability of Job Characteristics as Predictors of Absenteeism Over a Six-Year Period," *Personnel Psychology,* Spring 1998, pp. 165–90.

8. See R. B. Dunham, "Measurement and Dimensionality of Job Characteristics," *Journal of Applied Psychology,* August 1976, pp. 404–09; J. L. Pierce and R. B. Dunham, "Task Design: A Literature Review," *Academy of Management Review,* January 1976, pp. 83–97; D. M. Rousseau, "Technological Differences in Job Characteristics, Employee Satisfaction, and Motivation: A Synthesis of Job Design Research and Sociotechnical Systems Theory," *Organizational Behavior and Human Performance,* October 1977, pp. 18–42; and Y. Fried and G. R. Ferris, "The Dimensionality of Job Characteristics: Some Neglected Issues," *Journal of Applied Psychology,* August 1986, pp. 419–26.

9. Fried and Ferris, "The Dimensionality of Job Characteristics."

10. See, for instance, Fried and Ferris, "The Dimensionality of Job Characteristics;" and M. G. Evans and D. A. Ondrack, "The Motivational Potential of Jobs: Is a Multiplicative Model Really Necessary?" in S. L. McShane (ed.), *Organizational Behavior, ASAC Conference Proceedings,* vol. 9, part 5, Halifax, Nova Scotia, 1988, pp. 31–39.

11. R. B. Tiegs, L. E. Tetrick, and Y. Fried, "Growth Need Strength and Context Satisfactions as Moderators of the Relations of the Job Characteristics Model," *Journal of Management,* September 1992, pp. 575–93.

12. C. A. O'Reilly and D. F. Caldwell, "Informational Influence as a Determinant of Perceived Task Characteristics and Job Satisfaction," *Journal of Applied Psychology,* April 1979, pp. 157–65; R. V. Montagno, "The Effects of Comparison Others and Prior Experience on Responses to Task Design," *Academy of Management Journal,* June 1985, pp. 491–98; and P. C. Bottger and I. K-H. Chew, "The Job Characteristics Model and Growth Satisfaction: Main Effects of Assimilation of Work Experience and Context Satisfaction," *Human Relations,* June 1986, pp. 575–94.

13. Hackman, "Work Design," pp. 132–33.

14. G. R. Salancik and J. Pfeffer, "A Social Information Processing Approach to Job Attitudes and Task Design," *Administrative Science Quarterly,* June 1978, pp. 224–53; J. G. Thomas and R. W. Griffin, "The Power of Social Information in the Workplace," *Organizational Dynamics,* Autumn 1989, pp. 63–75; and M. D. Zalesny and J. K. Ford, "Extending the Social Information Processing Perspective: New Links to Attitudes, Behaviors, and Perceptions," *Organizational Behavior and Human Decision Processes,* December 1990, pp. 205–46.

15. J. R. Hackman, "Work Design," in J. R. Hackman and J. L. Suttle, *Improving Life at Work* (Santa Monica, CA: Goodyear, 1977), pp. 115–20.

16. J. P. Wanous, "Individual Differences and Reactions to Job Characteristics," *Journal of Applied Psychology,* October 1974, pp. 616–22; and H. P. Sims and A. D. Szilagyi, "Job Characteristic Relationships: Individual and Structural Moderators," *Organizational Behavior and Human Performance,* June 1976, pp. 211–30.

17. M. Fein, "The Real Needs and Goals of Blue Collar Workers," *The Conference Board Record,* February 1972, pp. 26–33.

18. See, for instance, J. Thomas and R. W. Griffin, "The Social Information Processing Model of Task Design: A Review of the Literature," *Academy of Management Journal,* October 1983, pp. 672–82; and M. D. Zalesny and J. K. Ford, "Extending the Social Information Processing Perspective: New Links to Attitudes, Behaviors, and Perceptions," *Organizational Behavior and Human Decision Processes,* December 1990, pp. 205–46; and G. W. Meyer, "Social Information Processing and Social Networks: A Test of Social Influence Mechanisms," *Human Relations,* September 1994, pp. 1013–45.

19. See, for example, T. H. Berry, *Managing the Total Quality Transition* (New York: McGraw Hill, 1991); D. Ciampa, *Total Quality* (Reading, MA: Addison-Wesley, 1992); W. H. Schmidt and J. P. Finnegan, *The Race Without a Finish Line* (San Francisco: Jossey-Bass, 1992); and T. B. Kinni, "Process Improvement," *Industry Week,* January 23, 1995, pp. 52–58.

20. M. Sashkin and K. J. Kiser, *Putting Total Quality Management to Work* (San Francisco: Berrett-Koehler, 1993), p. 44.

21. M. Hammer and J. Champy, *Reengineering the Corporation: A Manifesto for Business Revolution* (New York: HarperBusiness, 1993). See also J. Champy, *Reengineering Management: The Mandate for New Leadership* (New York: HarperBusiness, 1995); and M. Hammer and S. A. Stanton, *The Reengineering Revolution* (New York: HarperBusiness, 1995).

22. R. Karlgaard, "ASAP Interview: Mike Hammer," *Forbes ASAP,* September 13, 1993, p. 70.

23. Ibid.

24. "The Age of Reengineering," *Across the Board,* June 1993, p. 29.

25. Ibid., p. 33.

26. See, for instance, D. M. Upton, "The Management of Manufacturing Flexibility," *California Management Review,* Winter 1994, pp. 72–89; G. Bylinksy, "The Digital Factory," *Fortune,* November 14, 1994, pp. 96–100; and P. Coy, "The Technology Paradox," *Business Week,* March 6, 1995, pp. 76–84.

27. S. Moffat, "Japan's New Personalized Production," *Fortune,* October 22, 1990, p. 44.

28. See E. Norton, "Small, Flexible Plants May Play Crucial Role in U.S. Manufacturing," *Wall Street Journal,* January 13, 1993, p. A1.

29. See, for instance, P. E. Ross, "Software as Career Threat," *Forbes,* May 22, 1995, pp. 240–46; S. Schafer "Software That Thinks," *INC. Technology,* December 2, 1996, pp. 109–10; and J. W. Verity, "Coaxing Meaning Out of Raw Data," *Business Week*, February 3, 1997, pp. 134–38.

30. See, for example, M. Milford, "Du Pont Shuts the Door on Private Offices," *New York Times,* February 23, 1997, p. 31; B. Nussbaum, "Blueprints for Business," *Business Week,* November 3, 1997, pp. 112–22; D. Bencivenga, "A Humanistic Approach to Space," *HRMagazine,* March 1998, pp. 68–78; and C. Howard, "It's the Same Job, After All," *Canadian Business,* June 26/July 10, 1998, pp. 125–26.

31. See F. Becker and F. Steele, *Workplace By Design* (San Francisco: Jossey-Bass, 1995).

32. J. Pfeffer, *Organizations and Organization Theory* (Boston: Pitman, 1982), p. 261.

33. S. Lohr, "Hey, Who Took the Office Doors?" *New York Times,* August 11, 1997, p. C7.

34. Ibid.

35. See, for instance, B. Nussbaum, "Blueprints for Business."

36. See, for example, L. S. Festinger, S. Schachter, and K. Back, *Social Pressures in Informal Groups* (Stanford, CA: Stanford University Press, 1950).

37. See, for example, R. L. Zweigenhaft, "Personal Space in the Faculty Office Desk Placement and the Student-Faculty Interaction," *Journal of Applied Psychology,* August 1976, pp. 529–32; D. E. Campbell, "Interior Office Design and Visitor Response," *Journal of Applied Psychology,* December 1979, pp. 648–53; P. C. Morrow and J. C. McElroy, "Interior Office Design and Visitor Response: A Constructive Replication," *Journal of Applied Psychology,* October 1981, pp. 646–50; and G. R. Oldham, "Effects of Changes in Workspace Partitions and Spatial Density on Employee Reactions: A Quasi-Experiment," *Journal of Applied Psychology,* May 1988, pp. 253–58.

38. S. Lohr, "Hey, Who Took the Office Doors?" p. C7.

39. Ibid.; and D. Bencivenga, "A Humanistic Approach to Space."

40. L. Gallagher, "Death to the Cubicle!" *Forbes,* September 7, 1998, p. 54; and M. Henricks, "Musical Chairs," *Entrepreneur,* April 1999, pp. 77–79.

41. "Office 'Hoteling' Isn't as Inn as Futurists Once Thought," *Wall Street Journal,* September 2, 1997, p. A1; and P. Weinberg, "The Space Race," *Report on Business Magazine,* November 1997, pp. 134–38.

42. R. A. Baron, "The Physical Environment of Work Settings: Effects on Task Performance, Interpersonal Relations, and Job Satisfaction," in B. M. Staw and L. L. Cummings, (eds.), *Research in Organizational Behavior,* vol. 16 (Greenwich, CT: JAI Press, 1994), p. 33.

43. J. I. Porras and P. J. Robertson, "Organizational Development: Theory, Practice, and Research," in M. D. Dunnette and L. M. Hough, (eds.), *Handbook of Industrial & Organizational Psychology,* 2nd ed., vol. 3 (Palo Alto, CA: Consulting Psychologists Press, 1992), p. 734.

44. E. Proper, "Surroundings Affect Worker Productivity," *Industry Week,* June 8, 1998, p. 14.

45. Ibid.

46. S. Lohr, "Hey, Who Took the Office Doors?" p. C7.

47. J. E. Rigdon, "Using Lateral Moves to Spur Employees," *Wall Street Journal,* May 26, 1992, p. B1.

48. B. G. Posner, "Role Changes," *INC.,* February 1990, pp. 95–98.

49. C. Garfield, "Creating Successful Partnerships with Employees," *At Work,* May/June 1992, p. 8.

50. Ibid.

51. See, for instance, data on job enlargement described in M. A. Campion and C. L. McClelland, "Follow-Up and Extension of the Interdisciplinary Costs and Benefits of Enlarged Jobs," *Journal of Applied Psychology,* June 1993, pp. 339–51.

52. Related in personal communication with the author.

53. J. R. Hackman and G. R. Oldham, *Work Redesign* (Reading, MA: Addison Wesley, 1980).

54. Cited in *U.S. News & World Report,* May 31, 1993, p. 63.

55. See, for example, J. R. Hackman and G. R. Oldham, *Work Redesign;* J. B. Miner, *Theories of Organizational Behavior* (Hinsdale, IL: Dryden Press, 1980), pp. 231–66; R. W. Griffin, "Effects of Work Redesign on Employee Perceptions, Attitudes, and Behaviors: A Long-Term Investigation," *Academy of Management Journal,* June 1991, pp. 425–35; and J. L. Cotton, *Employee Involvement* (Newbury Park, CA: Sage, 1993), pp. 141–72.

56. J. R. Hackman, "Work Design," in J. R. Hackman and J. L. Suttle (eds.), *Improving Life at Work* (Santa Monica, CA: Goodyear, 1977), pp. 132–33.

57. R. W. Griffin and G. C. McMahan, "Motivation Through Job Design," in J. Greenberg (ed.), *Organizational Behavior: The State of the Science* (Hillsdale, NJ: Lawrence Erlbaum Associates, 1994), pp. 36–38.

58. J. R. Hackman, "The Design of Work Teams," in J. W. Lorsch (ed.), *Handbook of Organizational Behavior* (Upper Saddle River, NJ: Prentice Hall, 1987), pp. 324–27.

59. See, for example, P. T. Kilborn, "In Their Quest for Efficiency, Factories Scrap 5-Day Week," *New York Times,* June 4, 1996, p. A1.

60. Cited in M. Verespej, "Just Note the Difference," *Industry Week,* August 17, 1998, p. 16.

61. G. Fuchsberg, "Four-Day Workweek Has Become a Stretch for Some Employees," *Wall Street Journal*, August 3, 1994, p. A1.

62. Reported in ibid.

63. E. J. Calvasina and W. R. Boxx, "Efficiency of Workers on the Four-Day Workweek," *Academy of Management Journal*, September 1975, pp. 604–10.

64. See, for example, J. C. Latack and L. W. Foster, "Implementation of Compressed Work Schedules: Participation and Job Redesign as Critical Factors for Employee Acceptance," *Personnel Psychology*, Spring 1985, pp. 75–92; and J. W. Seybolt and J. W. Waddoups, "The Impact of Alternative Work Schedules on Employee Attitudes: A Field Experiment," paper presented at the Western Academy of Management Meeting, Hollywood, CA, April 1987.

65. J. C. Goodale and A. K. Aagaard, "Factors Relating to Varying Reactions to the 4-Day Work Week," *Journal of Applied Psychology*, February 1975, pp. 33–38.

66. L. Rubis, "Fourth of Full-Timers Enjoy Flexible Hours," *HRMagazine*, June 1998, pp. 26–28.

67. Ibid.

68. D. R. Dalton and D. J. Mesch, "The Impact of Flexible Scheduling on Employee Attendance and Turnover," *Administrative Science Quarterly*, June 1990, pp. 370–87; and K. S. Kush and L. K. Stroh, "Flextime: Myth or Reality," *Business Horizons*, September–October 1994, p. 53.

69. See, for example, D. A. Ralston and M. F. Flanagan, "The Effect of Flextime on Absenteeism and Turnover for Male and Female Employees," *Journal of Vocational Behavior*, April 1985, pp. 206–17; D. A. Ralston, W. P. Anthony, and D. J. Gustafson, "Employees May Love Flextime, But What Does It Do to the Organization's Productivity?" *Journal of Applied Psychology*, May 1985, pp. 272–79; J. B. McGuire and J. R. Liro, "Flexible Work Schedules, Work Attitudes, and Perceptions of Productivity," *Public Personnel Management*, Spring 1986, pp. 65–73; P. Bernstein, "The Ultimate in Flextime: From Sweden, by Way of Volvo," *Personnel*, June 1988, pp. 70–74; and D. R. Dalton and D. J. Mesch, "The Impact of Flexible Scheduling on Employee Attendance and Turnover," *Administrative Science Quarterly*, June 1990, pp. 370–87.

70. Cited in E. M. Friedman (ed.), "Almanac: A Statistical and Informational Snapshot of the Business World Today," *INC's The State of Small Business 1997*, p. 121.

71. H. Schacter, "Slaves of the New Economy," *Canadian Business*, April 1996, p. 89.

72. S. Shellenbarger, "Two People, One Job: It Can Really Work," *Wall Street Journal*, December 7, 1994, p. B1.

73. "Job-Sharing: Widely Offered, Little Used," *Training*, November 1994, p. 12.

74. S. Shellenbarger, "Two People, One Job."

75. See, for example, T. H. Davenport and K. Pearlson, "Two Cheers for the Virtual Office," *Sloan Management Review*, Summer 1998, pp. 61–65; E. J. Hill, B. C. Miller, S. P. Weiner, and J. Colihan, "Influences of the Virtual Office on Aspects of Work and Work/Life Balance," *Personnel Psychology*, Autumn 1998, pp. 667–83; and S. Fister, "A Lure For Labor," *Training*, February 1999, pp. 57–62.

76. Cited in S. Shallenbarger, "Madison Avenue May Need to Alter Image of '90s Telecommuter," *Wall Street Journal*, August 20, 1997, p. B1.

77. "Telecommuting as a Way of Life," *Fortune*, January 12, 1998, p. 94.

78. Cited in R. W. Judy and C. D'Amico, *Workforce 2020* (Indianpolis: Hudson Institute, 1997), p. 58.

79. "Telecommuting in Europe," *Manpower Argus*, April 1997, p. 9.

80. Cited in R. W. Judy and C. D'Amico, *Workforce 2020*, p. 58.

81. R. Hearn, "First Banker in Space," *Canadian Business*, August 1997, p. 15.

82. E. C. Baig, "Saying Adios to the Office," *Business Week*, October 12, 1998, pp. 152–53; A. Tergesen, "Making Stay-at Homes Feel Welcome," *Business Week*, October 12, 1998, pp. 155–56; and C. A. L. Dannhauser, "The Invisible Worker," *Working Woman*, November 1998, p. 38.

83. S. Silverstein, "Telecommuting Boomlet Has Few Follow-Up Calls," *Los Angeles Times*, May 16, 1994, p. A1.

THE
ORGANIZATION
SYSTEM

After listening to my employees, I have to conclude that I have only three types of people working for me: Stars, All-Stars, and Superstars! How is it possible for all my people to be above average?

—An Anonymous Boss

Recent newspaper stories lead with headlines like: "Boeing to Lay Off 28,000." "Sears Cuts Workforce by 50,000." "Chase-Chemical Merger to Eliminate 12,000 Jobs." But there's another parallel story that isn't getting as much ink: An increasing number of employers are facing a serious shortage of skilled workers.[1] A strong economy, overzealous downsizing programs, and inadequate skill levels of many new job entrants are putting a premium on getting and holding on to quality skilled employees. Aetna Inc., for instance, cut 5,000 workers when it merged with U.S. Healthcare in 1996. Two years later it realized the cuts were too deep. Customers and providers faced lengthy delays. So it was back in the labor market, looking for new employees. Similarly, Bell Atlantic North offered its union members an attractive severance package in order to reduce the number of line installers and clerical staff. To the company's surprise, 14,000 workers accepted the package. Meanwhile, the company found itself grossly understaffed as demand surged for wire-related lines to operate faxes, modems, and additional phones. So Bell Atlantic North found itself actively searching to hire thousands of new workers.

This demand for skilled workers is motivating executives to bend over backward to accommodate valued employees. Ira Phillips is one such executive. Owner and president of Quoizel, an importer and manufacturer of lamps and lighting fixtures, he recently moved his company from Long Island, New York, to Charleston, South Carolina.[2] Realizing the difficulty of replacing his experienced production staff (see photo of three Quoizel production workers), even though they were only semiskilled and modestly paid, Phillips covered the full cost of moving 125 of them to South Carolina.

Human Resource Policies and Practices

16

These examples illustrate the message of this chapter: Human resource policies and practices—such as employee selection, union–management relations, and retention programs–influence organizational effectiveness.[3] We begin our discussion with the subject of hiring.

SELECTION PRACTICES

The objective of effective selection is to match individual characteristics (ability, experience, etc.) with the requirements of the job.[4] When management fails to get a proper match, both employee performance and satisfaction suffer. In this search to achieve the right individual–job fit, where does management begin? The answer is to assess the demands and requirements of the job. The process of assessing the activities within a job is called *job analysis*.

JOB ANALYSIS

Job analysis involves developing a detailed description of the tasks involved in a job, determining the relationship of a given job to other jobs, and ascertaining the knowledge, skills, and abilities necessary for an employee to successfully perform the job.[5]

How is this information attained? Exhibit 16-1 describes the more popular job analysis methods.

Information gathered by using one or more of the job analysis methods results in the organization being able to create a **job description** and **job specification**. The former is a written statement of what a jobholder does, how it is done, and why

AFTER READING THIS CHAPTER, YOU SHOULD BE ABLE TO

1. Contrast job descriptions with job specifications
2. Identify the key skills for effective interviewing
3. List the advantages of performance simulation tests over written tests
4. Define four general skill categories
5. Describe how career planning has changed since the 1980s
6. Explain the purposes of performance evaluation
7. Describe actions that can improve the performance evaluation process
8. Clarify how the existence of a union affects employee behavior
9. Describe characteristics of a family-friendly workplace
10. Identify the content in a typical diversity training program

EXHIBIT

16-1

Popular Job Analysis Methods

Observation. An analyst watches employees directly or reviews films of workers on the job.

Interviews. Selected job incumbents are extensively interviewed, and the results of a number of interviews are combined into a single job analysis.

Diaries. Job incumbents record their daily activities, and the amount of time spent on each, in a diary or log.

Questionnaires. Incumbents check or rate the items they perform in their jobs from a long list of possible task items.

job analysis

Developing a detailed description of the tasks involved in a job, determining the relationship of a given job to other jobs, and ascertaining the knowledge, skills, and abilities necessary for an employee to perform the job successfully.

job description

A written statement of what a jobholder does, how it is done, and why it is done.

job specification

States the minimum acceptable qualifications that an employee must possess to perform a given job successfully.

it is done. It should accurately portray job content, environment, and conditions of employment. The job specification states the minimum acceptable qualifications that an employee must possess to perform a given job successfully. It identifies the knowledge, skills, and abilities needed to do the job effectively. So job descriptions identify characteristics of the job, while job specifications identify characteristics of the successful job incumbent.

The job description and specification have historically been important documents for guiding the selection process. The job description can be used to describe the job to potential candidates. The job specification keeps the attention of those doing the selection on the list of qualifications necessary for an incumbent to perform a job and assists in determining whether or not candidates are qualified. However, there are signs that these documents may be declining in importance. Because job analysis is a static view of the job as it currently exists, job descriptions and specifications are also static documents. To facilitate flexibility, organizations are increasingly hiring for organizational needs rather than for specific individual jobs.[6] Organizations want their permanent employees to be able to do a variety of tasks and to be able to move smoothly from project to project and from one team to another. In such a climate, organizations will tend to seek new employees who, in addition to job-relevant skills, have personalities and attitudes that fit with the organization's culture and who display organizational citizenship behaviors. Traditional job analysis can identify current job-relevant skills but is inadequate for identifying these other contextual factors that managers are increasingly looking for in new employees.

SELECTION DEVICES

What do application forms, interviews, employment tests, background checks, and personal letters of recommendation have in common? Each is a device for obtaining information about a job applicant that can help the organization determine whether or not the applicant's skills, knowledge, and abilities are appropriate for the job in question. In this section, we review the more important of these selection devices—interviews, written tests, and performance simulation tests.

Interviews In Korea, Japan, and many other Asian countries, employee interviews traditionally have not been part of the selection process. Decisions were made almost entirely on the basis of exam scores, scholastic accomplishments, and letters of recommendation. This is not the case, however, throughout most of the world. It's probably correct to say that most of us don't know anyone who has gotten a job without at least one interview. You may have an acquaintance who got a part-time or summer job through a close friend or relative without having to go through an interview, but such instances are rare. Of all the selection devices that organizations use to differentiate candidates, the interview continues to be the one most frequently used.[7] Even companies in Asian countries have begun to rely on employee interviews as a screening device.[8]

Not only is the interview widely used, it also seems to carry a great deal of weight. That is, the results tend to have a disproportionate amount of influence on the selection decision. The candidate who performs poorly in the employment interview is likely to be cut from the applicant pool, regardless of his or her experience, test scores, or letters of recommendation. Conversely, "all too often, the person most polished in job-seeking techniques, particularly those used in the interview process, is the one hired, even though he or she may not be the best candidate for the position."[9]

These findings are important because of the unstructured manner in which the selection interview is frequently conducted. The unstructured interview— short in duration, casual, and made up of random questions—has been proven to be an ineffective selection device.[10] The data gathered from such interviews are typically biased and often unrelated to future job performance. Without structure, a number of biases can distort results. These biases include interviewers tending to favor applicants who share their attitudes, giving unduly high weight to negative information, and allowing the order in which applicants are interviewed to influence evaluations.[11] By having interviewers use a standardized set of questions, providing interviewers with a uniform method of recording information, and standardizing the rating of the applicant's qualifications, the variability in results across applicants is reduced and the validity of the interview as a selection device is greatly enhanced.

The evidence indicates that interviews are most valuable for assessing an applicant's intelligence, level of motivation, and interpersonal skills.[12] When these qualities are related to job performance, the validity of the interview as a selection device is increased. For example, these qualities have demonstrated relevance for performance in upper managerial positions. This may explain why applicants for senior management positions typically undergo dozens of interviews with executive recruiters, board members, and other company executives before a final decision is made. It can also explain why organizations that design work around teams may similarly put applicants through an unusually large number of interviews.

In practice, most organizations use interviews for more than a "prediction-of-performance" device.[13] Companies as diverse as Southwest Airlines, Disney, Microsoft, and Procter & Gamble use the interview to assess applicant–organization fit. So in addition to specific, job-relevant skills, organizations are looking at candidates' personality characteristics, personal values, and the like to find individuals that fit with the organization's culture and image.

Written Tests   Typical written tests are tests of intelligence, aptitude, ability, interest, and integrity. Long popular as selection devices, they have generally declined in use since the late 1960s, especially in the United States. The reason is that such tests have frequently been characterized as discriminating, and many organizations have not validated, or cannot validate, such tests as being job related.

Selection Interviewing

The interview is made up of four stages. It begins with *preparation,* followed by the *opening,* a period of *questioning and discussion*, and a *conclusion.*[14]

1. *Preparation.* Before meeting the applicant, review his or her application form and résumé. Also review the job description and job specification of the position for which the applicant is interviewing.

   Next, structure the agenda for the interview. Specifically, use the standardized questions provided to you or prepare a set of questions you want to ask the applicant. Choose questions that can't be merely answered with only a yes or no. Avoid leading questions that telegraph the desired response (such as "Would you say you have good interpersonal skills?") and bipolar questions that require the applicant to select an answer from only two choices (such as "Do you prefer working with people or working alone?"). In most cases, questions relating to marital and family status, age, race, religion, sex, ethnic background, credit rating, and arrest record are prohibited by law in the United States unless you can demonstrate that they are in some way related to job performance. So avoid them. In place of asking "Are you married?" or "Do you have children?" you might ask "Are there any reasons why you might not be able to work overtime several times a month?" Of course, to avoid discrimination, you have to ask this question of both male and female candidates. Since the best predictor of future behavior is past behavior, the best questions tend to be those that focus on previous experiences that are relevant to the current job. Examples might include: "What have you done in previous jobs that demonstrates your creativity?" "On your last job, what was it that you most wanted to accomplish but didn't? Why didn't you?"

2. *Opening.* Assume that the applicant is tense and nervous. If you're going to get valid insights into what the applicant is really like, you'll need to put him or her at ease. Introduce yourself. Be friendly. Begin with a few simple questions or statements that can break the ice.

   Once the applicant is fairly relaxed, you should provide a brief orientation. Preview what topics will be discussed, how long the interview will take, and explain if you'll be taking notes. Encourage the applicant to ask questions.

3. *Questioning and Discussion.* The questions you developed during the preparation stage will provide a general road map to guide you. Make sure you cover them all. Additional questions should arise from the answers to the standardized questions. Select follow-up questions that naturally flow from the answers given.

   Follow-up questions should seek to probe more deeply into what the applicant says. If you feel that the applicant's response is superficial or inadequate, seek elaboration. Encourage greater response by saying, "Tell me more about that issue." To clarify information, you could say, "You said working overtime was OK *sometimes.* Can you tell me specifically when you'd be willing to work overtime?" If the applicant doesn't directly answer your question, follow up by repeating the question or paraphrasing it. Finally, never underestimate the power of silence in an interview. One of the biggest errors that inexperienced interviewers make is that they talk too much. Pause for at least a few seconds after the applicant appears to have finished an answer. Your silence encourages the applicant to continue talking.

4. *Concluding.* Once you're through with the questions and discussions, you're ready to wrap up the interview. Let the applicant know this fact with a statement such as, "Well, that covers all the questions I have. Is there anything about the job or our organization that I haven't answered for you?" Then let the applicant know what's going to happen next. When can he or she expect to hear from you? Will you write or phone? Are there likely to be more follow-up interviews?

   Before you consider the interview complete, write your evaluation while it is fresh in your mind. Ideally, you kept notes or recorded the applicant's answers to your questions and made comments of your impressions. Now that the applicant is gone, take the time to assess the applicant's responses.

Tests in intellectual ability, spatial and mechanical ability, perceptual accuracy, and motor ability have been shown to be moderately valid predictors for many semiskilled and unskilled operative jobs in industrial organizations.[15] Intelligence tests have proven to be particularly good predictors for jobs that require cognitive complexity.[16] Japanese automakers, when staffing plants in the United States, have relied heavily on written tests to predict candidates who will be high performers.[17] Getting a job with Toyota, for instance, can take up to three days of testing and interviewing. Written tests typically focus on skills such as reading, mathematics, mechanical dexterity, and ability to work with others.

As ethical problems have increased in organizations, integrity tests have gained popularity. These are paper-and-pencil tests that measure factors such as dependability, carefulness, responsibility, and honesty. The evidence is impressive that these tests are powerful in predicting supervisory ratings of job performance and counterproductive employee behavior on the job such as theft, discipline problems, and excessive absenteeism.[18]

Performance Simulation Tests   What better way is there to find out if an applicant can do a job successfully than by having him or her do it? That's precisely the logic of performance simulation tests.

Performance simulation tests have increased in popularity during the past two decades. Undoubtedly the enthusiasm for these tests comes from the fact that they are based on job analysis data and, therefore, they more easily meet the requirement of job relatedness than do most written tests.

The two best-known performance simulation tests are work sampling and assessment centers. The former is suited to routine jobs, whereas the latter is relevant for the selection of managerial personnel.

Work sampling tests are hands-on simulations of part or all of the job that must be performed by applicants. By carefully devising work samples based on job analysis data, management determines the knowledge, skills, and abilities needed for each job. Then each work sample element is matched with a corresponding job performance element. Work samples are widely used in the hiring of skilled workers, such as welders, machinists, carpenters, and electricians. Job candidates for production jobs at BMW's factory in South Carolina are given work sample tests.[19] They're given 90 minutes to perform a variety of typical work tasks on a specially built simulated assembly line.

work sampling
Creating a miniature replica of a job to evaluate the performance abilities of job candidates.

The results from work sample experiments are impressive. Studies almost consistently demonstrate that work samples yield validities superior to written aptitude and personality tests.[20]

A more elaborate set of performance simulation tests, specifically designed to evaluate a candidate's managerial potential, is administered in **assessment centers**. In assessment centers, line executives, supervisors, and/or trained psychologists evaluate candidates as they go through one to several days of exercises that simulate real problems that they would confront on the job.[21] Based on a list of descriptive dimensions that the actual job incumbent has to meet, activities might include interviews, in-basket problem-solving exercises, leaderless group discussions, and business decision games. For instance, a candidate might be required to play the role of a manager who must decide how to respond to 10 memos in his or her in-basket within a two-hour period.

assessment centers
A set of performance simulation tests designed to evaluate a candidate's managerial potential.

How valid is the assessment center as a selection device? The evidence on the effectiveness of assessment centers is impressive. They have consistently demonstrated results that predict later job performance in managerial positions.[22]

"It's First Impressions That Count"

This statement is true. When we meet someone for the first time, we notice a number of things about that person—physical characteristics, clothes, firmness of handshake, gestures, tone of voice, and the like. We then use these impressions to fit the person into ready-made categories. And this early categorization, formed quickly and on the basis of minimal information, tends to hold greater weight than impressions and information received later.

The best evidence on first impressions comes from research on employment interviews. Findings clearly demonstrate that first impressions count. For instance, the primacy effect is potent. That is, the first information presented affects later judgments more than information presented later.[23]

Research on applicant appearance confirms the power of first impressions.[24] Studies have looked at assessments made of applicants before the actual interview—that brief period in which the applicant walks into an interview room, exchanges greetings with the interviewer, sits down, and engages in minor chit-chat. The evidence indicates that the way applicants walk, talk, dress, and look can have a great impact on the interviewer's evaluation of applicant qualifications. Facial attractiveness seems to be particularly influencial. Applicants who are highly attractive are evaluated as more qualified for a variety of jobs than persons who are unattractive.

A final body of confirmative research finds that interviewers' postinterview evaluations of applicants conform, to a substantial degree, to their preinterview impressions.[25] That is, those first impressions carry considerable weight in shaping the interviewers' final evaluations, regardless of what actually transpired in the interview itself. This latter conclusion assumes that the interview elicits no highly negative information.

TRAINING AND DEVELOPMENT PROGRAMS

Competent employees don't remain competent forever. Skills deteriorate and can become obsolete. That's why organizations spend billions of dollars each year on formal training. For instance, it was reported that U.S. corporations with 100 or more employees spent $60.7 billion in one recent year on formal training for 50 million workers.[26] Xerox, as a case in point, spends more than $300 million each year on training and retraining its employees.[27]

TYPES OF TRAINING

Training can include everything from teaching employees basic reading skills to advanced courses in executive leadership. The following summarizes four general skill categories—basic literacy, technical, interpersonal, and problem solving. In addition, we briefly discuss ethics training.

Basic Literacy Skills A recent report by the U.S. Department of Education found that 90 million American adults have limited literacy skills, and about 40 million can read little or not at all![28] Most workplace demands require a tenth or eleventh grade reading level, but about 20 percent of Americans between the ages of 21 and 25 can't read at even an eighth grade level.[29] And in many Third World countries, few workers can read or have gone beyond the equivalent of the third grade.

Organizations are increasingly having to provide basic reading and math skills for their employees. For instance, William Dudek runs a small manufacturing firm on Chicago's north side.[30] His 35 employees make metal clips, hooks, and clasps used in household appliances and automotive components. When

Dudek tried to introduce some basic quality management principles in his plant, he noticed that many of his employees seemed to disregard the written instructions, and only a few could calculate percentages or plot a simple graph. After confirming his employees' lack of basic skills, he hired an instructor and had classes in English and mathematics taught to his employees in the firm's cafeteria. Dudek said that this training, which cost him $15,000 in its first year, made his employees more efficient and that they now work better as a team.

Technical Skills   Most training is directed at upgrading and improving an employee's technical skills. Technical training has become increasingly important today for two reasons—new technology and new structural designs.

Jobs change as a result of new technologies and improved methods. For instance, many auto repair personnel have had to undergo extensive training to fix and maintain recent models with computer-monitored engines, electronic stabilizing systems, and other innovations. Similarly, computer-controlled equipment has required millions of production employees to learn a whole new set of skills.

In addition, technical training has become increasingly important because of changes in organization design. As organizations flatten their structures, expand their use of teams, and break down traditional departmental barriers, employees need to learn a wider variety of tasks.

Financial services firm Merrill Lynch is upgrading its stockbrokers' technical skills by teaching them how to conduct trades on the Internet. Although the company's full-service stockbrokers are not currently involved in Internet trading, Merrill Lynch wants them to be proficient in using the new technology. The company believes that with the explosion in online trading, full-service customers may want to trade on the Internet in the future, and it wants its stockbrokers to be prepared to do so when that time comes.

Interpersonal Skills   Almost all employees belong to a work unit. To some degree, their work performance depends on their ability to effectively interact with their co-workers and their boss. Some employees have excellent interpersonal skills, but others require training to improve theirs. This includes learning how to be a better listener, how to communicate ideas more clearly, and how to be a more effective team player.

Problem-Solving Skills   Managers, as well as many employees who perform nonroutine tasks, have to solve problems on their job. When people require these skills but are deficient in them, they can participate in problem-solving training. This would include activities to sharpen their logic, reasoning, and problem-defining skills, as well as their abilities to assess causation, develop alternatives, analyze alternatives, and select solutions. Problem-solving training has become a basic part of almost every organizational effort to introduce self-managed teams or implement TQM.

What About Ethics Training?   A recent survey finds that about 75 percent of employees working in the 1,000 largest U.S. corporations receive ethics training.[31] But the evidence is not clear on whether you can teach ethics.

Critics argue that ethics are based on values, and value systems are fixed at an early age. By the time employers hire people, their ethical values have already been established. The critics also claim that ethics cannot be formally "taught" but must be learned by example.

Supporters of ethics training argue that values can be learned and changed after early childhood. And even if they couldn't, ethics training would be effective because it helps employees to recognize ethical dilemmas and become more aware of the ethical issues underlying their actions, and it reaffirms an organization's expectations that members will act ethically.

TRAINING METHODS

Training methods are most readily classified as formal or informal and on-the-job or off-the-job training.

Historically, training meant *formal training* that's planned in advance and has a structured format. However, recent evidence indicates that organizations are increasingly relying on *informal training*—unstructured, unplanned, and easily adapted to situations and individuals—for teaching skills and keeping employees current.[32] In reality, most informal training is nothing other than employees helping each other out. They share information and solve work-related problems with one another. Maybe the most important outcome of this trend is that many managers are now supportive of what used to be considered "idle chatter." At a Siemens plant in North Carolina, for instance, management now recognizes that people needn't be on the production line to be working.[33] Discussions around the water cooler or in the cafeteria weren't, as managers thought, about nonwork topics such as sports or politics. They largely focused on solving work-related problems. So now Siemens's management encourages such casual meetings.

On-the-job training includes job rotation, apprenticeships, understudy assignments, and formal mentoring programs. But the primary drawback of these on-the-job training methods is that they often disrupt the workplace. So organizations invest in *off-the-job training*. The $60 billion figure we cited earlier for training costs was largely spent on the formal, off-the-job variety. What types of training might this include? The most popular is live classroom lectures. But it also encompasses videotapes, public seminars, self-study programs, Internet courses, satellite-beamed television classes, and group activities that use role plays and case studies. One of the most famous off-the-job training programs is the two-week course offered at McDonald's Hamburger University.[34] Ham U's curriculum combines operations enhancement, equipment management, and interpersonal skills training for restaurant managers and franchisees. And it's all done in a protected environment that maximizes learning while minimizing frustration on real customers. Most of us have experienced that "slow burn" when we have to deal with a clerk, cashier, or

The Grand Hyatt in Shanghai uses off-the-job training to teach its Chinese staff the high standards of customer service the hotel provides at its locations worldwide. In this photo, new hires are trained in the art of serving tea in one of the hotel's dining areas. Hyatt believes that its investment in training employees to give guests exceptional service will give it a competitive advantage over other Chinese hotels, where service is below international standards.

other service employee who is undergoing on-the-job training. They take up our valuable time while a supervisor tries to explain or show an employee how particular tasks are to be done.

INDIVIDUALIZE FORMAL TRAINING TO FIT THE EMPLOYEE'S LEARNING STYLE

The way that you process, internalize, and remember new and difficult material isn't necessarily the same way that I do. This fact means that effective formal training should be individualized to reflect the learning style of the employee.[35]

Some examples of different learning styles include reading, watching, listening, and participating. Some people absorb information better when they read about it. They're the kind of people who can learn to use computers by sitting in their study and reading manuals. Some people learn best by observation. They watch others and then emulate the behaviors they've seen. Such people can watch someone use a computer for a while and then copy what they've seen. Listeners rely heavily on their auditory senses to absorb information. They would prefer to learn how to use a computer by listening to an audiotape. People who prefer a participating style learn by doing. They want to sit down, turn on the computer, and gain hands-on experience by practicing.

You can translate these styles into different learning methods. To maximize learning, readers should be given books or other reading material to review; watchers should get the opportunity to observe individuals modeling the new skills either in person or on video; listeners will benefit from hearing lectures or audiotapes; and participants will benefit most from experiential opportunities in which they can simulate and practice the new skills.

These different learning styles are obviously not mutually exclusive. In fact, good teachers recognize that their students learn differently and, therefore, provide multiple learning methods. They assign readings before class; give lectures; use visual aids to illustrate concepts; and have students participate in group projects, case analyses, role plays, and experiential learning exercises. If you know the preferred style of an employee, you can design his or her formal training program to optimize this preference. If you don't have that information, it's probably best to design the program to use a variety of learning styles. Overreliance on a single style places individuals who don't learn well from that style at a disadvantage.

CAREER DEVELOPMENT

Few human resource issues have changed as much in the past decade or two as the role of the organization in its employees' careers.[36] It has gone from paternalism—in which the organization took nearly complete responsibility for managing its employees' careers—to supporting individuals as they take personal responsibility for their future. And careers, themselves, have gone from a series of upward moves with increasing income, authority, status, and security to one in which people adapt quickly, learn continuously, and change their work identities over time.

For much of this century, companies recruited young workers with the intent that they would spend their entire career inside that single organization. For those with the right credentials and motivation, they created promotion paths dotted with ever-increasing responsibility. Employers would provide the training and opportunities, and employees would respond by demonstrating loyalty and hard work. This arrangement has undergone serious decay. High uncertainty now limits the ability of organizations to accurately forecast future needs. Management seeks flexibility over permanence. Meanwhile, flattened hierarchies have reduced

EXHIBIT

16-2

NON SEQUITUR BY WILEY

YEAH... BUT YOU'VE GOT TO ADMIT, IT'S MORE FUN THAN THE TRADITIONAL PINK SLIP

©1996 Washington Post Writers Group

WILEY 9-12

E-mail: SEQUITOON@aol.com

Source: Non Sequitur by Wiley. September 12, 1996. Washington Post Writers Group.

promotion opportunities. The result is that, today, career planning is something increasingly being done by individual employees rather than by their employers. It has become the employee's responsibility to keep his or her skills, abilities, and knowledge current and to prepare for tomorrow's new tasks.

The Organization's Responsibilities What, if any, responsibility does the organization have for career development under these new rules? Amoco Corp.'s career development program is a model for modern companies.[37] It's designed around employee self-reliance and to help employees reflect on their marketability both inside and outside the Chicago-based oil company. All workers are encouraged to participate in a half-day introduction to the program and full-day self-assessment and self-development sessions. The company supports its employees by providing information—a worldwide electronic job-posting system, a network of career advisers, and a worldwide directory of Amoco employees and their skills from which company managers can search for candidates for job openings. But the whole program is voluntary and assumes that it's the employee's responsibility to maintain his or her employability.

The essence of a progressive career development program is built on providing support for employees to continually add to their skills, abilities, and knowledge. This support includes:

1. *Clearly communicating the organization's goals and future strategies.* When people know where the organization is headed, they're better able to develop a personal plan to share in that future.
2. *Creating growth opportunities.* Employees should have the opportunity to get new, interesting, and professionally challenging work experiences.
3. *Offering financial assistance.* The organization should offer tuition reimbursement to help employees keep current.
4. *Providing the time for employees to learn.* Organizations should be generous in providing paid time off from work for off-the-job training. Additionally, workloads should not be so demanding that they preclude employees from having the time to develop new skills, abilities, and knowledge.

The Employee's Responsibilities Today's employees should manage their own careers like entrepreneurs managing a small business. They should think of themselves as self-employed, even if employed in a large organization.[38] In a world of "free agency," the successful career will be built on maintaining flexibility and keeping skills and knowledge up-to-date. The following suggestions are consistent with the view that you, and only you, hold primary responsibility for your career.[39]

1. *Know yourself.* Know your strengths and weaknesses. What talents can you bring to an employer? Personal career planning begins by being honest with yourself.
2. *Manage your reputation.* Without appearing as a braggart, let others both inside and outside your current organization know about your achievements. Make yourself and your accomplishments visible.
3. *Build and maintain network contacts.* In a world of high mobility, you need to develop contacts. Join national and local professional associations, attend conferences, and network at social gatherings.
4. *Keep current.* Develop those specific skills and abilities that are in high demand. Avoid learning organization-specific skills that can't be transferred quickly to other employers.
5. *Balance your specialist and generalist competencies.* You need to stay current within your technical specialty. But you also need to develop general competencies that give you the versatility to react to an ever-changing work environment. Overemphasis in a single functional area or even in a narrow industry can limit your mobility.
6. *Document your achievements.* Employers are increasingly looking to what you've accomplished rather than the titles you've held. Seek jobs and assignments that will provide increasing challenges and that will also offer objective evidence of your competencies.
7. *Keep your options open.* Always have contingency plans prepared that you can call on when needed. You never know when your group will be eliminated, your department downsized, your project canceled, or your company acquired in a takeover. "Hope for the best but be prepared for the worst" may be a cliché, but it's still not bad advice.

French computer services firm CAP Gemini Sogeti gives its software engineers and technicians challenging work experiences and provides them with the tools they need to keep current. The company's intranet, called Knowledge Galaxy, puts critical resources and expertise within each employee's reach. It even installed an Internet cafe at its Paris headquarters, shown here, so employees can surf the Net during their breaks. But CAP Gemini assumes that it's the employees' responsibility to develop their skills and keep current with their technical specialty as well as with the trends in the fast-changing software industry.

PERFORMANCE EVALUATION

Would you study differently or exert a different level of effort for a college course graded on a pass-fail basis than for one in which letter grades from A to F are used? When I ask that question of students, I usually get an affirmative answer. Students typically tell me that they study harder when letter grades are at stake. Additionally, they tell me that when they take a course on a pass-fail basis, they tend to do just enough to ensure a passing grade.

This finding illustrates how performance evaluation systems influence behavior. Major determinants of your in-class behavior and out-of-class studying effort in college are the criteria and techniques your instructor uses to evaluate your performance. Of course, what applies in the college context also applies to employees at work. In this section, we show how the choice of a performance evaluation system and the way it's administered can be an important force influencing employee behavior.

PURPOSES OF PERFORMANCE EVALUATION

Performance evaluation serves a number of purposes in organizations (see Exhibit 16-3 for survey results on primary uses of evaluations).[40] Management uses evaluations for general *human resource decisions.* Evaluations provide input

Use	Percent*
Compensation	85.6
Performance feedback	65.1
Training	64.3
Promotion	45.3
Human resource planning	43.1
Retention/discharge	30.3
Research	17.2

EXHIBIT 16-3

*Based on responses from 600 organizations.

Source: Based on "Performance Appraisal: Current Practices and Techniques," *Personnel*, May–June 1984, p. 57.

into such important decisions as promotions, transfers, and terminations. Evaluations *identify training and development needs*. They pinpoint employee skills and competencies that are currently inadequate but for which programs can be developed to remedy. Performance evaluations can be used as a *criterion against which selection and development programs are validated*. Newly hired employees who perform poorly can be identified through performance evaluation. Similarly, the effectiveness of training and development programs can be determined by assessing how well those employees who have participated do on their performance evaluation. Evaluations also fulfill the purpose of *providing feedback to employees* on how the organization views their performance. Furthermore, performance evaluations are used as the *basis for reward allocations*. Decisions as to who gets merit pay increases and other rewards are frequently determined by performance evaluations.

Each of these functions of performance evaluation is important. Yet their importance to us depends on the perspective we're taking. Several are clearly relevant to human resource management decisions. But our interest is in organizational behavior. As a result, we shall be emphasizing performance evaluation in its role as a mechanism for providing feedback and as a determinant of reward allocations.

PERFORMANCE EVALUATION AND MOTIVATION

In Chapter 6, considerable attention was given to the expectancy model of motivation. We argued that this model currently offers one of the best explanations of what influences the amount of effort an individual will exert on his or her job. A vital component of this model is performance, specifically the effort–performance and performance–reward linkages.

But what defines *performance*? In the expectancy model, it's the individual's performance evaluation. To maximize motivation, people need to perceive that the effort they exert leads to a favorable performance evaluation and that the favorable evaluation will lead to the rewards that they value.

Following the expectancy model of motivation, if the objectives that employees are expected to achieve are unclear, if the criteria for measuring those objectives are vague, and if the employees lack confidence that their efforts will lead to a satisfactory appraisal of their performance or believe that there will be an unsatisfactory payoff by the organization when their performance objectives are achieved, we can expect individuals to work considerably below their potential.

WHAT DO WE EVALUATE?

The criteria or criterion that management chooses to evaluate, when appraising employee performance, will have a major influence on what employees do. Two examples illustrate this.

In a public employment agency, which served workers seeking employment and employers seeking workers, employment interviewers were appraised by the number of interviews they conducted. Consistent with the thesis that the evaluating criteria influence behavior, interviewers emphasized the *number* of interviews conducted rather than the *placements* of clients in jobs.[41]

A management consultant specializing in police research noticed that, in one community, officers would come on duty for their shift, proceed to get into their police cars, drive to the highway that cut through the town, and speed back and forth along this highway for their entire shift. Clearly this fast cruising had little to do with good police work, but this behavior made considerably more sense once the consultant learned that the community's city council used mileage on police vehicles as an evaluative measure of police effectiveness.[42]

These examples demonstrate the importance of criteria in performance evaluation. This, of course, begs the question: What should management evaluate? The three most popular sets of criteria are individual task outcomes, behaviors, and traits.

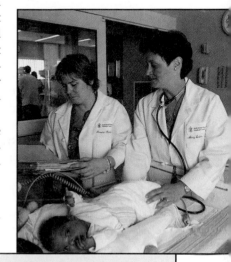

In addition to their clinical knowledge, nurses are evaluated on behaviors such as building caring and trusting relationships with patients and family members and providing emotional support for medical team members. These behaviors improve the overall performance of nurses like Mary Quinn (right), a critical-care neonatal specialist at Beth Israel Deaconess Medical Center in Boston. Working on a team that resuscitates infants, Quinn must confer with and console parents facing difficult decisions about their critically ill babies.

Individual Task Outcomes   If ends count rather than means, then management should evaluate an employee's task outcomes. Using task outcomes, a plant manager could be judged on criteria such as quantity produced, scrap generated, and cost per unit of production. Similarly, a salesperson could be assessed on overall sales volume in his or her territory, dollar increase in sales, and number of new accounts established.

Behaviors   In many cases, it's difficult to identify specific outcomes that can be directly attributable to an employee's actions. This is particularly true of personnel in staff positions and individuals whose work assignments are intrinsically part of a group effort. In the latter case, the group's performance may be readily evaluated, but the contribution of each group member may be difficult or impossible to identify clearly. In such instances, it is not unusual for management to evaluate the employee's behavior. Using the previous examples, behaviors of a plant manager that could be used for performance evaluation purposes might include promptness in submitting his or her monthly reports or the leadership style that the manager exhibits. Pertinent salesperson behaviors could be average number of contact calls made per day or sick days used per year.

Note that these behaviors needn't be limited to those directly related to individual productivity.[43] As we pointed out in our previous discussion on organizational citizenship behavior (see specifically Chapters 1 and 4), helping others, making suggestions for improvements, and volunteering for extra duties make work groups and organizations more effective. So including subjective or contextual factors in a performance evaluation—as long as these factors contribute to organizational effectiveness—may not only make sense; they may also improve coordination, teamwork, cooperation, and overall organizational performance.

Traits   The weakest set of criteria, yet one that is still widely used by organizations, is individual traits.[44] We say they are weaker than either task outcomes or behaviors because they are farthest removed from the actual performance of the job itself. Traits such as having "a good attitude," showing "confidence," being "dependable," "looking busy," or possessing "a wealth of experience" may or may not be highly correlated with positive task outcomes, but only the naive would ignore the reality that such traits are frequently used in organizations as criteria for assessing an employee's level of performance.

WHO SHOULD DO THE EVALUATING?

Who should evaluate an employee's performance? The obvious answer would seem to be his or her immediate boss! By tradition, a manager's authority typically has included appraising subordinates' performance. The logic behind this tradition seems to be that since managers are held responsible for their employees' performance, it only makes sense that these managers do the evaluating of their performance. But that logic may be flawed. Others may actually be able to do the job better.

Immediate Superior   As we implied, about 95 percent of all performance evaluations at the lower and middle levels of the organization are conducted by the employee's immediate boss.[45] Yet a number of organizations are recognizing the drawbacks to using this source of evaluation. For instance, many bosses feel unqualified to evaluate the unique contributions of each of their employees. Others resent being asked to "play God" with their employees' careers. Additionally, with many of today's organizations using self-managed teams, telecommuting, and other organizing devices that distance bosses from their employees, an employee's immediate superior may not be a reliable judge of that employee's performance.

> *About 95 percent of all performance evaluations at the lower and middle levels of the organization are conducted by the employee's immediate boss.*

Peers   Peer evaluations are one of the most reliable sources of appraisal data. Why? First, peers are close to the action. Daily interactions provide them with a comprehensive view of an employee's job performance. Second, using peers as raters results in a number of independent judgments. A boss can offer only a single evaluation, but peers can provide multiple appraisals. And the average of several ratings is often more reliable than a single evaluation. On the downside, peer evaluations can suffer from co-workers' unwillingness to evaluate one another and from biases based on friendship or animosity.

Self-Evaluation   Having employees evaluate their own performance is consistent with values such as self-management and empowerment. Self-evaluations get high marks from employees themselves; they tend to lessen employees' defensiveness about the appraisal process; and they make excellent vehicles for stimulating job performance discussions between employees and their superiors. However, as you might guess, they suffer from overinflated assessment and self-serving bias. Moreover, self-evaluations are often low in agreement with superiors' ratings.[46] Because of these serious drawbacks, self-evaluations are probably better suited to developmental uses than evaluative purposes.

Immediate Subordinates   A fourth judgment source is an employee's immediate subordinates. For instance, Datatec Industries, a maker of in-store computer systems, uses this form of appraisal.[47] The company's president says it's consistent with the firm's core values of honesty, openness, and employee empowerment.

Immediate subordinates' evaluations can provide accurate and detailed information about a manager's behavior because the evaluators typically have frequent contact with the evaluatee. The obvious problem with this form of rating is fear of reprisal from bosses given unfavorable evaluations. Therefore, respondent anonymity is crucial if these evaluations are to be accurate.

360-Degree Evaluations The latest approach to performance evaluation is the use of 360-degree evaluations.[48] It provides for performance feedback from the full circle of daily contacts that an employee might have, ranging from mailroom personnel to customers to bosses to peers (see Exhibit 16-4). The number of appraisals can be as few as three or four evaluations or as many as 25; with most organizations collecting five to ten per employee.

A recent survey shows that about 12 percent of American organizations are using full 360-degree programs but the trend is growing.[49] Companies currently using this approach include Alcoa, Du Pont, Levi Strauss, Honeywell, UPS, Sprint, Amoco, AT&T, and W.L. Gore & Associates.

What's the appeal of 360-degree evaluations? They fit well into organizations that have introduced teams, employee involvement, and TQM programs. By relying on feedback from co-workers, customers, and subordinates, these organizations are hoping to give everyone more of a sense of participation in the review process and gain more accurate readings on employee performance.

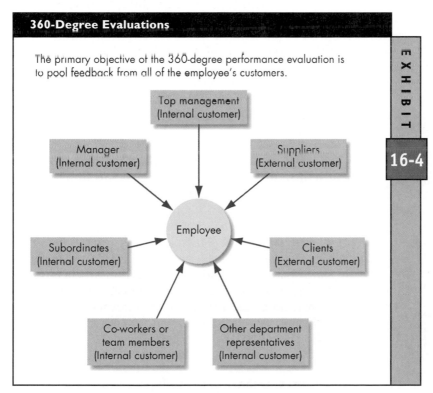

360-Degree Evaluations

The primary objective of the 360-degree performance evaluation is to pool feedback from all of the employee's customers.

EXHIBIT 16-4

Top management (Internal customer)

Manager (Internal customer)

Suppliers (External customer)

Employee

Subordinates (Internal customer)

Clients (External customer)

Co-workers or team members (Internal customer)

Other department representatives (Internal customer)

Source: Adapted from *Personnel Journal*, November 1994, p. 100.

Glossary terms (margin)

critical incidents

Evaluating those behaviors that are key in making the difference between executing a job effectively and executing it ineffectively.

graphic rating scales

An evaluation method in which the evaluator rates performance factors on an incremental scale.

behaviorally anchored rating scales

An evaluation method in which actual job-related behaviors are rated along a continuum.

METHODS OF PERFORMANCE EVALUATION

The previous sections explained *what* we evaluate and *who* should do the evaluating. Now we ask: *How* do we evaluate an employee's performance? That is, what are the specific techniques for evaluation? This section reviews the major performance evaluation methods.

Written Essays Probably the simplest method of evaluation is to write a narrative describing an employee's strengths, weaknesses, past performance, potential, and suggestions for improvement. The written essay requires no complex forms or extensive training to complete. But the results often reflect the ability of the writer. A good or bad appraisal may be determined as much by the evaluator's writing skill as by the employee's actual level of performance.

Critical Incidents **Critical incidents** focus the evaluator's attention on those behaviors that are key in making the difference between executing a job effectively and executing it ineffectively. That is, the appraiser writes down anecdotes that describe what the employee did that was especially effective or ineffective.

The key here is that only specific behaviors, not vaguely defined personality traits, are cited. A list of critical incidents provides a rich set of examples from which the employee can be shown those behaviors that are desirable and those that call for improvement.

Graphic Rating Scales One of the oldest and most popular methods of evaluation is the use of **graphic rating scales**. In this method, a set of performance factors, such as quantity and quality of work, depth of knowledge, cooperation, loyalty, attendance, honesty, and initiative, is listed. The evaluator then goes down the list and rates each on incremental scales. The scales typically specify five points, so a factor such as *job knowledge* might be rated 1 ("poorly informed about work duties") to 5 ("has complete mastery of all phases of the job").

Why are graphic ratings scales so popular? Though they don't provide the depth of information that essays or critical incidents do, they are less time consuming to develop and administer. They also allow for quantitative analysis and comparison.

Vidcon Enterprises owners Kerry Schultz (top left) and Kevin Schultz use a computer-based performance evaluation program so the managers of their seven video and convenience stores have a consistent technique for employee reviews. The evaluation consists of a graphic rating scale that rates employees on a scale from I to 5. It covers II performance factors such as job knowledge, initiative, and oral and written communication. Each factor is weighted according to its importance to an employee's job function.

Behaviorally Anchored Rating Scales Behaviorally anchored rating scales (BARS) combine major elements from the critical incident and graphic rating scale approaches: The appraiser rates the employees based on items along a continuum, but the points are examples of actual behavior on the given job rather than general descriptions or traits.

BARS specify definite, observable, and measurable job behavior. Examples of job-related behavior and performance dimensions are found by asking participants to give specific illustrations of effective and ineffective behavior regarding each performance dimension. These behavioral examples are then translated into a set of performance dimensions, each dimension having varying levels of performance. The results of this process are behavioral descriptions, such as *anticipates, plans, executes, solves immediate problems, carries out orders,* and *handles emergency situations.*

Multiperson Comparisons Multiperson comparisons evaluate one individual's performance against the performance of one or more others. It is a relative rather than an absolute measuring device. The three most popular comparisons are group order ranking, individual ranking, and paired comparisons.

The **group order ranking** requires the evaluator to place employees into a particular classification, such as top one-fifth or second one-fifth. This method is often used in recommending students to graduate schools. Evaluators are asked whether the student ranks in the top 5 percent of the class, the next 5 percent, the next 15 percent, and so forth. But when used by managers to appraise employees, managers deal with all their subordinates. Therefore, if a rater has 20 employees, only four can be in the top fifth and, of course, four must also be relegated to the bottom fifth.

The **individual ranking** approach rank-orders employees from best to worst. If the manager is required to appraise 30 employees, this approach assumes that the difference between the first and second employee is the same as that between the twenty-first and twenty-second. Even though some of the employees may be closely grouped, this approach allows for no ties. The result is a clear ordering of employees, from the highest performer down to the lowest.

The **paired comparison** approach compares each employee with every other employee and rates each as either the superior or the weaker member of the pair. After all paired comparisons are made, each employee is assigned a summary ranking based on the number of superior scores he or she achieved. This approach ensures that each employee is compared against every other, but it can obviously become unwieldy when many employees are being compared.

Multiperson comparisons can be combined with one of the other methods to blend the best from both absolute and relative standards. For example, in an effort to deal with grade inflation, Dartmouth College a few years back changed its transcripts to include not only a letter grade but also class size and class average.[50] So a prospective employer or graduate school can now look at two students who each got a B in their physical geology courses and draw considerably different conclusions about each because next to one grade it says the average grade was a C, while next to the other it says the average grade was a B+. Obviously, the former student performed relatively better than did the latter.

SUGGESTIONS FOR IMPROVING PERFORMANCE EVALUATIONS

The performance evaluation process is a potential minefield of problems. For instance, evaluators can make leniency, halo, and similarity errors, or use the process for political purposes. They can unconsciously inflate evaluations (positive leniency), understate performance (negative leniency), or allow the assessment of one characteristic to unduly influence the assessment of other characteristics (the halo error). Some appraisers bias their evaluations by unconsciously favoring people who have qualities and traits similar to themselves (the similarity error). And, of course, some evaluators see the evaluation process as a political opportunity to overtly reward or punish employees they like or dislike. While there are no protections that will *guarantee* accurate performance evaluations, the following suggestions can significantly help to make the process more objective and fair.

Emphasize Behaviors Rather Than Traits Many traits often considered to be related to good performance may, in fact, have little or no performance relationship. For example, traits such as loyalty, initiative, courage, reliability, and self-expression are intuitively appealing as desirable characteristics in employees. But the relevant question is: Are individuals who are evaluated as high on those traits higher performers than those who rate low? We can't answer this question

group order ranking

An evaluation method that places employees into a particular classification such as quartiles.

individual ranking

An evaluation method that rank-orders employees from best to worst.

paired comparison

An evaluation method that compares each employee with every other employee and assigns a summary ranking based on the number of superior scores that the employee achieves.

easily. We know that there are employees who rate high on these characteristics and are poor performers. We can find others who are excellent performers but do not score well on traits such as these. Our conclusion is that traits such as loyalty and initiative may be prized by managers, but there is no evidence to support that certain traits will be adequate synonyms for performance in a large cross section of jobs.

Another weakness of trait evaluation is the judgment itself. What is "loyalty"? When is an employee "reliable"? What you consider "loyalty," I may not. So traits suffer from weak interrater agreement.

Document Performance Behaviors in a Diary   Diaries help evaluators to better organize information in their memory. The evidence indicates that by keeping a diary of specific critical incidents for each employee, evaluations tend to be more accurate and less prone to rating errors.[51] Diaries, for instance, tend to reduce leniency and halo errors because they encourage the evaluator to focus on performance-related behaviors rather than traits.

Use Multiple Evaluators   As the number of evaluators increases, the probability of attaining more accurate information increases. If rater error tends to follow a normal curve, an increase in the number of appraisers will tend to find the majority congregating about the middle. You see this approach being used in athletic competitions in such sports as diving and gymnastics. A set of evaluators judges a performance, the highest and lowest scores are dropped, and the final performance evaluation is made up from the cumulative scores of those remaining. The logic of multiple evaluators applies to organizations as well.

If an employee has had ten supervisors, nine having rated her excellent and one poor, we can discount the value of the one poor evaluation. Therefore, by moving employees about within the organization so as to gain a number of evaluations or by using multiple assessors (as provided in 360-degree appraisals), we increase the probability of achieving more valid and reliable evaluations.

Evaluate Selectively   Appraisers should evaluate in only those areas in which they have some expertise.[52] If raters make evaluations on only those dimensions on which they are in a good position to rate, we increase the interrater agreement and make the evaluation a more valid process. This approach also recognizes that different organizational levels often have different orientations toward ratees and observe them in different settings. In general, therefore, we would recommend that appraisers should be as close as possible, in terms of organizational level, to the individual being evaluated. Conversely, the more levels that separate the evaluator and evaluatee, the less opportunity the evaluator has to observe the individual's behavior and, not surprisingly, the greater the possibility for inaccuracies.

Train Evaluators   If you can't *find* good evaluators, the alternative is to *make* good evaluators. There is substantial evidence that training evaluators can make them more accurate raters.[53]

Common errors such as halo and leniency have been minimized or eliminated in workshops in which managers practice observing and rating behaviors. These workshops typically run from one to three days, but allocating many hours to training may not always be necessary. One case has been cited in which both halo and leniency errors were decreased immediately after exposing evaluators to explanatory training sessions lasting only five minutes.[54] But the effects of training do appear to diminish over time.[55] This suggests the need for regular refresher sessions.

Provide Employees with Due Process   The concept of *due process* can be applied to appraisals to increase the perception that employees are treated fairly.[56] Three features characterize due process systems: (1) Individuals are provided with adequate notice of what is expected of them; (2) all relevant evidence to a proposed violation is aired in a fair hearing so individuals affected can respond; and (3) the final decision is based on the evidence and free from bias.

There is considerable evidence that evaluation systems often violate employees' due process by providing them with infrequent and relatively general performance feedback, allowing them little input into the appraisal process, and knowingly introducing bias into performance ratings. However, when due process has been part of the evaluation system, employees report positive reactions to the appraisal process, perceive the evaluation results as more accurate, and express increased intent to remain with the organization.

PROVIDING PERFORMANCE FEEDBACK

For many managers, few activities are more unpleasant than providing performance feedback to employees.[57] In fact, unless pressured by organizational policies and controls, managers are likely to ignore this responsibility.[58]

Why the reluctance to give performance feedback? There seem to be at least three reasons. First, managers are often uncomfortable discussing performance weaknesses directly with employees. Given that almost every employee could stand to improve in some areas, managers fear a confrontation when presenting negative feedback. This apparently even applies when people give negative feedback to a computer! Bill Gates reports that Microsoft conducted a project that required users to rate their experience with a computer. "When we

> For many managers, few activities are more unpleasant than providing performance feedback to employees.

had the computer the users had worked with ask for an evaluation of its performance, the responses tended to be positive. But when we had a second computer ask the same people to evaluate their encounters with the first machine, the people were significantly more critical. Their reluctance to criticize the first computer 'to its face' suggested that they didn't want to hurt its feelings, even though they knew it was only a machine."[59] Second, many employees tend to become defensive when their weaknesses are pointed out. Instead of accepting the feedback as constructive and a basis for improving performance, some employees challenge the evaluation by criticizing the manager or redirecting blame to someone else. A survey of 151 area managers in Philadelphia, for instance, found that 98 percent of these managers encountered some type of aggression after giving employees negative appraisals.[60] Finally, employees tend to have an inflated assessment of their own performance. Statistically speaking, half of all employees must be below-average performers. But the evidence indicates that the average employee's estimate of his or her own performance level generally falls around the 75th percentile.[61] So even when managers are providing good news, employees are likely to perceive it as not good enough!

The solution to the performance feedback problem is not to ignore it but to train managers in how to conduct constructive feedback sessions. An effective review—one in which the employee perceives the appraisal as fair, the manager as sincere, and the climate as constructive—can result in the employee leaving the interview in an upbeat mood, informed about the performance areas in which he or she needs to improve, and determined to correct the deficiencies.[62] In addition, the performance review should be designed more as a counseling activity than a judgment process. This can best be accomplished by allowing the review to evolve out of the employee's own self-evaluation.

WHAT ABOUT TEAM PERFORMANCE EVALUATIONS?

Performance evaluation concepts have been almost exclusively developed with only individual employees in mind. This reflects the historic belief that individuals are the core building block around which organizations are built. But as we've described throughout this book, more and more organizations are restructuring themselves around teams. In those organizations using teams, how should they evaluate performance? Four suggestions have been offered for designing a system that supports and improves the performance of teams.[63]

1. *Tie the team's results to the organization's goals.* It's important to find measurements that apply to important goals that the team is supposed to accomplish.
2. *Begin with the team's customers and the work process the team follows to satisfy customers' needs.* The final product the customer receives can be evaluated in terms of the customer's requirements. The transactions between teams can be evaluated based on delivery and quality. And the process steps can be evaluated based on waste and cycle time.
3. *Measure both team and individual performance.* Define the roles of each team member in terms of accomplishments that support the team's work process. Then assess each member's contribution and the team's overall performance. Remember that individual skills are necessary for team success but are not sufficient for good team performance.[64]
4. *Train the team to create its own measures.* Having the team define its objectives and those of each member ensures everyone understands their role on the team and helps the team develop into a more cohesive unit.

THE UNION-MANAGEMENT INTERFACE

labor union

An organization, made up of employees, that acts collectively to protect and promote employee interests.

Labor unions are a vehicle by which employees act collectively to protect and promote their interests. Currently, in the United States, less than 15 percent of the workforce belongs to and is represented by a union. This number is considerably higher in other countries. For instance, the comparable figures for Canada and Australia are 37 percent and 41 percent, respectively.

For employees who are members of a labor union, wage levels and conditions of employment are explicitly articulated in a contract that is negotiated, through collective bargaining, between representatives of the union and the organization's management. Where a labor union exists, it influences a number of organizational activities.[65] Recruitment sources, hiring criteria, work schedules, job design, redress procedures, safety rules, and eligibility for training programs are examples of activities that are influenced by unions. American labor unions, having to contend with declining job markets in industries in which they were historically strong—such as steel, autos, and rubber—have focused their attention in recent years on improving stagnant wages, discouraging corporate downsizings, minimizing the outsourcing of jobs, and coping with job obsolescence.[66]

The most obvious and pervasive area of labor's influence is wage rates and working conditions. Where unions exist, performance evaluation systems tend to be less complex because they play a relatively small part in reward decisions.

The Union's Impact on Employee Performance and Job Satisfaction

Union contract provisions for performance outcome contingencies

Union training programs, apprenticeships, leadership experience

Union restrictions on amount produced, speed of work, overtime, type of work allowed, productivity bargaining, specification of leader role

Union contract provisions, open information on outcome distributions, equitable distributions

EXHIBIT 16-5

Situational constraints or facilitators

Motivation × Ability → Performance → Outcome attainment and job satisfaction

Source: T. H. Hammer, "Relationships Between Local Union Characteristics and Worker Behavior and Attitudes," *Academy of Management Journal*, December 1978, p. 573.

Wage rates, when determined through collective bargaining, emphasize seniority and downplay performance differences.

Exhibit 16-5 shows what impact a union has on an employee's performance and job satisfaction. The union contract affects motivation through determination of wage rates, seniority rules, layoff procedures, promotion criteria, and security provisions. Unions can influence the competence with which employees perform their jobs by offering special training programs to their members, by requiring apprenticeships, and by allowing members to gain leadership experience through union organizational activities. The actual level of employee performance will be further influenced by collective bargaining restrictions placed on the amount of work produced, the speed with which work can be done, overtime allowances per worker, and the kind of tasks a given employee is allowed to perform.

The research evaluating the specific effect of unions on productivity is mixed.[67] Some studies found that unions had a positive effect on productivity as a result of improvements in labor–management relations as well as improvements in the quality of the labor force. In contrast, other studies have shown that unions negatively impact on productivity by reducing the effectiveness of some productivity enhancing managerial practices and by contributing to a poorer labor–management climate. The evidence, then, is too inconsistent to draw any meaningful conclusions.

Are union members more satisfied with their jobs than their nonunion counterparts? The answer to this question is more complicated than a simple Yes or No. The evidence consistently demonstrates that unions have only indirect effects on job satisfaction.[68] They increase pay satisfaction but negatively affect satisfaction with the work itself (by decreasing job scope perceptions), satisfaction with co-workers and supervision (through less favorable perceptions of supervisory behavior), and satisfaction with promotions (through the lower importance placed on promotions).

INTERNATIONAL HUMAN RESOURCE PRACTICES: SELECTED ISSUES

Many of the human resource policies and practices discussed in this chapter have to be modified to reflect societal differences.[69] To illustrate this point, let's briefly look at the problem of selecting managers for foreign assignments and the importance of performance evaluation in different cultures.

SELECTION

The global corporation increasingly needs managers who have experience in diverse cultures and who are sensitive to the challenges of international operations. At Ford Motor Co., for instance, an international assignment is a requirement for a rising executive's career. But many domestic managers don't have the attitudes or characteristics associated with successful international executives. One selection technique that an increasing number of companies are using is the Overseas Assignment Inventory (OAI). This 85-item questionnaire assesses 15 predictors: motivations, expectations, open-mindedness, respect for others' beliefs, trust in people, flexibility, tolerance, personal control, patience, adaptability, self-confidence/initiative, sense of humor, interpersonal interest, interpersonal harmony, and spouse/family communication. Results are compared against a database of more than 10,000 previous test takers. Research indicates that using the OAI as a prescreening device eliminates about 40 percent of traditional overseas assignment problems.[70]

PERFORMANCE EVALUATION

We previously examined the role that performance evaluation plays in motivation and in affecting behavior. Caution must be used, however, in generalizing across cultures. Why? Because many cultures are not particularly concerned with performance appraisal or, if they are, they don't look at it the same way as do managers in the United States or Canada.

Let's look at four cultural dimensions: individualism/collectivism, a person's relationship to the environment, time orientation, and focus of responsibility.

Individualistic cultures such as the United States emphasize formal performance evaluation systems to a greater degree than informal systems. They advocate, for instance, written evaluations performed at regular intervals, the results of which are shared with employees and used in the determination of rewards. On the other hand, collectivist cultures that dominate Asia and much of Latin America are characterized by more informal systems—downplaying formal feedback and disconnecting reward allocations from performance ratings.

U.S. and Canadian organizations hold people responsible for their actions because people in these countries believe that they can dominate their environment. In Middle Eastern countries, on the other hand, performance evaluations aren't likely to be widely used since managers in these countries tend to see people as subjugated to their environment.

Some countries, such as the United States, have a short-term time orientation. Performance evaluations are likely to be frequent in such a culture—at least once a year. In Japan, however, where people hold a long-term time frame, performance appraisals may occur only every five or ten years.

Israel's culture values group activities much more than does the United States or Canada. So, while North American managers emphasize the individual in performance evaluations, their counterparts in Israel are much more likely to emphasize group contributions and performance.

MANAGING DIVERSITY IN ORGANIZATIONS

David Morris and his father, Saul, started Habitat International in 1981. Located in Rossville, Georgia, the company manufacturers a grasslike indoor-outdoor carpet. From the beginning, the Morrises hired refugees from Cambodia, Bosnia, and Laos, many of whom didn't speak English. But when a social service worker suggested in 1984 that the company hire mentally challenged people, Saul balked. Hiring someone with a condition such as Down's syndrome seemed too chancy. But David thought otherwise. He talked his dad into giving it a try.[71]

The first group of eight mentally disabled workers came in with their job coach from the social-services agency and went straight to work boxing mats. Two weeks later, says Saul, employees were coming to him and wondering why the company couldn't "hire more people like this, who care, do their work with pride, and smile."

Today, 75 percent of Habitat's employees have some kind of disability. People with schizophrenia, for instance, are driving forklifts next to employees with autism or cerebral palsy. Meanwhile, the Morris father-son team are doing good things for both these people and for themselves. The disabled employees have enhanced self-esteem and are now self-sufficient enough to be off government aid; and the Morrises enjoy the benefits from a dedicated, hard-working labor force. "We have practically zero absenteeism and very little turnover," says David.

Habitat International illustrates the role of employee selection in increasing diversity. But effective diversity programs go well beyond merely hiring a diverse workforce. They also include creating family-friendly workplaces, providing diversity training, and developing mentoring programs. These seem to be common characteristics among major organizations that have developed reputations as diversity leaders—including American Express, Bankamerica, Du Pont, Johnson & Johnson, Lucent Technologies, Marriott International, and Xerox.[72]

Selecting employees with physical and mental disabilities brings diversity to Habitat International's workforce. Habitat's experience with disabled workers has been so positive that owners David and Saul Morris are working with human resources managers at other firms to help them establish their own programs in hiring people with disabilities.

FAMILY-FRIENDLY WORKPLACES

Forty-six percent of the U.S. workforce is now female. More and more fathers want to actively participate in the care and raising of their children. As the baby boom generation ages, many are finding themselves having to care for elderly parents. These three facts translate into an increasing number of employees who are attempting to juggle family obligations along with their job responsibilities. In response, companies such as MBNA America, Motorola, First Tennesse Bank, Hewlett-Packard, Baxter International, and Sequent Computer Systems are leading the way in establishing themselves as **family-friendly workplaces**.[73] These are organizations that have instituted programs to reduce the conflict between work and family obligations.[74] They offer an umbrella of programs such as paid pater-

family-friendly workplace

Companies that offer an umbrella of work/family programs such as on-site day care, child care and elder care referrals, flexible hours, compressed workweeks, job sharing, telecommuting, temporary part-time employment, and relocation assistance for employees' family members.

nity and adoption leave, on-site day care, child care and elder care referrals, use of sick leave for children's illnesses, flexible work hours, four-day workweeks, job sharing, telecommuting, temporary part-time employment, and relocation assistance for employees' family members.[75]

Creating a family-friendly work climate was initially motivated by management's concern with improving employee morale and productivity and reducing absenteeism. For instance, a recent survey of U.S. corporations found that 25 percent of employees with children under age 12 miss at least eight days of work annually because of child care problems.[76] As a more specific example, 60 percent of employees at Quaker Oats admit to being absent at least three days a year because of children's illnesses, and 56 percent say they're unable to attend company-related functions or to work overtime because of child care problems.[77]

So has the family-friendly workplace movement achieved its goals? Yes and no! There are few data to support any significant increase in productivity. But the evidence does indicate that creating a family-friendly workplace makes it easier for employers to recruit and retain first-class workers.[78] There are also substantial observational data to suggest that it limits family-related distractions and reduces absenteeism.[79]

DIVERSITY TRAINING

The centerpiece of most diversity programs is training. For instance, a recent survey found that, among companies with diversity initiatives, 93 percent used training as part of their programs.[80] Diversity training programs are generally intended to provide a vehicle for increasing awareness and examining stereotypes. Participants learn to value individual differences, increase their cross-cultural understanding, and confront stereotypes.[81]

Participants in diversity training programs learn to value individual differences, increase their cross-cultural understanding, and confront stereotypes.

The typical program lasts from half a day to three days in length and includes role-playing exercises, lectures, discussions, and group experiences. For example, a training exercise at Hartford Insurance that sought to increase sensitivity to aging asked participants to respond to the following four questions: (1) If you didn't know how old you are, how old would you guess you are? In other words, how old do you feel inside? (2) When I was 18, I thought middle age began at age ____. (3) Today, I think middle age begins at age ____. (4) What would be your first reaction if someone called you "an older worker"?[82] Answers to these questions were then used to analyze age-related stereotypes. In another program designed to raise awareness of the power of stereotypes, each participant was asked to write an anonymous paper detailing all groups—women, born-again Christians, blacks, gays, Hispanics, men—to which they had attached stereotypes.[83] They were also asked to explain why they'd had trouble working with certain groups in the past. Based on responses, guest speakers were brought into the class to shatter the stereotypes directed at each group. This was followed by extensive discussion.

MENTORING PROGRAMS

mentor

A senior employee who sponsors and supports a less experienced employee (a protégé).

We previously discussed mentors briefly in Chapter 2. **Mentoring** refers to a relationship between a junior (a protégé) and a senior (in terms of age or experience) that exists primarily to support the personal development and career advancement of the junior person. The mentoring role includes coaching, counseling, and sponsorship.[84] As coaches, mentors help to develop their protégés' skills. As counselors, mentors provide support and help bolster the protégés' self-confidence. As sponsors, mentors actively intervene on behalf of their protégés, lobby to get them visible assignments, and politick to get them rewards such as promotions and salary increases.

Kent Sutherland and Sam Walton (of Wal-Mart fame) developed a mentoring relationship that shaped Sutherland's life.[85] Sutherland met Walton when the former was just 23 and fresh out of college. At the time, he was a sales representative for the health care products firm Becton Dickinson. The two met on Sutherland's third visit to Wal-Mart headquarters, and Walton took an immediate liking to the young man because, as a mutual acquaintance put it, "I think he saw something of himself in him." For seven years, the two met intermittently. They'd talk business and Walton would share his wisdom on how to create and build successful companies. Now 40, and an entrepreneur with several businesses of his own, Sutherland says, "I feel he had a tremendous impact by motivating me to do things a different way than I might have."

Is mentoring important? For those who want to get ahead, it seems to be. Business school graduates who have had mentors early in their career are promoted faster, make higher salaries, and are more satisfied with their career progress later in life.[86] And more than half the men who make it to executive positions report they had a mentor along the way.[87]

Formal mentoring programs are particularly important for minorities and women. Why? Because the evidence indicates that individuals from these groups are less likely to be informally chosen as protégés than are white males and, thus, are less likely to accrue the benefits of mentorship.[88] Mentors tend to select protégés who are similar to themselves on criteria such as background, education, gender, race, ethnicity, and religion. "People naturally move to mentor and can more easily communicate with those with whom they most closely identify."[89] In the United States, for instance, upper-management positions in most organizations have been traditionally staffed by white males, so it's hard for minorities and women to be selected as protégés. In addition, in terms of cross-gender mentoring, senior male managers may select male protégés to minimize problems such as sexual attraction or gossip. So organizations have responded by replacing informal mentoring relationships with formal programs and providing training and coaching for potential mentors of special groups such as minorities and women.

SUMMARY AND IMPLICATIONS FOR MANAGERS

An organization's human resource policies and practices represent important forces for shaping employee behavior and attitudes. In this chapter, we specifically discussed the influence of selection practices, training and development programs, performance evaluation systems, and the existence of a union.

SELECTION PRACTICES

An organization's selection practices will determine who gets hired. If properly designed, they will identify competent candidates and accurately match them to the job and the organization. The use of the proper selection devices will increase the probability that the right person will be chosen to fill a slot.

While employee selection is far from a science, some organizations fail to design their selection systems so as to maximize the likelihood that the right person–job fit will be achieved. When errors are made, the chosen candidate's performance may be less than satisfactory. Training may be necessary to improve the candidate's skills. At the worst, the candidate will prove unacceptable and a replacement will need to be found. Similarly, when the selection process results in the hiring of less qualified candidates or individuals who don't fit into the organization, those chosen are likely to feel anxious, tense, and uncomfortable. This, in turn, is likely to increase dissatisfaction with the job.

TRAINING AND DEVELOPMENT PROGRAMS

Training programs can affect work behavior in two ways. The most obvious is by directly improving the skills necessary for the employee to successfully complete his or her job. An increase in ability improves the employee's potential to perform at a higher level. Of course, whether that potential becomes realized is largely an issue of motivation.

A second benefit from training is that it increases an employee's self-efficacy. As you'll remember from Chapter 6, self-efficacy is a person's expectation that he or she can successfully execute the behaviors required to produce an outcome.[90] For employees, those behaviors are work tasks and the outcome is effective job performance. Employees with high self-efficacy have strong expectations about their abilities to perform successfully in new situations. They're confident and expect to be successful. Training, then, is a means to positively affect self-efficacy because employees may be more willing to undertake job tasks and exert a high level of effort. Or in expectancy terms (see Chapter 6), individuals are more likely to perceive their effort as leading to performance.

We also discussed career development in this chapter. We noted the significant decline in formal programs intended to guide an employee's career within a single organization. But employees still value career planning and development. So organizations can increase employee commitment, loyalty, and satisfaction by encouraging and guiding employees in developing a self-managed career plan, and by clearly communicating the organization's goals and future strategies, giving employees growth experiences, offering financial assistance to help employees keep their knowledge and skills current, and providing paid time off from work for off-the-job training.

PERFORMANCE EVALUATION

A major goal of performance evaluation is to assess accurately an individual's performance contribution as a basis for making reward allocation decisions. If the performance evaluation process emphasizes the wrong criteria or inaccurately appraises actual job performance, employees will be over- or underrewarded. As demonstrated in Chapter 6, in our discussion of equity theory, this can lead to negative consequences such as reduced effort, increases in absenteeism, or search for alternative job opportunities. In addition, the content of the performance evaluation has been found to influence employee performance and satisfaction.[91] Specifically, performance and satisfaction are increased when the evaluation is based on behavioral, results-oriented criteria, when career issues as well as performance issues are discussed, and when the employee has an opportunity to participate in the evaluation.

UNION-MANAGEMENT INTERFACE

The existence of a union in an organization adds another variable in our search to explain and predict employee behavior. The union has been found to be an important contributor to employees' perceptions, attitudes, and behavior.

The power of the union surfaces in the collective bargaining agreement that it negotiates with management. Much of what an employee can and cannot do on the job is formally stipulated in this agreement. In addition, the informal norms that union cohesiveness fosters can encourage or discourage high productivity, organizational commitment, and morale.

Layoffs Are an Indication of Management Failures

D uring the past decade, very few weeks went by without some large corporation announcing a major downsizing. Regardless of the spin an organization puts on downsizing, the reality is that layoffs are a sign of management failure.[1]

Management lays off employees when it has erred in estimating market demand, when it hasn't anticipated some critical development or created adequate contingency plans. Coming face-to-face with its own mistakes, management tries to solve its dilemma by cutting costs. And it's a lot easier and faster to cut staff than close down plants or sell off equipment.

Layoffs should be a solution of absolute last resort. From a social-responsibility standpoint, layoffs destroy lives. From the organization's standpoint, they destroy the mutual trust and respect needed to make a company successful. At a time when finding and keeping the right people is more important than ever to a company's success, layoffs are prima facia evidence that management has failed.

While often overlooked, there are typically other ways to manage labor costs without resorting to layoffs. Management can be more vigilant on the hiring side. Don't hire people unless you're solidly convinced that they'll be needed for the long term. For short-term increases in labor demand, management can rely on overtime and temporary hires. Management can also commit the organization to a sustained growth strategy. Springfield Remanufacturing Corp., for instance, commits itself to grow at 10 to 15 percent a year, through good times and bad, which acts to shield its workforce against layoffs. Finally, if overstaffing occurs, management should try to think creatively. Ben & Jerry's, as a case in point, leased out some of its employees temporarily to other organizations in Vermont. When business picked up, the employees returned to the ice-cream firm.

[1]See J. Stack, "Mad About Layoffs," *INC.*, May 1996, pp. 21–22.

L ayoffs are normal, inevitable, often even a necessary condition of doing business in today's economy. Companies have to eliminate jobs, even in good times, to remain competitive. These layoffs help companies to be more competitive in the long term, to protect the interests of stockholders, and to prevent bigger layoffs in the future.

Regardless of how good management is at planning, no management is so prescient that it can consistently make accurate forecasts of demand for its products or services. As one expert noted, "No company knows what its customers will demand, what its products will be, or even in exactly what business it will be five years hence. How can such a company offer its employees more than interim employment?"[2] So layoffs are inevitable in a dynamic environment. And why use layoffs as a means to cut costs? Because for most firms, its workforce represents the bulk of its variable costs. When the business cycle turns down, or when competitive actions reduce demand, or when new technologies and processes require less people, only an irresponsible management team would fail to cut costs and reduce its labor force.

Organizations confront new competitors and have to adapt to major breakthroughs in technology. Add in the normal ups and downs of business cycles, and no firm any longer is immune from having to impose layoffs. Although layoffs should be viewed as a last-resort strategy, there are times when a company has no choice but to downsize, regardless of who's to blame or what the consequences may be. So layoffs are not a sign of management failures. Quite the contrary. It is professional managers who shirk their responsibility to keep their organization "lean and mean" who are the failures. They have failed in their role of guardian of the organization's assets and to uphold their obligation to maximize shareholder wealth.

[2]Ibid., p. 22.

1. What is job analysis? How is it related to those the organization hires?

2. What are assessment centers? Why do you think they might be more effective for selecting managers than traditional written tests?

3. Contrast formal and informal training.

4. What can organizations do to help employees develop their careers?

5. What can individuals do to foster their own career development?

6. Why do organizations evaluate employees?

7. What are the advantages and disadvantages of the following performance evaluation methods: (1) written essays, (b) graphic rating scales, and (c) behaviorally anchored rating scales?

8. How can management effectively evaluate individuals when they work as part of a team?

9. How can an organization's performance evaluation system affect employee behavior?

10. What impact do unions have on an organization's reward system?

1. How could the phrase "the best predictor of future behavior is past behavior" guide you in managing human resources?

2. Describe a training program you might design to help employees develop their interpersonal skills. How would that program differ from one you designed to improve employee ethical behavior?

3. What relationship, if any, is there between job analysis and performance evaluation?

4. What problems, if any, can you see developing as a result of using 360-degree evaluations?

5. Your company's president has asked you to identify things your firm might do to improve its track record for hiring and keeping female managers. What suggestions would you make? Do any of your suggestions discriminate against male employees?

Team Exercise | Evaluating Performance and Providing Feedback

Objective

To experience the assessment of performance and observe the providing of performance feedback.

Time

Approximately 30 minutes.

Procedure

A class leader is to be selected. He or she may be either a volunteer or someone chosen by your instructor. The class leader will preside over the class discussion and perform the role of manager in the evaluation review.

Your instructor will leave the room. The class leader is then to spend up to 15 minutes helping the class to evaluate your instructor. Your instructor understands that this is only a class exercise and is prepared to accept criticism (and, of course, any praise you may want to convey). Your instructor also recognizes that the leader's evaluation is actually a composite of many students' input. So be open and honest in your evaluation and have confidence that your instructor will not be vindictive.

Research has identified seven performance dimensions to the college instructor's job: (1) instructor knowledge, (2) testing procedures, (3) student–teacher relations, (4) organizational skills, (5) communication skills, (6) subject relevance, and (7) utility of assignments. The discussion of your instructor's performance should focus on these seven dimensions. The leader may want to take notes for personal use but will not be required to give your instructor any written documentation.

When the 15-minute class discussion is complete, the leader will invite the instructor back into the room. The performance review will begin as soon as the instructor walks through the door, with the class leader becoming the manager and the instructor playing himself or herself.

When completed, class discussion will focus on performance evaluation criteria and how well your class leader did in providing performance feedback.

Ethical Dilemma | What's the Right Balance Between Work and Family?

More employees are bringing family matters into their working lives, and more managers are trying to accommodate them. As the line between work and family blurs, managers must address a number of questions. What's your position on each of the following questions? Compare your answers with others in your class.

1. Is it OK for someone to bring his or her baby to work on an emergency basis?

2. Should a boss ask subordinates if they want to buy Girl Scout cookies from her daughter?

3. Is it OK for a worker to interrupt a conversation with a subordinate or peer to take a call from her spouse? How about from her children? How about from her best friend?

4. A worker is asked to spend several months away from home to solve a problem at a factory. He can fly home on the weekends at the company's expense. Should the company pay for accommodations that would allow his wife and two children to accompany him?

5. Is it discriminating against employees *without* families for employers to give preferences and additional benefits to those employees who have families?

Internet Search Exercises

1. Assess the national trend of the legal status of (a) lie detectors and (b) handwriting analysis as selection devices. If the information is available, what is the legal status of these tools in your own state or province?

2. Find 10 current job listings from 10 different organizations for new college graduates.

PHLIP Companion Web Site

We invite you to visit the Robbins homepage on the Prentice Hall Web site at **www.prenhall.com/robbins** for our on-line study guide, current events, links to related Web sites, and more.

Case Incident | Is This Any Way to Run a Business?

SAS Institute Inc. is probably the least-well-known major software company in the world. The company makes statistical analysis software (hence, the acronym SAS). And it's growing very rapidly. From 1,900 employees five years ago, it now has 5,400. But SAS is not your typical software company. It's not your typical *anything* company!

At its headquarters, just outside Raleigh, North Carolina, there is a 36,000-square-foot gym for employees. There's a large, hardwood aerobic floor; two full-length basketball courts, pool tables, a private, skylight yoga room, and workout areas are also provided. Outside, there are soccer and softball fields. Massages are available several times a week, and classes are offered in golf, African dance, tennis, and tai chi. The company also operates the largest on-site day care facility in North Carolina. To encourage families to eat lunch together, the SAS cafeteria supplies baby seats and high chairs. To encourage families to eat dinner together, the company has a seven-hour workday, five days a week. Unlike many work-obsessive software firms, most SAS employees leave the office by 5 P.M. Management likes to call its workplace culture "relaxed."

The list of employee amenities at SAS goes on and on. Unlimited soda, coffee, tea, and juice. One-week paid vacation between Christmas and New Year's Day. An on-site health clinic staffed with six nurse practitioners and two physicians. Zero cost to employees for health insurance. Dirty workout clothes laundered overnight at no charge. Casual dress every day. Elder care advice and referrals. Unlimited sick days, and use of sick days to care for sick family members.

Is this any way to run a business? Management thinks so. SAS's strategy is to make it impossible for people not to do their work. Even though the company provides no stock options and salaries are no better than competitive rates, the company has built an unbelievably loyal workforce. While competitors typically have turnover rates above 30 percent, SAS's rate has never been higher than 5 percent. Management claims that it saves $67 million a year just in employee replacement costs such as recruitment, interviews, moving costs for new hires, and lost work time. That gives it an extra $12,500 per year per employee to spend on benefits.

Just in case anyone wonders if the company makes any money, we'll add the following. SAS is owned by just two people—Jim Goodnight and John Sall. *Forbes* magazine recently listed Goodnight, with $3 billion, as number 43 on its list of the 400 richest people in America. Sall, with $1.5 billion, was number 110.

Questions

1. One critic calls SAS "a big brother approach to managing people." Is the company too paternalistic? Can a company *be* too paternalistic?

2. When, if ever, do family-friendly practices become paternalistic?

3. What negatives, if any, would you find working for SAS?

4. Are progressive HR practices such as those at SAS a *cause* or *result* of high profits? Discuss.

5. Microsoft is an unbelievably successful software company. But no one would ever call its culture relaxed. It is frantic. Employees regularly put in 12 - to 14-hour days, six and seven days a week. How does Microsoft keep people? Do you think SAS and Microsoft attract different types of employees? Explain.

Source: Based on C. Fishman, "Sanity Inc.," *Fast Company*, January 1999, pp. 85–96.

End Notes

1. N. Bernstein, "Oops, That's Too Much Downsizing," *Business Week*, June 8, 1998, p. 38; and C. Fishman, "The War for Talent," *Fast Company*, August 1998, pp. 104–08.
2. P. Siekman, "The Hunt for Good Factory Workers," *Fortune*, June 22, 1998, pp. 138B-J.
3. See B. Becker and B. Gerhart, "The Impact of Human Resource Management on Organizational Performance: Progress and Prospects," *Academy of Management Journal*, August 1996, pp. 779–801; J. T. Delaney and M. A. Huselid, "The Impact of Human Resource Management Practices on the Perceptions of Organizational Performance," *Academy of Management Journal*, August 1996, pp. 949–69; and M. A. Huselid, S. E. Jackson, and R. S. Schuler, "Technical and Strategic Human Resource Management Effectiveness as Determinants of Firm Performance," *Academy of Management Journal*, February 1997, pp. 171–88.
4. See, for instance, C. T. Dortch, "Job–Person Match," *Personnel Journal*, June 1989, pp. 49–57; and S. Rynes and B. Gerhart, "Interviewer Assessments of Applicant 'Fit': An Exploratory Investigation," *Personnel Psychology*, Spring 1990, pp. 13–34.
5. See, for example, J. V. Ghorpade, *Job Analysis: A Handbook for the Human Resource Director* (Englewood Cliffs, NJ: Prentice Hall, 1988).
6. D. E. Bowen, G. E. Ledford Jr., and B. R. Nathan, "Hiring for the Organization, Not the Job," *Academy of Management Executive*, November 1991, pp. 35–51; E. E. Lawler III, "From Job-Based to Competency-Based Organizations," *Journal of Organizational Behavior*, January 1994, pp. 3–15; and D. M. Cable and T. A. Judge, "Interviewers' Perceptions of Person–Organization Fit and Organizational Selection Decisions," *Journal of Applied Psychology*, August 1997, pp. 546–61.
7. L. Yoo-Lim, "More Companies Rely on Employee Interviews," *Business Korea*, November 1994, pp. 22–23.
8. Ibid.
9. T. J. Hanson and J. C. Balestreri-Spero, "An Alternative to Interviews," *Personnel Journal*, June 1985, p. 114. See also T. W. Dougherty, D. B. Turban, and J. C. Callender, "Confirming First Impressions in the Employment Interview: A Field Study of Interviewer Behavior," *Journal of Applied Psychology*, October 1994, pp. 659–65.
10. See A. I. Huffcutt and W. Arthur Jr., "Hunter and Hunter (1984) Revisited: Interview Validity for Entry-Level Jobs," *Journal of Applied Psychology*, April 1994, pp. 184–90; M. A. McDaniel, D. L. Whetzel, F. L. Schmidt, and S. D. Maurer, "The Validity of Employment Interviews: A Comprehensive Review and Meta-Analysis," *Journal of Applied Psychology*, August 1994, pp. 599–616; J. M. Conway, R. A. Jako, and D. F. Goodman, "A Meta-Analysis of Interrater and Internal Consistency Reliability of Selection Interviews," *Journal of Applied Psychology*, October 1995, pp. 565–79; M. A. Campion, D. K. Palmer, and J. E. Campion, "A Review of Structure in the Selection Interview," *Personnel Psychology*, Autumn 1997, pp. 655–702; and F. L. Schmidt and J. E. Hunter, "The Validity and Utility of Selection Methods in Personnel Psychology: Practical and Theoretical Implications of 85 Years of Research Findings," *Psychological Bulletin*, September 1998, pp. 262–74.
11. R. L. Dipboye, *Selection Interviews: Process Perspectives* (Cincinnati: South-Western Publishing, 1992), pp. 42–44.

12. W. F. Cascio, *Applied Psychology in Personnel Management,* 4th ed. (Englewood Cliffs, NJ: Prentice Hall, 1991), p. 271.

13. See G. A. Adams, T. C. Elacqua, and S. M. Colarelli, "The Employment Interview as a Sociometric Selection Technique," *Journal of Group Psychotherapy,* Fall 1994, pp. 99–113; R. L. Dipboye, "Structured and Unstructured Selection Interviews: Beyond the Job–Fit Model," *Research in Personnel Human Resource Management,* Vol. 12, 1994, pp. 79–123; and B. Schneider, D. B. Smith, S. Taylor, and J. Fleenor, "Personality and Organizations: A Test of the Homogeneity of Personality Hypothesis," *Journal of Applied Psychology,* June 1998, pp. 462–70.

14. This box is based on W. C. Donaghy, *The Interview: Skills and Applications* (Glenview, IL: Scott, Foresman, 1984), pp. 245–80; J. M. Jenks and B. L. P. Zevnik, "ABCs of Job Interviewing," *Harvard Business Review,* July–August 1989, pp. 38–42; E. D. Pulakos and N. Schmitt, "Experience-Based and Situational Interview Questions: Studies of Validity," *Personnel Psychology,* Summer 1995, pp. 289–308; and C. Hirschman, "Playing the High-Stakes Hiring Game," *HRMagazine,* March 1998, pp. 80–86.

15. E. E. Ghiselli, "The Validity of Aptitude Tests in Personnel Selection," *Personnel Psychology,* Winter 1973, p. 475.

16. R. J. Herrnstein and C. Murray, *The Bell Curve: Intelligence and Class Structure in American Life* (New York: Free Press, 1994); and M. J. Ree, J. A. Earles, and M. S. Teachout, "Predicting Job Performance: Not Much More Than g," *Journal of Applied Psychology,* August 1994, pp. 518–24.

17. J. Flint, "Can You Tell Applesauce From Pickles?" *Forbes,* October 9, 1995, pp. 106–08.

18. D. S. Ones, C. Viswesvaran, and F. L. Schmidt, "Comprehensive Meta-Analysis of Integrity Test Validities: Findings and Implications for Personnel Selection and Theories of Job Performance," *Journal of Applied Psychology,* August 1993, pp. 679–703; P. R. Sackett and J. E. Wanek, "New Developments in the Use of Measures of Honesty, Integrity, Conscientiousness, Dependability, Trustworthiness, and Reliability for Personnel Selection," *Personnel Psychology,* Winter 1996, pp. 787–829; and Schmidt and Hunter, "The Validity and Utility of Selection Methods in Personnel Psychology."

19. P. Carbonara, "Hire for Attitude, Train for Skill," *Fast Company,* Greatest Hits, Vol. 1, 1997, p. 68.

20. J. J. Asher and J. A. Sciarrino, "Realistic Work Sample Tests: A Review," *Personnel Psychology,* Winter 1974, pp. 519–33; and I. T. Robertson and R. S. Kandola, "Work Sample Tests: Validity, Adverse Impact and Applicant Reaction," *Journal of Occupational Psychology,* Spring 1982, pp. 171–82.

21. See, for instance, A. C. Spychalski, M. A. Quinones, B. B. Gaugler, and K. Pohley, "A Survey of Assessment Center Practices in Organizations in the United States, *Personnel Psychology,* Spring 1997, pp. 71–90.

22. B. B. Gaugler, D. B. Rosenthal, G. C. Thornton, and C. Benson, "Meta-Analysis of Assessment Center Validity," *Journal of Applied Psychology,* August 1987, pp. 493–511; and G. C. Thornton, *Assessment Centers in Human Resource Management* (Reading, MA: Addison-Wesley, 1992).

23. R. E. Carlson, "Effect of Interview Information in Altering Valid Impressions," *Journal of Applied Psychology,* February 1971, pp. 66–72; and M. London and M. D. Hakel, "Effects of Applicant Stereotypes, Order, and Information on Interview Impressions," *Journal of Applied Psychology,* April 1974, pp. 157–62.

24. N. R. Bardack and F. T. McAndrew, "The Influence of Physical Attractiveness and Manner of Dress on Success in a Simulated Personnel Decision," *Journal of Social Psychology,* August 1985, pp. 777–78; and R. Bull and N. Rumsey, *The Social Psychology of Facial Appearance* (London: Springer-Verlag, 1988).

25. T. W. Dougherty, R. J. Ebert, and J. C. Callender, "Policy Capturing in the Employment Interview," *Journal of Applied Psychology,* February 1986; and T. M. Macan and R. L. Dipboye, "The Relationship of the Interviewers' Preinterview Impressions to Selection and Recruitment Outcomes," *Personnel Psychology,* Autumn 1990, pp. 745–69.

26. Cited in *Training,* October 1998, p. 48.

27. Cited in J. C. Szabo, "Training Workers for Tomorrow," *Nation's Business,* March 1993, pp. 22–32.

28. Cited in M. Hequet, "The Union Push for Lifelong Learning," *Training,* March 1994, p. 31.

29. Reported in *From School to Work* (Princeton, NJ: Educational Testing Service, 1990).

30. J. C. Szabo, "Honing Workers' Basic Skills," *Nation's Business,* May 1994, p. 69.

31. G. R. Weaver, L. K. Trevino, and P. L. Cochran, "Corporate Ethics Practices in the Mid-1990's: An Empirical Study of the Fortune 1000," *Journal of Business Ethics,* February 1999, pp. 283–94.

32. H. Frazis, M. Gittleman, M. Horrigan, and M. Joyce, "Results From the 1995 Survey of Employer-Provided Training," *Monthly Labor Review,* June 1998, pp. 4–5.

33. S. J. Wells, "Forget the Formal Training. Try Chatting at the Water Cooler," *New York Times,* May 10, 1998, p. BU-11.

34. D. Schaaf, "Inside Hamburger University," *Training,* December 1994, pp. 18–24.

35. D. A. Kolb, "Management and the Learning Process," *California Management Review,* Spring 1976, pp. 21–31; and B. Filipczak, "Different Strokes: Learning Styles in the Classroom," *Training,* March 1995, pp. 43–48.

36. D. T. Hall, "Protean Careers of the 21st Century," *Academy of Management Executive,* November 1996, pp. 8–16; M. B. Arthur and D. Rousseau, "A New Career Lexicon for the 21st Century," *Academy of Management Executive,* November 1996, pp. 28–39; D. T. Hall and Associates (ed.), *The Career Is Dead—Long Live the Career* (San Francisco: Jossey-Bass, 1996); M. Cianni and D. Wnuck, "Individual Growth and Team Enhancement: Moving Toward a New Model of Career Development," *Academy of Management Executive,* February 1997, pp. 105–15; and D. Bencivenga, "Employers & Workers Come to Terms," *HRMagazine,* June 1997, pp. 91–97.

37. M. Hequet, "Flat and Happy?" *Training,* April 1995, pp. 29–34.

38. G. Johns, *Organizational Behavior: Understanding and Managing Life at Work,* 4th ed. (New York: HarperCollins, 1996), p. 622.

39. Based on P. Hirsch, *Pack Your Own Parachute: How to Survive Mergers, Takeovers, and Other Corporate Disasters* (Reading, MA: Addison-Wesley, 1987); R. Henkoff, "Winning the New Career Game," *Fortune,* July 12, 1993, pp. 46–49; and H. Lancaster, "As Company Programs Fade, Workers Turn to Guild-Like Groups," *Wall Street Journal,* January 16, 1996, p. B1.

40. See J. N. Cleveland, K. R. Murphy, and R. E. Williams, "Multiple Uses of Performance Appraisal: Prevalence and Correlates," *Journal of Applied Psychology*, February 1989, pp. 130–35; J. F. Milliman, B. Nathan, and A. M. Mohrman, "Conflicting Appraisal Purposes of Managers and Subordinates and Their Effect on Performance and Satisfaction"; paper presented at the National Academy of Management meeting; Miami, Florida, 1991; and J. F. Milliman, S. Nason, K. Lowe, N-H. Kim, and P. Huo, "An Empirical Study of Performance Appraisal Practices in Japan, Korea, Taiwan, and the U.S.," in D. P. Moore (ed.), *Academy of Management Best Paper Proceedings* (Vancouver, BC, 1995).

41. P. M. Blau, *The Dynamics of Bureaucracy,* rev. ed. (Chicago: University of Chicago Press, 1963).

42. "The Cop-Out Cops," *National Observer,* August 3, 1974.

43. See W. C. Borman and S. J. Motowidlo, "Expanding the Criterion Domain to Include Elements of Contextual Performance," in N. Schmitt and W. C. Borman (eds.), *Personnel Selection in Organizations* (San Francisco: Jossey-Bass, 1993), pp. 71–98; W. H. Bommer, J. L. Johnson, G. A. Rich, P. M. Podsakoff, and S. B. MacKenzie, "On the Interchangeability of Objective and Subjective Measures of Employee Performance: A Meta-Analysis," *Personnel Psychology,* Autumn 1995, pp. 587–605.

44. A. H. Locher and K. S. Teel, "Appraisal Trends," *Personnel Journal,* September 1988, pp. 139–45.

45. G. P. Latham and K. N. Wexley, *Increasing Productivity Through Performance Appraisal* (Reading, MA: Addison-Wesley, 1981), p. 80.

46. See review in R. D. Bretz, Jr., G. T. Milkovich, and W. Read, "The Current State of Performance Appraisal Research and Practice: Concerns, Directions, and Implications," *Journal of Management,* June 1992, p. 326.

47. "Appraisals: Reverse Reviews," *INC.,* October 1992, p. 33.

48. See, for instance, R. Lepsinger and A. D. Lucia, "360° Feedback and Performance Appraisal," *Training,* September 1997, pp. 62–70; A. Furnham and P. Stringfield, "Congruence in Job-Performance Ratings: A Study of 360° Feedback Examining Self, Manager, Peers, and Consultant Ratings," *Human Relations,* April 1998, pp. 517–30; M. K. Mount, T. A. Judge, S. E. Scullen, M. R. Sytsma and S. A. Hezlett, "Trait, Rater and Level Effects in 360-Degree Performance Ratings," *Personnel Psychology,* Autumn 1998, pp. 557–76; and W. W. Tornow and M. London (eds.), *Maximizing the Value of 360-Degree Feedback* (San Francisco: Jossey-Bass, 1998).

49. Cited in D. A. Waldman, L. E. Atwater, and D. Antonioni, "Has 360 Degree Feedback Gone Amok?" *Academy of Management Executive,* May 1998, p. 86.

50. D. Goldin, "In a Change of Policy, and Heart, Colleges Join Fight Against Inflated Grades," *The New York Times,* July 4, 1995, p. Y-10.

51. A. S. DeNisi and L. H. Peters, "Organization of Information in Memory and the Performance Appraisal Process: Evidence From the Field," *Journal of Applied Psychology,* December 1996, pp. 717–37.

52. See, for instance, J. W. Hedge and W. C. Borman, "Changing Conceptions and Practices in Performance Appraisal," in A. Howard (ed.), *The Changing Nature of Work* (San Francisco: Jossey-Bass, 1995), pp. 453–59.

53. See, for instance, D. E. Smith, "Training Programs for Performance Appraisal: A Review," *Academy of Management Review,* January 1986, pp. 22–40; T. R. Athey and R. M. McIntyre, "Effect of Rater Training on Rater Accuracy: Levels-of-Processing Theory and Social Facilitation Theory Perspectives," *Journal of Applied Psychology,* November 1987, pp. 567–72; and D. J. Woehr, "Understanding Frame-of-Reference Training: The Impact of Training on the Recall of Performance Information," *Journal of Applied Psychology,* August 1994, pp. 525–34.

54. H. J. Bernardin, "The Effects of Rater Training on Leniency and Halo Errors in Student Rating of Instructors," *Journal of Applied Psychology,* June 1978, pp. 301–08.

55. Ibid.; and J. M. Ivancevich, "Longitudinal Study of the Effects of Rater Training on Psychometric Error in Ratings," *Journal of Applied Psychology,* October 1979, pp. 502–08.

56. M. S. Taylor, K. B. Tracy, M. K. Renard, J. K. Harrison, and S. J. Carroll, "Due Process in Performance Appraisal: A Quasi-Experiment in Procedural Justice," *Administrative Science Quarterly,* September 1995, pp. 495–523.

57. J. S. Lublin, "It's Shape-Up Time for Performance Reviews," *Wall Street Journal,* October 3, 1994, p. B1.

58. Much of this section is based on H. H. Meyer, "A Solution to the Performance Appraisal Feedback Enigma," *Academy of Management Executive,* February 1991, pp. 68–76.

59. B. Gates, *The Road Ahead* (New York: Viking, 1995), p. 86.

60. T. D. Schelhardt, "It's Time to Evaluate Your Work, and All Involved Are Groaning," *Wall Street Journal,* November 19, 1996, p. A1.

61. R. J. Burke, "Why Performance Appraisal Systems Fail," *Personnel Administration,* June 1972, pp. 32–40.

62. B. R. Nathan, A. M. Mohrman, Jr., and J. Milliman, "Interpersonal Relations as a Context for the Effects of Appraisal Interviews on Performance and Satisfaction: A Longitudinal Study," *Academy of Management Journal,* June 1991, pp. 352–69. See also B. D. Cawley, L. M. Keeping, and P. E. Levy, "Participation in the Performance Appraisal Process and Employee Reactions: A Meta-Analytic Review of Field Investigations," *Journal of Applied Psychology,* August 1998, pp. 615–33.

63. J. Zigon, "Making Performance Appraisal Work for Teams," *Training,* June 1994, pp. 58–63.

64. E. Salas, T. L. Dickinson, S. A. Converse, and S. I. Tannenbaum, "Toward an Understanding of Team Performance and Training," in R. W. Swezey and E. Salas (eds.), *Teams: Their Training and Performance* (Norwood, NJ: Ablex, 1992), pp. 3–29.

65. Much of the material in this section was adapted from T. H. Hammer, "Relationship Between Local Union Characteristics and Worker Behavior and Attitudes," *Academy of Management Journal,* December 1978, pp. 560–77.

66. See B. B. Auster and W. Cohen, "Rallying the Rank and File," *U.S. News & World Report,* April 1, 1996, pp. 26–28; and M. A. Verespej, "Wounded and Weaponless," *Industry Week,* September 16, 1996, pp. 46–58.

67. J. B. Arthur and J. B. Dworkin, "Current Topics in Industrial and Labor Relations Research and Practice," *Journal of Management,* September 1991, pp. 530–32.

68. See, for example, C. J. Berger, C. A. Olson, and J. W. Boudreau, "Effects of Unions on Job Satisfaction: The Role of Work-Related Values and Perceived Rewards," *Organizational Behavior and Human Performance,* December 1983, pp. 289–324; and M. G. Evans and D. A. Ondrack, "The Role of Job Outcomes and Values in Understanding

the Union's Impact on Job Satisfaction: A Replication," *Human Relations,* May 1990, pp. 401–18.

69. See, for instance, M. Mendonca and R. N. Kanungo, "Managing Human Resources: The Issue of Cultural Fit," *Journal of Management Inquiry,* June 1994, pp. 189–205; and N. Ramamoorthy and S. J. Carroll, "Individualism/ Collectivism Orientations and Reactions Toward Alternative Human Resource Management Practices," *Human Relations,* May 1998, pp. 571–88.

70. W. Lobdell, "Who's Right for an Overseas Position?" *World Trade,* April–May 1990, pp. 20–26.

71. N. B. Henderson, "An Enabling Work Force," *Nation's Business,* June 1998, p. 93.

72. See L. Urresta and J. Hickman, "The Diversity Elite," *Fortune,* August 3, 1998, pp. 114–22.

73. K. H. Hammonds, "Work and Family," *Business Week,* September 15, 1997, pp. 96–99; A. T. Palmer, "Who's Minding the Baby? The Company," *Business Week,* April 26, 1999, p. 32; and M. B. Grover, "Daddy Stress," *Forbes,* September 6, 1999, pp. 202–08.

74. Based on R. G. Netemeyer, J. S. Boles, and R. McMurrian, "Development and Validation of Work–Family Conflict and Family–Work Conflict Scales," *Journal of Applied Psychology,* August 1996, pp. 400–10.

75. See, for instance, S. A. Lobel and E. E. Kossek, "Human Resource Strategies to Support Diversity in Work and Personal Lifestyle: Beyond the 'Family-Friendly' Organization," in E.E. Kossek and S. A. Lobel, *Managing Diversity* (Cambridge, MA: Blackwell, 1996), pp. 221–44; M. N. Martinez, "An Inside Look at Making the Grade," *HRMagazine,* March 1998, pp. 61–66; and S. Branch, "The 100 Best Companies to Work For in America," *Fortune,* January 11, 1999, pp. 118–40.

76. Cited in "Childcare Is First Demand in U.S. Workplace," *Manpower Argus,* April 1998, p. 6.

77. Cited in M. A. Verespej, "People-First Policies," *Industry Week,* June 21, 1993, p. 20.

78. S. Shellenbarger, "Data Gap," *Wall Street Journal,* June 21, 1993, p. R6.

79. S. Hand and R. A. Zawacki, "Family-Friendly Benefits: More Than a Frill," *HRMagazine,* October 1994, pp. 79–84; and R. Dogar, "Corporate Relief for Desperate Parents," *Working Woman,* March 1995, pp. 15–16.

80. Cited in "Survey Shows 75% of Large Corporations Support Diversity Programs," *Fortune,* July 6, 1998, p. S14.

81. See, for example, S. Nelton, "Nurturing Diversity," *Nation's Business,* June 1995, pp. 25–27; J. K. Ford and S. Fisher, "The Role of Training in a Changing Workplace and Workforce: New Perspectives and Approaches," in E. E. Kossek and S. A. Lobel (eds.), *Managing Diversity* (Cambridge, MA: Blackwell Publishers, 1996), pp. 164–93.

82. B. Hynes-Grace, "To Thrive, Not Merely Survive," in Textbook Authors Conference Presentations (Washington, DC: October 21, 1992), sponsored by the American Association of Retired Persons, p. 12.

83. "Teaching Diversity: Business Schools Search for Model Approaches," *Newsline,* Fall 1992, p. 21.

84. See, for example, K. E. Kram, *Mentoring at Work: Developmental Relationships in Organizational Life* (Glenview, IL: Scott, Foresman, 1985); and G. T. Chao and P. D. Gardner, "Formal and Informal Mentorships: A Comparison of Mentoring Functions and Contrast with Nonmentored Counterparts," *Personnel Psychology,* Spring 1992, pp. 1–16.

85. E. O. Wells, "The Mentors," *INC.,* June 1998, pp. 48–60.

86. G. Dreher and R. Ash, "A Comparative Study of Mentoring Among Men and Women in Managerial, Professional, and Technical Positions," *Journal of Applied Psychology,* October 1990, pp. 539–46; and W. Whitely, T. Dougherty, and G. Dreher, "Relationship of Career Mentoring and Socioeconomic Origin to Managers' and Professionals' Early Career Progress," *Academy of Management Journal,* June 1991, pp. 331–51.

87. Reported in Johns, *Organizational Behavior: Understanding and Managing Life at Work,* p. 620.

88. See, for example, B. R. Ragins, "Barriers to Mentoring: The Female Manager's Dilemma," *Human Relations,* January 1989, pp. 1–22; B. R. Ragins and D. McFarlin, "Perceptions of Mentor Roles in Cross-Gender Mentoring Relationships," *Journal of Vocational Behavior,* December 1990, pp. 321–39; and D. A. Thomas, "The Impact of Race on Managers' Experiences of Developmental Relationships: An Intra-Organizational Study," *Journal of Organizational Behavior,* November 1990, pp. 539–46.

89. J. A. Wilson and N. S. Elman, "Organizational Benefits of Mentoring," *The Executive,* November 1990, p. 90.

90. A. Bandura, "Self-Efficacy: Towards a Unifying Theory of Behavioral Change," *Psychological Review,* March 1977, pp. 191–215; and P. C. Earley, "Self or Group? Cultural Effects of Training on Self-Efficacy and Performance," *Administrative Science Quarterly,* March 1994, pp. 89–117.

91. Nathan, Mohrman, Jr., and Milliman, "Interpersonal Relations as a Context for the Effects of Appraisal Interviews on Performance and Satisfaction: A Longitudinal Study;" and Cawley, Keeping, and Levy, "Participation in the Performance Appraisal Process and Employee Reactions."

part four

THE ORGANIZATION SYSTEM

Mitsubishi Motors recently announced that it lost $846 million for the fiscal year—nearly triple what had previously been expected. In contrast to competitors such as Honda and DaimlerChrysler, this major Japanese car manufacturer has serious problems. The company's heavy reliance on weak truck and bus markets in Asia and its inability to quickly respond to the hot demand for minivans and sport-utility vehicles have contributed to its financial losses. But the real culprit is the deeply rooted Mitsubishi culture. Its tradition-based culture is better suited to the automobile industry that existed in the 1970s than the one that exists today. Katsuhiko Kawasoe, Mitsubishi Motors' new president (see photo), is clearly a man on the hot seat. He's got to try to change this culture.[1]

The automobile division of Mitsubishi Heavy Industries is much like the rest of the company. It has cloistered itself from the real world of competition. While other Japanese firms have broken from the country's long-held beliefs on the importance of tradition and history, Mitsubishi continues to move at its own pace. For instance, most other Japanese companies have discarded the notion of lifetime employment, realizing it's no longer realistic in a highly competitive world marketplace. Not Mitsubishi. It continues, almost arrogantly, to do things its way. When the chairman of Mitsubishi Heavy was recently asked about laying off people, he replied, "Employment is more important than profits! We are not concerned with return on equity ... if foreign investors don't see merit in our stock, they can sell it." Which, not surprisingly, they have!

A consultant who works with Mitsubishi says the company is being held back by the lack of incentives and market pressure on management. In short, nobody is holding management accountable. When something goes wrong, managers simply intone: It would be un-Japanese to fire anyone or to close plants. But that isn't stopping other Japanese companies. And, unfortunately, the future doesn't look particularly better for Mitsubishi. New

Organizational Culture

recruits aren't lectured on the importance of competition or profits. Rather, company executives continue to talk about Mitsubishi's "special place in history" and duty to country.

A strong organizational culture provides employees with a clear understanding of "the way things are done around here." It provides stability to an organization. But, as evidenced at Mitsubishi, it can also be a major barrier to change. In this chapter, we show that every organization has a culture and, depending on its strength, it can have a significant influence on the attitudes and behaviors of organization members.

INSTITUTIONALIZATION: A FORERUNNER OF CULTURE

The idea of viewing organizations as cultures—where there is a system of shared meaning among members—is a relatively recent phenomenon. Until the mid-1980s, organizations were, for the most part, simply thought of as rational means by which to coordinate and control a group of people. They had vertical levels, departments, authority relationships, and so forth. But organizations are more. They have personalities too, just like individuals. They can be rigid or flexible, unfriendly or supportive, innovative or conservative. General Electric offices and people *are* different from the offices and people at General Mills. Harvard and MIT are in the same business—education—and separated only by the width of the Charles River, but each has a unique feeling and character beyond its structural characteristics. Organizational theorists now acknowledge this by recognizing

LEARNING OBJECTIVES

AFTER READING THIS CHAPTER, YOU SHOULD BE ABLE TO

1. Describe institutionalization and its relationship to organizational culture

2. Define the common characteristics making up organizational culture

3. Contrast strong and weak cultures

4. Identify the functional and dysfunctional effects of organizational culture on people and the organization

5. Explain the factors determining an organization's culture

6. List the factors that maintain an organization's culture

7. Clarify how culture is transmitted to employees

8. Outline the various socialization alternatives available to management

the important role that culture plays in the lives of organization members. Interestingly, though, the origin of culture as an independent variable affecting an employee's attitudes and behavior can be traced back more than 50 years ago to the notion of **institutionalization**.[2]

When an organization becomes institutionalized, it takes on a life of its own, apart from its founders or any of its members. Ross Perot created Electronic Data Systems (EDS) in the early 1960s, but he left in 1987 to found a new company, Perot Systems. EDS has continued to thrive despite the departure of its founder. Sony, Eastman Kodak, Gillette, McDonald's, and Disney are examples of organizations that have existed beyond the life of their founder or any one member.

Additionally, when an organization becomes institutionalized, it becomes valued for itself, not merely for the goods or services it produces. It acquires immortality. If its original goals are no longer relevant, it doesn't go out of business. Rather, it redefines itself. When the demand for Timex's watches declined, the Timex Corp. merely redirected itself into the consumer electronics business—making, in addition to watches, clocks, computers, and health care products such as digital thermometers and blood pressure testing devices. Timex took on an existence that went beyond its original mission to manufacture low-cost mechanical watches.

> *When an organization takes on institutional permanence, acceptable modes of behavior become largely self-evident to its members.*

Institutionalization operates to produce common understandings among members about what is appropriate and, fundamentally, meaningful behavior.[3] So when an organization takes on institutional permanence, acceptable modes of behavior become largely self-evident to its members. As we'll see, this is essentially the same thing that organizational culture does. So an understanding of what makes up an organization's culture, and how it is created, sustained, and learned will enhance our ability to explain and predict the behavior of people at work.

WHAT IS ORGANIZATIONAL CULTURE?

A number of years back, I asked an executive to tell me what he thought *organizational culture* meant and he gave me essentially the same answer that a Supreme Court Justice once gave in attempting to define pornography: "I can't define it, but I know it when I see it." This executive's approach to defining organizational culture isn't acceptable for our purposes. We need a basic definition to provide a point of departure for our quest to better understand the phenomenon. In this section, we propose a specific definition and review several peripheral issues that revolve around this definition.

A DEFINITION

There seems to be wide agreement that **organizational culture** refers to a system of shared meaning held by members that distinguishes the organization from other organizations.[4] This system of shared meaning is, on closer examination, a set of key characteristics that the organization values. The research suggests that there are seven primary characteristics that, in aggregate, capture the essence of an organization's culture.[5]

1. *Innovation and risk taking.* The degree to which employees are encouraged to be innovative and take risks.

2. *Attention to detail*. The degree to which employees are expected to exhibit precision, analysis, and attention to detail.
3. *Outcome orientation*. The degree to which management focuses on results or outcomes rather than on the techniques and processes used to achieve these outcomes.
4. *People orientation*. The degree to which management decisions take into consideration the effect of outcomes on people within the organization.
5. *Team orientation*. The degree to which work activities are organized around teams rather than individuals.
6. *Aggressiveness*. The degree to which people are aggressive and competitive rather than easygoing.
7. *Stability*. The degree to which organizational activities emphasize maintaining the status quo in contrast to growth.

Innovation and attention to detail are key characteristics of Gillette Company's organizational culture. Gillette's development of new shaving breakthroughs like the Sensor razor involves thousands of shaving tests and design modifications. The company's team of research scientists use microscopes to examine razor blades at atomic level and high-speed video to capture the act of a blade cutting a single whisker. Gillette's CEO Alfred Zeien (in suit) devotes 2.2 percent of the firm's annual sales to research and development—about twice the average of other consumer product companies. Zeien predicts that his huge investment in R&D will result in 50 percent of Gillette's sales coming from products introduced within the past five years.

Each of these characteristics exists on a continuum from low to high. Appraising the organization on these seven characteristics, then, gives a composite picture of the organization's culture. This picture becomes the basis for feelings of shared understanding that members have about the organization, how things are done in it, and the way members are supposed to behave. Exhibit 17-1 demonstrates how these characteristics can be mixed to create highly diverse organizations

CULTURE IS A DESCRIPTIVE TERM

Organizational culture is concerned with how employees perceive the characteristics of an organization's culture, not with whether or not they like them. That is, it's a descriptive term. This is important because it differentiates this concept from that of job satisfaction.

Research on organizational culture has sought to measure how employees see their organization: Does it encourage teamwork? Does it reward innovation? Does it stifle initiative?

In contrast, job satisfaction seeks to measure affective responses to the work environment. It's concerned with how employees feel about the organization's expectations, reward practices, and the like. Although the two terms undoubtedly have overlapping characteristics, keep in mind that the term *organizational culture* is descriptive, while *job satisfaction* is evaluative.

DO ORGANIZATIONS HAVE UNIFORM CULTURES?

Organizational culture represents a common perception held by the organization's members. This was made explicit when we defined culture as a system of *shared* meaning. We should expect, therefore, that individuals with different backgrounds or at different levels in the organization will tend to describe the organization's culture in similar terms.[6]

EXHIBIT

17-1

Organization A

This organization is a manufacturing firm. Managers are expected to fully document all decisions; and "good managers" are those who can provide detailed data to support their recommendations. Creative decisions that incur significant change or risk are not encouraged. Because managers of failed projects are openly criticized and penalized, managers try not to implement ideas that deviate much from the status quo. One lower-level manager quoted an often used phrase in the company: "If it ain't broke, don't fix it."

There are extensive rules and regulations in this firm that employees are required to follow. Managers supervise employees closely to ensure there are no deviations. Management is concerned with high productivity, regardless of the impact on employee morale or turnover.

Work activities are designed around individuals. There are distinct departments and lines of authority, and employees are expected to minimize formal contact with other employees outside their functional area or line of command. Performance evaluations and rewards emphasize individual effort; although seniority tends to be the primary factor in the determination of pay raises and promotions.

Organization B

This organization is also a manufacturing firm. Here, however, management encourages and rewards risk taking and change. Decisions based on intuition are valued as much as those that are well rationalized. Management prides itself on its history of experimenting with new technologies and its success in regularly introducing innovative products. Managers or employees who have a good idea are encouraged to "run with it." And failures are treated as "learning experiences." The company prides itself on being market driven and rapidly responsive to the changing needs of its customers.

There are few rules and regulations for employees to follow, and supervision is loose because management believes that its employees are hardworking and trustworthy. Management is concerned with high productivity but believes that this comes through treating its people right. The company is proud of its reputation as being a good place to work.

Job activities are designed around work teams and team members are encouraged to interact with people across functions and authority levels. Employees talk positively about the competition between teams. Individuals and teams have goals, and bonuses are based on achievement of these outcomes. Employees are given considerable autonomy in choosing the means by which the goals are attained.

Acknowledgment that organizational culture has common properties does not mean, however, that there cannot be subcultures within any given culture. Most large organizations have a dominant culture and numerous sets of subcultures.[7]

A **dominant culture** expresses the core values that are shared by a majority of the organization's members. When we talk about an organization's culture, we are referring to its dominant culture. It is this macro view of culture that gives an organization its distinct personality.[8] **Subcultures** tend to develop in large organizations to reflect common problems, situations, or experiences that members face. These subcultures are likely to be defined by department designations and geographical separation. The purchasing department, for example, can have a subculture that is uniquely shared by members of that department. It will include the **core values** of the dominant culture plus additional values unique to members of the purchasing department. Similarly, an office or unit of the organization that is physically separated from the organization's main operations may take on a different personality. Again, the core values are essentially retained but modified to reflect the separated unit's distinct situation.

If organizations had no dominant culture and were composed only of numerous subcultures, the value of organizational culture as an independent variable would be significantly lessened because there would be no uniform interpretation of what represented appropriate and inappropriate behavior. It is the

dominant culture

Expresses the core values that are shared by a majority of the organization's members.

subcultures

Minicultures within an organization, typically defined by department designations and geographical separation.

core values

The primary or dominant values that are accepted throughout the organization.

"shared meaning" aspect of culture that makes it such a potent device for guiding and shaping behavior. That's what allows us to say that Microsoft's culture values aggressiveness and risk taking;[9] and then to use that information to better understand the behavior of Microsoft executives and employees. But we cannot ignore the reality that many organizations also have subcultures that can influence the behavior of members.

FROM CONCEPTS *TO* SKILLS

How to "Read" an Organization's Culture

The ability to read and assess an organization's culture can be a valuable skill.[10] If you're looking for a job, you'll want to choose an employer whose culture is compatible with your values and in which you'll feel comfortable. If you can accurately assess a prospective employer's culture before you make your decision, you may be able to save yourself a lot of grief and reduce the likelihood of making a poor choice. Similarly, you'll undoubtedly have business transactions with numerous organizations during your professional career. You'll be trying to sell a product or service, negotiate a contract, arrange a joint venture, or merely be seeking out who in an organization controls certain decisions. The ability to assess another organization's culture can be a definite plus in successfully completing these pursuits.

For the sake of simplicity, we'll approach the problem of reading an organization's culture from that of a job applicant. We'll assume you're interviewing for a job. Here's a list of things you can do to help learn about a potential employer's culture:

- Do your homework ahead of time. Get names of former employees from friends or acquaintances, and talk with them. Also talk with members of professional trade associations to which the organization's employees belong and executive recruiters who deal with the organization. Look for clues in stories told in annual reports and other organizational literature; and check out the organization's Web sites for evidence of high turnover or recent management shake-ups.
- Observe the physical surroundings. Pay attention to signs, pictures, style of dress, length of hair, degree of openness between offices, and office furnishings and arrangements.
- With whom did you meet? How did they expect to be addressed?
- How would you characterize the style of the people you met? Formal? Casual? Serious? Jovial?

- Does the organization have formal rules and regulations printed in a personnel policy manual? If so, how detailed are these policies?
- Ask questions of the people with whom you meet. The most valid and reliable information tends to come from asking the same questions of many people (to see how closely their responses align). Questions that will give you insights into organizational processes and practices might include:
- What's the background of the founders?
- What's the background of current senior managers? What are their functional specializations? Were they promoted from within or hired from outside?
- How does the organization integrate new employees? Is there an orientation program? Training? If so, could you describe these features?
- How does your boss define his or her job success? (Amount of profit? Serving customers? Meeting deadlines? Acquiring budget increases?)
- How would you define fairness in terms of reward allocations?
- Can you identify some people here who are on the "fast track"? What do you think has put them on the fast track?
- Can you identify someone who seems to be considered a deviant in the organization? How has the organization responded to this person?
- Can you describe a decision that someone made here that was well received?
- Can you describe a decision that didn't work out well? What were the consequences for the decision maker?
- Could you describe a crisis or critical event that has occurred recently in the organization? How did top management respond? What was learned from this experience?

STRONG VS. WEAK CULTURES

It has become increasingly popular to differentiate between strong and weak cultures.[11] The argument here is that strong cultures have a greater impact on employee behavior and are more directly related to reduced turnover.

In a **strong culture**, the organization's core values are both intensely held and widely shared.[12] The more members who accept the core values and the greater their commitment to those values is, the stronger the culture is. Consistent with this definition, a strong culture will have a great influence on the behavior of its members because the high degree of sharedness and intensity creates an internal climate of high behavioral control. For example, Seattle-based Nordstrom has developed one of the strongest service cultures in the retailing industry. Nordstrom employees know in no uncertain terms what is expected of them and these expectations go a long way in shaping their behavior.

One specific result of a strong culture should be lower employee turnover. A strong culture demonstrates high agreement among members about what the organization stands for. Such unanimity of purpose builds cohesiveness, loyalty, and organizational commitment. These qualities, in turn, lessen employees' propensity to leave the organization.[13]

CULTURE VS. FORMALIZATION

A strong organizational culture increases behavioral consistency. In this sense, we should recognize that a strong culture can act as a substitute for formalization.

In Chapter 14, we discussed how formalization's rules and regulations act to regulate employee behavior. High formalization in an organization creates predictability, orderliness, and consistency. Our point is that a strong culture achieves the same end without the need for written documentation. Therefore, we should view formalization and culture as two different roads to a common destination. The stronger an organization's culture, the less management need be concerned with developing formal rules and regulations to guide employee behavior. Those guides will be internalized in employees when they accept the organization's culture.

Mercedes-Benz executives took national culture into account in making its sports utility vehicle in Tuscaloosa, Alabama. It was the first time Mercedes used a non-German workforce and a plant outside of Germany to produce a vehicle. At its U.S. plant, Mercedes' executives abandoned the strict hierarchy of its typical production line in Germany and replaced it with an egalitarian approach that would appeal to its U.S. workers, shown here. They designed the plant so employees could stop the assembly line to correct problems, formed employee teams to discuss problems with German trainers, and gave workers polo shirts with their names embroidered on the pockets to give them a sense of ownership.

ORGANIZATIONAL CULTURE VS. NATIONAL CULTURE

We opened this chapter by describing the challenges facing Mitsubishi's new president as he tries to change his company's organizational culture. But we also saw how Japan's national culture was closely intertwined with Mitsubishi's corporate culture. Throughout this book we've argued that national differences—that is, national cultures—must be taken into account if accurate predictions are to be made about organizational behavior in different countries. It seems appropriate at this point, then, to ask the question: Does national culture override an organization's culture? Is an IBM facility in Germany, for example, more likely to reflect German ethnic culture or IBM's corporate culture?

The research indicates that national culture has a greater impact on employees than does their organization's culture.[14] German employees at an IBM facility in Munich, therefore, will be influenced more by German culture than by IBM's culture. This means that as influential as organizational culture is in shaping employee behavior, national culture is even more influential.

The preceding conclusion has to be qualified to reflect the self-selection that goes on at the hiring stage.[15] A British multinational corporation, for example, is likely to be less concerned with hiring the "typical Italian" for its Italian operations than in hiring an Italian who fits with the corporation's way of doing things. We should expect, therefore, that the employee selection process will be used by multinationals to find and hire job applicants who are a good fit with their organization's dominant culture, even if such applicants are somewhat atypical for members of their country.

WHAT DO CULTURES DO?

We've alluded to organizational culture's impact on behavior. We've also explicitly argued that a strong culture should be associated with reduced turnover. In this section, we will more carefully review the functions that culture performs and assess whether culture can be a liability for an organization.

CULTURE'S FUNCTIONS

Culture performs a number of functions within an organization. First, it has a boundary-defining role; that is, it creates distinctions between one organization and others. Second, it conveys a sense of identity for organization members. Third, culture facilitates the generation of commitment to something larger than one's individual self-interest. Fourth, it enhances social system stability. Culture is the social glue that helps hold the organization together by providing appropriate standards for what employees should say and do. Finally, culture serves as a sense-making and control mechanism that guides and shapes the attitudes and behavior of employees. It is this last function that is of particular interest to us.[16] As the following quote makes clear, culture defines the rules of the game:

> *Culture is the social glue that helps hold the organization together.*

> Culture by definition is elusive, intangible, implicit, and taken for granted. But every organization develops a core set of assumptions, understandings, and implicit rules that govern day-to-day behavior in the workplace. . . . Until newcomers learn the rules, they are not accepted as full-fledged members of the organization. Transgressions of the rules on the part of high-level executives or front-line employees result in universal disapproval and powerful penalties. Conformity to the rules becomes the primary basis for reward and upward mobility.[17]

The role of culture in influencing employee behavior appears to be increasingly important in today's workplace.[18] As organizations have widened spans of control, flattened structures, introduced teams, reduced formalization, and empowered employees, the *shared meaning* provided by a strong culture ensures that everyone is pointed in the same direction.

The shared meaning provided by Yahoo! Inc.'s strong corporate culture is stated in the company's motto—"Do what's crazy, but not stupid." The motto guides employees as they develop entertaining programs and services that grab the attention of today's Internet users. Employee creativity is key to keeping Yahoo! the leading search engine on the Internet. Yahoo! hires young Net enthusiasts who thrive in an informal setting where there are few rules and regulations to stifle the creative process.

As we show later in this chapter, who receives a job offer to join the organization, who is appraised as a high performer, and who gets the promotion are strongly influenced by the individual–organization "fit"—that is, whether the applicant or employee's attitudes and behavior are compatible with the culture. It's not a coincidence that employees at Disney theme parks appear to be almost universally attractive, clean, and wholesome looking, with bright smiles. That's the image Disney seeks. The company selects employees who will maintain that image. And once on the job, a strong culture, supported by formal rules and regulations, ensures that Disney theme-park employees will act in a relatively uniform and predictable way.

CULTURE AS A LIABILITY

We are treating culture in a nonjudgmental manner. We haven't said that it's good or bad, only that it exists. Many of its functions, as outlined, are valuable for both the organization and the employee. Culture enhances organizational commitment and increases the consistency of employee behavior. These are clearly benefits to an organization. From an employee's standpoint, culture is valuable because it reduces ambiguity. It tells employees how things are done and what's important. But we shouldn't ignore the potentially dysfunctional aspects of culture, especially a strong one, on an organization's effectiveness.

Barrier to Change Culture is a liability when the shared values are not in agreement with those that will further the organization's effectiveness. This is most likely to occur when an organization's environment is dynamic. When an environment is undergoing rapid change, an organization's entrenched culture may no longer be appropriate. So consistency of behavior is an asset to an organization when it faces a stable environment. It may, however, burden the organization and make it difficult to respond to changes in the environment. This helps to explain the challenges that executives at companies such as Mitsubishi, General Motors, Eastman Kodak, Kellogg, and Boeing have had in recent years in adapting to upheavals in their environment. These companies have strong cultures that worked well for them in the past. But these strong cultures become barriers to change when "business as usual" is no longer effective (see "Myth or Science?" box).

Barrier to Diversity Hiring new employees who, because of race, gender, disability, or other differences, are not like the majority of the organization's members creates a paradox.[19] Management wants new employees to accept the organization's core cultural values. Otherwise, these employees are unlikely to fit in or be accepted. But at the same time, management wants to openly acknowledge and demonstrate support for the differences that these employees bring to the workplace.

Strong cultures put considerable pressure on employees to conform. They limit the range of values and styles that is acceptable. In some instances, such as the widely publicized Texaco case (which was settled on behalf of 1,400 employees for $176 million) in which senior managers made disparaging remarks about minorities, a strong culture that condones prejudice can even undermine formal corporate diversity policies.[20]

Organizations seek out and hire diverse individuals because of the alternative strengths these people bring to the workplace. Yet these diverse behaviors and strengths are likely to diminish in strong cultures as people attempt to fit in.

"Success Breeds Success"

This statement is not always true. Generally speaking, success creates positive momentum. People like being associated with a successful team or organization, which allows winning teams and organizations to get the best new recruits. Microsoft's incredible success in the 1990s made it a highly desirable place to work. It had its pick among the "best and the brightest" job applicants when filling job slots. Success led to further successes. Microsoft's experience is generalizable across decades to other companies. In the 1960s, when General Motors controlled nearly 50 percent of the U.S. automobile market, GM was the most sought after employer by newly minted M.B.A.s. In the early 1990s, Motorola was routinely described as one of the best managed and successful companies in America, and it was able to attract the best and the brightest engineers and professionals.

But success often breeds failure, especially in organizations with strong cultures.[21] Organizations that have tremendous successes begin to believe in their own invulnerability. They often become arrogant. They lose their competitive edge. Their strong cultures reinforce past practices and make change difficult. "Why change? It worked in the past. If it ain't broke, don't fix it."

The corporate highway is littered with companies that let arrogance undermine previous successes. JC Penney and Sears once ruled the retail department-store market. Their executives considered their markets immune to competition. Beginning in the mid-1970s, Wal-Mart did a pretty effective job of humbling Penney's and Sears's managements. GM executives, safe and cloistered in their Detroit headquarters, ignored the aggressive efforts by Japanese auto firms to penetrate its markets. The result? GM's market share has been in a free fall for three decades. Interestingly, Toyota, once one of those aggressive Japanese firms that was successfully stealing market share from GM, itself became a casualty of its own successes. During the first half of the 1990s, having been slow to respond to the recreational vehicle market and stuck with a cumbersome vehicle development process, Toyota experienced a serious loss in market share and profit margins.[22] Motorola may have been the high-tech darling of the early 1990s, when it dominated world markets for semiconductors and analog cellular phones, but the company became arrogant. It stumbled badly in the digital market, failed to listen to the needs of its customers, and overextended itself in Asia. In 1998, it took a $1.95 billion write-off and cut its workforce by 15,000.[23]

Strong cultures, therefore, can be liabilities when they effectively eliminate those unique strengths that people of different backgrounds bring to the organization. Moreover, strong cultures can also be liabilities when they support institutional bias or become insensitive to people who are different.

Barrier to Acquisitions and Mergers Historically, the key factors that management looked at in making acquisition or merger decisions were related to financial advantages or product synergy. In recent years, cultural compatibility has become the primary concern.[24] While a favorable financial statement or product line may be the initial attraction of an acquisition candidate, whether the acquisition actually works seems to have more to do with how well the two organizations' cultures match up.

A number of acquisitions consummated in the 1990s already have failed. And the primary cause is conflicting organizational cultures.[25] For instance, AT&T's 1991 acquisition of NCR was a disaster. AT&T's unionized employees objected to working in the same building as NCR's nonunion staff. Meanwhile, NCR's conservative, centralized culture didn't take kindly to AT&T's insistence on calling supervisors "coaches" and removing executives' office doors. By the time AT&T finally sold NCR, the failure of the deal had cost AT&T more than $3 billion. Similarly, Word-

Perfect Corp. bought Novell Inc. in 1994 to give it a viable word-processing product to compete against Microsoft. But employees and managers from the two organizations could never see eye to eye on important issues. When WordPerfect was sold to Corel Corp. in 1996, Novell got $1 billion less than it had paid just two years earlier.

Sometimes, astute executives can see the culture problems during the "dating" stage and cancel the marriage before tying the knot. That's what happened in the recent merger plans between American Home Products and Monsanto.[26] Despite the potential advantages from research efficiencies and a larger pool of scientific talent, it became clear to executives at both firms that trying to merge a frugal, rigidly run company like American Home with a high-spending, risk-taking one like Monsanto was a potential disaster in the making.

CREATING AND SUSTAINING CULTURE

An organization's culture doesn't pop out of thin air. Once established, it rarely fades away. What forces influence the creation of a culture? What reinforces and sustains these forces once they're in place? We answer both of these questions in this section.

HOW A CULTURE BEGINS

An organization's current customs, traditions, and general way of doing things are largely due to what it has done before and the degree of success it has had with those endeavors. This leads us to the ultimate source of an organization's culture: its founders.[27]

The founders of an organization traditionally have a major impact on that organization's early culture. They have a vision of what the organization should be. They are unconstrained by previous customs or ideologies. The small size that typically characterizes new organizations further facilitates the founders' imposition of their vision on all organizational members.

The process of culture creation occurs in three ways.[28] First, founders only hire and keep employees who think and feel the way they do. Second, they indoctrinate and socialize these employees to their way of thinking and feeling. And finally, the founders' own behavior acts as a role model that encourages employees to identify with them and thereby internalize their beliefs, values, and assumptions. When the organization succeeds, the founders' vision becomes seen as a primary determinant of that success. At this point, the founders' entire personalities become embedded in the culture of the organization.

The culture at Hyundai, the giant Korean conglomerate, is largely a reflection of its founder Chung Ju Yung. Hyundai's fierce, competitive style and its disciplined, authoritarian nature are the same characteristics often used to describe Chung. Other contemporary examples of founders who have had an immeasurable impact on their organization's culture would include Bill Gates at Microsoft, Akio Morita at Sony, David Packard at Hewlett-Packard, Herb Kelleher at Southwest Airlines, Fred Smith at Federal Express, Mary Kay at Mary Kay Cosmetics, and Richard Branson at the Virgin Group.

KEEPING A CULTURE ALIVE

Once a culture is in place, there are practices within the organization that act to maintain it by giving employees a set of similar experiences.[29] For example, many of the human resource practices discussed in the pre-

Akio Morita, Sony Corporation's co-founder, had such a tremendous influence on the company's culture that people referred to him as Mr. Sony. Morita was described as a passsionate lover of music and art, a workaholic, a great socializer, a brilliant observer of people's behavior, and a man with unbounding energy, a relentless drive, and a determined focus. Morita applied these qualities in pursuing his vision of creating a brand name for products that appealed to people worldwide. He chose a short, catchy name for his company so people everywhere could easily pronounce and remember it. Morita began his globalization strategy in the United States, where he moved his family so he could study American culture and increase Sony's chance of success. Today Sony is recognized throughout the world as a leading brand name.

OB *in the News*

Learning the Disney Culture

The Walt Disney Company has an employee development group that puts on programs for all employees. The mission of this group is to design and facilitate quality educational programs and services that promote the professional and personal development of its employees, maintain The Walt Disney Company image, corporate culture, and history, create synergistic opportunities, and enhance employee morale and motivation.

The foundation of the Disney programs is based on two courses:

Welcome to Disney—Act I. This is a seven-hour orientation program, which introduces new employees to the company, its traditions, diverse business activities, and future goals.

Welcome to Disney—Act II. Working with Integrity. This is the second part of the company's orientation program. Lasting four hours, it covers two topics: (1) Standards of Business Conduct and (2) Respect: Disney's Key to Success.

In addition to these two programs, the company offers others on planning and time management, writing skills, behavioral style, and communication. For instance, the four-hour program entitled "What's Your Behavioral Style?" includes completion of a personality profile to help employees better understand themselves and others. Employees "identify ways to be more successful with different work styles and minimize potential conflicts with others. You'll also discover how to work with certain behavioral styles and how to become more effective in the workplace."

Source: From "The Employee Development Calendar," The Disney University; January–March 1999.

vious chapter reinforce the organization's culture. The selection process, performance evaluation criteria, training and career development activities, and promotion procedures ensure that those hired fit in with the culture, reward those who support it, and penalize (and even expel) those who challenge it. Three forces play a particularly important part in sustaining a culture: selection practices, the actions of top management, and socialization methods. Let's take a closer look at each.

Selection   The explicit goal of the selection process is to identify and hire individuals who have the knowledge, skills, and abilities to perform the jobs within the organization successfully. Typically, more than one candidate will be identified who meets any given job's requirements. When that point is reached, it would be naive to ignore that the final decision as to who is hired will be significantly influenced by the decision maker's judgment of how well the candidates will fit into the organization. This attempt to ensure a proper match, whether purposely or inadvertently, results in the hiring of people who have values essentially consistent with those of the organization, or at least a good portion of those values.[30] Additionally, the selection process provides information to applicants about the organization. Candidates learn about the organization and, if they perceive a conflict between their values and those of the organization, they can self-select themselves out of the applicant pool. Selection, therefore, becomes a two-way street, allowing employer or applicant to abrogate a marriage if there appears to be a mismatch. In this way, the selection process sustains an organization's culture by selecting out those individuals who might attack or undermine its core values.

Applicants for entry-level positions in brand management at Procter & Gamble (P&G) experience an exhaustive application and screening process. Their interviewers are part of an elite cadre who have been selected and trained extensively via lectures, videotapes, films, practice interviews, and role plays to identify applicants who will successfully fit in at P&G. Applicants are interviewed in depth for such qualities as their ability to "turn out high volumes of excellent work," "identify and understand problems," and "reach thoroughly substantiated and well-reasoned conclusions that lead to action." P&G values rationality and seeks applicants who think that way. College applicants receive two interviews and a general knowledge test on campus before being flown back to Cincinnati for three more one-on-one interviews and a group interview at lunch. Each encounter seeks corroborating evidence of the traits that the firm believes correlate highly with "what counts" for success at P&G.[31] Applicants for positions at Compaq Computer are carefully chosen for their ability to fit into the company's teamwork-oriented culture. As one executive put it, "We can find lots of people who are competent. . . . The No. 1 issue is whether they fit into the way we do business."[32] At Compaq, that means job candidates who are easy to get along with and who feel comfortable with the company's consensus management style. To increase the likelihood that loners and those with big egos get screened out, it's not unusual for an applicant to be interviewed by 15 people, who represent all departments of the company and a variety of seniority levels.[33]

Top Management   The actions of top management also have a major impact on the organization's culture.[34] Through what they say and how they behave, senior executives establish norms that filter down through the organization as to whether risk taking is desirable; how much freedom managers should give their employees; what is appropriate dress; what actions will pay off in terms of pay raises, promotions, and other rewards; and the like.

For example, look at Xerox Corp.[35] Its chief executive from 1961 to 1968 was Joseph C. Wilson. An aggressive, entrepreneurial type, he oversaw Xerox's staggering growth on the basis of its 914 copier, one of the most successful products in American history. Under Wilson, Xerox had an entrepreneurial environment, with an informal, high-camaraderie, innovative, bold, risk-taking culture. Wilson's replacement as CEO was C. Peter McColough, a Harvard M.B.A. with a formal management style. He instituted bureaucratic controls and a major change in Xerox's culture. When McColough stepped down in 1982, Xerox had become stodgy and formal, with lots of politics and turf battles and layers of watchdog managers. His replacement was David T. Kearns. He believed the culture he inherited hindered Xerox's ability to compete. To increase the company's competitiveness, Kearns trimmed Xerox down by cutting 15,000 jobs, delegated decision making downward, and refocused the organization's culture around a simple theme: boosting the quality of Xerox products and services. By his actions and those of his senior managerial cadre, Kearns conveyed to everyone at Xerox that the company valued and rewarded quality and efficiency. When Kearns retired in 1990, Xerox still had its problems. The copier business was mature and Xerox had fared badly in developing computerized office systems. The next CEO, Paul Allaire, again sought to reshape Xerox's culture. Specifically, he reorganized the corporation around a worldwide marketing department, unified product development and manufacturing divisions, and replaced half of the company's top-management team with outsiders. Allaire sought to reshape Xerox's culture to focus on innovative thinking and outhustling the competition. The present CEO, G. Richard Thoman, replaced Allaire in the spring of 1999. He came to Xerox from IBM in 1997. Not surprisingly, given his experiences at IBM,

The actions of Herbert Kelleher, Southwest Airlines' chief executive, have a strong influence on the company's casual, fun-loving culture. He stars in the company's orientation film, where new employees see their leader singing and dancing. Kelleher models the lighthearted behavior he expects of his employees so they, in turn, know it's okay that part of providing exceptional customer service is to have fun with the airlines' passengers.

Thoman's focus is on technology. He envisions reshaping Xerox into a fast-moving provider of high-tech services all built around digital documents.

Socialization No matter how good a job the organization does in recruitment and selection, new employees are not fully indoctrinated in the organization's culture. Maybe most important, because they are unfamiliar with the organization's culture, new employees are potentially likely to disturb the beliefs and customs that are in place. The organization will, therefore, want to help new employees adapt to its culture. This adaptation process is called **socialization**.[36]

All Marines must go through boot camp, where they "prove" their commitment. Of course, at the same time, the Marine trainers are indoctrinating new recruits in the "Marine way." New Sanyo employees go through an intensive five-month training program (trainees eat and sleep together in company-subsidized dorms and are required to vacation together at company-owned resorts) where they learn the Sanyo way of doing everything—from how to speak to superiors to proper grooming and dress.[37] The company considers this program essential for transforming young employees, fresh out of school, into dedicated *kaisha senshi*, or corporate warriors. Starbucks, the rapidly growing gourmet-coffee chain, doesn't go to the extreme that Sanyo does, but it seeks the same outcome.[38] All new employees go through 24 hours of training. Just for an entry-level job in a retail store making coffee? Yes! Classes cover everything necessary to turn new employees into brewing consultants. They learn the Starbucks philosophy, the company jargon (including phrases such as "half-decaf double tall almond skim mocha"), and even how to help customers make decisions about beans, grind, and espresso machines. The result is employees who understand Starbucks' culture and who project an enthusiastic and knowledgeable interface with customers.

As we discuss socialization, keep in mind that the most critical socialization stage is at the time of entry into the organization. This is when the organization seeks to mold the outsider into an employee "in good standing." Those employees who fail to learn the essential or pivotal role behaviors risk being labeled "nonconformists" or "rebels," which often leads to expulsion. But the organization will be socializing every employee, though maybe not as explicitly, throughout his or her entire career in the organization. This further contributes to sustaining the culture.

Socialization can be conceptualized as a process made up of three stages: prearrival, encounter, and metamorphosis.[39] The first stage encompasses all the learning that occurs before a new member joins the organization. In the second stage, the new employee sees what the organization is really like and confronts the possibility that expectations and reality may diverge. In the third stage, the relatively long-lasting changes take place. The new employee masters the skills required for his or her job, successfully performs his or her new roles, and makes the adjustments to his or her work group's values and norms.[40] This three-stage process impacts on the new employee's work productivity, commitment to the organization's objectives, and eventual decision to stay with the organization. Exhibit 17-2 depicts this process.

The **prearrival stage** explicitly recognizes that each individual arrives with a set of values, attitudes, and expectations. These cover both the work to be done and the organization. For instance, in many jobs, particularly professional work, new members will have undergone a considerable degree of prior socialization in training and in school. One major purpose of a business school, for example, is to socialize business students to the attitudes and behaviors that business firms want. If business executives believe that successful employees value the

socialization
The process that adapts employees to the organization's culture.

prearrival stage
The period of learning in the socialization process that occurs before a new employee joins the organization.

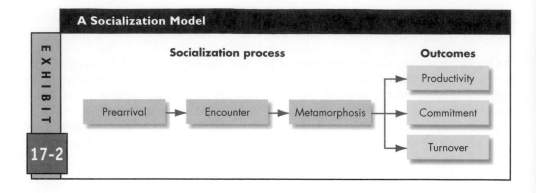

EXHIBIT 17-2

A Socialization Model

Socialization process | Outcomes

Prearrival → Encounter → Metamorphosis →

Productivity

Commitment

Turnover

profit ethic, are loyal, will work hard, and desire to achieve, they can hire individuals out of business schools who have been premolded in this pattern. But prearrival socialization goes beyond the specific job. The selection process is used in most organizations to inform prospective employees about the organization as a whole. In addition, as noted previously, the selection process also acts to ensure the inclusion of the "right type"—those who will fit in. "Indeed, the ability of the individual to present the appropriate face during the selection process determines his ability to move into the organization in the first place. Thus, success depends on the degree to which the aspiring member has correctly anticipated the expectations and desires of those in the organization in charge of selection."[41]

encounter stage

The stage in the socialization process in which a new employee sees what the organization is really like and confronts the possibility that expectations and reality may diverge.

Upon entry into the organization, the new member enters the **encounter stage**. Here the individual confronts the possible dichotomy between her expectations—about her job, her co-workers, her boss, and the organization in general—and reality. If expectations prove to have been more or less accurate, the encounter stage merely provides a reaffirmation of the perceptions gained earlier. However, this is often not the case. Where expectations and reality differ, the new employee must undergo socialization that will detach her from her previous assumptions and replace them with another set that the organization deems desirable. At the extreme, a new member may become totally disillusioned with the actualities of her job and resign. Proper selection should significantly reduce the probability of the latter occurrence.

metamorphosis stage

The stage in the socialization process in which a new employee changes and adjusts to the job, work group, and organization.

Finally, the new member must work out any problems discovered during the encounter stage. This may mean going through changes—hence, we call this the **metamorphosis stage**. The options presented in Exhibit 17-3 are alternatives designed to bring about the desired metamorphosis. Note, for example, that the more management relies on socialization programs that are formal, collective, fixed, serial, and emphasize divestiture, the greater the likelihood that newcomers' differences and perspectives will be stripped away and replaced by standardized and predictable behaviors. Careful selection by management of newcomers' socialization experiences can—at the extreme—create conformists who maintain traditions and customs, or inventive and creative individualists who consider no organizational practice sacred.

We can say that metamorphosis and the entry socialization process are complete when the new member has become comfortable with the organization and his job. He has internalized the norms of the organization and his work group, and understands and accepts these norms. The new member feels accepted by his peers as a trusted and valued individual, is self-confident that he has the competence to complete the job successfully, and understands the system—not only his

EXHIBIT

17-3

Entry Socialization Options

Formal vs. Informal The more a new employee is segregated from the ongoing work setting and differentiated in some way to make explicit his or her newcomer's role, the more formal socialization is. Specific orientation and training programs are examples. Informal socialization puts the new employee directly into his or her job, with little or no special attention.

Individual vs. Collective New members can be socialized individually. This describes how it's done in many professional offices. They can also be grouped together and processed through an identical set of experiences, as in military boot camp.

Fixed vs. Variable This refers to the time schedule in which newcomers make the transition from outsider to insider. A fixed schedule establishes standardized stages of transition. This characterizes rotational training programs. It also includes probationary periods, such as the eight- to ten-year "associate" status used by accounting and law firms before deciding on whether or not a candidate is made a partner. Variable schedules give no advanced notice of their transition timetable. Variable schedules describe the typical promotion system, where one is not advanced to the next stage until he or she is "ready."

Serial vs. Random Serial socialization is characterized by the use of role models who train and encourage the newcomer. Apprenticeship and mentoring programs are examples. In random socialization, role models are deliberately withheld. The new employee is left on his or her own to figure things out.

Investiture vs. Divestiture Investiture socialization assumes that the newcomer's qualities and qualifications are the necessary ingredients for job success, so these qualities and qualifications are confirmed and supported. Divestiture socialization tries to strip away certain characteristics of the recruit. Fraternity and sorority "pledges" go through divestiture socialization to shape them into the proper role.

Source: Based on J. Van Maanen, "People Processing: Strategies of Organizational Socialization," *Organizational Dynamics*, Summer 1978, pp. 19–36; and E. H. Schein, "Organizational Culture," *American Psychologist*, February 1990, p. 116.

own tasks, but the rules, procedures, and informally accepted practices as well. Finally, he knows how he will be evaluated, that is, what criteria will be used to measure and appraise his work. He knows what is expected, and what constitutes a job "well done." As Exhibit 17-2 shows, successful metamorphosis should have a positive impact on the new employee's productivity and his commitment to the organization, and reduce his propensity to leave the organization.

SUMMARY: HOW CULTURES FORM

Exhibit 17-4 summarizes how an organization's culture is established and sustained. The original culture is derived from the founder's philosophy. This, in turn, strongly influences the criteria used in hiring. The actions of the current top management set the general climate of what is acceptable behavior and what is not. How employees are to be socialized will depend both on the degree of success achieved in matching new employees' values to those of the organization's in the selection process and on top management's preference for socialization methods.

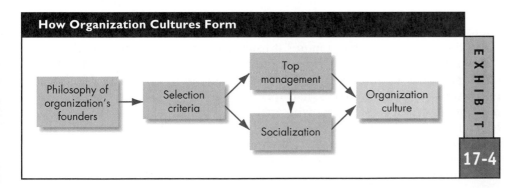

How Organization Cultures Form

EXHIBIT

17-4

HOW EMPLOYEES LEARN CULTURE

Culture is transmitted to employees in a number of forms, the most potent being stories, rituals, material symbols, and language.

STORIES

During the days when Henry Ford II was chairman of the Ford Motor Co., one would have been hard pressed to find a manager who hadn't heard the story about Mr. Ford reminding his executives, when they got too arrogant, that "it's my name that's on the building." The message was clear: Henry Ford II ran the company!

Nordstrom employees are fond of the following story. It strongly conveys the company's policy toward customer returns: When this specialty retail chain was in its infancy, a customer came in and wanted to return a set of automobile tires. The sales clerk was a bit uncertain how to handle the problem. As the customer and sales clerk spoke, Mr. Nordstrom walked by and overheard the conversation. He immediately interceded, asking the customer how much he had paid for the tires. Mr. Nordstrom then instructed the clerk to take the tires back and provide a full cash refund. After the customer had received his refund and left, the perplexed clerk looked at the boss. "But, Mr. Nordstrom, we don't sell tires!" "I know," replied the boss, "but we do whatever we need to do to make the customer happy. I mean it when I say we have a no-questions-asked return policy." Nordstrom then picked up the telephone and called a friend in the auto parts business to see how much he could get for the tires.

Stories such as these circulate through many organizations. They typically contain a narrative of events about the organization's founders, rule breaking, rags-to-riches successes, reductions in the workforce, relocation of employees, reactions to past mistakes, and organizational coping.[42] These stories anchor the present in the past and provide explanations and legitimacy for current practices.[43] For the most part, these stories develop spontaneously. But some organizations actually try to manage this element of culture learning. For instance, Krispy Kreme, a large doughnut maker out of North Carolina, has a full-time "minister of culture" whose primary responsibility is to tape interviews with customers and employees.[44] The stories these people tell are then put in the company's video magazine that describes Krispy Kreme's history and values.

RITUALS

rituals

Repetitive sequences of activities that express and reinforce the key values of the organization, which goals are most important, which people are important, and which are expendable.

Rituals are repetitive sequences of activities that express and reinforce the key values of the organization, which goals are most important, and which people are important and which are expendable.[45]

College faculty members undergo a lengthy ritual in their quest for permanent employment—tenure. Typically, the faculty member is on probation for six years. At the end of that period, the member's colleagues must make one of two choices: extend a tenured appointment or issue a one-year terminal contract. What does it take to obtain tenure? It usually requires satisfactory teaching performance, service to the department and university, and scholarly activity. But, of course, what satisfies the requirements for tenure in one department at one university may be appraised as inadequate in another. The key is that the tenure decision, in essence, asks those who are tenured to assess whether the candidate has demonstrated, based on six years of performance, whether he or she fits in. Colleagues who have been socialized properly will have proved themselves worthy of being granted tenure. Every year, hundreds of faculty members at colleges and universities are denied tenure. In some cases, this action is a result of poor

EXHIBIT

17-5

"I don't know how it started, either. All I know is that it's part of our corporate culture."

Drawing by Mick Stevens in *The New Yorker*, October 3, 1994. Copyright © 1994 by The New Yorker Magazine, Inc. Reprinted by permission.

performance across the board. More often, however, the decision can be traced to the faculty member's not doing well in those areas that the tenured faculty believe are important. The instructor who spends dozens of hours each week preparing for class and achieves outstanding evaluations by students but neglects his or her research and publication activities may be passed over for tenure. What has happened, simply, is that the instructor has failed to adapt to the norms set by the department. The astute faculty member will assess early on in the probationary period what attitudes and behaviors his or her colleagues want and will then proceed to give them what they want. And, of course, by demanding certain attitudes and behaviors, the tenured faculty have made significant strides toward standardizing tenure candidates.

One of the best-known corporate rituals is Mary Kay Cosmetics' annual award meeting.[46] Looking like a cross between a circus and a Miss America pageant, the meeting takes place over a couple of days in a large auditorium, on a stage in front of a large, cheering audience, with all the participants dressed in glamorous evening clothes. Saleswomen are rewarded with an array of flashy gifts—gold and diamond pins, fur stoles, pink Cadillacs—based on success in achieving sales quota. This "show" acts as a motivator by publicly recognizing outstanding sales performance. In addition, the ritual aspect reinforces Mary Kay's personal determination and optimism, which enabled her to overcome personal hardships, found her own company, and achieve material success. It conveys to her salespeople that reaching their sales quota is important and that through hard work and encouragement they too can achieve success.

MATERIAL SYMBOLS

The headquarters of Alcoa doesn't look like your typical head office operation. As we noted in Chapter 15, there are few individual offices. It is essentially made up of cubicles, common areas, and meeting rooms. This informal corporate headquarters conveys to employees that Alcoa values openness, equality, creativity, and flexibility.

Some corporations provide their top executives with chauffeur-driven limousines and, when they travel by air, unlimited use of the corporate jet. Others may not get to ride in limousines or private jets but they might still get a car and air transportation paid for by the company. Only the car is a Chevrolet (with no driver) and the jet seat is in the economy section of a commercial airliner.

The layout of corporate headquarters, the types of automobiles top executives are given, and the presence or absence of corporate aircraft are a few examples of material symbols. Others include the size of offices, the elegance of furnishings, executive perks, and dress attire.[47] These material symbols convey to employees who is important, the degree of egalitarianism desired by top management, and the kinds of behavior (e.g., risk taking, conservative, authoritarian, participative, individualistic, social) that are appropriate.

LANGUAGE

Many organizations and units within organizations use language as a way to identify members of a culture or subculture. By learning this language, members attest to their acceptance of the culture and, in so doing, help to preserve it.

The following are examples of terminology used by employees at Dialog, a California-based data redistributor: *accession number* (a number assigned to each individual record in a database); *KWIC* (a set of key-words-in-context); and *relational operator* (searching a database for names or key terms in some order). Librarians are a rich source of terminology foreign to people outside their profession. They sprinkle their conversations liberally with acronyms such as ARL (Association for Research Libraries), OCLC (a center in Ohio that does cooperative cataloging), and OPAC (for on-line patron accessing catalog). If you're a new employee at Boeing, you'll find yourself learning a whole unique vocabulary of acronyms, including BOLD (Boeing on-line data); CATIA (computer-graphics-aided, three-dimensional interactive application); MAIDS (manufacturing assembly and installation data system); POP (purchased outside production); and SLO (service-level objectives).[48]

Organizations, over time, often develop unique terms to describe equipment, offices, key personnel, suppliers, customers, or products that relate to their business. New employees are frequently overwhelmed with acronyms and jargon that, after six months on the job, have become fully part of their language. Once assimilated, this terminology acts as a common denominator that unites members of a given culture or subculture.

Employees at Tattoo, a marketing services agency in San Francisco, use special words to convey the company's unique culture. They call Tattoo's three floors of office space the "hive" because it buzzes with activity as employees move between the floors to work on different client projects. They refer to themselves as "Tattools," because the company discourages formal job titles and other symbols of formal authority. Unlike most marketing firms that use market research studies and focus groups for developing brand campaigns, Tattoo uses an intuitive approach it calls "living the brand." Employees call client presentations "collages," a blending of music and visuals intended to show the sensory and emotional aspects of a brand.

MATCHING PEOPLE WITH CULTURES

There is now a substantive body of evidence to demonstrate that organizations attempt to select new members who fit well with the organization's culture.[49] And most job candidates similarly try to find organizations where their values and personality will fit in.

Recent research by Goffee and Jones provides some interesting insights on different organizational cultures and guidance to prospective employees.[50] They have identified four distinct cultural types. Let's take a look at their cultural framework and how you can use it to select an employer where you'll best fit in.

Goffee and Jones argue that two dimensions underlie organizational culture. The first they call *sociability*. This is a measure of friendliness. High sociability means people do kind things for one another without expecting something in return and relate to each other in a friendly, caring way. In terms of our definition of organizational culture presented at the beginning of this chapter, sociability is consistent with a high people orientation, high team orientation, and focus on processes rather than outcomes. The second is *solidarity*. It's a measure of task orientation. High solidarity means people can overlook personal biases and rally behind common interests and common goals. Again, referring back to our earlier definition, solidarity is consistent with high attention to detail and high aggressiveness. Exhibit 17-6 illustrates a matrix with these two dimensions rated as either high or low. They create four distinct culture types:

Networked culture (high on sociability; low on solidarity). These organizations view members as family and friends. People know and like each other. People willingly give assistance to others and openly share information. The major negative aspect associated with this culture is that the focus on friendships can lead to a tolerance for poor performance and creation of political cliques.

Mercenary culture (low on sociability; high on solidarity). These organizations are fiercely goal focused. People are intense and determined to meet goals. They have a zest for getting things done quickly and a powerful sense of purpose. Mercenary cultures aren't just about winning; they're about destroying the enemy. This focus on goals and objectivity also leads to a minimal degree of politicking. The downside of this culture is that it can lead to an almost inhumane treatment of people who are perceived as low performers.

Fragmented culture (low on sociability; low on solidarity). These organizations are made up of individualists. Commitment is first and foremost to individual members and their job tasks. There is little or no identification with the organization. In fragmented cultures, employees are judged solely on their productivity and the quality of their work. The major negatives in these cultures are excessive critiquing of others and an absence of collegiality.

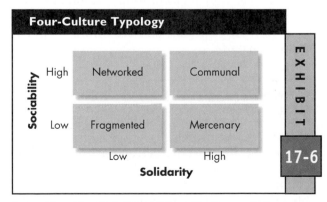

Four-Culture Typology

	Low	High
Sociability High	Networked	Communal
Sociability Low	Fragmented	Mercenary

Solidarity

EXHIBIT 17-6

Source: Adapted from R. Goffee and G. Jones, *The Character of a Corporation* (New York: Harper Business, 1998), p. 21.

Communal culture (high on sociability; high on solidarity). This final category values both friendship and performance. People have a feeling of belonging but there is still a ruthless focus on goal achievement. Leaders of these cultures tend to be inspirational and charismatic, with a clear vision of the organizations' future. The downside of these cultures is that they often consume one's total life. Their charismatic leaders frequently look to create disciples rather than followers, resulting in a work climate that is almost cultlike.

Unilever and Heineken are examples of networked cultures. Heineken, for example, has over 30,000 employees but retains the feeling of friendship and family that is more typical among small firms. The company's highly social culture produces a strong sense of belonging and often a passionate identification with its product. Are you cut out for a networked culture? You are if you possess good social skills and empathy; you like to forge close, work-related friendships; you thrive in a relaxed and convivial atmosphere; and you're not obsessed with efficiency and task performance.

Mars, Campbell Soup, and Japanese heavy-equipment manufacturer Komatsu are classic mercenary cultures. At Mars, for instance, meetings are almost totally concerned with work issues. There's little tolerance for socializing or small talk. You're well matched to a mercenary culture if you're goal oriented; thrive on competition, like clearly structured work tasks, enjoy risk taking, and are able to deal openly with conflict.

Most top-tier universities and law firms take on the properties of fragmented cultures. Professors at major universities, for instance, are judged on their research and scholarship. Senior professors with big reputations don't need to be friendly to their peers or attend social functions to retain their status. Similarly, law partners who bring in new clients and win cases need to expend little energy getting to know co-workers or being visible in the office. You're likely to fit in well in a fragmented culture if you're independent; have a low need to be part of a group atmosphere; are analytical rather than intuitive; and have a strong sense of self that is not easily undermined by criticism.

Examples of communal cultures would include Hewlett-Packard, Johnson & Johnson, and consulting firm Bain & Co. Hewlett-Packard is large and very goal focused, yet it has a strong family feel. The "HP Way" is a set of values that the company has enumerated that governs how people should behave and interact with each other. The HP Way's values of trust and community encourages loyalty to the company. And the company returns that loyalty to employees as long as they perform well. Who fits into communal cultures? You might if you have a strong need to identify with something bigger than yourself, enjoy working in teams, and are willing to put the organization above family and personal life.

SUMMARY AND IMPLICATIONS FOR MANAGERS

Exhibit 17-7 depicts organizational culture as an intervening variable. Employees form an overall subjective perception of the organization based on such factors as degree of risk tolerance, team emphasis, and support of people. This overall perception becomes, in effect, the organization's culture or personality. These favorable or unfavorable perceptions then affect employee performance and satisfaction, with the impact being greater for stronger cultures.

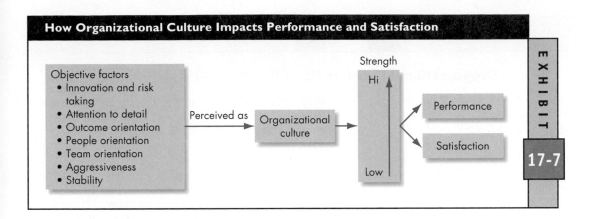

How Organizational Culture Impacts Performance and Satisfaction

EXHIBIT 17-7

Objective factors
- Innovation and risk taking
- Attention to detail
- Outcome orientation
- People orientation
- Team orientation
- Aggressiveness
- Stability

Perceived as → Organizational culture →

Strength
Hi → Low

Performance

Satisfaction

Just as people's personalities tend to be stable over time, so too do strong cultures. This makes strong cultures difficult for managers to change. When a culture becomes mismatched to its environment, management will want to change it. But as the Point-Counterpoint debate for this chapter demonstrates, changing an organization's culture is a long and difficult process. The result, at least in the short term, is that managers should treat their organization's culture as relatively fixed.

One of the more important managerial implications of organizational culture relates to selection decisions. Hiring individuals whose values don't align with those of the organization is likely to lead to employees who lack motivation and commitment and who are dissatisfied with their jobs and the organization.[51] Not surprisingly, employee "misfits" have considerably higher turnover rates than individuals who perceive a good fit.[52]

We should also not overlook the influence socialization has on employee performance. An employee's performance depends to a considerable degree on knowing what he should or should not do. Understanding the right way to do a job indicates proper socialization. Furthermore, the appraisal of an individual's performance includes how well the person fits into the organization. Can he or she get along with co-workers? Does he or she have acceptable work habits and demonstrate the right attitude? These qualities differ between jobs and organizations. For instance, on some jobs, employees will be evaluated more favorably if they are aggressive and outwardly indicate that they are ambitious. On another job, or on the same job in another organization, such an approach may be evaluated negatively. As a result, proper socialization becomes a significant factor in influencing both actual job performance and how it's perceived by others.

Organizational Cultures Can't Be Changed

An organization's culture is made up of relatively stable characteristics. It develops over many years and is rooted in deeply held values to which employees are strongly committed. In addition, there are a number of forces continually operating to maintain a given culture. These would include written statements about the organization's mission and philosophy, the design of physical spaces and buildings, the dominant leadership style, hiring criteria, past promotion practices, entrenched rituals, popular stories about key people and events, the organization's historic performance evaluation critieria, and the organization's formal structure.

Selection and promotion policies are particularly important devices that work against cultural change. Employees chose the organization because they perceived their values to be a "good fit" with the organization. They become comfortable with that fit and will strongly resist efforts to disturb the equilibrium. The terrific difficulties that organizations such as General Motors, AT&T, and the U.S. Postal Service have had in trying to reshape their cultures attest to this dilemma. These organizations historically tended to attract individuals who desired situations that were stable and highly structured. Those in control in organizations will also select senior managers who will continue the current culture. Even attempts to change a culture by going outside the organization to hire a new chief executive are unlikely to be effective. The evidence indicates that the culture is more likely to change the executive than the other way around.

Our argument should not be viewed as saying that culture can *never* be changed. In the unusual case when an organization confronts a survival-threatening crisis—a crisis that is universally acknowledged as a true life-or-death situation—members of the organization will be responsive to efforts at cultural change. However, anything less than a crisis is unlikely to be effective in bringing about cultural change.

Changing an organization's culture is extremely difficult, but cultures *can* be changed. The evidence suggests that cultural change is most likely to take place when most or all of the following conditions exist:

A dramatic crisis. This is the shock that undermines the status quo and calls into question the relevance of the current culture. Examples of these crises might be a surprising financial setback, the loss of a major customer, or a dramatic technological breakthrough by a competitor.

Turnover in leadership. New top leadership, which can provide an alternative set of key values, may be perceived as more capable of responding to the crisis.

Young and small organizations. The younger the organization is, the less entrenched its culture will be. Similarly, it's easier for management to communicate its new values when the organization is small.

Weak culture. The more widely held a culture is and the higher the agreement among members on its values, the more difficult it will be to change. Conversely, weak cultures are more amenable to change than strong ones.

If the preceding conditions exist, the following actions may lead to change: New stories and rituals need to be set in place by top management; employees should be selected and promoted who espouse the new values; the reward system needs to be changed to support the new values; and current subcultures need to be undermined through transfers, job rotation, and terminations.

Under the best of conditions, these actions won't result in an immediate or dramatic shift in the culture. This is because, in the final analysis, cultural change is a lengthy process—measured in years rather than in months. But cultures can be changed!

1. What's the difference between job satisfaction and organizational culture?

2. Can an employee survive in an organization if he or she rejects its core values? Explain.

3. How can an outsider assess an organization's culture?

4. What defines an organization's subcultures?

5. Contrast organizational culture with national culture.

6. How can culture be a liability to an organization?

7. How does a strong culture affect an organization's efforts to improve diversity?

8. What benefits can socialization provide for the organization? For the new employee?

9. How is language related to organizational culture?

10. Describe four cultural types and the characteristics of employees who fit best with each.

Questions for Critical Thinking

1. Contrast individual personality and organizational culture. How are they similar? How are they different?

2. Is socialization the same as brainwashing? Explain.

3. If management sought a culture characterized as innovative and autonomous, what might its socialization program look like?

4. Can you identify a set of characteristics that describes your college's culture? Compare them with several of your peers. How closely do they agree?

5. "We should be opposed to the manipulation of individuals for organizational purposes, but a degree of social uniformity enables organizations to work better." Do you agree or disagree with this statement? What are its implications for organizational culture? Discuss.

Team Exercise | **Rate Your Classroom Culture**

Listed here are 14 statements. Using the five-item scale (from strongly agree to strongly disagree), respond to each statement by circling the number that best represents your opinion.

	Strongly Agree	Agree	Neutral	Disagree	Strongly Disagree
1. I feel comfortable challenging statements made by my instructor.	5	4	3	2	1
2. My instructor heavily penalizes assignments that are not turned in on time.	1	2	3	4	5
3. My instructor believes that "final results are what count."	1	2	3	4	5
4. My instructor is sensitive to my personal needs and problems.	5	4	3	2	1
5. A large portion of my grade depends on how well I work with others in the class.	5	4	3	2	1

	Strongly Agree	Agree	Neutral	Disagree	Strongly Disagree
6. I often feel nervous and tense when I come to class.	1	2	3	4	5
7. My instructor seems to prefer stability over change.	1	2	3	4	5
8. My instructor encourages me to develop new and different ideas.	5	4	3	2	1
9. My instructor has little tolerance for sloppy thinking.	1	2	3	4	5
10. My instructor is more concerned with how I came to a conclusion than the conclusion itself.	5	4	3	2	1
11. My instructor treats all students alike.	1	2	3	4	5
12. My instructor frowns on class members helping each other with assignments.	1	2	3	4	5
13. Aggressive and competitive people have a distinct advantage in this class.	1	2	3	4	5
14. My instructor encourages me to see the world differently.	5	4	3	2	1

Calculate your total score by adding up the numbers you circled. Your score will fall between 14 and 70.

A high score (49 or above) describes an open, risk-taking, supportive, humanistic, team-oriented, easygoing, growth-oriented culture. A low score (35 or below) describes a closed, structured, task-oriented, individualistic, tense, and stability-oriented culture. Note that differences count. So a score of 60 indicates a more open culture than one that scores 50. Also, realize that one culture isn't preferable over the other. The "right" culture depends on you and your preferences for a learning environment.

Form teams of five to seven members each. Compare your scores. How closely do they align? Discuss and resolve discrepancies. Based on your team's analysis, what type of student do you think would perform best in this class?

Ethical Dilemma	**Cultural Factors and Unethical Behavior**

An organization's culture socializes people. It subtly conveys to members that certain actions are acceptable, even though they are illegal. For instance, when executives at General Electric, Westinghouse, and other manufacturers of heavy electrical equipment illegally conspired to set prices in the early 1960s, the defendants invariably testified that they came new to their jobs, found price fixing to be an established way of life, and simply entered into it as they did into other aspects of their job. One GE manager noted that every one of his bosses had directed him to meet with the competition: "It had become so common and gone on for so many years that I think we lost sight of the fact that it was illegal."*

The strength of an organization's culture has an influence on the ethical behavior of its managers. A strong culture will exert more influence on managers than a weak one. If the culture is strong and supports high ethical standards, it should have a very powerful positive influence on a manager's ethical behavior.

However, in a weak culture, managers are more likely to rely on subcultural norms to guide their behavior. So work groups and departmental standards will more strongly influence ethical behavior in organizations that have weak overall cultures.

It is also generally acknowledged that the content of a culture affects ethical behavior. Assuming this is true, what would a culture look like that would shape high ethical standards? What could top management do to strengthen that culture? Do you think it's possible for a manager with high ethical standards to uphold those standards in an organizational culture that tolerates, or even encourages, unethical practices?

---

*As described in P. C. Yeager, "Analyzing Corporate Offenses: Progress and Prospects," in W. C. Frederick and L. E. Preston (eds.), *Business Ethics: Research Issues and Empirical Studies* (Greenwich, CT: JAI Press, 1990), p. 174.

Internet Search Exercises

1. Identify a merger or acquisition that has run into trouble (or been dissolved) in the past year and in which the primary problem identified was incompatible cultures. Describe and discuss which specific elements of the cultures led to the problem.

2. As e-commerce explodes around the globe it becomes increasingly critical for companies operating in this arena to be sensitive to the use of culturally specific jargon, references and symbols on their Web sites. Provide four examples of culturally specific jargon, references, or symbols that you find on company Web sites. Be sure to include at least two non-U.S. examples. Using your examples, please answer the following questions. Why do organizations use jargon? How can it be useful in helping organizational employees learn their company's culture? How can it impede international transactions?

PHLIP Companion Web Site

We invite you to visit the Robbins homepage on the Prentice Hall Web site at **www.prenhall.com/robbins** for our on-line study guide, current events, links to related Web sites, and more.

Case Incident | Shaking Up P&G

Durk Jager is a man on a mission. As the newly appointed CEO of Procter & Gamble, he is determined to make P&G a more conflict-friendly organization.

Jager has some ambitious goals for P&G. At the top of the list is to significantly boost sales volume. In 1997, he said he wanted the company, best known for products such as Tide, Crest, and Crisco, to double sales to $70 billion by the year 2005. But the company's strong cultlike culture tends to "Procter-ize" people, says Jager. P&G people are too insular, risk averse, and slow to make decisions. According to Jager, the problem has a lot to do with keeping people isolated inside P&G's twin-towers' headquarters in Cincinnati. The company recruits job candidates from a variety of backgrounds, puts them through a relatively standardized training program, and then insulates them at company headquarters. After awhile, they begin to sound alike, think alike—even look alike, he says.

Jager's career path is unusual for P&G. While he's been with the company for nearly 30 years, he's spent most of his time outside Cincinnati. A Dutchman by birth, he joined P&G as an assistant brand manager in Holland. After 12 years, he was transferred to Japan as an advertising manager and was later promoted to general manager. He grew up totally removed from Cincinnati's central bureaucracy. So, in spite of all his years with the company, he has an outsider's perspective.

Asked to describe Jager, those who know him describe him as a "loner," "hard-driving," "tough," and a person who "doesn't mince words." He has a reputation for shaking things up. As such, he might be just the right man for his new job.

P&G is a company in which managers have a passion for memo writing and dissent is rarely tolerated. Employees may be wasting up to half their time on "non-value-added work," such as memo writing, he says. During a recent talk with employees in Japan, for instance, one worker complained to Jager that he had to continually create new management review charts, often with the same information in several different forms. The employee thought he was wasting a lot of his time.

Jager is determined to change P&G's culture. He wants to make the company faster on its feet, more innovative, and more conflict friendly. "Great ideas generally come from conflict—a dissatisfaction with the status quo. I'd like to have an organization where there are rebels."

Questions

1. How was the P&G culture shaped?

2. Using the four-culture typology described in this chapter, what type of culture do you think P&G is currently? What type is Jager trying to change it to?

3. If you were Jager, what would you do to change this culture? Be specific.

4. Do you think Jager will succeed? Explain your position.

Source: T. Parker-Pope, "New CEO Preaches Rebellion for P&G's 'Cult'," *Wall Street Journal*, December 11, 1998, p. B1; K. Brooker, "Can Procter & Gamble Change Its Culture, Protect Its Market Share, and Find the Next Tide?" *Fortune*, April 26, 1999, pp. 146–52; and D. Canedy, "P&G to Cut 15,000 Jobs and Shut Down 10 Plants," *New York Times*, June 10, 1999, p. C2

Video Case	The Jagged Edge

SMALL BUSINESS 2000

If someone told you to "take a hike," you might be offended. If someone told one of the Quenemoen sisters, the owners of Jagged Edge, to take a hike, they might just grab their climbing gear and go for it. Margaret and Paula Quenemoen have built a business that evolves around their love of the outdoors. Many people attempt to turn hobbies or personal interests into businesses—some succeed and some fail. Jagged Edge, by all accounts, is a successful venture. What is really interesting about this company is the working environment that has emerged.

Many things can affect the culture of a business. To understand the culture at Jagged Edge, it might be best to better understand the women who run it and what makes them tick. Margaret comes across as being a survivor. In fact, although the company is oriented toward being an environmentally conscious manufacturer of outdoor clothing, Margaret founded it for a more fundamental reason. She was broke and needed to earn some money—and earn it fast. As you will learn firsthand, Margaret is not easily discouraged and is very committed to the things in which she believes. Paula Quenemoen is also very driven but perhaps in a different way than her sister. Paula joined her sister after spending several years studying in China and other parts of Asia. Paula brings to the company the spiritual influence of this experience.

Paula and Margaret do not run Jagged Edge by themselves. In building a staff, they seem to have worked hard at finding individuals who are in some way similar to themselves. This does not mean that they cloned themselves, but they have sought out employees that have some interests in common with them. The obvious common interest is mountain climbing and hiking, but it's not the only possibility. As you watch this case, try to develop an understanding of the culture of this company. Think about why people would want to work at Jagged Edge and how comfortable you might feel working in a company like this one.

Questions

1. You learned about Paula and Margaret's personal beliefs and some things they have done in their lives. How do you think the sisters influence the personality and culture of the company?

2. Paula told us about a factory in China with which she does business on a handshake, without any formal contracting. She even sends cash in advance of receiving finished goods. What do you think about this practice? Why do you think Jagged Edge does business this way?

3. It seems like the staff at Jagged Edge not only works together, but sometimes they play together too. What do you think are some of the advantages and disadvantages of the work/recreation commonality that many employees share? How might this affect the culture of the company?

1. N. Weinberg, "A Setting Sun?" *Forbes*, April 20, 1998, pp. 118–24.

2. P. Selznick, "Foundations of the Theory of Organizations," *American Sociological Review*, February 1948, pp. 25–35.

3. See L. G. Zucker, "Organizations as Institutions," in S. B. Bacharach (ed.), *Research in the Sociology of Organizations* (Greenwich, CT: JAI Press, 1983), pp. 1–47; A. J. Richardson, "The Production of Institutional Behaviour: A Constructive Comment on the Use of Institutionalization Theory in Organizational Analysis," *Canadian Journal of Administrative Sciences*, December 1986, pp. 304–16; L. G. Zucker, *Institutional Patterns and Organizations: Culture and Environment* (Cambridge, MA: Ballinger, 1988); and R. L. Jepperson, "Institutions, Institutional Effects, and Institutionalism," in W. W. Powell and P. J. DiMaggio (eds.), *The New Institutionalism in Organizational Analysis* (Chicago: University of Chicago Press, 1991), pp. 143–63.

4. See, for example, H. S. Becker, "Culture: A Sociological View," *Yale Review*, Summer 1982, pp. 513–27; and E. H. Schein, *Organizational Culture and Leadership* (San Francisco: Jossey-Bass, 1985), p. 168.

5. This seven-item description is based on C. A. O'Reilly III, J. Chatman, and D. F. Caldwell, "People and Organizational Culture: A Profile Comparison Approach to Assessing Person–Organization Fit," *Academy of Management Journal*, September 1991, pp. 487–516; and J. A. Chatman and K. A. John, "Assessing the Relationship Between Industry Characteristics and Organizational Culture: How Different Can You Be?" *Academy of Management Journal*, June 1994, pp. 522–53. For a description of other popular measures, see A. Xenikou and A. Furnham, "A Correlational and Factor Analytic Study of Four Questionnaire Measures of Organizational Culture," *Human Relations*, March 1996, pp. 349–71.

6. The view that there will be consistency among perceptions of organizational culture has been called the "integration" perspective. For a review of this perspective and conflicting approaches, see D. Meyerson and J. Martin, "Cultural Change: An Integration of Three Different Views," *Journal of Management Studies*, November 1987, pp. 623–47; and P. J. Frost, L. F. Moore, M. R. Louis, C. C. Lundberg, and J. Martin (eds.), *Reframing Organizational Culture* (Newbury Park, CA: Sage Publications, 1991).

7. See J. M. Jermier, J. W. Slocum, Jr., L. W. Fry, and J. Gaines, "Organizational Subcultures in a Soft Bureaucracy: Resistance Behind the Myth and Facade of an Official Culture," *Organization Science*, May 1991, pp. 170–94; S. A. Sackmann, "Culture and Subcultures: An Analysis of Organizational Knowledge," *Administrative Science Quarterly*, March 1992, pp. 140–61; R. F. Zammuto, "Mapping Organizational Cultures and Subcultures: Looking Inside and Across Hospitals," paper presented at the 1995 National Academy of Management Conference, Vancouver, BC, August 1995; and G. Hofstede, "Identifying Organizational Subcultures: An Empirical Approach," *Journal of Management Studies*, January 1998, pp. 1–12.

8. T. A. Timmerman, "Do Organizations Have Personalities?" paper presented at the 1996 National Academy of Management Conference; Cincinnati, OH, August 1996.

9. S. Hamm, "No Letup—and No Apologies," *Business Week*, October 26, 1998, pp. 58–64.

10. Ideas in this box were influenced by A. L. Wilkins, "The Culture Audit: A Tool for Understanding Organizations," *Organizational Dynamics*, Autumn 1983, pp. 24–38; H. M. Trice and J. M. Beyer, *The Cultures of Work Organizations* (Upper Saddle River, NJ: Prentice Hall, 1993), pp. 358–62; H. Lancaster, "To Avoid a Job Failure, Learn the Culture of a Company First," *Wall Street Journal*, July 14, 1998, p. B1; and M. Belliveau, "4 Ways to Read a Company," *Fast Company*, October 1998, p. 158.

11. See, for example, G. G. Gordon and N. DiTomaso, "Predicting Corporate Performance From Organizational Culture," *Journal of Management Studies*, November 1992, pp. 793–98.

12. Y. Wiener, "Forms of Value Systems: A Focus on Organizational Effectiveness and Cultural Change and Maintenance," *Academy of Management Review*, October 1988, p. 536.

13. R. T. Mowday, L. W. Porter, and R. M. Steers, *Employee-Organization Linkages: The Psychology of Commitment, Absenteeism, and Turnover* (New York: Academic Press, 1982).

14. See N. J. Adler, *International Dimensions of Organizational Behavior*, 3rd ed. (Cincinnati, OH: Southwestern, 1997), pp. 61–63.

15. S. C. Schneider, "National vs. Corporate Culture: Implications for Human Resource Management," *Human Resource Management*, Summer 1988, p. 239.

16. See C. A. O'Reilly and J. A. Chatman, "Culture as Social Control: Corporations, Cults, and Commitment," in B. M. Staw and L. L. Cummings (eds.), *Research in Organizational Behavior*, vol. 18 (Greenwich, CT: JAI Press, 1996), pp. 157–200.

17. T. E. Deal and A. A. Kennedy, "Culture: A New Look Through Old Lenses," *Journal of Applied Behavioral Science*, November 1983, p. 501.

18. J. Case, "Corporate Culture," *INC.*, November 1996, pp. 42–53.

19. See C. Lindsay, "Paradoxes of Organizational Diversity: Living Within the Paradoxes," in L. R. Jauch and J. L. Wall (eds.), *Proceedings of the 50th Academy of Management Conference* (San Francisco, 1990), pp. 374–78; and T. Cox, Jr., *Cultural Diversity in Organizations: Theory, Research & Practice* (San Francisco: Berrett-Koehler, 1993), pp. 162–70.

20. K. Labich, "No More Crude at Texaco," *Fortune*, September 6, 1999, pp. 205–12.

21. D. Miller, "What Happens After Success: The Perils of Excellence," *Journal of Management Studies*, May 1994, pp. 11–38.

22. N. Weinberg, "Shaking Up an Old Giant," *Forbes*, May 20, 1996, pp. 68–80.

23. D. Roth, "From Poster Boy to Whipping Boy: Burying Motorola," *Fortune*, July 6, 1998, p. 28.

24. A. F. Buono and J. L. Bowditch, *The Human Side of Mergers and Acquisitions: Managing Collisions Between People, Cultures, and Organizations* (San Francisco: Jossey-Bass, 1989); Y. Weber and D. M. Schweiger, "Top Management Culture Conflict in Mergers and Acquisitions: A Lesson From Anthropology," *The International Journal of Conflict Management*, January 1992, pp. 1–17; S. Cartwright and C. L. Cooper, "The Role of Culture Compatibility in Successful Organizational Marriages," *Academy of Management Executive*, May 1993, pp. 57–70; D. Carey and D. Ogden, "A Match Made in Heaven? Find Out Before You Merge," *Wall Street Journal*, November 30, 1998, p. A22; and R. J. Grossman, "Irreconcilable Differences," *HRMagazine*, April 1999, pp. 42–48.

25. Carleton, "Cultural Due Diligence," p. 70; and Carey and Ogden, "A Match Made in Heaven?"

26. Carey and Ogden, "A Match Made in Heaven?"

27. E. H. Schein, "The Role of the Founder in Creating Organizational Culture," *Organizational Dynamics*, Summer 1983, pp. 13–28.

28. E. H. Schein, "Leadership and Organizational Culture," in F. Hesselbein, M. Goldsmith, and R. Beckhard, (eds.), *The Leader of the Future* (San Francisco: Jossey-Bass, 1996), pp. 61–62.

29. See, for example, J. R. Harrison and G. R. Carroll, "Keeping the Faith: A Model of Cultural Transmission in Formal Organizations," *Administrative Science Quarterly*, December 1991, pp. 552–82.

30. B. Schneider, "The People Make the Place," *Personnel Psychology*, Autumn 1987, pp. 437–53; D. E. Bowen, G. E. Ledford, Jr., and B. R. Nathan, "Hiring for the Organization, Not the Job," *Academy of Management Executive*, November 1991, pp. 35–51; B. Schneider, H. W. Goldstein, and D. B. Smith, "The ASA Framework: An Update," *Personnel Psychology*, Winter 1995, pp. 747–73; A.L. Kristof, "Person–Organization Fit: An Integrative Review of Its Conceptualizations, Measurement, and Implications," *Personnel Psychology*, Spring 1996, pp. 1–49; D. M. Cable and T. A. Judge, "Interviewers' Perceptions of Person–Organization Fit and Organizational Selection Decisions," *Journal of Applied Psychology*, August 1997, pp. 546–61; and J. Schaubroeck, D. C. Ganster, and J. R. Jones, "Organization and Occupation Influences in the Attraction-Selection-Attrition Process," *Journal of Applied Psychology*, December 1998, pp. 869–91.

31. R. Pascale, "The Paradox of 'Corporate Culture': Reconciling Ourselves to Socialization," *California Management Review*, Winter 1985, pp. 26–27.

32. "Who's Afraid of IBM?" *Business Week*, June 29, 1987, p. 72.

33. Ibid.

34. D. C. Hambrick and P. A. Mason, "Upper Echelons: The Organization as a Reflection of Its Top Managers," *Academy of Management Review*, April 1984, pp. 193–206; B. P. Niehoff, C. A. Enz, and R. A. Grover, "The Impact of Top-Management Actions on Employee Attitudes and Perceptions," *Group & Organization Studies*, September 1990, pp. 337–52; and H. M. Trice and J. M. Beyer, "Cultural Leadership in Organizations," *Organization Science*, May 1991, pp. 149–69.

35. "Culture Shock at Xerox," *Business Week*, June 22, 1987, pp. 1, 6–10; T. Vogel, "At Xerox, They're Shouting 'Once More into the Breach,'" *Business Week*, July 23, 1990, pp.

62–63; and D. Brady, "Xerox," *Business Week*, April 12, 1999, pp. 93–100.

36. See, for instance, N. J. Allen and J. P. Meyer, "Organizational Socialization Tactics: A Longitudinal Analysis of Links to Newcomers' Commitment and Role Orientation," *Academy of Management Journal*, December 1990, pp. 847–58; J. P. Wanous, *Organizational Entry*, 2nd ed. (New York: Addison-Wesley, 1992); G. T. Chao, A. M. O'Leary-Kelly, S. Wolf, H. J. Klein, and P. D. Gardner, "Organizational Socialization: Its Content and Consequences," *Journal of Applied Psychology*, October 1994, pp. 730–43; J. S. Black and S. J. Ashford, "Fitting In or Making Jobs Fit: Factors Affecting Mode of Adjustment for New Hires," *Human Relations*, April 1995, pp. 421–37; B. E. Ashforth, A. M. Saks, and R. T. Lee, "Socialization and Newcomer Adjustment: The Role of Organizational Context," *Human Relations*, July 1998, pp. 897–926.

37. J. Impoco, "Basic Training, Sanyo Style," *U.S. News & World Report*, July 13, 1992, pp. 46–48.

38. B. Filipczak, "Trained by Starbucks," *Training*, June 1995, pp. 73–79; and S. Gruner, "Lasting Impressions," *INC.*, July 1998, p. 126.

39. J. Van Maanen and E. H. Schein, "Career Development," in J. R. Hackman and J. L. Suttle (eds.), *Improving Life at Work* (Santa Monica, CA: Goodyear, 1977) pp. 58–62.

40. D. C. Feldman, "The Multiple Socialization of Organization Members," *Academy of Management Review*, April 1981, p. 310.

41. Van Maanen and Schein, "Career Development," p. 59.

42. D. M. Boje, "The Storytelling Organization: A Study of Story Performance in an Office-Supply Firm," *Administrative Science Quarterly*, March 1991, pp. 106–26; and C. H. Deutsch, "The Parables of Corporate Culture," *The New York Times*, October 13, 1991, p. F25.

43. A. M. Pettigrew, "On Studying Organizational Cultures," *Administrative Science Quarterly*, December 1979, p. 576.

44. "Job Titles of the Future: Minister of Culture," *Fast Company*, September 1998, p. 64.

45. See K. Kamoche, "Rhetoric, Ritualism, and Totemism in Human Resource Management," *Human Relations*, April 1995, pp. 367–85.

46. Cited in J. M. Beyer and H. M. Trice, "How an Organization's Rites Reveal Its Culture," *Organizational Dynamics*, Spring 1987, p. 15.

47. A. Rafaeli and M. G. Pratt, "Tailored Meanings: On the Meaning and Impact of Organizational Dress," *Academy of Management Review*, January 1993, pp. 32–55.

48. "DCACronyms," April 1997, Rev. D; published by The Boeing Co.

49. See footnote 30.

50. This section is based on R. Goffee and G. Jones, *The Character of a Corporation: How Your Company's Culture Can Make or Break Your Business* (New York: HarperBusiness, 1998).

51. J. A. Chatman, "Matching People and Organizations: Selection and Socialization in Public Accounting Firms," pp. 459–84; and B. Z. Posner, "Person–Organization Values Congruence: No Support for Individual Differences as a Moderating Influence," *Human Relations*, April 1992, pp. 351–61.

52. J. E. Sheridan, "Organizational Culture and Employee Retention," *Academy of Management Journal*, December 1992, pp. 1036–56.

It's Impossible *Not* to Do Your Work: Human Resource Practices at the Sanest Company in America

What is it like to have a job where you can eat lunch with your kids, enjoy unlimited sick days, and go home every day at 5 o'clock? Employees at SAS Institute, a software firm in Cary, North Carolina, think it's great. When programming manager Martin Bourque arrived at SAS 10 years ago, "I'd never seen anything like this in my career," he says. "Here, what you accomplish is more important than how you appear."[1]

A privately owned $1 billion dollar company founded by Jim Goodnight, SAS thrives on a culture of sanity. In contrast to the grueling hours, dull surroundings, and high-stakes politics of some technology firms, SAS offers employees a 35-hour workweek; three day care centers (two on-site and one off); an enormous gym with pool tables, Ping-Pong™ tables, basketball courts, and laundry service for sweaty work-out clothes; separate dance and yoga studios; an on-site health clinic with a staff of 30; free health insurance; on-site massages; family benefits for domestic partners; unlimited sick days including days to care for other family members; and, every Wednesday, hundreds of pounds of free M&Ms, plain and peanut. SAS has been so successful at making its atmosphere conducive to normal family life, in fact, that today 51 percent of its managers are women.

SAS's head of human resources, David Russo, says all this sanity is "part of a soundly designed strategy . . . Jim's idea is that if you hire adults and treat them like adults, then they'll behave like adults."[2] And, it seems to be working. The firm experiences extremely low turnover and almost fanatical loyalty among its 6,200 employees worldwide. And, in an atmosphere designed to make it both easy and satisfying to get the job done, politics and power struggles are greatly reduced.

There is accountability, however, even though the company's hierarchy is so flat that it has no formal organization chart. When SAS grows, it tends to add new divisions rather than taller hierarchies of management. After nearly 25 years in existence, SAS still can boast that most of its front-line employees are only two or three levels away from Jim Goodnight.

Spectacularly successful at developing data-management software, SAS counts among its clients 98 of the 100 largest public companies in the United States, including Marriott Hotels, Merck & Co., and Pfizer. SAS software is also the tool the U.S. government uses to calculate the Consumer Price Index.

Study Questions

As you watch the SAS Institute video segment, look for ways the firm's human resource policies contribute to its culture, to the way jobs are designed, and to its organizational structure. Specifically, answer the following questions:

1. How would you characterize SAS Institute's span of control and its degree of centralization? How do you think these aspects of its organizational structure help account for its employee-friendly environment?

2. What can you conclude about the physical design of SAS's workspaces? How do they balance the needs for privacy and interaction? Do you think the physical environment of SAS contributes to its employees' productivity? Why or why not?

3. Contrast SAS Institute's 35-hour workweek with some of the family-friendly options employed at other firms. Why do you think SAS chose a traditional work schedule for the vast majority of its employees?

4. Managers at SAS not only oversee the work—they also do it. How do you think this management style influences the firm's distinctive culture? Do you think it makes for effective controls? Why or why not?

Source: [1]Charles Fishman, "Sanity Inc.," *Fast Company*, January 1999, pp. 87. [2]Fishman, p. 89.

part five

ORGANIZATIONAL DYNAMICS

I t began in 1972 at a small automotive mirror factory in rural Tennessee. And, at the time, it was considered revolutionary. By 1976, it was hailed as one of the most significant success stories in American business. We're talking about the Bolivar Project.[1]

The mirror factory in question was located in Bolivar, Tennessee (hence, the name *Bolivar Project*). It was one of many factories operated by Harman Automotive Inc. The owner and CEO of Harman Automotive at the time, Sidney Harman, was concerned with the general anger and alienation that American workers were expressing toward their jobs. He considered the problem to be corporate America's belief that employees should be treated like replaceable pieces of machinery. Harman saw workers differently. He thought if you treated workers like adults, they'd act like adults. So in a bold experiment, he decided he would change the way the Bolivar plant was structured and managed.

The jobs at Bolivar had been unpleasant at best. The plant was old and ramshackle. With its fiery metal casting lines, it was a hellish environment for most workers. And relations between management and the union were often tense. But in cooperation with the plant's union, Harman enthusiastically set out to make Bolivar a model for worker empowerment.

The essence of the Bolivar Project was that the employees would control their own work lives. Most of the decisions previously made by supervisors would now be made by the employees themselves. For instance, the workers redesigned their jobs to smooth out workloads and limit interruptions that cut into productivity. Consistent with the belief that adults are responsible, employees who filled their production quotas early

Organizational Change and Stress Management

could take self-improvement classes taught on-site or were free to go home. In addition, Harman set up a credit union for employees, pioneered a stock ownership plan, and created a plant newspaper to keep employees informed and allow them to formally air their concerns.

The project received a huge amount of publicity. Its early successes are widely attributed to having encouraged major automakers and others to begin drawing workers into a wide range of decisions formerly reserved for managers. But while initial reports out of Bolivar were positive, in reality it was having serious troubles. Managers claimed to be supportive of the changes, yet most found it difficult to give up authority. And allowing employees the freedom to go home early if they met their production quotas proved a disaster. It created tension between those in jobs who could finish three or four hours early by working in teams, and others in which human presence was required for the entire shift. Workers began cutting corners on quality so they could leave early. And the plant began attracting the worst kind of job applicants. Their first question once they were hired was not "Which machine should I run?" but "When can I go home?"

The Bolivar plant closed in 1998. Its demise was due to many factors, including the Bolivar Project. The plant changed ownership several times and the new owners often had little interest in worker empowerment. And although it was an early model for today's empowered workplace, Bolivar illustrates several potential problems that confront organizational change efforts. For instance, managers, as well as employees, have to be fully committed. And care needs to be taken to ensure that changes don't unfairly favor some groups of employees over others.

T his chapter is about change and stress. We describe environmental forces that are requiring managers to implement comprehensive change programs. We also consider why people and organizations often resist change and how this

LEARNING OBJECTIVES

AFTER READING THIS CHAPTER, YOU SHOULD BE ABLE TO

1. Describe forces that act as stimulants to change

2. Contrast first-order and second-order change

3. Summarize sources of individual and organizational resistance to change

4. Identify properties of innovative organizations

5. List characteristics of a learning organization

6. Describe potential sources of stress

7. Explain individual difference variables that moderate the stress–outcome relationship

resistance can be overcome. We review various processes for managing organizational change. We also discuss contemporary change issues for today's managers. Then we move to the topic of stress. We elaborate on the sources and consequences of stress. Finally, we conclude this chapter with a discussion of what individuals and organizations can do to better manage stress levels.

FORCES FOR CHANGE

More and more organizations today face a dynamic and changing environment. This, in turn, is requiring these organizations to adapt. "Change or die!" is the rallying cry among today's managers worldwide. Exhibit 18-1 summarizes six specific forces that are acting as stimulants for change.

In a number of places in this book, we've discussed the *changing nature of the workforce*. For instance, almost every organization is having to adjust to a multicultural environment. Human resource policies and practices have to change in order to attract and keep this more diverse workforce. And many companies are having to spend large amounts of money on training to upgrade reading, math, computer, and other skills of employees.

As noted in Chapter 15, *technology* is changing jobs and organizations. The substitution of computer control for direct supervision, for instance, is resulting in wider spans of control for managers and flatter organizations. Sophisticated information technology is also making organizations more responsive. Companies such as AT&T, Motorola, General Electric, and Ford can now develop, make, and distribute their products in a fraction of the time it took them a decade ago. And, as organizations have had to become more adaptable, so too have their employees. As we noted in our discussion of groups and organization design, many jobs are being reshaped. Individuals doing narrow, specialized, and routine jobs are being replaced by work teams whose members can perform multiple tasks and actively participate in team decisions.

EXHIBIT 18-1

Forces for Change

Force	Examples
Nature of the workforce	■ More cultural diversity ■ Increase in professionals ■ Many new entrants with inadequate skills
Technology	■ Faster and cheaper computers ■ TQM programs ■ Reengineering programs
Economic shocks	■ Asian real estate collapse ■ Russian devaluation of the ruble ■ Changes in oil prices
Competition	■ Global competitors ■ Mergers and consolidations ■ Growth of e-commerce
Social trends	■ Attitude toward smokers ■ Delayed marriages by young people ■ Popularity of sport-utility vehicles
World politics	■ Collapse of Soviet Union ■ Opening of markets in China ■ Black rule of South Africa

We live in an "age of discontinuity." In the 1950s and 1960s, the past was a pretty good prologue to the future. Tomorrow was essentially an extended trend line from yesterday. That's no longer true. Beginning in the early 1970s, with the overnight quadrupling of world oil prices, *economic shocks* have continued to impose changes on organizations. In recent years, for instance, economic problems in Russia, Asia, and Latin America have rocked world stock markets and forced banks such as Chase Manhattan to take heavy losses. Similarly, when oil prices dropped from $22 a barrel to $13 in the late 1990s, many oil service companies went bankrupt.

Competition is changing. The global economy means that competitors are as likely to come from across the ocean as from across town. Heightened competition also means that established organizations need to defend themselves against both traditional competitors that develop new products and services and small, entrepreneurial firms with innovative offerings. Successful organizations will be the ones that can change in response to the competition. They'll be fast on their feet, capable of developing new products rapidly and getting them to market quickly. They'll rely on short production runs, short product cycles, and an ongoing stream of new products. In other words, they'll be flexible. They will require an equally flexible and responsive workforce that can adapt to rapidly and even radically changing conditions.

Take a look at *social trends* during the past generation. They suggest changes to which organizations have to adjust. For instance, there has been a clear trend in marriage and divorce during the past two decades. Young people are delaying marriage, and half of all marriages are ending in divorce. One obvious result of this social trend is an increasing number of single households and demand for housing by singles. If you're in the house-building business, this is an important factor in determining the size and design of homes. Similarly, the expansion of single households has increased demand for single-portion quantities of frozen meals, which is highly relevant to organizations such as ConAgra's Healthy Choice division or Pillsbury's Green Giant.

We've called for seeing OB in a global context throughout this book. While business schools have been preaching a global perspective since the early 1980s, no one—not even the strongest proponents of globalization—could have imagined how *world politics* would change in recent years. A few examples make the point: the reunification of Germany, the breakup of the Soviet Union, the end of aparthied in South Africa, and the opening of markets in China. Almost every major U.S. defense contractor, for instance, has had to rethink its business and make serious changes in response to the demise of the Soviet Union and a shrinking Pentagon budget. Companies such as Hughes Electronics, Lockheed Martin, Raytheon, and Northrop Grumman have each cut tens of thousands of jobs in the past decade.

MANAGING PLANNED CHANGE

A group of employees who work for a small telemarketer confronted the owner: "It's very hard for most of us to maintain rigid 8-to-5 workhours," said their spokeswoman. "Each of us has significant family and personal responsibilities. And rigid hours don't work for us. We're going to begin looking for someplace else to work if you don't set up flexible workhours." The owner listened thoughtfully to the group's ultimatum and agreed to its request. The next day the owner introduced a flextime plan for his employees.

A major automobile manufacturer spent several billion dollars to install state-of-the-art robotics. One area that would receive the new equipment was quality control. Sophisticated computer-controlled equipment would be put in place to significantly improve the company's ability to find and correct defects. Since the new equipment would dramatically change the jobs of the people working in the quality control area, and since management anticipated considerable employee resistance to the new equipment, executives were developing a program to help people become familiar with the equipment and to deal with any anxieties they might be feeling.

Both of the previous scenarios are examples of **change**. That is, both are concerned with making things different. However, only the second scenario describes a planned change. In this section, we want to clarify what we mean by planned change, describe its goals, contrast first-order and second-order change, and consider who is responsible for bringing about **planned change** in an organization.

Many changes in organizations are like the one that occurred with the telemarketer—they just happen. Some organizations treat all change as an accidental occurrence. However, we're concerned with change activities that are proactive and purposeful. In this chapter, we address change as an intentional, goal-oriented activity.

What are the goals of planned change? Essentially there are two. First, it seeks to improve the ability of the organization to adapt to changes in its environment. Second, it seeks to change employee behavior.

If an organization is to survive, it must respond to changes in its environment. When competitors introduce new products or services, government agencies enact new laws, important sources of supply go out of business, or similar environmental changes take place, the organization needs to adapt. Efforts to stimulate innovation, empower employees, and introduce work teams are examples of planned change activities directed at responding to changes in the environment.

Since an organization's success or failure is essentially due to the things that its employees do or fail to do, planned change also is concerned with changing the behavior of individuals and groups within the organization. In this chapter, we review a number of techniques that organizations can use to get people to behave differently in the tasks they perform and in their interactions with others.

It also helps to think of planned change in terms of order of magnitude.[2] **First-order change** is linear and continuous. It implies no fundamental shifts in the assumptions that organizational members hold about the world or how the organization can improve its functioning. In contrast, **second-order change** is a multidimensional, multilevel, discontinuous, radical change involving reframing of assumptions about the organization and the world in which it operates. Mikio Kitano, director of all production engineering at Toyota, is introducing first-order change in his company.[3] He's pursuing slow, subtle, incremental changes in production processes to improve the efficiency of Toyota's plants. On the other hand, Boeing's top executives have recently committed themselves to radically reinventing their company.[4] Responding to a massive airline slump, aggressive competition from Airbus, and the threat of Japanese competitors, this second-order change process at Boeing includes slashing costs by up to 30 percent, reducing the time it takes to make a 737 from 13 months to 6 months, dramatically cutting inventories, putting the company's entire workforce through a four-day course in "competitiveness," and bringing customers and suppliers into the once secret process of designing new planes.

Theodore Waitt, founder and chief executive of Gateway, Inc., in Sioux City, South Dakota, made a goal-oriented change to ensure the growth of his computer firm. Gateway primarily sells computers directly to consumers. But to increase revenues, Waitt wants to expand into the small and mid-size business markets. To do so, Gateway needs employees with expertise in areas such as Web site setup and design. Unable to attract people for 250 job openings in Sioux City, Waitt moved Gateway's headquarters to San Diego, where he could recruit the high-tech talent the firm needs to implement its growth strategy.

Who in organizations are responsible for managing change activities? The answer is **change agents**. Change agents can be managers or nonmanagers, employees of the organization or outside consultants.

Typically we look to senior executives as agents of change. CEO Hugh Mc-Call has been a primary change agent at NationsBank. Mikio Kitano is one at Toyota. The primary change agent at Microsoft is its CEO, Bill Gates.

For major change efforts, top managers are increasingly turning to temporary outside consultants with specialized knowledge in the theory and methods of change. Consultant change agents can offer a more objective perspective than insiders can. However, they are disadvantaged in that they often have an inadequate understanding of the organization's history, culture, operating procedures, and personnel. Outside consultants are also more willing to initiate second-order changes—which can be a benefit or a disadvantage—because they don't have to live with the repercussions. In contrast, internal staff specialists or managers, especially those who've spent many years with the organization, are often more cautious because they fear offending long-term friends and associates.

first-order change

Linear and continuous change.

second-order change

Change that is multidimensional, multilevel, discontinuous, and radical.

change agents

Persons who act as catalysts and assume the responsibility for managing change activities.

WHAT CAN CHANGE AGENTS CHANGE?

What can a change agent change? The options essentially fall into four categories: structure, technology, physical setting, and people.[5] (See Exhibit 18-2.) *Changing structure* involves making an alteration in authority relations, coordination mechanisms, job redesign, or similar structural variables. Changing *technology* encompasses modifications in the way work is processed and in the methods and equipment used. Changing the *physical setting* covers altering the space and layout arrangements in the workplace. Changing *people* refers to changes in employee attitudes, skills, expectations, perceptions, and/or behavior.

CHANGING STRUCTURE

In Chapter 14, we discussed structural issues such as work specialization, span of control, and various organizational designs. But organizational structures are not set in concrete. Changing conditions demand structural changes. As a result, the change agent might need to modify the organization's structure.

An organization's structure is defined by how tasks are formally divided, grouped, and coordinated. Change agents can alter one or more of the key elements in an organization's design. For instance, departmental responsibilities can be combined, vertical layers removed, and spans of control widened to make the organization flatter and less bureaucratic. More rules and procedures can be implemented to increase standardization. An increase in decentralization can be made to speed up the decision-making process.

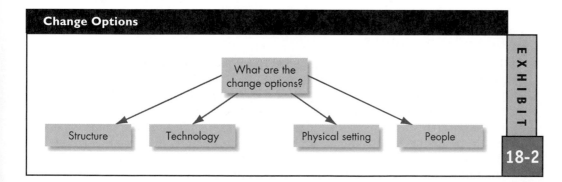

Change Options

What are the change options?

Structure Technology Physical setting People

EXHIBIT 18-2

Change agents can also introduce major modifications in the actual structural design. This might include a shift from a simple structure to a team-based structure or the creation of a matrix design. Change agents might consider redesigning jobs or work schedules. Job descriptions can be redefined, jobs enriched, or flexible work hours introduced. Still another option is to modify the organization's compensation system. Motivation could be increased by, for example, introducing performance bonuses or profit sharing.

CHANGING TECHNOLOGY

Most of the early studies in management and organizational behavior dealt with efforts aimed at technological change. At the turn of the century, for example, scientific management sought to implement changes based on time-and-motion studies that would increase production efficiency. Today, major technological changes usually involve the introduction of new equipment, tools, or methods; automation; or computerization.

Competitive factors or innovations within an industry often require change agents to introduce new equipment, tools, or operating methods. For example, steelmakers today are building small mini-mills rather than sprawling manufacturing complexes. The former are built to make specific products and are much more efficient than their large counterparts.

Automation is a technological change that replaces people with machines. It began in the industrial revolution and continues as a change option today. Examples of automation are the introduction of automatic mail sorters by the U.S. Postal Service and robots on automobile assembly lines.

As noted in previous chapters, the most visible technological change in recent years has been expanding computerization. Most organizations now have sophisticated management information systems that link the organization's employees regardless of where they're located. And the office of 2001 is dramatically different from its counterpart of 1981, predominantly because of computerization. This is typified by desktop microcomputers that can run hundreds of business software packages and network systems that allow these computers to communicate with one another.

CHANGING THE PHYSICAL SETTING

The layout of work space should not be a random activity. Typically, management thoughtfully considers work demands, formal interaction requirements, and social needs when making decisions about space configurations, interior design, equipment placement, and the like.

For example, by eliminating walls and partitions, and opening up an office design, it becomes easier for employees to communicate with each other. Similarly, management can change the quantity and types of lights, the level of heat or cold, the levels and types of noise, and the cleanliness of the work area, as well as interior design dimensions such as furniture, decorations, and color schemes.

CHANGING PEOPLE

The final area in which change agents operate is in helping individuals and groups within the organization to work more effectively together. This category typically involves changing the attitudes and behaviors of organizational members through processes of communication, decision making, and problem solving. As you'll see later in this chapter, the concept of *organizational development* has come to encompass an array of interventions designed to change people and the nature and quality of their work relationships. We review these people-changing interventions in our discussion of organizational development.

RESISTANCE TO CHANGE

One of the most well-documented findings from studies of individual and organizational behavior is that organizations and their members resist change. In a sense, this is positive. It provides a degree of stability and predictability to behavior. If there weren't some resistance, organizational behavior would take on characteristics of chaotic randomness. Resistance to change can also be a source of functional conflict. For example, resistance to a reorganization plan or a change in a product line can stimulate a healthy debate over the merits of the idea and result in a better decision. But there is a definite downside to resistance to change. It hinders adaptation and progress.

Resistance to change doesn't necessarily surface in standardized ways. Resistance can be overt, implicit, immediate, or deferred. It is easiest for management to deal with resistance when it is overt and immediate. For instance, a change is proposed and employees quickly respond by voicing complaints, engaging in a work slowdown, threatening to go on strike, or the like. The greater challenge is managing resistance that is implicit or deferred. Implicit resistance efforts are more subtle—loss of loyalty to the organization, loss of motivation to work, increased errors or mistakes, increased absenteeism due to "sickness"—and, hence, more difficult to recognize. Similarly, deferred actions cloud the link between the source of the resistance and the reaction to it. A change may produce what appears to be only a minimal reaction at the time it is initiated, but then resistance surfaces weeks, months, or even years later. Or a single change that in and of itself might have little impact becomes the straw that breaks the camel's back. Reactions to change can build up and then explode in some response that seems totally out of proportion to the change action it follows. The resistance, of course, has merely been deferred and stockpiled. What surfaces is a response to an accumulation of previous changes.

Let's look at the sources of resistance. For analytical purposes, we've categorized them by individual and organizational sources. In the real world, the sources often overlap.

INDIVIDUAL RESISTANCE

Individual sources of resistance to change reside in basic human characteristics such as perceptions, personalities, and needs. The following summarizes five reasons why individuals may resist change. (See Exhibit 18-3.)

Habit Every day, when you go to work or school, do you continually use the same route and streets? Probably. If you're like most people, you find a single route and you use it regularly.

As human beings, we're creatures of habit. Life is complex enough; we don't need to consider the full range of options for the hundreds of decisions we have to make every day. To cope with this complexity, we all rely on habits or programmed responses. But when confronted with change, this tendency to re-

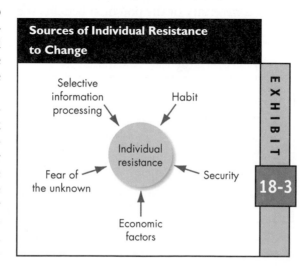

Sources of Individual Resistance to Change

Selective information processing

Habit

Individual resistance

Fear of the unknown

Security

Economic factors

EXHIBIT 18-3

spond in our accustomed ways becomes a source of resistance. So when your department is moved to a new office building across town, it means you're likely to have to change many habits: waking up 10 minutes earlier, taking a new set of streets to work, finding a new parking place, adjusting to the new office layout, developing a new lunchtime routine, and so on.

Security People with a high need for security are likely to resist change because it threatens their feelings of safety. When Sears announces it's laying off 20,000 people or Ford introduces new robotic equipment, many employees at these firms may fear that their jobs are in jeopardy.

Economic Factors Another source of individual resistance is concern that changes will lower one's income. Changes in job tasks or established work routines also can arouse economic fears if people are concerned that they won't be able to perform the new tasks or routines to their previous standards, especially when pay is closely tied to productivity.

Fear of the Unknown Changes substitute ambiguity and uncertainty for the known. The transition from high school to college is typically such an experience. By the time we're seniors in high school, we understand how things work. You might not have liked high school, but at least you understood the system. Then you move on to college and face a whole new and uncertain system. You have traded the known for the unknown and the fear or insecurity that goes with it.

Employees in organizations hold the same dislike for uncertainty. If, for example, the introduction of TQM means production workers will have to learn statistical process control techniques, some may fear they'll be unable to do so. They may, therefore, develop a negative attitude toward TQM or behave dysfunctionally if required to use statistical techniques.

Selective Information Processing As we learned in Chapter 5, individuals shape their world through their perceptions. Once they have created this world, it resists change. So individuals are guilty of selectively processing information in order to keep their perceptions intact. They hear what they want to hear. They ignore information that challenges the world they've created. To return to the production workers who are faced with the introduction of TQM, they may ignore the arguments their managers make in explaining why a knowledge of statistics is necessary or the potential benefits the change will provide them.

Source: Dilbert by Scott Adams. August 3, 1996. DILBERT reprinted by permission of United Feature Syndicate, Inc.

ORGANIZATIONAL RESISTANCE

Organizations, by their very nature, are conservative.[6] They actively resist change. You don't have to look far to see evidence of this phenomenon. Government agencies want to continue doing what they have been doing for years, whether the need for their service changes or remains the same. Organized religions are deeply entrenched in their history. Attempts to change church doctrine require great persistence and patience. Educational institutions, which exist to open minds and challenge established doctrine, are themselves extremely resistant to change. Most school systems are using essentially the same teaching technologies today as they were 50 years ago. The majority of business firms, too, appear highly resistant to change.

Six major sources of organizational resistance have been identified.[7] They are shown in Exhibit 18-5.

Structural Inertia Organizations have built-in mechanisms to produce stability. For example, the selection process systematically selects certain people in and certain people out. Training and other socialization techniques reinforce specific role requirements and skills. Formalization provides job descriptions, rules, and procedures for employees to follow.

The people who are hired into an organization are chosen for fit; they are then shaped and directed to behave in certain ways. When an organization is confronted with change, this structural inertia acts as a counterbalance to sustain stability.

Limited Focus of Change Organizations are made up of a number of interdependent subsystems. You can't change one without affecting the others. For example, if management changes the technological processes without simultaneously modifying the organization's structure to match, the change in technology is not likely to be accepted. So limited changes in subsystems tend to get nullified by the larger system.

Group Inertia Even if individuals want to change their behavior, group norms may act as a constraint. An individual union member, for instance, may be willing to accept changes in his job suggested by management. But if union norms dictate resisting any unilateral change made by management, he's likely to resist.

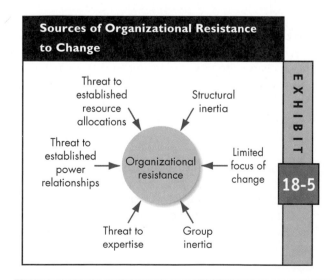

Sources of Organizational Resistance to Change

Threat to established resource allocations → Organizational resistance

Structural inertia → Organizational resistance

Threat to established power relationships → Organizational resistance

Limited focus of change → Organizational resistance

Threat to expertise → Organizational resistance

Group inertia → Organizational resistance

EXHIBIT 18-5

Threat to Expertise Changes in organizational patterns may threaten the expertise of specialized groups. The introduction of decentralized personal computers, which allow managers to gain access to information directly from a company's mainframe, is an example of a change that was strongly resisted by many information systems departments in the early 1980s. Why? Because decentralized end-user computing was a threat to the specialized skills held by those in the centralized information systems departments.

Threat to Established Power Relationships Any redistribution of decision-making authority can threaten long-established power relationships within the organization. The introduction of participative decision making or self-managed work teams is the kind of change that is often seen as threatening by supervisors and middle managers.

Threat to Established Resource Allocations Those groups in the organization that control sizable resources often see change as a threat. They tend to be content with the way things are. Will the change, for instance, mean a reduction in their budgets or a cut in their staff size? Those that most benefit from the current allocation of resources often feel threatened by changes that may affect future allocations.

OVERCOMING RESISTANCE TO CHANGE

Six tactics have been suggested for use by change agents in dealing with resistance to change.[8] Let's review them briefly.

Education and Communication Resistance can be reduced through communicating with employees to help them see the logic of a change. This tactic basically assumes that the source of resistance lies in misinformation or poor communication: If employees receive the full facts and get any misunderstandings cleared up, resistance will subside. Communication can be achieved through one-on-one discussions, memos, group presentations, or reports. Does it work? It does, provided that the source of resistance is inadequate communication and that management–employee relations are characterized by mutual trust and credibility. If these conditions don't exist, the change is unlikely to succeed.

Participation It's difficult for individuals to resist a change decision in which they participated. Prior to making a change, those opposed can be brought into the decision process. Assuming that the participants have the expertise to make a meaningful contribution, their involvement can reduce resistance, obtain commitment, and increase the quality of the change decision. However, against these advantages are the negatives: potential for a poor solution and great time consumption.

Facilitation and Support Change agents can offer a range of supportive efforts to reduce resistance. When employee fear and anxiety are high, employee counseling and therapy, new-skills training, or a short paid leave of absence may facilitate adjustment. The drawback of this tactic is that, as with the others, it is time consuming. Additionally, it's expensive, and its implementation offers no assurance of success.

Negotiation Another way for the change agent to deal with potential resistance to change is to exchange something of value for a lessening of the resistance. For instance, if the resistance is centered in a few powerful individuals, a specific reward package can be negotiated that will meet their individual needs. Negotiation as a tactic may be necessary when resistance comes from a powerful source. Yet one cannot ignore its potentially high costs. Additionally, there is the risk that, once a change agent negotiates with one party to avoid resistance, he or she is open to the possibility of being blackmailed by other individuals in positions of power.

Manipulation and Co-optation Manipulation refers to covert influence attempts. Twisting and distorting facts to make them appear more attractive, withholding undesirable information, and creating false rumors to get employees to accept a change are all examples of manipulation. If corporate management threatens to close down a particular manufacturing plant if that plant's employees fail to accept an across-the-board pay cut, and if the threat is actually untrue, management is using manipulation. Co-optation, on the other hand, is a form of both manipulation and participation. It seeks to "buy off"

By involving her employees in decorating their new offices, Betsy Nichol helped them adjust to the company's relocation to New York City. Nichol, president of Nichol & Co., Ltd., a small public relations and marketing firm, helped reduce the stress and anxiety of the relocation by giving employees cameras and company time to take pictures that reflect the architecture and diverse workforce of New York City. She framed one photo from each employee and involved all employees in deciding where the photos would be displayed. The project helped employees to connect to their new environment and "made everyone appreciate the city where we work," says Nichol.

the leaders of a resistance group by giving them a key role in the change decision. The leaders' advice is sought, not to seek a better decision, but to get their endorsement. Both manipulation and co-optation are relatively inexpensive and easy ways to gain the support of adversaries, but the tactics can backfire if the targets become aware that they are being tricked or used. Once discovered, the change agent's credibility may drop to zero.

Coercion Last on the list of tactics is coercion, that is, the application of direct threats or force upon the resisters. If the corporate management mentioned in the previous discussion really is determined to close a manufacturing plant if employees don't acquiesce to a pay cut, then coercion would be the label attached to its change tactic. Other examples of coercion are threats of transfer, loss of promotions, negative performance evaluations, and poor letters of recommendation. The advantages and drawbacks of coercion are approximately the same as those mentioned for manipulation and co-optation.

THE POLITICS OF CHANGE

No discussion of resistance to change would be complete without a brief mention of the politics of change. Because change invariably threatens the status quo, it inherently implies political activity.[9]

Internal change agents typically are individuals high in the organization who have a lot to lose from change. They have, in fact, risen to their positions of authority by developing skills and behavioral patterns that are favored by the organization. Change is a threat to those skills and patterns. What if they are no longer the ones the organization values? This creates the potential for others in the organization to gain power at their expense.

Politics suggests that the impetus for change is more likely to come from outside change agents, employees who are new to the organization (and have less invested in the status quo), or from managers slightly removed from the main power structure. Those managers who have spent their entire careers with a single organization and eventually achieve a senior position in the hierarchy are often major impediments to change. Change, itself, is a very real threat to their status and position. Yet they may be expected to implement changes to demonstrate that they're not merely caretakers. By acting as change agents, they can symbolically convey to various constituencies—stockholders, suppliers, employees, customers—that they are on top of problems and adapting to a dynamic environment. Of course, as you might guess, when forced to introduce change, these long-time power holders tend to implement first-order changes. Radical change is too threatening.

Power struggles within the organization will determine, to a large degree, the speed and quantity of change. You should expect that long-time career executives will be sources of resistance. This, incidentally, explains why boards of directors that recognize the imperative for the rapid introduction of second-order change in their organizations frequently turn to outside candidates for new leadership.[10]

FROM CONCEPTS *TO* SKILLS

Assessing the Climate for Change

Why do some change programs succeed and others fail? One major factor is change readiness.[11] Research by Symmetrix, a Massachusetts consulting firm, identified 17 key elements to successful change. The more affirmative answers you get to the following questions, the greater the likelihood that change efforts will succeed.

1. Is the sponsor of change high up enough to have power to effectively deal with resistance?
2. Is day-to-day leadership supportive of the change and committed to it?
3. Is there a strong sense of urgency from senior management about the need for change and is it shared by the rest of the organization?
4. Does management have a clear vision of how the future will look different from the present?
5. Are there objective measures in place to evaluate the change effort and are reward systems explicitly designed to reinforce them?
6. Is the specific change effort consistent with other changes going on within the organization?
7. Are functional managers willing to sacrifice their personal self-interest for the good of the organization as a whole?
8. Does management pride itself on closely monitoring changes and actions taken by competitors?
9. Is the importance of the customer and a knowledge of customer needs well accepted by everyone in the workforce?
10. Are managers and employees rewarded for taking risks, being innovative, and looking for new solutions?
11. Is the organizational structure flexible?
12. Are communication channels open both downward and upward?
13. Is the organization's hierarchy relatively flat?
14. Has the organization successfully implemented major changes in the recent past?
15. Is employee satisfaction and trust in management high?
16. Is there a high degree of cross-boundary interactions and cooperation between units in the organization?
17. Are decisions made quickly, taking into account a wide variety of suggestions?

APPROACHES TO MANAGING ORGANIZATIONAL CHANGE

Now we turn to several popular approaches to managing change: Lewin's classic three-step model of the change process; action research; and organizational development.

LEWIN'S THREE-STEP MODEL

Kurt Lewin argued that successful change in organizations should follow three steps: **unfreezing** the status quo, *movement* to a new state, and **refreezing** the new change to make it permanent.[12] (See Exhibit 18-6.) The value of this model can be seen in the following example when the management of a large oil company decided to reorganize its marketing function in the western United States.

The oil company had three divisional offices in the West, located in Seattle, San Francisco, and Los Angeles. The decision was made to consolidate the divisions into a single regional office to be located in San Francisco. The reorganization meant transferring over 150 employees, eliminating some duplicate managerial positions, and instituting a new hierarchy of command. As you might guess, a move of this magnitude was difficult to keep secret. The rumor of its occurrence preceded the announcement by several months. The decision itself was made unilaterally. It came from the executive offices in New York. Those people affected had no say whatsoever in the choice. For those in Seattle or Los Angeles, who may have disliked the decision and its consequences—the problems inherent in transferring to another city, pulling youngsters out of school, making new friends, having new co-workers, undergoing the reassignment of responsibilities—their only recourse was to quit. In actuality, less than 10 percent did.

The status quo can be considered to be an equilibrium state. To move from this equilibrium—to overcome the pressures of both individual resistance and group conformity—unfreezing is necessary. It can be achieved in one of three ways. (See Exhibit 18-7.) The **driving forces**, which direct behavior away from the status quo, can be increased. The **restraining forces**, which hinder movement from the existing equilibrium, can be decreased. A third alternative is to *combine the first two approaches.*

The oil company's management could expect employee resistance to the consolidation. To deal with that resistance, management could use positive incentives to encourage employees to accept the change. For instance, increases in pay can be offered to those who accept the transfer. Very liberal moving expenses can be paid by the company. Management might offer low-cost mortgage funds to allow employees to buy new homes in San Francisco. Of course, management

unfreezing

Change efforts to overcome the pressures of both individual resistance and group conformity.

refreezing

Stabilizing a change intervention by balancing driving and restraining forces.

driving forces

Forces that direct behavior away from the status quo.

restraining forces

Forces that hinder movement away from the status quo.

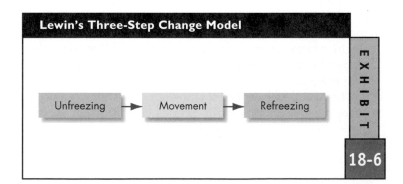

Lewin's Three-Step Change Model

Unfreezing → Movement → Refreezing

EXHIBIT 18-6

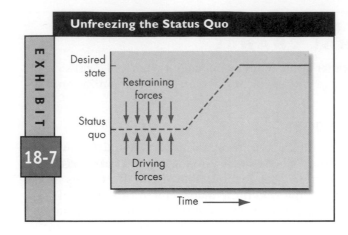

EXHIBIT

18-7

Unfreezing the Status Quo

Desired state

Restraining forces

Status quo

Driving forces

Time →

might also consider unfreezing acceptance of the status quo by removing restraining forces. Employees could be counseled individually. Each employee's concerns and apprehensions could be heard and specifically clarified. Assuming that most of the fears are unjustified, the counselor could assure the employees that there was nothing to fear and then demonstrate, through tangible evidence, that restraining forces are unwarranted. If resistance is extremely high, management may have to resort to both reducing resistance and increasing the attractiveness of the alternative if the unfreezing is to be successful.

Once the consolidation change has been implemented, if it is to be successful, the new situation needs to be refrozen so that it can be sustained over time. Unless this last step is taken, there is a very high chance that the change will be short-lived and that employees will attempt to revert to the previous equilibrium state. The objective of refreezing, then, is to stabilize the new situation by balancing the driving and restraining forces.

How could the oil company's management refreeze its consolidation change? By systematically replacing temporary forces with permanent ones. For instance, management might impose a permanent upward adjustment of salaries. The formal rules and regulations governing behavior of those affected by the change should also be revised to reinforce the new situation. Over time, of course, the work group's own norms will evolve to sustain the new equilibrium. But until that point is reached, management will have to rely on more formal mechanisms.

ACTION RESEARCH

action research

A change process based on systematic collection of data and then selection of a change action based on what the analyzed data indicate.

Action research refers to a change process based on the systematic collection of data and then selection of a change action based on what the analyzed data indicate.[13] Their importance lies in providing a scientific methodology for managing planned change.

The process of action research consists of five steps: diagnosis, analysis, feedback, action, and evaluation. You'll note that these steps closely parallel the scientific method.

The change agent, often an outside consultant in action research, begins by gathering information about problems, concerns, and needed changes from members of the organization. This *diagnosis* is analogous to the physician's search to find what specifically ails a patient. In action research, the change agent asks questions, interviews employees, reviews records, and listens to the concerns of employees.

Diagnosis is followed by *analysis*. What problems do people key in on? What patterns do these problems seem to take? The change agent synthesizes this information into primary concerns, problem areas, and possible actions.

Action research includes extensive involvement of the change targets. That is, the people who will be involved in any change program must be actively involved in determining what the problem is and participating in creating the solution. So the third step—*feedback*—requires sharing with employees what has been found from steps one and two. The employees, with the help of the change agent, develop action plans for bringing about any needed change.

Now the *action* part of action research is set in motion. The employees and the change agent carry out the specific actions to correct the problems that have been identified.

The final step, consistent with the scientific underpinnings of action research, is *evaluation* of the action plan's effectiveness. Using the initial data gathered as a benchmark, any subsequent changes can be compared and evaluated.

Action research provides at least two specific benefits for an organization. First, it's problem focused. The change agent objectively looks for problems and the type of problem determines the type of change action. While this may seem intuitively obvious, a lot of change activities aren't done this way. Rather, they're solution centered. The change agent has a favorite solution—for example, implementing flextime, teams, or a management by objectives program—and then seeks out problems that his or her solution fits. Second, because action research so heavily involves employees in the process, resistance to change is reduced. In fact, once employees have actively participated in the feedback stage, the change process typically takes on a momentum of its own. The employees and groups that have been involved become an internal source of sustained pressure to bring about the change.

ORGANIZATIONAL DEVELOPMENT

No discussion of managing change would be complete without including organizational development. **Organizational development (OD)** is not an easily defined single concept. Rather, it's a term used to encompass a collection of planned-change interventions built on humanistic-democratic values that seek to improve organizational effectiveness and employee well-being.[14]

The OD paradigm values human and organizational growth, collaborative and participative processes, and a spirit of inquiry.[15] The change agent may be directive in OD; however, there is a strong emphasis on collaboration. Concepts such as power, authority, control, conflict, and coercion are held in relatively low esteem among OD change agents. The following briefly identifies the underlying values in most OD efforts.

organizational development (OD)

A collection of planned-change interventions, built on humanistic-democratic values, that seeks to improve organizational effectiveness and employee well-being.

1. *Respect for people*. Individuals are perceived as being responsible, conscientious, and caring. They should be treated with dignity and respect.
2. *Trust and support*. The effective and healthy organization is characterized by trust, authenticity, openness, and a supportive climate.
3. *Power equalization*. Effective organizations deemphasize hierarchical authority and control.
4. *Confrontation*. Problems shouldn't be swept under the rug. They should be openly confronted.
5. *Participation*. The more that people who will be affected by a change are involved in the decisions surrounding that change, the more they will be committed to implementing those decisions.

What are some of the OD techniques or interventions for bringing about change? In the following pages, we present five interventions that change agents might consider using.

Change agent George Fisher, CEO of Eastman Kodak, is applying the underlying values of organizational development in boosting employee morale and reigniting the company's growth. When Fisher took the top job at Kodak, the company was suffering from a series of restructurings, a dispirited workforce, a rigid hierarchy, and huge debts. While past Kodak CEOs tended to be autocratic and inaccessible, Fisher (right in photo) is rebuilding the company through respect for people, trust and support, openness, the sharing of power, and participation.

Sensitivity Training It can go by a variety of names—laboratory training, **sensitivity training**, encounter groups, or T-groups (training groups)—but all refer to a method of changing behavior through unstructured group interaction.[16] Members are brought together in a free and open environment in which participants discuss themselves and their interactive processes, loosely directed by a professional behavioral scientist. The group is process oriented, which means that individuals learn through observing and participating rather than being told. The professional creates the opportunity for participants to express their ideas, beliefs, and attitudes. He or she does not accept—in fact, overtly rejects—any leadership role.

The objectives of the T-groups are to provide the subjects with increased awareness of their own behavior and how others perceive them, greater sensitivity to the behavior of others, and increased understanding of group processes. Specific results sought include increased ability to empathize with others, improved listening skills, greater openness, increased tolerance of individual differences, and improved conflict resolution skills.

If individuals lack awareness of how others perceive them, then the successful T-group can affect more realistic self-perceptions, greater group cohesiveness, and a reduction in dysfunctional interpersonal conflicts. Furthermore, it will ideally result in a better integration between the individual and the organization.

sensitivity training

Training groups that seek to change behavior through unstructured group interaction.

survey feedback

The use of questionnaires to identify discrepancies among member perceptions; discussion follows and remedies are suggested.

Survey Feedback One tool for assessing attitudes held by organizational members, identifying discrepancies among member perceptions, and solving these differences is the **survey feedback** approach.[17]

Everyone in an organization can participate in survey feedback, but of key importance is the organizational family—the manager of any given unit and those employees who report directly to him or her. A questionnaire is usually completed by all members in the organization or unit. Organization members may be asked to suggest questions or may be interviewed to determine what issues are relevant. The questionnaire typically asks members for their perceptions and attitudes on a broad range of topics, including decision-making practices; communication effectiveness; coordination between units; and satisfaction with the organization, job, peers, and their immediate supervisor.

The data from this questionnaire are tabulated with data pertaining to an individual's specific "family" and to the entire organization and distributed to employees. These data then become the springboard for identifying problems and clarifying issues that may be creating difficulties for people. Particular attention is given to the importance of encouraging discussion and ensuring that discussions focus on issues and ideas and not on attacking individuals.

Finally, group discussion in the survey feedback approach should result in members identifying possible implications of the questionnaire's findings. Are people listening? Are new ideas being generated? Can decision making, interpersonal relations, or job assignments be improved? Answers to questions such as these, it is hoped, will result in the group agreeing upon commitments to various actions that will remedy the problems that are identified.

Process Consultation No organization operates perfectly. Managers often sense that their unit's performance can be improved, but they're unable to identify what can be improved and how it can be improved. The purpose of **process consultation** is for an outside consultant to assist a client, usually a manager, "to perceive, understand, and act upon process events" with which he or she must deal.[18] These might include work flow, informal relationships among unit members, and formal communication channels.

Process consultation (PC) is similar to sensitivity training in its assumption that organizational effectiveness can be improved by dealing with interpersonal problems and in its emphasis on involvement. But PC is more task directed than sensitivity training.

Consultants in PC are there to "give the client 'insight' into what is going on around him, within him, and between him and other people."[19] They do not solve the organization's problems. Rather, the consultant is a guide or coach who advises on the process to help the client solve his or her own problems.

The consultant works with the client in *jointly* diagnosing what processes need improvement. The emphasis is on *jointly* because the client develops a skill at analyzing processes within his or her unit that can be continually called on long after the consultant is gone. Additionally, by having the client actively participate in both the diagnosis and the development of alternatives, there will be greater understanding of the process and the remedy and less resistance to the action plan chosen.

Importantly, the process consultant need not be an expert in solving the particular problem that is identified. The consultant's expertise lies in diagnosis and developing a helping relationship. If the specific problem uncovered requires technical knowledge outside the client's and consultant's expertise, the consultant helps the client to locate such an expert and then instructs the client in how to get the most out of this expert resource.

Team Building As we've noted in numerous places throughout this book, organizations are increasingly relying on teams to accomplish work tasks. **Team building** utilizes high-interaction group activities to increase trust and openness among team members.[20]

Team building can be applied within groups or at the intergroup level where activities are interdependent. For our discussion, we emphasize the intragroup level and leave intergroup development to the next section. As a result, our interest concerns applications to organizational families (command groups), as well as to committees, project teams, self-managed teams, and task groups.

process consultation
Consultant gives a client insights into what is going on around the client, within the client, and between the client and other people; identifies processes that need improvement.

team building
High interaction among team members to increase trust and openness.

[*Team building increases trust and openness among team members.*]

Not all group activity has interdependence of functions. To illustrate, consider a football team and a track team:

> Although members on both teams are concerned with the team's total output, they function differently. The football team's output depends synergistically on how well each player does his particular job in concert with his teammates. The quarterback's performance depends on the performance of his linemen and receivers, and ends on how well the quarterback throws the ball, and so on. On the other hand, a track team's performance is determined largely by the mere addition of the performances of the individual members.[21]

Team building is applicable to the case of interdependence, such as in football. The objective is to improve coordinative efforts of members, which will result in increasing the team's performance.

The activities considered in team building typically include goal setting, development of interpersonal relations among team members, role analysis to clarify each member's role and responsibilities, and team process analysis. Of course, team building may emphasize or exclude certain activities depending on the purpose of the development effort and the specific problems with which the team is confronted. Basically, however, team building attempts to use high interaction among members to increase trust and openness.

It may be beneficial to begin by having members attempt to define the goals and priorities of the team. This will bring to the surface different perceptions of what the team's purpose may be. Following this, members can evaluate the team's performance—how effective is the team in structuring priorities and achieving its goals? This should identify potential problem areas. This self-critique discussion of means and ends can be done with members of the total team present or, where large size impinges on a free interchange of views, may initially take place in smaller groups followed up by the sharing of their findings with the total team.

Team building can also address itself to clarifying each member's role on the team. Each role can be identified and clarified. Previous ambiguities can be brought to the surface. For some individuals, it may offer one of the few opportunities they have had to think through thoroughly what their job is all about and what specific tasks they are expected to carry out if the team is to optimize its effectiveness.

Still another team-building activity can be similar to that performed by the process consultant, that is, to analyze key processes that go on within the team to identify the way work is performed and how these processes might be improved to make the team more effective.

Intergroup Development   A major area of concern in OD is the dysfunctional conflict that exists between groups. As a result, this has been a subject to which change efforts have been directed.

intergroup development

OD efforts to change the attitudes, stereotypes, and perceptions that groups have of each other.

Intergroup development seeks to change the attitudes, stereotypes, and perceptions that groups have of each other. For example, in one company, the engineers saw the accounting department as composed of shy and conservative types, and the human resources department as having a bunch of "ultra-liberals who are more concerned that some protected group of employees might get their feelings hurt than with the company making a profit." Such stereotypes can have an obviously negative impact on the coordinative efforts between the departments.

Although there are several approaches for improving intergroup relations,[22] a popular method emphasizes problem solving.[23] In this method, each group meets independently to develop lists of its perception of itself, the other group, and how it believes the other group perceives it. The groups then share their lists, after which similarities and differences are discussed. Differences are clearly articulated, and the groups look for the causes of the disparities.

Are the groups' goals at odds? Were perceptions distorted? On what basis were stereotypes formulated? Have some differences been caused by misunderstandings of intentions? Have words and concepts been defined differently by each group? Answers to questions such as these clarify the exact nature of the conflict. Once the causes of the difficulty have been identified, the groups can move to the integration phase—working to develop solutions that will improve relations between the groups.

Subgroups, with members from each of the conflicting groups, can now be created for further diagnosis and to begin to formulate possible alternative actions that will improve relations.

CONTEMPORARY CHANGE ISSUES FOR TODAY'S MANAGERS

Talk to managers. Read the popular business periodicals. What you'll find is that two issues have risen above the rest as current change topics. They are stimulating organizational *innovation* and creating a *learning organization*. In the following pages, we take a look at these topics. Then we address the question: Is managing change culture bound?

INNOVATION

The relevant question is: How can an organization become more innovative? The standard toward which many organizations strive is that achieved by the 3M Co.[24] It has built a reputation as one of the most innovative organizations in the world by consistently developing new products over a very long period of time. 3M has a stated objective that 30 percent of its sales are to come from products less than four years old. In one recent year alone, 3M launched more than 500 new products.

What's the secret of 3M's success? What can other organizations do to clone 3M's track record for innovation? While there is no guaranteed formula, certain characteristics surface again and again when researchers study innovative organizations. We've grouped them into structural, cultural, and human resource categories. Our message to change agents is that they should consider introducing these characteristics into their organization if they want to create an innovative climate. Before we look at these characteristics, however, let's clarify what we mean by innovation.

ATI Technologies in Toronto, Canada, is recognized as the hottest 3-D chipmaker in the computer industry. It makes the 3-D computer chips that give reality to computer games like Quake II and Half-Life. Company co-founder Kwok Yuen Ho, shown here, keeps ATI's steady flow of innovations moving by regularly talking with employees to hear about their creative insights. Because product-cycle turnaround is critical in the chipmaking industry, Ho double-teams engineers, a technique that has cut turnaround time in half, enabling ATI to release a new generation version in under nine months.

Definition   We said change refers to making things different. **Innovation** is a more specialized kind of change. Innovation is a new idea applied to initiating or improving a product, process, or service.[25] So all innovations involve change, but not all changes necessarily involve new ideas or lead to significant improvements. Innovations in organizations can range from small incremental improvements, such as RJR Nabisco's extension of the Oreo product line to include double stuffs and chocolate-covered Oreos, up to radical breakthroughs, such as Jeff Bezo's idea in 1994 to create an on-line bookstore (Amazon.com). Keep in mind

innovation

A new idea applied to initiating or improving a product, process, or service.

that while our examples are mostly of product innovations, the concept of innovation also encompasses new production process technologies, new structures or administrative systems, and new plans or programs pertaining to organizational members.

Sources of Innovation *Structural variables* have been the most studied potential source of innovation.[26] A comprehensive review of the structure–innovation relationship leads to the following conclusions.[27] First, organic structures positively influence innovation. Because they're lower in vertical differentiation, formalization, and centralization, organic organizations facilitate the flexibility, adaptation, and cross-fertilization that make the adoption of innovations easier. Second, long tenure in management is associated with innovation. Managerial tenure apparently provides legitimacy and knowledge of how to accomplish tasks and obtain desired outcomes. Third, innovation is nurtured where there are slack resources. Having an abundance of resources allows an organization to afford to purchase innovations, bear the cost of instituting innovations, and absorb failures. Finally, interunit communication is high in innovative organizations.[28] These organizations are high users of committees, task forces, cross-functional teams, and other mechanisms that facilitate interaction across departmental lines.

Innovative organizations tend to have similar *cultures*. They encourage experimentation. They reward both successes and failures. They celebrate mistakes. At Hewlett-Packard, for instance, top management has successfully built a corporate culture that supports people who try something that doesn't work out.[29] Unfortunately, in too many organizations, people are rewarded for the absence of failures rather than for the presence of successes. Such cultures extinguish risk taking and innovation. People will suggest and try new ideas only where they feel such behaviors exact no penalties. Managers in innovative organizations recognize that failures are a natural by-product of venturing into the unknown. When Babe Ruth set his record for home runs in one season, he also led the league in strikeouts. And he is remembered for the former, not the latter!

> [*Innovative organizations encourage experimentation . . . reward both successes and failures . . . and celebrate mistakes.*]

Within the *human resources* category, we find that innovative organizations actively promote the training and development of their members so that they keep current, offer high job security so employees don't fear getting fired for making mistakes, and encourage individuals to become champions of change. Once a new idea is developed, **idea champions** actively and enthusiastically promote the idea, build support, overcome resistance, and ensure that the innovation is implemented.[30] The evidence indicates that champions have common personality characteristics: extremely high self-confidence, persistence, energy, and a tendency to take risks. Idea champions also display characteristics associated with transformational leadership. They inspire and energize others with their vision of the potential of an innovation and through their strong personal conviction in their mission. They are also good at gaining the commitment of others to support their mission. In addition, idea champions have jobs that provide considerable decision-making discretion. This autonomy helps them introduce and implement innovations in organizations.[31]

Given the status of 3M as a premier product innovator, we would expect it to have most of the properties we've identified. And it does. The company is so highly decentralized that it has many of the characteristics of small, organic organizations. The structure relies on extensive redundancy. For instance, every divi-

idea champions

Individuals who take an innovation and actively and enthusiastically promote the idea, build support, overcome resistance, and ensure it is implemented.

sion, department, and product group has its own labs—many of which are deliberately duplicating the work of others. And consistent with the need for cross-fertilization of ideas, the company holds internal trade shows where divisions will show their technologies to employees of other divisions. All of 3M's scientists and managers are challenged to "keep current." Idea champions are created and encouraged by allowing scientists and engineers to spend up to 15 percent of their time on projects of their own choosing. And if a 3M scientist comes up with a new idea but finds resistance within the researcher's own division, he or she can apply for a $50,000 grant from an internal venture-capital fund to further develop the idea. The company encourages its employees to take risks—and rewards the failures as well as the successes. And 3M's management has the patience to see ideas through to successful products. It invests nearly 7 percent of company sales revenue (more than $1 billion a year) in research and development, yet management tells its R&D people that *not everything is going to work*. It also fosters a culture that allows people to defy their supervisors. For instance, each new employee and his or her supervisor take a one-day orientation class where, among other things, stories are told of victories won by employees despite the opposition of their boss. Finally, 3M is a model of corporate stability. The average tenure for company officers is 32 years, overall annual employee turnover is a miniscule 3 percent, and the company still prides itself on being an employer for life. Financial analysts, in fact, have recently criticized the company for being *too* stable. In particular, they take issue with management's unwillingness to cut costs through employee layoffs. Management's response is that it's this stability that underpins its innovative culture and allows it to keep its brightest scientists.

CREATING A LEARNING ORGANIZATION

What TQM was to the 1980s and reengineering was to the early 1990s, the learning organization has become today. It has developed a groundswell of interest from managers and organization theorists looking for new ways to successfully respond to a world of interdependence and change.[32] In this section, we describe what a learning organization looks like and methods for managing learning.

What's a Learning Organization?   A **learning organization** is an organization that has developed the continuous capacity to adapt and change. Just as individuals learn, so too do organizations. "All organizations learn, whether they consciously choose to or not—it is a fundamental requirement for their sustained existence."[33] However, some organizations, such as Xerox, Corning, Federal Express, Ford, General Electric, and Wal-Mart, just do it better than others.

Most organizations engage in what has been called **single-loop learning**.[34] When errors are detected, the correction process relies on past routines and present policies. In contrast, learning organizations use **double-loop learning**. When an error is detected, it's corrected in ways that involve the modification of the organization's objectives, policies, and standard routines. Like second-order change described at the beginning of this chapter, double-loop learning challenges deep-rooted assumptions and norms within an organization. In this way, it provides opportunities for radically different solutions to problems and dramatic jumps in improvement.

Exhibit 18-8 summarizes the five basic characteristics of a learning organization. It's an organization where people put aside their old ways of thinking, learn to be open with each other, understand how their organization really works, form a plan or vision that everyone can agree upon, and then work together to achieve that vision.[35]

learning organization
An organization that has developed the continuous capacity to adapt and change.

single-loop learning
Errors are corrected using past routines and present policies.

double-loop learning
Errors are corrected by modifying the organization's objectives, policies, and standard routines.

EXHIBIT

18-8

Characteristics of a Learning Organization

1. There exists a shared vision on which everyone agrees.
2. People discard their old ways of thinking and the standard routines they use for solving problems or doing their jobs.
3. Members think of all organizational processes, activities, functions, and interactions with the environment as part of a system of interrelationships.
4. People openly communicate with each other (across vertical and horizontal boundaries) without fear of criticism or punishment.
5. People sublimate their personal self-interest and fragmented departmental interests to work together to achieve the organization's shared vision.

Source: Based on P. M. Senge, *The Fifth Discipline* (New York: Doubleday, 1990).

Proponents of the learning organization envision it as a remedy for the three fundamental problems inherent in traditional organizations: fragmentation, competition, and reactiveness.[36] First, *fragmentation* based on specialization creates "walls" and "chimneys" that separate different functions into independent and often warring fiefdoms. Second, an overemphasis on *competition* often undermines collaboration. Members of the management team compete with one another to show who is right, who knows more, or who is more persuasive. Divisions compete with one another when they ought to cooperate to share knowledge. Team project leaders compete to show who is the best manager. And third, *reactiveness* misdirects management's attention to problem solving rather than creation. The problem solver tries to make something go away, while a creator tries to bring something new into being. An emphasis on reactiveness pushes out innovation and continuous improvement and, in its place, encourages people to run around "putting out fires."

It may help to better understand what a learning organization is if you think of it as an *ideal* model that builds on a number of *previous OB concepts*. No company has successfully achieved all the characteristics described in Exhibit 18-8. As such, you should think of a learning organization as an ideal to strive toward rather than a realistic description of structured activity. Notice, too, how learning organizations draw on previous OB concepts such as TQM, organizational culture, the boundaryless organization, functional conflict, and transformational leadership. For instance, the learning organization adopts TQM's commitment to continuous improvement. Learning organizations are also characterized by a specific culture that values risk taking, openness, and growth. It seeks "boundarylessness" through breaking down barriers created by hierarchical levels and fragmented departmentation. A learning organization supports the importance of disagreements, constructive criticism, and other forms of functional conflict. And transformational leadership is needed in a learning organization to implement the shared vision.

Managing Learning How do you change an organization to make it into a continual learner? What can managers do to make their firms learning organizations?

Establish a strategy. Management needs to make explicit its commitment to change, innovation, and continuous improvement.

Redesign the organization's structure. The formal structure can be a serious impediment to learning. By flattening the structure, eliminating or combining departments, and increasing the use of cross-functional teams, interdependence is reinforced and boundaries between people are reduced.

Reshape the organization's culture. As noted earlier, learning organizations are characterized by risk taking, openness, and growth. Management sets the tone for the organization's culture both by what it says (strategy) and what it does (behavior). Managers need to demonstrate by their actions that taking risks and admitting failures are desirable traits. That means rewarding people who take chances and make mistakes. And management needs to encourage functional conflict. "The key to unlocking real openness at work," says one expert on learning organizations, "is to teach people to give up having to be in agreement. We think agreement is so important. Who cares? You have to bring paradoxes, conflicts, and dilemmas out in the open, so collectively we can be more intelligent than we can be individually."[37]

An Example: The U.S. Army   The U.S. Army isn't the typical example that comes to mind when you think of what a learning organization might look like. But think again.[38]

The army's environment has changed dramatically since the days of the Vietnam conflict. For one thing, the Soviet threat, which was a major justification for the army's military buildup, is largely gone. Army soldiers are more likely to be involved in feeding children in Somalia, peacekeeping in Haiti, or helping put out forest fires in the Pacific Northwest than fighting a war. And its new mission is reflected in its budget. The army's annual appropriation dropped from $90 billion in 1989 to $64 billion in 1998. Meanwhile, the number of troops in uniform have been downsized from 780,000 to 480,000. Clearly, it's no longer "business as usual" in the U.S. Army.

The army's high command has redesigned its structure to reflect its new mission. The old army was said to be an organization "designed by geniuses to be run by idiots." That rigid, hierarchical, command-and-control structure was fine when the army's single purpose was combat related. Authority was centralized at the Pentagon, and orders were passed down to the field. Officers weren't expected to innovate or make adjustments. But that type of structure doesn't fit with the changing role of the military. The new army is putting into place an adaptive and flexible structure to match its more varied objectives.

Along with the new structure is a major program to make the army's culture more egalitarian. Everyone from PFCs to brigadier generals has gone through team training to learn how to make decisions in the field and even to question authority (a previously unheard of idea). Senior officers are required to go through something called the After Action Review (AAR)—a public performance appraisal—where decisions are openly critiqued by subordinates. The potential for public embarrassment in an AAR would never have been allowed in the old army.

The bottom line is that the U.S. Army is becoming a learning organization. It's

As part of its efforts to become a learning organization, the U.S. Army is experimenting with programs that boost morale for troops in combat. One pilot program allows men and women to use videoconferencing to visit with their loved ones. When Army Lieutenant Frank Holmes, shown here, was stationed in Bosnia, he visited with his wife and three-week-old daughter in Fort Bragg, North Carolina, via videophone. The pilot videoconferencing program "was the single greatest morale boost for my troops in a long time," said Holmes's commanding officer.

developing soldiers, especially officers, who can adapt rapidly to different tasks and missions. The new army seeks to be able to quickly improvise in complex and ambiguous situations. Its soldiers will be prepared to play a multiple set of changing roles—fighting, peacekeeping, peacemaking, humanitarian rescue, nation building, or whatever—and be able to change those roles quickly as need.

MANAGING CHANGE: IT'S CULTURE BOUND!

A number of change issues we've discussed are culture bound. To illustrate, let's briefly look at five questions: (1) Do people believe change is possible? (2) If it's possible, how long will it take to bring it about? (3) Is resistance to change greater in some cultures than in others? (4) Does culture influence how change efforts will be implemented? (5) Do successful idea champions do things differently in different cultures?

Do people believe change is possible? Remember that cultures vary in terms of beliefs about their ability to control their environment. In cultures where people believe that they can dominate their environment, individuals will take a proactive view of change. This, for example, would describe the United States and Canada. In many other countries, such as Iran and Saudi Arabia, people see themselves as subjugated to their environment and, thus, will tend to take a passive approach toward change.

If change is possible, how long will it take to bring it about? A culture's time orientation can help us answer this question. Societies that focus on the long term, such as Japan, will demonstrate considerable patience while waiting for positive outcomes from change efforts. In societies with a short-term focus, such as the United States and Canada, people expect quick improvements and will seek change programs that promise fast results.

Is resistance to change greater in some cultures than in others? Resistance to change will be influenced by a society's reliance on tradition. Italians, as an example, focus on the past, while Americans emphasize the present. Italians, therefore, should generally be more resistant to change efforts than their American counterparts.

Does culture influence how change efforts will be implemented? Power distance can help with this issue. In high-power-distance cultures, such as the Philippines or Venezuela, change efforts will tend to be autocratically implemented by top management. In contrast, low-power-distance cultures value democratic methods. We'd predict, therefore, a greater use of participation in countries such as Denmark and Israel.

Finally, do successful idea champions do things differently in different cultures? The evidence indicates that the answer is Yes.[39] People in collectivist cultures, in contrast to individualistic cultures, prefer appeals for cross-functional support for innovation efforts; people in high-power-distance cultures prefer champions to work closely with those in authority to approve innovative activities before work is conducted on them; and the higher the uncertainty avoidance of a society, the more champions should work within the organization's rules and procedures to develop the innovation. These findings suggest that effective managers will alter their organization's championing strategies to reflect cultural values. So, for instance, while idea champions in the United States might succeed by ignoring budgetary limitations and working around confining procedures, champions in Venezuela, Greece, Italy, or other cultures high in uncertainty avoidance will be more effective by closely following budgets and procedures.

WORK STRESS AND ITS MANAGEMENT

Most of us are aware that employee stress is an increasing problem in organizations. We hear about postal workers killing co-workers and supervisors and then we learn job-related tensions were a major cause. Friends tells us they're stressed out from greater workloads and having to work longer hours because of downsizing at their company. We read surveys in which employees complain about the stress created in trying to balance work and family responsibilities. In this section we'll look at the causes and consequences of stress, and then consider what individuals and organizations can do to reduce it. (See Exhibit 18-9 for a ranking of jobs based on stress scores.)

WHAT IS STRESS?

Stress is *a dynamic condition in which an individual is confronted with an opportunity, constraint, or demand related to what he or she desires and for which the outcome is perceived to be both uncertain and important.*[40] This is a complicated definition. Let's look at its components more closely.

Stress is not necessarily bad in and of itself. While stress is typically discussed in a negative context, it also has a positive value. It is an opportunity when it offers potential gain. Consider, for example, the superior performance that an athlete or stage performer gives in "clutch" situations. Such individuals often use stress positively to rise to the occasion and perform at or near their maximum.

More typically, stress is associated with **constraints** and **demands**. The former prevent you from doing what you desire. The latter refers to the loss of

stress

A dynamic condition in which an individual is confronted with an opportunity, constraint, or demand related to what he or she desires and for which the outcome is perceived to be both uncertain and important.

constraints

Forces that prevent individuals from doing what they desire.

demands

The loss of something desired.

The Most Stressful Jobs

How do jobs rate in terms of stress? The following shows how selected occupations ranked in an evaluation of 250 jobs. Among the criteria used in the rankings were overtime, quotas, deadlines, competitiveness, physical demands, environmental conditions, hazards encountered, initiative required, stamina required, win-lose situations, and working in the public eye.

Rank Score		Stress Score	Rank Score		Stress Score
1.	U.S. president	176.6	47.	Auto salesperson	56.3
2.	Firefighter	110.9	50.	College professor	54.2
3.	Senior executive	108.6	60.	School principal	51.7
6.	Surgeon	99.5	103.	Market research analyst	42.1
10.	Air traffic controller	83.1	104.	Personnel recruiter	41.8
12.	Public relations executive	78.5	113.	Hospital administrator	39.6
16.	Advertising account executive	74.6	119.	Economist	38.7
17.	Real estate agent	73.1	122.	Mechanical engineer	38.3
20.	Stockbroker	71.7	124.	Chiropractor	37.9
22.	Pilot	68.7	132.	Technical writer	36.5
25.	Architect	66.9	149.	Retail salesperson	34.9
31.	Lawyer	64.3	173.	Accountant	31.1
33.	General physician	64.0	193.	Purchasing agent	28.9
35.	Insurance agent	63.3	229.	Broadcast technician	24.2
42.	Advertising salesperson	59.9	245.	Actuary	20.2

EXHIBIT 18-9

something desired. So when you take a test at school or you undergo your annual performance review at work, you feel stress because you confront opportunities, constraints, and demands. A good performance review may lead to a promotion, greater responsibilities, and a higher salary. But a poor review may prevent you from getting the promotion. An extremely poor review might even result in your being fired.

Two conditions are necessary for potential stress to become actual stress.[41] There must be uncertainty over the outcome and the outcome must be important. Regardless of the conditions, it's only when there is doubt or uncertainty regarding whether the opportunity will be seized, the constraint removed, or the loss avoided that there is stress. That is, stress is highest for those individuals who perceive that they are uncertain as to whether they will win or lose and lowest for those individuals who think that winning or losing is a certainty. But importance is also critical. If winning or losing is an unimportant outcome, there is no stress. If keeping your job or earning a promotion doesn't hold any importance to you, you have no reason to feel stress over having to undergo a performance review.

UNDERSTANDING STRESS AND ITS CONSEQUENCES

What causes stress? What are its consequences for individual employees? Why is it that the same set of conditions that creates stress for one person seems to have little or no effect on another person? Exhibit 18-11 provides a model that can help to answer questions such as these.[42]

The model identifies three sets of factors—environmental, organizational, and individual—that act as *potential* sources of stress. Whether they become *ac-*

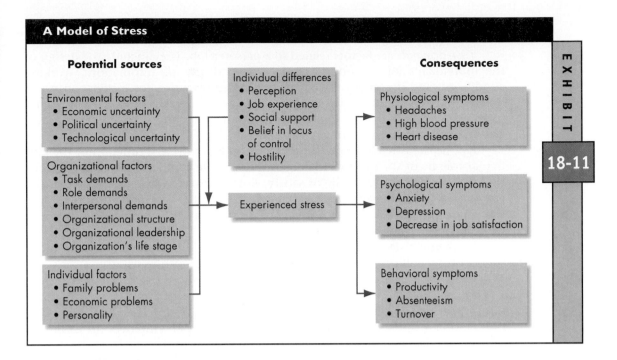

A Model of Stress

Potential sources

Environmental factors
- Economic uncertainty
- Political uncertainty
- Technological uncertainty

Organizational factors
- Task demands
- Role demands
- Interpersonal demands
- Organizational structure
- Organizational leadership
- Organization's life stage

Individual factors
- Family problems
- Economic problems
- Personality

Individual differences
- Perception
- Job experience
- Social support
- Belief in locus of control
- Hostility

Experienced stress

Consequences

Physiological symptoms
- Headaches
- High blood pressure
- Heart disease

Psychological symptoms
- Anxiety
- Depression
- Decrease in job satisfaction

Behavioral symptoms
- Productivity
- Absenteeism
- Turnover

EXHIBIT

18-11

tual stress depends on individual differences such as job experience and personality. When stress is experienced by an individual, its symptoms can surface as physiological, psychological, and behavioral outcomes.

POTENTIAL SOURCES OF STRESS

As the model in Exhibit 18–11 shows, there are three categories of potential stressors: environmental, organizational, and individual. Let's take a look at each.[43]

Environmental Factors   Just as environmental uncertainty influences the design of an organization's structure, it also influences stress levels among employees in that organization. Changes in the business cycle create *economic uncertainties*. When the economy is contracting, for example, people become increasingly anxious about their security. *Political uncertainties* don't tend to create stress among North Americans as they do for employees in countries such as Haiti or Iraq. The obvious reason is that the United States and Canada have stable political systems in which change is typically implemented in an orderly manner. Yet political threats and changes, even in countries such as the United States and Canada, can be stress inducing. For instance, threats by Quebec to separate from Canada and become a distinct, French-speaking country increase stress among many Canadians, especially among Quebecers with little or no skills in the French language. *Technological uncertainty* is a third type of environmental factor that can cause stress. Because new innovations can make an employee's skills and experience obsolete in a very short period of time, computers, robotics, automation, and similar forms of technological innovation are a threat to many people and cause them stress.

Organizational Factors   There is no shortages of factors within the organization that can cause stress. Pressures to avoid errors or complete tasks in a limited time period, work overload, a demanding and insensitive boss, and unpleasant co-workers are a few examples. We've categorized these factors around task, role, and interpersonal demands; organizational structure; organizational leadership; and the organization's life stage.[44]

Task demands are factors related to a person's job. They include the design of the individual's job (autonomy, task variety, degree of automation), working conditions, and the physical work layout. Assembly lines, for instance, can put pressure on people when their speed is perceived as excessive. Similarly, working in an overcrowded room or in a visible location where interruptions are constant can increase anxiety and stress.

Role demands relate to pressures placed on a person as a function of the particular role he or she plays in the organization. Role conflicts create expectations that may be hard to reconcile or satisfy. Role overload is experienced when the employee is expected to do more than time permits. Role ambiguity is created when role expectations are not clearly understood and the employee is not sure what he or she is to do.

Interpersonal demands are pressures created by other employees. Lack of social support from colleagues and poor interpersonal relationships can cause considerable stress, especially among employees with a high social need.

Organizational structure defines the level of differentiation in the organization, the degree of rules and regulations, and where decisions are made. Excessive rules and lack of participation in decisions that affect an employee are examples of structural variables that might be potential sources of stress.

Organizational leadership represents the managerial style of the organization's senior executives. Some chief executive officers create a culture characterized by tension, fear, and anxiety. They establish unrealistic pressures to perform in the short run, impose excessively tight controls, and routinely fire employees who don't "measure up."

Organizations go through a cycle. They're established, they grow, become mature, and eventually decline. An *organization's life stage*—that is, where it is in this four-stage cycle—creates different problems and pressures for employees. The establishment and decline stages are particularly stressful. The former is characterized by a great deal of excitement and uncertainty, while the latter typically requires cutbacks, layoffs, and a different set of uncertainties. Stress tends to be least in maturity where uncertainties are at their lowest ebb.

Individual Factors The typical individual works about 40 to 50 hours a week. But the experiences and problems that people encounter in those other 120-plus nonwork hours each week can spill over to the job. Our final category, then, encompasses factors in the employee's personal life. Primarily, these factors are family issues, personal economic problems, and inherent personality characteristics.

National surveys consistently show that people hold *family* and personal relationships dear. Marital difficulties, the breaking off of a relationship, and discipline troubles with children are examples of relationship problems that create stress for employees that aren't left at the front door when they arrive at work.

Economic problems created by individuals overextending their financial resources is another set of personal troubles that can create stress for employees and distract their attention from their work. Regardless of income level—people who make $80,000 a year seem to have as much trouble handling their finances as those who earn $18,000—some people are poor money managers or have wants that always seem to exceed their earning capacity.

Studies in three diverse organizations found that stress symptoms reported prior to beginning a job accounted for most of the variance in stress symptoms reported nine months later.[45] This led the researchers to conclude that some people may have an inherent tendency to accentuate negative aspects of the world in general. If true, then a significant individual factor influencing stress is a person's basic dispositional nature. That is, stress symptoms expressed on the job may actually originate in the person's *personality*.

Stressors Are Additive   A fact that tends to be overlooked when stressors are reviewed individually is that stress is an additive phenomenon.[46] Stress builds up. Each new and persistent stressor adds to an individual's stress level. So a single stressor may be relatively unimportant in and of itself, but if it's added to an already high level of stress, it can be "the straw that breaks the camel's back." If we want to appraise the total amount of stress an individual is under, we have to sum up his or her opportunity stresses, constraint stresses, and demand stresses.

INDIVIDUAL DIFFERENCES

Some people thrive on stressful situations, while others are overwhelmed by them. What is it that differentiates people in terms of their ability to handle stress? What individual difference variables moderate the relationship between *potential* stressors and *experienced* stress? At least five variables—perception, job experience, social support, belief in locus of control, and hostility—have been found to be relevant moderators.

In Chapter 5, we demonstrated that employees react in response to their perception of reality rather than to reality itself. *Perception*, therefore, will moderate the relationship between a potential stress condition and an employee's reaction to it. For example, one person's fear that he'll lose his job because his company is laying off personnel may be perceived by another as an opportunity to get a large severance allowance and start his own business. So stress potential doesn't lie in objective conditions; it lies in an employee's interpretation of those conditions.

The evidence indicates that *experience* on the job tends to be negatively related to work stress. Why? Two explanations have been offered.[47] First is the idea of selective withdrawal. Voluntary turnover is more probable among people who experience more stress. Therefore, people who remain with the organization longer are those with more stress-resistant traits, or those who are more resistant to the stress characteristics of their organization. Second, people eventually develop coping mechanisms to deal with stress. Because this takes time, senior members of the organization are more likely to be fully adapted and should experience less stress.

There is increasing evidence that *social support*—that is, collegial relationships with co-workers or supervisors—can buffer the impact of stress.[48] The logic underlying this moderating variable is that social support acts as a palliative, mitigating the negative effects of even high-strain jobs.

Locus of control was introduced in Chapter 4 as a personality attribute. Those

Social interaction with co-workers helps reduce the high-stress jobs of employees at Qualcomm, a San Diego firm that pioneered digital wireless technology. Qualcomm makes it easy for employees to develop collegial relationships with co-workers. Part of Qualcomm's campus environment is devoted to a sand volleyball court, where employees can take a break from work and reenergize themselves by joining a pickup volleyball game.

with an internal locus of control believe they control their own destiny. Those with an external locus believe their lives are controlled by outside forces. Evidence indicates that internals perceive their jobs to be less stressful than do externals.[49] When internals and externals confront a similar stressful situation, the internals are likely to believe that they can have a significant effect on the results. They, therefore, act to take control of events. In contrast, externals are more likely to be passive and feel helpless.

Some people's personality includes a high degree of hostility and anger. These people are chronically suspicious and mistrustful of others. Evidence indicates that this *hostility* significantly increases a person's stress and risk for heart disease.[50] More specifically, people who are quick to anger, maintain a persistently hostile outlook, and project a cynical mistrust of others are more likely to experience stress in situations.

CONSEQUENCES OF STRESS

Stress shows itself in a number of ways. For instance, an individual who is experiencing a high level of stress may develop high blood pressure, ulcers, irritability, difficulty in making routine decisions, loss of appetite, accident proneness, and the like. These can be subsumed under three general categories: physiological, psychological, and behavioral symptoms.[51]

Physiological Symptoms　Most of the early concern with stress was directed at physiological symptoms. This was predominantly due to the fact that the topic was researched by specialists in the health and medical sciences. This research led to the conclusion that stress could create changes in metabolism, increase heart and breathing rates, increase blood pressure, bring on headaches, and induce heart attacks.

The link between stress and particular physiological symptoms is not clear. There are few, if any, consistent relationships.[52] This is attributed to the complexity of the symptoms and the difficulty of objectively measuring them. But of greater relevance is the fact that physiological symptoms have the least direct relevance to students of OB. Our concern is with behaviors and attitudes. Therefore, the two other categories of symptoms are more important to us.

Psychological Symptoms　Stress can cause dissatisfaction. Job-related stress can cause job-related dissatisfaction. Job dissatisfaction, in fact, is "the simplest and most obvious psychological effect" of stress.[53] But stress shows itself in other psychological states—for instance, tension, anxiety, irritability, boredom, and procrastination.

The evidence indicates that when people are placed in jobs that make multiple and conflicting demands or in which there is a lack of clarity as to the incumbent's duties, authority, and responsibilities, both stress and dissatisfaction are increased.[54] Similarly, the less control people have over the pace of their work, the greater the stress and dissatisfaction. While more research is needed to clarify the relationship, the evidence suggests that jobs that provide a low level of variety, significance, autonomy, feedback, and identity to incumbents create stress and reduce satisfaction and involvement in the job.[55]

Behavioral Symptoms　Behaviorally related stress symptoms include changes in productivity, absence, and turnover, as well as changes in eating habits, increased smoking or consumption of alcohol, rapid speech, fidgeting, and sleep disorders.

There has been a significant amount of research investigating the stress–performance relationship. The most widely studied pattern in the stress–performance literature is the inverted-U relationship.[56] This is shown in Exhibit 18-12.

The logic underlying the inverted U is that low to moderate levels of stress stimulate the body and increase its ability to react. Individuals then often perform their tasks better, more intensely, or more rapidly. But too much stress places unattainable demands or constraints on a person, which result in lower performance. This inverted-U pattern may also describe the reaction to stress over time, as well as to changes in stress intensity. That is, even moderate levels of stress can have a negative influence on performance over the long term as the continued intensity of the stress wears down the individual and saps his or her energy resources. An athlete may be able to use the positive effects of stress to obtain a higher performance during every Saturday's game in the fall season, or a sales executive may be able to psych herself up for her presentation at the annual

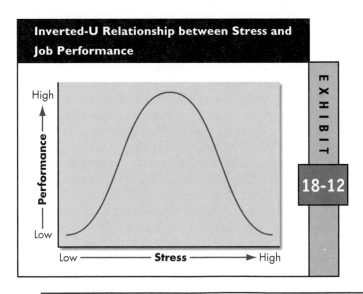

Inverted-U Relationship between Stress and Job Performance

EXHIBIT

18-12

national meeting. But moderate levels of stress experienced continually over long periods of time, as typified by the emergency room staff in a large urban hospital, can result in lower performance. This may explain why emergency room staffs at such hospitals are frequently rotated and why it is unusual to find individuals who have spent the bulk of their career in such an environment. In effect, to do so would expose the individual to the risk of "career burnout."

In spite of the popularity and intuitive appeal of the inverted-U model, it doesn't get a lot of empirical support.[57] At this point in time, managers should be careful in assuming this model accurately depicts the stress–performance relationship.

MANAGING STRESS

From the organization's standpoint, management may not be concerned when employees experience low to moderate levels of stress. The reason, as we showed earlier, is that such levels of stress may be functional and lead to higher employee performance. But high levels of stress, or even low levels sustained over long periods of time, can lead to reduced employee performance and, thus, require action by management.

While a limited amount of stress may benefit an employee's performance, don't expect employees to see it that way. From the individual's standpoint, even low levels of stress are likely to be perceived as undesirable. It's not unlikely, therefore, for employees and management to have different notions of what constitutes an acceptable level of stress on the job. What management considers as "a positive stimulus that keeps the adrenalin running" may be seen as "excessive pressure" by the employee. Keep this in mind as we discuss individual and organizational approaches toward managing stress.[58]

Individual Approaches   An employee can take personal responsibility for reducing his or her stress level. Individual strategies that have proven effective include implementing time management techniques, increasing physical exercise, relaxation training, and expanding the social support network.

Many people manage their time poorly. The things they have to accomplish in any given day or week are not necessarily beyond completion if they manage their time properly. The well-organized employee, like the well-organized student, can often accomplish twice as much as the person who is poorly organized. So an understanding and utilization of basic *time management* principles can help individuals better cope with tensions created by job demands.[59] A few of the more well-known time management principles are (1) making daily lists of activities to be accomplished; (2) prioritizing activities by importance and urgency; (3) scheduling activities according to the priorities set; and (4) knowing your daily cycle and handling the most demanding parts of your job during the high part of your cycle when you are most alert and productive.[60]

Noncompetitive physical exercise such as aerobics, walking, jogging, swimming, and riding a bicycle have long been recommended by physicians as a way to deal with excessive stress levels. These forms of *physical exercise* increase heart capacity, lower at-rest heart rate, provide a mental diversion from work pressures, and offer a means to "let off steam."[61]

Individuals can teach themselves to reduce tension through *relaxation techniques* such as meditation, hypnosis, and biofeedback. The objective is to reach a state of deep relaxation, where one feels physically relaxed, somewhat detached from the immediate environment, and detached from body sensations.[62] Fifteen or twenty minutes a day of deep relaxation releases tension and provides a person with a pronounced sense of peacefulness. Importantly, significant changes in heart rate, blood pressure, and other physiological factors result from achieving the deep relaxation condition.

As we noted earlier in this chapter, having friends, family, or work colleagues to talk to provides an outlet when stress levels become excessive. Expanding your *social support network*, therefore, can be a means for tension reduction. It provides you with someone to hear your problems and to offer a more objective perspective on the situation. Research also demonstrates that social support moderates the stress–burnout relationship.[63] That is, high support reduces the likelihood that heavy work stress will result in job burnout.

Organizational Approaches Several of the factors that cause stress—particularly task and role demands, and organizational structure—are controlled by management. As such, they can be modified or changed. Strategies that management might want to consider include improved personnel selection and job placement, use of realistic goal setting, redesigning of jobs, increased employee involvement, improved organizational communication, and establishment of corporate wellness programs.

While certain jobs are more stressful than others, we learned earlier in this chapter that individuals differ in their response to stress situations. We know, for example, that individuals with little experience or an external locus of control tend to be more prone to stress. *Selection and placement* decisions should take these facts into consideration. Obviously, while management shouldn't restrict hiring to only experienced individuals with an internal locus, such individuals may adapt better to high-stress jobs and perform those jobs more effectively.

We discussed *goal setting* in Chapter 6. Based on an extensive amount of research, we concluded that individuals perform better when they have specific and challenging goals and receive feedback on how well they are progressing toward these goals. The use of goals can reduce stress as well as provide motivation. Specific goals that are perceived as attainable clarify performance expectations. Additionally, goal feedback reduces uncertainties as to actual job performance. The result is less employee frustration, role ambiguity, and stress.

Redesigning jobs to give employees more responsibility, more meaningful work, more autonomy, and increased feedback can reduce stress because these factors give the employee greater control over work activities and lessen dependence on others. But as we noted in our discussion of work design, not all employees want enriched jobs. The right redesign, then, for employees with a low need for growth might be less responsibility and increased specialization. If individuals prefer

Company-sponsored yoga classes help Autodesk's employees improve their mental and physical wellness. Autodesk, a leading developer of computer-aided design software based in San Rafael, California, also eases employee stress by allowing them to bring their pets to work and by granting six-week paid sabbaticals every four years.

structure and routine, reducing skill variety should also reduce uncertainties and stress levels.

Role stress is detrimental to a large extent because employees feel uncertain about goals, expectations, how they'll be evaluated, and the like. By giving these employees a voice in those decisions that directly affect their job performances, management can increase employee control and reduce this role stress. So managers should consider *increasing employee involvement* in decision making.[64]

Increasing formal *organizational communication* with employees reduces uncertainty by lessening role ambiguity and role conflict. Given the importance that perceptions play in moderating the stress–response relationship, management can also use effective communications as a means to shape employee perceptions. Remember that what employees categorize as demands, threats, or opportunities are merely an interpretation, and that interpretation can be affected by the symbols and actions communicated by management.

wellness programs

Organizationally supported programs that focus on the employee's total physical and mental condition.

Our final suggestion is to offer organizationally supported **wellness programs**. These programs focus on the employee's total physical and mental condition.[65] For example, they typically provide workshops to help people quit smoking, control alcohol use, lose weight, eat better, and develop a regular exercise program. The assumption underlying most wellness programs is that employees need to take personal responsibility for their physical and mental health. The organization is merely a vehicle to facilitate this end.

Organizations, of course, aren't altruistic. They expect a payoff from their investment in wellness programs. And most of those firms that have introduced wellness programs have found significant benefits. For instance, Johnson & Johnson calculated the following annual savings in insurance premiums when an employee exchanges bad habits for healthy ones: quitting smoking ($1,110); starting to exercise ($260); lowering cholesterol from 240 to 190 milligrams ($1,200); and slimming down from obese to normal weight ($177).[66]

SUMMARY AND IMPLICATIONS FOR MANAGERS

The need for change has been implied throughout this text. "A casual reflection on change should indicate that it encompasses almost all our concepts in the organizational behavior literature. Think about leadership, motivation, organizational environment, and roles. It is impossible to think about these and other concepts without inquiring about change."[67]

If environments were perfectly static, if employees' skills and abilities were always up-to-date and incapable of deteriorating, and if tomorrow was always exactly the same as today, organizational change would have little or no relevance to managers. But the real world is turbulent, requiring organizations and their members to undergo dynamic change if they are to perform at competitive levels.

Managers are the primary change agents in most organizations. By the decisions they make and their role-modeling behaviors, they shape the organization's change culture. For instance, management decisions related to structural design, cultural factors, and human resource policies largely determine the level of innovation within the organization. Similarly, management decisions, policies, and practices will determine the degree to which the organization learns and adapts to changing environmental factors.

We found that the existence of work stress, in and of itself, need not imply lower performance. The evidence indicates that stress can be either a positive or negative influence on employee performance. For many people, low to moderate amounts of stress enable them to perform their jobs better, by increasing their work intensity, alertness, and ability to react. However, a high level of stress, or even a moderate amount sustained over a long period of time, eventually takes its toll and performance declines. The impact of stress on satisfaction is far more straightforward. Job-related tension tends to decrease general job satisfaction.[68] Even though low to moderate levels of stress may improve job performance, employees find stress dissatisfying.

Managing Change Is an Episodic Activity

Organizational change is an episodic activity. That is, it starts at some point, proceeds through a series of steps, and culminates in some outcome that those involved hope is an improvement over the starting point. It has a beginning, a middle, and an end.

Lewin's three-step model represents a classic illustration of this perspective. Change is seen as a break in the organization's equilibrium. The status quo has been disturbed, and change is necessary to establish a new equilibrium state. The objective of refreezing is to stabilize the new situation by balancing the driving and restraining forces.

Some experts have argued that organizational change should be thought of as balancing a system made up of five interacting variables within the organization—people, tasks, technology, structure, and strategy. A change in any one variable has repercussions on one or more of the others. This perspective is episodic in that it treats organizational change as essentially an effort to sustain an equilibrium. A change in one variable begins a chain of events that, if properly managed, requires adjustments in the other variables to achieve a new state of equilibrium.

Another way to conceptualize the episodic view of looking at change is to think of managing change as analogous to captaining a ship. The organization is like a large ship traveling across the calm Mediterranean Sea to a specific port. The ship's captain has made this exact trip hundreds of times before with the same crew. Every once in a while, however, a storm will appear, and the crew has to respond. The captain will make the appropriate adjustments—that is, implement changes—and, having maneuvered through the storm, will return to calm waters. Like this ship's voyage, managing an organization should be seen as a journey with a beginning and an end, and implementing change as a response to a break in the status quo and needed only in occasional situations.

The episodic approach may be the dominant paradigm for handling organizational change, but it has become obsolete. It applies to a world of certainty and predictability. The episodic approach was developed in the 1950s and 1960s, and it reflects the environment of those times. It treats change as the occasional disturbance in an otherwise peaceful world. However, this paradigm has little resemblance to today's environment of constant and chaotic change.

If you want to understand what it's like to manage change in today's organizations, think of it as equivalent to permanent white-water rafting.[1] The organization is not a large ship but more akin to a 40-foot raft. Rather than sailing a calm sea, this raft must traverse a raging river made up of an uninterrupted flow of permanent white-water rapids. To make things worse, the raft is manned by 10 people who have never worked together or traveled the river before, much of the trip is in the dark, the river is dotted by unexpected turns and obstacles, the exact destination of the raft is not clear, and at irregular intervals the raft needs to pull to shore, where some new crew members are added and others leave. Change is a natural state and managing change is a continual process. That is, managers never get the luxury of escaping the white-water rapids.

The stability and predictability characterized by the episodic perspective no longer captures the world we live in. Disruptions in the status quo are not occasional, temporary, and followed by a return to an equilibrium state. There is, in fact, no equilibrium state. Managers today face constant change, bordering on chaos. They're being forced to play a game they've never played before, governed by rules that are created as the game progresses.

---

[1]This perspective is based on P. B. Vaill, *Managing as a Performing Art: New Ideas for a World of Chaotic Change* (San Francisco: Jossey-Bass, 1989).

1. What is meant by the phrase "we live in an age of discontinuity"?

2. "Resistance to change is an irrational response." Do you agree or disagree? Explain.

3. Why is participation considered such an effective technique for lessening resistance to change?

4. Why does change so frequently become a political issue in organizations?

5. How does Lewin's three-step model of change deal with resistance to change?

6. What changes can an organization that has a history of "following the leader" make to foster innovation?

7. "Learning organizations attack fragmentation, competitiveness, and reactiveness." Explain this statement.

8. What characteristics distinguish organizational development?

9. How are opportunities, constraints, and demands related to stress? Give an example of each.

10. What can organizations do to reduce employee stress?

1. How have changes in the workforce during the past 20 years affected organizational policies?

2. "Managing today is easier than at the turn of the century because the years of real change took place between the Civil War and World War I." Do you agree or disagree? Discuss.

3. Are all managers change agents? Discuss.

4. Discuss the link between learning theories discussed in Chapter 2 and the issue of organizational change.

5. Discuss the link between second-order change and double-loop learning.

Team Exercise   The Beacon Aircraft Company

Objectives

1. To illustrate how forces for change and stability must be managed in organizational development programs.

2. To illustrate the effects of alternative change techniques on the relative strength of forces for change and forces for stability.

The Situation

The marketing division of the Beacon Aircraft Company has gone through two reorganizations in the past two years. Initially, its structure changed from a functional to a matrix form. But the matrix structure did not satisfy some functional managers. They complained that the structure confused the authority and responsibility relationships.

In reaction to these complaints, the marketing manager revised the structure back to the functional form. This new structure maintained market and project groups, which were managed by project managers with a few general staff personnel, but no functional specialists were assigned to these groups.

After the change, some problems began to surface. Project managers complained that they could not obtain adequate assistance from functional staff members. It not only took more time to obtain necessary assistance, but it also created problems in establishing stable relationships with functional staff members. Since these problems affected their services to customers, project managers demanded a change in the organizational structure—probably again toward a matrix structure. Faced with these complaints and demands from project managers, the vice president is pondering another reorganization. He has requested an outside consultant to help him in the reorganization plan.

The Procedure

1. Divide yourselves into groups of five to seven and take the role of consultants.

2. Each group identifies the driving and resisting forces found in the firm. List these forces in the spaces provided.

Driving Forces

_____

_____

_____

_____

Resisting Forces

_____

_____

_____

_____

3. Each group develops a set of strategies for increasing the driving forces and another set for reducing the resisting forces.

4. Each group prepares a list of changes it wants to introduce.

5. The class reassembles and hears each group's recommendations.

Source: Adapted from Kae H. Chung and Leon C. Megginson, *Organizational Behavior*, Copyright © 1981 by Kae H. Chung and Leon Megginson. Reprinted by permission of HarperCollins Publishers, Inc.

Internet Search Exercises

1. Describe what five companies are doing to help their employees reduce stress. What commonalities and differences did you find among the five? Do you believe that these programs are worthwhile?

2. Find five companies whose primary business is helping organizations to manage change. What common characteristics, if any, did you find in the programs these companies offer?

PHLIP Companion Web Site

We invite you to visit the Robbins homepage on the Prentice Hall Web site at **www.prenhall.com/robbins** for our on-line study guide, current events, links to related Web sites, and more.

Case Incident | Wisconsin Art & Greetings

At first Tammy Reinhold didn't believe the rumors. Now that the rumors were confirmed, she was in denial. "I can't believe it," she said. "I've worked as a greeting-card artist here for 17 years. I love what I do. Now they tell me that I'm going to have to do all my work on a computer."

Tammy was not alone in her fear. The company's other two artists, Mike Tomaski and Maggie Lyall, were just as concerned. Each had graduated from art school near the top of their class. They came to work for Wisconsin Art & Greetings right out of school—Mike in 1976, Tammy in 1983, and Maggie in 1988. They chose the company, which had been around for more

than 50 years, because of its reputation as a good place to work. The company also had never had a layoff.

Wisconsin Art & Greetings is a small maker of greeting cards and specialty wrapping paper. It has modest resources and modest ambitions. Management has always pursued progress slowly. Maybe that's why it was so late in introducing computerized technology to its production operations. And why now it decided that it no longer wanted its artists to do hand-rendered work. Management had bought three high-powered Mac computers and equipped them with the latest graphics and photo-manipulation software including Photoshop, Quark, and Illustrator.

Courtland Gray, the company's owner, called Tammy, Mike, and Maggie into his office this morning. He told them about the changes that were going to be made. Gray acknowledged that the three were going to have a lot to learn to be able to do all their work on computers. But he stressed that the changes would dramatically speed up the art-production and photo-layout processes and eventually result in significant cost savings. He offered to send the three to a one-week course in Dallas specifically designed to train artists in the new technology. He also said he expected all of the company's art and photo operations to be completely digitalized within three months.

Tammy was not stupid. She'd been following the trends in graphic art. More and more work was being done on computers. She just thought, as did Mike and Maggie, that she might escape having to learn these programs. After all, Wisconsin Art is not Hallmark. But Tammy was wrong. Technology was coming to Wisconsin Art & Greetings and there wasn't much she could do about it—other than complain or look for another job!

Questions

1. Explain Tammy's resistance.

2. Evaluate the way Courtland Gray handled this change.

3. What, if anything, would you have done differently if you had been Gray?

Video Case	Boardroom Incorporated

There is one thing that most managers in today's business world can be 100 percent certain of: The environment their company operates in—and the company itself—will go through many changes over time. If the only factors that managers had to worry about were those over which they had complete control, you might argue that they could keep things the same and maybe do as they pleased. But this is not the case. Companies often operate in environments over which they have little control. Technology is continuously changing, competitors are trying new things, and customers change their preferences and demand different products. Internal to a company, employees change too. Attitudes toward work are not fixed. Priorities change based on things that happen in the workplace and because of things that happen in people's lives outside of the workplace.

Boardroom Inc. knows about change. This company has grown from being a family-based business in the founder's basement to a company that employs over 80 people and generates over $100 million in annual sales. Until now, the company has been headed by its founder Marty Edelston. Soon, he will step aside and hand the operation over to a team made up of his three children and a gentleman who has been with the company for over 15 years. What will this mean for Boardroom Inc.? It's hard to say. One thing is for sure, instead of being run and guided by a single force, Marty Edelston's, the company will now be managed by a group of four. We can expect that the new leaders will have some new ideas for the company and that they may manage it with different priorities than Marty had.

As you watch this segment, think about what you would do if you were on the new management team. The company has a tremendous history and appears to be strong in both financial and market terms—people want Boardroom's products. But, as you have learned, nothing stands still. Think about how the new management team, long-time employees, and customers might respond to the change in leadership at Boardroom Inc.

Questions

1. Identify some things that you think may be external factors that affect Boardroom Inc. How might these things affect the company? If you were a member of the management team of this company, how would you react; what would you do?

2. We learned that Boardroom Inc. will soon undergo a change in leadership. What do you think of the approach the company is taking to prepare for this transition? If you were a consultant to the company, what else might you recommend in regard to the forthcoming change in leadership?

3. We can expect that some things may stay the same after the new management team takes over at Boardroom Inc., but some things will undoubtedly change. What types of things do you think might change? How do you think the staff, many of whom have worked for Marty Edelston for a long time, will react to changes that the new managers make? What might the new management team do to help the staff understand and adjust to these changes?

1. B. J. Feder, "The Little Project That Couldn't," *New York Times*, February 21, 1998, p. B1.
2. A. Levy, "Second-Order Planned Change: Definition and Conceptualization," *Organizational Dynamics*, Summer 1986, pp. 4–20.
3. K. L. Miller, "The Factory Guru Tinkering With Toyota," *Business Week*, May 17, 1993, pp. 95–97.
4. J. S. McClenahen, "Condit Takes a Hike," *Industry Week*, December 2, 1996, pp. 12–16.
5. Based on H. J. Leavitt, "Applied Organization Change in Industry," in W. Cooper, H. Leavitt, and M. Shelly (eds.), *New Perspectives on Organization Research* (New York: John Wiley, 1964); and P. J. Robertson, D. R. Roberts, and J. I. Porras, "Dynamics of Planned Organizational Change: Assessing Empirical Support for a Theoretical Model," *Academy of Management Journal*, June 1993, pp. 619–34.
6. R. H. Hall, *Organizations: Structures, Processes, and Outcomes*, 4th ed. (Englewood Cliffs, NJ: Prentice Hall, 1987), p. 29.
7. D. Katz and R.L. Kahn, *The Social Psychology of Organizations*, 2nd ed. (New York: John Wiley & Sons, 1978), pp. 714–15.
8. J. P. Kotter and L. A. Schlesinger, "Choosing Strategies for Change," *Harvard Business Review*, March–April 1979, pp. 106–14.
9. D. Buchanan and R. Badham, "Politics and Organizational Change: The Lived Experience," *Human Relations*, May 1999, pp. 609–30.
10. See, for instance, W. Ocasio, "Political Dynamics and the Circulation of Power: CEO Succession in U.S. Industrial Corporations, 1960–1990," *Administrative Science Quarterly*, June 1994, pp. 285–312.
11. This box is based on T. A. Stewart, "Rate Your Readiness to Change," *Fortune*, February 7, 1994, pp. 106–10.
12. K. Lewin, *Field Theory in Social Science* (New York: Harper & Row, 1951).
13. See, for example, A. B. Shani and W. A. Pasmore, "Organization Inquiry: Towards a New Model of the Action Research Process," in D. D. Warrick (ed.), *Contemporary Organization Development: Current Thinking and Applications* (Glenview, IL: Scott, Foresman, 1985), pp. 438–48.
14. For a sampling of various OD definitions, see J. I. Porras and P. J. Robertson, "Organizational Development: Theory, Practice, and Research," in M. D. Dunnette and L. M. Hough (eds.), *Handbook of Industrial & Organizational Psychology*, 2nd ed., vol. 3 (Palo Alto: Consulting Psychologists Press, 1992), pp. 721–23.
15. See, for instance, W. A. Pasmore and M. R. Fagans, "Participation, Individual Development, and Organizational Change: A Review and Synthesis," *Journal of Management*, June 1992, pp. 375–97; T. G. Cummings and C. G. Worley, *Organization Development and Change*, 5th ed. (Minneapolis: West, 1993); and W. W. Burke, *Organization Development: A Process of Learning and Changing*, 2nd ed. (Reading, MA: Addison-Wesley, 1994).
16. R. T. Golembiewski and A. Blumberg, eds., *Sensitivity Training and the Laboratory Approach*, 2nd ed. (Itasca, IL: Peacock, 1973).
17. J. E. Edwards and M. D. Thomas, "The Organizational Survey Process: General Steps and Practical Considerations," in P. Rosenfeld, J. E. Edwards, and M. D. Thomas (eds.), *Improving Organizational Surveys: New Directions, Methods, and Applications* (Newbury Park, CA: Sage, 1993), pp. 3–28.
18. E. H. Schein, *Process Consultation: Its Role in Organizational Development*, 2nd ed. (Reading, MA: Addison-Wesley, 1988), p. 9.
19. Ibid.
20. W. Dyer, *Team Building: Issues and Alternatives* (Reading, MA: Addison-Wesley, 1994).
21. N. Margulies and J. Wallace, *Organizational Change: Techniques and Applications* (Glenview, IL: Scott, Foresman, 1973), pp. 99–100.
22. See, for example, E. H. Neilsen, "Understanding and Managing Intergroup Conflict," in J. W. Lorsch and P. R. Lawrence (eds.), *Managing Group and Intergroup Relations* (Homewood, IL: Irwin-Dorsey, 1972), pp. 329–43.
23. R. R. Blake, J. S. Mouton, and R. L. Sloma, "The Union–Management Intergroup Laboratory: Strategy for Resolving Intergroup Conflict," *Journal of Applied Behavioral Science*, no. 1 (1965), pp. 25–57.
24. Discussions of the 3M Co. in this chapter are based on T. Stevens, "Tool Kit for Innovators," *Industry Week*, June 5, 1995; T. A. Stewart, "3M Fights Back," *Fortune*, February 5, 1996, pp. 94–99; B. O'Reilly, "The Secrets of America's Most Admired Corporations: New Ideas, New Products," *Fortune*, March 3, 1997, pp. 60–64; B. Filipczak, "Innovation Drivers," *Training*, May 1997, p. 36; M. Conlin, "Too Much Doodle?" *Forbes*, October 19, 1998, pp. 54–55; and D. Weimer, "3M: The Heat Is on the Boss," *Business Week*, March 15, 1999, pp. 82–84.
25. See, for instance, A. Van de Ven, "Central Problems in the Managment of Innovation," *Management Science*, vol. 32, 1986, pp. 590–607; and R. M. Kanter, "When a Thousand Flowers Bloom: Structural, Collective and Social Conditions for Innovation in Organizations," in B. M. Staw and L. L. Cummings (eds.), *Research in Organizational Behavior*, vol. 10 (Greenwich, CT: JAI Press, 1988), pp. 169–211.
26. F. Damanpour, "Organizational Innovation: A Meta-Analysis of Effects of Determinants and Moderators," *Academy of Management Journal*, September 1991, p. 557.
27. Ibid., pp. 555–90.
28. See also P. R. Monge, M. D. Cozzens, and N. S. Contractor, "Communication and Motivational Predictors of the Dynamics of Organizational Innovation," *Organization Science*, May 1992, pp. 250–74.
29. J. H. Sheridan, "Lew Platt: Creating a Culture for Innovation," *Industry Week*, December 19, 1994, pp. 26–30.
30. J. M. Howell and C. A. Higgins, "Champions of Change," *Business Quarterly*, Spring 1990, pp. 31–32; and D. L. Day, "Raising Radicals: Different Processes for Championing Innovative Corporate Ventures," *Organization Science*, May 1994, pp. 148–72.
31. Howell and Higgins, "Champions of Change."
32. See, for example, D. Q. Mills and B. Friesen, "The Learning Organization," *European Management Journal*, June

1992, pp. 146–56; M. Dodgson, "Organizational Learning: A Review of Some Literatures," *Organization Studies*, vol. 14, no. 3, 1993; D. A. Garvin, "Building a Learning Organization," *Harvard Business Review*, July–August 1993, pp. 78–91; C. Argyris and D. A. Schoen, *Organizational Learning II* (Reading, MA: Addison-Wesley, 1996); the special edition on organizational learning in *Organizational Dynamics*, Autumn 1998; and A. M. Webber, "An Interview with Peter Senge: Learning for a Change," *Fast Company*, May 1999, pp. 178–88.

33. D. H. Kim, "The Link Between Individual and Organizational Learning," *Sloan Management Review*, Fall 1993, p. 37.

34. C. Argyris and D. A. Schon, *Organizational Learning* (Reading, MA: Addison-Wesley, 1978).

35. B. Dumaine, "Mr. Learning Organization," *Fortune*, October 17, 1994, p. 148.

36. F. Kofman and P. M. Senge, "Communities of Commitment: The Heart of Learning Organizations," *Organizational Dynamics*, Autumn 1993, pp. 5–23.

37. B. Dumaine, "Mr. Learning Organization," p. 154.

38. L. Smith, "New Ideas from the Army (Really)," *Fortune*, September 19, 1994, pp. 203–12; and L. Baird, P. Holland, and S. Deacon, "Imbedding More Learning into the Performance Fast Enough to Make a Difference," *Organizational Dynamics*, Spring 1999, pp. 19–32.

39. See S. Shane, S. Venkataraman, and I. MacMillan, "Cultural Differences in Innovation Championing Strategies," *Journal of Management*, vol. 21, no. 5, 1995, pp. 931–52.

40. Adapted from R. S. Schuler, "Definition and Conceptualization of Stress in Organizations," *Organizational Behavior and Human Performance*, April 1980, p. 189. For an updated review of definitions, see R. L. Kahn and P. Byosiere, "Stress in Organizations," in M. D. Dunnette and L. M. Hough, (eds.) *Handbook of Industrial and Organizational Psychology*, 2nd ed., vol. 3 (Palo Alto, CA: Consulting Psychologists Press, 1992), pp. 573–80.

41. Ibid., p. 191.

42. This model is based on D. F. Parker and T. A. DeCotiis, "Organizational Determinants of Job Stress," *Organizational Behavior and Human Performance*, October 1983, p. 166, S. Parasuraman and J. A. Alutto, "Sources and Outcomes of Stress in Organizational Settings: Toward the Development of a Structural Model," *Academy of Management Journal*, June 1984, p. 333; and Kahn and Byosiere, "Stress in Organizations," p. 592.

43. This section is adapted from C. L. Cooper and R. Payne, *Stress at Work* (London: John Wiley, 1978); Parasuraman and Alutto, "Sources and Outcomes of Stress in Organizational Settings," pp. 330–50; and S. Cartwright and C. L. Cooper, *Managing Workplace Stress* (Thousand Oaks, CA: Sage, 1997).

44. See, for example, D. R. Frew and N. S. Bruning, "Perceived Organizational Characteristics and Personality Measures as Predictors of Stress/Strain in the Work Place," *Journal of Management*, Winter 1987, pp. 633–46; and M. L. Fox, D. J. Dwyer, and D. C. Ganster, "Effects of Stressful Job Demands and Control of Physiological and Attitudinal Outcomes in a Hospital Setting," *Academy of Management Journal*, April 1993, pp. 289–318.

45. D. L. Nelson and C. Sutton, "Chronic Work Stress and Coping: A Longitudinal Study and Suggested New Direc-

tions," *Academy of Management Journal*, December 1990, pp. 859–69.

46. H. Selye, *The Stress of Life*, rev. ed. (New York: McGraw-Hill, 1956).

47. S. J. Motowidlo, J. S. Packard, and M. R. Manning, "Occupational Stress: Its Causes and Consequences for Job Performance," *Journal of Applied Psychology*, November 1987, pp. 619–20.

48. See, for instance, S. Jayaratne, D. Himle, and W. A. Chess, "Dealing with Work Stress and Strain: Is the Perception of Support More Important Than Its Use?" *The Journal of Applied Behavioral Science*, vol. 24, no. 2, 1988, pp. 191–202; R. C. Cummings, "Job Stress and the Buffering Effect of Supervisory Support," *Group & Organization Studies*, March 1990, pp. 92–104; and M. R. Manning, C. N. Jackson, and M. R. Fusilier, "Occupational Stress, Social Support, and the Cost of Health Care," *Academy of Management Journal*, June 1996, pp. 738–50.

49. See L. R. Murphy, "A Review of Organizational Stress Management Research," *Journal of Organizational Behavior Management*, Fall–Winter 1986, pp. 215–27.

50. R. Williams, *The Trusting Heart: Great News About Type A Behavior* (New York: Times Books, 1989).

51. Schuler, "Definition and Conceptualization of Stress," pp. 200–205; and Kahn and Byosiere, "Stress in Organizations," pp. 604–10.

52. See T. A. Beehr and J. E. Newman, "Job Stress, Employee Health, and Organizational Effectiveness: A Facet Analysis, Model, and Literature Review," *Personnel Psychology*, Winter 1978, pp. 665–99; and B. D. Steffy and J. W. Jones, "Workplace Stress and Indicators of Coronary-Disease Risk," *Academy of Management Journal*, September 1988, pp. 686–98.

53. Steffy and Jones, "Workplace Stress and Indicators of Coronary-Disease Risk," p. 687.

54. C. L. Cooper and J. Marshall, "Occupational Sources of Stress: A Review of the Literature Relating to Coronary Heart Disease and Mental Ill Health," *Journal of Occupational Psychology*, vol. 49, no. 1 (1976), pp. 11–28.

55. J. R. Hackman and G. R. Oldham, "Development of the Job Diagnostic Survey," *Journal of Applied Psychology*, April 1975, pp. 159–70.

56. See, for instance, J. M. Ivancevich and M. T. Matteson, *Stress and Work* (Glenview, IL: Scott, Foresman, 1981); R. D. Allen, M. A. Hitt, and C. R. Greer, "Occupational Stress and Perceived Organizational Effectiveness in Formal Groups: An Examination of Stress Level and Stress Type," *Personnel Psychology*, Summer 1982, pp. 359–70; and L. A. Muse and S. G. Harris, "The Relationship Between Stress and Job Performance: Has the Inverted U Theory Had a Fair Test?" Paper presented at the Southern Management Asssociation meeting, 1998.

57. S. E. Sullivan and R. S. Bhagat, "Organizational Stress, Job Satisfaction and Job Performance: Where Do We Go From Here?" *Journal of Management*, June 1992, pp. 361–64; and M. Westman and D. Eden, "The Inverted-U Relationship Between Stress and Performance: A Field Study," *Work & Stress*, Spring 1996, pp. 165–73.

58. The following discussion has been influenced by J. E. Newman and T. A. Beehr, "Personal and Organizational Strategies for Handling Job Stress," *Personnel Psychology*,

Spring 1979, pp. 1–38; J. M. Ivancevich and M. T. Matteson, "Organizational Level Stress Management Interventions: A Review and Recommendations," *Journal of Organizational Behavior Management*, Fall–Winter 1986, pp. 229–48; M. T. Matteson and J. M. Ivancevich, "Individual Stress Management Interventions: Evaluation of Techniques," *Journal of Management Psychology*, January 1987, pp. 24–30; and J. M. Ivancevich, M. T. Matteson, S. M. Freedman, and J. S. Phillips, "Worksite Stress Management Interventions," *American Psychologist*, February 1990, pp. 252–61.

59. T. H. Macan, "Time Management: Test of a Process Model," *Journal of Applied Psychology*, June 1994, pp. 381–91.

60. See, for example, M. E. Haynes, *Practical Time Management: How to Make the Most of Your Most Perishable Resource* (Tulsa, OK: PennWell Books, 1985).

61. J. Kiely and G. Hodgson, "Stress in the Prison Service: The Benefits of Exercise Programs," *Human Relations*, June 1990, pp. 551–72.

62. E. J. Forbes and R. J. Pekala, "Psychophysiological Effects of Several Stress Management Techniques," *Psychological Reports*, February 1993, pp. 19–27; and G. Smith, "Meditation, the New Balm for Corporate Stress," *Business Week*, May 10, 1993, pp. 86–87.

63. D. Etzion, "Moderating Effects of Social Support on the Stress–Burnout Relationship," *Journal of Applied Psychology*, November 1984, pp. 615–22; and Jackson, Schwab, and Schuler, "Toward an Understanding of the Burnout Phenomenon."

64. S. E. Jackson, "Participation in Decision Making as a Strategy for Reducing Job-Related Strain," *Journal of Applied Psychology*, February 1983, pp. 3–19.

65. See, for instance, R. A. Wolfe, D. O. Ulrich, and D. F. Parker, "Employee Health Management Programs: Review, Critique, and Research Agenda," *Journal of Management*, Winter 1987, pp. 603–15; D. L. Gebhardt and C. E. Crump, "Employee Fitness and Wellness Programs in the Workplace," *American Psychologist*, February 1990, pp. 262–72; and C. E. Beadle, "And Let's Save 'Wellness.' It Works," *New York Times*, July 24, 1994, p. F9.

66. S. Tully, "America's Healthiest Companies," *Fortune*, June 12, 1995, p. 104.

67. P. S. Goodman and L. B. Kurke, "Studies of Change in Organizations: A Status Report," in P. S. Goodman (ed.), *Change in Organizations* (San Francisco: Jossey-Bass, 1982), pp. 1–2.

68. Kahn and Byosiere, "Stress in Organizations," pp. 605–08.

S ee the Wind Blow' at Waterford Crystal: Change and Innovation at the World's Finest Glassmaker

The history of glassmaking in Ireland is lost in the mists of time. But Waterford Crystal as it exists today began in Ireland amid the ruins of World War II, not far from the site of an eighteenth century glass factory that was the first establishment to carry the Waterford name. Begun on a small scale with workers trained by Eastern European craftsmen, the firm now dwarfs its original premises and stands for the highest quality in luxury crystal products worldwide. Computer technology has been added to master craftsmanship on the factory floor, and over the last five years the company's sales, mostly to Waterford's largest customer, the United States, have more than doubled.

According to Diarmuid Ryan, Waterford's Director of Human Resources, today's Waterford reaches back to a long tradition of quality shared with the original, short-lived, glassmaking firm. The Waterford of 1799 sought to "merit the approbation of their customers," and today the firm's mission is "to delight the world with beautiful gifts."

You might expect that a company whose traditions go back so far would experience little change. In fact, not only has Waterford recently survived a bitter strike and a major downsizing effort, but it has also cherished and nurtured a spirit of innovation and acceptance of change. Change has come not just in terms of bringing computer technology into its factory and adding outsourcing to its manufacturing strategy, but also in the company's structure and its product lines. Indeed, new products like the millennium line account for most of Waterford's incremental sales.

When it comes to change and innovation at Waterford, Diarmuid Ryan foresees even more to come. Based on recent successes in collaborating with contemporary fashion designers to develop new products, Waterford expects its own future designers may come from the world of fashion rather than from the traditional source, the factory floor. After all, what Ryan looks for in Waterford's creative employees is an innate ability to change or, as he puts it, to "see the wind blow."

Study Questions

As you watch the Waterford video segment, listen for indications of how well Waterford has dealt with the recent downsizing and how well it is responding to the rapid creation of new products. Decide whether you think the company is managing change well, and whether it is positioned for even greater change in the future. Specifically, answer the following questions:

1. Waterford often hires several members of the same family in the relatively small community in which it is located. Given the heavy impact on family and community of any major loss of jobs in the factory, what steps do you think the firm should have taken before it let any workers go?

2. Do you agree with Ryan that change is easier for a firm when its survival is on the line, and harder when the business is successful? Why or why not?

3. Waterford seeks to hire people with the innate ability to change and create innovation on their own. How can they accomplish this? In what other ways can innovation be encouraged?

4. Ryan describes the company's efforts to communicate more information about costs and revenues and to "explain, explain, explain, followed by train, train, train." How do you think craft workers can benefit from this kind of information?

The Historical Evolution of Organizational Behavior

Why study history? Oliver Wendell Holmes answered that question succinctly when he said, "When I want to understand what is happening today or try to decide what will happen tomorrow, I look back." By looking back at the history of organizational behavior, you gain a great deal of insight into how the field got to where it is today. It'll help you understand, for instance, how management came to impose rules and regulations on employees, why many workers in organizations do standardized and repetitive tasks on assembly lines, and why a number of organizations in recent years have replaced their assembly lines with team-based work units. In this appendix, you'll find a brief description of how the theory and practice of organizational behavior have evolved.

So where do we start? Human beings and organized activities have been around for thousands of years, but we needn't go back beyond the eighteenth or nineteenth century to find OB's roots.

Early Practices

There is no question that hundreds of people helped to plant the "seeds" from which the OB "garden" has grown.[1] Three individuals, however, were particularly important in promoting ideas that would eventually have a major influence in shaping the direction and boundaries of OB: Adam Smith, Charles Babbage, and Robert Owen.

Adam Smith

Adam Smith is more typically cited by economists for his contributions to classical economic doctrine, but his discussion in *The Wealth of Nations*,[2] published in 1776, included a brilliant argument on the economic advantages that organizations and society would reap from the division of labor (also called work specialization). Smith used the pin-manufacturing industry for his examples. He noted that 10 individuals, each doing a specialized task, could produce about 48,000 pins a day among them. He proposed, however, that if each were working separately and independently, the 10 workers together would be lucky to make 10 pins in one day. If each had to draw the wire, straighten it, cut it, pound heads for each pin, sharpen the point, and solder the head and pin shaft, it would be quite a feat to produce 10 pins a day!

Smith concluded that division of labor raised productivity by increasing each worker's skill and dexterity, by saving time that is commonly lost in changing tasks, and by encouraging the creation of labor-saving inventions and machinery. The extensive development of assembly-line production processes during the twentieth century was undoubtedly stimulated by the economic advantages of work specialization cited over two centuries ago by Adam Smith.

CHARLES BABBAGE

Charles Babbage was a British mathematics professor who expanded on the virtues of division of labor first articulated by Adam Smith. In his book *On the Economy of Machinery and Manufactures*,[3] published in 1832, Babbage added the following to Smith's list of the advantages that accrue from division of labor:

1. It reduces the time needed for learning a job.
2. It reduces the waste of material during the learning stage.
3. It allows for the attainment of high skill levels.
4. It allows a more careful matching of people's skills and physical abilities with specific tasks.

Moreover, Babbage proposed that the economies from specialization should be as relevant to doing mental work as physical labor. Today, for example, we take specialization for granted among professionals. When we have a skin rash, we go to a dermatologist. When we buy a home, we consult a lawyer who specializes in real estate. The professors you encounter in your business school classes specialize in areas such as tax accounting, entrepreneurship, marketing research, and organizational behavior. These applications of division of labor were unheard of in eighteenth-century England. But contemporary organizations around the world—in both manufacturing and service industries—make wide use of division of labor.

ROBERT OWEN

Robert Owen was a Welsh entrepreneur who bought his first factory in 1789, at the age of 18. He is important in the history of OB because he was one of the first industrialists to recognize how the growing factory system was demeaning to workers.

Repulsed by the harsh practices he saw in factories—such as the employment of young children (many under the age of 10), 13-hour workdays, and miserable working conditions—Owen became a reformer. He chided factory owners for treating their equipment better than their employees. He criticized them for buying the best machines but then employing the cheapest labor to run them. Owen argued that money spent on improving labor was one of the best investments that business executives could make. He claimed that showing concern for employees both was profitable for management and would relieve human misery.

For his time, Owen was an idealist. What he proposed was a utopian workplace that would reduce the suffering of the working class. He was more than a hundred years ahead of his time when he argued, in 1825, for regulated hours of work for all, child labor laws, public education, company-furnished meals at work, and business involvement in community projects.[4]

The Classical Era

The classical era covered the period from about 1900 to the mid-1930s. It was during this period that the first general theories of management began to evolve. The classical contributors—who include Frederick Taylor, Henri Fayol, Max Weber, Mary Parker Follett, and Chester Barnard—laid the foundation for contemporary management practices.

SCIENTIFIC MANAGEMENT

The typical United Parcel Service (UPS) driver today makes 120 stops during his or her work shift. Every step on that driver's daily route has been carefully studied by UPS industrial engineers to maximize efficiency. Every second taken up by stoplights, traffic, detours, doorbells, walkways, stairways, and coffee breaks has been documented by UPS engineers so as to cut wasted time. It's no accident, for instance, that all UPS drivers tap their horns when they approach a stop in hopes that the customer will hurry to the door seconds sooner. It's also no accident that all UPS drivers walk to a customer's door at the brisk pace of three feet per second and knock first lest seconds be lost searching for the doorbell.

Today's UPS drivers are following principles that were laid down 90 years ago by Frederick W. Taylor in his *Principles of Scientific Management*.[5] In this book, Taylor described how the scientific method could be used to define the "one best way" for a job to be done. In this section, we review his work.

As a mechanical engineer at the Midvale and Bethlehem Steel companies in Pennsylvania, Taylor was consistently appalled at the inefficiency of workers. Employees used vastly different techniques to do the same job. They were prone to "taking it easy" on the job. Taylor believed that worker output was only about one third of what was possible. Therefore, he set out to correct the situation by applying the scientific method to jobs on the shop floor. He spent more than two decades pursuing with a passion the "one best way" for each job to be done.

It's important to understand what Taylor saw at Midvale Steel that aroused his determination to improve the way things were done in the plant. At the time, there were no clear concepts of worker and management responsibilities. Virtually no effective work standards existed. Employees purposely worked at a slow pace. Management decisions were of the "seat-of-the-pants" variety, based on hunch and intuition. Workers were placed on jobs with little or no concern for matching their abilities and aptitudes with the tasks they were required to do. Most important, management and workers considered themselves to be in continual conflict. Rather than cooperating to their mutual benefit, they perceived their relationship as a zero-sum game—any gain by one would be at the expense of the other.

Taylor sought to create a mental revolution among both the workers and management by defining clear guidelines for improving production efficiency. He defined four principles of management, listed in Exhibit A-1; he argued that following these

TAYLOR'S FOUR PRINCIPLES OF MANAGEMENT

1. Develop a science for each element of an individual's work. (Previously, workers used the "rule-of-thumb" method.)

2. Scientifically select and then train, teach, and develop the worker. (Previously, workers chose their own work and trained themselves as best they could.)

3. Heartily cooperate with the workers so as to ensure that all work is done in accordance with the principles of the science that has been developed. (Previously, management and workers were in continual conflict.)

4. Divide work and responsibility almost equally between management and workers. Management takes over all work for which it is better suited than the workers. (Previously, almost all the work and the greater part of the responsibility were thrown upon the workers.)

principles would result in the prosperity of both management and workers. Workers would earn more pay, and management more profits.

Probably the most widely cited example of scientific management has been Taylor's pig iron experiment. The average daily output of 92-pound pigs loaded onto rail cars was 12.5 tons per worker. Taylor was convinced that by scientifically analyzing the job to determine the one best way to load pig iron, the output could be increased to between 47 and 48 tons per day.

Taylor began his experiment by looking for a physically strong subject who placed a high value on the dollar. The individual Taylor chose was a big, strong Dutch immigrant, whom he called Schmidt. Schmidt, like the other loaders, earned $1.15 a day, which even at the turn of the century, was barely enough for a person to survive on. As the following quotation from Taylor's book demonstrates, Taylor used money—the opportunity to make $1.85 a day—as the primary means to get workers like Schmidt to do exactly as they were told:

> "Schmidt, are you a high-priced man?" "Vell, I don't know vat you mean." "Oh, yes you do. What I want to know is whether you are a high-priced man or not." "Vell, I don't know vat you mean." "Oh, come now, you answer my questions. What I want to find out is whether you are a high-priced man or one of

these cheap fellows here. What I want to know is whether you want to earn $1.85 a day or whether you are satisfied with $1.15, just the same as all those cheap fellows are getting." "Did I vant $1.85 a day? Vas dot a high-priced man? Vell, yes. I vas a high-priced man."[6]

Using money to motivate Schmidt, Taylor went about having him load the pig irons, alternating various job factors to see what impact the changes had on Schmidt's daily output. For instance, on some days Schmidt would lift the pig irons by bending his knees, whereas on other days he would keep his legs straight and use his back. He experimented with rest periods, walking speed, carrying positions, and other variables. After a long period of scientifically trying various combinations of procedures, techniques, and tools, Taylor succeeded in obtaining the level of productivity he thought possible. By putting the right person on the job with the correct tools and equipment, by having the worker follow his instructions exactly, and by motivating the worker through the economic incentive of a significantly higher daily wage, Taylor was able to reach his 48-ton objective.

Another Taylor experiment dealt with shovel sizes. Taylor noticed that every worker in the plant used the same-sized shovel, regardless of the material he was moving. This made no sense to Taylor. If there was an optimum weight that would maximize a worker's shoveling output over an entire day, then Taylor thought the size of the shovel should vary depending on the weight of the material being moved. After extensive experimentation, Taylor found that 21 pounds was the optimum shovel capacity. To achieve this optimum weight, heavy material like iron ore would be moved with a small-faced shovel and light material like coke with a large-faced shovel. Based on Taylor's findings, supervisors would no longer merely tell a worker to "shovel that pile over there." Depending on the material to be moved, the supervisor would now have to determine the appropriate shovel size and assign that size to the worker. The result, of course, was again significant increases in worker output.

Using similar approaches in other jobs, Taylor was able to define the one best way for doing each job. He could then, after selecting the right people for the job, train them to do it precisely in this one best way. To motivate workers, he favored incentive wage plans. Overall, Taylor achieved consistent improvements in productivity in the range of 200 percent or more. He reaffirmed the role of managers to plan and control and that of workers to perform as they were instructed. *The Principles of Scientific Management*, as well as papers that Taylor wrote and presented, spread his ideas not only in the United States, but also in France, Germany, Russia, and Japan. One of the biggest boosts in interest in scientific management in the United States came during a 1910 hearing on railroad rates before the Interstate Commerce Commission. Appearing before the commission, an efficiency expert claimed that railroads could save a million dollars a day (equivalent to about $16 million a day in 2000 dollars) through the application of scientific management! The early acceptance of scientific management techniques by U.S. manufacturing companies, in fact, gave them a comparative advantage over foreign firms that made U.S. manufacturing efficiency the envy of the world—at least for 50 years or so!

ADMINISTRATIVE THEORY

Administrative theory describes efforts to define the universal functions that managers perform and principles that constitute good management practice. The major contributor to administrative theory was a French industrialist named Henri Fayol.

Writing at about the same time as Taylor, Fayol proposed that all managers perform five management functions: They plan, organize, command, coordinate, and control.[7] The importance of this simple insight is underlined when we acknowledge that almost every introductory management textbook today uses these same five functions, or a very close variant of them, as a basic framework for describing what managers do.

In addition, Fayol described the practice of management as something distinct from accounting, finance, production, distribution, and other typical business functions. He argued that management was an activity common to all human undertakings in business, in government, and even in the home. He then proceeded to state 14 principles of management that could be taught in schools and universities. These principles are shown in Exhibit A-2.

EXHIBIT A-2

FAYOL'S 14 PRINCIPLES OF MANAGEMENT

1. *Division of Work*. This principle is the same as Adam Smith's "division of labor." Specialization increases output by making employees more efficient.

2. *Authority*. Managers must be able to give orders. Authority gives them this right. Along with authority, however, goes responsibility. Whenever authority is exercised, responsibility arises.

3. *Discipline*. Employees must obey and respect the rules that govern the organization. Good discipline is the result of effective leadership, a clear understanding between management and workers regarding the organization's rules, and the judicious use of penalties for infractions of the rules.

4. *Unity of Command*. Every employee should receive orders from only one superior.

5. *Unity of Direction*. Each group of organizational activities that have the same objective should be directed by one manager using one plan.

6. *Subordination of Individual Interests to the General Interests*. The interests of any one employee or group of employees should not take precedence over the interests of the organization as a whole.

7. *Remuneration*. Workers must be paid a fair wage for their services.

8. *Centralization*. Centralization refers to the degree to which subordinates are involved in decision making. Whether decision making is centralized (to management) or decentralized (to subordinates) is a question of proper proportion. The problem is to find the optimum degree of centralization for each situation.

9. *Scalar Chain*. The line of authority from top management to the lowest ranks represents the scalar chain. Communications should follow this chain. However, if following the chain creates delays, cross-communications can be allowed if agreed to by all parties and superiors are kept informed.

10. *Order*. People and materials should be in the right place at the right time.

11. *Equity*. Managers should be kind and fair to their subordinates.

12. *Stability of Tenure of Personnel*. High employee turnover is inefficient. Management should provide orderly personnel planning and ensure that replacements are available to fill vacancies.

13. *Initiative*. Employees who are allowed to originate and carry out plans will exert high levels of effort.

14. *Esprit de Corps*. Promoting team spirit will build harmony and unity within the organization.

STRUCTURAL THEORY

While Taylor was concerned with management at the shop level (or what we today would describe as the job of a supervisor) and Fayol focused on general management functions, the German sociologist Max Weber (pronounced *Vay-ber*) was developing a theory of authority structures and describing organizational activity as based on authority relations.[8] He was one of the first to look at management and organizational behavior from a structural perspective.

Weber described an ideal type of organization that he called a bureaucracy. Bureaucracy was a system characterized by division of labor, a clearly defined hierarchy, detailed rules and regulations, and impersonal relationships. Weber recognized that this "ideal bureaucracy" didn't exist in reality but, rather, represented a selective reconstruction of the real world. He meant it to be taken as a basis for theorizing about work and how work could be done in large groups. His theory became the design prototype for large organizations. The detailed features of Weber's ideal bureaucratic structure are outlined in Exhibit A-3.

EXHIBIT A-3

WEBER'S IDEAL BUREAUCRACY

1. *Job Specialization.* Jobs are broken down into simple, routine, and well-defined tasks.

2. *Authority Hierarchy.* Offices or positions are organized in a hierarchy, each lower one being controlled and supervised by a higher one.

3. *Formal Selection.* All organizational members are to be selected on the basis of technical qualifications demonstrated by training, education, or formal examination.

4. *Formal Rules and Regulations.* To ensure uniformity and to regulate the actions of employees, managers must depend heavily on formal organizational rules.

5. *Impersonality.* Rules and controls are applied uniformly, avoiding involvement with personalities and personal preferences of employees.

6. *Career Orientation.* Managers are professional officials rather than owners of the units they manage. They work for fixed salaries and pursue their careers within the organization.

"SOCIAL MAN" THEORY

People such as Taylor, Fayol, and Weber could be faulted for forgetting that human beings are the central core of every organization and that human beings are social animals. Mary Parker Follett and Chester Barnard were two theorists who saw the importance of the social aspects of organizations. Their ideas were born late in the scientific management period but didn't achieve any large degree of recognition until the 1930s.[9]

Mary Parker Follett Mary Parker Follett was one of the earliest writers to recognize that organizations could be viewed from the perspective of individual and group behavior.[10] A transitionalist writing during the time when scientific management dominated, Follett was a social philosopher who proposed more people-oriented ideas. Her ideas had clear implications for organizational behavior. Follett thought that organizations should be based on a group ethic rather than individualism. Individual potential, she argued, remained only potential until released through group association. The manager's job was to harmonize and coordinate group efforts. Managers and workers should view themselves as partners—as part of a common group. Therefore, managers should rely more on their expertise and knowledge than on the formal authority of their position to lead subordinates.

Follett's humanistic ideas have influenced the way we look at motivation, leadership, power, and authority today. In fact, Japanese organization and management styles, which came into vogue in North America and Europe in the late 1970s, are indebted to Follett. They place a heavy emphasis on group togetherness and team effort.

Chester Barnard Like Henri Fayol, Chester Barnard was a practitioner. He joined the American Telephone and Telegraph system in 1909 and became president of New Jersey Bell in 1927. Barnard had read Weber and was influenced by his writings. But unlike Weber, who had a mechanistic and impersonal view of organizations, Barnard saw organizations as social systems that require human cooperation. He expressed his views in *The Functions of the Executive*,[11] published in 1938.

Barnard viewed organizations as made up of people who have interacting social relationships. Managers' major roles were to communicate and to stimulate subordinates to high levels of effort. A major part of an organization's success, as Barnard saw it, depended on obtaining cooperation from its personnel. Barnard also argued that success depended on maintaining good relations with people and institutions outside the organization with whom the organization regularly interacted. By recognizing the organization's dependence on investors, suppliers, customers, and other external constituencies, Barnard introduced the idea that managers had to examine the environment and then adjust the organization to maintain a state of equilibrium. So, for instance, regardless of how efficient an organization's production might be, if management failed to ensure a continuous input of materials and supplies or to find markets for its outputs, then the organization's survival would be threatened. Much of the contemporary interest in how the environment affects organizations and their employees can be traced to ideas initially suggested by Barnard.

The Behavioral Era

The "people side" of organizations came into its own during the period we'll call the behavioral era. As we show, this era was marked by the human relations movement and the widespread application in organizations of behavioral science research. While this behavioral era really didn't begin to roll until the 1930s, two earlier events deserve brief mention because they played an important part in the application and development of organizational behavior. These are the birth of the "personnel office" around 1900 and the creation of the field of industrial psychology with the publication of Hugo Münsterberg's textbook in 1913.

THE BIRTH OF THE "PERSONNEL OFFICE"

In response to the growth of trade unionism at the turn of the century, a few firms—for example, H.J. Heinz, Colorado Fuel & Iron, and International Harvester—created the position of "welfare secretary." Welfare secretaries were supposed to assist workers by suggesting improvements in working conditions, housing, medical care, educational facilities, and recreation. These people, who were the forerunners of today's personnel or human resource management directors, acted as a buffer between the organization and its employees. The B. F. Goodrich Co. developed the first employment department in 1900, but its responsibilities consisted only of hiring. In 1902, the National Cash Register Company established the first comprehensive labor department responsible for wage administration, grievances, employment and working conditions, health conditions, recordkeeping, and worker improvement.

THE BIRTH OF INDUSTRIAL PSYCHOLOGY

Hugo Münsterberg created the field of industrial psychology with the publication of his text *Psychology and Industrial Efficiency*[12] in 1913. In it, he argued for the scientific study of human behavior to identify general patterns and to explain individual differences. Interestingly, Münsterberg saw a link between scientific management and industrial psychology. Both sought increased efficiency through scientific work analyses and through better alignment of individual skills and abilities with the demands of various jobs.

Münsterberg suggested the use of psychological tests to improve employee selection, the value of learning theory in the development of training methods, and the study of human behavior in order to understand what techniques are most effective for motivating workers. Much of our current knowledge of selection techniques, employee training, work design, and motivation is built on Münsterberg's work.

THE MAGNA CARTA OF LABOR

Following the stock market crash of 1929, the United States and much of the world's economy entered the Great Depression. To help relieve the effects of the depression on the U.S. labor force, President Franklin D. Roosevelt supported the Wagner Act, which was passed in 1935. This act recognized unions as the authorized representatives of workers, able to bargain collectively with employers in the interests of their members. The Wagner Act would prove to be the Magna Carta of labor. It legitimized the role of trade unions and encouraged rapid growth in union membership. In response to this legislation, managers in industry became much more open to finding new ways to handle their employees. Having lost the battle to keep unions out of their factories, management began to try to improve working conditions and seek better relations with its workforce. A set of studies done at Western Electric's Hawthorne plant would be the prime stimulus for the human relations movement that swept American industry from the late 1930s through the 1950s.

HUMAN RELATIONS

The essence of the human relations movement was the belief that the key to higher productivity in organizations was increasing employee satisfaction. In addition to the Hawthorne studies, three people played important roles in conveying the message of human relations: Dale Carnegie, Abraham Maslow, and Douglas McGregor. In this section, we briefly review each man's contribution. But first, we'll describe the very influential Hawthorne studies.

The Hawthorne Studies Without question, the most important contribution to the human relations movement within organizational behavior came out of the Hawthorne studies undertaken at the Western Electric Company's Hawthorne Works in Cicero, Illinois. These studies, originally begun in 1924 but eventually expanded and carried on through the early 1930s, were initially devised by Western Electric industrial engineers to examine the effect of various illumination levels on worker productivity. Control and experimental groups were established. The experimental group was presented with varying illumination intensities, while the control group worked under a constant intensity. The engineers had expected individual output to be directly related to the intensity of light. However, they found that as the light level was increased in the experimental group, output for both groups rose. To the surprise of the engineers, as the light level was dropped in the experimental group, productivity continued to increase in both groups. In fact, a productivity decrease was observed in the experimental group only when the light intensity had been reduced to that of moonlight. The engineers concluded that illumination intensity was not directly related to group productivity, but they could not explain the behavior they had witnessed.

The Western Electric engineers asked Harvard professor Elton Mayo and his associates in 1927 to join the study as consultants. Thus began a relationship that would last through 1932 and encompass numerous experiments covering the redesign of jobs, changes in the length of the workday and workweek, introduction of rest periods, and individual versus group wage plans.[13] For example, one experiment was designed to evaluate the effect of a group piecework incentive pay system on group productivity. The results indicated that the incentive plan had less effect on a worker's output than did group pressure and acceptance and the concomitant security. Social norms or standards of the group, therefore, were concluded to be the key determinants of individual work behavior.

Scholars generally agree that the Hawthorne studies had a large and dramatic impact on the direction of organizational behavior and management practice. Mayo's conclusions were that behavior and sentiments were closely related, that group influences significantly affected individual behavior, that group standards established individual worker output, and that money was less a factor in determining output than were group standards, group sentiments, and security. These conclusions led to a new emphasis on the human factor in the functioning of organizations and the attainment of

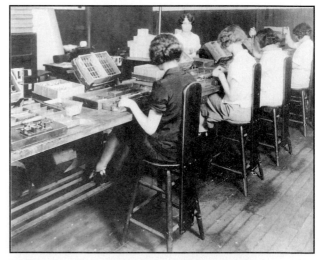

These women were part of the experiments at the Hawthorne plant of Western Electric. The Hawthorne studies dramatized that a worker was not a machine and scientific management's "one best way" approach had to be modified to recognize the effects of individual and group behavior.

their goals. They also led to increased paternalism by management.

The Hawthorne studies have not been without critics. Attacks have been made on their procedures, analyses of findings, and the conclusions they drew.[14] However, from a historical standpoint, it's of little importance whether the studies were academically sound or their conclusions justified. What is important is that they stimulated an interest in human factors.

Dale Carnegie Dale Carnegie's book *How to Win Friends and Influence People*[15] was read by millions during the 1930s, 1940s, and 1950s. During this same period, tens of thousands of managers and aspiring managers attended his management speeches and seminars. So Carnegie's ideas deserve attention because of the wide audience they commanded.

Carnegie's essential theme was that the way to success was through winning the cooperation of others. He advised his audience to (1) make others feel important through a sincere appreciation of their efforts; (2) strive to make a good first impression; (3) win people to their way of thinking by letting others do the talking, being sympathetic, and "never telling a man he is wrong"; and (4) change

Abraham Maslow (1908–1970), a humanistic psychologist, gave us one of the most widely recognized theories of motivation. Maslow proposed that people possess an innate inclination to develop their potential and seek self-actualization.

people by praising their good traits and giving the offender the opportunity to save face.[16]

Abraham Maslow Few students of college age have not been exposed to the ideas of Abraham Maslow. A humanistic psychologist, Maslow proposed a theoretical hierarchy of five needs: physiological, safety, social, esteem, and self-actualization.[17] From a motivation standpoint, Maslow argued that each step in the hierarchy must be satisfied before the next can be activated, and that once a need was substantially satisfied, it no longer motivated behavior. Moreover, he believed that self-actualization—that is, achieving one's full potential—was the summit of a human being's existence. Managers who accepted Maslow's hierarchy attempted to alter their organizations and management practices to reduce barriers to employees' self-actualization.

Douglas McGregor Douglas McGregor is best known for his formulation of two sets of assumptions—Theory X and Theory Y—about human nature.[18] Briefly, Theory X rests on an essentially negative view of people. It assumes that they have little ambition, dislike work, want to avoid responsibility, and need to be closely directed to work effectively. Theory Y, on the other hand, rests on a positive view of people. It assumes they can exercise self-direction, accept responsibility, and consider work to be as natural as rest or play. McGregor personally believed that Theory Y assumptions better captured the true nature of workers and should guide management practice. As a result, he argued that managers should free up their employees to unleash their full creative and productive potential.

BEHAVIORAL SCIENCE THEORISTS

The final category within the behavioral era encompasses a group of researchers who, as Taylor did in scientific management, relied on the scientific method for the study of organizational behavior. Unlike members of the human relations movement, the behavioral science theorists engaged in objective research of human behavior in organizations. They carefully attempted to keep their personal beliefs out of their work. They sought to develop rigorous research designs that could be replicated by other behavioral scientists in the hope that a science of organizational behavior could be built.

A full review of the contributions made by behavioral science theorists would cover hundreds of pages, since their work makes up a large part of today's foundations of organizational behavior. But to give you the flavor of their work, we'll briefly summarize the contributions of a few of the major theorists.

Jacob Moreno Jacob Moreno created an analytical technique—called sociometry—for studying group interactions.[19] Members of a group were asked whom they liked or disliked, and with whom they wished to work or not work. From these data, collected in interviews, Moreno was able to construct sociograms that identified attraction, repulsion, and indifference patterns among group members. Moreno's sociometric analysis has been used in organizations to create cohesive and high-performing work teams.

B. F. Skinner Few behavioral scientists' names are more familiar to the general public than that of B. F. Skinner. His research on operant conditioning and behavior modification had a significant effect

Using operant conditioning chambers like those in this photo, B. F. Skinner experimented with giving food to rats and pigeons in order to test the effects of rewards on behavior.

on the design of organizational training programs and reward systems.[20]

Essentially, Skinner demonstrated that behavior is a function of its consequences. He found that people will most likely engage in desired behavior if they are rewarded for doing so; these rewards are most effective if they immediately follow the desired response; and behavior that is not rewarded, or is punished, is less likely to be repeated.

David McClelland Psychologist David McClelland tested the strength of individual achievement motivation by asking subjects to look at a set of somewhat ambiguous pictures and to write their own story about each picture. Based on these projective tests, McClelland found he was able to differentiate people with a high need to achieve—individuals who had a strong desire to succeed or achieve in relation to a set of standards—from people with a low need to achieve.[21] His research has been instrumental in helping organizations better match people with jobs and in redesigning jobs for high achievers so as to maximize their motivation potential. In addition, McClelland and his associates successfully trained individuals to increase their achievement drive. For instance, in India, people who underwent achievement training worked longer hours, initiated more new business ventures, made greater investments in productive assets, employed a larger number of employees, and saw a greater increase in their gross incomes than did a similar group who did not undergo achievement training.

Fred Fiedler Leadership is one of the most important and extensively researched topics in organizational behavior. The work of Fred Fiedler on the subject is significant for its emphasis on the situational aspects of leadership as well as for its attempt to develop a comprehensive theory of leadership behavior.[22]

From the mid-1960s through the late 1970s, Fiedler's contingency model dominated leadership research. He developed a questionnaire to measure an individual's inherent leadership orientation and identified three contingency variables that, he argued, determined what type of leader behavior is most effective. In testing his model, Fiedler and his associates studied hundreds of groups. Dozens of researchers have attempted to replicate his results. Although some of the predictions from the model have not stood up well under closer analysis, Fielder's model has been a major influence on current thinking and research about leadership.

Frederick Herzberg With the possible exception of the Hawthorne studies, no single stream of research has had a greater impact on undermining the recommendations of scientific management than the work of Frederick Herzberg.[23]

Herzberg sought an answer to the question: What do individuals want from their jobs? He asked hundreds of people that question in the late 1950s and then carefully analyzed their responses. He concluded that people preferred jobs that offered opportunities for recognition, achievement, responsibility, and growth. Managers who concerned themselves with things such as company policies, employee pay, creating narrow and repetitive jobs, and developing favorable working conditions might placate their workers, but they wouldn't motivate them. According to Herzberg, if managers want to motivate their people, they should redesign jobs to allow workers to perform more and varied tasks. Much of the contemporary interest in enriching jobs and improving the quality of work life can be traced to Herzberg's research.

J. Richard Hackman and Greg Oldham While Herzberg's conclusions were greeted with enthusiasm, the methodology he used for arriving at those conclusions was far less enthusiastically embraced. It would be the work of J. Richard Hackman and Greg Oldham in the 1970s that would provide an explanation of how job factors influence employee motivation and satisfaction and that would offer a valid framework for analyzing jobs.[24] Hackman and Oldham's research also uncovered the core job dimensions—skill variety, task identity, task significance, autonomy, and feedback—that have stood up well as guides in the design of jobs. More specifically, Hackman and Oldham found that among individuals with strong growth needs, jobs that score high on these five core dimensions lead to high employee performance and satisfaction.

OB Today: A Contingency Perspective

We've attempted to demonstrate in this appendix that the present state of organizational behavior encompasses ideas introduced dozens, and sometimes hundreds, of years ago. So don't think of one era's concepts as replacing an earlier era's; rather, view them as *extensions* and *modifications* of earlier ideas. As United Parcel Service demonstrates, many of Taylor's scientific management principles can be applied today with impressive results. Of course, that doesn't mean that those principles will work as well in other organizations. If there is anything we've learned over the last 35 years, it's that few ideas—no matter how attractive—are applicable to all organizations or to all jobs or to all types of employees. Today, organizational behavior must be studied and applied in a contingency framework.

Baseball fans know that a batter doesn't *always* try for a home run. It depends on the score, the inning, whether runners are on base, and similar contingency variables. Similarly, you can't say that students always learn more in small classes than in large ones. An extensive body of educational research tells us that *contingency* factors such as course content and teaching style of the instructor influence the relationship between class size and learning effectiveness. Applied to organizational behavior, contingency theory recognizes that there is no "one best way" to manage people in organizations and no single set of simple principles that can be applied universally.[25]

A contingency approach to the study of OB is intuitively logical. Why? Because organizations obviously differ in size, objectives, and environmental uncertainty. Similarly, employees differ in values, attitudes, needs, and experiences. So it would be surprising to find that there are universally applicable principles that work in *all* situations. But, of course, it's one thing to say "it all depends" and another to say *what* it all depends upon.

The most popular OB topics for research investigation in recent years have been theories of motivation, leadership, work design, and job satisfaction.[26] But while the 1960s and 1970s saw the development of new theories, the emphasis since has been on refining existing theories, clarifying previous assumptions, and identifying relevant contingency variables.[27] That is, researchers have been trying to identify the "what" variables and which ones are relevant for understanding various behavioral phenomena. This essentially reflects the maturing of OB as a scientific discipline. The near-term future of OB research is likely to continue to focus on fine-tuning current theories so as to better help us understand those situations in which they're most likely to be useful.

Summary

While the seeds of organizational behavior were planted more than 200 years ago, current OB theory and practice are essentially products of the twentieth century.

Frederick Taylor's principles of scientific management were instrumental in engineering precision and standardization into people's jobs. Henri Fayol defined the universal functions that all managers perform and the principles that constitute good management practice. Max Weber developed a theory of authority structures and described organizational activity based on authority relations.

The "people side" of organizations came into its own in the 1930s, predominantly as a result of the Hawthorne studies. These studies led to a new emphasis on the human factor in organizations and increased paternalism by management. In the late 1950s, managers' attention was caught by the ideas of people such as Abraham Maslow and Douglas McGregor, who proposed that organization structures and management practices had to be altered so as to bring out the full productive potential of employees. Motivation and leadership theories offered by David McClelland, Fred Fiedler, Frederick Herzberg, and other behavioral scientists during the 1960s and 1970s provided managers with still greater insights into employee behavior.

Almost all contemporary management and organizational behavior concepts are contingency based. That is, they provide various recommendations dependent upon situational factors. As a maturing discipline, current OB research is emphasizing the refinement of existing theories.

End Notes

1. See, for instance, D. A. Wren, *The Evolution of Management Thought*, 4th ed. (New York: John Wiley & Sons, 1994), especially Chapters 13–18.
2. A. Smith, *An Inquiry into the Nature and Causes of the Wealth of Nations* (New York: Modern Library, 1937; orig. pub. 1776).
3. C. Babbage, *On the Economy of Machinery and Manufactures* (London: Charles Knight, 1832).
4. R. A. Owen, *A New View of Society* (New York: E. Bliss & White, 1825).
5. F. W. Taylor, *Principles of Scientific Management* (New York: Harper & Brothers, 1911).
6. Ibid., p. 44.
7. H. Fayol, *Industrial and General Administration* (Paris: Dunod, 1916).
8. M. Weber, *The Theory of Social and Economic Organizations*, ed. T. Parsons, trans. A. M. Henderson and T. Parsons (New York: Free Press, 1947).
9. Wren, *The Evolution of Management Thought*, Chapter 14.
10. See, for example, M. P. Follett, *The New State: Group Organization the Solution of Popular Government* (London: Longmans, Green & Co., 1918). See also the review forum on Mary Parker Follett in *Organization*, February 1996, pp. 147–80.
11. C. I. Barnard, *The Functions of the Executive* (Cambridge, MA: Harvard University Press, 1938).
12. H. Münsterberg, *Psychology and Industrial Efficiency* (Boston: Houghton Mifflin, 1913).
13. E. Mayo, *The Human Problems of an Industrial Civilization* (New York: Macmillan, 1933); and F. J. Roethlisberger and W. J. Dickson, *Management and the Worker* (Cambridge, MA: Harvard University Press, 1939).
14. See, for example, A. Carey, "The Hawthorne Studies: A Radical Criticism," *American Sociological Review*, June 1967, pp. 403–16; R. H. Franke and J. Kaul, "The Hawthorne Experiments: First Statistical Interpretations," *American Sociological Review*, October 1978, pp. 623–43; B. Rice, "The Hawthorne Defect: Persistence of a Flawed Theory," *Psychology Today*, February 1982, pp. 70–74; J. A. Sonnenfeld, "Shedding Light on the Hawthorne Studies," *Journal of Occupational Behavior*, April 1985, pp. 111–30; and S. R. G. Jones, "Was There a Hawthorne Effect?" *American Journal of Sociology*, November 1992, pp. 451–68.
15. D. Carnegie, *How to Win Friends and Influence People* (New York: Simon & Schuster, 1936).
16. Wren, *The Evolution of Management Thought*, p. 336.
17. A. Maslow, *Motivation and Personality* (New York: Harper & Row, 1954).

18. D. McGregor, *The Human Side of Enterprise* (New York: McGraw-Hill, 1960).

19. J. L. Moreno, "Contributions of Sociometry to Research Methodology in Sociology," *American Sociological Review*, June 1947, pp. 287–92.

20. See, for instance, B. F. Skinner, *Science and Human Behavior* (New York: Free Press, 1953); and B. F. Skinner, *Beyond Freedom and Dignity* (New York: Knopf, 1972).

21. D. C. McClelland, *The Achieving Society* (New York: Van Nostrand Reinhold, 1961); and D. C. McClelland and D. G. Winter, *Motivating Economic Achievement* (New York: Free Press, 1969).

22. F. E. Fiedler, *A Theory of Leadership Effectiveness* (New York: McGraw-Hill, 1967).

23. F. Herzberg, B. Mausner, and B. Snyderman, *The Motivation to Work* (New York, John Wiley, 1959); and F. Herzberg, *The Managerial Choice: To Be Efficient or to Be Human*, rev. ed. (Salt Lake City: Olympus, 1982).

24. J. R. Hackman and G. R. Oldham, "Development of the Job Diagnostic Survey," *Journal of Applied Psychology*, April 1975, pp. 159–70.

25. See, for instance, J. M. Shepard and J. G. Hougland, Jr., "Contingency Theory: 'Complex Man' or 'Complex Organization'?" *Academy of Management Review*, July 1978, pp. 413–27; and H. L. Tosi, Jr. and J. W. Slocum, Jr., "Contingency Theory: Some Suggested Directions," *Journal of Management*, Spring 1984, pp. 9–26.

26. C. A. O'Reilly III, "Organizational Behavior: Where We've Been, Where We're Going," in M. R. Rosenzweig and L. W. Porter (eds.), *Annual Review of Psychology*, vol. 42 (Palo Alto, CA: Annual Reviews, Inc., 1991), pp. 429–30.

27. Ibid., pp. 427–58.

APPENDIX B

Research in Organizational Behavior

Some years back, a friend of mine was all excited because he had read about the findings from a research study that finally, once and for all, resolved the question of what it takes to make it to the top in a large corporation. I doubted there was any simple answer to this question but, not wanting to dampen his enthusiasm, I asked him to tell me about what he had read. The answer, according to my friend, was *participation in college athletics*. To say I was skeptical of his claim is a gross understatement, so I asked him to tell me more.

The study encompassed 1,700 successful senior executives at the 500 largest U.S. corporations. The researchers found that half of these executives had played varsity-level college sports.[1] My friend, who happens to be good with statistics, informed me that since fewer than 2 percent of all college students participate in intercollegiate athletics, the probability of this finding occurring by mere chance is less than one in 10 million! He concluded his analysis by telling me that, based on this research, I should encourage my management students to get into shape and to make one of the varsity teams.

My friend was somewhat perturbed when I suggested that his conclusions were likely to be flawed. These executives were all males who attended college in the 1940s and 1950s. Would his advice be meaningful to females in the twenty-first century? These executives also weren't your typical college students. For the most part, they had attended elite private colleges such as Princeton and Lehigh, where a large proportion of the student body participates in intercollegiate sports. And these "jocks" hadn't necessarily played football or basketball; many had participated in golf, tennis, baseball, cross-country running, crew, rugby, and similar minor sports. Moreover, maybe the researchers had confused the direction of causality. That is, maybe individuals with the motivation and ability to make it to the top of a large corporation are drawn to competitive activities like college athletics.

My friend was guilty of misusing research data. Of course, he is not alone. We are all continually bombarded with reports of experiments that link certain substances to cancer in mice and surveys that show changing attitudes toward sex among college students, for example. Many of these studies are carefully designed, with great caution taken to note the implications and limitations of the findings. But some studies are poorly designed, making their conclusions at best suspect, and at worst meaningless.

Rather than attempting to make you a researcher, the purpose of this appendix is to increase your awareness as a consumer of behavioral research. A knowledge of research methods will allow you to appreciate more fully the care in data collection that underlies the information and conclusions presented in this text. Moreover, an understanding of research methods will make you a more skilled evaluator of those OB studies you will encounter in business and professional journals. So an appreciation of behavioral research is important because (1) it's the foundation upon which the theories in this text are built, and (2) it will benefit you in future years when you read reports of research and attempt to assess their value.

Purpose of Research

Research is concerned with the systematic gathering of information. Its purpose is to help us in our search for the truth. While we will never find ultimate truth—in our case, that would be to know precisely how any person would behave in any organizational context—ongoing research adds to our body of OB knowledge by supporting some theories, contradicting others, and suggesting new theories to replace those that fail to gain support.

Research Terminology

Researchers have their own vocabulary for communicating among themselves and with outsiders. The following briefly defines some of the more popular terms you're likely to encounter in behavioral science studies.[2]

Variable   A *variable* is any general characteristic that can be measured and that changes in either amplitude, intensity, or both. Some examples of OB variables found in this text are job satisfaction, employee productivity, work stress, ability, personality, and group norms.

Hypothesis   A tentative explanation of the relationship between two or more variables is called a *hypothesis*. My friend's statement that participation in college athletics leads to a top executive position in a large corporation is an example of a hypothesis. Until confirmed by empirical research, a hypothesis remains only a tentative explanation.

Dependent Variable   A *dependent variable* is a response that is affected by an independent variable. In terms of the hypothesis, it is the variable that the researcher is interested in explaining. Referring back to our opening example, the dependent variable in my friend's hypothesis was executive succession. In organizational behavior research, the most popular dependent variables are productivity, absenteeism, turnover, job satisfaction, and organizational commitment.[3]

Independent Variable   An *independent variable* is the presumed cause of some change in the dependent variable. Participating in varsity athletics was the independent variable in my friend's hypothesis. Popular independent variables studied by OB researchers include intelligence, personality, job satisfaction, experience, motivation, reinforcement patterns, leadership style, reward allocations, selection methods, and organization design.

You may have noticed we said that job satisfaction is frequently used by OB researchers as both a dependent and an independent variable. This is not an error. It merely reflects that the label given to a variable depends on its place in the hypothe-

sis. In the statement "Increases in job satisfaction lead to reduced turnover," job satisfaction is an independent variable. However, in the statement "Increases in money lead to higher job satisfaction," job satisfaction becomes a dependent variable.

Moderating Variable   A *moderating variable* abates the effect of the independent variable on the dependent variable. It might also be thought of as the contingency variable: If X (independent variable), then Y (dependent variable) will occur, but only under conditions Z (moderating variable). To translate this into a real-life example, we might say that if we increase the amount of direct supervision in the work area (X), then there will be a change in worker productivity (Y), but this effect will be moderated by the complexity of the tasks being performed (Z).

Causality   A hypothesis, by definition, implies a relationship. That is, it implies a presumed cause and effect. This direction of cause and effect is called *causality*. Changes in the independent variable are assumed to cause changes in the dependent variable. However, in behavioral research, it's possible to make an incorrect assumption of causality when relationships are found. For example, early behavioral scientists found a relationship between employee satisfaction and productivity. They concluded that a happy worker was a productive worker. Follow-up research has supported the relationship but disconfirmed the direction of the arrow. The evidence more correctly suggests that high productivity leads to satisfaction rather than the other way around.

Correlation Coefficient   It's one thing to know that there is a relationship between two or more variables. It's another to know the *strength* of that relationship. The term *correlation coefficient* is used to indicate that strength, and is expressed as a number between -1.00 (a perfect negative relationship) to $+1.00$ (a perfect positive correlation).

When two variables vary directly with one another, the correlation will be expressed as a positive number. When they vary inversely—that is, one increases as the other decreases—the correlation will be expressed as a negative number. If the two variables vary independently of each other, we say that the correlation between them is zero.

For example, a researcher might survey a group of employees to determine the satisfaction of each with his or her job. Then, using company absenteeism reports, the researcher could correlate the job satisfaction scores against individual attendance records to determine whether employees who are more satisfied with their jobs have better attendance records than their counterparts who indicated lower job satisfaction. Let's suppose the researcher found a correlation coefficient between satisfaction and attendance of +0.50. Would that be a strong association? There is, unfortunately, no precise numerical cutoff separating strong and weak relationships. A standard statistical test would need to be applied to determine whether or not the relationship was a significant one.

A final point needs to be made before we move on: A correlation coefficient measures only the strength of association between two variables. A high value does *not* imply causality. The length of women's skirts and stock market prices, for instance, have long been noted to be highly correlated, but one should be careful not to infer that a causal relationship between the two exists. In this instance, the high correlation is more happenstance than predictive.

Theory The final term we introduce in this section is *theory*. Theory describes a set of systematically interrelated concepts or hypotheses that purports to explain and predict phenomena. In OB, theories are also frequently referred to as *models*. We use the two terms interchangeably.

There are no shortages of theories in OB. For instance, we have theories to describe what motivates people, the most effective leadership styles, the best way to resolve conflicts, and how people acquire power. In some cases, we have half a dozen or more separate theories that purport to explain and predict a given phenomenon. In such cases, is one right and the others wrong? No! They tend to reflect science at work—researchers testing previous theories, modifying them, and, when appropriate, proposing new models that may prove to have higher explanatory and predictive powers. Multiple theories attempting to explain common phenomena merely attest that OB is an active discipline, still growing and evolving.

Evaluating Research

As a potential consumer of behavioral research, you should follow the dictum of *caveat emptor*—let the buyer beware! In evaluating any research study, you need to ask three questions.[4]

Is it valid? Is the study actually measuring what it claims to be measuring? Many psychological tests have been discarded by employers in recent years because they have not been found to be valid measures of the applicants' ability to successfully do a given job. The validity issue is relevant to all research studies. So, if you find a study that links cohesive work teams with higher productivity, you want to know how each of these variables was measured and whether it is actually measuring what it is supposed to be measuring.

Is it reliable? Reliability refers to consistency of measurement. If you were to have your height measured every day with a wooden yardstick, you'd get highly reliable results. On the other hand, if you were measured each day by an elastic tape measure, there would probably be considerable disparity between your height measurements from one day to the next. Your height, of course, doesn't change from day to day. The variability is due to the unreliability of the measuring device. So if a company asked a group of its employees to complete a reliable job satisfaction questionnaire, and then repeat the questionnaire six months later, we'd expect the results to be very similar—provided nothing changed in the interim that might significantly affect employee satisfaction.

Is it generalizable? Are the results of the research study generalizable to groups of individuals other than those who participated in the original study? Be aware, for example, of the limitations that might exist in research that uses college students as subjects. Are the findings in such studies generalizable to full-time employees in real jobs? Similarly, how generalizable to the overall work population are the results from a study that assesses job stress among 10 nuclear power plant engineers in the hamlet of Mahone Bay, Nova Scotia?

Research Design

Doing research is an exercise in trade-offs. Richness of information typically comes with reduced generalizability. The more a researcher seeks to control for confounding variables, the less realistic his or her results are likely to be. High precision, generalizability, and control almost always translate into higher costs. When researchers make choices about whom they'll study, where their research will be done, the methods they'll use to collect data, and so on, they must make some concessions. Good research designs are not perfect, but they do carefully reflect the questions being addressed. Keep these facts in mind as we review the strengths and weaknesses of five popular research designs: case studies, field surveys, laboratory experiments, field experiments, and aggregate quantitative reviews.

Case Study   You pick up a copy of Soichiro Honda's autobiography. In it he describes his impoverished childhood; his decisions to open a small garage, assemble motorcycles, and eventually build automobiles; and how this led to the creation of one of the largest and most successful corporations in the world. Or you're in a business class and the instructor distributes a 50-page handout covering two companies: Dell Computer and Apple Computer. The handout details the two firms' histories, describes their product lines, production facilities, management philosophies, and marketing strategies, and includes copies of their recent balance sheets and income statements. The instructor asks the class members to read the handout, analyze the data, and determine why Dell has been more successful in recent years than Apple.

Soichiro Honda's autobiography and the Dell and Apple handouts are case studies. Drawn from real-life situations, case studies present an in-depth analysis of one setting. They are thorough descriptions, rich in details about an individual, a group, or an organization. The primary source of information in case studies is obtained through observation, occasionally backed up by interviews and a review of records and documents.

Case studies have their drawbacks. They're open to the perceptual bias and subjective interpretations of the observer. The reader of a case is captive to what the observer/case writer chooses to include and exclude. Cases also trade off generalizability for depth of information and richness of detail. Since it's always dangerous to generalize from a sample of one, case studies make it difficult to prove or reject a hypothesis. On the other hand, you can't ignore the in-depth analysis that cases often provide. They are an excellent device for initial exploratory research and for evaluating real-life problems in organizations.

Field Survey   A lengthy questionnaire was created to assess the use of ethics policies, formal ethics structures, formalized activities such as ethics training, and executive involvement in ethics programs among billion-dollar corporations. The public affairs or corporate communications office of all *Fortune* 500 industrial firms and 500 service corporations were contacted to get the name and address of the "officer most responsible for dealing with ethics and conduct issues" in each firm. The questionnaire, with a cover letter explaining the nature of the study, was mailed to these 1,000 officers. Of the total, 254 returned a completed questionnaire, for a response rate just above 25 percent. The results of the survey found, among other things, that 77 percent had formal codes of ethics and 54 percent had a single officer specifically assigned to deal with ethics and conduct issues.[5]

The preceding study illustrates a typical field survey. A sample of respondents (in this case, 1,000 corporate officers in the largest U.S. publicly held corporations) was selected to represent a larger group that was under examination (billion-dollar U.S. business firms). The respondents were then surveyed using a questionnaire or interviewed to collect data on particular characteristics (the content and structure of ethics programs and practices) of interest to the researchers. The standardization of response items allows for data to be easily quantified, analyzed, and summarized, and for the researchers to make inferences from the representative sample about the larger population.

The field survey provides economies for doing research. It's less costly to sample a population than to obtain data from every member of that population. (There are, for instance, more than 5,000 U.S. business firms with sales in excess of a billion dollars; and some of these are privately held, don't release financial data to the public, and are therefore excluded from the *Fortune* list). Moreover, as the ethics study illustrates, field surveys provide an efficient way to find out how people feel about issues or how they say they behave. These data can then be easily quantified. But the field survey has a number of potential weaknesses. First, mailed questionnaires rarely obtain 100 percent returns. Low response rates call into question whether conclusions based on respondents' answers are generalizable to nonrespondents. Second, the format is better at tapping respondents' attitudes and perceptions than behaviors. Third, responses can suffer from social desirability, that is, people saying what they think the researcher wants to hear. Fourth, since field surveys are designed to focus on specific issues, they're a relatively poor means of acquiring depth of information. Finally, the quality of the generalizations is largely a factor of the population chosen. Responses from executives at *Fortune* 500 firms, for instance, tell us nothing about small- or medium-sized firms or not-for-profit organizations. In summary, even a well-designed field survey trades off depth of information for breadth, generalizability, and economic efficiencies.

Laboratory Experiment The following study is a classic example of the laboratory experiment. A researcher, Stanley Milgram, wondered how far individuals would go in following commands. If subjects were placed in the role of a teacher in a learning experiment and told by an experimenter to administer a shock to a learner each time that learner made a mistake, would the subjects follow the commands of the experimenter? Would their willingness to comply decrease as the intensity of the shock was increased?

To test these hypotheses, Milgram hired a set of subjects. Each was led to believe that the experiment was to investigate the effect of punishment on memory. Their job was to act as teachers and administer punishment whenever the learner made a mistake on the learning test.

Punishment was administered by an electric shock. The subject sat in front of a shock generator with 30 levels of shock—beginning at zero and pro-

gressing in 15-volt increments to a high of 450 volts. The demarcations of these positions ranged from "Slight Shock" at 15 volts to "Danger: Severe Shock" at 450 volts. To increase the realism of the experiment, the subjects received a sample shock of 45 volts and saw the learner—a pleasant, mild-mannered man about 50 years old—strapped into an "electric chair" in an adjacent room. Of course, the learner was an actor, and the electric shocks were phony, but the subjects didn't know this.

Taking his seat in front of the shock generator, the subject was directed to begin at the lowest shock level and to increase the shock intensity to the next level each time the learner made a mistake or failed to respond.

When the test began, the shock intensity rose rapidly because the learner made many errors. The subject got verbal feedback from the learner: At 75 volts, the learner began to grunt and moan; at 150 volts, he demanded to be released from the experiment; at 180 volts, he cried out that he could no longer stand the pain; and at 300 volts, he insisted that he be let out, yelled about his heart condition, screamed, and then failed to respond to further questions.

Most subjects protested and, fearful they might kill the learner if the increased shocks were to bring on a heart attack, insisted they could not go on with their job. Hesitations or protests by the subject were met by the experimenter's statement, "You have no choice, you must go on! Your job is to punish the learner's mistakes." Of course, the subjects did have a choice. All they had to do was stand up and walk out.

The majority of the subjects dissented. But dissension isn't synonymous with disobedience. Sixty-two percent of the subjects increased the shock level to the maximum of 450 volts. The average level of shock administered by the remaining 38 percent was nearly 370 volts.[6]

In a laboratory experiment such as that conducted by Milgram, an artificial environment is created by the researcher. Then the researcher manipulates an independent variable under controlled conditions. Finally, since all other things are held equal, the researcher is able to conclude that any change in the dependent variable is due to the manipulation or change imposed on the independent variable. Note that, because of the controlled conditions, the researcher is able to imply causation between the independent and dependent variables.

The laboratory experiment trades off realism and generalizability for precision and control. It provides a high degree of control over variables and precise measurement of those variables. But findings from laboratory studies are often difficult to generalize to the real world of work. This is because the artificial laboratory rarely duplicates the intricacies and nuances of real organizations. Additionally, many laboratory experiments deal with phenomena that cannot be reproduced or applied to real-life situations.

Field Experiment   The following is an example of a field experiment. The management of a large company is interested in determining the impact that a four-day workweek would have on employee absenteeism. To be more specific, management wants to know if employees working four 10-hour days have lower absence rates than similar employees working the traditional five-day week of eight hours each day. Because the company is large, it has a number of manufacturing plants that employ essentially similar workforces. Two of these are chosen for the experiment, both located in the greater Cleveland area. Obviously, it would not be appropriate to compare two similar-sized plants if one is in rural Mississippi and the other is in urban Copenhagen because factors such as national culture, transportation, and weather might be more likely to explain any differences found than changes in the number of days worked per week.

In one plant, the experiment was put into place—workers began the four-day week. At the other plant, which became the control group, no changes were made in the employees' five-day week. Absence data were gathered from the company's records at both locations for a period of 18 months. This extended time period lessened the possibility that any results would be distorted by the mere novelty of changes being implemented in the experimental plant. After 18 months, management found that absenteeism had dropped by 40 percent at the experimental plant, and by only 6 percent in the control plant. Because of the design of this study, management believed that the larger drop in absences at the experimental plant was due to the introduction of the compressed workweek.

The field experiment is similar to the laboratory experiment, except it is conducted in a real organization. The natural setting is more realistic than the laboratory setting, and this enhances validity but hinders control. Additionally, unless control groups are maintained, there can be a loss of control if extraneous forces intervene—for example, an employee strike, a major layoff, or a corporate restructuring. Maybe the greatest concern with field studies has to do with organizational selection bias. Not all organizations are going to allow outside researchers to come in and study their employees and operations. This is especially true of organizations that have serious problems. Therefore, since most published studies in OB are done by outside researchers, the selection bias might work toward publication of studies conducted almost exclusively at successful and well-managed organizations.

Our general conclusion is that, of the four research designs we've discussed, the field experiment typically provides the most valid and generalizable findings and, except for its high cost, trades off the least to get the most.[7]

Aggregate Quantitative Reviews   What's the overall effect of organizational behavior modification (O.B. Mod) on task performance? There have been a number of field experiments that have sought to throw light on this question. Unfortunately, the large range of effect from these various studies makes it hard to generalize.

To try to reconcile these diverse findings, two researchers reviewed all the empirical studies they could find on the impact of O.B. Mod on task performance over a 20-year period.[8] After discarding reports that had inadequate information, nonquantitative data, or didn't meet all conditions associated with principles of behavioral modification, the researchers narrowed their set to 19 studies that included data on 2,818 individuals. Using an aggregating technique called *meta-analysis*, the researchers were able to synthesize the studies quantitatively and conclude that the average person's task performance will rise from the 50th percentile to the 67th percentile after an O.B. Mod intervention.

The O.B. Mod–task performance review done by these researchers illustrates the use of meta-analysis, a quantitative form of literature review that enables researchers to look at validity findings from a comprehensive set of individual studies, and then apply a formula to them to determine if they consistently produced similar results.[9] If results prove to be consistent, researchers may conclude more confidently that validity is generalizable. Meta-analysis is a means for overcoming the potentially imprecise interpretations of qualitative reviews and to synthesize variations in quantitative studies. Additionally, the technique enables researchers to identify potential moderating variables between an independent and a dependent variable.

In the past 20 years, there's been a surge in the popularity of this research method. Why? It appears to offer a more objective means for doing traditional literature reviews. While the use of meta-analysis requires researchers to make a number of judgment calls, which can introduce a considerable amount of subjectivity into the process, there is no arguing that meta-analysis reviews have now become widespread in the OB literature.

Ethics in Research

Researchers are not always tactful or candid with subjects when they do their studies. For instance, questions in field surveys may be perceived as embarrassing by respondents or as an invasion of privacy. Also, researchers in laboratory studies have been known to deceive participants as to the true purpose of their experiment "because they felt deception was necessary to get honest responses."[10]

The "learning experiments" conducted by Stanley Milgram were widely criticized by psychologists on ethical grounds. He lied to subjects, telling them his study was investigating learning, when, in fact, he was concerned with obedience. The shock machine he used was a fake. Even the "learner" was an accomplice of Milgram's who had been trained to act as if he were hurt and in pain.

Professional associations such as the American Psychological Association, the American Sociological Association, and the Academy of Management have published formal guidelines for the conduct of research. Yet the ethical debate continues. On one side are those who argue that strict ethical controls can damage the scientific validity of an experiment and cripple future research. Deception, for example, is often necessary to avoid contaminating results. Moreover, proponents of minimizing ethical controls note that few subjects have been appreciably harmed by deceptive experiments. Even in Milgram's highly manipulative experiment, only 1.3 percent of the subjects reported negative feelings about their experience. The other side of this debate focuses on the rights of participants. Those favoring strict ethical controls argue that no procedure should ever be emotionally or physically distressing to subjects, and that, as professionals, researchers are obliged to be completely honest with their subjects and to protect the subjects' privacy at all costs.

Now, let's take a look at a sampling of ethical questions relating to research. Do you think Milgram's experiment was unethical? Would you judge it unethical for a company to anonymously survey its employees with mail questionnaires on their intentions to quit their present job? Would your answer be any different if the company coded the survey responses to identify those who didn't reply so they could send them follow-up questionnaires? Would it be unethical for management to hide a video camera on the production floor to study group interaction patterns (with the goal of using the data to design more effective work teams) without first telling employees that they were subjects of research?

Summary

The subject of organizational behavior is composed of a large number of theories that are research based. Research studies, when cumulatively integrated, become theories, and theories are proposed and followed by research studies designed to validate them. The concepts that make up OB, therefore, are only as valid as the research that supports them.

The topics and issues in this text are for the most part largely research derived. They represent the result of systematic information gathering rather than merely hunch, intuition, or opinion. This doesn't mean, of course, that we have all the answers to OB issues. Many require far more corroborating evidence. The generalizability of others is limited by the research methods used. But new information is being created and published at an accelerated rate. To keep up with the latest findings, we strongly encourage you to regularly review the latest research in organizational behavior. The more academic work can be found in journals such as the *Academy of Management Journal*, *Academy of Management Review*, *Administrative Science Quarterly*, *Human Relations*, *Journal of Applied Psychology*, *Journal of Management*, and *Leadership Quarterly*. For more practical interpretations of OB research findings, you may want to read the *Academy of Management Executive*, *California Management Review*, *Harvard Business Review*, *Organizational Dynamics*, and *Sloan Management Review*.

End Notes

1. J. A. Byrne, "Executive Sweat," *Forbes*, May 20, 1985, pp. 198–200.
2. This discussion is based on material presented in E. Stone, *Research Methods in Organizational Behavior* (Santa Monica, CA: Goodyear, 1978).
3. B. M. Staw and G. R. Oldham, "Reconsidering Our Dependent Variables: A Critique and Empirical Study," *Academy of Management Journal*, December 1978, pp. 539–59; and B. M. Staw, "Organizational Behavior: A Review and Reformulation of the Field's Outcome Variables," in M. R. Rosenzweig and L. W. Porter (eds.), *Annual Review of Psychology*, vol. 35 (Palo Alto, CA: Annual Reviews, 1984), pp. 627–66.
4. R. S. Blackburn, "Experimental Design in Organizational Settings," in J. W. Lorsch (ed.), *Handbook of Organizational Behavior* (Englewood Cliffs, NJ: Prentice Hall, 1987), pp. 127–28.
5. G. R. Weaver, L. K. Trevino, and P. L. Cochran, "Corporate Ethics Practices in the Mid-1990's: An Empirical Study of the Fortune 1000," *Journal of Business Ethics*, February 1999, pp. 283–94.
6. S. Milgram, *Obedience to Authority* (New York: Harper & Row, 1974). For a critique of this research, see T. Blass, "Understanding Behavior in the Milgram Obedience Experiment: The Role of Personality, Situations, and Their Interactions," *Journal of Personality and Social Psychology*, March 1991, pp. 398–413.
7. See, for example, W. N. Kaghan, A. L. Strauss, S. R. Barley, M. Y. Brannen, and R. J. Thomas, "The Practice and Uses of Field Research in the 21st Century Organization," *Journal of Management Inquiry*, March 1999, pp. 67–81.
8. A. D. Stajkovic and F. Luthans, "A Meta-Analysis of the Effects of Organizational Behavior Modification on Task Performance, 1975–1995," *Academy of Management Journal*, October 1997, pp. 1122–49.
9. See, for example, R. A. Guzzo, S. E. Jackson, and R. A. Katzell, "Meta-Analysis Analysis," in L. L. Cummings and B. M. Staw (eds.), *Research in Organizational Behavior*, vol. 9 (Greenwich, CT: JAI Press, 1987), pp. 407–42; A. L. Beaman, "An Empirical Comparison of Meta-Analytic and Traditional Reviews," *Personality and Social Psychology Bulletin*, June 1991, pp. 252–57; K. Zakzanis, "The Reliability of Meta Analytic Review," *Psychological Reports*, August 1998, pp. 215–22; and F. L. Schmidt and J. E. Hunter, "Comparison of Three Meta-Analysis Methods Revisited: An Analysis of Johnson, Mullen, and Salas (1995)," *Journal of Applied Psychology*, February 1999, pp. 144–48.
10. For more on ethical issues in research, see T. L. Beauchamp, R. R. Faden, R. J. Wallace, Jr., and L. Walters (eds.), *Ethical Issues in Social Science Research* (Baltimore, MD: Johns Hopkins University Press, 1982); and D. Baumrind, "Research Using Intentional Deception," *American Psychologist*, February 1985, pp. 165–74.

ILLUSTRATION CREDITS

INDEXES

Name Index

A

Ability *An individual's capacity to perform the various tasks in a job*, 36–39, 53
of group members, 226
intellectual, 37–38
and job fit, 38–39
motivation and, 173–74
physical, 38
of team members, 264–65
A-B (attitude-behavior) relationship, 72–73
Absenteeism *The failure to report to work*, 20–21 (*see also* Gender; Work tasks)
flextime and, 463
job satisfaction and, 78
perception and, 146
reducing through lotteries, 48
rewarding attendance and, 48–49
Accommodating *The willingness of one party in a conflict to place the opponent's interests above his or her own*, 390
Achievement need *The drive to excel, to achieve in relation to a set of standards, to strive to succeed*, 162, 163, 175
culture and, 176
skill-based pay plans and, 203
Achievement-oriented leader, 324, 325
Acquisitions, organizational culture as barrier to, 517–18
Action research *A change process based on systematic collection of data and then selection of a change action based on what the analyzed data indicate*, 552–53
Actions vs. words, 288, 303
Active listening, 303
Adjourning stage *The final stage in group development for temporary groups, characterized by concern with wrapping up activities rather than task performance*, 219
Administrative theory, 585
Administrators, 2
Affect *A broad range of feelings that people experience*, 104

Affective component of an attitude *The emotional or feeling segment of an attitude*, 68
Affiliation need *The desire for friendly and close interpersonal relationships*, 162, 163
Age
as employee characteristic, 34–35
learning by older workers and, 47
Aggregate quantitative reviews, in research, 599–600
Agreeableness *A personality dimension that describes someone who is good-natured, cooperative, and trusting*, 95
Alexithymia, 107
Allocation of resources norms, 231
Alternative development, in decision making, 139
Ambiguity, tolerance for, 141
Analytic decision-making style, 141
Anger, stress and, 568
Anthropology *The study of societies to learn about human beings and their activities*, 11
Appearance, in employment interviews, 480
Appearance norms, 230
Application forms, 476
Arbitrator *A third party to a negotiation who has the authority to dictate an agreement*, 402
Architecture, work design and, 444–45
Army (*see* U.S. Army)
Arrangement, of work space, 457
Asch's conformity studies, 231–32
Assessment centers *A set of performance simulation tests designed to evaluate a candidate's managerial potential*, 479
Attendance, rewarding, 48–49
Attentional processes, 43
Attitudes *Evaluative statements or judgments concerning objects, people, or events*, 68 (*see also* Attitude surveys)
A-B relationship and, 72–73

changing of, 75
cognitive dissonance and, 71–72
components of, 68
consistency and, 70–71
job satisfaction and, 61
perception and, 122
self-perception and, 73
types of, 68–69
workforce diversity and, 75–76
worldwide job-related needs, 70
Attitude surveys *Eliciting responses from employees through questionnaires about how they feel about their jobs, work groups, supervisors, and the organization*, 74
Attribution theory *When individuals observe behavior, they attempt to determine whether it is internally or externally caused*, 125–26
Authoritative command, as conflict management technique, 392
Authority *The rights inherent in a managerial position to give orders and to expect the orders to be obeyed*, 417
delegating, 421
Authority structures, 224
Autocratic leadership style, 335
Automobile industry
Bolivar Project and, 538–39
boundaryless organization in, 428
conflict with unions, 396
job satisfaction and, 80
Autonomy *The degree to which the job provides substantial freedom and discretion to the individual in scheduling the work and in determining the procedures to be used in carrying it out*, 447
Availability heuristic *The tendency for people to base their judgments on information that is readily available to them*, 139
Avoiding *The desire to withdraw from or suppress a conflict*, 390
as conflict management technique, 392, 403

Fringe benefits, 204
Frustration-regression dimension, of ERG theory, 161
Functional conflict *Conflict that supports the goals of the group and improves its performance*, 385, 393–95
Functional, departmentalization, 416
Fundamental attribution error *The tendency to underestimate the influence of external factors and overestimate the influence of internal factors when making judgments about the behavior of others*, 126

G

Gainsharing *An incentive plan in which improvements in group productivity determine the total amount of money that is allocated*, 199–200
Gender (*see also* Workforce diversity)
 communication barriers and, 296–97
 emotions and, 107–8
 as employee characteristic, 35
 leadership capabilities and, 331
 negotiation and, 400–401
Generation X work ethic values, 64, 65
Geography, departmentalization and, 416
Globalization, 13, 262 (*see also* Cross-cultural differences)
 boundaryless organization and, 428–29
 generation X work values and, 65
Goals
 motivation and, 155
 organization and achievement of, 2
 rewards and, 171
 of teams, 268
Goal setting, stress management and, 571
Goal-setting theory *The theory that specific and difficult goals, with goal/feedback, lead to higher performance*, 166–67, 175
 MBO and, 190–91

Grapevine *The organization's informal communication network*, 291–93
 communication skills and, 303
Graphic rating scales *An evaluation method in which the evaluator rates performance factors on an incremental scale*, 490
Group(s) *Two or more individuals, interacting and interdependent, who have come together to achieve particular objectives*, 216–17 (*see also* Work group)
 behavior, 216
 cohesiveness of, 237, 238
 communication within, 284–85
 composition of, 235–37
 conditions favoring, 241
 conflict and, 393, 405
 decision making in, 240–43, 244–45
 evaluating effectiveness of, 246
 external conditions imposed on, 224–25
 formal leadership in, 227
 formal small-group networks, 290–91
 inertia and change in, 547
 learning effective group behavior, 411
 member resources of, 226
 norms in, 230–32
 performance of, 246–47
 power coalitions in, 360–61
 prison experiment and, 229–30
 processes of, 238–39
 pros and cons of, 248
 punctuated equilibrium model for temporary, 220–21
 reasons for joining, 218
 roles in, 227–30
 satisfaction and, 247
 size of, 234–35
 sociometry for analyzing, 221–23, 590
 status and, 232–34
 structure of, 226–37
 tasks of, 239–40
 work group behavior and, 223
Group demography *The degree to which members of a group share a common demographic attribute, such as age, sex, race, educational level, or length of service in the*

organization, and the impact of this attribute on turnover, 236–37
Group development, five-stage model of, 219–20
Group goals, 167
Group order ranking *An evaluation method that places employees into a particular classification such as quartiles*, 491
Groupshift *A change in decision risk between the group's decision and the individual decision that members within the group would make; can be either toward conservatism or greater risk*, 242–43
Groupthink *Phenomenon in which the norm for consensus overrides the realistic appraisal of alternative courses of action*, 242–43
Growth needs, 161

H

Habit, change and, 545–46
Halo effect *Drawing a general impression about an individual on the basis of a single characteristic*, 127–28
Hand gestures, culture and meaning of, 299
Happiness (*see also* Job satisfaction)
 productivity and, 77
Harassment (*see* Sexual harassment)
Hawthorne studies, 77, 588–89
Heredity, personality and, 92–93
Hersey and Blanchard's situational theory, 322
Herzberg's two-factor theory, 158–60, 590–91
Heuristics *Judgmental shortcuts in decision making*, 139
 availability heuristic, 139
 representative heuristic, 139–40
Hierarchy of needs theory *There is a hierarchy of five needs— physiological, safety, social, esteem, and self-actualization; as each need is substantially satisfied, the next need becomes dominant*, 156–57, 175–76, 589

M

Machiavellianism *Degree to which an individual is pragmatic, maintains emotional distance, and believes that ends can justify means*, 97
Malcolm Baldrige National Quality Award, 260
Management
functions of, 2–3
human resource, 5
leadership and, 313–14
organizational culture and, 520–21
participative, 194
roles of, 3–5
skills of, 4–5
of teams, 271–73
traditional, 5
Management by objectives (MBO) *A program that encompasses specific goals, participatively set, for an explicit time period, with feedback on goal progress*, 189–91
Managerial Grid *A nine-by-nine matrix outlining 81 different leadership styles*, 317
Managers *Individuals who achieve goals through other people*, 2
effective vs. successful activities of, 5–6
people skills of, 6
time allocation by, 5–6
Manipulation, resistance to change and, 549
Manipulative leadership style, 335
Manufacturing
flexible systems and, 454–55
specialization in, 414
Marital status, as employee characteristic, 36
Maslow's hierarchy of needs theory, 156–57, 175–76, 589
Material symbols, culture learned through, 525–26
Matrix structure *A structure that creates dual lines of authority; combines functional and product departmentalization*, 424–25
Mature teams, 273
MBO (*see* Management by objectives [MBO])

McClelland's theory of needs *Achievement, power, and affiliation are three important needs that help explain motivation*, 162–64
Meaning (*see also* Attribution theory; Culture)
communication and, 284
language use and, 287–88
shared cultural, 515, 516
Mechanistic model *A structure characterized by extensive departmentalization, high formalization, a limited information network, and centralization*, 429
Mechanistic structure, flexibility and, 438
Media richness model, 295
Mediator *A neutral third party who facilitates a negotiated solution by using reasoning, persuasion, and suggestions for alternatives*, 402
Mental skills (*see* Intellectual ability)
Mentoring *A senior employee who sponsors and supports a less experienced employee (a protégé)*, 498–99
Mentoring programs, 51
Mercenary culture, 527, 528
Mergers, organizational culture as barrier to, 517–18
Message *What is communicated*, 286
Metaanalysis, 599–600
Metamorphosis stage *The stage in the socialization process in which a new employee changes and adjusts to the job, work group, and organization*, 522–23
Mexico, cultural values of, 67
Milgram experiment, 598–99
Minorities (*see* Workforce diversity)
Model *An abstraction of reality; simplified representation of some real-world phenomenon*, 19
decision-style, 140–41
of OB, 19–23, 24
of rational decision-making, 132–33
Money, as motivator, 179, 188

Monitor role, 3, 4
Moods *Feelings that tend to be less intense than emotions and that lack a contextual stimulus*, 104
Moral development (*see* Ethical behavior)
Moral leadership, 334–35
Motivating potential score *A predictive index suggesting the motivating potential in a job*, 448–49
Motivation *The processes that account for an individual's intensity, direction, and persistence of effort toward attaining a goal*, 155–56
ability, opportunity, and, 173–74
cognitive evaluation theory of, 164–66
contemporary theories of, 160–74
of contingent workers, 206
culture and, 175–76
of diversified workforce, 206–7
early theories of, 156–60
emotions and, 110–11
employee involvement programs and, 193–98
employee recognition programs and, 192–93
equity theory of, 168–71
ERG theory of, 161–62
expectancy theory of, 171–73
flexible benefits and, 204–5
goal-setting theory of, 166–67
in group, 284–85
hierarchy of needs theory and, 156–57
implications for managers, 208
integrating contemporary theories of, 174–75
of low-skilled service workers, 207
management by objectives and, 189–91
McClelland's theory of needs, 162–64
money and, 179, 188
of people doing highly repetitive tasks, 207–8
performance evaluation and, 486
power of theories, 178
of professionals, 205–6
reinforcement theory of, 167–68

intuition vs. systematic study of, 7–8
model of, 19–23, 24
personality attributes influencing, 96–100
Organizational change, 538–39
action research and, 552–53
Lewin's three-step model and, 551–52
organizational development and, 553–57
Organizational chart, 441–42
Organizational citizenship behavior (OCB) *Discretionary behavior that is not part of an employee's formal job requirements, but that nevertheless promotes the effective functioning of the organization*, 21, 80, 96
Organizational commitment *The degree to which an employee identifies with a particular organization and its goals, and wishes to maintain membership in the organization*, 69
Organizational context, of groups, 220
Organizational culture *A common perception held by the organization's members, a system of shared meaning*, 508–9
change in, 530, 533
creating and sustaining, 518–23
definition of, 510–11
as descriptive term, 511
employee learning of, 524–26
vs. formalization, 514
institutionalization and, 509–10
vs. national culture, 514–15
performance and satisfaction impacts of, 529
political behavior and, 367
"reading" and assessing, 513
strong vs. weak, 514
unethical behavior and, 533–34
uniform, 511–13
work groups and, 225
Organizational development (OD) *A collection of planned-change interventions, built on humanistic-democratic values, that seeks to improve*

organizational effectiveness and employee well-being, 553–57
Organizational structure *How job tasks are formally divided, grouped, and coordinated*, 412–13, 414
centralization, decentralization, and, 419–20
chain of command and, 417–18
departmentalization and, 415–17
design of, 425–29
employees and, 434–36
flexibility of design and, 438
formalization and, 420–22
implicit models of, 437
organizational designs and, 422–25
reasons for differences in, 429–33
redesigning for learning, 560
span of control and, 418–19
stress and, 566
work specialization and, 414–15
Organization life stage, stress and, 566
Organizing *Determining what tasks are to be done, who is to do them, how the tasks are to be grouped, who reports to whom, and where decisions are to be made*, 2
Outcomes (*see* Reward[s])
Outsiders, as conflict stimulation technique, 392

P

Paired comparison *An evaluation method that compares each employee with every other employee and assigns a summary ranking based on the number of superior scores that the employee achieves*, 491
Paralinguistics, 294
Participation, resistance to change and, 548
Participative leadership, 324, 325, 335
Participative management *A process in which subordinates share a significant degree of decision-making power with their immediate superiors*, 194

Path-goal theory *The theory that a leader's behavior is acceptable to subordinates insofar as they view it as a source of either immediate or future satisfaction*, 324–25
Pay
executive, 211
motivation and, 170, 179
skill-based, 201–3
variable, 198–201
PDCA cycle (*see* Plan-Do-Check-Act [PDCA] cycle)
Peer evaluations, 488
"People-first" strategies, 26
People skills, 16
Perceived conflict *Awareness by one or more parties of the existence of conditions that create opportunities for conflict to arise*, 388
Perception *A process by which individuals organize and interpret their sensory impressions in order to give meaning to their environment*, 121–31
communication barriers and, 300
factors influencing, 122–24
and individual decision making, 131–32
person, 124–31
selective, 287
stress and, 567
Performance (*see also* Motivation)
expectancy theory and, 171–73
group cohesiveness and, 238
of groups, 246–47
job satisfaction and, 77–79
organizational culture and, 529
organizational structure and, 434–36
pay for, 200
personality and, 96
rewards and, 171–72, 175
Performance bonuses (*see* Bonuses)
Performance evaluation, 485–94
decision making and, 142
evaluator and, 488–89
improving, 491–93
in international human resources, 496
methods of, 490–91
motivation and, 486
perception and, 130

Prescribed clusters *Formal groups such as departments, work teams, task forces, or committees,* 221
Primary traits, 94, 113
Principles of Scientific Management (Taylor), 583–85
Prison experiment, 229–30
Privacy, in work space, 457–58
Problem *A discrepancy between some current state of affairs and some desired state,* 131
Problem identification, 138–39
Problem solving
    as conflict management technique, 392
    culture and, 143
    information management and, 470
Problem-solving skills, of team members, 264–65
Problem-solving teams *Groups of 5 to 12 employees from the same department who meet for a few hours each week to discuss ways of improving quality, efficiency, and the work environment,* 259–60
Procedural justice *The perceived fairness of the process used to determine the distribution of rewards,* 170–71
Process conflict *Conflict over how work gets done,* 385
Process consultation *Consultant gives a client insights into what is going on around the client, within the client, and between the client and other people; identifies processes that need improvement,* 555
Process departmentalization, 416–17
Process value analysis *Determination to what degree each organizational process adds value to the organization's distinctive competencies,* 453
Product departmentalization, 416
Production-oriented leader *One who emphasizes technical or task aspects of the job,* 316–17
Productivity *A performance measure that includes effectiveness and efficiency,* 20

age and, 34–35
employee characteristics and, 33–34
empowerment and, 375
flextime and, 463
group cohesiveness and, 238
reengineering and, 14–15
satisfaction and, 77–79
specialization and, 415
work space design and, 458–59
Professional associations, ethics guidelines of, 600
Professionals, motivation of, 205–6
Profit-sharing plans *Organizationwide programs that distribute compensation based on some established formula designed around a company's profitability,* 199
Programmed routines, decision making and, 142
Projection *Attributing one's own characteristics to other people,* 128
Promotions, political behavior and, 367
Protestant work ethic values, 64, 65–66
Psychological contract *An unwritten agreement that sets out what management expects from the employee, and vice versa,* 228
Psychological stress responses, 568
Psychology *The science that seeks to measure, explain, and sometimes change the behavior of humans and other animals,* 9–10
Psychology and Industrial Efficiency (Münsterberg), 587
Punctuated equilibrium model *Temporary groups go through transitions between inertia and activity,* 220–21
Punishment, 44
Pygmalion effect, 131

Q
Quality management, 14–15, 271–72, 451–53
Quality circle *A work group of employees who meet regularly to discuss their quality problems, investigate causes,*

recommend solutions, and take corrective actions, 195–96
    in practice, 197–98
Quality of life *A national culture attribute that emphasizes relationships and concern for others,* 66
    culture and, 176
Quality management, 14–15, 271–72, 451–53
Quantity of life *A national culture attribute describing the extent to which societal values are characterized by assertiveness and materialism,* 66
    motivation theory and, 175

R
Rational *Refers to choices that are consistent and value maximizing,* 132
Rational decision-making model *A decision-making model that describes how individuals should behave in order to maximize some outcome,* 132–33, 143
Rationality myth, 103
Reactiveness, 560
Realistic job previews, 148
Recognition (*see* Employee recognition programs)
Reengineering *A process that reconsiders how work would be done and the organization structured if they were being created from scratch,* 15, 452–54
    worker obsolescence and, 455
Reference groups *Important groups to which individuals belong or hope to belong and with whose norms individuals are likely to conform,* 231
Referent power *Influence based on possession by an individual of desirable resources or personal traits,* 355
Refreezing *Stabilizing a change intervention by balancing driving and restraining forces,* 551
Regulations, formal organizational, 224–25
Reinforcement processes, 43
    negative reinforcement, 43–44
    positive reinforcement, 43

Self-managed work teams *Groups of 10 to 15 people who take on responsibilities of their former supervisors*, 260–61

Self-management *Learning techniques that allow individuals to manage their own behavior so that less external management control is necessary*, 51

Self-monitoring *A personality trait that measures an individual's ability to adjust his or her behavior to external, situational factors*, 98

Self-perception theory *Attitudes are used after the fact to make sense out of an action that has already occurred*, 73

Self-serving bias *The tendency for individuals to attribute their own successes to internal factors while putting the blame for failures on external factors*, 127

Semantics, as communication barrier, 299

Sensitivity training *Training groups that seek to change behavior through unstructured group interaction*, 554

Serial vs. random socialization, 523

Service workers, motivation of low-skilled, 207

Sexual harassment *Unwelcome advances, requests for sexual favors, and other verbal or physical conduct of a sexual nature*, 361–62

Shaping behavior *Systematically reinforcing each successive step that moves an individual closer to the desired response*, 43–44

Shared meaning, of culture, 515, 516

Short-term orientation *A national culture attribute that emphasizes the past and present, respect for tradition, and fulfilling social obligation*, 66

Sick pay, 48–49

Simple structure *A structure characterized by a low degree of departmentalization, wide spans of control, authority centralized in a single person, and little formalization*, 422–23

Single-loop learning *Errors are corrected using past routines and present policies*, 559

Situation
perception and, 124
personality and, 93

Situational leadership theory (SLT) *A contingency theory that focuses on followers' readiness*, 322

Size
of groups, 234–35
of teams, 266
of work space, 457

Skill-based pay plans *Pay levels are based on how many skills employees have or how many jobs they can do*, 201–3

Skills
attitudes, changing, 75
change climate, assessing, 550
communication, 302–4
creative thinking, 134
delegating authority, 421
disciplinary, 50
emotions, reading, 107
enriching jobs, 461
group member, 226
interviewing, 478
motivating special groups, 205–8
motivation, general, 208
negotiating, 400
organizational culture, reading, 513
politicking, 368
team players, shaping, 270–71
trust, building, 339

Skill variety *The degree to which the job requires a variety of different activities*, 447, 448

Smoothing, as conflict management technique, 392

Sociability, organizational culture and, 527

Social alliances (*see* Friendship group)

Social arrangement norms, 230

Social facilitation effect *The tendency for performance to improve or decline in response to the presence of others*, 239

Social information processing (SIP) model *Employees adopt attitudes and behaviors in response to the social cues provided by others with whom they have contact*, 449–50

Socialization *The process that adapts employees to the organization's culture*
entry options, 523
model of, 522
organizational culture and, 521–23

Social-learning theory *People can learn through observation and direct experience*, 42–43
training programs and, 50

Social loafing *The tendency for individuals to expend less effort when working collectively than when working individually*, 234–35
synergy and, 238
of teams, 269

"Social man" theory, 586–87

Social needs, culture and, 176

Social network mapping (*see* Sociometry)

Social networks *A specific set of linkages among a defined set of individuals*, 221

Social psychology *An area within psychology that blends concepts from psychology and sociology and that focuses on the influence of people on one another*, 11

Social support, stress and, 567

Social trends, organizational change and, 540, 541

Sociogram *A diagram that graphically maps the preferred social interactions obtained from interviews or questionnaires*, 221

Sociology *The study of people in relation to their fellow human beings*, 11

Sociometry *An analytical technique for studying group interactions*, 221, 590

Software, worker obsolescence and, 455–56

Span of control *The number of subordinates a manager can*

Terminal values *Desirable end-states of existence; the goals that a person would like to achieve during his or her lifetime*, 63

Tests (*see also* Written tests) of intellectual abilities, 38–39

T-groups (training groups), 554

Theory X *The assumption that employees dislike work, are lazy, dislike responsibility, and must be coerced to perform*, 157–58, 197, 589

Theory Y *The assumption that employees like work, are creative, seek responsibility, and can exercise self-direction*, 157–58, 197, 589

Thinking styles, 140–41

Third-party negotiation, 402–3

Three-component model of creativity *Proposition that individual creativity requires expertise, creative-thinking skills, and intrinsic task motivation*, 134–35

Three-dimensional environment model, 432–33

360-degree performance evaluation, 489

Three-step change model (*see* Lewin's three-step model)

Time constraints, decision making and, 142–43

Time management principles, 570

Total quality management (TQM) *A philosophy of management driven by the constant attainment of customer satisfaction through continuous improvement of all organizational processes*, 15
reengineering and, 451–53
teams and, 271–72

Traditional management, 5

Traditional view of conflict *The belief that all conflict is harmful and must be avoided*, 384

Training
for diversity, 498
individualizing, 483
for leadership, 342
methods of, 482–83
for specialization, 415
of team members, 270–71

Training programs, 50, 480–83
types of, 480–82
for workplace diversity, 75–76

Traits (*see* Personality traits)

Trait theories of leadership *Theories that consider personality, social, physical, or intellectual traits to differentiate leaders from nonleaders*, 113, 314–15

Transactional leaders *Leaders who guide or motivate their followers in the direction of established goals by clarifying role and task requirements*, 329–30

Transformational leaders *Leaders who provide individualized consideration and intellectual stimulation, and who possess charisma*, 329–30

Troubleshooters, team leaders as, 334

Trust *A positive expectation that another will not act opportunistically*, 336–40
building, 339
deterrence-based, 338
identification-based, 340
knowledge-based, 339–40
leadership and, 337–38
political behavior and, 367
types of, 338–40

Turnover *The voluntary and involuntary permanent withdrawal from an organization*, 21
group composition and, 237
job satisfaction and, 78–79
among low-skilled service workers, 207
sociometry and, 223
tenure and, 36

Two-factor theory *Intrinsic factors are related to job satisfaction, while extrinsic factors are associated with dissatisfaction*, 158–60, 591

Type A personality *Aggressive involvement in a chronic, incessant struggle to achieve more and more in less and less time and, if necessary, against the opposing efforts of other things or other people*, 99–100, 101

Type B personality, 99–100

U

Uncertainty avoidance *A national culture attribute describing the extent to which a society feels threatened by uncertain and ambiguous situations and tries to avoid them*, 66
culture and, 176

Unconditioned stimulus and response, 40–41

Unfreezing *Change efforts to overcome the pressures of both individual resistance and group conformity*, 551

Union (*see* Labor union)

Unity of command *A subordinate should have only one superior to whom he or she is directly responsible*, 417–18

University of Michigan leadership studies, 316–17

Upward communication, 289–90

Utilitarianism *Decisions are made to provide the greatest good for the greatest number*, 144

Utopianism, 583

V

Values *Basic convictions that a specific mode of conduct or end-state of existence is personally or socially preferable to an opposite or converse mode of conduct or end-state of existence*, 62–68
culture and, 66–68
importance of, 62
job satisfaction and, 61, 62–68
loyalty, ethical behavior, and, 65–66
in today's workforce, 64–65
types of, 62–65

Value system *A hierarchy based on a ranking of an individual's values in terms of their intensity*, 62

Variable-interval schedule *Rewards are initiated after a fixed or constant number of responses*, 45

Variable-pay programs *A portion of an employee's pay is based on some individual and/or organizational measure of performance*, 198–201